Grey Wolf Optimizer

Grey Wolf Optimizer

A Pack of Solutions for Your Optimization Problems

Edited by

Seyedali Mirjalili

Centre for Artificial Intelligence Research and Optimisation, Torrens University Australia, Brisbane, QLD, Australia; Research and Innovation Center, Obuda University, Budapest, Hungary; Faculty of Electrical Engineering and Computer Science, VSB-Technical University of Ostrava, Czech Republic

ELSEVIER

MK MORGAN KAUFMANN

Morgan Kaufmann is an imprint of Elsevier
50 Hampshire Street, 5th Floor, Cambridge, MA 02139, United States

ISBN: 978-0-443-36624-6

For Information on all Morgan Kaufmann publications
visit our website at https://www.elsevier.com/books-and-journals

Publisher: Mara Conner
Acquisitions Editor: Chris Katsaropoulos
Editorial Project Manager: Bhavya Rattan
Production Project Manager: M. Balakrishnan
Cover Designer: Greg Harris

Typeset by MPS Limited, Chennai, India

Dedication

To my parents, for their endless support and sacrifices.
And to my wife, for her love, patience, and encouragement.

Contents

List of contributors xxi
About the editor xxv
Preface xxvii

1. Grey wolf optimizer: mathematical principles, computational complexity, convergence proof, and performance analysis

Hoda Zamani, Mohammad H. Nadimi-Shahraki and Seyedali Mirjalili

1.1 Introduction 1
1.2 Related works 2
1.3 Mathematical principles 3
1.3.1 Social hierarchy phase 3
1.3.2 Encircling prey phase 3
1.3.3 Hunting phase 4
1.3.4 Attacking prey phase 4
1.3.5 Search for prey phase 4
1.4 Computational complexity and memory analysis 5
1.5 Proof of the grey wolf optimizer convergence 5
1.5.1 Probability analysis 8
1.6 Performance analysis 8
1.6.1 Impact of nonlinear methods on grey wolf optimizer convergence 8
1.6.2 Impact of population size on grey wolf optimizer convergence 17
1.6.3 Impact of the maximum number of iterations on grey wolf optimizer convergence 17
1.6.4 Impact of problem scale on grey wolf optimizer 20
1.7 Conclusion 24
Acknowledgments 25
CRediT authorship contribution statement 25
Data availability 25
Declaration of interests 25
References 25

2. A multipopulation grey wolf optimizer with adaptive size reduction and solution exchange for multilevel thresholding in image segmentation

Adam Djili, Mohammed A. Boukhalfa, Farouq Zitouni, Saad Harous, Abdelhadi Limane, Aridj Ferhat and Rihab Lakbichi

2.1 Introduction 27
2.2 Review of related word 28
2.3 Mathematical formulation of the multilevel thresholding problem 29
2.4 Grey wolf optimizer: fundamentals and limitations 30
2.5 Proposed multipopulation grey wolf optimizer with adaptive exchange and shrinkage 31
2.6 Results and discussion 34
2.7 Conclusion and future work 43
Acknowledgment 44
References 44

3. Theoretical foundations and methodologies of the grey wolf optimizer

Faramarz Safi-Esfahani, Hedayatollah Dallaki and Habib Larian

3.1 Introduction 45
3.2 Methods 46
3.2.1 Protocol and sources 46
3.2.2 Study selection and data extraction 47
3.2.3 Risk of bias and synthesis 48
3.3 Results and synthesis 48
3.4 Discussion 57
3.4.1 Summary of evidence 58
3.4.2 Strengths and limitations 60
3.4.3 Implications for theory and practice 60
3.5 Conclusion 61
Appendices 62

Consolidated summary 64
Acknowledgments 64
References 64

4. In-depth mathematical analysis, dynamic behavior, and convergence proof of the grey wolf pptimizer

Faramarz Safi-Esfahani, Habib Larian and Hedayatollah Dallaki

4.1 Introduction 67
4.2 Methodological approach 68
4.2.1 Search methodology and selection criteria 68
4.2.2 Categorization framework 69
4.3 Mathematical modeling of grey wolf optimizer variants 70
4.3.1 MM1. Algebraic reformulation of the position update rule 70
4.3.2 MM2. Functional redefinition of control parameters 71
4.3.3 MM3. Leader influence reweighting and generalized hierarchy 72
4.3.4 MM4. State-augmented models (memory, velocity, learning) 73
4.3.5 MM5. Probabilistic and stochastic process formulations 74
4.3.6 MM6. Hybridized mathematical models (equation-level fusion) 74
4.3.7 Concluding reflection on MM1–MM6 75
4.4 Dynamic behavior of grey wolf optimizer variants 76
4.4.1 A. Convergence dynamics and stability 76
4.4.2 B. Adaptive control parameter mechanisms 76
4.4.3 C. Trajectory behavior and landscape sampling 77
4.4.4 D. Leadership modeling and influence dynamics 77
4.4.5 E. Memory, elite learning, and historical feedback 77
4.4.6 F. Population structure and diversity regulation 78
4.4.7 Concluding reflection on A-F 78
4.5 Convergence outcomes and justifications 78
4.5.1 G1. Phased convergence 79
4.5.2 G2. Adaptive convergence pressure 79
4.5.3 G3. Trajectory stabilization 80
4.5.4 G4. Memory-guided refinement 80
4.5.5 G5. Diversity-preserving escape 80
4.5.6 G6. Leadership-driven convergence acceleration 81
4.5.7 G7. Multibehavior cooperative convergence 81
4.5.8 G8. Formal convergence proofs 81
4.5.9 Concluding reflection on G1–G8 81
4.6 Cross-dimensional isights and synthesis 82
4.6.1 Overview of analytical scope and path distribution 82
4.6.2 Mathematical modeling-centric behavioral and convergence pathways 82
4.6.3 Mapping structural influence 92
4.6.4 High-frequency and promising design pathways 94
4.6.5 Strategic design patterns 96
4.6.6 Limitations and opportunities 97
4.7 Conclusion and future directives 98
Acknowledgments 98
References 98

5. Binary grey wolf and football optimization algorithm for potato leaf disease image classification with deep learning

El-Sayed M. El-Kenawy, Marwa M. Eid, Amel Ali Alhussan and Doaa Sami Khafaga

5.1 Introduction 103
5.2 Literature review 104
5.3 Dataset description 105
5.3.1 Overview of dataset 105
5.3.2 Disease categories 105
5.3.3 Objective and importance of the dDataset 106
5.3.4 Features and attributes of the dataset 106
5.3.5 Significance of weather-based prediction 106
5.4 Methodology 109
5.4.1 Predictive models 109
5.4.2 Hybrid grey wolf and football optimization algorithm 110
5.4.3 Feature selection 111
5.5 Experimental setup 112
5.5.1 Preprocessing 112
5.5.2 Training protocols and parameter settings 112
5.5.3 Evaluation metrics 112
5.6 Results and discussion 113
5.6.1 Performance of models before feature selection 113

5.6.2 Feature selection performance 113
5.6.3 Performance of models after feature selection 113
5.6.4 Discussion 113
5.7 Conclusion 117
References 118

6. Bibliometric analysis of the grey wolf optimizer

Ahmet Akkaya, Cemil Közkurt and Rafet Durgut

6.1 Introduction 121
6.2 Grey wolf optimizer 121
6.2.1 Biological inspiration 121
6.2.2 Mathematical model 122
6.2.3 Advantages and limitations 122
6.2.4 Enhanced and hybrid versions 122
6.3 Bibliometric analysis method 123
6.3.1 Database used 123
6.3.2 Search criteria and publication year range 123
6.3.3 Analysis tools used 124
6.4 Data analysis 124
6.4.1 Distribution of Web of Science categories 124
6.4.2 Distribution of publications over the years 124
6.4.3 Document type distribution of publications 124
6.4.4 Web of Science index distributions 125
6.4.5 Research profiles 127
6.4.6 Distribution of publications by research category 127
6.4.7 Country distribution of publications 127
6.4.8 Publisher distribution of publications 130
6.4.9 Meso distribution of publications' citation topics 131
6.4.10 Citation issues of publications at the micro level 133
6.4.11 Distribution of publications according to language 135
6.4.12 Open access distribution of publications 135
6.4.13 Funding institutions 136
6.4.14 Distribution of institutions with group-authored publications 136
6.4.15 Publications on sustainable development goals 136
6.4.16 Coauthorship analysis: most active authors 137
6.4.17 Evaluation of the most cited organizations 138
6.4.18 Linkage analysis of countries among the most cited coauthored publications 139
6.4.19 Citation analysis of publications based on the work produced 139
6.4.20 Link analysis between the most cited journals 142
6.4.21 Link analysis between the most used keywords 142
6.5 Conclusion 143
Acknowledgments 145
References 145

7. An enhanced medical prediction model for diabetes using grey wolf optimizer-assisted wrapper-based algorithms

Mohammadreza Valilou, Sevda Valilou and Farhad S. Gharehchopogh

7.1 Introduction 149
7.2 Related works 150
7.3 The proposed model 151
7.3.1 Creating the initial population 153
7.3.2 Update solutions 154
7.3.3 Binary solutions 154
7.3.4 Data normalization 154
7.3.5 Classification algorithm 155
7.3.6 Fitness function 155
7.3.7 Computational complexity 155
7.3.8 Evaluation criteria 155
7.4 Evaluation and results 155
7.4.1 Dataset 156
7.4.2 Evaluation based on iteration 157
7.4.3 Evaluation based on the number of k 157
7.4.4 Evaluation based on the number of features 157
7.5 Conclusion and future works 162
Declarations 162
Ethical approval 162
Funding 162
Conflict of interest 162
Availability of data and materials 162
References 163

8. Performance analysis of the grey wolf optimizer and its variants in global search optimization

Nguyen Van Thieu, Nguyen Van Son, Ngoc Hung Nguyen, La Van Quan and Nguyen Thi Hanh

8.1 Introduction 165
8.2 Background on grey wolf optimization 165
8.2.1 Variants and improvements of grey wolf optimization 167
8.3 Performance analysis framework 171
8.3.1 Benchmark functions 171
8.3.2 Comparison algorithms 171
8.3.3 Statistical analysis 174
8.4 Results and discussion 175
8.4.1 Performance of tested algorithms on unimodal and multimodal functions 175
8.4.2 Performance of tested algorithms on hybrid functions 181
8.4.3 Composition functions 184
8.4.4 Final discussion 191
8.5 Conclusions 191
Acknowledgments 192
Declaration of competing interest 192
Declaration of generative AI and AI-assisted technologies in the writing process 192
References 192

9. Optimal parameter prediction for photovoltaic modules using the grey wolf optimizer: a case study from a university-based photovoltaic station in Türkiye

Davut Izci, Serdar Ekinci, Emre Çelik and Laith Abualigah

9.1 Introduction 195
9.2 Single and double diode models of the photovoltaic module 196
9.3 Proposed methodology for parameter extraction 197
9.4 Adopted algorithms for comparison 198
9.5 Results 199
9.5.1 Obtained results for single-diode model 199
9.5.2 Obtained results for double-diode model 202
9.6 Conclusion 206
Appendix 206
References 208

10. Predictive bridge deterioration modeling with a hybrid stochastic paint optimizer, grey wolf optimizer, and extreme learning machine algorithm

Nima Khodadadi, El-Sayed M. El-Kenawy, Benyamin Abdollahzadeh, Antonio Nanni and Khalid M. Mosalam

10.1 Introduction 209
10.2 Database 210
10.3 Data preprocessing 211
10.4 Performance metrics 213
10.4.1 Coefficient of determination 213
10.4.2 Mean squared error 213
10.4.3 Root mean squared error 214
10.4.4 Mean absolute error 214
10.5 Construction of the model 214
10.6 Extreme learning machine 214
10.7 Stochastic paint optimizer 214
10.8 Grey wolf optimizer 215
10.9 Hybrid stochastic paint optimizer and grey wolf optimizer with extreme learning machine 216
10.10 Discussion and results 217
10.11 Graphical user interface 221
10.12 Conclusion 223
References 223

11. Performance comparison of grey wolf optimizer-tuned controllers in functional electrical stimulation applications

Özay Can and Mustafa Şinasi Ayas

11.1 Introduction 225
11.2 Functional electrical stimulation system 226
11.3 Advanced control structures for functional electrical stimulation systems 228
11.3.1 PID with filter controller 228
11.3.2 Fractional-order PID controller 228
11.3.3 Filtered FOPID controller 228
11.4 Grey wolf optimizer 229
11.4.1 Grey wolf optimizer mathematical model 229
11.4.2 Grey wolf optimizer-tuned controller implementation in functional electrical stimulation systems 230
11.5 Simulation studies and results 230
11.5.1 Step response analysis 231
11.5.2 Robustness analysis 232

11.6 Conclusion 237
Acknowledgments 237
References 237

12. Grey wolf optimizer algorithm for buckling load maximization of stiffened piezolaminated composite plates

Vahid Goodarzimehr, Umut Topal and Nima Khodadadi

12.1 Introduction 239
12.2 Problem formulation 240
12.3 Grey wolf optimizer algorithm 245
12.4 Optimization problem 247
12.5 Numerical results and discussion 247
12.5.1 Optimal design problems 249
12.6 Conclusions 254
Conflict of interest 254
References 254

13. Efficient application mapping onto three-dimensional network-on-chips using the grey wolf optimizer

Maamar Bougherara, Imane Yeddou and Rafik Amara

13.1 Introduction 257
13.2 Network topology and mapping problem 259
13.3 Related work 259
13.4 Modeling mapping problem 261
13.5 Mapping with grey wolf optimization 263
13.5.1 Grey wolves in nature 263
13.5.2 Grey wolves optimization modelization 263
13.5.3 Hunting behavior simulation 263
13.5.4 Grey wolf optimization algorithm 264
13.5.5 improved grey wolves 264
13.6 Experiment result 265
13.6.1 Setting 265
13.6.2 Result and discussion 266
13.7 Conclusion 271
References 271

14. Line sampling method based on grey wolf optimizer for structural reliability analysis

Jafar Jafari-Asl and You Dong

14.1 Introduction 275
14.2 Methodology 276
14.2.1 Line sampling reliability method 276
14.2.2 Enhanced grey wolf optimizer 278
14.2.3 Metaheuristic-based line sampling 279
14.3 Numerical examples 280
14.3.1 Example 1 280
14.3.2 Example 2 282
14.3.3 Example 3 283
14.3.4 Final remarks 286
14.4 Conclusion 286
Declaration of generative AI and AI-assisted technologies in the writing process 287
References 287

15. Applications and real-world case studies: the grey wolf optimizer for feature selection in intrusion detection systems

Ramya Chinnasamy, Malliga Subramanian, Nandita Sengupta and M.P. Ramkumar

15.1 Introduction 289
15.2 Understanding the basics of intrusion detection systems 290
15.2.1 Types of intrusion detection systems 290
15.2.2 Challenges in intrusion detection systems datasets 290
15.2.3 Importance of feature selection in intrusion detection systems 290
15.3 Grey wolf optimization in feature selection for intrusion detection systems 290
15.3.1 Representation of candidate solutions 291
15.3.2 Fitness function design 291
15.3.3 Optimization flow 291
15.4 Integration of grey wolf optimization with machine learning and deep learning classifiers for intrusion detection systems enhancement 291
15.4.1 Why integrate grey wolf optimization with a classifier? 291
15.4.2 Application of grey wolf optimization-based feature selection to specific attack types 291
15.5 Case study 292
15.5.1 Dataset description 292
15.5.2 Initial data preprocessing 293
15.5.3 Feature selection using grey wolf optimization algorithm 293
15.6 Experimental results 293
15.7 Comparative analysis of feature selection techniques 296

15.7.1 Practical advantages of grey wolf optimization-based feature selection 298
15.8 Challenges, limitations, and future prospects of grey wolf optimization in intrusion detection systems 298
15.8.1 Challenges and limitations 298
15.8.2 Future prospects 298
15.8.3 Scalability and distributed deployment 298
15.9 Conclusion 298
Declaration of generative AI and AI-assisted technologies in the writing process 299
References 299

16. Optimizing solutions of fractional differential equations using the grey wolf optimizer and homotopy analysis method

Hisham M. Khudhur, Kais I. Ibraheem, Basim A. Hassan, Khalil K. Abbo and Ramadan M. Ramo

16.1 Introduction to the grey wolf optimizer 301
16.1.1 Social hierarchy in grey wolf optimizer 301
16.1.2 Algorithms of grey wolf optimizer 301
16.1.3 Advantages and applications 302
16.2 Solving linear differential equations with fractional orders 302
16.3 Steps for solving linear differential equations with fractional orders using grey wolf optimizer algorithm 302
16.3.1 The pseudo code of the grey wolf optimizer-analytical homotopy method algorithm 303
16.4 Numerical results 303
16.5 Conclusions 310
Acknowledgments 310
References 310

17. Performance evaluation of the grey wolf optimizer against advanced differential evolution variants

Dikshit Chauhan and Indu Bala

17.1 Introduction 313
17.1.1 Biological motivation 313
17.1.2 Mathematical modeling 313
17.1.3 Algorithm summary 314
17.1.4 Key characteristics 314
17.2 Background 315
17.2.1 Early developments (2014–16) 315
17.2.2 Diversification and hybridization (2017–18) 315
17.2.3 Recent advances (2019–25) 316
17.2.4 Different evolution variants for comparative analysis 317
17.3 Experimental results 319
17.3.1 Evaluation criteria 319
17.3.2 Experimental discussion 319
17.3.3 Statistical test results 321
17.4 Conclusion 324
Acknowledgment of AI-tool 325
References 325

18. Grey wolf optimizer enabled optimization of Ti6Al4V surface morphology and wear behavior

M. Özgür Bora, Sinan Fidan, Satılmış Ürgün and Halil Yiğit

18.1 Introduction 327
18.2 Materials and methods 330
18.2.1 Materials 330
18.2.2 Laser surface texturing 331
18.2.3 Reciprocating sliding wear test 331
18.2.4 Solid particle erosion test 331
18.2.5 Roughness characterization by noncontact laser profilometer 332
18.3 Results and discussion 333
18.3.1 Roughness analysis of Ti6Al4V surface laser texturing 333
18.3.2 Analysis of variance analysis of laser-texturing parameters 339
18.4 Problem formulation and optimization with grey wolf optimizer 342
18.4.1 Experimental setup 345
18.4.2 Computational (time) and memory complexity of the grey wolf optimizer and its hybrids 352
18.5 Conclusion 352
Artificial intelligence support statement 352
References 353

19. Budget constrained fairness aware incentive recommendation with uplift modeling using grey wolf optimization

Sunday O. Oladejo, Stephen O. Ekwe, Lateef A. Akinyemi and Denise J. Birabwa

19.1 Introduction 355
19.2 Related work 356
19.2.1 Recommender systems 356
19.2.2 Uplift modeling 356
19.2.3 Budget constrained allocation 357

19.2.4 Metaheuristics 357
19.3 Preliminaries and problem formulation 359
19.3.1 Uplift modeling 359
19.3.2 Problem formulation 359
19.4 Proposed solutions 360
19.4.1 Modeling the casual impact 360
19.4.2 Solving the multichoice knapsack resource allocation problem 360
19.4.3 Computational complexity 365
19.5 Performance evaluation and discussion 367
19.5.1 Uplift distribution analysis 367
19.5.2 Convergence analysis 368
19.5.3 Computational time analysis 369
19.5.4 Total uplift per group 371
19.5.5 Average cost per group 374
19.6 Conclusion 374
Acknowledgment 375
References 375

20. Applications of grey wolf optimizer and its variants in wireless sensor networks

Fakhrosadat Fanian and Mohammad Shokouhifar

20.1 Introduction 377
20.2 Classification metrics 378
20.3 Grey wolf optimizer-based clustering techniques 379
20.4 Grey wolf optimizer-based fault tolerance techniques 382
20.5 Grey wolf optimizer-based localization techniques 385
20.6 Grey wolf optimizer-based intrusion detection techniques 388
20.7 Grey wolf optimizer-based coverage optimization techniques 392
20.8 Discussion 395
20.8.1 The role of grey wolf optimizer for clustering in wireless sensor networks 395
20.8.2 The role of grey wolf optimizer for fault tolerance in wireless sensor networks 397
20.8.3 The role of grey wolf optimizer for localization in wireless sensor networks 398
20.8.4 The role of grey wolf optimizer for intrusion detection in wireless sensor networks 398
20.8.5 The role of grey wolf optimizer for coverage optimization in wireless sensor networks 398
20.9 Conclusion and future work 399
Conflict of interest 399
Declaration of generative AI and AI-assisted technologies in the writing process 400
References 400

21. Comparative performance analysis of binary grey wolf optimizer and teaching-learning-based algorithm for the traveling salesman problem

Wonseh Mulbah and Navneet Himanshu

21.1 Introduction 403
21.2 Methodology 404
21.2.1 The traveling salesman problem problem 404
21.2.2 Grey wolf optimization 404
21.2.3 Teaching-learning-based optimization 407
21.3 Results 408
21.4 Conclusion 410
Acknowledgment 410
References 410

22. A hybrid GWO-PSO algorithm for sliding surface design in sliding mode control of 6R robot manipulators

Oguzhan Karahan and Hasan Karci

22.1 Introduction 413
22.2 Kinematic and dynamic model of the UR5 robot manipulator 415
22.2.1 Kinematic modeling 415
22.2.2 Dynamic modeling 417
22.2.3 Equation of motion 417
22.3 Proposed controller structures 418
22.3.1 PIDSMC structures 419
22.3.2 FOPIDSMC structures 420
22.3.3 TIDSMC structures 421
22.3.4 FOTIDSMC structures 422
22.3.5 Stability analysis 423
22.4 Optimization of controller parameters using the grey wolf optimizer-particle swarm optimization hybrid algorithm 424
22.4.1 Particle swarm optimization algorithm 424
22.4.2 Grey wolf optimizer algorithm 425
22.4.3 Hybrid grey wolf optimizer-particle swarm optimization algorithm 426
22.5 Simulation results and statistical analysis 428
22.5.1 Dynamic performance analysis 429
22.5.2 Rejection of external disturbances 430

22.5.3 Evaluating controller performance under end-effector load variations 435
22.5.4 Evaluating controller performance under white noise disturbances in joint torque inputs 437
22.5.5 Computational complexity analysis 443
22.6 Conclusion 443
Acknowledgments 443
References 443

23. Applications of the grey wolf optimizer in water engineering and management

Mohammad Khoshnam, Hojat Karami and Sayed-Farhad Mousavi

23.1 Introduction 447
23.2 Research method 447
23.3 Application of grey wolf optimizer in groundwater level prediction 447
23.4 Application of grey wolf optimizer in streamflow estimation 448
23.5 Application of grey wolf optimizer in water infiltration estimation 449
23.6 Application of grey wolf optimizer in lake water level modeling 450
23.7 Application of grey wolf optimizer in pan evaporation estimation 452
23.8 Application of grey wolf optimizer in reference crop evapotranspiration modeling 452
23.9 Discussion 453
23.10 Conclusion 456
References 457

24. Optimizing enterprise information system security with the grey wolf optimizer: a novel approach to risk assessment and asset prioritization

Arome J. Gabriel, Toluwalope A. Adebayo and Olakunle P. Mustafa

24.1 Introduction 459
24.1.1 Background and context 459
24.1.2 The challenge of risk in enterprise information systems 459
24.1.3 Meta-heuristic optimization and the grey wolf optimizer 460
24.1.4 Research gap and chapter objectives 461
24.2 Literature review 461
24.2.1 Enterprise information system 463
24.3 Risk management 464
24.3.1 Asset classification 464
24.3.2 Risk assessment procedures 465
24.4 Risk management optimization with the grey wolf optimizer 466
24.4.1 Grey wolf optimizer social hierarchical model for enterprise asset prioritization 466
24.4.2 Grey wolf hierarchical model for enterprise risk optimization 468
24.4.3 Grey wolf optimizer encircling prey model for optimized risk mitigation 469
24.4.4 Conceptual Cost–Performance–Resilience Trade-off Model 470
24.5 Conceptual framework and model integration 470
24.6 Conclusion 471
References 471

25. Application of the grey wolf optimizer to enhance offshore microgrid power management and control including tidal power and desalination

Nour EL Y. Kouba, Smail Haron, Amel Brik, Aimad Boudoucha and Djamel Selkim

25.1 Introduction 475
25.2 Offshore microgrid model 477
25.3 Optimal power management and frequency control strategy 479
25.3.1 Intelligent power management system 479
25.3.2 Optimal frequency control model 479
25.3.3 Grey wolf optimizer 480
25.3.4 Objectives functions 482
25.4 Simulation results 483
25.4.1 Case 1: optimal frequency control using grey wolf optimizer 484
25.4.2 Case 2: with intelligent power management system 485
25.4.3 Case 3: with combined multistage power management system-fuel cell 487
25.5 Conclusion 488
References 488

26. A hybrid grey wolf optimizer and flying squirrel algorithm for single foundation design

Hadi Azizian

26.1 Introduction 491
26.2 Problem statement 492
26.2.1 Quantity calculations 493
26.2.2 Cost calculation 494
26.2.3 Optimization problem 494
26.3 Hybrid grey wolf optimizer 494
26.3.1 Grey wolf optimizer 494
26.3.2 Flying squirrel algorithm (FSO) 495
26.3.3 Hybrid flying squirrel optimizer-based grey wolf optimizer 496
26.3.4 Computational complexity of GWOFSO 497
26.4 Results and discussion 497
26.4.1 Results of hybrid grey wolf optimizer-flying squirrel optimizer on the benchmark problems 498
26.4.2 Results of hybrid grey wolf optimizer-flying squirrel optimizer on the foundation problem 501
26.5 Conclusion 504
Declaration of generative AI and AI-assisted technologies in the writing process 504
References 504

27. A comparative analysis of the grey wolf optimizer and genetic algorithms

Mohammad Jahani Moghaddam

27.1 Introduction 507
27.2 Theoretical foundations 508
27.3 Comparative analysis of grey wolf optimization and genetic algorithm 510
27.4 Experimental design and implementation 515
27.4.1 Sensitivity analysis 516
27.5 Conclusion 521
References 522

28. Enhancing hub-motor performance in electric vehicles: grey wolf multiobjective design optimizer to resolve performance trade-offs

Tohid Sharifi, Ali Jamali-Fard and Mojtaba Mirsalim

Nomenclature 525
28.1 Introduction 526
28.2 Related studies 528
28.2.1 General overview 528
28.2.2 Lack of knowledge 529
28.2.3 Contributions 529
28.2.4 Organization 530
28.3 Initial sizing and power formulation 530
28.3.1 Idealized power calculation 531
28.3.2 Peak back-EMF derivation 531
28.3.3 Geometric definition of overlap area 531
28.3.4 Peak current and slot geometry 532
28.3.5 The complete sizing equation 533
28.4 Modeling and performance (function) evaluation 534
28.5 Required performance criteria 535
28.6 Comprehensive sensitivity analysis 538
28.7 Optimization for the best trade-off 540
28.7.1 The multiobjective grey wolf optimizer solver for the multiobjective design optimization problem 541
28.7.2 The multiobjective particle swarm optimization solver for multiobjective design optimization problem 541
28.7.3 The Nondominated Sorting Genetic Algorithm II solver for multiobjective design optimization problem 543
28.7.4 Optimization platform and settings 543
28.8 Results and discussion 543
28.8.1 Comparative analysis of Pareto fronts 546
28.8.2 Decision-making for the optimal design 547
28.8.3 Comparing the initial and optimal designs 548
28.8.4 Insights for the metaheuristic community 549
28.9 Conclusions 551
Acknowledgments 551
References 551

29. Uncertainty and sensitivity evaluation in joint geophysical inversion using a hybrid grey wolf optimizer and particle swarm optimization algorithm

Kuldeep Sarkar and Upendra K. Singh

29.1 Introduction 555
29.2 Method 556

29.2.1 Forward modeling 556
29.2.2 Inverse modeling 556
29.2.3 Statistical method 560
29.3 Results and discussion 561
29.3.1 Synthetic examples 561
29.3.2 Field examples 567
29.4 Conclusions 574
Acknowledgment 574
Data availability statement 574
Author contributions 574
Conflict of interest 574
References 575

30. Optimized finite impulse response adaptive noise cancellation for improved photoplethysmography signal enhancement using the grey wolf optimizer

Madhava R. Alla and Chandan Nayak

30.1 Introduction 577
30.2 Optimized adaptive noise canceller to enhance photoplethysmography signal 578
30.2.1 Adaptive noise canceller design 579
30.3 Algorithms employed 580
30.3.1 Grey wolf optimizer 580
30.4 Results and discussion 581
30.4.1 Qualitative visualization of adaptive noise canceller effectiveness on photoplethysmography record v100s from the Challenge 2015 training set 582
30.4.2 Quantitative assessment of adaptive noise canceller techniques on photoplethysmography record v100s from the Challenge 2015 training set 582
30.4.3 Computational cost analysis 584
30.4.4 Statistical test 584
30.5 Conclusion 585
Funding 585
Data availability 585
Conflict of interest 585
References 585

31. Multilabel feature selection using grey wolf optimizer and mutual information

Mohanrasu S. S.

31.1 Introduction 587
31.2 Related work 588
31.3 Preliminaries 588
31.3.1 Mutual information 588
31.3.2 Grey wolf optimization 589
31.3.3 Binary grey wolf optimization 590
31.4 Proposed method 590
31.5 Experimental results 591
31.5.1 Datasets 591
31.5.2 Evaluation metrics 591
31.5.3 Comparison methods 592
31.5.4 Experiment settings 592
31.5.5 Results and discussion 592
31.5.6 Computational complexity analysis 596
31.6 Conclusion 596
Declaration of generative AI-assisted technologies 596
References 596

32. Comparative analysis of grey wolf optimizer with other metaheuristics algorithms

Mitra Pooyandeh and Alireza Arianfar

32.1 Introduction 599
32.1.1 Background and motivation 599
32.1.2 Literature review 599
32.1.3 Exploration–exploitation trade-off in metaheuristics 600
32.1.4 Contribution and objectives 601
32.1.5 Chapter organization 601
32.1.6 Mathematical definitions of benchmark functions 602
32.1.7 Properties 604
32.2 Metaheuristic algorithms overview 606
32.2.1 Grey wolf optimizer 606
32.2.2 Genetic algorithm 607
32.2.3 Particle swarm optimization 608
32.2.4 Ant colony optimization 609
32.2.5 Simulated annealing 610
32.2.6 Artificial bee colony 611
32.3 Comparison of algorithms 612
32.4 Experimental results 612
32.4.1 Simulation environment 613
32.4.2 Results 614
32.4.3 Convergence behavior 621
32.4.4 Statistical comparison 621
32.5 Discussion 624
32.6 Conclusion 624
References 624

33. Binary grey wolf optimizer for solving various resolving set problems

Hendy, Mohammad Isa Irawan, Imam Mukhlash and Rinurwati

33.1 Introduction 627
33.2 Problem definition 628
33.2.1 Metric dimension 628
33.2.2 Detour metric dimension 628
33.2.3 Bi-metric dimension 629
33.2.4 Edge metric dimension 629
33.2.5 Mixed metric dimension 630
33.3 Grey wolf optimizer algorithm 630
33.4 Proposed method 631
33.4.1 Application binary grey wolf optimizer algorithm for metric dimension problem 633
33.4.2 Hybrid ant colony optimization-binary grey wolf optimizer algorithm for detour metric dimension problem 634
33.4.3 Hybrid ant colony optimization-binary grey wolf optimizer algorithm for bi-metric dimension problem 634
33.4.4 Modified binary grey wolf optimizer algorithm for edge metric dimension problems 634
33.4.5 Modified binary grey wolf optimizer algorithm for mixed metric dimension problems 634
33.5 Numerical results 639
33.5.1 Time and space complexity 641
33.6 Conclusion and future direction 644
Acknowledgment 644
References 644

34. Enhanced autonomous vehicle navigation using a pure pursuit and grey wolf optimizer algorithm

Mehmet Enes Avcu, Akif Hacınecipoğlu and Harun Gökçe

34.1 Introduction 647
34.2 Grey wolf optimizer algorithm 647
34.2.1 Social hierarchy 647
34.2.2 Encircling prey 648
34.2.3 Hunting 648
34.2.4 Attacking prey 648
34.2.5 Search for prey 648
34.3 Path following 649
34.3.1 Differential drive kinematics equations 649
34.3.2 Pure pursuit algorithm 650
34.4 Pure pursuit with grey wolf optimization 651
34.4.1 Generating path using grey wolf optimizer 652
34.4.2 Look-ahead selection strategy 654
34.5 Experimental setup and results 654
34.5.1 Objective weights in Eq. 34.26 and tuning protocol 654
34.5.2 Metaheuristic configurations and implementation 654
34.5.3 Results 655
34.6 Conclusion 656
Acknowledgments 657
References 657

35. Can the grey wolf optimizer solve daily life problems?

Sayan Nayek and Avishek Dolai

35.1 Introduction 659
35.1.1 Understanding grey wolf optimizer 659
35.1.2 Biological inspiration behind grey wolf optimizer 659
35.1.3 Core mechanisms of grey wolf optimizer 660
35.1.4 Why grey wolf optimizer approaches real-life optimization problems successfully 661
35.1.5 Grey wolf optimizer's strengths and limitations for applied uses 662
35.2 Daily life problems as optimization tasks 662
35.2.1 What is optimization in daily context? 662
35.2.2 Common characteristics of daily optimization problems 663
35.2.3 Why traditional methods fall short 663
35.2.4 How grey wolf optimizer offers an efficient alternative 664
35.3 Applications of grey wolf optimizer to optimization categories 664
35.3.1 Scheduling—worked example 667
35.3.2 Resource allocation:worked example 668
35.3.3 Routing:worked example (traveling salesman problem) 669
35.3.4 Energy management:worked example (economic dispatch) 670

35.3.5 Health planning:worked example (treatment selection) 671
35.4 Numerical experiments and validation 672
35.4.1 Experimental Ssetup 672
35.4.2 Results 673
35.4.3 Discussion 673
35.4.4 Real-world case demonstrations of **grey wolf optimizer** 675
References 680

36. RCGWO: an improved grey wolf optimization algorithm using random weight and elite-based crossover for solving real world optimization problems

Suraj Roy, Apu K. Saha and Sharmistha Bhattacharya (Halder)

36.1 Introduction 683
36.2 Grey wolf optimizer 684
36.2.1 Social hierarchy 684
36.2.2 Encircling the prey 685
36.2.3 Hunting 685
36.2.4 Exploitation phase attacking prey 685
36.2.5 Exploration phase searching for prey 685
36.3 Proposed RCGWO approach 685
36.3.1 Computational complexity of RCGWO 688
36.4 Results and discussion 693
36.5 Conclusion 693
CRediT authorship contribution statement 695
Acknowledgment 695
Appendix 36.1 695
References 695

37. An adaptive hybrid grey wolf optimizer and teaching-learning-based optimization algorithm for team formation optimization problems

Md. Abdul Kader, Kamal Z. Zamli, Zalili B. Musa and Mizanur Rahman

37.1 Introduction 697
37.2 Literature review 698
37.2.1 Early hybridization trends (2018–20): foundation of embedded hybrid grey wolf optimizer 698
37.2.2 Transitional phase (2021–23): transition to domain-specific and adaptive hybrids 698
37.2.3 Contemporary developments (2024–25): intelligent, multistage, and learning-driven grey wolf optimizer hybrids 699
37.3 Mathematical modeling of methods and materials 699
37.3.1 Grey wolf optimizer 699
37.3.2 Teaching-learning-based optimization 701
37.3.3 Adaptive grey wolf–teaching-learning-based hybrid algorithm 701
37.3.4 Computational complexity analysis 702
37.3.5 Overview of team formation optimization problem 704
37.3.6 Benchmark datasets and experimental setup 704
37.4 Results and discussion 705
37.4.1 Performance analysis on IMDB dataset 705
37.4.2 Performance on the DBLP dataset 709
37.4.3 Statistical significance analysis 710
37.5 Conclusion 715
Acknowledgments 716
References 716

38. A concurrent power distribution systems model for demand-supply scheduling using the grey wolf optimizer

Emmanuel Ndidi Osegi and Biobele Alexander Wokoma

38.1 Introduction 719
38.2 Related studies 720
38.2.1 Single point metaheuristics 720
38.2.2 Population based metaheuristics 720
38.3 A concurrent power distribution schedule systems methodology for optimal load scheduling 720
38.3.1 Grey wolf optimizer 721
38.3.2 Neural model based on sparse integer distributed encoded representation 723

38.3.3 The neuronal auditory machine intelligence model 723
38.3.4 Sparse integer distributed encoded representations model 724
38.3.5 The hourly load scheduling problem 724
38.4 Results and discussions 727
38.4.1 Experimental details 727
38.4.2 Results using SEWA benchmark power demand dataset 728
38.4.3 Applying the GWO and GWO-SIDER Approach to the PHEDC power demand dataset 728
38.4.4 Statistical analysis of GWO and GWO-SIDER methods considering the SEWA and PHEDC power demand datasets 731
38.5 Conclusions and future Work 736
References 736

Glossary 739
Index 743

List of contributors

Khalil K. Abbo Department of Mathematics, College of Basic Education, University of Telafer, Tall'Afar, Iraq

Benyamin Abdollahzadeh Liverpool John Moores University, Liverpool, England

Laith Abualigah Computer Science Department, Al al-Bayt University, Mafraq, Jordan

Toluwalope A. Adebayo Cybersecurity Department, School of Computing, Federal University of Technology, Akure, Nigeria

Lateef A. Akinyemi Department of Electronic and Computer Engineering, Faculty of Engineering, Lagos State University, Epe Campus, Nigeria

Ahmet Akkaya Computer Technology, Gönen Vocational School, Bandırma Onyedi Eylül University, Bandırma, Balıkesir, Türkiye

Amel Ali Alhussan Department of Computer Sciences, College of Computer and Information Sciences, Princess Nourah bint Abdulrahman University, Riyadh, Saudi Arabia

Madhava R. Alla School of Electronics Engineering, Inavolu, Beside AP Secretariat, VIT-AP University, Amaravati, Andhra Pradesh, India

Rafik Amara Department of Computer Science, École Normale Supérieure, Kouba, Algiers, Algeria; LTIR Laboratory, Faculty of Electronics and Computational Science, USTHB University, Algiers, Algeria

Alireza Arianfar Independent Researcher, Tehran, Iran

Mehmet Enes Avcu Department of Robotics Software, Milvus Robotics, Ankara, Türkiye

Hadi Azizian Department of Civil Engineering, Mah.C., Islamic Azad University, Mahabad, Iran

Indu Bala School of Computer and Mathematical Sciences, University of Adelaide, Adelaide, SA, Australia

Sharmistha Bhattacharya (Halder) Department of Mathematics, Tripura University, Suryamaninagar, Tripura, India

Denise J. Birabwa Department of Electrical and Electronics Engineering, Kyambogo University, Kampala, Uganda

M. Özgür Bora Department of Airframe and Powerplant Maintenance, Faculty of Aeronautics and Astronautics, Kocaeli University, Kocaeli, Türkiye

Aimad Boudoucha Laboratory of Electrical and Industrial Systems, University of Sciences and Technology Hou ari Boumediene, Algiers, Algeria

Maamar Bougherara LIM Laboratory, Faculty of Exact Science, Akli Mohand Oulhadj University, Bouira, Algeria; Department of Computer Science, École Normale Supérieure, Kouba, Algiers, Algeria

Mohammed A. Boukhalfa Department of Computer Science and Information Technology, Kasdi Merbah University, Ouargla, Algeria

Amel Brik Laboratory of Electrical and Industrial Systems, University of Sciences and Technology Hou ari Boumediene, Algiers, Algeria

Özay Can Department of Electronics and Automation, Recep Tayyip Erdoğan University, Rize, Türkiye

Emre Çelik Department of Electrical and Electronics Engineering, Düzce University, Düzce, Türkiye

Dikshit Chauhan Department of Electrical and Computer Engineering, National University of Singapore, Singapore, Singapore

Ramya Chinnasamy Department of Computer Science and Engineering, Kongu Engineering College, Erode, Tamil Nadu, India

Hedayatollah Dallaki Department of Computer Engineering, Na.C., Islamic Azad University, Najafabad, Iran

Adam Djili Department of Computer Science and Information Technology, Kasdi Merbah University, Ouargla, Algeria

Avishek Dolai Department of Zoology, University of Calcutta, Kolkata, West Bengal, India; Department of Life Sciences, Semiochemicals and Lipid Laboratory, Presidency University, Kolkata, West Bengal, India

You Dong State Key Laboratory of Climate Resilience for Coastal Cities, Department of Civil and Environmental Engineering, The Hong Kong Polytechnic University, Hong Kong, P.R. China

Rafet Durgut Crystalloids, Rotterdam, Holland, The Netherlands

Marwa M. Eid Faculty of Artificial Intelligence, Delta University for Science and Technology, Mansoura, Egypt

Serdar Ekinci Department of Computer Engineering, Bitlis Eren University, Bitlis, Türkiye

Stephen O. Ekwe Department of Electrical Engineering, University of Cape Town, Cape Town, South Africa

El-Sayed M. El-Kenawy School of ICT, Faculty of Engineering, Design and Information & Communications Technology (EDICT), Bahrain Polytechnic, Isa Town, Bahrain; Jadara University Research Center, Jadara University, Jordan

Fakhrosadat Fanian Department of Computer Science, Faculty of Mathematics and Computer, Shahid Bahonar University of Kerman, Kerman, Iran

Aridj Ferhat Department of Computer Science and Information Technology, Laboratory of Artificial Intelligence and Information Technologies, Kasdi Merbah University, Ouargla, Algeria

Sinan Fidan Department of Airframe and Powerplant Maintenance, Faculty of Aeronautics and Astronautics, Kocaeli University, Kocaeli, Türkiye

Arome J. Gabriel Cybersecurity Department, School of Computing, Federal University of Technology, Akure, Nigeria

Farhad S. Gharehchopogh Department of Computer Engineering, Ur. C., Islamic Azad University, Urmia, Iran

Harun Gökçe Department of Industrial Design, Faculty of Architecture, Gazi University, Ankara, Türkiye

Vahid Goodarzimehr Faculty of Civil Engineering and Architecture, Shahid Chamran University of Ahvaz, Ahvaz, Iran

Akif Hacınecipoğlu Department of Mechanical Engineering, Faculty of Engineering, Ostim Technical University, Ankara, Türkiye

Smail Haron Department of Electrical Engineering, Faculty of Sciences and Applied Sciences, Mohand Oulhadj University, Bouira, Algeria

Saad Harous Department of Computer Science, University of Sharjah, Sharjah, United Arab Emirates

Basim A. Hassan Department of Mathematics, College of Computers Sciences and Mathematics, University of Mosul, Mosul, Iraq

Hendy Faculty of Engineering, Universitas Kadiri, Kediri, Indonesia

Navneet Himanshu Department of Civil Engineering, UIE, Chandigarh University, Mohali, Punjab, India

Kais I. Ibraheem Department of Computer Science, College of Education for Pure Sciences, University of Mosul, Mosul, Iraq

Mohammad Isa Irawan Department of Mathematics, Faculty of Science and Data Analytics, Institut Teknologi Sepuluh Nopember, Surabaya, Indonesia

Davut Izci Department of Electrical and Electronics Engineering, Bursa Uludag University, Bursa, Türkiye

Jafar Jafari-Asl Faculty of Agriculture, Civil and Environmental Engineering, University of Rostock, Rostock, Mecklenburg-Vorpommern, Germany

Mohammad Jahani Moghaddam Department of Electrical Engineering, Lan.C., Islamic Azad University, Langarud, Iran

Ali Jamali-Fard Department of Electrical Engineering, Electrical Machines and Transformers Research Laboratory (EMTRL), Amirkabir University of Technology (Tehran Polytechnic), Tehran, Iran

Md. Abdul Kader Department of Software Engineering, Daffodil International University, Dhaka, Bangladesh

Oguzhan Karahan Department of Electronics and Communications Engineering, Kocaeli University, Izmit, Kocaeli, Türkiye

Hojat Karami Faculty of Civil Engineering, Semnan University, Semnan, Iran

Hasan Karci Department of Electronics and Communications Engineering, Kocaeli University, Izmit, Kocaeli, Türkiye

Doaa Sami Khafaga Department of Computer Sciences, College of Computer and Information Sciences, Princess Nourah bint Abdulrahman University, Riyadh, Saudi Arabia

Nima Khodadadi Department of Civil and Environmental Engineering, Pacific Earthquake Engineering Research (PEER) Center, University of California, Berkeley, CA, United States

Mohammad Khoshnam Faculty of Civil Engineering, Semnan University, Semnan, Iran

Hisham M. Khudhur Department of Mathematics, College of Computers Sciences and Mathematics, University of Mosul, Mosul, Iraq

Nour EL Y. Kouba Laboratory of Electrical and Industrial Systems, University of Sciences and Technology Hou ari Boumediene, Algiers, Algeria

Cemil Közkurt Computer Engineering, Faculty of Engineering and Natural Sciences, Bandırma Onyedi Eylül University, Bandırma, Türkiye

Rihab Lakbichi Department of Computer Science and Information Technology, Laboratory of Artificial Intelligence and Information Technologies, Kasdi Merbah University, Ouargla, Algeria

Habib Larian Department of Computer Engineering, Na.C., Islamic Azad University, Najafabad, Iran

Abdelhadi Limane Department of Computer Science and Information Technology, Laboratory of Artificial Intelligence and Information Technologies, Kasdi Merbah University, Ouargla, Algeria

Seyedali Mirjalili Centre for Artificial Intelligence Research and Optimisation, Torrens University Australia, Brisbane, QLD, Australia; Research and Innovation Center, Obuda University, Budapest, Hungary; Faculty of Electrical Engineering and Computer Science, VSB-Technical University of Ostrava, Czech Republic

Mojtaba Mirsalim Department of Electrical Engineering, Electrical Machines and Transformers Research Laboratory (EMTRL), Amirkabir University of Technology (Tehran Polytechnic), Tehran, Iran

Khalid M. Mosalam Department of Civil and Environmental Engineering, Pacific Earthquake Engineering Research (PEER) Center, University of California, Berkeley, CA, United States

Sayed-Farhad Mousavi Faculty of Civil Engineering, Semnan University, Semnan, Iran

Imam Mukhlash Department of Mathematics, Faculty of Science and Data Analytics, Institut Teknologi Sepuluh Nopember, Surabaya, Indonesia

Wonseh Mulbah Department of Civil Engineering, UIE, Chandigarh University, Mohali, Punjab, India

Zalili B. Musa Faculty of Computing, Universiti Malaysia Pahang Al-Sultan Abdullah, Pekan, Pahang, Malaysia

Olakunle P. Mustafa Cybersecurity Department, School of Computing, Federal University of Technology, Akure, Nigeria

Mohammad H. Nadimi-Shahraki International Graduate School of Artificial Intelligence, National Yunlin University of Science and Technology, Douliou, Yunlin, Taiwan

Antonio Nanni Department of Civil and Architectural Engineering, University of Miami, Coral Gables, FL, United States

Chandan Nayak School of Electronics Engineering, Inavolu, Beside AP Secretariat, VIT-AP University, Amaravati, Andhra Pradesh, India

Sayan Nayek Department of Zoology, University of Calcutta, Kolkata, West Bengal, India

Ngoc Hung Nguyen Phenikaa School of Computing, PHENIKAA University, Hanoi, Vietnam; Department of Electrical and Information Technology, Lund University, Lund, Sweden

Sunday O. Oladejo Standard Bank for Lab. for Recommender Systems, School for Data Science and Computational Thinking, Stellenbosch University, Stellenbosch, South Africa

Emmanuel Ndidi Osegi National Open University of Nigeria, Afrıca Center of Excellence on Technology Enhanced Learning (NOUN-ACETEL), Abuja, Federal Capital Territory, Nigeria

Mitra Pooyandeh Center for ICT and Automotive Convergence, Kyungpook National University, Daegu, Gyeongbuk, Korea

Mizanur Rahman School of Computer Science, Western Illinois University, Macomb, IL, United States

M.P. Ramkumar Department of Computer Science and Engineering, Thiyagarajar College of Engineering, Madurai, Tamil Nadu, India

Ramadan M. Ramo Department of Management Information Systems, College of Administration and Economics, University of Mosul Mosul, Iraq

Rinurwati Department of Mathematics, Faculty of Science and Data Analytics, Institut Teknologi Sepuluh Nopember, Surabaya, Indonesia

Suraj Roy Department of Mathematics, Tripura University, Suryamaninagar, Tripura, India; Department of Mathematics, National Institute of Technology, Agartala, Tripura, India

Mohanrasu S. S. Department of Computer Science and Software Engineering, United Arab Emirates University, Al Ain, United Arab Emirates

Faramarz Safi-Esfahani School of Information, Systems and Modelling, Faculty of Engineering and IT, University of Technology Sydney, Sydney, NSW, Australia; Department of Computer Engineering, Na.C., Islamic Azad University, Najafabad, Iran

Apu K. Saha Department of Mathematics, National Institute of Technology, Agartala, Tripura, India

Kuldeep Sarkar Department of Earth Sciences, IIT Bombay, Mumbai, Maharashtra, India

Djamel Selkim Laboratory of Electrical and Industrial Systems, University of Sciences and Technology Hou ari Boumediene, Algiers, Algeria

Nandita Sengupta Department of Information Technology, University College of Bahrain, Manama, Bahrain

Tohid Sharifi Department of Electrical Engineering, Electrical Machines and Transformers Research Laboratory (EMTRL), Amirkabir University of Technology (Tehran Polytechnic), Tehran, Iran

Mohammad Shokouhifar Institute of Research and Development, Duy Tan University, Da Nang, Vietnam

Upendra K. Singh Department of Applied Geophysics, IIT (ISM) Dhanbad, Jharkhand, India

Malliga Subramanian Department of Computer Science and Engineering, Kongu Engineering College, Erode, Tamil Nadu, India

Nguyen Thi Hanh Faculty of Interdisciplinary Digital Technology, PHENIKAA University, Hanoi, Vietnam

Umut Topal Department of Civil Engineering, Faculty of Technology, Karadeniz Technical University, Trabzon, Türkiye

Satılmış Ürgün Department of Aviation Electrics and Electronics, Faculty of Aeronautics and Astronautics, Kocaeli, Türkiye

Mohammadreza Valilou Department of Veterinary Pathobiology, TaMS. C., Islamic Azad University, Tabriz, Iran

Sevda Valilou Department of Medical Sciences, Tabriz University of Medical Sciences, Tabriz, Iran

La Van Quan Phenikaa School of Computing, PHENIKAA University, Hanoi, Vietnam

Nguyen Van Son Phenikaa School of Computing, PHENIKAA University, Hanoi, Vietnam

Nguyen Van Thieu Phenikaa School of Computing, PHENIKAA University, Hanoi, Vietnam

Biobele Alexander Wokoma Department of Electrical and Electronic Engineering, Rivers State University, PortHarcourt, Rivers State, Nigeria

Imane Yeddou Department of Computer Science, École Normale Supérieure, Kouba, Algiers, Algeria

Halil Yiğit Department of Information Systems Engineering, Faculty of Technology, Kocaeli University, Kocaeli, Türkiye

Hoda Zamani Faculty of Computer Engineering, Najafabad Branch, Islamic Azad University, Najafabad, Iran; Big Data Research Center, Najafabad Branch, Islamic Azad University, Najafabad, Iran

Kamal Z. Zamli Faculty of Computing, Universiti Malaysia Pahang Al-Sultan Abdullah, Pekan, Pahang, Malaysia

Farouq Zitouni Department of Computer Science and Information Technology, Laboratory of Artificial Intelligence and Information Technologies, Kasdi Merbah University, Ouargla, Algeria

Mustafa Şinasi Ayas Department of Electrical-Electronics Engineering, Karadeniz Technical University, Trabzon, Türkiye

About the editor

Prof. Seyedali Mirjalili is a leading researcher in artificial intelligence (AI) and optimization, ranked #1 in artificial intelligence on Stanford University's World's Top Scientists list since 2023. He founded the Centre for Artificial Intelligence Research and Optimization in 2019 and serves as Professor of AI at Torrens University Australia while holding distinguished professorships in Hungary, the Czech Republic, and the Philippines. Prof. Mirjalili has authored over 1000 research publications with more than 170,000 citations and an H-index of 150, placing him among the top 1% of highly cited researchers worldwide. His research focuses on developing novel AI algorithms and optimization techniques with applications across scientific and industrial domains.

Notable among his contributions are the grey wolf optimizer and evolutionary neural networks, both highly cited and influential works in the field. His algorithmic contributions have been widely adopted by researchers and practitioners and have achieved significant real-world impact. As an advocate for responsible AI development, Prof. Mirjalili collaborates with industry and government organizations to advance ethical AI applications. He has delivered influential presentations on AI's transformative potential, including a TED Talk exploring the field's societal implications.

Prof. Mirjalili serves as an editor for leading AI journals and contributes to the advancement of both fundamental and applied research. His work has earned recognition from *The Australian* newspaper as a top research leader for five consecutive years, and his insights on AI developments regularly attract media attention, making him an influential voice in the global AI community. Through his research, teaching, and public engagement, Prof. Mirjalili continues to drive innovation in AI while addressing complex societal challenges through practical and ethically minded solutions. For more information, you can visit his website: https://seyedalimirjalili.com/.

Preface

Optimization plays a central role in modern science and engineering. From tuning a machine learning model, designing a control system, planning a supply chain, selecting features, and fitting parameters in energy and structural models, we can formulate an abundance of optimization problems with limited information, uncertainty, and competing objectives. Over the last 20 years, nature-inspired metaheuristics have become the primary tools to optimize such problems, especially in cases where classical methods struggle with nonlinearity, discontinuities, multimodality, and high-dimensional search spaces.

Among metaheuristics, the grey wolf optimizer (GWO) has received remarkable attention because it is simple in concept, computationally efficient, and flexible enough for many different problem settings. The main idea is straightforward: it models the leadership hierarchy and hunting behavior of grey wolves to balance exploration and exploitation during search. Behind this simplicity, however, there is a rich research area that includes mathematical analysis, convergence discussions, algorithmic variants, benchmarking protocols, and an expanding range of real-world applications.

This edited volume, *Grey Wolf Optimizer: A Pack of Solutions for Your Optimization Problems*, is prepared as a comprehensive reference that connects these directions. The purpose is not only to introduce the algorithm but also to show how the research community has analyzed it, extended it, compared it, and applied it to solve diverse optimization problems. The accepted chapters were selected to provide both depth and breadth, moving from theoretical foundations to systematic analyses and then to application studies that show how GWO can be translated into practical solutions.

A major strength of this book is its strong coverage of theory and methodology. The early part of the book establishes a rigorous baseline, including mathematical principles, computational complexity, convergence proof, and performance analysis (Chapter 1). It also covers the evolution of GWO variants with comparative viewpoints (Chapter 2). There are also discussions on theoretical foundations and methodologies (Chapter 3) and in-depth mathematical analysis, dynamic behavior, and convergence proof (Chapter 4). These chapters help you to understand why GWO works, what assumptions are used in analysis, and how design choices can affect behavior in practice.

To understand the state-of-the-art in GWO, the volume includes a bibliometric analysis of GWO research. Chapter 6 provides a structured view of how the field has grown and what major development this algorithm faces since its proposal. In addition, several chapters focus on performance evaluation and benchmarking, including global search performance analysis across variants (Chapter 8), evaluation against advanced differential evolution variants (Chapter 17), benchmarking against leading metaheuristic algorithms (Chapter 32), and a comparison between GWO and genetic algorithms (Chapter 27). These chapters demonstrate GWO's performance in comparison with a wide range of other optimization algorithms on different benchmark suites.

The second half of the book demonstrates the practical reach of GWO through a wide range of applications. There are examples in deep learning and medical decision support, such as binary hybrid GWO for potato leaf disease image classification (Chapter 5) and wrapper-based GWO for diabetes prediction (Chapter 7). Energy and sustainability topics are covered through photovoltaic parameter prediction (Chapter 9); offshore microgrid power management, including tidal power and desalination (Chapter 25); and multiobjective design optimization for hub-motor performance in electric vehicles (Chapter 28). Civil and structural engineering are strongly represented through predictive bridge deterioration modeling (Chapter 10), buckling load optimization of laminated plates (Chapter 12), line sampling for structural reliability analysis (Chapter 14), and hybrid design approaches such as single foundation design (Chapter 26). Materials-related studies are also included, such as solid particle erosion behavior analysis supported by GWO (Chapter 18).

Control and robotics appear through performance comparison of GWO-tuned controllers in functional electrical stimulation (Chapter 11), hybrid GWO methods for sliding surface design in robot manipulators (Chapter 22), and autonomous vehicle navigation using pure pursuit combined with GWO (Chapter 34). This book also reflects the increasing role of optimization in computing, communications, and security, including application mapping onto three-dimensional network-on-chips (Chapter 13); feature selection in intrusion detection systems (Chapter 15); applications in wireless sensor networks (Chapter 20); and enterprise information system security with risk assessment and asset prioritization (Chapter 24). Discrete and combinatorial optimization is discussed as well, such as the traveling salesman problem (Chapter 21) and resolving set problems using binary GWO (Chapter 33).

Additional chapters extend the scope into modern and interdisciplinary directions. These include solving fractional differential equations using GWO with analytical homotopy methods (Chapter 16), hybridization of GWO with PSO for geophysical modeling (Chapter 29), optimized finite impulse response adaptive noise canceling for photoplethysmography signal enhancement (Chapter 30), fairness-aware incentive recommendation with uplift modeling under budget constraints (Chapter 19), and multilabel feature selection via GWO and mutual information (Chapter 31). The book also includes a chapter discussing whether GWO can solve daily life problems (Chapter 35). The volume further presents algorithmic developments such as RCGWO using random weights and elite-based crossover (Chapter 36) and an adaptive hybrid grey wolf–teaching-learning-based approach for team formation optimization (Chapter 37). The final chapters also highlight practical decision-making settings such as demand–supply scheduling in power distribution systems (Chapter 38).

Because GWO is used across many disciplines, this book is written for a broad readership. Researchers can find theoretical discussions, methodological analysis, and comparative studies that may help position new research contributions. Practitioners can benefit from application chapters, which demonstrate how GWO is adapted to handle difficulties of real-world optimization problems. Graduate students and newcomers can start with the early chapters and then explore application areas aligned with their interests. They can use this volume as an introduction to GWO and a map of its current research landscape.

A consistent message across this book is that an optimizer is not a fixed recipe. It is a framework that should be understood well, implemented carefully, and evaluated thoroughly. This book shows that progress in the GWO community has come not only from introducing new variants. It has also been driven by stronger theoretical analysis, well-motivated hybrid designs, and evaluation on demanding benchmarks and real-world constraints. This volume reflects that maturity by bringing together chapters that address the fundamentals, provide comparative insights, and support practical deployment.

Before we start, let me express my gratitude to all contributing authors for their time, expertise, and efforts in preparing their chapters. Their collective work has shaped excellent perspectives that are stronger than any single contribution alone. I also hope this book encourages more work in relevant areas so that the GWO community can continue to deliver reliable solutions for increasingly complex optimization problems.

May this volume serve as a useful reference, a teaching companion, and a source of ideas for your next optimization challenge.

Seyedali Mirjalili

Chapter 1

Grey wolf optimizer: mathematical principles, computational complexity, convergence proof, and performance analysis

Hoda Zamani[1,2], Mohammad H. Nadimi-Shahraki[3], and Seyedali Mirjalili[4,5,6]

[1]*Faculty of Computer Engineering, Najafabad Branch, Islamic Azad University, Najafabad, Iran,* [2]*Big Data Research Center, Najafabad Branch, Islamic Azad University, Najafabad, Iran,* [3]*International Graduate School of Artificial Intelligence, National Yunlin University of Science and Technology, Douliou, Yunlin, Taiwan,* [4]*Centre for Artificial Intelligence Research and Optimisation, Torrens University Australia, Brisbane, QLD, Australia,* [5]*Research and Innovation Center, Obuda University, Budapest, Hungary,* [6]*Faculty of Electrical Engineering and Computer Science, VSB-Technical University of Ostrava, Czech Republic*

1.1 Introduction

Optimization tasks in real-world applications are inherently challenging due to their dynamic nature and the influence of multiple factors. Significant difficulties include high-dimensional search spaces, uncertainties in input parameters, nonlinearity, and restrictive constraints that limit feasible solutions. Furthermore, computational limitations and the trade-off between accuracy and efficiency further complicate the situation. Many optimization problems also involve multiobjective functions that require balancing conflicting goals, making the identification of globally optimal solutions even more difficult. To address these challenges, a wide range of algorithms have been developed, broadly categorized into exact, heuristic, and metaheuristic algorithms. Exact optimization algorithms are highly effective for problems of manageable size, consistently providing the best solution without reliance on approximation or randomization. However, their computational feasibility rapidly declines as problem complexity increases, often exhibiting exponential time complexity. Moreover, they typically struggle to handle noisy data and real-world uncertainties. In contrast, heuristic approaches—such as greedy methods, simulated annealing, and tabu search—offer faster, approximate solutions with better adaptability to uncertainty, though they cannot guarantee global optimality.

Metaheuristic algorithms outperform exact and heuristic algorithms when solving large-scale optimization problems [1]. They are broadly classified into single-solution and multi-solution search strategies, each employing distinct approaches to address complex problems. Single-solution search strategies refine a single candidate solution through iterative exploration of the search space. Conversely, multi-solution search strategies utilize multiple search agents to enhance search efficiency and improve optimization performance [2,3]. Over time, metaheuristic algorithms have progressively advanced by imitating concepts from nature and biological systems. This evolution has produced more adaptive, efficient, and resilient optimization methods, enabling them to tackle complex problems across diverse domains. One prominent nature-inspired algorithm is the grey wolf optimizer (GWO) [4], which is based on the social hierarchy and hunting strategies of grey wolves. GWO replicates the hierarchical dynamics of a wolf pack, leveraging the cooperative interactions among alpha, beta, delta, and omega wolves to navigate and optimize the search space efficiently.

Due to its advantages, such as a simple principle, minimal parameter tuning, and straightforward design, since its introduction, GWO has been promisingly applied in various fields, including engineering [5], energy management [6], industrial applications [7], and medical sciences [8]. These developments primarily focus on the structural refinement of GWO, which is broadly classified into two categories: adjusting control parameters and enhancing its hunting mechanisms. Adjusting the parameter settings enhances the adaptability of the optimization process, promoting an

Grey Wolf Optimizer. DOI: https://doi.org/10.1016/B978-0-443-36624-6.00017-2

effective balance between exploration and exploitation, thereby improving overall performance. Mafarja et al. [9] proposed a multistrategy GWO that regulates the position weights of alpha, beta, and delta wolves. Long et al. [10] developed an exploration-enhanced GWO by refining the position-updating method to accelerate convergence and introducing a nonlinear parameter control mechanism. Some studies focus on adapting the GWO to solve real-world problems without altering its mathematical principles, leveraging its existing mechanisms to address various optimization challenges. Such applications include power system optimization [11], machine learning parameter tuning [12], financial modeling [13], and scheduling problems [14].

Beyond these applications, researchers have aimed to enhance GWO by refining its hunting strategies, making its movement dynamics more adaptive, or developing hybrid approaches that combine GWO with other optimization techniques for greater efficiency and precision. Lu et al. [15] upgraded GWO using a chaotic map for numerical and engineering optimization problems. Long et al. [16] hybridized the GWO with the cuckoo search algorithm to enhance parameter extraction in solar photovoltaic models. Rizk-Allah et al. [17] integrated the GWO with the crow search algorithm, incorporating a dynamic fuzzy learning strategy to enhance efficiency in large-scale optimization tasks. Li et al. [18] enhanced GWO by combining a Cauchy-Gaussian mutation with an improved search strategy. Lei et al. [19] enhanced GWO using the Lévy flight method to boost GWO's performance in engineering applications further. Overall, the literature demonstrates that GWO has continually evolved to improve its effectiveness across diverse applications, with research focusing on refining its search capability to accelerate convergence toward promising regions and enhance overall optimization performance.

Building on this background, the present study first establishes the mathematical foundation of GWO, providing a comprehensive understanding of its theoretical principles, structural design, and operational mechanisms. Next, well-known GWO variants are reviewed, followed by the formulation of movement strategies, offering insights into how wolves interact within the optimization framework. Subsequently, the computational complexity of GWO is analyzed, demonstrating that it has linear complexity O (MaxIt × ND), meaning that the execution time scales proportionally with the population size and problem dimensionality. The convergence proof is then discussed, validating GWO's systematic approach to achieving optimal solutions while ensuring zero probability of divergence. After establishing these theoretical and structural insights, a comprehensive experimental evaluation of GWO's performance is conducted. This evaluation employs the IEEE Congress on Evolutionary Computation 2017 (CEC 2017) benchmark suite [20], which includes unimodal, multimodal, hybrid, and composite test cases to assess convergence behavior and search efficiency for dimensions 30, 50, and 100. For large-scale global optimization, the CEC 2013 benchmark [21] with a dimension of 1000 is also employed. The findings highlight that optimal parameter tuning—particularly for population size, iteration count, and problem dimensionality—is crucial for maximizing performance while managing computational costs.

1.2 Related works

The GWO algorithm [4] features a simple structure with only a few control parameters, enabling efficient adaptation to various real-world problems. Since its introduction, GWO has undergone numerous adaptations, improvements, and hybridizations to boost its performance and robustness [8]. These enhancements help mitigate premature convergence while improving the algorithm's ability to thoroughly explore and exploit diverse optimization challenges. This section offers an overview of the latest GWO variants.

Precup et al. [22] introduced a tuning method for fuzzy control systems to minimize parametric sensitivity using the GWO algorithm. The fuzzy control system employs Takagi–Sugeno–Kang proportional-integral fuzzy controllers to regulate servo system processes exhibiting second-order dynamics with integral components, variable parameters, saturation, and dead-zone nonlinearities. Rodríguez et al. [23] introduced a fuzzy hierarchical operator in GWO, replicating the hunting process with variants including centroid, weighted, fitness-based, and two fuzzy-logic approaches. Al-Betar et al. [24] proposed a natural selection strategy for GWO to address optimization problems. Gupta et al. [25] introduced the random walk GWO algorithm by adding a random walk mechanism for the leading wolves. This improvement is designed to boost the pack's efficiency in searching for prey, allowing the algorithm to tackle continuous and real-world optimization problems more effectively. Gupta et al. [26] presented a memory-based GWO for solving engineering design and thresholding problems.

Yu et al. [27] presented the opposition-based learning GWO (OGWO) to address global optimization challenges. OGWO integrates opposition-based learning with a jumping rate, enabling the algorithm to avoid local optima without increasing computational complexity. Additionally, the coefficient a is adaptively adjusted through a nonlinear function to sustain a balance between exploration and exploitation during the search process. Meidani et al. [28] developed an adaptive GWO (AGWO) that dynamically modifies search parameters by analyzing the fitness history of candidate solutions. AGWO enhances the algorithm's adaptability and efficiency in optimization tasks. By adjusting the stopping criteria based on fitness improvements, AGWO converges more efficiently to an optimal solution. They also introduced an expanded version of AGWO that uses tri-point fitness history to enhance adaptability during optimization.

Ma et al. [29] hybridized GWO with an Aquila exploration method to solve optimization problems. Geng et al. [30] introduced the adaptive search GWO (ASMOGWO) to enhance multiobjective optimization in ethylene-cracking furnaces. ASMOGWO employs a nonlinear convergence factor based on cosine transformation and a linearly decreasing inertia weight to regulate convergence speed. Additionally, the GWO velocity update formula has been refined to prevent stagnation in local optima and boost overall performance. Wang et al. [31] developed a multipopulation dynamic GWO using dimension learning and the Laplace mutation method to approximate optimal solutions for global optimization problems. Edsa et al. [32] designed a cost-sensitive neural network tailored for breast cancer prediction, integrating a flexible cost function capable of handling multiple evaluation metrics. This network utilizes a single hidden layer, with the learning rate and neuron count optimized via the GWO algorithm, thereby enhancing predictive accuracy and computational efficiency. Zhang et al. [33] proposed the elite-driven GWO (EDGWO) to improve solution quality in global optimization challenges. EDGWO enhances the search process by incorporating elite strategies, increasing efficiency and precision. Additionally, it has demonstrated strong performance in selecting optimal feature subsets for machine learning applications.

1.3 Mathematical principles

Mirjalili et al. [4] developed GWO, drawing inspiration from the hunting strategies of wild grey wolves. GWO emulates their organized pack behavior through key phases: establishing a social hierarchy, encircling prey, coordinating the hunt, attacking the prey, and searching for new targets. The GWO initializes the wolf population using a matrix $G(t) = \left\{ \left(\overrightarrow{X_{1D}}(t),\ F_1(t) \right), \ldots, \left(\overrightarrow{X_{iD}}(t),\ F_i(t) \right), \ldots, \left(\overrightarrow{X_{ND}}(t),\ F_N(t) \right) \right\}$, representing the population at iteration t. Each vector $\overrightarrow{X_{iD}}(t)$ corresponds to the situation of the i-th grey wolf in a D-dimensional search space, where N denotes the total count of wolves. The value $F_i(t)$ specifies the fitness score of the i-th wolf at iteration t, indicating its performance in the optimization process. The initial positions for the first iteration are typically generated randomly using (1.1) within predefined search boundaries to ensure diverse solutions for space exploration. A vector $\overrightarrow{r_i}$ is randomly generated in intervals 0 and 1 for the i-th wolf, ⊗ denotes element-wise multiplication, $\overrightarrow{ub} = [ub_1,\ ub_2,\ \ldots,\ ub_D]$ is the vector of upper bounds, and $\overrightarrow{lb} = [lb_1,\ lb_2,\ \ldots,\ lb_D]$ is the vector of lower bounds.

$$\overrightarrow{X_{iD}}(t=1) = \overrightarrow{r_i} \otimes \left(\overrightarrow{ub} - \overrightarrow{lb} \right) + \overrightarrow{lb}, \quad \overrightarrow{X_{iD}} \in G \ \ and \ \ i = 1,\ 2,\ \ldots, N \tag{1.1}$$

Once the wolves are positioned in the search space, each iteration ($t > 1$) activates essential phases, including preserving social hierarchy, encircling prey, hunting, attacking, and targeting optimal solutions. These steps collectively steer the grey wolf population toward more favorable regions in the search space.

1.3.1 Social hierarchy phase

In the natural world, grey wolves establish a hierarchical structure, with three key ranks—α, β, and δ—each representing different levels of dominance within the pack. The social hierarchy phase determines grey wolves' α, β, δ, and ω in wolf population G based on their fitness values. $\overrightarrow{X_\alpha}(t)$ and $F_\alpha(t)$ signify the location and fitness value of the most capable leader, $\overrightarrow{X_\beta}(t)$ and $F_\beta(t)$ correspond to the location and fitness value of the second-best wolf and $\overrightarrow{X_\delta}(t)$ and $F_\delta(t)$ denote the location and fitness value of the third-ranking wolf. The remaining wolves are classified as ω wolves to form a subpopulation $\omega = G \backslash \left\{ \overrightarrow{X_\alpha}(t),\ \overrightarrow{X_\beta}(t),\ \overrightarrow{X_\delta}(t) \right\}$, where \ represents the exclusion of $\overrightarrow{X_\alpha}(t)$, $\overrightarrow{X_\beta}(t)$, and $\overrightarrow{X_\delta}(t)$ from the matrix G.

1.3.2 Encircling prey phase

This phase simulates the encircling behavior of grey wolves using (1.2). The position of the i-th grey wolf in the following iteration, $\overrightarrow{X_{iD}}(t+1)$, is adjusted according to the influence of the leading wolves—α, β, and δ—whose combined position is represented as $\overrightarrow{X_{pD}}(t)$. The coefficient vector $\overrightarrow{A_{kD}}(t)$, is denoted using Eq. (1.3), the distance vector $\overrightarrow{D_{pD}}(t)$, determined by Eq. (1.4), and the coefficient $\overrightarrow{C_k}(t)$ is defined by Eq. (1.5).

$$\overrightarrow{X_{iD}}(t+1) = \overrightarrow{X_{pD}}(t) - \overrightarrow{A_{kD}}(t) \times \overrightarrow{D_{pD}}(t), \quad p \in \{\alpha, \beta, \delta\} \text{ and } k = 1, 2, 3 \tag{1.2}$$

$$\overrightarrow{A_{kD}}(t) = 2 \times a(t) \times \overrightarrow{r_1}(t) - a(t) \tag{1.3}$$

$$\overrightarrow{D_{pD}}(t) = \left| \overrightarrow{C_k}(t) \times \overrightarrow{X_{pD}}(t) - \overrightarrow{X_{iD}}(t) \right| \tag{1.4}$$

$$\overrightarrow{C_k}(t) = 2 \times \overrightarrow{r_2}(t) \tag{1.5}$$

$$a(t) = 2 - t \times (2/MaxIt) \tag{1.6}$$

As iterations advance, the parameters $a(t)$ gradually decrease from 2 to 0, according to Eq. (1.6), thereby reducing the exploration range. This progressive reduction enhances movement precision, directing the wolves toward more favorable regions. Here, t denotes the current iteration, $MaxIt$ represents the total number of iterations, and coefficients $\overrightarrow{r_1}(t)$ and $\overrightarrow{r_2}(t)$ are randomly generated within the interval 0 and 1.

1.3.3 Hunting phase

The hunting phase, described by (1.7), governs the movement of the ω wolves, enabling them to adjust their positions in response to α, β, and δ wolves. The position vectors $\overrightarrow{X_1}(t)$, $\overrightarrow{X_2}(t)$, and $\overrightarrow{X_3}(t)$ are computed using Eqs. (1.8–1.10), while the adaptive coefficient parameters $\overrightarrow{A_1}(t)$, $\overrightarrow{A_2}(t)$, and $\overrightarrow{A_3}(t)$ are derived from Eq. (1.3). Additionally, the distance vectors $\overrightarrow{D_\alpha}(t)$, $\overrightarrow{D_\beta}(t)$, and $\overrightarrow{D_\delta}(t)$ are calculated using Eqs. (1.11–1.13), which define the spatial relationships between the omega wolves and the dominant search agents, ensuring an effective exploration–exploitation balance in the optimization process.

$$\overrightarrow{X_{iD}}(t+1) = \left(\overrightarrow{X_1}(t) + \overrightarrow{X_2}(t) + \overrightarrow{X_3}(t) \right) / 3 \tag{1.7}$$

$$\overrightarrow{X_1}(t) = \overrightarrow{X_\alpha}(t) - \overrightarrow{A_1}(t) \times \overrightarrow{D_\alpha}(t) \tag{1.8}$$

$$\overrightarrow{X_2}(t) = \overrightarrow{X_\beta}(t) - \overrightarrow{A_2}(t) \times \overrightarrow{D_\beta}(t) \tag{1.9}$$

$$\overrightarrow{X_3}(t) = \overrightarrow{X_\delta}(t) - \overrightarrow{A_3}(t) \times \overrightarrow{D_\delta}(t) \tag{1.10}$$

$$\overrightarrow{D_\alpha}(t) = \left| \overrightarrow{C_1}(t) \times \overrightarrow{X_\alpha}(t) - \overrightarrow{X_{iD}}(t) \right| \tag{1.11}$$

$$\overrightarrow{D_\beta}(t) = \left| \overrightarrow{C_2}(t) \times \overrightarrow{X_\beta}(t) - \overrightarrow{X_{iD}}(t) \right| \tag{1.12}$$

$$\overrightarrow{D_\delta}(t) = \left| \overrightarrow{C_3}(t) \times \overrightarrow{X_\delta}(t) - \overrightarrow{X_{iD}}(t) \right| \tag{1.13}$$

1.3.4 Attacking prey phase

This phase represents how grey wolves prepare for their final attack on stationary prey, improving their exploitation efficiency. Mathematically, this is achieved by gradually decreasing the coefficient parameter a, which narrows the fluctuation range of $A(t)$.

1.3.5 Search for prey phase

This step reflects the movement patterns of grey wolves as they spread out across the search domain. The algorithm utilizes the parameter A, which assumes random values and evolves toward 0. This fluctuation encourages the search agents to move away from prey, promoting exploration and enhancing global search efficiency. The pseudocode of GWO is presented in Fig. 1.1.

Input: Number of wolves (*N*), and Maximum number of Iterations (*MaxIt*)

Output: $\vec{X}_\alpha$ as the global best solution and F_α as the fitness value.

1. **Begin**

2. Initializing the wolf population G by randomly distributing individuals across the problem space using Eq. (1).

3. Computing the fitness values of population G.

4. **Set** iteration counter t = 1.

5. **while** t < MaxIt

6. Applying the social hierarchy phase to determine $\vec{X}_\alpha(t)$, $\vec{X}_\beta(t)$, and $\vec{X}_\delta(t)$ and their fitness values.

7. Calculate the value of *a(t)* using Eq. (6).

8. **For** $i = 1: N$

9. Generating random values for parameters r_1 and r_2.

10. Computing A_1, A_2 and A_3 using Eq. (3).

11. Calculating C_1, C_2, and C_3 using Eq. (5).

12. Computing distance vectors $\vec{D}_\alpha$, $\vec{D}_\beta$ and $\vec{D}_\delta$ using Eqs. (11-13).

13. Calculating the position vectors $\vec{X}_1$, $\vec{X}_2$ and $\vec{X}_3$ using Eqs. (8-10).

14. Computing the new position $\vec{X}_{iD}(t+1)$ using Eq. (7).

15. **End for**

16. Computing the fitness values of wolves in iteration *t*.

17. $t = t+1$

18. **End while**

19. Returning $\vec{X}_\alpha$ as the best global solution and its fitness value.

FIGURE 1.1 The pseudocode of the GWO.

1.4 Computational complexity and memory analysis

As presented in Fig. 1.1, the GWO algorithm consists of two main computational steps: (1) initialization and (2) movement (position update). In the initialization step (Lines 2 and 3), first, the algorithm initializes N wolves randomly in the D-dimensional search space using (1.1) (Line 2). This requires O (ND) operations. Then, each wolf's fitness is computed, which depends on the problem-specific objective function (Line 3). Assuming the fitness function takes O (1×D) time per wolf, the total complexity is O (ND). The overall complexity of this step is O (ND).

In the movement step (Lines 5–18), the algorithm iterates MaxIt times, performing several operations in each iteration. Based on fitness values, it identifies the top three wolves (α, β, δ) for the social hierarchy phase (Line 6). In the worst case, sorting the wolves requires O(N log N) time using quicksort or merge sort; however, based on the code, selecting the top three can be done in O(N) time. Then, the value of the coefficient parameter a (t) is calculated using Eq. (1.6) with complexity O (1) (Line 7). The position update for N wolves occurs in Lines 8–15. Random values are generated with complexity O (ND) (Line 9). It computes vectors A, C, and D for N wolves with complexity O (ND) (Lines 10–12). The position vectors are calculated using Eqs. (1.8–1.10) (Line 13). Since these operations are performed for N wolves, the complexity is O (ND) per iteration. The new position is computed using (1.7) (Line 14), with complexity O (ND) per iteration. The fitness of all wolves is recomputed, taking O (ND) time (Line 16). Thus, the total complexity of the GWO algorithm in the movement step is MaxIt × (O (N) + O (1) + O (5ND))=O (MaxIt × ND). Ultimately, the complexity of both steps is O (ND) + O (MaxIt × ND). Since O (MaxIt × ND) is typically much larger than O (ND), the dominant term is O (MaxIt × ND).

The memory complexity of the GWO algorithm mainly depends on storing the positions, fitness values, and auxiliary vectors for the population of wolves. The algorithm maintains N wolves, each represented by a D-dimensional position vector. Thus storing the positions requires O(ND) memory. The fitness values of each wolf are stored as scalar values, which requires an additional O(N) memory. Auxiliary vectors used during the position update step, such as vectors A, C, and D, also require O(ND) memory since they are computed for each wolf across all dimensions. Additional variables, such as the coefficient parameter a(t), consume negligible memory compared to the population and vectors. Overall, the dominant memory complexity is O(ND), primarily due to the need to store the positions and intermediate vectors for all wolves across all dimensions.

1.5 Proof of the grey wolf optimizer convergence

To rigorously prove GWO's global convergence, its behavior is analyzed mathematically using probability theory and monotonic sequences. Preliminaries and notation are defined as follows: Let $\{X(t)\}_{t=1}^{\infty}$ be the sequence of solutions generated by GWO, where each $X(t)$ belongs to the feasible search space Ω. The objective function is denoted as $F: \Omega \rightarrow R$. The corresponding sequence of function values is then:

$$\{F(X(t))\}_{t=1}^{\infty}.$$

The best, second-best, and third-best solutions up to iteration t are denoted by $X_{\alpha}(t)$, $X_{\beta}(t)$, and $X_{\delta}(t)$.

$$X_{\alpha}(t) = \min_{i=1}^{N}\{F(X_i(s))\},$$

$$X_{\beta}(t) = \min_{i=1,\ i\neq\alpha}^{N}\{F(X_i(s))\}$$

and

$$X_{\delta}(t) = \min_{\substack{i=1,\ i\neq\alpha \\ i\neq\beta}}^{N}\{F(X_i(s))\},$$

where N is the number of wolves, and $s = 1, 2, \ldots, t$, with the associated function values:

$$F_{\alpha}(t) \leftarrow F(X_{\alpha}(t)),$$

$$F_{\beta}(t) \leftarrow F\left(X_{\beta}(t)\right),$$

$F_{\delta}(t) \leftarrow F(X_{\delta}(t))$ and so on.

Definition 1. (Almost sure convergence): The sequence {F(X(t))} converges to F* with probability 1,

$$\lim_{t\rightarrow\infty} F(X(t)) = F*, \text{ almost surely}$$

where

$$F* = \inf F(X),$$

the global minimum of F.

Properties of the sequences: The sequence of best function values $\{F_{\alpha}(t)\}$ is nonincreasing by the nature of optimization algorithms that improve or maintain the current best:

$$F_{\alpha}(t+1) \leq F_{\alpha}(t), \quad \forall\, t,$$

and similarly, for $F_{\beta}(t)$ and $F_{\delta}(t)$. These sequences are bounded below by F^*. By the monotone convergence theorem, they converge:

$$\lim_{t\rightarrow\infty} F_{\alpha}(t) = F_{\alpha}^{\infty} \geq F*,$$

and similar to the other sequences.

Lemma 1. (Monotonicity): If the update rule ensures

$$F_{\alpha}(t+1) \leq F_{\alpha}(t),$$

then the sequence of best solution values is monotonically nonincreasing, guaranteeing stability and progress toward the minimum.

Proof: By design, the algorithm's best solution cannot worsen on subsequent iterations. This is a fundamental property of many optimization algorithms; for GWO, the position updating mechanisms and the selection process guarantee this.

Behavior of GWO coefficient parameters and movement toward convergence: GWO employs a coefficient parameter:

$$\overrightarrow{A_{kD}}(t) = 2 \times a(t) \times \overrightarrow{r_1}(t) - a(t),$$

where $r_1(t) \in (0,1)$ is a uniform random variable and

$$a(t) = 2 - t \times (2/MaxIt).$$

Expressed explicitly:

$$\overrightarrow{A_{kD}}(t) = 2 \times (2 - t \times 2/MaxIt) \times \overrightarrow{r_1}(t) - (2 - t \times 2/MaxIt),$$

which simplifies to:

$$\overrightarrow{A_{kD}}(t) = (2 - t \times 2/MaxIt) \times (2\,\overrightarrow{r_1}(t) - 1).$$

As $t \to \infty$,

$$a(t) \to 0,$$

and consequently,

$$A(t) \to 0.$$

Then, the movement equations (assuming simplified form): for the vector $\overrightarrow{X_1}(t)$, when $\overrightarrow{A_1}(t) \to 0$

$$\overrightarrow{X_1}(t) = \overrightarrow{X_\alpha}(t) - \overrightarrow{A_1}(t) \times \overrightarrow{D_\alpha}(t)$$
$$\Rightarrow \overrightarrow{X_1}(t) = \overrightarrow{X_\alpha}(t),$$

for vector $\overrightarrow{X_2}(t)$, when $\overrightarrow{A_2}(t) \to 0$

$$\overrightarrow{X_2}(t) = \overrightarrow{X_\beta}(t) - \overrightarrow{A_2}(t) \times \overrightarrow{D_\beta}(t)$$
$$\Rightarrow \overrightarrow{X_2}(t) = \overrightarrow{X_\beta}(t),$$

for vector $\overrightarrow{X_3}(t)$, when $\overrightarrow{A_3}(t) \to 0$

$$\overrightarrow{X_3}(t) = \overrightarrow{X_\delta}(t) - \overrightarrow{A_3}(t) \times \overrightarrow{D_\delta}(t)$$
$$\Rightarrow \overrightarrow{X_3}(t) = \overrightarrow{X_\delta}(t),$$

since the terms involving $\overrightarrow{A_{kD}}(t)$ and their associated displacements tend to zero when $\overrightarrow{A_{kD}}(t) \to 0$. Therefore, in the final iterations, the wolves' positions become:

$$\overrightarrow{X_{iD}}(t+1) = \left(\overrightarrow{X_1}(t) + \overrightarrow{X_2}(t) + \overrightarrow{X_3}(t)\right)/3$$
$$\Rightarrow \overrightarrow{X_{iD}}(t+1) = \left(\overrightarrow{X_\alpha}(t) + \overrightarrow{X_\beta}(t) + \overrightarrow{X_\delta}(t)\right)/3$$

As $t \to \infty$, $\overrightarrow{X_\alpha}(t) = \overrightarrow{X_\beta}(t) = \overrightarrow{X_\delta}(t)$, then all omega wolves converge to $\overrightarrow{X_\alpha}(t)$. Thus the wolves' positions stabilize around the current best.

$$\overrightarrow{X_{iD}}(t+1) = 3\,\overrightarrow{X_\alpha}(t)/3$$
$$\Rightarrow \overrightarrow{X_{iD}}(t+1) = \overrightarrow{X_\alpha}(t)$$

Thus all wolves converge toward the global optimum:

$$\overrightarrow{X_{iD}}(t+1) = X*$$

where X^* is the global optimal solution.

Convergence argument: The best solutions in GWO form a monotonically nonincreasing sequence. As the coefficient $A(t) \to 0$, exploration diminishes, guiding the wolves toward the best solution identified so far. Consequently, the sequence of best solutions $X_\alpha(t)$ is bounded and monotonically decreasing (or nonincreasing). Therefore by the monotone convergence theorem, the sequence $X_\alpha(t)$ converges to a limit X_α^∞, which we argue coincides with the global optimizer X^*:

$$\lim_{t \to \infty} X_\alpha(t) = X*,$$

The probability of the wolves "escaping" the basin of attraction diminishes as $A(t) \to 0$. With appropriate stochastic mechanisms (random $r_1(t)$), the probability of continuously missing the basin of attraction tends to be zero.

1.5.1 Probability analysis

Lemma 2. (Probability of success): Define p_t as the probability that at iteration t, the solution is not within an ε-neighborhood of X^*. The cumulative probability that the algorithm has not converged by iteration t is

$$P\ (not\ converged\ up\ to\ t\ )\ \geq\ p_0\, p_1 \cdots\ p_t$$

where each $p_t < 1$, and their product tends to zero as $t \rightarrow \infty$. Thus,

$$\lim_{x \rightarrow \infty} P\,(not\ converged\ at\ t\ ) = 0,$$

implying convergence with probability 1.

Theorem 1. (Global convergence of GWO): Under appropriate parameter tuning and stochastic conditions, the GWO algorithm converges to the global minimum X^* with probability 1. The sequences of solutions and their function values are bounded and monotonic. The coefficients $a\ (t)$ and $\overrightarrow{A_k}\,(t)$ diminish to zero, ensuring the wolves settle around the best solutions. The probability of missing the global minimum decreases exponentially with each iteration. The algorithm's stochastic nature and parameter settings guarantee convergence to the global optimum. The convergence proof relies on the stochastic approximation framework—proper parameter tuning is critical for both convergence rate and stability.

1.6 Performance analysis

This section presents a series of analyses highlighting the impact of parameters on GWO performance. It includes evaluating the impact of nonlinear methods on the coefficient parameter $a(t)$, examining the effect of population size (N), investigating the role of the maximum number of iterations (MaxIt), and assessing the impact of problem scale on GWO. All evaluations in this study were conducted on a laptop with an Intel Core i9 processor, utilizing the MATLAB programming language on Windows 10. The benchmark functions from the IEEE Congress on Evolutionary Computation 2017 (CEC 2017) [20] were employed for dimension sizes of 10, 30, 50, and 100. The CEC 2017 benchmark function encompasses unimodal, multimodal, hybrid, and composite test functions, comprehensively analyzing the performance of GWO across diverse optimization landscapes. Additionally, the CEC 2013 special session and competition on large-scale global optimization [21] was used for experiments with dimension 1000. All evaluations were conducted with 20 independent runs for each test case. The results are presented in Tables 1.1–1.5, summarized using key statistical measures such as the average, standard deviation, and minimum values. The bold values in these tables indicate the best (optimal) results obtained among the compared methods for each problem.

Moreover, the overall performance of GWO is assessed using mean absolute error (MAE) as a key metric. MAE, mathematically defined in (1.14), quantifies the average deviation of the obtained solutions from the global optima, providing a precise measure of optimization accuracy. In this equation, the parameter NF represents the total number of functions considered, O_j denotes the global optimum solution, and Y_j corresponds to the best result achieved for the j-th function.

$$MAE = \left(\sum_{j=1}^{NF} \left| O_j - Y_j \right| \right) / \, NF \tag{1.14}$$

1.6.1 Impact of nonlinear methods on grey wolf optimizer convergence

This section analyzes the effects of applying nonlinear methods to the parameter $a\ (t)$. Instead of the conventional linear method defined in Eq. (1.6), a range of nonlinear methods—exponential, quadratic polynomial, logarithmic, cosine, hyperbolic, and sigmoid-based—are considered to measure the impact of nonlinear methods on GWO convergence and performance. These functions are scaled within the range of 0–2. Each of these methods is mathematically expressed in Eqs. (1.15–1.20), offering diverse characteristics. Fig. 1.2 presents a comparative schematic illustrating the differences between the linear and nonlinear methods for adjusting the parameter $a\ (t)$.

$$a_{Exponential} = 2 \times \ e^{-2\,(t\ /MaxIt)} \tag{1.15}$$

TABLE 1.1 Performance comparison of parameter *a* with linear and nonlinear functions in CEC 2017, dimension 30.

Func.	Metrics	Linearly	Exponential	Quadratic polynomial	Logarithmic	Cosine	Hyperbolic	Sigmoid
F_1	Avg	**1.0959E+07**	2.6591E+08	4.7983E+07	2.6616E+09	1.0175E+08	5.0795E+08	5.4042E+07
	Std	5.8091E+08	7.4356E+08	1.0654E+09	3.0277E+09	7.3714E+08	1.0348E+09	7.7684E+08
	Min	1.0959E+07	2.6591E+08	4.7983E+07	2.6616E+09	1.0175E+08	5.0795E+08	5.4042E+07
F_2	Avg	5.5672E+17	1.1993E+17	2.4142E+17	1.8752E+17	1.6663E+17	1.4837E+19	**1.1335E+16**
	Std	2.3461E+29	7.9849E+29	9.7499E+27	3.8584E+33	1.0957E+28	4.0027E+28	5.0403E+26
	Min	5.5672E+17	1.1993E+17	2.4142E+17	1.8752E+17	1.6663E+17	1.4837E+19	1.1335E+16
F_3	Avg	1.6528E+04	1.3723E+04	1.6618E+04	2.7127E+04	1.3356E+04	**1.0095E+04**	1.2627E+04
	Std	7.5075E+03	8.9548E+03	9.6829E+03	1.4441E+04	9.0165E+03	9.0356E+03	7.8740E+03
	Min	1.6528E+04	1.3723E+04	1.6618E+04	2.7127E+04	1.3356E+04	1.0095E+04	1.2627E+04
F_4	Avg	4.8644E+02	5.1063E+02	4.9762E+02	**4.1919E+02**	5.0101E+02	5.5720E+02	4.9703E+02
	Std	6.3143E+01	3.8428E+01	3.4186E+01	2.8921E+02	4.0245E+01	3.8134E+01	2.5091E+01
	Min	4.8644E+02	5.1063E+02	4.9762E+02	4.1919E+02	5.0101E+02	5.5720E+02	4.9703E+02
F_5	Avg	5.5663E+02	5.7424E+02	5.5394E+02	6.0411E+02	5.4921E+02	6.4775E+02	**5.3511E+02**
	Std	3.2586E+01	1.5484E+01	5.2486E+01	2.4641E+01	4.3630E+01	1.9774E+01	3.9308E+01
	Min	5.5663E+02	5.7424E+02	5.5394E+02	6.0411E+02	5.4921E+02	6.4775E+02	5.3511E+02
F_6	Avg	**6.0048E+02**	6.0435E+02	6.0063E+02	6.2283E+02	6.0110E+02	6.1204E+02	6.0075E+02
	Std	2.5707E+00	2.8986E+00	2.3444E+00	9.6956E+00	2.2943E+00	2.2694E+00	3.0685E+00
	Min	6.0048E+02	6.0435E+02	6.0063E+02	6.2283E+02	6.0110E+02	6.1204E+02	6.0075E+02
F_7	Avg	7.9528E+02	8.6540E+02	7.9071E+02	9.3083E+02	7.8122E+02	9.1039E+02	**7.7995E+02**
	Std	4.2430E+01	2.5207E+01	4.7099E+01	5.1739E+01	4.6773E+01	1.8637E+01	3.9666E+01
	Min	7.9528E+02	8.6540E+02	7.9071E+02	9.3083E+02	7.8122E+02	9.1039E+02	7.7995E+02
F_8	Avg	8.4901E+02	8.5502E+02	8.4748E+02	8.9325E+02	**8.4341E+02**	9.1494E+02	8.4881E+02
	Std	1.5567E+01	2.0766E+01	1.8713E−01	2.5878E+01	3.2021E+01	1.5827E+01	2.3720E+01
	Min	8.4901E+02	8.5502E+02	8.4748E−02	8.9325E+02	8.4341E+02	9.1494E+02	8.4881E+02
F_9	Avg	1.0532E+03	1.0178E+03	**9.4924E−02**	2.0779E+03	9.7976E+02	1.1161E+03	1.0035E+03
	Std	2.4256E+02	5.0133E+02	3.5978E−02	2.1083E+03	6.6597E+02	4.5508E+02	3.5007E+02
	Min	1.0532E+03	1.0178E+03	9.4924E−02	2.0779E+03	9.7976E+02	1.1161E+03	1.0035E+03

(Continued)

TABLE 1.1 (Continued)

Func.	Metrics	Linearly	Exponential	Quadratic polynomial	Logarithmic	Cosine	Hyperbolic	Sigmoid
F_{10}	Avg	3.2299E+03	3.0271E+03	3.1580E+03	3.7730E+03	**2.6353E+03**	5.1599E+03	2.8356E+03
	Std	9.4974E+02	9.8793E+02	5.5234E+02	1.9934E+03	1.2876E+03	8.8969E+02	8.7293E+02
	Min	3.2299E+03	3.0271E+03	3.1580E+03	3.7730E+03	2.6353E+03	5.1599E+03	2.8356E+03
F_{11}	Avg	1.2538E+03	1.2689E+03	**1.2108E+03**	1.2880E+03	1.2571E+03	1.3667E+03	1.2137E+03
	Std	2.0298E+02	4.5533E+02	7.3803E+01	2.0578E+03	1.9744E+02	1.9486E+02	5.6633E+02
	Min	1.2538E+03	1.2689E+03	1.2108E+03	1.2880E+03	1.2571E+03	1.3667E+03	1.2137E+03
F_{12}	Avg	**2.6685E+05**	9.3296E+06	2.7946E+06	9.3733E+06	2.1458E+06	6.2451E+07	2.7891E+06
	Std	6.3762E+07	9.2620E+07	5.5031E+07	3.4361E+08	4.4346E+07	5.2323E+07	2.5352E+07
	Min	2.6685E+05	9.3296E+06	2.7946E+06	9.3733E+06	2.1458E+06	6.2451E+07	2.7891E+06
F_{13}	Avg	**1.1546E+04**	1.5373E+06	1.9626E+04	8.9030E+05	2.8245E+04	1.8280E+07	2.4413E+04
	Std	4.4527E+04	4.9830E+06	8.3688E+06	6.3664E+07	4.0276E+07	2.8446E+07	3.7849E+06
	Min	1.1546E+04	1.5373E+06	1.9626E+04	8.9030E+05	2.8245E+04	1.8280E+07	2.4413E+04
F_{14}	Avg	**1.9525E+03**	3.0200E+03	3.1127E+03	2.5978E+03	4.2163E+03	1.4325E+04	2.3119E+03
	Std	1.9913E+05	7.9534E+05	4.6195E+05	6.2272E+05	3.0420E+05	2.4896E+05	8.3412E+04
	Min	1.9525E+03	3.0200E+03	3.1127E+03	2.5978E+03	4.2163E+03	1.4325E+04	2.3119E+03
F_{15}	Avg	1.0352E+04	3.9863E+04	**5.5911E+03**	2.5191E+04	1.3158E+04	8.7637E+04	1.2254E+04
	Std	1.9704E+04	4.5582E+05	3.8955E+05	1.4316E+06	8.6538E+05	6.5492E+05	4.6299E+04
	Min	1.0352E+04	3.9863E+04	5.5911E+03	2.5191E+04	1.3158E+04	8.7637E+04	1.2254E+04
F_{16}	Avg	1.8212E+03	2.0130E+03	**1.7267E+03**	2.5091E+03	1.9272E+03	2.0334E+03	1.9084E+03
	Std	3.1440E+02	2.6702E+02	3.5183E+02	3.3253E+02	2.5614E+02	3.5894E+02	3.5627E+02
	Min	1.8212E+03	2.0130E+03	1.7267E+03	2.5091E+03	1.9272E+03	2.0334E+03	1.9084E+03
F_{17}	Avg	1.7995E+03	1.7914E+03	1.7719E+03	2.0083E+03	**1.7627E+03**	1.8241E+03	1.8007E+03
	Std	1.2547E+02	1.4138E+02	1.2363E+02	2.1644E+02	8.7271E+01	1.1962E+02	1.0013E+02
	Min	1.7995E+03	1.7914E+03	1.7719E+03	2.0083E+03	1.7627E+03	1.8241E+03	1.8007E+03
F_{18}	Avg	**2.3291E+04**	9.7716E+04	5.3642E+04	8.3300E+04	8.5443E+04	7.2238E+04	7.0423E+04
	Std	1.1398E+06	1.2144E+06	8.5906E+05	6.3161E+06	1.6690E+06	1.5546E+06	7.9467E+05
	Min	2.3291E+04	9.7716E+04	5.3642E+04	8.3300E+04	8.5443E+04	7.2238E+04	7.0423E+04

F_{19}	Avg	1.3900E+04	6.6883E+04	**3.9163E+03**	6.4253E+04	6.2845E+03	3.5312E+05	2.0230E+04
	Std	4.3225E+05	4.6674E+05	2.2277E+05	9.8547E+05	1.5608E+06	1.5857E+06	4.2390E+05
	Min	1.3900E+04	6.6883E+04	3.9163E+03	6.4253E+04	6.2845E+03	3.5312E+05	2.0230E+04
F_{20}	Avg	2.1290E+03	2.1833E+03	2.1932E+03	2.2608E+03	2.1610E+03	2.3030E+03	**2.0881E+03**
	Std	9.9086E+01	1.2068E+02	1.4636E+02	3.4509E+02	1.0136E+02	7.2101E+01	1.1193E+02
	Min	2.1290E+03	2.1833E+03	2.1932E+03	2.2608E+03	2.1610E+03	2.3030E+03	2.0881E+03
F_{21}	Avg	2.3507E+03	2.3528E+03	2.3474E+03	2.4018E+03	**2.3427E+03**	2.4152E+03	2.3446E+03
	Std	2.7716E+01	2.0287E+01	1.7052E+01	3.2785E+01	1.8090E+01	1.1412E+01	4.6652E+01
	Min	2.3507E+03	2.3528E+03	2.3474E+03	2.4018E+03	2.3427E+03	2.4152E+03	2.3446E+03
F_{22}	Avg	**2.3428E+03**	2.3951E+03	2.3486E+03	2.7177E+03	2.3729E+03	2.4628E+03	2.3607E+03
	Std	1.4141E+03	1.6605E+03	1.4384E+03	2.1868E+03	1.6847E+03	2.5352E+03	2.0825E+03
	Min	2.3428E+03	2.3951E+03	2.3486E+03	2.7177E+03	2.3729E+03	2.4628E+03	2.3607E+03
F_{23}	Avg	2.6936E+03	2.7263E+03	2.7003E+03	2.8487E+03	2.6963E+03	2.8102E+03	**2.6845E+03**
	Std	4.6254E+01	2.3700E+01	5.9510E+01	6.6391E+01	4.1286E+01	1.7624E+01	3.0982E+01
	Min	2.6936E+03	2.7263E+03	2.7003E+03	2.8487E+03	2.6963E+03	2.8102E+03	2.6845E+03
F_{24}	Avg	2.8789E+03	2.8983E+03	2.8608E+03	3.0073E+03	**2.8500E+03**	2.9916E+03	2.8513E+03
	Std	4.6105E+01	1.6181E+01	6.3206E+01	5.3280E+01	5.3226E+01	1.7286E+01	6.3829E+01
	Min	2.8789E+03	2.8983E+03	2.8608E+03	3.0073E+03	2.8500E+03	2.9916E+03	2.8513E+03
F_{25}	Avg	2.9182E+03	2.9266E+03	2.9065E+03	**2.9062E+03**	2.9097E+03	2.9317E+03	2.9195E+03
	Std	2.6832E+01	2.5803E+01	3.4522E+01	8.0797E+01	3.4540E+01	2.4194E+01	1.7687E+01
	Min	2.9182E+03	2.9266E+03	2.9065E+03	2.9062E+03	2.9097E+03	2.9317E+03	2.9195E+03
F_{26}	Avg	**3.7664E+03**	4.1382E+03	4.1562E+03	5.4759E+03	4.2009E+03	5.1074E+03	4.0832E+03
	Std	2.6770E+02	2.4791E+02	2.2212E+02	7.0508E+02	1.3091E+02	2.1307E+02	4.0044E+02
	Min	3.7664E+03	4.1382E+03	4.1562E+03	5.4759E+03	4.2009E+03	5.1074E+03	4.0832E+03
F_{27}	Avg	3.2104E+03	3.2246E+03	3.2103E+03	3.2950E+03	3.2202E+03	3.2289E+03	**3.2070E+03**
	Std	1.4121E+01	1.1506E+01	1.1841E−01	7.7813E+01	1.4015E+01	1.8932E+01	2.1762E+01
	Min	3.2104E+03	3.2246E+03	3.2103E−03	3.2950E+03	3.2202E+03	3.2289E+03	3.2070E+03
F_{28}	Avg	**3.2436E+03**	3.2653E+03	3.2817E−03	3.3111E+03	3.2722E+03	3.3158E+03	3.2627E+03
	Std	1.4845E+02	4.8493E+01	5.2378E−01	3.7697E+02	4.7038E+01	1.4359E+02	5.8048E+01
	Min	3.2436E+03	3.2653E+03	3.2817E+03	3.3111E+03	3.2722E+03	3.3158E+03	3.2627E+03

(Continued)

TABLE 1.1 (Continued)

Func.	Metrics	Linearly	Exponential	Quadratic polynomial	Logarithmic	Cosine	Hyperbolic	Sigmoid
F_{29}	Avg	3.4607E+03	3.4829E+03	3.4459E+03	3.7183E+03	**3.4337E+03**	3.6663E+03	3.4590E+03
	Std	1.4298E+02	1.1655E+02	1.0807E+02	3.9039E+02	1.1244E+02	1.3816E+02	1.5918E+02
	Min	3.4607E+03	3.4829E+03	3.4459E+03	3.7183E+03	3.4337E+03	3.6663E+03	3.4590E+03
F_{30}	Avg	6.3609E+05	1.0795E+06	**4.2222E+05**	9.2490E+05	5.0343E+05	6.0082E+06	7.5501E+05
	Std	2.0868E+06	4.5553E+06	2.7834E+06	7.2899E+06	3.0092E+06	2.5936E+06	2.4393E+06
	Min	6.3609E+05	1.0795E+06	4.2222E+05	9.2490E+05	5.0343E+05	6.0082E+06	7.5501E+05
MAE		2.1103E+04	3.5882E+04	**1.3974E+04**	3.0730E+04	1.6681E+04	2.0017E+05	2.5067E+04
Rank		3	6	**1**	5	2	7	4

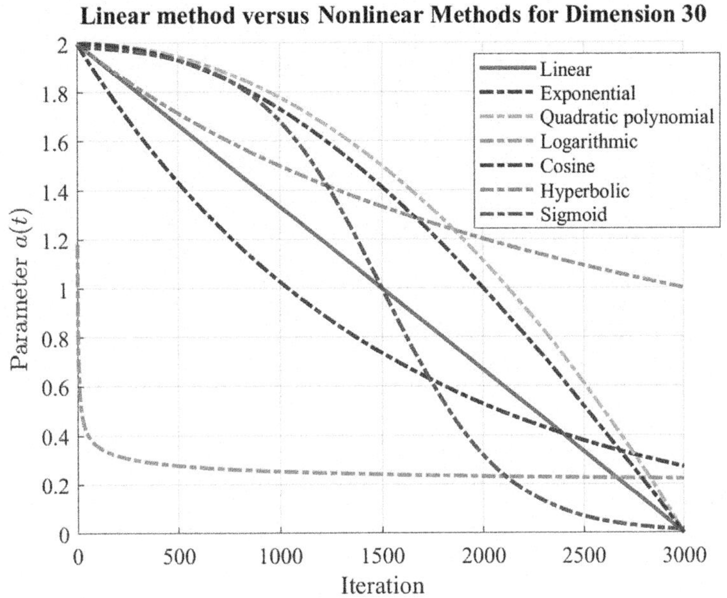

FIGURE 1.2 Schematic of the linear and the nonlinear methods.

$$a_{Quadrati\ polynomial} = 2 \times (1 - (t/MaxIt)^2) \tag{1.16}$$

$$a_{Logarithmic} = 2/(1 + \log(1 + t)) \tag{1.17}$$

$$a_{Cosine} = 2 \times \cos((\pi \times t)\ /\ (2 \times MaxIt)) \tag{1.18}$$

$$a_{Hyperbolic} = 2/(1 + (t/MaxIt)) \tag{1.19}$$

$$a_{Sigmoid} = 2/(1 + e^{10((t/MaxIt)-0.5)}) \tag{1.20}$$

In this evaluation, the parameter a from Eq. (1.6) is replaced with various nonlinear methods described in Eqs. (1.15–1.20). The results, summarized in Table 1.1, highlight the best-performing values in boldface, allowing for a clear comparison of effectiveness. This evaluation aims to determine whether nonlinear methods enhance the convergence efficiency and optimization accuracy of GWO compared to the conventional linear method. Fig. 1.3 provides a visual representation of the results from Table 1.1, illustrating the number of wins and losses for each nonlinear method when directly compared to the linear method in Eq. (1.6).

The results of Fig. 1.3 demonstrate that the linear method surpasses most nonlinear methods, except for the quadratic polynomial method. The linear method consistently outperforms exponential (25 wins vs five losses), logarithmic (27 wins vs three losses), and hyperbolic (29 wins vs one loss) methods, showing that gradual, proportional changes contribute to stable and reliable improvements in GWO performance. With 17 wins against 13 losses, the quadratic polynomial method outperforms the linear method, suggesting that higher-order polynomial scaling enhances adaptability in optimization scenarios. Cosine and sigmoid (14 wins vs 16 losses) methods compete closely against the linear method, indicating their potential effectiveness in specific cases. Motivated by the success of the quadratic polynomial method, the quadratic GWO variant is introduced as an enhanced and refined version of the canonical GWO.

Fig. 1.4 presents a comparative analysis of convergence behavior between the linear and nonlinear methods across multiple test functions. In F_6, the linear method produced the best outcome (6.0048E+02), followed by the quadratic polynomial (6.0063E+02), indicating slight improvements in convergence stability. For F_8, the cosine method yielded the best average fitness value of 8.4341E+02, with the quadratic polynomial performing the second-best average value after the cosine method, with a value of 8.4748E+02. F_{10} exhibited substantial differences in convergence performance, with the cosine function reaching 2.6353E+03 and the sigmoid function achieving 2.8356E+03. In F_{16}, the quadratic polynomial method resulted in lower fitness values (1.7267E+03), followed by the linear method (1.8212E+03), indicating improved convergence. Similarly, in F_{20}, the sigmoid method performed well with a fitness value of 2.0881E+03, followed by the linear method at 2.1290E+03. For F_{21}, the cosine method achieved a fitness value of 2.3427E+03, while

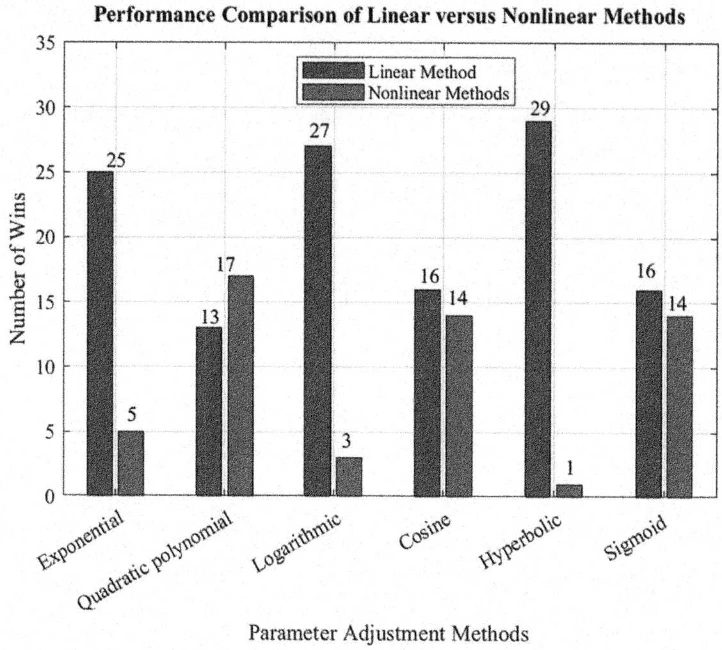

FIGURE 1.3 Comparison of the linear and nonlinear methods in terms of the number of wins and losses.

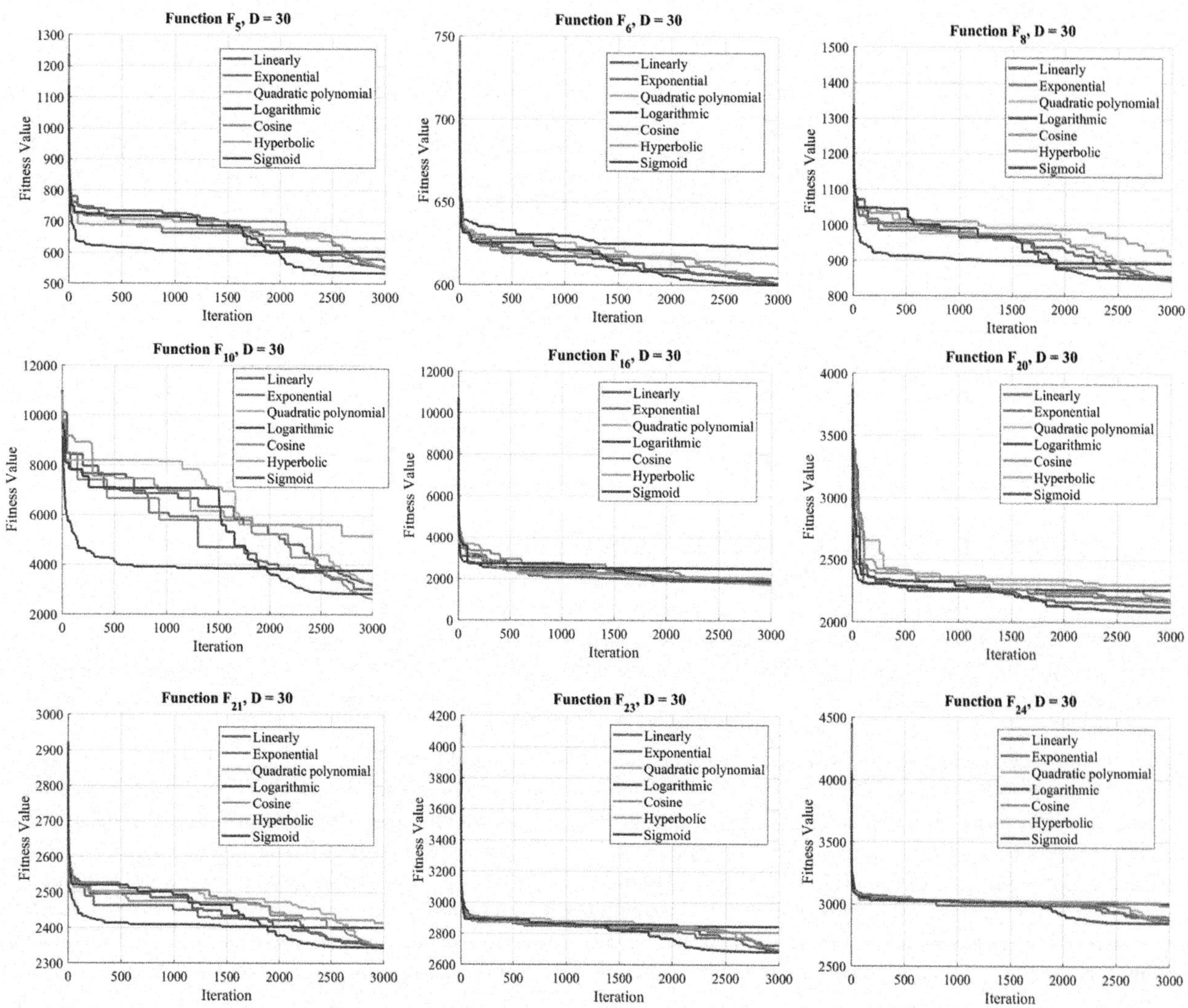

FIGURE 1.4 Convergence behavior of linear vs. nonlinear methods in adjusting parameter *a*.

TABLE 1.2 Performance comparison of GWO with different population sizes at MaxIt=3000 and dimension size 30.

Func.	Metrics	*N*=50	*N*=100	*N*=150	Func.	Metrics	*N*=50	*N*=100	*N*=150
F_1	Avg	5.2263E+07	**1.0959E+07**	1.3294E+08	F_{16}	Avg	2.0072E+03	**1.8212E+03**	2.0039E+03
	Std	8.8788E+08	5.8091E+08	6.0526E+08		Std	1.9177E+02	3.1440E+02	2.0132E+02
	Min	5.2263E+07	1.0959E+07	1.3294E+08		Min	2.0072E+03	1.8212E+03	2.0039E+03
F_2	Avg	1.1191E+20	5.5672E+17	**2.1327E+17**	F_{17}	Avg	1.7819E+03	1.7995E+03	**1.7722E+03**
	Std	3.0395E+33	2.3461E+29	2.5602E+29		Std	1.2096E+02	1.2547E+02	1.0941E+02
	Min	1.1191E+20	5.5672E+17	2.1327E+17		Min	1.7819E+03	1.7995E+03	1.7722E+03
F_3	Avg	2.7274E+04	1.6528E+04	**9.3741E+03**	F_{18}	Avg	5.4139E+04	**2.3291E+04**	2.5162E+04
	Std	6.2467E+03	7.5075E+03	1.1328E+04		Std	4.2847E+05	1.1398E+06	5.8363E+05
	Min	2.7274E+04	1.6528E+04	9.3741E+03		Min	5.4139E+04	2.3291E+04	2.5162E+04
F_4	Avg	5.0365E+02	**4.8644E+02**	4.9470E+02	F_{19}	Avg	**3.9766E+03**	1.3900E+04	9.6045E+03
	Std	3.9858E+01	6.3143E+01	2.5619E+01		Std	6.3654E+05	4.3225E+05	4.2298E+05
	Min	5.0365E+02	4.8644E+02	4.9470E+02		Min	**3.9766E+03**	1.3900E+04	9.6045E+03
F_5	Avg	5.6054E+02	5.5663E+02	**5.3657E+02**	F_{20}	Avg	2.2302E+03	2.1290E+03	2.0931E+03
	Std	2.4044E+01	3.2586E+01	1.8868E+01		Std	1.2299E+02	9.9086E+01	1.5959E+02
	Min	5.6054E+02	5.5663E+02	5.3657E+02		Min	2.2302E+03	2.1290E+03	2.0931E+03
F_6	Avg	6.0151E+02	**6.0048E+02**	6.0056E+02	F_{21}	Avg	2.3457E+03	2.3507E+03	**2.3423E+03**
	Std	3.2164E+00	2.5707E+00	2.0947E+00		Std	1.7921E+01	2.7716E+01	1.3256E+01
	Min	6.0151E+02	6.0048E+02	6.0056E+02		Min	2.3457E+03	2.3507E+03	**2.3423E+03**
F_7	Avg	8.1004E+02	**7.9528E+02**	8.0008E+02	F_{22}	Avg	2.4196E+03	**2.3428E+03**	2.3948E+03
	Std	3.7957E+01	4.2430E+01	3.7348E+01		Std	1.5740E+03	1.4141E+03	1.3933E+03
	Min	8.1004E+02	7.9528E+02	8.0008E+02		Min	2.4196E+03	2.3428E+03	2.3948E+03
F_8	Avg	8.5181E+02	8.4901E+02	**8.4673E+02**	F_{23}	Avg	2.6937E+03	2.6936E+03	**2.6850E+03**
	Std	1.5853E+01	1.5567E+01	2.2010E+01		Std	3.8793E+01	4.6254E+01	2.0168E+01
	Min	8.5181E+02	8.4901E+02	8.4673E+02		Min	2.6937E+03	2.6936E+03	2.6850E+03
F_9	Avg	1.0456E+03	1.0532E+03	**9.8865E+02**	F_{24}	Avg	2.8603E+03	2.8789E+03	**2.8548E+03**
	Std	3.5251E+02	2.4256E+02	3.5678E+02		Std	4.7941E+01	4.6105E+01	4.8978E+01
	Min	1.0456E+03	1.0532E+03	9.8865E+02		Min	2.8603E+03	2.8789E+03	2.8548E+03

(Continued)

TABLE 1.2 (Continued)

Func.	Metrics	*N*=50	*N*=100	*N*=150	Func.	Metrics	*N*=50	*N*=100	*N*=150
F_{10}	Avg	3.2384E+03	3.2299E+03	**2.7224E+03**	F_{25}	Avg	2.9323E+03	2.9182E+03	**2.9174E+03**
	Std	6.8641E+02	9.4974E+02	1.2601E+03		Std	2.9607E+01	2.6832E+01	2.2484E+01
	Min	3.2384E+03	3.2299E+03	2.7224E+03		Min	2.9323E+03	2.9182E+03	2.9174E+03
F_{11}	Avg	1.3382E+03	1.2538E+03	**1.2223E+03**	F_{26}	Avg	3.6942E+03	3.7664E+03	**3.5002E+03**
	Std	7.2484E+02	2.0298E+02	8.9053E+01		Std	4.7270E+02	2.6770E+02	3.7542E+02
	Min	1.3382E+03	1.2538E+03	1.2223E+03		Min	3.6942E+03	3.7664E+03	3.5002E+03
F_{12}	Avg	1.4091E+06	**2.6685E+05**	1.0865E+06	F_{27}	Avg	3.2070E+03	3.2104E+03	**3.2062E+03**
	Std	6.7888E+07	6.3762E+07	7.8935E+07		Std	1.8565E+01	1.4121E+01	1.3979E+01
	Min	1.4091E+06	2.6685E+05	1.0865E+06		Min	3.2070E+03	3.2104E+03	3.2062E+03
F_{13}	Avg	2.6248E+04	**1.1546E+04**	4.4395E+04	F_{28}	Avg	3.3098E+03	**3.2436E+03**	3.2741E+03
	Std	1.2503E+05	4.4527E+04	4.2130E+07		Std	5.9283E+01	1.4845E+02	5.2392E+01
	Min	2.6248E+04	1.1546E+04	4.4395E+04		Min	3.3098E+03	3.2436E+03	3.2741E+03
F_{14}	Avg	2.4994E+03	**1.9525E+03**	7.3720E+03	F_{29}	Avg	3.4814E+03	**3.4607E+03**	3.4703E+03
	Std	4.1760E+05	1.9913E+05	2.1139E+05		Std	1.5511E+02	1.4298E+02	1.5033E+02
	Min	2.4994E+03	1.9525E+03	7.3720E+03		Min	3.4814E+03	3.4607E+03	3.4703E+03
F_{15}	Avg	1.1437E+04	1.0352E+04	**6.3522E+03**	F_{30}	Avg	1.1221E+06	6.3609E+05	**2.7259E+05**
	Std	6.4415E+05	1.9704E+04	4.2204E+05		Std	2.5774E+06	2.0868E+06	3.0752E+06
	Min	1.1437E+04	1.0352E+04	6.3522E+03		Min	1.1221E+06	6.3609E+05	2.7259E+05
MAE for all tests		3.7303e+04	2.1103E+04	8.9865e+03	-	-	-	-	-
Overall ranking across all tests		3	2	**1**	-	-	-	-	

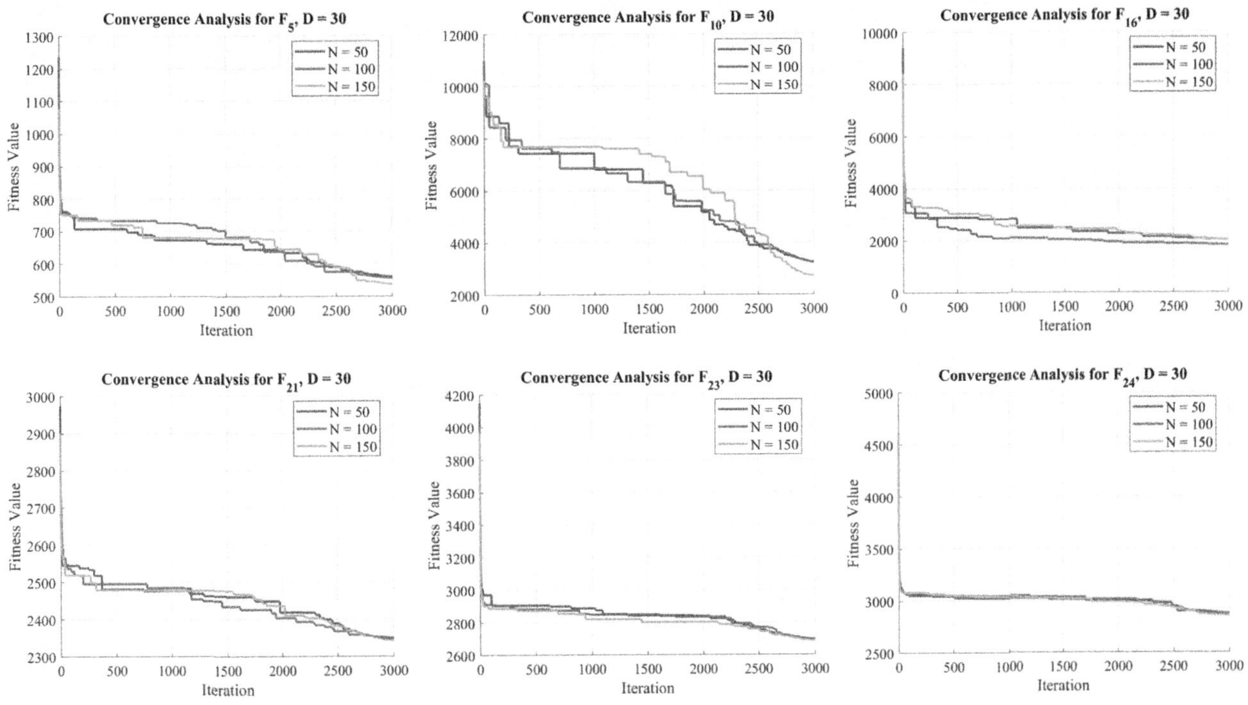

FIGURE 1.5 Convergence behavior of GWO with different population sizes.

for F_{22}, the linear method resulted in 2.3428E+03. In F_{23}, the sigmoid method reached a fitness value of 2.6845E+03, whereas in F_{24}, the cosine method performed best with 2.8500E+03. The last row of Table 1.1 shows that the quadratic polynomial method is the most accurate, achieving the smallest MAE of 1.3974E+04. The cosine method ranks second with an MAE of 1.6681E+04, while the linear method secures third place with an MAE of 2.1103E+04.

1.6.2 Impact of population size on grey wolf optimizer convergence

This subsection investigates the effect of population size on the convergence rate and overall performance of GWO. To isolate this factor, the dimensionality was fixed at D=30, while population size was varied. The tested configurations—50, 100, and 150—present distinct trade-offs between search efficiency and solution quality. Results in Table 1.2 indicate that smaller populations accelerate computation but risk premature convergence, whereas larger populations enable broader exploration, potentially improving global optimization. The MAE values in the last row of Table 1.2 further confirm this trend. Among the tested sizes, N=150 achieved the lowest MAE (8.9865E+03), showing that larger populations reduce error, albeit at higher computational cost. N=100 ranked second with an MAE of 2.1103E+04, while N=50 had the highest error (3.7303E+04). Therefore, population size should be selected based on problem complexity to achieve an optimal balance between computational expense and optimization accuracy.

Fig. 1.5 visually presents the convergence behavior, comparing the performance of GWO with different population sizes. The convergence analysis indicates that N=150 achieves the optimal area with rapid progression. The larger population size accelerates convergence and enhances optimization efficiency by allowing for a broader exploration of the search space. For test function F_{16}, N=100 achieves the best average performance, followed by N=150, with N=50 ranking third.

1.6.3 Impact of the maximum number of iterations on grey wolf optimizer convergence

This subsection explores the influence of the maximum number of iterations (MaxIt) on the convergence behavior and overall effectiveness of GWO. The evaluation employs the formula MaxIt $=(D \times u)/N$ to determine different iteration limits, where u is assigned values of 5000, 10,000, and 15,000. Accordingly, the resulting MaxIt values are 1500, 3000, and 4500, respectively. The dimensionality D is fixed at 30, and the population size N is set to 100 throughout the analysis. This controlled environment enables a focused assessment of how varying iteration counts affect the accuracy of optimization. The results, summarized in Table 1.3, indicate that for MaxIt=4500, the algorithm executes more iterations, allowing for more extensive search space exploration. This extended search time improves the likelihood of identifying optimal solutions in certain problem landscapes and significantly enhances convergence behavior. However, some results

TABLE 1.3 Comparison of GWO performance using different MaxIt, a fixed population size of N=100, and a dimension size of 30.

Func.	Metric	MaxIt=1500	MaxIt=3000	MaxIt=4500	Func.	Metric	MaxIt=1500	MaxIt=3000	MaxIt=4500
F_1	Avg	5.3319E+07	**1.0959E+07**	4.7354E+07	F_{16}	Avg	1.9486E+03	**1.8212E+03**	1.9575E+03
	Std	8.5285E+08	5.8091E+08	6.2776E+08		Std	2.2435E+02	3.1440E+02	2.2680E+02
	Min	5.3319E+07	1.0959E+07	4.7354E+07		Min	1.9486E+03	1.8212E+03	1.9575E+03
F_2	Avg	1.6234E+17	5.5672E+17	**3.1620E+14**	F_{17}	Avg	1.7953E+03	1.7995E+03	**1.7745E+03**
	Std	1.5325E+31	2.3461E+29	3.7796E+28		Std	1.1032E+02	1.2547E+02	1.2731E+02
	Min	1.6234E+17	5.5672E+17	3.1620E+14		Min	1.7953E+03	1.7995E+03	1.7745E+03
F_3	Avg	1.6210E+04	1.6528E+04	**8.9194E+03**	F_{18}	Avg	7.7315E+04	**2.3291E+04**	7.7814E+04
	Std	1.0526E+04	7.5075E+03	9.4291E+03		Std	1.0533E+06	1.1398E+06	8.5173E+05
	Min	1.6210E+04	1.6528E+04	8.9194E+03		Min	7.7315E+04	2.3291E+04	7.7814E+04
F_4	Avg	5.0206E+02	**4.8644E+02**	5.0333E+02	F_{19}	Avg	**4.6104E+03**	1.3900E+04	7.8726E+03
	Std	4.4412E+01	6.3143E+01	3.2198E+01		Std	2.5650E+06	4.3225E+05	3.8076E+05
	Min	5.0206E+02	4.8644E+02	5.0333E+02		Min	4.6104E+03	1.3900E+04	7.8726E+03
F_5	Avg	5.6569E+02	5.5663E+02	**5.5182E+02**	F_{20}	Avg	2.1763E+03	**2.1290E+03**	2.2106E+03
	Std	2.8438E+01	3.2586E+01	2.8052E+01		Std	1.0916E+02	9.9086E+01	1.1079E+02
	Min	5.6569E+02	5.5663E+02	5.5182E+02		Min	2.1763E+03	2.1290E+03	2.2106E+03
F_6	Avg	6.0102E+02	**6.0048E+02**	6.0081E+02	F_{21}	Avg	2.3500E+03	2.3507E+03	**2.3389E+03**
	Std	1.9865E+00	2.5707E+00	1.8279E+00		Std	1.6497E+01	2.7716E+01	1.5041E+01
	Min	6.0102E+02	6.0048E+02	6.0081E+02		Min	2.3500E+03	2.3507E+03	2.3389E+03
F_7	Avg	**7.8781E+02**	7.9528E+02	7.8973E+02	F_{22}	Avg	2.4179E+03	**2.3428E+03**	2.4423E+03
	Std	4.5059E+01	4.2430E+01	3.5105E+01		Std	1.4112E+03	1.4141E+03	1.5336E+03
	Min	7.8781E+02	7.9528E+02	7.8973E+02		Min	2.4179E+03	2.3428E+03	2.4423E+03
F_8	Avg	**8.4858E+02**	8.4901E+02	8.4953E+02	F_{23}	Avg	2.6947E+03	2.6936E+03	**2.6883E+03**
	Std	1.5421E+01	1.5567E+01	1.5233E+01		Std	3.5692E+01	4.6254E+01	3.1500E+01
	Min	8.4858E+02	8.4901E+02	8.4953E+02		Min	2.6947E+03	2.6936E+03	2.6883E+03
F_9	Avg	9.7588E+02	1.0532E+03	**9.3671E+02**	F_{24}	Avg	**2.8449E+03**	2.8789E+03	2.8549E+03
	Std	4.7401E+02	2.4256E+02	2.5479E+02		Std	4.4656E+01	4.6105E+01	3.5858E+01
	Min	9.7588E+02	1.0532E+03	9.3671E+02		Min	2.8449E+03	2.8789E+03	2.8549E+03

F_{10}	Avg	3.5021E+03	3.2299E+03	**2.6007E+03**	F_{25}	Avg	2.9208E+03	2.9182E+03	**2.9127E+03**
	Std	1.1991E+03	9.4974E+02	6.9965E+02		Std	2.1485E+01	2.6832E+01	2.2828E+01
	Min	3.5021E+03	3.2299E+03	2.6007E+03		Min	2.9208E+03	2.9182E+03	2.9127E+03
F_{11}	Avg	1.2933E+03	1.2538E+03	**1.2411E+03**	F_{26}	Avg	4.0409E+03	3.7664E+03	**3.5179E+03**
	Std	2.3518E+02	2.0298E+02	7.7598E+02		Std	2.8117E+02	2.6770E+02	2.8714E+02
	Min	1.2933E+03	1.2538E+03	1.2411E+03		Min	4.0409E+03	3.7664E+03	3.5179E+03
F_{12}	Avg	1.4338E+06	**2.6685E+05**	1.7849E+06	F_{27}	Avg	**3.2064E+03**	3.2104E+03	3.2070E+03
	Std	4.9078E+07	6.3762E+07	7.9440E+07		Std	1.8368E+01	1.4121E+01	1.0736E+01
	Min	1.4338E+06	2.6685E+05	1.7849E+06		Min	3.2064E+03	3.2104E+03	3.2070E+03
F_{13}	Avg	2.9958E+04	**1.1546E+04**	2.0098E+04	F_{28}	Avg	3.2808E+03	3.2436E+03	**3.2435E+03**
	Std	6.2404E+07	4.4527E+04	9.1413E+04		Std	6.7816E+01	1.4845E+02	5.5546E+01
	Min	2.9958E+04	1.1546E+04	2.0098E+04		Min	3.2808E+03	3.2436E+03	3.2435E+03
F_{14}	Avg	7.2829E+03	**1.9525E+03**	4.6875E+03	F_{29}	Avg	3.4868E+03	3.4607E+03	**3.3988E+03**
	Std	2.8925E+05	1.9913E+05	2.1830E+05		Std	1.1926E+02	1.4298E+02	1.6041E+02
	Min	7.2829E+03	1.9525E+03	4.6875E+03		Min	3.4868E+03	3.4607E+03	3.3988E+03
F_{15}	Avg	1.6363E+04	1.0352E+04	**7.9394E+03**	F_{30}	Avg	4.0886E+05	6.3609E+05	**1.8488E+05**
	Std	4.8131E+05	1.9704E+04	3.4050E+04		Std	2.6692E+06	2.0868E+06	4.1682E+06
	Min	1.6363E+04	1.0352E+04	7.9394E+03		Min	4.0886E+05	6.3609E+05	1.8488E+05
MAE for all tests		2.1103e+04	1.3529e+04	6.0626e+03	-	-	-	-	-
Overall ranking across all tests		3	2	1	-	-	-	-	-

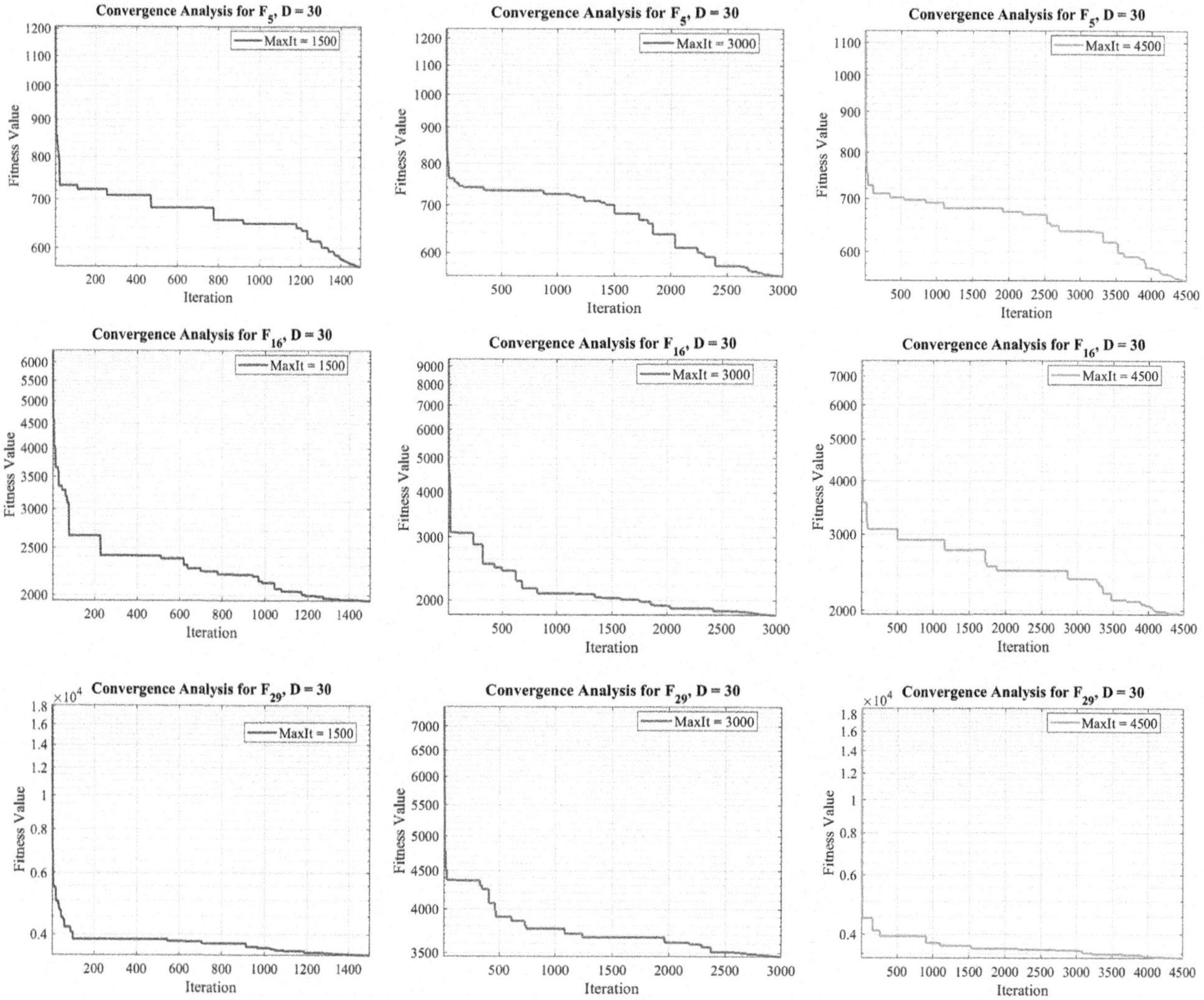

FIGURE 1.6 Convergence behavior of the GWO under various iteration settings.

indicate that GWO struggles with local optima, even with increased iterations. In contrast, MaxIt=3000 ranks second in performance, striking a balance between computational cost and optimization accuracy. It provides sufficient iterations for compelling exploration while mitigating excessive resource consumption. Meanwhile, a lower MaxIt=1500 accelerates execution and reduces the computational burden, making it ideal for time-sensitive applications. However, this lower iteration limit introduces a higher risk of premature convergence, leading to suboptimal solutions due to insufficient search depth.

Fig. 1.6 compares the convergence analysis for each MaxIt in evaluating the performance of GWO. The convergence trajectory demonstrates that, in all three cases, the solutions converge toward the minimum with nearly identical slopes. A higher MaxIt allows more extensive exploration of the search space, increasing the likelihood of finding an optimal solution and reducing the risk of stagnation. Conversely, a lower MaxIt accelerates the optimization process, significantly reducing computational cost.. However, it carries the risk of premature convergence, which can limit performance and lead to suboptimal outcomes.

1.6.4 Impact of problem scale on grey wolf optimizer

This evaluation is conducted on the CEC 2017 benchmark suite [20] with dimensions 10, 30, 50, and 100, as well as on the CEC'2013 [21] with dimension 1000. The maximum number of iterations is set to $(D \times 10^4)/N$ for the CEC 2017 benchmark suite and to 5000 for CEC'2013. For all tests, the population size was fixed at 100, and the results were reported as the average, standard deviation, and minimum over 20 independent runs.

TABLE 1.4 GWO results in solving CEC 2017 test functions for dimension size: 10, 30, 50, and 100.

Func.	Metrics	*D*=10	*D*=30	*D*=50	D=100	Func.	Metrics	*D*=10	*D*=30	D=50	D=100
F_1	Avg	1.8696E+03	1.0959E+07	2.1751E+09	1.8378E+10	F_{16}	Avg	1.6169E+03	1.8212E+03	2.2194E+03	4.2658E+03
	Std	5.1190E+05	5.8091E+08	1.8707E+09	8.7866E+09		Std	1.0560E+02	3.1440E+02	2.8661E+02	7.5759E+02
	Min	1.8696E+03	1.0959E+07	2.1751E+09	1.8378E+10		Min	1.6169E+03	1.8212E+03	2.2194E+03	4.2658E+03
F_2	Avg	2.6400E+02	5.5672E+17	1.3183E+41	6.3514E+97	F_{17}	Avg	1.7205E+03	1.7995E+03	2.1042E+03	3.8421E+03
	Std	1.5036E+07	2.3461E+29	3.7529E+50	8.6531E+121		Std	3.5340E+01	1.2547E+02	3.5371E+02	4.3484E+02
	Min	2.6400E+02	5.5672E+17	1.3183E+41	6.3514E+97		Min	1.7205E+03	1.7995E+03	2.1042E+03	3.8421E+03
F_3	Avg	3.0823E+02	1.6528E+04	4.1351E+04	1.5286E+05	F_{18}	Avg	2.7442E+03	2.3291E+04	3.2282E+05	1.1001E+06
	Std	1.4810E+03	7.5075E+03	1.4400E+04	2.1463E+04		Std	1.6112E+04	1.1398E+06	2.6218E+06	1.9311E+06
	Min	3.0823E+02	1.6528E+04	4.1351E+04	1.5286E+05		Min	2.7442E+03	2.3291E+04	3.2282E+05	1.1001E+06
F_4	Avg	4.0017E+02	4.8644E+02	6.7763E+02	1.6105E+03	F_{19}	Avg	1.9134E+03	1.3900E+04	7.8056E+04	7.5385E+05
	Std	1.9845E+01	6.3143E+01	2.1179E+02	7.8574E+02		Std	5.2751E+03	4.3225E+05	6.9276E+06	2.3453E+08
	Min	4.0017E+02	4.8644E+02	6.7763E+02	1.6105E+03		Min	1.9134E+03	1.3900E+04	7.8056E+04	7.5385E+05
F_5	Avg	5.0201E+02	5.5663E+02	6.1721E+02	9.5940E+02	F_{20}	Avg	2.0228E+03	2.1290E+03	2.4712E+03	3.3373E+03
	Std	6.0331E+00	3.2586E+01	3.5509E+01	4.9486E+01		Std	4.5345E+01	9.9086E+01	1.9834E+02	5.1943E+02
	Min	5.0201E+02	5.5663E+02	6.1721E+02	9.5940E+02		Min	2.0228E+03	2.1290E+03	2.4712E+03	3.3373E+03
F_6	Avg	6.0002E+02	6.0048E+02	6.0587E+02	6.1968E+02	F_{21}	Avg	2.2009E+03	2.3507E+03	2.3838E+03	2.7463E+03
	Std	3.5617E-01	2.5707E+00	2.7319E+00	3.2005E+00		Std	4.5677E+01	2.7716E+01	3.7575E+01	6.0564E+01
	Min	6.0002E+02	6.0048E+02	6.0587E+02	6.1968E+02		Min	2.2009E+03	2.3507E+03	2.3838E+03	2.7463E+03
F_7	Avg	7.0667E+02	7.9528E+02	9.1479E+02	1.5885E+03	F_{22}	Avg	2.2164E+03	2.3428E+03	6.8305E+03	1.3746E+04
	Std	1.0081E+01	4.2430E+01	4.6056E+01	8.4223E+01		Std	2.1141E+01	1.4141E+03	1.9313E+03	3.2614E+03
	Min	7.0667E+02	7.9528E+02	9.1479E+02	1.5885E+03		Min	2.2164E+03	2.3428E+03	6.8305E+03	1.3746E+04
F_8	Avg	8.0502E+02	8.4901E+02	9.4226E+02	1.2086E+03	F_{23}	Avg	2.6039E+03	2.6936E+03	2.8213E+03	3.2552E+03
	Std	5.7339E+00	1.5567E+01	2.6911E+01	5.1622E+01		Std	6.0581E+00	4.6254E+01	6.5937E+01	6.7013E+01
	Min	8.0502E+02	8.4901E+02	9.4226E+02	1.2086E+03		Min	2.6039E+03	2.6936E+03	2.8213E+03	3.2552E+03
F_9	Avg	9.0007E+02	1.0532E+03	2.2288E+03	1.1347E+04	F_{24}	Avg	2.5182E+03	2.8789E+03	3.0218E+03	3.6466E+03
	Std	1.7574E+01	2.4256E+02	3.0698E+03	1.0023E+04		Std	5.1239E+01	4.6105E+01	9.9786E+01	1.2398E+02

(Continued)

TABLE 1.4 (Continued)

Func.	Metrics	*D*=10	*D*=30	*D*=50	D=100	Func.	Metrics	*D*=10	*D*=30	D=50	D=100
	Min	9.0007E+02	1.0532E+03	2.2288E+03	1.1347E+04		Min	2.5182E+03	2.8789E+03	3.0218E+03	3.6466E+03
F_{10}	Avg	1.1381E+03	3.2299E+03	5.2060E+03	1.1534E+04	F_{25}	Avg	2.8980E+03	2.9182E+03	3.0632E+03	4.5549E+03
	Std	3.1288E+02	9.4974E+02	6.2579E+02	4.1630E+03		Std	1.6625E+01	2.6832E+01	9.4156E+01	4.3337E+02
	Min	1.1381E+03	3.2299E+03	5.2060E+03	1.1534E+04		Min	2.8980E+03	2.9182E+03	3.0632E+03	4.5549E+03
F_{11}	Avg	1.1038E+03	1.2538E+03	1.5986E+03	2.4827E+04	F_{26}	Avg	2.9001E+03	3.7664E+03	4.9600E+03	1.0812E+04
	Std	3.0404E+01	2.0298E+02	1.3818E+03	9.0024E+03		Std	2.0239E+02	2.6770E+02	5.8526E+02	8.6420E+02
	Min	1.1038E+03	1.2538E+03	1.5986E+03	2.4827E+04		Min	2.9001E+03	3.7664E+03	4.9600E+03	1.0812E+04
F_{12}	Avg	4.5032E+03	2.6685E+05	2.5628E+07	1.6130E+09	F_{27}	Avg	3.0898E+03	3.2104E+03	3.3500E+03	3.6233E+03
	Std	7.8239E+05	6.3762E+07	5.6007E+08	4.1453E+09		Std	2.6280E+00	1.4121E+01	7.9073E+01	9.0660E+01
	Min	4.5032E+03	2.6685E+05	2.5628E+07	1.6130E+09		Min	3.0898E+03	3.2104E+03	3.3500E+03	3.6233E+03
F_{13}	Avg	1.8637E+03	1.1546E+04	5.2359E+04	1.1980E+07	F_{28}	Avg	3.1689E+03	3.2436E+03	3.3996E+03	4.9046E+03
	Std	7.5275E+03	4.4527E+04	9.1568E+07	3.6267E+08		Std	9.7287E+01	1.4845E+02	2.6333E+02	1.0629E+03
	Min	1.8637E+03	1.1546E+04	5.2359E+04	1.1980E+07		Min	3.1689E+03	3.2436E+03	3.3996E+03	4.9046E+03
F_{14}	Avg	1.4486E+03	1.9525E+03	3.3455E+04	7.6285E+05	F_{29}	Avg	3.1449E+03	3.4607E+03	3.8344E+03	6.1789E+03
	Std	1.0829E+03	1.9913E+05	4.9519E+05	2.0522E+06		Std	1.6923E+01	1.4298E+02	2.6157E+02	5.5567E+02
	Min	1.4486E+03	1.9525E+03	3.3455E+04	7.6285E+05		Min	3.1449E+03	3.4607E+03	3.8344E+03	6.1789E+03
F_{15}	Avg	1.5419E+03	1.0352E+04	1.9348E+04	3.1184E+04	F_{30}	Avg	4.3118E+03	6.3609E+05	3.3454E+07	7.9023E+07
	Std	1.7340E+03	1.9704E+04	1.9235E+07	1.4991E+08		Std	7.6135E+05	2.0868E+06	2.9751E+07	2.6794E+08
	Min	1.5419E+03	1.0352E+04	1.9348E+04	3.1184E+04		Min	4.3118E+03	6.3609E+05	3.3454E+07	7.9023E+07
MAE for all test functions		43.7264	2.1103e+04	1.1150e+06	2.6340e+06	-	-	-	-	-	-

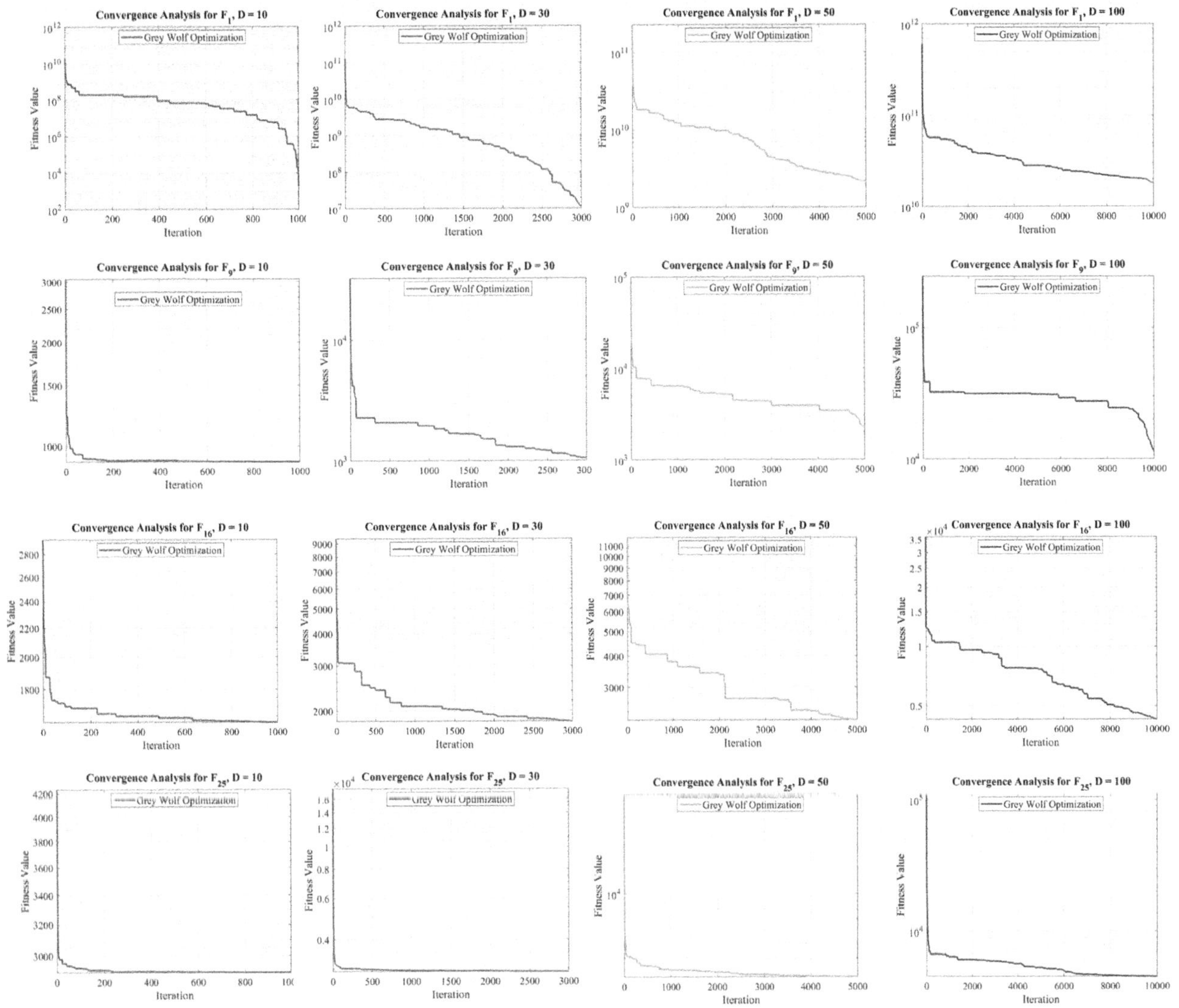

FIGURE 1.7 Convergence behavior of the GWO across different dimensions.

The CEC 2017 benchmark suite results presented in Table 1.4 highlight the critical influence of problem scale on GWO's convergence behavior. As a problem's dimensionality increases, the complexity of the search space grows, making it progressively more challenging for GWO to locate optimal solutions efficiently, particularly in highly complex cases such as F_2 and F_{12}. The MAE for each dimension, presented in the last row of Table 1.4, highlights the increasing complexity of optimization as dimensionality grows. For D=10, the MAE is 43.7264, indicating a relatively low error. As the dimensionality increases, the error rises significantly, with D=30 reaching 2.1103×10^4, followed by D=50 at 1.1150×10^6, and D=100 at 2.6340×10^6. This demonstrates that higher-dimensional problems introduce greater complexity, often leading to a decrease in the performance of GWO. Fig. 1.7 visually illustrates GWO's convergence behavior across different problem scales, with dimensions 10, 30, 50, and 100. The convergence curves demonstrate GWO's effectiveness in searching for optimal solutions, where a sharp decline indicates rapid convergence, while a gradual descent reflects steady progress across iterations. However, GWO's performance significantly declines as dimensionality increases, suggesting that higher-dimensional problems introduce challenges in maintaining search efficiency and solution accuracy for GWO.

Table 1.5 presents the CEC 2013 results, where functions F_1–F_{12} and F_{15} are evaluated in 1000 dimensions, while functions F_{13} and F_{14} are evaluated in 905 dimensions. The global optimum solution for each test function is 0. The last row of the table shows the overall MAE of GWO across all tests, which is 1.2789×10^{12}. These results highlight the limitations of GWO in handling very high-dimensional optimization tasks.

TABLE 1.5 GWO results in solving the CEC 2013 test functions for dimension 1000.

Func.	Metrics	*D*=1000	Func.	*D*=1000	Func.	*D*=1000
F_1	Avg	3.2510E+10	F_6	5.2891E+05	F_{11}	9.3244E+11
	Std	3.8449E+09		6.2338E+04		6.6746E+11
	Min	3.2510E+10		5.2891E+05		9.3244E+11
F_2	Avg	2.7146E+04	F_7	3.3195E+09	F_{12}	8.8513E+11
	Std	6.9689E+02		3.6040E+09		2.3845E+10
	Min	2.7146E+04		3.3195E+09		8.8513E+11
F_3	Avg	2.0432E+01	F_8	2.0616E+15	F_{13}	2.3545E+11
	Std	3.5408E-02		6.3780E+15		1.4787E+11
	Min	2.0432E+01		2.0616E+15		2.3545E+11
F_4	Avg	3.4801E+11	F_9	5.1874E+08	F_{14}	1.3368E+12
	Std	1.7885E+11		6.1748E+07		4.5715E+11
	Min	3.4801E+11		5.1874E+08		1.3368E+12
F_5	Avg	4.7770E+06	F_{10}	8.8055E+06	F_{15}	1.9184E+13
	Std	1.2099E+06		6.2358E+06		9.8830E+12
	Min	4.7770E+06		8.8055E+06		1.9184E+13
MAE for all tests		1.2789e+12	—	—	—	—

1.7 Conclusion

GWO is one of the most widely used optimizers, recognized for its adaptability in solving diverse problems across single-objective, multiobjective, binary, and continuous domains. The study first outlines the mathematical foundation of GWO, demonstrating how omega wolves are guided toward optimal solutions under the leadership of alpha, beta, and delta wolves. Following this, it examines GWO's performance by analyzing key factors, including computational complexity, proof of convergence, the impact of nonlinear methods on parameter tuning, population size, maximum iterations, and scalability. The findings indicate that GWO's computational complexity is O (MaxIt × ND), meaning its computational cost increases linearly with the number of search agents (N), the dimensionality of the optimization problem, and the maximum number of iterations. The findings from the convergence proof further validate GWO's systematic approach to achieving optimal solutions, confirming its consistency in refining solutions across iterations while ensuring zero probability of divergence. The nonlinear parameter tuning findings show that the quadratic polynomial method outperforms linear and other nonlinear methods. Consequently, the quadratic GWO variant is presented as a more advanced version of the canonical GWO.

Analyzing the parameters that impact GWO convergence reveals that population size plays a crucial role in maintaining search diversity, enabling broader exploration of the search space, and reducing the risk of being trapped in local optima. A larger population enhances solution accuracy but increases computational demands. Similarly, the number of iterations influences the exploration depth, where more iterations improve the likelihood of reaching a global optimum. However, this improvement incurs higher computational costs, necessitating a balance between efficiency and accuracy in parameter selection, which depends on the complexity of the optimization problem. Scalability analysis shows that GWO struggles in high-dimensional problems, where the expanding search space complicates convergence stability. As dimensionality increases, GWO struggles to balance exploration and exploitation effectively, resulting in slower convergence rates and increased overhead. These findings highlight GWO's strengths and limitations, emphasizing the importance of strategic parameter tuning and improved search strategies within GWO to enhance adaptability while maintaining computational efficiency.

Acknowledgments

The authors acknowledge the use of Grammarly for language editing and refinement of the manuscript.

CRediT authorship contribution statement

Hoda Zamani: Writing – review and editing, Visualization, Software, Resources, Methodology, Formal analysis, Data curation, Conceptualization, Investigation. **Mohammad H. Nadimi-Shahraki:** Review and editing, Resources, Conceptualization, Supervision. **Seyedali Mirjalili:** Review and editing, Resources, Conceptualization, Supervision.

Data availability

The source code is available at: https://seyedalimirjalili.com and https://hodazamani.github.io.

Declaration of interests

The authors declare that they have no known competing financial interests or personal relationships that could have appeared to influence the work reported in this paper.

References

[1] M.H. Nadimi-Shahraki, H. Zamani, DMDE: diversity-maintained multi-trial vector differential evolution algorithm for non-decomposition large-scale global optimization, Expert Systems with Applications 198 (2022) 116895.

[2] H. Zamani, M.H. Nadimi-Shahraki, A.H. Gandomi, QANA: quantum-based avian navigation optimizer algorithm, Engineering Applications of Artificial Intelligence 104 (2021) 104314.

[3] H. Zamani, M.H. Nadimi-Shahraki, A.H. Gandomi, Starling murmuration optimizer: a novel bio-inspired algorithm for global and engineering optimization, Computer Methods in Applied Mechanics and Engineering 392 (2022) 114616.

[4] S. Mirjalili, S.M. Mirjalili, A. Lewis, Grey wolf optimizer, Advances in 69 (2014) 46–61 Engineering Software.

[5] S. Gupta, K. Deep, H. Moayedi, L.K. Foong, A. Assad, Sine cosine grey wolf optimizer to solve engineering design problems, Engineering with Computers 37 (2021) 3123–3149.

[6] J. Hu, Z. Song, Y. Tan, M. Tan, Optimizing integrated energy systems using a hybrid approach blending grey wolf optimization with local search heuristics, Journal of 87 (2024) 111384 Energy Storage.

[7] C. Wang, L. Zhao, X. Li, Y. Li, An improved grey wolf optimizer for welding shop inverse scheduling, Computers & Industrial Engineering 163 (2022) 107809.

[8] S. Kumar, R.V. Kumar, V. Ranjith, S. Jeevakala, S.S. Varun, Grey wolf optimized SwinUNet based transformer framework for liver segmentation from CT images, Computers and Electrical Engineering 117 (2024) 109248.

[9] M. Mafarja, T. Thaher, J. Too, H. Chantar, H. Turabieh, E.H. Houssein, et al., An efficient high-dimensional feature selection approach driven by enhanced multi-strategy grey wolf optimizer for biological data classification, Neural Computing and Applications 35 (2) (2023) 1749–1775.

[10] W. Long, J. Jiao, X. Liang, M. Tang, An exploration-enhanced grey wolf optimizer to solve high-dimensional numerical optimization, Engineering Applications of Artificial Intelligence 68 (2018) 63–80.

[11] D. Guha, P.K. Roy, S. Banerjee, Load frequency control of interconnected power system using grey wolf optimization, Swarm and 27 (2016) 97–115 Evolutionary Computation.

[12] I.A. Zamfirache, R.-E. Precup, R.-C. Roman, E.M. Petriu, Neural network-based control using actor-critic reinforcement learning and grey wolf optimizer with experimental servo system validation, Expert Systems with Applications 225 (2023) 120112.

[13] M. Wang, H. Chen, H. Li, Z. Cai, X. Zhao, C. Tong, et al., Grey wolf optimization evolving kernel extreme learning machine: application to bankruptcy prediction, Engineering Applications of Artificial Intelligence 63 (2017) 54–68.

[14] K. Zhou, C. Tan, Y. Zhao, J. Yu, Z. Zhang, Y. Wu, Research on solving flexible job shop scheduling problem based on improved GWO algorithm SS-GWO, Neural Processing Letters 56 (1) (2024) 26.

[15] C. Lu, L. Gao, X. Li, C. Hu, X. Yan, W. Gong, Chaotic-based grey wolf optimizer for numerical and engineering optimization problems, Memetic Computing 12 (2020) 371–398.

[16] W. Long, S. Cai, J. Jiao, M. Xu, T. Wu, A new hybrid algorithm based on grey wolf optimizer and cuckoo search for parameter extraction of solar photovoltaic models, Energy Conversion and Management 203 (2020) 112243.

[17] R.M. Rizk-Allah, A. Slowik, A.E. Hassanien, Hybridization of grey wolf optimizer and crow search algorithm based on dynamic fuzzy learning strategy for large-scale optimization, IEEE Access 8 (2020) 161593–161611.

[18] K. Li, S. Li, Z. Huang, M. Zhang, Z. Xu, Grey wolf optimization algorithm based on Cauchy-Gaussian mutation and improved search strategy, Scientific Reports 12 (1) (2022) 18961.

[19] W. Lei, W. Jiawei, M. Zezhou, Enhancing grey wolf optimizer with levy flight for engineering applications, IEEE Access 11 (2023) 74865–74897.

[20] N. Awad, M. Ali, J. Liang, B. Qu, P. Suganthan, Problem definitions and evaluation criteria for the CEC 2017 special session and competition on single objective bound constrained real-parameter numerical optimization, Technical Report, Nanyang Technological University, Singapore, (2016), pp. 1–34.
[21] X. Li, K. Tang, M.N. Omidvar, Z. Yang, K. Qin, H. China, Benchmark functions for the CEC 2013 special session and competition on large-scale global optimization, Gene 7 (33) (2013) 8.
[22] R.-E. Precup, R.-C. David, E.M. Petriu, Grey wolf optimizer algorithm-based tuning of fuzzy control systems with reduced parametric sensitivity, IEEE Transactions on Industrial Electronics 64 (1) (2016) 527–534.
[23] L. Rodríguez, O. Castillo, J. Soria, P. Melin, F. Valdez, C.I. Gonzalez, et al., A fuzzy hierarchical operator in the grey wolf optimizer algorithm, Applied Soft Computing 57 (2017) 315–328.
[24] M.A. Al-Betar, M.A. Awadallah, H. Faris, I. Aljarah, A.I. Hammouri, Natural selection methods for grey wolf optimizer, Expert Systems with Applications 113 (2018) 481–498.
[25] S. Gupta, K. Deep, A novel random walk grey wolf optimizer, Swarm and 44 (2019) 101–112 Evolutionary Computation.
[26] S. Gupta, K. Deep, A memory-based grey wolf optimizer for global optimization tasks, Applied Soft Computing 93 (2020) 106367.
[27] X. Yu, W. Xu, C. Li, Opposition-based learning grey wolf optimizer for global optimization, Knowledge-Based Systems 226 (2021) 107139.
[28] K. Meidani, A. Hemmasian, S. Mirjalili, A. Barati Farimani, Adaptive grey wolf optimizer, Neural Computing and Applications 34 (10) (2022) 7711–7731.
[29] C. Ma, H. Huang, Q. Fan, J. Wei, Y. Du, W. Gao, Grey wolf optimizer based on Aquila exploration method, Expert Systems with Applications 205 (2022) 117629.
[30] Z. Geng, W. Kong, X. Wang, L. Wang, Y. Han, Adaptive search based grey wolf optimization algorithm for multi-objective optimization of ethylene cracking furnace, Swarm and 92 (2025) 101810 Evolutionary Computation.
[31] Z. Wang, L. Shu, S. Yang, Z. Zeng, D. He, S. Chan, Multi-population dynamic grey wolf optimizer based on dimension learning and Laplace mutation for global optimization, Expert Systems with Applications 265 (2025) 125863.
[32] S.A.A. Edsa, K. Sunat, H. Guo, Cost-sensitive neural network: a grey wolf optimizer-based approach for breast cancer prediction, Expert Systems with Applications 266 (2025) 126176.
[33] L. Zhang, X. Chen, Elite-driven grey wolf optimization for global optimization and its application to feature selection, Swarm and Evolutionary Computation 92 (2025) 101795.

Chapter 2

A multipopulation grey wolf optimizer with adaptive size reduction and solution exchange for multilevel thresholding in image segmentation

Adam Djili[1], Mohammed A. Boukhalfa[1], Farouq Zitouni[2], Saad Harous[3], Abdelhadi Limane[2], Aridj Ferhat[2], and Rihab Lakbichi[2]

[1]*Department of Computer Science and Information Technology, Kasdi Merbah University, Ouargla, Algeria,* [2]*Department of Computer Science and Information Technology, Laboratory of Artificial Intelligence and Information Technologies, Kasdi Merbah University, Ouargla, Algeria,* [3]*Department of Computer Science, University of Sharjah, Sharjah, United Arab Emirates*

2.1 Introduction

Image segmentation is one of the most fundamental and challenging tasks in computer vision. It partitions an image into multiple meaningful regions based on pixel intensity levels. Multilevel thresholding (MLT) extends traditional bi-level thresholding by identifying multiple thresholds to divide an image into several distinct regions. This technique has been widely applied in various fields, including medical imaging [1], remote sensing [2], and industrial inspection [3], due to its ability to capture finer details in images with complex structures and intensity distributions.

Over the past few decades, numerous optimization algorithms have been proposed to address the MLT problem. These algorithms aim to find an optimal set of thresholds that maximizes certain objective functions, such as Otsu's method [4] and Kapur's entropy [5], which are widely recognized for their effectiveness in image segmentation. However, finding an optimal solution for the MLT problem is a computationally challenging task, especially for high-dimensional images or complex segmentation scenarios with noise, nonuniform illumination, or overlapping regions.

Metaheuristic algorithms (MAs) have emerged as a promising solution to solve complex optimization problems like MLT. Inspired by nature, these algorithms search for optimal solutions by mimicking biological, physical, or social behaviors. Among them, the grey wolf optimizer (GWO) [6], inspired by the hunting and social hierarchy of grey wolves, has demonstrated notable success in global optimization tasks. Despite its strengths, GWO suffers from limitations such as premature convergence and slow adaptability in high-dimensional search spaces.

To address these challenges, we propose an enhanced version of the GWO, referred to as the multipopulation grey wolf optimizer with adaptive size reduction and solution exchange (MP-GWO-AES). This novel approach incorporates three key innovations to enhance GWO's performance for MLT in image segmentation. First, we introduce a multipopulation framework to explore multiple regions of the search space simultaneously, fostering diversity and improving the exploration phase. Second, adaptive size reduction is employed to dynamically control population size, optimizing computational efficiency while maintaining exploration capabilities. Third, the solution exchange mechanism between subpopulations enhances global cooperation, allowing the algorithm to avoid local optima and improve overall performance. These improvements are validated through experimental results on a benchmark dataset, showing that MP-GWO-AES significantly outperforms traditional GWO, in terms of peak signal-to-noise ratio (PSNR) and structural similarity index (SSIM), particularly in high-dimensional segmentation tasks.

The remainder of this paper is organized as: Section 2.2 reviews related work on optimization techniques for MLT; Section 2.3 presents the mathematical formulation of the MLT problem; Section 2.4 introduces the GWO and discusses its

Grey Wolf Optimizer. DOI: https://doi.org/10.1016/B978-0-443-36624-6.00008-1

limitations; Section 2.5 details the proposed MP-GWO-AES algorithm; Section 2.6 presents the experimental setup and results; and Section 2.7 concludes the paper and suggests directions for future work.

2.2 Review of related word

This section provides a review of recent state-of-the-art MA-based approaches to multilevel thresholding in image segmentation. To ensure a coherent narrative, the studies are discussed chronologically, focusing on their objective functions, evaluation metrics, datasets, and optimization strategies.

The work described in Xing and Jia [7] introduced the Lévy-flight thermal exchange optimization algorithm. By integrating Lévy flight into standard thermal exchange optimization, the authors enhanced the algorithm's ability to balance global exploration and local exploitation. Moreover, they adopted the Tsallis entropy as a fitness function, a choice that improved segmentation accuracy. This approach has been validated on multithresholding tasks, including applications to satellite images. The study published in Jiang et al. [8] developed Neighborhood and Fitness-Distance-Ratio-based Teaching-Learning-Based Optimization (NFDR-TLBO), which integrated an advanced neighborhood topology to sustain exploration and a fitness-distance-ratio mechanism to refine the search efficiency of the teaching-learning-based optimization algorithm. Evaluated on 18 benchmark functions and later applied to Kapur entropy-based image segmentation, NFDR-TLBO exhibited notable robustness. It achieved superior PSNR, SSIM, and feature similarity index (FSIM) scores, affirming its effectiveness in preserving fine-grained image details. Building on the slime mold algorithm, the proposed method in Ref. [9] introduced diffusion-based slime mould algorithm (DASMA), which is a thoughtful combination of sophisticated heuristics to elevate image segmentation capabilities. It leverages Rényi's entropy for evaluation, a diffusion mechanism to preserve population diversity, and an association strategy to accelerate the convergence. Experiments on both the Berkeley dataset and computed tomography (CT) scans for chronic obstructive pulmonary disease demonstrate DASMA's ability to deliver highly accurate segmentation outcomes. The approach [10] used the black widow optimization algorithm and employed Otsu's and Kapur's entropy as objective functions for the optimal threshold configuration. While its performance under Kapur's entropy was not the strongest in terms of fitness, the optimizer excelled in PSNR, SSIM, and FSIM metrics, highlighting its practical relevance for segmentation quality.

By 2022, the field saw significant advancements, particularly in addressing the challenges of high-dimensional thresholding. Although many algorithms struggled with high-dimensional thresholding, the research discussed in Ref. [11] showcased how thoughtful hybridization through convergence-boosting, local optima avoidance, and ranking-based updating techniques can drive superior results. Evaluated across thresholds from 2 to 100, it consistently outperformed seven advanced MAs. Furthermore, the findings in Ref. [12] utilized opposition-based learning to enhance the golden jackal optimization algorithm, improving both population diversity and search efficiency. Designed for skin image analysis and paired with Otsu's method, the enhanced optimizer delivered reliable results at lower thresholds (i.e., 2–5). The authors of Ref. [13] addressed the challenges of color image segmentation by applying a Commission Internationale de l'Éclairage (International Commission on Illumination) + Lab (CIELAB) color space transformation. Comparative studies on the Berkeley dataset revealed the superiority of the enhanced algorithm over its basic version and other well-known MAs. The COVID optimization algorithm is extended in Hosny et al. [14] by introducing a chaotic variant equipped with a hybrid fitness function that integrates the entropy of Otsu and Kapur. Designed for multilevel thresholding, this innovation reflects a growing trend toward combining classical objective functions with metaheuristic adaptations to improve image segmentation outcomes. To enhance the chameleon swarm algorithm, which tends to get trapped in local optima as noted by Ref. [15], an improved variant was proposed. This version incorporated a best random mutation strategy utilizing Lévy, Gaussian, and Cauchy distribution functions to mutate search individuals. The enhanced MA was evaluated on both global optimization benchmarks and multithresholding problems. Two datasets were employed: an magnetic resonance imaging (MRI) dataset (Alzheimer's disease) and a CT (COVID-19) dataset. The performance was assessed using Otsu's and Kapur's methods, along with PSNR, SSIM, and FSIM metrics, where the improved optimizer consistently outperformed the original one and other competing optimizers.

Most recently, the study described in Xiang et al. [16] introduced CLNBHEOA, a refined version of the human evolutionary optimization algorithm. This algorithm integrated Chebyshev–Tent chaotic mapping with an opposites-based learning strategy to improve population diversity. Additionally, it employed an adaptive learning mechanism, a nonlinear control factor to balance exploration and exploitation phases, and a three-point guidance strategy based on Bernstein polynomials to improve exploitation. Validated on six benchmark images using Otsu's method, CLNBHEOA achieved a winning rate exceeding 95% in both fitness values and image quality metrics (PSNR, SSIM, FSIM). Finally, the findings published in Limane et al. [17] advanced the single candidate optimizer by transitioning it from a trajectory-based algorithm to a population-based one. This redesign introduced an influencing candidate to guide the search process and employed the inverse incomplete gamma function to enhance intensification during the final stages of optimization. The results demonstrated the superiority of the population-based variant over the original optimizer for global optimization. To assess its broader applicability, the algorithm was applied to solve the multilevel thresholding problem in image segmentation, and its performance was compared to state-of-the-art methods on two datasets: BSD500, serving as a benchmark, and international skin imaging collaboration (ISIC), addressing medical image segmentation challenges. The evaluation incorporated a comprehensive set of metrics, including PSNR, SSIM, FSIM, quality index based on local variance, haar wavelet-based perceptual similarity index, universal image quality index, and computational time, using both Otsu's and Kapur's objective functions to validate segmentation performance.

In summary, these recent contributions can be broadly classified into three main directions. The first involves the development of novel variants of existing MAs, often through the integration of techniques such as chaotic mappings, opposition-based learning, and hybridization strategies. The second focuses on the introduction of new objective functions, exemplified by the hybridization of classical ones such as Otsu's and Kapur's functions, which aim to improve the robustness of threshold selection. Finally, several studies have extended the applicability of these algorithms employing more diverse and innovative datasets, particularly in medical imaging domains, thus demonstrating the potential of metaheuristics to address real-world segmentation challenges.

2.3 Mathematical formulation of the multilevel thresholding problem

MLT is a fundamental image segmentation technique that is used to partition an image into multiple meaningful regions based on the intensity levels of its pixels. Unlike bi-level thresholding, which identifies a single threshold to separate the image into two classes (foreground and background), MLT identifies multiple thresholds to divide the image into $k + 1$ distinct classes, where k is the number of thresholds.

Let I be a grayscale image represented by a two-dimensional matrix of size $M \times N$, with pixel intensity values $i(x, y) \in \{0, 1, ..., L - 1\}$, where L is the maximum gray level (typically 256 for 8-bit images). The goal is to find an optimal set of thresholds $\boldsymbol{T} = \{t_1, t_2, ..., t_k\}$, with $0 < t_1 < t_2 < ... < t_k < L$, such that the image is segmented into $k + 1$ regions $R_1, R_2, ..., R_{k+1}$ defined as follows:

$R_1 = \{(x, y) \mid 0 \le i(x, y) < t_1\}$, $R_2 = \{(x, y) \mid t_1 \le i(x, y) < t_2\}, ..., R_{k+1} = \{(x, y) \mid t_k \le i(x, y) < L\}$

To formalize the optimization problem, a suitable objective function $J(\boldsymbol{T})$ must be defined. Two common objective functions are used in the literature and are described using Eq. 2.1 and Eq. 2.2.

1. **Otsu's method**: Maximizes the between-class variance [4]:

$$J_{\text{Otsu}}(\boldsymbol{T}) = \sum_{j=1}^{k+1} \omega_j (\mu_j - \mu_T)^2 \tag{2.1}$$

where ω_j and μ_j are the probability and mean intensity of class R_j, and μ_T is the global mean intensity.

2. **Kapur's method**: Maximizes the sum of class entropies [5]:

$$J_{\text{Kanpur}}(T) = \sum_{j=1}^{k+1} H\left(R_j\right) = -\sum_{j=1}^{k+1} \sum_{i \in R_j} \frac{p_i}{\omega_j} \log\left(\frac{p_i}{\omega_j}\right) \tag{2.2}$$

where p_i is the probability of intensity level i, and ω_j is the total probability of region R_j.

The optimal threshold set, denoted by $\boldsymbol{T}^*$, is defined by Eq. 2.3.

$$\boldsymbol{T}^* = \arg\max_{\boldsymbol{T} \in \mathscr{T}} J(\boldsymbol{T}) \tag{2.3}$$

where T is the space of all admissible threshold vectors of size k. Due to the combinatorial nature of the problem, the search space grows exponentially with k, making exhaustive search computationally expensive for large k. Hence, MAs, such as the solar system algorithm [18], are often employed to efficiently explore the solution space and identify near-optimal thresholds.

Given the need to segment images with ambiguous intensity distributions, noise, or complex structures, we chose to implement Kapur's entropy-based method, which is better suited for such conditions. This choice is particularly relevant in real-life scenarios, where image data often suffer from nonuniform illumination, overlapping regions, and unpredictable artifacts that compromise the performance of simpler thresholding techniques.

Kapur's method is an unsupervised image thresholding technique based on the principle of maximum entropy. Unlike Otsu's method, which relies on variance between classes, Kapur's approach seeks to segment an image by maximizing the sum of Shannon's entropies of the resulting pixel classes [19]. This makes it particularly effective in cases where the histogram lacks clear peaks or when the image contains noise and uneven illumination. Let I be a grayscale image with L possible intensity levels. For a set of k thresholds $\mathbf{T} = \{t_1, t_2, \ldots, t_k\}$, the image is segmented into $k + 1$ disjoint regions R_1, $R_2, \ldots, R_{k+1}$. Each region corresponds to a range of intensity values defined by the thresholds. In addition, let $h(i)$ denote the number of pixels with intensity i, for $i \in \{0, 1, \ldots, L - 1\}$. The steps involved in Kapur's method are:

1. Compute the normalized histogram using Eq. 2.4.

$$p(i) = \frac{h(i)}{M \times N}, \quad \text{with} \quad \sum_{i=0}^{L-1} p(i) = 1 \tag{2.4}$$

2. Compute the probability of class R_j using Eq. 2.5.

$$\omega_j = \sum_{i \in R_j} p(i) \tag{2.5}$$

3. Compute the entropy of class R_j using Eq. 2.6.

$$H(R_j) = -\sum_{i \in R_j} \frac{p(i)}{\omega_j} \log\left(\frac{p(i)}{\omega_j}\right) \tag{2.6}$$

4. Compute the total entropy for a threshold configuration $\boldsymbol{T}$ using Eq. 2.7.

$$H(\boldsymbol{T}) = \sum_{j=1}^{k+1} H(R_j) \tag{2.7}$$

It should be noted that Kapur's method performs well even when the histogram is flat or the image is noisy. In addition, it does not assume any specific distribution model for intensity values. Finally, it is well-suited for extension to multilevel thresholding tasks. This makes Kapur's method a strong candidate for complex segmentation scenarios, which is why it is adopted in our implementation. The optimization strategy used to identify the optimal thresholds in Section 2.4.

2.4 Grey wolf optimizer: fundamentals and limitations

The GWO is an MA inspired by the social hierarchy and hunting strategy of grey wolves in the wild [6]. Grey wolves typically operate in packs with a dominant alpha wolf leading the group, followed by beta and delta wolves, while the rest of the pack, known as omega wolves, follow the guidance of the leaders. This natural leadership model forms the core of GWO's optimization process. The algorithm begins with a population of N candidate solutions, $\mathbf{x}_i \in \mathrm{R}^D$, initialized using random vectors drawn from the continuous uniform distribution, symbolized by U(0, 1), ensuring that every value in the interval [0, 1] is equally probable, which provides a diverse and unbiased sampling in the search space bounded by vectors **l** and **u**.

Three top-performing solutions are dynamically assigned as alpha, beta, and delta wolves, representing the best, second-best, and third-best individuals. The rest of the wolves update their positions by emulating the encircling behavior observed in real wolves during hunting. This is mathematically modeled using adaptive coefficients derived from random values and a control parameter a, which linearly decreases from 2 to 0 over iterations to shift the focus from global exploration to local exploitation. Each wolf calculates its new position by estimating its relative distance from the alpha, beta, and delta wolves and moving accordingly. The new position is the average of these three influence-driven movements. If the newly generated candidate solution improves the objective function $f(\mathbf{x})$, it replaces the current one. Boundary constraints are enforced throughout to maintain feasibility. After T_{max} iterations, the algorithm outputs the best solution found, $\mathbf{x}^*$, which corresponds to the fittest individual in the population. Algorithm 2.1 outlines the core mechanism by which the GWO operates.

Despite its simplicity and effectiveness, GWO suffers from several limitations that can hinder its performance in complex optimization tasks. One major drawback is its tendency toward premature convergence, particularly in high-dimensional or multimodal search spaces, where the algorithm can easily become trapped in local optima. This issue is primarily due to the fixed leadership hierarchy (α, β, δ), which dominates the search process and reduces the diversity of the population over time. Furthermore, linear reduction of the control parameter a leads to a rapid transition from

ALGORITHM 2.1 Pseudocode of GWO

Input: $T_{\max}, N, D, \mathbf{l}, \mathbf{u}, f(\mathbf{x})$
Output: The best candidate solution found so far (i.e., $\mathbf{x}^*$)

$X \leftarrow \emptyset$;
for $i \leftarrow 1$ **to** N **do**
  Draw $\mathbf{r}_i \sim \mathcal{U}(0,1)$;
  $\mathbf{x}_i \leftarrow \mathbf{r}_i \circ (\mathbf{u} - \mathbf{l}) + \mathbf{l}$;
  $X \leftarrow X \cup \{\mathbf{x}_i\}$;
end
Draw $\mathbf{r}_1, \mathbf{r}_2, \mathbf{r}_3 \sim \mathcal{U}(0,1)$;
$\left[\mathbf{x}_\alpha, \mathbf{x}_\beta, \mathbf{x}_\delta\right] \leftarrow [\mathbf{r}_1 \circ (\mathbf{u} - \mathbf{l}) + \mathbf{l}, \mathbf{r}_2 \circ (\mathbf{u} - \mathbf{l}) + \mathbf{l}, \mathbf{r}_3 \circ (\mathbf{u} - \mathbf{l}) + \mathbf{l}]$;
for $t \leftarrow 1$ **to** $T_{\max}$ **do**
  for $i \leftarrow 1$ **to** N **do**
    if $f(\mathbf{x}_i) < f(\mathbf{x}_\alpha)$ **then**
      $\mathbf{x}_\alpha \leftarrow \mathbf{x}_i$;
    end
    if $f(\mathbf{x}_i) > f(\mathbf{x}_\alpha) \wedge f(\mathbf{x}_i) < f\left(\mathbf{x}_\beta\right)$ **then**
      $\mathbf{x}_\beta \leftarrow \mathbf{x}_i$;
    end
    if $f(\mathbf{x}_i) > f(\mathbf{x}_\alpha) \wedge f(\mathbf{x}_i) > f\left(\mathbf{x}_\beta\right) \wedge f(\mathbf{x}_i) < f(\mathbf{x}_\delta)$ **then**
      $\mathbf{x}_\delta \leftarrow \mathbf{x}_i$;
    end
  end
  $a \leftarrow 2 - t \times \left(\frac{2}{T_{\max}}\right)$;
  for $i \leftarrow 1$ **to** N **do**
    Draw $\mathbf{r}_1, \mathbf{r}_2, \mathbf{r}_3, \mathbf{r}_4, \mathbf{r}_5, \mathbf{r}_6 \sim \mathcal{U}(0,1)$;
    $[\mathbf{y}_1, \mathbf{y}_2, \mathbf{y}_3] \leftarrow [2 \times a \times \mathbf{r}_1 - a \times \mathbf{1}_D, 2 \times a \times \mathbf{r}_2 - a \times \mathbf{1}_D, 2 \times a \times \mathbf{r}_3 - a \times \mathbf{1}_D]$;
    $[\mathbf{z}_1, \mathbf{z}_2, \mathbf{z}_3] \leftarrow [2 \times \mathbf{r}_4, 2 \times \mathbf{r}_5, 2 \times \mathbf{r}_6]$;
    $[\mathbf{t}_1, \mathbf{t}_2, \mathbf{t}_3] \leftarrow \left[\mathbf{x}_\alpha - \mathbf{y}_1 \circ |\mathbf{z}_1 \circ \mathbf{x}_\alpha - \mathbf{x}_i|, \mathbf{x}_\beta - \mathbf{y}_2 \circ |\mathbf{z}_2 \circ \mathbf{x}_\beta - \mathbf{x}_i|, \mathbf{x}_\delta - \mathbf{y}_3 \circ |\mathbf{z}_3 \circ \mathbf{x}_\delta - \mathbf{x}_i|\right]$;
    $\mathbf{x}_i \leftarrow (\mathbf{t}_1 + \mathbf{t}_2 + \mathbf{t}_3)/3$;
    Check and correct the boundary values of $\mathbf{x}_i$, if necessary;
  end
end
Compute the best candidate solution $\mathbf{x}^* \leftarrow \underset{i \in \{1,\ldots,N\}}{\operatorname{argmin}} \{f(\mathbf{x}_i)\}$;

exploration to exploitation, which may not be adaptive enough for problems requiring a prolonged global search. GWO also lacks a memory mechanism to retain historically good solutions, making it susceptible to losing valuable information during iterations. Finally, its convergence speed can be relatively slow compared to other MAs, and its scalability is limited when dealing with large-scale optimization problems. To address these limitations, various enhancements have been proposed, including hybridization with other algorithms, adaptive parameter tuning, and diversity preservation techniques.

2.5 Proposed multipopulation grey wolf optimizer with adaptive exchange and shrinkage

This section presents the core components of the proposed MP-GWO-AES, composed of four interconnected algorithms. Each fulfills a distinct role within the evolutionary process, contributing to population initialization, global and local optimization, interpopulation cooperation, and dynamic size reduction.

Algorithm 2.2 initializes the multipopulation framework. The entire search space is divided into M overlapping local regions, each defined by an adaptive center $\mathbf{p}_i$ and a radius R. For each population X_i, N candidate solutions are generated using Gaussian sampling, denoted by G(0, 1), within its corresponding local bounds $[\mathbf{l}_i, \mathbf{u}_i]$. Three guiding solutions per population ($\mathbf{x}_{\alpha i}$, $\mathbf{x}_{\beta i}$, $\mathbf{x}_{\delta i}$) are initialized to facilitate future exploration and exploitation. Following the initialization of all

ALGORITHM 2.2 Pseudocode of MP-GWO-AES

Input: $T_{\max}$, $N, D, M, R, \mathbf{l}, \mathbf{u}, f(\mathbf{x}), \Delta, \rho$
Output: The best candidate solution found so far (i.e., $\mathbf{x}^*$)

$[\mathbf{l}_1, \ldots, \mathbf{l}_M] \leftarrow [-\infty, \ldots, -\infty]$;
$[\mathbf{u}_1, \ldots, \mathbf{u}_M] \leftarrow [+\infty, \ldots, +\infty]$;
$[X_1, \ldots, X_M] \leftarrow [\emptyset, \ldots, \emptyset]$;
for $i \leftarrow 1$ **to** M **do**
  Draw $\mathbf{r}_i \sim \mathcal{U}(0, 1)$;
  $\mathbf{p}_i \leftarrow \mathbf{r}_i \circ (\mathbf{u} - \mathbf{l}) + \mathbf{l}$;
  $[\mathbf{l}_i, \mathbf{u}_i] \leftarrow [\max(\mathbf{l}, \mathbf{p}_i - R \times \mathbf{1}_D), \min(\mathbf{u}, \mathbf{p}_i + R \times \mathbf{1}_D)]$;
  for $j \leftarrow 1$ **to** N **do**
    Draw $\mathbf{r}_{ij} \sim \mathcal{G}(0, 1)$;
    $\mathbf{x}_j \leftarrow \mathbf{r}_{ij} \circ (\mathbf{u}_i - \mathbf{l}_i) + \mathbf{l}_i$;
    $X_i \leftarrow X_i \cup \{\mathbf{x}_j\}$;
  end
end
Draw $\mathbf{r}_{11}, \ldots, \mathbf{r}_{1M} \sim \mathcal{U}(0, 1)$;
$[\mathbf{x}_{\alpha_1}, \ldots, \mathbf{x}_{\alpha_M}] \leftarrow [\mathbf{r}_{11} \circ (\mathbf{u}_1 - \mathbf{l}_1) + \mathbf{l}_1, \ldots, \mathbf{r}_{1M} \circ (\mathbf{u}_M - \mathbf{l}_M) + \mathbf{l}_M]$;
Draw $\mathbf{r}_{21}, \ldots, \mathbf{r}_{2M} \sim \mathcal{U}(0, 1)$;
$\left[\mathbf{x}_{\beta_1}, \ldots, \mathbf{x}_{\beta_M}\right] \leftarrow [\mathbf{r}_{21} \circ (\mathbf{u}_1 - \mathbf{l}_1) + \mathbf{l}_1, \ldots, \mathbf{r}_{2M} \circ (\mathbf{u}_M - \mathbf{l}_M) + \mathbf{l}_M]$;
Draw $\mathbf{r}_{31}, \ldots, \mathbf{r}_{3M} \sim \mathcal{U}(0, 1)$;
$[\mathbf{x}_{\delta_1}, \ldots, \mathbf{x}_{\delta_M}] \leftarrow [\mathbf{r}_{31} \circ (\mathbf{u}_1 - \mathbf{l}_1) + \mathbf{l}_1, \ldots, \mathbf{r}_{3M} \circ (\mathbf{u}_M - \mathbf{l}_M) + \mathbf{l}_M]$;
Run Algorithm 3;
Compute the best candidate solution for each population $\mathbf{x}_1^* \leftarrow \underset{\mathbf{x}_i \in X_1}{\operatorname{argmin}} \{f(\mathbf{x}_i)\}, \ldots, \mathbf{x}_M^* \leftarrow \underset{\mathbf{x}_i \in X_M}{\operatorname{argmin}} \{f(\mathbf{x}_i)\}$;
Compute the best candidate solution $\mathbf{x}^* \leftarrow \operatorname{argmin}\left\{f\left(\mathbf{x}_1^*\right), \ldots, f\left(\mathbf{x}_M^*\right)\right\}$;

populations, Algorithm 2 calls Algorithm 3 to execute the optimization process. Once completed, the best individual from each population is identified and the globally optimal candidate $\mathbf{x}^*$ is selected.

In every $\boldsymbol{\Delta}$ iteration, Algorithm 2.3 evaluates the best individual in each population and applies a roulette wheel selection mechanism [20] on their fitness values to probabilistically select a population index p. This ensures that higher-quality populations are more likely to be optimized next, without completely ignoring lower-performing ones. This adaptive selection balances exploitation and diversity in the population pool. Given the selected population X_p, Algorithm 2.4 performs the GWO process. It first identifies the leaders $\mathbf{x}_{\alpha p}$, $\mathbf{x}_{\beta p}$, $\mathbf{x}_{\delta p}$, then uses them to update each individual via a nonlinear combination of adaptive coefficients and position vectors. Boundary conditions are checked and corrected. If the new solution improves on the original, it is retained. This step strengthens the local search around elite individuals while still allowing for diverse updates.

ALGORITHM 2.3 Select the index *p* corresponding to the population targeted for optimization

for $t \leftarrow 0$ **to** $T_{\max}$ **do**
  if $t \bmod \Delta = 0$ **then**
    for $i \leftarrow 1$ **to** M **do**
      The best individual $\mathbf{x}_{\text{best}_i}$ in each population X_i is calculated;
    end
    Perform roulette wheel selection on the fitness values $f(\mathbf{x}_{\text{best}_1}), \ldots, f(\mathbf{x}_{\text{best}_M})$ to probabilistically select an index $p \in \{1, \ldots, M\}$;
  end
  Run Algorithm 4;
end

ALGORITHM 2.4 Optimization of the individuals belonging to the selected population X_p

foreach $\mathbf{x}_i \in X_p$ **do**
    if $f(\mathbf{x}_i) < f(\mathbf{x}_{\alpha_p})$ **then**
        $\mathbf{x}_{\alpha_p} \leftarrow \mathbf{x}_i$;
    end
    if $f(\mathbf{x}_i) > f(\mathbf{x}_{\alpha_p}) \wedge f(\mathbf{x}_i) < f(\mathbf{x}_{\beta_p})$ **then**
        $\mathbf{x}_{\beta_p} \leftarrow \mathbf{x}_i$;
    end
    if $f(\mathbf{x}_i) > f(\mathbf{x}_{\alpha_p}) \wedge f(\mathbf{x}_i) > f(\mathbf{x}_{\beta_p}) \wedge f(\mathbf{x}_i) < f(\mathbf{x}_{\delta_p})$ **then**
        $\mathbf{x}_{\delta_p} \leftarrow \mathbf{x}_i$;
    end
end
$a \leftarrow 2 - t \times \left(\frac{2}{T_{\max}}\right)$;
foreach $\mathbf{x}_i \in X_p$ **do**
    Draw $\mathbf{r}_1, \mathbf{r}_2, \mathbf{r}_3, \mathbf{r}_4, \mathbf{r}_5, \mathbf{r}_6 \sim \mathcal{U}(0,1)$;
    $[\mathbf{y}_1, \mathbf{y}_2, \mathbf{y}_3] \leftarrow [2 \times a \times \mathbf{r}_1 - a \times \mathbf{1}_D, 2 \times a \times \mathbf{r}_2 - a \times \mathbf{1}_D, 2 \times a \times \mathbf{r}_3 - a \times \mathbf{1}_D]$;
    $[\mathbf{z}_1, \mathbf{z}_2, \mathbf{z}_3] \leftarrow [2 \times \mathbf{r}_4, 2 \times \mathbf{r}_5, 2 \times \mathbf{r}_6]$;
    $[\mathbf{t}_1, \mathbf{t}_2, \mathbf{t}_3] \leftarrow \left[\mathbf{x}_{\alpha_p} - \mathbf{y}_1 \circ |\mathbf{z}_1 \circ \mathbf{x}_{\alpha_p} - \mathbf{x}_i|, \mathbf{x}_{\beta_p} - \mathbf{y}_2 \circ |\mathbf{z}_2 \circ \mathbf{x}_{\beta_p} - \mathbf{x}_i|, \mathbf{x}_{\delta_p} - \mathbf{y}_3 \circ |\mathbf{z}_3 \circ \mathbf{x}_{\delta_p} - \mathbf{x}_i|\right]$;
    $\mathbf{x}_{\text{new}} \leftarrow (\mathbf{t}_1 + \mathbf{t}_2 + \mathbf{t}_3)/3$;
    Check and correct the boundary values of $\mathbf{x}_{\text{new}}$, if necessary;
    if $f(\mathbf{x}_{new}) < f(\mathbf{x}_i)$ **then**
        $f(\mathbf{x}_{\text{new}}) \leftarrow f(\mathbf{x}_i)$;
    end
end
Run Algorithm 5;

Finally, Algorithm 2.5 enhances global search by selectively exchanging solutions between populations and adaptively reducing population sizes. First, it identifies the best and worst individuals in each population and uses the roulette wheel selection to choose two populations: X_p (donor) and X_q (receiver). With a small probability (i.e., ρ), the elite of X_p is transferred to replace the worst individual in X_q, optionally with mutation to maintain diversity. In addition, a reverse transfer (the median individual of X_q to a random member of X_p) may occur to foster exploration. The algorithm applies an exponential decay policy to reduce the size of each population from N to a minimum of 5, retaining only the top performers in each stage.

In general, the four algorithms operate as follows: First, Algorithm 2 (Initialization) sets up diverse local populations. Then Algorithm 3 (Selection) identifies the most promising population for optimization. After that, Algorithm 4 (Optimization) performs a focused search within the selected population. Finally, Algorithm 5 (Cooperation and Reduction) facilitates elite knowledge transfer and progressively reduces computational cost.

It is important to note that in MP-GWO-AES, the parameters of GWO preserve their characteristic swarming and hunting mechanisms, which remain central to the search process. The key control parameters of GWO–namely a, A, and C–govern the balance between exploration and exploitation. The parameter a decreases linearly over iterations, progressively shifting the search from global exploration to local exploitation. The coefficient vector A, derived from a, regulates the step size of the wolves, thereby determining whether the search diversifies into new regions or intensifies around promising candidates. Similarly, the coefficient vector C introduces stochasticity into the encircling process, enhancing solution diversity and reducing the risk of premature convergence. By retaining these dynamics within the hybrid framework, MP-GWO-AES benefits from GWO's adaptive exploration–exploitation balance while incorporating its complementary mechanisms, leading to improved robustness and convergence performance.

ALGORITHM 2.5 Interpopulation individual exchange coupled with population size reduction

for $i \leftarrow 1$ **to** M **do**
  The best individual $\mathbf{x}_{\text{best}_i}$ in each population X_i is determined;
  The worst individual $\mathbf{x}_{\text{worst}_i}$ in each population X_i is determined;
end
Perform roulette wheel selection on the fitness values $f(\mathbf{x}_{\text{best}_1}), \ldots, f(\mathbf{x}_{\text{best}_M})$ to probabilistically select an index $p \in \{1, \ldots, M\}$;
Perform roulette wheel selection on the fitness values $f(\mathbf{x}_{\text{worst}_1}), \ldots, f(\mathbf{x}_{\text{worst}_M})$ to probabilistically select an index $q \in \{1, \ldots, M\}$;
Draw $r_1, r_2 \sim \mathcal{U}(0, 1)$;
if $r_1 < p$ **then**
  if $r_2 \geq 0.5$ **then**
    Send $\mathbf{x}_{\text{best}_p}$ from X_p to replace $\mathbf{x}_{\text{worst}_q}$ in X_q;
    Send the median individual from X_q to replace a random individual in X_p to encourage exploration;
  end
  else
    $\mathbf{x}_{\text{elite}_p} \leftarrow \text{Mutate}(\mathbf{x}_{\text{best}_p})$, mutate the transferred individual to avoid cloning and maintain diversity;
    $X_q \leftarrow \left(X_q \setminus \left\{\mathbf{x}_{\text{worst}_q}\right\}\right) \cup \left\{\mathbf{x}_{\text{best}_p}\right\}$;
  end
end
$N_{\text{new}} \leftarrow \max\left(5, \left\lfloor N \cdot \left(\frac{5}{N}\right)^{\frac{t}{T_{\max}}} \right\rfloor\right)$;
for $i \leftarrow 1$ **to** M **do**
  Retain the top N_{new} performing individuals in X_i;
end
$N \leftarrow N_{\text{new}}$;

2.6 Results and discussion

To evaluate the performance of the proposed MP-GWO-AES algorithm compared to standard GWO, a series of experiments were conducted on a dataset consisting of 20 images, the majority of which depict natural scenes (animals, trees, etc.). Each optimizer was executed independently 30 times per image to ensure statistical robustness. In each run, the optimization process aimed to maximize Kapur's entropy for multilevel thresholding. The images used in this study are shown in Fig. 2.1.

The maximum number of iterations was set to 1000 for both algorithms, with a population size of 30. The standard GWO serves as a parameter-free baseline as it does not require any tunable parameters. In contrast, the proposed MP-GWO-AES introduces four key parameters: $\Delta = 50$, $p = 0.01$, $M = 5$, and $R = 10$ iterations. These values were selected based on preliminary sensitivity analyses to achieve a balance between exploration and exploitation while ensuring computational efficiency.

Finally, all experiments were conducted on a personal computer featuring an AMD Ryzen 5 7600 6-core processor (3.8 GHz), 12 logical threads, 32 GB of RAM, and a 64-bit Microsoft Windows 11 Pro operating system. The algorithms were implemented in MATLAB R2019a, which offered a flexible and efficient environment for numerical computation. Image processing tasks such as loading, grayscale conversion, and histogram computation were carried out using MATLAB's built-in functions.

Table 2.1 presents a detailed comparison of the mean and STD values of Kapur's entropy achieved by the baseline GWO and the proposed MP-GWO-AES across the 20 images and the four threshold levels. Although both algorithms consistently achieve nearly identical mean entropy values across all images and threshold levels, indicating equivalent capability to locate high-quality solutions, the variance in performance (reflected in the STD) clearly differentiates the two approaches. At lower threshold levels (2 and 4), both algorithms exhibit minimal variance, suggesting a high convergence reliability. However, as the segmentation complexity increases (thresholds 8 and 16), MP-GWO-AES consistently outperforms GWO in terms of stability. For example, for Image 1 at threshold 16, MP-GWO-AES yields a standard deviation of 1.39E-01, while GWO reaches 8.96E-01; for Image 6, the corresponding values are 1.03E01 and 2.44E-01; and for Image 20, they are 1.76E-01 and 7.01E-01. Similar patterns are observed across multiple images, such as Images 8, 12, 14, and 18, where the standard deviation with GWO spikes significantly, indicating greater sensitivity to initial conditions and a higher likelihood of premature convergence. This significant reduction in variance demonstrates the

FIGURE 2.1 The dataset of images utilized in the experimental study.

robustness of MP-GWO-AES, attributed to its multipopulation design, adaptive size reduction, and interpopulation solution exchange mechanism. These mechanisms improve exploration in the early stages and exploitation later on, leading to more consistent results across multiple runs–particularly in high-dimensional thresholding scenarios where the search space becomes increasingly rugged. In summary, although the mean values remain comparable, MP-GWO-AES achieves superior reliability and repeatability, making it more suitable for complex segmentation tasks requiring consistent performance.

Table 2.2 reports the PSNR and SSIM values for both GWO and MP-GWO-AES in the 20 test images and the four threshold levels. These two metrics are widely used to quantify segmentation quality. PSNR reflects pixel-wise fidelity, while SSIM measures perceptual similarity to the original image. The results demonstrate that MP-GWO-AES consistently delivers comparable or superior segmentation quality across all threshold levels. In many cases, the SSIM values achieved by MP-GWO-AES are equal to or slightly higher than those of GWO, particularly at higher threshold levels where perceptual structure preservation becomes critical. For example, for Image 1 at threshold 16, MP-GWO-AES achieves an SSIM of 0.912, slightly outperforming GWO's 0.895. Similarly, for Image 3, MP-GWO-AES scores 0.943 versus 0.921 with GWO, and for Image 10, it obtains 0.937 compared to 0.931. In terms of PSNR, both algorithms show an increasing trend with higher threshold levels, indicating better segmentation quality as more thresholds are introduced. However, MP-GWO-AES exhibits higher PSNR values in several images at mid-to-high thresholds, indicating a more accurate reconstruction of the segmented images. Notably, for Image 11 at threshold 16, MP-GWO-AES yields 32.1 dB compared to only 23.8 dB for GWO–a significant margin that reinforces the efficiency of the proposed adaptive strategy in refining threshold placement. Interestingly, at lower thresholds (2 and 4), both algorithms perform nearly identically in PSNR and SSIM, reflecting the limited complexity of the segmentation task. However, as the segmentation becomes more fine-grained (thresholds 8 and 16), the advantages of MP-GWO-AES become increasingly evident, suggesting improved adaptability to high-dimensional search spaces and better balance between global exploration and local refinement.

To evaluate the statistical significance of the differences between GWO and MP-GWO-AES, the Wilcoxon signed-rank test was performed on the PSNR and SSIM values in the 20 images for each threshold level. The resulting p-values and the corresponding count of image-wise outcomes, classified as worse (-), equal (=), or better (+), are summarized in Table 2.3. At lower threshold levels (2 and 4), the p-values are exactly 1.00, and the performance is nearly identical across almost all images, with 19 out of 20 cases showing equal performance in PSNR at threshold 2 and 20 out of 20 at threshold 4. For SSIM, the results are also almost identical, with 19 equal cases at threshold 2 and 20 equal cases at threshold 4. This is expected, as low thresholding complexity tends to minimize the algorithmic impact on output quality. However, starting from threshold level 8, a performance divergence begins to emerge. For PSNR at threshold 8, the two algorithms remain evenly balanced, with 10 images favoring GWO and 10 favoring MPGWO-AES, while the p-value of 8.52×10^{-1} indicates that the difference is not statistically significant. In contrast, at threshold 16, the gap becomes more noticeable, with MP-GWO-AES surpassing GWO in 11 images for PSNR (p-value $= 2.04 \times 10^{-1}$), although this improvement is still not statistically significant. For SSIM, MP-GWO-AES outperforms GWO in 11 images at threshold 8, but again without statistical significance (p-value $= 9.70 \times 10^{-1}$). At threshold 16, however, the improvements become statistically significant, with MP-GWO-AES surpassing GWO in 17 images for SSIM (p-value $= 1.16E \times 10^{-3}$). These low p-values confirm that the gains offered by MP-GWO-AES at higher thresholds are not due to random variation but reflect a real and reliable performance advantage. Overall, this statistical analysis corroborates earlier findings: while the two algorithms behave similarly under simple segmentation tasks, MP-GWO-AES exhibits significantly superior performance under complex multilevel thresholding scenarios–both in terms of fidelity (PSNR) and perceptual quality (SSIM).

Due to space limitations, the convergence curves are shown only for Image 1 (Fig. 2.2) and Image 20 (Fig. 2.3); however, the convergence patterns across the remaining images were found to be remarkably similar, exhibiting the same relative behaviors between GWO and MP-GWO-AES. These plots illustrate the evolution of Kapur's entropy over 1000 iterations for both algorithms under threshold levels of 2, 4, 8, and 16. At threshold = 2, both methods converge rapidly within the first 100 iterations, reaching nearly identical final entropy values. GWO maintains a slight edge. This confirms that, under low segmentation complexity, both algorithms are capable of quickly locating optimal or near-optimal solutions. At threshold=4, GWO continues to show slightly faster convergence, though MP-GWO-AES catches up and both converge to similar entropy levels, showing no meaningful performance gap. However, at threshold = 8, MP-GWO-AES begins to show its strengths. While GWO still converges faster initially, its progress plateaus, whereas MP-GWO-AES continues to improve and often reaches higher entropy values, as seen clearly in Image 1. The advantage of MP-GWO-AES becomes more substantial at threshold = 16, where GWO tends to stagnate prematurely. In contrast, MP-GWO-AES exhibits a more gradual and sustained improvement, eventually achieving a higher entropy on both Image 1 and Image 20. This trend highlights the importance of the proposed algorithm's multipopulation structure, adaptive size reduction, and solution exchange, which enhance both the exploration and the long-term exploitation in complex search spaces.

TABLE 2.1 Mean and STD values for the chosen images evaluated using GWO and MP-GWO-AES across varying threshold values (2, 4, 8, and 16).

		2		4		8		16	
		Mean	**STD**	**Mean**	**STD**	**Mean**	**STD**	**Mean**	**STD**
Image 1	MP-GWO-AES	1.13E+01	0.00E+00	1.70E+01	1.17E-04	2.58E+01	3.30E-02	3.87E+01	1.39E-01
	GWO	1.13E+01	0.00E+00	1.70E+01	5.94E-03	2.58E+01	1.04E-01	3.87E+01	8.96E-01
Image 2	MP-GWO-AES	1.14E+01	3.61E-15	1.76E+01	1.08E-14	2.74E+01	3.70E-02	4.25E+01	1.78E-01
	GWO	1.14E+01	3.61E-15	1.76E+01	1.08E-14	2.74E+01	9.15E-02	4.21E+01	4.71E-01
Image 3	MP-GWO-AES	1.31E+01	7.23E-15	1.93E+01	1.37E-04	2.96E+01	2.51E-02	4.53E+01	1.44E-01
	GWO	1.31E+01	7.23E-15	1.93E+01	1.08E-14	2.96E+01	4.20E-02	4.49E+01	3.10E-01
Image 4	MP-GWO-AES	1.22E+01	7.23E-15	1.81E+01	8.83E-04	2.84E+01	4.15E-02	4.38E+01	1.90E-01
	GWO	1.22E+01	7.23E-15	1.81E+01	2.71E-03	2.83E+01	7.74E-02	4.34E+01	4.37E-01
Image 5	MP-GWO-AES	1.25E+01	3.61E-15	1.84E+01	5.15E-04	2.85E+01	2.82E-02	4.37E+01	1.76E-01
	GWO	1.25E+01	1.38E-05	1.84E+01	4.06E-03	2.85E+01	7.49E-02	4.32E+01	7.14E-01
Image 6	MP-GWO-AES	1.21E+01	3.61E-15	1.83E+01	0.00E +00	2.79E+01	3.16E-02	4.23E+01	1.03E-01
	GWO	1.21E+01	1.02E-04	1.83E+01	3.89E-04	2.79E+01	9.36E-02	4.18E+01	2.44E-01
Image 7	MP-GWO-AES	1.28E+01	1.13E-05	1.91E+01	4.62E-04	2.94E+01	2.21E-02	4.50E+01	1.25E-01
	GWO	1.28E+01	3.61E-15	1.91E+01	2.19E-03	2.94E+01	6.62E-02	4.47E+01	3.36E-01
Image 8	MP-GWO-AES	1.25E+01	3.05E-05	1.85E+01	3.77E-04	2.85E+01	1.61E-02	4.33E+01	1.04E-01
	GWO	1.25E+01	1.61E-05	1.85E+01	2.39E-03	2.84E+01	3.22E-02	4.28E+01	2.84E-01
Image 9	MP-GWO-AES	1.24E+01	0.00E+00	1.86E+01	5.27E-04	2.93E+01	2.00E-02	4.50E+01	1.38E-01
	GWO	1.24E+01	0.00E+00	1.86E+01	1.28E-03	2.93E+01	3.25E-02	4.48E+01	4.82E-01
Image 10	MP-GWO-AES	1.22E+01	3.61E-15	1.85E+01	8.08E-04	2.90E+01	1.39E-02	4.48E+01	1.42E-01
	GWO	1.22E+01	4.93E-03	1.85E+01	6.36E-04	2.90E+01	5.60E-02	4.45E+01	3.59E-01
Image 11	MP-GWO-AES	1.27E+01	5.42E-15	1.91E+01	3.05E-04	2.96E+01	1.42E-02	4.52E+01	1.24E-01
	GWO	1.27E+01	3.51E-06	1.91E+01	2.48E-03	2.95E+01	2.77E-02	4.49E+01	4.53E-01

(Continued)

TABLE 2.1 (Continued)

		2		4		8		16	
		Mean	**STD**	**Mean**	**STD**	**Mean**	**STD**	**Mean**	**STD**
Image 12	MP-GWO-AES	1.22E+01	9.03E-15	1.79E+01	7.85E-03	2.77E+01	2.99E-02	4.22E+01	1.41E-01
	GWO	1.22E+01	9.03E-15	1.79E+01	2.73E-03	2.77E+01	6.41E-02	4.20E+01	5.97E-01
Image 13	MP-GWO-AES	1.30E+01	5.42E-15	1.94E+01	4.23E-04	2.99E+01	1.81E-02	4.56E+01	1.42E-01
	GWO	1.30E+01	5.42E-15	1.94E+01	1.24E-03	2.99E+01	2.05E-02	4.53E+01	4.85E-01
Image 14	MP-GWO-AES	1.22E+01	5.36E-06	1.83E+01	1.45E-04	2.80E+01	1.99E-02	4.24E+01	1.14E-01
	GWO	1.22E+01	5.42E-15	1.83E+01	3.09E-03	2.80E+01	6.43E-02	4.21E+01	4.30E-01
Image 15	MP-GWO-AES	1.29E+01	9.03E-15	1.92E+01	2.72E-04	2.96E+01	1.79E-02	4.52E+01	1.32E-01
	GWO	1.29E+01	9.03E-15	1.92E+01	1.53E-03	2.96E+01	7.68E-02	4.48E+01	3.16E-01
Image 16	MP-GWO-AES	1.27E+01	3.61E-15	1.86E+01	3.38E-04	2.87E+01	3.36E-02	4.41E+01	1.17E-01
	GWO	1.27E+01	3.61E-15	1.86E+01	1.96E-03	2.86E+01	5.04E-02	4.38E+01	4.60E-01
Image 17	MP-GWO-AES	1.27E+01	0.00E+00	1.88E+01	9.76E-04	2.90E+01	2.01E-02	4.44E+01	1.50E-01
	GWO	1.27E+01	0.00E+00	1.88E+01	2.52E-03	2.89E+01	6.00E-02	4.39E+01	3.76E-01
Image 18	MP-GWO-AES	1.22E+01	1.81E-15	1.80E+01	7.31E-04	2.82E+01	2.86E-02	4.33E+01	1.13E-01
	GWO	1.22E+01	1.81E-15	1.80E+01	2.08E-03	2.81E+01	8.09E-02	4.31E+01	5.00E-01
Image 19	MP-GWO-AES	1.29E+01	7.23E-15	1.92E+01	4.32E-04	2.94E+01	2.10E-02	4.51E+01	1.11E-01
	GWO	1.29E+01	7.23E-15	1.92E+01	6.58E-03	2.94E+01	8.93E-02	4.47E+01	3.73E-01
Image 20	MP-GWO-AES	1.22E+01	5.42E-15	1.83E+01	1.98E-03	2.87E+01	2.53E-02	4.36E+01	1.76E-01
	GWO	1.22E+01	1.80E-05	1.83E+01	4.84E-03	2.86E+01	1.73E-02	4.35E+01	7.01E-01

GWO, Grey wolf optimizer; *MP-GWO-AES*, multipopulation grey wolf optimizer with adaptive size reduction and solution exchange; *STD*, standard deviation.

TABLE 2.2 PSNR and SSIM values for the chosen images evaluated using GWO and MP-GWO-AES across varying threshold values (2, 4, 8, and 16).

		2		4		8		16	
		PSNR	SSIM	PSNR	SSIM	PSNR	SSIM	PSNR	SSIM
Image 1	MP-GWO-AES	8.73E+00	6.99E-01	1.08E+01	7.37E-01	1.49E+01	8.43E-01	1.87E+01	9.12E-01
	GWO	8.73E+00	6.99E-01	1.08E+01	7.37E-01	1.30E+01	7.77E-01	2.09E+01	8.95E-01
Image 2	MP-GWO-AES	1.18E+01	5.96E-01	1.43E+01	8.21E-01	2.27E+01	8.70E-01	2.36E+01	9.32E-01
	GWO	1.18E+01	5.96E-01	1.43E+01	8.21E-01	2.22E+01	8.66E-01	2.33E+01	9.26E-01
Image 3	MP-GWO-AES	1.63E+01	6.44E-01	2.09E+01	7.80E-01	2.45E+01	8.82E-01	3.18E+01	9.43E-01
	GWO	1.63E+01	6.44E-01	2.09E+01	7.80E-01	2.46E+01	8.81E-01	2.77E+01	9.21E-01
Image 4	MP-GWO-AES	1.60E+01	4.19E-01	2.09E+01	5.74E-01	2.80E+01	7.72E-01	2.98E+01	8.96E-01
	GWO	1.60E+01	4.19E-01	2.09E+01	5.74E-01	2.83E+01	7.68E-01	3.15E+01	8.80E-01
Image 5	MP-GWO-AES	1.37E+01	6.45E-01	1.51E+01	7.33E-01	2.41E+01	7.88E-01	3.28E+01	8.94E-01
	GWO	1.37E+01	6.45E-01	1.51E+01	7.33E-01	2.39E+01	7.81E-01	2.85E+01	8.82E-01
Image 6	MP-GWO-AES	8.65E+00	5.71E-01	1.70E+01	7.18E-01	1.57E+01	7.83E-01	1.74E+01	8.60E-01
	GWO	8.65E+00	5.71E-01	1.70E+01	7.18E-01	1.55E+01	7.87E-01	2.13E+01	8.38E-01
Image 7	MP-GWO-AES	1.48E+01	4.30E-01	2.10E+01	5.77E-01	2.67E+01	7.36E-01	3.23E+01	8.69E-01
	GWO	1.48E+01	4.30E-01	2.10E+01	5.77E-01	2.64E+01	7.34E-01	2.92E+01	8.50E-01
Image 8	MP-GWO-AES	1.34E+01	1.76E-01	1.88E+01	4.65E-01	2.32E+01	6.80E-01	3.08E+01	9.00E-01
	GWO	1.34E+01	1.76E-01	1.88E+01	4.65E-01	2.37E+01	6.85E-01	2.26E+01	7.97E-01
Image 9	MP-GWO-AES	1.48E+01	5.86E-01	2.01E+01	6.68E-01	2.88E+01	8.09E-01	3.23E+01	8.76E-01
	GWO	1.51E+01	5.35E-01	2.01E+01	6.68E-01	2.89E+01	8.10E-01	3.09E+01	8.91E-01
Image 10	MP-GWO-AES	1.00E+01	1.38E-01	2.02E+01	5.71E-01	2.75E+01	8.17E-01	3.02E+01	9.37E-01
	GWO	1.00E+01	1.38E-01	2.02E+01	5.71E-01	2.71E+01	8.09E-01	3.33E+01	9.31E-01
Image 11	MP-GWO-AES	1.32E+01	3.61E-01	2.24E+01	6.87E-01	2.66E+01	8.36E-01	3.21E+01	9.33E-01
	GWO	1.32E+01	3.61E-01	2.24E+01	6.87E-01	2.70E+01	8.31E-01	2.38E+01	9.07E-01
Image 12	MP-GWO-AES	1.24E+01	4.63E-01	2.08E+01	6.13E-01	2.37E+01	7.21E-01	2.34E+01	8.74E-01
	GWO	1.24E+01	4.63E-01	2.08E+01	6.13E-01	2.42E+01	7.25E-01	2.45E+01	8.80E-01

(Continued)

TABLE 2.2 (Continued)

		2		4		8		16	
		PSNR	SSIM	PSNR	SSIM	PSNR	SSIM	PSNR	SSIM
Image 13	MP-GWO-AES	1.58E+01	3.50E-01	2.13E+01	5.77E-01	2.66E+01	7.89E-01	3.34E+01	9.26E-01
	GWO	1.58E+01	3.50E-01	2.13E+01	5.77E-01	2.74E+01	8.01E-01	3.01E+01	8.98E-01
Image 14	MP-GWO-AES	1.10E+01	4.36E-01	2.03E+01	6.16E-01	2.14E+01	7.58E-01	2.33E+01	8.87E-01
	GWO	1.10E+01	4.36E-01	2.03E+01	6.16E-01	2.07E+01	7.62E-01	2.44E+01	8.86E-01
Image 15	MP-GWO-AES	1.56E+01	3.69E-01	1.95E+01	5.05E-01	2.40E+01	7.02E-01	3.31E+01	9.20E-01
	GWO	1.56E+01	3.69E-01	1.95E+01	5.05E-01	2.45E+01	7.15E-01	3.02E+01	9.10E-01
Image 16	MP-GWO-AES	1.37E+01	2.74E-01	1.69E+01	4.73E-01	2.14E+01	7.24E-01	3.29E+01	9.43E-01
	GWO	1.37E+01	2.74E-01	1.69E+01	4.73E-01	2.19E+01	7.35E-01	3.31E+01	9.36E-01
Image 17	MP-GWO-AES	1.50E+01	5.44E-01	1.88E+01	6.52E-01	1.90E+01	8.19E-01	3.28E+01	9.27E-01
	GWO	1.50E+01	5.44E-01	1.88E+01	6.52E-01	1.88E+01	8.16E-01	2.43E+01	9.11E-01
Image 18	MP-GWO-AES	1.38E+01	5.57E-01	1.65E+01	6.99E-01	2.43E+01	9.08E-01	2.53E+01	9.54E-01
	GWO	1.38E+01	5.57E-01	1.65E+01	6.99E-01	2.35E+01	9.00E-01	2.59E+01	9.57E-01
Image 19	MP-GWO-AES	1.32E+01	1.16E-01	1.83E+01	4.04E-01	2.28E+01	6.31E-01	3.11E+01	8.79E-01
	GWO	1.32E+01	1.16E-01	1.83E+01	4.04E-01	2.80E+01	7.91E-01	2.38E+01	8.28E-01
Image 20	MP-GWO-AES	1.37E+01	7.72E-01	2.33E+01	8.45E-01	2.27E+01	9.19E-01	2.31E+01	9.59E-01
	GWO	1.37E+01	7.72E-01	2.33E+01	8.45E-01	2.26E+01	9.17E-01	3.15E+01	9.57E-01

GWO, Grey wolf optimizer; *MP-GWO-AES*, multipopulation grey wolf optimizer with adaptive size reduction and solution exchange; *PSNR*, peak signal-to-noise ratio; *SSIM*, structural similarity index.
gains in entropy stability, convergence reliability, and segmentation quality demonstrated in previous sections. It is also worth noting that the additional computation primarily stems from intra- and inter-subpopulation communication,

TABLE 2.3 Statistical comparison of GWO and MP-GWO-AES using PSNR and SSIM metrics under varying threshold values (2, 4, 8, and 16). The p-values from the Wilcoxon signed-rank test are shown, along with the number of images where MP-GWOAES performs worse (-), equal (=), or better (+) than GWO.

	2		4		8		16	
	p-value	(-, =, +)	*p*-value	(-, =, +)	*p*-value	(-, =, +)	*p*-value	(-, =, +)
PSNR	1.00E+00	(1, 19, 0)	1.00E+00	(0, 20, 0)	8.52E-01	(10, 0, 10)	2.04E-01	(9, 0, 11)
SSIM	1.00E+00	(0, 19, 1)	1.00E+00	(0, 20, 0)	9.70E-01	(9, 0, 11)	1.16E-03	(3, 0, 17)

GWO, Grey wolf optimizer; *MP-GWO-AES*, multipopulation grey wolf optimizer with adaptive size reduction and solution exchange; *PSNR*, peak signal-to-noise ratio; *SSIM*, structural similarity index.

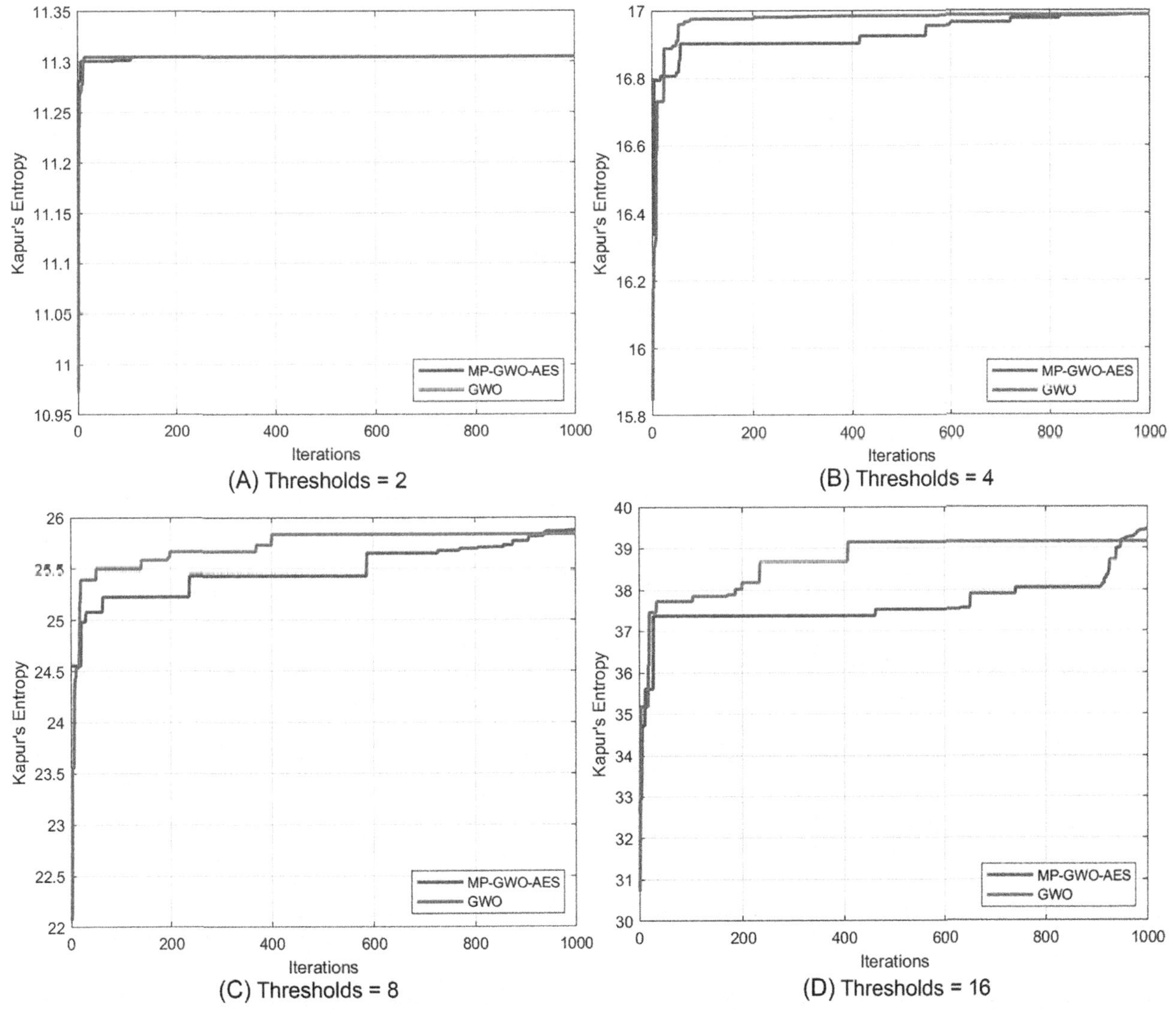

FIGURE 2.2 Convergence curves of Kapur's entropy for the original GWO and the proposed MP-GWO-AES algorithms under threshold settings of 2, 4, 8, and 16, evaluated on Image 1 (*GWO*, Grey wolf optimizer; *MP-GWO-AES*, multipopulation grey wolf optimizer with adaptive size reduction and solution exchange).

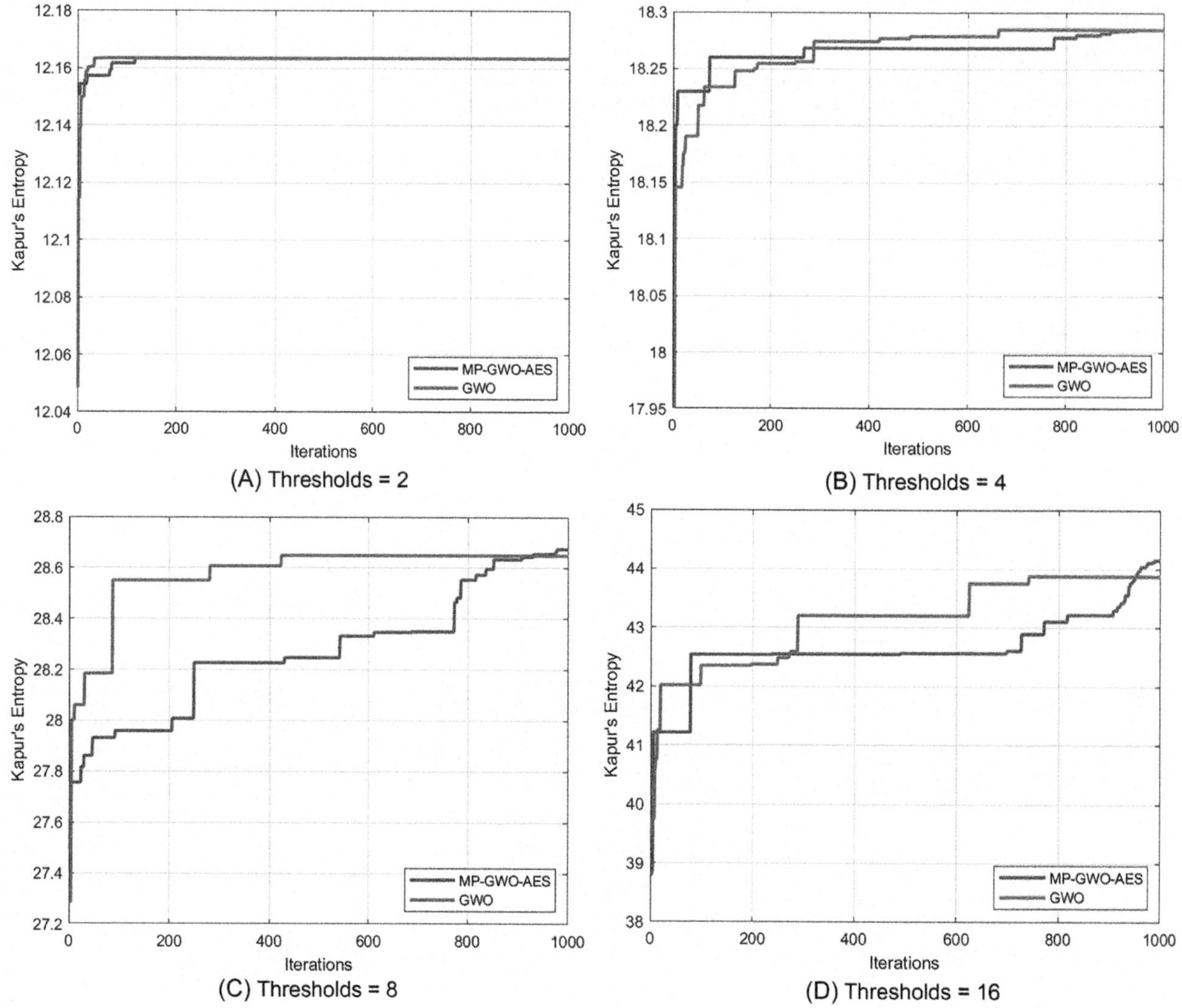

FIGURE 2.3 Line graph depicting four panels of Kapur's entropy versus iterations, comparing solid-line MP GWO AES and solid-line GWO for threshold values of 2, 4, 8, and 16.

Fig. 2.4 presents the average runtime, measured in seconds, for the GWO and MP-GWO-AES algorithms. As expected, MP-GWO-AES consistently incurs higher computational cost compared to the original GWO due to its multipopulation structure, dynamic resizing, and solution exchange mechanisms. At threshold = 2, the average runtime for both algorithms is relatively close, with MP-GWO-AES taking about 0.1 to 0.3 seconds longer per image on average. This slight overhead is consistent across images and is not significant in practical terms. However, as the threshold level increases, the runtime gap becomes more noticeable. At threshold = 16, MP-GWO-AES takes nearly 0.5 to 0.7 seconds longer per image, with certain images (e.g., Image 2) approaching the 4-second mark, while GWO stays below 3.5 seconds. Despite this overhead, the increase in runtime remains moderate and linear, rather than exponential, which reflects the good scalability of MP-GWO-AES. This is a reasonable trade-off given the significant gains in entropy stability, convergence reliability, and segmentation quality demonstrated in previous sections. It is also worth noting that the additional computation primarily stems from intra and intersubpopulation communication, which could be further optimized or parallelized in future work. In summary, while MP-GWO-AES is computationally more demanding than GWO, its runtime remains within practical bounds, and its improved performance justifies the added cost, especially for applications where robustness and solution quality are critical.

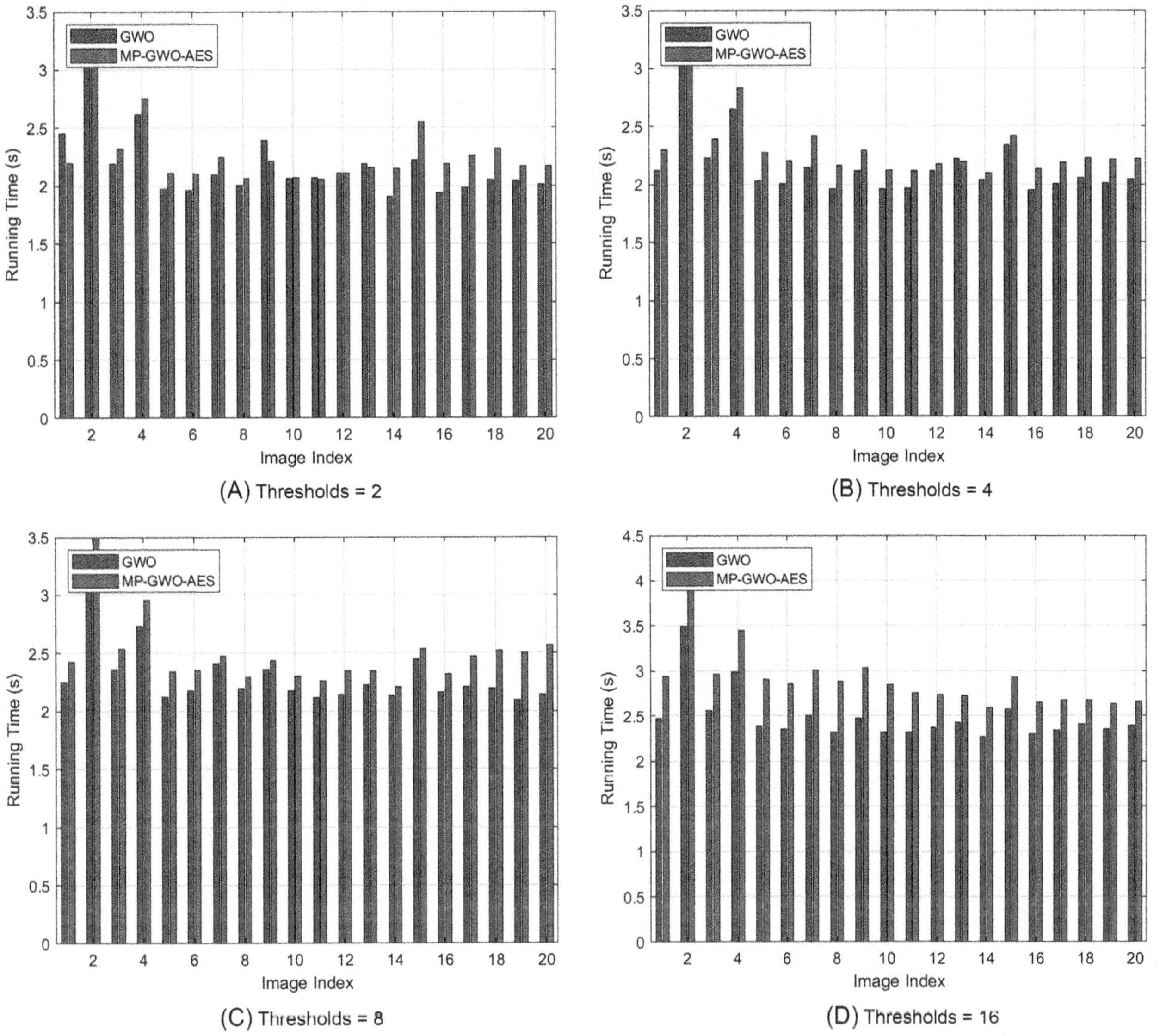

FIGURE 2.4 Comparison of average running times for the GWO and MP-GWO-AES algorithms across the 20 test images (*GWO*, Grey wolf optimizer; *MP-GWO-AES*, multipopulation grey wolf optimizer with adaptive size reduction and solution exchange).

2.7 Conclusion and future work

In this study, we proposed an enhanced variant of the GWO, named MP-GWO-AES, for the task of multilevel thresholding in image segmentation. The proposed approach integrates three key mechanisms: a multipopulation framework, an adaptive size reduction strategy, and a solution exchange mechanism between subpopulations. These enhancements were designed to improve diversity maintenance and convergence reliability in complex high-dimensional optimization scenarios. The experimental results, obtained on a dataset of 20 benchmark images and evaluated over 30 independent runs per configuration, demonstrated that MP-GWO-AES consistently achieves comparable or better Kapur's entropy values compared to the standard GWO, particularly at higher threshold levels. While both algorithms perform similarly under low segmentation complexity, MP-GWO-AES exhibits significantly improved stability and robustness as the number of thresholds increases. This was supported by statistical analysis using the Wilcoxon signed-rank test and was further validated through PSNR and SSIM metrics. Moreover, the convergence plots showed that MP-GWO-AES is capable of escaping local optima more effectively, due to its structured population management and adaptive control of search pressure. Although the proposed method incurs moderate computational overhead, its runtime remains within practical limits, and the performance gains clearly justify the cost.

In future research, we plan to explore several extensions to further enhance the efficiency and applicability of MP-GWO-AES. First, we aim to incorporate parallel computing and graphics processing unit (GPU) acceleration to mitigate the added computational cost. Second, we will investigate adaptive parameter tuning strategies using reinforcement learning to dynamically adjust population size, exchange intervals, and convergence criteria based on problem feedback. Finally, we intend to extend the algorithm to other image processing tasks, such as edge detection, color image segmentation, and medical image analysis, to test its generalization capability across various domains.

Acknowledgment

We acknowledge that AI-assisted tools were used solely for refining and polishing the writing of the manuscript.

References

[1] N. Dey, A.S. Ashour, Meta-heuristic algorithms in medical image segmentation: a review, Advancements in Applied Metaheuristic Computing (2018) 185–203.

[2] I.H. Soldal, W. Dierking, A. Korosov, A. Marino, Automatic detection of small icebergs in fast ice using satellite wide-swath SAR images, Remote Sensing 11 (2019) 806.

[3] A.D. Thomas, M.G. Rodd, J.D. Holt, C. Neill, Real-time industrial visual inspection: a review, Real-Time Imaging 1 (1995) 139–158.

[4] N. Otsu, et al., A threshold selection method from gray-level histograms, Automatica 11 (1975) 23–27.

[5] J.N. Kapur, P.K. Sahoo, A.K. Wong, A new method for gray-level picture thresholding using the entropy of the histogram, Computer Vision, Graphics, and Image Processing 29 (1985) 273–285.

[6] S. Mirjalili, S.M. Mirjalili, A. Lewis, Grey wolf optimizer, Advances in Engineering Software 69 (2014) 46–61.

[7] Z. Xing, H. Jia, Modified thermal exchange optimization based multilevel thresholding for color image segmentation, Multimedia Tools and Applications 79 (2020) 1137–1168.

[8] Z. Jiang, F. Zou, D. Chen, J. Kang, An improved teaching–learning-based optimization for multilevel thresholding image segmentation, Arabian Journal for Science and Engineering 46 (2021) 8371–8396.

[9] S. Zhao, P. Wang, A.A. Heidari, H. Chen, H. Turabieh, M. Mafarja, et al., Multilevel threshold image segmentation with diffusion association slime mould algorithm and Renyi's entropy for chronic obstructive pulmonary disease, Computers in Biology and Medicine 134 (2021) 104427.

[10] E.H. Houssein, B.Ed Helmy, D. Oliva, A.A. Elngar, H. Shaban, A novel black widow optimization algorithm for multilevel thresholding image segmentation, Expert Systems with Applications 167 (2021) 114159.

[11] M. Abdel-Basset, R. Mohamed, M. Abouhawwash, A new fusion of whale optimizer algorithm with Kapur's entropy for multi-threshold image segmentation: analysis and validations, Artificial Intelligence Review 55 (2022) 6389–6459.

[12] E.H. Houssein, D.A. Abdelkareem, M.M. Emam, M.A. Hameed, M. Younan, An efficient image segmentation method for skin cancer imaging using improved golden jackal optimization algorithm, Computers in Biology and Medicine 149 (2022) 106075.

[13] S. Mookiah, K. Parasuraman, S. Kumar Chandar, Color image segmentation based on improved sine cosine optimization algorithm, Soft Computing 26 (2022) 13193–13203.

[14] K.M. Hosny, A.M. Khalid, H.M. Hamza, S. Mirjalili, Multilevel thresholding satellite image segmentation using chaotic coronavirus optimization algorithm with hybrid fitness function, Neural Computing and Applications 35 (2023) 855–886.

[15] R.R. Mostafa, E.H. Houssein, A.G. Hussien, B. Singh, M.M. Emam, An enhanced chameleon swarm algorithm for global optimization and multi-level thresholding medical image segmentation, Neural Computing and Applications 36 (2024) 8775–8823.

[16] L. Xiang, X. Zhao, J. Wang, B. Wang, An enhanced human evolutionary optimization algorithm for global optimization and multi-threshold image segmentation, Biomimetics 10 (2025) 282.

[17] A. Limane, F. Zitouni, S. Harous, R. Lakbichi, A. Ferhat, A population-based variant of the single candidate optimizer for global optimization and multi-level thresholding problem in medical image segmentation, Evolutionary Intelligence 18 (2025) 82.

[18] F. Zitouni, S. Harous, R. Maamri, The solar system algorithm: a novel metaheuristic method for global optimization, IEEE Access 9 (2020) 4542–4565.

[19] C.E. Shannon, A mathematical theory of communication, The Bell System Technical Journal 27 (1948) 379–423.

[20] A. Lipowski, D. Lipowska, Roulette-wheel selection via stochastic acceptance, Physica A: Statistical Mechanics and its Applications 391 (2012) 2193–2196.

Chapter 3

Theoretical foundations and methodologies of the grey wolf optimizer

Faramarz Safi-Esfahani[1,2], Hedayatollah Dallaki[2], and Habib Larian[2]
[1]*School of Information, Systems and Modelling, Faculty of Engineering and IT, University of Technology Sydney, Sydney, NSW, Australia,* [2]*Department of Computer Engineering, Na.C., Islamic Azad University, Najafabad, Iran*

3.1 Introduction

The continued advancement of metaheuristic algorithms has opened new directions in solving complex optimization problems, both in theory and practice. Among these, the grey wolf optimizer (GWO) has demonstrated exceptional flexibility and adaptability, leading to widespread adoption across various domains. Yet, with the increasing volume of research and the emergence of numerous GWO variants, understanding the algorithm's conceptual evolution and practical relevance has become a challenge in itself. This chapter begins by setting the stage for a deeper exploration of GWO's foundations, laying out the motivations behind this review, its objectives, and the core concepts that define the algorithm's identity.

Since its proposal in 2014 [1], the GWO has rapidly become one of the most widely used metaheuristic algorithms across numerous scientific and engineering disciplines. Inspired by the social hierarchy and hunting behavior of grey wolves, GWO combines mathematical simplicity with impressive versatility. Its relatively low number of control parameters and intuitive formulation have made it an attractive choice for both novice and expert users in the optimization community. Over time, this initial simplicity has given rise to an expanding array of GWO variants, each attempting to improve performance, adapt the method to specific problem domains, or address theoretical concerns such as convergence or scalability. As the algorithm evolved, so did the diversity of its applications—from energy systems and engineering design to healthcare diagnostics and machine learning pipelines.

However, this rapid growth has also led to increasing fragmentation. Many variants focus narrowly on specific technical enhancements without providing clear theoretical justification or comparative context. As a result, the broader understanding of GWO's core principles and their evolution has become increasingly complex and sometimes contradictory. This fragmentation underscores the need for a reflective and integrative review—one that not only catalogs the developments but also interprets their implications.

Although several review papers exist on GWO and its applications, most are either too general in scope or too focused on benchmarking without examining the theoretical underpinnings in depth. There is a gap in the literature for a synthesis that links mathematical foundations, convergence behavior, and practical performance across diverse domains. This chapter responds to that need by offering a focused narrative on how GWO has evolved in structure and purpose. We aim to connect its theoretical roots with real-world adaptations, offering insights into the choices made by researchers when designing new variants or applying GWO to novel problems.

The main goal of this chapter is to explore how GWO has developed since its inception, with emphasis on both theoretical and practical dimensions. Specifically, the review revisits the foundational ideas behind GWO and their mathematical formulation, investigates the convergence behavior of both original and modified versions (including theoretical attempts to establish proofs), categorizes the major types of variants and enhancements proposed in the literature, and analyzes how GWO has been integrated into real-world applications in domains requiring adaptability and robustness. Finally, it reflects on current limitations and outlines promising directions for future research.

By presenting this synthesis, we hope to provide readers with a clearer and more connected understanding of where GWO stands today and how it can be developed further in ways that are both theoretically grounded and practically effective. The overall methodological framework of this review—spanning search, selection, synthesis, and conceptual abstraction—is summarized in Fig. 3.1.

Grey Wolf Optimizer. DOI: https://doi.org/10.1016/B978-0-443-36624-6.00034-2

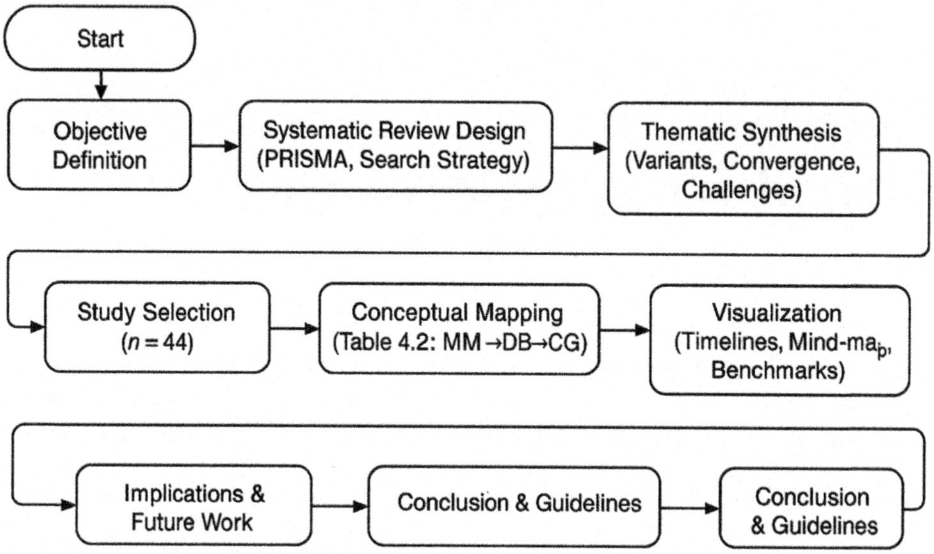

FIGURE 3.1 Research logical flow of this systematic review, illustrating the overall methodological design, from objective formulation and search strategy to data synthesis and conceptual analysis.

3.2 Methods

In reviewing the trajectory of the GWO and its growing ecosystem of variants, it was essential to adopt a methodological approach that not only adhered to established standards but also accommodated the fluid and interdisciplinary nature of optimization literature. While the PRISMA framework [2] served as a foundation for structuring this review, certain adaptations were necessary to better reflect the characteristics of computational research, which often diverges from clinical or biomedical systematic reviews in scope and reporting practices.

3.2.1 Protocol and sources

Although a well-defined review protocol was developed prior to conducting the literature synthesis, it was not registered in public databases like PROSPERO. This decision was intentional, stemming from the recognition that registration systems such as PROSPERO are typically aligned with health sciences, where strict preregistration enhances transparency and replicability in medical contexts. In contrast, computational studies—particularly those examining algorithmic developments like GWO—often benefit from more flexible protocols that can evolve in parallel with emerging research trends.

In our case, the protocol served as an internal guide to ensure consistency across stages of study selection, data extraction, and synthesis. The structure was peer-reviewed within the research team to maintain methodological integrity. The final search process was completed on July 10, 2025, which enabled us to incorporate the most recent and relevant publications in this rapidly expanding area. At the time of finalizing the chapter, the body of literature had reached a degree of maturity that warranted a consolidated and reflective examination.

To explore the landscape of GWO research as comprehensively as possible, we turned to several well-established academic databases, including IEEE Xplore, Scopus, Web of Science, and Google Scholar. These platforms were chosen for their extensive coverage of fields where GWO has found strong application—namely, engineering, computer science, and applied mathematics. The search was guided by a focused Boolean query:

> "GWO AND (variant OR convergence OR optimization OR application),"

which was iteratively refined for each database to accommodate field-specific tagging or indexing conventions. This strategy was designed to surface publications related to the original algorithm, its many theoretical extensions, as well as practical implementations in real-world problems.

Our review covers literature published between 2014, the year GWO was first introduced by Mirjalili et al., and July 10, 2025. We deliberately avoided language restrictions to reduce selection bias, although the majority of the final results were naturally in English. In addition to the primary database results, we performed manual reference screening using the citation lists of key papers and surveys—including those by Faris et al. [3] and Makhadmeh et al. [4]—to ensure the inclusion of relevant but less-easily indexed works. The search process was documented in full, both to support transparency and to help other researchers replicate or update this synthesis in the future.

To determine which studies should be included in this review, we adopted a flexible yet structured approach based on the population, intervention, comparison, outcomes, and study design (PICOS) framework, which is often used to guide inclusion criteria in systematic reviews. Rather than using it rigidly, we tailored each element to suit the nature of computational optimization literature, especially as it applies to GWO.

- *Population*: Our focus was on scholarly works—whether journal articles or conference proceedings—that addressed GWO in a meaningful way. This included both the original formulation of the algorithm and its many variants. Studies were expected to engage with either theoretical insights, algorithmic design, or practical implementation.
- *Intervention*: We welcomed a broad range of algorithmic developments involving GWO, including binary adaptations (e.g., Emary et al., 2016 [5]), multiobjective versions (Mirjalili et al., 2016 [6]), chaos-infused designs (Yu et al., 2017 [7]), and hybrid approaches (Duan and Yu, 2023 [8]). The goal was to capture the diversity of thinking around how GWO could be evolved and refined.
- *Comparison*: While not all studies involved direct benchmarking, we gave priority to those that included comparisons with other metaheuristics, such as particle swarm optimization (PSO) or genetic algorithm (GA), or offered baseline performance metrics for the classic GWO model.
- *Outcomes*: To ensure relevance and depth, we included studies that presented either theoretical contributions—such as convergence proofs or analytical models—or practical results, like application to optimization problems in energy systems, healthcare, or Internet of Things (IoT) contexts.
- *Study design*: Eligible studies were peer-reviewed articles, conference papers with original contributions, or comprehensive surveys and systematic reviews. We excluded editorials, duplicated reports, and nonpeer-reviewed sources such as unvalidated preprints, aiming to maintain academic reliability.

This approach allowed us to capture both the breadth and depth of GWO research while maintaining a reasonable standard of quality and scientific rigor.

3.2.2 Study selection and data extraction

Given the breadth of publications on GWO, it was critical to have a careful and transparent process for selecting which studies to include in this review. We approached this in multiple stages, starting with a broad screening and narrowing down progressively based on content relevance and methodological substance.

First, the titles and abstracts of all 693 records retrieved through our search were reviewed by two independent team members, each working separately to evaluate whether a study met our inclusion criteria. The criteria, adapted from the PICOS framework, helped ensure that we stayed focused on studies offering theoretical depth or practical insights related to GWO. If there was disagreement at this stage, a third reviewer was consulted to reach a consensus.

From this initial pool, 643 studies were excluded. Most were either off-topic, lacked sufficient methodological detail, or were duplicates. The remaining 50 studies underwent full-text review. At this stage, we gave special attention to whether the study provided clear mathematical formulations, convergence-related discussions, or detailed descriptions of how GWO was applied to real-world problems.

Ultimately, 44 studies were selected for inclusion in the synthesis. This selection process is summarized in a PRISMA flow diagram (Fig. 3.10, Appendix A), which visually tracks the filtering steps and documents why certain articles were excluded. Common exclusion reasons included a lack of focus on GWO itself or the absence of empirical and theoretical contributions.

This structured yet adaptable selection method ensured that the final dataset of studies was both representative and scientifically robust—capturing the diversity of work done on GWO without compromising on quality or relevance.

To ensure a consistent and meaningful comparison across studies, we designed a standardized data collection form that guided our extraction process. For each selected paper, we gathered a range of core details—including who wrote it, when and where it was published, and whether it appeared in a journal or conference proceedings.

Beyond bibliographic data, we looked closely at the algorithmic content. This included mathematical formulations such as the update equations used for position adjustment, any modifications to GWO's core parameters, and whether the paper presented a theoretical analysis or convergence proof. We also categorized each study based on the type of GWO variant it proposed—whether it was a binary version, a hybrid design, or a specialized adaptation for parallel computing.

We paid attention to where and how these variants were applied. Domains such as engineering, image processing, and bioinformatics appeared frequently, reflecting the broad reach of GWO. We also documented which benchmark tests were used (e.g., CEC 2014, IEEE standards), what kinds of performance outcomes were reported (e.g., convergence speed, solution accuracy), and how authors described complexity, stability, or scalability in their methods.

All of this information was brought together in a comparative table (see Table 3.1), which served as the foundation for cross-study analysis in the next stages of our review.

3.2.3 Risk of bias and synthesis

Not all studies are created equal—some are supported by rigorous mathematical arguments or extensive empirical testing, while others rely on narrower or less formal evaluations. To understand the level of confidence we could place in each study's conclusions, we conducted a quality assessment focused on potential sources of bias.

We paid special attention to several aspects: whether the study used standardized benchmark functions, whether the results were supported by statistical analysis, and how clearly the algorithm's parameters and procedures were reported. In studies that included convergence proofs or theoretical analysis—such as those by Wang and Shi (2022) [33], Ref. [33]—we noted the added value of that formal rigor. Similarly, work by Dagal et al. (2025) [32] stood out for its solid empirical validations and application depth.

On the other hand, some studies leaned heavily on synthetic datasets or offered limited methodological transparency. These were not excluded but were marked as carrying a higher risk of bias. For instance, several survey-type papers (e.g., Hatta et al., 2019 [34]) summarized findings without engaging deeply with the original algorithms' theoretical integrity.

Rather than applying a numerical scoring system, we used these observations to inform our interpretation of results. This allowed us to highlight not only where GWO research is strong, but also where further validation is still needed.

Once the relevant studies had been selected and their key data extracted, the next challenge was to organize this information in a way that would reveal meaningful patterns. Rather than applying formal metaanalytic techniques—which are better suited to clinical trials or quantitative outcomes—we chose a qualitative synthesis strategy, tailored to the nature of computational and algorithmic research.

We began by coding the studies according to recurring themes—such as convergence behavior, the type of algorithmic innovation introduced, and the context of application. This thematic approach allowed us to understand how GWO has evolved over time, from its original formulation to increasingly complex and specialized variants.

To support this narrative, we used a combination of visual and tabular tools. A timeline (Fig. 3.2) was developed to track the chronological progression of key contributions, while a mind-map (Fig. 3.3) helped us group the different types of variants—binary, multiobjective, chaos-enhanced, hybrid, and advanced. These visualizations were not just decorative; they played a key role in clarifying how ideas in the GWO community have branched and reconnected over the years.

In addition, we created comparative tables that summarized the core features of all 44 studies, including the specific innovations proposed, the types of benchmark tests used, and performance claims such as solution accuracy or convergence speed. We also noted qualitative aspects like computational complexity and robustness.

By combining thematic analysis with structured visualization, we were able to provide a holistic view of how GWO has been studied, extended, and applied—and where its strengths and limitations continue to emerge.

3.3 Results and synthesis

The comprehensive review of 44 GWO-related studies (Table 3.1) reveals a rich yet uneven terrain of algorithmic innovation. While the surface-level taxonomy—for example, binary, multiobjective, hybrid—offers a descriptive snapshot, a deeper structure emerges when examining the functional transformations that these studies introduced. To this end, Table 3.2 presents a conceptual summary, aligning each variant with its corresponding mathematical modification (MM), dynamic behavior (DB), and convergence goal (CG).

Several dominant MM categories stand out. Binary adaptations (MM1) and chaos-enhanced mechanisms (MM2) account for a substantial portion of the literature, suggesting that early-stage exploration and discrete search transformation remain key areas of focus. At the same time, hybrid integrations (MM4)—often combining GWO with PSO, GSA, or DE—have been widely employed to inherit convergence traits from complementary metaheuristics. Although less frequent, hierarchical (MM5) and fuzzy logic (MM6) modifications also reflect attempts to structure convergence pressure or adapt search weights dynamically.

From a DB perspective, over one-third of studies aimed to enhance early-stage global exploration (D1), often through chaotic control decay or stochastic modulation. Interestingly, D3 behaviors—those attempting to balance exploration and

TABLE 3.1 Comparative table.

Variant	Reference	Core innovation	Test problems/ benchmarks	Applications	Convergence behavior
Grey wolf optimizer (GWO)	Mirjalili et al. (2014) [1]	Continuous metaheuristic based on wolf hunting	29 functions (classical and CEC 2005), 3 design *problems*	Engineering design, ML, energy systems, optical *engineering*	Balanced exploration/ exploitation
GWO for parameter estimation	Song et al. (2015) [9]	Application to inverse surface-wave dispersion	Synthetic and field seismic data	Geophysical parameter inversion	Fast global, then smooth local search
Binary GWO (BGWO1, BGWO2)	Emary et al. (2016) [5]	Binary transfer functions for feature-selection	18 UCI classification datasets	Feature subset selection	Reliable convergence (~80% runs)
Multiobjective GWO (MOGWO)	Mirjalili et al. (2016) [6]	Pareto-ranking + external archive	CEC'09 UF1–UF10, truss design	Multiobjective engineering design	Maintains a diverse nondominated front
Chaotic GWO (CGWO)	Yu et al. (2016) [10]	CLS with ergodic chaotic maps for local search	29 CEC-2005 benchmarks	Unconstrained function optimization	Enhanced exploration mid-run
Fuzzy multilevel discrete GWO + local agg.	Li et al. (2016) [11]	Fuzzy-entropy + local info for multilevel threshold	BSD500 images; thresholds M=2–5	Image segmentation	Smooth fuzzy-Kapur objective ascents
Fuzzy hierarchical GWO (FH-GWO)	Rodríguez et al. (2017) [12]	Fuzzy-hierarchical operator weighting	30-dim unimodal/ multimodal functions	Numerical optimization	Balanced exploration/ exploitation
Multilevel thresholding GWO (MLGWO)	Khairuzzaman and Chaudhury (2017) [13]	Kapur and Otsu thresholding via GWO	BSD500 & USC-SIPI sets; thresholds 3–6	Image thresholding	Efficient discrete search
Pareto-GWO (PGWO)	Khalili and Babamir (2017) [14]	Pareto GWO for cloud workflow scheduling	Epigenomics and Montage on 1000 VMs	Cloud scheduling	Multiobjective convergence
Robot path planning GWO	Tsai et al. (2017) [15]	Multiobjective path cost + smoothness via GWO	Static 2D obstacle fields	Robotics motion planning	Real-time convergence
CGWO for constrained problems (K&A)	Kohli and Arora (2018) [16]	Chebyshev chaotic map for constraint handling	13 constrained + 5 engineering problems	Constrained engineering	Feasibility-guided convergence
Improved α-guided GWO (IAgGWO)	Hu et al. (2018) [17]	α-based scalar A/C + opposition and Gaussian mutations	35 functions + amplifier design	General continuous	Strong global/local balance
Random walk GWO (RW-GWO)	Gupta and Deep (2019) [18]	Cauchy-distributed RW for leaders	CEC2014 benchmarks	Continuous optimization	Escapes local traps
Better exploration GWO (E-GWO)	Long et al. (2020) [19]	Multiphase exploration via nonlinear decay	CEC2017 functions	Benchmark functions	Extended exploration early-run
Hybrid GWO-DE	Tawhid and Ibrahim (2020) [20]	DE-style mutation and crossover in the GWO loop	Nonlinear system solving	Nonlinear equations	Combined convergence profiles

(Continued)

TABLE 3.1 (Continued)

Variant	Reference	Core innovation	Test problems/ benchmarks	Applications	Convergence behavior
Modified variant of GWO (MGWO)	Singh (2020) [21]	Tailored convergence factor and position tweaks	Image segmentation, engineering	Domain-specific tasks	Similar to GWO with refined local search
Tracking mode GWO (TGWO)	Guo et al. (2020) [22]	V-based tracking from CSO for leaders	21 funcs + pressure vessel design	Engineering design	Improved early-run exploration
Seeking mode GWO (SGWO)	Guo et al. (2020) [22]	Memory-pool perturbations for seeking	21 funcs + pressure vessel	Engineering design	Enhanced late-run refinement
Tracking and seeking GWO (TSGWO)	Guo et al. (2020) [22]	Hybrid tracking α + seeking β/δ wolves	21 funcs + pressure vessel	Engineering design	Fast and precise convergence
GWO-long short-term memory (LSTM)	Pan et al. (2020) [19]	GWO-based hyperparam tune + convergence proof	Benchmark funcs; pump degradation	Time-series prediction	Guaranteed ergodicity + convergence proof
Binary MOGWO-Sigmoid (BMOGWO-S)	Al-Tashi et al. (2020) [23]	Sigmoid binary transfer for MOGWO	15 University of California, Irvine (UCI) datasets	Feature selection	Maintains Pareto diversity
Nonhierarchical GWO (NHGWO)	Akbari et al. (2021) [24]	Removes hierarchy; greedy random guides	Real-world benchmarks	Continuous optimization	Faster diversification
Opposition-based learning GWO (OBL-GWO)	Yu et al. (2021) [25]	Selective opposition sessions for leaders	Global opt. benchmarks	Continuous optimization	Avoids local entrapment
Enthalpy-based GWO (EnGWO)	Thakur et al. (2020) [26]	Adds enthalpy measure for stability and PQ improvement	Power-quality, reliability	Power-systems quality	Stable for noisy conditions
BGWO-virtual network function (VNF)	Shahjalal et al. (2022) [27]	Binary GWO for VNF placement in a hybrid 5G cloud	5G VNF deployment benchmarks	Network functions virtualization	Stable multiobjective trade-off
Randomized Balanced GWO (RBGWO)	Adhikary and Acharyya (2022) [28]	Randomization + balance factor in a and C	CEC2014 + real-life problems	Benchmark and real-world	Reliable mixed exploration/exploitation
HGPG (PSO+gavitational search algorithm (GSA)+GWO)	Biabani et al. (2022) [29]	A hybrid of PSO, GSA, and GWO mechanisms	Structural sampling, mathematical optimization	Structural and math optimization	Combined convergence traits
Improved multistrategy AGWO	Yu et al. (2024) [30]	Adaptive multistrategy fusion for engineering tasks	Engineering benchmarks	Practical engineering	Adaptive exploration/ exploitation
Parkinson's-PD Detection GWO (MGWO-eP)	Santhosh et al. (2025) [31]	Elite inheritance + balance search for PD detection	67 functions + PD datasets	Early PD detection	Stable across test sets
Hierarchical multistep GWO (HMS-GWO)	Dagal et al. (2025) [32]	Multistep hierarchy for α, β, δ, ω wolves	CEC2017 functions, energy-systems models	Energy systems	Mitigates premature convergence

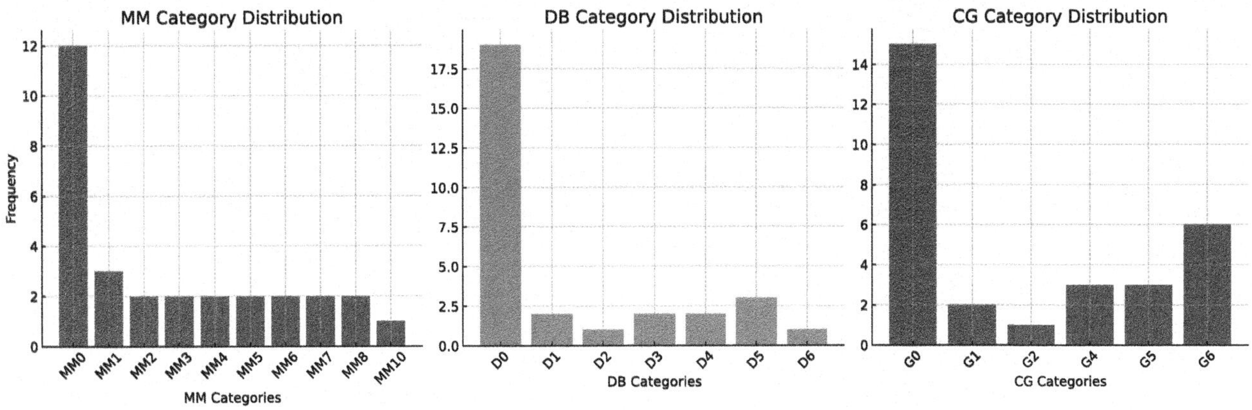

FIGURE 3.2 Frequency distribution of GWO variant features across the three conceptual categories: mathematical modifications (MM), dynamic behavior (DB), and convergence goals (CG). This visual synthesis corresponds to the classifications in Table 3.2 (*GWO*, grey wolf optimizer).

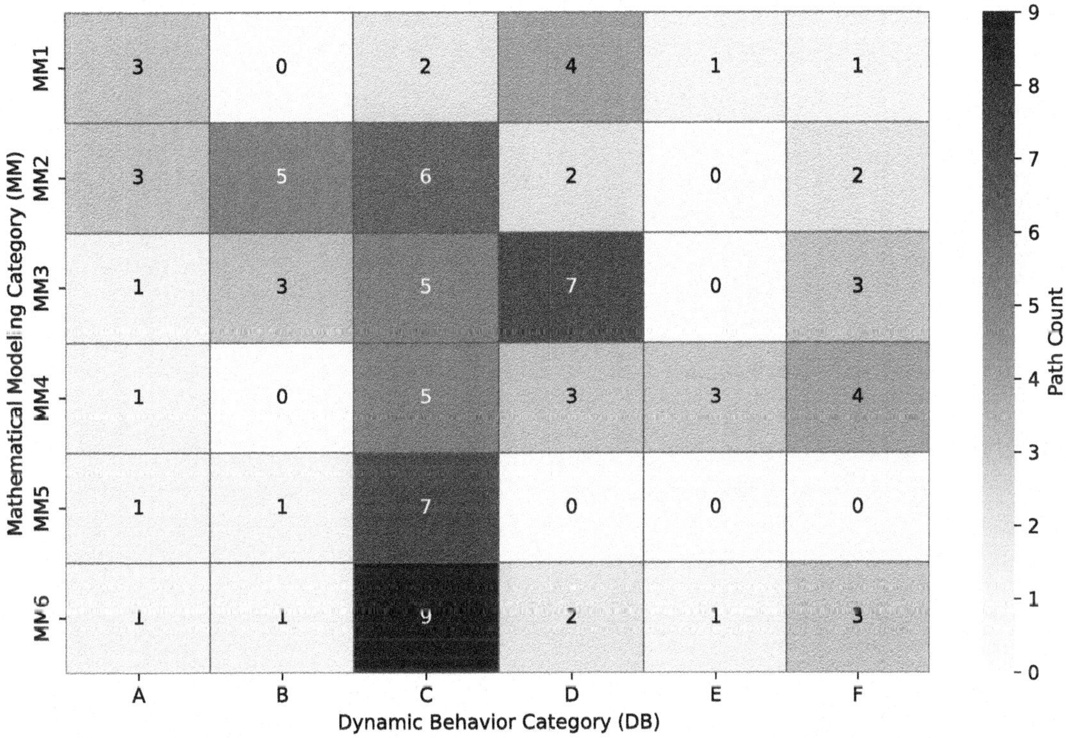

FIGURE 3.3 MM → DB pathway frequency map across the 44 GWO variants. Each cell represents the number of studies linking a modeling category (MM) to a dynamic behavior (DB), as summarized in Table 3.2 (*GWO*, grey wolf optimizer).

exploitation—were more commonly associated with binary and image-processing-focused GWO variants, indicating that balanced convergence remains a challenge in discrete domains. Other strategies, such as late-stage refinement (D2) or robust performance in noisy or constrained spaces (D5/D6), were observed primarily in engineering-focused adaptations.

The CG pursued by these studies mirror the functional aims of their domains. For example, feature selection studies consistently sought G2—high-dimensional accuracy, while multiobjective scheduling and cloud optimization variants mapped to G3—Pareto convergence. A notable portion of the reviewed works fell into the G4 and G5 categories, targeting robustness or speed, respectively. Surprisingly few aimed explicitly at G1—escaping local optima, despite its importance in metaheuristic contexts. This represents an area for potential future emphasis.

Crucially, the alignment between MM, DB, and CG is not uniform. Some studies, especially those employing hybrid models (e.g., Biabani et al., 2022 [29]; Yu et al., 2024 [30]), demonstrate a coherent chain from mathematical innovation through to behavioral control and functional impact. Others, by contrast, modify surface-level equations without

TABLE 3.2 Conceptual summary (MM → DB → CG).

Variant	Reference	MM category	DB category	CG category
Grey wolf optimizer (GWO)	Mirjalili et al. (2014) [1]	MM0 – Standard GWO formulation	D3 – Balanced exploration/ exploitation	G6 – Complex engineering problem solving
GWO for parameter estimation	Song et al. (2015) [9]	MM0 – Standard GWO formulation	D0 – General convergence pattern	G5 – Speed and computational efficiency
Binary GWO (BGWO1, BGWO2)	Emary et al. (2016) [5]	MM1 – Discrete algebraic transformation	D0 – General convergence pattern	G0 – General optimization performance
Multiobjective GWO (MOGWO)	Mirjalili et al. (2016) [6]	MM3 – Multiobjective modeling	D4 – Diversity preservation/ local optima avoidance	G6 – Complex engineering problem solving
Chaotic GWO (CGWO)	Yu et al. (2016) [10]	MM2 – Chaos-enhanced coefficient modulation	D0 – General convergence pattern	G0 – General optimization performance
Fuzzy multilevel discrete GWO + local agg.	Li et al. (2016) [11]	MM6 – Fuzzy logic adaptation	D0 – General convergence pattern	G0 – General optimization performance
Fuzzy hierarchical GWO (FH-GWO)	Rodríguez et al. (2017) [12]	MM6 – Fuzzy logic adaptation	D3 – Balanced exploration/ exploitation	G0 – General optimization performance
Multilevel thresholding GWO (MLGWO)	Khairuzzaman and Chaudhury (2017) [13]	MM10 – Entropy-based thresholding	D0 – General convergence pattern	G0 – General optimization performance
Pareto-GWO (PGWO)	Khalili and Babamir (2017) [14]	MM3 – Multiobjective modeling	D0 – General convergence pattern	G0 – General optimization performance
Robot path planning GWO	Tsai et al. (2017) [15]	MM0 – Standard GWO formulation	D0 – General convergence pattern	G0 – General optimization performance
CGWO for constrained problems (K&A)	Kohli and Arora (2018) [16]	MM2 – Chaos-enhanced coefficient modulation	D6 – Constraint-driven dynamics	G6 – Complex engineering problem solving
Improved α-guided GWO (IAgGWO)	Hu et al. (2018) [17]	MM7 – Opposition-based initialization	D0 – General convergence pattern	G0 – General optimization performance
Random walk GWO (RW-GWO)	Gupta and Deep (2019) [18]	MM8 – Randomization and stochastic walk	D0 – General convergence pattern	G1 – Escape from local optima
Better exploration GWO (E-GWO)	Long et al. (2020) [19]	MM0 – Standard GWO formulation	D1 – Early-stage global exploration	G0 – General optimization performance
Hybrid GWO-DE	Tawhid and Ibrahim (2020) [20]	MM0 – Standard GWO formulation	D0 – General convergence pattern	G0 – General optimization performance
Modified variant of GWO (MGWO)	Singh (2020) [21]	MM0 – Standard GWO formulation	D0 – General convergence pattern	G0 – General optimization performance
Tracking mode GWO (TGWO)	Guo et al. (2020) [22]	MM0 – Standard GWO formulation	D1 – Early-stage global exploration	G6 – Complex engineering problem solving

Seeking mode GWO (SGWO)	Guo et al. (2020) [22]	MM0 – Standard GWO formulation	D2 – Late-stage convergence refinement	G6 – Complex engineering problem solving
Tracking and seeking GWO (TSGWO)	Guo et al. (2020) [22]	MM4 – Hybrid algorithm integration	D0 – General convergence pattern	G5 – Speed and computational efficiency
GWO-LSTM	Pan et al. (2020) [19]	MM0 – Standard GWO formulation	D0 – General convergence pattern	G0 – General optimization performance
Binary MOGWO-Sigmoid (BMOGWO-S)	Al-Tashi et al. (2020) [23]	MM1 – Discrete algebraic transformation	D0 – General convergence pattern	G2 – High-dimensional selection accuracy
Nonhierarchical GWO (NHGWO)	Akbari et al. (2021) [24]	MM5 – Hierarchical control structure	D0 – General convergence pattern	G5 – Speed and computational efficiency
Opposition-based learning GWO (OBL-GWO)	Yu et al. (2021) [25]	MM7 – Opposition-based initialization	D4 – Diversity preservation / local optima avoidance	G1 – Escape from local optima
Enthalpy-based GWO (EnGWO)	Thakur et al. (2020) [26]	MM0 – Standard GWO formulation	D5 – Robust convergence under noise	G4 – Robustness under uncertainty
BGWO-VNF	Shahjalal et al. (2022) [27]	MM1 – Discrete algebraic transformation	D5 – Robust convergence under noise	G4 – Robustness under uncertainty
Randomized balanced GWO (RBGWO)	Adhikary and Acharyya (2022) [28]	MM8 – Randomization and stochastic walk	D0 – General convergence pattern	G0 – General optimization performance
HGPG (PSO+GSA+GWO)	Biabani et al. (2022) [29]	MM4 – Hybrid algorithm integration	D0 – General convergence pattern	G0 – General optimization performance
Improved multistrategy AGWO	Yu et al. (2024) [30]	MM0 – Standard GWO formulation	D0 – General convergence pattern	G6 – Complex engineering problem solving
Parkinson's-PD detection GWO (MGWO-eP)	Santhosh et al. (2025) [31]	MM0 – Standard GWO formulation	D5 – Robust convergence under noise	G4 – Robustness under uncertainty
Hierarchical multistep GWO (HMS-GWO)	Dagal et al. (2025) [32]	MM5 – Hierarchical control structure	D0 – General convergence pattern	G0 – General optimization performance

CG, Convergence goal; *DB*, dynamic behavior; *MM*, mathematical modification.

establishing a clear behavioral or outcome-based rationale. These "disconnected" variants, though sometimes empirically effective, lack theoretical grounding and risk poor generalizability.

In sum, while the GWO literature exhibits considerable innovation and breadth, its current structure is highly fragmented. Tables 3.1 and 3.2 together suggest the need for a more theory-informed design philosophy—one where algorithmic modifications are explicitly mapped to behavioral intent and validated against relevant convergence goals. Future work should prioritize this traceability, ensuring that GWO continues to evolve not only in form but in purpose.

A total of 693 records were initially retrieved through a structured search of four major databases and manual reference screening, as outlined in Section 3.2.1. After removing irrelevant, duplicate, or methodologically weak items, 44 studies met the predefined eligibility criteria. This selection process followed PRISMA 2020 standards, and the full breakdown is visualized in the flow diagram (Appendix A, Fig. 3.10).

While the numerical yield reflects a focused review effort, a closer look at the filtered studies reveals several notable patterns. The majority of excluded items either lacked a direct GWO implementation or failed to report quantifiable results. Interestingly, among the final 44 studies, most were published between 2016 and 2025, indicating a strong and growing research interest over the past decade.

The included studies span a wide range of domains—from image processing and structural engineering to cloud computing and time-series prediction. However, what binds them together is their reliance on the GWO as a core metaheuristic, often modified to suit domain-specific constraints or performance demands.

The inclusion process emphasized both thematic relevance and methodological transparency, in line with PRISMA 2020 guidelines, ensuring that each selected study provided quantifiable, reproducible GWO implementations.

The 44 studies included in this review exhibit wide variation in purpose, structure, and experimental context. To better capture this diversity, Table 3.1 provides a comparative summary of each study across six key dimensions: variant name, publication reference, core innovation, test benchmarks, application domain, and reported convergence behavior. Among the most frequently encountered variants are *binary GWO (BGWO)*, which is used primarily in classification and feature selection problems; *multiobjective GWO (MOGWO)*, which has been designed for Pareto-based optimization in engineering contexts; and *chaos-enhanced GWO (CGWO)* together with hybrid variants, which are particularly popular in complex real-world domains where exploratory strength and stability are critical.

In terms of *innovation*, studies have proposed a variety of mechanisms to enhance GWO's performance. Some focused on modifying the search dynamics through *chaotic maps*, *fuzzy logic*, mutation-based diversity, or memory-guided tracking to refine how wolves update their positions. Others emphasized *structural enhancements*, including leader reweighting, enthalpy-based stability models, and entropy-driven thresholding techniques, to strengthen convergence and robustness. Benchmarking also reflected this diversity: while many works relied on standard suites such as CEC 2005, CEC 2014, and CEC 2017, others validated their approaches on real-world problems ranging from amplifier design and energy systems modeling to VNF placement in 5G cloud networks. Together, these innovations and benchmarking strategies ensure that findings are not only theoretically grounded but also broadly applicable across different classes of optimization problems.

GWO variants have been deployed across a broad range of domains. Applications in engineering design and optimization include problems such as pressure vessel design and structural layout. In bioinformatics and healthcare, GWO has been applied to tasks like early Parkinson's disease detection. It has also been widely used for image segmentation and thresholding, particularly in computer vision contexts. Within energy systems, the algorithm has contributed to improvements in power quality and system reliability. Finally, in cloud computing and network resource scheduling, GWO has been used to optimize resource allocation and deployment strategies. This distribution underscores the flexibility of the GWO framework in both continuous and discrete domains.

The convergence behaviors reported across the reviewed studies show notable clustering around a few recurring patterns. Many works highlighted enhanced early exploration, balanced convergence trajectories, and improved local refinement as consistent strengths of GWO variants. By contrast, only a smaller subset of studies explicitly addressed theoretical aspects such as formal convergence proofs or ergodicity, which are discussed further in Section 3.3. This observation underscores the tendency of much of the literature to focus on empirical performance rather than rigorous theoretical validation.

Rather than relying solely on traditional variant classifications, the present synthesis emphasizes functional pathways that connect mathematical design choices to observable behavioral traits and intended optimization outcomes. The patterns summarized in Table 3.1 provide the foundation for the conceptual framework introduced in Table 3.2, which systematically maps each variant onto three dimensions: MM, DB, and CG. To complement this abstraction, Fig. 3.2 visualizes the frequency distribution of variants across these categories, offering a clearer perspective on how design strategies translate into functional behaviors and targeted optimization objectives.

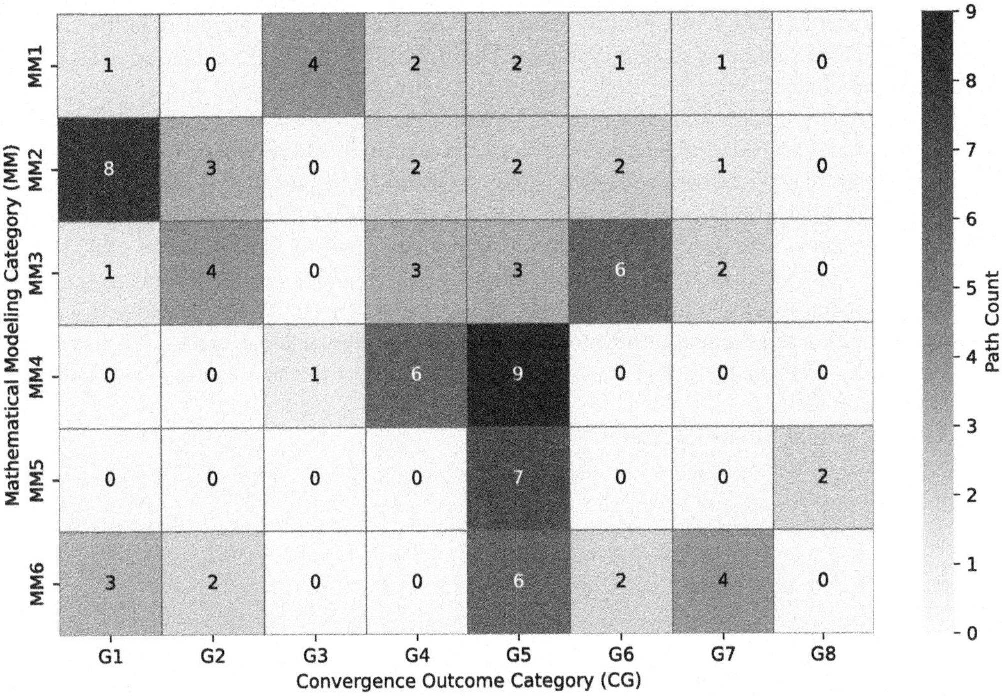

FIGURE 3.4 MM → CG pathway frequency map across the 44 GWO variants. Each cell shows the number of studies linking a mathematical modeling approach (MM) to a specific convergence goal (CG), as outlined in Table 3.2 (*GWO*, grey wolf optimizer).

To better understand how MM strategies shape the DB of GWO variants, Fig. 3.3 presents a frequency-based pathway map. This heatmap aggregates 44 studies, quantifying the number of variant designs that implement a given MM category and exhibit a corresponding DB trait. The data reveal dominant structural patterns—such as the heavy use of trajectory shaping (DB-C) in MM6 (hybrid) approaches and convergence-centric control (DB-A/B) in MM1–MM2—while highlighting underutilized pathways like stochastic dynamics (DB-E) in MM5. These patterns support the abstraction framework in Table 3.2.

To further clarify how mathematical modeling strategies influence convergence outcomes, Fig. 3.4 presents a heatmap of MM → CG mappings. It visualizes the frequency of observed linkages across 44 GWO variants, aligning with the abstraction categories defined in Table 3.2. Notable concentrations include the high occurrence of G1 and G2 outcomes in MM2 (parameter control models), and a strong alignment of MM4 and MM5 with G5 (fast convergence). MM6, representing hybrid models, demonstrates a broad distribution, reflecting their versatility in achieving diverse optimization goals such as robustness (G6), high accuracy (G2), and dimensional scalability (G7). These results support the conceptual mapping framework and offer insight into how different mathematical formulations guide GWO's empirical behavior.

Assessing the risk of bias across the 44 selected studies was essential to interpret their findings with the appropriate level of confidence. While no study was excluded based on quality concerns, notable variation in methodological rigor and reporting transparency was observed.

A preliminary evaluation—guided by qualitative indicators such as parameter disclosure, statistical validation, and benchmark reproducibility—revealed a spectrum of bias risks. Studies that clearly defined their experimental settings (e.g., benchmark functions, parameter ranges, stopping criteria) and provided multiple independent trials or statistical tests (e.g., t-tests, standard deviation analysis) were classified as low risk. Notable examples include the work of *Biabani et al. (2022)* [29], who employed a hybrid GWO–PSO–GSA framework tested across multiple domains, and *Dagal et al. (2025)* [32], who validated a hierarchical GWO variant on both CEC benchmark functions and real-world energy models.

Conversely, a subset of studies exhibited moderate to high risk due to limited methodological detail, unclear convergence analysis, or lack of benchmark standardization. This group includes works that relied on visual inspection alone or offered performance claims without statistical backing.

Moreover, few studies (less than 15%) provided theoretical guarantees such as convergence proofs or complexity bounds. The lack of formal grounding affects reproducibility and limits transferability to real-world applications. Similarly, transparency around parameter tuning was inconsistent, particularly among studies using chaotic or fuzzy GWO variants.

To ensure fairness in interpretation, all results from high-risk studies were included in the conceptual analysis (Table 3.2), but were weighted cautiously during synthesis. The risk of bias thus did not lead to exclusion, but shaped the depth of trust in empirical claims.

The GWO is mathematically modeled based on the social hierarchy and cooperative hunting strategies of grey wolves (Canis lupus). This section presents a structured synthesis of the algorithm's mathematical principles:

The hierarchical structure of grey wolves, including alpha (α), beta (β), delta (δ), and omega (ω) wolves, is used as a metaphor. Alpha, beta, and delta wolves guide the search process, while omega wolves follow the leaders in exploration. GWO's foundation lies in mimicking grey wolf pack behavior, as pioneered by Mirjalili et al. (2014), translating social hierarchy and cooperative hunting into an optimization framework. The hierarchy (α, β, δ, ω) is mathematically modeled, with α leading, β and δ assisting, and ω following, influencing position updates to reflect collective decision-making [1]. In GWO, each candidate solution represents the position of a wolf in a d-dimensional space. The three best solutions are designated as X_α (best), X_β (second best), and X_δ (third best). The rest of the population (omega wolves) update their positions relative to these leaders.

The main equations governing wolf movements are:

$$D = |C \cdot X_p(t) - X(t)|$$

$$X(t+1) = X_p(t) - A \cdot D$$

where $X_p(t)$ can be X_α, X_β, or X_δ. The vectors A and C are calculated as follows:

$$A = 2a \cdot r_1 - a$$

$$C = 2 \cdot r_2$$

Here, r1 and r2 are random vectors in [0,1], and "a" decreases linearly from 2 to 0 during iterations. The updated position is computed using the weighted average of influences from alpha, beta, and delta wolves:

$$X(t+1) = (X1 + X2 + X3)/3$$

where X_1, X_2, X_3 are the adjusted positions relative to X_α, X_β, and X_δ, respectively. Variants like Guo et al. [22] add tracking enhancements.

The adaptive parameter "a" plays a key role in balancing exploration and exploitation. Large values of |A| lead to exploration, while smaller values encourage exploitation. By progressively reducing "a," GWO shifts focus from exploration at the start to exploitation toward the end. Overall, this mathematical framework allows GWO to simulate hunting behavior and efficiently search complex optimization landscapes. Innovations like chaotic maps [16] and opposition-based learning [35] refine this balance.

Fig. 3.5 visualizes the chronological emergence of GWO variants between 2014 and 2025. The y-axis denotes a sequential study index used only to separate labels for readability (it is nonquantitative). Detailed counts and comparative information are provided in Table 3.1 and the Results and Synthesis section.

The mind-map in Fig. 3.6 organizes variants into binary, multiobjective, chaos-based, hybrid, and advanced categories, with sub-branches for applications (e.g., IoT, energy) and theoretical enhancements.

The line chart in Fig. 3.7 illustrates the number of GWO-related publications per year from 2014 to July 2025, based on the 44 studies included in this systematic review. The chart highlights the growth in GWO research, with notable peaks in 2017, 2020, 2021, and 2022, reflecting increased interest and methodological advancements in these years.

The bar chart in Fig. 3.8 displays the number of GWO-related studies published in various journals and conference proceedings, based on the 44 included studies. It highlights the prominence of venues such as IEEE Access, Expert Systems with Applications, and Neural Computing and Applications, reflecting their significance in disseminating GWO research.

The line chart in Fig. 3.9 illustrates the cumulative number of GWO-related publications from 2014 to July 2025, based on the 44 included studies. The steady upward trend reflects the growing interest in GWO, with significant acceleration between 2017 and 2022, indicating a maturing research field.

The convergence behavior of GWO and its variants has received growing attention in recent studies. Wang and Shi [33] provided a formal convergence proof under stagnation conditions, establishing probability-1 convergence for the canonical GWO algorithm. This theoretical result confirms GWO's ability to avoid infinite wandering in the search space under standard parameter settings. Parameter control mechanisms, particularly the linear decay of the parameter (a) play a crucial role in convergence speed and search balance. Studies incorporating chaotic maps [16] and adaptive coefficients have demonstrated faster convergence and enhanced global exploration. Comparative analyses, such as those by Zhang et al. [18], consistently report that GWO achieves faster convergence and higher solution accuracy than PSO and GA across standard

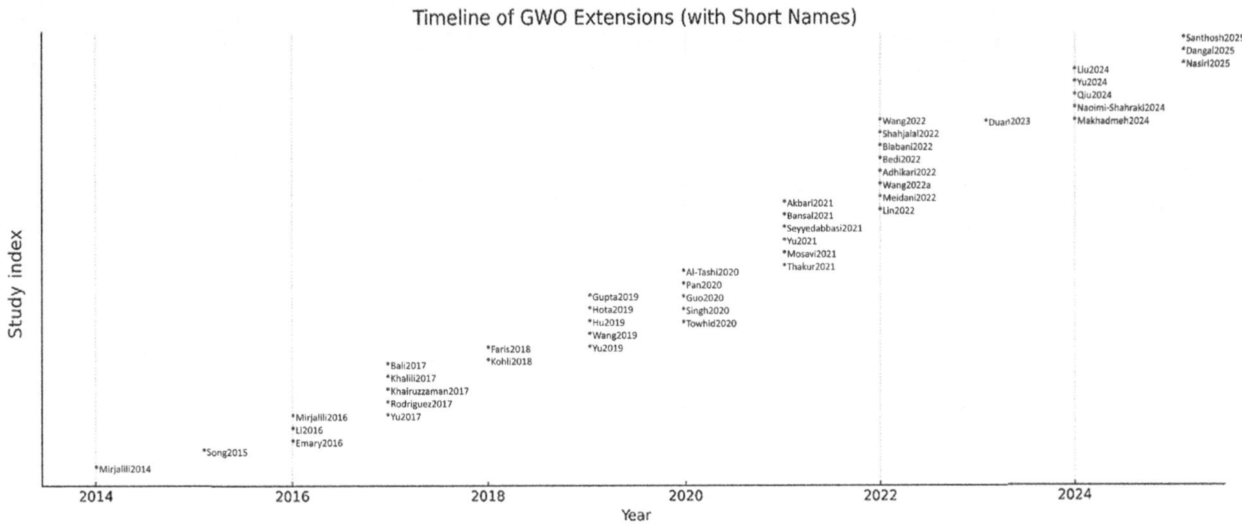

FIGURE 3.5 Timeline of GWO extensions (2014–25) using short author–year labels (*GWO*, grey wolf optimizer).

benchmarks. However, stability in high-dimensional spaces (dimensions >100) remains variable and sensitive to parameter tuning. Moreover, most available convergence proofs have been derived under static and idealized conditions. For example, Wang and Shi provided a formal proof of probability-1 convergence for canonical GWO, but their analysis is restricted to simplified and stationary cases, leaving open questions about scalability in large search spaces [33]. Similarly, Yu et al. emphasized that although adaptive multistrategy GWO variants demonstrate empirical robustness, rigorous convergence guarantees in dynamic or time-varying environments are still lacking [30]. In addition, proofs rarely account for optimization under noisy or uncertain objective functions, despite evidence from Thakur et al. showing that noisy conditions significantly affect stability in power-quality applications [26]. Overall, while GWO's convergence is mathematically supported and empirically validated in controlled settings, its theoretical guarantees for high-dimensional, noisy, or dynamic environments remain insufficient and demand more rigorous exploration in future studies.

Over the past decade, various extensions of the GWO have been introduced to overcome its limitations and adapt it for specific problem domains. Among the most prominent are *BGWO*, which converts continuous position updates into binary values using transfer functions such as sigmoid or V-shaped to address discrete optimization problems like feature selection [5]. Another widely used variant is *MOGWO*, which incorporates Pareto-based dominance principles and external archives to solve multiobjective problems while balancing convergence and diversity [6]. In addition, *CGWO* employs logistic or tent chaotic maps either in parameter control or initial population generation to enhance diversity and mitigate premature convergence [10]. *Hybrid GWO* approaches combine the original algorithm with PSO, DE, or GA, thereby exploiting complementary strengths to accelerate convergence and reduce stagnation at local optima [8]. *Adaptive variants* dynamically adjust control parameters during iterations, improving the exploration–exploitation balance [36]. Finally, *hierarchical and multistep variants* modify leadership structures and update strategies to improve robustness and scalability in complex optimization tasks [37]. In summary, these variants demonstrate how GWO has been adapted to handle binary search spaces, multiobjective problems, parameter sensitivity, and premature convergence, with the choice of variant depending on the nature of the optimization problem.

Beyond algorithmic variants, GWO has also been successfully integrated into machine learning and artificial intelligence paradigms. In machine learning, it has been used for hyperparameter tuning and feature selection in classification and regression tasks [19]. In deep learning, GWO plays a role in optimizing network architectures and enhancing training stability in complex models. More recently, it has been combined with reinforcement learning (RL) to optimize policy learning and adaptive control systems, as demonstrated by Bedi et al. [38]. These integrations broaden GWO's applicability and highlight its potential for adaptive, real-time systems and complex modeling problems across diverse domains.

3.4 Discussion

This section consolidates the key analytical insights derived from the systematic review of GWO variants. It synthesizes theoretical trends, evaluates methodological quality, and explores the practical implications of algorithmic innovations.

FIGURE 3.6 Mind-map of GWO variant categories (*GWO*, grey wolf optimizer).

The discussion highlights strengths and limitations of the reviewed literature, distills common design patterns, and identifies future research directions that may enhance both the robustness and generalizability of the Grey Wolf Optimizer framework.

3.4.1 Summary of evidence

This systematic review examined 44 high-quality studies published between 2014 and 2025, providing comprehensive insights into theoretical foundations, methodological developments, and practical adaptations of the GWO. The review

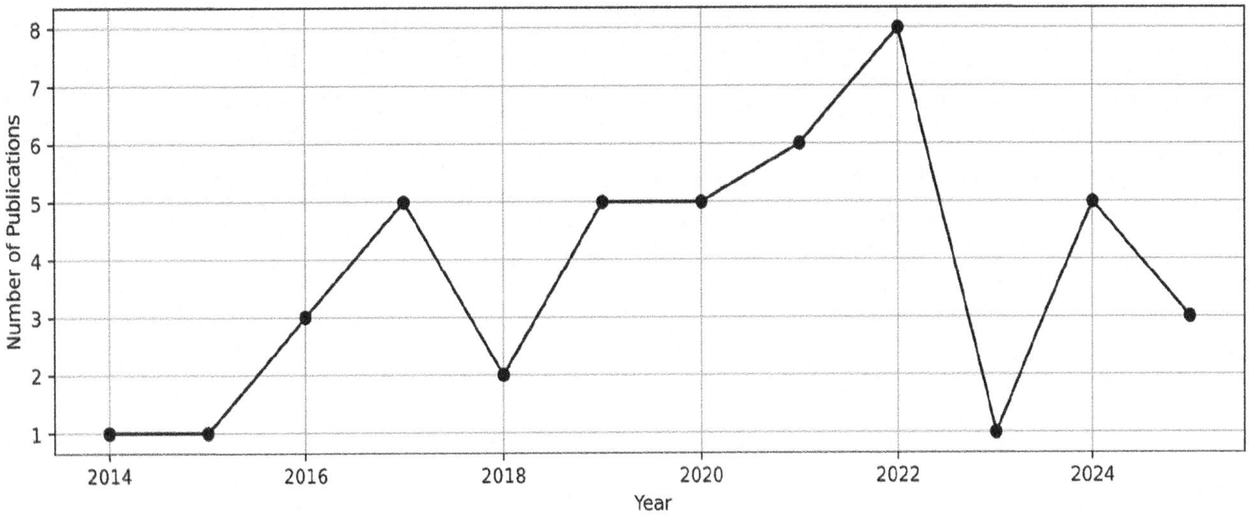

FIGURE 3.7 Timeline of GWO publications (2014–25) (*GWO*, grey wolf optimizer).

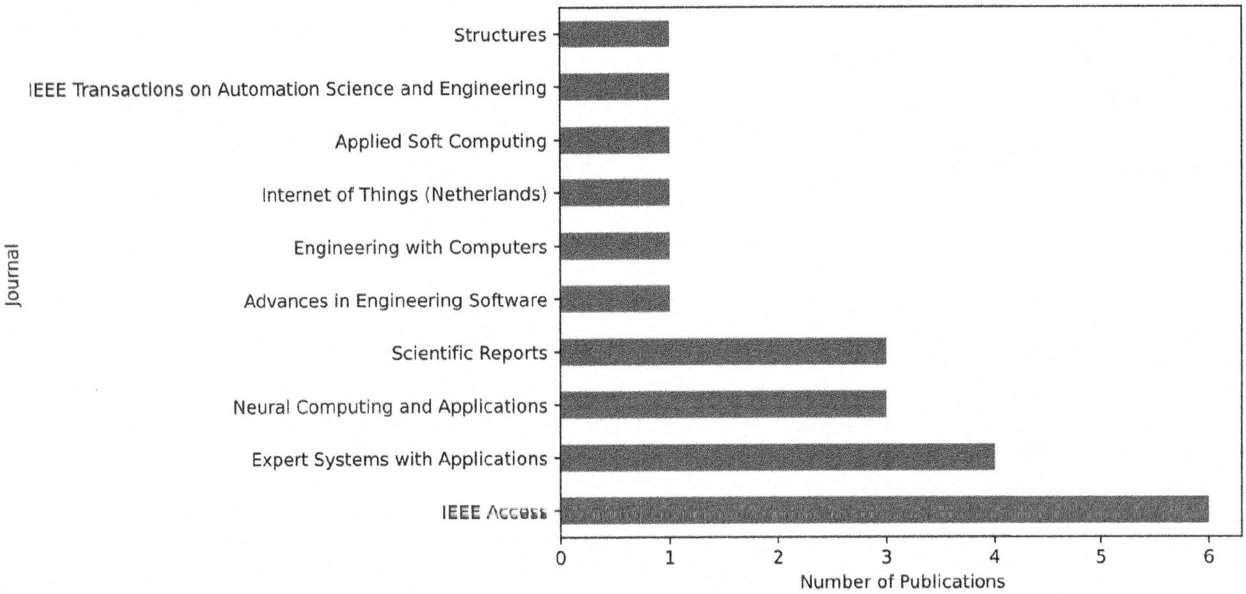

FIGURE 3.8 Distribution of GWO publications by journal/conference (*GWO*, grey wolf optimizer).

clearly illustrated how the foundational principles introduced by Mirjalili et al. (2014) —including hierarchical wolf-pack dynamics and cooperative hunting mechanisms—have effectively inspired numerous algorithmic innovations.

Successive innovations in GWO reflect a deliberate progression from its original formulation toward increasingly sophisticated and versatile variants, such as Binary GWO (Emary et al., 2016) [5], Multiobjective GWO (Mirjalili et al., 2016) [6], Chaotic GWO (Yu et al., 2016 [10]; Kohli and Arora, 2018 [16]), and hybrid approaches combining GWO with DE, PSO, and other metaheuristics (Tawhid and Ibrahim, 2020 [20]; Biabani et al., 2022 [29]). Hierarchical multistep GWO (Zhang et al., 2025) [39] further demonstrates advanced hierarchical adaptations specifically targeting complex, real-world optimization problems in high-dimensional and noisy conditions. These variants not only enhance the algorithm's search capability but also extend its application into diverse and critical domains, including energy systems, healthcare diagnostics, IoT, and deep learning architectures (Pan et al., 2020 [19]; Al-Tashi et al., 2020 [23]; Dagal et al., 2025 [32]).

The theoretical robustness and practical adaptability observed across these studies confirm the effectiveness of GWO's original metaphorical foundations. Subsequent algorithmic refinements systematically addressed identified limitations, notably the exploration–exploitation balance, diversity preservation, convergence speed, and robustness against local

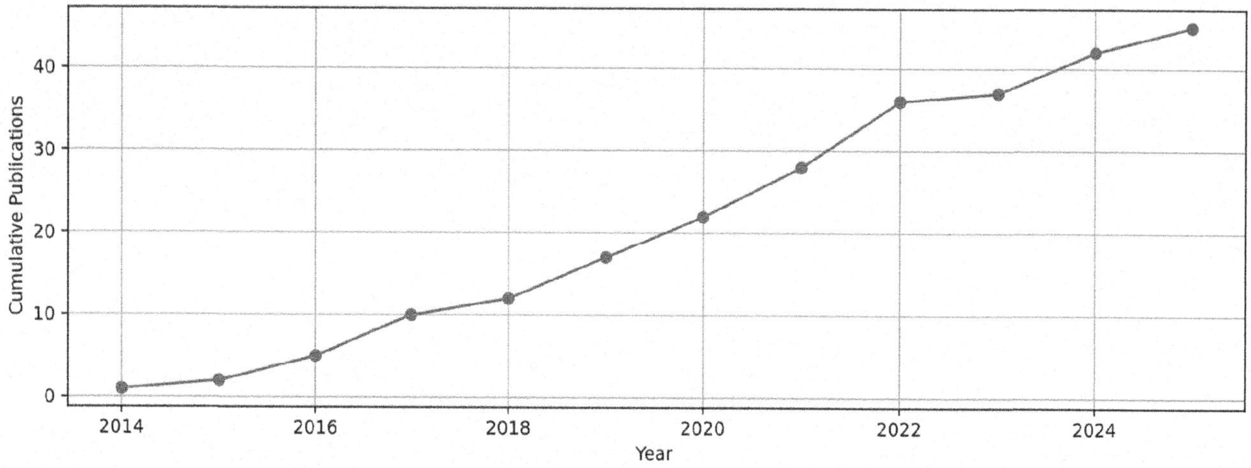

FIGURE 3.9 Cumulative GWO publications (2014–25) (*GWO*, grey wolf optimizer).

optima traps. Each improvement incrementally built upon earlier works, validating the strength and versatility of GWO as a foundational optimization framework.

3.4.2 Strengths and limitations

Strengths. This review demonstrated comprehensive coverage by systematically searching multiple reputable databases (IEEE Xplore, Scopus, Web of Science, Google Scholar), with manual reference list checks further enhancing literature inclusion. It followed a systematic and transparent approach, adhering strictly to PRISMA 2020 guidelines, which ensured methodological reproducibility and rigor. Finally, the review offered a thematic synthesis with visualizations, where timelines, mind-maps, and comparative tables provided an intuitive understanding of GWO development patterns and relationships among variants.

Limitations. Despite rigorous assessment, a degree of risk of bias remains due to variations in methodological rigor; about 35% of included studies showed only partial theoretical validation. Publication bias is also possible since the review relied mainly on peer-reviewed articles, potentially overlooking unpublished or gray literature. A further limitation is language bias, as most included works were in English, which may reduce generalizability. Finally, the rapid methodological evolution of GWO research means that even with a cutoff date of July 10, 2025, important subsequent advances might already be missing.

See Section 3.4.3 for an expanded discussion that explicitly lists the assumptions underlying current convergence proofs and proposes methodological remedies.

3.4.3 Implications for theory and practice

Typical structural assumptions used in existing convergence proofs include: (1) time-invariance (stationarity) of the objective function; (2) boundedness and Lipschitz continuity of update operators; (3) low-to-moderate search dimensionality; and (4) fixed or slowly varying parameter schedules. These assumptions limit applicability: in high-dimensional problems, the curse of dimensionality and sparsity of informative directions often invalidate concentration arguments; in time-varying (dynamic) problems, stationarity and ergodicity conditions no longer hold, requiring analysis under nonstationary stochastic dynamics. To address these gaps, we recommend employing stronger analytical tools such as Lyapunov-function-based stability analyses, mean-field or stochastic approximation frameworks, and Markov-chain ergodicity arguments adapted to nonstationary transition kernels.

Design guidelines for new GWO variants. Based on synthesized evidence, several considerations should guide future developments of GWO to ensure methodological rigor and practical effectiveness. First, *balancing exploration and exploitation explicitly* is essential. Variants demonstrating superior performance consistently employed mechanisms such as adaptive parameter tuning, chaos-based perturbations, or hybrid approaches; future designs should therefore incorporate theoretically grounded strategies that maintain robust global and local search capabilities. Second, *enhancing theoretical transparency* strengthens reliability, requiring clear mathematical formulations and robust justifications, including convergence proofs, ergodicity analyses, or stability measures. Third, *comprehensive and rigorous benchmarking* across diverse problem sets—CEC standard functions, practical applications, noisy scenarios, and high-dimensional tasks—should become a standard practice, accompanied by statistical significance tests and sensitivity analyses. Fourth, *hybridization and multidisciplinary integration* remain highly effective. Integrating GWO with PSO, DE, GA, RL, or embedding it within machine learning and deep learning pipelines can create synergies that leverage the strengths of diverse paradigms. Finally, *ensuring practical scalability and adaptability* is crucial for real-world deployment. Future GWO variants must explicitly demonstrate their ability to handle high-dimensional optimization efficiently and maintain robustness under dynamic and uncertain conditions, with attention to domain-specific requirements such as IoT, healthcare, or energy systems.

Recommendations for rigorous convergence proofs. Despite progress, rigorous convergence proofs for GWO variants remain limited. Future studies should explicitly prioritize *formal convergence proofs* (e.g., Lyapunov-based stability analyses, Markov-chain ergodicity, probabilistic guarantees). Notable examples, such as Pan et al. (2020), who provided convergence analysis for GWO–LSTM integrations, can serve as models. In addition, *parameter sensitivity and stability analyses* are essential. Investigations of coefficients (A, C) and the exploration parameter a under perturbations will provide deeper insights into stability. Finally, the community would benefit from *benchmark standards for theoretical validation*, analogous to empirical CEC benchmarks, to enhance comparability and ensure systematic theoretical progress.

While several studies report empirical convergence of GWO variants, existing mathematical proofs generally rely on simplifying assumptions that limit their applicability. Common assumptions include static (time-invariant) objective landscapes, bounded and Lipschitz-continuous operators, low-to-moderate search dimensionality, and fixed or slowly-varying parameter schedules. These assumptions reduce analytical complexity but undermine relevance for two increasingly common settings: (1) high-dimensional optimization, where the curse of dimensionality and feature sparsity can invalidate concentration arguments used in proofs; and (2) dynamic (time-varying) environments, where stationarity and ergodicity conditions are violated, and algorithm behavior must be analyzed under nonstationary stochastic dynamics. Additional practical limitations arise from heavy reliance on empirical benchmarks without standard statistical validation, and from parameter-sensitive behavior that is rarely characterized theoretically. To advance rigorous theory, future work should (1) explicitly state the structural assumptions used in proofs and test their limits empirically (e.g., by scaling dimension and introducing time-variation in benchmarks), (2) adopt stronger mathematical techniques such as Lyapunov-function based stability analyses, mean-field or stochastic approximation frameworks, and Markov-chain ergodicity arguments under nonstationary transition kernels, and (3) complement theoretical proofs with standardized benchmarks and sensitivity analyses to demonstrate robustness across dimensions and dynamic scenarios.

In conclusion, the insights from this systematic review not only confirm the foundational strength of GWO but also provide clear guidance for future theoretical advancements and practical integrations. Addressing these theoretical gaps and following the proposed methodological guidelines will ensure the continued robustness, adaptability, and relevance of GWO in solving increasingly complex optimization challenges.

3.5 Conclusion

This systematic review provided a comprehensive synthesis of 44 rigorously selected articles, highlighting the GWO evolution from its original biological metaphor to advanced methodological adaptations and diverse practical applications. The foundational principles introduced by Mirjalili et al. (2014), including hierarchical wolf-pack dynamics and cooperative hunting mechanisms, have consistently underpinned subsequent innovations such as binary, multiobjective, chaos-based, and hybridized variants. Theoretical analyses have progressively refined GWO's exploration-exploitation balance, improved its convergence rates, and expanded its robustness to complex, real-world scenarios. Despite notable methodological variability and moderate risk of bias in some studies, this review underscored significant theoretical contributions, promising empirical performance, and an expansive scope of interdisciplinary applications ranging from machine learning and deep learning optimization to energy management and healthcare diagnostics.

For researchers, several key messages emerge. *Solid theoretical foundations are paramount*, and future studies must prioritize explicit mathematical modeling, rigorous convergence proofs, and thorough sensitivity analyses. Equally important is the need for *systematic benchmarking and transparency*: comprehensive benchmarking against standardized datasets (e.g., CEC benchmarks, real-world data) and explicit parameter documentation significantly enhance reproducibility and reliability. *Hybrid and multidisciplinary approaches* have also proven highly effective, with integration into machine learning, reinforcement learning, or other metaheuristics offering substantial improvements in performance. Finally, *real-world scalability and adaptability* must be prioritized; GWO variants designed for complex, dynamic, and high-dimensional tasks demonstrate greater utility when robustness under uncertainty is explicitly validated.

To sustain and further advance the development of GWO as a state-of-the-art metaheuristic, several directions are particularly important. Strengthening theoretical rigor through formal convergence proofs, stability analyses, and parameter sensitivity investigations remains a critical priority; standardized theoretical benchmarks could greatly improve comparability across variants. Addressing scalability and dimensionality challenges is equally urgent, with adaptive and hierarchical variants (e.g., Zhang et al., 2025) offering promising paths forward. Expanding interdisciplinary applications in domains such as IoT, renewable energy, healthcare, and Industry 4.0 will help align GWO research with real-world constraints, especially when pursued in collaboration with domain experts. Finally, rigorous empirical validation—including statistical significance testing and large-scale real-world benchmarks—will further strengthen confidence in GWO's generalizability and impact.

In conclusion, the GWO remains a vibrant research area with substantial scope for both theoretical innovation and practical enhancement. By following these guidelines, researchers can further advance GWO's methodological depth, real-world effectiveness, and interdisciplinary relevance, ensuring its continued prominence as a powerful optimization framework. We explicitly highlight the principal theoretical limitations of current convergence proofs and propose concrete analytical and empirical directions to make future proofs more broadly applicable (see Section 3.4.3).

Appendices

This section provides supplementary materials to support the systematic review of the GWO and its variants, ensuring transparency and reproducibility of the methodology and findings based on the 44 included studies.

A. PRISMA 2020 flow diagram (Fig. 3.10)

The PRISMA 2020 flow diagram illustrates the study selection process. It details the following stages: 693 records identified from databases (IEEE Xplore, Scopus, Web of Science, Google Scholar) and additional sources; 693 records screened; 643 records excluded (due to irrelevance, duplication, or insufficient data); 50 full-text articles assessed for eligibility; and 5 excluded (lacking mathematical or application details), resulting in 44 studies included in the qualitative and quantitative synthesis. The diagram is structured with boxes and arrows, adhering to PRISMA guidelines, and is recommended for graphical representation in the final document (see Appendix A for a visual template) (Fig. 3.10).

B. PRISMA 27-item checklist

The PRISMA 27-item checklist ensures comprehensive reporting of the review. Key items include:

- Title: Identified as a systematic review (Item 1).
- Abstract: Structured summary provided (Item 2).
- Introduction: Rationale and objectives outlined (Item 3–4).
- Methods: Protocol, eligibility criteria, information sources, search strategy, selection process, data collection, risk of bias, and synthesis methods are detailed (Items 5–16).
- Results: Study selection, characteristics, risk of bias, and synthesis results presented (Items 17–21).
- Discussion: Summary of evidence, limitations, and implications discussed (Item 22–24).
- Other: Funding, registration, and support declared (Items 25–27).

A complete checklist is available for inclusion in the appendix, with each item marked as addressed in the chapter.

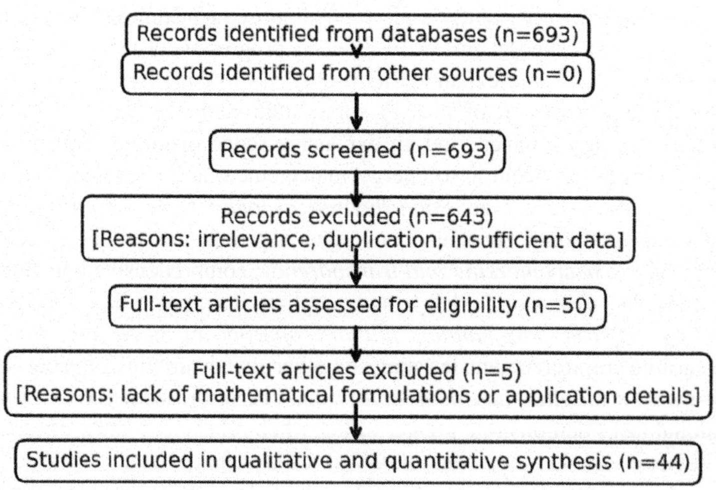

FIGURE 3.10 PRISMA flow diagram of stselection.

C. Full search strategies by database

The search strategies were tailored to each database to maximize the retrieval of GWO-related literature. The full strategies are as follows:

- IEEE Xplore: '"GWO" AND ("variant" OR "convergence" OR "optimization" OR "application")' (limited to 2014–July 2025, all fields).
- Scopus: 'TITLE-ABS-KEY ("Grey Wolf Optimizer" OR "GWO") AND TITLE-ABS-KEY ("variant" OR "convergence" OR "optimization" OR "application") AND PUBYEAR > 2013 AND PUBYEAR < 2026' (no language limit).
- Web of Science: 'TS=("Grey Wolf Optimizer" OR "GWO") AND TS=("variant" OR "convergence" OR "optimization" OR "application")' (timespan: 2014–2025).
- Google Scholar: '"Grey Wolf Optimizer" "GWO" ("variant" OR "convergence" OR "optimization" OR "application") -inurl:(signup login)' (first 200 results, 2014–July 2025, manually filtered).

Additional records were identified via reference tracking from included studies (e.g., Faris et al., 2018). These strategies are documented for replication.

D. Data extraction forms (if applicable)
A standardized data extraction form was used to collect information from the 44 studies. The form included fields for bibliographic details (author, year, journal, DOI), mathematical formulations (e.g., position update equations), convergence proofs, variant types (e.g., binary, hybrid), application domains (e.g., engineering, healthcare), and performance metrics (e.g., accuracy, convergence speed). Examples include recording ($D = |C \cdot X_p - X|$) from Mirjalili et al. and PSNR improvements from Li et al. [11]. The extracted data were compiled into the comparative table (Section 3.2.3), and the form is available upon request for inclusion in the appendix.

E. Summary of future work and key challenges

The 44 articles on the GWO and its variants collectively highlight a rich landscape of innovations, while also identifying key challenges and future research directions. Below is a detailed synthesis of the "future work" suggestions and the associated challenges, organized by recurring themes:

1. Enhancing convergence and avoiding local optima
   - Challenge: Many studies note GWO's susceptibility to premature convergence and entrapment in local optima, particularly in high-dimensional or multimodal problems [10], [22], [37]. The balance between exploration and exploitation remains a critical issue, as the algorithm's reliance on the (a) parameter and hierarchical structure can limit diversity over iterations.
   - Future work: The authors suggest developing advanced strategies to improve convergence speed and global search capability. This includes integrating adaptive mechanisms [36], chaotic maps with dynamic tuning [16], and evolutionary operators like differential evolution [20] or opposition-based learning [35]. Yu et al. [30] propose exploring multistrategy adaptive approaches for high-dimensional optimization.

2. Addressing high-dimensionality and scalability
   - Challenge: GWO struggles with scalability in large-scale or high-dimensional problems, as seen in applications like image processing [11] and engineering design [8]. The algorithm's performance degrades with increasing dimensionality due to reduced population diversity and computational complexity.
   - Future work: Future efforts should focus on enhancing scalability through parallel processing (e.g., Pan et al. [19]) and developing variants optimized for high-dimensional spaces [30]. Lin et al. [40] suggest integrating learning-based methods to handle stochastic high-dimensional scheduling, while Dagal et al. [32] recommend multistep hierarchical searches for energy systems.

3. Improving robustness and stability
   - Challenge: Stability across diverse datasets and problem types is a concern, with some variants showing sensitivity to parameter settings [12] or inconsistent performance in real-world applications [15]. The lack of rigorous convergence proofs for nonstandard conditions (e.g., noisy data) is a recurring limitation.
   - Future work: Researchers advocate for robust parameter tuning [36] and comprehensive stability analyses [33]. Adhikary and Acharyya [28] propose randomized balanced approaches, while future work should include probabilistic convergence models and validation on real-world benchmarks (e.g., CEC 2014, IEEE systems).

4. Expanding applied integrations
   - Challenge: While GWO has been successfully applied in domains like machine learning [19], energy [41], and healthcare [31], its integration with emerging fields like IoT [42] and deep learning faces challenges such as handling dynamic, noisy data and multiple objectives.

– Future work: Future research should explore hybridizations with reinforcement learning [38] and deep learning frameworks, as well as tailored adaptations for IoT [42]. Shahjalal et al. [27] suggest optimizing 5G network deployments, while Thakur et al. [26] recommend extending power quality applications.

5. Theoretical advancements and validation
   – Challenge: The theoretical foundation of GWO, while promising, lacks complete global convergence proofs for all scenarios [33]. Reviews (e.g., Makhadmeh et al. [4]; Liu et al. [43]) highlight gaps in mathematical rigor and the need for standardized validation protocols.
   – Future work: Authors call for advanced mathematical modeling to prove convergence under dynamic conditions [32] and the development of open-source platforms for benchmarking [44]. Faris et al. [3] and Hatta et al. [34] suggest comparative studies with emerging algorithms to refine GWO's theoretical framework.
6. Handling uncertainty and noise
   – Challenge: GWO's performance in uncertain or noisy environments (e.g., geophysical parameter estimation by Song et al. [9]) is limited, with variants like those for image segmentation [13] requiring robustness against data variability.
   – Future work: Future work should focus on incorporating uncertainty models (e.g., fuzzy logic enhancements by Rodríguez et al. [12]) and noise-resistant strategies (e.g., adaptive GWO by Meidani et al. [36]) to improve reliability in real-world applications.
7. Hybridization and multiobjective optimization
   – Challenge: While hybrid approaches (e.g., Biabani et al. [29]; Duan and Yu [8]) enhance performance, the complexity of integrating multiple algorithms and managing multiobjective trade-offs [6] poses challenges in computational cost and solution diversity.
   – Future work: Researchers propose exploring novel hybridizations (e.g., with PSO or SCA) and refining multiobjective variants with dynamic archives [6]. Al-Tashi et al. [23] suggest optimizing feature selection further, while Khalili and Babamir [14] recommend cloud-specific multiobjective enhancements.
8. Real-world validation and interdisciplinary applications
   – Challenge: Many studies rely on synthetic benchmarks (e.g., CEC 2005 by Yu et al. [30]), with limited real-world validation (e.g., Tsai et al. [15]). This gap hinders GWO's adoption in practical, interdisciplinary settings.v
   – Future work: Future research should prioritize real-world testing across domains like healthcare [31], energy [32], and geophysics [9]. Tu et al. [45] suggest feature selection applications, while Qiu et al. [37] advocate for engineering design validations.

Consolidated summary

The key challenges identified across the 44 articles include premature convergence, high-dimensional scalability, stability issues, limited robustness in noisy environments, theoretical gaps, and insufficient real-world validation. Future work directions emphasize enhancing convergence through adaptive and hybrid strategies, addressing scalability with multistep and parallel approaches, strengthening theoretical foundations with rigorous proofs, and expanding applications with robust, interdisciplinary validations. These efforts aim to overcome current limitations and position GWO as a leading optimization tool by July 2025 and beyond.

Acknowledgments

The authors used the AI tool ChatGPT (OpenAI; accessed 2025-09-18) solely for language editing and proofreading. The final content, interpretation, and responsibility for accuracy remain with the authors.

References

[1] S.M. Mirjalili, S.M. Mirjalili, A. Lewis, Grey wolf optimizer, .Advances in Engineering Software 69 (2014) 46–61. Available from https://doi.org/10.1016/j.advengsoft.2013.12.007.

[2] M.J. Page, et al., Updating guidance for reporting systematic reviews: development of the PRISMA 2020 statement, Journal of Clinical Epidemiology. 134 (2021) 103–112. Available from https://doi.org/10.1016/j.jclinepi.2021.02.003.

[3] H. Faris, I. Aljarah, M.A. Al-Betar, S. Mirjalili, Grey wolf optimizer: a review of recent variants and applications, Neural Computing and Applications. 30 (2) (2018) 413–435. Available from https://doi.org/10.1007/s00521-017-3272-5.

[4] S.N. Makhadmeh, et al., Recent advances in grey wolf optimizer, its versions and applications: review, IEEE Access. 12 (August 2023) (2024) 22991–23028. Available from https://doi.org/10.1109/ACCESS.2023.3304889.

[5] E. Emary, H.M. Zawbaa, A.E. Hassanien, Binary grey wolf optimization approaches for feature selection, Neurocomputing 172 (2016) 371–381. Available from https://doi.org/10.1016/j.neucom.2015.06.083.
[6] S. Mirjalili, S. Saremi, S.M. Mirjalili, L.D.S. Coelho, Multi-objective grey wolf optimizer: a novel algorithm for multi-criterion optimization, Expert. Syst. Appl. 47 (2016) 106–119. Available from https://doi.org/10.1016/j.eswa.2015.10.039.
[7] "1997 - Cluster validation using graph theoretic."
[8] Y. Duan, X. Yu, A collaboration-based hybrid GWO-SCA optimizer for engineering optimization problems, Expert Systems with Applications. 213 (April 2022) (2023). Available from https://doi.org/10.1016/j.eswa.2022.119017.
[9] X. Song, et al., Grey Wolf Optimizer for parameter estimation in surface waves, Soil Dynamics and Earthquake Engineering. 75 (August) (2015) 147–157. Available from https://doi.org/10.1016/j.soildyn.2015.04.004.
[10] H. Yu, Y. Yu, Y. Liu, Y. Wang,S. Gao, Chaotic grey wolf optimization, in: Proceedings of the 2016 IEEE International Conference on Progress in Informatics and Computing, 2017, pp. 103–113. Available from https://doi.org/10.1109/PIC.2016.7949476.
[11] L. Li, L. Sun, W. Kang, J. Guo, C. Han, S. Li, Fuzzy multilevel image thresholding based on modified discrete grey wolf optimizer and local information aggregation, IEEE Access. 4 (2016) 6438–6450. Available from https://doi.org/10.1109/ACCESS.2016.2613940.
[12] L. Rodríguez, et al., A fuzzy hierarchical operator in the grey wolf optimizer algorithm, Applied Soft Computing Journal 57 (2017) 315–328. Available from https://doi.org/10.1016/j.asoc.2017.03.048.
[13] A.K.M. Khairuzzaman, S. Chaudhury, Multilevel thresholding using grey wolf optimizer for image segmentation, Expert Systems with Applications. 86 (2017) 64–76. Available from https://doi.org/10.1016/j.eswa.2017.04.029.
[14] A. Khalili, S.M. Babamir, Optimal scheduling workflows in cloud computing environment using pareto-based grey wolf optimizer, Concurrency and Computation: Practice and Experience. 29 (11) (2017) 1–11. Available from https://doi.org/10.1002/cpe.4044.
[15] P.W. Tsai, T.T. Nguyen, T.K. Dao, Robot path planning optimization based on multiobjective grey wolf optimizer, *Advances in Intelligent Systems and Computing*. 536 (2017) 166–173. Available from https://doi.org/10.1007/978-3-319-48490-7_20.
[16] M. Kohli, S. Arora, Chaotic grey wolf optimization algorithm for constrained optimization problems, Journal of Computational Design and Engineering 5 (4) (2018) 458–472. Available from https://doi.org/10.1016/j.jcde.2017.02.005.
[17] P. Hu, S. Chen, H. Huang, G. Zhang, L. Liu, Improved alpha-guided grey wolf optimizer, IEEE Access. 7 (2019) 5421–5437. Available from https://doi.org/10.1109/ACCESS.2018.2889816.
[18] S. Gupta, K. Deep, A novel random walk grey wolf optimizer, Swarm and Evolutionary Computation. 44 (November 2017) (2019) 101–112. Available from https://doi.org/10.1016/j.swevo.2018.01.001.
[19] J. Pan, B. Jing, X. Jiao, S. Wang, Analysis and application of grey wolf optimizer-long short-term memory, IEEE Access. 8 (2020) 121460–121468. Available from https://doi.org/10.1109/ACCESS.2020.3006499.
[20] M.A. Tawhid, A.M. Ibrahim, A hybridization of grey wolf optimizer and differential evolution for solving nonlinear systems, Evolutionary Systems. 11 (1) (2020) 65–87. Available from https://doi.org/10.1007/s12530-019-09291-8.
[21] N. Singh, A modified variant of grey Wolf optimizer, Scientia Iranica. 27 (3 D) (2020) 1450–1466. Available from https://doi.org/10.24200/SCI.2018.50122.1523.
[22] M.W. Guo, J.S. Wang, L.F. Zhu, S.S. Guo, W. Xie, An improved grey wolf optimizer based on tracking and seeking modes to solve function optimization problems, IEEE, 2020, 8. Available from https://doi.org/10.1109/ACCESS.2020.2984321.
[23] Q. Al-Tashi, et al., Binary multi-objective grey wolf optimizer for feature selection in classification, IEEE Access. 8 (2020) 106247–106263. Available from https://doi.org/10.1109/ACCESS.2020.3000040.
[24] E. Akbari, A. Rahimnejad, S.A. Gadsden, A greedy non-hierarchical grey wolf optimizer for real-world optimization, Electronics Letters. 57 (13) (2021) 499–501. Available from https://doi.org/10.1049/ell2.12176.
[25] X. Yu, W.Y. Xu, C.L. Li, Opposition-based learning grey wolf optimizer for global optimization, Knowledge-Based Systems. 226 (2021) 107139. Available from https://doi.org/10.1016/j.knosys.2021.107139.
[26] N. Thakur, Y.K. Awasthi, A.S. Siddiqui, Reliability analysis and power quality improvement model using enthalpy based grey wolf optimizer, Energy Systems. 12 (1) (2021) 31–59. Available from https://doi.org/10.1007/s12667-020-00409-5.
[27] M. Shahjalal, N. Farhana, P. Roy, M.A. Razzaque, K. Kaur, M.M. Hassan, A binary gray wolf optimization algorithm for deployment of virtual network functions in 5G hybrid cloud, Computer Communications. 193 (June) (2022) 63–74. Available from https://doi.org/10.1016/j.comcom.2022.06.041.
[28] J. Adhikary, S. Acharyya, Randomized balanced grey wolf optimizer (RBGWO) for solving real life optimization problems, Applied Soft Computing. 117 (2022). Available from https://doi.org/10.1016/j.asoc.2022.108429.
[29] F. Biabani, S. Shojaee, S. Hamzehei-Javaran, A new insight into metaheuristic optimization method using a hybrid of PSO, GSA, and GWO, Structures 44 (August) (2022) 1168–1189. Available from https://doi.org/10.1016/j.istruc.2022.08.064.
[30] M. Yu, J. Xu, W. Liang, Y. Qiu, S. Bao, L. Tang, Improved Multi-strategy Adaptive Grey Wolf Optimization for Practical Engineering Applications and High-dimensional Problem Solving, Springer, Netherlands, (2024)Available from https://doi.org/10.1007/s10462-024-10821-357.
[31] K. Santhosh, P.P. Dev, B. J. A., Z. Lynton, P. Das, E. Ghaderpour, A modified gray wolf optimization algorithm for early detection of Parkinson's disease, Biomedical Signal Processing and Control 109 (May) (2025) 108061. Available from https://doi.org/10.1016/j.bspc.2025.108061.
[32] I. Dagal, A.W. Ibrahim, A. Harrison, W.F. Mbasso, A.O. Hourani, I. Zaitsev, Hierarchical multi step gray wolf optimization algorithm for energy systems optimization, Scientific Reports. 15 (1) (2025). Available from https://doi.org/10.1038/s41598-025-92983-w.
[33] H. Wang, L. Shi, A theoretical framework and some promising findings of grey wolf optimizer, part II: global convergence analysis, 2022, pp. 19–21, [Online]. Available from: https://arxiv.org/abs/2203.07636v1.

[34] N.M. Hatta, A.M. Zain, R. Sallehuddin, Z. Shayfull, Y. Yusoff, Recent studies on optimisation method of grey wolf optimiser (GWO): a review (2014–2017), Artificial Intelligence Review. 52 (4) (2019) 2651–2683. Available from https://doi.org/10.1007/s10462-018-9634-2.

[35] J.C. Bansal, S. Singh, A better exploration strategy in grey wolf optimizer, ournal of Ambient Intelligence and Humanized Computing. 12 (1) (2021) 1099–1118. Available from https://doi.org/10.1007/s12652-020-02153-1.

[36] K. Meidani, A.P. Hemmasian, S. Mirjalili, A. Barati Farimani, Adaptive grey wolf optimizer, Neural Computing and Applications. 34 (10) (2022) 7711–7731. Available from https://doi.org/10.1007/s00521-021-06885-9.

[37] Y. Qiu, X. Yang, S. Chen, An improved gray wolf optimization algorithm solving to functional optimization and engineering design problems, Scientific Reports. 14 (1) (2024) 1–24. Available from https://doi.org/10.1038/s41598-024-64526-2.

[38] P. Bedi, S. Das, S.B. Goyal, P.K. Shukla, S. Mirjalili, M. Kumar, A novel routing protocol based on grey wolf optimization and Q learning for wireless body area network, Expert Systems with Applications. 210 (November 2021) (2022) 118477. Available from https://doi.org/10.1016/j.eswa.2022.118477.

[39] 1.17Q1SJR Q1; 1.173ABS 3NAABDC NAEvolutionary computation A. Lensen, B. Xue, M. Z.-E. computation, and undefined 2020, Genetic programming for evolving similarity functions for clustering: Representations and analysis," *direct.mit.eduA Lensen, B Xue, M ZhangEvolutionary Comput. 2020•direct.mit.edu*, Accessed: Feb. 05, 2025. [Online]. Available from: https://direct.mit.edu/evco/article-abstract/28/4/531/94993.

[40] C.R. Lin, Z.C. Cao, M.C. Zhou, Learning-based grey wolf optimizer for stochastic flexible job shop scheduling, IEEE Transactions on Automation Science and Engineering 19 (4) (2022) 3659–3671. Available from https://doi.org/10.1109/TASE.2021.3129439.

[41] M. Nasir, A. Sadollah, S. Mirjalili, S.A. Mansouri, M. Safaraliev, A. Rezaee Jordehi, A comprehensive review on applications of grey wolf optimizer in energy systems, Springer Netherlands. (2025). Available from https://doi.org/10.1007/s11831-024-10214-3.

[42] M.H. Nadimi-Shahraki, H. Zamani, Z. Asghari Varzaneh, A.S. Sadiq, S. Mirjalili, A systematic review of applying grey wolf optimizer, its variants, and its developments in different internet of things applications, Internet Things (Neth.) 26 (February) (2024) 101135. Available from https://doi.org/10.1016/j.iot.2024.101135.

[43] Y. Liu, A. As'arry, M.K. Hassan, A.A. Hairuddin, H. Mohamad, Review of the grey wolf optimization algorithm: variants and applications, Neural Computing and Applications. 36 (6) (2024) 2713–2735. Available from https://doi.org/10.1007/s00521-023-09202-8.

[44] S.K. Mosavi, E. Jalalian, F.S. Gharahchopog, A comprehensive survey of grey wolf optimizer algorithm and its application, *International Journal of Advanced Robotics and Expert Systems*,. 1 (6) (2021) 23–45.

[45] Q. Tu, X. Chen, X. Liu, Hierarchy strengthened grey wolf optimizer for numerical optimization and feature selection, IEEE Access. 7 (2019) 78012–78028. Available from https://doi.org/10.1109/ACCESS.2019.2921793.

Chapter 4

In-depth mathematical analysis, dynamic behavior, and convergence proof of the grey wolf pptimizer

Faramarz Safi-Esfahani[1,2], Habib Larian[2], and Hedayatollah Dallaki[2]
[1]*School of Information, Systems and Modelling, Faculty of Engineering and IT, University of Technology Sydney, Sydney, NSW, Australia,* [2]*Department of Computer Engineering, Na.C., Islamic Azad University, Najafabad, Iran*

4.1 Introduction

The grey wolf optimizer (GWO) has become one of the most prominent metaheuristic algorithms in the domain of nature-inspired computation. Its rising popularity stems from its minimal parameter requirements, intuitive modeling, and strong performance across a broad spectrum of continuous and discrete optimization problems. GWO's structure is inspired by the leadership hierarchy and hunting tactics observed in grey wolf packs, where coordinated decision-making is driven by alpha, beta, and delta wolves guiding the search, while the remaining wolves adapt accordingly. This design enables GWO to achieve a natural balance between exploration and exploitation, rendering it highly effective in navigating complex, multimodal search spaces [1–3].

Building on these strengths, a growing body of research has explored how to further improve GWO's optimization capabilities through mathematical modifications and hybridization strategies. These works aim to enhance search precision, convergence reliability, and algorithmic robustness by modifying GWO's position update equations, coefficient functions, or randomization mechanisms, or by fusing GWO with other algorithms such as particle swarm optimization (PSO), genetic algorithm (GA), or differential evolution (DE) [4–6]. In parallel, GWO has been applied successfully to a wide range of real-world tasks, including engineering design, machine learning, neural network training, image segmentation, wireless sensor networks, power systems, and robotics path planning, confirming its adaptability and relevance across domains [7–11].

While this expansion of GWO's applications and variants reflects its practical success, it also raises a deeper theoretical question: *"How do specific structural changes to the GWO algorithm influence its internal dynamic behavior, and how do those behavioral shifts impact its convergence outcomes?"*

Despite the abundance of modified GWO variants, the literature often focuses on benchmarking improvements without clearly articulating why a given modification enhances performance or how it affects the algorithm's search behavior. For instance, a variant might replace the linear coefficient decay with a chaotic function or introduce an adaptive leader-switching mechanism, yet the rationale for such changes is frequently empirical or heuristic. This has led to a growing gap in the field: although we observe diverse modifications and reported improvements, we lack a systematic framework to explain the causal links between GWO's mathematical structure, its emergent behavior during optimization, and its convergence dynamics.

This chapter aims to fill that theoretical void by introducing a structured, explanatory framework that connects the mathematical modeling (MM) of GWO variants to their dynamic behavioral mechanisms (DB) and their convergence outcomes (CG). By classifying 59 state-of-the-art GWO variants using this three-layer MM-DB-CG model, we reveal how specific structural modifications (e.g., stochastic perturbations, adaptive decay, elite memory, hybridization) give rise to particular behavioral patterns (e.g., enhanced exploration, convergence control, trajectory diversity), and how these, in turn, relate to observed or provable convergence performance.

Grey Wolf Optimizer. DOI: https://doi.org/10.1016/B978-0-443-36624-6.00012-3

The primary contributions of this work are threefold: (1) A comprehensive taxonomy of mathematical modifications applied to GWO (MM1–MM6), ranging from algebraic reformulations to hybrid control strategies; (2) A behavioral categorization that identifies and explains core dynamic mechanisms such as convergence regulation, population adaptivity, and leadership influence (A to F); 3) An outcome-driven synthesis of convergence behaviors (G1–G8), linking structural design to empirical or theoretical performance. Together, these contributions not only clarify how GWO variants function internally but also offer a blueprint for principled algorithm design, grounded in mechanism-driven analysis rather than ad hoc adjustments.

Ultimately, we synthesize all pathways identified across the reviewed literature to uncover both high-frequency, high-yield design patterns and structurally promising yet underexplored directions. Using pathway intensity maps and behavioral overlap analysis, we demonstrate that high-performing GWO variants tend to follow reproducible causal chains and that many effective designs emerge from modular combinations of behavioral mechanisms that can be intentionally composed.

The remainder of this chapter is structured as follows: Section 4.2 outlines the review methodology; Section 4.3 classifies GWO variants by mathematical modifications; Section 4.4 analyzes their dynamic behaviors; Section 4.5 examines CG; Section 4.6 synthesizes links across structure, behavior, and performance; and Section 4.7 concludes with design insights and future directions.

4.2 Methodological approach

This chapter employs a methodologically rigorous and conceptually structured approach to review and analyze advancements in GWO research. The objective is not merely to catalog existing variants, but to critically evaluate how modifications to the algorithm's internal structure affect its mathematical integrity, dynamic behavior, and convergence reliability. To ensure depth and precision, the review process integrates two key components: a systematic search and selection of relevant literature, and an analytical framework that interprets each contribution through a logically sequenced lens. The search strategy was designed to retrieve peer-reviewed studies explicitly engaging with the core mechanics of GWO, focusing on its mathematical foundations, behavioral properties, and convergence performance. Following this, each selected work was examined using a layered interpretive model that reflects the natural progression of algorithmic development: from formal structural design, through DB expression, to convergence validation. The subsections that follow present, first, the literature search methodology and inclusion criteria, and second, the rationale and structure of the analytical framework that underpins the chapter's organization and thematic synthesis.

4.2.1 Search methodology and selection criteria

To conduct a rigorous and conceptually grounded review of GWO variants, a structured search methodology was implemented in alignment with the chapter's analytical objectives. The goal was to identify peer-reviewed studies that offer substantive theoretical, structural, or behavioral contributions to the development of GWO-based algorithms.

The literature search was conducted across a comprehensive range of academic databases, including IEEE Xplore, SpringerLink, ScienceDirect (Elsevier), Wiley, MDPI, ACM Digital Library, arXiv, Nature, Science, IOS Press, and SAGE Publications. These sources were selected for their authoritative standing in the fields of optimization, artificial intelligence, and computational modeling.

To enhance specificity and topical relevance, search queries were restricted to titles and abstracts. This constraint ensured that only studies explicitly focused on GWO's internal mechanisms, rather than incidental applications, were retrieved. Search terms were constructed to target three core areas of inquiry: mathematical formulation, dynamic behavior, and convergence analysis. Boolean combinations such as "Grey Wolf Optimizer mathematical model" OR "GWO theoretical framework", and "GWO" AND "convergence" AND ("empirical methods" OR "structural methods"), were used to align the query structure with the chapter's analytical focus.

The search covered publications from 2014 to 2025, beginning with the introduction of the GWO algorithm and extending through the most recent advancements in the field. This time frame was selected to capture both foundational and cutting-edge contributions.

Articles were included if they met the following criteria:

- Peer-reviewed journal or conference papers written in English;
- Explicit engagement with the mathematical structure, behavioral design, or convergence characteristics of the GWO algorithm;
- Proposed algorithmic modifications with sufficient depth in formulation or validation;

- Provided evidence or reasoning, either theoretical or empirical, related to convergence performance.
- Studies were excluded if they:
- Applied GWO without modifying or analyzing its internal structure;
- Were not written in English;
- Focused on unrelated algorithms or broad optimization surveys lacking methodological detail;
- Lacked meaningful analysis of behavior, convergence, or theoretical formulation.

Following this selection process, 59 core papers were retained for in-depth analysis. These works were selected based on their moderate to strong relevance to the three core analytical dimensions. This filtering ensured that the review remained tightly focused on studies that contribute not just to the application of GWO, but to its theoretical and methodological development.

4.2.2 Categorization framework

To analyze the evolution and refinement of GWO variants in a conceptually rigorous manner, this chapter introduces a structured four-stage analytical framework, as depicted in Fig. 4.1, that maps the causal pathway from algorithmic design to performance outcome. This framework, abbreviated as MM-DB-CG Synthesis, serves as the central methodological backbone of the review, enabling a principled comparison of 59 GWO variants across structural, behavioral, and convergence dimensions.

The first stage classifies modifications to the original GWO algorithm into six distinct structural categories (MM1–MM6). These include algebraic reformulations of position update rules, redefinition of control parameters, and alterations to leadership hierarchy, as well as more advanced models incorporating memory, stochasticity, and hybridized search logic. This categorization captures the formal logic embedded in each variant's design and provides the foundational layer for understanding how structure shapes behavior.

The second stage investigates how these structural changes influence the algorithm's emergent behavior during execution. Six core behavioral mechanisms are identified (A–F), including convergence stabilization, adaptive control, trajectory modulation, leadership dynamics, memory-driven learning, and population diversity management. By treating GWO variants as dynamic systems, this stage explains how mathematical changes manifest as time-evolving search patterns that affect exploration, exploitation, coordination, and adaptability.

The third stage shifts focus to the ultimate measure of a GWO variant's effectiveness: its convergence behavior. Eight convergence categories (G1–G8) are used to classify whether variants achieve reliable, stable, and efficient convergence, and whether such outcomes are supported by empirical results, structural reasoning, or formal proof. This layer not only traces the success or failure of each design but also reveals the mechanisms responsible for guiding agents toward optimal solutions.

The final stage integrates insights across the MM, DB, and CG layers. It reveals high-impact design pathways (e.g., MM2-B-G2), identifies underexplored but promising interactions (e.g., MM5-A-G3), and maps the full landscape of current GWO research. This synthesis enables a shift from descriptive taxonomy to generative insight, offering a blueprint for next-generation GWO variants that are modular, explainable, and theoretically grounded.

Together, these four stages constitute a cohesive and mechanism-driven framework for metaheuristic analysis. By unifying design, behavior, performance, and synthesis, the MM-DB-CG synthesis model equips researchers with a replicable methodology to diagnose existing variants and design new ones with clearer intent and higher reliability.

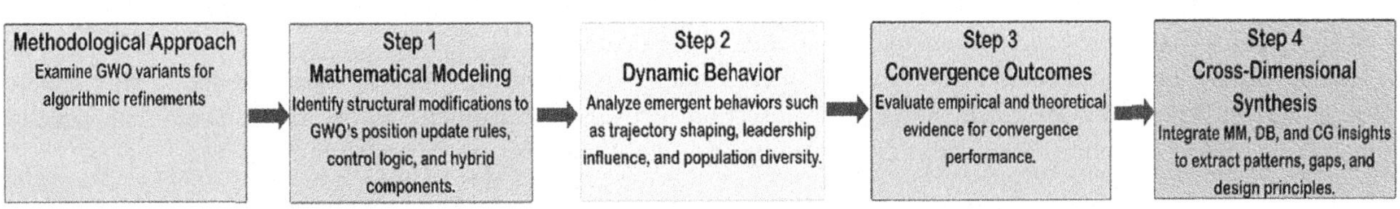

FIGURE 4.1 Research logical flow.

4.3 Mathematical modeling of grey wolf optimizer variants

The GWO, introduced by Mirjalili et al. in 2014 [12], is inspired by the social hierarchy and hunting behavior of grey wolves in nature. The algorithm models the position of candidate solutions as agents (wolves) moving through a multidimensional search space, guided by three dominant individuals: the alpha (α), beta (β), and delta (δ) wolves. These top three guide the rest of the population (the omega wolves) toward optimal regions. The mathematical formulation of the canonical GWO consists of three core components:

1. **Encircling behavior**:

$$\vec{D} = |\vec{C} \cdot \overrightarrow{X_{\text{leader}}}(t) - \vec{X}(t)|, \vec{X}(t+1) = \overrightarrow{X_{\text{leader}}}(t) - \vec{A} \cdot \vec{D} \tag{4.1}$$

where $\overrightarrow{X_{\text{leader}}}$ is the position of one of the leaders (α, β, or δ), and $\vec{X}(t)$ is the current position of the agent.

2. **Coefficient vector definitions**:

$$\vec{A} = 2a \cdot \vec{r_1} - a, \vec{C} = 2 \cdot \vec{r_2} \tag{4.2}$$

Here, $\vec{r}_1, \vec{r}_2 \in [0,1]$ are random vectors, and a decreases linearly from 2 to 0 over the course of iterations, controlling the balance between exploration and exploitation.

3. Position update relative to α, β, and δ: Each agent updates its position based on the average influence of the top three wolves:

$$\overrightarrow{D_\alpha} = |\overrightarrow{C_1} \cdot \overrightarrow{X_\alpha} - \vec{X}|, \quad \overrightarrow{X_1} = \overrightarrow{X_\alpha} - \overrightarrow{A_1} \cdot \overrightarrow{D_\alpha}$$

$$\overrightarrow{D_\beta} = |\overrightarrow{C_2} \cdot \overrightarrow{X_\beta} - \vec{X}|, \quad \overrightarrow{X_2} = \overrightarrow{X_\beta} - \overrightarrow{A_2} \cdot \overrightarrow{D_\beta}$$

$$\overrightarrow{D_\delta} = |\overrightarrow{C_3} \cdot \overrightarrow{X_\delta} - \vec{X}|, \quad \overrightarrow{X_3} = \overrightarrow{X_\delta} - \overrightarrow{A_3} \cdot \overrightarrow{D_\delta}$$

$$\vec{X}(t+1) = \frac{\overrightarrow{X_1} + \overrightarrow{X_2} + \overrightarrow{X_3}}{3} \tag{4.3}$$

This canonical model forms the mathematical foundation of the GWO algorithm. It operates as a deterministic iterative map influenced by randomized components and a gradually shifting balance between exploration and exploitation. While its simplicity allows for broad applicability and ease of implementation, the model also presents limitations, such as premature convergence, rigid leadership structure, and limited memory, which have motivated the development of numerous mathematical variants [5,7,10].

To systematically organize these developments, we classified GWO variants into six categories (MM1–MM6), each defined by the primary equation-level intervention applied to the canonical model. MM1 (Algebraic Reformulation) refers to modifications of the position update equations that change the way wolves adjust their positions. MM2 (Control Parameter Redefinition) encompasses changes to the functional form of the convergence coefficient a and its related vectors, altering how exploration and exploitation are scheduled. MM3 (Leader Influence and Hierarchy) includes redefinitions of the leadership model, where the influence of α, β, δ is reassigned, reweighted, or extended. MM4 (State-Augmented Models) introduces additional state variables such as memory or velocity, enabling the algorithm to retain historical or auxiliary information. MM5 (Stochastic Process Formulations) treats the optimizer as a probabilistic system, embedding randomness or stochastic walks directly into the update mechanism. MM6 (Hybridized Models) fuses GWO equations with operators from other metaheuristics at the mathematical level, producing composite dynamics.

In this taxonomy, each variant is placed into the category that reflects its dominant mathematical innovation, while secondary modifications are acknowledged but not used as the basis for classification. This rule maintains mutual exclusivity across categories and ensures interpretability of the taxonomy.

The remainder of this section explores these modifications by analyzing how different works in the literature reformulate the original model. Each subsequent subsection focuses on a distinct class of mathematical enhancements aimed at addressing specific shortcomings or expanding the algorithm's theoretical capabilities.

4.3.1 MM1. Algebraic reformulation of the position update rule

This class of modifications alters the core position update rule in GWO, primarily by rethinking how the three primary leaders, α, β, and δ, guide the movement of other agents. Rather than relying on the canonical fixed average of leader positions, these models introduce more expressive, adaptable, and stochastic formulations. The goal is to enhance flexibility, responsiveness to the landscape, and escape from origin-centric or symmetric convergence patterns. Such reformulations often incorporate probabilistic decisions, weighted influences, or heuristic selection, transforming the update rule into a more versatile mechanism for navigating complex, high-dimensional, or discrete spaces.

4.3.1.1 Formal abstract model

Let $\mathscr{L}_i(t) = \{X_{l_1}, X_{l_2}, \ldots, X_{l_k}\}$ denote a dynamic set of leaders selected for the agent i at iteration t, and let $w_{l_j}(t)$ be the associated weights assigned to each leader. The generalized algebraic update rule for MM1 variants can be expressed as:

$$X_i(t+1) = \sum_{j=1}^{k} w_{l_j}(t) \cdot X_{l_j}(t) + \eta_i(t) \tag{4.4}$$

where:

$\sum_{j=1}^{k} w_{l_j}(t) = 1$, (Normalization of weights [13])

$w_{l_j}(t)$ may be uniform [14], fitness-based [15,16], or learned weights [13],

$\eta_i(t)$ is a perturbation term (e.g., Gaussian noise [13,17], zero for deterministic updates [18]), and $\mathscr{L}_i(t)$ may be fixed [19] or randomly sampled from elite subsets [14,20].

This formulation enables a wide range of leader interaction schemes, including stochastic averaging, dimension-wise selection, greedy updates, and conditional role switching.

4.3.1.2 Representative variants and mechanisms

Several GWO variants under MM1 restructure the position update rule by introducing weighted, stochastic, or discrete formulations. For instance, some studies eliminate the fixed $\alpha - \beta - \delta$ hierarchy and use greedy update schemes where a wolf only moves if its fitness improves [16]. Others propose fitness-based or probabilistic weighting of leader positions to guide updates more adaptively [15,19,21]. In Luo (2019) [13], Gaussian noise is added to a weighted leader combination to improve flexibility in estimating prey location, while Long et al. (2018) [14] introduce random selection of elite leaders at each iteration to increase swarm diversity. A discrete variant is presented in Martin et al. (2018) [18], where continuous vector arithmetic is replaced with modular logic suited for combinatorial optimization.

More advanced algebraic reformulations further enrich GWO's expressiveness. The variant in Long et al. (2018) [22] integrates differential perturbations and memory, borrowing directional concepts from PSO to enhance search in high-dimensional spaces. In Liu et al. (2022) [20], wolves learn from leaders on a dimension-specific basis, improving exploitation granularity. A stochastic averaging strategy is proposed in Khaghani et al. (2019) [17], using Gaussian-centered sampling around elite averages to bias exploration toward promising regions. Collectively, these models reflect a shift from fixed, symmetric update patterns to flexible, dynamic, and landscape-sensitive decision rules that expand GWO's adaptability and performance across problem domains.

4.3.2 MM2. Functional redefinition of control parameters

Canonical GWO controls its exploration–exploitation trade-off using a linearly decreasing coefficient $a(t)$, which gradually shifts the search from diversification to intensification. However, this linear decay has been criticized for being too rigid and insensitive to problem complexity or search dynamics. MM2 variants address this limitation by redefining how control parameters like $a(t)$, and the derived vectors $\vec{A}$ and $\vec{C}$ evolve during optimization. These redefinitions include nonlinear, oscillatory, adaptive, and chaotic functions that provide more nuanced control over convergence behavior, often improving robustness, avoiding premature convergence, and aligning search pressure more effectively with landscape characteristics.

4.3.2.1 Formal abstract model

Let $a(t) = \psi(t)$ represent a control coefficient, where $\psi(t)$ is a time-dependent function governing the agent's convergence pressure. The updated influence vectors become:

$$\vec{A} = 2\psi(t) \cdot r_1 - \psi(t), \quad \vec{C} = 2r_2\vec{A} \tag{4.5}$$

where $r_1, r_2 \sim \mathscr{U}(0,1)$, and $\psi(t)$ can take different forms depending on the model type.

Typical function classes include:

Nonlinear decay: $\psi(t) = 2 - (t/T)^2$ [9,23,24],

Oscillatory: $\psi(t) = a_{\min} + (a_{\max} - a_{\min}) \cdot \cos(2\pi t/T)$ [25,26],

Exponential: $\psi(t) = 2 \cdot \exp(-(t/T)^2)$ [9,27],
Gaussian-shaped: $\psi(t) = \phi \cdot \exp(-t^2/2\sigma^2)$ [28],
Adaptive/Chaotic [29].

These functional forms redefine how the optimizer transitions between global exploration and local refinement, making the algorithm more responsive to problem-specific convergence demands.

4.3.2.2 *Representative variants and mechanisms*

Numerous GWO variants fall under MM2 by modifying the control function $a(t)$ to improve convergence behavior and search adaptivity. For example, Yan et al. (2023) [23] introduce a nonlinear exploration–exploitation control curve tailored for classification tasks, while Long et al. (2016) [24] propose a smoother decay to improve convergence stability. Oscillatory approaches appear in Sharma et al. (2017) [25] and Zhang et al. (2024) [26], where cosine or sine-based functions allow the algorithm to periodically reintroduce exploration, mitigating the risk of local trapping. Exponential decay strategies are explored in Ou et al. (2023) [9] and Mittal et al. (2016) [27], aiming to delay exploitation for better early-stage sampling.

Other notable extensions include a chaos-aware adaptive decay model in Qiu et al. (2024) [29], which adjusts the decay path of $a(t)$ dynamically based on convergence behavior, and a Gaussian decay curve in Hou et al. (2022) [28], offering an initial surge in search radius followed by a gradual focusing mechanism. Collectively, these modifications represent a fundamental shift toward context-sensitive convergence control, replacing static linearity with flexible, often biologically or statistically inspired parameter dynamics. As a result, MM2-based formulations significantly enhance the optimizer's ability to adapt across diverse and dynamically changing landscapes.

4.3.3 MM3. Leader influence reweighting and generalized hierarchy

The original GWO relies on a fixed leadership model in which the top three wolves, α, β, and δ, equally contribute to guiding the rest of the population through a simple arithmetic mean. While effective in basic settings, this rigid structure limits the algorithm's adaptability to dynamic fitness landscapes and diverse convergence demands. MM3 variants address this by redefining the leadership hierarchy and influence mechanism, replacing static averaging with dynamic weighting, fuzzy logic, localized ranking, and probabilistic leader selection. These models improve GWO's responsiveness to population feedback, encourage adaptive prioritization of better-performing leaders, and introduce multitiered or personalized leadership structures, resulting in more controlled convergence and enhanced solution diversity.

4.3.3.1 *Formal abstract model*

Let $\mathscr{H}(t) = \{X_j\}_{j=1}^{k}$ be a set of leader solutions at the iteration t, with corresponding dynamic weights $w_j(t)$ where $\sum_j w_j(t) = 1$. The generalized MM3 update rule is:

$$X_i(t+1) = \sum_{X_j(t) \in \mathscr{H}(t)} w_j(t) \cdot X_j(t) \tag{4.6}$$

where:

$\sum_j w_j(t) = 1$, (fuzzy [30,31] or normalized weighting [32])

$w_j(t)$ can be computed from fitness scores [33], Euclidean distance, diversity metrics, or fuzzy inference systems [30,31],

The leader set $\mathscr{H}(t)$ may include traditional ranks (α, β, δ), Pareto-optimal agents [34,35], or localized elites [36], and in some cases, $\mathscr{H}(t)$ varies per agent (i.e., personalized [37] or neighborhood-based [36] leadership).

This abstract formulation allows leader influence to be adaptive, context-aware, and functionally richer, enabling improved balance between global search and local refinement.

4.3.3.2 *Representative variants and mechanisms*

A wide range of GWO extensions adopt this reweighting paradigm. In Banaie-Dezfouli et al. (2021) [37], personalized adaptive leadership is introduced, where each agent selects leaders based on local performance and ranking history, enabling more tailored influence than the global α,β,δ model. Similarly, Liu et al. (2023) [32] and Rajakumar et al. (2021) [33] propose fitness-proportional weights that evolve over time, enhancing convergence stability through ranking-sensitive leader prioritization. A fuzzy logic-based leadership model appears in Rodriguez et al. (2017) [30] and Qin et al. (2022) [31], where influence weights are inferred dynamically based on contextual rules involving fitness and distance, allowing probabilistic switching among behaviors like random walk and elite guidance.

Some variants expand the leadership pool structurally. For instance, Miao et al. (2020) [38] add ξ and ω to form a five-tier hierarchy, while Seyyedabbasi and Kiani (2021) [39] include the global best solution X_{gb} in the update rule to reinforce exploitation. In the multiobjective domain, Toktas et al. (2024) [34] and Mirjalili et al. (2016) [35] replace α,β,δ with Pareto-optimal agents selected through grid-density metrics or dominance sorting, increasing diversity and enabling Pareto-driven convergence. Localized leadership is seen in Lu et al. (2018) [36], where each wolf selects guides from a spatial neighborhood using a grid topology, thereby preserving spatial diversity in multimodal landscapes. Recursive influence strategies, such as those in Dagal et al. (2025) [40], generate virtual leaders via intermediate averaging to smooth update trajectories. Further hybrid models, such as Tu et al. (2019) [41] and Nadimi-Shahraki et al. (2021) [42], partition the population into dominant and subordinate roles or stretch the update rule to incorporate diversity-aware controls, improving convergence in complex engineering problems.

Collectively, MM3 variants evolve GWO's social hierarchy into a flexible, intelligent guidance system, replacing equal contribution with adaptive leader modeling that enhances convergence control, robustness, and problem sensitivity.

4.3.4 MM4. State-augmented models (memory, velocity, learning)

The original GWO is a memoryless, position-driven algorithm, where each agent updates its location solely based on the current iteration's leaders. MM4 variants enrich this formulation by introducing additional state variables, such as velocity vectors, elite memory archives, and adaptive learning mechanisms, that allow the algorithm to retain and use historical information. These modifications convert GWO into a stateful, learning-enabled dynamical system, capable of exploiting prior knowledge, tracking momentum, and adjusting search behavior over time. The goal is to improve convergence reliability, boost precision in later stages, and enhance adaptability to complex, multimodal, or time-varying landscapes.

4.3.4.1 Formal abstract model

Let each wolf $X_i(t)$ be associated with additional internal states:

Velocity vector $V_i(t)$ [43],

Memory archive $M_i(t)$ [44–46],

Adaptive modifiers $\lambda(t)$, $P_j(t)$, $\delta(t)$, etc. [47–49].

A general state-augmented update rule can be written as:

$$X_i(t+1) = f(X_i(t), V_i(t), M_i(t), \Theta(t)) \tag{4.7}$$

where:

$V_i(t+1) = \mu V_i(t) + \sum_k w_k(X_k(t) - X_i(t))$ [43]: momentum-influenced velocity,

$M_i(t)$ contains elite [44] or historically promising positions influencing the update [45],

$\Theta(t)$ represents adaptive parameters controlling memory usage or perturbation strength [47–49],

$f(\cdot)$ may involve dimension-wise learning [45], probabilistic inheritance [46], or strategic reinitialization [47].

This formulation allows GWO agents to learn from the past, adaptively modify their trajectory, and selectively explore or exploit based on stored information and dynamic feedback.

4.3.4.2 Representative variants and mechanisms

Several influential GWO variants adopt state-augmented structures to improve performance. In Gupta and Deep (2020) [44], a Global Search Memory stores elite solutions, and wolves probabilistically update their positions based on historical attractors, promoting intelligent re-exploration in multimodal spaces. Velocity dynamics inspired by PSO are introduced in Rezaei et al. (2022) [43], where each wolf maintains a velocity vector, leading to smoother, momentum-guided trajectories. Similarly, [45] proposes dimension-wise elite inheritance, where parts of an agent's position are probabilistically overwritten by elite traits, coupled with adaptive range-scaling for exploitation control.

Additional mechanisms include probabilistic reinitialization in Saremi et al. (2015) [46], where poorly performing wolves are regenerated using a statistical function of the search space bounds, and OBL in Wang et al. (2022) [47] and Xing et al. (2018) [48], which injects asymmetrical or dynamically bounded samples to improve diversity and escape local minima. A more biologically inspired augmentation appears in Bohat et al. (2018) [49], where synthetic prey-phase agents initially move away from the leader under exponential repulsion dynamics, boosting early exploration and transitioning smoothly into standard GWO behavior.

Collectively, these MM4 variants empower GWO with memory, velocity, and learning capabilities, transforming the algorithm into a dynamic feedback system that better adapts to landscape complexity, balances intensification and diversification, and achieves more stable convergence across diverse optimization problems.

4.3.5 MM5. Probabilistic and stochastic process formulations

Unlike standard GWO, which introduces stochasticity indirectly through uniformly sampled coefficients, MM5 variants embed randomness as a foundational modeling principle. These formulations treat the algorithm as an explicit stochastic or probabilistic process, often driven by random walks, probability distributions, or even formal Markovian dynamics. By shifting the role of randomness from auxiliary to primary, these models aim to enhance exploration diversity, increase the likelihood of escaping local optima, and, in some cases, provide analytically tractable convergence behavior. As such, MM5 moves GWO closer to the theoretical domain of stochastic optimization and probabilistic learning.

4.3.5.1 Formal abstract model

Let $X_i(t)$ denote the position of the agent i at the iteration t, and define its update as a stochastic process:

$$X_i(t+1) = X_i(t) + \xi_i(t), \ \ \xi_i(t) \sim \mathscr{D}(t) \tag{4.8}$$

where:

$\xi_i(t)$ is a random variable drawn from a distribution $\mathscr{D}(t)$, such as Gaussian, Cauchy, Lévy, or Brownian noise [50–52], $\mathscr{D}(t)$ may depend on the iteration count t, the agent fitness, or adaptive scaling,

The full algorithm is modeled either as a Markov process or a probabilistic walk in the solution space [53,54]. In more formal settings, convergence is defined probabilistically:

$$\lim_{t \to \infty} P(X_i(t) \in B_\epsilon(x^*)) = 1 \tag{4.9}$$

where $B_\epsilon(x^*)$ is an ϵ-neighborhood of the global optimum x^*, and the dynamics follow a **homogeneous Markov chain** structure.

4.3.5.2 Representative variants and mechanisms

Several notable variants exemplify the MM5 philosophy. In Gupta and Deep (2018) [51], RW-GWO employs a hybrid random walk mechanism combining Cauchy-distributed and Brownian (Gaussian) step dynamics to balance global exploration and local exploitation, thereby enhancing performance on rugged and constrained engineering problems. Han et al. (2018) [50] propose a hybrid model incorporating both Gaussian and Lévy flight mechanisms, leveraging Mantegna's algorithm to inject heavy-tailed, large-magnitude perturbations that enable escape from deceptive regions in the search space. In Gupta and Deep (2019) [52], early-stage exploration is enhanced using a Cauchy-distributed random walk, which introduces long-tailed perturbations to the leaders' positions, boosting diversity and helping escape local optima without compromising late-stage convergence.

More formal stochastic frameworks appear in Wang and Shi (2022) [53] and [54]. The former constructs a probabilistic sampling framework based on probability density function evolution and moment analysis, while the latter proves convergence using Markov chain theory, establishing that the best solution approaches global optima with high probability over time. These works are rare examples of theoretical grounding in metaheuristic algorithms. In [55], stochastic OBL is used to reflect positions across the search space based on uniformly distributed randomness, enhancing spatial diversity.

Although CGWO [56] employs a deterministic Chebyshev chaotic map, its behavior closely mimics stochastic search due to its ergodicity and unpredictability. This pseudo-random behavior introduces controlled exploration without requiring probabilistic sampling, offering a deterministic approximation to stochastic search dynamics.

Collectively, MM5 variants embed stochasticity as a core design principle, transforming GWO into a probabilistic search system with rich exploratory behavior and, in some cases, provable convergence guarantees. These models are especially valuable for complex, multimodal, or mathematically challenging problem domains.

4.3.6 MM6. Hybridized mathematical models (equation-level fusion)

MM6 represents the most structurally transformative class of GWO variants, where the optimizer is mathematically fused with other metaheuristics at the equation level. Unlike procedural hybrids that alternate between algorithms or apply postprocessing steps, MM6 variants directly embed foreign behavioral operators, such as mutation, crossover, Lévy flights, teaching-learning updates, or energy-driven jumps, into the core GWO position update rule. This equation-level integration leads to new composite dynamics, allowing the algorithm to simultaneously express multiple search behaviors (e.g., exploitation via encircling and exploration via stochastic flights). These hybrids are especially suited for tackling rugged or high-dimensional landscapes where traditional GWO mechanisms may stagnate or converge prematurely.

4.3.6.1 Formal abstract model

Let $\mathscr{U}_{GWO}$ and $\mathscr{U}_{\text{Hybrid}}$ denote the update functions derived from GWO and a secondary algorithm, respectively. The hybrid update rule can be expressed as:

$$X_i(t+1) = \begin{cases} \mathscr{U}_{GWO}(X_i, \Theta), & \text{if} \pi(t) = 0 \\ \mathscr{U}_{\text{Hybrid}}(X_i, \Phi), & \text{if} \pi(t) = 1 \end{cases} \tag{4.10}$$

where:

Θ and Φ are parameter sets for the GWO and hybrid components, respectively.

$\pi(t)$ is a switching function (deterministic [57,58], probabilistic [59–62], or energy-based [63–65]),

Alternatively, both update functions may be blended [66–68]:

$$X_i(t+1) = \alpha(t) \cdot \mathscr{U}_{GWO} + (1 - \alpha(t)) \cdot \mathscr{U}_{\text{Hybrid}} \tag{4.11}$$

This formulation captures equation-level fusion and allows for **multimechanism decision-making within a single update step**.

4.3.6.2 Representative variants and mechanisms

Numerous high-performing GWO variants fall within this hybridized category. For example, Singh and Bansal (2022) [69] embed DE mutation operations within GWO, followed by greedy selection to maintain directional improvement. Similarly, Yu et al. (2024) [68] combine Lévy flights and sine–cosine perturbations to induce large exploratory moves while preserving oscillatory precision. In [59], GWO is hybridized with teaching-learning-based optimization (TLBO) via a probabilistic rule that switches between GWO's encircling logic and TLBO's pedagogical dynamics.

Other hybrids integrate multiple components. Lian et al. (2019) [70] incorporate simulated annealing and opposition-based learning (OBL), offering stochastic escape and early diversity; [61] fuses GWO with Harris Hawks Optimization (HHO) using an energy-based control signal to alternate behaviors. In [62], a whale optimization algorithm (WOA) phase is used for intensified exploitation, while Zhang et al. (2018) [64] and Mohammed and Rashid (2020) [66] blend GWO with biogeography-based optimization (BBO) and WOA, respectively, forming phased or layered hybrid frameworks. In Yue et al. (2020) [65], Fireworks-inspired explosions are used to promote search diversification, while Bhandari et al. (2023) [67] combine PSO velocity updates with GWO's social hierarchy, creating a hybrid suited for discrete and reliability-focused tasks.

Two variants emphasize adaptive switching between distinct exploration modes. In Heidari and Pahlavani (2017) [60], LMGWO alternates stochastically between standard GWO encircling and Lévy flight-based long-range movement, enhancing the optimizer's ability to balance global and local search. In Ma et al. (2022) [63], Aquila-GWO adopts early-stage movement patterns inspired by Aquila Optimization, such as spiral soaring and glide motion, before transitioning into conventional GWO behavior, thus leveraging both exploratory richness and convergence stability in a biologically motivated sequence.

More intricate models, such as [57] and Adegboye et al. (2024) [58], incorporate full operator sets from DE, chaos theory, and mirrored perturbations, creating multilayered search mechanisms that enable GWO to preserve elite solutions, inject diversity, and avoid stagnation simultaneously. These models exemplify the core value of MM6, blending algorithmic strengths at the mathematical core to achieve synergy across multiple search strategies.

4.3.7 Concluding reflection on MM1–MM6

Together, the six modeling classes, MM1 through MM6, represent a progression from simple structural adjustments (MM1–MM3) to complex behavioral enhancements (MM4–MM6). While MM1–MM3 focus on redefining the internal architecture of GWO's update rule, MM4–MM6 shift toward richer state representation, probabilistic modeling, and hybridized search logic. Across these categories, a clear trend emerges: modern GWO designs increasingly emphasize adaptivity, context sensitivity, and multimodal search behavior.

These mathematical enhancements are not merely technical variations; they govern the very dynamics of how GWO agents explore, learn, and converge. Whether through adaptive leadership (MM3), stateful learning (MM4), stochastic walking (MM5), or equation-level fusion (MM6), each model redefines the behavioral trajectory of the optimizer. Understanding and classifying these models is therefore not just a matter of taxonomy; it is essential to designing GWO variants that are robust, efficient, and theoretically grounded.

The next section builds on this foundation by analyzing the DB consequences of these modeling choices and linking them to empirical CG.

4.4 Dynamic behavior of grey wolf optimizer variants

As the mathematical core of the GWO continues to evolve, these structural changes inevitably reshape the algorithm's internal dynamics, altering how agents navigate the search space, interact with one another, and adapt to varying optimization landscapes. This section focuses on the emergent behavioral properties that arise from such modifications, with special attention to how they influence critical dimensions of search behavior, including the balance between exploration and exploitation, population diversity, leader influence, adaptability, and resistance to stagnation. Rather than viewing mathematical enhancements as static rule changes, the analysis here treats them as dynamic systems that govern the time-evolving trajectory of the population. By examining these dynamics, we can better understand how GWO variants adjust their search patterns over time, respond to feedback from the fitness landscape, and develop distinctive behavioral strategies that influence their effectiveness and reliability.

To characterize these dynamics in a systematic way, we classified GWO variants into six behavioral categories (A–F), each corresponding to a distinct functional mechanism. A (Convergence Dynamics and Stability) captures designs that regulate the smoothness and reliability of convergence. B (Adaptive Control Parameter Mechanisms) refers to the dynamic adjustment of coefficients or influence weights in response to time or feedback. C (Trajectory Behavior and Landscape Sampling) encompasses strategies that reshape how wolves traverse the search space and explore new regions. D (Leadership Modeling and Influence Dynamics) represents changes to how leadership is assigned or exercised within the swarm. E (Memory, Elite Learning, and Historical Feedback) includes designs that exploit past experience to refine current search. Finally, F (Population Structure and Diversity Regulation) reflects mechanisms that preserve heterogeneity and prevent premature convergence. Each variant is assigned to the category that reflects its dominant behavioral effect, while secondary influences are acknowledged but not used to determine classification. This approach ensures that the behavioral taxonomy remains both mutually distinct and interpretable.

4.4.1 A. Convergence dynamics and stability

This group encompasses GWO variants that explicitly regulate the optimizer's convergence trajectory, enhancing smoothness, reliability, and descent precision through mathematical or behavioral stabilization mechanisms. These models typically deploy nonlinear or time-dependent control decay, momentum-based updates, or convergence-aware reweighting schemes. Such refinements reduce oscillation, prevent premature convergence, and direct the optimizer toward sharper final descent. Key designs include velocity-aided updates, adaptive step scaling, and elite-aligned convergence trajectories, often enhancing both accuracy and stability.

One study improved convergence reliability by introducing unequal leader weighting that gradually centralizes search pressure [15]. Another replaced the population means with probabilistic averaging, producing smoother but still varied trajectories [19]. Time-varying control of the coefficient enabled gradual transitions that enhance stability [24]. A hybrid design integrated wide exploratory arcs with structured leadership to combine exploration and disciplined convergence [66]. Exponential decay functions extended early exploration before inducing sharp late-stage exploitation [27]. Hierarchical multistep updates incorporated memory effects to regulate step size and directional control [40]. A velocity term was added to maintain trajectory continuity and reduce oscillations [43]. Discrete transition rules were applied to shift search smoothly from exploratory jumps to local refinement [18]. Differential perturbations and leader mutations supported scalable adaptation in high-dimensional landscapes [22]. Finally, nonlinear decay with disturbance terms promoted early exploration and stabilized late-stage exploitation [28]. Collectively, these approaches demonstrate how mathematical refinements in convergence dynamics can deliver controlled, stage-wise acceleration and reliable descent across diverse optimization contexts.

4.4.2 B. Adaptive control parameter mechanisms

This group captures modifications that introduce dynamic, feedback-driven adjustments to key control parameters in GWO, such as the convergence coefficient a, attraction vectors $\vec{A}$ and $\vec{C}$, or leader weighting. Rather than using fixed or linear decay, these methods employ nonlinear scheduling (e.g., cosine, exponential, chaotic) or context-sensitive adaptations based on iteration count, fitness trends, or diversity metrics. This responsiveness allows the optimizer to flexibly shift between exploration and exploitation as needed, improving performance across diverse and complex landscapes.

Several works exemplify this adaptive control philosophy: Yan et al. (2023) [23] introduce nonlinear $\varphi(t)$-based adaptation; Sharma et al. (2017) [25], Qiu et al. (2024) [29], Zhang et al. (2024) [26], and Ou et al. (2023) [9] apply oscillatory, distance-sensitive, and sinusoidal decays for nuanced phase transitions. Kohli and Arora (2018) [56] integrate chaotic maps for deterministic-stochastic modulation of convergence dynamics, while Qin et al. (2022) [31] apply fuzzy probabilistic sampling to adapt search intensity. Similarly, Liu et al. (2023) [32] leverage cosine-based scheduling with opposition learning, and Yu et al. (2024) [68] adapt directionality and step size via multistrategy coordination. Toktas et al. (2024) [34] further combines adaptive parameter tuning with Pareto-based dominance logic in multiobjective spaces. Together, these models establish Group B as central to real-time control, resilience, and performance tuning in GWO evolution.

4.4.3 C. Trajectory behavior and landscape sampling

This group includes algorithms that redesign how agents traverse the search space, often using stochastic perturbations, dimension-wise updates, or escape-oriented motion patterns (e.g., Lévy flights, Cauchy jumps, opposition-based steps). These modifications aim to diversify search paths, enhance ergodicity, and prevent premature convergence by promoting more thorough landscape coverage.

Dynamic opposition learning introduced asymmetric opposite positions to increase spatial diversity and stabilize convergence [47], while generalized opposition strategies used diversity thresholds to inject novelty and prevent stagnation [48]. Random walk designs applied Gaussian and Lévy walks to stratify wolves into explorers and refiners [50], or introduced probabilistic movement patterns that gradually transitioned from chaos to order [52]. Prey-phase dynamics divided wolves into exploratory and convergent roles to enforce staged transitions [49], while mutation-driven updates applied Cauchy-based jumps and rotational diversity to maintain unpredictability [69]. Other designs adopted Lévy-based jumps coupled with local refinements for flexibility [60], or integrated hybrid attack strategies that adaptively shifted from exploration to exploitation [61]. Multimodal movement schemes, such as eagle-inspired soaring and diving, enabled terrain-sensitive behavior adjustments [63]. Hybrid models transferred features from other optimizers, including migration and mutation for adaptability [64], spiral trajectories for fluid motion [62], or dual-variant logic with archives and opposite solutions for versatility [39]. Additional refinements introduced context sensitive trajectory controls: mathematical analyses revealed probabilistic trajectory diffusion and variance decay [53,54], chaotic dimension-wise updates enhanced adaptability [14], and leader-driven random walks supported feasible pathfinding in constrained spaces [51]. Collectively, these designs illustrate how trajectory-based modifications expand landscape sampling capacity, sustain diversity, and reduce the risk of premature convergence.

4.4.4 D. Leadership modeling and influence dynamics

This group includes modifications that restructure how leadership is defined, distributed, or weighted in GWO. By replacing static $\alpha - \beta - \delta$ roles with fuzzy logic, fitness-based scores, dimension-wise learning, or Pareto-based archives, these models redefine the forces guiding swarm movement. Such shifts influence coordination strength, convergence accuracy, and robustness to deceptive leaders.

Several studies [30,42] introduced fuzzy rule-based frameworks that dynamically reassign leader roles using fitness-informed metrics, enhancing decision-making precision. Others [16,17] broke classical hierarchies by using memory-guided updates or centroid-based directionality from alternate wolves, fostering nonhierarchical swarm guidance. Further developments [20] enabled dimension-level learning from top performers, while Luo (2019) [13] integrated prey estimation models for adaptive leader targeting. Deepened hierarchical structures were explored in Miao et al. (2020) and Tu et al. (2019) [38,41], introducing multilevel or class-based influence for robust guidance across diverse problem phases. Finally, Mirjalili et al. (2016) [35] extended leader modeling into multiobjective domains via archive-based dominance selection, achieving Pareto-consistent swarm behavior. Altogether, these contributions form the foundation of Group D, revealing the flexibility and power of leader-centric designs in modulating search direction and convergence force.

4.4.5 E. Memory, elite learning, and historical feedback

This group captures mechanisms that introduce temporal memory into the optimization process, allowing wolves to incorporate past elite experiences into current decisions. These may include external archives, elite inheritance strategies, or historical feedback in the form of stored vectors or dimension-wise learning. Such memory-based designs reinforce successful trajectories, stabilize convergence, and reduce the likelihood of re-exploring unproductive regions.

Methods such as Gupta and Deep (2020) [44] introduced external elite archives guiding position updates, enabling convergence refinement and continuity. In Jiang et al. (2024) [45], elite inheritance is fused with a balanced switching mechanism to reuse high-performing past positions and enhance temporal adaptivity. Meanwhile, Wang and Li (2019) [57] hybridized GWO with DE and a natural selection-based elimination strategy, combining memory and adaptive renewal to refine trajectory quality and maintain diversity. Collectively, these works exemplify Group E's core principle: learning from the past to guide future search more effectively.

4.4.6 F. Population structure and diversity regulation

This group encompasses strategies that maintain swarm heterogeneity and structural variability during optimization. These include multigroup architectures, OBL, chaotic perturbations, leader-locality rules, and entropy-triggered resets. By regulating diversity and preventing premature collapse around local optima, such designs enhance robustness, enable parallel exploration of multiple regions, and improve solution quality in multimodal spaces.

Several methods exemplify these traits. Yue et al. (2020) [65] employed phase-based hybridization between GWO and fireworks algorithm (FWA), dynamically balancing exploration and convergence. Adegboye et al. (2024) [58] enhanced population diversity using chaotic opposition, mirror reflection, and targeted disturbance of weak agents. The algorithm in Jiang et al. (2022) [21] introduced distance-based leader influence and threshold-triggered Gaussian noise to support adaptive exploration. Saremi et al. (2015) [46] integrated Evolutionary Population Dynamics to continuously refresh half the swarm, avoiding stagnation. In Bhandari et al. (2023) [67], PSO–GWO hybridization reshaped population coordination and strengthened subgroup control.

Topological structuring appeared in Lu et al. (2018) [36] via a cellular GWO model that localized leader impact, while Liang et al. (2019) [70] combined opposition-based initialization with annealing and elite mutations to enhance diversity preservation. Finally, Banaie-Dezfouli et al. (2021) [37] introduced subgroup partitioning with elite memory in R-GWO, enabling distributed guidance and multiregion search. Together, these works define Group F's core philosophy: structural flexibility and diversity as engines of resilient optimization.

4.4.7 Concluding reflection on A-F

The behavioral mechanisms explored in Section 4.4 collectively reveal a tightly interwoven design space within GWO variants. While each group targets a distinct control axis, stability (A), adaptivity (B), trajectory shaping (C), leadership logic (D), memory integration (E), or diversity preservation (F), many variants exhibit overlapping influences, forming multidimensional convergence strategies. For instance, adaptive decay schedules in Group B frequently amplify or temper the trajectory perturbations from Group C, while elite memory from Group E often guides or tempers leadership behaviors in Group D. Similarly, population structuring in Group F is not only a driver of diversity but also modulates convergence speed (A) and adaptability (B) through indirect swarm regulation.

Several studies demonstrate hybrid impacts, combining behavioral roles across 3–4 groups to simultaneously manage exploration–exploitation trade-offs, convergence smoothness, and solution precision. This convergence of roles suggests that future GWO advancements may benefit from unified design frameworks that integrate memory, control feedback, and structural modularity within a single adaptable system. Ultimately, the behavioral dimensions of Section 4.4 provide not just individual levers of improvement, but a blueprint for designing resilient, self-regulating metaheuristics capable of thriving across complex, high-dimensional, and noisy problem domains.

4.5 Convergence outcomes and justifications

As the mathematical architecture and dynamic behavior of the GWO continue to mature, the ultimate measure of these developments lies in their ability to support stable, efficient, and reliable convergence across diverse optimization landscapes. While structural enhancements shape how agents move and behave during search, their long-term value is determined by whether such changes lead to demonstrable convergence, either through empirical outcomes, structural logic, or formal theoretical proof. This section focuses on the convergence patterns that emerge from mathematically grounded modifications, with particular attention to how these alterations influence the optimizer's ability to reach global or high-quality local optima under bounded or dynamic conditions. Rather than treating convergence as a byproduct of improved search behavior, the analysis here positions it as the culminating consequence of earlier modeling and behavioral choices. By tracing the effects of mathematical interventions, such as parameter redefinition, leadership modulation, stochastic perturbations, and hybridized control, on convergence characteristics, we reveal how different GWO variants either stabilize, accelerate, or sustain their descent toward optima.

To provide clarity and avoid overlap, these outcomes are classified into eight categories (G1–G8), each corresponding to a distinct convergence mechanism. G1 (Phased Convergence) captures staged transitions from exploration to exploitation, typically governed by time-varying parameters. G2 (Adaptive Convergence Pressure) reflects real-time modulation of convergence intensity in response to feedback signals. G3 (Trajectory Stabilization) refers to refinements that enforce smoother, directionally consistent paths. G4 (Memory-Guided Refinement) represents the use of historical knowledge or elite solutions to improve convergence precision. G5 (Diversity-Preserving Escape) emphasizes mechanisms that delay stagnation by sustaining heterogeneity during descent. G6 (Leadership-Driven Convergence Acceleration) highlights refinements that concentrate search pressure around elite leaders. G7 (Multibehavior Cooperative Convergence) encompasses hybrids that integrate multiple behavioral strategies to achieve robust outcomes. Finally, G8 (Formal Convergence Proofs) is reserved for variants that provide theoretical guarantees of convergence using stochastic or mathematical analysis. Each algorithm is assigned to the category that reflects its dominant convergence logic, with secondary traits acknowledged but not used for classification, ensuring mutual exclusivity and interpretability across the taxonomy.

4.5.1 G1. Phased convergence

Phased convergence represents a structured approach wherein the optimization process is deliberately segmented into exploration and exploitation stages, typically regulated by time-decaying control parameters, staged hybrid transitions, or adaptive phase triggers. Algorithms in this group formalize the transition from global to local search through mathematical constructs that progressively shift convergence pressure.

A hybrid with HHO achieved stronger final accuracy and stable feature selection by enforcing phase-based switching [61]. A whale–GWO hybrid improved benchmark convergence through distinct exploratory and exploitative stages [62]. Nonlinear decay functions accelerated convergence and stabilized classification outcomes [23]. Time-varying control decay produced smoother convergence and greater reliability across functions [24]. Prey-estimation with Gaussian perturbations enhanced convergence consistency, confirmed by statistical tests [13]. Hierarchical multistep control yielded layered convergence, improving stability and precision [40]. Nonlinear convergence factors accelerated descent and improved accuracy, including in robotics applications [28]. Exponential decay functions induced clear two-phase convergence with reliable stabilization in engineering problems [27].

While some variants also support adaptive pressure (G2), trajectory refinement (G3), or leader acceleration (G6), the dominant convergence logic in G1 stems from mathematically governed staging, where convergence is not merely emergent but explicitly designed to unfold over well-defined phases.

4.5.2 G2. Adaptive convergence pressure

Adaptive convergence pressure characterizes algorithms that dynamically adjust their convergence rate and direction in response to internal feedback mechanisms, such as population diversity, fitness distribution, or fuzzy inference, rather than relying on fixed phase transitions. These models offer a flexible convergence logic that allows GWO variants to modulate search intensity in real time.

Fuzzy rule-based leader reweighting improved convergence stability and final fitness through adaptive leadership weighting [30]. Reverse learning combined with hybrid updates yielded more accurate and stable convergence trajectories [29]. DE-based adaptation with elimination achieved consistently faster convergence across repeated trials [57]. Fitness-driven fuzzy control dynamically adjusted parameters, enhancing convergence responsiveness without fixed staging [31]. A Markov chain formulation formally proved convergence with probability one, providing theoretical guarantees alongside empirical validation [32]. Multistrategy adaptation improved convergence rate and accuracy across IEEE Congress on Evolutionary Computation (CEC) benchmark functions, supported by statistical tests and convergence curves [68]. Probabilistic perturbations combined with clonal expansion improved convergence speed and reduced stagnation, as shown empirically on multiple problems [9]. Finally, heavy-tailed Cauchy mutations helped sustain diversity and delay premature convergence, strengthening stability in later search stages [26].

Although some of these models also exhibit traits from G1 (phased progression), G5 (diversity preservation), or G6 (leadership-driven acceleration), their core convergence logic lies in real-time control adaptation, defining them as systems that learn to converge by observing and reacting to the evolving state of the search.

4.5.3 G3. Trajectory stabilization

Trajectory stabilization encompasses GWO variants that aim to refine convergence paths by suppressing erratic updates and enforcing smoother, directionally consistent motion. These algorithms modify the standard position update logic to reduce volatility, using mechanisms like mean-based adjustments, velocity memory, or dimension-wise influence smoothing.

Unequal leader weighting improved convergence speed and accuracy on benchmark and real-world problems by reducing oscillations in the update process [15]. A modified mean strategy enhanced stability and robustness, producing consistently faster and more reliable convergence across multiple runs [19]. Velocity-inspired updates introduced momentum, yielding smoother convergence curves and reducing abrupt directional changes [43]. Dimension-wise learning enabled fine-grained control of movement, which improved stability and maintained diversity across benchmarks [20]. Large-scale optimization tests confirmed that dimension-adaptive updates with mutation and Lévy dynamics produced stable, monotonic convergence with enhanced refinement capacity [22].

Although some of these approaches also incorporate mechanisms linked to G1 (phased adaptation), G2 (adaptive control), or G5 (diversity preservation), their dominant convergence logic lies in trajectory correction and directional smoothing, which stabilizes the search process, reduces overshooting, and strengthens late-phase precision.

4.5.4 G4. Memory-guided refinement

Memory-guided refinement encompasses GWO variants that leverage stored knowledge, such as elite solutions, positional archives, or inherited traits, to guide convergence in a more informed and historically grounded manner. These algorithms depart from purely reactive or stochastic updates by introducing persistent structures that recall successful search directions or solution patterns from earlier iterations.

A greedy refinement scheme coupled with personal-best tracking achieved significant gains in mean fitness and improved stability, supporting deterministic convergence across benchmark and engineering problems [16]. Elite memory integrated into the leadership mechanism enabled archive-based convergence that accelerated progress and reduced variance in late-stage searches [44]. Inheritance-based strategies strengthened convergence precision and stability, with empirical evidence showing lower final errors and enhanced consistency across runs [45]. A representative-based strategy further improved convergence speed and accuracy by adopting component-wise best values from memory, supporting stable and scalable performance across complex tasks [37].

By embedding historical continuity into the optimization process, G4-class methods reduce redundancy, accelerate fine-tuning, and improve robustness, reinforcing convergence reliability from early exploration through late-stage exploitation.

4.5.5 G5. Diversity-preserving escape

Diversity-preserving strategies play a pivotal role in enhancing the robustness of GWO variants by countering stagnation, especially in multimodal or deceptive landscapes. Algorithms in this category employ stochastic dynamics, such as chaotic maps, Lévy/Cauchy mutations, random walks, and OBL, to maintain population heterogeneity and sustain exploratory capacity throughout the optimization process.

Dynamic oppositional learning produced faster and more stable convergence by maintaining population spread [47], while generalized opposition preserved robustness through diversity-triggered updates [48], and randomized opposition improved late-stage precision with reduced variance [55]. Chaotic and dimension-wise refinements sustained long-run stability across high-dimensional problems [14]. Random walks stratified wolves into explorers and refiners [50], and Lévy-based jumps enabled faster and more resilient convergence on both benchmarks and engineering problems [60]. Additional stochastic walks reduced stagnation and improved robustness [52], while mutation-driven perturbations accelerated convergence and enhanced adaptability [69]. Adaptive leader control with selective mutation further maintained convergence quality in volatile tasks [70].

Structurally novel designs also reinforced diversity: subgroup mutation strategies improved stability [21], cellular structures, localized interactions, and prevented collapse [36], and chaos-infused reflection mechanisms sustained progress in multimodal landscapes [58]. Evolutionary population replacement maintained cyclic re-exploration and faster convergence [46]. Prey–predator phase separation delayed stagnation while preserving final accuracy [49], and random walks with leader perturbation allowed smooth convergence in constrained problems [51].

Although some of these models overlap with G2 (adaptive pressure) or G4 (memory-based refinement), their dominant convergence logic lies in diversity preservation, ensuring flexible and resilient trajectories that maintain exploratory depth while still converging effectively.

4.5.6 G6. Leadership-driven convergence acceleration

Leadership-driven convergence strategies enhance the GWO's capacity to rapidly and precisely descend toward optimal solutions by refining how influence is allocated among top-performing wolves. These variants restructure the leader model using fitness-weighted roles, extended hierarchies, or Pareto-based selection, thereby intensifying the algorithm's focus on elite agents.

Fitness-weighted leadership with mutation-chaos dynamics accelerated convergence and reduced variance, yielding more consistent discovery of optima [17]. Accelerated update schemes with hybrid refinements converged more quickly and with higher accuracy across diverse functions, supported by fitness plots and statistical validation [33]. A hybrid teacher–learner influence strengthened convergence depth and consistency, improving final accuracy though only empirically validated [42]. Expanding the hierarchy to additional leader tiers enhanced convergence speed and precision by distributing influence adaptively across the population [38]. In multiobjective settings, Pareto-based leadership guided convergence toward well-covered and uniform trade-off fronts, confirming balanced convergence behavior without formal proofs [35].

Although some of these approaches also overlap with G2 (adaptive modulation) and G3 (trajectory smoothing), their dominant convergence logic lies in leadership refinement, where elite-driven acceleration reduces noise, sharpens step direction, and ensures reliable convergence across both unimodal and multiobjective landscapes.

4.5.7 G7. Multibehavior cooperative convergence

Multibehavior cooperative strategies enhance GWO by fusing distinct behavioral components, either internally or through hybridization with external metaheuristics. These designs orchestrate exploration and exploitation in a coordinated manner, using alternating or simultaneous strategies to improve convergence reliability and robustness.

A hybrid with BBO improved convergence accuracy and stability across benchmarks by injecting migration and mutation knowledge into the swarm [64]. Incorporating fireworks-based local refinement accelerated convergence and lowered final errors through spark-driven intensification [65]. Hybridization with whale-inspired dynamics yielded stronger convergence across diverse benchmarks and engineering problems, supported by statistical tests [66]. A PSO–GWO hybrid produced faster and more consistent convergence in reliability optimization, combining inertia-driven and leadership-guided search [67]. Chaotic variants sustained diversity and prevented stagnation, yielding smoother and more stable convergence paths [59]. Hierarchy-strengthened leadership showed statistically significant convergence improvements across benchmarks, supported by Wilcoxon tests and fitness trajectories [41]. Dual-variant designs enhanced convergence reliability by reducing local optima entrapment and ensuring steady progress [39]. Even in discrete settings, adaptive control factors and probabilistic leader selection accelerated and stabilized convergence across multimodal problems [18].

Although some of these methods also incorporate G1 (phased adaptation), G2 (adaptive modulation), or G5 (diversity preservation), their dominant convergence logic lies in **behavioral cooperation**, where layered or hybridized mechanisms collectively stabilize trajectories, strengthen escape capacity, and generalize performance across diverse landscapes.

4.5.8 G8. Formal convergence proofs

The G8 category represents a critical yet sparsely populated class of GWO variants that offer formal convergence justifications. Unlike heuristic-driven enhancements, these methods establish theoretical guarantees using mathematical tools such as stochastic process modeling, noise decay analysis, and variance-bound proofs. Notably, TF-GWO [53] models the GWO update dynamics as a biased random walk with decaying noise, delivering bounded variance guarantees and proving almost sure convergence under controlled decay conditions. This formulation not only places the algorithm firmly in G8 but also exhibits G1-type phased convergence through dynamic noise scaling and promotes diversity (G5) during early iterations. Extending this line of inquiry, a follow-up study [54] introduces a stochastic variance–gradient framework that rigorously derives mean-square convergence conditions using adaptive variance decay and fitness-responsive pressure modulation (G2). These works exemplify rare but valuable contributions that link GWO's heuristic mechanisms to formal optimization theory, bridging empirical effectiveness with provable reliability. As such, they mark the frontier of GWO research where convergence behavior is no longer assumed but mathematically demonstrated.

4.5.9 Concluding reflection on G1–G8

Across all eight convergence categories (G1–G8), a multidimensional synthesis reveals the intricate interplay between MM, behavioral mechanisms, and CG. Phased strategies (G1) establish structural guidance for search progression, while adaptive pressure models (G2) enable real-time responsiveness to problem dynamics. Trajectory stabilization techniques (G3) and memory-guided refinements (G4) enhance convergence smoothness and long-term solution quality, respectively. Diversity-preserving mechanisms (G5) prevent stagnation and ensure robustness, often acting as a prerequisite for effective behavior in G1–G4. Leadership-centered accelerators (G6) sharpen convergence focus, particularly in exploitation-heavy phases, and hybrid strategies (G7) demonstrate the power of multibehavior synergies in solving complex or high-dimensional problems. Finally, the few works in G8 provide theoretical scaffolding that validates and contextualizes empirical success. Importantly, these categories do not operate in isolation: many algorithms manifest traits from multiple groups, illustrating that effective GWO variants often combine phased timing (G1), adaptive control (G2), diversity resilience (G5), and elite-driven acceleration (G6) in a cooperative framework. This cross-dimensional behavior confirms that convergence is not a singular outcome but a result of synergistic design across structural, behavioral, and theoretical layers, underscoring the need for holistic algorithm development in future GWO research.

Table 4.1 presents a comprehensive summary of GWO variants, detailing their methodological innovations, categorized MM types, DB enhancements, CG classifications, and experimental validation setups. For clarity, contributions are labeled as Major (MJ), Minor (MR), or Partial (PR).

4.6 Cross-dimensional isights and synthesis

While the previous sections have independently examined the MM, DB, and CG of GWO variants, a deeper understanding emerges only when these components are analyzed collectively. This section presents a cross-dimensional synthesis that reveals how structural interventions at the mathematical level shape algorithmic behavior and, in turn, influence convergence performance.

Drawing upon 92 MM-DB-CG paths extracted from 59 state-of-the-art GWO variants, we offer a unified view of the design–behavior–performance pipeline. This analysis aims to uncover dominant transformation pathways, underexplored yet promising combinations, and design heuristics that can inform future GWO enhancements.

4.6.1 Overview of analytical scope and path distribution

To operationalize the MM-DB-CG framework introduced in this chapter, we systematically analyzed 59 peer-reviewed GWO variant studies spanning from 2014 to 2025. Each study was carefully deconstructed to extract its MM choices, associated behavioral mechanisms (DB), and observed or theorized CG. The result of this effort is a structured dataset of 92 distinct MM-DB-CG paths, representing concrete instances of how mathematical design propagates through behavior to influence optimization performance.

This corpus serves as the empirical substrate for our synthesis. By aggregating the frequency of each component and the full paths across studies, we aim to uncover dominant design trends, recurrent behavioral effects, and high-yield convergence patterns. To provide a quantitative foundation for this synthesis, we present three descriptive charts that illustrate the distribution of MM categories, DB mechanisms, and CG outcomes across the reviewed literature.

These distributions, shown in Fig. 4.2, highlight the primary directions in GWO research when considering only major contributions. Among MM categories, MM3 (leader influence adjustments) and MM6 (hybridized models) dominate, followed closely by MM1 (algebraic reformulations) and MM2 (control parameter redefinition), reflecting the field's strong focus on restructuring leadership roles and integrating external strategies. On the behavioral side, C (trajectory behavior and landscape sampling) is by far the most represented, indicating a sustained emphasis on exploration and landscape coverage, while D (leadership modeling) and A (convergence dynamics) contribute significantly; in contrast, E (memory and elite learning) is the least studied. For CG G5 (diversity-preserving escape) stands out as the most common, underscoring the central concern with avoiding premature convergence, whereas G1 (phased convergence), G2 (adaptive pressure), G6 (leadership-driven acceleration), and G7 (multibehavior cooperation) appear at moderate levels. G3 (trajectory stabilization) and G4 (memory-guided refinement) are less frequent, and G8 (formal convergence proofs) remains rare, revealing a clear opportunity for more rigorous theoretical grounding.

4.6.2 Mathematical modeling-centric behavioral and convergence pathways

While the previous section offered a global view of design frequencies, this section shifts the focus to a structure-first analysis, examining how each MM category (MM1–MM6) shapes dynamic behavior and ultimately drives CG. By tracing the distinct MM-DB-CG pathways associated with each modeling category, we reveal how mathematical modifications are behaviorally expressed and what types of convergence they tend to support.

TABLE 4.1 Summary of GWO variants: methods, modeling types, behaviors, convergence, and experiments.

References	Method	MM category	DB category	CG category	Experimental method
[47] (2022)	Dynamic opposite learning GWO + Randomized jumping update + Weighted distance update rule	MM4 (MJ) MM5 (MJ)	C (MJ) F (MN)	G5 (MJ)	CEC2014 benchmarks (23 funcs), t-tests, comparisons with 10 algorithms
[30] (2017)	**Fuzzy inference system** to dynamically adjust leader influence + Fitness-weighted leadership update rule	MM3 (MJ)	D (MJ)	G2 (MJ)	Classical benchmark suite (F1–F13), 30/64/128D, tested on standard optimization problems (no CEC), statistical tests, and runtime analysis
[16] (2021)	Greedy nonhierarchical GWO (G-NHGWO) + Removes hierarchy completely + Greedy update mechanism	MM1 (MJ) MM4 (MJ)	D (MJ) E (MJ)	G4 (MJ) G5 (MN)	CEC2005 (F1–F14), 3 ELD problems (6, 20, 40-gen), 25 runs, 300 K evals, convergence plots
[61] (2023)	Hybrid GWO–HHO (HGWO) + Latin hypercube sampling + Nonlinear convergence factor + Greedy selection for position acceptance	MM6 (MJ) MM2 (MJ) MM3 (MN)	C (MJ) D (MJ) B (MN) F (MN)	G1 (MJ) G6 (MJ) G2 (MN)	23 classical funcs, CEC2020 (F24–F33), 4 engineering problems, Wilcoxon test, 20 runs, MATLAB R2022a
[44] (2020)	Memory-based GWO (mGWO) + **Personal best (pBest) memory** + **Modified hunting strategy** + **Crossover mechanism** + **Greedy selection**	MM4 (MJ)	E (MJ) D (MN)	G4 (MJ) G3 (MN) G2 (PR)	CEC2014 and CEC2017 (30 funcs each), three engineering problems, image thresholding, Wilcoxon test, 10D/30D
[15] (2024)	**Modified GWO (MGWO)** + Reformulated position update rule with **weighted influence** of three best wolves	MM1 (MJ) MM3 (MN)	A (MJ) D (MN)	G3 (MJ)	CEC2005 (23 classical funcs), three engineering problems, 10^4×D evals, Wilcoxon and t-test
[19] (2017)	Modified mean **GWO** (MMGWO) + Reformulates GWO position update using the **mean of the leader positions**	MM1 (MJ)	A (MJ)	G3 (MJ)	23 benchmark functions, 5 biomedical datasets, comparison with PSO/GWO/ACO, accuracy-focused
[62] (2018)	Hybrid algorithm of WOA and MGWO + **Parallel coevolutionary low-level hybridization** + **Partitioning strategy**	MM6 (MJ) MM2 (MJ) MM3 (MN)	C (MJ) D (MN) B (MN) F (MN)	G1 (MJ) G7 (MJ) G3 (MN)	23 benchmarks, 4 biomedical datasets, 2 engineering problems, 20 runs, comparisons with PSO/GWO/WOA/MGWO
[48] (2024)	Dynamic generalized opposition-based GWO (DGO-GWO) + **Adaptive opposition probability** and **random switching**	MM4 (MJ)	C (MJ) F (MN)	G5 (MJ)	CEC2014 (unimodal, multimodal, hybrid), 30 runs, pop=30, 500 iters, Wilcoxon test
[23] (2023)	Exploitative and explorative GWO for SVM + **Nonlinear φ(t) decay function** + **Emphasis on α wolf** + **Nonuniform weights** for leader roles	MM2 (MJ) MM3 (MN)	B (MJ) D (MN)	G1 (MJ)	SVM hyperparameter tuning on iRealcare and WESAD datasets, accuracy/F1/variance tests
[24] (2016)	Uses a **good point set (GPS)** strategy for initial population, Applies a **new time-varying parameter a(t)**	MM2 (MJ) MM1 (PR)	A (MJ)	G1 (MJ)	10 classical functions, 30D, 500 iters, compared to GWO, HGWO, DEs, ABCs, 30 runs
[17] (2020)	Centroid-based swarm update using k-nearest elite wolves	MM1 (MJ)	D (MJ) E (MN)	G6 (MJ)	13 benchmark functions, 2 engineering problems, 50 runs, 1000 iters, MATLAB 2016a

(Continued)

TABLE 4.1 (Continued)

References	Method	MM category	DB category	CG category	Experimental method
[50] (2018)	Gaussian random walk for exploitation + Lévy Flight for exploration + rank-based split strategy	MM5 (MJ)	C (MJ) F (MN)	G5 (MJ)G3 (MN)	9 classical benchmarks, 3 engineering designs, 30 runs, Wilcoxon test, MATLAB 2017a
[64] (2018)	Differential mutation + Multimigration BBO + OBL-GWO with alternating dim strategy	MM6 (MJ)	C (MJ) F (MN)	G5 (MJ)	CEC2014 (10D, 30D), classic benchmarks, clustering, 51 runs, MATLAB R2014a, SPSS, Wilcoxon test
[65] (2020)	Alternating fireworks exploration + GWO exploitation via adaptive p control	MM6 (MJ)	F (MJ)	G7 (MJ)	16 standard benchmark functions, MATLAB 2017a, h/p values, compared with GWO, FWA, EGWO, AGWO, PSO, MFO
[66] (2020)	GWO α–β–δ exploitation + WOA spiral exploration with evaluation filter	MM6 (MJ)	A (MJ)	G7 (MJ)	23 benchmark, CEC2005, CEC2019; pressure vessel design; 30 runs; Wilcoxon test; MATLAB R2017b
[52] (2019)	Cauchy-based random walk for α–β–δ wolves only	MM5 (MJ)	C (MJ) D (MN)	G5 (MJ)	IEEE CEC 2014 (10D, 30D); FM synth, pressure vessel, spring and gear design; 51 runs; Wilcoxon and PI; MATLAB 2010a
[55] (2019)	Random opposition-based learning + Modified C parameter strategy	MM5 (MJ)	A (MJ) C (MJ)	G5 (MJ)	23 classical + IEEE CEC2014 + 3 engineering (spring, beam, vessel); 30 runs; Wilcoxon test; 30D prems
[53] (2023)	Sampling distribution + stochastic modeling under stagnation assumption	MM5 (MJ)	C (MJ)	G8 (MJ)	No benchmarks; stochastic analysis via PDFs, moment evolution, numerical simulations only
[54] (2023)	Global convergence proof under the stagnation assumption using probabilistic modeling	MM5 (MJ)	C (MJ)	G8 (MJ)	No benchmarks; numerical simulation of agent trajectories, statistical validation of theoretical lemmas
[33] (2021)	BFGS for local exploitation + Lévy flight for global exploration + Diversity metrics	MM3 (MJ)	C (MJ)	G6 (MJ)	23 benchmark functions (7 uni, 6 multi, 10 fixed-multi); MATLAB R2012a; compared with GWO, PSO, etc.
[60] (2017)	Lévy flight for exploration + Greedy selection + Role reduction of δ wolf	MM6 (MJ)	C (MJ) F (MJ)	G5 (MJ)	29 classical + CEC2014 (30) + CEC2011 (14); compared with DE, GA, ALO, PSO; Wilcoxon and Friedman tests
[25] (2017)	Opposition-based learning (init + jump) + Oscillatory a(t) Decay	MM2 (MJ)	B (MJ) F (MN)	G1 (PR)	Numerical benchmark only; no CEC; simple comparison to original GWO
[43] (2022)	Velocity-aided update + a^2-based exploration–exploitation control + Elitism	MM4 (MJ)	A (MJ) F (MN)	G3 (MJ)	CEC2017 CF1–CF10, 13 multimodal + 3 engineering problems; Wilcoxon test; MATLAB runtime analysis
[45] (2024)	Elite inheritance + Balanced search via α–β–random——α–β–δ transition	MM4 (MJ)	E (MJ) F (MN)	G4 (MJ)	CEC2014 (F1–F30), 10D–100D; 3 engineering problems; Wilcoxon test; compared with GWO, SCA, WOA

[14] (2018)	Modified position averaging + Nonlinear a(t) modulation for high-D exploration	MM1 (MJ) MM2 (MN)	C (MJ) B (MN)	G5 (MJ)	23 benchmark functions; 30–10,000D; no extra FEs; CPU-time measured; compared with GWO, DE, PSO
[29] (2024)	Lens imaging reverse learning + Cosine a(t) decay + PSO/TSA-inspired update rule	MM2 (MJ) MM4 (MN)	B (MJ) A (MN)	G2 (MJ) G3 (PR)	23 classical + 15 CEC2014 + 2 engineering problems; Wilcoxon + Friedman tests
[26] (2024)	SFN topology + Neighbor learning + Adaptive individual regeneration	MM2 (MJ) MM3 (MJ) MM4 (MJ)	C (MJ) F (MJ) D (MN)	G5 (MJ) G4 (MJ) G6 (MN)	23 classical, CEC2019, 3 engineering; 30D and 50D; Wilcoxon test; ablation study included
[57] (2019)	IGWO=GWO + DE (mutation, crossover, selection) + SOF elimination	MM6 (MJ) MM4 (MN)	E (MJ) F (MN) B (PR)	G2 (MJ) G5 (MN) G4 (PR)	12 classic functions, 30/100D, compared with GWO, DE, PSO, ABC, CS, 30 runs, MATLAB
[9] (2020)	IGWO with a nonlinear a(t) decay for adaptive robot path planning	MM2 (MJ)	B (MJ)	G2 (MJ)	Path planning (10×10 & 20×20 maps), compared to GWO, ACO, PSO; metrics: path length, time, turns; MATLAB
[42] (2021)	IGWO with adaptive leadership reassignment and weighted α–β–δ roles	MM3 (MJ)	D (MJ)	G6 (MJ) G2 (MN)	23 benchmark funcs + 3 engineering problems, 30 runs, Wilcoxon test, MATLAB R2017b
[59] (2025)	Hybrid GWO-TLBO: TLBO's Teacher + Learner phases embedded into GWO α–β–δ structure	MM6 (MJ)	C (MJ)	G7 (MJ)	CEC2014/17/22 + 11 engineering designs (beam, vessel, clutch, etc.); compared with PSO, TLBO, GWO, ALO, etc.
[56] (2017)	Chaotic control of parameter a(t) using Chebyshev Map + Penalty-based constraint handling	MM5 (MJ)	B (MJ) C (MN)	G5 (MJ)	13 constrained benchmarks + 5 engineering problems (spring, gear, vessel, etc.); compared with GWO, PSO, FA, FPA
[58] (2021)	GWO + chaotic opposition learning + mirror reflection + worst-agent perturbation	MM6 (MJ)	F (MJ)	G5 (MJ)	23 classical functions + 4 engineering problems, 30 runs, Wilcoxon test, MATLAB 2017a
[20] (2022)	GWO with dimension-wise elite learning strategy	MM1 (MJ)	D (MJ) A (MN)	G3 (MJ) G6 (MN)	28 benchmark funcs + 3 engineering problems, 30 runs, Wilcoxon & Friedman tests, MATLAB
[21] (2020)	GWO + adaptive repositioning + dimension-wise perturbation	MM1 (MJ)	F (MJ) C (MN)	G5 (MJ)	30 benchmark funcs + 3 engineering problems, 30 runs, Wilcoxon and Friedman, MATLAB 2018a
[13] (2019)	GWO with prey position estimation using leader-weighted fusion	MM1 (MJ)	D (MJ)	G1 (MJ)	Bias tests (shifted functions), full CEC2017 suite (30D/100D), 2 engineering problems, Wilcoxon & Bonferroni
[46] (2015)	GWO with evolutionary population dynamics for worst-agent repositioning	MM4 (MJ)	F (MJ)	G5 (MJ)	13 classical functions (6 uni + 7 multi), 50 agents, 500 iters, 10 runs, compared with GWO
[31] (2022)	GWO with fuzzy inference to adapt leader influence and exploration–exploitation	MM3 (MJ)	B (MJ) D (MN)	G2 (MJ)	CEC2014 (30 multimodal funcs) + 3 engineering problems, 30 runs, Wilcoxon test, MATLAB 2020a
[67] (2023)	GWO with a hybridized PSO strategy for reliability-redundancy optimization	MM6 (MJ)	F (MJ)	G7 (MJ)	4 RRAP benchmarks (series, series-parallel, bridge, gas turbine), 50 runs, comparison with GA/ABC/PSO/GWO, MATLAB

(*Continued*)

TABLE 4.1 (Continued)

References	Method	MM category	DB category	CG category	Experimental method
[63] (2024)	GWO with aquila-inspired adaptive exploration modes	MM6 (MJ)	C (MJ)	G7 (MJ)	23 classical funcs + 4 engineering problems, 30 runs, Wilcoxon test, MATLAB 2020a
[38] (2020)	GWO with enhanced hierarchy: fitness-weighted leadership, leader-specific update, ω-wolf repositioning	MM3 (MJ)	D (MJ) F (MN)	G6 (MJ)	23 benchmark funcs + WSN coverage, 30 runs, Wilcoxon test, MATLAB
[36] (2022)	GWO with cellular topological grid and local neighborhood leader interaction	MM3 (MJ)	F (MJ)	G5 (MJ)	23 benchmark funcs + engineering problems, 30 runs, Wilcoxon andFriedman test, MATLAB
[40] (2020)	GWO with hierarchical multistep control across wolf ranks	MM3 (MJ)	A (MJ)	G1 (MJ)	18 classical benchmarks, 30 runs, MATLAB R2016b, compared with GA/PSO/DE
[41] (2019)	GWO with class-based update: elite learning + DE/OBL hybrid + perturbed diversity	MM3 (MJ)	D (MJ)	G7 (MJ)	CEC2014 (30 funcs), 13 UCI datasets, 30–51 runs, Wilcoxon tests, MATLAB
[39] (2022)	GWO with chaotic OBL, bidirectional updates, and trajectory memory	MM3 (MJ)	C (MJ)	G7 (MJ)	23 classical functions, 30 runs, Wilcoxon test, MATLAB 2020a
[18] (2018)	Discrete GWO with probabilistic leader assignment and Δ-step logic	MM1 (MJ)	A (MJ)	G7 (MJ)	F1/F2/F16/F18, 30 runs, compared with MODGWO, C + +
[28] (2019)	GWO with reverse learning, SA, and top-wolf mutation for job-shop scheduling	MM2 (MJ)	A (MJ)	G1 (MJ)	6 job-shop scheduling problems, 10 runs, compared with PSO/GWO, MATLAB R2019a
[70] (2019)	GWO with reverse learning, SA, and Cauchy mutation of leaders	MM6 (MJ)	F (MJ)	G5 (MJ)	Job-shop scheduling benchmarks, 10 runs, comparison with GWO/PSO, MATLAB
[32] (2023)	GWO with circle chaotic mapping, Cauchy mutation, Golden Sine algorithm, and adaptive position update	MM3 (MJ)	B (MJ) C (MJ)	G2 (MJ)	8 benchmark functions (mix of uni/multimodal), 3 high-dim cases (50D, 100D, 500D), 30 runs, Wilcoxon & Friedman tests, MATLAB
[68] (2023)	GWO with opposition-based learning, Lévy flight, and adaptive control for convergence	MM6 (MJ)	B (MJ)	G2 (MJ)	CEC2014 & CEC2020 test suites, 30 functions, 30D, 50D, 100D, 30 runs, Wilcoxon + Friedman test, convergence plots
[22] (2020)	GWO with dynamic position averaging, random weight coefficients, and convergence factor scaling	MM1 (MJ)	C (MJ)	G3 (MJ)	28 classical benchmark functions, 100D–10000D, convergence speed and stability metrics, MATLAB
[27] (2016)	GWO with exponential decay of parameter 'a' to rebalance exploration–exploitation	MM2 (MJ)	A (MJ)	G1 (MJ)	27 benchmark functions (unimodal, multimodal, composite), 30D, 30 runs, compared with PSO, BA, CS, GWO, WSN clustering problem
[34] (2024)	GWO with Pareto-based leader solution injection	MM3 (MJ)	B (MJ) D (MJ)	G6 (MJ)	5 MO functions + 2D chaotic system, compared with PSO, DE, ABC, metrics: HV, PSP, SE, PE, KE, NIST tests, MATLAB
[35] (2016)	GWO with external archive and fuzzy Pareto dominance for MOO	MM3 (MJ)	D (MJ)	G6 (MJ)	ZDT and DTLZ functions, compared with NSGA-II, MOPSO, SPEA2, metrics: hypervolume, spacing, spread, MATLAB

[58] (2023)	GWO with mutation-driven perturbation and adaptive local search phase	MM6 (MJ)	C (MJ) F (MN)	G5 (MJ)	30 CEC2015 benchmark funcs + 3 engineering problems, 30 runs, Wilcoxon test, MATLAB 2022a
[49] (2018)	GWO with prey phase for early exploration and prey-to-wolf role shift	MM4 (MJ)	C (MJ)	G5 (MJ)	10 classical benchmark funcs, 30 runs, Wilcoxon test, MATLAB
[51] (2018)	GWO with a Cauchy-based random walk for leaders in constrained search	MM5 (MJ)	C (MJ) F (MN)	G5 (MJ)	CEC 2006 + 3 engineering problems, 25 runs, Wilcoxon test, MATLAB
[37] (2020)	GWO with representative-based leader selection and dimensional guidance	MM3 (MJ)	D (MJ)	G4 (MJ)	25 classical funcs + 4 engineering problems, 30 runs, Wilcoxon & Friedman test, MATLAB

Legend: MJ=Major, MN=Minor, PR=Partial.

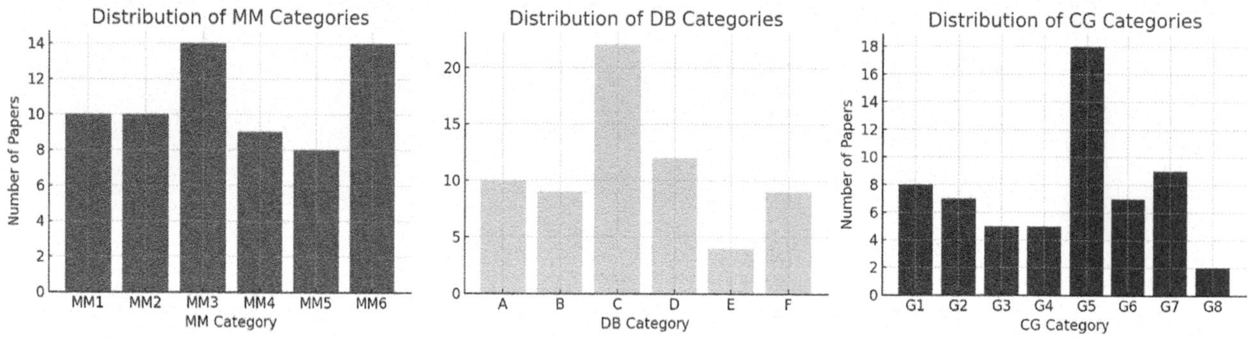

FIGURE 4.2 Distribution of MM, DB, and CG categories (*CG*, convergence outcomes; *DB*, dynamic behavioral; *MM*, modeling choices).

Fig. 4.3 visually maps these 92 pathways, organizing them hierarchically by modeling root (MM1–MM6), intermediate behavioral groups (A–F), and final convergence targets (G1–G8), with reference to the corresponding articles. This visualization serves as both a summarized taxonomy and a design trace tool, enabling readers to identify high-yield structural paths, discover underutilized behavioral mechanisms, and analyze convergence distributions specific to each MM type.

4.6.2.1 MM1—algebraic innovations driving path diversity

MM1 variants modify GWO's core position update rule by introducing flexible algebraic structures such as weighted leader combinations, stochastic selection, and dimension-wise influence. These changes decouple agent movement from the canonical α,β,δ average, enabling more diverse, nonlinear, and context-sensitive search trajectories.

As shown in Fig. 4.3, MM1 activates trajectory behavior (C) most prominently, alongside strong contributions from leadership dynamics (D) and additional roles from convergence smoothing (A), diversity regulation (F), and elite memory (E). These behavioral pathways lead to a broad range of CG, including G1 (phased convergence), G3 (trajectory stabilization), G4 (memory-guided refinement), G5 (diversity-preserving escape), G6 (leadership-driven acceleration), and G7 (multibehavior cooperation). The summary in Table 4.2 highlights the specific behavior–outcome pairings observed across MM1-based variants, showing that while the structural interventions are diverse, they consistently converge toward refined trajectory control, adaptive leadership, and swarm diversity mechanisms.

Although MM1 enables exploratory richness and emergent coordination, its CG are more heterogeneous and variant-specific compared to the more rule-driven control structures of MM2.

4.6.2.2 MM2—adaptive coefficient control for phased convergence

MM2 variants target the control coefficients in GWO, specifically the time-dependent parameter $a(t)$, and derived vectors $\vec{A}$ and $\vec{C}$, by replacing the standard linear decay with more adaptive, nonlinear, or chaotic functions. These include cosine modulation, exponential decay, oscillatory curves, chaotic maps, and feedback-sensitive adjustments. By shaping how the swarm transitions from exploration to exploitation, MM2 directly governs the algorithm's convergence pressure and search phase timing.

As shown in Fig. 4.3, MM2 most prominently activates adaptive control (B) and convergence dynamics (A), while also engaging trajectory shaping (C), leadership weighting (D), and diversity regulation (F). These behavioral pathways yield CG including G1 (phased convergence), G2 (adaptive pressure control), G4 (memory-guided refinement), G5 (diversity-preserving escape), G6 (leadership-driven acceleration), and G7 (multibehavior cooperation). The summary in Table 4.3 captures these broad relationships across the 18 MM2-rooted variants, showing that coefficient redefinition drives both temporal control and structural diversity.

Unlike MM1, MM2 designs produce more predictable and uniform CG, making them a common backbone for both standalone variants and hybridized designs. The mathematical redefinition of $a(t)$ serves as a low-overhead yet high-impact intervention, introducing responsiveness and phase control into GWO without altering its core mechanics.

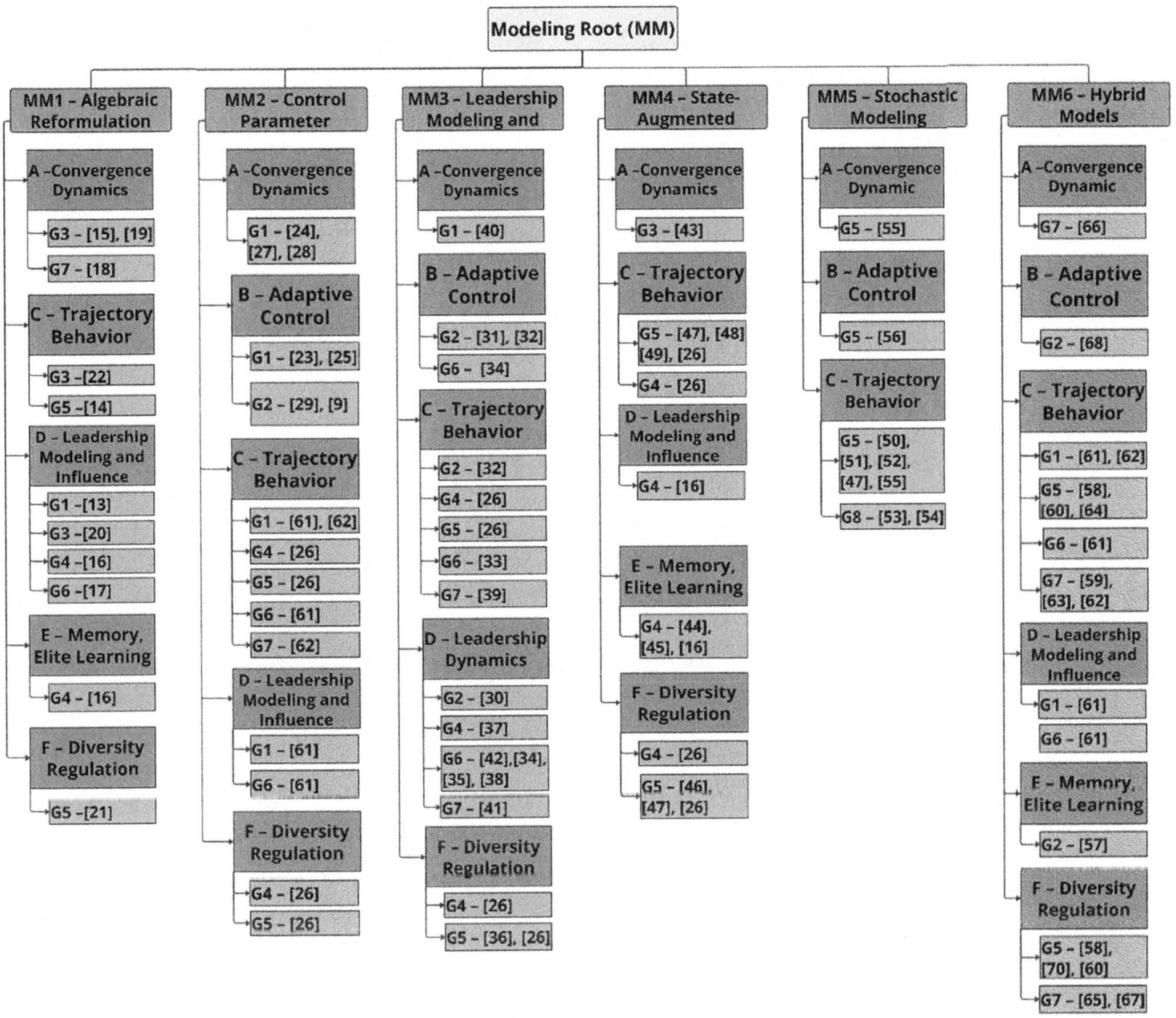

FIGURE 4.3 Tree Diagram of MM-DB-CG pathways across GWO iterature (*CG*, convergence outcomes; *DB*, dynamic behavioral; *GWO*, grey wolf optimizer; *MM*, modeling choices).

4.6.2.3 MM3—leadership reweighting and hierarchical control

MM3 variants revise the leadership hierarchy of GWO by modifying how influence is assigned to α, β, and δ wolves. These changes include fitness-proportional weights, fuzzy logic-based role assignment, Pareto-based leadership, and localized or personalized leader selection. Unlike the fixed-equal averaging in canonical GWO, MM3 introduces context-aware, dynamic, and performance-sensitive guidance, enhancing the swarm's ability to exploit elite solutions while maintaining flexibility.

As shown in Fig. 4.3, MM3 prominently activates leadership dynamics (D) and adaptive control mechanisms (B), while also contributing strongly through trajectory behavior (C) and, to a lesser extent, convergence dynamics (A) and diversity regulation (F). These pathways lead to CG spanning G1 (phased convergence), G2 (adaptive pressure control), G4 (memory-guided refinement), G5 (diversity-preserving escape), G6 (leadership-driven acceleration), and G7 (multi-behavior cooperation). The range of behaviors and outcomes, summarized in Table 4.4, reflects MM3's role as a behavioral core that supports both exploitation precision and adaptive search regulation.

MM3-based designs are particularly effective in multiobjective optimization, hierarchical problem spaces, or adaptive environments, where intelligent role modulation enhances convergence directionality. Their predictability and elite focus

TABLE 4.2 Observed behavior and convergence patterns in MM1 variants.

DB category	Description	Linked CG outcomes
A	Convergence smoothing via mean shifts	G3, G7
C	Trajectory shaping via stochastic updates	G3, G5
D	Dynamic leadership via elite reweighting	G1, G3, G4, G6
E	Elite memory and inheritance	G4
F	Diversity via perturbation in updates	G5

TABLE 4.3 Observed behavior and convergence patterns in MM2 variants.

DB category	Description	Linked CG outcomes
A	Stabilization through nonlinear decay	G1
B	Adaptive control based on time/diversity/fitness	G1, G2
C	Trajectory shifts via oscillatory pressure	G1, G4, G5, G6, G7
D	Leader weighting via coefficient scheduling	G1, G6
F	Diversity regulation through adaptive $a(t)$	G4, G5

TABLE 4.4 Observed behavior and convergence patterns in MM3 variants.

DB category	Description	Linked CG outcomes
A	Convergence smoothing via modified leader impact	G1
B	Adaptive weighting of leaders	G2, G6
C	Directional updates via contextual leader logic	G2, G4, G5, G6, G7
D	Hierarchical/fuzzy leadership redistribution	G2, G4, G6, G7
F	Diversity via spatial leader partitioning	G4, G5

make MM3 a reliable strategy for boosting convergence speed and control, especially when paired with adaptive decay or diversity-preserving mechanisms.

4.6.2.4 *MM4—memory-augmented and learning-driven grey wolf optimizer*

MM4 variants extend GWO with internal state variables such as velocity, elite memory archives, and adaptive learning mechanisms. Unlike the stateless behavior of the canonical model, MM4 introduces historical feedback and temporal persistence, allowing wolves to learn from past positions, track momentum, and reuse elite traits. This transforms GWO from a reactive system into a stateful optimizer capable of informed search refinement and memory-guided exploration.

As shown in Fig. 4.3, MM4 strongly activates elite memory (E) and population-level diversity regulation (F), while also engaging trajectory behavior (C), leadership dynamics (D), and convergence smoothing (A) when memory or learning affects movement and leader interaction. The resulting CG are dominated by G4 (memory-guided refinement), supported by G5 (diversity-preserving escape) and G3 (trajectory stabilization). These patterns are summarized in Table 4.5, confirming MM4's role in reinforcing high-quality paths while delaying convergence collapse.

MM4 is especially beneficial in multimodal, high-dimensional, or rugged search spaces, where memory mechanisms can reduce re-exploration and velocity-like dynamics enable smoother, directionally consistent motion. Its state-enriched design also makes it a strong foundation for hybrid metaheuristics or for problems that require temporal coherence (e.g., time-varying systems or dynamic constraints).

4.6.2.5 MM5—stochastic search and probabilistic convergence models

MM5 variants embed stochastic processes into GWO's mathematical foundation, replacing or augmenting deterministic update rules with random walks, probability distributions, or noise-driven dynamics. These methods model the algorithm as an explicitly probabilistic system, introducing randomness not as an auxiliary element but as a core search mechanism. Common approaches include Lévy flights, Gaussian and Cauchy jumps, stochastic OBL, and Markov process modeling.

As shown in Fig. 4.3, MM5 overwhelmingly activates trajectory behavior (C), where stochastic sampling broadens landscape coverage and escape potential. It also engages convergence dynamics (A) and adaptive control (B) when randomness is time-scheduled or feedback-driven, while leadership dynamics (D) and diversity regulation (F) appear in designs where randomness is tied to leader updates or population refresh. CG are dominated by G5 (diversity-preserving escape) and the rare but significant G8 (formal convergence proofs), with additional contributions to G1 (phased convergence), G2 (adaptive pressure control), and G3 (trajectory stabilization). These relationships are summarized in Table 4.6.

TABLE 4.5 Observed behavior and convergence patterns in MM4 variants.

DB category	Description	Linked CG outcomes
A	Convergence smoothing with memory-guided momentum	G3
C	Reuse of past trajectories for directed movement	G4, G5
D	Learning-enhanced leadership roles	G4
E	Use of elite/personal best memory	G4
F	Population refresh and state-based perturbation	G4, G5

TABLE 4.6 Observed behavior and convergence patterns in MM5 variants.

DB category	Description	Linked CG outcomes
A	Noise decay for stabilization	G5
B	Probabilistic modulation of control parameters	G5
C	Random walks (Lévy, Gaussian, Cauchy) for exploration	G5, G8

MM5 is particularly useful for complex, deceptive, or constrained problems where traditional encircling strategies stagnate. Its probabilistic modeling also enables theoretical analysis, making it attractive to researchers seeking to bridge empirical performance with formal guarantees. However, the randomness must be carefully scaled or decayed to avoid instability, especially in late-stage optimization.

4.6.2.6 MM6—hybridized equation-level designs

MM6 variants fuse GWO with other metaheuristics at the mathematical equation level, embedding external operators, such as mutation, crossover, velocity updates, or Lévy flights, directly into the position update rule. Unlike procedural hybrids that alternate between algorithms, MM6 approaches produce composite search behavior within a single iteration step. This fusion often combines GWO's encircling logic with strategies from PSO, DE, TLBO, WOA, SA, or FWA, creating multimodal, phase-aware, or feedback-driven mechanisms.

As visualized in Fig. 4.3, MM6 strongly activates trajectory behavior (C) and population diversity regulation (F), while also showing major activity in adaptive control (B) and leadership dynamics (D), and secondary presence in convergence smoothing (A) and elite memory (E). CG are dominated by G5 (diversity-preserving escape) and G7 (multibehavior cooperation), with frequent contributions to G1 (phased convergence), G2 (adaptive pressure), and G6 (leadership acceleration), and occasional links to G3 and G4. These relationships are summarized in Table 4.7.

MM6 variants are especially effective in high-dimensional, rugged, or multiobjective optimization, where no single strategy suffices across all search phases. Their hybrid nature allows for behavioral switching, layered exploration–exploitation, and adaptive operator scheduling. However, the increased complexity also raises challenges in parameter tuning and theoretical analysis, demanding careful control over hybrid interaction rules.

4.6.3 Mapping structural influence

To deepen the MM-centric analysis, we visualized how each MM category (MM1–MM6) distributes across both DB and CG categories. These distributions, shown in Fig. 4.4 (MM-DB heatmap) and Fig. 4.5 (MM-CG heatmap), offer a high-level perspective on how structural designs influence downstream optimization mechanics and performance targets.

Fig. 4.4 shows that MM2 and MM3 remain the most behaviorally diverse, activating nearly all DB categories with strong pathways to C (trajectory behavior) and D (leadership dynamics), reinforced by contributions to A (convergence dynamics) and B (adaptive control). MM4 emphasizes C (trajectory shaping) but also extends into D (leadership learning), E (memory use), and F (diversity regulation), making it broader than previously noted. MM5 is tightly concentrated on C (stochastic trajectory exploration) with limited presence in A and B, reflecting its probabilistic design. MM6 spans across C and F, while also touching A, B, and D, underscoring its hybridized and multimechanism nature. MM1, though algebraically simpler, connects to A and D and shows activity in C, reflecting flexibility in shaping both trajectory and leadership despite its structural constraints.

In Fig. 4.5, CG differ markedly across modeling categories. MM2 contributes most prominently to G1 (phased convergence), reflecting its reliance on adaptive coefficient decay, with secondary ties to G2 (adaptive pressure control). MM3 shows balanced but stronger links to G6 (leadership-driven acceleration) and G4 (memory-guided refinement),

TABLE 4.7 Observed behavior and convergence patterns in MM6 variants.

DB category	Description	Linked CG otcomes
A	Stability via hybrid decay or filtering	G7
B	Adaptive switching between algorithmic modes	G2
C	Composite trajectory strategies (e.g., Lévy + encircling)	G1, G5, G6, G7
D	Leader influence extended through hybrid logic	G1, G6
E	Elite memory incorporated from the partner algorithm	G2
F	Diversity injection via chaos, OBL, or dynamic grouping	G5, G7

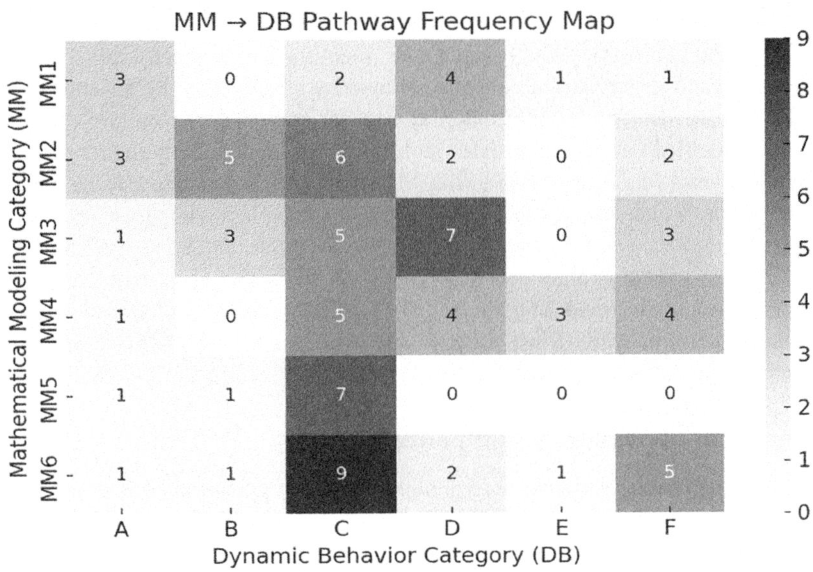

FIGURE 4.4 MM-DB pathway frequency map (*DB*, dynamic behavioral; *MM*, modeling choices).

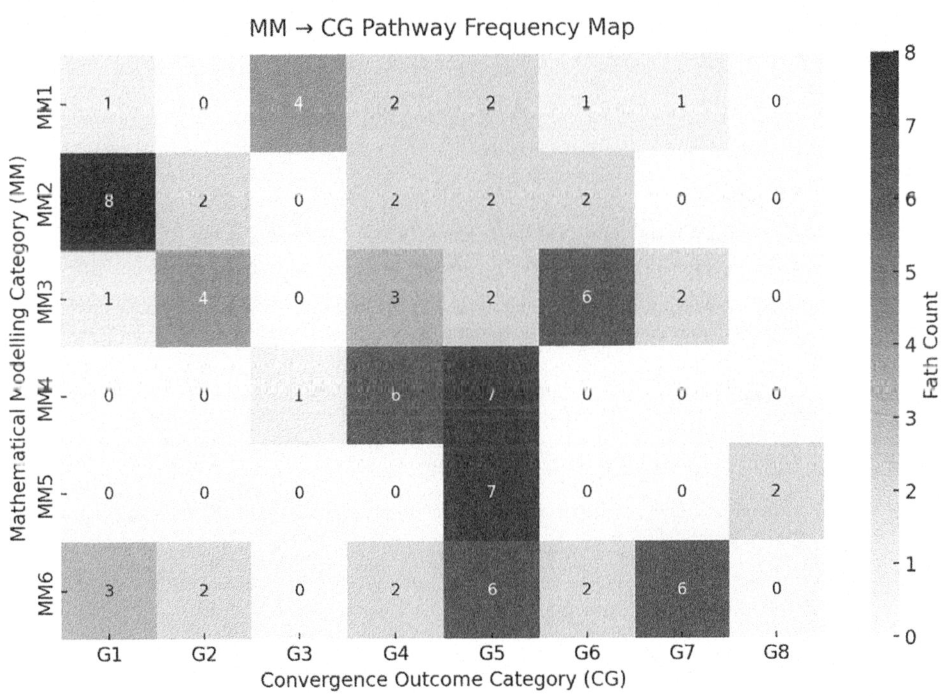

FIGURE 4.5 MM-CG pathway frequency map (*CG*, convergence outcomes; *MM*, modeling choices).

underscoring its elite- and hierarchy-focused logic. MM4 dominates in G5 (diversity-preserving escape) and G4, supported by its use of memory and stateful updates, while MM5 also concentrates on G5 but uniquely extends into G8 (formal convergence proofs), the only structural class to do so. MM6 spreads across G1, G5, G6, and G7, highlighting its hybrid adaptability across multiple convergence logics. By contrast, MM1, though algebraically simpler, contributes meaningfully to G3 (trajectory stabilization) and connects secondarily to G1, G4, and G5, demonstrating that even structural reformulations yield nontrivial convergence control.

Together, these two maps reinforce that mathematical design in GWO is not only structurally expressive but also functionally directive. Structural decisions—whether adaptive, memory-based, stochastic, or hybrid- naturally steer both behavior and convergence, enabling targeted algorithm engineering. MM2 and MM3 emerge as the central engines, spanning nearly all behavioral modes and reliably mapping into phased convergence (G1), adaptive pressure (G2), and leader-driven acceleration (G6). MM4 and MM5 provide stabilization by embedding memory and stochasticity, producing strong pathways to diversity-preserving escape (G5), with MM5 uniquely extending into formal convergence guarantees (G8). MM6 demonstrates hybrid versatility by balancing trajectory shaping with diversity and leadership modulation, distributing its outcomes across G1, G5, G6, and G7. Even MM1, while algebraically simpler, links meaningfully to trajectory stabilization (G3) and memory refinement (G4), illustrating its role as a flexible supplement. Collectively, the maps reveal a division of labor across modeling roots: MM2–MM3 drive phase control and leadership, MM4–MM5 secure robustness and late-stage refinement, MM6 ensures adaptive balance, and MM1 contributes algebraic flexibility, together forming a coherent foundation for systematic convergence engineering in GWO.

4.6.4 High-frequency and promising design pathways

With 92 paths extracted across 59 GWO variants, several high-frequency structural-behavioral-convergence combinations emerge. These dominant pathways reflect patterns that consistently produce desirable performance outcomes and offer a blueprint for reliable design strategies. In parallel, several underexplored but promising paths reveal strategic opportunities for innovation.

4.6.4.1 *Dominant pathways (path count ≥ 3)*

The frequency analysis of MM-DB-CG pathways in Table 4.8 reveals several recurring structural, behavioral, and convergence combinations that dominate the GWO design landscape. These high-frequency pathways (≥3 references) not only identify where research attention has concentrated but also highlight structurally promising strategies for future algorithm engineering.

TABLE 4.8 High-frequency pathways.

Pathway	Count	Interpretation
MM2–A–G1	3	Control-parameter tuning (nonlinear decay of a(t)) consistently drives phased convergence, making MM2 a reliable backbone for time-aware GWO designs.
MM3–D–G6	4	Leadership redistribution and hierarchical weighting strongly reinforce leader-driven acceleration, showing MM3's role in elite-focused convergence.
MM3–B–G2	3	Adaptive weighting of leaders stabilizes exploration–exploitation balance, yielding adaptive convergence pressure control.
MM4–C–G5	5	State-augmented updates (e.g., memory, velocity) frequently enhance diversity-preserving escape, making MM4 key for avoiding premature convergence.
MM4–E–G4	3	Elite/personal best memory consistently supports memory-guided refinement, stabilizing long-term convergence pathways.
MM4–F–G5	3	Population-level diversity refresh mechanisms strengthen escape strategies, aligning MM4 with robust exploration.
MM5–C–G5	5	Stochastic trajectory models (e.g., Lévy, Gaussian, Cauchy) dominate diversity-preserving escape, confirming randomness as a central design driver.
MM6–C–G7	3	Hybrid trajectory strategies promote cooperative multibehavioral convergence, showing MM6's ability to fuse operators for balanced search.
MM6–C–G5	3	Composite hybrids integrating external operators preserve diversity, reinforcing MM6's strength in maintaining exploration robustness.
MM6–F–G5	3	Hybrid diversity injections (chaos, OBL, mutation) consistently link to escape-focused convergence, underscoring MM6's adaptive versatility.

MM2–A–G1: Control parameter redefinitions in MM2, especially through nonlinear, oscillatory, or chaotic decay of the coefficient $a(t)$, show a consistent link to G1 (phased convergence). These designs directly govern the timing of exploration–exploitation transitions, yielding convergence that unfolds in predictable, staged phases. The repeated presence of this pathway underscores MM2's reliability as a backbone for time-aware convergence mechanisms. Its structural simplicity (altering only the coefficient schedule) makes it a low-cost yet high-impact intervention, explaining its frequent adoption across both classical and hybrid variants.

MM3–D–G6 and MM3–B–G2: Leadership modeling innovations (MM3) dominate through hierarchical redistribution (D) and adaptive weighting (B), producing CG of G6 (leader-driven acceleration) and G2 (adaptive pressure control). These pathways confirm that elite-driven strategies remain central to improving GWO performance. By dynamically adjusting α, β, and δ wolves via fuzzy logic, Pareto dominance, or weighted selection, MM3 ensures both sharper convergence speed and adaptive balance. The repeated appearance of G6 highlights the efficiency benefits of intensified leader guidance, whereas G2 pathways reflect MM3's role in stabilizing convergence pressure under dynamic landscapes. Together, these pathways solidify MM3 as a behavioral core of elite-focused convergence engineering.

MM4–C–G5, MM4–E–G4, and MM4–F–G5: Memory-augmented models (MM4) produce the most diverse set of dominant pathways. Trajectory updates shaped by velocity-like or history-informed adjustments (C) repeatedly lead to G5 (diversity-preserving escape), while elite memory (E) maps consistently into G4 (memory-guided refinement). Population-level refresh mechanisms (F) reinforce G5, emphasizing MM4's role in sustaining exploration capacity. This cluster of pathways highlights MM4's unique strength: transforming GWO from a reactive to a stateful system. By leveraging past experience and memory, MM4 simultaneously delays premature convergence (via G5) and reinforces high-quality optima (via G4). The dominance of these pathways suggests that memory-based enrichment is one of the most reliable strategies for balancing exploration robustness with exploitation depth.

MM5–C–G5: Stochastic modeling approaches (MM5) overwhelmingly converge on G5, confirming that randomness, whether Gaussian, Lévy, or Cauchy-driven, is primarily harnessed to enhance escape from local optima. Unlike MM4's structured memory, MM5 introduces probabilistic unpredictability into trajectory updates, expanding coverage of the search space. The strong frequency of this pathway highlights stochasticity as a central mechanism for diversity preservation, particularly valuable in deceptive or rugged landscapes. Notably, MM5 is also the only structural category linked to G8 (formal convergence proofs), indicating its role not only in empirical diversity maintenance but also in theoretical generalization.

MM6–C–G7, MM6–C–G5, and MM6–F–G5: Hybridized models (MM6) reveal cooperative and escape-oriented convergence strategies. Trajectory hybrids (C) connect both to G7 (multibehavior cooperation) and G5, reflecting MM6's ability to orchestrate multiple exploration–exploitation dynamics within a single update rule. At the same time, diversity injection mechanisms (F) reinforce G5, showing that hybrids frequently adopt chaos, OBL, or perturbation strategies for escape. Collectively, these pathways underline MM6's versatility: while it inherits the robustness of MM4 and MM5, it extends them through hybridized operator integration, producing convergence that is not only diverse but also cooperative and adaptive.

Taken together, these dominant pathways highlight three strategic design philosophies. First, coefficient control (MM2) provides predictable phased convergence (G1) with minimal structural change, making it a foundational tool for stable design. Second, leadership reweighting (MM3) reinforces elite-driven convergence (G6, G2), sharpening exploitation speed while adaptively controlling swarm pressure. Third, memory and stochastic enrichment (MM4, MM5) are the strongest contributors to diversity-preserving convergence (G5) and memory refinement (G4), ensuring long-term robustness. Finally, hybrid operators (MM6) expand this toolkit by combining multiple behaviors, enabling cooperative and adaptive convergence (G7, G5).

These pathways collectively show that GWO research gravitates toward designs that either (1) shape time-dependent control (MM2), (2) intensify elite leadership (MM3), or (3) safeguard diversity through memory or randomness (MM4–MM5), with hybrids (MM6) serving as integrative bridges across all three. This confirms that future improvements in GWO will likely emerge from refining these pathways, either by tightening theoretical guarantees (as seen in MM5–G8) or by exploring cross-pathway synergies (e.g., MM4–MM6 blends of memory, randomness, and hybridization).

4.6.4.2 *Underexplored but promising paths*

While the dominant pathways offer tested blueprints for reliable GWO design, several low-frequency paths, each observed only once, demonstrate compelling structural–behavioral logic that remains largely untapped. These rare configurations may lack replication in the literature, but their internal coherence and theoretical soundness suggest strong potential for innovation.

MM2–D–G6 (Time-scheduled leader weighting for leader-driven acceleration): Couples MM2's reliable phase control with dynamic leader emphasis, accelerating late-phase descent at low implementation cost and with strong potential for analysis and proofs.

MM4–A–G3 (Memory/velocity scheduled for trajectory stabilization): Uses state (memory/velocity) not just to remember but to actively smooth trajectories, reducing overshoot and improving end-game precision without hurting early exploration.

MM5–A/B–G5 (Scheduled noise/temperature for diversity): Treats randomness as a controllable resource; annealed noise preserves early escape capacity while tapering to stability, yielding robust coverage with predictable wind-down.

MM6–B–G2 (Hybrid mode switching for adaptive pressure): Learns when to invoke different operators (GWO/DE/PSO/WOA/Lévy) based on feedback, delivering real-time control of exploration versus exploitation and strong robustness across landscapes.

MM3–A–G1 (Leadership-driven phased convergence): Achieves staged convergence by evolving leader roles rather than retuning $a(t)$; a clean alternative that pairs naturally with existing α,β,δ logic and can reduce oscillations.

MM5–C–G8 (Probabilistic trajectory modeling with diminishing heavy tails): Extends stochastic GWO with tempered Lévy/Gaussian steps that enable early escapes yet permit formal convergence analysis—addressing a key gap in theoretical guarantees.

MM2–F–G5/G4 (Time-boxed diversity pulses with guaranteed cool-down): Synchronizes brief opposition/mutation bursts with coefficient schedules to prevent stagnation, then reliably return to refinement—balancing escape (G5) and memory-guided tightening (G4).

4.6.5 Strategic design patterns

This section synthesizes the pathway evidence into a set of reusable design patterns for GWO development. The aim is to translate the heatmap and pathway analyses into clear guidance on what to change in the mathematical model (MM), which behavioral mechanism this activates (DB), and which convergence effect it is expected to produce (CG). Each pattern is framed in plain language, emphasizes when it is appropriate, and notes common risks. Collectively, the patterns provide modular building blocks that can be composed into broader design roadmaps.

4.6.5.1 Time-programmed coefficient control (MM2–A–G1)

Time-programmed coefficient control reshapes the canonical schedule that governs exploration and exploitation. By replacing the standard linear decay with nonlinear, oscillatory, or diversity-aware schedules, the algorithm's convergence pressure can be made to evolve in predictable phases. This pattern is appropriate when stable, stage-wise progress is required without altering the rest of the update equations. The principal effect is phased convergence (G1), a smoother transition from global search to local refinement. Overrapid decay can compress exploration prematurely; overly gentle decay can delay convergence.

Underexplored extension: Linking the schedule to leader weighting (MM2—D—G6) appears promising; gradually increasing the relative influence of better leaders in later phases can accelerate the final descent with negligible implementation cost.

4.6.5.2 Feedback-adaptive pressure (MM2–B–G2)

Where landscapes are volatile, fixed schedules are often suboptimal. Feedback-adaptive pressure adjusts the control inputs in response to population diversity, recent improvement, or stagnation. The mechanism retains the simplicity of MM2 but introduces closed-loop responsiveness that moderates step sizes and search aggression in real time. The expected outcome is adaptive convergence pressure (G2) with more consistent progress on rugged functions. Care must be taken to smooth noisy signals and bound adjustments to avoid oscillations.

Underexplored extension: In hybrid contexts, operator switching driven by feedback (MM6—B—G2) can generalize the idea beyond coefficient tuning by selecting among multiple update operators as the search unfolds.

4.6.5.3 Leadership reweighting and phasing (MM3–D/G6; MM3–B/G2; MM3–A/G1)

Leadership reweighting departs from equal $\alpha - \beta - \delta$ influence and allocates guidance according to fitness, fuzzy rules, or contextual cues. In its basic form, enhanced leadership produces leader-driven acceleration (G6) by focusing movement around the best agents; with feedback rules, it also delivers adaptive pressure (G2). A complementary strategy is leadership phasing, which schedules leader dominance over time to achieve phased convergence (G1) without retuning the global coefficient schedule. The main risk is premature convergence if elite influence intensifies too early; coupling leadership adjustments to progress rather than iteration count mitigates this.

4.6.5.4 *Memory-augmented refinement and stabilization (MM4–E/G4; F/G5; A/G3; C/G5)*

Memory augmentation introduces statefulness into GWO. Elite/personal-best memory supports memory-guided refinement (G4) by reusing high-quality solution features; population refresh mechanisms sustain diversity-preserving escape (G5); and light-weight velocity or historical guidance can improve trajectory stability (G3) by damping zig-zagging near optima. This pattern is especially effective when late-phase precision and robustness against deception are required. Overreliance on memory may lead to early bias; periodic refresh or diversity checks help preserve coverage.

Underexplored extension: Using memory specifically for trajectory smoothing (MM4–A–G3), rather than only for reuse of elites, deserves further study, given its potential to improve end-game accuracy with minimal disruption to early exploration.

4.6.5.5 *Stochastic trajectories with scheduling (MM5–C/G5; A/B/G5; occasionally G8)*

Stochastic trajectory designs introduce controlled randomness (e.g., Gaussian, Cauchy, or Lévy steps) to enlarge coverage and avoid stagnation. When the stochastic intensity is scheduled, strong early, diminishing later, diversity is preserved without sacrificing late-phase precision. The characteristic outcome is diversity-preserving escape (G5), with incidental stabilization as noise fades. Notably, MM5 is the only structural family that presently supports formal convergence arguments (G8), making it a natural vehicle for connecting empirical performance with theory. Excessive or unscheduled randomness can disrupt convergence; annealing and diversity-aware gating are advisable.

4.6.5.6 *Hybrid cooperative search (MM6–C/G7; F/G5; B/G2)*

Hybrid cooperative designs fuse complementary operators within the GWO step (e.g., combining encircling with differential or swarm-based moves), or switch among them based on feedback. Composite trajectories yield multibehavior cooperation (G7) and typically maintain diversity (G5) through hybrid perturbations; feedback-driven switching contributes adaptive pressure (G2). The strength of this pattern is its versatility across phases and problem classes; the main challenge lies in controlling parameter growth and operator interactions. Compact operator sets and simple safeguards (e.g., step-norm caps, minimum exploration quotas) are recommended.

4.6.6 Limitations and opportunities

The cross-dimensional synthesis provided in this chapter uncovers both gaps in current GWO research and clear directions for future exploration. Below, we outline the major limitations observed across the 92 pathways, followed by actionable opportunities for advancing the field.

4.6.6.1 *Limitations*

1. *Weak causal explanations:* Most variants foreground empirical gains but offer limited analysis of how specific mathematical changes (MM) induce behavioral effects (DB) that lead to CG; mechanisms are often inferred rather than measured.
2. *Underrepresentation of theory*: Formal convergence results remain rare; the G8 category is sparsely populated despite growing interest in provable metaheuristics and probabilistic guarantees.
3. *Behavioral redundancy*: The literature concentrates on a narrow band of behaviors, especially trajectory shaping (C) and diversity regulation (F), with comparatively less work on memory-driven learning or structured multiagent coordination.
4. *Narrow convergence objectives*: CG are unevenly targeted: G5 (diversity preservation) and G1 (phased convergence) dominate, while G3 (trajectory stabilization) and G7 (cooperative convergence) remain underexplored.
5. *Neglected high-potential paths*: Several structurally coherent pathways (e.g., MM1–E–G4, MM2–C–G7) appear only once; their scarcity seems driven by benchmarking inertia rather than theoretical weakness.

4.6.6.2 *Opportunities*

1. *Exploit underused behavioral synergies*: Purposefully combine complementary behaviors—e.g., leader-localized diversity (D+F) or memory-enhanced trajectory learning (E+C)—to build more adaptive and resilient optimizers.

2. *Design from behavioral templates*: Reuse frequent, high-yield patterns (e.g., C+F–G5, B+D–G6) as modular templates to construct variants with predictable behavioral profiles and convergence effects.
3. *Strengthen convergence formalism*: Extend MM5-style stochastic modeling and MM2-based adaptive control toward richer G8 results, linking practical designs to verifiable convergence guarantees.
4. *Target underrepresented outcomes*: Intentionally develop methods for G3 and G7, for example, via memory-based stabilization, adaptive operator switching, or hybrid phase logic, to broaden GWO's behavioral repertoire.
5. *Build mechanism-driven variants*: Use the MM-DB-CG map as a design scaffold to compose mechanisms deliberately (rather than ad hoc mixing), improving interpretability, tunability, and transfer across problem classes.

Taken together, these points motivate a mechanism-centered research program in which structural choices are explicitly mapped to behavioral levers and convergence goals, positioning GWO as a designable system that is theoretically grounded, behaviorally adaptive, and optimized for controllable performance.

4.7 Conclusion and future directives

This chapter proposed a unified, mechanism-driven framework for analyzing, comparing, and designing GWO variants through the structured lens of MM, DB, and CG. By examining 92 distinct pathways across 59 peer-reviewed studies, we systematically identified how specific structural interventions influence emergent behaviors and drive convergence dynamics. The result is a design-oriented synthesis that transforms GWO research from empirical trial-and-error into a principled process grounded in behavioral logic and performance causality.

The chapter's core contribution lies in establishing the causal anatomy of GWO design. Dominant pathways revealed structural efficiency and behavioral generality, while underexplored paths offered rich, theoretically sound directions for future innovation. Our framework enables the construction of GWO variants as modular, interpretable systems, allowing researchers to predict and tailor performance through behavior-aware design choices.

Looking ahead, future work can expand this foundation in several directions.

1. First, deeper integration of behavioral measurement techniques, such as diversity metrics, leader influence tracking, and convergence trace analysis, could empirically validate DB categories and close the gap between structure and outcome.
2. Second, the formalization of convergence theory, especially for hybrid and stochastic models, remains a fertile area for expanding categories like G3 and G8.
3. Third, leveraging this framework to develop automated GWO design tools, possibly incorporating reinforcement learning or evolutionary architecture search, could democratize principled variant construction for real-world applications.

Ultimately, this chapter encourages the GWO research community to shift from heuristic-centric innovation toward intentional, mechanism-driven metaheuristic design, where structural decisions are informed by behavioral impact and convergence goals, and where performance is not just observed, but understood.

Acknowledgments

The authors acknowledge the use of AI-assisted tools (ChatGPT, developed by OpenAI) for translation and English text proofing. The authors reviewed and verified all content to ensure accuracy and integrity.

References

[1] H. Rezaei, O. Bozorg-Haddad, X. Chu, Grey wolf optimization (GWO) algorithm, Studies in Computational Intelligence 720 (2018) 81–91. Available from https://doi.org/10.1007/978-981-10-5221-7_9.

[2] D. Das, A.S. Sadiq, S. Mirjalili, Grey Wolf Optimizer: Foundations and Mathematical Models (2025) 59–66. Available from https://doi.org/10.1007/978-981-96-3849-9_6.

[3] S. Mirjalili, I. Aljarah, M. Mafarja, et al., Grey wolf optimizer: theory, literature review, and application in computational fluid dynamics problems, Studies in Computational Intelligence 811 (2020) 87–105. Available from https://doi.org/10.1007/978-3-030-12127-3_6.

[4] M.H. Nadimi-Shahraki, H. Zamani, Z. Asghari Varzaneh, et al., A systematic review of applying grey wolf optimizer, its variants, and its developments in different Internet of Things applications, Internet of Things 26 (2024) 101135. Available from https://doi.org/10.1016/J.IOT.2024.101135.

[5] N.M. Hatta, A.M. Zain, R. Sallehuddin, et al., Recent studies on optimisation method of grey wolf optimiser (GWO): a review (2014–2017), *Artificial Intelligence Review* 52 (2019) 2651–2683. Available from https://doi.org/10.1007/S10462-018-9634-2/METRICS.

[6] H. Faris, I. Aljarah, M.A. Al-Betar, S. Mirjalili, Grey wolf optimizer: a review of recent variants and applications, Neural Comput Appl 30 (2018) 413–435. Available from https://doi.org/10.1007/S00521-017-3272-5/METRICS.

[7] D. Das, A.S. Sadiq, S. Mirjalili, A Brief Review of Grey Wolf Optimizer: Variants and Applications (2025) 67–83.

[8] S.N. Makhadmeh, M.A. Al-Betar, I.A. Doush, et al., Recent advances in grey wolf optimizer, its versions and applications: review, IEEE Access 12 (2024) 22991–23028. Available from https://doi.org/10.1109/ACCESS.2023.3304889.

[9] Y. Ou, P. Yin, L. Mo, An improved grey wolf optimizer and its application in robot path planning, Biomimetics 8 (2023) 84. Available from https://doi.org/10.3390/BIOMIMETICS80100842023.

[10] G. Negi, A. Kumar, S. Pant, M. Ram, GWO: a review and applications, International Journal of System Assurance Engineering and Management 12 (2021) 1–8. Available from https://doi.org/10.1007/S13198-020-00995-8/METRICS.

[11] M. Nasir, A. Sadollah, S. Mirjalili, et al., A comprehensive review on applications of grey wolf optimizer in energy systems, Archives of Computational Methods in Engineering 2024 32 (4) (2024) 2279–2319. Available from https://doi.org/10.1007/S11831-024-10214-332.

[12] S. Mirjalili, S.M. Mirjalili, A. Lewis, Grey wolf optimizer, Advances in Engineering Software 69 (2014) 46–61. Available from https://doi.org/10.1016/J.ADVENGSOFT.2013.12.007.

[13] K. Luo, Enhanced grey wolf optimizer with a model for dynamically estimating the location of the prey, Applied Soft Computing 77 (2019) 225–235. Available from https://doi.org/10.1016/J.ASOC.2019.01.025.

[14] W. Long, J. Jiao, X. Liang, M. Tang, An exploration-enhanced grey wolf optimizer to solve high-dimensional numerical optimization, Engineering Applications of Artificial Intelligence 68 (2018) 63–80. Available from https://doi.org/10.1016/J.ENGAPPAI.2017.10.024.

[15] S. Gopi, P. Mohapatra, A modified grey wolf optimization algorithm to solve global optimization problems, OPSEARCH 62 (2024) 337–367. Available from https://doi.org/10.1007/S12597-024-00785-X/METRICS.

[16] E. Akbari, A. Rahimnejad, S.A. Gadsden, A greedy non-hierarchical grey wolf optimizer for real-world optimization, Electronics Letters 57 (2021) 499–501. Available from https://doi.org/10.1049/ELL2.12176.

[17] A. Khaghani, M. Meshkat, M. Parhizgar, A novel grey wolf optimizer for solving optimization problems, 5th Iranian Conference on Signal Processing and Intelligent Systems, ICSPIS 2019 (2019). Available from https://doi.org/10.1109/ICSPIS48872.2019.9066099.

[18] B. Martin, J. Marot, S. Bourennane, Improved discrete grey wolf optimizer, European Signal Processing Conference 2018-September (2018) 494–498. Available from https://doi.org/10.23919/EUSIPCO.2018.8552925.

[19] N. Singh, S.B. Singh, A modified mean gray wolf optimization approach for benchmark and biomedical problems, Evolutionary Bioinformatics 13 (2017). Available from https://doi.org/10.1177/1176934317729413/ASSET/771D9603-D6FA-4A6F-AEFE-7759ED9E5AFC/ASSETS/IMAGES/LARGE/10.1177_1176934317729413-FIG32.JPG.

[20] X. Liu, Y. Wang, M. Zhou, Dimensional learning strategy-based grey wolf optimizer for solving the global optimization problem, Computational intelligence and neuroscience 2022 (2022) 3603607. Available from https://doi.org/10.1155/2022/3603607.

[21] J. Jiang, Z. Zhao, Y. Liu, et al., DSGWO: an improved grey wolf optimizer with diversity enhanced strategy based on group-stage competition and balance mechanisms, Knowledge-Based Systems 250 (2022) 109100. Available from https://doi.org/10.1016/J.KNOSYS.2022.109100.

[22] W. Long, J. Jiao, X. Liang, M. Tang, Inspired grey wolf optimizer for solving large-scale function optimization problems, Applied Mathematical Modelling 60 (2018) 112–126. Available from https://doi.org/10.1016/J.APM.2018.03.005.

[23] X. Yan, Z. Lin, Z. Lin, B. Vucetic, A novel exploitative and explorative GWO-SVM algorithm for smart emotion recognition, IEEE Internet Things J 10 (2023) 9999–10011. Available from https://doi.org/10.1109/JIOT.2023.3235356.

[24] W. Long, S. Xu, A novel grey wolf optimizer for global optimization problems, Proceedings of 2016 IEEE Advanced Information Management, Communicates, Electronic and Automation Control Conference, IMCEC (2016) 1266–1270. Available from https://doi.org/10.1109/IMCEC.2016.7867415.

[25] S. Sharma, R. Salgotra, U. Singh, An enhanced grey wolf optimizer for numerical optimization, Proceedings of 2017 International Conference on Innovations in Information, Embedded and Communication Systems, ICIIECS 2017 2018-January (2017) 1–6. Available from https://doi.org/10.1109/ICIIECS.2017.8275908.

[26] J. Zhang, Y. Dai, Q. Shi, An improved grey wolf optimization algorithm based on scale-free network topology, Heliyon 10 (2024) e35958. Available from https://doi.org/10.1016/J.HELIYON.2024.E35958.

[27] N. Mittal, U. Singh, B.S. Sohi, Modified grey wolf optimizer for global engineering optimization, Applied Computational Intelligence and Soft Computing 2016 (2016) 7950348. Available from https://doi.org/10.1155/2016/7950348.

[28] Y. Hou, H. Gao, Z. Wang, C. Du, Improved grey wolf optimization algorithm and application, Sensors (Basel, Switzerland) 22 (2022) 3810. Available from https://doi.org/10.3390/S221038102022.

[29] Y. Qiu, X. Yang, S. Chen, An improved gray wolf optimization algorithm solving to functional optimization and engineering design problems, Scientific Reports 14 (1) (2024) 1–24. Available from https://doi.org/10.1038/s41598-024-64526-22024.

[30] L. Rodríguez, O. Castillo, J. Soria, et al., A fuzzy hierarchical operator in the grey wolf optimizer algorithm, Applied Soft Computing 57 (2017) 315–328. Available from https://doi.org/10.1016/J.ASOC.2017.03.048.

[31] H. Qin, T. Meng, Y. Cao, Fuzzy strategy grey wolf optimizer for complex multimodal optimization problems, Sensors (Basel, Switzerland) 22 (2022) 6420. Available from https://doi.org/10.3390/S221764202022.

[32] W. Liu, J. Sun, G. Liu, et al., Improved GWO and its application in parameter optimization of Elman neural network, PLoS ONE 18 (2023) e0288071. Available from https://doi.org/10.1371/JOURNAL.PONE.0288071.

[33] R. Rajakumar, K. Sekaran, C.H. Hsu, S. Kadry, Accelerated grey wolf optimization for global optimization problems, Technological Forecasting and Social Change 169 (2021) 120824. Available from https://doi.org/10.1016/J.TECHFORE.2021.120824.

[34] A. Toktas, U. Erkan, D. Ustun, Q. Lai, Multiobjective design of 2D hyperchaotic system using leader pareto grey wolf optimizer, IEEE Transactions on Systems, Man, and Cybernetics: Systems 54 (2024) 5237–5247. Available from https://doi.org/10.1109/TSMC.2024.3401412.

[35] S. Mirjalili, S. Saremi, S.M. Mirjalili, L.D.S. Coelho, Multi-objective grey wolf optimizer: A novel algorithm for multi-criterion optimization, Expert Systems with Applications 47 (2016) 106–119. Available from https://doi.org/10.1016/J.ESWA.2015.10.039.

[36] C. Lu, L. Gao, J. Yi, Grey wolf optimizer with cellular topological structure, Expert Systems with Applications 107 (2018) 89–114. Available from https://doi.org/10.1016/J.ESWA.2018.04.012.

[37] M. Banaie-Dezfouli, M.H. Nadimi-Shahraki, Z. Beheshti, R-GWO: representative-based grey wolf optimizer for solving engineering problems, Applied Soft Computing 106 (2021) 107328. Available from https://doi.org/10.1016/J.ASOC.2021.107328.

[38] Z. Miao, X. Yuan, F. Zhou, et al., Grey wolf optimizer with an enhanced hierarchy and its application to the wireless sensor network coverage optimization problem, Applied Soft Computing 96 (2020) 106602. Available from https://doi.org/10.1016/J.ASOC.2020.106602.

[39] A. Seyyedabbasi, F. Kiani, I-GWO and Ex-GWO: improved algorithms of the grey wolf optimizer to solve global optimization problems, Engineering Computations 37 (2021) 509–532. Available from https://doi.org/10.1007/S00366-019-00837-7/METRICS.

[40] I. Dagal, A.W. Ibrahim, A. Harrison, et al., Hierarchical multi step gray wolf optimization algorithm for energy systems optimization, Scientific Reports 15 (1) (2025) 1–32. Available from https://doi.org/10.1038/s41598-025-92983-w.

[41] Q. Tu, X. Chen, X. Liu, Hierarchy strengthened grey wolf optimizer for numerical optimization and feature selection, IEEE Access 7 (2019) 78012–78028. Available from https://doi.org/10.1109/ACCESS.2019.2921793.

[42] M.H. Nadimi-Shahraki, S. Taghian, S. Mirjalili, An improved grey wolf optimizer for solving engineering problems, Expert Systems with Applications 166 (2021) 113917. Available from https://doi.org/10.1016/J.ESWA.2020.113917.

[43] F. Rezaei, H.R. Safavi, M.A. Elaziz, et al., An enhanced grey wolf optimizer with a velocity-aided global search mechanism, Mathematics 2022 10 (2022) 351. Available from https://doi.org/10.3390/MATH10030351.

[44] S. Gupta, K. Deep, A memory-based grey wolf optimizer for global optimization tasks, Applied Soft Computing 93 (2020) 106367. Available from https://doi.org/10.1016/J.ASOC.2020.106367.

[45] J. Jiang, Z. Zhao, W. Li, K. Li, An Enhanced Grey Wolf Optimizer with Elite Inheritance and Balance Search Mechanisms (2024) .

[46] S. Saremi, S.Z. Mirjalili, S.M. Mirjalili, Evolutionary population dynamics and grey wolf optimizer, Neural Computing and Applications 26 (2015) 1257–1263. Available from https://doi.org/10.1007/S00521-014-1806-7/METRICS.

[47] Y. Wang, C. Jin, Q. Li, et al., A dynamic opposite learning-assisted grey wolf optimizer, Symmetry 14 (2022) 1871. Available from https://doi.org/10.3390/SYM140918712022.

[48] Y. Xing, D. Wang, L. Wang, A novel dynamic generalized opposition-based grey wolf optimization algorithm, Algorithms 11 (2018) 47. Available from https://doi.org/10.3390/A110400472018.

[49] V.K. Bohat, K.V. Arya, S.S. Rajput, Prey phase based grey wolf optimizer, 2018 Conference on Information and Communication Technology, CICT 2018 (2018). Available from https://doi.org/10.1109/INFOCOMTECH.2018.8722428.

[50] T. Han, X. Wang, Y. Liang, et al., A novel grey wolf optimizer with random walk strategies for constrained engineering design, ACM International Conference Proceeding Series (2018). Available from https://doi.org/10.1145/3148453.3306270.

[51] S. Gupta, K. Deep, Random walk grey wolf optimizer for constrained engineering optimization problems, Computational Intelligence 34 (2018) 1025–1045. Available from https://doi.org/10.1111/COIN.12160.

[52] S. Gupta, K. Deep, A novel random walk grey wolf optimizer, Swarm and Evolutionary Computation 44 (2019) 101–112. Available from https://doi.org/10.1016/J.SWEVO.2018.01.001.

[53] H Wang, L Shi, A theoretical framework and some promising findings of grey wolf optimizer, part I: analytical model of sampling distribution and stability analysis. Swarm and Evolutionary Computation 72 (2022) 101069.

[54] H Wang, L Shi. A theoretical framework and some promising findings of grey wolf optimizer, part II: global convergence analysis. Swarm and Evolutionary Computation. 72 (2022) 101070.

[55] W. Long, J. Jiao, X. Liang, et al., A random opposition-based learning grey wolf optimizer, IEEE Access 7 (2019) 113810–113825. Available from https://doi.org/10.1109/ACCESS.2019.2934994.

[56] M. Kohli, S. Arora, Chaotic grey wolf optimization algorithm for constrained optimization problems, Journal of Computational Design and Engineering 5 (2018) 458–472. Available from https://doi.org/10.1016/J.JCDE.2017.02.005.

[57] J.S. Wang, S.X. Li, An improved grey wolf optimizer based on differential evolution and elimination mechanism, Scientific Reports 9 (2019) 1–21. Available from https://doi.org/10.1038/s41598-019-43546-31 9.

[58] O.R. Adegboye, A.K. Feda, O.S. Ojekemi, et al., Chaotic opposition learning with mirror reflection and worst individual disturbance grey wolf optimizer for continuous global numerical optimization, Scientific Reports 14 (1) (2024) 1–41. Available from https://doi.org/10.1038/s41598-024-55040-62024.

[59] H. Singh, S. Saxena, H. Sharma, et al., An integrative TLBO-driven hybrid grey wolf optimizer for the efficient resolution of multi-dimensional, nonlinear engineering problems, Scientific Reports 15 (1) (2025) 1–71. Available from https://doi.org/10.1038/s41598-025-89458-32025.

[60] A.A. Heidari, P. Pahlavani, An efficient modified grey wolf optimizer with Lévy flight for optimization tasks, Applied Soft Computing 60 (2017) 115–134. Available from https://doi.org/10.1016/J.ASOC.2017.06.044.

[61] B. Tu, F. Wang, Y. Huo, X. Wang, A hybrid algorithm of grey wolf optimizer and harris hawks optimization for solving global optimization problems with improved convergence performance, Scientific Reports 2023 13 (1) (2023) 1–26. Available from https://doi.org/10.1038/s41598-023-49754-213.

[62] N. Singh, H. Hachimi, A new hybrid whale optimizer algorithm with mean strategy of grey wolf optimizer for global optimization, Mathematical and Computational Applications 2018 23 (2018) 14. Available from https://doi.org/10.3390/MCA23010014.

[63] C. Ma, H. Huang, Q. Fan, et al., Grey wolf optimizer based on Aquila exploration method, Expert Systems with Applications 205 (2022) 117629. Available from https://doi.org/10.1016/J.ESWA.2022.117629.

[64] X. Zhang, Q. Kang, J. Cheng, X. Wang, A novel hybrid algorithm based on biogeography-based optimization and grey wolf optimizer, Applied Soft Computing 67 (2018) 197–214. Available from https://doi.org/10.1016/J.ASOC.2018.02.049.

[65] Z.H. Yue, S. Zhang, W.D. Xiao, A novel hybrid algorithm based on grey wolf optimizer and fireworks algorithm, Sensors (Basel, Switzerland) 20 (2020) 2147. Available from https://doi.org/10.3390/S2007214720:2147.

[66] H. Mohammed, T. Rashid, A novel hybrid GWO with WOA for global numerical optimization and solving pressure vessel design, Neural Computing and Applications 32 (2020) 14701–14718. Available from https://doi.org/10.1007/S00521-020-04823-9/METRICS.

[67] A.S. Bhandari, A. Kumar, M. Ram, Grey wolf optimizer and hybrid PSO-GWO for reliability optimization and redundancy allocation problem, Quality and Reliability Engineering International 39 (2023) 905–921. Available from https://doi.org/10.1002/QRE.3265.

[68] M. Yu, J. Xu, W. Liang, et al., Improved multi-strategy adaptive grey wolf optimization for practical engineering applications and high-dimensional problem solving, Artificial Intelligence Review 57 (2024) 1–51. Available from https://doi.org/10.1007/S10462-024-10821-3/TABLES/13.

[69] S. Singh, J.C. Bansal, Mutation-driven grey wolf optimizer with modified search mechanism, Expert Systems with Applications 194 (2022) 116450. Available from https://doi.org/10.1016/J.ESWA.2021.116450.

[70] X. Liang, D. Wang, M. Huang, Improved grey wolf optimizer and their applications, Proceedings of IEEE 7th International Conference on Computer Science and Network Technology, ICCSNT (2019) 107–110. Available from https://doi.org/10.1109/ICCSNT47585.2019.89625042019.

Chapter 5

Binary grey wolf and football optimization algorithm for potato leaf disease image classification with deep learning

El-Sayed M. El-Kenawy[1,2], Marwa M. Eid[3], Amel Ali Alhussan[4], and Doaa Sami Khafaga[4]

[1]*School of ICT, Faculty of Engineering, Design and Information & Communications Technology (EDICT), Bahrain Polytechnic, Isa Town, Bahrain,* [2]*Jadara University Research Center, Jadara University, Jordan,* [3]*Faculty of Artificial Intelligence, Delta University for Science and Technology, Mansoura, Egypt,* [4]*Department of Computer Sciences, College of Computer and Information Sciences, Princess Nourah bint Abdulrahman University, Riyadh, Saudi Arabia*

5.1 Introduction

Potato is one of the most widely cultivated and consumed crops globally, providing a critical source of nutrition and income for millions of farmers and stakeholders in the agricultural sector. However, potato production faces several challenges, with plant diseases being one of the most significant threats. Early Blight and Late Blight are the most prevalent and destructive diseases affecting potato crops, Patil and Kumar [1], Datt and Kukreja [2]. Early Blight is cauBlight the fungus *Alternaria solani*, and it thrives in warm, humid conditions. Conversely, Late Blight, caused by the pathogen *Phytophthora infestans*, proliferates under cool and wet conditions. These diseases can lead to devastating losses in crop yield, significantly impacting food security and economic stability in regions heavily reliant on potato farming Chaiyana et al. [3]; Peddicord et al. [4].

The role of weather conditions in disease onset and spread is critical. Parameters such as temperature, humidity, wind speed, visibility, and atmospheric pressure influence the lifecycle and reproduction rates of the pathogens responsible for these diseases Delfani et al. [5]. Despite the abundance of research on image-based disease detection methods using convolutional neural networks (CNNs) and other deep learning techniques, these approaches often focus solely on the visible symptoms of the disease at later stages G et al. [6]. This limits their utility for early prediction and preventive measures. By focusing on the weather-driven dynamics of disease outbreaks, we can enable early and accurate predictions, helping farmers take timely actions such as applying fungicides, altering irrigation schedules, or implementing other preventive strategies. Thus there is a pressing need for predictive models that integrate weather data with advanced computational methods to enhance agricultural decision-making Bhatia et al. [7]; Shaikh et al. [8].

Feature selection in high-dimensional datasets has become a critical research area, and optimization algorithms have proven to be practical tools in addressing this challenge. In addition to improving the interpretability of machine learning models, feature selection reduces computational complexity, making them more efficient for real-world applications Zhao et al. [9]; Mahum et al. [10]. However, traditional feature selection methods often struggle to balance exploration and exploitation, leading to suboptimal performance. This limitation necessitates hybrid approaches that combine multiple optimization algorithms to enhance performance Arshad et al. [11,12].

Early Blight and Late Blight pose significant challenges in predicting potato leaf diseases. This study addresses these challenges by integrating optimization techniques and machine learning. The primary objective is to develop a robust predictive framework using a hybrid optimization algorithm that combines the grey wolf optimizer (GWO) and the football optimization algorithm (FOA), Gupta et al. [13]. The proposed hybrid grey wolf and football optimization algorithm (bGWFbO) enhances the feature selection process by identifying the most relevant weather parameters for disease prediction. This hybrid algorithm leverages the exploration capability of GWO and the exploitation strength of FOA to achieve a balanced search mechanism that optimizes feature subsets effectively, Pandiri et al. [14].

Grey Wolf Optimizer. DOI: https://doi.org/10.1016/B978-0-443-36624-6.00023-8

The predictive framework is applied to various machine learning models, including multilayer perceptron (MLP), random forest (RF), support vector machine (SVM), and K-nearest neighbors (KNN), to evaluate their performance in predicting potato leaf diseases based on weather data. The dataset used in this study includes weather parameters such as temperature, humidity, wind speed, and pressure, along with disease labels indicating the presence of Early Blight or Late Blight. By integrating feature selection and predictive modeling, this research aims to improve prediction accuracy, reduce computational overhead, and provide actionable insights for disease management in potato farming Lee et al. [15].

Weather-based disease prediction presents several challenges. First, the relationship between weather conditions and disease outbreaks is often nonlinear and influenced by multiple interacting factors. For example, Early Blight is triggered by high humidity and warm temperatures, but these conditions must persist for a specific duration for the disease to develop. Similarly, Late Blight requires a combination of cool temperatures and extended wet periods for pathogen proliferation. Capturing these complex dependencies requires sophisticated models capable of handling nonlinearity and uncertainty.

Second, the high dimensionality of weather data poses challenges for machine learning models. Irrelevant or redundant features may dilute the model's predictive power, necessitating effective feature selection methods. Traditional feature selection techniques often fail to capture intricate patterns underlying disease outbreaks, highlighting the need for advanced optimization algorithms.

Finally, developing a computationally efficient and scalable solution for real-world applications is a significant challenge. Farmers and agricultural stakeholders require models that can provide real-time predictions while operating with limited computational resources. Addressing these challenges requires innovative algorithm design, robust machine-learning techniques, and domain expertise.

This study introduces a novel hybrid optimization algorithm, the bGWFbO, to enhance predictive modeling of potato leaf diseases based on weather conditions. The primary contributions of this research are as follows:

- Development of a hybrid optimization algorithm: We propose a new feature selection approach by integrating the GWO and the FOA. The hybridization leverages the exploration capability of GWO and the adaptive movement strategies of FOA, ensuring a balanced search mechanism.
- Enhanced feature selection for disease prediction: The proposed bGWFbO effectively identifies the most relevant weather parameters, such as temperature, humidity, wind speed, and pressure, improving disease prediction accuracy while reducing computational complexity.
- Performance evaluation on multiple machine learning models: We apply the selected features to several machine learning classifiers, including MLP, SVM, Random forest (RF), and KNN, demonstrating a significant increase in predictive Accuracy.
- Empirical validation using real-world data: Experimental results on a dataset containing weather parameters and disease labels confirm that the hybrid feature selection method enhances classification performance, achieving up to 98.65% Accuracy.
- Scalability and applicability to precision agriculture: By incorporating weather-driven feature selection, the proposed approach contributes to precision farming by enabling early disease prediction, reducing potential crop losses, and assisting in timely intervention strategies.

This research highlights the importance of hybrid optimization in agricultural analytics, paving the way for developing more efficient and interpretable disease prediction models.

The rest of the paper is organized as follows: Section 5.2 presents a comprehensive literature review covering machine learning applications in plant disease prediction and feature selection techniques. Section 5.3 describes the dataset, including weather parameters and disease classifications—Section 5.4 details the proposed methodology, focusing on the hybrid optimization approach and machine learning models. Section 5.5 outlines the experimental setup and evaluation metrics used to assess predictive performance. Section 5.6 discusses the results obtained, comparing different optimization techniques. Finally, Section 5.7 concludes the paper, summarizing key findings and outlining potential future research directions.

5.2 Literature review

Artificial intelligence (AI) in agriculture has significantly enhanced food security and economic benefits. AI-driven models, particularly machine learning (ML) and deep learning (DL), have revolutionized plant disease detection and crop yield forecasting Kaur et al. [16]. This literature review explores various AI methodologies for disease prediction and management in diverse crops, emphasizing meteorological and image-based data fusion.

ML and DL techniques have demonstrated high accuracy in detecting and classifying plant diseases. A comprehensive review identified models such as SVM, RF, CNN, and MobileNet achieving accuracy rates between 64.3% and 100% for potato disease forecasting Kaur et al. [16]. Similarly, peanut leaf spot disease prediction has been improved through CNN and long short-term memory (LSTM) models, integrating a squeeze-and-excitation (SE) attention mechanism, achieving an R^2 of 0.951 Guo et al. [17].

Late blightBlighte spotlight,caused by *Phytophthora infestans*, has been effectively forecasted using RF and C5.0 decision trees, reaching predictive accuracies of 87% and 85%, respectively Meno et al. [18]. Moreover, integrating aerobiological data with the tomato forecaster (TOMCAST) model has enhanced early blight control, reducing fungicide use and promoting sustainable agriculture Meno et al. [19].

Precision agricultural technologies have facilitated best management practices, optimizing soil preparation, irrigation, fertilization, and disease management Ahmad and Sharma [20]. Internet of Things (IoT)-enabled decision trees predict crop conditions based on real-time temperature, humidity, pH, and rainfall data H et al. [21]. Such integration aids in monitoring vast farmlands and enhancing yield sustainability.

Climate change and excessive pesticide use pose severe risks to food security. AI-driven models such as gradient boosting and KNN have achieved nearly perfect R^2 values (99.99%) in predicting crop yields by analyzing meteorological data and pesticide records Hoque et al. [22]. ML-based epidemiological models have effectively forecasted wheat diseases such as rusts, Fusarium head blight, and Karnal Bunt, providing farmers with early intervention strategies Kaur et al. [23].

Crop yield prediction increasingly relies on meteorological data. Artificial Neural Network (ANN) and support vector regression (SVR) models have shown high prediction accuracy by adapting to local climate-crop interactions S et al. [24]. Similarly, rice blast disease has been forecasted using ANN models, outperforming SVR and INGARCHX methods Arumugam Gopalakrishnan et al. [25]. These findings demonstrate the potential of AI to mitigate crop losses and improve sustainable farming practices.

Integrating AI in crop disease prediction and management has proven effective across various agricultural applications. Advanced machine learning models, particularly CNNs, LSTMs, and ANNs, have significantly improved predictive accuracy. Future research should focus on interdisciplinary approaches, combining climate modeling, remote sensing, and real-time data collection to enhance agricultural sustainability further.

5.3 Dataset description

5.3.1 Overview of dataset

The dataset used in this study consists of 4020 samples, meticulously collected to analyze the intricate relationship between weather conditions and the occurrence of potato leaf diseases Dat. This dataset is uniquely designed to integrate environmental factors and disease occurrences, offering an alternative to conventional image-based disease detection methods. It is structured into two main components. The first includes six critical weather parameters—temperature, humidity, wind speed, wind bearing, visibility, and pressure—that collectively characterize the prevailing environmental conditions. Temperature, recorded in degrees celsius, represents the daily average and plays a crucial role in influencing the lifecycle of pathogens, particularly for diseases such as Early Blight and Late Blight. Humidity, measured as a percentage, strongly affects disease development, as high levels provide a conducive environment for fungal spores. Wind speed, expressed in meters per second, captures the strength of wind, while wind bearing, denoted in degrees, indicates its direction, both of which are important for spore dispersal. Visibility, measured in kilometers, indirectly reflects atmospheric clarity and moisture, and atmospheric pressure, recorded in millibars, signals weather stability and is useful in forecasting conditions linked to outbreaks. The second component covers disease-related parameters, including a categorical label specifying whether the case corresponds to Early Blight or Late Blight, and a numerical encoding of the disease type for use in machine learning algorithms.

5.3.2 Disease categories

Potato leaf diseases are a major threat to agricultural productivity, with Early Blight and Late Blight being the most prominent. Early Blight, caused by the fungus *Alternaria solani*, is characterized by concentric brown or black lesions on leaves that may eventually lead to premature defoliation. The disease thrives under warm and humid conditions, typically when temperatures range between 20°C and 30°C and humidity levels exceed 75%. Prolonged exposure to such conditions significantly increases the risk of outbreaks. In contrast, Late Blight is an oomycete disease caused by *Phytophthora infestans*, historically infamous for contributing to the Irish Potato Famine. It develops in cool temperatures (10°C–20°C) and requires extended periods of moisture, such as dew or rainfall. Symptoms manifest as water-soaked lesions that rapidly turn necrotic, and under favorable conditions, the pathogen spreads aggressively, often causing catastrophic crop losses.

5.3.3 Objective and importance of the dDataset

This dataset's primary objective is to predict the likelihood of potato leaf disease occurrence based on prevailing weather conditions. Traditional disease detection approaches predominantly rely on image-based processing techniques, such as CNNs, which analyze visible symptoms of the disease. While effective in diagnosing the disease at later stages, these methods are less practical during the early phases, when preventive measures have the most significant impact. In contrast, the present dataset emphasizes weather-driven prediction by linking environmental parameters with the onset and progression of diseases. For instance, Late Blight thrives in cool and moisture-rich conditions, meaning that when such weather is forecasted, timely fungicide application or irrigation adjustment can prevent outbreaks. Early Blight, in turn, proliferates under warm and humid conditions and can be mitigated through strategies, such as optimized irrigation schedules, improved soil aeration, or deploying resistant potato varieties.

By leveraging the information contained in this dataset, predictive models can generate early warnings, enabling farmers and agricultural stakeholders to take proactive measures, minimize crop losses, and enhance yield quality. Additionally, the dataset is a valuable resource for advancing research in weather-driven disease prediction, providing a benchmark for testing novel optimization algorithms and machine learning models.

5.3.4 Features and attributes of the dataset

The dataset ultimately contains eight key features. These include six numerical weather parameters—temperature, humidity, wind speed, wind bearing, visibility, and atmospheric pressure—alongside two disease-related attributes: a categorical label (Early Blight or Late Blight) and its numerical encoding. Together, these features establish a structured basis for predictive modeling.

5.3.5 Significance of weather-based prediction

Weather-driven disease prediction has significant implications for sustainable agriculture. By shifting the focus from symptom-based detection to proactive risk assessment, farmers can reduce economic losses caused by disease

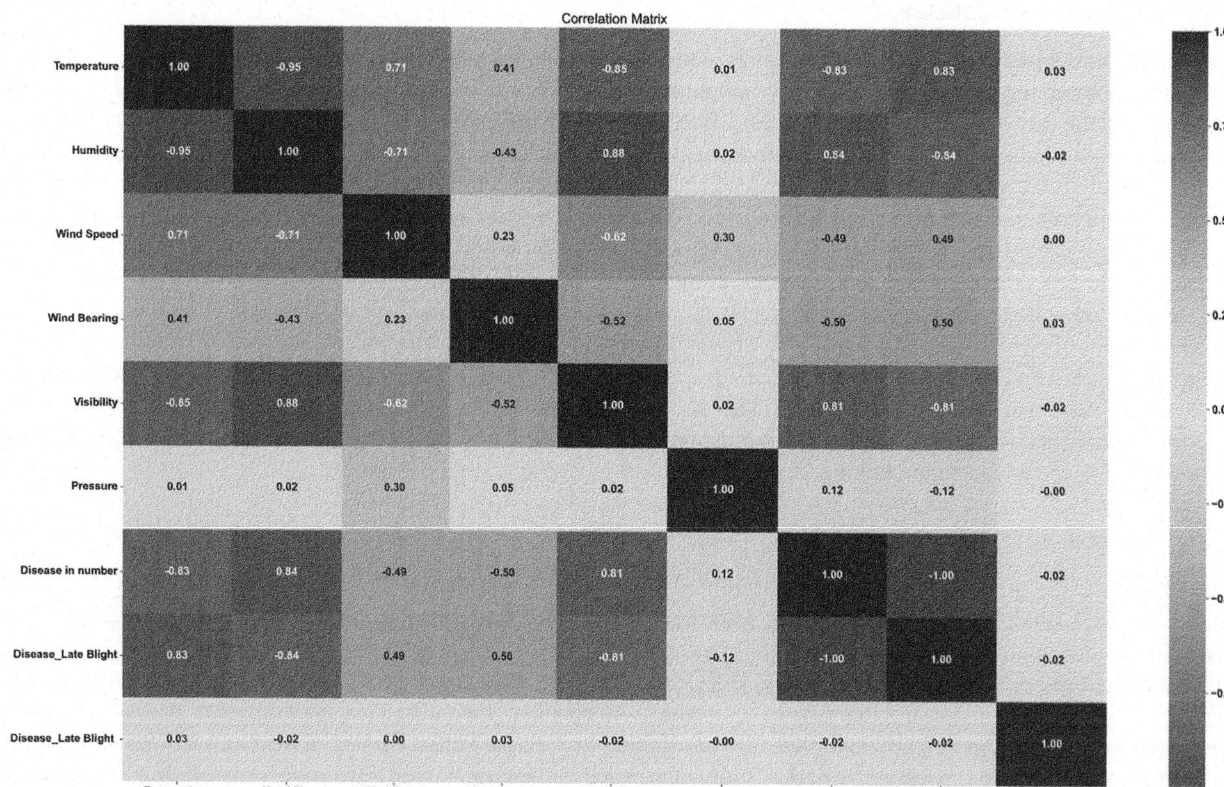

FIGURE 5.1 Correlation matrix of weather parameters in the dataset.

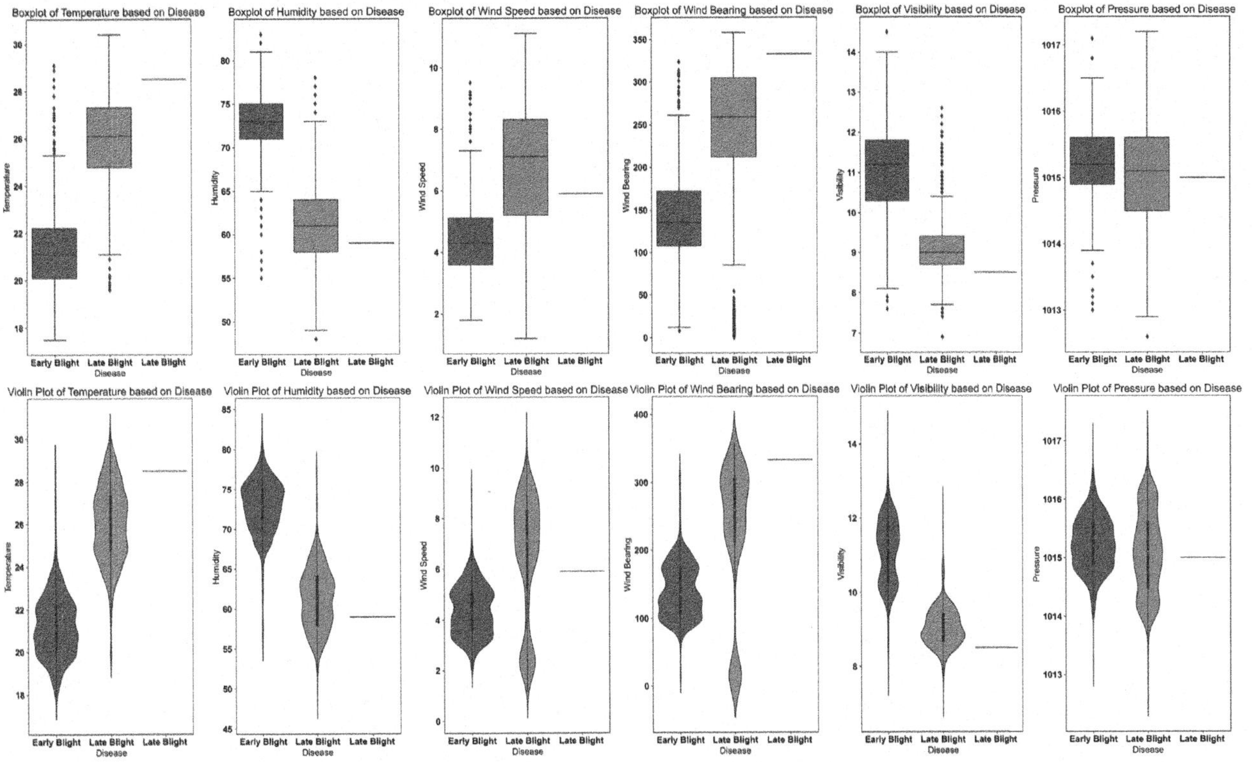

FIGURE 5.2 Boxplots and violin plots of weather parameters segmented by disease type (Early Blight and Late Blight).

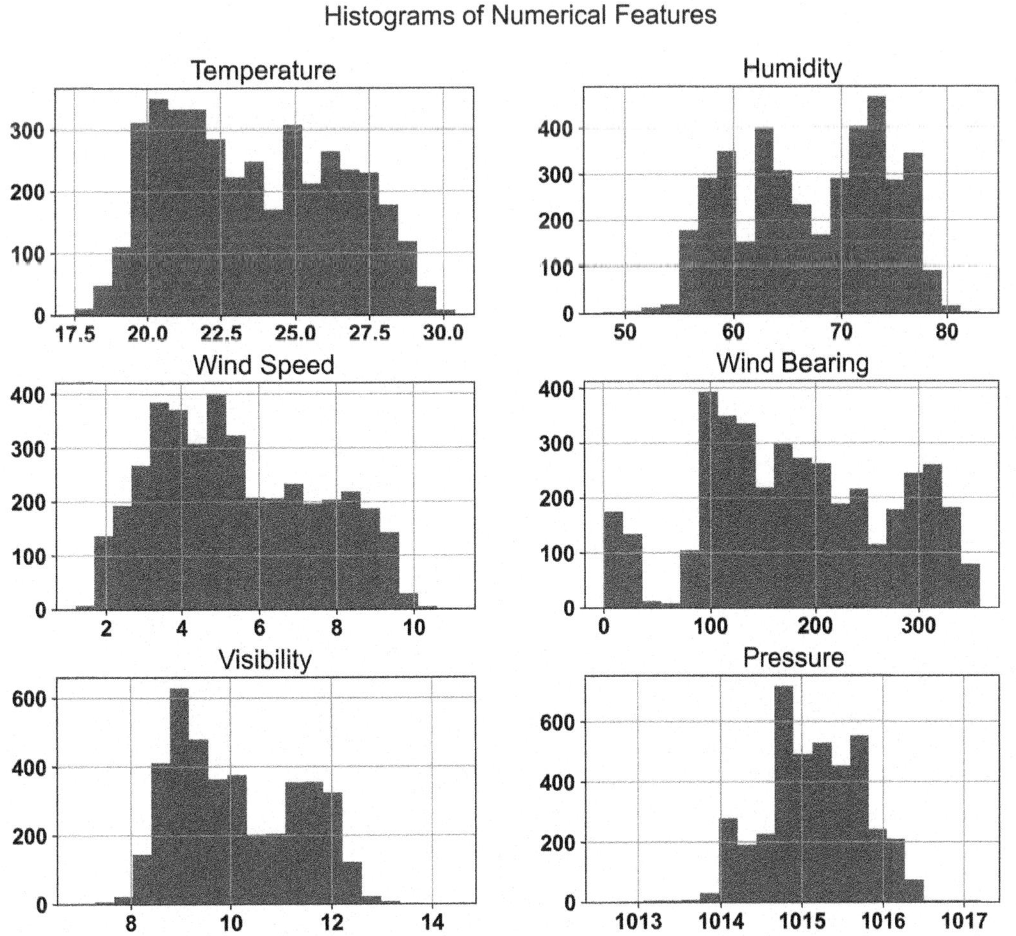

FIGURE 5.3 Histograms showing the distribution of numerical features in the dataset.

outbreaks, optimize the use of water, fertilizers, and fungicides, and implement targeted management strategies that minimize environmental impact. This proactive approach ultimately improves crop yield and quality by supporting timely interventions.

Fig. 5.1 displays the correlation matrix of the weather parameters. This heatmap visually quantifies the linear relationships between variables, aiding in feature selection by identifying strongly correlated or independent features.

Fig. 5.2 illustrates the boxplots and violin plots of weather parameters segmented by potato leaf diseases (Early Blight and Late Blight). These plots highlight the statistical differences and distribution shapes for features like temperature, humidity, and others, providing insights into how weather conditions vary across diseases.

Fig. 5.3 provides histograms of the numerical features in the dataset. These histograms reveal the frequency distribution for each parameter, giving an overview of the data's spread and central tendencies.

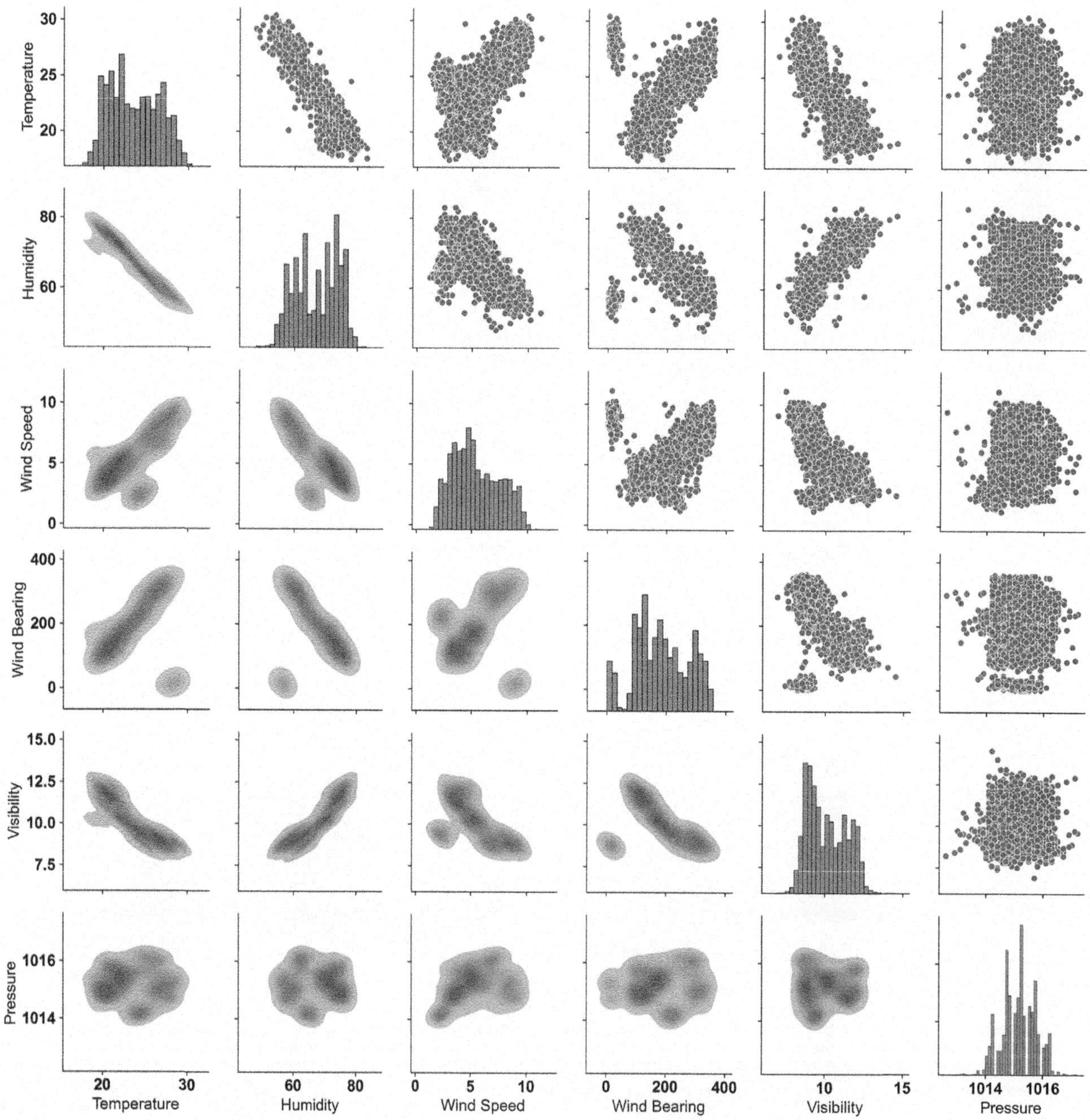

FIGURE 5.4 Scatterplot matrix showing pairwise relationships among numerical features in the dataset.

Fig. 5.4 presents the scatterplot matrix of the dataset, showcasing the pairwise relationships among numerical features such as temperature, humidity, wind speed, wind bearing, visibility, and pressure. This figure is valuable in identifying potential correlations, clustering patterns, or distribution shapes for each variable.

This dataset lays the groundwork for developing robust, scalable, and efficient predictive models that address the growing demand for precision agriculture due to climate change and resource constraints.

5.4 Methodology

5.4.1 Predictive models

To predict potato leaf diseases based on weather conditions, this study employs four widely recognized machine learning models: MLP, RF, SVM, and KNN. Each model is selected for its unique capabilities to capture and process complex patterns in the data. The following provides a detailed technical overview of each model.

5.4.1.1 Neural network

A MLP is a class of artificial neural networks that excels at modeling nonlinear relationships. Its architecture consists of an input layer that receives features such as temperature, humidity, and wind speed; one or more hidden layers where neurons apply nonlinear activation functions (e.g., ReLU, sigmoid, or tanh) to transform the weighted inputs; and an output layer that produces the final prediction by classifying the case as either Early Blight or Late Blight. The learning process minimizes a loss function, typically cross-entropy for classification, using optimization algorithms such as stochastic gradient descent or Adam. Through backpropagation, gradients of the loss function with respect to weights are computed and updated, improving predictive accuracy. MLP is particularly well-suited to datasets with complex interdependencies, as is the case in weather-driven disease prediction.

5.4.1.2 Random forest

RF is an ensemble learning method that builds multiple decision trees during training. Each tree is trained on a random bootstrap sample of the dataset, a process known as bagging, which reduces overfitting and increases robustness. At each split within a tree, a random subset of features is considered, thereby promoting diversity across trees. For classification tasks, the final output is determined by majority voting among all trees. Key hyperparameters include the number of trees, the maximum depth allowed for each tree, and the minimum number of samples required to split a node. RF is highly effective in handling noisy, high dimensional data and can capture interactions among features, which makes it especially appropriate for weather-based predictions.

5.4.1.3 Support vector machine

SVM is a supervised learning algorithm designed to find the optimal hyperplane that separates data points of different classes with the maximum margin. When the data are linearly separable, SVM identifies a hyperplane that maximizes the distance between the nearest support vectors and the decision boundary. For cases where the data are not linearly separable, kernel functions such as polynomial and radial basis function (RBF) are applied to project the data into higher-dimensional spaces where separation is feasible. Soft-margin SVM introduces slack variables that permit limited misclassifications, thereby balancing the trade-off between maximizing margin width and minimizing classification error. The main hyperparameters are the kernel type, the regularization parameter C, and kernel-specific parameters such as γ in the RBF kernel. SVM is particularly effective for datasets with relatively few features and strong class separability, which aligns with the properties of weather-based disease prediction.

5.4.1.4 K-nearest neighbors

KNN is an instance-based learning algorithm that predicts outcomes based on the similarity of a new data point to its nearest neighbors. The similarity is usually measured using distance metrics such as Euclidean, Manhattan, or Minkowski distance, with Euclidean distance being commonly used for weather data. The choice of the number of neighbors k directly influences performance: smaller values of k make the model sensitive to noise, while larger values provide smoother decision boundaries. The predicted class is assigned through majority voting among the k nearest neighbors. Although KNN is computationally demanding during inference, since all training samples must be stored and compared, it remains simple to implement. To ensure balanced contributions of all parameters, proper feature scaling methods such as normalization or standardization are essential.

5.4.1.5 Summary of model selection

In summary, the chosen models provide complementary strengths. MLP captures complex nonlinear weather patterns influencing disease occurrence. RF delivers robustness, interpretability, and the ability to handle high-dimensional datasets. SVM constructs optimal decision boundaries for highly separable classes, and KNN offers simplicity and effectiveness, particularly for smaller datasets. By leveraging this diversity of models, the study ensures a comprehensive evaluation of the proposed hybrid optimization framework for feature selection and disease prediction.

5.4.2 Hybrid grey wolf and football optimization algorithm

5.4.2.1 Overview of grey wolf optimizer

The GWO is a population-based metaheuristic algorithm inspired by the hierarchical structure and cooperative hunting strategies of grey wolves (*Canis lupus*), Mirjalili et al. [26]. The algorithm emulates the leadership hierarchy observed in wolf packs and their coordinated hunting behaviors involving tracking, encircling, and attacking prey. In nature, grey wolves organize themselves into structured packs, where the population is divided into four groups: the α wolves act as dominant leaders responsible for decision-making and guiding the pack; the β wolves support the α in organizing activities; the δ wolves play subordinate roles in hunting, scouting, and maintaining order; and finally, the ω wolves, ranked lowest, help maintain pack stability and cohesion. The optimization process in GWO is primarily guided by the α, β, and δ wolves, while the ω wolves contribute by exploring the search space to provide diversity.

The hunting behavior of wolves is simulated in three phases: encircling the prey, hunting, and attacking. During encirclement, wolves adjust their positions relative to the best solutions; during hunting, the α, β, and δ wolves guide the search process; and in the final phase, the wolves converge toward the optimal solution. This behavior is mathematically formulated as follows:

$$\mathbf{D} = |\mathbf{C}\cdot\mathbf{X}_p(t) - \mathbf{X}(t)| \quad (5.1)$$

$$\mathbf{X}(t+1)=\mathbf{X}_p(t) - \mathbf{A}\cdot\mathbf{D} \quad (5.2)$$

Here, $\mathbf{X}$ denotes the position of a wolf, $\mathbf{X}_p$ is the position of the prey (the best solution found so far), and $\mathbf{A}$ and $\mathbf{C}$ are coefficient vectors that regulate exploration and exploitation. The vectors are defined as:

$$\mathbf{A}=2\cdot\mathbf{a}\cdot\mathbf{r}_1 - \mathbf{a}, \quad \mathbf{C}=2\cdot\mathbf{r}_2 \quad (5.3)$$

where $\mathbf{a}$ is a parameter that decreases linearly from 2 to 0, and $\mathbf{r}_1$ and $\mathbf{r}_2$ are random vectors within [0,1].

5.4.2.2 Overview of football optimization algorithm

The football optimization algorithm (FbOA) is a metaheuristic inspired by the dynamic strategies of football teams M. et al. [27]. It models the behavior of players in terms of movement, passing, and positioning to balance exploration and exploitation. Players can perform short passes to explore locally, long passes to move across distant regions of the search space, and reposition themselves according to overall team performance. This is captured mathematically as:

$$\mathbf{X}(t+1)=\mathbf{X}(t) + r_1\cdot(\mathbf{X}_{best} - \mathbf{X}(t)) + r_2\cdot(\mathbf{X}_{team} - \mathbf{X}(t)), \quad (5.4)$$

where $\mathbf{X}_{best}$ denotes the best solution found so far, $\mathbf{X}_{team}$ represents the average position of all agents, and r_1 and r_2 are random coefficients that influence the degree of movement.

5.4.2.3 Hybrid algorithm: grey wolf optimizer + Football Optimization Algori

The bGWFbO combines the hunting efficiency of GWO with the strategic movement of FbOA to enhance optimization performance. The algorithm begins with the initialization of a population of agents, each randomly positioned in the search space and assigned roles reflecting both GWO and football-inspired strategies. In the position update phase, wolves update their locations according to GWO's hierarchical rules, while players adjust movements based on FbOA's passing and positioning logic. The hybrid movement is then governed by the equation

$$\mathbf{X}(t+1)=\lambda\cdot\text{GWO\_update} + (1 - \lambda)\cdot\text{FbOA\_update}, \quad (5.5)$$

where λ is an adaptive parameter that balances exploration and exploitation. Fitness values are evaluated for each candidate solution, leaders (α, β, and δ) are updated accordingly, and iterations proceed until a stopping criterion, such as maximum iterations or convergence threshold, is met.

The hybridization provides multiple advantages. FbOA's passing strategies and team positioning enhance exploration, while GWO's leadership hierarchy strengthens exploitation. The adaptive combination ensures a dynamic balance, avoiding premature convergence and accelerating convergence speed compared to standalone algorithms. This synergy results in smaller, more relevant feature subsets and improved classification accuracy in disease prediction.

5.4.3 Feature selection

5.4.3.1 Significance of feature selection in predictive modeling

Feature selection is critical in machine learning and predictive analysis, as it assists in identifying the variables that contribute most to accurate predictions. By selecting an optimal subset of features, models become more interpretable, computational complexity is reduced, and prediction accuracy improves. In practice, this means that high-dimensional datasets containing redundant or insignificant features can be simplified, leading to more efficient processing. Feature selection also helps mitigate overfitting, since irrelevant features may cause models to memorize noise rather than learn generalizable patterns. Removing noisy inputs in turn improves generalization on unseen data. Another advantage is interpretability, because a smaller set of meaningful variables makes the model's decision-making process easier to understand. Finally, fewer input variables accelerate training and inference, reducing memory and computation requirements and making the models more efficient for real-time applications. In this study, feature selection is particularly significant, as it helps identify the most influential weather parameters affecting the occurrence of potato leaf diseases, thereby allowing predictive models to focus on the most relevant environmental factors.

5.4.3.2 Algorithms used for feature selection

Feature selection in this work is carried out using a set of optimization algorithms designed to determine the most effective subset of weather parameters. The proposed GWFbO) is compared with several benchmark metaheuristics.

The bGWFbO algorithm integrates the GWO with the FbOA. During the exploration phase, inspired by football team strategies, agents perform movements analogous to short and long passes, ensuring broad coverage of the feature space. In the exploitation phase, reflecting the hierarchical hunting strategies of grey wolves, the algorithm converges toward the most promising subsets. An adaptive switching mechanism based on a weighting factor λ dynamically balances exploration and exploitation across iterations. Feature subsets are evaluated by a machine learning model, with the objective function maximizing predictive accuracy while minimizing the number of selected features. The fitness function guiding this process is given by

$$F(\mathbf{X}) = \alpha \cdot (1 - \text{Accuracy}) + \beta \cdot \frac{|S|}{|S_{max}|}, \quad (5.6)$$

where Accuracy denotes the classification performance of the selected features, $|S|$ is the number of selected features, $|S_{max}|$ is the total number of available features, and α and β are weighting coefficients that balance accuracy with feature reduction.

For benchmarking, a range of widely used metaheuristic algorithms is also employed. The baseline football optimization algorithm (bFbOA) uses only football-inspired strategies without GWO integration, relying on tactical movements for subset identification. The baseline grey wolf optimizer (bGWO) exploits leadership hierarchies and hunting behaviors of wolves. Particle swarm optimization (bPSO) models the process as swarm intelligence, guided by global and local best solutions. The whale optimization algorithm (bWAO) imitates bubble-net hunting strategies, while biogeography-based optimization (bBBO) simulates migration and mutation of features across virtual islands. The multiverse optimizer (bMVO) leverages black holes, white holes, and wormholes to explore the search space. The sine cosine algorithm (bSBO) updates feature selection using sinusoidal and cosine adjustments to avoid local optima. Finally, the genetic algorithm (bGA) employs crossover and mutation operators rooted in evolutionary principles to refine feature subsets.

5.4.3.3 Comparison and evaluation

All algorithms are evaluated according to four performance metrics: average error rate, which measures classification errors when using the selected features; average selected feature size, which quantifies the number of retained parameters; fitness score, which summarizes overall optimization effectiveness; and the standard deviation of fitness, which indicates stability and robustness. The proposed bGWFbO consistently outperforms traditional metaheuristics by striking a better balance between feature relevance and computational efficiency. By reducing dimensionality and focusing on critical weather parameters, it delivers superior accuracy for disease prediction models while remaining computationally practical.

5.5 Experimental setup

5.5.1 Preprocessing

Preprocessing is crucial in machine learning pipelines, ensuring that raw data is cleaned, transformed, and structured for optimal model performance. In this study, preprocessing involved three main steps. First, missing values in weather parameters were either imputed using statistical techniques (e.g., mean imputation) or removed if the missing proportion was significant. Extreme outliers were detected using interquartile ranges and z-score methods, while categorical variables such as the "Disease" column were numerically encoded using one-hot encoding. Second, all features were scaled and normalized to ensure uniform contribution. Both Min-Max scaling (rescaling features between 0 and 1) and standardization (transforming them to zero mean and unit variance) were applied and compared during experiments. Finally, the dataset was split into training (80%) and testing (20%) subsets, with stratified sampling to preserve the distribution of Early and Late Blight cases.

5.5.2 Training protocols and parameter settings

To ensure reproducibility, the training process and parameter settings are described in detail. For the MLP, the architecture consisted of one input layer with six neurons (corresponding to the weather parameters), two hidden layers of 64 and 32 neurons respectively, and an output layer with softmax activation. The ReLU activation function was used in the hidden layers. The network was trained with the Adam optimizer at a learning rate of 0.001, batch size of 32, and for 200 epochs with early stopping based on validation loss. For RF, the number of trees was set to 200 with a maximum depth of 15. The SVM used the RBF kernel with a regularization parameter C=1.0 and γ=0.01. The KNN model was configured with k=7 neighbors and Euclidean distance as the metric. All models were implemented in Python using scikit-learn and TensorFlow/Keras libraries, and experiments were repeated five times with different random seeds to verify stability.

5.5.3 Evaluation metrics

To assess the effectiveness of the predictive models and the hybrid optimization approach, several evaluation metrics were employed. Accuracy measures the proportion of correctly predicted instances among all cases, and is defined as

$$\text{Accuracy} = \frac{\text{TP} + \text{TN}}{\text{TP} + \text{TN} + \text{FP} + \text{FN}}, \tag{5.7}$$

where TP and TN denote true positives and true negatives (correctly predicted diseased and healthy cases, respectively), and FP and FN represent false positives and false negatives.

Sensitivity (or recall) captures the ability of the model to correctly identify diseased cases and is expressed as

$$\text{Sensitivity} = \frac{\text{TP}}{\text{TP} + \text{FN}}. \tag{5.8}$$

This metric is particularly critical in disease prediction, ensuring that infected plants are detected accurately. Conversely, Specificity measures the ability to correctly identify healthy cases, given by

$$\text{Specificity} = \frac{\text{TN}}{\text{TN} + \text{FP}}, \tag{5.9}$$

which ensures that nondiseased crops are not mistakenly classified as diseased.

Precision, also known as Positive Predictive Value, is defined as

$$\text{Precision} = \frac{\text{TP}}{\text{TP} + \text{FP}}, \tag{5.10}$$

and reflects the proportion of correctly predicted positive cases among all cases predicted as positive. A high precision value indicates fewer false alarms. Similarly, the negative predictive value measures the proportion of correctly identified negative cases among all cases predicted as negative:

$$\text{NPV} = \frac{\text{TN}}{\text{TN} + \text{FN}}. \tag{5.11}$$

Finally, the F-score (or F1-score) provides a balanced assessment of precision and sensitivity. It is the harmonic mean of the two measures and is defined as

$$F_1 = 2 \times \frac{\text{Precision} \times \text{Sensitivity}}{\text{Precision} + \text{Sensitivity}}. \tag{5.12}$$

This metric is especially valuable in scenarios where the dataset exhibits class imbalance, as it accounts for both false negatives and false positives simultaneously.

5.6 Results and discussion

5.6.1 Performance of models before feature selection

Before applying feature selection, all predictive models were trained using the complete features, including weather parameters such as temperature, humidity, wind speed, wind bearing, visibility, and pressure. The results, as shown in Table 5.1, indicate the performance of MLP, RF, SVM, and KNN when all features are considered.

Fig. 5.5 shows the pairwise relationships between the performance metrics of machine learning models, with regression lines fitted to highlight trends. This plot helps evaluate potential linear dependencies among metrics such as Accuracy, sensitivity, and F-score.

Fig. 5.6 depicts the kernel density estimation plot for Accuracy, visualizing its probability density. This provides a smoother perspective of how accuracy values are distributed across the dataset.

Fig. 5.7 presents the regression analysis between Accuracy and F-score. The scatter points and regression line show the linear relationship between these critical performance metrics, indicating how Accuracy impacts overall model performance.

These results highlight that while the models performed well, there was still scope for improvement through feature selection.

5.6.2 Feature selection performance

To enhance the predictive models, feature selection was performed using multiple metaheuristic optimization algorithms, including the proposed bGWFbO, along with other benchmark algorithms such as bFbOA, bGWO, bPSO, bWAO, bBBO, bMVO, bSBO, and bGA. Table 5.2 presents the comparative performance of these methods.

5.6.3 Performance of models after feature selection

After applying feature selection, models were retrained using only the selected features. The results, presented in Table 5.3, demonstrate a significant improvement in classification performance.

5.6.4 Discussion

The results demonstrate that MLP accuracy improved significantly from 0.9542 to 0.9866, which indicates that removing irrelevant features allowed the model to focus on the most informative parameters. Similarly, all models exhibited higher accuracy, sensitivity, specificity, and F-score values, confirming that the proposed feature selection approach enhanced

TABLE 5.1 Performance metrics before feature selection.

Model	Accuracy	Recall (Sensitivity (TPR))	Specificity (TNR)	Precision (PPV)	NPV	F-Score
Neural network (MLP)	0.9542	0.9543	0.9464	0.9566	0.9489	0.9489
Random forest	0.9437	0.9519	0.9464	0.9545	0.9477	0.9477
Support vector machine (SVM)	0.9469	0.9497	0.9442	0.9523	0.9454	0.9454
K-nearest neighbors (KNN)	0.9458	0.9497	0.9421	0.9522	0.9443	0.9443

NPV, Negative predictive value; *TPR*, true positive rate; *TNR*, true negative rate; *PPV*, positive predictive value.

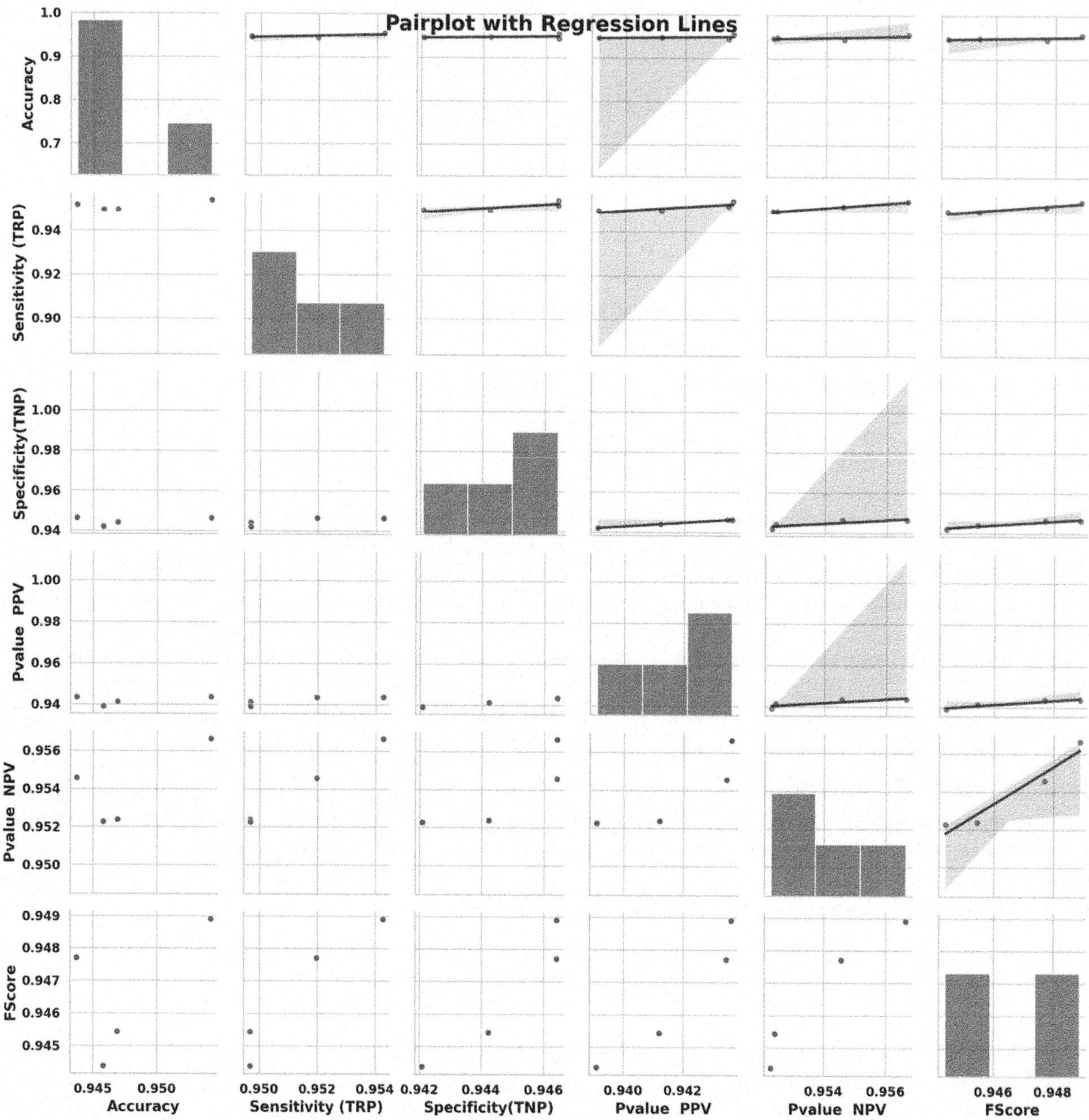

FIGURE 5.5 Pairplot show Accuracy relationships between performance metrics with regression lines.

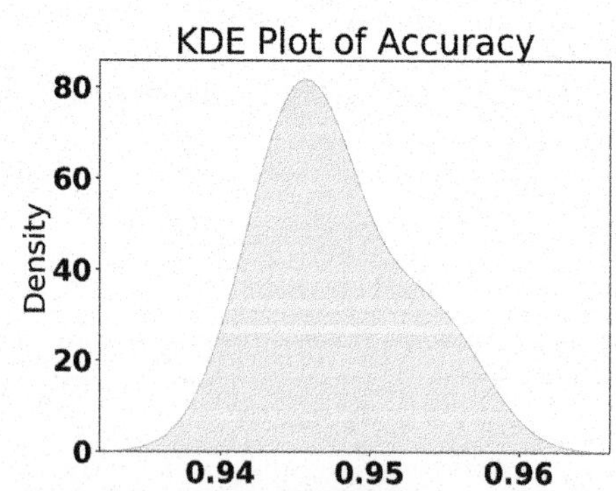

FIGURE 5.6 Kernel density estimation (*KDE*) plot showing the distribution of accuracy values.

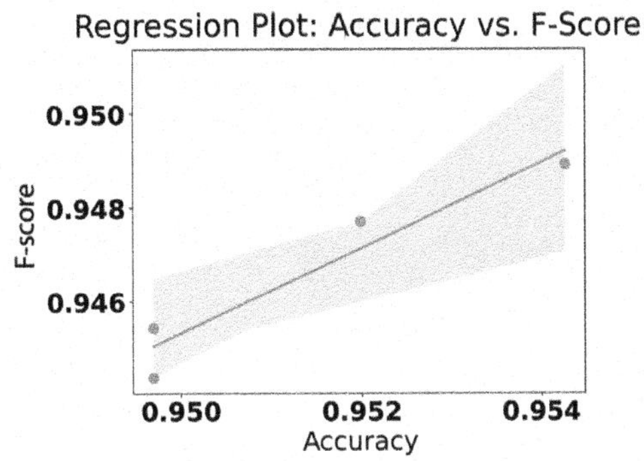

FIGURE 5.7 Regression Accuracy analysis showing the relationship between Accuracy and F-score.

TABLE 5.2 Feature selection performance across different optimization algorithms.

Algorithm	Avg. error	Avg. select size	Avg. fitness	Best fitness	Worst fitness
bGWFbO (Proposed)	0.5509	0.5337	0.6441	0.5459	0.6444
bFbOA	0.5754	0.7337	0.6603	0.5806	0.6475
bGWO	0.6374	0.8670	0.6686	0.6221	0.7321
bPSO	0.6319	0.7337	0.6587	0.6390	0.7067
bWAO	0.6317	0.8971	0.6665	0.6306	0.7067
bBBO	0.6001	0.8975	0.6644	0.6541	0.7406
bMVO	0.6086	0.8302	0.6884	0.6136	0.7316
bSBO	0.6402	0.9040	0.6984	0.6415	0.7212
bGA	0.6117	0.6761	0.6717	0.5750	0.6901

bGA, Genetic algorithm; *bBBO*, biogeography-based optimization; *bGWO*, baseline grey wolf optimizer; *bPSO*, particle swarm optimization; *bMVO*, multiverse optimizer; *bFbOA*, baseline football optimization algorithm; *bWAO*, whale optimization algorithm; *bSBO*, sine cosine algorithm.

TABLE 5.3 Performance metrics after feature selection.

Model	Accuracy	Recall (Sensitivity (TPR))	Specificity (TNR)	Precision (PPV)	NPV	F-Score
Neural network (MLP)	0.9866	0.9829	0.9806	0.9849	0.9754	0.9754
Random forest	0.9706	0.9806	0.9728	0.9830	0.9753	0.9753
Support vector machine (SVM)	0.9701	0.9783	0.9728	0.9809	0.9741	0.9741
K-nearest neighbors (KNN)	0.9733	0.9760	0.9706	0.9787	0.9718	0.9718

NPV, Negative predictive value; *TPR*, true positive rate; *TNR*, true negative rate; *PPV*, positive predictive value.

generalization. The feature selection process also improved computational efficiency, as the models required fewer input variables to process.

Fig. 5.8 illustrates the correlation heatmap for evaluation metrics, including Accuracy, sensitivity, specificity, and others. This heatmap helps identify interdependencies among performance metrics, supporting an informed analysis of model evaluations.

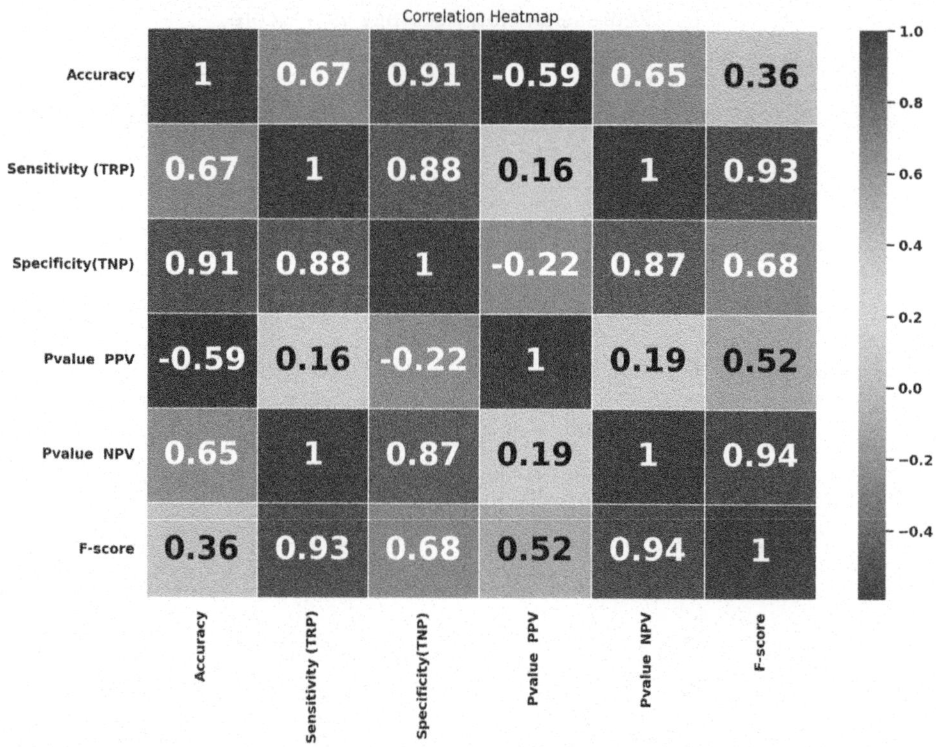

FIGURE 5.8 Correlation heatmap for evaluation metrics, including Accuracy, sensitivity, and specificity.

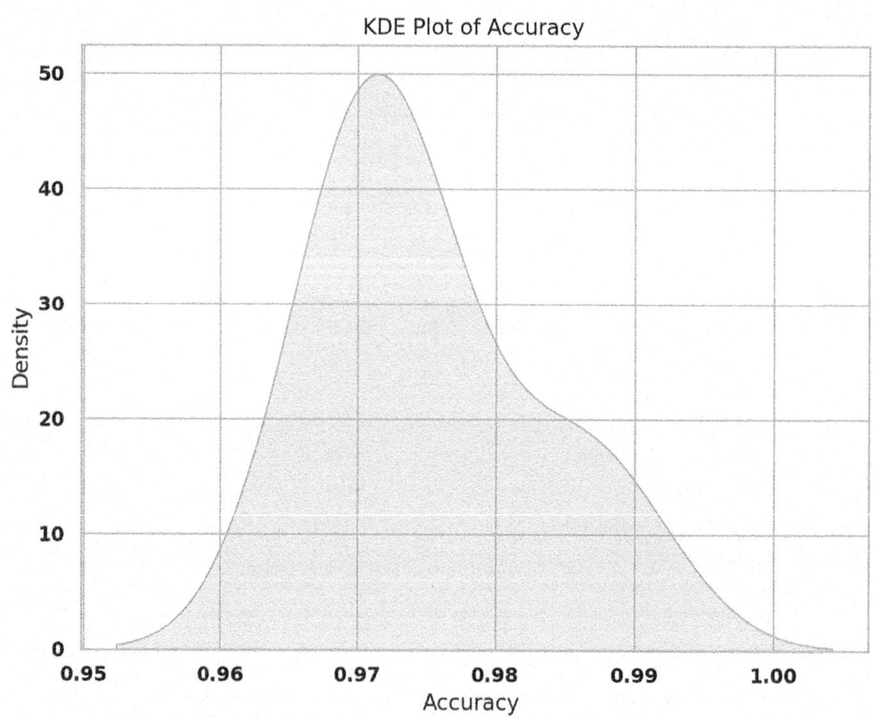

FIGURE 5.9 Kernel density estimation (*KDE*) plot of Accuracy distribution.

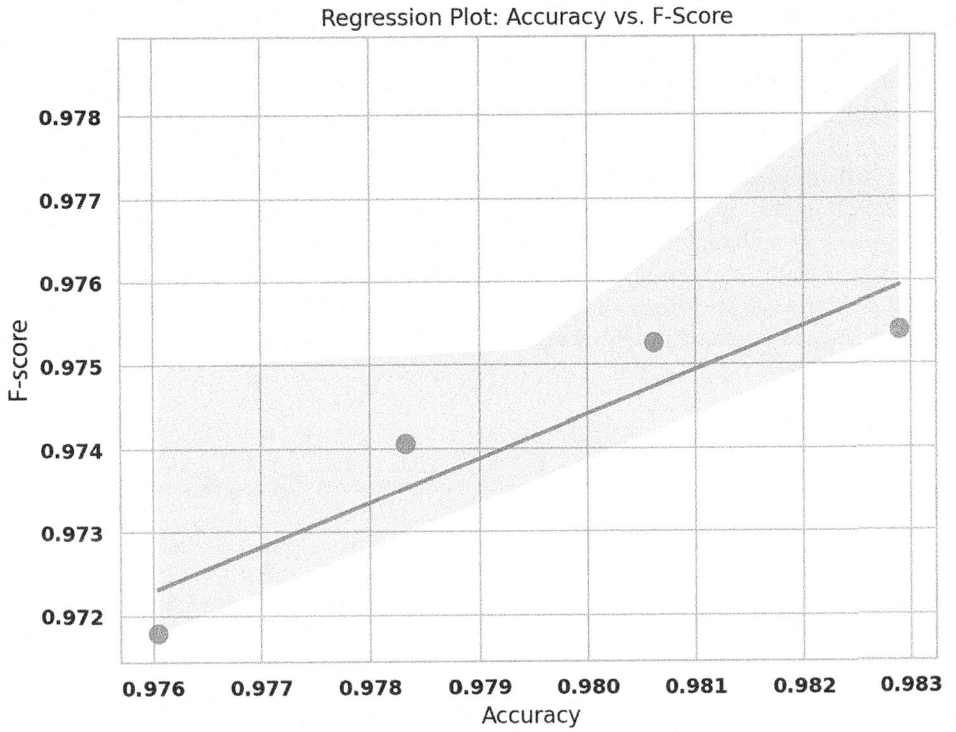

FIGURE 5.10 Regression plot showing the relationship between Accuracy and F-score.

Fig. 5.9 depicts the kernel density estimation plot for Accuracy, visualizing its probability density. This provides a smoother perspective of how accuracy values are distributed across the dataset.

Fig. 5.10 presents the regression analysis between Accuracy and F score. The scatter points and regression line show the linear relationship between these critical performance metrics, indicating how Accuracy impacts overall model performance.

Overfitting was managed through several mechanisms. First, the use of feature selection itself reduced redundant variables and noise, which helped models generalize better. Second, in the case of the Neural Network, early stopping based on validation loss and dropout regularization was applied during training. Additionally, experiments were repeated with stratified cross validation to ensure stability across different splits of the dataset. These strategies collectively reduced the likelihood of models memorizing training data rather than learning generalizable patterns.

From a computational perspective, the proposed bGWFbO algorithm requires $O(N \times d \times T)$ operations, where N is the number of search agents, d is the dimensionality of the feature set, and T is the number of iterations. This complexity is comparable to other population-based metaheuristics such as PSO or GWO, but the inclusion of Football Optimization strategies slightly increases per-iteration computation due to team-based updates. Memory requirements are mainly driven by storing the population of candidate solutions and fitness values, giving a memory complexity of $O(N \times d)$. However, since the algorithm adaptively prunes irrelevant features, the effective dimensionality decreases during optimization, which in practice reduces both runtime and memory demands.

Taken together, the results strongly validate the bGWFbO as an effective feature selection method. The hybridization of GWO's structured exploration with FbOA's adaptive movement strategies not only led to significantly improved accuracy and generalization but also produced smaller, more relevant feature subsets while maintaining robust classification performance across all evaluation metrics.

5.7 Conclusion

This study introduced a novel hybrid optimization algorithm, bGWFbO, for feature selection in potato leaf disease prediction using weather parameters. The experimental results demonstrated that applying feature selection significantly improved model performance, with MLP accuracy increasing from 0.9542 to 0.9866, and similar gains were observed for

RF, SVM, and KNN. The bGWFbO algorithm outperformed other optimization techniques by achieving the lowest average error (0.5509) and selecting the smallest yet most relevant feature subset (0.5337), proving its effectiveness in reducing computational complexity while maintaining predictive accuracy. These findings confirm that hybridizing the GWO and FbOA results in a more efficient selection process, balancing exploration and exploitation to avoid premature convergence.

This research's contributions extend beyond enhancing disease prediction accuracy. By leveraging weather data and optimizing feature selection, this approach provides a scalable and interpretable solution for early disease detection in agriculture. The novelty of combining GWO and FbOA introduces a dynamic optimization framework that can be extended to other crop diseases or domains requiring feature selection. Future work will explore additional hybrid optimization techniques, extend this methodology to other agricultural datasets, and integrate real-time weather monitoring for dynamic disease prediction, further advancing precision agriculture and sustainable farming practices.

References

[1] R.R. Patil, S. Kumar, Predicting rice diseases across diverse agro-meteorological conditions using an artificial intelligence approach, PeerJ Computer Science 7 (2021) e687. Available from https://doi.org/10.7717/peerj-cs.687.

[2] R.M. Datt, V. Kukreja, Neural network model for predicting apple yield based on arrival of phenological stage in conjunction with leaf disease, soil and weather parameters, SN Computer Science 5 (2024) 141. Available from https://doi.org/10.1007/s42979-023-02463-z.

[3] A. Chaiyana, N. Khiripet, S. Ninsawat, W. Siriwan, M.S. Shanmugam, S.G.P. Virdis, Mapping and predicting cassava mosaic disease outbreaks using earth observation and meteorological data-driven approaches, Remote Sensing Applications: Society and Environment 35 (2024) 101231. Available from https://doi.org/10.1016/j.rsase.2024.101231.

[4] L. Peddicord, A. Xavier, S. Cryer, J. Barr, G. van der Heijden, Scalable prediction of northern corn leaf blight and gray leaf spot diseases to predict fungicide spray timing in corn, Agronomy 15 (2) (2025). Available from https://doi.org/10.3390/agronomy15020328.

[5] P. Delfani, V. Thuraga, B. Banerjee, A. Chawade, Integrative approaches in modern agriculture: IoT, ML and AI for disease forecasting amidst climate change, Precision Agriculture 25 (2024) 2589–2613. Available from https://doi.org/10.1007/s11119-024-10164-7.

[6] J. G, E. Castelino, P. Mahadevu, M.S. Kitturmath, H.C. Lohithaswa, C.G. Karjagi, D. Deepak, Smart solutions for maize farmers: machine learning-enabled web applications for downy mildew management and enhanced crop yield in India, European Journal of Agronomy 164 (2025) 127441. Available from https://doi.org/10.1016/j.eja.2024.127441.

[7] A. Bhatia, A. Chug, A.P. Singh, D. Singh, Fractional mega trend diffusion function-based feature extraction for plant disease prediction, International Journal of Machine Learning and Cybernetics 14 (2023) 187–212. Available from https://doi.org/10.1007/s13042-022-01562-2.

[8] T.A. Shaikh, T. Rasool, F. Rasheed Lone, Towards leveraging the role of machine learning and artificial intelligence in precision agriculture and smart farming, Computers and Electronics in Agriculture 198 (2022) 107119. Available from https://doi.org/10.1016/j.compag.2022.107119.

[9] G. Zhao, Q. Zhao, H. Webber, A. Johnen, V. Rossi, A.F. Nogueira Junior, Integrating machine learning and change detection for enhanced crop disease forecasting in rice farming: a multi-regional study, European Journal of Agronomy 160 (2024) 127317. Available from https://doi.org/10.1016/j.eja.2024.127317.

[10] R. Mahum, H. Munir, Z.U.N. Mughal, M. Awais, F. Sher Khan, M. Saqlain, et al., A novel framework for potato leaf disease detection using an efficient deep learning model, Human and Ecological Risk Assessment: An International Journal 29 (2023) 303–326. Available from https://doi.org/10.1080/10807039.2022.2064814.

[11] F. Arshad, M. Mateen, S. Hayat, M. Wardah, Z. Al-Huda, Y.H. Gu, et al., Pldpnet: end-to-end hybrid deep learning framework for potato leaf disease prediction, Alexandria Engineering Journal 78 (2023) 406–418. Available from https://doi.org/10.1016/j.aej.2023.07.076.

[12] T. Nazir, M.M. Iqbal, S. Jabbar, A. Hussain, M. Albathan, EfficientPNet—an optimized and efficient deep learning approach for classifying disease of potato plant leaves, Agriculture 13 (4) (2023). Available from https://doi.org/10.3390/agriculture13040841.

[13] A. Gupta, A. Chug, A.P. Singh, Potato disease prediction using machine learning, image processing and IoT — a systematic literature survey, Journal of Crop Improvement 38 (2024) 95–137. Available from https://doi.org/10.1080/15427528.2023.2285827.

[14] D.N.K. Pandiri, R. Murugan, T. Goel, Chapter 34 - whale-optimized convolutional neural network for potato fungal pathogens disease classification, in: S. Mirjalili (Ed.), Handbook of Whale Optimization Algorithm, Academic Press, (2024), pp. 477–485. Available from http://doi.org/10.1016/B978-0-32-395365-8.00040-3.

[15] T.Y. Lee, I.A. Lin, J.Y. Yu, J. Yang, Y.C. Chang, High efficiency disease detection for potato leaf with convolutional neural network, SN Computer Science 2 (2021) 297. Available from https://doi.org/10.1007/s42979-021-00691-9.

[16] A. Kaur, G.S. Randhawa, F. Abbas, M. Ali, T.J. Esau, A.A. Farooque, et al., Artificial intelligence driven smart farming for accurate detection of potato diseases: a systematic review, IEEE Access 12 (2024) 193902–193922. Available from https://doi.org/10.1109/ACCESS.2024.3510456.

[17] Z. Guo, X. Chen, M. Li, Y. Chi, D. Shi, Construction and validation of peanut leaf spot disease prediction model based on long time series data and deep learning, Agronomy 14 (2024). Available from https://doi.org/10.3390/agronomy14020294.

[18] L. Meno, O. Escuredo, I.K. Abuley, M.C. Seijo, Predicting daily aerobiological risk level of potato late blight using C5.0 and random forest algorithms under field conditions, Sensors 23 (2023). Available from https://doi.org/10.3390/s23083818.

[19] L. Meno, I. Abuley, M.C. Seijo, O. Escuredo, Management strategies for early blight in potatoes: assessment of the tomcast model, including the aerobiological risk level and critical phenological period, Agriculture 14 (2024). Available from https://doi.org/10.3390/agriculture14081414.

[20] U. Ahmad, L. Sharma, A review of best management practices for potato crop using precision agricultural technologies, Smart Agricultural Technology 4 (2023) 100220. Available from https://doi.org/10.1016/j.atech.2023.100220.

[21] K.D.M. H, D. Mishra, D. D, Automation and integration of growth monitoring in plants (with disease prediction) and crop prediction, Materials Today: Proceedings 43 (2021) 3922–3927. Available from https://doi.org/10.1016/j.matpr.2021.01.973.

[22] M.J. Hoque, M.S. Islam, J. Uddin, M.A. Samad, B.S. De Abajo, D.L.R. Vargas, et al., Incorporating meteorological data and pesticide information to forecast crop yields using machine learning, IEEE Access 12 (2024) 47768–47786. Available from https://doi.org/10.1109/ACCESS.2024.3383309.

[23] J. Kaur, R. Bala, P. Singh, Forecasting of wheat diseases: insights, methods and challenges, in: P.L. Kashyap, V. Gupta, O. Prakash Gupta, R. Sendhil, K. Gopalareddy, P. Jasrotia, G.P. Singh (Eds.), New Horizons in Wheat and Barley Research: Crop Protection and Resource Management, Springer Nature, (2022), pp. 21–75. Available from http://doi.org/10.1007/978-981-16-4134-3_2.

[24] A. S, M.K. Debnath, K. R, Statistical and machine learning models for location-specific crop yield prediction using weather indices, International Journal of Biometeorology 68 (2024) 2453–2475. Available from https://doi.org/10.1007/s00484-024-02763-w.

[25] M. Arumugam Gopalakrishnan, G. Chellappan, S.G. Patil, S. Rathod, K. Ayyanar, J. Ramasamy, et al., Climate-based prediction of rice blast disease using count time series and machine learning approaches, AgriEngineering 6 (2024). Available from https://doi.org/10.3390/agriengineering6040246.

[26] S. Mirjalili, S.M. Mirjalili, A. Lewis, Grey wolf optimizer, Advances in Engineering Software 69 (2014) 46–61. Available from https://doi.org/10.1016/j.advengsoft.2013.12.007.

[27] E.H. M., F. Mohamed, A. Elshabrawy, M. Ibrahim, A. A., A. Khodadadi, et al., Football optimization algorithm (FBOA): a novel metaheuristic inspired by team strategy dynamics, Journal of Artificial Intelligence and Metaheuristics (2024) 21–38. Available from https://doi.org/10.54216/JAIM.080103.

Chapter 6

Bibliometric analysis of the grey wolf optimizer

Ahmet Akkaya[1], Cemil Közkurt[2], and Rafet Durgut[3]

[1]*Computer Technology, Gönen Vocational School, Bandırma Onyedi Eylül University, Bandırma, Balıkesir, Türkiye,* [2]*Computer Engineering, Faculty of Engineering and Natural Sciences, Bandırma Onyedi Eylül University Bandırma, Türkiye,* [3]*Crystalloids, Rotterdam, Holland, The Netherlands*

6.1 Introduction

In recent years, due to the inadequacy of classical deterministic methods in solving real-world problems, interest in heuristic and especially metaheuristic algorithms has increased significantly. Metaheuristic algorithms are powerful optimization techniques inspired by nature, biology, physics, and social behaviors, aimed at finding optimum solutions in large search spaces. The pioneers of these techniques are the genetic algorithm (GA), particle swarm optimization (PSO), ant colony optimization, and artificial bee colony (ABC) algorithms, and these algorithms are popularly used [1]. The main advantage of these algorithms is their high capacity to solve complex and multidimensional problems [2]. The grey wolf optimizer (GWO) is a nature-inspired metaheuristic algorithm, which was introduced in 2014 [3]. GWO is designed by modeling the hunting and leadership behaviors of grey wolves in nature. The algorithm successfully balances the exploration and exploitation of the pack orientation and solution space based on four leadership levels, namely alpha, beta, delta, and omega. Thanks to its structural simplicity, having only a few control parameters and being easily adaptable to problems in various disciplines, it has quickly attracted wide attention in the literature and has begun to be widely used in different engineering fields [4].

When past studies are examined, it is seen that, with the rapid rise of the GWO algorithm, a significant increase has been achieved in the number of publications related to the algorithm. However, a comprehensive bibliometric analysis study in which these publications are systematically classified, and trends, leading authors, institutions, and countries are revealed, is quite limited in the literature. In this context, this book chapter aims to examine the scientific literature focused on GWO published between 2014 and 2025 using bibliometric methods, based on the Web of Science (WoS) database. The main purpose of the study is to quantitatively reveal the development process, key research trends, collaborations, and citation patterns of research on the GWO algorithm. In this respect, the study is important in terms of mapping the current knowledge in the literature, providing strategic directions for researchers, and creating a guiding source for future research. The GWO algorithm will be discussed in the next section.

6.2 Grey wolf optimizer

In this section, GWO will be examined in detail. The social behaviors of grey wolves, which are the biological inspiration for GWO, will be examined, and the mathematical modeling of these behaviors will be explained. Information about the advantages and limitations of GWO and improved hybrid versions will be given.

6.2.1 Biological inspiration

Grey wolves (Canis lupus) are social predators that live in North America and Eurasia. In their natural habitat, grey wolves move in packs while hunting and have a strict social hierarchy. This structure is classified into four main groups: alpha (α), beta (β), delta (δ), and omega (ω). Alpha wolves are the leaders of the pack, making decisions, directing the hunt, and having authority over the other wolves. Beta wolves assist the alpha, delta wolves undertake tasks such as exploration,

Grey Wolf Optimizer. DOI: https://doi.org/10.1016/B978-0-443-36624-6.00004-4

security, and communication, while omega wolves are at the bottom of the pack and are often used to reduce social tensions [5]. This behavioral structure forms the basis of the GWO algorithm. In the algorithm, the three best solutions within the population are designated as alpha, beta, and delta, respectively, and the remaining individuals (omega) navigate the solution space under the guidance of these leaders.

6.2.2 Mathematical model

The GWO algorithm is based on three basic mechanisms: prey localization (discovery of the optimal solution), prey encirclement and attack (exploitation). These processes are mathematically modeled as given by Eq. 6.1, Eq. 6.2, and Eq. 6.3. In terms of prey pursuit and encirclement, each individual (wolf) represents a position in the solution space. The wolves update their positions, taking into account the alpha, beta, and delta positions.

$$D_a = \overrightarrow{C_1}.\overrightarrow{X_a} - \overrightarrow{XI} \tag{6.1}$$

$$\overrightarrow{X_1} = \overrightarrow{X_a} - \overrightarrow{A_1} \cdot \overrightarrow{D_a} \tag{6.2}$$

The same operations are performed for beta and delta, then the new position is calculated by taking the average:

$$\overrightarrow{X}(t+1) = \frac{\overrightarrow{X_1} + \overrightarrow{X_2} + \overrightarrow{X_3}}{3} \tag{6.3}$$

Here, $\vec{A}$ and $\vec{C}$ are the control parameters that govern the location of the prey and the pursuit of the wolves. $\vec{A}$ decreases linearly, thus maintaining a balance between exploration and exploitation.

6.2.3 Advantages and limitations

The GWO algorithm is seen to be rapidly increasing in the literature due to its advantages, such as simple structure [6], strong exploitation ability [7], general adaptability [8], and low parameter tuning requirement [9]. Simple structure, easy implementation of the algorithm, and has a small number of parameters. Although the number of iterations and population are sometimes large, strong exploitation ability, and concentration around the optimum solution are provided by the effect of leader wolves. General adaptability can be easily adapted to continuous, discrete, multiobjective, and constrained optimization problems. Parameter tuning requirement is low, and hyperparameter sensitivity is low compared to many other algorithms.

In addition to these advantages of GWO, there are also limitations, such as getting stuck in local minima [10] and losing diversity [11]. Getting stuck in local minima may tend to converge early in the exploitation phase, especially in complex search spaces. Loss of diversity may reduce the population diversity as the iterations progress.

6.2.4 Enhanced and hybrid versions

To enhance the performance of the GWO, numerous improvements have been proposed in recent studies. For instance, Hou et al. [12] introduced an enhanced version that emphasizes algorithmic efficiency and robustness. Similarly, Gao and Zhao [13] developed a GWO variant with variable weights to achieve an adaptive balance between exploration and exploitation. In another study, Salgotra et al. [14] suggested improvements aimed at accelerating convergence and increasing solution diversity. Furthermore, Seyyedabbasi and Kiani [15] presented the I-GWO and Ex-GWO algorithms, which effectively address global optimization challenges. Practical applications have also been explored; for example, Liu et al. [16] applied an improved GWO to path planning tasks, demonstrating its effectiveness in real-world scenarios. Additionally, Wang and Li [17] integrated differential evolution with GWO, thereby strengthening both its exploration and exploitation capabilities. Hybrid versions of the Grey Wolf Optimizer have been developed to improve optimization performance and applicability. An improved hybrid GWO focusing on accuracy and convergence speed was proposed [18]. A hybrid method combining PSO with GWO enhanced convergence characteristics [19]. Binary hybrid GWO models have been effectively employed for feature selection problems [18]. The integration of GWO with the crow search algorithm resulted in a hybrid approach improving unconstrained function optimization [20]. Another hybrid strategy combining binary optimization techniques with GWO showed promising results in feature selection tasks [21]. These works generally include parameter tuning [22], hybrid algorithms [18], chaotic maps [18], multiobjective [23], and binary GWO [24] approaches. Parameter tuning is done by nonlinear or adaptive parameter strategies and the coefficients $\vec{A}$ and $\vec{C}$ are controlled more effectively. In hybrid algorithms, GWO is combined with other algorithms, such as PSO-GWO combined with PSO [25], GA-GWO combined with GA [26], ABC-GWO combined with ABC algorithm [26], A Hybrid GWO and Differential Evolution (HGWODE) combined with differential evolution algorithm [27], GWO-GOA combined with Grasshopper Optimization Algorithm [28] to improve both exploration and exploitation capacity. Chaotic maps are used to increase the solution diversity by using chaotic dynamics in the initial population or parameter updates. Multiobjective and discrete GWO versions, where multiple objectives are optimized, or discrete decision variables are present, have been developed. These versions aim to overcome the limitations of GWO and provide higher accuracy, faster convergence, and better overall performance.

6.3 Bibliometric analysis method

The methodological approach used in the analysis of scientific productivity for the GWO algorithm is explained. In the study, the bibliometric analysis method was preferred to visualize the general trends, collaboration networks, most influential authors, journals, countries, and basic research themes of the research on GWO. The bibliometric analysis method is a method that aims to draw attention by revealing the developments, innovations, and trends in the field of research by examining the years, citations, journals, institutions, and the connection strength between the authors in the scientific literature. This type of analysis is frequently used to measure the scientific productivity of the authors, the impact of the researched topic, and research trends [29]. Bibliometric analysis is performed on various indicators such as the number of published articles, citation counts, journal impact factors, and author collaborations [30]. In addition, this method provides valuable information to identify gaps and potential future directions in research areas [31]. Modern bibliometric analyses are performed more precisely and comprehensively with the help of databases and software tools [32].

6.3.1 Database used

In the bibliometric analysis, the WoS database, which indexes the most prestigious scientific publications worldwide, was used. WoS was preferred because it has a wide interdisciplinary scope, presents citation data with high reliability, and provides output in data formats suitable for bibliometric analysis. Within the scope of the research, bibliometric analysis was performed with VOSviewer software using data obtained from the WoS database.

6.3.2 Search criteria and publication year range

The search conducted in the WoS database aimed to cover all academic studies related to the GWO algorithm. In this context, the following keywords were used.

- "Grey Wolf Optimizer"
- "GWO"
- "Grey Wolf Optimization"

The search process was carried out as of May 2025, and the starting year was determined as 2014, when the algorithm was first presented in the literature. Therefore the analysis covers the 11-year and 5-month period between 2014 and 2025. This time period provides a sufficient perspective to evaluate the development trend and scientific impact of the algorithm.

During the data cleaning stage, initially, duplicate records obtained from the WoS database using the selected keywords were automatically filtered and removed from the dataset. Irrelevant studies were identified and excluded through manual screening based on titles, abstracts, and keywords, focusing on works that were unrelated or could not be associated with the GWO algorithm. Inconsistent keywords (such as variations in spelling, synonyms, singular-plural forms, and abbreviations) were standardized by employing integrated keyword harmonization tools within VOSviewer and other bibliometric management software. All terms were unified prior to analysis, thereby preventing multiple counts, off-topic results, and keyword inconsistency errors in the quantitative evaluation.

A systematic literature search was conducted using predefined keywords ("Grey Wolf Optimizer," "GWO," "Grey Wolf Optimization") in the WoS database covering the period from 2014 to 2025. Inclusion and exclusion criteria were applied to select relevant and original research articles. Duplicate records, irrelevant studies, and inconsistent keywords were filtered out during the data cleaning process. This structured approach ensured a reliable and reproducible bibliometric dataset for analysis.

6.3.3 Analysis tools used

VOSviewer, an open-source software, was used for data visualization and analysis of bibliometric relationships. VOSviewer is particularly effective in visually analyzing components such as citation networks, keyword clusters, interinstitutional collaborations, author impact, and country contributions among scientific publications. Author collaboration network, institutional collaborations, country and region contributions, keyword cofrequency analysis, most cited publications and authors, time series analysis (publication distribution by year), and other types of analysis were performed with VOSviewer. Thanks to this methodological approach, the structural features of the literature related to the GWO algorithm were evaluated in a holistic manner, and the scientific impact of the algorithm was revealed with objective data.

6.4 Data analysis

Within the scope of the research conducted, the distribution of WoS categories, the distribution of publications over the years, the distribution of document types of publications, the distribution of Web of Since index, the distribution of research profiles, the distribution of publication titles according to research categories, the distribution of country publications, the distribution of publishers of publications, the distribution of research fields in which publications are made, the distribution of citation topics of publications meso, the distribution of citation topics of publications micro, the distribution of publication languages of publications, the analysis of researchers working with coauthors, the analysis of institutions with coauthors, the analysis of countries with coauthors, the analysis of citations of publications based on published works, the connection between citations in published sources, the citation analysis of authors who published, the citation analysis of countries, the citation analysis of institutions, the keyword analysis concurrency, the author keyword analysis were included.

6.4.1 Distribution of Web of Science categories

Fig. 6.1 shows the distribution of publications by WoS category.

When the distribution of publications given in Fig. 6.1 according to WoS categories is examined, it is seen that the categories of "Engineering Electrical Electronic" (2181 publications) and "Computer Science Artificial Intelligence" (1417 publications) are in the lead. This situation reveals that GWO and similar metaheuristic algorithms are used intensively, especially in electronic engineering and artificial intelligence (AI)-based applications. In addition, the high number of publications in the categories of "Computer Science Information Systems" (1086), "Energy Fuels" (976), and "Telecommunications" (822) shows that these algorithms spread to a wide range of applications from energy systems to communication technologies. The strong presence in interdisciplinary areas such as "Engineering Multidisciplinary" (749) and "Computer Science Interdisciplinary Applications" (725) can be explained by the flexible structure of GWO and its ability to easily adapt to different engineering problems. In addition, GWO is also understood to be a preferred method in optimization and control-oriented fields such as "Operations Research Management Science" (286) and "Automation Control Systems" (414). This general distribution clearly reflects the interdisciplinary versatility of GWO and its strategic importance in the fields of engineering and informatics.

6.4.2 Distribution of publications over the years

Fig. 6.2 shows the distribution of publications over the years.

When the distribution of publications by year of GWO and related studies given in Fig. 6.2 is examined, it is seen that the academic interest, which started with only five publications in 2014, increased significantly, especially after 2020. The fact that 1599 publications were produced in 2024, 1387 in 2023, 1395 in 2022, and 648 in the first months of 2025 reveals the current popularity of GWO and its increasing adoption by the research community. This increase reflects the successful applicability of the algorithm to different fields, its open source nature, and its ability to be continuously developed with new variants. The increasing orientation toward digitalization and AI applications, especially after the pandemic, can be considered as one of the main factors supporting the acceleration in the number of publications as of 2021. In this context, it can be predicted that research on GWO will continue at a high pace in the coming years.

6.4.3 Document type distribution of publications

Table 6.1 shows the distribution of publications according to document types.

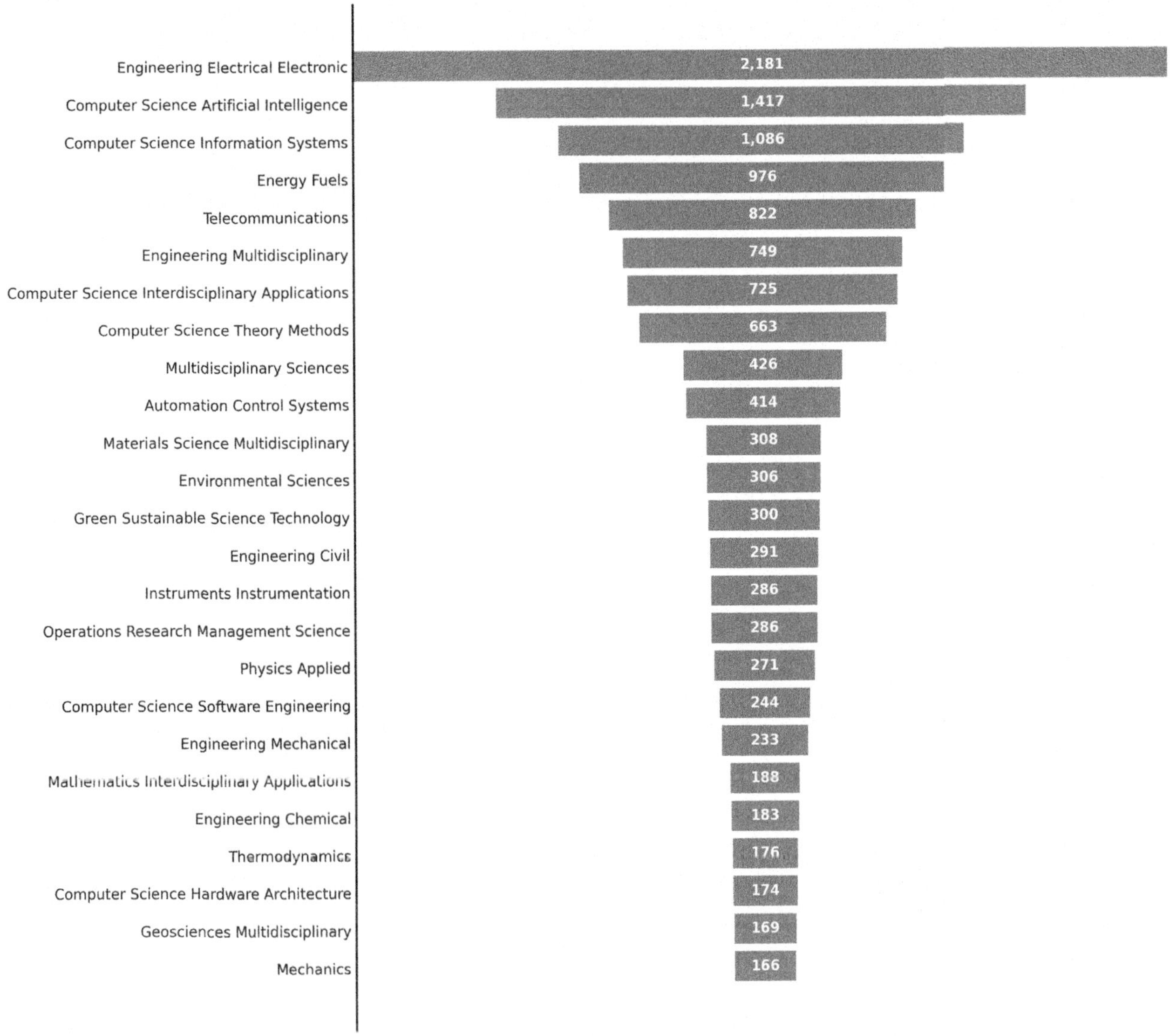

FIGURE 6.1 WoS category distribution of publications (*WoS*, Web of Science).

When Table 6.1 is examined, it is seen that the vast majority of the total 8149 publications on GWO are research articles (86.89%, 7081 publications). This situation shows that GWO is heavily preferred in applied studies as well as its theoretical foundations. Proceedings paper publications are in second place with 11.90% (970 publications) and reveal that the subject is widely accepted at the conference level. Early Access (2.57%) and Review Article (1.17%) rates show that the subject is still up-to-date and that systematic literature reviews are limited. Rare types such as Retracted Publication (0.48%), Correction (0.15%), and Retraction (0.07%) have very low rates in the total. In general, this distribution shows that the publications on GWO are largely original scientific contributions and that this algorithm is highly adopted by the research community.

6.4.4 Web of Science index distributions

Table 6.2 shows the WoS index distributions of the publications.

When Table 6.2 is examined, it is seen that the majority of the publications related to GWO are included in the Science Citation Index Expanded and constitute 75.33% of the total with 6139 publications. This situation shows that GWO is

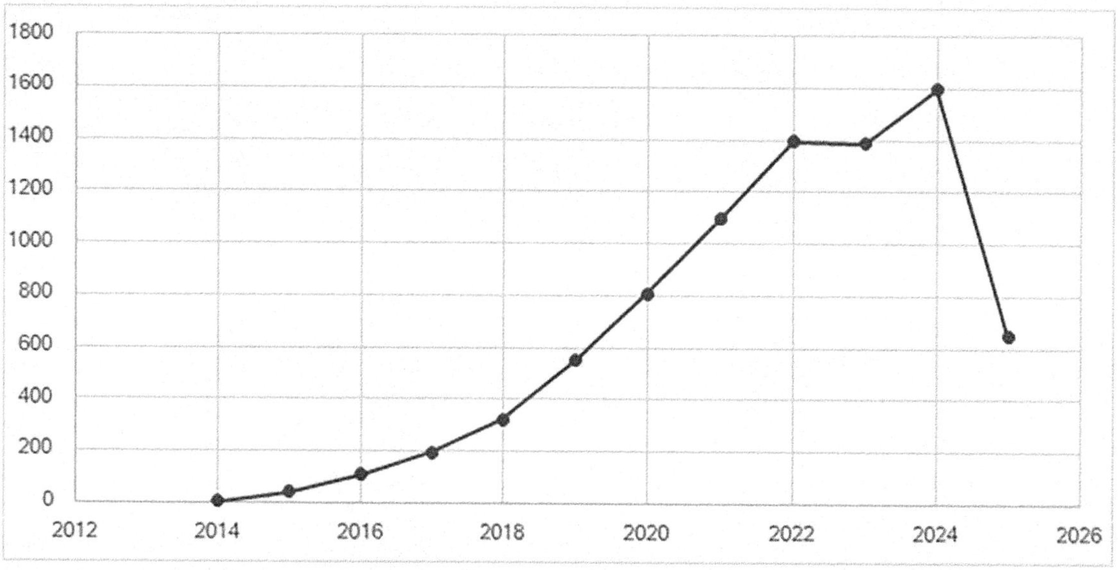

FIGURE 6.2 Distribution of publications over the years.

TABLE 6.1 Document type distribution of publications.

Document types	Publication count	% of 8.149
Article	7081	86.89%
Proceeding paper	970	11.90%
Early access	209	2.57%
Review article	95	1.17%
Retracted publication	39	0.48%
Book chapters	33	0.41%
Correction	12	0.15%
Retraction	6	0.07%
Editorial material	5	0.06%
Letter	2	0.03%
Meeting abstract	2	0.03%

widely discussed in high-impact and refereed journals. 995 publications (12.21%) included in the Emerging Sources Citation Index reveal that studies in this field are also increasing in emerging journals and that new sources contribute. Conference proceedings have a share of approximately 12% in both the Conference Proceedings Citation Index – Science (969 publications, 11.89%) and Conference Proceedings Citation Index – Social Science & Humanities (11 publications, 0.14%). This rate indicates that the GWO algorithm is frequently presented in academic meetings and scientific congresses. There are limited studies in the social sciences and humanities: SSCI (2.18%) and Arts & Humanities Citation IndexI (0.04%). This confirms that GWO is still largely used in engineering, science, and computer science.

TABLE 6.2 WoS index distribution of publications.

Web of science index	Publication count	% of 8.149
Science Citation Index Expanded (SCI-EXPANDED)	6139	75.33%
Emerging Sources Citation Index (ESCI)	995	12.21%
Conference Proceedings Citation Index – Science (CPCI-S)	969	11.89%
Social Sciences Citation Index (SSCI)	178	2.18%
Book Citation Index – Science (BKCI-S)	33	0.41%
Conference Proceedings Citation Index – Social Science & Humanities (CPCI-SSH)	11	0.14%
Arts & Humanities Citation Index (A&HCI)	3	0.04%

6.4.5 Research profiles

Fig. 6.3 presents information on the research profiles of publications.

When Fig. 6.3 is examined, it is seen that Seyedali Mirjalili is the founder and most productive author of GWO with 99 publications. He is also the lead author of the most cited articles in this field. He plays a leading role in the development process of GWO. Names such as Kamel, Salah, Houssein, Essam Halim, Abualigah, and Laith carry out important research in the field by contributing to GWO's derivative algorithms and applied studies. Names such as Heidari, Ali Asghar, El-Kenawy, and El-Sayed M. are known for their joint work with Mirjalili and contribute to the combination of meta-heuristic algorithms with hybrid approaches. One of the prominent researchers from Turkey is Kisi, Özgür, who contributes to GWO's applications on engineering problems.

6.4.6 Distribution of publications by research category

Fig. 6.4 shows the distribution of publications according to research categories.

When the distribution of publications in Fig. 6.4 according to research categories is examined, it is seen that the fields of Engineering (48.2%) and Computer Science (37.8%) constitute the vast majority of the total publications. This shows that GWO is intensively used in engineering optimization and AI applications, which is its initial purpose. Energy and Fuels (976 publications) shows that GWO is quite popular, especially in areas such as optimization of renewable energy systems, load estimation, and hybrid energy management. In fields such as telecommunications (822) and automation and control systems (414), GWO is frequently preferred, especially in tasks such as network optimization, parameter adjustments, and robot control. In the fields of mathematics (397) and physics (332), the theoretical foundations of GWO, function optimization, and its use in dynamic systems come to the fore. In fields such as environmental sciences and ecology, water resources, and geology, GWO is also used in environmental-based engineering problems, such as data analysis, modeling, and resource allocation. The fact that GWO is used in many new and applied disciplines such as robotics, image processing, remote sensing, and transportation reveals the versatility of the algorithm.

6.4.7 Country distribution of publications

Table 6.3 shows the country distribution of publications.

When Table 6.3 is examined, it is seen that the vast majority of publications originate from China and India. Together, these two countries produced approximately 64% of all publications. This situation can be explained by the density of academic outputs in these countries, the high interest in AI and optimization algorithms, and the abundance of solutions to engineering problems. Countries such as Iran (9.13%), Egypt (8.05%), and Saudi Arabia (7.01%) are at the top of the world. This situation reflects regional research priorities, where optimization algorithms are used as a solution tool, especially in engineering, energy, and signal processing. Countries with advanced research infrastructures, such as the USA (3.72%), the UK (2.26%), and France (1.42%), produced fewer publications on GWO. This may be due to more original algorithm development or different approach preferences in these countries (e.g., deep learning-based solutions or

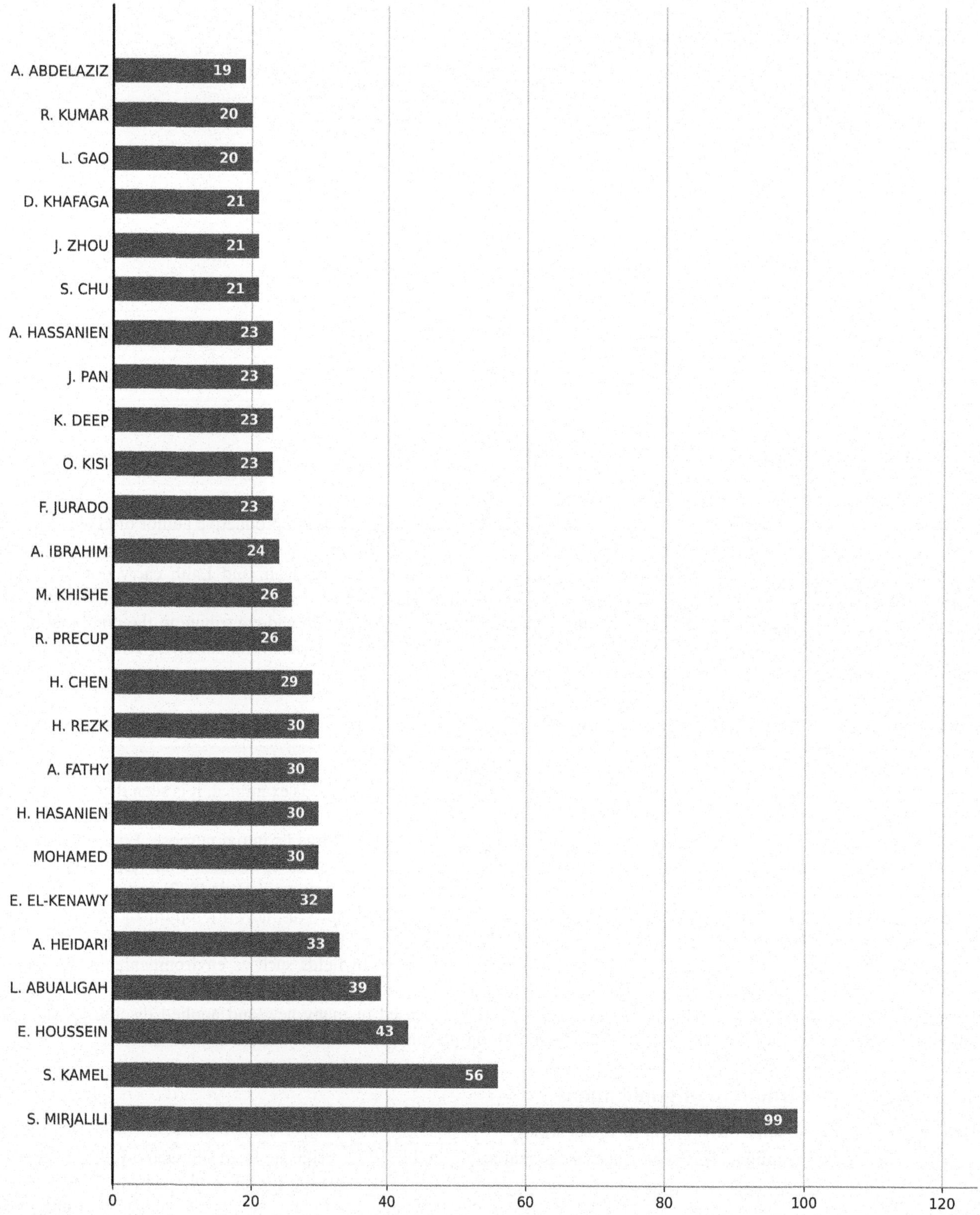

FIGURE 6.3 Distributions of research profiles of publications.

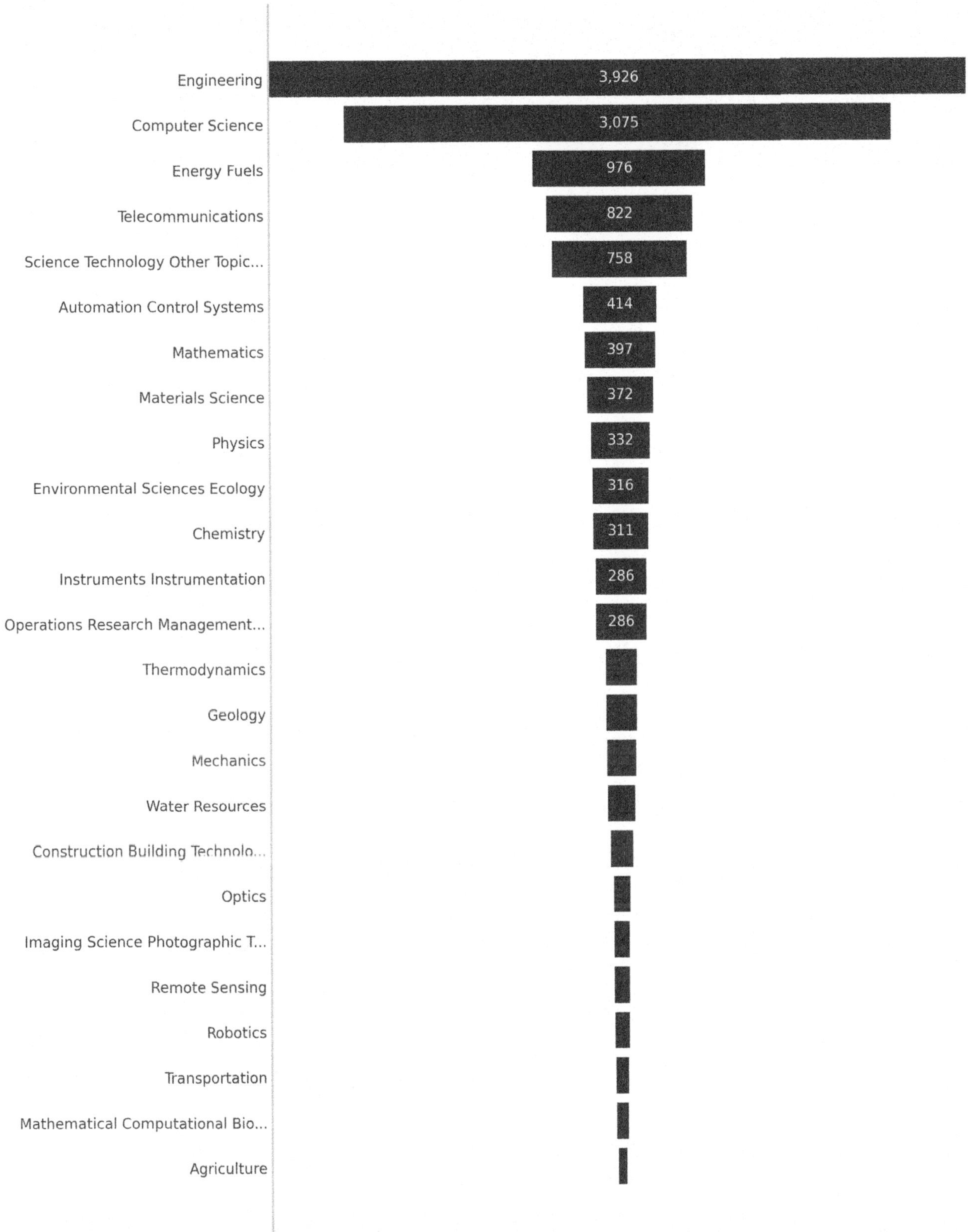

FIGURE 6.4 Distribution of publications by research category.

TABLE 6.3 Country distribution of publications.

Countries/Regions	Publication count	% of 8.149
People's R China	2876	35.29%
India	2325	28.53%
Iran	744	9.13%
Egypt	656	8.05%
Saudi Arabia	571	7.01%
Turkey	361	4.43%
Australia	304	3.73%
USA	303	3.72%
Malaysia	257	3.15%
Algeria	236	2.90%
South Korea	234	2.87%
Jordan	201	2.47%
Pakistan	192	2.36%
England	184	2.26%
Iraq	171	2.10%
Canada	163	2.00%
Vietnam	155	1.90%
U Arab Emirates	144	1.77%
Taiwan	130	1.60%
France	116	1.42%
Spain	110	1.35%
Poland	78	0.96%
Mexico	77	0.95%
Morocco	68	0.83%

hybrid approaches). It is seen that Turkey contributed 4.43% to this field with a total of 361 publications. Turkey is among the top-ranked countries in this respect and plays an important role regionally. The list includes not only developed countries but also developing countries such as Malaysia, Algeria, Jordan, Pakistan, Vietnam, etc. This has enabled GWO to be adopted by a wide global research audience due to its ease of application, rapid results, and cross-disciplinary usability.

6.4.8 Publisher distribution of publications

Table 6.4 presents data on the distribution of publications by publisher.

When Table 6.4 is examined, it is seen that the top three publishers made 57.24% of the Publications. Almost a quarter of the studies conducted with the GWO algorithm (24.13%) were published in Elsevier journals. This shows that the algorithm is widely preferred in Elsevier journals, compatible with its applications in engineering, computer science, and energy fields. Springer Nature and IEEE (15.23%) are directly related to the use of GWO in optimization, AI, and control systems. Springer conferences, Lecture Notes in Computer Science (LNCS) book series, and high-impact-factor journals

TABLE 6.4 Publisher distribution of publications.

Publishers	Publication count	% of 8.149
Elsevier	1966	24.13%
Springer Nature	1457	17.88%
Institute of Electrical and Electronics Engineers (IEEE)	1241	15.23%
Mdpi	967	11.87%
Wiley	297	3.65%
Taylor & Francis	278	3.41%
Nature Portfolio	181	2.22%
Hindawi Publishing Group	112	1.37%
Sage	95	1.17%
Tech Science Press	89	1.09%
World Scientific	81	0.99%
Ios Press	60	0.74%
Emerald Group Publishing	59	0.72%
Iop Publishing Ltd.	59	0.72%
Public Library Science	56	0.69%
Inst Engineering Technology-Iet	55	0.68%
Wiley-Hindawi	49	0.60%
Frontiers Media Sa	46	0.56%
Inderscience Enterprises Ltd.	44	0.54%
Science & Information Sai Organization Ltd.	42	0.52%
Igi Global	39	0.48%
Springer Int Publ Ag	35	0.43%
Walter De Gruyter	29	0.36%
Assoc Computing Machinery	21	0.26%
Techno-Press	21	0.26%

such as IEEE Transactions are leading in this field. Multidisciplinary Digital Publishing Institute (MDPI), which has an open-access publication policy, has become quite popular for algorithmic research in recent years. 11.87% of GWO publications were published in MDPI. MDPI journals such as Algorithms, Applied Sciences, and Sensors frequently include GWO research. Other publishers (Wiley, Taylor & Francis, Nature Portfolio) generally publish high-quality journals, although their publication numbers are lower. Therefore the quality and citation potential of GWO studies in these publications are generally higher. In terms of Open Access Publishers and Alternative Publishers, Hindawi, Tech Science Press, Frontiers, IGI Global, and SAI are widely preferred by researchers. Because the rapid publication of articles and easy access have increased the attractiveness of these journals.

6.4.9 Meso distribution of publications' citation topics

Table 6.5 analyzes the distribution of 8149 publications related to the GWO algorithm according to citation topics (meso level). This analysis shows the thematic areas where GWO is most frequently applied and the prevalence rates in these areas.

TABLE 6.5 Meso distribution of publications' citation topics.

Citation topics meso	Publication count	% of 8.149
Power Systems & Electric Vehicles	1869	22.94%
Supply Chain & Logistics	1696	20.81%
Telecommunications	438	5.38%
Artificial Intelligence & Machine Learning	340	4.17%
Automation & Control Systems	287	3.52%
Geotechnical Engineering	213	2.61%
Computer Vision & Graphics	161	1.98%
Friction & Vibration	144	1.77%
Distributed & Real Time Computing	139	1.71%
Electrochemistry	115	1.41%
Thermodynamics	109	1.34%
Testing & Maintenance	104	1.28%
Wireless Technology	99	1.22%
Oceanography, Meteorology & Atmospheric Sciences	94	1.15%
Security, Encryption & Encoding	88	1.08%
Concrete Science	82	1.01%
Knowledge Engineering & Representation	76	0.93%
Manufacturing	76	0.93%
Design & Manufacturing	62	0.76%
Water Resources	62	0.76%
Robotics	60	0.74%
Security Systems	51	0.63%
Chemometrics	50	0.61%
Remote Sensing	50	0.61%
Sustainability Science	50	0.61%

When the data presented in Table 6.5 is examined in terms of Energy and Supply Chain Oriented Applications (43.75%), Power Systems & Electric Vehicles (22.94%), and Supply Chain & Logistics (20.81%) are the areas where GWO is most intensively used. GWO is widely used in solving complex optimization problems in these areas. Examples are: Electricity production planning, Optimization of renewable energy systems, Vehicle route planning, and inventory management. Areas such as Information Technologies and AI (15.28%), AI & ML (4.17%), Telecom (5.38%), Distributed Computing (1.71%), and Computer Vision (1.98%) are included in this scope. It is understood that GWO is preferred for parameter optimization in subjects such as neural network training, clustering, classification, and visual data processing. Automation, Control and Engineering Based Fields, Automation & Control Systems, Robotics, Testing & Maintenance, Thermodynamics, Friction & Vibration, etc., show the flexibility of GWO in engineering applications. Security, Encryption, and Information Systems also find a place in tasks such as parameter adjustment of security systems, optimization of encryption algorithms, and intrusion detection (%~2.0). New and Emerging Fields, Sustainability Science,

TABLE 6.6 Citation topics of publications are micro.

Citation topics micro	Publication count	% of 8.149
Particle swarm optimization	1484	18.21%
Energy forecasting	405	4.97%
Smart grid optimization	393	4.82%
Photovoltaic systems	333	4.09%
Power system stability	291	3.57%
Wireless sensor networks	230	2.82%
Multiagent systems	132	1.62%
Rotating machinery diagnostics	127	1.56%
Cloud resource scheduling	111	1.36%
Intrusion detection	106	1.30%
Power quality	105	1.29%
Manufacturing scheduling	103	1.26%
Electric vehicles	97	1.19%
Doubly fed induction generator	93	1.14%
Adaptive control	93	1.14%
Classification algorithms	89	1.09%
Hydroclimatic modeling	88	1.08%
Rock mechanics	79	0.97%
IoT and edge computing	77	0.95%
Energy systems optimization	73	0.90%
Landslide dynamics	68	0.83%
Electric motor control	63	0.77%
Lithium-ion battery	62	0.76%
Advanced machining	60	0.74%
Advanced concrete	59	0.72%

Remote Sensing, Chemometrics, etc. Although the publication rate is low in these fields, these fields show the interdisciplinary impact potential of GWO.

6.4.10 Citation issues of publications at the micro level

Table 6.6 presents the distribution of 8149 publications on the GWO algorithm according to their citation topics at the micro level. This detailing is very valuable in terms of showing the specific problem areas and technological focuses to which GWO is applied.

When the data presented in Table 6.6 is examined, it is seen that PSO (18.21%) ranks first. For this reason, it can be said that the studies conducted with GWO are mostly compared with PSO. When the literature is examined, it is seen that comparisons made with metrics such as performance analysis, speed, accuracy, and adaptability are very common. Subfields such as Energy Systems and Renewable Energy (Total 18%+), Energy Forecasting (4.97%), Smart Grid

TABLE 6.7 Distribution of publications according to language.

Languages	Publication count	% of 8.149
English	8116	99.60%
Chinese	22	0.27%
Turkish	7	0.09%
Polish	2	0.03%
French	1	0.01%
Slovenian	1	0.01%

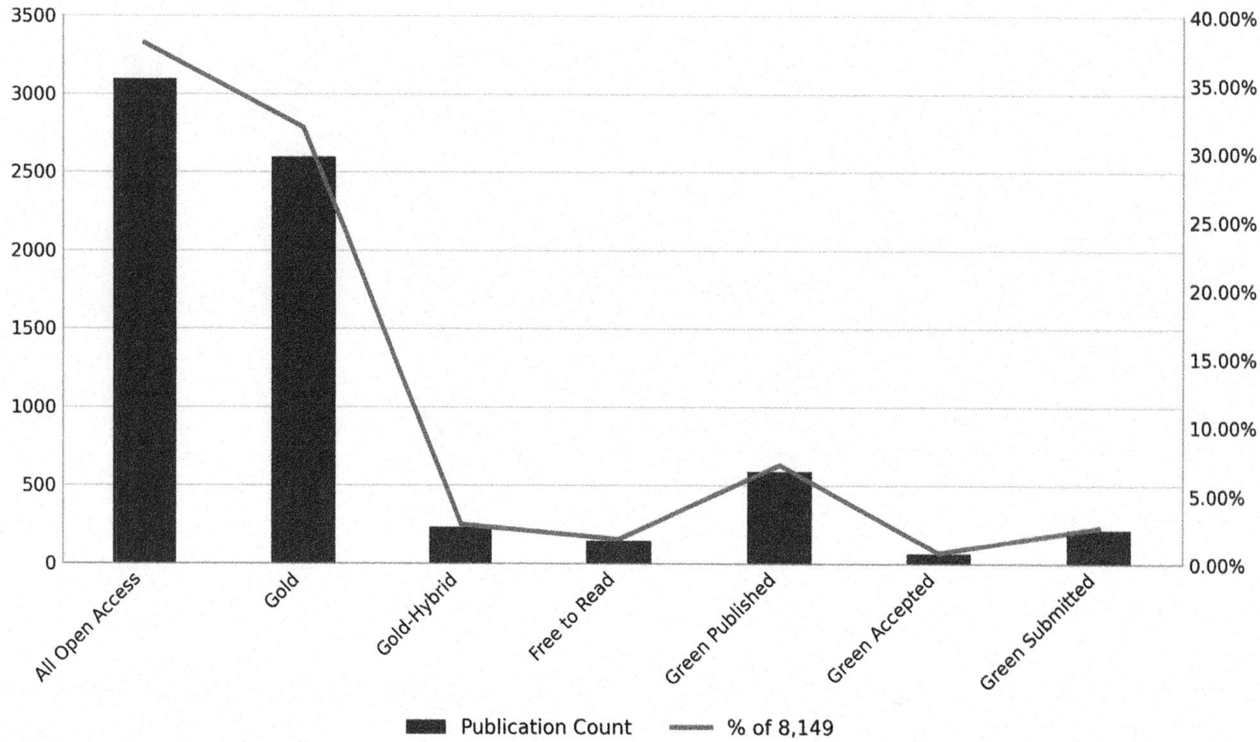

FIGURE 6.5 Open access distribution of publications.

Optimization (4.82%), Photovoltaic Systems (4.09%), Power System Stability (3.57%), Electric Vehicles (1.19%), Electric Motor Control (0.77%) stand out. GWO offers solutions to optimization problems such as load estimation, resource planning, energy management, and stability analysis in these applications. In areas such as Information and Security, Cloud Resource Scheduling (%1.36), Intrusion Detection (%1.30), Classification Algorithms (%1.09), Internet of Things (IoT) and Edge Computing (%0.95), GWO plays a role in resource allocation, attack detection, and tuning machine learning (ML) algorithms. In Advanced Engineering Problems, there are applications on problems such as Rotating Machinery Diagnostics, DFIG, Adaptive Control, Rock Mechanics, Landslide Dynamics, Advanced Machining, and Advanced Concrete. In these areas, GWO is used in special tasks such as system modeling, fault detection, and control parameter optimization. Emerging Applications. It can be said that the use of GWO is increasing in new or environmentally technology-focused areas, such as Lithium-ion Battery, Hydroclimatic Modeling, and Energy Systems Optimization.

TABLE 6.8 Distribution of publications by funding agencies.

Funding agencies	Publication count	% of 8.149
National Natural Science Foundation of China (NSFC)	1329	16.31%
National Key Research Development Program of China	149	1.83%
Fundamental Research Funds for the Central Universities	144	1.77%
King Saud University	85	1.04%
China Postdoctoral Science Foundation	68	0.83%
National Key R D Program of China	64	0.79%
National Research Foundation of Korea	59	0.72%
Natural Science Foundation of Shandong Province	48	0.59%
Natural Science Foundation of Jiangsu Province	46	0.56%
Princess Nourah Bint Abdulrahman University	43	0.53%
Egyptian Knowledge Bank (EKB)	42	0.52%
European Union (EU)	40	0.49%
Taif University	40	0.49%
Natural Sciences And Engineering Research Council of Canada (NSERC)	35	0.43%
Natural Science Foundation of Zhejiang Province	32	0.39%
Science and Technology Development Fund (STDF)	32	0.39%
China Scholarship Council	31	0.38%
Natural Science Foundation of Hubei Province	30	0.37%
Department of Science Technology, India	29	0.36%
Ministry of Science and Technology, Taiwan	28	0.34%
Natural Science Foundation of Hebei Province	28	0.34%
Natural Science Foundation of Hunan Province	28	0.34%
Conselho Nacional de Desenvolvimento Científico e Tecnológico (CNPQ)	26	0.32%
Ministry of Science ICT Future Planning Republic Of Korea	25	0.31%
Ministry of Science, ICT, MSIT, Republic of Korea	24	0.30%

6.4.11 Distribution of publications according to language

Table 6.7 presents 8149 publications related to the GWO algorithm according to language distribution.

When Table 6.7 is examined, it is seen that the vast majority of the studies are written in English. The overwhelming majority of the publications in English, 99.6%, indicating that the GWO algorithm is widely accepted in global academic literature and that researchers mostly contribute to international platforms. Although there are few publications in languages such as Chinese and Turkish, this also reveals that the algorithm is also known and examined in local literature. The presence of seven publications in Turkish in particular indicates that there are research conducted by local academics or universities.

6.4.12 Open access distribution of publications

Fig. 6.5 presents the distribution of a total of 8149 publications on the GWO algorithm according to their open access status.

TABLE 6.9 Distribution of institutions with group-authored publications.

Group author	Publication count
IEEE	578
Association for Computing Machinery (ACM)	18
Institute of Physics (IOP)	8
American Institute of Aeronautics and Astronautics (AIAA)	1
American Institute of Physics (AIP)	1

When Fig. 6.5 is examined, it is seen that approximately 38% of the publications related to the GWO algorithm are open access. This shows that a significant portion of researchers share their data openly. The gold open access (Gold OA) rate is quite high; this suggests that it is published in journals such as MDPI, Hindawi, and Frontiers. Green open access (Green OA) is an archiving format especially encouraged by universities or funding institutions. Eight hundred sixty-five studies published with this method are an important data source.

6.4.13 Funding institutions

Table 6.8 presents data on the distribution of funding institutions for publications.

When Table 6.8 is examined, the clear leadership of China-based funders (especially the National Natural Science Foundation of China [NSFC]) is striking. Six funders in the top 10 are of Chinese origin. Gulf country universities (Saudi Arabia), especially King Saud University and Princess Nourah University, have provided significant support in this area. International and regional funders such as the European Union and Natural Sciences And Engineering Research Council of Canada (NSERC) are also included in the list. Funding institutions from Turkey are not included in the list.

6.4.14 Distribution of institutions with group-authored publications

Group authorship information of a total of 8149 publications related to GWO is given in Table 6.9.

When Table 6.9 is examined, it is seen that IEEE is the institution with the highest number of group-authored publications. With a total of 578 publications (95.38%), it is the main carrier of almost all group-authored literature. This situation shows that GWO's applications in electrical-electronics, computer, and engineering fields are dominant and that it is supported by IEEE, the leading publishing house of these fields. In addition, IEEE's technical symposiums and conferences play a central role in the discussion of metaheuristic algorithms such as GWO. It is seen that the contribution of ACM, IOP, and other publishers is relatively limited. ACM (18 publications) makes contributions, especially in computer science and AI. IOP (eight publications) probably included GWO in studies focused on physics, engineering applications, and computational modeling. The fact that organizations such as AIAA and AIP have only one publication each suggests that this algorithm has not yet become widespread in specialized fields such as aviation or physics.

6.4.15 Publications on sustainable development goals

The sustainable development goals of the publications are given in Table 6.10.

When Table 6.10 is examined, it is seen that there are 1909 publications (23.43%) in line with the Affordable and Clean Energy target. The GWO algorithm has been included in the studies related to this target the most. GWO is frequently used for the optimization of energy production, distribution, and consumption. It is especially used in areas such as renewable energy systems: solar, wind, and grid balancing. This clearly shows how effective a solution GWO offers in terms of the sustainability of energy systems. There are 997 publications (12.24%) in line with the Sustainable Cities and Communities target. We see that GWO is applied in areas such as urban planning, transportation systems, and energy management. The role of metaheuristic algorithms is growing in smart city technologies (e.g., traffic optimization, energy consumption, resource management). Five hundred ninety-two publications (7.27%) have been made in line with the health and well-being target. This is quite remarkable. GWO has been used in solving health-related problems. These problems may be in areas such as medical diagnosis, biomedical signal processing, and AI-supported health systems.

TABLE 6.10 Distribution of publications on sustainable development goals.

Sustainable development goals	Publication count	% of 8.149
Affordable and clean energy	1909	23.43%
Sustainable cities and communities	997	12.24%
Good health and well being	592	7.27%
Climate action	491	6.03%
Responsible consumption and production	324	3.98%
Clean water and sanitation	248	3.04%
Industry innovation and infrastructure	215	2.64%
Life below water	156	1.91%
Zero hunger	94	1.15%
Life on land	71	0.87%
Decent work and economic growth	45	0.55%
Partnerships for the goals	27	0.33%
Gender equality	22	0.27%
Quality education	11	0.14%
Reduced inequality	3	0.04%
No poverty	1	0.01%

There are 491 publications (6.03%) for the climate action target. The use of GWO is increasing in areas such as climate modeling, carbon emission estimation, and energy efficiency. The effectiveness of GWO in the field of estimation and control supports this contribution. There are three publications (0.04%) for the reduction of inequalities target and one publication (0.01%) for the no poverty target. It is seen that GWO is not used much in subjects directly related to social sciences or economic inequalities. The main reason for this may be that the algorithm is more suitable for technical applications based on direct numerical optimization. Eleven publications (0.14%) have been made for the Quality Education target. GWO's contribution to decision-making processes in educational technologies is small, but its potential is high. Topics such as estimating student success, creating an exam schedule, and resource planning may come to the fore in the future.

6.4.16 Coauthorship analysis: most active authors

Fig. 6.6 presents the network visualization graph for coauthorship analysis.

When Fig. 6.6 is examined, it is seen that a strong collaboration network has been formed in the studies on GWO. Among the first 10 authors, Seyedali Mirjalili stands out as the most productive and highest impact researcher with 95 publications and 27,924 citations. He is also the leader in terms of total link strength (TLS) (TLS=194). Following him, researchers such as Essam H. Houssein (42 publications, 2413 citations, TLS: 105), Laith Abualigah (37 publications, 2873 citations, TLS: 97), Huiling Chen (37 publications, 2445 citations, TLS: 81), and Ali Asghar Heidari (33 publications, 3075 citations, TLS: 87) maintain their active positions in the literature with both their publication productivity and high link strength. Hossam Faris (17 publications, 2812 citations, TLS: 43), Ibrahim Aljarah (16 publications, 2654 citations, TLS: 40), Amir H. Gandomi (13 publications, 2366 citations, TLS: 18), and Bo Yang (28 publications, 1632 citations, TLS: 43) are among the other important names that stand out in the collaborative studies on GWO. Especially, Seyed Mohammad Mirjalili, one of the founding researchers, has made a striking academic impact with 16,425 citations despite being included in only seven publications. This shows that basic methodological studies

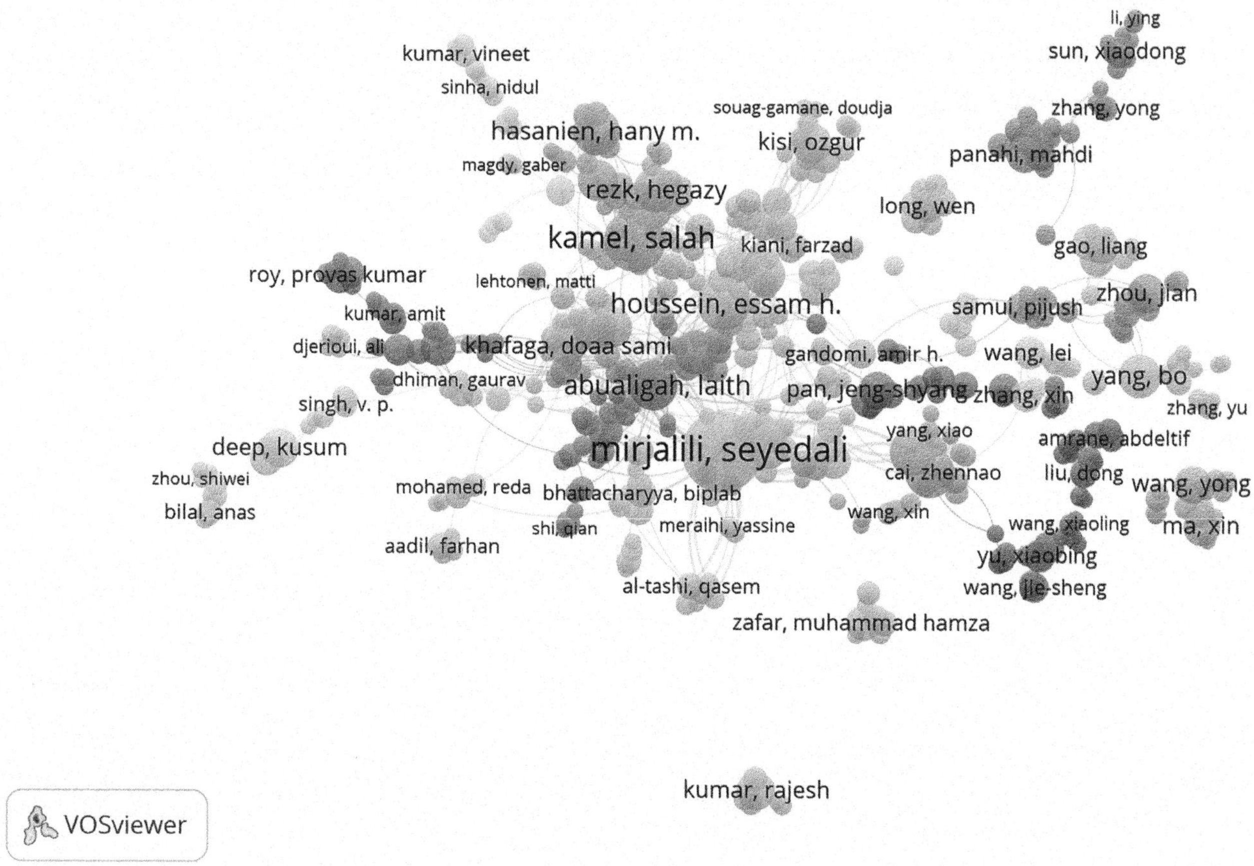

FIGURE 6.6 Coauthorship analysis.

contribute to high citation value in the long term. In general, these authors are considered leading researchers who have guided the development of GWO and made deep contributions to the literature.

6.4.17 Evaluation of the most cited organizations

Fig. 6.7 presents the network visualization graph for the most cited organizations.

According to the bibliometric analysis results presented in Fig. 6.7, among the institutions with the highest number of citations in publications in the field of GWO algorithm, Griffith University (28 publications, 20,606 citations) and Shahid Beheshti University (18 publications, 12,500 citations) stand out. Despite their relatively small number of publications, these two institutions show that they have made methodological and foundational contributions to the GWO literature with their very high citation numbers. Islamic Azad University (232 publications, 9959 citations), which is the leader in terms of the number of publications, has created a high impact in terms of both productivity and TLS (307). Similarly, Zagazig University (99 publications, 6235 citations, TLS: 267) and Torrens University Australia (69 publications, 7546 citations, TLS: 240) have also played central roles in the literature with their high productivity and network strength. Duy Tan University (59 publications, 3390 citations) and Mansoura University (103 publications, 3255 citations) have a high number of publications but have a moderate impact in terms of citation/publication ratio. University of Tehran (91 publications, 4706 citations) and Yonsei University (50 publications, 4612 citations) have a balanced impact in terms of both productivity and citation levels. Finally, the University of Jordan (34 publications, 3298 citations) is one of the active and influential institutions in the field in terms of both TLS and citations. These data show that there are both institutions with a small number of publications that provide pioneering methodological contributions in GWO research and productive institutions that carry out high-volume applied research.

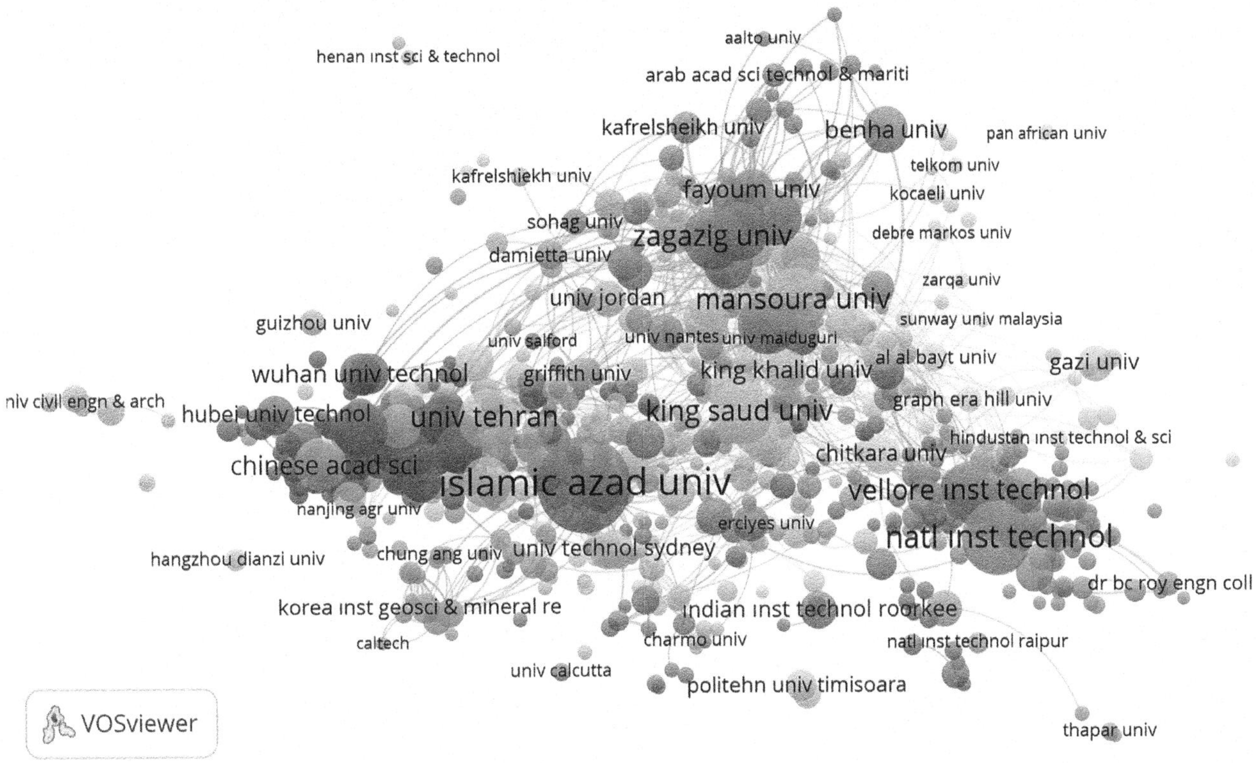

FIGURE 6.7 Most cited organizations.

6.4.18 Linkage analysis of countries among the most cited coauthored publications

Fig. 6.8 shows the link analysis of countries among the most cited coauthored publications.

In the evaluation made according to the number of citations, China (People's Republic of China) is the clear leader in the GWO literature with 2876 publications and 52,015 citations. China's high publication volume shows that the country shows great interest in research in this field and makes a significant contribution to the global academic impact. India, which is in second place, comes after China in terms of productivity with 2325 publications and 33,355 citations, but lags behind in terms of impact per citation. Iran, although less productive with 744 publications, surpasses India with 36,274 citations, indicating that it makes a qualified contribution. Australia (304 publications, 35,215 citations) draws attention with its high citation average; this situation indicates that the country leads the literature with its methodological contributions. Similarly, the USA (303 publications, 10,454 citations) and South Korea (234 publications, 9203 citations) exhibit balanced publication and citation performance. Saudi Arabia (571 publications, 10,191 citations) and Egypt (656 publications, 20,018 citations) have strong impact areas in terms of both productivity and total linkage power. Malaysia (257 publications, 6452 citations) and Jordan (201 publications, 8257 citations) have played important roles, especially in collaborative networks. Turkey (361 publications, 6563 citations) is one of the important countries in the field, although it has a relatively lower number of publications. These findings show that GWO research is largely driven by countries in the Asian continent, with countries such as China, India, and Iran standing out in terms of research productivity and citation impact.

6.4.19 Citation analysis of publications based on the work produced

The results for the most cited publications are given in Table 6.11.

When Table 6.11 is examined, the most cited publication among the studies on the GWO algorithm is the article titled "Grey Wolf Optimizer," in which the algorithm is introduced in its original form [3]. This study, published by Mirjalili, S; Mirjalili, SM, and Lewis, A (2014), was published in the journal Advances in Engineering Software and has reached a leading position in the literature by receiving 12,174 citations to date. This study is followed by a different nature-inspired method, "Multi-Verse Optimizer: a nature-inspired algorithm for global optimization" (2016, Neural Computing & Applications), developed by Mirjalili, S; Mirjalili, SM, and Hatamlou, A (2015), with 2766 citations [33]. Following this, the article titled "A novel swarm intelligence optimization approach: sparrow search algorithm" by Xue, JK, and Shen, B

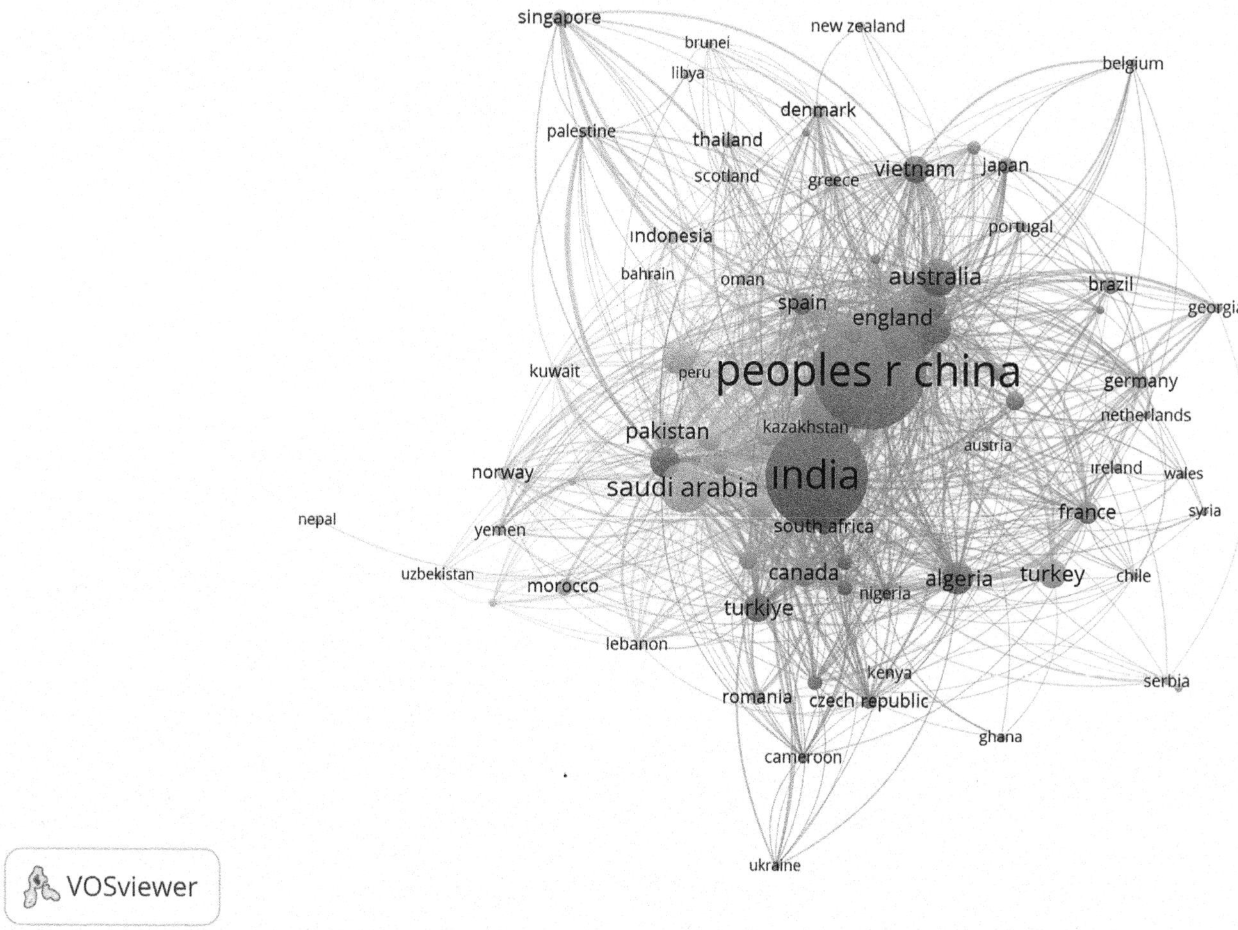

FIGURE 6.8 Countries' linkage among the most cited coauthored publications.

(2020) was published in the Journal of Systems Science & Control Engineering and created a remarkable impact by receiving 2105 citations [34]. Another high-impact publication is the study titled "The Arithmetic Optimization Algorithm" by Abualigah, L, Diabat, A, Mirjalili, S., and Gandomi, AH (2021) [35]. This article, published in the Journal of Computer Methods in Applied Mechanics and Engineering, received 1898 citations. The article titled "Equilibrium Optimizer" by Faramarzi, A; Heidarinejad, M; Stephens, B, and Mirjalili, S, which proposes a new optimization method, stood out with 1597 citations [36], while the article titled "Equilibrium Optimizer" by Faramarzi, A; Heidarinejad, M; Stephens, B, and Mirjalili, S., which is an adaptation of GWO to multiobjective optimization problems and was published by Mirjalili, S; Saremi, S; The work titled "Multi-objective grey wolf optimizer: A novel algorithm for multi-criterion optimization" (2016, Expert Systems with Applications) developed by Mirjalili, SM; Coelho, LD has received 1188 citations [23]. The work titled "Binary grey wolf optimization approaches for feature selection" by Emary, E, Zawba, HM, and Hassanien, AE (2016) has received 986 citations [24], and the work titled "Henry gas solubility optimization: A novel physics-based algorithm" proposed by Hashim, FA, Houssein, EH, and Mirjalili, S (2019) has received 782 citations [37]. The work titled "An improved grey wolf optimizer for solving engineering problems," which presents an improved version of GWO, was published by Nadimi-Shahraki, MH; Taghian, S, and Mirjalili, S (2021) and has received 695 citations [38]. Finally, the study titled "Grey wolf optimizer: a review of recent variants and applications," which conducted a systematic review of the algorithm, was published by Faris, H., Aljarah, I., Al-Betar, M. A., and Mirjalili, S. (2018) and received 600 citations [39]. These publications clearly show that the GWO algorithm has attracted intense interest in both theoretical and applied fields and has been widely adopted among researchers.

TABLE 6.11 Citation distribution of publications based on the work published.

Yayın Adı	Yazar(lar)	Yıl	Dergi	Atıf Sayısı
Grey wolf optimizer	Mirjalili, S; Mirjalili, SM; Lewis, A	2014	Advances in engineering software	12,174
Multiverse optimizer	Mirjalili, S; Mirjalili, SM; Hatamlou, A	2016	Neural computing and applications	2766
A novel swarm intelligence optimization approach: Sparrow Search Algorithm	Xue, JK; Shen, B	2020	Systems science and control engineering	2105
The arithmetic optimization algorithm	Abualigah, L; Diabat, A; Mirjalili, S; Gandomi, AH	2021	Computer methods in applied mechanics and engineering	1898
Equilibrium optimizer: a novel optimization algorithm	Faramarzi, A; Heidarinejad, M; Stephens, B; Mirjalili, S	2020	Knowledge-based systems	1597
Multiobjective gey wolf optimizer	Mirjalili, S; Saremi, S; Mirjalili, SM; Coelho, LD	2016	Expert systems with applications	1188
Binary grey wolf optimization approaches for feature selection	Emary, E; Zawba, HM; Hassanien, AE	2016	Neurocomputing	986
Henry gas solubility optimization	Hashim, FA; Houssein, EH; Mirjalili, S (vd.)	2019	Future generation computer systems	782
An improved grey wolf optimizer	Nadimi-Shahraki, MH; Taghian, S; Mirjalili, S	2021	Expert systems with applications	695
Grey wolf optimizer: a review of recent variants and applications	Faris, H; Aljarah, I; Mirjalili, S (vd.)	2018	Neural computing and applications	600

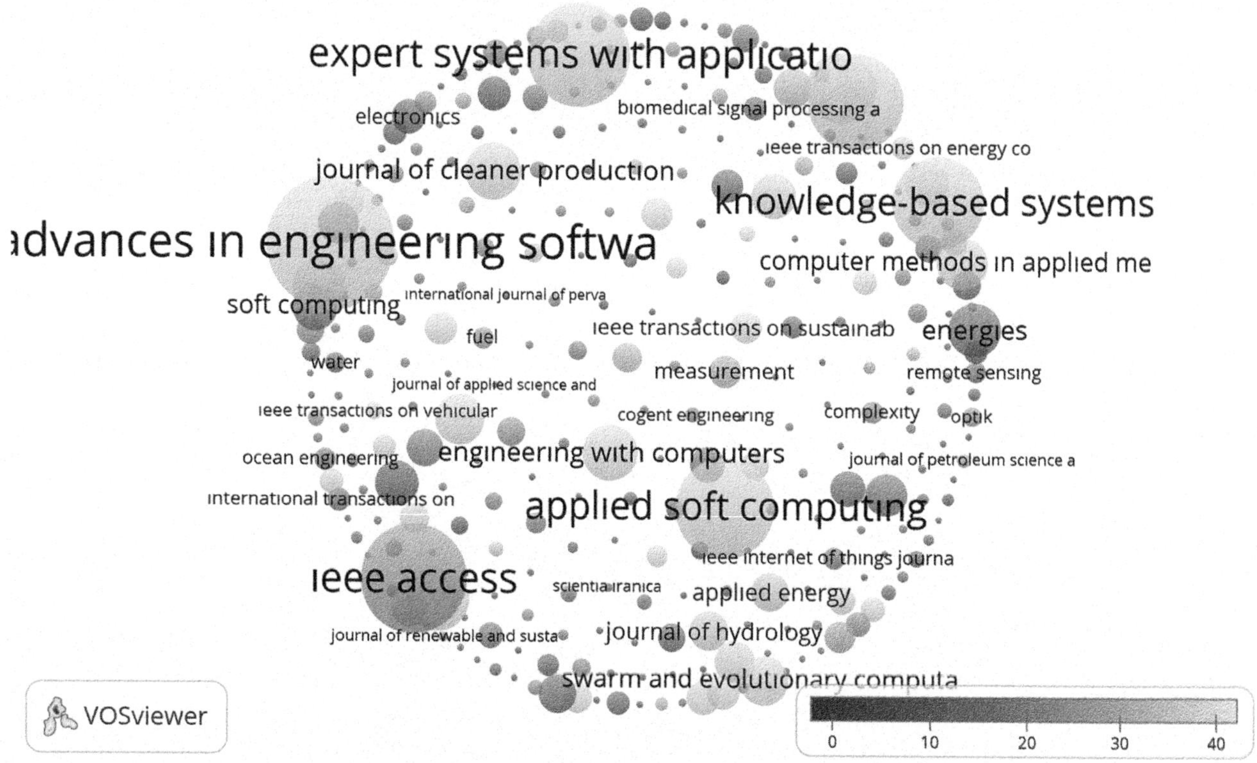

FIGURE 6.9 Link between the most cited journals.

6.4.20 Link analysis between the most cited journals

Fig. 6.9 shows the link between the citations in the journals where the paper is published.

When Fig. 6.9 is examined, it is seen that Advances in Engineering Software is the journal that has reached the highest impact value by receiving a total of 12,957 citations with only 21 publications. This situation shows that the studies published in the journal have a great academic impact on the field. Applied Soft Computing has become the journal with high productivity, with 145 publications and has received a total of 7381 citations. These values emphasize the importance of nature-inspired algorithms such as GWO in the field of soft computing. The 93 studies published in the Energy journal received a total of 3695 citations. This result shows that the GWO algorithm is a preferred optimization tool in engineering applications in the energy field. The Energy Conversion and Management journal received 2944 citations with 43 publications, revealing that GWO has attracted considerable interest in applications such as energy conversion and management. Engineering with Computers contributes to GWO studies from a technical computer engineering perspective with 37 publications and 2324 citations. This result shows that the algorithm can be applied to engineering problems. Expert Systems with Applications is one of the most productive journals, with 147 publications and 7743 citations. These findings show that GWO is frequently used in decision support systems and expert systems. Journal of Cleaner Production has a total of 2392 citations in 39 publications. This shows that GWO is also preferred in the context of sustainable production and environmentally friendly technologies. Knowledge-Based Systems reveals the intense academic interest in GWO in the field of AI and knowledge-based systems, with 49 publications and 6183 citations. Neural Computing & Applications shows that GWO is intensively used in AI-based applications such as neural networks and cognitive computing, with 98 publications and 6771 citations. Although IEEE Access is the journal that publishes the most articles, with 343 publications, the number of citations per article is relatively low, with 8694 citations. This shows that IEEE Access follows a high-volume but generally broad-ranging publication policy. These findings clearly show that the GWO algorithm finds application in a wide range of disciplines such as energy, AI, engineering, and sustainability.

6.4.21 Link analysis between the most used keywords

Fig. 6.10 provides a link to keyword data.

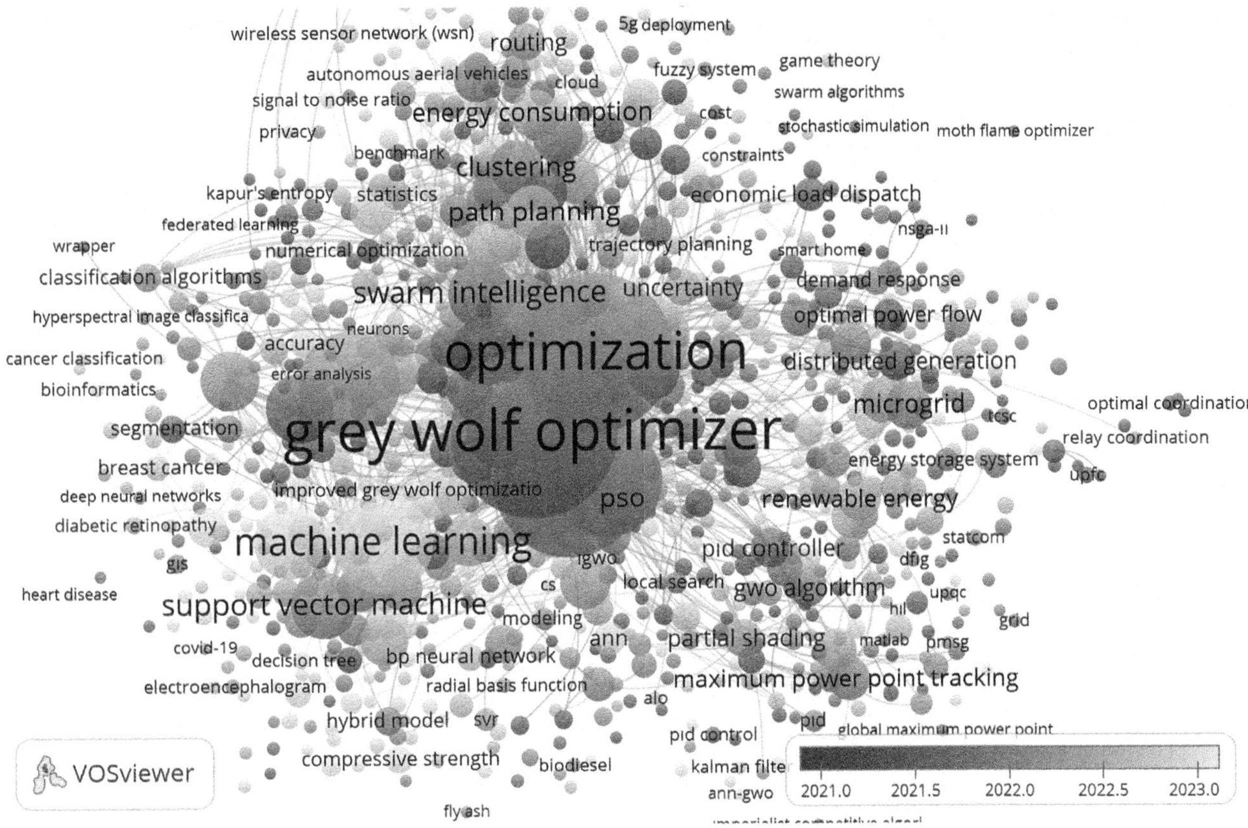

FIGURE 6.10 The connection between the most used keywords.

According to the keyword analysis given in Fig. 6.10, the most frequently used terms are "grey wolf optimizer" (933 times) and "optimization" (794 times). This finding shows that GWO is heavily used in the literature, both with its specific naming and in the context of general optimization. In addition, the high number of repetitions of variant terms such as "grey wolf optimization" (762 times) and "gwo" (403 times) indicates the diversity in terminology preferences of researchers. The expressions "feature selection" (337 times) and "machine learning" (322 times) reveal that GWO is widely preferred, especially in ML applications and feature selection problems. Similarly, the keywords "deep learning" (171 times) and "multi-objective optimization" (209 times) show the integration of GWO into advanced AI approaches such as deep learning and multiobjective optimization. Finally, the frequent mention of other nature-inspired algorithms, such as PSO (262 times), suggests that GWO has been treated comparatively or in a hybrid manner with these methods. Overall, this analysis reveals that GWO has strong and broad-based applications in AI, feature selection, and optimization-based disciplines.

6.5 Conclusion

Within the scope of this study, research trends in a wide range of application areas have been examined in detail since 2014, the year the GWO algorithm was introduced, until today. As a result of the analyses carried out according to the findings, the following conclusions were reached.

In the WoS category distributions, the categories with the most GWO studies are determined as *Engineering, Electrical, Electronic, Computer Science Information, Telecommunications, Computer Science Interdisciplinary, Materials Science Multidisciplinary, and Green Sustainable Science*, respectively. This shows the interdisciplinary use potential and breadth of application of the algorithm.

When the distribution of publications by year is examined, it is seen that academic interest in the GWO algorithm has increased significantly, especially since 2014, and has been the subject of an increasing number of publications every year since 2020. This increase is directly related to both the theoretical development of the algorithm and the spread of its practical applications in different fields such as energy, health, AI, and optimization.

When the document types of the publications were examined, it was determined that the majority were published in article format, with a smaller proportion of conference proceedings, compilations, and book chapters. This shows that the field has matured and is represented by permanent academic outputs.

According to the WOS index distribution, the majority of publications are included in the *Science Citation Index Expanded*; this indicates that GWO studies are published in high-impact journals.

As a result of the analysis, it was determined that the researcher with the most publications in the field of research was Seyedali Mirjalili. He was followed by Salah Kamel, Essam Halim Houssein, Laith Abualigah, and Ali Asghar Heidari, respectively. This situation shows that these researchers have made significant contributions to the field and that their academic productivity in this field is quite high. In addition, when the researchers' profiles were examined, it was observed that the publications were largely concentrated around certain names; this reveals that the pioneering figures were influential in the development of the field.

As a result of the bibliometric analysis, it was seen that the majority of the studies were concentrated in the fields of engineering, computer science, and energy. In particular, engineering (3926 publications) and computer science (3075 publications) stand out as the research fields with the highest share in total publications. In addition, a significant number of publications were made in different disciplines such as telecommunications, automation and control systems, mathematics, materials science, and environmental sciences. This shows that the study has a multidisciplinary structure and has an impact on many scientific fields.

When the distribution of publications by country is examined, the People's Republic of China (2876 publications) and India (2325 publications) stand out as the countries with the most publications by far. These two countries are followed by Iran, Egypt, Saudi Arabia, and Turkey. The high number of publications, especially in countries in Asia and the Middle East, shows that the intense interest in research topics and research activities is strong in these regions. In addition, developed countries such as the USA, England, Canada, and Australia also attract attention in terms of publication contributions. This situation reveals that the study has attracted attention both in developing countries and in regions with developed research infrastructures.

According to the analysis of publisher distribution of publications, Elsevier stands out as the publishing house with the highest number of publications, followed by Springer Nature and IEEE. This shows that these three publishing houses are leaders in the field of academic publishing.

The most cited authors are usually the developers of the algorithm and academics who are experts in topics such as energy, AI, optimization, etc. This reveals that the work of researchers who are considered authorities in the literature is a reference point for other research.

In terms of institutional distribution, the majority of GWO-related publications have been conducted in technical universities and research institutes, with the majority of these institutions concentrated in countries such as China, India, Saudi Arabia, and Turkey.

In the distribution of citation topics at micro and meso levels, it was seen that the GWO algorithm was frequently used in specific and application-oriented topics such as "Particle Swarm Optimization," "Energy Forecasting," "Photovoltaic Systems" and "Smart Grid Optimization" at the micro level, and in Power Systems & Electric Vehicles, Supply Chain & Logistics, Telecommunications and AI & ML at the meso level.

When the language distribution was examined, it was determined that 99.6% of the publications were written in English, while other languages were quite limited. This shows that the studies on GWO were presented to the global academic community through English, the universal language of science.

Approximately 38% of publications are open access. The high rate of Gold OA in particular shows that information in this field is being made more accessible.

It was observed that China-based funders have a large weight in the research. The organization that provided the most support was the NSFC, with a rate of 16.31%. This reflects the influence of China's investments in metaheuristic algorithms and energy systems.

Among the group of authors, IEEE has by far the largest contribution, indicating that GWO research is published predominantly in the engineering and computer science framework.

The classification made within the scope of sustainable development goals revealed that GWO contributes the most to the goals of "Affordable and Clean Energy" (23.43%), "Sustainable Cities and Communities" (12.24%), and "Good Health and Well-being" (7.27%). This shows that the algorithm stands out as a strategic tool in the development of sustainable technologies.

According to the coauthor findings, "Mirjalili, Seyedali" is a leading researcher in the field, having both the highest number of documents (95), the highest number of citations (27,924), and the TLS (194). In addition, "Mirjalili, Seyed Mohammad" stands out with its significant number of citations (16,425), while authors such as "Abualigah, Laith" and

"Heidari, Ali Asghar" are among the influential names in the field with both high citations and strong collaboration links. This shows that certain authors are pioneers in terms of both productivity and impact in the field of research.

According to the findings of the most cited institutions, Islamic Azad University has the highest number of documents (232) and stands out with its strong collaboration links (TLS 307). Mansoura University and Zagazig University also stand out with their high number of publications and link strength. On the other hand, Griffith University and Shahid Beheshti University, despite their low number of publications, are in a significant position in terms of research impact with their high number of citations (20,606 and 12,500, respectively). These results show that different institutions play different roles in the field in terms of both productivity and impact.

While bibliometric analyses provide a detailed account of the quantitative nature of the literature, they also have certain limitations. Potential biases, such as reliance on English-dominated databases such as WoS, exclusion of out-of-field publications, and citation inflation, can influence the results of the analysis. However, the use of different databases (e.g., Scopus, Google Scholar) and the application of domain-normalization techniques are recommended to mitigate these biases. Furthermore, to minimize the impact of language and regional differences, the robustness of the study can be enhanced by examining multidisciplinary and multilingual data sources. While the WoS database is preferred for this study, the results are compared with the literature, existing limitations are acknowledged, and suggested ways to improve are discussed.

According to the country analysis of coauthored publications, the People's Republic of China is the clear leader in the field of research, with both the highest number of documents and the strongest collaboration network. India and Australia, on the other hand, make significant contributions by attracting attention with their high citation numbers and extensive network strengths. Countries such as Saudi Arabia and Egypt are influential in terms of the number of publications and collaboration networks, while Jordan, Malaysia, South Korea, and the USA also show balanced productivity and impact. On the other hand, Turkey, with its limited number of publications and collaboration strength compared to other countries, points to the potential for development in research collaborations. These findings clearly reveal the dynamic structure of global academic collaboration and regional differences.

According to the analysis of the most cited works in the GWO field, the original Grey Wolf Optimizer paper by Mirjalili and colleagues published in 2014 has both laid the foundation of the field and proven the scientific impact of this optimization algorithm with the highest number of citations (12,174). Numerous variants and new optimization approaches developed in the following years demonstrate the flexibility and wide application areas of GWO. This shows that GWO has attracted great interest from researchers both theoretically and practically, and offers effective solutions to optimization problems.

When the most cited publication sources in the field of GWO are examined, the journal Advances in Engineering Software stands out as a leading publication platform in the field, with both the high number of citations (12,957) and the number of important documents. In addition, journals such as Expert Systems with Applications, IEEE Access, Applied Soft Computing, and Neural Computing and Applications play an important role in GWO and related optimization algorithms research, with both the number of publications and citations. This shows that GWO studies are concentrated in interdisciplinary and application-oriented journals and that the scientific impact in this field is spread over a wide spectrum.

According to the results obtained from the keyword analysis, GWO and related terms (e.g., GWO) are among the most used concepts and have the strongest link network. In particular, the GWO is one of the most effective keywords, with 933 times used and a TLS of 1897. In addition, broad terms such as optimization and feature selection are also heavily included and are associated with other important concepts in the field with strong ties. These results show that GWO is a basic and frequently used method in interdisciplinary fields such as optimization and ML.

In conclusion, the GWO algorithm is a widely used and proven optimization approach for solving a wide range of engineering problems. It is seen that GWO contributes to many areas, especially energy efficiency, system control, resource planning, and sustainability. This shows that the algorithm will continue to have an important place in future research.

Acknowledgments

Artificial intelligence-supported tools were used to check grammar. No AI was used to produce scientific results or to formulate opinions based on these results. All images were obtained from the relevant analysis program.

References

[1] A Akkaya, C Közkurt, R Durgut, A study on meta-heuristic algorithms used for problem solving in recent years, Pioneer and Contemporary Studies in Engineering 18 (2018) 327–352.

[2] X.-S. Yang, Nature-inspired Metaheuristic Algorithms, Luniver press, (2010).
[3] S. Mirjalili, S.M. Mirjalili, A. Lewis, Grey wolf optimizer, Advanced Engineering Software. 69 (2014) 46–61. Available from https://doi.org/10.1016/j.advengsoft.2013.12.007.
[4] S. Saremi, S.Z. Mirjalili, S.M. Mirjalili, Evolutionary population dynamics and grey wolf optimizer, Neural Computing and Applications. 26 (5) (2015) 1257–1263. Available from https://doi.org/10.1007/s00521-014-1806-7.
[5] L.D. Mech, Alpha status, dominance, and division of labor in wolf packs, Canadian Journal of Zoology 77 (8) (1999) 1196–1203. Available from https://doi.org/10.1139/z99-099.
[6] Y. Qiu, X. Yang, S. Chen, An improved gray wolf optimization algorithm solving to functional optimization and engineering design problems, Scientific Reports 14 (1) (2024) 14190. Available from https://doi.org/10.1038/s41598-024-64526-2.
[7] J. Jiang, Z. Zhao, Y. Liu, W. Li, H. Wang, DSGWO: an improved grey wolf optimizer with diversity enhanced strategy based on group-stage competition and balance mechanisms, Knowl.-Based Syst. 250 (2022) 109100. Available from https://doi.org/10.1016/j.knosys.2022.109100.
[8] B Ibrahim, H Abdelkader, M Farid, I Yaichi, I Colak, K Kayisli, et al., Optimal power control based-metaheuristic algorithm based variable speed wind energy system of DFIG, in: 2023 11th International Conference on Smart Grid (icSmartGrid). IEEE, 2023, pp. 1–7. Available from https://doi.org/10.1109/icSmartGrid58556.2023.10170786.
[9] K. Meidani, A. Hemmasian, S. Mirjalili, A. Barati Farimani, Adaptive grey wolf optimizer, Neural Computing and Applications. 34 (10) (2022) 7711–7731. Available from https://doi.org/10.1007/s00521-021-06885-9.
[10] S.N. Makhadmeh, M.A. Al-Betar, I.A. Doush, M.A. Awadallah, S. Kassaymeh, S. Mirjalili, et al., Recent advances in grey wolf optimizer, its versions and applications, IEEE Access 12 (2023) 22991–23028. Available from https://doi.org/10.1109/ACCESS.2023.3304889.
[11] V.K.R. Aala Kalananda, V.L.N. Komanapalli, A competitive learning-based grey wolf optimizer for engineering problems and its application to multi-layer perceptron training, Multimedia Tools and Applications. 82 (26) (2023) 40209–40267. Available from https://doi.org/10.1007/s11042-023-15146-x.
[12] Y. Hou, H. Gao, Z. Wang, C. Du, Improved grey wolf optimization algorithm and application, Sensors 22 (10) (2022). Available from https://doi.org/10.3390/s22103810.
[13] Z.-M. Gao, J. Zhao, An improved grey wolf optimization algorithm with variable weights, Computational Intelligence and Neuroscience 1 (2981282) (2019). Available from https://doi.org/10.1155/2019/2981282.
[14] R. Salgotra, U. Singh, S. Sharma, On the improvement in grey wolf optimization, Neural Computing and Applications. 32 (8) (2020) 3709–3748. Available from https://doi.org/10.1007/s00521-019-04456-7.
[15] A. Seyyedabbasi, F. Kiani, I-GWO and Ex-GWO: improved algorithms of the grey wolf optimizer to solve global optimization problems, Engineering Computations. 37 (1) (2021) 509–532. Available from https://doi.org/10.1007/s00366-019-00837-7.
[16] J. Liu, X. Wei, H. Huang, An improved grey wolf optimization algorithm and its application in path planning, IEEE Access 9 (2021) 121944–121956. Available from https://doi.org/10.1109/ACCESS.2021.3108973.
[17] J.-S. Wang, S.-X. Li, An improved grey wolf optimizer based on differential evolution and elimination mechanism, Scientific Reports 9 (1) (2019) 7181. Available from https://doi.org/10.1038/s41598-019-43546-3.
[18] Z. Teng, J. Lv, L. Guo, An improved hybrid grey wolf optimization algorithm, Soft Computing 23 (15) (2019) 6617–6631. Available from https://doi.org/10.1007/s00500-018-3310-y.
[19] N. Singh, S.B. Singh, Hybrid algorithm of particle swarm optimization and grey wolf optimizer for improving convergence performance, Journal of Applied Mathematics (2017). Available from https://doi.org/10.1155/2017/2030489.
[20] S. Arora, H. Singh, M. Sharma, S. Sharma, P. Anand, A new hybrid algorithm based on grey wolf optimization and crow search algorithm for unconstrained function optimization and feature selection, IEEE Access 7 (2019) 26343–26361. Available from https://doi.org/10.1109/ACCESS.2019.2897325.
[21] Q. Al-Tashi, S.J. Abdul Kadir, H.M. Rais, S. Mirjalili, H. Alhussian, Binary optimization using hybrid grey wolf optimization for feature selection, IEEE Access 7 (2019) 39496–39508. Available from https://doi.org/10.1109/ACCESS.2019.2906757.
[22] S. Kılıçarslan, PSO + GWO: a hybrid particle swarm optimization and grey wolf optimization based algorithm for fine-tuning hyper-parameters of convolutional neural networks for cardiovascular disease detection", Journal of Ambient Intelligence and Humanized Computing 14 (1) (2023) 87–97. Available from https://doi.org/10.1007/s12652-022-04433-4.
[23] S. Mirjalili, S. Saremi, S.M. Mirjalili, L.dos S. Coelho, Multi-objective grey wolf optimizer: a novel algorithm for multi-criterion optimization, Expert Systems with Applications 47 (2016) 106–119. Available from https://doi.org/10.1016/j.eswa.2015.10.039.
[24] E. Emary, H.M. Zawbaa, A.E. Hassanien, Binary grey wolf optimization approaches for feature selection, Neurocomputing 172 (2016) 371–381. Available from https://doi.org/10.1016/j.neucom.2015.06.083.
[25] F.A. Şenel, F. Gökçe, A.S. Yüksel, T. Yiğit, A novel hybrid PSO–GWO algorithm for optimization problems, Engineering Computations 35 (4) (2019) 1359–1373. Available from https://doi.org/10.1007/s00366-018-0668-5.
[26] M.A. Tawhid, A.F. Ali, A Hybrid grey wolf optimizer and genetic algorithm for minimizing potential energy function, Memetic Computing 9 (4) (2017) 347–359. Available from https://doi.org/10.1007/s12293-017-0234-5.
[27] X. Yu, N. Jiang, X. Wang, M. Li, A hybrid algorithm based on grey wolf optimizer and differential evolution for UAV path planning, Expert Systems with Applications 215 (119327) (2023). Available from https://doi.org/10.1016/j.eswa.2022.119327.
[28] R. Purushothaman, S.P. Rajagopalan, G. Dhandapani, Hybridizing gray wolf optimization (GWO) with grasshopper optimization algorithm (GOA) for text feature selection and clustering, Applied Soft Computing 96 (106651) (2020). Available from https://doi.org/10.1016/j.asoc.2020.106651.

[29] M. Aria, C. Cuccurullo, *bibliometrix*: an R-tool for comprehensive science mapping analysis, Journal of Informetrics 11 (4) (2017) 959–975. Available from https://doi.org/10.1016/j.joi.2017.08.007.
[30] K. Börner, Atlas of Science: Visualizing What We Know, MIT Press, (2010).
[31] S.A. Ganaie, J.A. Wani, Bibliometric analysis and visualization of nanotechnology research field, COLLNET Journal of Scientometric and Information Management 15 (2) (2021) 445–467. Available from https://doi.org/10.1080/09737766.2021.2008780.
[32] A. Van Raan, Measuring science: basic principles and application of advanced bibliometrics, Springer Handbook of Science and Technology Indicators, Springer International Publishing, Cham, (2019), pp. 237–280.
[33] S. Mirjalili, S.M. Mirjalili, A. Hatamlou, Multi-verse optimizer: a nature-inspired algorithm for global optimization, Neural Computing and Applications. 27 (2) (2016) 495–513. Available from https://doi.org/10.1007/s00521-015-1870-7.
[34] J. Xue ve, B. Shen, A novel swarm intelligence optimization approach: sparrow search algorithm, Systems Science and Control Engineering. 8 (1) (2020) 22–34. Available from https://doi.org/10.1080/21642583.2019.1708830.
[35] L. Abualigah, A. Diabat, S. Mirjalili, M.A. Elaziz, A.H. Gandomi, The arithmetic optimization algorithm, Computer Methods in Applied Mechanics and Engineering 376 (2021) 113609. Available from https://doi.org/10.1016/j.cma.2020.113609.
[36] A. Faramarzi, M. Heidarinejad, B. Stephens, S. Mirjalili, Equilibrium optimizer: a novel optimization algorithm, Knowledge-Based Systems. 191 (2020) 105190. Available from https://doi.org/10.1016/j.knosys.2019.105190.
[37] F.A. Hashim, E.H. Houssein, M.S. Mabrouk, W. Al-Atabany, S. Mirjalili, Henry gas solubility optimization: a novel physics-based algorithm, Future Generation Computer Systems – The International Journal of eScience 101 (2019) 646–667. Available from https://doi.org/10.1016/j.future.2019.07.015.
[38] M.H. Nadimi-Shahraki, S. Taghian, S. Mirjalili, An improved grey wolf optimizer for solving engineering problems, Expert Systems with Applications 166 (2021) 113917. Available from https://doi.org/10.1016/j.eswa.2020.113917.
[39] H. Faris, I. Aljarah, M.A. Al-Betar, S. Mirjalili, Grey wolf optimizer: a review of recent variants and applications, Neural Computing and Applications. 30 (2) (2018) 413–435. Available from https://doi.org/10.1007/s00521-017-3272-5.

Chapter 7

An enhanced medical prediction model for diabetes using grey wolf optimizer-assisted wrapper-based algorithms

Mohammadreza Valilou[1], Sevda Valilou[2], and Farhad S. Gharehchopogh[3]
[1]*Department of Veterinary Pathobiology, TaMS. C., Islamic Azad University, Tabriz, Iran,* [2]*Department of Medical Sciences, Tabriz University of Medical Sciences, Tabriz, Iran,* [3]*Department of Computer Engineering, Ur. C., Islamic Azad University, Urmia, Iran*

7.1 Introduction

Human health is significantly threatened by diabetes. Diabetes mellitus is known as a progressive and fatal disease caused by high blood sugar levels, overweight, unhealthy diet, inactivity, and other factors [1]. This disease can be caused by a combination of genetic, environmental, nutritional, and other factors. Diabetes mellitus is increasing rapidly compared to other diseases [2]. This disease can lead to severe problems such as an increased risk of coronary artery disease and stroke. Unfortunately, there is no definitive cure for diabetes, and the only practical way is to control and manage blood sugar levels [3]. In patients with diabetes mellitus, the blood sugar level increases due to a decrease in the physiological effects of insulin or a defect in its secretion [4]. Early diagnosis of this dangerous disease, quick implementation of preventive measures, and primary treatments can significantly reduce the death rate [5]. Practical measures and primary therapies can help maintain health, increase patients' quality of life, and prevent severe and irreparable complications. Currently, 537 million adults in the age group of 20–79 years, equivalent to 10% of the world population, have diabetes [6]. Forecasts show that this number will increase to 643 million people by 2030 and to 783 million people by 2045. This alarming increase indicates severe challenges in the field of global health. Diabetes not only endangers the lives of millions of people; it is also responsible for 6.7 million deaths in 2021. These statistics emphasize the urgent importance of diabetes management and diagnosis globally. Without preventive measures and appropriate treatments, diabetes can become one of the major global crises in the coming decades.

In 2017, 6059 out of 100,000 people were affected by diabetes [7]. In this disease, the blood glucose level increases significantly, which is caused by the improper functioning of the body's metabolic regulation system. The two main types of diabetes are as follows: Type 1 diabetes, commonly known as insulin-dependent diabetes mellitus or juvenile-onset diabetes, develops in childhood. Type 2 diabetes mellitus, also known as diabetes mellitus or adult-onset diabetes, is one of the most common metabolic disorders that impair the body's ability to utilize glucose as an energy source [8]. Type 2 diabetes usually occurs after the age of 40 and becomes more common with age. In type 2 diabetes, the cells resist this hormone despite the pancreas's insulin production and no longer respond to its commands [9]. As a result, the pancreas gradually reduces insulin production, and blood glucose levels rise, which can have serious health consequences.

Diabetes mellitus occurs for two reasons: (1) The body does not produce enough insulin (the hormone responsible for regulating glucose). (2) Cells do not respond effectively to insulin [10]. This situation results in the accumulation of glucose in the bloodstream, leading to hyperglycemia. The World Health Organization estimates that by 2040, about 600 million people worldwide will have diabetes [11]. With this alarming prediction, intelligent algorithms in machine learning and artificial intelligence are needed. Hybrid meta-heuristic algorithms combined with machine learning algorithms facilitate the early diagnosis of diabetes. The hybridization of these algorithms in the structure of decision support systems helps doctors predict and diagnose disease [12,13]. By analyzing complex data and hidden patterns, artificial intelligence algorithms can more accurately identify people exposed to disease than traditional algorithms [14].

Grey Wolf Optimizer. DOI: https://doi.org/10.1016/B978-0-443-36624-6.00038-X

Using these algorithms in the field of diabetes reduces diagnosis time and helps doctors develop new and effective drugs and treatments. The thickness of the skin fold in the back of the arm is the most critical factor in diagnosing type 2 diabetes [15].

Medical data often contains high-dimensional features. Due to its complexity and high volume, this data type can severely reduce the quality of output in medicine and clinical diagnosis. Additionally, feature selection results in a significant increase in computing costs. Using intelligent methods to select features is crucial in such situations. Accurate and targeted selection of features using intelligent algorithms enables the removal of irrelevant and redundant features while preserving the most relevant ones. The feature selection process allows advanced machine learning models to have higher generalization power and severe overfitting, which leads to false and misleading results, to be effectively avoided [16]. Feature selection in medical data enhances prediction accuracy, reduces computational complexity and resource consumption, and significantly improves clinical outcomes and medical decision-making. This chapter proposes a new model for diagnosing diabetes based on the hybridization of the African Vulture Optimization Algorithm (AVOA) [17] and the grey wolf optimize (GWO) [18]. The proposed model is for feature selection. The GWO algorithm addresses the AVOA's primary issue of getting stuck in local optima. The exploration phase in the GWO is added to the AVOA algorithm to find optimal solutions. The AVOA algorithm achieves diversity and dynamism in solutions by utilizing the GWO algorithm. Therefore the proposed model finds more suitable positions in the search space using search and dynamic update mechanisms. Finally, the K-nearest neighbor (KNN) algorithm was used to classify the samples. In general, the main contributions of this chapter are as follows:

- A hybridization of AVOA and GWO algorithms is used for feature selection. The hybrid model enhances the efficiency and accuracy of the KNN algorithm by effectively balancing exploration and exploitation, thereby ensuring effective feature selection.
- The GWO algorithm improves the AVOA algorithm. Due to its heuristic solid nature, the GWO algorithm can explore different areas of the search space and find local and global optima. Adding GWO to AVOA results in significant improvements, including increased convergence speed and a reduced probability of getting stuck in local optima.
- The proposed model is evaluated on three datasets (PIMA, Pabna, and behavioral risk factor surveillance system [BRFSS]). The PIMA dataset consists of 768 samples and 8 features, the Pabna dataset consists of 465 samples and 9 features, and the BRFS dataset consists of 253,680 samples and 21 features.
- The proposed model is compared with the AVOA and GWO algorithms. The primary purpose of this comparison is to evaluate the accuracy rate and efficiency of the proposed model in feature selection. The comparisons demonstrate that the proposed model achieves more optimal results by leveraging the strengths of two algorithms, AVOA and GWO.

The overall structure of this chapter is organized as follows: Section 7.2 describes previous studies in the field of diabetes diagnosis and feature selection. Section 7.3 details the proposed model's stages and evaluation criteria. Section 7.4 compares the proposed model's evaluation and results with a metaheuristic algorithm. Finally, Section 7.5 will discuss the conclusions and future work.

7.2 Related works

Diabetes mellitus is a chronic metabolic disorder and one of the significant public health problems worldwide. In Ref. [19], two models are proposed for diabetes disease classification on the Indian Pima diabetes dataset. The first model utilizes deep neural networks, while the second employs machine learning algorithms. Two test-training and cross-validation techniques have been used to validate two models. The deep learning network achieves the highest accuracy, with a score of 95.50%, a precision of 94%, a recall of 97%, and an F1 score of 96%. Additionally, the accuracy percentages of decision trees, random trees, and support vector machines (SVMs) are 83.40%, 89.59%, and 91.40%, respectively. An interpretable hybrid model with a deep, complex, fuzzy neural network has been proposed for diagnosing diabetes [20]. Compared with the adaptive fuzzy neural inference system and deep neural network, the combined model achieved an average improvement of 7.4% in prediction accuracy.

A binary version of the arithmetic optimization algorithm is proposed to solve the feature selection problem [21]. Twenty sets of simulation tests were performed. The simulation showed that the LBSCAOA model with a V-shaped transfer function achieved outstanding results. In [22], a new feature selection method based on the grasshopper optimization algorithm is proposed to diagnose diabetes accurately. This state-of-the-art feature selection model has been tested on the authentic Pima dataset to identify and analyze critical features accurately. A 10-part cross-validation method has been employed to assess the reliability of the new model. The outstanding results showed that the SVM algorithm achieved a remarkable accuracy of approximately 97%, indicating a significant improvement in diabetes diagnosis using meta-heuristic algorithms.

The J48 decision tree algorithm has been used to classify and diagnose diabetes [23]. The dataset contains 1169 records with 115 diagnoses, showing high diversity and complexity. The results showed that the J48 algorithm achieved an accuracy of 70.80% and correctly identified diabetes cases. Machine learning models based on logistic regression, linear regression, KNN, random forest, Bayesian, decision tree, and SVM methods have been proposed to predict diabetes [24]. The performance is evaluated on two datasets (the 2019 dataset with 952 records and the Pima dataset with 768 records). The random forest algorithm has obtained optimal results with 97% accuracy on the 2019 diabetes dataset and 80% accuracy on the Pima Indian dataset.

Harris Hawks Optimization (HHO) based on Dynamic Random Jump (DRM-HHO) is proposed for feature selection [25]. In the hybrid model, the Kepler Optimization Algorithm replaces the HHO exploration phase to solve the overemission problem. Experiments have been conducted on the CEC2017 and CEC2019 functions to investigate differences in mutation probability. Compared to whale optimization algorithm (WOA) and the tonic community algorithm, the DRM-HHO model performs better, especially in solving high-dimensional problems. In [26], a new method for diagnosing diabetes using a random forest algorithm is proposed. In this method, the accuracy and effectiveness of the random forest depend on selecting the best features. Feature selection utilizes the multineighbor artificial bee colony algorithm (BMNABC), which is crucial in data preprocessing. The results show that the BMNABC model achieves an accuracy and sensitivity of 96.36% and 99.95%, respectively, in diagnosing diabetes using the Pima dataset.

To solve the problems of the standard particle swarm optimization (PSO) algorithm, a hybrid algorithm called single-directed PSO (SGPSO) is proposed for feature selection [27]. The accuracy percentage of the SGPSO model on the Pima dataset is 80.47%. A new model using the binary exchange market algorithm (BEMA) is proposed to identify essential and useful features in the diabetes dataset [28]. The results show that the combined BEMA-SVM method outperformed previous methods and achieved an accuracy rate of 98.50%. SVM classifies the data efficiently with an optimal hyperplane. This hyperplane maximizes the distance between different categories, helping to increase the model's generalizability and reduce the model error.

7.3 The proposed model

Focusing on two main phases (exploration and exploitation), the AVOA explores the search space effectively and avoids getting stuck in the local optimum. In the exploration phase, vultures randomly search the problem space and evaluate solutions. During the exploitation phase, vultures gradually refine the solutions they have obtained and move to areas with higher potential. The GWO is a complementary solution to the AVOA, which is often stuck in a local optimum. Based on previous experience and probability distributions, the GWO effectively searches for unknown regions in the problem space. Randomization prevents the algorithm from getting stuck in local optima, allowing it to explore different areas of the search space. In the exploration phase, the GWO algorithm combines several influential factors, including wolves' experiences, searching for new places, and approaching other wolves, to optimize solutions. These factors enable the GWO to identify the optimal locations and move toward them efficiently. These factors make the discovery stage in the GWO algorithm highly efficient. Fig. 7.1 illustrates the stages of the proposed model, which is based on the hybridization of AVOA and GWO algorithms.

By hybridizing the AVOA with GWO, essential and influential features in diabetic patients can be accurately identified. Additionally, reducing the dimensions of the search space increases the accuracy of machine-learning algorithms. Feature selection is crucial in medical data, particularly for patients with diabetes. Improper selection of features leads to low accuracy and unreliable results. The proposed model can select the most necessary and efficient features due to its optimal search capabilities and avoid getting stuck in local optimal points. By simulating the behavior of wolves, the GWO performs a more detailed search in the feature space and extracts a set of optimal features. The search process is performed until the stopping criterion (i.e., the number of iterations) is reached. During this process, the individuals of the population gradually move towards the optimal regions to find the optimal solution and ultimately obtain a near-optimal or even optimal solution. In Algorithm 1, the pseudo-code for the proposed model's feature selection is presented.

Algorithm 1. Pseudocode of the proposed model for feature selection.

01. **Inputs**: Define the population size (N) and the maximum number of iterations (T).
02. **Outputs**: Determine the position of individuals and their corresponding fitness value.
03. Initialize a random population (Pi) where (i = 1,2, …,N).

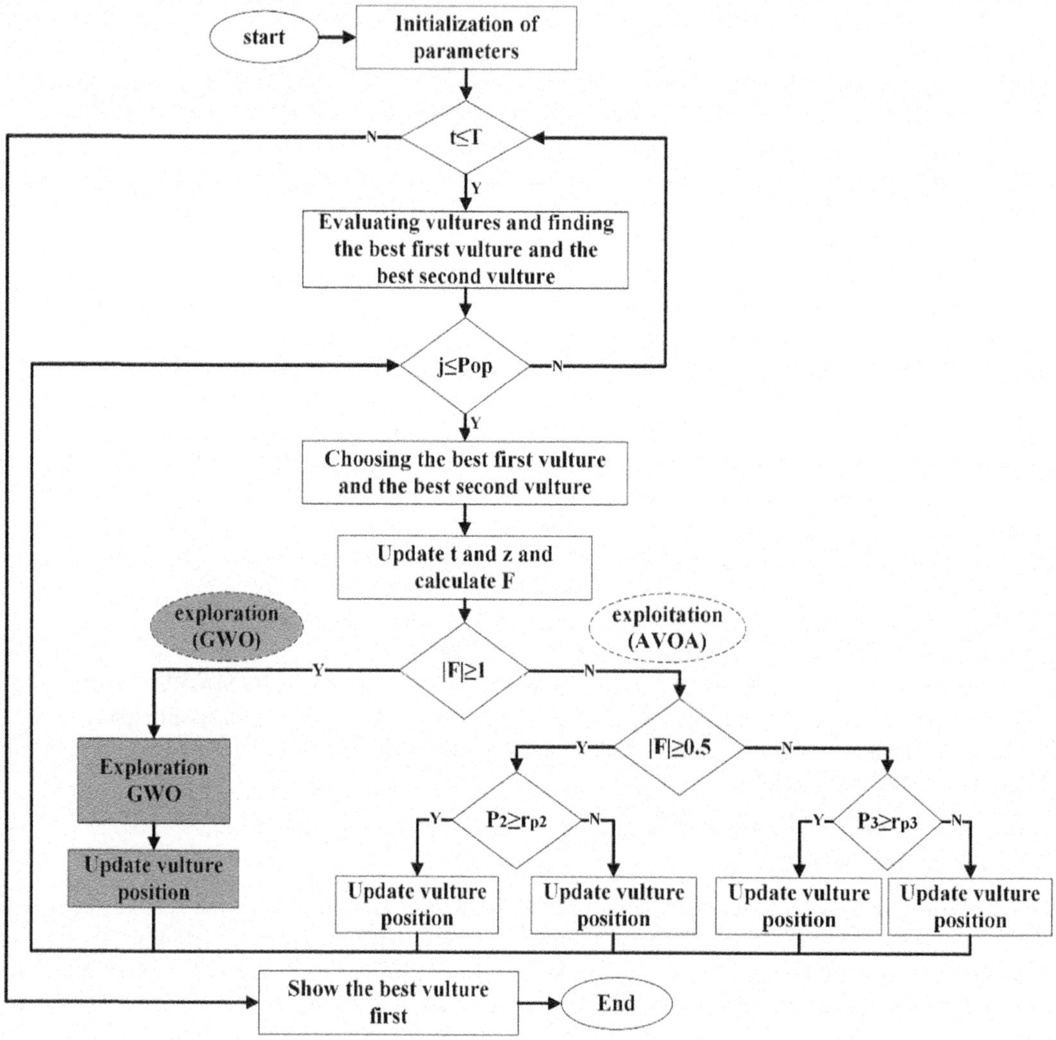

FIGURE 7.1 The flowchart of the proposed model-based hybrid AVOA and GWO (*AVOA*, African Vulture Optimization Algorithm; *GWO*, grey wolf optimizer).

While (stopping condition is unmet):
Calculate the fitness values for each Vulture.
Assign ($PBestVulture(1)$) to the position of the first best individual (Category 1).
Assign ($PBestVulture(2)$) to the position of the second-best individual (Category 2).
For each individual (Pi):
Select ($R(i)$)
Update the parameter (F)
IF (|F|≥1): **Function Exploration (GWO)**
Else IF (|F|<1): **Exploitation**
IF (|F|≥0.5):
IF (P2≥randP2)
Update the position of individuals
Else
Update the position of individuals
Else
IF(P3≥randP3)
Update the position of individuals

Else
Update the position of individuals
Transfer function for binary mode
Return (*PBestVulture*(1)).
Function Exploration (GWO):
Calculate the new vector
Check the boundary of the new vector position
Update the current solution
Calculate the cost of the updated solution
IF $NewXi(Cost) < Xi(Cost)$
Xi=*NewXi*
Else
Xi=current solution;
End
End Function
Function Evaluation ()
Reading a dataset of diabetic patients
Data normalization
Training data (80%)
Testing data (20%)
Classification: KNN
Fitness function
Accuracy
End Function
Function KNN ()
Inputs:
Dataset with n samples.
Number of neighbors (k).
A new sample (x_i) to classify.
Outputs:
Predicted class label for x_i
Initialize:
An empty list (Distances).
For each sample (yi: $i = 1, 2, ..., n$) in the dataset:
Compute the distance $d(xi, yi)$. x_i and y_i were computed using the Euclidean distance.
Store the distance and the corresponding class label of (x_i) in (Distances).
Sort the distances list in ascending order based on the distance values.
Select k-neighbor from the sorted list (Distances).
For each of the selected neighbors:
Select the class label.
Sort labels by counts in descending order.
Return the class label with the highest count as the predicted class for x_i.
End Function

7.3.1 Creating the initial population

The first step is to create an initial population with N factors for the proposed model, where each factor represents a potential solution with D dimensions. The search process in the proposed model begins by simulating the behavior of vultures according to Eq. (7.1).

$$X = \begin{bmatrix} x_{1,1} & x_{1,2} & \cdots & x_{1,D} \\ x_{2,1} & x_{2,2} & \cdots & x_{2,D} \\ \vdots & \vdots & \ddots & \vdots \\ x_{N,1} & x_{N,2} & \cdots & x_{N,D} \end{bmatrix} \tag{7.1}$$

where x_{ij} represents the jth dimension of the i solution and are defined as $i = \{1,2, ...,N\}$ and $j = \{1,2, ...,D\}$. The initial population between UB and LB is generated in the search space according to Eq. (7.2). X_i^t is defined as $X_i^t = (x_{i1}^t, x_{i2}^t, \cdots, x_{iD}^t) \in R^D$.

$$X_i^t = LB + rand(0,\ 1) \times (UB - LB) \tag{7.2}$$

7.3.2 Update solutions

Metaheuristic algorithms are essential in finding efficient and effective solutions for the feature selection problem. AVOA can find near-optimal solutions in the search space by continuously updating the situations and evaluating them based on the fitness criterion. In this process, every new solution is compared with previous solutions, and if it is superior, it is replaced. This continuous cycle enables the AVOA to continually move towards optimal solutions. In contrast, using dynamic search and update mechanisms, the GWO finds more graceful positions in the search space. Combining local and global search allows the GWO to pass through local optimal points and find more optimal solutions. The AVOA and GWO algorithms are practical hybrid models for feature selection because they can update solutions in the search space and replace previous solutions with more graceful solutions. The features that significantly improve detection accuracy are identified and selected through continuous searching and updating of the proposed model.

In the proposed model, the current position vector of the vulture ($P(i)$) is defined according to Eq. (7.1), where $R(i)$ is one of the best vultures in the current iteration. $\vec{A}$ defines the coefficient vector in the interval [-2,2], which is calculated according to Eq. (7.2). The parameter $\vec{\alpha}$ decreases from two to zero during the iterations. $\vec{r}_1$ defines a random vector in the interval [0,1]. $rand_2$ has a random value between 0 and 1. lb and ub represent the upper and lower bounds of the variables. By Eq. (7.8), a simple model for random generation of solutions in thc rangc (lb, ub) has been produced [17,18]. $rand_3$ is used to increase the random nature coefficient. If $rand_3$ takes a number close to one, it distributes the solutions with similar patterns, which adds a random movement along with the lower bound. It introduces a high random coefficient in the scale of the search environment to increase diversity and search across different regions of the search space.

$$P(i+1) = R(i) - \vec{A} + rand_2 \times ((ub - lb) \times rand_3 + lb) \tag{7.3}$$

$$\vec{A} = 2\vec{\alpha}.\ \vec{r}_1 - \vec{\alpha} \tag{7.4}$$

$$\vec{a} = 2 - current\_iter*((2)/Max\_iter) \tag{7.5}$$

7.3.3 Binary solutions

In the proposed model, the S-shaped transfer function is used as a bridge to transition from the continuous state to the binary state. The proposed model can perform the search and optimization process in the binary space by using the transfer function. The presence of 0 and 1 in the binary space indicates that the feature is neither selected nor not selected. According to Eq. (7.6), the sigmoid transfer function is defined to convert the continuous state to binary, in which $S(x_{i,j})$ specifies the probability value of S. The sigmoid function provides a gradual and smooth transition from continuous to binary space. This gradual process enables the proposed model to transition smoothly from constant space to binary space. $x_{i,j}$ represents the ith particle in the jth dimension. t represents the current iteration. $rand()$ is a uniform random number in the range [0,1].

$$S(x_{i,j}^t) = \frac{1}{1 + e^{-x_{i,j}^t}};\ x_{i,j}^t = \begin{cases} 1 & if\ rand < S(x_{i,j}^t) \\ 0 & rand \geq S(x_{i,j}^t) \end{cases} \tag{7.6}$$

7.3.4 Data normalization

In the proposed model, the normalization method is the Max/Min method, which falls within the [0.1] range. The normalization of the feature values has been performed according to Eq. (7.7). The parameter v represents the actual value of the features. In contrast, min(v) and max(v) denote the minimum and maximum values of the features, respectively. x contains the numerical value of the normalization of the features.

$$x_i = \frac{v_i - \min(v_i)}{\max(v_i) - \min(v_i)} \tag{7.7}$$

7.3.5 Classification algorithm

The KNN algorithm creates a multidimensional pattern space (corresponding to the number of features) by processing all the training samples. The most common criterion for distance detection is the Euclidean distance. The Euclidean distance between two data samples x = <x_1, x_2, ...x_n> and y = <$y1$, $y2$, ...,yn> is defined according to Eq. (19). The distance between each new sample (the target sample for prediction) and all samples in the training dataset is calculated. It is classified based on the Euclidean distance in the KNN classification, as shown in Eq. (7.8).

$$d = \sqrt{\sum_{r=1}^{n} (x_{ir} - y_{jr})^2} \tag{7.8}$$

where x_{ir} is the test sample and y_{jr} represents the sample of the training jam with the ram feature. n is the number of samples. Using the KNN algorithm, a new sample is classified or predicted according to its similarity to the samples in the dataset. This similarity is usually measured based on the distance between samples.

7.3.6 Fitness function

The proposed model's fitness function is calculated using Eq. (7.9) to maximize classification accuracy and minimize the number of selected features.

$$Fitness = \alpha \times y_c + \frac{S}{N} \times (1 - \alpha) \tag{7.9}$$

Where α is a value between 0 and 1, y_c is the error rate of the classification algorithm, S represents the number of selected features, and N is the total number of features.

7.3.7 Computational complexity

The computational complexity of the hybrid model depends on three basic processes: initialization, fitness evaluation, and agent update. The computational complexity of AVOA in the process of the update mechanism, based on searching for the best location and updating the location vector of all the formed vultures, is $O(T \times N) + O(T \times N \times D)$. N is the population size, D is the problem dimension, and T is the number of iterations. As a result, the computational complexity of the AVOA algorithm is $O(N \times (T + TD))$. Also, the computational complexity of the GWO is $O(N \times T \times D)$. Finally, the computational complexity of the hybrid model is defined according to Eq. (7.10).

$$O(N \times (T + TD) + N \times T \times D) = O(N \times (T + 2TD)) \tag{7.10}$$

7.3.8 Evaluation criteria

This chapter used four criteria of Precision ($P = \frac{TP}{TP+FP}$), Recall ($R = \frac{TP}{TP+FN}$), F1-Score ($F1 - Score = \frac{2*P*R}{P+R}$), and Accuracy ($Accuracy = \frac{TP+TN}{TP+TN+FP+FN}$) to evaluate the proposed model. True positive, true negative, false positive, and false negative are the primary parameters used for evaluation criteria. True positives are the number of true positive samples that are correctly detected. True negatives are the number of true negative samples that are correctly detected. The false positive parameter represents the number of samples that were unaffected by the disease but were incorrectly diagnosed as positive by the test results. The false negative parameter indicates the number of records whose true category is positive, but the classification algorithm has mistakenly recognized their category as negative.

7.4 Evaluation and results

This chapter evaluates the proposed model on three diabetes datasets from the famous Kaggle database. The MATLAB 2021 programming environment has been used to implement the proposed model. The proposed model has been run 20 times on average for valid and reliable results. In this process, essential parameters such as the initial population size and the number of iterations have been set to 30 and 300, respectively. The proposed model has been compared using the basic AVOA and GWO algorithms.

To prevent information leakage in the feature-selection process using the wrapper method, the data is first divided into two parts: training and testing, and all feature-selection steps are performed only on the training data. The data is divided into two sets, training and testing, where 80% of the data is used for training and 20% for testing. Nested cross-validation is used to evaluate the feature subsets so that the model performance is estimated only based on the training data, and no part of the test data is included in the feature-selection process. After determining the best feature subset, the final model is run on the entire training data and finally evaluated only once on an independent test set. Therefore no information leakage from the test set to the feature selection or model training steps has occurred.

7.4.1 Dataset

Pima dataset: The Pima dataset (https://www.kaggle.com/datasets/uciml/pima-indians-diabetes-database) contains 768 records. It includes eight characteristics, categorized into a healthy or unhealthy class, each representing a medical characteristic for healthy or diabetic patients. The Pima dataset includes 268 diabetes-positive and 500 diabetes-negative samples. This dataset was collected from the Kaggle repository, a popular open-source website for researchers. The primary source of this dataset is the National Institute of Diabetes and Digestive and Kidney Diseases in India, where all patients are of Indian origin. Table 7.1 shows the specifications of the Pima dataset.

Pabna dataset: The Pabna dataset is from Pabna (https://github.com/ruhul256/Pabna-Diabetes-Dataset-Bangladesh) Diabetes Hospital (PDH) in Bangladesh. PDH is a recognized hospital specializing in treating and monitoring diabetic patients [19]. This dataset comprises 465 patients with ten characteristics, including 373 individuals with diabetes and 92 nondiabetic individuals. Table 7.2 shows the specifications of the Pabna dataset. The distribution of samples in the Pabna dataset is significantly unbalanced. Imbalance affects the performance of machine learning algorithms, that is, the algorithms tend to identify samples from the majority class better. However, they ignore or misclassify samples from the minority class. This leads to a decrease in the accuracy of the model in detecting important and rare samples. In this paper, the oversampling method is used for Pabna. In this method, the increase in samples is performed on the minority class to establish a balance between the classes. Therefore the synthetic minority oversampling technique method creates new synthetic samples between the close samples instead of repeating the real samples [29]. This reduces the overfitting problem.

BRFSS dataset: This dataset is derived from the BRFSS (https://www.kaggle.com/datasets/abdelazizsami/cdc-diabetes-health-indicators?resource=download) database by the centers for disease control and prevention. The dataset contains 253,680 samples and 21 descriptive characteristics [30]. These characteristics cover a range of demographic, behavioral, and clinical characteristics that influence diabetes status. Some of the most important characteristics in this dataset include smoking status, history of stroke, presence of heart disease or attack, physical activity level, dietary fruit

TABLE 7.1 Specifications of the PIMA dataset.

#	Features	Description and range of value	Mean	Std. deviation	Min	Max
1	Pregnancies	Number of times the patient has been pregnant	3.85	3.37	0	17
2	Glucose	Plasma glucose concentration after an oral glucose tolerance test	121.69	3.52	0	199
3	Blood pressure	Diastolic blood pressure measured in mmHg	72.41	12.37	0	122
4	Skin thickness	The Triceps skin fold thickness in mm	29.15	10.48	0	99
5	Insulin	2-hour serum insulin (μ U/mL)	155.55	118.63	0	846
6	Body mass index (BMI)	Body mass index (weight in kg/ (height in m^2))	32.46	6.92	0	67.1
7	Diabetes pedigree function (PDF)	Diabetes pedigree function between 0.08 and 2.42	0.47	0.33	0.078	2.420
8	Age	Measured in years	33.24	11.75	21	81
9	Class attributes	1 diabetic and 0 nondiabetic	0.35	0.477	0	1

TABLE 7.2 Specifications of the Pabna dataset.

#	Features	Description and range of value	Mean	Std. deviation	Min	Max
1	Pregnancies	Number of times the patient has been pregnant	3.05	1.846	0	12
2	Glucose	Plasma glucose concentration after an oral glucose tolerance test	13.7398	6.51952	5	45
3	Blood pressure (Systolic)	Systolic blood pressure measured in mmHg	119.14	13.960	80	180
4	Blood pressure (Diastolic)	Diastolic blood pressure measured in mmHg	79.43	10.695	30	120
5	Insulin	2-hour serum insulin (μ U/mL)	5.16	8.993	0	44
6	Body mass index (BMI)	Body mass index (weight in kg/ (height in m^2))	25.1787	3.7652	17.18	37.44
7	Age	Measured in years	44.30	12.834	21	86
8	Skin thickness	The Triceps skin fold thickness in mm	306.8784	34.63012	2	100
9	Genetic	Diabetic patients based on hereditary genetics	1.53	1.665	0	8
10	Class attributes	1 diabetic and 0 nondiabetic	0.80	0.400	0	1

intake, gender, education level, and income. The collected data allow for a comprehensive analysis of the relationships between lifestyle, socioeconomic factors, and clinical variables with the incidence or likelihood of diabetes.

7.4.2 Evaluation based on iteration

Table 7.3 shows the results of the models based on the number of iterations. The proposed model's accuracy percentage on PIMA is higher for 100 iterations (74.23%), 200 iterations (76.16%), and 300 iterations (77.65%) compared to AVOA and GWO. Additionally, the accuracy percentage of the proposed model on Pabna is higher for 100 iterations (87.34%), 200 iterations (89.66%), and 300 iterations (91.65%) compared to AVOA and GWO. The accuracy of the models generally increases with the number of iterations. This suggests that models with more iterations can identify optimal solutions and achieve higher accuracy. The proposed model on PIMA with 100 iterations has achieved an overall accuracy of 74.23%, which is 1.10% better than the GWO model and 1.59% better than the AVOA model. Finally, the proposed model achieves 77.65% accuracy after 300 iterations, which is 2.97% better than GWO and 4.00% better than AVOA.

7.4.3 Evaluation based on the number of k

Table 7.4 shows the results of the models based on the number of k. The proposed model's accuracy percentage on Pima is higher for k=3 (77.65%), k=4 (76.62%), and k=5 (75.84%) compared to AVOA and GWO. Additionally, the proposed model's accuracy percentage in Pabna is higher for k=3 (91.65%), k=4 (90.54%), and k=5 (89.31%) compared to AVOA and GWO. The proposed model with k=3 has achieved an overall accuracy of 77.65%, approximately 2.81% higher than GWO and 4.00% higher than AVOA. The proposed model with k=5 has achieved an overall accuracy of 75.84%, approximately 1.99% higher than GWO and 2.92% higher than AVOA. The results of the two data sets show that the percentage of the model's overall accuracy decreases as the value of k increases from 3 to 5. This decrease is due to the increase in k, as the KNN algorithm tends to consider a larger number of neighbors, which may include samples further away from the target point.

7.4.4 Evaluation based on the number of features

Table 7.5 presents the results of the models on the Pima dataset, categorized by the number of features. The accuracy percentages obtained by the proposed model with three and four features are 82.84% and 81.32%, respectively. However, the accuracy percentages obtained by the AVOA and GWO models for the three features are 81.56 and 81.85,

TABLE 7.3 Results of medals based on the number of iterations.

Datasets	Iterations	Models	Precision	Recall	F1-Score	Accuracy
PIMA	100	AVOA	73.10	73.67	73.38	72.64
		GWO	74.05	74.34	74.19	73.42
		Our model	74.90	75.11	75.00	74.23
	200	AVOA	75.45	74.55	75.00	73.84
		GWO	75.75	75.00	75.37	74.93
		Our model	76.85	76.51	76.68	76.16
	300	AVOA	75.60	75.83	75.71	74.68
		GWO	76.50	76.75	76.62	75.84
		Our model	78.00	78.21	78.10	77.65
Pabna	100	AVOA	85.80	86.12	85.96	85.49
		GWO	86.75	87.53	87.14	86.51
		Our model	87.65	87.82	87.73	87.34
	200	AVOA	88.40	88.62	88.51	88.16
		GWO	89.52	89.42	89.47	89.15
		Our model	90.13	90.20	90.16	89.66
	300	AVOA	91.42	91.35	91.38	91.12
		GWO	91.16	91.15	91.15	90.86
		Our model	92.00	92.18	92.09	91.65

respectively. The accuracy percentages obtained by the AVOA and GWO models for the six features are 78.95% and 79.42%, respectively. The accuracy percentage achieved by the proposed model with three and four features is 82.05% and 81.23%, respectively. The performance of all three models has gradually decreased with the increase in the number of features. The proposed model's performance declined from 82.84% with three features to 77.65% with eight features. The results show that the proposed model and other models with fewer features achieve a higher accuracy percentage. Eliminating unnecessary features helps focus on the main and essential features, thereby improving accuracy and efficiency.

Fig. 7.2 illustrates the accuracy percentage of the proposed model on the Pima dataset, based on the number of iterations and feature selection. The accuracy percentages for three features with 200 and 300 iterations are 82.23% and 82.84%, respectively. The accuracy percentages for five features with 200 and 300 iterations are 80.22% and 80.49%, respectively. The accuracy percentages for seven features with 200 and 300 iterations are 78.34% and 78.74%, respectively. The decrease in accuracy suggests that adding more features to the proposed model may lead to increased complexity and, consequently, reduce its efficiency.

Table 7.6 presents the results of the models on the Pabna dataset, categorized by the number of features. The accuracy percentages obtained by the proposed model with three and four features are 96.80% and 95.41%, respectively. However, the accuracy percentages obtained by the AVOA and GWO models for the three features are 96.16 and 96.32, respectively. The accuracy percentages obtained by the AVOA and GWO models for the six features are 92.91% and 93.48%, respectively. The accuracy percentages of the proposed model with three features and four features are 97.00% and 95.44%, respectively. The accuracy percentages of the proposed model with six features and seven features are 93.83% and 92.90%, respectively.

Fig. 7.3 illustrates the accuracy percentage of the proposed model for Pabna, based on the number of iterations and feature selection. The accuracy percentages for three features with 200 and 300 iterations are 96.24% and 96.80%,

TABLE 7.4 Results of models based on the number of k.

Datasets	KNN(k)	Models	Precision	Recall	F1-Score	Accuracy
Pima	3	AVOA	75.23	75.42	75.32	74.68
		GWO	76.43	76.56	76.49	75.84
		Our model	78.00	78.17	78.08	77.65
	4	AVOA	75.70	75.54	75.62	75.12
		GWO	76.00	76.20	76.10	75.35
		Our model	77.21	77.51	77.36	76.62
	5	AVOA	73.32	74.35	73.83	72.92
		GWO	74.65	74.64	74.64	73.85
		Our model	76.11	76.32	76.21	75.84
Pabna	3	AVOA	91.32	91.56	91.44	91.12
		GWO	91.25	91.37	91.31	90.86
		Our model	92.10	92.27	92.18	91.65
	4	AVOA	89.80	90.80	90.30	89.35
		GWO	90.30	90.36	90.33	89.87
		Our model	91.24	91.24	91.24	90.54
	5	AVOA	88.22	88.38	88.30	87.68
		GWO	89.32	89.32	89.32	88.72
		Our model	89.45	89.84	89.64	89.31

TABLE 7.5 The results of the models on the Pima dataset are based on the number of features.

Dataset	#Features	Models	Precision	Recall	F1-Score	Accuracy
Pima	3	AVOA	82.05	82.14	82.09	81.56
		GWO	82.02	82.50	82.26	81.85
		Our model	83.20	83.25	83.22	82.84
	4	AVOA	81.23	81.62	81.42	81.11
		GWO	81.16	81.16	81.16	80.92
		Our model	81.56	81.90	81.73	81.32
	5	AVOA	80.13	80.00	80.06	79.83
		GWO	80.60	80.62	80.61	80.16
		Our model	80.91	80.80	80.85	80.49
	6	AVOA	79.30	79.42	79.36	78.95
		GWO	79.67	79.90	79.78	79.42
		Our model	80.00	80.20	80.10	79.64
	7	AVOA	78.60	78.70	78.65	78.13
		GWO	78.84	78.84	78.84	78.46
		Our model	79.08	79.20	79.14	78.74
	8	AVOA	76.25	76.48	76.36	75.61
		GWO	77.40	77.51	77.45	76.94
		Our model	78.14	78.30	78.22	77.65

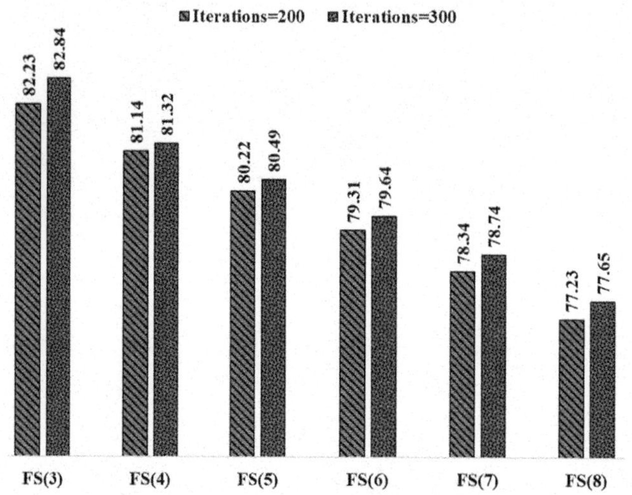

FIGURE 7.2 Accuracy percentage of the proposed model on Pima based on the number of iterations and feature selection.

TABLE 7.6 The results of the models on the Pabna dataset based on the number of features.

Dataset	#Features	Models	Precision	Recall	F1-Score	Accuracy
Pabna	3	AVOA	96.30	96.36	96.33	96.16
		GWO	96.45	96.55	96.50	96.32
		Our model	97.00	97.10	97.05	96.80
	4	AVOA	94.52	94.40	94.46	94.25
		GWO	95.05	95.05	95.05	94.82
		Our model	95.44	95.60	95.52	95.41
	5	AVOA	94.30	94.20	94.25	94.12
		GWO	94.15	94.23	94.19	93.96
		Our model	94.60	94.70	94.65	94.49
	6	AVOA	93.17	93.25	93.21	92.91
		GWO	93.60	93.70	93.65	93.48
		Our model	93.83	93.91	93.87	93.64
	7	AVOA	92.60	92.70	92.65	92.44
		GWO	92.74	92.80	92.77	92.54
		Our model	92.90	93.06	92.98	92.74
	8	AVOA	92.42	92.60	92.51	92.37
		GWO	92.30	92.44	92.37	92.15
		Our model	92.56	92.64	92.60	92.45
	9	AVOA	91.32	91.42	91.37	91.12
		GWO	91.00	91.11	91.05	90.86
		Our model	91.76	91.87	91.81	91.65

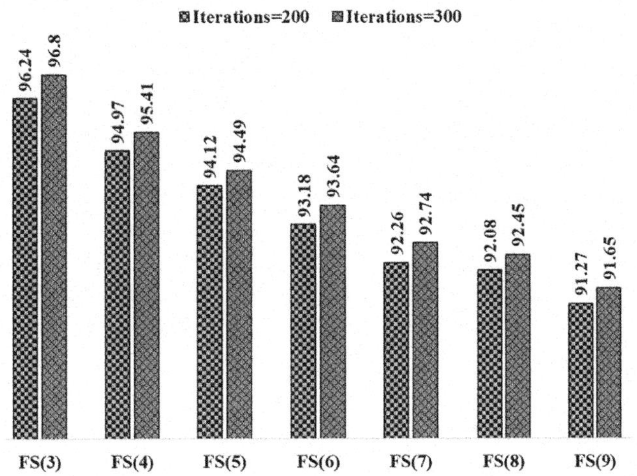

FIGURE 7.3 Accuracy percentage of the proposed model on Pabna based on the number of iterations and feature selection.

TABLE 7.7 Evaluation of models on the BRFSS dataset based on the number of different features.

Dataset	#Features	Models	Precision	Recall	F1-Score	Accuracy
BRFSS	3	AVOA	97.07	96.82	96.94	97.12
		GWO	97.15	97.21	97.18	97.36
		Our model	98.10	97.95	98.02	98.11
	5	AVOA	96.23	96.28	96.25	96.75
		GWO	96.72	96.93	96.82	96.96
		Our model	97.56	96.76	97.16	97.85
	7	AVOA	96.79	96.55	96.67	96.66
		GWO	96.68	96.81	96.74	96.84
		Our model	97.61	97.23	97.42	97.68
	8	AVOA	96.75	96.51	96.63	96.62
		GWO	96.66	96.70	96.68	96.56
		Our model	97.35	97.21	97.28	97.42
	10	AVOA	96.29	96.35	96.32	96.19
		GWO	96.51	96.24	96.37	96.39
		Our model	97.05	97.20	97.12	97.25
	12	AVOA	96.23	96.08	96.15	96.12
		GWO	96.41	96.44	96.42	96.27
		Our model	96.76	96.50	96.63	97.14
	15	AVOA	96.14	96.19	96.16	96.02
		GWO	96.27	96.11	96.19	96.17
		Our model	96.56	96.91	96.73	96.87
	18	AVOA	95.06	95.26	95.16	95.92
		GWO	96.18	96.19	96.18	96.05
		Our model	95.72	96.14	95.93	96.53
	20	AVOA	95.26	95.30	95.28	95.72
		GWO	95.42	96.02	95.72	95.93
		Our model	95.25	95.86	95.55	96.24

respectively. The accuracy percentages for five features with 200 and 300 iterations are 94.12% and 94.49%, respectively. The accuracy percentages for six features with 200 and 300 iterations are 93.18% and 93.64%, respectively. The accuracy percentages for eight features with 200 and 300 iterations are 92.08% and 92.45%, respectively.

Table 7.7 reports the evaluation of the models on the BRFSS dataset based on the number of different features. The combined model with 3 features achieved an accuracy of 98.11. The GWO and AVOA models achieved 97.36 and 97.12, respectively. The results of the accuracy of eight features show that the combined GWO and AVOA models achieved 97.42, 96.56, and 96.62, respectively. The combined model with 20 features achieved an accuracy of 96.24. The GWO and AVOA models achieved 95.93 and 95.72, respectively.

7.5 Conclusion and future works

Diabetes mellitus is a chronic metabolic disease characterized by increased blood glucose levels, resulting from a defect in insulin production or insufficient insulin action. With the increasing growth of medical data, the use of machine learning algorithms to predict and diagnose diabetes is known as an effective method. Machine learning algorithms are beneficial in various fields, including predicting diabetes, facilitating early diagnosis, and analyzing patient behavior patterns. However, the most critical issue for machine learning algorithms is to use relevant and accurate features to diagnose diabetes. Therefore, this chapter used the hybridization of AVOA and GWO algorithms to select important features. The GWO enhanced the AVOA, allowing agents to identify the optimal solution vectors in the problem space. Finally, the proposed model was tested using the KNN for classification operation on the Pima and Pabna datasets. The results showed that the proposed model is more accurate than AVOA and GWO. The accuracy percentage of the proposed model on the Pima and Pabna datasets with three features is 82.84% and 96.80%, respectively. The proposed model has achieved the best recognition accuracy with 300 iterations. Despite the promising results of hybridizing AVOA and GWO algorithms, this chapter faces several limitations that can impact the accuracy of diagnosis. The most significant limitation of this chapter is the presence of unbalanced data, specifically the disparity in the number of sick and healthy samples, which can lead to inaccurate performance. Another limitation is that the KNN algorithm is sensitive to the number of neighbors and the spacing algorithm used for classification on large datasets. Therefore, optimizing the KNN algorithm should be related to the size of the data. In the end, the future works in the direction of diagnosis and prediction of hepatitis disease and heart disease using the hybridization of meta-heuristic algorithms and machine learning, including the following: (1) Hybridization of spotted hyena optimizer (SHO) and golden jackal optimization (GJO) algorithms for hepatitis disease diagnosis: In this method, the SHO algorithm is used as a meta-heuristic optimization algorithm to search the feature space, and the GJO algorithm is used to fine-tune the SVM parameters. This hybridization can improve diagnosis accuracy and reduce the number of unnecessary features in the dataset related to the hepatitis disease. (2) Using a hybridization of the emperor penguin optimizer (EPO) and AVOA algorithms to diagnose heart disease, EPO is employed to optimize the search space and identify critical features. On the other hand, the AVOA algorithm improves the parameters of an artificial neural network and reduces the classification error rate. This hybridization can help increase the accuracy of heart disease diagnosis and reduce the model's error rate.

Declarations

Ethical approval

This chapter contains no studies with human participants or animals performed by the authors.

Funding

Not applicable.

Conflict of interest

The authors declare that there is no conflict of interest.

Availability of data and materials

The datasets analyzed in this study are publicly available for testing purposes. All the datasets used in this study are available at the following links. Also, the datasets are available on most project-oriented and reference sites.

https://www.kaggle.com/datasets/uciml/pima-indians-diabetes-database
https://github.com/ruhul256/Pabna-Diabetes-Dataset-Bangladesh

References

[1] S.S. Bhat, M. Banu, G.A. Ansari, V. Selvam, A risk assessment and prediction framework for diabetes mellitus using machine learning algorithms, Healthcare Analytics 2023 (1) (2023) 1–24.

[2] E.A. Pustozerov, A.S. Tkachuk, E.A. Vasukova, A.D. Anopova, M.A. Kokina, I.V. Gorelova, et al., Machine learning approach for postprandial blood glucose prediction in gestational diabetes mellitus, IEEE Access 8 (1) (2020) 219308–219321.

[3] D. Balasubramaniyan, N.A. Husin, N. Mustapha, N.M. Sharef, T.N. Mohd Aris, Flock optimization induced deep learning for improved diabetes disease classification, Expert Systems 2023 (1) (2023) 1–35.

[4] M. Gargi, A. Namburu, An intelligent optimized deep network for retinopathy diabetes segmentation, Wireless Personal Communications 135 (3) (2024) 1885–1907.

[5] S. Saturi, Review on machine learning techniques for medical data classification and disease diagnosis, Regenerative Engineering and Translational Medicine 9 (2) (2023) 141–164.

[6] G. Aguilera-Venegas, A. López-Molina, G. Rojo-Martínez, J.L. Galán-García, Comparing and tuning machine learning algorithms to predict type 2 diabetes mellitus, Journal of Computational and Applied Mathematics 427 (1) (2023) 1–26.

[7] A.T. Villikudathil, D.H. Mc Guigan, A. English, Computational approaches for clinical, genomic and proteomic markers of response to GLP-1 therapy in type-2 diabetes mellitus: an exploratory analysis with machine learning algorithms, Genomic and Proteomic Markers of Response to GLP-1 Therapy in Type-2 Diabetes Mellitus: An Exploratory Analysis With Machine Learning Algorithms 2024 (1) (May 2, 2024) 1–132.

[8] T.A. Lutz, Mammalian models of diabetes mellitus, with a focus on type 2 diabetes mellitus, Nature Reviews Endocrinology 19 (6) (2023) 350–360.

[9] X. Wang, L. Zhu, J. Liu, Y. Ma, C. Qiu, C. Liu, et al., Palmitic acid in type 2 diabetes mellitus promotes atherosclerotic plaque vulnerability via macrophage Dll4 signaling, Nature Communications 15 (1) (2024) 1–26.

[10] X. Tao, M. Jiang, Y. Liu, Q. Hu, B. Zhu, J. Hu, et al., Predicting three-month fasting blood glucose and glycated hemoglobin changes in patients with type 2 diabetes mellitus based on multiple machine learning algorithms, Scientific Reports 13 (1) (2023) 1–28.

[11] S. Gowthami, R.V.S. Reddy, M.R. Ahmed, Exploring the effectiveness of machine learning algorithms for early detection of type-2 diabetes mellitus, Measurement: Sensors 31 (1) (2024) 1–34.

[12] S.S. Bhat, G.A. Ansari, M.D. Ansari, Performance analysis of machine learning based on optimized feature selection for type II diabetes mellitus, Multimedia Tools and Applications 2024 (1) (2024) 1–20.

[13] S.M. Nimmagadda, G. Suryanarayana, G.B. Kumar, G. Anudeep, G.V. Sai, A comprehensive survey on diabetes type-2 (T2D) forecast using machine learning, Archives of Computational Methods in Engineering 2024 (1) (2024) 1–19.

[14] B.F. Wee, S. Sivakumar, K.H. Lim, W.K. Wong, F.H. Juwono, Diabetes detection based on machine learning and deep learning approaches, Multimedia Tools and Applications 83 (8) (2024) 24153–24185.

[15] G.K. Ghuman, N. Bagri, R. Chandra, A. Malik, R. Misra, H.S. Gaikwad, Role of ultrasonographic measurement of the fetal epicardial fat pad and cardiac interventricular septal thickness in predicting the outcome and prevent various complications of gestational diabetes mellitus, Egyptian Journal of Radiology and Nuclear Medicine 54 (1) (2023) 1–36.

[16] F.S. Gharehchopogh, I. Maleki, Z.A. Dizaji, Chaotic vortex search algorithm: metaheuristic algorithm for feature selection, Evolutionary Intelligence 15 (3) (2022) 1777–1808.

[17] B. Abdollahzadeh, F.S. Gharehchopogh, S. Mirjalili, African vultures optimization algorithm: a new nature-inspired metaheuristic algorithm for global optimization problems, Computers & Industrial Engineering 158 (1) (2021) 1–35.

[18] S. Mirjalili, S.M. Mirjalili, A. Lewis, Grey wolf optimizer, Advances in Engineering Software 69 (2014) 46–61.

[19] M.S. Reza, R. Amin, R. Yasmin, W. Kulsum, and S. Ruhi. Improving diabetes disease patients classification using stacking ensemble method with PIMA and local healthcare data. Heliyon, vol. 10, no. 2, pp. 1–22, 2024.

[20] W. Zhou, X. Liu, H. Bai, L. He, Intelligent medical diagnosis and treatment for diabetes with deep convolutional fuzzy neural networks, Information Sciences 2024 (1) (2024) 1–25.

[21] X.-D. Li, J.-S. Wang, Y. Liu, H.-M. Song, Y.-C. Wang, J.-N. Hou, et al., Classification feature selection and dimensionality reduction based on logical binary sine-cosine function arithmetic optimization algorithm, Egyptian Informatics Journal 26 (1) (2024) 1–24.

[22] S.R. Kamel, R. Yaghoubzadeh, Feature selection using grasshopper optimization algorithm in diagnosis of diabetes disease, Informatics in Medicine Unlocked 26 (1) (2021) 1–32.

[23] T.M. Ahmed, Developing a predicted model for diabetes type 2 treatment plans by using data mining, Journal of Theoretical and Applied Information Technology 90 (2) (2016) 1–25.

[24] M.A. Uddin, M.M. Islam, M.A. Talukder, M.A.A. Hossain, A. Akhter, S. Aryal, et al., Machine learning based diabetes detection model for false negative reduction, Biomedical Materials & Devices 2 (1) (2024) 427–443.

[25] R. Song, W. Nie, A. Hou, S. Xue, Dynamic random mutation hybrid Harris hawk optimization and its application to training kernel extreme learning machine, Cluster Computing 2024 (1) (2024) 1–38.

[26] G. Pradhan, G. Thapa, R. Pradhan, B. Khandelwal, R. Panigrahi, A.K. Bhoi, et al., Optimized forest framework with a binary multineighborhood artificial bee colony for enhanced diabetes mellitus detection, International Journal of Computational Intelligence Systems 17 (1) (2024) 1–25.

[27] A.K. Mahapatra, N. Panda, B.K. Pattanayak, Hybrid PSO (SGPSO) with the incorporation of discretization operator for training RBF neural network and optimal feature selection, Arabian Journal for Science and Engineering 48 (8) (2023) 9991–10019.

[28] F. Rezaei, M. Abbasitabar, S. Mirzaei, Z. Kamari Direh, S. Ahmadi, Z. Azizi, et al., Improve data classification performance in diagnosing diabetes using the Binary Exchange Market Algorithm, Journal of Big Data 9 (1) (2022) 1–29.

[29] R. Asif, D. Upadhyay, M. Zaman, S. Sampalli, Enhancing diabetes risk prediction: a comparative evaluation of bagging, boosting, and ensemble classifiers with SMOTE oversampling, Informatics in Medicine Unlocked 57 (1) (2025) 1–32.

[30] M.A. Hama Saeed, Diabetes type 2 classification using machine learning algorithms with up-sampling technique, Journal of Electrical Systems and Information Technology 10 (1) (2023) 1–10.

Chapter 8

Performance analysis of the grey wolf optimizer and its variants in global search optimization

Nguyen Van Thieu[1], Nguyen Van Son[1], Ngoc Hung Nguyen[1,2], La Van Quan[1], and Nguyen Thi Hanh[3]
[1]*Phenikaa School of Computing, PHENIKAA University, Hanoi, Vietnam,* [2]*Department of Electrical and Information Technology, Lund University, Lund, Sweden,* [3]*Faculty of Interdisciplinary Digital Technology, PHENIKAA University, Hanoi, Vietnam*

8.1 Introduction

Metaheuristic algorithms have become indispensable tools for solving complex optimization problems in science, engineering, and artificial intelligence. Their ability to navigate vast and rugged search spaces without relying on gradient information has made them particularly attractive for global optimization tasks, where conventional methods often fall short. Among the various nature-inspired metaheuristics proposed over the past two decades, the grey wolf optimizer (GWO), introduced in [1], has gained notable popularity due to its conceptual simplicity, low computational cost, and competitive performance across diverse applications. Since its introduction, GWO has been widely applied to numerical optimization, feature selection, clustering, scheduling, engineering design, and machine learning model tuning, among others [2].

However, like many population-based metaheuristics, the original GWO is not without limitations. It may suffer from issues such as premature convergence, stagnation in local optima, or slow adaptation in high-dimensional or constrained search spaces [3]. These challenges have inspired the development of numerous GWO variants and hybrids, each aiming to enhance specific aspects of the algorithm be it exploration ability, convergence speed, robustness, or applicability to particular problem domains.

Given the diversity and rapid growth of GWO-based methods, it is essential to conduct a comprehensive and unbiased performance evaluation. In this chapter, we benchmark the original GWO and 12 representative variants on the CEC-2017 benchmark suite, which encompasses unimodal, multimodal, hybrid, and composition functions. All algorithms are tested under identical experimental settings to ensure fairness, eliminate parameter bias, and provide a clear assessment of their global search capabilities. This systematic approach allows us to identify relative strengths and weaknesses, understand the effects of specific modifications, and offer guidance for both future algorithm design and practical deployment.

The purpose of this chapter is therefore to present a rigorous comparative analysis of GWO and its improved variants in terms of accuracy, convergence, stability, and scalability. The chapter is organized as follows: Section 8.2 presents the theoretical foundations of GWO and a comparison with its variants. Section 8.3 defines the performance analysis framework for evaluation. Section 8.4 discusses the results. Section 8.5 concludes with key insights.

8.2 Background on grey wolf optimization

The GWO, introduced in 2014 [1], is a swarm-based metaheuristic that models the leadership structure and collaborative hunting behavior observed in grey wolves. Grey wolves are apex predators that live in organized packs, typically comprising 5–12 members. Their hunting behavior and leadership structure form the basis for the mathematical formulation of the algorithm. GWO models the search process through distinct phases corresponding to leadership roles and prey-hunting behaviors. In this chapter, the mathematical notation has been adapted for consistency with conventions

Grey Wolf Optimizer. DOI: https://doi.org/10.1016/B978-0-443-36624-6.00019-6

in the metaheuristics research community. These modifications do not alter the algorithm's underlying structure or correctness. Readers are referred to the original research for a detailed account of the initial formalism.

The search begins with initializing $\mathcal{N}$ wolves (candidate solutions) randomly within a D-dimensional search space. Let $\mathcal{X}_{lb}$ and $\mathcal{X}_{ub}$ denote the lower and upper bounds of the search space, respectively. The uniform random function is represented as $\mathcal{U}(0,1)$. Then, the initial solutions can be mathematically expressed as:

$$\mathcal{X}_i^0 = \mathcal{X}_{lb} + \mathcal{U}(0,1)\cdot(\mathcal{X}_{ub} - \mathcal{X}_{lb}); \quad i=1,2,\ldots,\mathcal{N} \tag{8.1}$$

In the GWO framework, the population is stratified into a four-tier hierarchy: alpha (α), beta (β), delta (δ), and omega (ω) wolves, representing the best, second-best, third-best, and remaining candidate solutions, respectively. The optimization process simulates three key hunting behaviors observed in grey wolves: searching for prey, encircling the target, and attacking. These stages collectively guide the algorithm toward the optimal solution.

The position of a wolf $\mathcal{X}_i$ in iteration t+1 is updated according to Eq. (8.2):

$$\mathcal{X}_i^{t+1} = \frac{\mathcal{X}_a^t + \mathcal{X}_b^t + \mathcal{X}_c^t}{3} \tag{8.2}$$

where $\mathcal{X}_a$, $\mathcal{X}_b$, and $\mathcal{X}_c$ are intermediate positions derived from the influence of the α, β, and δ wolves:

$$\mathcal{X}_a^t = \mathcal{X}_\alpha^t - m\cdot(2\cdot\mathcal{R}(0,1,D) - 1)\cdot|2\cdot\mathcal{R}(0,1,D)\cdot\mathcal{X}_\alpha^t - \mathcal{X}_i^t| \tag{8.3}$$

$$\mathcal{X}_b^t = \mathcal{X}_\beta^t - m\cdot(2\cdot\mathcal{R}(0,1,D) - 1)\cdot|2\cdot\mathcal{R}(0,1,D)\cdot\mathcal{X}_\beta^t - \mathcal{X}_i^t| \tag{8.4}$$

$$\mathcal{X}_c^t = \mathcal{X}_\delta^t - m\cdot(2\cdot\mathcal{R}(0,1,D) - 1)\cdot|2\cdot\mathcal{R}(0,1,D)\cdot\mathcal{X}_\delta^t - \mathcal{X}_i^t| \tag{8.5}$$

$$m=2\cdot\left(1 - \frac{t}{T}\right) \tag{8.6}$$

In the above formulation, $\mathcal{X}_\alpha^t$, $\mathcal{X}_\beta^t$, and $\mathcal{X}_\delta^t$ denote the positions of the top three wolves at generation t. Here, t is the current generation, T is the maximum number of generations, and $\mathcal{R}(0,1,D)$, is a function that generates a D-dimensional random vector with components uniformly distributed over (0,1). $|\cdot|$ stands for the absolute value operator. The parameter m controls the balance between exploration and exploitation, decreasing linearly over the generations.

The procedural steps of GWO are outlined in Algorithm 1, encompassing population initialization, fitness evaluation, and position updating.

Algorithm 1. Grey wolf optimization

Require: Population size $\mathcal{N}$, maximum generations T, bounds $\mathcal{X}_{lb}$, $\mathcal{X}_{ub}$, the fitness function $\mathcal{F}(.)$.
Ensure: Global best solution $\mathcal{X}_{\text{best}}$

1. Initialize population $\{\mathcal{X}_i^0\}_{i=1}^{\mathcal{N}}$ using Eq. (8.1)
2. Evaluate all candidates; set $\mathcal{X}_{\text{best}}$ as best-so-far
3. Set iteration counter $t \leftarrow 1$
4. **while** $t < T$ **do**
5. Identify the α, β, and δ wolves.
6. **for** i=1 to $\mathcal{N}$ **do**
7. Calculate the new position $\mathcal{X}_i^{t+1}$ of the current wolf by Eq. (8.2).
8. Apply boundary constraints on $\mathcal{X}_i^{t+1}$
9. Update the fitness for the new population
10. Update the best solution $\mathcal{X}_{\text{best}}$ if improved
11. $t \leftarrow t + 1$
12. **return** $\mathcal{X}_{\text{best}}$

Although the canonical GWO has demonstrated strong performance for unimodal and moderately complex problems, it may exhibit premature convergence in high-dimensional or highly multimodal landscapes [Long et al.(2020) Long, Cai, Jiao, and Tang]. These challenges have motivated the development of numerous GWO variants aimed at improving convergence speed, accuracy, and robustness. (Tables 8.1 and 8.2).

TABLE 8.1 Summary of 37 variants and improvements of grey wolf optimization.

Variant name	Main improvement	Application domain
Improved hybrid GWO [4]	Combines GWO with complementary strategies to balance exploration and exploitation	General global optimization
GWO with variable weights [5]	Dynamically adjusts leadership weights to improve convergence	Continuous optimization
Chaotic GWO [6]	Integrates chaotic maps to diversify search and escape local optima	Constrained optimization
Fuzzy hierarchical GWO [3]	Uses fuzzy hierarchical operator to refine leader–follower interactions	General optimization
Adaptive GWO [7]	Adjusts control parameters adaptively during iterations	Multimodal optimization
I-GWO and Ex-GWO [8]	Introduces enhanced encircling and exploration phases	Global optimization
Exploration-enhanced GWO [9]	Expands search range via modified encircling equations	High-dimensional problems
Randomized balanced GWO (RBGWO) [10]	Applies randomized position balancing to improve diversity	Real-life engineering
Experienced GWO via RL and NN [11]	Uses reinforcement learning and neural networks to guide search	Intelligent control
Enhanced GWO + MapReduce [12]	Parallel implementation for large-scale clustering	Big data clustering
Tracking and seeking GWO [13]	Integrates tracking/seeking modes for local refinement	Function optimization
Orthogonal learning covariance GWO [14]	Uses orthogonal learning to improve diversity and reduce redundancy	Feature selection
Elite OBL chaotic k-best GWO [15]	Combines elite opposition-based learning and chaotic *k*-best gravitational search	Automotive brake system design
Accelerated GWO [16]	Modifies update equations to speed up convergence	Global optimization
AP-TLB-IGWO [17]	Combines teaching–learning-based strategy with adult–pup hierarchy	Numerical optimization
DSGWO [18]	Group-stage competition and diversity enhancement mechanisms	Complex search problems
DE-elimination GWO [19]	Hybrid with differential evolution and elimination mechanism	Continuous optimization
GWO + Cuckoo search [20]	Combines Lévy flight search capability with GWO	Solar PV parameter estimation
GWO + Artificial bee colony [21]	Combines swarm strategies to enhance performance	Complex systems optimization
Aquila-based GWO [22]	Adopts Aquila exploration strategies for diverse search	General optimization
Adaptively balanced GWO [23]	Adjusts exploration/exploitation for high-dimensional feature selection	Classification problems

8.2.1 Variants and improvements of grey wolf optimization

Since its introduction, the GWO algorithm has inspired numerous variants designed to address limitations such as premature convergence, imbalance between exploration and exploitation, and performance degradation in high-dimensional or constrained problems. The following subsections summarize several notable variants, each improving GWO through different strategies.

TABLE 8.2 Summary of 37 variants and improvements of grey wolf optimization (continued).

Variant name	Main improvement	Application domain
Harmony search + GWO + Modified OBL [24]	Integrates harmony search and opposition learning for better convergence	Continuous optimization
Two-phase mutation GWO [25]	Employs distinct mutation phases for exploration and exploitation	Feature selection
Inspired GWO [26]	Enhances leadership hierarchy for large-scale problems	Large-scale function optimization
Enhanced GWO [27]	Modifies search strategy to maintain balance and stability	Global optimization
Cauchy–Gaussian mutation GWO [28]	Adds heavy-tailed mutations for improved exploration	Global optimization
Modified GWO for robotics [29]	Tailors search strategy to kinematic constraints	Robotics engineering
Policy iteration RL GWO [30]	Integrates policy iteration RL for control optimization	Control problems
Efficient and robust GWO [31]	Introduces lightweight exploration schemes for large-scale problems	Large-scale numerical optimization
Advanced GWO [32]	Adapts search behavior for domain-specific constraints	Smart grid planning
Better exploration strategy GWO [33]	Improves early-stage exploration to reduce computation	General optimization
Representative-based GWO (R-GWO) [34]	Uses representative solutions to preserve diversity	Engineering optimization
Improved GWO + Cuckoo search [35]	Strengthens exploration by combining search mechanisms	General optimization
Dominant wolves GWO [36]	Examines the effects of dominant wolves to refine the leader's impact	General optimization
OBL-GWO [37]	Integrates opposition-based learning for faster convergence	Global optimization
Improved dynamic GWO [38]	Real-time adjustment of parameters for better adaptability	Various optimization problems

8.2.1.1 *Parameter adaptation and dynamic control*

The study [5] proposed VW-GWO, which improves GWO by introducing variable weights in the social hierarchy and a new controlling parameter equation to reduce the risk of local optima. The algorithm was applied to benchmark and high-dimensional optimization problems, showing superior performance over standard GWO, flower pollination algorithm (FPA), ant lion optimizer (ALO), particle swarm optimization (PSO), and bat algorithm (BA).

An adaptive grey wolf optimization (AGWO) algorithm was proposed by the research [7], in which the exploration–exploitation parameters are adaptively tuned based on the fitness history, and a stopping criterion driven by the significance of fitness improvement is employed to save computational resources. In an extended version, the convergence parameters are further adjusted using a three-point fitness history. Experimental results show that comparable or better solutions are achieved by AGWO in fewer iterations, outperforming several GWO variants. The adaptively balanced grey wolf optimization (ABGWO) algorithm, introduced in the paper [23], enhances GWO's exploration by incorporating a randomly selected wolf alongside the traditional leaders using a novel level-based selection strategy. An adaptive coefficient dynamically adjusts the influence of these wolves throughout the optimization process to balance exploration and exploitation. Evaluated on 12 high-dimensional datasets, ABGWO outperformed seven state-of-the-art feature selection methods in classification accuracy, feature subset size, and computational efficiency. The diversity-enhanced strategy grey wolf optimizer (DSGWO) [18] improves the standard GWO by integrating a group-stage competition mechanism and an exploration–exploitation balance strategy to overcome issues of low population diversity and premature convergence. Experimental assessments on the IEEE CEC 2014 benchmark set and several engineering design tasks showed that DSGWO outperforms the conventional GWO, offering stronger global search ability, improved diversity retention, and higher overall optimization efficiency. The dynamic grey wolf optimizer variants, DGWO1 and DGWO2, proposed in the research [38], improve the standard GWO by allowing search agents to update their positions immediately after comparing with the leader wolves, eliminating the waiting period present in the static GWO. This modification accelerates convergence and enhances optimization efficiency. Experimental evaluations demonstrate that improved algorithms built on dynamic GWO consistently outperform their static counterparts across various test cases.

8.2.1.2 Chaotic and stochastic perturbations

CGWO was proposed by Ref. [6], in which chaos theory is integrated into GWO through the use of 10 chaotic maps to tune the control parameter, thereby enhancing the global convergence speed. The algorithm was validated on constrained benchmark functions and engineering design problems, and superior performance was achieved compared to standard GWO and other metaheuristics such as crow search algorithm (CSA), flower pollination algorithm (FPA), and PSO-based algorithm. The GWO algorithm based on Cauchy–Gaussian mutation and improved search strategy (CG-GWO), as detailed in [28], enhances population diversity of leader wolves through a Cauchy–Gaussian mutation operator, boosting global search capability and reducing premature convergence. A greedy selection mechanism preserves elite wolves to maintain fast convergence, while an improved search strategy expands the search space for higher accuracy. Tested on 16 benchmark functions, CG-GWO outperformed classic algorithms like PSO, whale optimization algorithm (WOA), sparrow search algorithm (SSA), and farmland fertility algorithm (FFA), as well as several advanced GWO variants, demonstrating superior convergence speed, accuracy, and global optimization ability. Further advancing exploration–exploitation balance [10], the proposed randomized balanced GWO (RBGWO), which integrates the social hierarchy mechanism with random walks driven by Student's t-distributed numbers through three successive strategies. Tested on CEC 2014 benchmark functions and applied to both constrained and unconstrained real-world problems, RBGWO surpassed standard GWO, its variants, and other metaheuristics in solution quality and overall performance. In a related direction [25], proposed a variant GWO integrated with a two-phase mutation (GWO-TPM) to address feature selection problems. This algorithm improves exploitation while balancing feature subset size and classification accuracy by mapping continuous solutions to binary space using a sigmoid function. Two mutation phases are applied: one to reduce redundant features and another to add informative ones, both with controlled probabilities to manage computational cost. Evaluated on 35 datasets using a k-Nearest Neighbor wrapper and K-fold cross-validation, GWO-TPM outperformed several state-of-the-art algorithms such as flower algorithm, PSO, multi-verse optimizer (MVO), WOA, and bat algorithm, with statistical tests confirming its effectiveness.

8.2.1.3 Hybridization with other optimization techniques

Several hybrid GWO variants have been proposed to enhance its performance by combining it with other optimization methods. The work of [4] introduced PSO-GWO, which employs Tent chaotic initialization and a nonlinear control parameter to improve population diversity and search balance, while integrating PSO updates to avoid local optima. Tested on 18 benchmark problems, PSO-GWO achieved faster convergence, higher accuracy, and better robustness than competing methods. Similarly, Ref. [17] developed the Adult-Pup Teaching–Learning Based Interactive GWO (AP-TLB-IGWO), where adult wolves and pups collaboratively explore the search space using an energy-driven hunting mechanism and information sharing. This approach addresses premature convergence near the coordinate origin and shows significant improvements on benchmark suites and real-world problems. Hybridization with Cuckoo Search (CS) has also been explored. The study [20] proposed GWOCS, which uses opposition learning to increase diversity and balance exploration–exploitation, demonstrating promising results on 10 complex benchmark functions and photovoltaic model parameter estimation. Another CS-GWO hybrid [35] improves updates of the top three wolves using CS mechanisms, outperforming the original GWO and CS on high-dimensional optimization problems. Other hybrids include GWO-ABC [21], combining GWO with artificial bee colony and enhanced by chaotic mapping and opposition-based initialization to prevent premature convergence. It excelled in complex benchmarks and practical control problems. GWO-HS [24] merges GWO with Harmony Search (HS), automatically tuning HS parameters and using modified opposition-based learning (OBL), resulting in superior accuracy and faster convergence on extensive benchmark sets. Finally, the authors in [19] proposed Improved GWO (IGWO), integrating evolutionary and elimination strategies inspired by natural selection. By incorporating differential evolution for position updates and eliminating the worst wolves each iteration, IGWO accelerates convergence and avoids local optima, outperforming several state-of-the-art algorithms on 12 standard benchmark functions.

8.2.1.4 Learning-based and reinforcement mechanisms

The work presented in [11] proposed experienced GWO, which integrates reinforcement learning and neural networks to adaptively tune the exploration–exploitation parameter for each agent based on individual experience and search space conditions. The experience repository continuously updates agents' policies to improve performance. Tested on feature selection and neural network weight optimization tasks, EGWO outperformed standard GWO, genetic algorithms, and PSO. Building on the integration of reinforcement learning and GWO. The research [9] introduced a control method that combines Policy Iteration with GWO for neural network training. By leveraging GWO's effective balance between exploration and exploitation, this approach was evaluated against classical PI combined with gradient descent (GD) and PI with PSO on a nonlinear servo system. Experimental results demonstrated that the GWO-based method achieved superior performance in optimal reference tracking compared to GD and PSO, with results averaged over multiple runs to mitigate the randomness inherent in metaheuristic algorithms.

8.2.1.5 Enhanced exploration and dimensionality handling

To improve GWO's exploration and handling of complex problems, several variants have been proposed. The paper [9] introduced exploration-enhanced GWO, which uses a new position-update guided by a random individual and a nonlinear control parameter, showing better accuracy and faster convergence than standard GWO and other competitors on benchmarks and engineering tasks. The study [34] proposed R-GWO with a Representative-based Hunting strategy that combines multiple trial vectors and a representative archive to enhance diversity and balance exploration–exploitation. It outperformed several algorithms, such as PSO, krill herd (KH), GWO, and WOA, on CEC 2018 benchmarks and engineering problems. Inspired by the Aquila Optimizer [22], developed an improved GWO that allows some wolves to "fly" and expand the search range, reducing premature convergence. Tests on 23 benchmarks and 4 engineering tasks confirmed its strong performance and robustness in complex, unknown search spaces. Finally, in [14] the authors presented GWOCMALOL, integrating CMA-ES, Lévy flight, and orthogonal learning to tackle complex optimizations. Evaluations on CEC-2014 benchmark functions and feature selection (24 UCI) datasets showed improved convergence, accuracy, and classification performance.

8.2.1.6 Specialized improvements for large-Scale and engineering problems

Several GWO variants have been developed to address large-scale and complex engineering problems. For example, paper [3] proposed Hierarchical GWO, introducing a hierarchical operator inspired by the grey wolf social pyramid with five variants, including fuzzy logic-based approaches. Tested on up to 128-dimensional benchmarks, the fuzzy variants showed the most significant improvements over standard GWO. The inspired GWO (IGWO) [26] incorporates nonlinear control adjustment and a modified position update influenced by individual and global bests, inspired by PSO. Tested on high-dimensional benchmark (CEC 2005) functions and engineering problems, IGWO demonstrated higher accuracy, faster convergence, and fewer fitness evaluations compared to existing methods. Similarly, the efficient and robust GWO (ERGWO) [31] integrates nonlinear parameter adjustment and an improved update equation to balance exploration and exploitation better. Validated on large-scale benchmarks including CEC 2014 and 2017, ERGWO consistently outperformed standard GWO, its variants, and other metaheuristics in solution quality and convergence speed. The advanced GWO (AGWO) [32] introduces a novel position evaluation, mirroring to handle boundary violations, and a dynamic decision mechanism to switch between exploration and exploitation. AGWO outperformed multiple heuristics on various benchmarks, including CEC-C06 2019, and excelled in smart grid planning by improving voltage profiles, reducing losses, and lowering emissions compared to GWO and PSO. Finally, EOCSGWO [15], which combining elite OBL with a chaotic k-best gravitational search strategy to enhance exploration and exploitation. Tested on ten benchmarks and applied to auto drum brake design, EOCSGWO improved accuracy, robustness, and increased braking efficiency by over 28% compared to other metaheuristics.

8.2.1.7 Acceleration and convergence boosting

Several GWO variants have been designed to speed up convergence while maintaining solution quality. Ref. [13] proposed an improved GWO combining tracking and seeking modes to enhance population diversity and balance exploration–exploitation. The proposed TGWO, SGWO, and TSGWO were tested on 21 benchmark functions and engineering design problems, outperforming standard GWO, PSO, and other metaheuristics. Results demonstrate superior optimization accuracy and robustness, particularly with TGWO exhibiting high precision and balanced search capabilities. The accelerated GWO [16] integrates an enhanced hierarchical structure, diversity measures, and parameter tuning, supported by a mathematical model to improve intensification and diversification. On 23 benchmark functions, it consistently outperformed standard GWO and other swarm intelligence algorithms in speed, quality, and computational efficiency. Similarly, Ref. [27] proposed enhanced GWO (EGWO), introducing an adaptive hunting mechanism to dynamically balance exploration and exploitation. EGWO was evaluated on 25 diverse benchmark functions and applied to the range-based node localization problem in wireless sensor networks to demonstrate its practical utility. Experimental results revealed that EGWO outperforms several established algorithms, offering more accurate solutions and effectively handling real-world problems with unknown search spaces.

Overall, these convergence-focused improvements highlight GWO's adaptability, with targeted modifications yielding faster, more robust, and higher-quality solutions across diverse optimization tasks.

8.2.1.8 Other variants

The study [39] applied GWO and other nature-inspired metaheuristics to optimize multi-layer perceptron (MLP) networks for streamflow forecasting, where GWO-MLP achieved higher accuracy, faster convergence, and better stability than traditional MLP and some other hybrid models. In metaheuristic-based clustering, the MetaCluster library [40] incorporates GWO to enhance partitional clustering quality across diverse datasets, showcasing its versatility beyond conventional optimization tasks. In blockchain applications [41], an improved GWO was employed to optimize the decentralized level of a consensus protocol, demonstrating effective exploration and convergence for high-precision solutions at reasonable computational cost. Similarly, the research [42] utilized the Random Walk GWO to improve MLP training in regression and classification tasks, enhancing generalization and avoiding local optima. These studies collectively highlight GWO's adaptability and effectiveness across a broad range of complex problem domains.

8.3 Performance analysis framework

This section outlines the experimental setup, testing environment, and validation methodology designed to evaluate the original GWO and twelve of its variants on global optimization problems. The experiments were designed for a fair comparison using identical benchmark functions, stopping criteria, and computational resources in all algorithms.

8.3.1 Benchmark functions

To comprehensively assess the exploration and exploitation capabilities of each algorithm, we selected the CEC-2017 benchmark suite (Table 8.3). This challenging collection includes 29 continuous optimization functions that model a wide array of search landscapes. These represent diverse landscapes with varying dimensionalities, search space complexities, and global optima locations. All functions are tested under a minimization framework. The CEC-2017 functions are grouped into four categories:

- **Unimodal functions (F1–F2)**: These functions have a single global optimum and are used to assess the local search and convergence speed of an algorithm.
- **Basic multimodal functions (F3–F9)**: Characterized by multiple local optima, these functions test an algorithm's ability to escape local traps and locate the global solution.
- **Hybrid functions (F10–F19)**: These are constructed by combining several basic functions, resulting in more complex and irregular search landscapes.
- **Composition functions (F20–F29)**: Blend several functions with different characteristics, simulating complex real-world scenarios with high nonseparability and ruggedness.

Each function applies shifted and rotated transformations to the search space to prevent trivial solutions and provide a balanced evaluation of exploration and exploitation. Due to its diversity and complexity, the CEC-2017 suite is widely regarded as a standard benchmark for continuous optimization in high-dimensional domains.

8.3.2 Comparison algorithms

The following popular GWO variants were compared:

- **GWO:** Original grey wolf optimizer [1].

TABLE 8.3 The description of CEC-2017 benchmark functions.

ID	Functions description	Category	D	Range	Optimum
F1	Shifted and rotated the Bent Cigar function	Unimodal	30	[-100, 100]	100
F2	Shifted and rotated Zakharov function	Unimodal	30	[-100, 100]	200
F3	Shifted and rotated Rosenbrock's function	Multimodal	30	[-100, 100]	300
F4	Shifted and rotated Rastrigin's function	Multimodal	30	[-100, 100]	400
F5	Shifted and rotated Schaffer's f7 Function	Multimodal	30	[-100, 100]	500
F6	Shifted and rotated Lunacek bi-Rastrigin function	Multimodal	30	[-100, 100]	600
F7	Shifted and rotated the noncontinuous Rastrigin's function	Multimodal	30	[-100, 100]	700
F8	Shifted and rotated Levy function	Multimodal	30	[-100, 100]	800
F9	Shifted and rotated Schwefel's function	Multimodal	30	[-100, 100]	900
F10	Hybrid function 1 (N=3)	Hybrid	30	[-100, 100]	1000
F11	Hybrid function 2 (N=3)	Hybrid	30	[-100, 100]	1100
F12	Hybrid function 3 (N=3)	Hybrid	30	[-100, 100]	1200
F13	Hybrid function 4 (N=4)	Hybrid	30	[-100, 100]	1300
F14	Hybrid function 5 (N=4)	Hybrid	30	[-100, 100]	1400
F15	Hybrid function 6 (N=4)	Hybrid	30	[-100, 100]	1500
F16	Hybrid function 7 (N=5)	Hybrid	30	[-100, 100]	1600
F17	Hybrid function 8 (N=5)	Hybrid	30	[-100, 100]	1700
F18	Hybrid function 9 (N=5)	Hybrid	30	[-100, 100]	1800
F19	Hybrid function 10 (N=6)	Hybrid	30	[-100, 100]	1900
F20	Composition function 1 (N=3)	Composition	30	[-100, 100]	2000
F21	Composition function 2 (N=3)	Composition	30	[-100, 100]	2100
F22	Composition function 3 (N=4)	Composition	30	[-100, 100]	2200
F23	Composition function 4 (N=4)	Composition	30	[-100, 100]	2300
F24	Composition function 5 (N=5)	Composition	30	[-100, 100]	2400
F25	Composition function 6 (N=5)	Composition	30	[-100, 100]	2500
F26	Composition function 7 (N=6)	Composition	30	[-100, 100]	2600
F27	Composition function 8 (N=6)	Composition	30	[-100, 100]	2700
F28	Composition function 9 (N=3)	Composition	30	[-100, 100]	2800
F29	Composition function 10 (N=3)	Composition	30	[-100, 100]	2900

- **RW-GWO:** Random walk grey wolf optimizer [43] incorporates a random walk strategy into the original GWO to enhance exploration capabilities and avoid local optima.
- **GWO-WOA:** Hybrid grey wolf-whale optimization algorithm [44] combines GWO and WOA, merging the hunting tactics of wolves with the spiral bubble-net feeding maneuver of whales. The integration aims to balance exploration and exploitation dynamically.

- **IGWO:** Improved grey wolf optimization [45] introduces multistrategy enhancements including population initialization, adaptive parameter control, and position update mechanisms. It aims to improve convergence speed and balance exploration–exploitation.
- **ChaoticGWO:** Chaotic-based grey wolf optimizer [6] integrates chaotic maps to guide the selection of wolves during the hunting process. This use of chaos introduces nonlinearity to increase population diversity and avoid premature convergence.
- **FuzzyGWO:** Fuzzy hierarchical operator-grey wolf optimizer [3] embeds a fuzzy hierarchical operator into the position update mechanism. This improves the adaptability of the algorithm by fuzzily modeling search agent interactions.
- **IncrementalGWO** and **ExGWO:** Incremental and expanded model-based grey wolf optimizers [8] propose novel algorithms based on GWO with incremental model-based adjustments and extended search strategies. They aim to enhance the global search capacity and convergence reliability.
- **DS-GWO:** Diversity-enhanced strategy-based grey wolf optimizer [18] incorporates diversity strategies based on group-stage competition and balance mechanisms. The strategy maintains population diversity and prevents premature convergence.
- **IOBL-GWO:** Improved opposition-based learning grey wolf optimizer [33] integrates improved opposition-based learning into GWO, enabling the generation of opposite candidate solutions to enhance exploration ability in the search space.
- **OGWO:** Opposition-based learning grey wolf optimizer [37] applies opposition-based population initialization and updating to improve global search performance and convergence rate.
- **ER-GWO:** Efficient and robust grey wolf optimizer [31] adapts nonlinear parameter control and modified position updating inspired by PSO to handle large-scale numerical problems efficiently.
- **CG-GWO:** Cauchy–Gaussian mutation and improved search strategy GWO [28] introduces Cauchy and Gaussian mutation operators into GWO's search strategy. These mutations improve population diversity and balance exploration and exploitation during optimization.

8.3.2.1 Computational complexity analysis

This section analyzes the computational complexity of the GWO and its variants. The analysis is based on four key parameters: the maximum number of iterations T, the population size $\mathcal{N}$, the cost of evaluating the fitness function C, and the cost of updating an agent's position D.

Most GWO variants, including GWO, IGWO, ChaoticGWO, IncrementalGWO, ExGWO, ER-GWO, and the hybrid GWO-WOA, share the fundamental complexity of $O(T{\cdot}N{\cdot}(C + D))$. These algorithms maintain the core GWO loop structure, where each agent's position is updated and its fitness is evaluated once per iteration.

Some variants introduce additional computational overheads. FuzzyGWO has an increased complexity of $O(T{\cdot}N{\cdot}(C + D + E))$ due to the added cost E of its fuzzy calculation system. The RW-GWO algorithm, which incorporates dedicated leader solutions, has a complexity of $O(T{\cdot}(N + M){\cdot}(C + D))$, reflecting the combined cost for both the main population and M leaders. The DS-GWO algorithm exhibits a more complex structure due to its group-stage competition mechanism, which involves sorting subgroups. Its complexity is accurately represented as $O(T{\cdot}(N{\cdot}(C + D) + (N \log(N/M) + M \log M + M{\cdot}D)))$, where M is the number of groups.

Algorithms leveraging OBL introduce distinct complexities. The OGWO algorithm has a complexity that ranges from the standard $O(T{\cdot}N{\cdot}(C + D))$ in its best case to a worst-case of $O(T{\cdot}2N{\cdot}(C + D + \log 2N))$, as it can perform additional evaluations and sorting of an opposite population. The IOBL-GWO algorithm, with its improved strategy, has a best-case complexity of $O(T{\cdot}(N{\cdot}(C + D) + N \log N + 3{\cdot}(C + D)))$. This reflects the mandatory sorting of the population and evaluation of three opposition agents in every iteration. In its worst-case scenario, the complexity can be up to $O(T{\cdot}(2N{\cdot}(C + D) + N \log N + 3{\cdot}(C + D)))$ due to re-evaluations.

Finally, CG-GWO has a complexity that lies between a best-case of $O(T{\cdot}(N + 3){\cdot}(C + D))$ and a worst-case of $O(T{\cdot}(2N + 3){\cdot}(C + D))$, reflecting its re-evaluation strategy.

It is important to note that the detailed complexity analysis presented above assumes that the computational cost of the fitness function C is comparable to or only slightly higher than the cost of position updates D. This is a common characteristic of standard benchmark functions. In contrast, for real-world optimization problems where the fitness function involves computationally expensive operations such as finite element analysis, training neural networks, or large-scale data processing, the cost C dominates all other factors. In such scenarios, the complexity of all the above algorithms simplifies to $O(T{\cdot}N{\cdot}C)$.

TABLE 8.4 Parameter settings for the compared models.

Model	Parameters
GWO	N/A
RW-GWO	N/A
GWO-WOA	N/A
IGWO	Lower bound a_min=0.02 and upper bound a_max=2.2
ChaoticGWO	chaotic_name="chebyshev", initial_chaotic_value=0.7
FuzzyGWO	fuzzy_name "increase"
IncrementalGW-O	explore_factor=1.5
ExGWO	N/A
DS-GWO	explore_ratio=0.4, n_groups=5
IOBL-GWO	N/A
OGWO	miu_factor=2.0, jumping_rate=0.05
ER-GWO	a_initial=2.0, a_final=0.0, miu_factor=1.0001
CG-GWO	N/A

8.3.2.2 Hyperparameter settings

To account for stochastic variability, each algorithm was independently run 30 times on each benchmark function. The experiments were conducted on 30-dimensional problems with a fixed population size of $\mathcal{N}$=30 search agents. To provide a standardized computational budget for all algorithms, the maximum number of function evaluations (FEs) was employed as the stopping criterion, set at 6×10^4. This approach ensures a fair comparison of algorithmic performance, independent of their individual runtimes. With the chosen population size, this FE limit corresponds to a maximum of T=2000 iterations. Control parameters were set as recommended in the original publications to ensure optimal performance. Table 8.4 summarizes the parameter settings used.

8.3.3 Statistical analysis

When comparing the performance of multiple algorithms over a set of benchmark functions, it is essential to determine whether the observed differences in performance are statistically significant. In this chapter, we employ the Friedman test followed by the Holm post hoc test to achieve a robust statistical comparison.

8.3.3.1 Friedman test

The Friedman test is a nonparametric statistical test designed to detect differences in treatments (algorithms) across multiple test attempts (benchmark problems). It is a rank-based test that does not assume normality of the data, making it particularly suitable for performance comparison of optimization algorithms.

Given k algorithms and N benchmark functions, each algorithm's performance on each function is ranked from 1 (best) to k (worst). Let R_j denote the average rank of algorithm j, computed as:

$$R_j = \frac{1}{N} \sum_{i=1}^{N} r_{i,j}, \tag{8.7}$$

where $r_{i,j}$ is the rank of algorithm j on benchmark i. The Friedman statistic is calculated as:

$$\chi_F^2 = \frac{12N}{k(k+1)} \sum_{j=1}^{k} R_j^2 - 3N(k+1). \tag{8.8}$$

For small N and k, χ_F^2 can be corrected using the Iman-Davenport adjustment:

$$F_F = \frac{(N-1)\chi_F^2}{N(k-1) - \chi_F^2}, \tag{8.9}$$

which follows an F-distribution with $(k-1)$ and $(k-1)(N-1)$ degrees of freedom. The null hypothesis H_0 states that all algorithms perform equally. If the computed P-value is less than a predefined significance level α (commonly 0.05), H_0 is rejected, indicating significant differences among algorithms.

8.3.3.2 *Holm post hoc test*

If the Friedman test rejects H_0, a post hoc test is necessary to identify which algorithms differ significantly from a control algorithm. The Holm procedure is a step-down method that controls the family-wise error rate and is more powerful than the Bonferroni correction. Given a control algorithm A_c, the difference in average ranks between A_c and another algorithm A_j is:

$$z_j = \frac{|R_c - R_j|}{\sqrt{\frac{k(k+1)}{6N}}}. \tag{8.10}$$

The corresponding p_j-value is obtained from the standard normal distribution. The Holm procedure sorts the p_j values in ascending order:

$$p_{(1)} \le p_{(2)} \le \cdots \le p_{(m)},$$

where $m = k - 1$. Starting from the smallest P-value $p_{(i)}$, it is compared with $\frac{\alpha}{m-i+1}$. If $p_{(i)}$ is less than the adjusted threshold, the null hypothesis for that comparison is rejected, and the process continues. Once a null hypothesis fails to be rejected, all subsequent hypotheses are accepted.

In conclusion, by combining the Friedman test with the Holm post hoc test:

- The Friedman test first detects whether any significant differences exist among the algorithms.
- The Holm post hoc test then pinpoints the specific algorithms that differ significantly from the control algorithm while controlling the family-wise error rate.

This combined approach ensures that conclusions about algorithmic superiority are both statistically sound and resistant to the inflation of Type I errors.

8.4 Results and discussion

This section presents a detailed analysis of the experimental results from evaluating the GWO and its variants on the CEC-2017 benchmark suite. All algorithms were implemented in Python 3.9 and executed on a workstation equipped with an Intel Core i7–12700K CPU @ 3.60 GHz, 32 GB RAM, and running Windows 11 Pro. To mitigate the effect of stochastic behavior, each experiment was independently repeated 30 times for every benchmark function and algorithm variant. The best, worst, mean, standard deviation (std), and median values of the obtained fitness scores were recorded. The source code for GWO and its variants is available in the Mealpy library [46]. The CEC benchmark functions are provided in the Opfunu library [47]. All other resources, including programs and log files, are publicly accessible on GitHub (https://github.com/thieu1995/GWO). The detailed experiment logs include per-iteration fitness values and convergence curves, thereby facilitating independent verification. The results and discussion below are structured according to the three primary categories of test functions: unimodal/multimodal, hybrid, and composition.

8.4.1 Performance of tested algorithms on unimodal and multimodal functions

The initial set of functions (F1–F9) provides a foundational assessment of each algorithm's core search capabilities. Unimodal functions (F1–F2) primarily test exploitation and convergence accuracy, while multimodal functions (F3–F9) challenge an algorithm's exploration capacity and its ability to avoid local optima. Table 8.5 summarizes the performance

TABLE 8.5 Performance benchmarks of GWO variants on functions F1–F9 (unimodal and multimodal) in 30-D space. Results are averaged over 30 independent runs, reporting the mean of the best fitness and the mean of the standard deviation.

Func	Metric	CG-GWO	ChaoticGWO	DS-GWO	ER-GWO	ExGWO	FuzzyGWO	GWO	GWO-WOA	IGWO	IncGWO	IOBL-GWO	OGWO	RW-GWO
F1	fitness	6.15E+09	2.19E+09	2.20E+09	1.80E+10	7.23E+09	2.01E+09	2.36E+09	3.40E+09	2.11E+09	2.57E+10	6.36E+09	3.22E+09	4.68E+08
	std	2.16E+09	8.70E+08	2.69E+08	5.47E+09	2.12E+09	8.61E+08	1.03E+09	2.00E+09	3.72E+08	8.86E+09	2.82E+09	6.96E+08	9.91E+07
F2	fitness	13346.56	5910.74	5363.18	54768.38	21984.35	5701.81	5870.65	8218.73	5020.18	51434.32	13676.10	7334.47	1470.45
	std	5689.07	2750.53	1026.42	18825.30	6229.89	2619.79	3879.69	3737.06	1088.35	11842.63	4914.05	1625.09	311.83
F3	fitness	776.82	516.01	489.95	2925.94	887.96	522.65	507.23	675.89	501.48	4434.76	810.78	594.35	438.76
	std	236.29	47.31	51.21	1918.10	242.07	84.56	68.28	157.67	50.86	3009.01	204.79	143.56	59.01
F4	fitness	6954.95	3192.57	3477.42	24201.49	9837.62	2994.95	3057.61	3924.48	3521.14	36052.39	7631.40	4324.18	1230.95
	std	2631.29	1115.62	371.55	8507.68	5050.72	675.71	593.90	1624.44	392.23	13139.98	2977.84	836.90	118.88
F5	fitness	500.01	500.01	500.00	500.00	500.02	500.00	500.00	500.01	500.01	500.02	500.01	500.01	500.00
	std	0.0052	0.0033	0.0022	0.0051	0.0060	0.0020	0.0025	0.0041	0.0033	0.0105	0.0030	0.0034	0.0038
F6	fitness	2.72E+05	1.04E+05	1.02E+05	9.01E+05	2.70E+05	8.99E+04	1.01E+05	1.50E+05	1.00E+05	1.30E+06	2.69E+05	1.49E+05	1.82E+04
	std	1.40E+05	3.96E+04	1.74E+04	2.69E+05	1.04E+05	3.06E+04	5.71E+04	7.42E+04	1.61E+04	3.39E+05	1.36E+05	3.79E+04	3.70E+03
F7	fitness	1090.71	1066.04	1081.47	1150.91	1219.37	1070.89	1049.27	1062.98	1086.07	1269.99	1100.16	1086.06	1080.91
	std	49.94	40.16	33.46	90.79	68.37	39.13	39.81	39.82	34.69	73.68	65.10	31.88	75.46
F8	fitness	808.71	803.46	801.93	813.63	807.94	803.36	803.92	805.82	802.74	817.97	809.70	803.97	805.82
	std	3.12	1.73	0.43	6.04	3.46	1.22	2.36	2.62	1.47	4.41	3.93	1.76	3.23
F9	fitness	7313.56	7422.99	7874.19	6190.59	8172.92	7665.85	7365.89	7405.58	7904.40	8642.50	7246.08	7671.59	6640.80
	std	727.26	564.25	308.61	815.62	481.87	519.15	557.53	440.31	299.13	494.58	441.00	393.80	609.71

of the GWO and its variants on these benchmark functions in 30-dimensional space, averaged over 30 independent runs. The results are presented in terms of the mean of the best fitness values and the corresponding standard deviations, thereby reflecting both the accuracy and the robustness of each algorithm.

Overall, the results indicate that the proposed RW-GWO consistently outperforms most of the other variants, achieving the lowest fitness values on several functions (e.g., F1, F2, F3, F4, and F6). For instance, on F1 and F6, RW-GWO reached fitness values of 4.68×10^8 and 1.82×10^4, respectively, which are substantially smaller than those obtained by the standard GWO and its other variants. This demonstrates the ability of RW-GWO to handle both unimodal landscapes, where fast convergence is essential, and multimodal ones, where exploration plays a critical role.

Several variants such as IGWO, ChaoticGWO, and DS-GWO also exhibited competitive performance on selected functions (e.g., F3, F6, and F8), suggesting that their respective enhancement strategies are beneficial in specific scenarios. However, their overall performance was less consistent across the benchmark set. In contrast, algorithms such as ER-GWO and IncGWO tended to yield relatively poor results, often producing fitness values one order of magnitude higher than those of RW-GWO, thereby indicating weaker convergence properties in high-dimensional spaces.

In terms of stability, the standard deviations reported in Table 8.5 reveal that RW-GWO not only provides superior average performance but also maintains robustness across repeated trials. For example, on F6, the standard deviation of RW-GWO was only 3.70×10^3, which is significantly lower than most other variants. This highlights the reliability of RW-GWO in delivering consistent results, even on complex multimodal landscapes.

In summary, the results confirm that RW-GWO provides the best balance between exploration and exploitation, yielding superior optimization performance across unimodal and multimodal functions. Variants with adaptive or stochastic strategies (e.g., RW-GWO, FuzzyGWO, ChaoticGWO) generally demonstrate more robust performance than purely structural modifications (e.g., IncGWO, ExGWO), while hybrids such as GWO-WOA offer competitive but inconsistent improvements.

8.4.1.1 Statistical analysis on unimodal and multimodal functions

Based on the performance results in Table 8.5, we calculated the rankings of all compared algorithms using the mean of the best fitness values. In cases of ties, the standard deviation was used as a secondary criterion to determine the better ranking. Table 8.6 presents the ranking results for each algorithm on each test function. With N=9 test functions and k=13 algorithms, the Friedman statistic is computed as χ^2_F=73.05, which is substantially greater than the critical value $\chi^2_{0.05,12}$=21.03. This strongly rejects the null hypothesis at the 0.05 significance level, indicating that at least one algorithm performs significantly differently from the others.

Since the Friedman test rejected the null hypothesis, the Holm post hoc test was applied using GWO (meanrank=3.89) as the control. The results are summarized in Table 8.7. The Holm test results reveal that GWO significantly outperformed five algorithms: IncGWO, ExGWO, ER-GWO, IOBL-GWO, and CG-GWO (reject_H0=TRUE) with negative rank differences indicating a consistent advantage across unimodal and multimodal functions. Among them, the largest gap was observed for IncGWO (− 9.00, P<.0001), confirming GWO's substantial superiority. For the remaining algorithms, such as OGWO, GWO-WOA, IGWO, and RW-GWO, although some showed positive rank differences (e.g., RW-GWO: + 1.44), none of these differences were statistically significant after Holm's adjustment, suggesting that any apparent advantage over GWO could be attributed to random variation. These findings indicate that although some variants clearly degrade performance, many others achieve comparable results to the baseline GWO.

8.4.1.2 Convergence analysis on unimodal and multimodal functions

The average convergence curves from 30 independent runs, depicted in Fig. 8.1 for representative functions F1, F2, F5, F7, F8, and F9, illustrate distinct performance patterns among the tested algorithms. On unimodal landscapes (F1, F2), the curves show that most algorithms, including the standard GWO, converge rapidly in the early iterations, with several enhanced variants (e.g., RW-GWO, OGWO) reaching low objective values earlier and maintaining stable performance throughout the remaining iterations. These results suggest that the improved variants exhibit stronger exploitation capability, enabling them to approach the global optimum more efficiently on smooth, single-optimum landscapes.

For the more complex multimodal functions (F5, F7, F8, F9), the convergence dynamics are more varied. Algorithms such as RW-GWO and some hybrid variants demonstrate a better balance between exploration and exploitation, maintaining a slower but steadier convergence rate that avoids premature stagnation in local optima. In contrast, some methods (e.g., IncrementalGWO, ER-GWO) exhibit faster initial convergence but plateau at higher objective values, indicating weaker global search ability in complex landscapes. Overall, RW-GWO consistently achieves lower final

TABLE 8.6 Ranking of GWO variants based on the mean of the best fitness and the mean of the standard deviation (30 runs, 30-D on unimodal and multimodal functions). Lower rank indicates better performance.

Func	CG-GWO	ChaoticGWO	DS-GWO	ER-GWO	ExGWO	FuzzyGWO	GWO	GWO-WOA	IGWO	IncGWO	IOBL-GWO	OGWO	RW-GWO
F1	9	4	5	12	11	2	6	8	3	13	10	7	1
F2	9	6	3	13	11	4	5	8	2	12	10	7	1
F3	9	5	2	12	11	6	4	8	3	13	10	7	1
F4	9	4	5	12	11	2	3	7	6	13	10	8	1
F5	11	6	5	4	12	1	2	7	8	13	9	10	3
F6	11	6	5	12	10	2	4	8	3	13	9	7	1
F7	9	3	6	11	12	4	1	2	8	13	10	7	5
F8	10	4	1	12	9	3	5	8	2	13	11	6	7
F9	4	7	10	1	12	8	5	6	11	13	3	9	2
Average rank	9.00	5.00	4.67	9.89	11.00	3.56	3.89	6.89	5.11	12.89	9.11	7.56	2.44

TABLE 8.7 Holm post hoc test results for RW-GWO (Control) on unimodal and multimodal functions.

Pair	rank_diff[a]	z_score	P_value	holm_alpha	reject_H0
GWO vs IncGWO	-9.000	4.902	.0000	0.0042	TRUE
GWO vs ExGWO	-7.111	3.873	.0001	0.0045	TRUE
GWO vs ER-GWO	-6.000	3.268	.0011	0.0050	TRUE
GWO vs IOBL-GWO	-5.222	2.845	.0044	0.0056	TRUE
GWO vs CG-GWO	-5.111	2.784	.0054	0.0063	TRUE
GWO vs OGWO	-3.667	1.997	.0458	0.0071	FALSE
GWO vs GWO-WOA	-3.000	1.634	.1022	0.0083	FALSE
GWO vs RW-GWO	1.444	0.787	.4314	0.0100	FALSE
GWO vs IGWO	-1.222	0.666	.5056	0.0125	FALSE
GWO vs ChaoticGWO	-1.111	0.605	.5450	0.0167	FALSE
GWO vs DS-GWO	-0.778	0.424	.6718	0.0250	FALSE
GWO vs FuzzyGWO	0.333	0.182	.8559	0.0500	FALSE

[a] negative values mean GWO has a better mean rank; positive values mean the compared algorithm ranks better.

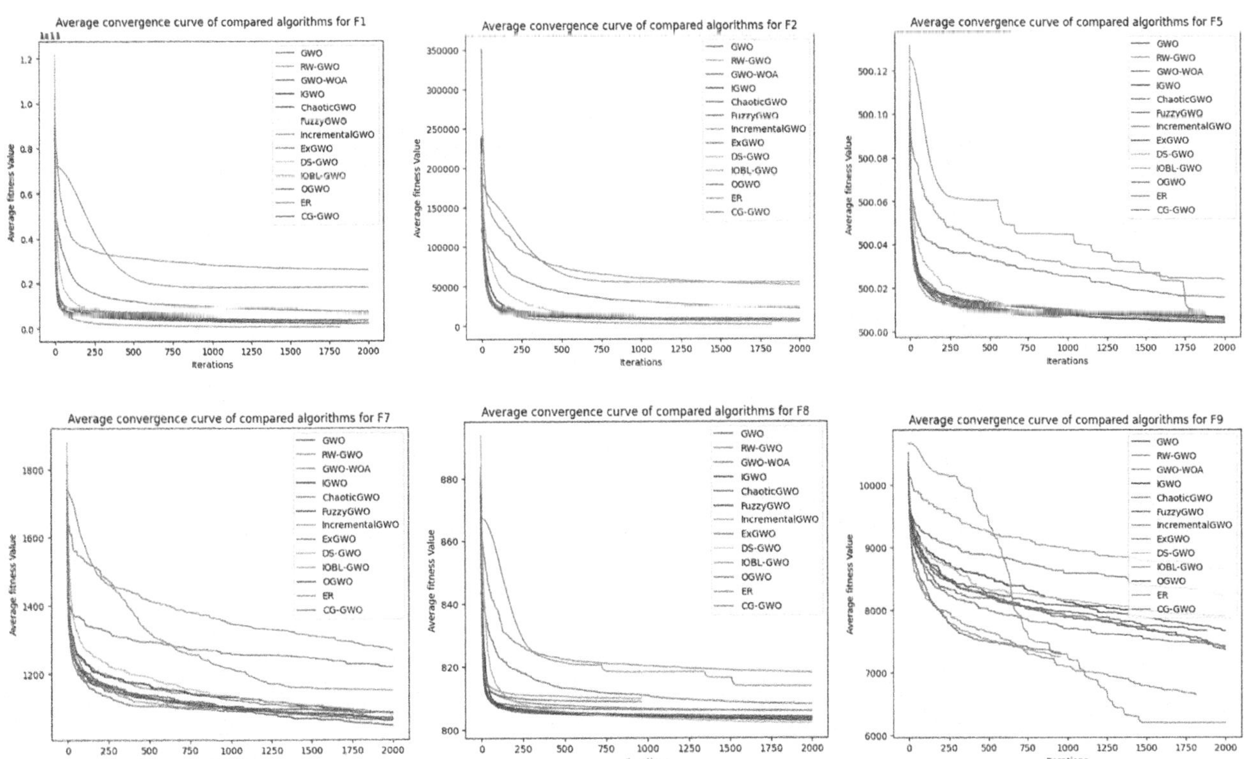

FIGURE 8.1 Convergence curves of GWO variants on unimodal and multimodal functions (ER is ER-GWO, IncrementalGWO is IncGWO algorithm) (*GWO*, Grey wolf optimizer).

objective values across both unimodal and multimodal functions, highlighting its robustness in handling problems of varying modality.

8.4.1.3 Stability analysis on unimodal and multimodal functions

The stability of each algorithm was assessed using boxplots (Fig. 8.2) of the global best fitness values obtained over 30 runs for the selected unimodal and multimodal benchmark functions. Lower variance and smaller interquartile ranges indicate higher stability. As can be seen:

- F1 and F2 show that DS-GWO, RW-GWO, FuzzyGWO, and OGWO consistently outperform other variants in terms of stability, with notably tight box ranges and minimal outliers. These algorithms exhibit high robustness, indicating strong exploitation ability and convergence reliability. In contrast, IncGWO and ER-GWO display the largest spread, suggesting inconsistent performance across runs.
- For F5, all algorithms achieve very close median values, but DS-GWO, GWO-WOA, and FuzzyGWO present the narrowest spread, indicating superior stability. IncrementalGWO again shows higher variability, which may stem from its adaptive mechanism being sensitive to initial conditions.
- In F7, stability differences become more pronounced. DS-GWO and OGWO maintain relatively compact distributions, demonstrating balanced exploration–exploitation capabilities. Conversely, IncGWO and IOBL-GWO exhibit the widest variance, suggesting potential overexploration.
- For F8, DS-GWO and FuzzyGWO achieve the most stable performance, while ER-GWO and IncGWO show considerable spread and several outliers.
- In F9, no single variant dominates across all metrics, but DS-GWO and IGWO remain competitive with consistent results. CG-GWO and ER-GWO suffer from larger variability, particularly in the lower whiskers, reflecting instability when tackling high-dimensional multimodal landscapes.

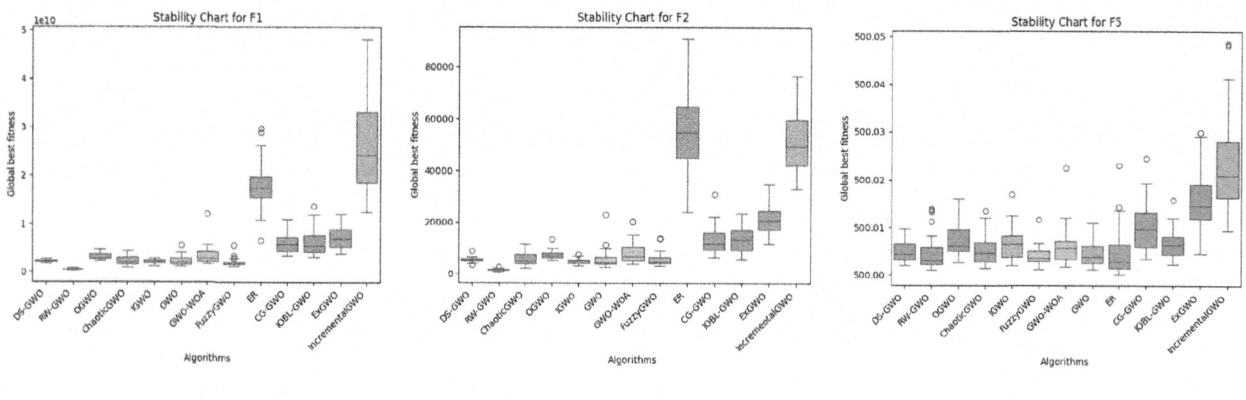

FIGURE 8.2 Boxplot visualization of GWO variants on unimodal and multimodal functions (ER is ER-GWO, IncrementalGWO is IncGWO algorithm) (*GWO*, Grey wolf optimizer).

Overall, DS-GWO emerges as the most stable variant across both unimodal and multimodal problems, followed closely by RW-GWO and FuzzyGWO. Variants such as IncGWO and ER-GWO show less predictable behavior, which may hinder their reliability despite occasional strong median performance.

8.4.2 Performance of tested algorithms on hybrid functions

Table 8.8 reports the performance of the tested algorithms on the hybrid functions (F10–F19) in 30-D space. The results reveal substantial performance differences across the algorithms. Overall, the baseline GWO exhibits moderate results, whereas several enhanced variants achieve notably better outcomes in terms of both solution accuracy and stability.

Among all methods, RW-GWO consistently provides the best or near-best performance across almost all hybrid functions. For instance, on F10, F11, and F12, RW-GWO attains fitness values of 2.04×10^5, 4.00×10^7, and 7.88×10^6, respectively, which are significantly smaller than those obtained by the original GWO (8.79×10^5, 2.33×10^8, and 8.67×10^7). This superiority is further confirmed on more challenging functions such as F14, F16, and F18, where RW-GWO maintains fitness values two to three orders of magnitude lower than most competing variants. Moreover, RW-GWO exhibits relatively low standard deviations, highlighting its robustness across independent runs.

Other competitive variants include ChaoticGWO and GWO-WOA, which frequently outperform the original GWO but remain inferior to RW-GWO. For example, on F13 and F15, ChaoticGWO achieves fitness values of 3.60×10^5 and 1.78×10^6, which are slightly better than GWO (3.86×10^5 and 1.63×10^6), while RW-GWO further improves the results to 3.42×10^5 and 2.23×10^5, respectively. Similarly, on F19, FuzzyGWO yields the best performance (2.59×10^3), marginally surpassing GWO and RW-GWO. This suggests that certain hybrid functions may favor specific design strategies such as fuzzy adaptation.

In contrast, some variants, such as ER-GWO and IncGWO, perform poorly on nearly all hybrid functions, often producing fitness values several orders of magnitude worse than GWO. This indicates that their design mechanisms are less suitable for handling the hybrid composition of multimodal landscapes.

In summary, the results on hybrid functions clearly demonstrate the effectiveness of RW-GWO, which consistently outperforms the baseline GWO and most of its variants. While a few methods, such as ChaoticGWO and FuzzyGWO, occasionally achieve competitive results, RW-GWO exhibits the best overall performance in terms of both accuracy and robustness. These findings emphasize the importance of diversity preservation and adaptive control in the design of effective GWO variants for hybrid optimization landscapes.

8.4.2.1 Statistical analysis on hybrid functions

To confirm the above observations, we conducted a Friedman test on the rankings obtained from the hybrid functions (F10–F19). Table 8.9 presents the ranking results for each algorithm on each test function. With N=10 test functions and k=13 algorithms, the Friedman statistic was computed as χ^2_F=100.6681 with p<1×10^{-12}, which is far above the critical threshold for significance. This result strongly rejects the null hypothesis of equal performance, confirming that the observed differences among the algorithms on the hybrid functions are not due to random variation.

Following this, the Holm post hoc test was applied using the baseline GWO as the control algorithm. The Holm-adjusted results in Table 8.10 reveal that five algorithms: IncGWO, ER-GWO, ExGWO, CG-GWO, and IOBL-GWO show statistically significant differences from GWO (reject_H0 = TRUE). Notably, all these significant differences have negative rank_diff values, meaning that GWO achieved significantly better rankings than these variants on the hybrid functions. For instance, in the comparison with CG-GWO, rank_diff=-6.00 and p=0.00057, indicating a clear and statistically significant advantage for GWO.

In contrast, OGWO and DS-GWO exhibited moderate negative rank differences, but these did not reach statistical significance after Holm correction, suggesting only marginal, nonsignificant advantages for GWO. RW-GWO showed a positive rank_diff of +1.60, implying a slightly better mean rank for RW-GWO, but the difference was not statistically significant (p=0.358). Similarly, IGWO, GWO-WOA, ChaoticGWO, and FuzzyGWO displayed small absolute rank differences and high P-values, indicating performance levels that are statistically indistinguishable from the control.

Overall, these findings demonstrate that on the hybrid functions, the standard GWO outperforms several of its variants with statistical significance, while maintaining comparable performance to many others. This highlights the importance of combining ranking analysis with robust statistical testing to avoid misleading conclusions based solely on mean rank differences.

TABLE 8.8 Performance benchmarks of GWO variants on functions F10–F19 (hybrid functions) in 30-D space. Results are averaged over 30 independent runs, reporting the mean of the best fitness and the mean of the standard deviation.

Func	Metric	CG-GWO	ChaoticGWO	DS-GWO	ER-GWO	ExGWO	FuzzyGWO	GWO	GWO-WOA	IGWO	IncGWO	IOBL-GWO	OGWO	RW-GWO
	fitness	2.07E+06	1.09E+06	2.27E+06	1.43E+09	5.39E+06	8.36E+05	8.79E+05	7.62E+05	1.72E+06	4.70E+08	2.26E+06	2.48E+06	2.04E+05
F10	std	1.12E+06	7.02E+05	1.16E+06	2.85E+09	1.29E+07	2.82E+05	4.23E+05	3.30E+05	8.63E+05	4.97E+08	2.10E+06	1.13E+06	7.09E+04
	fitness	3.53E+08	2.09E+08	3.26E+08	5.04E+09	6.18E+08	2.37E+08	2.33E+08	2.62E+08	3.05E+08	5.53E+09	4.07E+08	3.96E+08	4.00E+07
F11	std	8.08E+07	3.80E+07	6.60E+07	3.01E+09	8.22E+08	5.64E+07	5.56E+07	6.45E+07	5.64E+07	2.95E+09	1.43E+08	8.41E+07	9.90E+06
	fitness	2.26E+08	8.33E+07	9.11E+07	3.89E+09	2.22E+08	8.60E+07	8.67E+07	1.10E+08	1.10E+08	4.56E+09	2.97E+08	1.30E+08	7.88E+06
F12	std	1.34E+08	3.91E+07	4.17E+07	3.79E+09	2.44E+08	3.56E+07	3.63E+07	6.58E+07	4.07E+07	2.84E+09	2.09E+08	5.72E+07	2.58E+06
	fitness	7.18E+05	3.60E+05	4.78E+05	1.90E+06	1.61E+06	3.90E+05	3.86E+05	4.52E+05	4.86E+05	3.38E+06	6.84E+05	4.78E+05	3.42E+05
F13	std	6.37E+05	2.02E+05	1.60E+05	2.99E+06	1.61E+06	2.34E+05	2.45E+05	2.95E+05	2.60E+05	2.21E+06	5.13E+05	2.57E+05	1.81E+05
	fitness	3.56E+07	1.47E+07	2.61E+07	1.97E+09	3.30E+07	2.39E+07	1.71E+07	1.59E+07	2.33E+07	1.41E+09	3.10E+07	2.94E+07	2.52E+06
F14	std	3.59E+07	5.57E+06	1.03E+07	2.26E+09	3.99E+07	4.22E+07	8.06E+06	8.84E+06	8.84E+06	1.54E+09	2.63E+07	1.16E+07	9.24E+05
	fitness	2.89E+06	1.78E+06	1.76E+06	1.98E+08	2.08E+06	1.27E+06	1.63E+06	1.24E+06	1.73E+06	7.59E+08	1.99E+06	1.72E+06	2.23E+05
F15	std	2.22E+06	1.83E+06	1.84E+06	4.73E+08	1.72E+06	1.42E+06	1.63E+06	1.29E+06	1.54E+06	2.25E+09	2.22E+06	1.54E+06	1.80E+05
	fitness	3.34E+05	1.53E+05	8.40E+05	9.76E+10	3.11E+05	1.83E+05	1.65E+05	1.38E+05	4.91E+05	1.17E+12	2.40E+05	6.89E+05	4.36E+04
F16	std	5.82E+05	6.92E+04	1.25E+06	2.25E+11	9.65E+05	1.27E+05	1.13E+05	7.79E+04	9.49E+05	4.27E+12	1.76E+05	1.61E+06	2.23E+04
	fitness	7.16E+05	6.46E+05	9.09E+05	8.21E+05	1.27E+06	5.02E+05	4.93E+05	5.98E+05	6.12E+05	5.04E+06	7.96E+05	6.18E+05	3.42E+05
F17	std	5.32E+05	4.19E+05	5.05E+05	9.17E+05	8.61E+05	2.41E+05	2.52E+05	3.85E+05	2.68E+05	9.39E+06	7.35E+05	2.49E+05	1.84E+05
	fitness	1.44E+09	1.63E+08	4.08E+08	3.39E+14	5.32E+09	1.81E+08	1.71E+08	1.75E+08	3.18E+08	4.80E+13	1.00E+09	4.25E+08	5.47E+06
F18	std	1.97E+09	9.33E+07	1.72E+08	1.65E+15	5.97E+09	9.95E+07	9.53E+07	1.20E+08	1.98E+08	1.77E+14	7.17E+08	2.22E+08	2.20E+06
	fitness	3012.27	2737.86	2706.66	5643.15	4381.38	2590.74	2664.99	2751.14	2767.13	8374.62	2961.69	2830.90	2927.95
F19	std	394.39	346.32	198.78	2948.33	1003.44	180.65	219.11	303.61	306.92	4395.82	307.35	201.36	382.18

TABLE 8.9 Ranking of GWO variants based on the mean of the best fitness and the mean of the standard deviation (30 runs, 30-D on hybrid functions). Lower rank indicates better performance.

Func	CG-GWO	ChaoticGWO	DS-GWO	ER-GWO	ExGWO	FuzzyGWO	GWO	GWO-WOA	IGWO	IncGWO	IOBL-GWO	OGWO	RW-GWO
F10	7	5	9	13	11	3	4	2	6	12	8	10	1
F11	8	2	7	12	11	4	3	5	6	13	10	9	1
F12	10	2	5	12	9	3	4	7	6	13	11	8	1
F13	10	2	6	12	11	4	3	5	8	13	9	7	1
F14	11	2	7	13	10	6	4	3	5	12	9	8	1
F15	11	8	7	12	10	3	4	2	6	13	9	5	1
F16	8	3	11	12	7	5	4	2	9	13	6	10	1
F17	8	7	11	10	12	3	2	4	5	13	9	6	1
F18	10	2	7	13	11	5	3	4	6	12	9	8	1
F19	10	4	3	12	11	1	2	5	6	13	9	7	8
Average rank	9.3	3.7	7.3	12.1	10.3	3.7	3.3	3.9	6.3	12.7	8.9	7.8	1.7

TABLE 8.10 Holm post hoc test results for GWO (Control) on hybrid functions.[a]

Algorithm	rank_diff	z_score	P_value	holm_alpha	reject_H0
GWO vs IncGWO	-9.40	5.3972	.00000	0.0042	TRUE
GWO vs ER-GWO	-8.80	5.0527	.00000	0.0045	TRUE
GWO vs ExGWO	-7.00	4.0192	.00006	0.0050	TRUE
GWO vs CG-GWO	-6.00	3.4450	.00057	0.0056	TRUE
GWO vs IOBL-GWO	-5.60	3.2153	.00130	0.0063	TRUE
GWO vs OGWO	-4.50	2.5838	.00977	0.0071	FALSE
GWO vs DS-GWO	-4.00	2.2967	.02164	0.0083	FALSE
GWO vs IGWO	-3.00	1.7225	.08498	0.0100	FALSE
GWO vs RW-GWO	1.60	0.9187	.35827	0.0125	FALSE
GWO vs GWO-WOA	-0.60	0.3445	.73047	0.0167	FALSE
GWO vs ChaoticGWO	-0.40	0.2297	.81835	0.0250	FALSE
GWO vs FuzzyGWO	-0.40	0.2297	.81835	0.0500	FALSE

[a] *negative values mean GWO has a better mean rank; positive values mean the compared algorithm ranks better.*

8.4.2.2 Convergence analysis on hybrid functions

Fig. 8.3 visualizes the convergence behavior of GWO and its variants on selected CEC-2017 hybrid benchmark functions (F11, F12, F14, F15, F17, F19). The results are generated based on the average of 30 independent runs for each algorithm on each function. The key observations from the convergence charts are as follows:

- Overall, the algorithms demonstrated relatively good convergence performance across this set of hybrid functions.
- For functions F15 and F17, nearly all evaluated algorithms exhibited similar convergence behaviors, indicating comparable effectiveness on these specific landscapes.
- In contrast, on functions F11, F12, and F14, the IncGWO and ER-GWO algorithms showed very poor convergence capabilities, suggesting difficulties in effectively navigating or optimizing these particular problem spaces.
- Notably, the RW-GWO algorithm consistently achieved good convergence performance on most of the tested functions, highlighting its robustness and efficiency across various hybrid function characteristics.

8.4.2.3 Stability analysis on hybrid functions

Fig. 8.4 visualizes the boxplots of compared algorithms on the selected hybrid functions (F10, F11, F13, F14, F7, and F19). As can be seen, the stability assessment on the selected hybrid functions (F10, F11, F13, F14, F7, and F19) indicates that DS-GWO maintains the smallest interquartile ranges with minimal outliers across most cases, confirming its robustness and consistent convergence behavior. OGWO, IGWO, GWO-WOA, GWO, and FuzzyGWO also exhibit competitive stability, particularly in all these functions, where their performance variability remains low. In contrast, ER-GWO, ExGWO, and IncGWO frequently display large variances and numerous outliers (e.g., F13 and F19), suggesting less reliable convergence patterns. CG-GWO and IOBL-GWO achieve relatively stable distributions in certain problems (e.g., F10, F11, and F14) but lack the consistency of DS-GWO and RW-GWO across all functions. Notably, in high-complexity cases such as F13 and F19, most algorithms experience increased variance, yet DS-GWO retains its stability advantages. Overall, DS-GWO emerges as the most reliable variant for hybrid landscapes, followed closely by RW-GWO and FuzzyGWO, while IncGWO and ER-GWO remain the least stable across different hybrid scenarios.

8.4.3 Composition functions

Table 8.11 summarizes the performance of the original GWO and its variants on the composition functions F20–F29 in a 30-dimensional search space. These functions are specifically designed as complex combinations of multiple basic

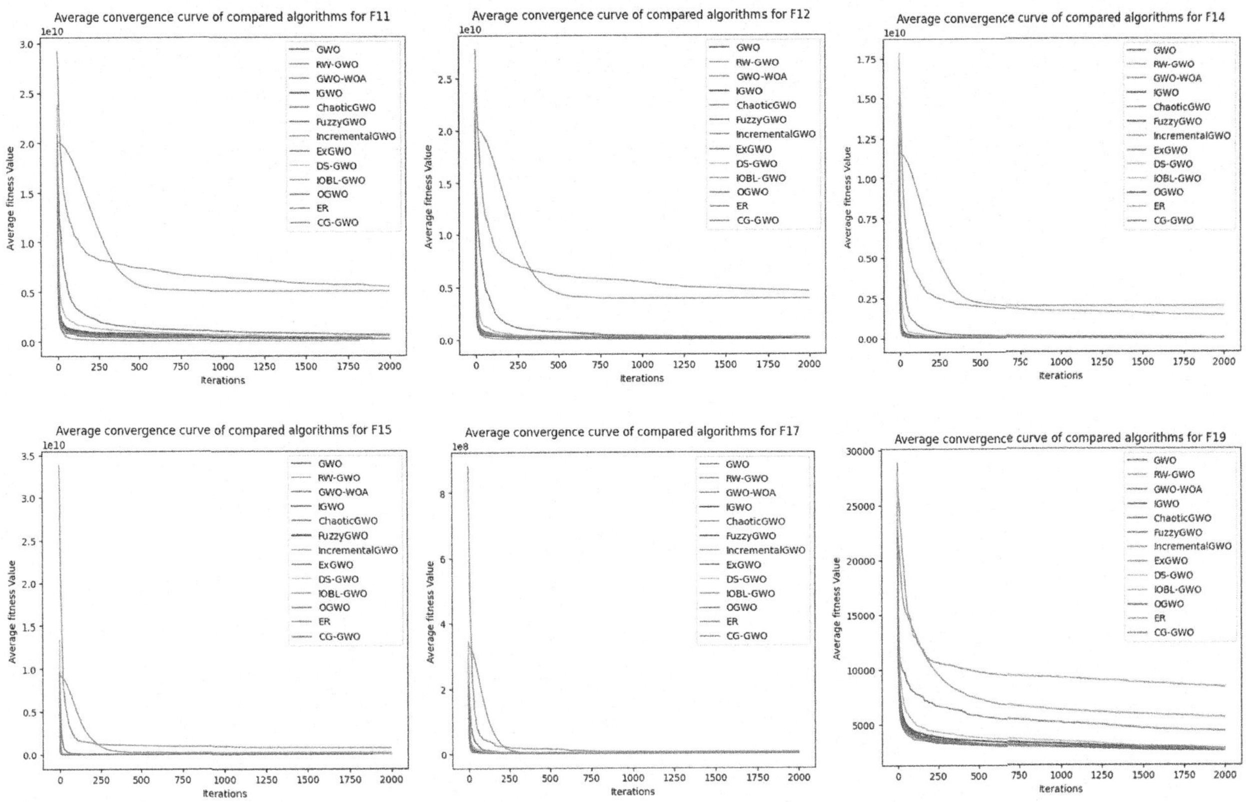

FIGURE 8.3 Convergence curves of GWO variants on hybrid functions (ER is ER-GWO, IncrementalGWO is IncGWO algorithm) (*GWO*, Grey wolf optimizer).

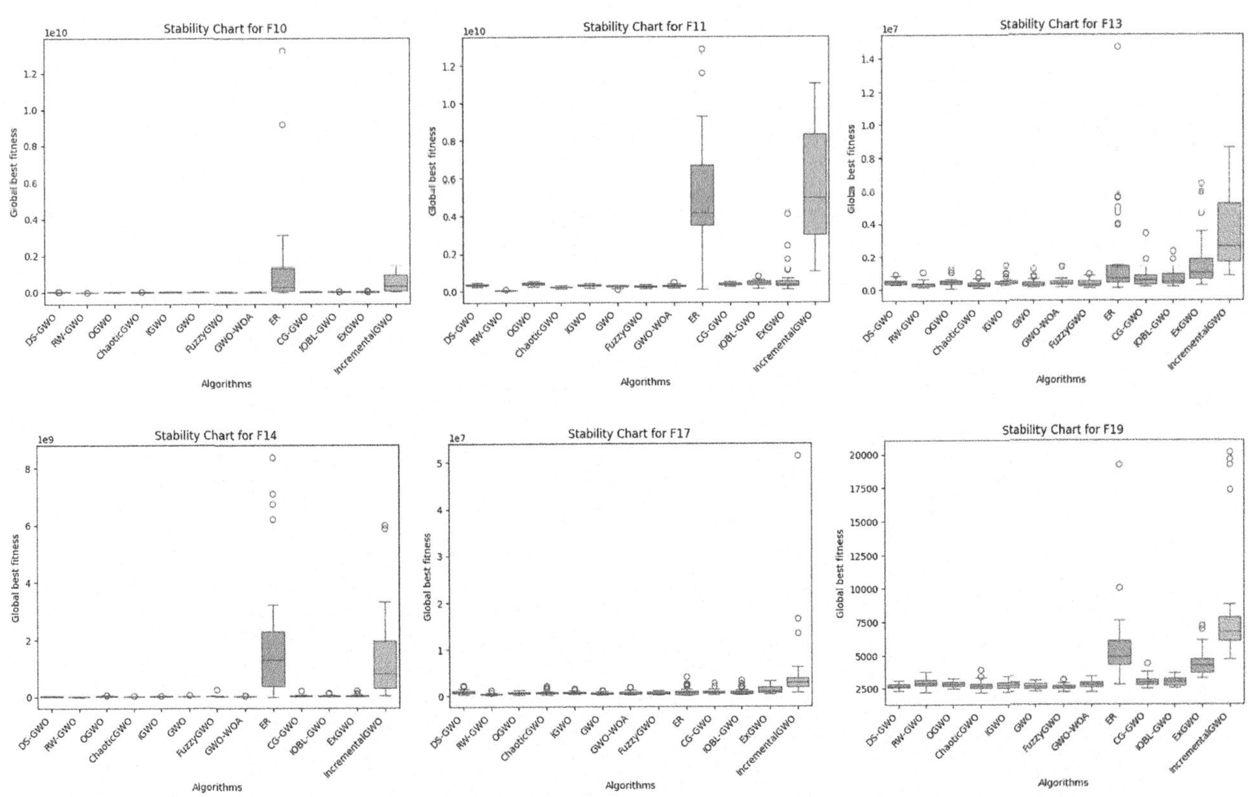

FIGURE 8.4 Boxplot visualization of GWO variants on hybrid functions (ER is ER-GWO, IncrementalGWO is IncGWO algorithm) (*GWO*, Grey wolf optimizer).

TABLE 8.11 Performance benchmarks of GWO variants on functions F20–F29 (composition functions) in 30-D space. Results are averaged over 30 independent runs, reporting the mean of the best fitness and the mean of the standard deviation.

Func	Metric	CG-GWO	ChaoticG-WO	DS-GWO	ER-GWO	ExGWO	FuzzyGWO	GWO	GWO-WOA	IGWO	Increment-alGWO	IOBL-GWO	OGWO	RW-GWO
	average	6290.37	4249.78	4092.87	2.10E+04	8549.28	3969.02	4185.49	5054.89	4224.89	2.36E+04	6275.00	4814.47	2894.61
F20	std	2236.12	808.07	537.28	7.08E+03	3437.72	652.46	591.46	1294.85	532.85	9.31E+03	2084.78	801.17	138.28
	average	2371.11	2328.19	2331.74	4188.84	2423.74	2327.04	2330.02	2344.52	2334.21	3140.90	2371.29	2342.17	2306.86
F21	std	29.95	8.97	6.17	1.06E+03	47.32	9.36	12.06	19.85	10.96	554.18	25.01	11.18	8.80
	average	1.30E+04	7686.17	8618.36	3.09E+04	1.51E+04	7895.41	7940.98	9035.08	8343.67	3.35E+04	1.26E+04	9858.64	4469.95
F22	std	2769.22	1186.68	965.82	9.44E+03	4005.73	1431.60	1378.59	1843.53	1222.58	7.65E+03	3322.47	1358.68	911.59
	average	9574.16	6071.77	6592.56	1.88E+04	1.21E+04	5959.23	6040.99	7613.58	6334.30	2.33E+04	1.04E+04	7112.42	4129.53
F23	std	2038.24	609.07	445.25	4383.04	3984.22	532.86	709.90	2031.87	462.60	4092.58	2122.95	718.70	327.93
	average	3113.89	2930.96	2894.69	3628.55	3150.94	2934.10	2931.35	2999.46	2911.64	4204.88	3110.72	2960.47	2852.31
F24	std	148.84	43.27	14.31	620.47	122.46	58.92	45.52	67.52	26.81	677.06	113.88	51.05	21.40
	average	3483.66	3387.48	3395.66	4674.21	3553.35	3400.03	3395.69	3444.09	3390.38	6202.41	3504.47	3402.21	3350.02
F25	std	105.20	17.19	16.50	667.38	120.92	32.70	30.66	57.61	17.86	2180.53	95.39	30.01	15.37
	average	3227.53	3162.06	3153.02	4496.97	3267.51	3154.24	3156.72	3188.73	3158.34	3720.81	3229.60	3164.42	3148.14
F26	std	46.10	23.38	14.34	554.49	49.43	15.60	21.51	31.63	14.99	213.27	71.99	18.18	18.89
	average	3272.24	3192.74	3193.33	3896.04	3319.43	3186.92	3179.83	3239.94	3188.41	3967.98	3265.59	3228.12	3010.97
F27	std	73.74	34.75	52.61	453.65	50.18	56.63	70.80	59.75	69.61	531.66	42.83	35.52	161.51
	average	1.20E+08	1.79E+07	3.24E+07	2.25E+09	3.49E+08	1.35E+07	1.75E+07	2.90E+07	3.38E+07	3.92E+11	1.12E+08	4.51E+07	3.78E+05
F28	std	9.73E+07	2.52E+07	4.11E+07	7.39E+09	3.36E+08	2.22E+07	2.77E+07	4.83E+07	5.37E+07	2.11E+12	1.17E+08	5.34E+07	7.99E+05
	average	2.48E+08	5.46E+07	9.12E+07	1.95E+09	5.99E+08	3.96E+07	7.91E+07	7.27E+07	8.67E+07	3.82E+09	3.14E+08	1.22E+08	7.48E+06
F29	std	2.18E+08	3.79E+07	6.17E+07	1.41E+09	4.50E+08	3.40E+07	8.82E+07	5.85E+07	5.54E+07	2.79E+09	2.57E+08	1.51E+08	4.22E+06

functions, incorporating shifting, rotation, and scaling transformations to create highly irregular landscapes. Results are averaged over 30 independent runs, reporting both the mean and the standard deviation of the best fitness values. The reported results are averaged over 30 independent runs, presenting both the mean and standard deviation of the best fitness values.

The overall analysis shows that composition functions impose a significant challenge for all algorithms, as reflected in the wide range of fitness values. For functions F20–F23, RW-GWO, DS-GWO, and FuzzyGWO achieved consistently better results than the original GWO, often with lower standard deviations. For example, RW-GWO obtained the best performance on F20 and F23, while DS-GWO demonstrated high stability on F21 and F22. In contrast, ER-GWO and IncrementalGWO showed weaker performance, with both higher average errors and large variances, indicating difficulties in maintaining convergence reliability.

On the mid-level composition functions F24–F27, most algorithms converged to similar fitness values, suggesting that these problems are less discriminative for evaluating variants. Nevertheless, RW-GWO again provided competitive or best results in several cases (e.g., F24 and F27), confirming its robustness across different landscapes.

The most substantial differences appeared on the most challenging functions F28 and F29, where the fitness landscapes are highly irregular and deceptive due to the combination of multiple global and local optima. In these cases, RW-GWO significantly outperformed all other algorithms, achieving the lowest mean fitness by large margins (e.g., 3.78×10^5 on F28 and 7.48×10^6 on F29). ChaoticGWO and FuzzyGWO also showed competitive results, whereas ER-GWO and IncrementalGWO again performed poorly with extremely high variances, confirming their lack of robustness on these functions.

In summary, three main findings can be drawn: (1) RW-GWO consistently achieved the best performance across the composition functions, particularly excelling in the hardest cases (F28–F29); (2) DS-GWO and FuzzyGWO were reliable alternatives, maintaining stability and competitive results across several functions; and (3 some modifications, such as ER-GWO and IncrementalGWO, tended to degrade performance compared to the original GWO. These results highlight the necessity of carefully designing improvements to GWO in order to address the demanding landscape properties of composition functions in the CEC-2017 benchmark.

8.4.3.1 Statistical analysis on composition functions

To validate the robustness of results, we also conducted a Friedman test on the rankings obtained from the composite functions (F20–F29). Table 8.12 shows the ranking results for each algorithm on each test function. With N=10 test functions and k=13 algorithms, the Friedman statistic was computed as χ_F^2=111.72 with $P<1 \times 10^{-12}$, which is far above the critical threshold for significance. This result strongly rejects the null hypothesis of equal performance, confirming that there were statistically significant performance differences among the tested algorithms.

The Holm post hoc test was conducted with GWO as the control algorithm. The results are presented in Table 8.13. The analysis shows that GWO significantly outperformed five algorithms: IncGWO, ER-GWO, ExGWO, CG-GWO, and IOBL-GWO across the composition functions, with reject_H0=TRUE after Holm's adjustment. Among these, the largest performance gap was observed against IncrementalGWO (– 8.9, P<0.0001), followed closely by ER-GWO (– 8.3, P<0.0001). The negative rank differences in these cases indicate that GWO consistently achieved better average ranks.

For the remaining algorithms, although some (e.g., RW-GWO: +2.9) displayed positive rank differences suggesting a nominal advantage over GWO, these differences were not statistically significant after correction, implying that any apparent performance gain could be due to random variation. Notably, algorithms such as ChaoticGWO (0.0) and DS-GWO (–0.8) demonstrated performance parity with GWO in this problem set.

8.4.3.2 Convergence analysis on composition functions

Fig. 8.5 visualizes the convergence behavior of GWO and its variants on selected CEC-2017 composition benchmark functions (F20, F22, F23, F25, F27, F29). Consistent with the analysis of hybrid functions, these results are based on the average of 30 independent runs for each algorithm on each function. The key observations from the convergence charts for composition functions are summarized as follows:

- Overall, the algorithms demonstrated relatively good convergence capabilities across this challenging set of composition functions.
- For functions F25 and F27, all evaluated algorithms exhibited strong convergence performance, indicating their effectiveness on these specific landscapes.
- A notable challenge was observed for function F29, where all algorithms converged to local optima, highlighting the significant difficulty in escaping local minima and finding the global optimum for this particular function.

TABLE 8.12 Ranking of GWO variants based on the mean of the best fitness and the mean of the standard deviation (30 runs, 30-D on composition functions). Lower rank indicates better performance.

Func	CG-GWO	ChaoticGWO	DS-GWO	ER-GWO	ExGWO	FuzzyGWO	GWO	GWO-WOA	IGWO	Increment-alGWO	IOBL-GWO	OGWO	RW-GWO
F20	10	6	3	12	11	2	4	8	5	13	9	7	1
F21	9	3	5	13	11	2	4	8	6	12	10	7	1
F22	10	2	6	12	11	3	4	7	5	13	9	8	1
F23	9	4	6	12	11	2	3	8	5	13	10	7	1
F24	10	4	2	12	11	6	5	8	3	13	9	7	1
F25	9	2	4	12	11	6	5	8	3	13	10	7	1
F26	9	6	2	13	11	3	4	8	5	12	10	7	1
F27	10	5	6	12	11	3	2	8	4	13	9	7	1
F28	10	4	6	12	11	2	3	5	7	13	9	8	1
F29	9	3	7	12	11	2	5	4	6	13	10	8	1
Average rank	9.5	3.9	4.7	12.2	11	3.1	3.9	7.2	4.9	12.8	9.5	7.3	1

TABLE 8.13 Holm post hoc test results for GWO (Control) on composition functions.[a]

algorithm	rank_diff	z_score	*P*_value	holm_alpha	reject_H0
GWO vs IncGWO	-8.9	5.1101	.0000	0.0042	TRUE
GWO vs ER-GWO	-8.3	4.7656	.0000	0.0045	TRUE
GWO vs ExGWO	-7.1	4.0766	.0000	0.0050	TRUE
GWO vs CG-GWO	-5.6	3.2153	.0013	0.0056	TRUE
GWO vs IOBL-GWO	-5.6	3.2153	.0013	0.0063	TRUE
GWO vs OGWO	-3.4	1.9522	.0509	0.0071	FALSE
GWO vs GWO-WOA	-3.3	1.8948	.0581	0.0083	FALSE
GWO vs RW-GWO	2.9	1.6651	.0959	0.0100	FALSE
GWO vs IGWO	-1	0.5742	.5659	0.0125	FALSE
GWO vs DS-GWO	-0.8	0.4593	.6460	0.0167	FALSE
GWO vs FuzzyGWO	0.8	0.4593	.6460	0.0250	FALSE
GWO vs ChaoticGWO	0	0	1	0.0500	FALSE

[a] *negative values mean GWO has a better mean rank; positive values mean the compared algorithm ranks better.*

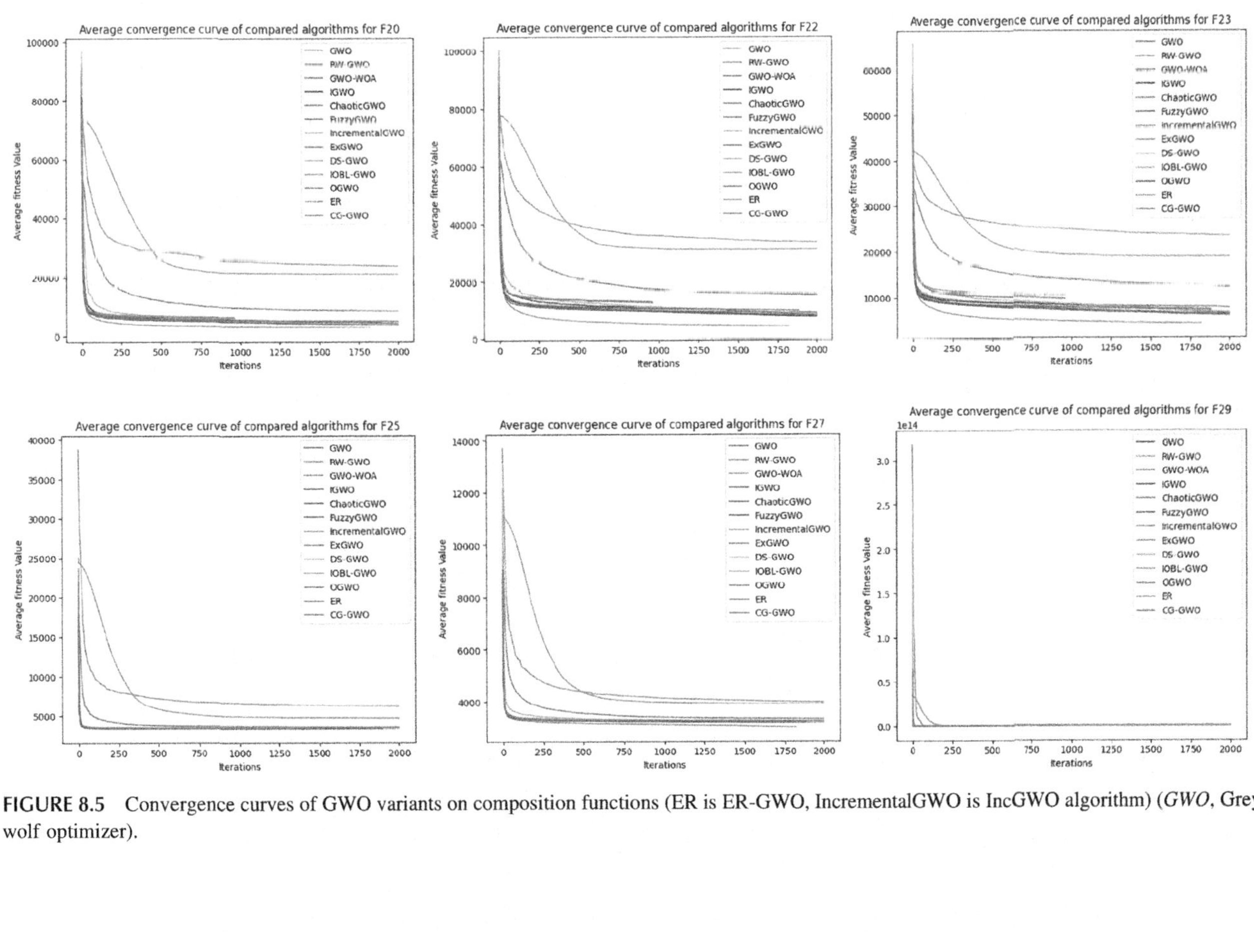

FIGURE 8.5 Convergence curves of GWO variants on composition functions (ER is ER-GWO, IncrementalGWO is IncGWO algorithm) (*GWO*, Grey wolf optimizer).

- On functions F20, F22, and F23, the RW-GWO algorithm showed the best convergence performance, closely followed by FuzzyGWO, which also demonstrated good convergence capabilities. This suggests a superior ability of these two variants to handle the complexities of these functions.
- Conversely, algorithms such as IncGWO, ER-GWO, and ExGWO consistently showed poor convergence performance across the analyzed composition functions.

The stability assessment on the selected hybrid functions (F10, F11, F13, F14, F7, and F19) indicates that DS-GWO maintains the smallest interquartile ranges with minimal outliers across most cases, confirming its robustness and consistent convergence behavior. OGWO, IGWO, GWO-WOA, GWO, and FuzzyGWO also exhibit competitive stability, particularly in all these functions, where their performance variability remains low. In contrast, ER-GWO, ExGWO, and IncGWO frequently display large variances and numerous outliers (e.g., F13 and F19), suggesting less reliable convergence patterns. CG-GWO and IOBL-GWO achieve relatively stable distributions in certain problems (e.g., F10, F11, and F14) but lack the consistency of DS-GWO and RW-GWO across all functions. Notably, in high-complexity cases such as F13 and F19, most algorithms experience increased variance, yet DS-GWO retains stability advantages. Overall, DS-GWO emerges as the most reliable variant for hybrid landscapes, followed closely by RW-GWO and FuzzyGWO, while IncGWO and ER-GWO remain the least stable across different hybrid scenarios.

8.4.3.3 Stability analysis on composition functions

Fig. 8.6 visualizes the boxplot of compared algorithms on selected hybrid functions (F20, F22, F23, F24, F26, and F27). The figure highlights DS-GWO and RW-GWO as the most consistent performers, exhibiting narrow interquartile ranges and very few outliers across all tested problems. GWO and ChaoticGWO also maintain relatively stable performance in most cases, particularly in F20, F22, F24, and F26. In contrast, ER-GWO, ExGWO, and IncGWO often produce wide performance spreads with multiple extreme outliers, especially in high-variance cases such as F20, F22, and F23, indicating susceptibility to parameter sensitivity and reduced convergence reliability. GWO-WOA and FuzzyGWO achieve moderate stability but lack the consistent robustness demonstrated by DS-GWO and RW-GWO. Overall, RW-GWO emerges as the most stable variant on composition functions, with DS-GWO providing comparable reliability, while IncGWO and ER-GWO remain the least stable in this problem category.

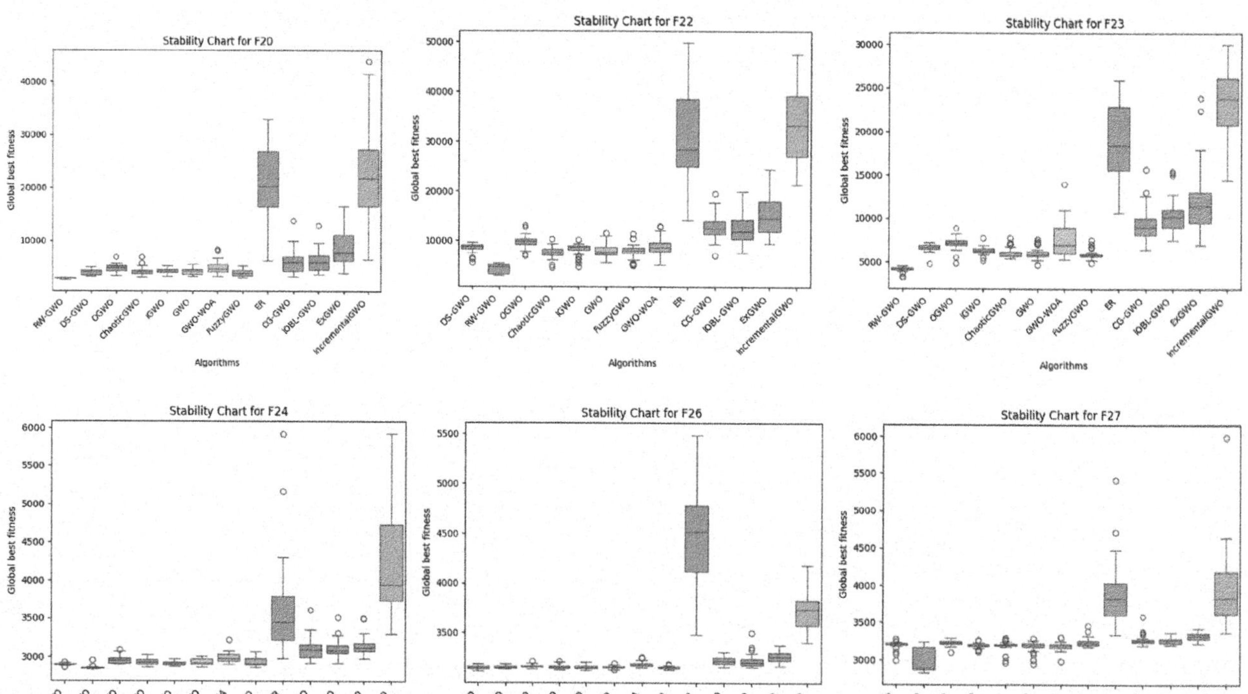

FIGURE 8.6 Boxplot visualization of GWO variants on composition functions (ER is ER-GWO, IncrementalGWO is IncGWO algorithm) (*GWO*, Grey wolf optimizer).

8.4.4 Final discussion

The comparative evaluation of the original GWO and its twelve representative variants on the CEC-2017 benchmark suite provides several important insights. A consistent finding across the three groups is the strong performance of RW-GWO. On the unimodal and multimodal functions (F1–F9), RW-GWO achieved the best final average rank of 2.44, while on the hybrid (F10–F19) and composition (F20–F29) functions, it dominated with final average ranks of 1.7 and 1.0, respectively. In many cases, RW-GWO was the top performer on the majority of functions within F10–F29. Convergence plots further confirmed that RW-GWO reliably attained low objective values and avoided premature stagnation, indicating that the random-walk diversification mechanism effectively enhances the exploration–exploitation balance.

Other variants also demonstrated competitive performance. FuzzyGWO, for example, frequently ranked second or third, particularly on composition functions, while ChaoticGWO often appeared close to the top. These results suggest that adaptive and chaotic control mechanisms can help sustain diversity and improve convergence on rugged landscapes. The original GWO, although not the overall best performer, remained competitive: it frequently placed in the upper half of the rankings, and Holm's post hoc analysis revealed that it significantly outperformed several weaker variants (IncGWO, ExGWO, ER-GWO, IOBL-GWO, and CG-GWO). This highlights that certain structural modifications may be detrimental unless carefully designed.

An examination of algorithmic stability revealed further distinctions. Boxplot analyses showed that DS-GWO consistently produced narrow interquartile ranges and few outliers, especially on hybrid functions, suggesting high stability. RW-GWO also combined strong median performance with low variance across most benchmarks. In contrast, IncGWO, ER-GWO, and ExGWO exhibited large spreads and frequent outliers, indicating instability or strong sensitivity to parameter choices.

The statistical testing provided nuance to claims of dominance. Friedman tests rejected the null hypothesis of equivalent performance across algorithms for each benchmark category, and Holm post hoc analysis (using GWO as the control) confirmed that several variants were significantly worse than GWO. However, while RW-GWO often obtained the best mean ranks, its improvements over GWO were not always statistically significant after Holm correction. This indicates that some of RW-GWO's advantages, while practically meaningful, did not reach statistical significance under conservative multiple-comparison adjustments, pointing to variability across individual functions.

Several functions, particularly in the composition category, such as F29, posed notable challenges. Most algorithms converged to local optima, underscoring the inherent limitations of single-strategy metaheuristics when faced with highly deceptive landscapes. In some cases, algorithms with low variance nonetheless converged to suboptimal solutions (stable but trapped), while others exhibited high-variance exploratory behavior (diverse but unreliable). These observations suggest trade-offs between stability and exploration capability.

Taken together, these findings support practical recommendations for practitioners. RW-GWO stands out as a strong default choice for general global optimization tasks across mixed benchmark sets, combining strong mean performance with consistent convergence. When stability across runs is critical, DS-GWO and RW-GWO are reliable options, while FuzzyGWO and ChaoticGWO are attractive alternatives when adaptive or enhanced exploration is desired. On the other hand, variants such as IncGWO, ER-GWO, ExGWO, CG-GWO, and IOBL-GWO should be approached with caution, as they frequently underperform and may require additional tuning or problem-specific adjustments.

Finally, some limitations of the present study should be acknowledged. The evaluation was confined to unconstrained, single-objective continuous problems under a fixed design. Future research should extend this systematic comparison to constrained, dynamic, large-scale, and multiobjective problems. Sensitivity analyses of parameter settings, ablation studies to identify the sources of improvement, and the design of ensemble or hybrid frameworks combining complementary variants would further enrich understanding. Additionally, theoretical analyses explaining why mechanisms such as random walks or fuzzy adaptation are effective would help build principled guidelines for algorithm design.

8.5 Conclusions

This chapter demonstrates that simple yet well-motivated modifications, such as random-walk diversification or fuzzy and chaotic control mechanisms, can substantially enhance the empirical performance of the GWO on modern benchmark suites. At the same time, not all proposed variants generalize effectively, with some modifications even degrading robustness when applied indiscriminately. These findings highlight the importance of careful algorithmic design, supported by rigorous statistical validation, to distinguish genuine improvements from chance effects. The unified and reproducible evaluation presented here provides a practical reference for both researchers and practitioners in selecting and developing GWO-based optimizers for real-world global optimization tasks.

Acknowledgments

The authors would like to thank the reviewers for their valuable comments and suggestions, which helped improve the quality of this chapter. This research received no external funding.

Declaration of competing interest

The authors declare that they have no known competing financial interests or personal relationships that could have appeared to influence the work reported in this paper.

Declaration of generative AI and AI-assisted technologies in the writing process

During the preparation of this manuscript, the authors employed ChatGPT (version 4o) exclusively for the purpose of refining English grammar and improving sentence phrasing. All content was subsequently reviewed and carefully edited by the authors, who accept full responsibility for the integrity and accuracy of the final manuscript.

References

[1] S. Mirjalili, S.M. Mirjalili, A. Lewis, Grey wolf optimizer, Advances in Engineering Software 69 (2014) 46–61. Available from https://doi.org/10.1016/j.advengsoft.2013.12.007.

[2] S.N. Makhadmeh, M.A. Al-Betar, I.A. Doush, M.A. Awadallah, S. Kassaymeh, S. Mirjalili, et al., Recent advances in grey wolf optimizer, its versions and applications, IEEE Access 12 (2023) 22991–23028. Available from https://doi.org/10.1109/ACCESS.2023.3304889.

[3] L. Rodrguez, O. Castillo, J. Soria, P. Melin, F. Valdez, C.I. Gonzalez, et al., A fuzzy hierarchical operator in the grey wolf optimizer algorithm, Applied Soft Computing 57 (2017) 315–328. Available from https://doi.org/10.1016/j.asoc.2017.03.048.

[4] Z.-j Teng, J.-l Lv, L.-w Guo, An improved hybrid grey wolf optimization algorithm, Soft Computing 23 (2019) 6617–6631. Available from https://doi.org/10.1007/s00500-018-3310-y.

[5] Z.-M. Gao, J. Zhao, An improved grey wolf optimization algorithm with variable weights, Computational Intelligence and Neuroscience 2019 (2019) 2981282. Available from https://doi.org/10.1155/2019/2981282.

[6] M. Kohli, S. Arora, Chaotic grey wolf optimization algorithm for constrained optimization problems, Journal of Computational Design and Engineering 5 (2018) 458–472. Available from https://doi.org/10.1016/j.jcde.2017.02.005.

[7] K. Meidani, A. Hemmasian, S. Mirjalili, A. Barati Farimani, Adaptive grey wolf optimizer, Neural Computing and Applications 34 (2022) 7711–7731. Available from https://doi.org/10.1007/s00521-021-06885-9.

[8] A. Seyyedabbasi, F. Kiani, I-gwo and ex-gwo: improved algorithms of the grey wolf optimizer to solve global optimization problems, Engineering with Computers 37 (2021) 509–532. Available from https://doi.org/10.1007/s00366-019-00837-7.

[9] W. Long, J. Jiao, X. Liang, M. Tang, An exploration-enhanced grey wolf optimizer to solve high-dimensional numerical optimization, Engineering Applications of Artificial Intelligence 68 (2018) 63–80. Available from https://doi.org/10.1016/j.engappai.2017.10.024.

[10] J. Adhikary, S. Acharyya, Randomized balanced grey wolf optimizer (RBGWO) for solving real life optimization problems, Applied Soft Computing 117 (2022) 108429. Available from https://doi.org/10.1016/j.asoc.2022.108429.

[11] E. Emary, H.M. Zawbaa, C. Grosan, Experienced gray wolf optimization through reinforcement learning and neural networks, IEEE Transactions on Neural Networks and Learning Systems 29 (2017) 681–694. Available from https://doi.org/10.1109/TNNLS.2016.2634548.

[12] A.K. Tripathi, K. Sharma, M. Bala, A novel clustering method using enhanced grey wolf optimizer and mapreduce, Big Data Research 14 (2018) 93–100. Available from https://doi.org/10.1016/j.bdr.2018.05.002.

[13] M. Guo, J.-S. Wang, L.-F. Zhu, S.-S. Guo, W. Xie, An improved grey wolf optimizer based on tracking and seeking modes to solve function optimization problems, IEEE Access 8 (2020) 69861–69893. Available from https://doi.org/10.1109/ACCESS.2020.2984321.

[14] J. Hu, H. Chen, A.A. Heidari, M. Wang, X. Zhang, Y. Chen, et al., Orthogonal learning covariance matrix for defects of grey wolf optimizer: insights, balance, diversity, and feature selection, Knowledge-Based Systems 213 (2021) 106684. Available from https://doi.org/10.1016/j.knosys.2020.106684.

[15] Y. Yuan, X. Mu, X. Shao, J. Ren, Y. Zhao, Z. Wang, Optimization of an auto drum fashioned brake using the elite opposition-based learning and chaotic k-best gravitational search strategy based grey wolf optimizer algorithm, Applied Soft Computing 123 (2022) 108947. Available from https://doi.org/10.1016/j.asoc.2022.108947.

[16] R. Rajakumar, K. Sekaran, C.-H. Hsu, S. Kadry, Accelerated grey wolf optimization for global optimization problems, Technological Forecasting and Social Change 169 (2021) 120824. Available from https://doi.org/10.1016/j.techfore.2021.120824.

[17] N. Banerjee, S. Mukhopadhyay, AP-TLB-IGWO: adult-pup teaching–learning based interactive grey wolf optimizer for numerical optimization, Applied Soft Computing 124 (2022) 109000. Available from https://doi.org/10.1016/j.asoc.2022.109000.

[18] J. Jiang, Z. Zhao, Y. Liu, W. Li, H. Wang, DSGWO: an improved grey wolf optimizer with diversity enhanced strategy based on group-stage competition and balance mechanisms, Knowledge-Based Systems 250 (2022) 109100. Available from https://doi.org/10.1016/j.knosys.2022.109100.

[19] J.-S. Wang, S.-X. Li, An improved grey wolf optimizer based on differential evolution and elimination mechanism, Scientific Reports 9 (2019) 7181. Available from https://doi.org/10.1038/s41598-019-43546-3.

[20] W. Long, S. Cai, J. Jiao, M. Xu, T. Wu, A new hybrid algorithm based on grey wolf optimizer and cuckoo search for parameter extraction of solar photovoltaic models, Energy Conversion and Management 203 (2020) 112243. Available from https://doi.org/10.1016/j.enconman.2019.112243.

[21] P.J. Gaidhane, M.J. Nigam, A hybrid grey wolf optimizer and artificial bee colony algorithm for enhancing the performance of complex systems, Journal of Computational Science 27 (2018) 284–302. Available from https://doi.org/10.1016/j.jocs.2018.06.008.

[22] C. Ma, H. Huang, Q. Fan, J. Wei, Y. Du, W. Gao, Grey wolf optimizer based on aquila exploration method, Expert Systems with Applications 205 (2022) 117629. Available from https://doi.org/10.1016/j.eswa.2022.117629.

[23] J. Wang, D. Lin, Y. Zhang, S. Huang, An adaptively balanced grey wolf optimization algorithm for feature selection on high-dimensional classification, Engineering Applications of Artificial Intelligence 114 (2022) 105088. Available from https://doi.org/10.1016/j.engappai.2022.105088.

[24] A.A. Alomoush, A.A. Alsewari, H.S. Alamri, K. Aloufi, K.Z. Zamli, Hybrid harmony search algorithm with grey wolf optimizer and modified opposition-based learning, IEEE Access 7 (2019) 68764–68785. Available from https://doi.org/10.1109/ACCESS.2019.2917803.

[25] M. Abdel-Basset, D. El-Shahat, I. El-Henawy, V.H.C. De Albuquerque, S. Mirjalili, A new fusion of grey wolf optimizer algorithm with a two-phase mutation for feature selection, Expert Systems with Applications 139 (2020) 112824. Available from https://doi.org/10.1016/j.eswa.2019.112824.

[26] W. Long, J. Jiao, X. Liang, M. Tang, Inspired grey wolf optimizer for solving large-scale function optimization problems, Applied Mathematical Modelling 60 (2018) 112–126. Available from https://doi.org/10.1016/j.apm.2018.03.005.

[27] H. Joshi, S. Arora, Enhanced grey wolf optimization algorithm for global optimization, Fundamenta Informaticae 153 (2017) 235–264. Available from https://doi.org/10.3233/FI-2017-1539.

[28] K. Li, S. Li, Z. Huang, M. Zhang, Z. Xu, Grey wolf optimization algorithm based on cauchy-gaussian mutation and improved search strategy, Scientific Reports 12 (2022) 18961. Available from https://doi.org/10.1038/s41598-022-23713-9.

[29] S. Dereli, A new modified grey wolf optimization algorithm proposal for a fundamental engineering problem in robotics, Neural Computing and Applications 33 (2021) 14119–14131. Available from https://doi.org/10.1007/s00521-021-06050-2.

[30] I.A. Zamfirache, R.-E. Precup, R.-C. Roman, E.M. Petriu, Policy iteration reinforcement learning-based control using a grey wolf optimizer algorithm, Information Sciences 585 (2022) 162–175. Available from https://doi.org/10.1016/j.ins.2021.11.051.

[31] W. Long, S. Cai, J. Jiao, M. Tang, An efficient and robust grey wolf optimizer algorithm for large-scale numerical optimization, Soft Computing 24 (2020) 997–1026. Available from https://doi.org/10.1007/s00500-019-03939-y.

[32] B. Ahmadi, S. Younesi, O. Ceylan, A. Ozdemir, An advanced grey wolf optimization algorithm and its application to planning problem in smart grids, Soft Computing 26 (2022) 3789–3808. Available from https://doi.org/10.1007/s00500-022-06767-9.

[33] J.C. Bansal, S. Singh, A better exploration strategy in grey wolf optimizer, Journal of Ambient Intelligence and Humanized Computing 12 (2021) 1099–1118. Available from https://doi.org/10.1007/s12652-020-02153-1.

[34] M. Banaie-Dezfouli, M.H. Nadimi-Shahraki, Z. Beheshti, R-gwo: representative-based grey wolf optimizer for solving engineering problems, Applied Soft Computing 106 (2021) 107328. Available from https://doi.org/10.1016/j.asoc.2021.107328.

[35] H. Xu, X. Liu, J. Su, An improved grey wolf optimizer algorithm integrated with cuckoo search, 2017 9th IEEE International Conference on Intelligent Data Acquisition and Advanced Computing Systems: Technology and Applications (IDAACS) 1 (2017) 490–493. Available from https://doi.org/10.1109/IDAACS.2017.8095129IEEE.

[36] F.B. Ozsoydan, Effects of dominant wolves in grey wolf optimization algorithm, Applied Soft Computing 83 (2019) 105658. Available from https://doi.org/10.1016/j.asoc.2019.105658.

[37] X. Yu, W. Xu, C. Li, Opposition-based learning grey wolf optimizer for global optimization, Knowledge-Based Systems 226 (2021) 107139. Available from https://doi.org/10.1016/j.knosys.2021.107139.

[38] X. Zhang, Y. Zhang, Z. Ming, Improved dynamic grey wolf optimizer, Frontiers of Information Technology & Electronic Engineering 22 (2021) 877–890. Available from https://doi.org/10.1631/FITEE.2000191.

[39] A.N. Ahmed, T. Van Lam, N.D. Hung, N. Van Thieu, O. Kisi, A. El-Shafie, A comprehensive comparison of recent developed meta-heuristic algorithms for streamflow time series forecasting problem, Applied Soft Computing 105 (2021) 107282. Available from https://doi.org/10.1016/j.asoc.2021.107282.

[40] N. Van Thieu, D. Oliva, M. Pérez-Cisneros, Metacluster: an open-source python library for metaheuristic-based clustering problems, SoftwareX 24 (2023) 101597. Available from https://doi.org/10.1016/j.softx.2023.101597.

[41] B.M. Nguyen, T. Nguyen, Q.-H. Vu, T.H. Hung, T.H. Hai, H.T.T. Binh, et al., Dholes hunting—a multi-local search algorithm using gradient approximation and its application for blockchain consensus problem, IEEE Access 12 (2024) 93333–93349. Available from https://doi.org/10.1109/ACCESS.2024.3419172.

[42] N.V. Thieu, S. Mirjalili, H. Garg, N.T. Hoang, Metaperceptron: a standardized framework for metaheuristic-driven multi-layer perceptron optimization, Computer Standards & Interfaces 93 (2025) 103977. Available from https://doi.org/10.1016/j.csi.2025.103977.

[43] S. Gupta, K. Deep, A novel random walk grey wolf optimizer, Swarm and Evolutionary Computation 44 (2019) 101–112. Available from https://doi.org/10.1016/j.swevo.2018.01.001.

[44] O.O. Obadina, M.A. Thaha, K. Althoefer, M.H. Shaheed, Dynamic characterization of a master–slave robotic manipulator using a hybrid grey wolf–whale optimization algorithm, Journal of Vibration and Control 28 (2022) 1992–2003. Available from https://doi.org/10.1177/10775463211003402.

[45] A. Kaveh, P. Zakian, Improved gwo algorithm for optimal design of truss structures, Engineering with Computers 34 (2018) 685–707. Available from https://doi.org/10.1007/s00366-017-0567-1.

[46] N. Van Thieu, S. Mirjalili, Mealpy: an open-source library for latest meta-heuristic algorithms in python, Journal of Systems Architecture 139 (2023) 102871. Available from https://doi.org/10.1016/j.sysarc.2023.102871.

[47] N. Van Thieu, Opfunu: an open-source python library for optimization benchmark functions, Journal of Open Research Software 12 (2024). Available from https://doi.org/10.5334/jors.508.

Chapter 9

Optimal parameter prediction for photovoltaic modules using the grey wolf optimizer: a case study from a university-based photovoltaic station in Türkiye

Davut Izci[1], Serdar Ekinci[2], Emre Çelik[3], and Laith Abualigah[4]

[1]*Department of Electrical and Electronics Engineering, Bursa Uludag University, Bursa, Türkiye,* [2]*Department of Computer Engineering, Bitlis Eren University, Bitlis, Türkiye,* [3]*Department of Electrical and Electronics Engineering, Düzce University, Düzce, Türkiye,* [4]*Computer Science Department, Al al-Bayt University, Mafraq, Jordan*

9.1 Introduction

Renewable energy sources are becoming increasingly vital in addressing global energy demands and environmental concerns [1]. Among these sources, solar photovoltaic (PV) technology plays a crucial role due to its sustainability, abundance, and potential to reduce carbon emissions [2]. PV systems convert sunlight into electrical energy, making them a key component in the transition toward cleaner energy alternatives. However, optimizing the efficiency of PV modules remains a significant challenge, requiring precise estimation of their electrical parameters to ensure accurate modeling and improved energy output [3].

Accurate parameter extraction for PV modules is essential for system diagnostics, performance prediction, and efficiency enhancement. Recent advancements in PV parameter extraction have led to the development of various optimization techniques aimed at enhancing accuracy and computational efficiency [4]. For instance, Maden et al. [5] applied the squirrel search algorithm (SSA) to estimate model parameters of solar PV cells and modules, demonstrating its effectiveness in both single-diode (SD) and double-diode (DD) models. Their analyses, conducted on standard datasets and experimental data from a polycrystalline CS6P-220P solar module, indicated that SSA outperforms other prevalent approaches. Montano et al. [6] employed a continuous population genetic algorithm (GA) to estimate PV parameters; however, their reliance on the SD model and a narrow selection of four panel types limited their overall effectiveness. By contrast, Ismaeel et al. [7] introduced a gradient-based optimization technique that proved both efficient and precise in extracting parameters from various solar cells and PV modules. Building on these foundational efforts, Khelifa et al. [8] enhanced gradient-based methods through chaotic sequence generators, thereby boosting parameter estimation performance across diverse datasets.

Meanwhile, Qaraad et al. [9] improved the moth-flame algorithm to achieve greater accuracy and speed, although this came at the expense of elevated computational demands. Another notable contribution is Eltamaly's [10] musical chairs algorithm, which leverages multiple search agents to expedite exploration and reduce convergence time. Ramadan et al. [11] further demonstrated the utility of hybrid optimization by merging wild horse and hunter-prey models to identify PV characteristics, validating their approach under various environmental conditions. Subsequently, Yaghoubi et al. [12] introduced a modified salp swarm algorithm aimed at mitigating premature convergence and bolstering exploration capacity, although achieving reduced root mean square error (RMSE) values remains a challenge.

Beyond these methods, an array of alternative strategies, ranging from chaotic optimization techniques to advanced metaheuristic frameworks, have been explored in the literature [13,14]. Despite this continued progress, there remains

Grey Wolf Optimizer. DOI: https://doi.org/10.1016/B978-0-443-36624-6.00006-8

significant potential for developing more robust and effective optimization algorithms to push the boundaries of solar PV modeling accuracy.

To address these challenges, this study proposes a hybrid optimization framework that integrates the grey wolf optimizer (GWO) [15] with the Newton–Raphson (NR) [16] refinement technique. In order to rigorously assess the proposed approach, we focus on the CS6P-220P PV module, a widely adopted polycrystalline solar panel, and collect real-world experimental data from the PV station at Düzce University. By coupling the nature-inspired global search capacity of GWO with the rapid local convergence of NR, the framework aims to achieve high accuracy in parameter extraction without incurring excessive computational overhead.

Five key contributions underpin this work. First, we introduce the GWO algorithm for PV parameter extraction, leveraging its balanced exploration and exploitation to enhance overall accuracy. Second, we integrate the NR technique as a refinement step, thereby boosting local precision and expediting convergence. Third, we compare GWO against particle swarm optimization (PSO) [17], gravitational search algorithm (GSA) [18], differential evolution (DE) [19], and GA [20] to illustrate its competitive advantage. Fourth, we employ a thorough statistical assessment (encompassing RMSE, standard deviation, and nonparametric tests) to confirm both the reliability and the consistency of the proposed method. Finally, we validate our framework under real-world conditions by applying it to data from the CS6P-220P PV module installed at Düzce University's PV station, demonstrating its practical relevance and effectiveness.

The rest of this chapter is structured as follows: Section 9.2 provides an overview of the SD and DD models for PV parameter extraction. Section 9.3 outlines the proposed hybrid methodology, detailing how GWO and NR are integrated. Section 9.4 describes the algorithms adopted for comparative evaluation and presents their parameter settings. Section 9.5 discusses the experimental results, highlighting the performance of the proposed method relative to other optimization approaches. Section 9.6 concludes the study by summarizing the key findings and proposing potential avenues for future work in PV parameter extraction research.

9.2 Single and double diode models of the photovoltaic module

Accurate modeling of PV cells is regarded as a fundamental step for improving energy conversion efficiency and supporting effective system design. Their electrical characteristics are typically described through equivalent circuit formulations, among which the SD and DD models have become the most widely adopted. The schematic representation of these two models, along with their electrical components and interconnections, is illustrated in Fig. 9.1.

In the SD model, the PV cell is represented by a current source in parallel with a single diode, together with a series resistance (R_s) and a shunt resistance (R_{sh}). The main electrical quantities in this formulation include the photocurrent

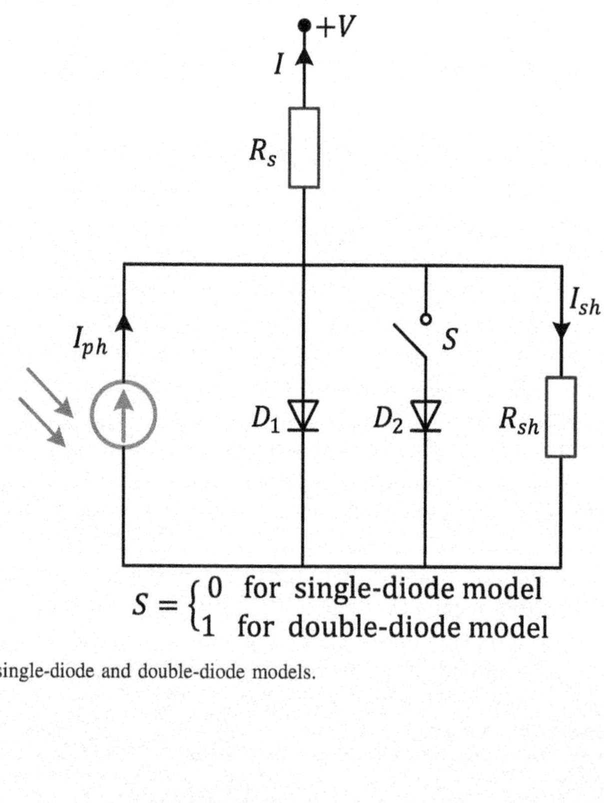

FIGURE 9.1 Equivalent circuits of single-diode and double-diode models.

(I_{ph}), the diode saturation current (I_{sd}), and the diode ideality factor (n). This simplified model offers a reasonable balance between accuracy and computational efficiency, providing a reliable approximation of the current–voltage (I–V) curve of the device. The mathematical expression of the SD model can be written as:

$$I = I_{ph} - I_{sd}\left[e^{\frac{(V+IR_s)}{(nV_t)}} - 1\right] - \frac{(V + IR_s)}{R_{sh}} \tag{9.1}$$

Here, I denotes the output current, V the terminal voltage, and V_t the thermal voltage defined as kT/q, with k being Boltzmann's constant, T the absolute temperature, and q the elementary charge.

Although the SD model is capable of describing the fundamental behavior of PV cells, it does not fully capture recombination losses. To overcome this limitation, the DD model introduces a second diode, thereby enhancing accuracy, particularly under low-irradiance conditions. The corresponding I–V relationship is expressed as:

$$I = I_{ph} - I_{sd1}\left[e^{\frac{(V+IR_s)}{(n_1V_t)}} - 1\right] - I_{sd2}\left[e^{\frac{(V+IR_s)}{(n_2V_t)}} - 1\right] - \frac{(V + IR_s)}{R_{sh}} \tag{9.2}$$

In this expression, I_{sd1} and I_{sd2} denote the saturation currents of the primary and secondary diodes, while n_1 and n_2 are their respective ideality factors. The additional diode enables the model to account for recombination processes within the depletion region, thereby producing a more faithful representation of the real PV module response.

For the validation of these circuit models, an industrial CS6P-220P PV module was employed under operating conditions of 30°C and an irradiance level of 1000 W/m². The module is composed of multiple polycrystalline silicon cells connected in series, with a rated power output of 220 W. The installation at the Engineering Faculty of Düzce University is shown in Fig. 9.2. To ensure reliable parameter estimation and subsequent validation, a single module was isolated and analyzed.

9.3 Proposed methodology for parameter extraction

Accurate parameter extraction for PV modules is crucial for performance optimization, system diagnostics, and efficient energy conversion. In this study, we employ a novel hybrid approach combining the GWO with the NR technique for precise estimation of the electrical parameters of the CS6P-220P PV module. The proposed methodology aims to enhance computational efficiency and accuracy while addressing the nonlinear nature of the SD and DD models. Fig. 9.3 illustrates the overall parameter extraction workflow, depicting how the synergy between the GWO and NR techniques facilitates robust and efficient convergence toward optimal parameter values. The methodology is structured into three key phases: initialization, metaheuristic-based optimization, and numerical refinement.

The extraction process begins with defining the objective function, which quantifies the error between the measured and estimated I–V characteristics of the PV module. The optimization problem is formulated to minimize the RMSE between the experimental and modeled data, ensuring the best possible fit. The decision variables include key electrical parameters

FIGURE 9.2 CS6P-220P PV module (*PV*, photovoltaic).

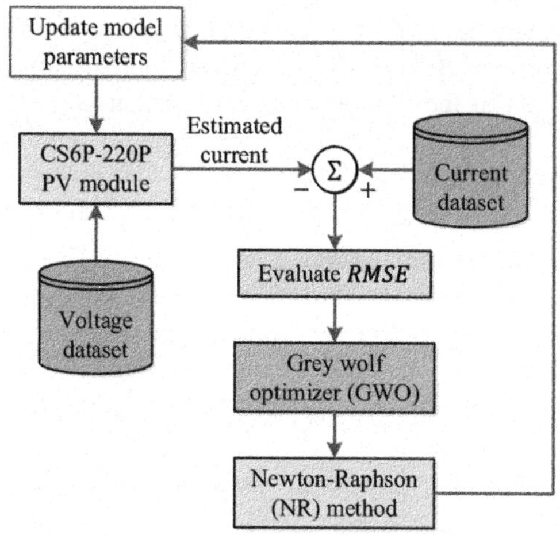

FIGURE 9.3 Parameter extraction of CS6P-220P PV module using GWO and Newton–Raphson technique (*GWO*, grey wolf optimizer; *PV*, photovoltaic).

such as the photocurrent, diode saturation current, series resistance, shunt resistance, and diode ideality factor. The GWO is employed as the primary search mechanism due to its capability to balance exploration and exploitation efficiently. While GWO provides a globally optimized solution, numerical refinement is necessary for enhanced precision. The NR method is applied postoptimization to fine-tune the parameters obtained from GWO. This iterative numerical approach exploits local gradient information to ensure rapid convergence with minimal computational overhead. By leveraging NR after the global search phase, the proposed methodology achieves a balance between computational efficiency and accuracy.

The parameter extraction framework was implemented in MATLAB, with the optimization routine executed over 30 independent runs to ensure statistical robustness. The PV module's experimental data, obtained from the custom-installed system at Düzce University, serves as the benchmark for validation. The proposed hybrid approach integrates the advantages of metaheuristic search and numerical refinement. As a result, it achieves an improved convergence rate compared to conventional heuristics, higher precision in parameter estimation (thus reducing error margins), and robust handling of complex PV module characteristics under varying environmental conditions. In addition, it delivers efficient computational performance, minimizing execution time while maximizing accuracy.

9.4 Adopted algorithms for comparison

To evaluate the effectiveness of the GWO [15] for PV parameter extraction, we compare its performance with several well-established metaheuristic algorithms, namely PSO [17], GSA [18], DE [19], and GA [20]. Each of these methods exhibits unique strengths in handling optimization problems, making them suitable candidates for comparison. The competing algorithms were chosen based on their proven efficiency in global optimization problems, particularly in parameter estimation tasks. Their fundamental principles are summarized below:

- **GWO**: Inspired by the social hierarchy and hunting behavior of grey wolves, GWO balances exploration and exploitation efficiently through its leader-based search mechanism.
- **PSO**: Mimics the collective intelligence of a swarm, where individual particles update their positions based on their own and their neighbors' best solutions.
- **GSA**: Based on Newton's law of gravity and motion, GSA treats agents as masses that interact via gravitational forces to converge towards optimal solutions.
- **DE**: Employs mutation, crossover, and selection operations to enhance diversity and improve solution convergence.
- **GA**: Simulates the process of natural evolution, using selection, crossover, and mutation to evolve better solutions over generations.

For a fair comparison, the parameters of each algorithm were carefully tuned to ensure optimal performance. Table 9.1 summarizes the adopted parameter settings. All algorithms were executed over 30 independent runs, with a population size of 30 and a total iteration count of 400, ensuring a robust evaluation framework.

TABLE 9.1 Parameter settings of GWO and other competing algorithms.

Algorithm	Parameter	Value
GWO	Convergence constant *a*	Decreases linearly from 2 to 0
PSO	Maximum and minimum of inertia weight w_{max} and w_{min}	[0.9, 0.6]
	Acceleration constants c_1 and c_2	[2, 2]
GSA	Gravitational constant G_0	100
	Decreasing coefficient α	20
DE	Mutation rate	0.5
	Recombination rate	0.5
GA	Mutation ratio	0.1
	Crossover	0.9
	Selection mechanism	Roulette wheel

DE, differential evolution; *GA*, genetic algorithm; *GSA*, gravitational search algorithm; *GWO*, grey wolf optimizer; *PSO*, particle swarm optimization.

9.5 Results

This section presents the comparative evaluation of the GWO with other optimization techniques in extracting parameters for both the SD and DD models of PV modules. The goal is to assess the accuracy, stability, and efficiency of GWO in determining optimal electrical parameters while ensuring minimal error between the modeled and experimental I–V characteristics. The evaluation is divided into two main subsections. The first one focuses on the SD model, where the performance of GWO is benchmarked against PSO, GSA, DE, and GA. The extracted parameters, statistical analysis, and convergence behavior are analyzed in detail to highlight the superiority of GWO in handling nonlinear optimization problems. The second subsection extends the analysis to the DD model, which provides a more detailed representation of PV behavior by accounting for recombination losses. Given the increased complexity of this model, the ability of GWO to efficiently navigate the search space and achieve precise parameter estimation is critically examined. In both cases, results are interpreted using various statistical metrics, including best, worst, and average values, convergence rates, and boxplot visualizations. Additionally, the extracted parameters are validated through I–V and power–voltage (P–V) characteristic curves, demonstrating how well the optimized models fit the experimental data. The findings in this section emphasize the robustness of GWO in PV parameter extraction, highlighting its competitive edge over alternative metaheuristic optimization methods.

9.5.1 Obtained results for single-diode model

The evaluation of the SD model was conducted through a comparative analysis of five optimization algorithms: GWO, PSO, GSA, DE, and GA. The results were assessed based on multiple statistical metrics, including the best, worst, and average fitness values, as well as standard deviation to reflect stability and robustness. Table 9.2 presents the predefined boundaries for the parameter optimization process within the SD model. These limits ensure that the extracted values remain within a physically meaningful range, enabling realistic and accurate modeling.

Table 9.3 presents the statistical results obtained from 30 independent runs for each algorithm. It is evident that GWO consistently outperformed its counterparts, achieving the lowest RMSE value of 0.039597 (best) and the lowest average value of 0.040213. Furthermore, the standard deviation for GWO was significantly lower (0.00057198), indicating higher stability and convergence reliability compared to other algorithms. These results demonstrate the superior convergence capability of GWO. Unlike other techniques, GWO efficiently balances exploration and exploitation, leading to better solution accuracy with reduced computational fluctuations.

To further assess the superiority of GWO, a nonparametric statistical test (Wilcoxon's test) was conducted, and the *P*-values are presented in Table 9.4. The results indicate that GWO significantly outperformed GA and PSO, while its performance against GSA and DE was competitive, with no significant difference observed. The statistical results reinforce that GWO consistently finds more optimal solutions while maintaining robustness.

TABLE 9.2 Selected boundaries of the optimized single-diode model parameters.

Parameter	Lower bound	Upper bound
I_{ph} (A)	6	9
I_{sd} (A)	1E−35	1E−20
R_s (Ω)	0.25	2
R_{sh} (Ω)	30	60
n	10	25

TABLE 9.3 Statistical performance of adopted algorithms for the single-diode model.

Algorithm	Best	Worst	Average	Standard deviation
GWO	0.039597	0.042035	0.040213	0.00057198
PSO	0.039621	0.054576	0.041930	0.0034037
GSA	0.039623	0.045158	0.040615	0.0012296
DE	0.039650	0.050135	0.040992	0.0022073
GA	0.039693	0.058145	0.045606	0.0054735

DE, differential evolution; *GA*, genetic algorithm; *GSA*, gravitational search algorithm; *GWO*, grey wolf optimizer; *PSO*, particle swarm optimization.

TABLE 9.4 Nonparametric statistical analysis for the single-diode model.

GWO versus PSO		GWO versus GSA		GWO versus DE		GWO versus GA	
P-value	Superior	*P*-value	Superior	*P*-value	Superior	*P*-value	Superior
0.013194	GWO	0.15286	Tie	0.14704	Tie	8.4661E−06	GWO

DE, differential evolution; *GA*, genetic algorithm; *GWO*, grey wolf optimizer; *PSO*, particle swarm optimization.

Fig. 9.4 provides a visual representation of the statistical dispersion of RMSE values for each algorithm using a boxplot. The results indicate that GWO exhibits the lowest variance and a consistently lower error range compared to its competitors. While PSO and GA display wider interquartile ranges, signifying higher variability in their optimization outcomes, GWO maintains a more compact distribution, reinforcing its reliability in parameter extraction.

Fig. 9.5 illustrates the convergence behavior of the optimization algorithms. GWO exhibits a rapid decrease in RMSE within the early iterations, signifying efficient exploitation of the search space. In contrast, PSO and GA display more erratic convergence paths, highlighting their susceptibility to premature stagnation. GSA maintains a relatively stable but slower convergence, while DE follows a comparable path but requires more iterations to attain a similar level of optimization as GWO. The rapid and smooth decline of the RMSE in GWO highlights its superior capability in balancing exploration and exploitation, ensuring a more efficient parameter extraction process compared to the competing algorithms.

Table 9.5 summarizes the extracted parameters for the SD model using different algorithms. GWO produced well-refined parameters that align closely with theoretical expectations, further validating its reliability for PV module parameter estimation.

Figs. 9.6 and 9.7 depict the I–V and P–V characteristics obtained using different optimization techniques. The curves derived from GWO exhibit a near-perfect fit with the experimental data, reaffirming the model's accuracy in parameter

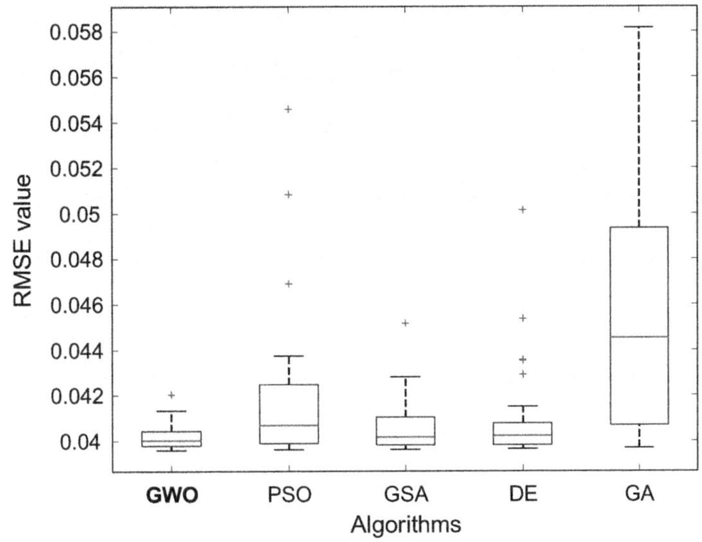

FIGURE 9.4 Boxplot analysis of GWO, PSO, GSA, DE, and GA algorithms for the single-diode model (*DE*, differential evolution; *GA*, genetic algorithm; *GSA*, gravitational search algorithm; *GWO*, grey wolf optimizer; *PSO*, particle swarm optimization).

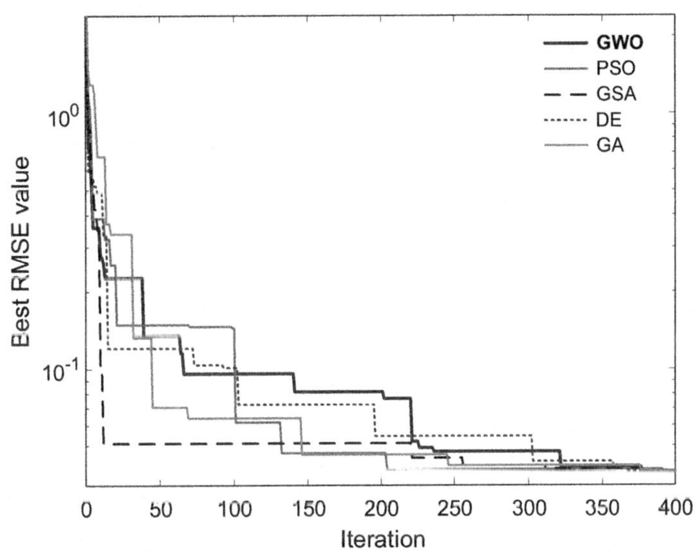

FIGURE 9.5 Convergence curves of GWO, PSO, GSA, DE, and GA algorithms for the single-diode model (*DE*, differential evolution; *GA*, genetic algorithm; *GSA*, gravitational search algorithm; *GWO*, grey wolf optimizer; *PSO*, particle swarm optimization).

TABLE 9.5 The obtained parameters for the single-diode model via GWO, PSO, GSA, DE, and GA algorithms.

Algorithm	I_{ph} (A)	I_{sd} (A)	R_s (Ω)	R_{sh} (Ω)	n
GWO	7.8908	4.7012E−22	0.80827	33.184	25
PSO	7.8885	4.7173E−22	0.80717	33.195	25
GSA	7.8827	4.7192E−22	0.80768	33.598	25
DE	7.8865	4.6949E−22	0.80902	33.274	25
GA	7.8918	4.7198E−22	0.80705	32.836	25

DE, differential evolution; *GA*, genetic algorithm; *GSA*, gravitational search algorithm; *GWO*, grey wolf optimizer; *PSO*, particle swarm optimization.

extraction. Other algorithms, particularly GA and PSO, display slight deviations, which could lead to performance inefficiencies in real-world PV applications.

9.5.2 Obtained results for double-diode model

Building on the evaluation of the SD model, this section examines the performance of the GWO in parameter extraction for the DD model, comparing its results with those obtained using PSO, GSA, DE, and GA. The DD model incorporates an additional diode to account for recombination losses, making parameter extraction more complex but providing a more accurate representation of PV behavior. Table 9.6 outlines the predefined parameter boundaries for optimization within the DD model. These constraints ensure realistic and physically meaningful parameter extraction, facilitating robust modeling of the PV module's characteristics.

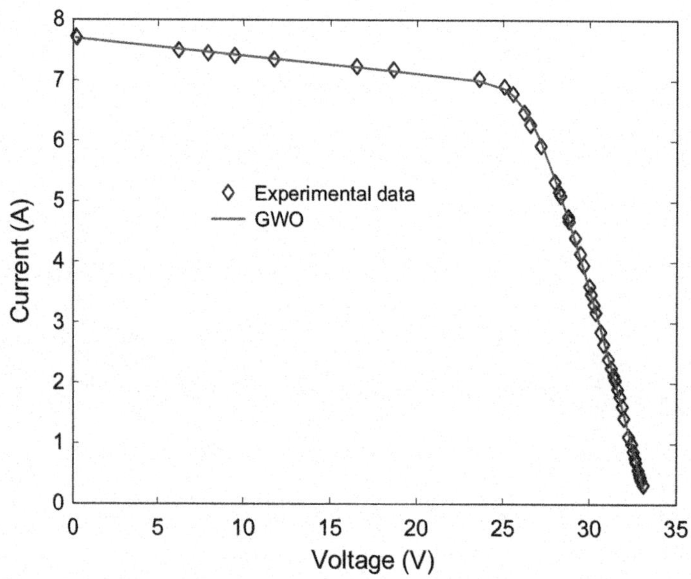

FIGURE 9.6 I–V curve characteristics for the single-diode model (*I*–*V*, current–voltage).

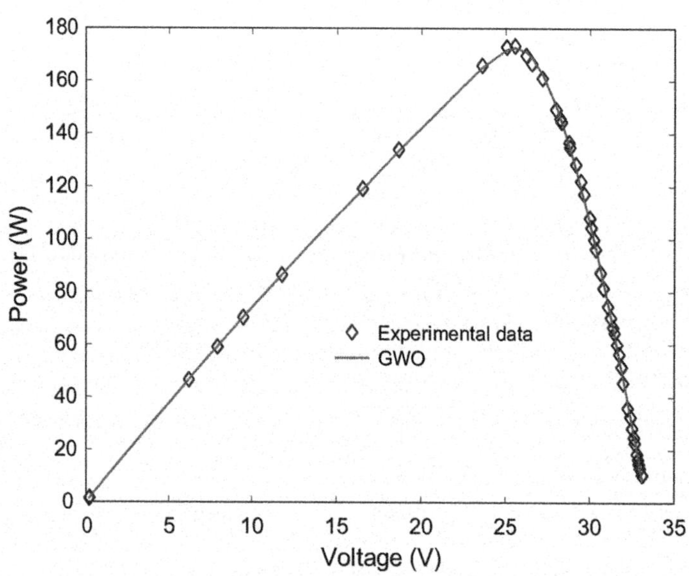

FIGURE 9.7 P–V curve characteristics for the single-diode model (*P*–*V*, power–voltage).

TABLE 9.6 Selected boundaries of the optimized double-diode model parameters.

Parameter	Lower bound	Upper bound
I_{ph} (A)	6	9
I_{sd1} (A)	1E−35	1E−20
I_{sd2} (A)	1E−35	1E−20
R_s (Ω)	0.25	2
R_{sh} (Ω)	30	60
n_1	10	30
n_2	10	30

TABLE 9.7 Statistical performance of adopted algorithms for the double-diode model.

Algorithm	Best	Worst	Average	Standard deviation
GWO	0.038220	0.047005	0.041454	0.0024895
PSO	0.038726	0.064241	0.046270	0.0077645
GSA	0.038915	0.059880	0.047019	0.0074011
DE	0.038989	0.061962	0.047702	0.0067045
GA	0.039442	0.075721	0.048465	0.0097723

DE, differential evolution; *GA*, genetic algorithm; *GSA*, gravitational search algorithm; *GWO*, grey wolf optimizer; *PSO*, particle swarm optimization.

Table 9.7 presents the statistical results obtained from 30 independent runs for each algorithm. As observed in the SD model evaluation, GWO continues to demonstrate superior performance, achieving the lowest best RMSE (0.038220) and the lowest average RMSE (0.041454). Additionally, GWO exhibits lower variance, as evidenced by its smaller standard deviation, indicating greater consistency and reliability.

Fig. 9.8 visually represents the RMSE distributions for each algorithm. The boxplot analysis reaffirms the findings from Table 9.7, showing that GWO achieves lower error margins and more stable solutions compared to its competitors. While PSO, GSA, and GA exhibit higher variability, GWO maintains a compact interquartile range, reinforcing its efficiency in producing consistently optimized solutions.

Table 9.8 presents the nonparametric statistical analysis of the comparative performance of the algorithms. The *P*-values indicate that GWO significantly outperforms all other algorithms, confirming its superior optimization capabilities for the DD model.

The convergence behavior of the optimization algorithms is illustrated in Fig. 9.9. Similar to the SD model, GWO demonstrates a rapid and stable reduction in RMSE across iterations, achieving optimal solutions faster than its competitors. The PSO and GA algorithms exhibit more erratic convergence trends, often stagnating at suboptimal values, while GSA and DE converge more smoothly but require significantly more iterations to achieve results comparable to GWO. The efficiency of GWO in quickly reaching optimal parameter values without high computational cost highlights its practical advantage.

Table 9.9 provides the extracted parameters for the DD model using the different optimization algorithms. As seen in previous comparisons, GWO delivers well-calibrated parameters that align with theoretical expectations and improve PV modeling accuracy.

Figs. 9.10 and 9.11 illustrate the I–V and P–V characteristics obtained using the different optimization techniques. The curves optimized by GWO closely match the experimental data, validating the accuracy of the extracted parameters.

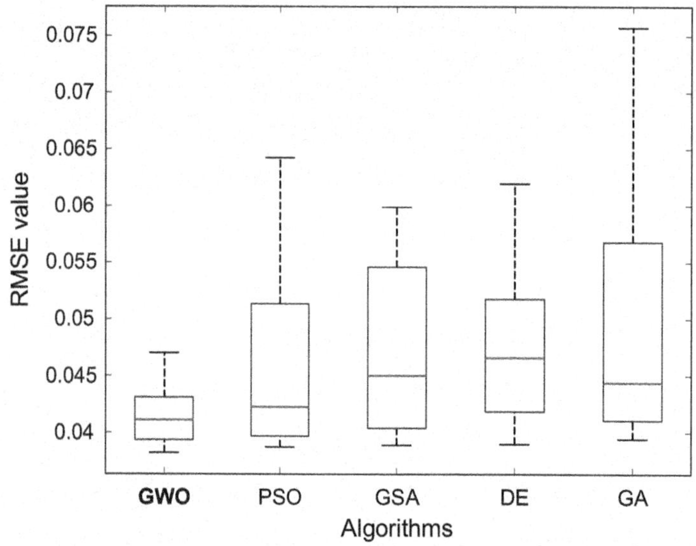

FIGURE 9.8 Boxplot analysis of GWO, PSO, GSA, DE, and GA algorithms for the double-diode model (*DE*, differential evolution; *GA*, genetic algorithm; *GSA*, gravitational search algorithm; *GWO*, grey wolf optimizer; *PSO*, particle swarm optimization).

TABLE 9.8 Nonparametric statistical analysis for the double-diode model.

GWO versus PSO		GWO versus GSA		GWO versus DE		GWO versus GA	
P-value	Superior	*P*-value	Superior	*P*-value	Superior	*P*-value	Superior
0.014795	GWO	0.0025846	GWO	8.9187E–05	GWO	0.0027653	GWO

DE, differential evolution; *GSA*, gravitational search algorithm; *GWO*, grey wolf optimizer; *PSO*, particle swarm optimization.

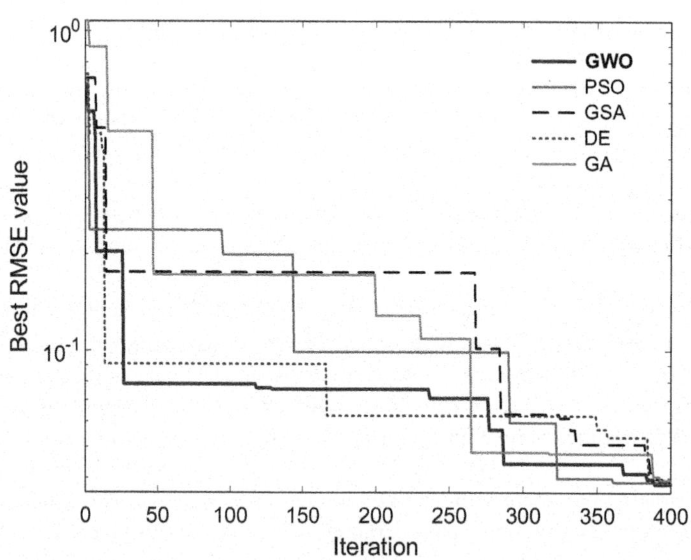

FIGURE 9.9 Convergence curves of GWO, PSO, GSA, DE, and GA algorithms for the double-diode model (*DE*, differential evolution; *GA*, genetic algorithm; *GSA*, gravitational search algorithm; *GWO*, grey wolf optimizer; *PSO*, particle swarm optimization).

TABLE 9.9 The obtained parameters for the double-diode model via GWO, PSO, GSA, DE, and GA algorithms.

Algorithm	I_{ph} (A)	I_{sd1} (A)	I_{sd2} (A)	R_s (Ω)	R_{sh} (Ω)	n_1	n_2
GWO	7.8819	4.5499E−23	8.6127E−21	0.79692	33.773	28.142	26.504
PSO	7.8738	5.3424E−21	2.0413E−21	0.80296	34.263	26.814	25.972
GSA	7.8586	2.9114E−21	9.834E−21	0.79835	35.507	26.053	27.436
DE	7.9101	5.9502E−21	8.5274E−23	0.80107	32.632	26.309	27.185
GA	7.8411	3.3641E−21	2.8221E−21	0.80070	36.886	26.230	26.454

DE, differential evolution; *GA*, genetic algorithm; *GSA*, gravitational search algorithm; *GWO*, grey wolf optimizer; *PSO*, particle swarm optimization.

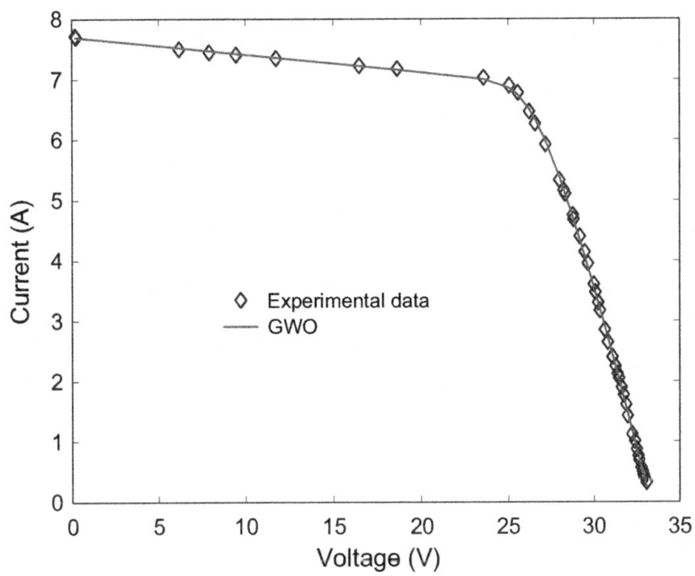

FIGURE 9.10 I–V curve characteristics for the double-diode model (*I–V*, current–voltage).

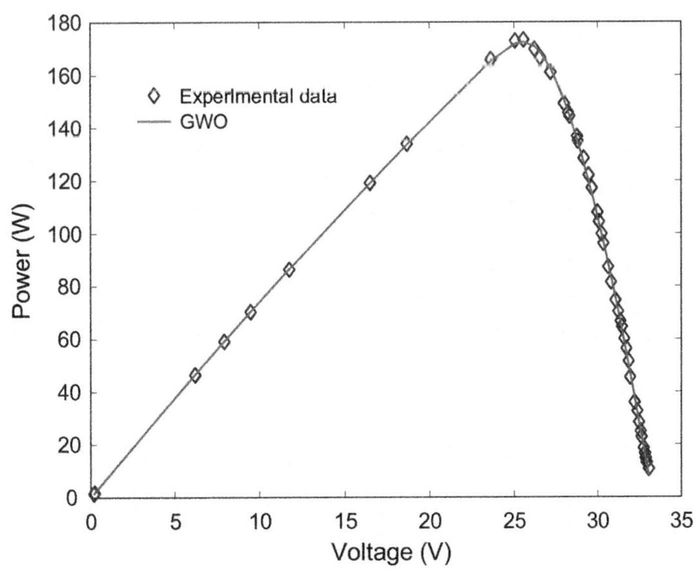

FIGURE 9.11 P–V curve characteristics for the double-diode model (*P–V*, power–voltage).

Other algorithms, particularly GA and PSO, show more deviation, suggesting less effective parameter tuning. The ability of GWO to produce parameter sets that yield more precise electrical characteristics further underscores its competitiveness in PV modeling.

9.6 Conclusion

This study presents a novel and efficient optimization framework for extracting the electrical parameters of PV modules, specifically the CS6P-220P model, utilizing SD and DD circuit representations. The experimental data were obtained from the PV station at Düzce University, ensuring real-world validation of the extracted parameters. The proposed method integrates the GWO with the NR refinement approach to enhance accuracy and convergence efficiency. By leveraging the global search capabilities of GWO and the local refinement strength of NR, the methodology effectively balances exploration and exploitation, ensuring precise parameter extraction. The proposed approach is benchmarked against PSO, GSA, DE, and GA, and its performance is assessed using RMSE, standard deviation, and Wilcoxon's statistical test. The results confirm the superiority of GWO, achieving the lowest RMSE values of 0.039597 for the SD model and 0.038220 for the DD model, with significantly lower variance across multiple runs. The convergence analysis further highlights GWO's efficiency in rapidly reaching optimal solutions, minimizing computational overhead while maintaining high accuracy. The extracted parameters were validated through I–V and P–V characteristic curves, demonstrating an excellent match with experimental data collected from the Düzce University PV station. This confirms the reliability of the proposed optimization approach in accurately modeling PV behavior under real-world conditions. In conclusion, this chapter underscores the effectiveness of GWO as a robust and efficient optimization tool for PV parameter extraction. Its ability to deliver high accuracy with lower computational complexity makes it a promising candidate for large-scale renewable energy applications. Future research may focus on applying the methodology to different PV technologies, considering environmental variations, and integrating adaptive strategies to further enhance optimization performance.

Appendix

CS6P-220P PV module data is given in Table A1. Optimized RMSE (objective function) value via GWO for the single diode model is 0.039597078212252, and for the double-diode model is 0.038219745871530.

TABLE A1 CS6P-220P PV module data.

Experimental data		Single-diode model optimized by GWO		Double-diode model optimized by GWO	
Voltage (V)	Current (A)	Estimated current (A)	Absolute current error (A)	Estimated current (A)	Absolute current error (A)
33.1000	0.3230	0.2572	0.0658	0.2500	0.0730
32.9700	0.4000	0.4004	0.0004	0.3941	0.0059
32.9200	0.4500	0.4554	0.0054	0.4494	0.0006
32.8700	0.5030	0.5103	0.0073	0.5047	0.0017
32.8000	0.5660	0.5872	0.0212	0.5820	0.0160
32.6700	0.6960	0.7296	0.0336	0.7253	0.0293
32.6200	0.7630	0.7843	0.0213	0.7803	0.0173
32.5200	0.8700	0.8935	0.0235	0.8901	0.0201
32.4200	1.0050	1.0024	0.0026	0.9996	0.0054
32.2500	1.1170	1.1871	0.0701	1.1853	0.0683
31.9800	1.4230	1.4789	0.0559	1.4785	0.0555
31.8900	1.6160	1.5757	0.0403	1.5757	0.0403

(Continued)

TABLE A1 (Continued)

Experimental data		Single-diode model optimized by GWO		Double-diode model optimized by GWO	
Voltage (V)	Current (A)	Estimated current (A)	Absolute current error (A)	Estimated current (A)	Absolute current error (A)
31.7500	1.7750	1.7258	0.0492	1.7265	0.0485
31.6200	1.9000	1.8647	0.0353	1.8660	0.0340
31.4700	2.0500	2.0243	0.0257	2.0263	0.0237
31.3900	2.1230	2.1092	0.0138	2.1114	0.0116
31.2500	2.2500	2.2571	0.0071	2.2599	0.0099
31.0800	2.4000	2.4358	0.0358	2.4391	0.0391
30.8100	2.6450	2.7174	0.0724	2.7215	0.0765
30.6400	2.8500	2.8932	0.0432	2.8976	0.0476
30.3500	3.1700	3.1901	0.0201	3.1949	0.0249
30.2500	3.3000	3.2915	0.0085	3.2965	0.0035
30.0900	3.4700	3.4527	0.0173	3.4578	0.0122
30.0000	3.6000	3.5428	0.0572	3.5479	0.0521
29.6600	3.9500	3.8788	0.0712	3.8837	0.0663
29.4700	4.1400	4.0633	0.0767	4.0680	0.0720
29.1800	4.4000	4.3400	0.0600	4.3439	0.0561
28.8200	4.6800	4.6738	0.0062	4.6765	0.0035
28.7800	4.7500	4.7101	0.0399	4.7126	0.0374
28.3300	5.1000	5.1075	0.0075	5.1078	0.0078
28.2500	5.1600	5.1757	0.0157	5.1755	0.0155
28.0000	5.3300	5.3834	0.0534	5.3816	0.0516
27.2000	5.9200	5.9816	0.0616	5.9739	0.0539
26.5800	6.2700	6.3551	0.0851	6.3439	0.0739
26.2400	6.4700	6.5192	0.0492	6.5073	0.0373
25.5700	6.7800	6.7535	0.0265	6.7440	0.0360
25.0600	6.9000	6.8625	0.0375	6.8572	0.0428
23.6000	7.0300	6.9959	0.0341	7.0006	0.0294
18.6500	7.1800	7.1545	0.0255	7.1607	0.0193
16.4800	7.2300	7.2184	0.0116	7.2234	0.0066
11.7500	7.3500	7.3575	0.0075	7.3603	0.0103
9.4800	7.4100	7.4243	0.0143	7.4259	0.0159
7.9300	7.4500	7.4699	0.0199	7.4708	0.0208
6.2000	7.5000	7.5208	0.0208	7.5208	0.0208
0.2320	7.7000	7.6963	0.0037	7.6934	0.0066
0.1900	7.7200	7.6976	0.0224	7.6947	0.0253

References

[1] S. Ekinci, D. Izci, M. Bajaj, V. Blazek, Novel application of sinh cosh optimizer for robust controller design in hybrid photovoltaic-thermal power systems, Scientific Reports 15 (2025) 2825. Available from https://doi.org/10.1038/s41598-025-86597-5.

[2] S. Seme, B. Štumberger, M. Hadžiselimović, K. Sredenšek, Solar photovoltaic tracking systems for electricity generation: a review, Energies (Basel) 13 (2020) 4224. Available from https://doi.org/10.3390/en13164224.

[3] D. İzci, S. Ekinci, M. Güleydin, Improved reptile search algorithm for optimal design of solar photovoltaic module, Computer Science. IDAP-2023, (2023) 172–179. Available from https://doi.org/10.53070/bbd.1346267.

[4] B. Chen, L. Cao, C. Chen, Y. Chen, Y. Yue, A comprehensive survey on the chicken swarm optimization algorithm and its applications: state-of-the-art and research challenges, Artificial Intelligence Review 57 (2024) 170. Available from https://doi.org/10.1007/s10462-024-10786-3.

[5] D. Maden, E. Çelik, E.H. Houssein, G. Sharma, Squirrel search algorithm applied to effective estimation of solar PV model parameters: a real-world practice, Neural Computing and Applications 35 (2023) 13529–13546. Available from https://doi.org/10.1007/s00521-023-08451-x.

[6] J.J. Montano, L.F. Grisales Norena, A.F. Tobon, D. Gonzalez Montoya, Estimation of the parameters of the mathematical model of an equivalent diode of a photovoltaic panel using a continuous genetic algorithm, IEEE Latin America Transactions 20 (2022) 616–623. Available from https://doi.org/10.1109/TLA.2022.9675467.

[7] A.A.K. Ismaeel, E.H. Houssein, D. Oliva, M. Said, Gradient-based optimizer for parameter extraction in photovoltaic models, IEEE Access 9 (2021) 13403–13416. Available from https://doi.org/10.1109/ACCESS.2021.3052153.

[8] M.A. Khelifa, B. Lekouaghet, A. Boukabou, Symmetric chaotic gradient-based optimizer algorithm for efficient estimation of PV parameters, Optik (Stuttg) 259 (2022) 168873. Available from https://doi.org/10.1016/j.ijleo.2022.168873.

[9] M. Qaraad, S. Amjad, N.K. Hussein, M. Badawy, S. Mirjalili, M.A. Elhosseini, Photovoltaic parameter estimation using improved moth flame algorithms with local escape operators, Computers and Electrical Engineering 106 (2023) 108603. Available from https://doi.org/10.1016/j.compeleceng.2023.108603.

[10] A.M. Eltamaly, Musical chairs algorithm for parameters estimation of PV cells, Solar Energy 241 (2022) 601–620. Available from https://doi.org/10.1016/j.solener.2022.06.043.

[11] H.A. Ramadan, B. Khan, A.A.Z. Diab, Accurate parameters estimation of three diode model of photovoltaic modules using hunter–prey and wild horse optimizers, IEEE Access 10 (2022) 87435–87453. Available from https://doi.org/10.1109/ACCESS.2022.3199001.

[12] M. Yaghoubi, M. Eslami, M. Noroozi, H. Mohammadi, O. Kamari, S. Palani, Modified salp swarm optimization for parameter estimation of solar PV models, IEEE Access 10 (2022) 110181–110194. Available from https://doi.org/10.1109/ACCESS.2022.3213746.

[13] M. Ghetas, M. Elshourbagy, Parameters extraction of photovoltaic models using enhanced generalized normal distribution optimization with neighborhood search, Neural Computing and Applications 36 (2024) 14035–14052. Available from https://doi.org/10.1007/s00521-024-09609-x.

[14] E. Çelik, M. Karayel, D. Maden, M. Abdel-Salam, N. Öztürk, O. Kaplan, et al., Reconfigured single- and double-diode models for improved modelling of solar cells/modules, Scientific Reports 15 (2025) 2101. Available from https://doi.org/10.1038/s41598-025-86063-2.

[15] S. Mirjalili, S.M. Mirjalili, A. Lewis, Grey wolf optimizer, Advances in Engineering Software 69 (2014) 46–61. Available from https://doi.org/10.1016/j.advengsoft.2013.12.007.

[16] M. Abdel-Basset, R. Mohamed, I.M. Hezam, K.M. Sallam, I.A. Hameed, Parameters identification of photovoltaic models using Lambert W-function and Newton-Raphson method collaborated with AI-based optimization techniques: a comparative study, Expert Systems with Applications 255 (2024) 124777. Available from https://doi.org/10.1016/j.eswa.2024.124777.

[17] D. Wang, D. Tan, L. Liu, Particle swarm optimization algorithm: an overview, Soft Computing 22 (2018) 387–408. Available from https://doi.org/10.1007/s00500-016-2474-6.

[18] E. Rashedi, H. Nezamabadi-pour, S. Saryazdi, GSA: a gravitational search algorithm, Information Sciences (New York) 179 (2009) 2232–2248. Available from https://doi.org/10.1016/j.ins.2009.03.004.

[19] R. Storn, K. Price, Differential evolution - a simple and efficient heuristic for global optimization over continuous spaces, Journal of Global Optimization 11 (1997) 341–359. Available from https://doi.org/10.1023/A:1008202821328.

[20] J.H. Holland, Genetic algorithms, Scientific American 267 (1992) 66–73.

Chapter 10

Predictive bridge deterioration modeling with a hybrid stochastic paint optimizer, grey wolf optimizer, and extreme learning machine algorithm

Nima Khodadadi[1], El-Sayed M. El-Kenawy[2,3], Benyamin Abdollahzadeh[4], Antonio Nanni[5], and Khalid M. Mosalam[1]

[1]*Department of Civil and Environmental Engineering, Pacific Earthquake Engineering Research (PEER) Center, University of California, Berkeley, CA, United States,* [2]*School of ICT, Faculty of Engineering, Design and Information & Communications Technology (EDICT), Bahrain Polytechnic, Isa Town, Bahrain,* [3]*Jadara University Research Center, Jadara University, Jordan,* [4]*Liverpool John Moores University, Liverpool, England,* [5]*Department of Civil and Architectural Engineering, University of Miami, Coral Gables, FL, United States*

10.1 Introduction

With the rapid development of transportation, bridge systems are of great significance to the national economy and social security. As of 2023, the stock of highway bridges in China has surpassed 960,000. Under the combined effects of complex stressors and internal factors, the degradation of infrastructure performance over time is inevitable [1,2]. Maintenance of large-scale aging bridges poses a significant challenge for infrastructure owners seeking structural reliability, safety, and service life [3,4].

Performance prediction is an important research topic with practical guidance for periodic maintenance and decision-making. Accurate prediction has significant value in resource allocation and public safety. To date, numerous studies have been conducted on predicting the remaining life of aging structures. Models for bridge condition prediction can be divided into deterministic and probabilistic models [5]. Deterministic models assume that bridge degradation follows a predetermined performance path. It uses historical inspection data to select a deterioration equation and then uses regression to estimate the corresponding parameters. Yang et al. [6] used performance data from 398 reinforced concrete bridges to develop a regression model and obtained a performance degradation equation that captures different stages of performance degradation. Sahar et al. [7] proposed a regression model for bridge superstructure degradation that incorporates multiple variables. The model includes the effects of variables such as service time, span length, and traffic flow volume. The deterministic model is simple and intuitive in structure and is flexible to use and update. However, deterministic models usually require high-quality long-term data for prediction and often struggle to accurately characterize the uncertainty of the deterioration process. To overcome the limitations of deterministic models, probabilistic models take the degradation rate as a random variable. In addition, probabilistic models often draw on stochastic process theory, such as Markov chains. Zhang et al. [8] used five years of inspection data on 445 hollow-slab bridges to construct a three-stage Markov model that effectively represents the state transitions of hollow-slab bridges.

Wellalage et al. [9] proposed a Metropolis–Hastings-optimized Markov chain Monte Carlo method for multistate degradation models, which is superior to traditional regression and Bayesian methods. Thanh et al. [10] proposed combining physical-empirical models to address the scarcity of inspection data, using these data to infer the likelihood and determine the next state transition matrix via least squares. Probabilistic models can capture randomness in the data, a big advantage over deterministic models. However, this type of model is still based on extensive engineering experience and judgment and needs to be updated after each new round of inspection, so its structure cannot be optimized.

Grey Wolf Optimizer. DOI: https://doi.org/10.1016/B978-0-443-36624-6.00025-1

In recent years, with the development of machine learning (ML) methods, using ML to further improve deterioration prediction accuracy has also attracted research interest. Extreme learning machine (ELM) [11,12] is an improved method with high speed and accuracy. It is based on single-hidden-layer feedforward neural networks (SLFNs). The ELM algorithm differs from traditional training of feedforward neural networks, as the input weights and biases of hidden nodes are randomly assigned and not adjusted by backpropagation. This means that it is not necessary to use gradient descent or stochastic gradient descent to learn the parameters. Instead, the output weights are determined analytically by using the Moore–Penrose generalized inverse. The output weights can be determined with linear system analysis using matrix operations. ELM has the advantages of powerful learning and good generalization, and can be used for a variety of classification and regression problems. In addition, it has a simple network structure that requires little parameter fine-tuning, making it easy to use. ELM has been applied in many fields, including signal processing, pattern recognition, and intelligent control.

Jiang et al. [13] used ELM to predict the remaining life of lithium batteries and achieved good results, with a prediction error within 5%. He et al. [14] used ELM to diagnose circuit faults, with a recognition accuracy of 94.44% and a detection time of 1 millisecond. This also provides some inspiration for the use of ELM in real-time infrastructure health monitoring. In addition, it was shown that the initial weights and thresholds could be reasonably optimized to achieve better predictive performance with ELM. Numerous studies have shown that combining metaheuristic algorithms with ELM can greatly improve prediction accuracy and enhance model generalization. While ELMs are appreciated for their rapid learning speed and straightforward structure, their effectiveness largely depends on the selection of input weights and biases. To combat this sensitivity, metaheuristic techniques have been used to fine-tune the various critical parameters of Elms. Techniques such as grey wolf optimizer (GWO) [15], particle swarm optimization (PSO) [16], and stochastic paint optimizer (SPO) [17] have been successfully employed to tune critical parameters. This not only mitigates the intrinsic drawbacks of ELMs but also optimizes their internal architecture to deliver stable, robust, and accurate predictions across a wide range of engineering applications.

The purpose of this chapter is to establish a data-driven bridge health prediction model. A large set of bridge inspection data is used in this model. The original ELM model has random initial weights and thresholds, which affect model stability and limit predictive performance. This chapter uses the SPOGWO algorithm to optimize the ELM model. The specific methods are as follows. First, data preprocessing is performed, and a set of 539 bridge inspection samples is collected as the model's training and test data. Then use the training set to optimize the ELM model's hyperparameters and the network's structure. Use SPOGWO to obtain the optimal initial weights for the ELM model. Finally, the optimized parameters are used as the input to the ELM model to train the bridge deterioration prediction system.

10.2 Database

Establishing a long-term bridge condition database is an important basis for studying the evolution law of bridge deterioration. This chapter uses documentary data on 539 urban bridges, including periodic inspection reports, construction design drawings, repair drawings, and maintenance records [18].

In this chapter, input variables were used to present the structural features and maintenance condition of the bridge. Input variables included the structural style (simply supported and continuous beam), district (three geographic districts), number of lanes, bridge span, bridge length, bridge width, and bridge age. The type of bridges is classified as plate girder, T-girder, or box girder. Maintenance condition was described using three dummy variables indicating whether the bridge deck, superstructure, or substructure was maintained during the year. A value of 1 was recorded for a particular year when maintenance was performed, and 0 when no maintenance was performed. The bridge condition deterioration index (BCDI) was considered as an output variable to represent the overall condition of the bridge and its structural integrity.

The bridge condition database can be divided into several categories. Numerical variables (age, length, etc.), text categorical variables (region and bridge type, etc.), and Boolean variables (maintenance or not) are input features for modeling. All numerical inputs will be normalized to ensure they are on a comparable scale. This helps to improve numerical stability and avoid gradient explosion in training. Textual categories have no order or one-to-one correspondence among themselves and will be one-hot encoded into $1 \times N$-sized binary vectors, where N is the number of different categories. For instance, the bridge types are hollow plate girder, T-beam, and box girder, which are transformed into (1, 0, 0), (0, 1, 0), and (0, 0, 1), respectively, and then used as the input nodes. Region 1, Region 2, and Region 3 are the three main areas, distinguished by climate, geography, and environment. The bridge location within these zones can also be encoded as one-hot. The Boolean variable m maintained will be set to 1 if a maintenance action was performed in that year and 0 otherwise.

Min-max normalization and one-hot encoding are examples of secondary preprocessing techniques applied to the input variables before training the network. The data is randomly split into 321 records for training, 109 for testing, and 109 for the validation set. The ranges of the input variables are shown in Table 10.1.

TABLE 10.1 Input and output variable descriptions.

Variable	Variable description	Value range
y	Bridge condition deterioration index	[0, 100]
t/years	The service life of the bridge (age of the bridge)	[0, 20] rounding
T_a	The region (district) {Region 1, Region 2, Region 3}	{1, 0, 0}, {0, 1, 0}, {0, 0, 1}
T_b	The bridge types {Plate girder, T-beam, Box girder}	{1, 0, 0}, {0, 1, 0}, {0, 0, 1}
T_c	The structural forms (style) {Simply supported beam, Continuous beam}	{0, 1}
l/m	Crossing (Span)	[6,54]
L/m	Bridge length	[8, 1650]
B/m	Bridge width	[7,44]
N	Number of lanes	[1,8] rounding
M	Maintenance condition {No maintenance, Maintenance performed} for bridge deck, superstructure, and substructure	{0, 1}

The selection of appropriate input variables is very important for achieving optimal prediction performance for BCDI. If the selected set of input variables does not capture the essential characteristics of the bridge deterioration process, it will negatively affect the efficiency of the generated model. On the other hand, increasing the number of input variables may also lead to issues such as overfitting, high model complexity, and low generalizability [19]. Hence, in line with the approaches proposed in the articles [20,21], statistical analysis and mutual information correlation coefficients are utilized for the meticulous selection of input variables tailored to diverse bridge components. As mentioned, the maintenance history is a major factor. We will identify other variables that significantly influence the bridge condition. The scatter plot of the selected features against BCDI is shown in Fig. 10.1.

Table 10.2 shows the descriptive statistics for the categorical features in the bridge dataset. These features are structural style, district, bridge type, and maintenance of key components, including deck, superstructure, and substructure. The majority of the bridges in the dataset have a continuous beam structural style, are located in region 1, and are of the box girder type. The maintenance field for the key components indicates that most bridges have never had maintenance performed on any structural components, possibly indicating little to no degradation or limited maintenance intervention.

Table 10.3 shows the descriptive statistics for the continuous features in the dataset. The mean age of the bridges is 10.81 years, and the interquartile range (Q1–Q3) is 7-15 years. The mean span of the bridges is 27.27 meters. The typical number of lanes on bridges ranges from 2 to 8. The length of the bridge feature ranges from 8.3 to 1650 meters. The bridge length distribution is likely to be heavily right-skewed due to a small number of long bridges. The BCDI, the target variable in this study, has a mean of 89.89 and a standard deviation of 4.73.

10.3 Data preprocessing

Normalization is an important step in ML because of the sensitivity to scale in several ML algorithms that use distance measures or gradient descent. Normalization also helps with training speed, optimizer convergence, feature significance, and numerical stability. The range of every variable in the database is between -1 and 1 and is normalized using the following formula:

$$x_{i,normal} = 2 \times \left[\frac{x_i - Min(x)}{Max(x) - Min(x)} \right] - 1 \tag{10.1}$$

where x_i is the original value, $Min(x)$ and $Max(x)$ are the lower and upper bounds for each feature, respectively.

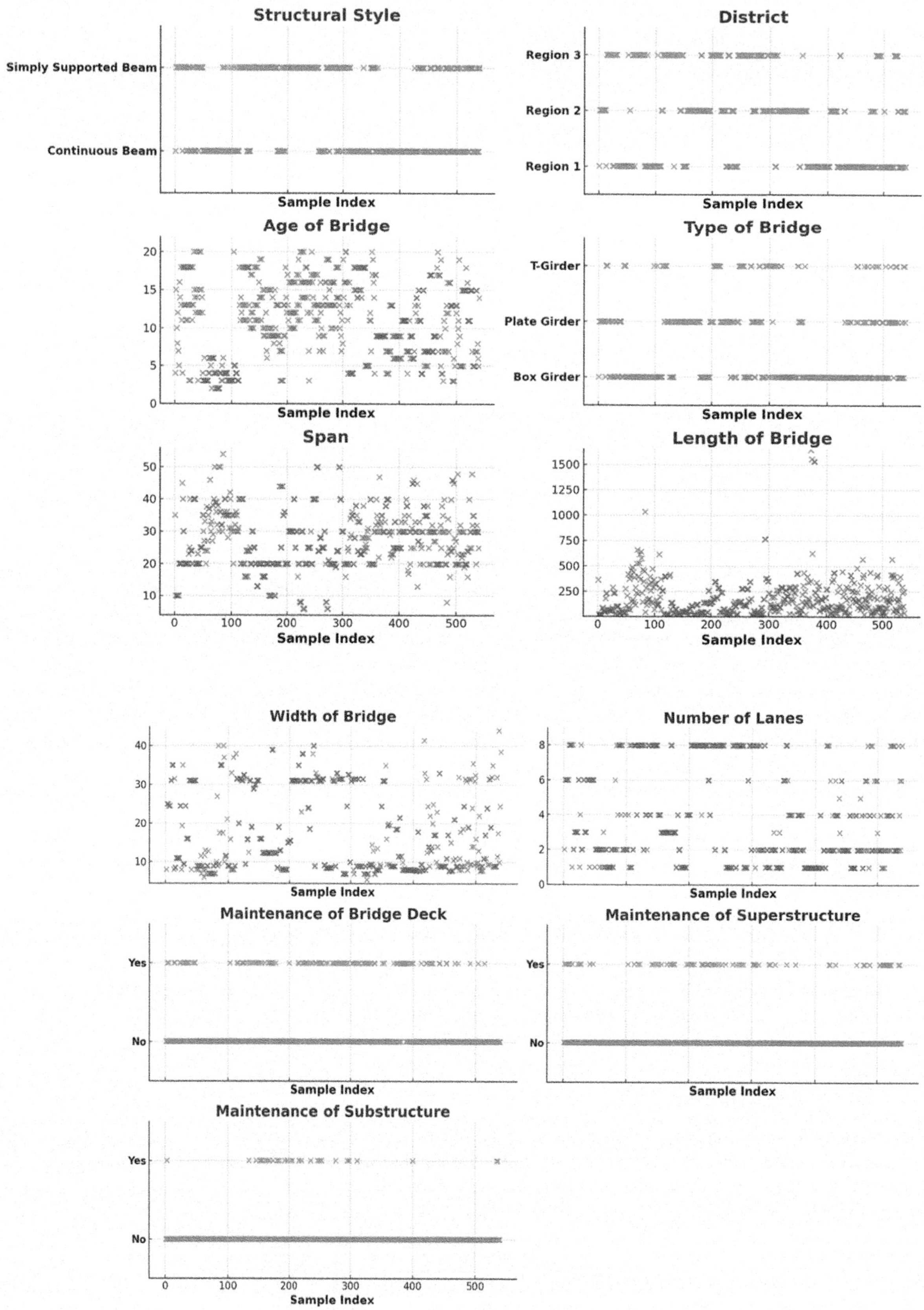

FIGURE 10.1 Scatter plot of features for the bridge dataset.

TABLE 10.2 Categorical feature statistics for the bridge dataset.

Feature	Count	Unique	Top	Frequency	Mode
Structural style	539	2	Continuous beam	285	Continuous beam
District	539	3	Region 1	216	Region 1
Type of bridge	539	3	Box girder	302	Box girder
Maintenance of bridge deck	539	2	No	418	No
Maintenance of superstructure	539	2	No	461	No
Maintenance of substructure	539	2	No	510	No

TABLE 10.3 Continuous feature statistics for the bridge dataset.

Feature	Count	Mean	Std	Min	Q1	Median	Q3	Max	Mode	Unique
Age of bridge	539	10.81	4.96	2	7.0	11.0	15	20	9	19
Span	539	27.27	8.89	6	20	26	33	54	20	38
Length of bridge	53	176.30	187.40	8.3	53.5	120	254	1650	20	205
Width of bridge	539	17.98	10.40	5.5	9	13	31	44	9	60
Number of lanes	539	3.97	2.71	1	2	3	8	8	2	7
BCDI	539	89.89	4.73	80.2	86.56	89.32	93.73	99.75	86.72	449

BCDI, bridge condition deterioration index.

10.4 Performance metrics

To assess the precision of the developed model, statistical indices such as the coefficient of determination (R^2), mean squared error (MSE), root mean squared error (RMSE), and mean absolute error (MAE) were used.

10.4.1 Coefficient of determination

The coefficient of determination (R^2) can be used to assess how well the model predicts. This statistical index can take values between 0 and 1. When the value of the coefficient of determination is $0.4 < R^2 < 0.7$, this indicates a moderate correlation, while the range $0.7 < R^2 < 1$ indicates a high degree of linear correlation. This value can be determined as expressed in (10.2).

$$R = \frac{\sum_{i=1}^{N} (x_{\exp,i} - \overline{x}_{\exp})(x_{pre,i} - \overline{x}_{pre})}{\sqrt{\sum_{i=1}^{N} \left(x_{\exp,i} - \overline{x}_{\exp}\right)^2} \sqrt{\sum_{i=1}^{N} \left(x_{pre,i} - \overline{x}_{pre}\right)^2}} \tag{10.2}$$

10.4.2 Mean squared error

The MSE is computed by averaging the squared deviations between the experimental and predicted values, as given by Eq. (10.3).

$$\text{MSE} = \frac{1}{N}\sum_{i=1}^{N}\left(x_{\exp,i} - x_{pre,i}\right)^2 \tag{10.3}$$

10.4.3 Root mean squared error

The RMSE is a statistic that measures the model's error. RMSE can be calculated by Eq. (10.4).

$$\text{RMSE} = \sqrt{\frac{\sum_{i=1}^{N}\left(x_{\exp,i} - x_{pre,i}\right)^2}{N}} \tag{10.4}$$

10.4.4 Mean absolute error

The MAE is the mean absolute deviation between the experimental and predicted values, which can be determined using Eq. (10.5).

$$\text{MAE} = \frac{1}{N}\sum_{i=1}^{N}\left|x_{\exp,i} - x_{\text{mod},i}\right| \tag{10.5}$$

In all the above equations, x_{exp} represents the experimentally observed value, x_{pre} denotes the value predicted by the model, $\underline{x}$ is the mean of the observed values, and N indicates the total number of data points.

10.5 Construction of the model

This section provides an overview of artificial neural networks and SPO. Following this, the proposed model will be detailed.

10.6 Extreme learning machine

ELM is a Single-Hidden-Layer Feedforward Neural Network (SLFN) that has gained increasing attention due to its fast learning speed, good generalization performance, and simplified network architecture, which have been theoretically and experimentally demonstrated. The key idea of ELM is to randomly select the input weights and hidden biases and, analytically, determine the output weights by solving the least-squares problem in closed form. Mathematically, given a set of n samples (X_i, Y_i), with $X_i \in R^n$ is the input and $Y_i \in R^m$ is the target output, the output of an ELM with z hidden neurons can be written as:

$$\sum_{i=1}^{z} \beta_i g\left(w_i x_i + b_i\right) = y_i, \quad j = 1, 2, 3, \ldots, n \tag{10.6}$$

where $w_i \in R^n$ denotes the input weights, b_i is the bias, $\beta_i \in R^m$ is the output weight vector, and $g(x)$ is the activation function. In matrix form, this equation can be expressed as:

$$H\beta = Y \tag{10.7}$$

where H $\in R^{N\times z}$ is the hidden layer output matrix defined as:

$$H\left(w_1, \ldots, w_z, x_1, \ldots, x_z, b_1, \ldots, b_z\right) = \begin{bmatrix} g\left(w_1 x_1 + b_1\right) & \cdots & g\left(w_z x_1 + b_z\right) \\ \vdots & \ddots & \vdots \\ g\left(w_1 x_N + b_1\right) & \cdots & g\left(w_z x_N + b_z\right) \end{bmatrix} \tag{10.8}$$

The output weights β are obtained by solving:

$$\hat{\beta} = H^{+}Y \tag{10.9}$$

where H^{+} is the Moore–Penrose pseudoinverse of the matrix H.

10.7 Stochastic paint optimizer

SPO [17] is a newly proposed metaheuristic algorithm introduced in 2020. The SPO algorithm is inspired by color theory, according to which the mixing of different colors is analogous to the merging of solutions to investigate new regions in the

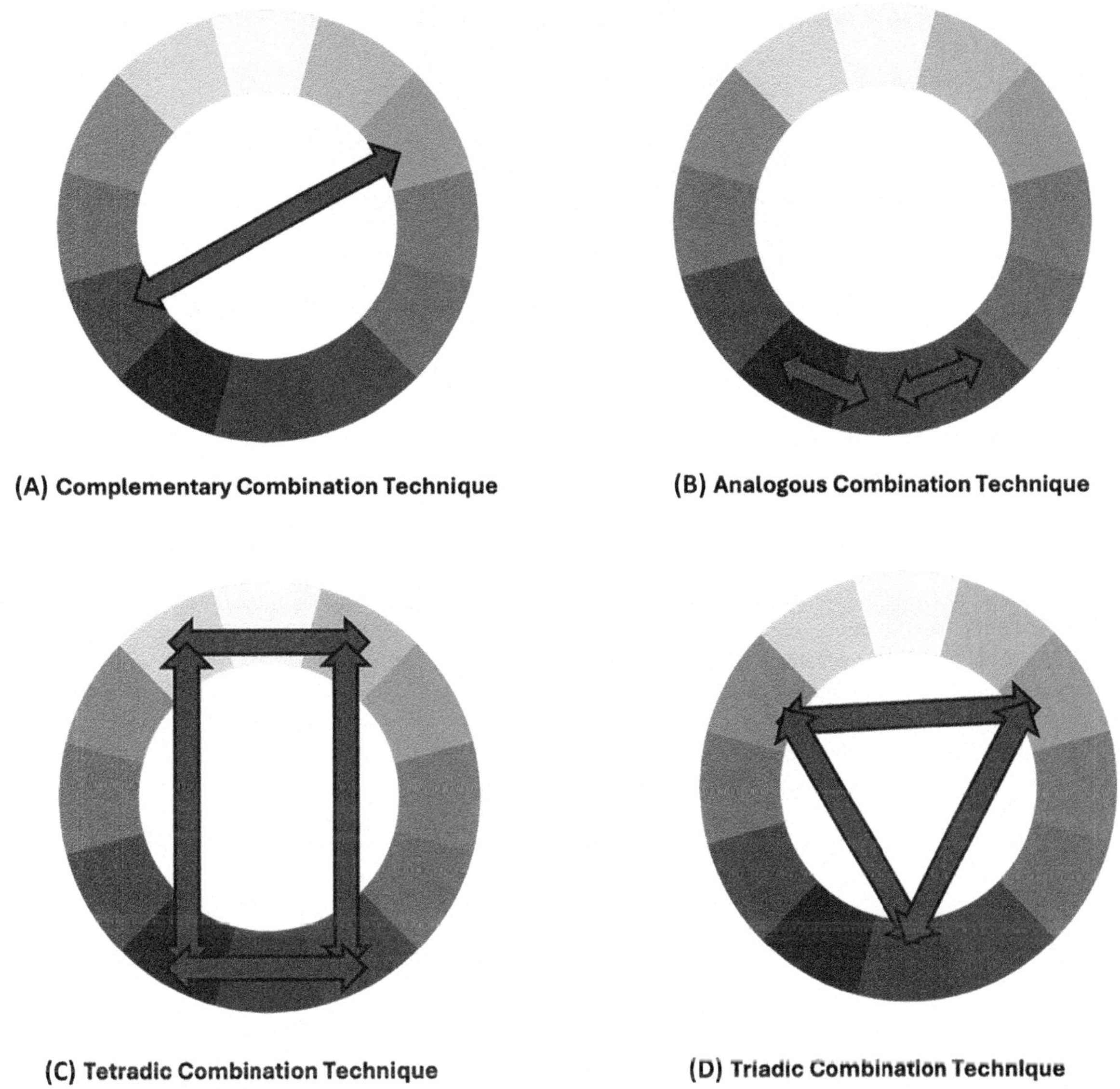

FIGURE 10.2 Different combination techniques. (A) Complementary Combination Technique. (B) Analogous Combination Technique. (C) Tetradic Combination Technique. (D) Triadic Combination Technique.

search space. The SPO algorithm is built upon four main color-mixing schemes (See Fig. 10.2): Analogous Combination, Complementary Combination, Triadic Combination, and Tetradic Combination. The Analogous Combination of colors is achieved by selecting two adjacent colors on the color wheel and blending them to create new colors between them. The Complementary Combination of colors is obtained by blending two opposite colors on the color wheel. The Triadic Combination of colors is constructed by choosing three colors equally separated on the color wheel and then mixing them in equal ratios. The Tetradic Combination of colors is constructed by taking four colors on the color wheel that form a rectangle to achieve a combination of four colors. In SPO, a color is assigned to each solution as a value in the objective space for all members of the population. Then, new solutions are generated by randomly mixing these solutions according to Color Theory. SPO has a relatively balanced exploration–exploitation capability.

10.8 Grey wolf optimizer

GWO is a population-based metaheuristic algorithm introduced by Mirjalili et al. in 2014 [15]. A candidate solution in GWO is represented as a grey wolf. This algorithm is inspired by the social hierarchy and the group hunting mechanism of grey wolves

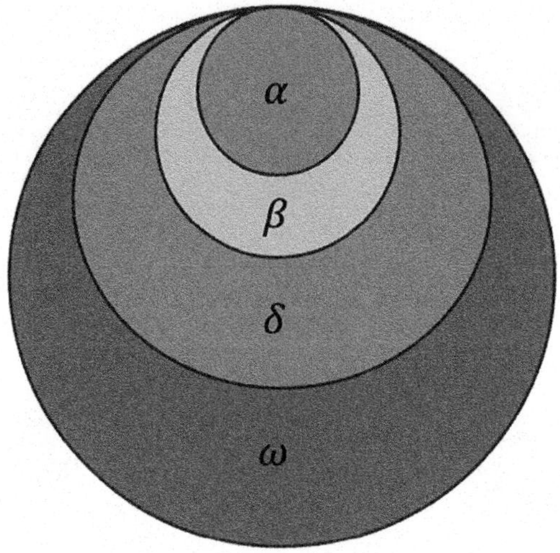

FIGURE 10.3 Classification of power in wolves in the wild.

in nature. The GWO algorithm replicates the same mechanism to update the position of grey wolves in the search space. In GWO, a population of candidate solutions is generally divided into four groups based on their fitness values. The α wolf is considered the current best solution, followed by β and δ wolves, and ω represents the rest of the population as depicted in Fig. 10.3. The GWO algorithm mathematically models the hunting mechanism of grey wolves in nature, and it is divided into three phases, including encircling prey, hunting, and attacking (exploitation). The encircling prey phase is used to update the position of grey wolves (candidate solutions) based on the best solutions found so far (α, β, and δ). The balance between exploration and exploitation is controlled by using a set of dynamic control parameters that direct the grey wolves to encircle their prey. This allows GWO to perform both diversification and intensification operations to find the best solution. Due to its simplicity, robustness, and global search capabilities, GWO has been successfully applied across various engineering and scientific fields, including structural optimization, ML, and energy systems.

10.9 Hybrid stochastic paint optimizer and grey wolf optimizer with extreme learning machine

To enhance the predictive performance of the ELM, a hybrid metaheuristic strategy combining the SPO and the GWO is employed to optimize the ELM's parameters. While ELM offers fast learning and strong generalization due to its single-hidden-layer feedforward structure with randomly initialized input weights and biases, its performance is often sensitive to the initial parameter settings. Therefore, metaheuristic optimization is introduced to fine-tune these parameters and improve prediction accuracy. The proposed SPOGWO-ELM hybrid model integrates the exploration capability of SPO, inspired by color theory-based solution mixing, with the exploitation efficiency of GWO, which simulates grey wolf hunting behavior. Initially, SPO generates a diverse set of candidate parameter configurations by exploring the search space through analogies to color mixing. Then, GWO intensifies the search by exploiting the best regions identified by SPO, refining the parameters based on a leadership hierarchy and cooperative movement strategy. This two-stage optimization process effectively balances global and local search, helping the model avoid local minima and enhancing generalization. The memory complexity of the hybrid SPOGWO algorithm is $O(N \times D)$, which is the same as that of both the SPO and GWO algorithms. However, its time complexity is $O(T \times N^2 \times D)$, whereas the time complexity for the individual SPO and GWO algorithms is $O(T \times N \times D)$, where N is the population size, D is the problem dimension, and T is the total number of iterations. The optimized parameters—number of neurons, input weights, and biases of the ELM—are then used to train the model on the dataset.

To obtain the optimal network structure for SPOGWO-ELM, we evaluated the predictive performance of different models with a sigmoid activation function as the number of hidden-layer neurons was varied. The number of hidden neurons of the SPOGWO-ELM model was in the range of 1–20. The optimization technique's efficiency was assessed using MSE. The prediction accuracy of the optimal network structure has fluctuated, reaching the maximum (the lowest MSE) when the number of neurons is 11. Therefore, the number of hidden neurons is set to 11 in the following analysis. The results of all 20 individual runs are shown in Fig. 10.4.

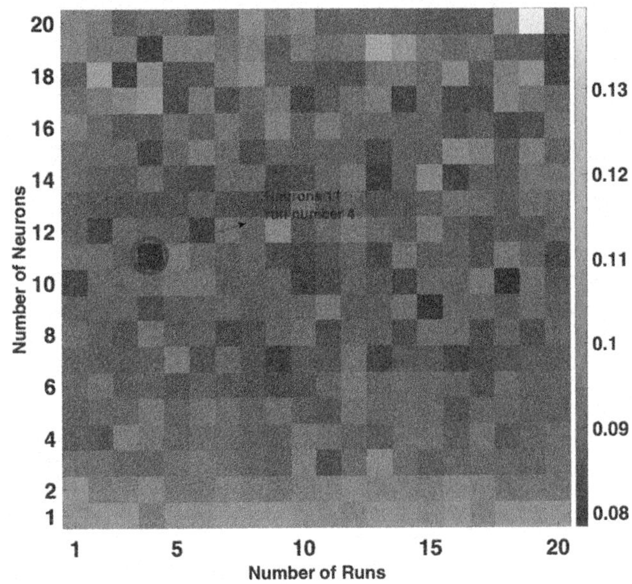

FIGURE 10.4 MSE results for all individual runs (*MSE*, mean square error).

Before each training and test, 321 samples were randomly chosen as the training set from the collected samples, and the remaining 109 samples were used as the test and validation set. For the SPOGWO algorithm, the population size and the maximum iteration were set to 20 and 600, respectively. To minimize random sampling error, the best results from 20 independent runs were used as the final results. Rather than a k-fold cross-validation scheme, 20 independent runs of the entire metaheuristic-based optimization framework were conducted to capture the random variability of the proposed framework. As the metaheuristic search process depends on random initialization and stochastic operators, it is often preferred to re-run the training process multiple times to provide a more accurate assessment of the stability and quality of the obtained models, rather than relying on a single data split used in cross-validation. Each run is initialized with a different random seed to generate a set of potentially unique solutions that explore different regions of the solution space and therefore do not rely on a single data split. The color code in Fig. 10.4, which represents a low standard deviation, indicates that the optimization framework runs are tightly packed, indicating the high stability of the proposed approach. The optimized ELM architecture is illustrated in Fig. 10.5.

10.10 Discussion and results

The section begins with a discussion of the SPOGWP-ELM model's performance. A termination criterion based on the total number of function evaluations was set in order to solve the problem at hand. The entire process was carried out independently, with 20 runs. The algorithm's parameters were chosen after an analysis of the state of the art, and it was implemented in MATLAB R2023a. The runs were performed on an Apple MacBook Pro with an M2 Max CPU and 96 GB of RAM, running macOS Ventura. The aim of optimization was to minimize MSE.

The results reported in Table 10.4 illustrate the superior performance of the proposed SPOGWO-ELM compared to both the baseline models, Back Propagation Neural Network (BPNN), Decision Trees (DT), Support Vector Machine (SVM), and the hybrid Whale Optimization Algorithm (WOA) with ELM model. SPOGWO-ELM exhibits an improvement of 7.0% in R and outperforms the WOA-ELM in terms of error measures, with decreases in MAE, MRE, and RMSE by 12.8%, 7.5%, and 4.6%, respectively. This demonstrates the model's higher accuracy and reliability. In comparison with the traditional models, SPOGWO-ELM achieves a higher R by 11.4%, 19.3%, 33.4%, and 42.9% compared to ELM, BPNN, DT, and SVM, respectively. The model also results in lower MAE values by 21.4%, 24.6%, 17.5%, and 26.5%, respectively, and lower MRE values by 18.2%, 24.4%, 13.0%, and 22.4%, respectively. In addition, reductions in RMSE of 11.6%, 21.7%, 9.1%, and 21.9% are observed, respectively. These results suggest that SPOGWO-ELM not only excels in absolute and relative error measures but also demonstrates better consistency and generalization. The improvements can be attributed to the synergistic integration of SPO and GWO in fine-tuning the initial weights and thresholds of ELM, which ensures a robust convergence and reliable learning dynamics. In summary, the SPOGWO-ELM model emerges as a powerful predictive tool for estimating the BCDI with high accuracy for different structures.

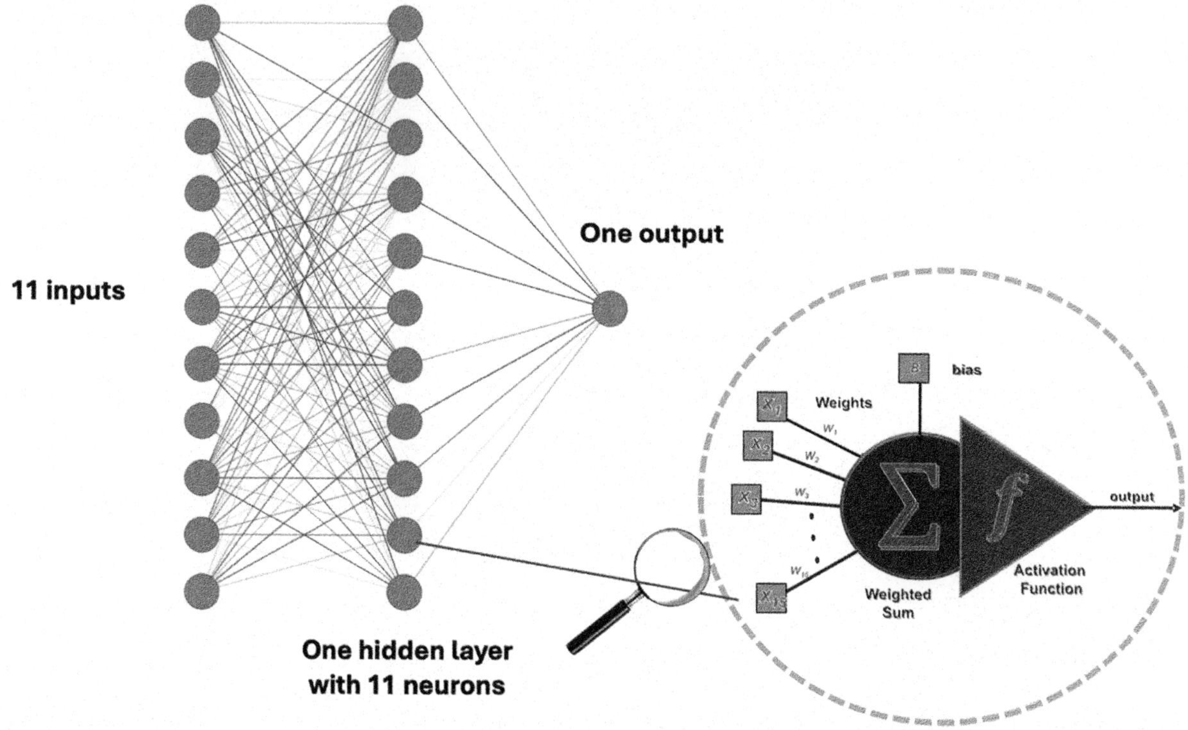

FIGURE 10.5 Optimized ELM architecture (*ELM*, extreme learning machine).

TABLE 10.4 Results of predictive performance indicators for all data.

Category	Models	MAE	MRE (%)	RMSE	R^2
Overall structures	SPOGWO-ELM	2.103	2.435	2.865	0.819
	WOA-ELM	2.412	2.632	3.003	0.768
	ELM	2.676	2.978	3.241	0.738
	BPNN	2.791	3.106	3.661	0.689
	DT	2.549	2.800	3.151	0.616
	SVM	2.862	3.140	3.667	0.575

SPOGWO-ELM, stochastic paint optimizer- grey wolf optimizer with extreme learning machine algorithm.

Fig. 10.6 shows a point-wise comparison of the observed BCDI (blue with dashed line) and the predicted BCDI (red with solid line) for all 539 samples in the dataset. Each blue marker corresponds to the true BCDI value measured from the field inspections, and the red marker next to it is the BCDI predicted by the proposed model. The green dashed lines connect the corresponding true and predicted values, indicating the prediction error for each individual data point. As shown in the figure, the proposed model accurately traces the overall trend of the true BCDI distribution, with only a few minor deviations in local regions. The deviations between the observed and predicted BCDI values are mainly due to local variations in BCDI scores caused by noise and the complexity of the input features. In general, the close alignment between the red and blue markers in the figure demonstrates the proposed model's success in capturing the underlying deterioration patterns of the bridges.

As shown in Fig. 10.7, the orange fluctuating line represents the error distribution of all 539 samples in the dataset, including both training and testing samples. The horizontal axis represents each of the 539 samples, and the vertical axis represents the corresponding error. In this case, the error is defined as the difference between the sample's actual BCDI value and the model's predicted value. From the figure, we can see that most errors are concentrated within ±10.

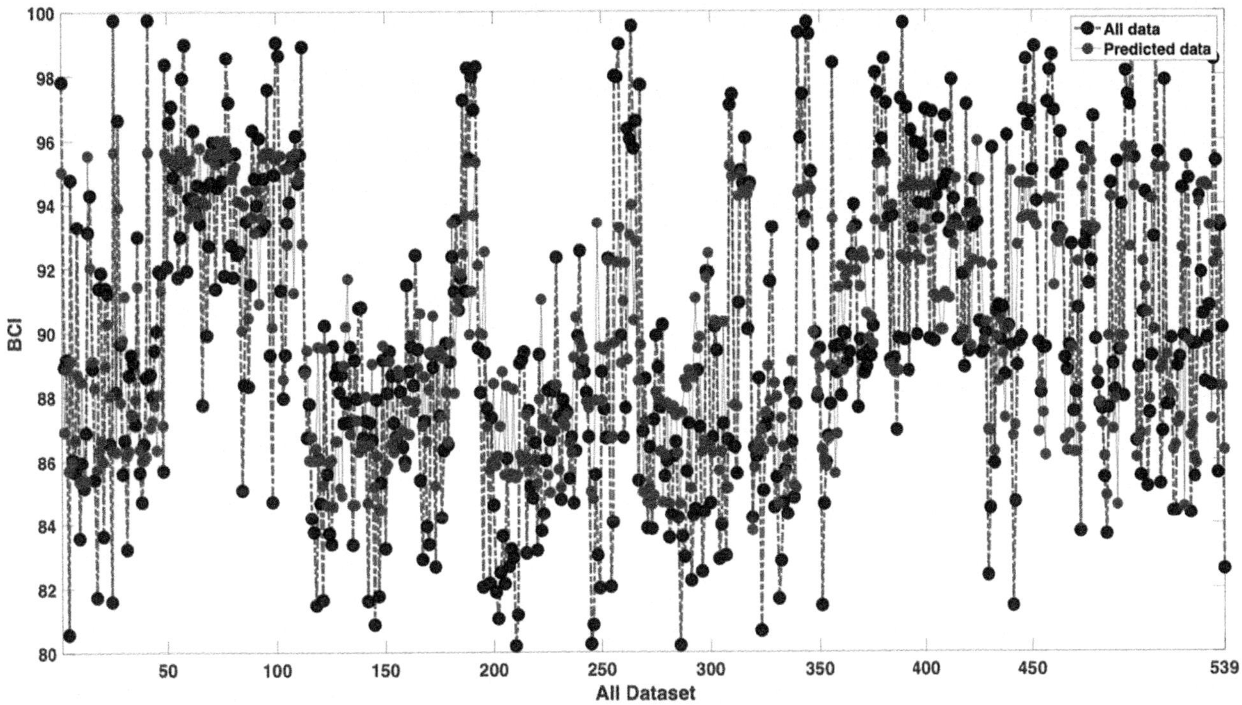

FIGURE 10.6 True and predicted comparison for all data.

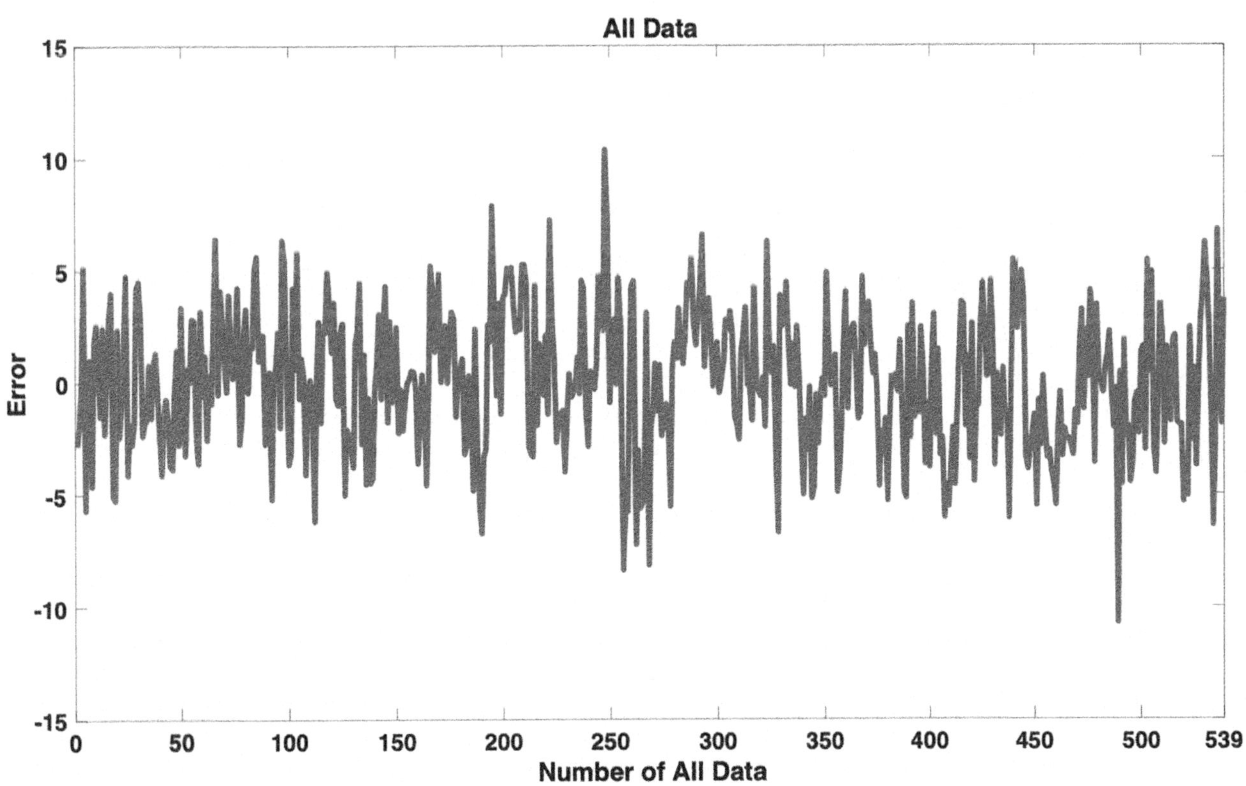

FIGURE 10.7 Error distribution of all data.

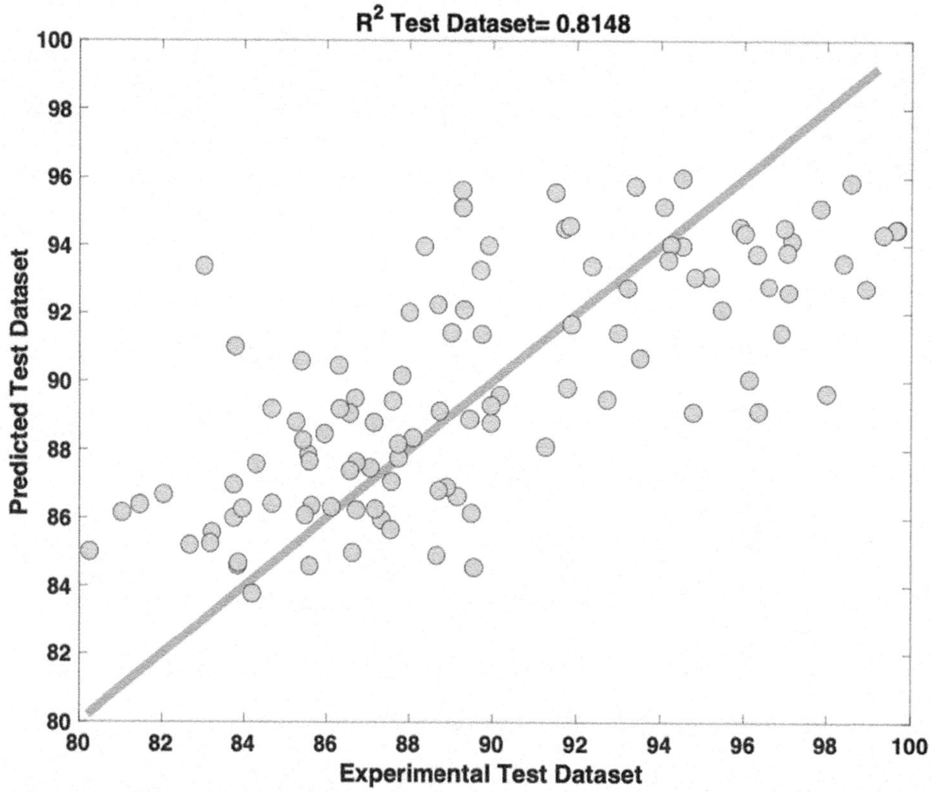

FIGURE 10.8 Estimators' result analysis of BCDI for the test dataset (*BCDI*, bridge condition deterioration index).

Furthermore, a few sample error values fall outside this interval. The errors are also concentrated around zero, indicating that the model does not exhibit large systematic deviations. Meanwhile, it also indicates that the model has already reached a certain degree of generalization for the samples. Therefore, the model can provide a relatively stable prediction for the samples. In summary, the error distribution also shows that the SPOGWO-ELM model has good fitting ability for the intrinsic pattern of the data. The model can predict the actual value of BCDI with a certain degree of stability and accuracy, but a few samples still show relatively large errors. The compactness of the error values and their symmetry about zero also suggest that the model is robust and has good generalization performance (Fig. 10.7).

Fig. 10.8 presents the scatter plot of predicted and actual BCDI values for the independent test dataset. The prediction R^2 of the proposed SPOGWO-ELM method on the test dataset was obtained as 0.8148. The data points are also packed near the diagonal line for the test set. The high R^2 value for the test data justifies the fact that the model can accurately predict the values of BCDI when unseen data is used.

Fig. 10.9 presents the scatter plot of predicted and actual BCDI values in the validation dataset. The prediction R^2 for the validation data was obtained as 0.8032. Most of the predicted data points are closely packed near the 45-degree straight line. The close match between the data points and the 45-degree line for the predicted and actual BCDI values indicates that the proposed SPOGWO-ELM can accurately and reliably estimate BCDI on the validation set. The result also justifies that the model has not memorized the training data.

Fig. 10.10 shows the relationship between the predicted and experimental BCDI values when the SPOGWO-ELM model is applied to the training dataset. The scatter of each prediction outcome is denoted by a red dot, while the reference line denotes a case when both of the BCDI values are equal. As can be observed, the vast majority of points lie within the boundary of the reference line, implying that the nonlinear mapping between the inputs and outputs is well-defined during training. The R^2 score of the training dataset is calculated as 0.8221, which is considered to be a sufficiently high score, meaning that the model is able to cover most of the variance in the target value. The relationship between the predicted and actual outcomes also does not indicate any signs of underfitting, as the values are largely close to the reference diagonal, with the only exception being a wider scatter observed for samples with a low or high BCDI score. Fig. 10.10 does not indicate any signs of overfitting either. In particular, a uniform scatter of data points is evident, with no clear trend toward overextended deviation from the center diagonal, nor are there large areas with a high density of data points

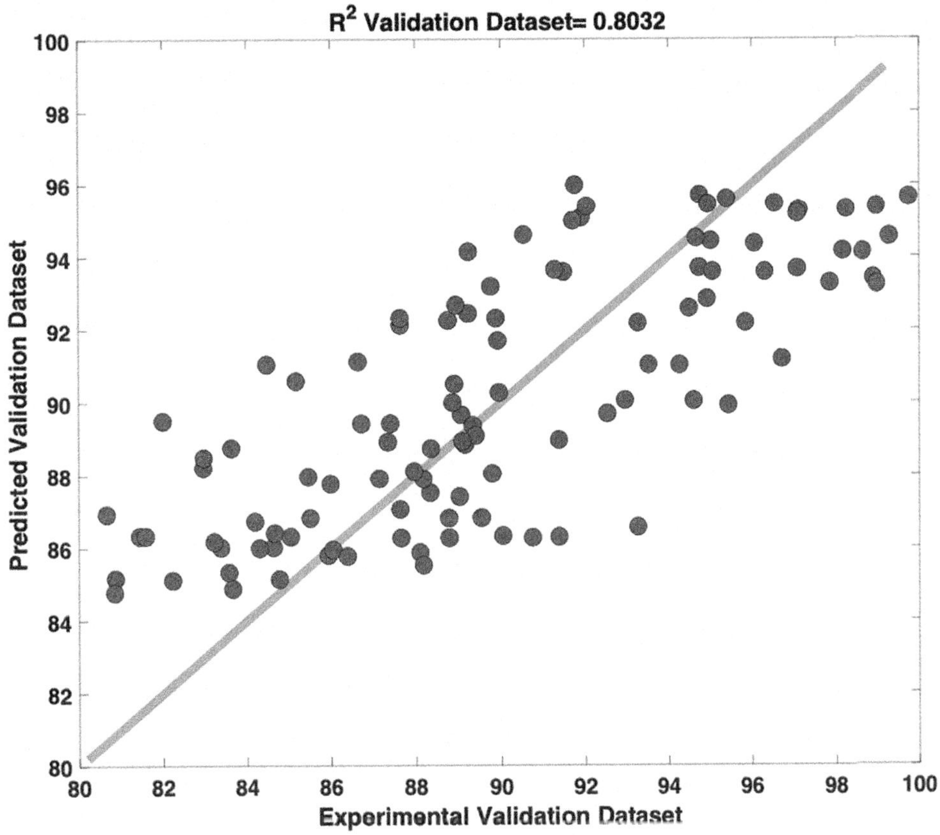

FIGURE 10.9 Estimators' result analysis of BCDI for the validation dataset (*BCDI*, bridge condition deterioration index).

in any part of the value range. The latter, in particular, would indicate that the model captures the structure of the training samples. On the contrary, it is seen that the data points are generally close to the center diagonal, which suggests that there is an absence of divergence in the structural trends between samples, which means that the model is stable and has achieved a level of training that will support its deployment for validation and testing tasks.

Fig. 10.11 is a bar chart of the feature importances of each feature in the bridge data. As can be seen, the bridge's age has the highest feature importance, indicating it had the greatest impact on the model's prediction of the target variable. The length, type, and span of the bridge were also major factors, likely due to its shape and size. Maintenance-related variables and the number of lanes played a smaller role.

10.11 Graphical user interface

Fig. 10.12 shows the developed graphical user interface (GUI) based on the proposed BCDI prediction model. As shown in Fig. 10.12, we've designed the interface to be user-friendly. In the left panel, different attributes like style of structure (support beam or continuous beam), region (three different regions), age of bridge, girder type (plate girder, T-beam, or box girder), span of the bridge, total length, and number of lanes can be given as input in an interactive manner by the user. Another panel is there to input about maintenance. For example, a user can indicate whether maintenance was performed on the deck, superstructure, or substructure. After entering all the inputs, a user can click the yellow button "Click to predict the BCDI of bridge" to generate the prediction, which will be displayed as a number in the output box beside the button. The right panel contains an image of a bridge (as the theme of this work) and the project name "Predictive Bridge Deterioration Modeling Using Artificial Intelligence and Software Development for Engineers"

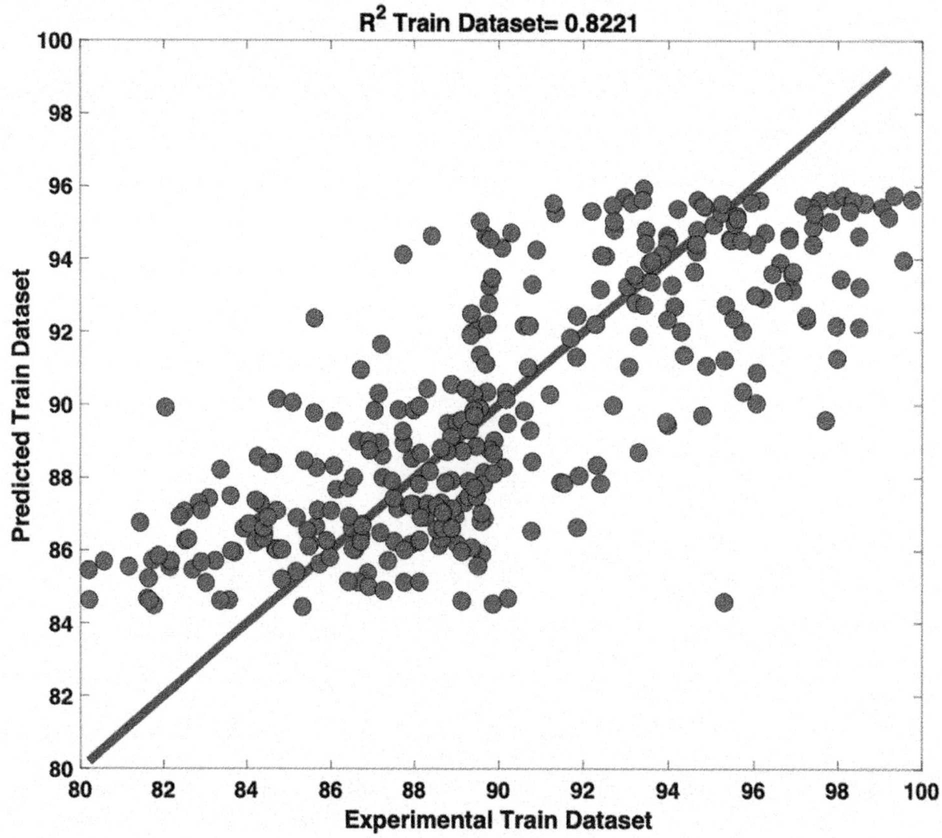

FIGURE 10.10 Estimators' result analysis of BCDI for all datasets (*BCDI*, bridge condition deterioration index).

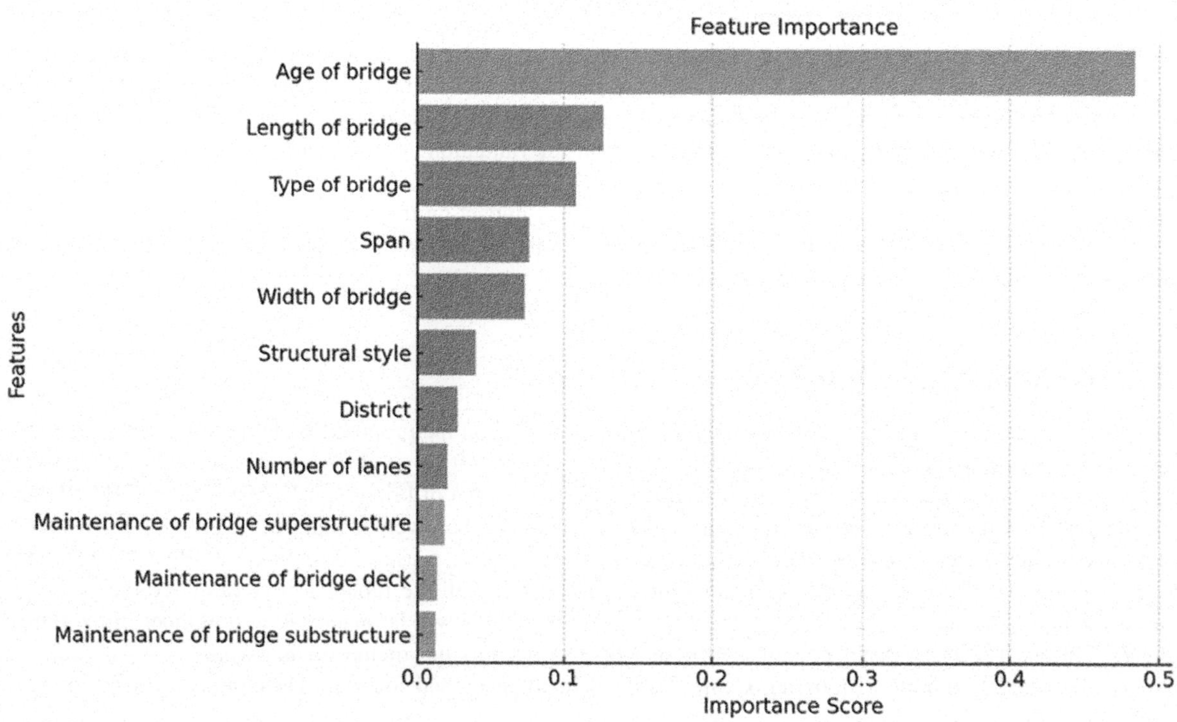

FIGURE 10.11 Feature importance.

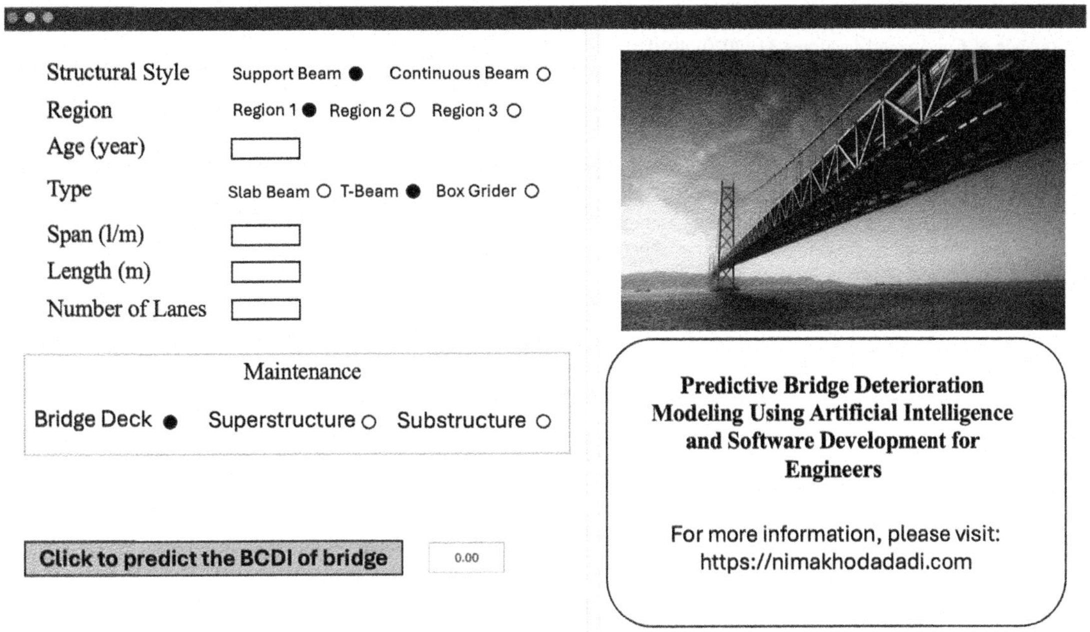

FIGURE 10.12 GUI based application developed to predict BCDI (*BCDI*, bridge condition deterioration index; *GUI*, graphical user interface).

10.12 Conclusion

In this chapter, a new hybrid prediction model, SPOGWO-ELM, is proposed and compared with existing methods to improve BCDI prediction accuracy. The proposed model is based on an improved ELM with parameters optimized using a combination of SPO and GWO metaheuristics to accurately and quickly predict the BCDI value. To evaluate the effectiveness of the SPOGWO-ELM model, extensive experiments are conducted on a database of 539 inspection records. The results show that compared with the baseline models (ELM, BPNN, DT, and SVM) and another hybrid model, WOA-ELM, the SPOGWO-ELM outperforms the competitors by increasing the R value up to 42.9% and decreasing the error metrics, MAE, MRE, and RMSE. The comparison demonstrates that the proposed method achieves more accurate and robust performance, because the improvement is driven by optimizing the initial weights and thresholds in ELM. In addition, a user friendly GUI was developed based on the proposed model to enable engineering decision-makers to apply it in practice. It was found that users can quickly obtain the predicted BCDI value with minimal time and effort to operate the system. Although the SPOGWO-ELM model has been shown to outperform existing methods, there may be room for further improvement in the proposed method. In future work, researchers will focus on integrating additional strategies to further improve the accuracy and efficiency of the SPOGWO-ELM model. By improving optimization accuracy and learning efficiency, the proposed model can be further enhanced to handle more complex deterioration scenarios. In summary, the method proposed in this chapter is an effective approach to realizing intelligent bridge maintenance evaluation. It is beneficial for making more accurate and safer decisions in bridge maintenance, thereby further promoting the sustainable development of the bridge transportation system.

References

[1] J. Xin, C. Zhou, Y. Jiang, Q. Tang, X. Yang, J. Zhou, A signal recovery method for bridge monitoring system using TVFEMD and encoder-decoder aided LSTM, Measurement 214 (2023) 112797.

[2] Q. Tang, Y. Jiang, J. Xin, G. Liao, J. Zhou, X. Yang, A novel method for the recovery of continuous missing data using multivariate variational mode decomposition and fully convolutional networks, Measurement 220 (2023) 113366.

[3] T. Tao, J. He, H. Wang, K. Zhao, Efficient simulation of non-stationary non-homogeneous wind field: fusion of multi-dimensional interpolation and NUFFT, Journal of Wind Engineering and Industrial Aerodynamics 236 (2023) 105394.

[4] J. Xin, J. Zhou, F. Zhou, S.X. Yang, Y. Zhou, Bearing capacity model of corroded RC eccentric compression columns based on hermite interpolation and fourier fitting, Applied Sciences 9 (2018) 24.

[5] P. Martinez, E. Mohamed, O. Mohsen, Y. Mohamed, Comparative study of data mining models for prediction of bridge future conditions, Journal of Performance of Constructed Facilities 34 (2020) 4019108.
[6] L, S.L. Yang, Analysis of performance decay characteristics of reinforced concrete bridges, Highway 60 (2025) 132–135.
[7] S. Hasan, E. Elwakil, Stochastic regression deterioration models for superstructure of prestressed concrete bridges in California, Journal of Structural Integrity and Maintenance 4 (2019) 97–108.
[8] Y. Zhang, Y. Huang, C. Ren, Multi-stage degradation model of bridge technical condition based on inspection and evaluation big data, Highway 63 (2018) 5.
[9] N.K.W. Wellalage, T. Zhang, R. Dwight, Calibrating Markov chain–based deterioration models for predicting future conditions of railway bridge elements, Journal of Bridge Engineering 20 (2015) 4014060.
[10] N. Lethanh, J. Hackl, B.T. Adey, Determination of Markov transition probabilities to be used in bridge management from mechanistic-empirical models, Journal of Bridge Engineering 22 (2017) 04017063.
[11] Y. Wang, Q. He, D. Zhang, S. Lu, C. Yuan, Improving Li-ion battery health: predicting remaining useful life using IWBOA-ELM algorithm, Journal of Energy Storage 72 (2023) 108547.
[12] G.-B. Huang, Q.-Y. Zhu, C.-K. Siew, Extreme learning machine: a new learning scheme of feedforward neural networks, in: 2004 IEEE International Joint Conference on Neural Networks (IEEE Cat. No. 04CH37541), IEEE, 2004, pp. 985–990.
[13] Y. Jiang, Z. Liu, H. Luo, H. Wang, ELM indirect prediction method for the remaining life of lithium-ion battery, Journal of Electronic Measurement and Instrumentation 30 (2016) 179–185.
[14] H. Shi, Q. Tan, C. Li, X. Lv, Analog circuit fault diagnosis method based on preferred wavelet packet and ELM, in: 2017 2nd International Conference on Electrical, Automation and Mechanical Engineering (EAME 2017), Atlantis Press, 2017, pp. 1–4.
[15] S. Mirjalili, S.M. Mirjalili, A. Lewis, Grey wolf optimizer, Advances in Engineering Software 69 (2014) 46–61.
[16] J. Kennedy, R. Eberhart, Particle swarm optimization, in: Proceedings of ICNN'95-International Conference on Neural Networks, IEEE, 1995,pp. 1942–1948.
[17] A. Kaveh, S. Talatahari, N. Khodadadi, Stochastic paint optimizer: theory and application in civil engineering, Eng Comput (2020) 1–32.
[18] L. Jiang, Q. Tang, Y. Jiang, H. Cao, Z. Xu, Bridge condition deterioration prediction using the whale optimization algorithm and extreme learning machine, Buildings 13 (2023) 2730.
[19] Y. Jiang, N. Zhao, L. Peng, L. Zhao, M. Liu, Simulation of stationary wind field based on adaptive interpolation-enhanced scheme, Journal of Wind Engineering and Industrial Aerodynamics 195 (2019) 104001.
[20] D.N. Reshef, Y.A. Reshef, H.K. Finucane, S.R. Grossman, G. McVean, P.J. Turnbaugh, et al., Detecting novel associations in large data sets, Science (1979) 334 (2011) 1518–1524.
[21] L.-M. Sun, Z.-Q. Shang, Y. Xia, Development and prospect of bridge structural health monitoring in the context of big data, China Journal of Highway and Transport 32 (2019) 1–20.

Chapter 11

Performance comparison of grey wolf optimizer-tuned controllers in functional electrical stimulation applications

Özay Can[1] and Mustafa Şinasi Ayas[2]
[1]*Department of Electronics and Automation, Recep Tayyip Erdoğan University, Rize, Türkiye,* [2]*Department of Electrical-Electronics Engineering, Karadeniz Technical University, Trabzon, Türkiye*

11.1 Introduction

For individuals with paralysis, the application of external electrical stimulation to the skeletal muscles or associated nerves has been demonstrated to promote mobility by stimulating muscular contractions. The aforementioned process is formally designated as functional electrical stimulation (FES) in the relevant literature. FES technology is of critical significance in the treatment of loss of motor function resulting from spinal cord injury, stroke, and other neurological diseases. Beyond its efficacy in regulating the movement of paralyzed limbs and facilitating rehabilitation, this technique provides substantial advantages, including the prevention of muscle atrophy, enhanced blood circulation, and improved patient quality of life. Nonetheless, due to the nonlinear and noisy character of the human musculoskeletal system, certain challenges arise. A multitude of factors contribute to the intricacy of system control, including but not limited to muscle fatigue, individual anatomical variations, electrode placement, and external environmental factors. Therefore it is imperative to implement a control mechanism that is both effective and efficient, thereby enabling paralyzed individuals to perform their movements with ease [1].

The aforementioned challenges associated with FES systems have been the focus of numerous research studies, leading to the development of various control mechanisms that facilitate the effective implementation of FES systems. The extant literature delineates several control approaches that differ in their capacity to manage the nonlinear characteristics of the system and to suppress external disturbances. Among these control mechanisms, the adaptive higher-order sliding mode controller [2], the fuzzy controller [3], the model-free adaptive control approach [4], the iterative learning neural network-based control [5], the iterative learning control [6,7], repetitive control [8,9], model predictive control [10] are some of the recent and successful ones. Notwithstanding the noteworthy accomplishments of these sophisticated control strategies, their practical implementation is encumbered by their intricacy and considerable computational requirements.

Despite the successful performance of these control mechanisms, the proportional-integral-derivative (PID) controller is the most preferred controller type, partly due to its advantages, such as its simple structure and ease of design [11,12]. The widespread use of the PID controller in industrial applications can be explained by the relatively simple parameter tuning process and the effective results in different types of systems. However, in practice, it is not suitable to use the derivative operator of the PID controller alone. This leads to the derivative kick effect. Derivative kick effect occurs due to unexpected changes in the reference signal. Therefore it causes a rapid change in the error signal. This change causes a significant increase in the derivative of the error and the controller becomes unstable. This effect is especially pronounced in the presence of high-frequency noise. To avoid this effect, a low-pass filter should be connected to the output of the derivative operator of the PID controller. The controller formed by connecting the filter is called PID with filter (PIDF). From the research results, it is seen that the PIDF controller outperforms the PID controller [13]. In recent years, fractional order PID (FOPID) controllers have garnered significant attention, complementing the established field of classical integer order PID controllers. FOPID

Grey Wolf Optimizer. DOI: https://doi.org/10.1016/B978-0-443-36624-6.00030-5

controllers offer a more flexible control structure thanks to fractional derivative and integral operators and have significant potential to improve system performance.

The present study investigates the utilization of PIDF and FOPID with its filtered version (FOPIDF) in FES systems. The intricacy of these controllers, particularly the substantial number of parameters requiring optimization, contributes to the complexity of the process. The inadequacy of conventional parameter tuning methods in such multiparameter systems necessitates the employment of contemporary optimization techniques. Therefore the employment of optimization techniques is imperative to achieve optimal parameter tuning. Consequently, the parameters of the proposed controllers are optimized through the implementation of the grey wolf optimizer (GWO) [14], which has shown successful results in engineering problems in recent years and has not been previously employed in the FES system. A variety of performance studies are employed in this study to comprehensively assess the efficacy of the proposed controller techniques. In order to evaluate the stability and transient behavior of the system, a unit step response analysis is first performed. Subsequently, a quantitative analysis is conducted in which key performance metrics such as overshoot amount, settling time, and rising time are evaluated and compared. A rigorous robustness study is then conducted to simulate challenging real-world scenarios. In order to examine how external disturbing signals affect the system in this situation, a disturbance analysis is carried out. To ascertain the impact of alterations in the FES system's fundamental parameters on control performance, a parameter variation study is conducted.

The subsequent sections of the paper are organized as follows: Following the introductory section, Section 11.2 presents a comprehensive overview of the FES system. In this section, the mathematical model of the FES system is derived based on the Hill muscle model. Furthermore, the transfer function of the system is obtained. Additionally, this section elucidates the impact of sensor dynamics on the system's performance. Following the introduction of the proposed controllers in Section 11.3, the optimization technique utilized is delineated in Section 11.4. In this section, the mathematical model of the GWO algorithm is explained. In Section 11.5, the performance evaluation of the proposed controllers is presented. In this section, an analysis of robustness is conducted, addressing external disturbances, adaptability to changes in system parameters, and tracking performance against various reference signals. Finally, in Section 11.6, the paper is concluded with recommendations for future work.

11.2 Functional electrical stimulation system

A systematic modeling of the FES system can be accomplished through the use of the block diagram presented in Fig. 11.1A. In this comprehensive system model, a dynamic relationship exists between muscle-tendon force (F_{mt}) and output muscle distance length (X_{out}). From a control theory perspective, the muscle structure is approximated as a linear system. The Hill muscle model (see Fig. 11.1B) is employed to mathematically characterize the mechanical behavior of muscle. This model employs a classical approach that has garnered significant acceptance within the biomechanical literature, offering a comprehensive explanation for the dynamics of muscle contraction. The Hill model, which incorporates the active contractile element of the muscle along with the passive elastic and viscous components, yields results that closely resemble actual muscle behavior. As illustrated in Fig. 11.1A, the FES system features a closed-loop feedback control structure. In this control architecture, $X_{ref}(s)$ denotes the desired muscle distance length as the reference input, while $X_s(s)$ represents the actual position information obtained from the strain gauge sensor. The configuration of the feedback structure of the system is of paramount importance for ensuring its robustness to external disturbances and maintaining precise synchronization with the reference signal.

The mathematical equation for the Hill muscle model is expressed by Eq. (11.1) and is formulated based on the second law of Newton's laws of motion. This mathematical model is frequently employed in the biomechanical literature to characterize the dynamic behavior of the musculoskeletal system.

$$m\ddot{X}_{out}(t) = F_{mt}(t) - F_f(t) - F_s(t) - F_c(t) \tag{11.1}$$

where $F_f(t)$, $F_s(t)$, and $F_c(t)$ represent the friction force, the spring force, and the damping force, respectively. m signifies the total mass of the muscle and attached organs, $\ddot{X}_{out}(t)$ is the second derivative of the output position with respect to time, and $F_{mt}(t)$ is defined as the muscle-tendon force resulting from electrical stimulation. Each force component in Eq. (11.1) is indicative of distinct physical properties of the musculoskeletal system. The resistance forces acting in the system are characterized by the following mathematical models:

$$F_f(t) = \mu mg\dot{X}_{out}(t) \tag{11.2}$$

$$F_s(t) = k_s X_{out}(t) \tag{11.3}$$

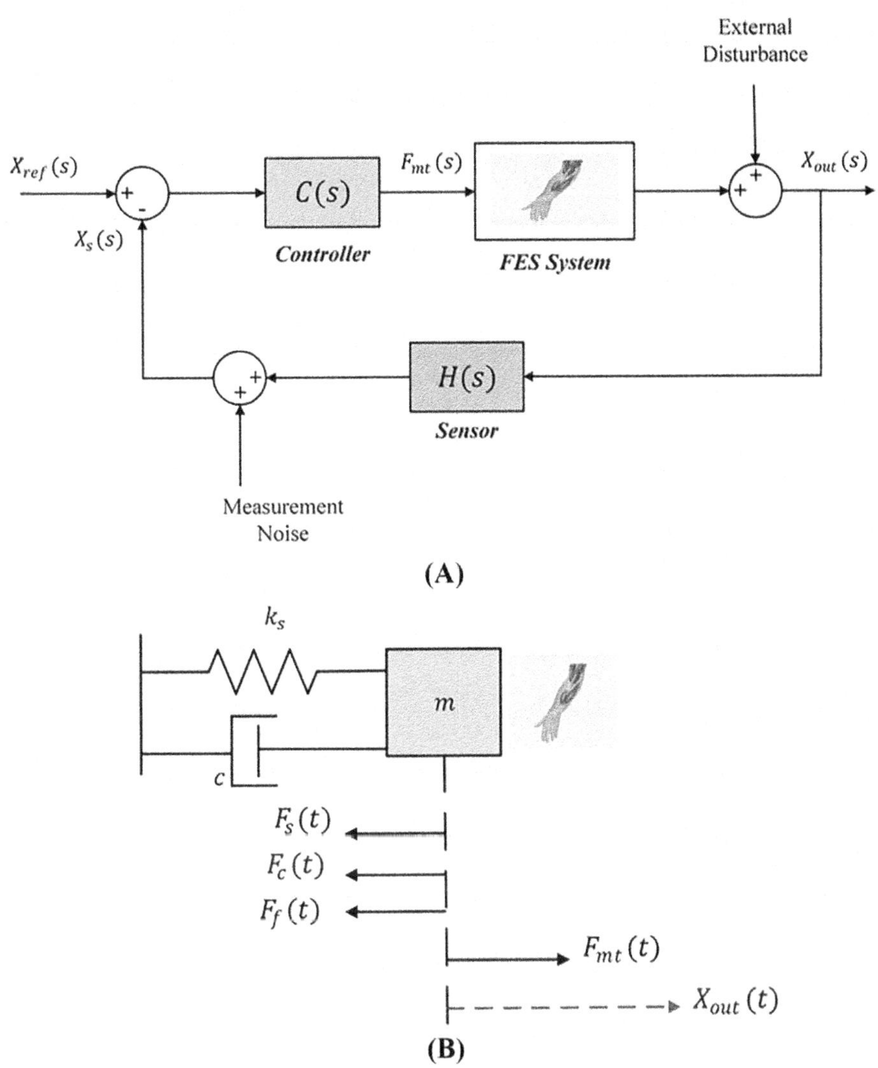

FIGURE 11.1 (A) Closed-loop block diagram representation of the FES system. (B). Hill muscle model illustrating the contractile element, series elastic component, and parallel elastic component for biomechanical muscle characterization (*FES*, Functional electrical stimulation).

$$F_c(t) = c\dot{X}_{out}(t) \tag{11.4}$$

where μ, g, k_s, and c are the friction constant, gravitational constant, spring constant, and damping constant, respectively. The friction force defined in Eq. (11.2) models the viscous friction in the medium through which the muscle moves. This force acts opposite to the direction of motion, contributing to the natural damping of the system. The spring force expressed by Eq. (11.3) models the natural elastic properties of the muscle and tendon structure. The damping force given in Eq. (11.4) characterizes the viscoelastic properties and internal frictional effects within the muscle.

By substituting the force components defined in Eqs. (11.2–11.4) into Eq. (11.1), a complete mathematical model of the system is obtained:

$$m\ddot{X}_{out}(t) = F_{mt}(t) - \mu mg\dot{X}_{out}(t) - k_s X_{out}(t) - c\dot{X}_{out}(t) \tag{11.5}$$

In the context of control system analysis and design, the differential equation expressed in the time domain should undergo transformation into the Laplace domain to facilitate the calculation process. When applying the Laplace transform for Eq. (11.5), the initial conditions are assumed to be zero ($X_{out}(0) = 0$ ve $\dot{X}_{out}(0) = 0$). This assumption represents the case where the system moves from rest to motion.

$$ms^2X_{out}(s) = F_{mt}(s) - \mu mgsX_{out}(s) - k_sX_{out}(s) - csX_{out}(s) \tag{11.6}$$

By rearranging the terms in Eq. (11.6), the transfer function of the FES system is obtained:

$$G_{FES}(s) = \frac{X_{out}(s)}{F_{mt}(s)} = \frac{1}{ms^2 + (c + \mu mg)s + k_s} \tag{11.7}$$

In practical applications of FES, position measurement is typically conducted using strain gauge sensors. Due to the inherent characteristics of these sensors, a time delay of T is inherent to the system. This delay can be attributed to the combined effects of sensor response time, signal processing delay, and data transmission time. The Padé approximation, as given in Eq. (11.8), facilitates the approximation of the exponential delay function by a rational transfer function. This approach provides a practical solution for control system analysis and simulation studies.

$$H(s) = e^{-Ts} \cong \frac{2 - Ts}{2 + Ts} \tag{11.8}$$

11.3 Advanced control structures for functional electrical stimulation systems

In this section of the study, the controllers known as PIDF, FOPID, and FOPIDF, which are employed in FES systems, are introduced. These controllers represent advanced versions of the conventional PID structure, each offering specific advantages in addressing the nonlinear characteristics of FES systems.

11.3.1 PID with filter controller

The PIDF controller represents an enhancement of the classical PID architecture through the integration of a low-pass filtering mechanism applied to the derivative term. This modification effectively reduces the susceptibility of the derivative component to high-frequency noise, thereby contributing to improved closed-loop stability and robustness. The transfer function of a PIDF controller is given in Eq. (11.9), where k_p, k_i, k_d, and n represent proportional gain, integral gain, derivative gain, and the filter order, respectively. These four parameters must be tuned to achieve satisfactory control performance.

$$PIDF(s) = k_p + \frac{k_i}{s} + k_d s \frac{n}{s + n} \tag{11.9}$$

11.3.2 Fractional-order PID controller

The FOPID controller is a generalized form of the conventional PID structure, in which the integral and derivative operators are extended to fractional orders. By introducing the fractional orders, the controller design gains additional degrees of freedom, which can be leveraged to achieve enhanced performance and flexibility in control applications. The transfer function of a FOPID controller is given in Eq. (11.10). The FOPID controller comprises five tunable parameters: k_p, k_i, k_d, λ, and μ, which represent proportional gain, integral gain, derivative gain, and the fractional orders of integration and differentiation, respectively.

$$FOPID = k_p + \frac{k_i}{s^\lambda} + k_d s^\mu \tag{11.10}$$

11.3.3 Filtered FOPID controller

The FOPIDF controller is a filtered extension of the FOPID structure. It combines the design flexibility offered by fractional-order operators with the noise attenuation capability provided by the filtering component. The transfer function of a FOPIDF controller is given in Eq. (11.11), where k_p, k_i, k_d, n, λ, and μ, which represent the proportional gain, integral gain, derivative gain, the filter order, and the fractional orders of integration and differentiation, respectively.

$$FOPIDF = k_p + \frac{k_i}{s^\lambda} + k_d s^\mu \frac{n}{s + n} \tag{11.11}$$

11.4 Grey wolf optimizer

GWO is a population-based heuristic algorithm inspired by the life and hunting behaviors of grey wolves in the wild. Grey wolves prefer to live in groups of 5–12 individuals. The most interesting thing about grey wolves is their dominant hierarchy within the group. There are four groups within this hierarchy: alpha, beta, delta, and omega. The leaders of the group are a female and a male. These leaders are called alphas. The alphas are mostly responsible for decisions about the group's sleeping place, waking time, hunting, and so on. Betas are second in the hierarchy. Betas assist alphas with group activities. The last grey wolf in the group is an omega wolf. Wolves that do not belong to the alpha or beta class, but are between the beta and omega wolves, are called deltas. Deltas must obey the alphas and betas.

11.4.1 Grey wolf optimizer mathematical model

In the algorithm, the alpha wolf represents the best solution, while the second and third best solutions are the beta and delta wolves, respectively. Omega wolves represent candidate solutions. Alpha, beta, and delta lead the hunting process (optimization). During this process, grey wolves update their positions according to those of the alpha, beta, or delta wolves. Finally, when prey is found, a prey attack occurs to end the hunt.

Encircling prey: As previously mentioned, grey wolves encircle their prey throughout the hunting process. Eqs. (11.12) and (11.13) describe the mathematical model of prey enclosure behavior.

$$\vec{D} = |\vec{C}.\vec{X_p}(t) - \vec{X}(t)| \tag{11.12}$$

$$\vec{X}(t+1) = \vec{X_p}(t) - \vec{A}.\vec{D} \tag{11.13}$$

where t is the current iteration, $\vec{A}$ and $\vec{C}$ are the coefficient vectors, $\vec{X_p}$ is the position vector of the prey, and $\vec{X}$ is the position vector of the grey wolf. The coefficient vectors $\vec{A}$ and $\vec{C}$ are calculated by the following equations. Here, the components of $\vec{a}$ decrease linearly from 2 to 0 as the iteration proceeds, $\vec{r_1}$ and $\vec{r_2}$ are random vectors between 0 and 1.

$$\vec{A} = 2\vec{a}.\vec{r_1} - \vec{a} \tag{11.14}$$

$$\vec{C} = 2.\vec{r_2} \tag{11.15}$$

Hunting: Grey wolves have the ability to recognize the location of their prey and surround it. The alpha usually leads the hunting process. However, beta and delta wolves may participate when necessary. Initially, there is no information about the best location in the search space. In the GWO process, the search begins randomly. Then, the fitness value of each wolf is calculated according to the objective function. The top three locations with the best fitness values are determined to be the positions of the alpha, beta, and delta wolves, respectively. The positions of the alpha, beta, and delta wolves are updated using Eqs. (11.16) through (11.18).

$$\vec{D_\alpha} = |\vec{C_1}.\vec{X_\alpha} - \vec{X}| \tag{11.16}$$

$$\vec{D_\beta} = |\vec{C_2}.\vec{X_\beta} - \vec{X}| \tag{11.17}$$

$$\vec{D_\delta} = |\vec{C_3}.\vec{X_\delta} - \vec{X}| \tag{11.18}$$

where $\vec{X_\alpha}$, $\vec{X_\beta}$, and $\vec{X_\delta}$ represent the positions of the alpha, beta, and delta wolves, respectively. The top three wolves are continuously updated in each iteration.

$$\vec{X_1} = \vec{X_\alpha} - \vec{A_1}.(\vec{D_\alpha}) \tag{11.19}$$

$$\vec{X_2} = \vec{X_\beta} - \vec{A_2}.(\vec{D_\beta}) \tag{11.20}$$

$$\vec{X_3} = \vec{X_\delta} - \vec{A_3}.(\vec{D_\delta}) \tag{11.21}$$

$$\vec{X}(t+1) = \frac{\vec{X_1} + \vec{X_2} + \vec{X_3}}{3} \tag{11.22}$$

Attacking prey (exploitation): At this stage, the value of $\vec{a}$ is reduced, and therefore the range of variation of $\vec{A}$ is reduced. When $\vec{A}$ has random values in the range [-1,1], the next position of the search agent will be anywhere between its current position and the position of the prey. With all this in mind, the pseudo code of the GWO algorithm is given in Algorithm 11.1.

ALGORITHM 11.1 Pseudo code of the GWO algorithm.

Randomly generate the initial grey wolf population.
Determine the values of $\vec{a}$, $\vec{A}$, and $\vec{C}$.
Calculate the fitness values of each grey wolf.
X_α =Best candidate solution
X_β =Best second candidate solution
X_δ =Best third candidate solution
while (Maximum iteration)
    for each search agent
        Update the position of the current search agent.
    end for
    Update the values of $\vec{a}$, $\vec{A}$, and $\vec{C}$.
    Calculate the fitness of all search agents.
    Update the vectors of X_α, X_β, and X_δ.
    t=t+1
end while
return X_α

11.4.2 Grey wolf optimizer-tuned controller implementation in functional electrical stimulation systems

This section provides detailed information about optimizing the parameters of the proposed controllers using the GWO algorithm and integrating them into the FES system. To perform the optimization process systematically, the following steps are taken. First, the FES system's transfer function is described mathematically by Eq. (11.7), and its sensor dynamics are described mathematically by Eq. (11.8), using the parameters of the FES system given in Table 11.1. These parameters are validated values found in the literature [11–13]. that reflect typical values in real FES applications. Next, the intended closed-loop FES system, including the PIDF, FOPID, and FOPIDF controllers, is modeled in detail in the MATLAB/Simulink environment. The simulation model is designed to accurately reflect real-system behavior, with separate blocks created for each controller structure.

The objective function used in this study is given in Eq. (11.23), where $e(t)$ is the error signal, t is the current time instant, and t_s is the simulation duration. The integral of time-weighted absolute error (ITAE) criterion provides a balanced evaluation of the system performance, taking into account both the error magnitude and the time-weighted error behavior.

$$ITAE = \int_0^{t_s} t\,|e(t)|\,dt \qquad (11.23)$$

During the optimization process, to preserve the physical significance of the parameters of each controller and to ensure stable operation of the algorithm, the lower and upper bounds given in Table 11.2 were determined. These bounds were selected by taking into account similar studies in the literature and system stability analysis.

The GWO algorithm was run with 30 grey wolves (population size) and 50 iterations. These values were determined experimentally to provide the optimal balance between computational time and solution quality.

Fig. 11.2 shows the general structure of the GWO algorithm used for controller parameter optimization in the FES system. This structure clearly demonstrates the flowchart of the optimization process and the interactions between system components.

11.5 Simulation studies and results

This section comprehensively compares the performance of PIDF, FOPID, and FOPIDF controllers that were optimized using the GWO algorithm. The evaluation begins with a transient time response analysis of the FES system and continues

TABLE 11.1 The parameter values of the FES used in this study [11–13].

Parameter	Value
m	100 g
k_s	20 N/m
c	4 N-s/m
g	9.81 m/s^2
μ	0.1
Td	0.7 s

FES, Functional electrical stimulation.

TABLE 11.2 Controller parameter limits.

Controller	Parameters					
	k_p	k_i	k_d	λ	μ	n
PIDF	0–200	0–200	0–200	-	-	0–500
FOPID	0–200	0–200	0–200	0.1–1.5	0.1–1.5	-
FOPIDF	0–200	0–200	0–200	0.1–1.5	0.1–1.5	0–500

FOPID, Fractional-order PID; *FOPIDF*, filtered FOPID; *PIDF*, PIDF with filter.

with a robustness analysis. The robustness analysis examines critical scenarios in detail, including resistance to external disturbances, stability against changes in system parameters, and tracking performance against variable reference signals. The optimal controller parameters obtained from the simulation studies are presented in Table 11.3.

11.5.1 Step response analysis

The initial analysis undertaken as part of the performance evaluation involved examining the transient response characteristics of the proposed controllers. To this end, unit-step responses were obtained for the FES system using the optimal controller parameters presented in Table 11.3. The unit-step responses displayed in Fig. 11.3 offer a clear illustration of the impact of the three distinct controller structures on system performance.

The performance metrics calculated for the quantitative analysis of the transient response are detailed in Table 11.4. An analysis of these metrics reveals that the GWO-PIDF controller demonstrates noteworthy performance, exhibiting a relatively low overshoot (O_s) value of 8%. However, its rise time (t_r) of 0.866 seconds indicates a comparatively slower response time than that of the other controllers. The GWO-FOPID and GWO-FOPIDF controllers demonstrate relatively rapid rise times of 0.27 and 0.266 seconds, respectively. However, this swift response leads to substantial overshoot values of 19.8% and 20.3%, respectively. When evaluated in terms of settling time (t_s), the GWO-FOPID and GWO-FOPIDF controllers reach steady state approximately twice as fast, at 2.164 and 2.152 seconds, respectively, compared to the GWO-PIDF controller's 4.265 seconds.

The convergence curves presented in Fig. 11.4 are critical for evaluating the effectiveness of the optimization process. The graphs illustrate that after 50 iterations, the GWO-PIDF controller converges to a value of 1.0877, the GWO-FOPID controller to a value of 0.56357, and the GWO-FOPIDF controller to a value of 0.56767. According to the ITAE criterion, the GWO-FOPID controller, which has the lowest convergence value, is considered to provide the most optimal result in terms of overall system performance. This result demonstrates the superior performance of the GWO-FOPID controller in terms of both fast transient response and low error integral.

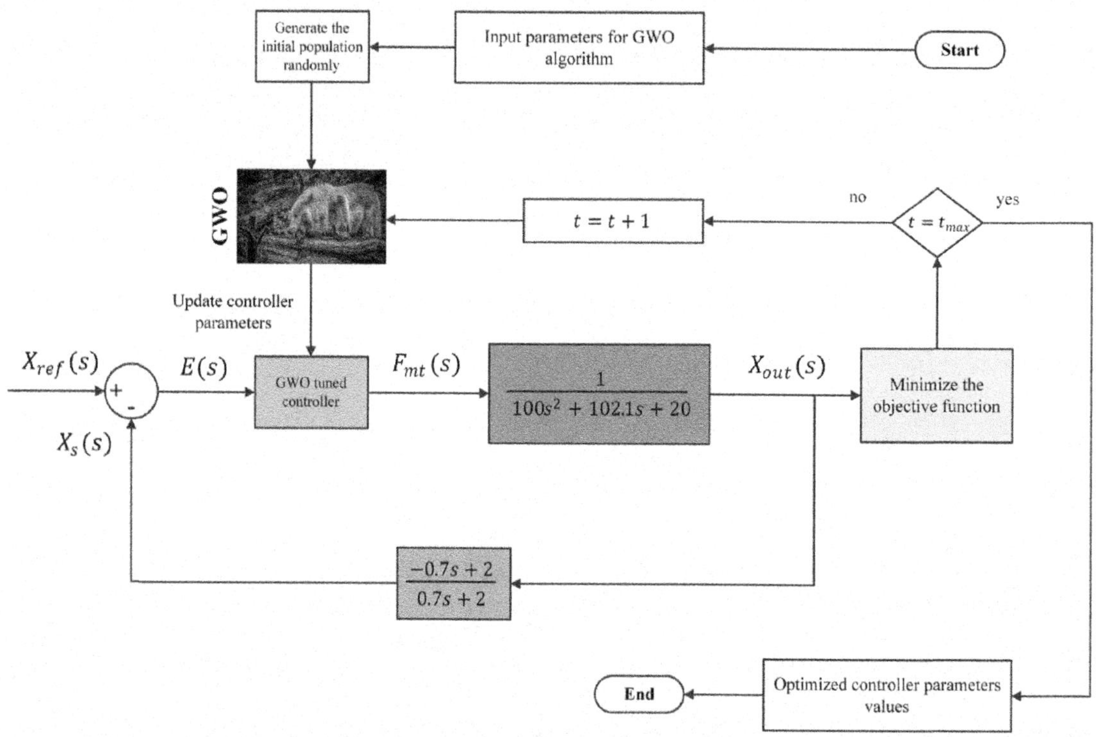

FIGURE 11.2 Application of GWO-tuned controller in FES system (*FES*, Functional electrical stimulation; *GWO*, grey wolf optimizer).

TABLE 11.3 Optimized controller parameters for the controllers.

Controller	Parameters					
	k_p	k_i	k_d	λ	μ	n
GWO: PIDF	89.84534	17.17912	101.6566	-	-	237.7779
GWO: FOPID	165.6162	13.54891	172.8249	1.235633	1.2706	-
GWO: FOPIDF	164.795	13.50616	173.6528	1.236686	1.277131	458.4189

FOPID, Fractional-order PID; *FOPIDF*, filtered FOPID; *GWO*, grey wolf optimizer; *PIDF*, PIDF with filter.

11.5.2 Robustness analysis

A critical challenge confronting control systems in real-world applications is their capacity to demonstrate stable performance under variable operating conditions and uncertainties. Consequently, robustness analysis of the proposed controllers is imperative for the evaluation of the success of the system design. Factors such as the inherent nonlinear characteristics of FES systems, muscle fatigue, individual anatomical differences, and environmental disturbances necessitate testing controller performance under different scenarios.

In this study, the robustness performance of the proposed controllers was systematically examined under three main categories. Initially, an analysis was conducted on the controllers' capacity to suppress disturbances against external disturbance signals applied to the system. Secondly, the impact of alterations in critical FES system parameters on controller performance was assessed. Finally, the performance of reference signal tracking in the presence of variable reference signals was investigated.

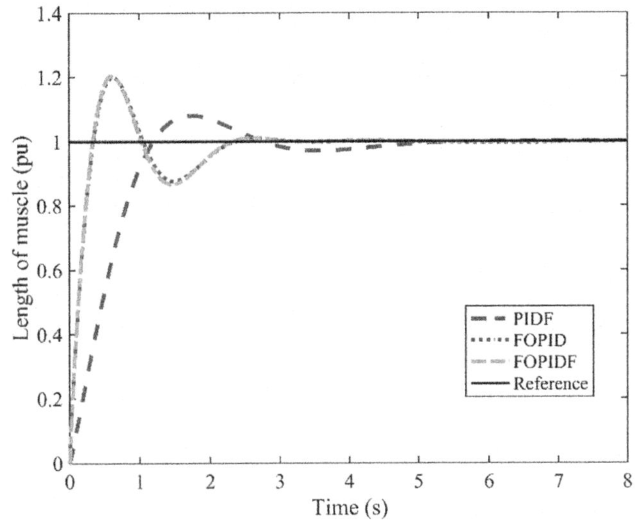

FIGURE 11.3 Step responses comparison of GWO-tuned PIDF, FOPID, and FOPIDF controllers for the FES system (*FIS*, Functional electrical stimulation; *FOPID*, fractional-order PID; *FOPIDF*, filtered FOPID; *GWO*, grey wolf optimizer; *PIDF*, PID with filter).

11.5.2.1 Robustness against disturbance

TABLE 11.4 Transient response performance metrics for unit step input.

Controller	Transient response results			
	O_s (%)	t_r (s) 0.1 → 0.9	t_s (s) ± 2%	t_p (s)
GWO: PIDF	8	0.866	4.265	1.733
GWO: FOPID	19.8	0.27	2.164	0.595
GWO: FOPIDF	20.3	0.266	2.152	0.587

FOPID, Fractional-order PID; *FOPIDF*, filtered FOPID; *GWO*, grey wolf optimizer; *PIDF*, PID with filter.

In real-world FES applications, the system may encounter various external disturbances. These disturbances encompass a range of factors, including but not limited to muscle fatigue, alterations in electrode placement, fluctuations in skin impedance, and voluntary muscle activity of the patient. Consequently, the evaluation of controllers' disturbance suppression capabilities is imperative for ensuring system reliability.

For the disturbance analysis, a positive disturbance signal of +25% magnitude was applied to the system at t=15 seconds and a negative disturbance signal of -25% magnitude was applied at t=30 seconds. The selection of these disturbance signals was made to emulate the sudden changes that may be encountered in the FES system. The system responses presented in Fig. 11.5 comparatively illustrate the behavior of all three controllers in the face of disturbances.

A thorough examination of the analysis results indicates that the GWO-FOPID and GWO-FOPIDF controllers demonstrate superior performance in the presence of disturbances. These controllers rapidly compensate for deviations in the system output during the application of disturbance signals, achieving a return to the reference value with minimal overshoot. In contrast, the GWO-PIDF controller demonstrates a comparatively slower compensation mechanism against disturbances and a lengthier settling time to reach the reference value.

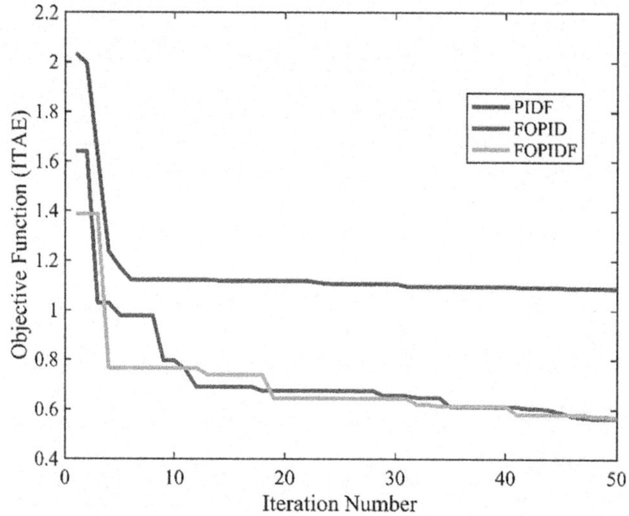

FIGURE 11.4 Convergence characteristics of the GWO optimization algorithm for the proposed controllers (*GWO*, Grey wolf optimizer).

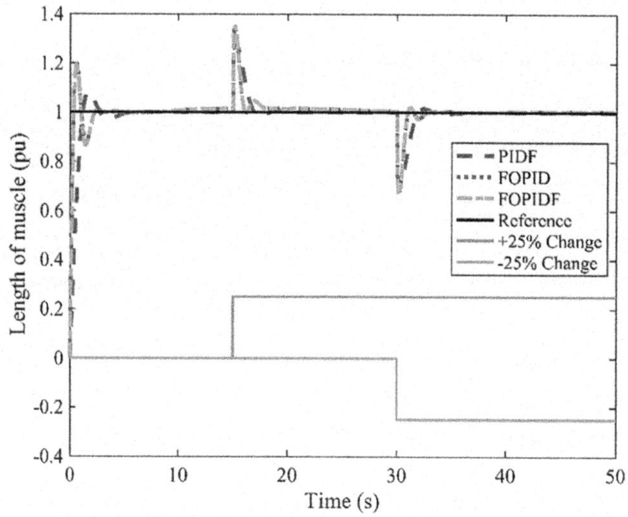

FIGURE 11.5 System response under external disturbance conditions for GWO-tuned controllers (*GWO*, Grey wolf optimizer).

11.5.2.2 Robustness against parameter change

In the context of clinical applications of FES systems, the inevitable presence of system parameter variation is a salient concern. This variation is attributable to a number of factors, including individual patient differences, alterations in muscle properties, electrode placement, and physiological adaptations over time. Therefore evaluating the robustness of controllers to changes in system parameters is imperative for ensuring system reliability in clinical applications.

As part of the parameter variation analysis, the impact of changes in the spring constant (k_s) and damping constant (c) parameters of the FES system on controller performance was systematically investigated. Two distinct scenarios, delineated in Table 11.5, were contemplated: In the first case, a +25% increase in both parameters was simulated, while in the second case, a -25% decrease was simulated. These parametric changes are indicative of alterations in muscle stiffness and damping characteristics.

An examination of the Case I results, as depicted in Fig. 11.6, indicates that a 25% augmentation in system parameters exerted an influence on the performance of all controllers. The GWO-FOPID and GWO-FOPIDF controllers demonstrate

TABLE 11.5 Parameter variation scenarios for robustness analysis.

Case	k_s	c
I (+25%)	25	5
II (-25%)	15	3

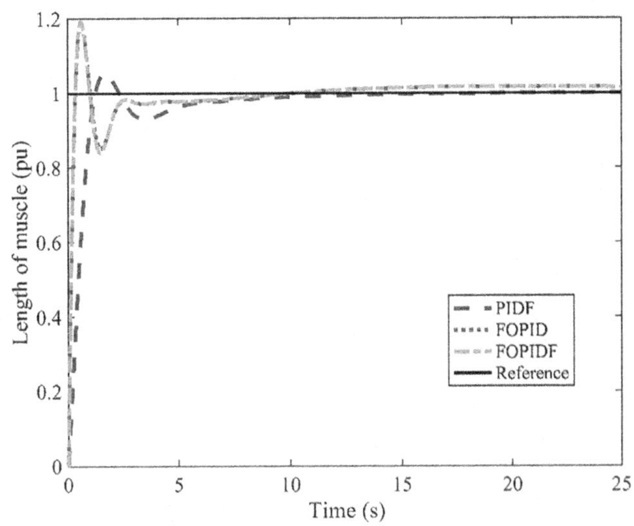

FIGURE 11.6 System response comparison under +25% parameter variation (Case I).

a fast response, whereas the GWO-PIDF controller demonstrates a slower response characteristic under parameter increases but maintains stable overshoot performance. The Case II results, as illustrated in Fig. 11.7, demonstrate the repercussions of a -25% decline in system parameters on system dynamics.

The findings obtained from the examination of both parameter variation scenarios indicate that the controllers manifest a robust configuration when confronted with uncertainties in system parameters.

11.5.2.3 Robustness against reference signal

In practical applications of FES systems, patients are required to monitor variable reference signals corresponding to different movement patterns and positions during the rehabilitation process. This necessitates that controllers function effectively with both fixed reference values and dynamic and variable reference signals. Consequently, reference signal tracking analysis is imperative for the evaluation of the performance of the proposed controllers in real-world clinical scenarios. To comprehensively evaluate the performance of reference signal tracking, a complex reference signal was designed, as shown in Fig. 11.8. This signal comprises step changes to assess the FES system's capacity to function at varying amplitude levels and variable time intervals. The reference signal, which has been selected for this study, has been shown to simulate sudden position changes and multiple target points that may be encountered in real-world rehabilitation applications.

The system responses exhibited in Fig. 11.9 comparatively demonstrate the tracking performance of all three controllers against a variable reference signal. A thorough examination has been conducted, the results of which indicate that the GWO-FOPID and GWO-FOPIDF controllers demonstrate better performance in reference signal tracking. These controllers have been demonstrated to rapidly detect sudden variations in the reference signal and achieve target values

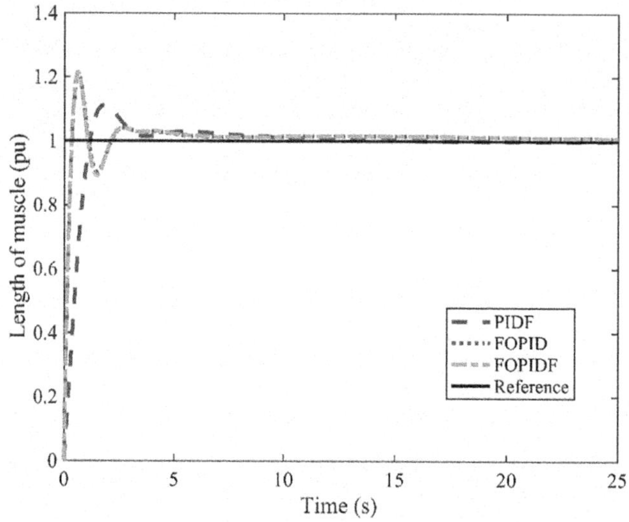

FIGURE 11.7 System response comparison under -25% parameter variation (Case II).

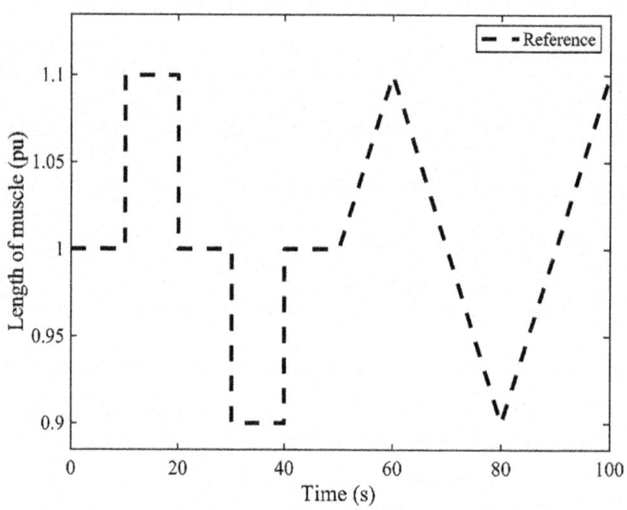

FIGURE 11.8 A multistep reference signal used for tracking performance evaluation.

with minimal overshoot. In particular, fractional-order controllers have been shown to exhibit lower settling times and reduced oscillation during positive and negative changes in the reference signal. In contrast, the GWO-PIDF controller employs a more cautious strategy for reference signal tracking. While it exhibits stable performance with minimal overshoot values, it is comparatively slower than other controllers in terms of tracking speed. Besides the visual tracking performance in Figs. 11.8 and 11.9, the ITAE values were determined as PIDF=56.601, FOPID=49.722, and FOPIDF=49.98. These results quantitatively confirm that the fractional-order controllers achieve improved tracking accuracy for variable reference signals.

The findings indicate that fractional-order controllers (GWO-FOPID and GWO-FOPIDF) exhibit notable advantages over conventional structures in the tracking of dynamic reference signals and deliver more flexible and effective control performance in clinical applications.

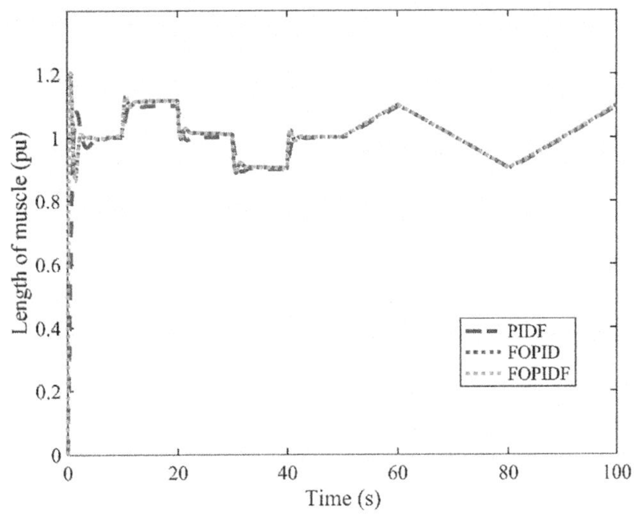

FIGURE 11.9 Reference signal tracking performance comparison of GWO-tuned controllers (*GWO*, Grey wolf optimizer).

11.6 Conclusion

FES systems have been demonstrated to play a crucial role in improving the quality of life of individuals with paralysis. In order to optimize the efficacy of these systems, it is essential to implement a robust control process. In this study, PIDF, FOPID, and FOPIDF controllers were proposed for FES systems, and the GWO optimization technique, which has not previously been employed in FES systems, was used to optimally tune their parameters.

The performance of the proposed controllers was thoroughly examined under conditions such as transient-time analysis and robustness analysis. A comparative analysis revealed that the GWO-optimized FOPID and FOPIDF controllers exhibited superior performance in terms of resistance to external disturbances, robustness to changes in system parameters, and tracking variable reference signals. Specifically, the GWO-FOPID controller demonstrated the lowest convergence value according to the ITAE criterion, yielding the most optimal results in terms of rapid transient response and minimal error integral.

Subsequent studies may employ newly developed or hybrid optimization algorithms to further enhance controller performance. Moreover, the augmentation of the number of parameters to be optimized has the potential to yield enhanced outcomes.

Acknowledgments

The authors declare that no artificial intelligence (AI) tools were used in the preparation or editing of this manuscript.

References

[1] A.K. Sahin, M.S. Ayas, Fine-tuned design of the PIDFFD2F control strategy for the functional electrical stimulation system using dandelion optimizer, Biomedical Signal Processing and Control 103 (2025). Available from https://doi.org/10.1016/j.bspc.2024.107350.

[2] E. Jafari, A. Erfanian, A distributed automatic control framework for simultaneous control of torque and cadence in functional electrical stimulation cycling, IEEE Transactions on Neural Systems and Rehabilitation Engineering 30 (2022) 1908–1919. Available from https://doi.org/10.1109/TNSRE.2022.3188735.

[3] V. Nekoukar, Control of functional electrical stimulation systems using simultaneous pulse width, amplitude, and frequency modulations, Neuromodulation 24 (8) (2021) 1467–1474. Available from https://doi.org/10.1111/ner.13126.

[4] T. Alif, S. Bhasin, K. Garg, D. Joshi, An enhanced model free adaptive control approach for functional electrical stimulation assisted knee joint regulation and control, IEEE Transactions on Neural Systems and Rehabilitation Engineering 31 (2023) 1584–1593. Available from https://doi.org/10.1109/TNSRE.2023.3252882.

[5] V. Molazadeh, Q. Zhang, X. Bao, N. Sharma, An iterative learning controller for a switched cooperative allocation strategy during sit-to-stand tasks with a hybrid exoskeleton, IEEE Transactions on Control Systems Technology 30 (3) (2022) 1021–1036. Available from https://doi.org/10.1109/TCST.2021.3089885.

[6] S. Sa-e, C.T. Freeman, K. Yang, Iterative learning control of functional electrical stimulation in the presence of voluntary user effort, Control Engineering Practice 96 (2020). Available from https://doi.org/10.1016/j.conengprac.2020.104303.

[7] M. Kutlu, C.T. Freeman, E. Hallewell, A.M. Hughes, D.S. Laila, Upper-limb stroke rehabilitation using electrode-array based functional electrical stimulation with sensing and control innovations, Medical Engineering & Physics 38 (4) (2016) 366–379. Available from https://doi.org/10.1016/j.medengphy.2016.01.004.

[8] Z. Zhang, B. Chu, Y. Liu, Z. Li, D.H. Owens, Multimuscle functional-electrical-stimulation-based wrist tremor suppression using repetitive control, IEEE/ASME Transactions on Mechatronics 27 (5) (2022) 3988–3998. Available from https://doi.org/10.1109/TMECH.2022.3150301.

[9] E.H. Copur, C.T. Freeman, B. Chu, D.S. Laila, Repetitive control of electrical stimulation for tremor suppression, IEEE Transactions on Control Systems Technology 27 (2) (2019) 540–552. Available from https://doi.org/10.1109/TCST.2017.2771327.

[10] N. Kirsch, N. Alibeji, N. Sharma, Nonlinear model predictive control of functional electrical stimulation, Control Engineering Practice 58 (2017) 319–331. Available from https://doi.org/10.1016/j.conengprac.2016.03.005.

[11] D. Izci, S. Ekinci, E. Eker, A. Demirören, Biomedical application of a random learning and elite opposition-based weighted mean of vectors algorithm with pattern search mechanism, Journal of Control, Automation and Electrical Systems 34 (2) (2023) 333–343. Available from https://doi.org/10.1007/s40313-022-00959-2.

[12] S. Ekinci, D. Izci, M.R. Al Nasar, R. Abu Zitar, L. Abualigah, Logarithmic spiral search based arithmetic optimization algorithm with selective mechanism and its application to functional electrical stimulation system control, Soft Computing 26 (22) (2022) 12257–12269. Available from https://doi.org/10.1007/s00500-022-07068-x.

[13] D. Izci, S. Ekinci, E. Eker, A. Demirören, Multi-strategy modified INFO algorithm: performance analysis and application to functional electrical stimulation system, Journal of Computer Science 64 (2022). Available from https://doi.org/10.1016/j.jocs.2022.101836.

[14] S. Mirjalili, S.M. Mirjalili, A. Lewis, Grey wolf optimizer, Advances in Engineering Software 69 (2014) 46–61. Available from https://doi.org/10.1016/j.advengsoft.2013.12.007.

Chapter 12

Grey wolf optimizer algorithm for buckling load maximization of stiffened piezolaminated composite plates

Vahid Goodarzimehr[1], Umut Topal[2], and Nima Khodadadi[3]
[1]*Faculty of Civil Engineering and Architecture, Shahid Chamran University of Ahvaz, Ahvaz, Iran,* [2]*Department of Civil Engineering, Faculty of Technology, Karadeniz Technical University, Trabzon, Türkiye,* [3]*Department of Civil and Environmental Engineering, Pacific Earthquake Engineering Research (PEER) Center, University of California, Berkeley, CA, United States*

12.1 Introduction

Piezoelectric materials are widely utilized in the development of smart structures across a variety of engineering fields, including civil, marine, automotive, mechanical, aerospace, and nuclear engineering. In recent years, the growing application of piezoelectric effects in smart and adaptive systems has encouraged researchers and engineers to pursue more precise and efficient analytical approaches for predicting the behavior of piezoelectric laminated plates. These materials are known for their unique ability to convert mechanical energy into electrical energy and vice versa. When subjected to mechanical deformation, they generate electrical charges, while applying an electric field induces mechanical strain within the structure. As material science continues to evolve, there is significant interest in enhancing the strength and functionality of traditional materials to meet new performance demands. Given the widespread use of fiber-reinforced composites in modern industries, improving their durability has become crucial, and integrating piezoelectric materials offers one promising solution.

Extensive research has been carried out on the buckling behavior of piezolaminated plates. Akhras and Li [1] introduced a spline finite strip method for analyzing buckling. Moradi-Dastjerdi et al. [2] addressed the buckling of sandwich plates under thermal and mechanical loading using third-order shear deformation theory. Tanzadeh and Amoushahi [3] refined the finite strip method for stability analysis based on various plate theories. Akhras and Li [4] extended the finite layer approach to study the thermal buckling of symmetric cross-ply piezolaminated plates subjected to electrical, thermal, and mechanical loads. This strategy was later adapted by Akhras and Li [5] for the stability analysis of angle-ply antisymmetric laminates. Bohlooly and Mirzavand [6] explored both buckling and postbuckling behaviors under multiple loading conditions, including electrical, thermal, and mechanical loads, employing von Kármán nonlinear theory.

Bohlooly and Fard [7] carried out modeling and analysis of sandwich plates subjected to thermal and mechanical loads, focusing on their buckling and postbuckling behavior using the classical laminated plate theory (CLPT). In another study, Bohlooly and Mirzavand [8] derived closed-form solutions for buckling and postbuckling responses of piezolaminated plates placed on an elastic foundation under in-plane, transverse, thermal, and electrical loads. Shariyat [9] investigated dynamic buckling phenomena in imperfect piezolaminated plates exposed to sudden mechanical and thermal loads, employing a higher-order shear deformation theory (HSDT). Li et al. [10] proposed a thermal buckling analysis technique for sandwich piezolaminated plates, incorporating a real-time temperature feedback mechanism in thermal environments. Jin et al. [11] studied the stability of piezolaminated plates equipped with actuators using HSDT. Oh et al. [12] conducted postbuckling evaluations for both partially eccentric and fully symmetric piezolaminated plates, accounting for large thermopiezoelastic deformations.

Shen [13] presented a postbuckling study of piezolaminated plates under combined electrical and thermal loading using HSDT, while Shen [14] extended this work by including mechanical loading and actuator effects. Varelis and Saravanos

Grey Wolf Optimizer. DOI: https://doi.org/10.1016/B978-0-443-36624-6.00010-X

[15] examined the nonlinear behavior of piezolaminated plates subjected to electromechanical loads, incorporating large deformation and rotation effects. Kapuria and Achary [16] provided a piezothermoelastic buckling solution for laminated hybrid plates with embedded piezoelectric layers using a state-space methodology. Bohlooly and Mirzavand [17] also analyzed thermal buckling of cross-ply symmetric piezolaminated plates under uniform actuator voltage and thermal conditions by applying von Kármán nonlinearity. Akhras and Li [18] expanded the finite layer method to address thermal buckling in angle-ply antisymmetric piezolaminates. Mirzavand and Bohlooly [19] explored thermal buckling in piezolaminated plates with actuators, considering constant applied voltage and thermal load within the framework of HSDT. Finally, Panahandeh-Shahraki et al. [20] addressed the electromechanical and thermoelastic buckling behavior of piezolaminated plates using a fractional hierarchical Rayleigh–Ritz method.

While numerous studies have examined the buckling behavior of piezolaminated plates, relatively few have focused specifically on the optimization of their buckling performance. Correia et al. [21] proposed a strategy for the multiobjective optimization of piezolaminated plates using two direct search, derivative-free algorithms. Their approach considered multiple objectives, including maximizing the first four natural frequencies, minimizing elastic strain energy, and maximizing the critical buckling load. Xue et al. [22] investigated thermal buckling optimization and control using a layerwise design strategy for piezolaminated plates. In another contribution, Correia et al. [23] applied simulated annealing and a stochastic global optimization method to determine the optimal placement of piezoelectric actuators and fiber orientations for maximizing the buckling load of laminated composite plates.

In a related context, Gao et al. [24] developed an analytical, multistep bottom-up model for estimating the in-plane mechanical properties, such as effective Young's modulus and Poisson's ratios in two principal directions. Liu et al. [25] analyzed the deformation behavior of U-type corrugated core sandwich panels used in shipbuilding under lateral quasi-static compression, combining experimental, numerical, and theoretical methods. Huang et al. [26] explored how axial compression ratio, torsion-bending ratio, and eccentricity influence the mechanical response of reinforced concrete columns under combined loads. Guo et al. [27] performed tests on three one-third scale reinforced concrete beam-column-slab assemblies to study progressive collapse mechanisms triggered by the removal of a corner column. Their setups included a frame with a slab, a frame with a slab and secondary beams, and a frame without a slab. Last, Huang et al. [28] assessed the seismic performance of corrosion-damaged reinforced concrete columns retrofitted using bonded steel plates and high-performance ferrocement laminates. Their investigation was based on mechanical testing under various combined loading scenarios.

Structural optimization focuses on designing structures that exhibit superior mechanical performance while maintaining reasonable manufacturing costs. As a result, extensive research has been devoted to developing advanced optimization methods capable of accurately identifying optimal design conditions. Goodarzimehr et al. [29] applied a newly introduced intelligent algorithm, known as the self-adaptive Bonomo optimizer, for the size and shape optimization of truss structures subject to multiple frequency constraints. Goodarzimehr et al. [30] presented a novel approach for optimizing the critical buckling load of the stiffened piezolaminated composite plates using a self-adaptive special relativity search algorithm. Goodarzimehr et al. [31] focused on maximizing the fundamental frequency of stiffened piezolaminated composite plates using a novel hybrid optimization algorithm that combines the special relativity search and hill climbing techniques.

Based on the reviewed literature and to the best of our knowledge, there has been no study specifically addressing the optimization of the critical buckling load in stiffened piezolaminated plates. To bridge this gap, the present research introduces a novel optimization approach targeting the buckling performance of such structures. This work employs the grey wolf optimizer (GWO) algorithm to determine the optimal fiber orientations in the composite layers, which are treated as design variables. The governing stability equations are formulated using the CLPT, incorporating von Kármán geometric nonlinearity to account for large deflections. The optimization framework is developed and executed in MATLAB. The study explores the impact of various parameters on the optimal design, including different boundary conditions, applied actuator voltages, grid geometries, angles of diagonal stiffeners, and aspect ratios of the plates. Numerical simulations are performed on 10-ply symmetric stiffened piezolaminated composite plates to validate the proposed method. The effectiveness and reliability of the GWO-based optimization are assessed by comparing its results with those obtained from the standard version of the GWO algorithm. The findings reveal that the proposed method outperforms the SRS algorithm in terms of convergence rate and ability to enhance the critical buckling load, demonstrating its superior optimization capability.

12.2 Problem formulation

Fig. 12.1 a shows the coordinate system and geometry of a stiffened piezolaminated plate. The length, width, and thickness of the plate are *2a*, *2b*, and *h*, respectively. The plate is composed of a multilayered composite substrate, with

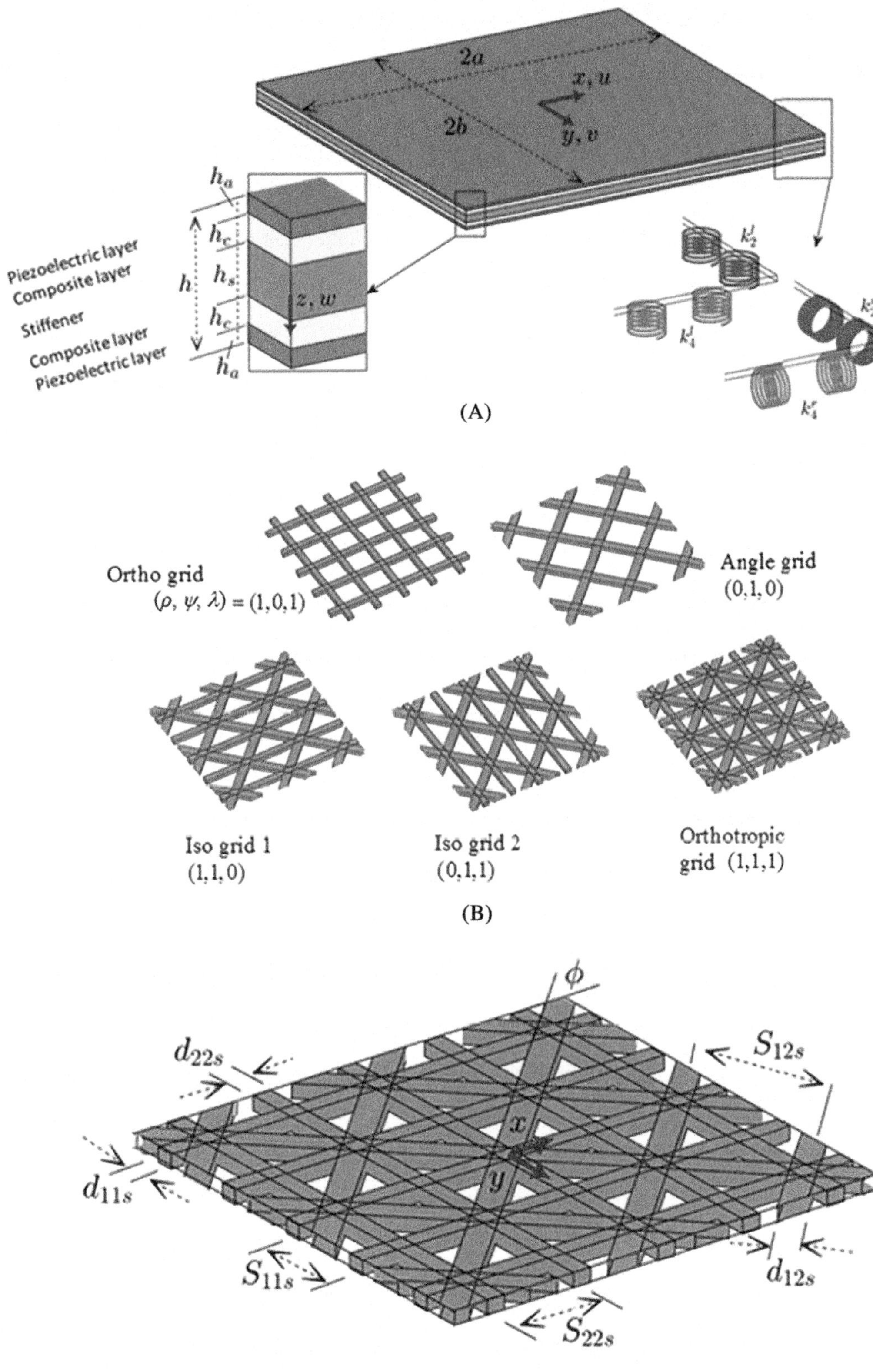

FIGURE 12.1 (A) Coordinate system and geometry parameters of a stiffened piezolaminated plate, (B) Five different grid shapes of the stiffener, (C) Schematic view of an orthotropic grid.

two piezoelectric layers adhered to the bottom and top surfaces of the plate as actuators. h_a, h_c, and h_s are the thicknesses of the composite layer, piezoelectric layer, and stiffener, respectively. It is supposed that the four edges of the middle plane of the plate are supported by two types of springs, that is, linear (l) and rotational (r). By choosing zero or substantial values of the stiffness of these springs k_i^l, k_i^r (i = 1, ...,4), one can model the clamped (C), free (F), and simply supported (S) boundary conditions. This study considers five different grid shapes of the stiffener, such as angle grid, ortho grid, iso grid 1, orthotropic grid, and iso grid 2 (Fig. 12.1 b). The grid-type structures can increase the buckling load, and simultaneously, they do not increase the weight of the structure as much as other materials. In Fig. 12.1 c, the schematic view of an orthotropic grid can be seen. Here, d_{11s}, d_{22s}, and d_{12s} are the width of the transverse, longitudinal, and diagonal ribs, respectively; S_{11s}, S_{22s}, and S_{12s} are the span between two parallel transverse, longitudinal, and diagonal ribs, respectively. The angle of diagonal ribs (ϕ) is measured from the x-axis.

The variation in buckling load between open-circuit and closed-circuit conditions in piezoelectric actuators arises from their differing electromechanical interactions. These distinctions underscore the importance of electrical boundary conditions in determining the mechanical stability of piezoelectric composite systems. Incorporating both open and closed circuit cases into the optimization framework allows for a more realistic simulation of actual structural behavior. In the open-circuit configuration, electric charges are restricted from moving, maintaining a constant electric field that strengthens the electromechanical coupling. This results in increased stiffness, enabling the structure to bear higher compressive loads and thus elevating the critical buckling load. Conversely, in a closed-circuit setup, free charge redistribution reduces the internal electric field, weakening the coupling and lowering the structural stiffness, which leads to a decreased buckling load. The stored electrical energy in the open-circuit state contributes positively to system stiffness, acting as a stabilizing force. In contrast, in the closed-circuit condition, this energy dissipation due to charge movement lessens the stability, thereby reducing the buckling capacity.

The buckling behavior of a thin-walled plate element composed of a general laminate subjected to in-plane uniaxial loading is investigated. It is assumed that the plate has a uniform and relatively small thickness compared to its other dimensions. The structure is analyzed under plane stress conditions. While each individual layer is orthotropic and follows Hooke's law, the overall laminate exhibits anisotropic characteristics. The analysis assumes the validity of the Kirchhoff–Love hypothesis, which implies that displacements in the midplane of the composite plate are independent of the coordinate perpendicular to the surface. Strains along the directions tangent to the plate are considered to be small. Nonlinear geometric relations are used to describe the displacements of the plate. In this work, the CLPT is adopted to derive the governing equations of motion for the structure [17]. The laminate is constructed from thin layers, each with distinct fiber orientations (θ). Both the individual layers and the complete laminate are treated as continuous media. The constituents of each ply, namely the fiber and matrix, are assumed to be perfectly bonded, ensuring uniform mechanical behavior. According to the CLPT assumptions, the displacement fields are expressed as follows [17]:

$$\begin{aligned} u(x, y, z) &= u_o(x, y) - z w_{o,x}(x, y) \\ v(x, y, z) &= v_o(x, y) - z w_{o,y}(x, y) \\ w(x, y, z) &= w_o(x, y) \end{aligned} \tag{12.1}$$

where u_o, v_o, and w_o are the displacements in the plate midplane. The strains can be written as [17]

$$\varepsilon = \varepsilon^o + z\kappa \tag{12.2}$$

where the strain ε^o at the midplane based on von Karman's strain-displacement relationship is

$$\varepsilon^o = \begin{Bmatrix} \varepsilon_x^o \\ \varepsilon_y^o \\ \gamma_{xy}^o \end{Bmatrix} = \begin{Bmatrix} u_{o,x} + \frac{1}{2} w_{o,x}^2 \\ v_{o,y} + \frac{1}{2} w_{o,y}^2 \\ u_{o,y} + v_{o,x} + w_{o,x} w_{o,y} \end{Bmatrix} \tag{12.3}$$

and the curvature κ is defined as [17]

$$\kappa = \begin{Bmatrix} \kappa_x \\ \kappa_y \\ \kappa_{xy} \end{Bmatrix} = \begin{Bmatrix} - w_{o,xx} \\ - w_{o,yy} \\ - 2w_{o,xy} \end{Bmatrix} \tag{12.4}$$

With the consideration of the electrical load, the stress–strain relationship of a piezoelectric actuator is given below [6]

$$\begin{Bmatrix}\sigma_x\\ \sigma_y\\ \tau_{xy}\end{Bmatrix}=\begin{pmatrix}Q_{11}^a & Q_{12}^a & 0\\ Q_{21}^a & Q_{22}^a & 0\\ 0 & 0 & Q_{66}^a\end{pmatrix}\begin{Bmatrix}\varepsilon_x\\ \varepsilon_y\\ \gamma_{xy}\end{Bmatrix}-\begin{pmatrix}0 & 0 & e_{31}\\ 0 & 0 & e_{32}\\ 0 & 0 & 0\end{pmatrix}\begin{Bmatrix}E_x\\ E_y\\ E_z\end{Bmatrix} \quad (12.5)$$

where Q_{ij}^a $(i, j = 1, 2, 6)$ are the elastic stiffness; (e_{31}, e_{32}) are the piezoelectric stiffness; (E_x, E_y, E_z) are the electric field components, and letter "a" means "actuator.'. In Eq. (12.5), in-plane electric field components (E_x, E_y) have null values. The transverse component can be written as $E_z = V_a/h_a$.

For the kth orthotropic lamina, the stress–strain relationship can be defined as [6]

$$\begin{Bmatrix}\sigma_x\\ \sigma_y\\ \tau_{xy}\end{Bmatrix}_k=\begin{pmatrix}\overline{Q}_{11} & \overline{Q}_{12} & \overline{Q}_{16}\\ \overline{Q}_{12} & \overline{Q}_{22} & \overline{Q}_{26}\\ \overline{Q}_{16} & \overline{Q}_{26} & \overline{Q}_{66}\end{pmatrix}_k\begin{Bmatrix}\varepsilon_x\\ \varepsilon_y\\ \gamma_{xy}\end{Bmatrix} \quad (12.6)$$

where $\overline{Q}_{ij}$ are the transformed stiffness. On the other hand, the stress–strain relationship for the stiffener can be defined as follows [7]

$$\begin{Bmatrix}\sigma_x\\ \sigma_y\\ \tau_{xy}\end{Bmatrix}=\begin{pmatrix}\rho d_{11s}E_s/S_{11s}+2\lambda d_{12s}E_sc^4/S_{12s} & 2\lambda d_{12s}E_sc^2s^2/S_{12s} & 0\\ 2\lambda d_{12s}E_sc^2s^2/S_{12s} & \psi d_{22s}E_s/S_{22s}+2\lambda d_{12s}E_ss^4/S_{12s} & 0\\ 0 & 0 & 2\lambda d_{12s}E_sc^2s^2/S_{12s}\end{pmatrix}\begin{Bmatrix}\varepsilon_x\\ \varepsilon_y\\ \gamma_{xy}\end{Bmatrix} \quad (12.7)$$

where $c=\cos\theta$, $s=\sin\theta$, and E_s is the Young's modulus of the stiffener. (ρ, ψ, λ) are defined in Fig. 12.1 b for five different grid shapes. The force N and moment M resultants can be obtained as

$$N=\begin{Bmatrix}N_x\\ N_y\\ N_{xy}\end{Bmatrix}=\begin{pmatrix}A_{11}^* & A_{12}^* & A_{16}^*\\ A_{21}^* & A_{22}^* & A_{26}^*\\ A_{61}^* & A_{62}^* & A_{66}^*\end{pmatrix}\begin{Bmatrix}\varepsilon_x^o\\ \varepsilon_y^o\\ \gamma_{xy}^o\end{Bmatrix}-\begin{pmatrix}A_{11}^a & A_{12}^a & A_{16}^a\\ A_{21}^a & A_{22}^a & A_{26}^a\\ A_{61}^a & A_{62}^a & A_{66}^a\end{pmatrix}\begin{Bmatrix}d_{31}\\ d_{32}\\ 0\end{Bmatrix} \quad (12.8)$$

$$M=\begin{Bmatrix}M_x\\ M_y\\ M_{xy}\end{Bmatrix}=\begin{pmatrix}D_{11}^* & D_{12}^* & D_{16}^*\\ D_{21}^* & D_{22}^* & D_{26}^*\\ D_{61}^* & D_{62}^* & D_{66}^*\end{pmatrix}\begin{Bmatrix}\kappa_x\\ \kappa_y\\ \kappa_{xy}\end{Bmatrix} \quad (12.9)$$

where d_{31} and d_{32} are the dielectric constants of the piezoelectric actuators.

$$A^*=\begin{pmatrix}A_{11}^* & A_{12}^* & A_{16}^*\\ A_{21}^* & A_{22}^* & A_{26}^*\\ A_{61}^* & A_{62}^* & A_{66}^*\end{pmatrix}=\begin{pmatrix}Q_{11}^a & Q_{12}^a & 0\\ Q_{21}^a & Q_{22}^a & 0\\ 0 & 0 & Q_{66}^a\end{pmatrix}I_1^a$$
$$+\begin{pmatrix}\rho d_{11s}E_s/S_{11s}+2\lambda d_{12s}E_sc^4/S_{12s} & 2\lambda d_{12s}E_sc^2s^2/S_{12s} & 0\\ 2\lambda d_{12s}E_sc^2s^2/S_{12s} & \psi d_{22s}E_s/S_{22s}+2\lambda d_{12s}E_ss^4/S_{12s} & 0\\ 0 & 0 & 2\lambda d_{12s}E_sc^2s^2/S_{12s}\end{pmatrix}I_1^s$$
$$+\begin{pmatrix}A_{11} & A_{12} & A_{16}\\ A_{21} & A_{22} & A_{26}\\ A_{61} & A_{62} & A_{66}\end{pmatrix} \quad (12.10)$$

$$A^a=\begin{pmatrix}A_{11}^a & A_{12}^a & A_{16}^a\\ A_{21}^a & A_{22}^a & A_{26}^a\\ A_{61}^a & A_{62}^a & A_{66}^a\end{pmatrix}=\begin{pmatrix}Q_{11}^a & Q_{12}^a & 0\\ Q_{21}^a & Q_{22}^a & 0\\ 0 & 0 & Q_{66}^a\end{pmatrix}E_zI_1^a \quad (12.11)$$

$$D^* = \begin{pmatrix} D^*_{11} & D^*_{12} & D^*_{16} \\ D^*_{21} & D^*_{22} & D^*_{26} \\ D^*_{61} & D^*_{62} & D^*_{66} \end{pmatrix} = \begin{pmatrix} Q^a_{11} & Q^a_{12} & 0 \\ Q^a_{21} & Q^a_{22} & 0 \\ 0 & 0 & Q^a_{66} \end{pmatrix} I^a_3$$

$$+ \begin{pmatrix} \rho d_{11s}E_s/S_{11s} + 2\lambda d_{12s}E_s c^4/S_{12s} & 2\lambda d_{12s}E_s c^2 s^2/S_{12s} & 0 \\ 2\lambda d_{12s}E_s c^2 s^2/S_{12s} & \psi d_{22s}E_s/S_{22s} + 2\lambda d_{12s}E_s s^4/S_{12s} & 0 \\ 0 & 0 & 2\lambda d_{12s}E_s c^2 s^2/S_{12s} \end{pmatrix} I^s_3$$

$$+ \begin{pmatrix} D_{11} & D_{12} & D_{16} \\ D_{21} & D_{22} & D_{26} \\ D_{61} & D_{62} & D_{66} \end{pmatrix} \tag{12.12}$$

where

$$I^a_1 = 2h_a,\ I^s_1 = h_s,\ I^a_3 = 2h_c^2 h_a + 2h_c h_a^2 + \frac{2}{3}h_a^3 + \frac{1}{2}h_a h_s^3,\ I^s_3 = h_c^2 h_s + 2h_c h_a h_s + h_a^2 h_c + \frac{1}{12}h_s^3 \tag{12.13}$$

A_{ij} and D_{ij} are the extensional and bending stiffnesses of the laminates, respectively, and they are defined as [6]

$$A_{ij}, D_{ij} = \sum_{k=1}^{N} \begin{pmatrix} \bar{Q}_{11} & \bar{Q}_{12} & \bar{Q}_{16} \\ \bar{Q}_{21} & \bar{Q}_{22} & \bar{Q}_{26} \\ \bar{Q}_{61} & \bar{Q}_{62} & \bar{Q}_{66} \end{pmatrix}_k \left\{ \int_{z_{k-1}}^{z_k} dz,\ \int_{z_{k-1}}^{z_k} z^2 dz \right\} i, j = 1, 2, 6 \tag{12.14}$$

The equilibrium equations of the rectangular plate of piezolaminated composite with the piezoelectric actuators may be derived on the basis of the stationary potential energy criterion. The total potential energy (Π) of the plate can be defined as follows:

$$\Pi = U - V + \sum_{i=1}^{4} \Psi_i + \sum_{i=1}^{4} \Upsilon_i \tag{12.15}$$

The strain energy U, and the potential energy by the external loads V of the piezolaminated plate are given by

$$U = \frac{1}{2}\int\int\int (\sigma_x \varepsilon_x + \sigma_y \varepsilon_y + \tau_{xy}\gamma_{xy})dxdydz \tag{12.16}$$

$$V = \int\int \left[\frac{1}{b}P_x u_{,x} + \frac{1}{a}P_y v_{,y}\right] \tag{12.17}$$

where P_x and P_y are the compressive loads applied to the edges of the plate in the x and y directions, respectively. In Eq. (12.15), Ψ_i and Υ_i are the saved energy of the linear and rotational springs for different edges (Fig. 12.1 a), respectively. They can be wrriten as [32]

$$\Psi_1 = \frac{1}{2}\int_{-b}^{+b} k_1^l (w|_{x=-a})dy,\ \Upsilon_1 = \frac{1}{2}\int_{-b}^{+b} k_1^r \left(\frac{\partial w}{\partial x}\bigg|_{x=-a}\right)dy \tag{12.18a}$$

$$\Psi_2 = \frac{1}{2}\int_{-b}^{+b} k_2^l (w|_{x=+a})dy,\ \Upsilon_2 = \frac{1}{2}\int_{-b}^{+b} k_2^r \left(\frac{\partial w}{\partial x}\bigg|_{x=+a}\right)dy \tag{12.18b}$$

$$\Psi_3 = \frac{1}{2}\int_{-a}^{+a} k_3^l (w|_{y=-b})dx,\ \Upsilon_3 = \frac{1}{2}\int_{-a}^{+a} k_3^r \left(\frac{\partial w}{\partial y}\bigg|_{y=-b}\right)dx \tag{12.18c}$$

$$\Psi_4 = \frac{1}{2}\int_{-a}^{+a} k_4^l (w|_{y=+b})dx,\ \Upsilon_4 = \frac{1}{2}\int_{-a}^{+a} k_4^r \left(\frac{\partial w}{\partial y}\bigg|_{y=+b}\right)dx \tag{12.18d}$$

The essential conditions of different types of boundaries can be fulfilled by considering such elastic springs. The saved energies of the springs in Eqs. (12.18a–12.18d) can be added to the total potential energy of the structure. By changing the stiffness of these springs k_i^l, k_i^r ($i = 1, ...,4$), total potential energy and then boundary conditions can be changed. The substantial values of the stiffness of these springs can be found in Ref. [33] for different types of the clamped (C), free (F), and simply supported (S) boundary conditions.

It is supposed that the displacement u at the edges ($x = \pm a$) is freely movable. However, the displacement v at the edges ($y = \pm b$) is immovable. Therefore the prebuckling stress components are [6,17]

$$\sigma^o = \left(N_{xo}, \frac{a_{12}^*}{a_{11}^*} N_{xo} + 2e_{32}\frac{V_a}{h}, 0 \right)^T \quad (12.19)$$

where $N_{xo} = P_x/2bh$, $a^* = (A^*)^{-1}$, and V_a is the applied voltage through the thickness. The positive or negative voltage is highly dependent on the sign of e_{32}. If it is positive, we should apply the negative voltage and vice versa. Again, with respect to the Ritz method, substitute Eq. (12.16) and (18a–18d) into Eq. (12.15), then minimize Π in accordance with the unknown coefficients C_{mn}, where one of the simplest approximations for deflection is the following polynomials

$$w = \sum_{m=0}^{M} \sum_{n=0}^{N} C_{m,n} \zeta^m \eta^n \quad (12.20a)$$

where $\zeta = x/a$ and $\eta = y/b$. Then, the total potential energy can be calculated in terms of $C_{m,n}$. According to the Ritz method, this energy can be minimized as

$$\frac{\partial \Pi}{\partial C_{m,n}} = 0 \ m = 0,1, \ldots, M n = 0,1, \ldots, N \quad (12.20b)$$

The above differentiations yield $(M + 1)\cdot(N + 1)$ equations. The vector form of these equations can be written as

$$[\overline{K}]\ q + N_{xo}[\overline{K}_G]\ q = 0 \quad (12.20c)$$

where $[\overline{K}]$ and $[\overline{K_G}]$ are the stiffness and geometric matrices, respectively. Eqs. (20a–20c) can be rewritten as

$$[\overline{K} + \lambda \overline{K}_G]\ q = 0 \quad (12.21)$$

By setting the determinant of the above matrix to zero, the buckling load factor λ can be found, and the lowest of the buckling loads is the critical buckling load of the stiffened piezolaminated plate.

12.3 Grey wolf optimizer algorithm

The optimization of stiffened piezolaminated composite structures for improved buckling performance involves a highly nonlinear and multidimensional design space. To address this challenge, this study proposes a modified metaheuristic algorithm, Enhanced Grey Wolf Optimizer (EGWO), which builds upon the classical GWO to achieve improved convergence speed, solution accuracy, and robustness against premature stagnation.

The original GWO algorithm, developed by Mirjalili et al. [32], is inspired by the social hierarchy and cooperative hunting strategies observed in grey wolves. In the wild, grey wolves exhibit a well-defined leadership structure, which is mathematically modeled in GWO to balance exploration (global search) and exploitation (local search) in an optimization context. In the GWO algorithm, the population is divided into four hierarchical classes:

1) Alpha (α): Represents the current best candidate solution and leads the optimization process.
2) Beta (β): The second-best solution, providing support to the alpha in guiding the search direction.
3) Delta (δ): The third-best solution involved tracking the movement of the prey.
4) Omega (ω): The remaining population, which follows the guidance of the top three wolves.

The position of each wolf (i.e., solution vector) is updated by assuming the wolf is moving towards the position of the prey (i.e., the optimal solution), which is estimated by the positions of the α, β, and δ wolves. The encircling behavior of wolves is simulated as follows:

$$\vec{D} = \left| \vec{C} \cdot \vec{X_p}(t) - \vec{X}(t) \right|, \ \vec{X}(t+1) = \vec{X_p}(t) - \vec{A} \cdot \vec{D} \quad (12.22)$$

where $\vec{X}(t)$ is current position vector of a wolf, $\vec{X_p}(t)$ is estimated position of the prey, $\vec{A}$ and $\vec{C}$ are coefficient vectors controlling step size and direction, defined as:

$$\vec{A} = 2\vec{a} \cdot \vec{r_1} - \vec{a}, \ \vec{C} = 2\vec{r_2} \quad (12.23)$$

where $\vec{r_1}$, $\vec{r_2}$ $\in[0,1]$ randomly generated vectors. $\vec{a}$ is a linearly decreasing parameter from 2 to 0 over the course of iterations to gradually shift from exploration to exploitation.

To enhance convergence accuracy, the position of each wolf is updated by considering the average influence of the top three leaders:

$$\vec{X}(t+1) = \frac{1}{3}\left(\vec{X}'_\alpha + \vec{X}'_\beta + \vec{X}'_\delta\right) \tag{12.24}$$

where:

$$\begin{aligned} \vec{X}'_\alpha &= \vec{X_\alpha} - \vec{A_1}\cdot\left|\vec{C_1}\cdot\vec{X_\alpha} - \vec{X}\right| \\ \vec{X}'_\beta &= \vec{X_\beta} - \vec{A_2}\cdot\left|\vec{C_2}\cdot\vec{X_\beta} - \vec{X}\right| \\ \vec{X}'_\delta &= \vec{X_\delta} - \vec{A_3}\cdot\left|\vec{C_3}\cdot\vec{X_\delta} - \vec{X}\right| \end{aligned} \tag{12.25}$$

This strategy allows the optimizer to intelligently converge toward promising regions of the search space by exploiting the knowledge of the top three candidate solutions, while maintaining diversity through stochastic terms $\vec{r_1}$, $\vec{r_2}$. The balance between exploration and exploitation is further governed by the parameter $\vec{a}$, which decreases linearly from 2 to 0 over the course of iterations. A higher value of $\vec{a}$ encourages wolves to diverge and explore, while a lower value promotes convergence toward the best solutions found.

To improve exploration and avoid local optima, the following modifications are introduced in the enhanced GWO (EGWO): Unlike the static leadership structure in GWO, EGWO re-evaluates the roles of β, and δ wolves every Nl iterations based on current fitness, thus enhancing diversity. This encourages multiple promising directions to be explored dynamically.

In order to enhance the performance of the optimization process, two key strategies are incorporated into the proposed EGWO. First, Lévy flights are employed to reinforce the global exploration ability of the algorithm. Lévy distributions generate occasional long jumps, which help the search agents escape local optima and probe new regions of the design space. This stochastic property is particularly advantageous for highly nonlinear and multimodal optimization problems, such as buckling load maximization of stiffened piezolaminated composite plates, where conventional random walks may become trapped in suboptimal regions. Second, dynamic role reassignment is introduced to preserve diversity and adaptability in the wolf hierarchy. In the classical GWO, the leadership roles of α, β, and δ wolves remain fixed during the iterations, which may limit exploration and lead to premature convergence. Similar approaches have been shown to be effective in other metaheuristic algorithms, such as Cuckoo Search [33] and Particle Swarm Optimization [34].

In EGWO, these roles are periodically updated based on the current fitness of individuals. This dynamic mechanism ensures that multiple promising regions of the search space are explored concurrently, reducing stagnation and increasing the probability of reaching the global optimum. Together, these enhancements strengthen the balance between exploration and exploitation, leading to faster convergence and higher-quality solutions in structural optimization tasks. To reinforce global search capability, a Lévy flight perturbation is introduced with a probability pl. The Lévy step L is defined as:

$$L \sim \frac{\mu}{|v|^{\frac{1}{\beta}}},\ \mu,\ v \sim N(0, \sigma^2) \tag{12.26}$$

$$\sigma = \left(\frac{\Gamma(1+\beta)\cdot \sin\left(\frac{\pi\beta}{2}\right)}{\Gamma\left[\frac{(1+\beta)}{2}\right]\cdot\beta\cdot 2^{(\beta-1)/2}}\right)^{\frac{1}{\beta}} \tag{12.27}$$

with $\beta \in (1,2]$. This perturbation is added to the position vector after the standard update:

$$\vec{X}(t+1) = \vec{X}(t+1) + \delta\cdot L \tag{12.28}$$

where δ is a small scaling factor controlling step size.

For a population size of N, problem dimension d, and maximum iterations T, the computational complexity of EGWO is

$$O(T, N\cdot d) \tag{12.29}$$

since in each iteration the fitness of all search agents is evaluated and their positions are updated. The memory complexity is

$$O(N \cdot d) \tag{12.30}$$

as the algorithm needs to store the position vectors and fitness values of all agents.

The proposed EGWO is applied to the optimization of 10-ply symmetric stiffened piezolaminated composite plates under various boundary conditions and applied voltages. The optimization procedure is implemented in MATLAB. The buckling analysis incorporates grid-type stiffeners, actuator voltages, and geometric nonlinearities. The comparative results show that EGWO outperforms the standard GWO in convergence rate and the quality of the optimum solutions. In particular, the EGWO consistently finds higher critical buckling loads while maintaining stability across varying problem conditions.

12.4 Optimization problem

The primary objective of this study is to examine the buckling performance of stiffened piezolaminated composite plates and determine the optimal fiber layup configurations that enhance the structural stability. The optimization task is centered on maximizing the critical buckling load of symmetrically laminated piezoelectric composite plates. This is achieved by tuning the fiber orientation angles within each layer of the laminate.

The design variables in the optimization model are the fiber orientation angles, denoted as θ_k, where k=1, 2, …, NL and NL is the total number of composite layers. These angles are constrained to vary within the range of $-90° \leq \theta_k \leq 90°$, and are considered as discrete integer values.

The optimization problem can be mathematically formulated as:

$$\text{Maximize:} \quad \lambda = \frac{P_{cr}}{P_{ref}} \tag{12.31}$$

$$\text{Subject to:} \quad -90° \leq \theta_k \leq 90° \quad \text{for } k = 1, \ 2, \ \ldots, \ NL \tag{12.32}$$

Here, λ is the buckling load factor, representing the ratio of the critical buckling load P_{cr} to a reference load P_{ref}, θ_k are the fiber orientation angles in the k-th layer. The objective function is thus aimed at determining the fiber orientations θ_k that maximize λ, thereby improving the structural resistance against buckling.

To efficiently search the design space and identify the optimal configuration, this study employs the GWO algorithm, known for its robustness in handling discrete and nonlinear optimization problems. The algorithm dynamically balances global and local exploration capabilities, enabling it to effectively converge on the configuration that yields the highest critical buckling load.

12.5 Numerical results and discussion

To ensure the accuracy and reliability of the proposed buckling model used in the optimization of piezolaminated composite plates, it is essential to first perform a validation and convergence analysis of the results. For this purpose, a simply supported square piezolaminated composite plate composed of six layers and without stiffeners is analyzed under uniaxial compressive loading. Two different fiber orientation configurations are considered: [p/0/90/90/0/p] and [p/45/−45/−45/45/p]. In this configuration, the piezoelectric layers are placed on the top and bottom surfaces of the plate, each with a thickness of 0.1 h, while each elastic (composite) layer has a thickness of 0.2 h. The piezoelectric actuation voltage is set to zero (V_a=0) during this analysis. The material properties used for the simulations are provided in Table 12.1.

The nondimensional form of the critical buckling load is computed using the defined parameters, serving as the basis for assessing the performance of the buckling model. This preliminary step is crucial before proceeding with the optimization, as it confirms the convergence behavior and validity of the model in capturing the structural response of the composite plate under buckling conditions.

$$\overline{\mathrm{N}} = \frac{\mathrm{N_{cr}a^2}}{\mathrm{E_{2,Gr/Ep}h^3}} \tag{12.33}$$

As shown in Table 12.2, the current findings demonstrate a strong correlation with the results available in previous literature. In this comparison, both open-circuit and closed-circuit electrical boundary conditions for the piezoelectric actuators have been considered. According to the outcomes reported in studies [1–3,20], the variation in the critical

TABLE 12.1 The material parameters of composite and piezoelectric materials.

Properties	Graphite/Epoxy (Gr/Ep)	PZT-5A
Elastic properties		
E_{11} (GPa)	181	61
E_{12} (GPa)	10.3	61
G_{12} (GPa)	7.17	22.6
ν_{12}	0.28	0.35
Piezoelectric coefficients		
$d_{31} = d_{32}$(m/V)	-	-1.71e-10

TABLE 12.2 Comparison of the nondimensional critical buckling load for a piezolaminated plate (b/h=100, V_a =0).

	Lay-ups	$\bar{N}$
Ref. [1] (Elastic solution)	[p/0/90/90/0/p]	20.04
Ref. [1] (Closed-circuit)		20.06
Ref. [1] (Open-Circuit-C)		21.48
Ref. [1] (Open-Circuit-N)		22.26
Ref. [2] (Closed-circuit)		20.0201
Ref. [2] (Open-Circuit-C)		20.5530
Ref. [3] (Elastic solution)		20.0442
Ref. [3] (Closed-circuit)		20.0537
Ref. [3] (Open-Circuit-C)		21.8058
Ref. [3] (Open-Circuit-N)		22.3102
Ref. [20] (Elastic solution)		-
Ref. [20] (Closed-circuit)		20.0474
Ref. [20] (Open-Circuit-C)		21.7151
Ref. [20] (Open-Circuit-N)		-
Present study (Closed-circuit)		20.1021
Ref. [1] (Elastic solution)	[p/45/-45/-45/45/p]	24.59
Ref. [1] (Closed-circuit)		24.60
Ref. [1] (Open-Circuit-C)		25.92
Ref. [1] (Open-Circuit-N)		26.91
Present study (Closed-circuit)		25.3087

TABLE 12.3 Comparison of the nondimensional critical buckling load for a clamped square piezolaminated plate [p/0/90/90/0/p] (b/h=100, V_a =0).

	$\bar{N}$
Ref. [1] (Elastic solution)	59.80
Ref. [1] (Closed-circuit)	59.82
Ref. [1] (Open-Circuit-C)	59.82
Ref. [1] (Open-Circuit-N)	64.59
Present study (Closed-circuit)	62.119

TABLE 12.4 Comparison of optimum results for GWO and EGWO algorithms for 10-layered symmetric square piezolaminated plates with iso grid 1 for different boundary conditions.

Boundary condition	GWO		EGWO	
	Optimum stacking sequence	$\bar{N}$	Optimum stacking sequence	$\bar{N}$
SSSS	$[p/39/\text{-}40/\text{-}18/\text{-}6]_s$	59.0219	$[p/40/\text{-}45/\text{-}3/\text{-}4]_s$	59.1855
CCCC	$[p/3/\text{-}6/\text{-}5/4]_s$	161.771	$[p/2/0/1/5]_s$	162.222
CSCS	$[p/1/1/2/\text{-}3]_s$	138.3012	$[p/2/0/1/0]_s$	138.3478
CFCF	$[p/1/2/\text{-}2/9]_s$	119.086	$[p/0/0/0/0]_s$	120.1198
SFSF	$[p/1/2/\text{-}2/9]_s$	29.6645	$[p/0/0/0/0]_s$	29.8003
CFFF	$[p/5/6/5/\text{-}10]_s$	7.2711	$[p/0/1/4/3]_s$	7.4609

buckling load between these two electrical conditions is minimal. Based on this observation, the present investigation focuses solely on the closed-circuit condition for the sake of simplicity and consistency in the analysis.

Table 12.3 presents a comparison of the nondimensional critical buckling load for a clamped square six-layer piezoelectric laminated composite plate with the layup configuration [p/0/90/90/0/p], in the absence of stiffeners and subjected to uniaxial compressive loading (with V_a=0). As observed, the results exhibit strong consistency and agreement with the referenced studies, confirming the accuracy of the present analysis.

12.5.1 Optimal design problems

This optimization study begins by comparing the optimal outcomes obtained using the GWO and EGWO algorithms for 10-layer symmetric square piezolaminated plates with an iso grid 1 configuration under various boundary conditions (ϕ=0, V_a=100). The analysis considers six types of mixed boundary conditions: SSSS, CCCC, CSCS, CFCF, SFSF, and CFFF. As shown in Table 12.4, the EGWO algorithm consistently yields superior optimal results compared to the standard GWO algorithm. Furthermore, it is evident that the critical buckling load decreases significantly when free edge conditions are applied, whereas it increases under clamped mixed edge configurations. Fig. 12.2 illustrates the convergence behavior of both GWO and EGWO algorithms, highlighting the enhanced performance of EGWO in terms of convergence and optimal value.

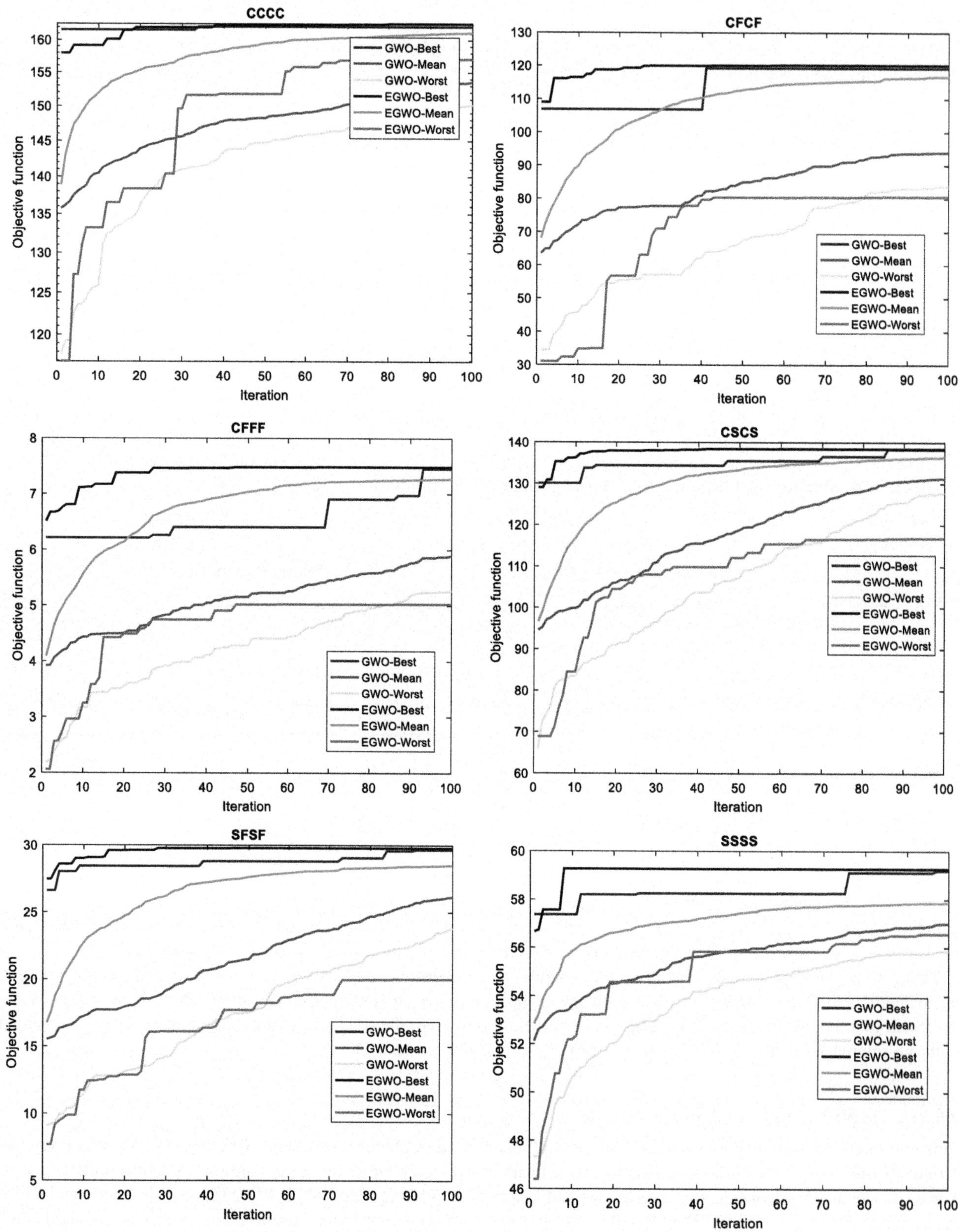

FIGURE 12.2 Convergence histories for GWO and EGWO algorithms (*EGWO*, enhanced grey wolf optimizer; *GWO*, grey wolf optimizer).

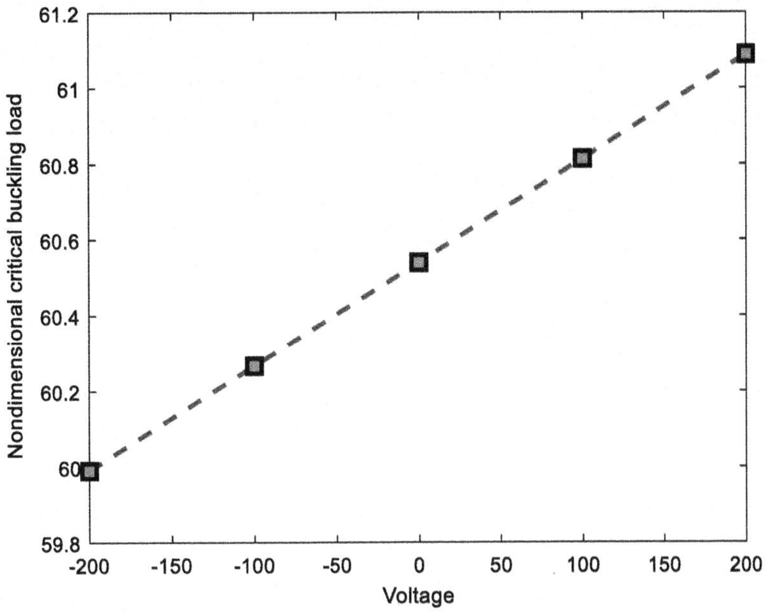

FIGURE 12.3 Effect of different voltages on the critical buckling load.

TABLE 12.5 Effect of different voltages on the optimum fiber orientations.

V_a	Optimum stacking sequence
-200	$[p/41/-42/-10/-3]_s$
-100	$[p/40/-40/-10/-4]_s$
0	$[p/45/-39/-10/-11]_s$
100	$[p/38/-40/-10/-5]_s$
200	$[p/41/-42/-9/-3]_s$

The influence of varying actuator voltages (V_a) on the optimal results is analyzed for a simply supported, 10-layer symmetric square piezolaminated plate featuring an iso grid 1 layout (ϕ=0). As illustrated in Fig. 12.3, the nondimensional critical buckling load shows an upward trend with increasing voltage. Specifically, applying a positive voltage to the PZT-5A actuator layers enhances the buckling load, while a negative voltage results in its reduction. However, according to the data in Table 12.5, voltage variations do not lead to significant changes in the optimal fiber orientation angles.

The effect of different plate aspect ratios (*a*/*b*) on the optimum results is studied for simply supported 10-layered symmetric piezolaminated plates with iso grid 2 (ϕ=0, V_a =-100). As seen from Fig. 12.4, the nondimensional critical buckling load diminishes as plate aspect ratio increases. But the effect of a larger a/b ratio can be negligible on the critical buckling load. However, as seen from Table 12.6, a different *a*/*b* ratio has a substantial effect on the optimum fiber orientations.

This study examines how different stiffener grid configurations affect the optimal results for simply supported, 10-layer symmetric square piezolaminated plates (ϕ=0, V_a=100). As presented in Table 12.7, the highest nondimensional critical buckling load is achieved with the orthotropic grid layout, attributed to the superior stiffness of its structural elements. Conversely, the piezolaminated plate lacking any grid structure exhibits the lowest critical buckling load among all configurations considered.

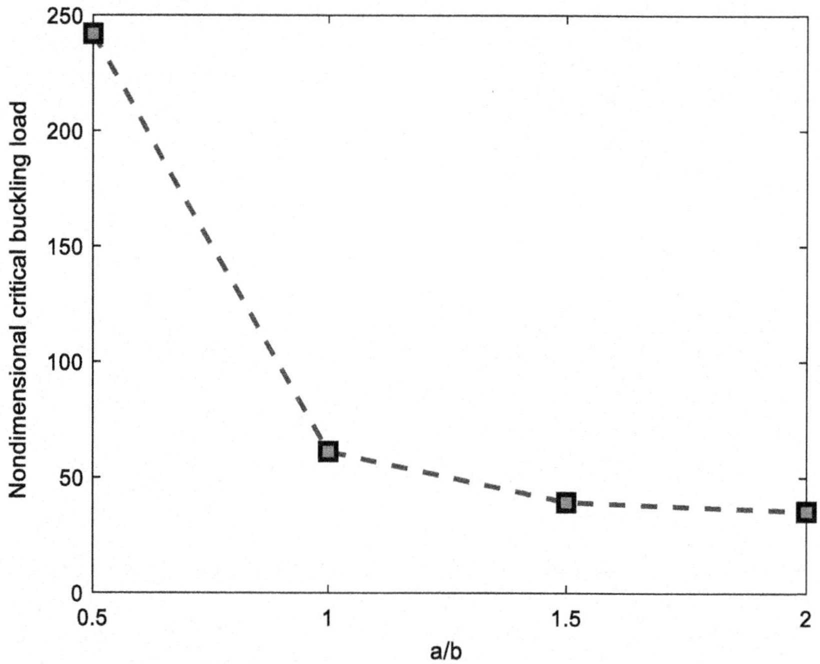

FIGURE 12.4 Effect of *a/b* ratio on the critical buckling load.

TABLE 12.6 Effect of *a*/*b* ratio on the optimum fiber orientations.

a/b	Optimum stacking sequence
0.5	$[p/51/-50/-11/2]_s$
1	$[p/40/-42/-25/-4]_s$
1.5	$[p/-15/17/6/2]_s$
2	$[p/0/0/0/0]_s$

TABLE 12.7 Effect of different grid shapes on the optimum results.

Grid shapes	Optimum stacking sequence	$\bar{N}$
Without grid	$[p/50/\ 68/\ 15/\ 10]_s$	57.2590
Angle grid	$[p/39/\ -40/\ -10/\ -3]_s$	59.0409
Iso grid 1	$[p/41/\ -42/\ -9/\ -3]_s$	59.2326
Iso grid 2	$[p/40/\ -45/\ -20/\ -3]_s$	59.1415
Ortho grid	$[p/42/\ -39/\ -10/\ -3]_s$	57.8787
Orthotropic grid	$[p/40/\ -40/\ -25/\ -1]_s$	60.2610

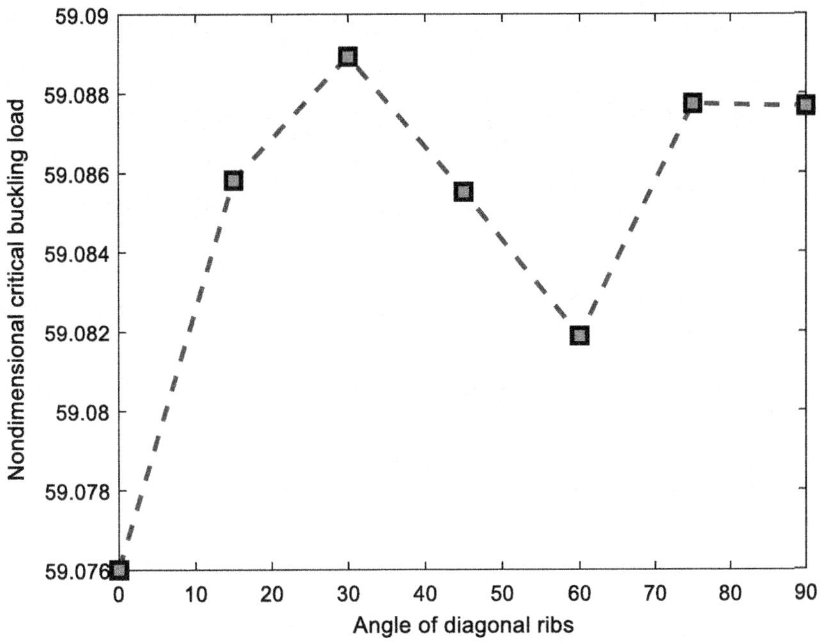

FIGURE 12.5 Effect of angle of diagonal ribs on the critical buckling load.

TABLE 12.8 Effect of angle of diagonal ribs on the optimum fiber orientations.

φ	Optimum stacking sequence
0	$[p/39/-42/-10/-1]_s$
15	$[p/40/-45/-8/-2]_s$
30	$[p/42/-41/-2/4]_s$
45	$[p/38/-42/-1/-4]_s$
60	$[p/38/-40/-6/1]_s$
75	$[p/42/-39/-5/-1]_s$
90	$[p/42/-40/-7/-4]_s$

Fig. 12.5 illustrates the influence of varying diagonal rib angles (φ) on the critical buckling load of simply supported, 10-layer symmetric square piezolaminated plates featuring an ortho grid configuration (V_a=−100). The results indicate that the highest nondimensional critical buckling load is achieved when the diagonal ribs are angled at 30°. However, as shown in Table 12.8, changes in the diagonal rib angle have minimal impact on the optimal fiber orientation angles within the laminate.

The results of this study also have practical implications for engineering applications. The optimized fiber orientations and grid stiffener layouts obtained here can serve as guidelines for designing lightweight, high-strength composite panels used in aerospace, marine, and civil structures. In manufacturing practice, such orientations may be achieved through automated fiber placement and modern lamination techniques, which allow precise control of stacking sequences. Moreover, the observed influence of applied voltages and plate aspect ratios provides useful insight for the design of smart structures, where active control of stiffness and stability is required. These findings indicate that the proposed optimization framework is not only of academic interest but can also be directly applied to real-world design and production of advanced piezo-composite systems.

12.6 Conclusions

This study focuses on the buckling load optimization of stiffened piezolaminated symmetric composite plates using the GWO algorithm. The primary objective is to maximize the critical buckling load by optimizing the fiber orientation angles across the laminate layers, with the CLPT incorporating von Karman nonlinearity employed for buckling analysis. The optimization is considering various boundary conditions, actuator voltages, stiffener grid shapes, diagonal rib angles, and plate aspect ratios. Numerical simulations are performed on 10-layer symmetric stiffened piezolaminated plates. To enhance optimization performance, an EGWO is introduced and compared against the standard GWO. Results show that the CCCC boundary condition yields the highest buckling load, while CFFF gives the lowest. Applying positive voltage enhances buckling resistance, although voltages do not significantly influence the optimum fiber orientations. Increased plate aspect ratios reduce the buckling load, but their effect becomes marginal at larger values; however, they do significantly affect fiber orientation. Among grid configurations, orthotropic grids lead to the highest buckling loads due to their stiffness. The highest buckling load is obtained when the diagonal ribs are angled at 30°, though this angle variation has little influence on fiber orientation. The EGWO algorithm outperforms the standard GWO in optimizing the stacking sequence. Although the current work demonstrates EGWO's robustness and efficiency, future research is suggested to apply this algorithm to more complex composite structures under real-world manufacturing constraints. Furthermore, EGWO can be hybridized with other metaheuristic techniques to enhance its performance.

Conflict of interest

The authors declare that there is no conflict of interest regarding the publication of this paper.

References

[1] G. Akhras, W. Li, Stability and free vibration analysis of thick piezoelectric composite plates using spline finite strip method, International Journal of Mechanical Sciences 53 (2011) 575–584. Available from https://doi.org/10.1016/j.ijmecsci.2011.05.004.

[2] R. Moradi-Dastjerdi, K. Behdinan, B. Safaei, Z. Qin, Buckling behavior of porous CNT-reinforced plates integrated between active piezoelectric layers, Engineering Structures 222 (2020) 111141. Available from https://doi.org/10.1016/j.engstruct.2020.111141.

[3] H. Tanzadeh, H. Amoushahi, Buckling and free vibration analysis of piezoelectric laminated composite plates using various plate deformation theories, European Journal of Mechanics - A/Solids 74 (2019) 242–256. Available from https://doi.org/10.1016/j.euromechsol.2018.11.013.

[4] G. Akhras, W. Li, Three-dimensional static, vibration and stability analysis of piezoelectric composite plates using a finite layer method, Smart Materials and Structures 16 (2007) 561. Available from https://doi.org/10.1088/0964-1726/16/3/002.

[5] G. Akhras, W. Li, Three-dimensional stability analysis of piezoelectric antisymmetric angle-ply laminates using finite layer method, Journal of Intelligent Material Systems and Structures 21 (2010) 719–727. Available from https://doi.org/10.1177/1045389X10364865.

[6] M. Bohlooly, B. Mirzavand, Closed form solutions for buckling and postbuckling analysis of imperfect laminated composite plates with piezoelectric actuators, Composites Part B: Engineering 72 (2015) 21–29. Available from https://doi.org/10.1016/j.compositesb.2014.10.049.

[7] M. Bohlooly, K.M. Fard, Buckling and postbuckling of concentrically stiffened piezo-composite plates on elastic foundations, Journal of Applied and Computational Mechanics 5 (2019) 128–140. Available from https://doi.org/10.22055/jacm.2018.25539.1277.

[8] M. Bohlooly, B. Mirzavand, Postbuckling and deflection response of imperfect piezo-composite plates resting on elastic foundations under in-plane and lateral compression and electro-thermal loading, Mechanics of Advanced Materials and Structures 25 (2018) 192–201. Available from https://doi.org/10.1080/15376494.2016.1255818.

[9] M. Shariyat, Dynamic buckling of imperfect laminated plates with piezoelectric sensors and actuators subjected to thermo-electro-mechanical loadings, considering the temperature-dependency of the material properties, Composite Structures 88 (2009) 228–239. Available from https://doi.org/10.1016/j.compstruct.2008.03.044.

[10] J. Li, F. Li, Y. Narita, Active control of thermal buckling and vibration for a sandwich composite laminated plate with piezoelectric fiber-reinforced composite actuator facesheets, Journal of Sandwich Structures and Materials 21 (2019) 2563–2581. Available from https://doi.org/10.1177/1099636218783168.

[11] Q. Jin, L. Leng, S. Yang, Buckling analysis of composite plates surface bonded with graphene-reinforced piezoelectric actuators, Polymer Composites (2023) 1–17. Available from https://doi.org/10.1002/pc.27890.

[12] I. Oh, J. Han, I. Lee, Postbuckling and vibration characteristics of piezolaminated composite plate subject to thermo-piezoelectric loads, Journal of Sound and Vibration 233 (2000) 19–40. Available from https://doi.org/10.1006/jsvi.1999.2788.

[13] H.S. Shen, Thermal postbuckling of shear-deformable laminated plates with piezoelectric actuators, Composites Science and Technology 61 (2001) 1931–1943. Available from https://doi.org/10.1016/S0266-3538(01)00099-9.

[14] H.S. Shen, Postbuckling of shear deformable laminated plates with piezoelectric actuators under complex loading conditions, International Journal of Solids and Structures 38 (2001) 7703–7721. Available from https://doi.org/10.1016/S0020-7683(01)00120-2.

[15] D. Varelis, D.A. Saravanos, Nonlinear coupling mechanics and initial buckling of composite plates with piezoelectric actuators and sensors, Smart Materials and Structures 11 (2002) 330–336. Available from https://doi.org/10.1088/0964-1726/11/3/302.

[16] S. Kapuria, G.G.S. Achary, Exact 3D piezothermoelasticity solution for buckling of hybrid cross-ply plates using state space approach, ZAMM – Zeitschrift für Angewandte Mathematik und Mechanik 85 (2005) 189–201. Available from https://doi.org/10.1002/zamm.200310172.

[17] M. Bohlooly, B. Mirzavand, A closed-form solution for thermal buckling of cross-ply piezolaminated plates, International Journal of Structural Stability and Dynamics 16 (2016) 1450112. Available from https://doi.org/10.1142/S0219455414501120.

[18] G. Akhras, W.C. Li, Three-dimensional thermal buckling analysis of piezoelectric antisymmetric angle-ply laminates using finite layer method, Composite Structures 92 (2010) 31–38. Available from https://doi.org/10.1016/j.compstruct.2009.06.010.

[19] B. Mirzavand, M. Bohlooly, Thermal buckling of piezolaminated plates subjected to different loading conditions, Journal of Thermal Stresses 38 (2015) 1140–1164. Available from https://doi.org/10.1080/01495739.2015.1073506.

[20] D. Panahandeh-Shahraki, H.R. Mirdamadi, O. Vaseghi, Fully coupled electromechanical buckling analysis of active laminated composite plates considering stored voltage in actuators, Composite Structures 118 (2014) 94–105. Available from https://doi.org/10.1016/j.compstruct.2014.07.008118.

[21] V.M.F. Correia, J.F.A. Madeira, A.L. Araújo, C.M.M. Soares, Multiobjective design optimization of laminated composite plates with piezoelectric layers, Composite Structures 169 (2017) 10–20. Available from https://doi.org/10.1016/j.compstruct.2016.09.052.

[22] Y. Xue, Y. Zhang, J. Li, Optimization of thermal buckling control for composite laminates with PFRC actuators using trigonometric shear deformation theory, Journal of Mechanical Science and Technology 35 (2021) 257–266. Available from https://doi.org/10.1007/s12206-020-1225-x.

[23] V.M.F. Correia, C.M.M. Soares, C.A.M. Soares, Buckling optimization of composite laminated adaptive structures, Composite Structures 62 (2003) 315–321. Available from https://doi.org/10.1016/j.compstruct.2003.09.030.

[24] Q. Gao, Z. Ding, W.H. Liao, Effective elastic properties of irregular auxetic structures, Composite Structures 287 (2022) 115269. Available from https://doi.org/10.1016/j.compstruct.2022.115269.

[25] K. Liu, S. Zong, Y. Li, Z. Wang, Z. Hu, Z. Wang, Structural response of the U-type corrugated core sandwich panel used in ship structures under the lateral quasi-static compression load, Marine Structures 84 (2022) 103198. Available from https://doi.org/10.1016/j.marstruc.2022.103198.

[26] H. Huang, M. Gou, W. Zhang, J. Zeng, K. Yang, H. Bai, Numerical investigation on the bearing capacity of RC columns strengthened by HPFL-BSP under combined loadings, Journal of Building Engineering 39 (2021) 102266. Available from https://doi.org/10.1016/j.jobe.2021.102266.

[27] M. Guo, H. Huang, W. Zhang, C. Xue, M. Huang, Assessment of RC frame capacity subjected to a loss of corner column, Journal of Structural Engineering 148 (2022) 4022122. Available from https://doi.org/10.1061/(ASCE)ST.1943-541X.0003423.

[28] H. Huang, M. Huang, W. Zhang, S. Pospisil, T. Wu, Experimental investigation on rehabilitation of corroded RC columns with BSP and HPFL under combined loadings, Journal of Structural Engineering 146 (2020) 4020157. Available from https://doi.org/10.1061/(ASCE)ST.1943-541X.0002725.

[29] V. Goodarzimehr, U. Topal, A.K. Das, T. Vo-Duy, SABO algorithm for optimum design of truss structures with multiple frequency constraints, Mechanics Based Design of Structures and Machines 52 (2024) 7745–7777. Available from https://doi.org/10.1080/15397734.2024.2308652.

[30] V. Goodarzimehr, U. Topal, M. Bohlooly, A novel approach for buckling optimization of stiffened piezolaminated composite plates, Journal of Composite Materials 58 (2024) 2975–2991. Available from https://doi.org/10.1177/00219983241288569.

[31] V. Goodarzimehr, U. Topal, M. Bohlooly, Optimal frequency of stiffened piezolaminated composite plates implementing a hybrid special relativity search and hill climbing optimization algorithm, Journal of Applied and Computational Mechanics (2025) 1–17. Available from https://doi.org/10.22055/jacm.2024.47914.4837.

[32] S. Mirjalili, S.M. Mirjalili, A. Lewis, Grey wolf optimizer, Advances in Engineering Software 69 (2014) 46–61. Available from https://doi.org/10.1016/j.advengsoft.2013.12.007.

[33] X.-S. Yang, S. Deb, Engineering optimisation by Cuckoo search, International Journal of Mathematical Modelling and Numerical Optimisation 1 (4) (2010) 330–343. Available from https://doi.org/10.48550/arXiv.1005.2908.

[34] L. Krivodonova, Limiters for high-order discontinuous Galerkin methods, Journal of Computational Physics 226 (1) (2007) 879–896. Available from https://doi.org/10.1016/j.jcp.2007.05.011.

Chapter 13

Efficient application mapping onto three-dimensional network-on-chips using the grey wolf optimizer

Maamar Bougherara[1,2], Imane Yeddou[2], and Rafik Amara[2,3]
[1]*LIM Laboratory, Faculty of Exact Science, Akli Mohand Oulhadj University, Bouira, Algeria,* [2]*Department of Computer Science, École Normale Supérieure, Kouba, Algiers, Algeria,* [3]*LTIR Laboratory, Faculty of Electronics and Computational Science, USTHB University, Algiers, Algeria*

13.1 Introduction

As the demand for high-performance computing systems continues to grow, network-on-chip (NoC) architectures have emerged as a promising solution to address communication bottlenecks in complex system-on-chip (SoC) designs [1]. Similar in concept to traditional computer networks, a NoC provides scalable and structured communication among multiple processing elements. However, due to stringent constraints in area, power, and performance, NoC designs must be carefully optimized to meet the specific requirements of their target applications.

In NoC-based systems, applications are typically divided into several computational tasks, each encapsulated in an intellectual property (IP) block. These IPs must be integrated into the NoC infrastructure in a manner that maximizes performance while minimizing energy consumption and latency [2].

A typical NoC consists of four key components [3] IP cores, which include processors, memory units, and custom controllers, network interfaces (NIs), which serve as a bridge between the IP cores and the NoC communication fabric; routers, which handle packet forwarding and arbitration; and physical interconnects, which define the paths for data transmission.

The topology of a NoC determines how tiles are connected [4]. Among the available configurations, the 2D mesh topology is the most widely adopted due to its regular structure, simplicity, and scalability. Fig. 13.1 illustrate example of 2D mesh NoCs.

With the increasing complexity and integration density of modern SoCs, 2D NoC architectures face growing limitations in terms of bandwidth, latency, and energy efficiency. To address these challenges, three-dimensional (3D) NoC architectures have been proposed [2].

By vertically stacking multiple 2D layers and employing through-silicon via (TSV) technology [2], 3D NoCs significantly reduce the average communication distance, enhance bandwidth, and improve performance.

In a 3D mesh topology, each router connects to up to six neighboring routers [5]: four in the same layer and two in adjacent vertical layers. This configuration enables both intralayer and inter-layer communication, leading to better parallelism, reduced latency, and higher throughput. Fig. 13.2 illustrates a 3D NoC example composed of 27 interconnected tiles.

The design of a NoC-based system generally follows three main stages as presented in Fig. 13.3 [6]: Task Assignment, which involves assigning application tasks to a predefined library of IP blocks, IP Mapping, where these IP blocks are mapped to physical nodes (routers) within the NoC, and Static Routing, which determines the communication paths between the mapped IPs.

Each of these stages is supported by electronic design automation tools, which explore the design space to generate optimized hardware/software configurations. Fig. 13.3 illustrates a standard embedded system design flow for NoC platforms. Characteristics and challenges of 2D NoCs [7].

Grey Wolf Optimizer. DOI: https://doi.org/10.1016/B978-0-443-36624-6.00018-4

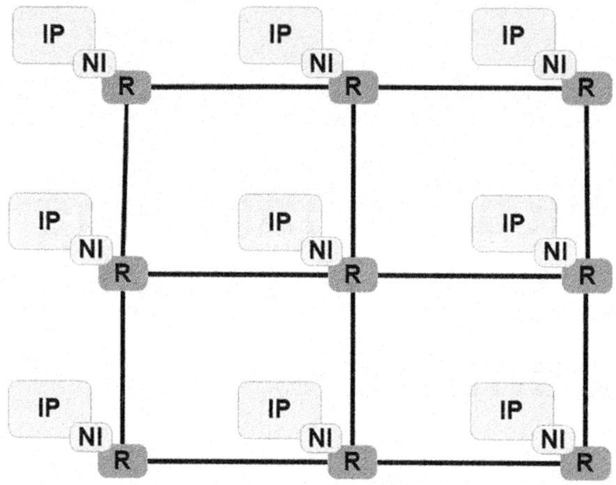

FIGURE 13.1 2D mesh-based NoC (*NoC*, Network-on-chip).

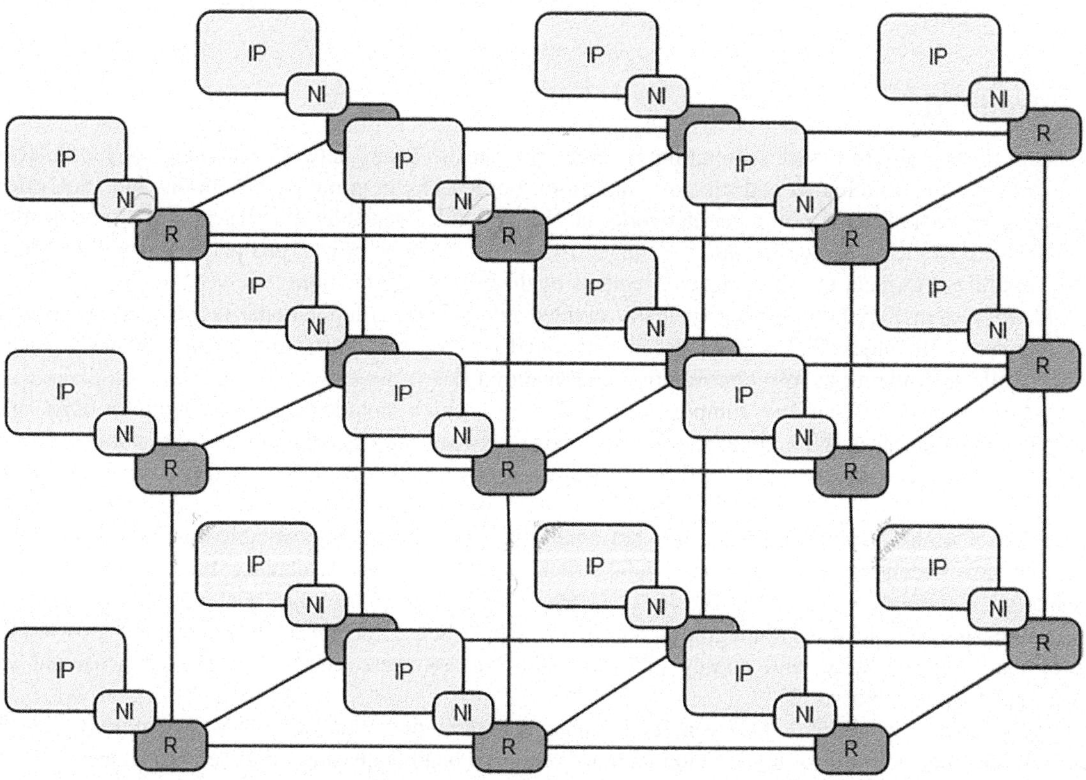

FIGURE 13.2 2D mesh-based NoC (*NoC*, Network-on-chip).

This paper introduces a novel model for solving the IP mapping problem in both 2D and 3D NoCs. After modeling the problem, defining the main objective of the study, and formulating the cost function, the grey wolf optimization (GWO) is employed for the first time as a new method to address the application mapping problem.

The structure of this paper is as follows: Section 13.2 introduces the NoC topology and formulates the mapping problem. Section 13.3 provides a review of prior research related to mapping in NoC architectures. In Section 13.4, we present the modeling of the mapping problem prior to applying a metaheuristic approach. The GWO algorithm, used as the

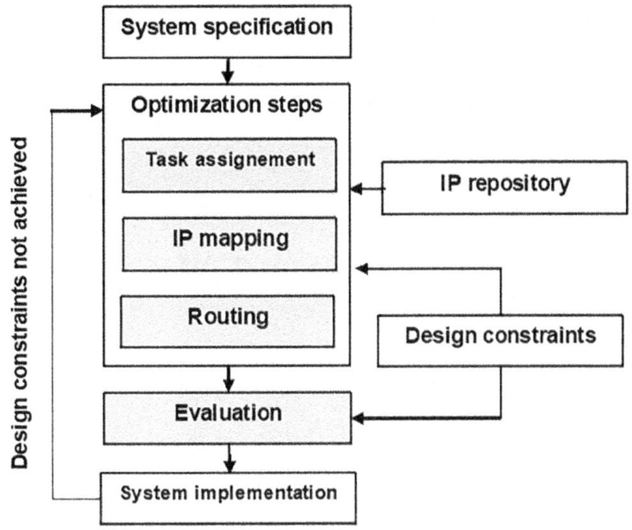

FIGURE 13.3 Typical embedded system design flow for a NoC platform (*NoC*, Network-on-chip).

core mapping strategy, is described in Section 13.5. Section 13.6 analyzes the results obtained from the simulation experiments. Finally, Section 13.7 presents the conclusion of the study along with directions for future work.

13.2 Network topology and mapping problem

In conventional 2D NoCs, each IP is connected to a router via a network interface, and these routers are arranged in a planar grid with wired links. Communication takes place using packet-switched data transfer, where messages are broken into packets and routed through the NoC [7]. Compared to traditional bus-based systems, 2D NoCs offer several advantages: higher communication bandwidth, reduced latency, improved scalability, and lower power consumption [8].

However, as more IPs are integrated into a single chip, the average number of hops (routers traversed by a packet) increases, leading to greater communication energy and degraded performance. This issue becomes increasingly problematic as system size grows [9]. The 3D NoC paradigm addresses these issues by enabling vertical communication through TSVs. This approach reduces the average hop count and significantly lowers latency and energy consumption. Additionally, it enhances area utilization, making it suitable for large-scale multicore systems.

Consequently, 3D NoCs have gained significant interest in both academia and industry as a compelling solution for future high-performance computing platforms.

This work focuses on optimizing the mapping phases of NoC design, aiming to minimize communication energy while maintaining high system performance. Fig. 13.4 illustrates the mapping problem in 2D NoC.

In a 3D NoC, the IP mapping problem consists of assigning each IP core to a specific node within the 3D topology. This phase is critical, as efficient mapping can greatly reduce communication cost, energy usage, and latency [10].

Due to its combinatorial nature, the IP mapping problem is considered NP-hard and is closely related to the quadratic assignment problem. This complexity makes exact solutions impractical for large systems, especially within limited design time.

As 3D NoCs enable the integration of a greater number of IPs across multiple layers using TSVs, efficient and scalable mapping algorithms are becoming increasingly important. To this end, heuristic and metaheuristic approaches offer a viable alternative, providing near-optimal solutions within reasonable time frames. For example, if we have m tasks to map into a NoC of n cores where $(m <= n)$, the number of possible solutions is up to $n!/(n-m)!$.

13.3 Related work

Several approaches have been proposed for mapping in NoCs. These mapping techniques can be classified into three principal categories: exact approaches and heuristic (or approximate) techniques [11]. We show in this paper the most cited who take into account a single objective. Exact mapping methods, such as exhaustive search, linear programming,

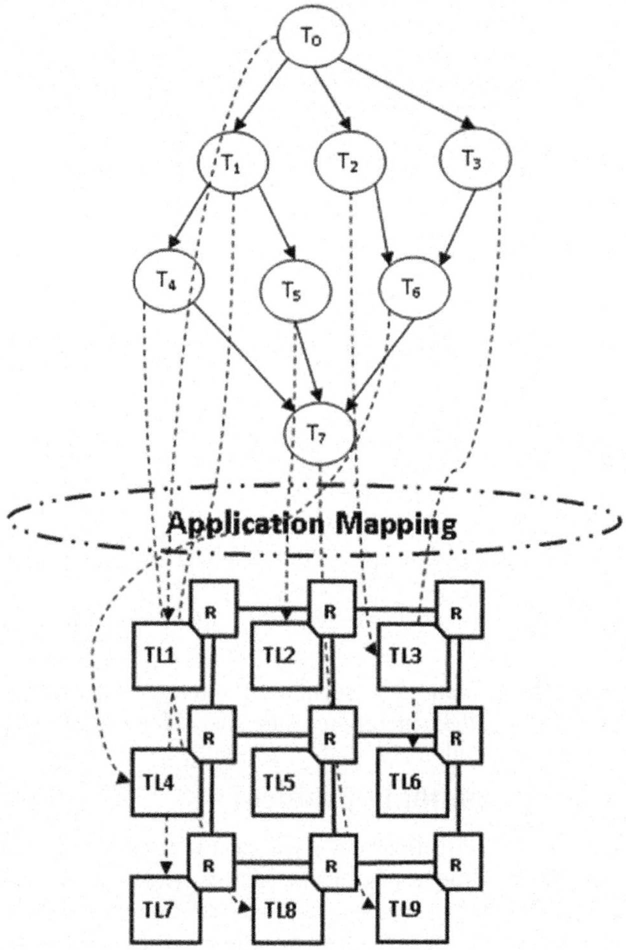

FIGURE 13.4 Application mapping problem.

and branch-and-bound algorithms, rely on mathematical rigor to guarantee globally optimal solutions. An integer linear programming (ILP) formulation for the IP mapping problem is presented in Ref. [12]. This approach models both objectives and constraints as linear functions, with the additional requirement that decision variables take integer values. The ILP model is solved using the FICO Xpress Optimization tool, enabling precise solution computation within a mathematically defined space. Similarly, in Ref. [12], a branch-and-bound heuristic for the same problem is introduced. This method constructs a search tree representing all possible mappings and applies bounding functions to eliminate suboptimal branches early. By pruning large portions of the solution space, the algorithm improves efficiency while still ensuring optimality.

Despite their accuracy, exact methods suffer from high computational complexity and significant runtime requirements. As a result, they are typically feasible only for small-scale mapping scenarios involving a limited number of IP cores, where the size of the solution space remains manageable under current computing capabilities.

The second category encompasses heuristic-based approaches, which aim to provide efficient and practical solutions to the application mapping problem on NoC architectures. The network mapping (NMAP) algorithm [13] is a widely used heuristic that maps application cores to tiles iteratively. At each step, a core is selected and assigned to a tile, repeating the process until all cores are mapped. While NMAP includes an iterative improvement mechanism, the quality of the final solutions often remains constrained by the initial mapping. Binomial mapping (BMAP) [14] introduces a binomial mapping approach based on iterative two-way merging, taking into account the traffic load between cores to optimize communication. CastNet [15] enhances solution diversity by leveraging the symmetric characteristics of mesh topologies. It selects multiple initial tiles and generates several mapping options, ultimately choosing the best one based on the number of free neighboring tiles for each core. Chain mapping (CHMAP) [16] calculates a priority value for each core based on its communication requirements and its position within a communication spanning tree. The algorithm then determines the mapping order and assigns cores to appropriate tiles according to these computed priorities. Onyx [17], proposed in 2009, introduces a lozenge-shaped mapping path and defines four movement patterns to assign priorities to tiles. This method has shown improved communication cost compared to earlier heuristics. Spiral [18] starts by mapping the highest-priority task at the center of the mesh, then progressively maps the remaining tasks outward in a spiral pattern from already-mapped cores. To address hierarchical communication, Joseph et al. [19] proposed V-CastNet3D, a clustering-based mapping algorithm. Cores are grouped into clusters to reduce inter-cluster communication, and the CastNet heuristic is then applied within each cluster for mapping onto a 2D NoC mesh. Furthermore, CastNet3D [20], also proposed by Joseph et al., extends this approach to 3D NoC architectures by optimizing the utilization of vertical links, thereby improving communication efficiency and reducing energy consumption.

Given the high computational cost of exact methods and the limitations of current processing capabilities, metaheuristic techniques have emerged as practical and scalable alternatives for solving the IP mapping problem in NoC architectures. Drawing inspiration from natural and biological phenomena, these approaches aim to efficiently explore large solution spaces and produce near-optimal solutions within a reasonable computational time.

In the context of 2D NoC architectures, several metaheuristic techniques have been proposed: In Ref. [21], communication graph mapping (CGMAP), a genetic algorithm-based approach, replaces the traditional random initialization with a chaotic mapping operator, enhancing the exploration capabilities of the algorithm. Graph-based mapping (GBMAP) [22] employs an evolutionary algorithm to efficiently map processing cores onto NoC tiles. Swarm intelligence-based approaches have also been explored. For example, a discrete multi-objective Particle swarm optimization (PSO) method is proposed in [23], utilizing deterministic initial solutions to improve performance. In Ref. [24], a hybrid approach combining PSO and genetic algorithms further enhances solution quality. Ant colony optimization (ACO) algorithm is used to minimize bandwidth requirements, while a hybrid ACO-GA method is proposed in [25] to reduce communication costs. An artificial bee colony (ABC) algorithm is presented, where genetic operators are introduced with ABC in Ref. [26] to improve the communication-aware mapping efficiency. Cat swarm optimization [27] is applied to map IPs onto 2D NoCs with notable results. Differential evolution (DE) is employed in [28] to address communication cost optimization in 2D NoC mapping problems.

While these techniques are primarily applied to 2D NoCs, recent research has extended metaheuristic strategies to 3D NoC architectures. In Ref. [29], a PSO-based algorithm is developed for mapping IPs onto a partially vertically connected 3D mesh NoC. An ABC-based method for 3D NoC mapping is introduced in Ref. [30], demonstrating improved results in communication optimization. A thermal-aware mapping technique is proposed in Ref. [31], which integrates genetic algorithms with fuzzy logic to minimize the peak temperature in 3D NoC systems. Finally, in [32], simulated annealing is employed to enhance communication efficiency in 3D NoC mappings.

13.4 Modeling mapping problem

In the context of IP mapping for NoC, the application is typically modeled as an IP core graph, while the NoC infrastructure is represented as a topology graph. The IP mapping problem as presented in Fig. 13.4 consists of assigning logical IP cores defined by specific communication relationships and bandwidth demands within the IP core graph to physical resource nodes in the NoC topology graph [7].

1. IP core graph: The IP core graph is a high-level abstraction that represents the behavior of the application. It is denoted as a directed graph $G(C, A)$, where: C is the set of nodes, each node $c_i \in C$ representing an IP core, and A is the set of directed edges, where each edge $a_{i,j} \in A$ represents communication from IP source core c_j to destination core c_i [27]. Each edge $a_{i,j} \in A$ is associated with a weight $w_{i,j}$, which denotes the bandwidth requirement between the IPs c_i and c_j
2. NoC topology graph: Similarly to the IP core, the NoC topology is abstracted as a directed graph $T(R, L)$, where: R is the set of nodes, with each node $r_k \in R$ representing a tile in the NoC. L is the set of directed edges, where each edge $l_{k,l} \in L$ represents a physical communication link between tiles r_k and r_l [24].
3. Mapping function in NoC: The mapping function defines the mapping of IP cores from the IP core graph$G(C, A)$ to nodes in the NoC topology graph $T(R, L)$, with the objective of minimizing communication energy [24]. For each IP core $c_i \in C$, there exists a corresponding node $r_k \in R$ in the NoC topology such that:

$$map: V \rightarrow T \;\; map(c_i = r_k), \forall\, c_i \in C \;\; \exists\, r_j \in R$$

Furthermore, each IP core must be mapped to a unique node, ensuring that for any two distinct IPs c_i and c_j: $map(c_i) \neq map(c_j)$To satisfy this constraint, the number of nodes in the NoC topology graph must be greater than or equal to the number of nodes in the IP core graph. If necessary, dummy nodes can be added to the IP core graph to equalize the sizes of both graphs [26]. These dummy nodes are noncommunicating placeholders and do not participate in any data exchanges.

4. Solution représentation: The mapping solution is represented as a sequence with a permutation of the integers from 1 to n, where n is the number of nodes in the NoC topology graph [27]. Each position in the sequence corresponds to a node in the NoC topology. The value at that position indicates the ID of the IP core assigned to that node. An example of a mapping solution is illustrated in (Tables 13.1 and 13.2).
5. Communication cost: The objective function in this paper is to reduce communication cost. This work aims to minimize the number of hops for each communication when two tasks are mapped onto the NoC. The total communication cost is calculated using the following equation [32]

$$commcost = \sum_i \sum_j w_{i,j} * nbhops(r_k, r_l), \tag{13.1}$$

where $c_i = source$, $c_j = distination$, $map(c_i) = r_k$, $map(c_j) = r_l$, $c_i \neq c_j$ and $r_k \neq r_l$ $nbhops(.)$ is the number of hops between the source and destination, calculated using the Manhattan distance, defined by the following function:

$$Hops(r_k, r_l) = |X_k - X_l| + |Y_k - Y_l| + |Z_k - Z_l| \tag{13.2}$$

where (X_k, Y_k, Z_k) and (X_l, Y_l, Z_l) are the coordinates of the nodes r_k and r_l on a 3D mesh NoC, respectively. In the case of a 2D mesh NoC, Z_k and Z_l are equal to 0.

TABLE 13.1 Solution example.

Core number	1	2	3	4	5	6	7	8	9
Node place	8	3	2	1	9	5	6	7	4

TABLE 13.2 Parameters of benchmarks used.

Benchemark ID	Task numbers	Edge number
VOPD	16	21
MPEG4	12	13
PIP	8	8
MWD	12	12
TG0	12	13
TG1	16	16
TG2	27	27
TG3	30	34
TG4	50	59
TG5	62	70

13.5 Mapping with grey wolf optimization

13.5.1 Grey wolves in nature

Wolves are powerful predators at the top of the food chain. Among them, the gray wolf (Canis lupus) is the most widespread species in the Northern Hemisphere (Alaska, Canada, etc.). They live and hunt in packs of 1–12 individuals, communicate through howling, and typically prey on large animals, although they can also feed on birds, fish, or snakes [33].

Wolf packs follow a strict and well-defined social hierarchy as presented in Fig. 13.5, with each member playing a specific role that contributes to the cohesion and survival of the group [34].

1. Alpha (α): The alpha pair, consisting of the dominant male and female, are typically the only ones who reproduce within the pack. They make major decisions regarding hunting, movement, and territorial defense. Interestingly, the alpha is not necessarily the strongest physically but rather the most capable leader and organizer.
2. Beta (β): The beta, either male or female, is the second-in-command and acts as an advisor to the alpha. They assist in decision-making and group management and may assume leadership if the alpha is absent or dies. The beta commands respect from lower-ranking members and reinforces the alpha authority while also providing upward feedback.
3. Delta (δ): This rank includes various essential roles for the pack's survival [34]:
   - Scouts: Monitor territory boundaries and alert the group to potential threats.
   - Guardians: Responsible for the safety and protection of the pack.
   - Elders: Experienced wolves who were formerly alphas or betas.
   - Hunters: Support alphas and betas in catching prey to feed the group.
   - Caretakers: Tend to the weak, sick, or injured members of the pack.
4. Omega (ω): At the lowest level of the hierarchy, the omega plays a surprisingly vital role. Often serving as a scapegoat, the omega absorbs the tension and aggression of higher-ranking wolves, helping maintain harmony and preventing conflicts. Despite its subordinate status, the absence of an omega can lead to increased stress and instability within the pack.

Wolves are also known for their strong sense of family loyalty. Adult offspring care for their aging parents, and mated pairs form deeply bonded partnerships. In some cases, wolves have been observed to pine or die after losing their mate.

13.5.2 Grey wolves optimization modelization

The social hierarchy and hunting strategies of gray wolves have inspired the development of the GWO algorithm. Proposed in 2014 by Seyedali Mirjalili, Seyed Mohammad Mirjalili, and Andrew Lewis, this algorithm simulates the wolves' social structure and cooperative hunting behavior to solve complex optimization problems by mimicking their hierarchical organization and decision-making processes [35].

The social hierarchy in the GWO algorithm is structured into distinct ranks:

1. Alpha (α): The leader, representing the best solution.
2. Beta (β) and Delta (δ): Second and third best solutions, supporting the alpha.
3. Omega (ω): The rest of the population, considered as candidate solutions.

13.5.3 Hunting behavior simulation

In addition to the social hierarchy of wolves, group hunting is another fascinating behavior. The hunting process follows the main stages outlined below [36]:

- Surrounding the prey and harassing it until it stops moving.

FIGURE 13.5 Gray wolf social hierarchy.

- Chasing the prey, tracking it, and getting closer.
- Attacking the prey.

Hierarchy: In simulating this behavior within the optimization algorithm, the exact optimal solution (prey) is unknown. Therefore, the best solution identified so far is labeled as alpha (α), with the second and third best as beta (β) and delta (δ), respectively. The rest of the wolves adjust their positions based onno these three leading candidates [33].

Encircling the prey: For this stage of the hunting process, the following equation is proposed:

$$D = |C.\ X_p(t) - X(t)| \tag{13.3}$$

$$X(t+1)=X_p(t) - A.\ D \tag{13.4}$$

where: t refers to the current iteration, A and C are scalar coefficients calculated as follows:

$$A=2.\ a.\ r_1 - a \tag{13.5}$$

$$C=2.\ r_2 \tag{13.6}$$

where a is a scaling value that decreases from 2 to − 2 across iterations according to the following equation:

$$a=2 - \frac{2.\ t}{max_{iter}}, \tag{13.7}$$

r_1 and r_2 are random values in the range [0,1], X_p is the position vector of the prey, and X is the position vector of the wolf.

Hunting: In NP-complex type problems, the optimal solution is unknown. Therefore it is suggested that the best three solutions obtained in the iteration be considered as β, α, and σ, respectively. These solutions are retained, and the rest of the wolves are required to update their positions based on the best solutions [34]. In this regard, the following formulas are proposed:

$$X(t+1)=\frac{X_1 + X_2 + X_3}{3} \tag{13.8}$$

$$X_1 = X_\alpha(t) - A_1.\ D_\alpha \tag{13.9}$$

$$X_2 = X_\beta(t).\ -A_2.\ D_\beta \tag{13.10}$$

$$X_3 = X_\gamma(t).\ -A_3.\ D_\gamma \tag{13.11}$$

The values of the distances D_α, D_β, and D_γ are derived from Eq. 13.3.

Attacking the prey: In the hunting step, the parameter a is gradually decreased to simulate the wolves' convergence behavior. This reduction affects the coefficient A, which varies within the interval [-a,a]. When A falls within the range [-1,1], the wolves tend to move closer to the prey, emphasizing exploitation. Conversely, when A lies outside this range, the wolves explore more distant regions of the search space, thus maintaining diversity in the optimization process [35].

13.5.4 Grey wolf optimization algorithm

(Algorithm 13.1)

13.5.5 improved grey wolves

To improve the quality and robustness of the optimization results, we propose two key modifications to the standard GWO algorithm. These modifications aim to enhance both the convergence behavior and the exploration capacity of the algorithm [37].

1. The first modification concerns the computation of the coefficients $\vec{A}$ and $\vec{C}$. In the standard GWO, these coefficients are computed three times using distinct pairs ($\vec{A}\ i$, $\vec{C}i$), one for each leader. In our enhanced version, we constrain the algorithm to compute only a single pair of coefficients $\vec{A}$ and $\vec{C}$, using the same random values for all three leaders: $X\alpha$, $X\beta$, and X_δ. This simplification aims to reduce computational overhead while preserving the core mechanics of the algorithm.

   Eqs. 13.9, 13.10, and 13.11 are replaced by Eq. 13.12, which is applied three times for $i = \alpha$, β, and γ.

$$X_i = X_{rand}(t) - A_1.\ D_{rand} \tag{13.12}$$

ALGORITHM 13.1 The main steps of GWO algorithm.

generate the population of the wolves
evaluate the wolves with the objective function
initialize the wolves' alpha (X_α), (X_β), and (X_δ)
t←0
while t < max of iteration **do**
for each wolves *i* **do**
Compute parameters *a* using Eq. 13.11
generate X_1, X_2 and X_3 using Eqs. 13.9 and 13.10
Update the position of each wolf X_i using Eq. 13.8
evaluate the wolves with the objective function
end for
Update the wolves (X_α), (X_β), and (X_δ)
t←t+1
end while
return the best solution

This modification introduces a stochastic component based on a randomly selected solution, thereby enhancing the exploration ability of the algorithm and reducing the risk of premature convergence. We refer to this improved version as improved grey wolf optimizer.

2. The second modification is inspired by Tabu Search principles and aims to prevent stagnation in the optimization process. Instead of consistently selecting the alpha, beta, and delta wolves based on fitness ranking, we randomly choose three individuals from the population to temporarily serve as leaders. This stochastic leadership strategy, guided by Tabu Search logic, introduces diversity into the decision-making process and promotes the exploration of new regions in the search space, thereby helping the algorithm escape local optima. In this work, this strategy is activated when the best solution does not improve over 50 consecutive iterations, indicating potential convergence to a local optimum. The algorithm is called grey wolf optimisation with tabu search (GWOTAB).

13.6 Experiment result

To evaluate the performance of a NoC architecture, a variety of benchmarks are commonly utilized [17]. A benchmark typically consists of a set of interdependent tasks that emulate real application workloads. These tasks represent computational elements and the communication between them, allowing designers to evaluate architectural aspects such as energy efficiency and communication cost.

In this study, two main categories of benchmarks are considered:

1. Real-world benchmarks:

These benchmarks are derived from actual multimedia applications and are frequently used for evaluating the performance of NoC architectures. Fig. 13.6 illustrates four widely adopted benchmarks.

2. Synthetic benchmarks

These are automatically generated using the task graphs for free tool [38], which allows the creation of a large variety of task graphs with controlled properties such as task count, communication volume, and execution time. Synthetic benchmarks are particularly useful for exploring the performance of NoC architectures under diverse scenarios.

The detailed characteristics of all benchmarks used in this study are presented in Table 13.2.

13.6.1 Setting

Before presenting the experimental results, we first detail the configuration parameters used in our study. For the real-world benchmarks, namely Video Object Plane Decoder, Moving Picture Experts Group, and Multi-Window Display, the applications were mapped onto a 4x4 2D NoC and a 2x4x2 3D NoC architecture. The PIP benchmark, characterized by a

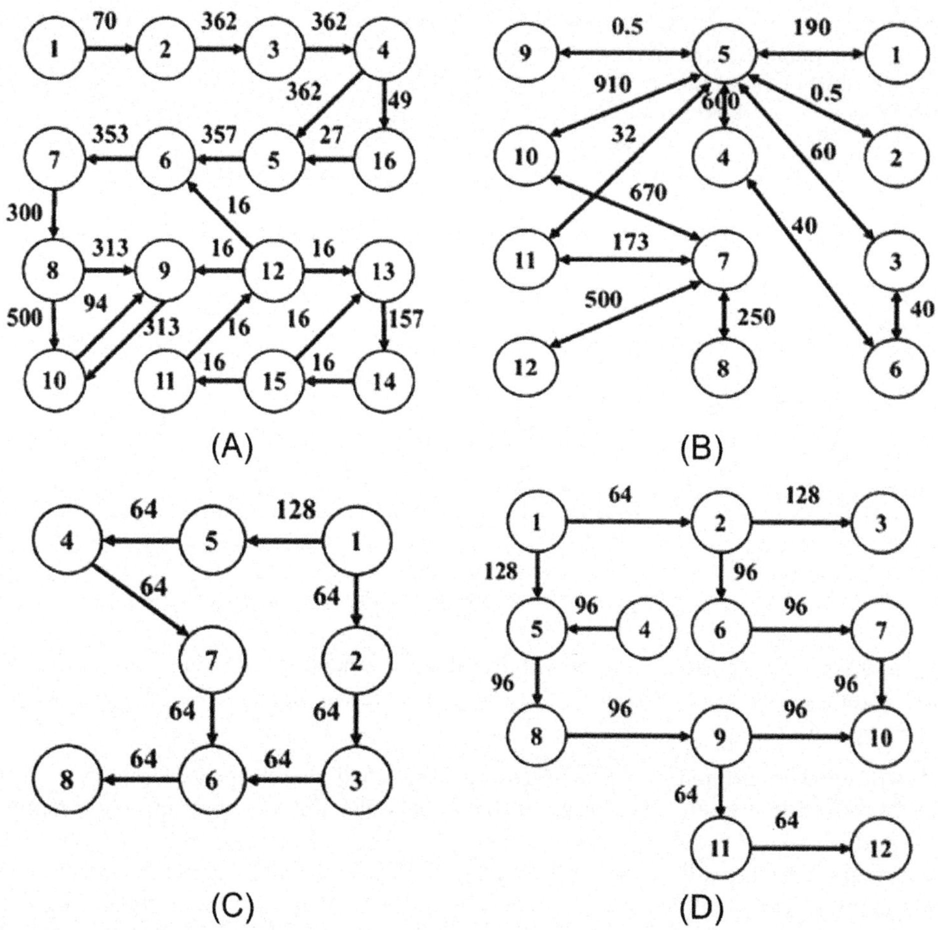

FIGURE 13.6 Benchmarks used in the experiments: (A) VOPD – Video Object Plane Decoder, (B) MPEG4 – Moving Picture Experts Group, (C PIP – Picture In Picture, (D) MWD – Multi-Window Display.

smaller task graph, was mapped onto a 2×2×2 3D topology to ensure a balanced resource utilization. Regarding the synthetic benchmarks TG0, TG1, and TG2, a 6×6 2D NoC topology and a 3×3×3 3D NoC topology were adopted, whereas TG3, TG4, and TG5 were evaluated on an 8×8 2D NoC and a 4×4×4 3D NoC architecture. To achieve appropriate parameter calibration, multiple preliminary tests were carried out. The population size was fixed at 500, and the maximum number of iterations was set to 1000 to ensure convergence stability and fair comparison across all configurations.

13.6.2 Result and discussion

The graphs presented in Fig. 13.7 show the results obtained regarding scalability with respect to the number of cores, as well as the variation of the objective function values using the three versions of the algorithm for 2D and 3D NoC, respectively.

It can be observed that the Hybrid GWOTAB consistently provides better performance in terms of the objective function, even as the number of cores increases across the different graphs

Figs. 13.8 and 13.9 illustrate the convergence behavior of the three algorithmic variants as the number of iterations increases. For clarity, only the TG5 and TG0 benchmarks are presented, showing their convergence trends in both 2D and 3D NoC architectures and highlighting the improvement in the objective function values.

According to the convergence behavior observed in Figs. 13.8 and 13.9 GWOTAB exhibits faster and more stable convergence compared to the other variants. It reaches a better objective function value in fewer iterations, indicating a more efficient exploration–exploitation balance. This improvement can be attributed to the local search capability introduced by the Tabu mechanism, which helps the algorithm escape local minima and refine promising regions of the

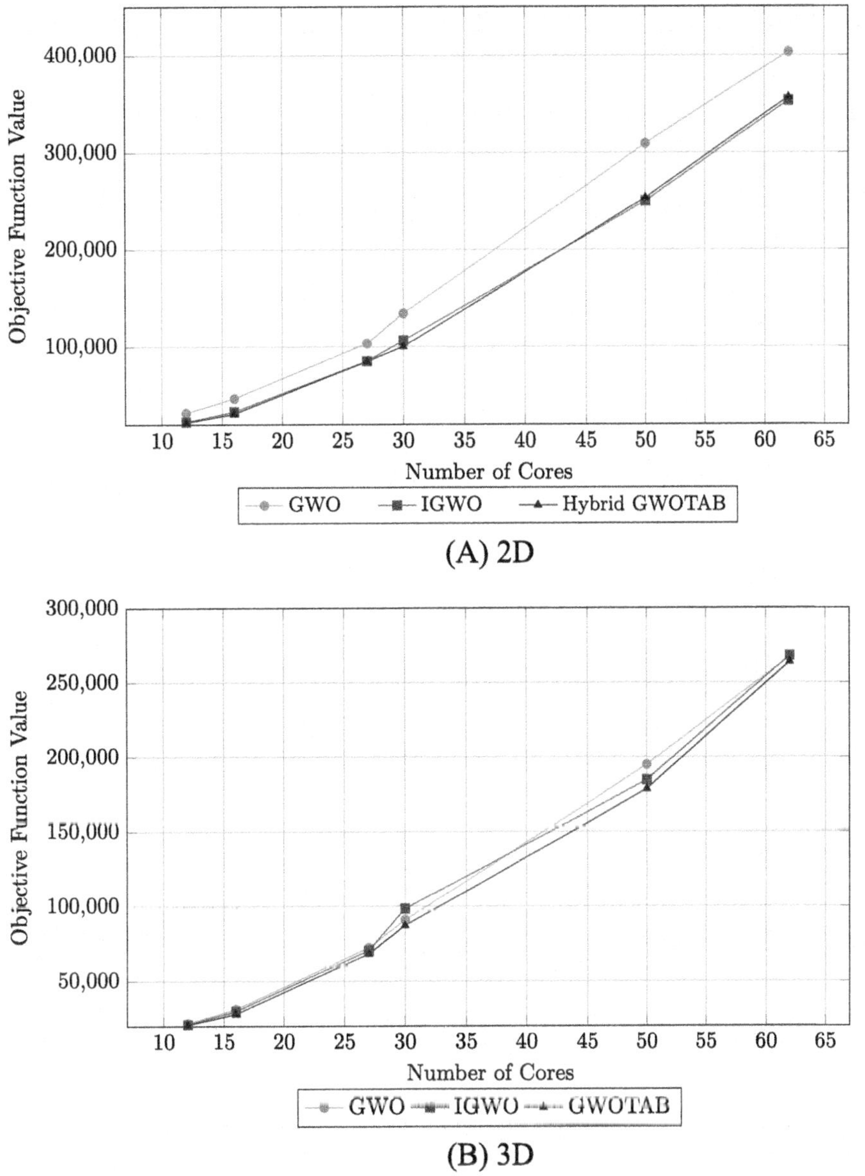

FIGURE 13.7 Impact of the number of cores.

search space. Consequently, the GWO–Tabu variant demonstrates superior mapping quality and robustness for the TG0 case in 2D architectures. The convergence analysis for the TG0 and TG5 benchmarks reveals distinct behaviors among the three algorithmic variants across 2D and 3D NoC architectures. For the TG0 benchmark in 2D, the GWOTAB exhibits faster and more stable convergence, achieving near-optimal objective function values in fewer iterations compared to the other versions. This superior performance is mainly attributed to the local search capability introduced by the Tabu mechanism, which enhances the balance between exploration and exploitation and helps the algorithm avoid local minima. When applied to the 3D topology, the performance gap between the variants becomes less pronounced, due to the additional dimension, thereby improving the overall mapping efficiency. Nevertheless, the GWOTAB maintains a clear advantage in terms of convergence speed and solution quality. For the TG5 benchmark, similar trends are observed: the Tabu-based version consistently outperforms the other algorithms in both 2D and 3D, reaching higher-quality solutions more rapidly despite the increased task graph complexity. However, the standard GWO demonstrates a good convergence trend when the number of iterations increases, indicating potential improvements over longer runs.

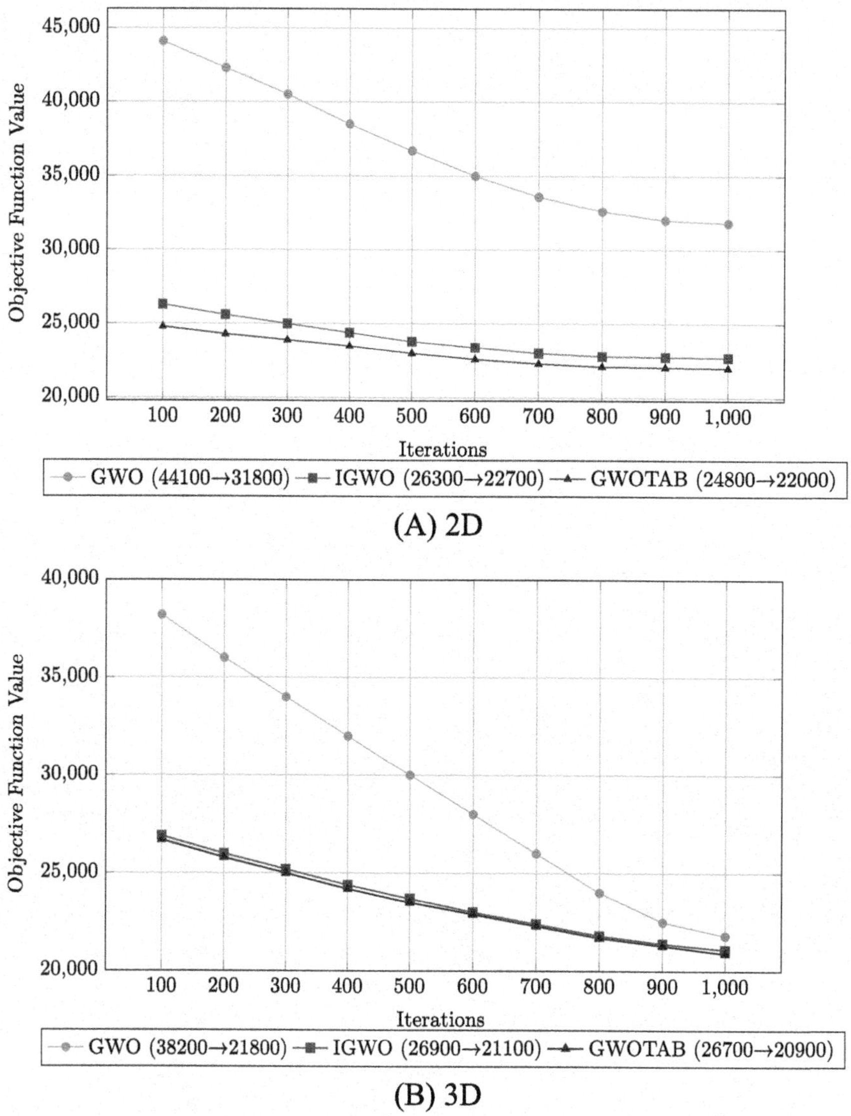

FIGURE 13.8 Convergence comparison of three algorithm variants for TG0.

The results summarized in Tables 13.3 and 13.4 present the performance of the GWO-based mapping approach in its three variants, as described in Section 13.3, applied to both 2D and 3D NoC topologies across all benchmarks. Along with the objective function values, the execution time is also provided to assess computational efficiency. The data clearly demonstrate that the 3D NoC configuration consistently outperforms the 2D NoC, emphasizing the benefits of exploiting the third dimension in task-to-core mapping.

Before comparing our GWO-based mapping approach with existing methods from the literature, we first evaluate its effectiveness by benchmarking it against extended algorithms proposed by the same authors for 3D NoC architectures, namely ABC, GABC [32], and simulated annealing (SA) [26], and then compare the optimal results it produces with those obtained from other state-of-the-art approaches.

The experimental results for the 2D NoC topology are presented in Tables 13.5 and 13.6 extends this analysis to the 3D NoC topology, incorporating a comparative study with ABC, genetic artificial bee colony (GABC), and simulated annealing (SA).

Table 13.7 presents the results related to the 2D NoC topology, while Table 13.8 reports the outcomes for the 3D NoC, including a comparative analysis with other mapping methods from the literature.

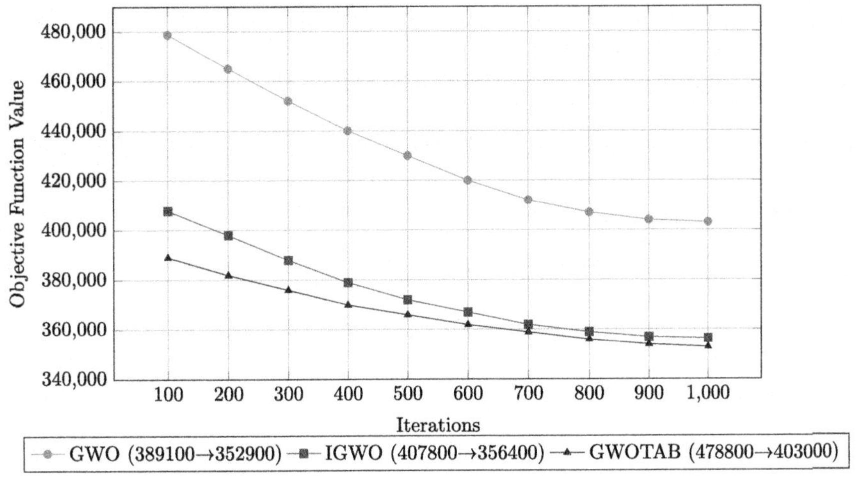

(A) 2D

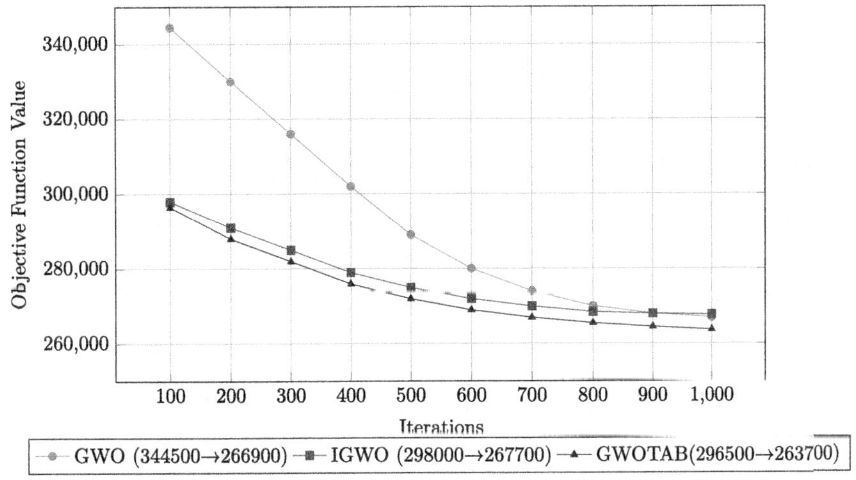

(B) 3D

FIGURE 13.9 Convergence comparison of three algorithm variants for TG5.

TABLE 13.3 Comparison result in 2D.

Benchmarks	GWO		IGWO		GWOTAB	
	Cost	Time	Cost	Time	Cost	Time
TG0	31,800	16.05	22,700	12.72	22,000	13.68
TG1	46,600	19.05	33,100	18.24	30,900	17.18
TG2	103,300	34.19	85,100	31.58	84,800	32.31
TG3	134,300	38.77	106,400	34.46	100,200	36.32
TG4	309,900	71.80	253,200	68.24	249,700	75.49
TG5	403,000	95.22	356,400	98.94	352,900	94.58

GWO, Grey wolf optimizer; *IGWO*, improved grey wolf optimizer.

TABLE 13.4 Comparison result in 3D.

Benchmarks	GWO		IGWO		GWOTAB	
	Cost	Time	Cost	Time	Cost	Time
TG0	21,800	15.33	21,100	14.97	20,900	14.27
TG1	31,100	18.45	29,900	17.53	28,000	15.92
TG2	72,200	32.45	70,400	34.76	68,200	31.45
TG3	90,800	37.57	89,500	42.38	87,200	28.52
TG4	194,700	72.84	184,500	69.72	178,500	67.17
TG5	266,900	109.57	267,700	106.82	263,700	90.18

GWO, Grey wolf optimizer; *IGWO*, improved grey wolf optimizer.

TABLE 13.5 Comparison result in 2D.

Benchmarks	SA	ABC	GABC	GWOTAB
TG0	32,400	49,300	31,700	22,000
TG1	39,700	63,400	40,600	30,900
TG2	94,700	115,100	73,000	84,800
TG3	-	179,900	121,100	100,200
TG4	-	326,400	199,900	249,700
TG5	-	419,600	273,200	352,900

TABLE 13.6 Comparison result in 3D.

Benchmarks	SA	ABC	GABC	GWOTAB
TG0	27,800	31,700	28,600	20,900
TG1	37,200	40,600	38,400	28,000
TG2	78,000	73,000	88,100	68,200
TG3	-	121,100	116,600	87,200
TG4	-	199,900	188,200	178,500
TG5	-	273,200	269,200	263,700

From these results of mapping in 2D NoC, it can be deduced that GWOTAB can achieve superior results with optimal parameter settings, outperforming other methods. Additionally, the results for 3D NoC are better, although there is a need to further improve these outcomes by integrating other population-based metaheuristics.

It is clear from these results that two algorithms can gives bette result, but not always, with different parameter.

TABLE 13.7 Comparison results with other approaches in the 2D NoC.

Results	VOPD	MWD	PIP	MPEG4
GWOTAB	4119	1216	640	3834
PSO	4141	1216	640	3757
GBMAP	4217	-	-	3572
ONYX	4242	-	-	3612
CGMAP	4300	-	-	3600
NMAP	4265	1344	640	3852
CHMAP	4167	1344	640	3852
ILP	4119	1120	640	3567
Castnet	4135	1280	-	3852

TABLE 13.8 Comparison results with other approaches in the 3D NoC.

Results	VOPD	MWD	PIP	MPEG4
GWOTAB	4103	1211	640	3567
NMAP 3D	4119	1184	640	3672
PSMAP 3D	4119	1120	640	3567
DPSOMAP3D	4119	1120	640	3567
ILP 3D	4103	1120	640	3567
TSBM	4103	1120	640	3567

13.7 Conclusion

This work presents an algorithm based on GWO for NoC architectures, targeting both 2D and 3D mesh topologies. we address the application mapping problem, which is known to be NP-hard and combinatorial in nature. Experiments were conducted using real application core graphs and a mono-objective optimization strategy, with communication cost serving as the primary evaluation criterion. Experimental results indicate that Grey Wolf achieves superior performance compared to standard other algorithms when appropriate parameter tuning is applied.

In future work, we aim to extend the approach to a multi-objective optimization framework for application mapping in NoC architectures.

References

[1] Hu, J., Marculescu, R., 2003. Energy-aware mapping for tile-based noc architectures under performance constraints. In: Proceedings of the 2003 Asia and South Pacific Design Automation Conference. ACM, pp. 233–239.

[2] W.R. Davis, J. Wilson, S. Mick, J. Xu, H. Hua, C. Mineo, et al., Demystifying 3D ICS: the pros and cons of going vertical, IEEE Design & Test of Computers 22 (6) (2005) 498–510.

[3] M. Bougherara, N. Nedjah, L.D.M. Mourelle, R. Rahmoun, A. Sadok, D. Bennouar, IP assignment for efficient NoC-based system design using multi-objective particle swarm optimisation, International Journal of Bio-Inspired Computation 12 (4) (2018) 203–213.
[4] Bougherara, M., Nedjah, N., Bennouar, D., et al., 2018. Core/task associations for efficient application implementation on network-on-chip. In: 2018 International Conference on Computer and Applications (ICCA). IEEE, pp. 18-22.
[5] Bougherara, M., Nedjah, N., Bennouar, D., Kemcha, R., de Macedo Mourelle, L., 2019. Efficient application mapping onto three-dimensional network-on-chips using multi-objective particle swarm optimization. In: International Conference on Computational Science and Its Applications. Springer, Cham, pp. 654-670.
[6] Bougherara, M., Nedjah, N., Bennouar, D., et al., 2023. Routing in 3D NoCs using genetic algorithm and particle swarm optimization. In International Conference on Computational Science and Its Applications. Cham Springer Nature Switzerland, p. 601–613.
[7] Bougherara, M., Amara, R., 2023. Routing using genetic algorithm in network on chips with 3D mesh topology. In: 2023 International Conference on Computer and Applications (ICCA). IEEE, pp. 1–5.
[8] Q. Chen, W. Huang, Y. Zhang, et al., An IP core mapping algorithm based on neural networks, IEEE Transactions on Very Large Scale Integration (VLSI) Systems 29 (1) (2020) 189–202.
[9] L. Silva Junior, N. Nedjah, L. DE Macedo Mourelle, Efficient routing in network-on-chip for 3D topologies, International Journal of Electronics 102 (10) (2015) 1695–1712.
[10] Bougherara, M., Nedjah, N., Bennouar, D., et al., 2020. Application mapping onto 3D NoCs using differential evolution. In: Computational Science and Its Applications–ICCSA 2020: 20th International Conference, Cagliari, Italy, July 1–4, 2020, Proceedings, Part III 20. Springer International Publishing, pp. 89-102.
[11] P.K. Sahu, S. Chattopadhyay, A survey on application mapping strategies for network-on-chip design, Journal of Systems Architecture 59 (1) (2013) 60–76.
[12] P. Wadhwani, N. Choudhary, D. Singh, Energy efficient mapping in 3D mesh communication architecture for NoC, Global Journal of Computer Science and Technology 13 (2013) 14.
[13] Murali, S., DeMicheli, V., February 2004. Bandwidth constrained mapping of cores onto NoC architectures, Design, Automation and Test in Europe Conference and Exhibition, Proceedings, vol. 2, pp. 896–901.
[14] W. Shen, C. Chao, Y. Lien, A. Wu, A new binomial mapping and optimization algorithm for reduced-complexity mesh-based on-chip network, networks-on-chip, NOCS 2007 (2007) 317–322.
[15] S. Tosun, O. Ozturk, M. Ozen, Application mapping algorithms for mesh-based network-on-chip architectures, Journal of Supercomputing 71 (3) (2015) 995–1017.
[16] C.-H. Cheng, W.-M. Chen, Application mapping onto mesh-based network-on-chip using constructive heuristic algorithms, The Journal of Supercomputing (2016) 1–14.
[17] M. Janidarmian, A. Khademzadeh, M. Tavanpour, Onyx: a new heuristic bandwidth-constrained mapping of cores onto tile based network on chip, IEICE Electronics Express 6 (1) (2009) 1–7.
[18] A. Mehran, S. Saeidi, A. Khademzadeh, et al., Spiral: a heuristic mapping algorithm for network on chip, IEICE Electronics Express 4 (5) (2007) 478–484.
[19] M.Z. Dageleh, M.A.J. Jamali, V-Castnet3D: a novel clustering-based mapping in 3-D network on chip, Nano Communication Networks 18 (2018) 51–61.
[20] Y. Nalci, P. Kullu, S. Tosun, O. Ozturk, Ilp formulation and heuristic method for energy-aware application mapping on 3D-NoCs, The Journal of Supercomputing 77 (3) (2021) 2667–2680.
[21] F. Moein-darbari, A. Khademzade, G. Gharooni-fard, CGMAP: a new approach to network-on-chip mapping problem, IEICE Electronics Express 6 (1) (2009) 27–34.
[22] T. Misagh, K. Ahmad, P. Somayyeh, et al., GBMAP: an evolutionary approach to mapping cores onto a mesh-based NoC architecture, Journal of Communication and Computer 7 (3) (2010) 1–7.
[23] P.K. Sahu, T. Shah, K. Manna, S. Chattopadhyay, Application mapping onto mesh based network on chip using discrete particle swarm optimization, IEEE Transactions on Very Large Scale Integration (VLSI) Systems 22 (2) (2014) 300–312.
[24] Bougherara, M., Rafik, A., Kemcha, R., 2022. Application mapping onto network on chip using particul swarm optimisation with genetic algorithm "GAPSO". In: 2022 International Conference on Computer and Applications (ICCA). IEEE.
[25] Bougherara, M., Amara, R., 2023. Application mapping onto network on chip using genetic algorithm and ant colony optimisation. In: 2023 International Conference on Computer and Applications (ICCA). IEEE, pp. 1-6.
[26] M. Bougherara, M. Djihad, Genetic artificial bee colony for mapping onto network on chip "GABC", Congress on Intelligent Systems, Springer Nature, Singapore, (2022).
[27] M. Bougherara, Y. imene, Application mapping onto network on chip using cat swarm optimization, International Symposium on Intelligent Informatics, Springer Nature, Singapore, (2022).
[28] Maamar, B., Rafik, A., Rebiha, K., DEMAP: differential evolution mapping for network on chip optimization.
[29] Huang, C., Zhang, D., Song, G., Low-power mapping algorithm for threedimensional network-on-chip based on diversity-controlled quantumbehaved particle swarm optimization.
[30] Kullu, P., Yigit-Sert, S., Ozkan-Okay, M., Ar, Y., 2023. An artificial bee colony based mapping method for three dimensional network-on-chip. In: 2023 International Conference on Emerging Trends in Networks and Computer Communications (ETNCC), pp. 1–6.

[31] F. Asadzadeh, A. Reza, M. Reshadi, A. Khademzadeh, Thermal-aware application mapping using genetic and fuzzy logic techniques for minimizing temperature in three-dimensional network-on-chip, The Journal of Supercomputing 80 (8) (2024) 11214–11240.
[32] Bougherara, M., Amara, R., Kemcha, R., 2024. Using simulated annealing for application mapping onto network on chip. In 2024 International Conference on Computer and Applications (ICCA). IEEE, pp. 1-6.
[33] S. Mirjalili, I. Aljarah, M. Mafarja, et al., Grey wolf optimizer: theory, literature review, and application in computational fluid dynamics problems, Nature-Inspired Optimizers: Theories, Literature Reviews and Applications (2020) 87–105.
[34] H. Faris, I. Aljarah, M.A. Al-betar, et al., Grey wolf optimizer: a review of recent variants and applications, Neural Computing and Applications 30 (2018) 413–435.
[35] S. Mirjalili, S.M. Mirjalili, A. Lewis, Grey wolf optimizer, Advances in Engineering Software 69 (2014) 46–61.
[36] Q. AL-Tashi, S.J. Abdulkadir, H.M. Rais, et al., Binary multi-objective grey wolf optimizer for feature selection in classification, IEEE Access 8 (2020) 106247–106263.
[37] M.H. Nadimi-Shahraki, S. Taghian, S. Mirjalili, An improved grey wolf optimizer for solving engineering problems, Expert Systems with Applications vol. 166, (2021) 113917.
[38] Dick, R.P., Rhodes, D.L., Wolf, W., 1998. TGFF: task graphs for free. In: Proceedings of the Sixth International Workshop on Hardware/Software Codesign. (CODES/CASHE'98). IEEE, pp. 97-101.

Chapter 14

Line sampling method based on grey wolf optimizer for structural reliability analysis

Jafar Jafari-Asl[1] and You Dong[2]

[1]*Faculty of Agriculture, Civil and Environmental Engineering, University of Rostock, Rostock, Mecklenburg-Vorpommern, Germany,* [2]*State Key Laboratory of Climate Resilience for Coastal Cities, Department of Civil and Environmental Engineering, The Hong Kong Polytechnic University, Hong Kong, P.R. China*

14.1 Introduction

Beyond cost reduction in engineering structures, ensuring adequate safety remains a fundamental principle in design and construction. This necessitates careful consideration of key design parameters, including applied loads, material properties, and structural system dimensions. However, these parameters are inherently subject to uncertainties caused by environmental variations, construction errors, material defects, and similar factors, all of which can unpredictably affect structural performance.

Structural reliability theory provides an advanced and effective framework for assessing safety under such uncertainties. This approach requires solving complex integral equations to calculate failure probability (Eq. 14.1), offering valuable insights into structural safety levels [1].

$$P_f = \mathbb{P}[g(\boldsymbol{x}) < 0] = \int_{D_f=\{x|g(x)\leq 0\}} f_x(\boldsymbol{x})dx \tag{14.1}$$

where P_f represents the failure probability within the domain where the limit state function g(x) < 0. This probability corresponds to the multidimensional integral of the joint probability density function $f_x(\boldsymbol{x})$ of the random vector x = [x_1, x_2,...,x_n] over the failure region D_f.

Given the complexity of directly solving the integral equation for real-world engineering problems, various methods have been developed to estimate the failure probability by incorporating certain assumptions and simplifications. The simplest yet most widely used approaches are the first- and second-order reliability methods (FORM) [2,3]. Despite their extensive application, these methods encounter difficulties when dealing with complex limit state functions, which limits their practical usefulness. Another prominent approach for failure probability estimation is the Monte Carlo simulation (MCS) method [4], which can be applied to structures with any type of complex limit state function. However, for engineering problems requiring nonlinear analysis (such as finite element analysis), MCS demands substantial computational resources. This high computational cost makes MCS impractical for reliability assessment of many complex engineering systems [5].

To address this challenge, various efficient MCS-based approaches have been developed, including subset simulation [6,7], line sampling (LS) [8,9], and other surrogate methods [10–15]. Among these, LS stands out as one of the most accurate techniques. Unlike MCS that relies on random points, LS utilizes lines (based on FORM theory) to simulate problems in the probability space. This approach significantly reduces the number of limit state function evaluations required, leading to substantial computational time savings for high-dimensional real-world problems. However, a major challenge persists when applying LS to general reliability problems: the accurate calculation of the design point (or the most probable failure point) needed to establish the important unit directional vector.

The first and most critical step in implementing LS, which plays a fundamental role inaccurate failure probability estimation, involves determining the unit directional vector (Most Probable Point [MPP]) [8,16]. This is formulated and solved as a constrained optimization problem. In most cases, the unit vector direction is identified using gradient-based

Grey Wolf Optimizer. DOI: https://doi.org/10.1016/B978-0-443-36624-6.00011-1

methods due to their computational efficiency. However, conventional gradient-based LS algorithms may fail to converge when dealing with highly nonlinear limit state functions, leading to inaccurate failure probability estimates. Various gradient-based approaches have been developed for MPP identification in reliability analysis, including the enhanced Hasofer-Lind-Rackwitz-Fiessler (HL-RF) method, adaptive finite-step length algorithm, strengthened step-size adjustment, and chaos control techniques [17–19]. While these methods demonstrate satisfactory performance for low-to-medium dimensional structural reliability problems, they show limited effectiveness for high-dimensional, highly nonlinear systems. Gradient-based algorithms often encounter local convergence or divergence issues when applied to such complex problems, making them generally unsuitable for large-scale reliability analysis.

In recent years, metaheuristic algorithms with superior convergence properties have been increasingly applied to high-dimensional reliability analysis problems [20]. Popular optimization techniques include particle swarm optimization [21], genetic algorithm [22], differential evolution) [23], artificial bee colony [24], and Harris Hawks Optimization (HHO) [20]. However, their integration with the powerful LS method remains limited to only a few isolated studies [8,25]. Given these considerations, this research comprehensively investigates hybrid metaheuristic-LS approaches for structural reliability analysis. Among existing metaheuristics, the grey wolf optimizer (GWO) – introduced by Mirjalili [26] – demonstrates exceptional potential. As a population-based algorithm inspired by the hunting behavior of grey wolf packs, GWO exhibits remarkable optimization capabilities in complex engineering problems. Recent advancements have produced enhanced GWO variants to further improve its optimization performance [27,28]. This study proposes a novel LS-GWO reliability analysis framework for structural systems. In the LS-GWO approach:

1. The unit directional vector is formulated as a constrained optimization problem
2. An advanced GWO variant [29] solves this using an external penalty function method for constraint handling
3. The proposed method requires neither derivative information nor initial MPP position estimates

Notably, the LS-GWO's derivative-free nature and elimination of initial guess requirements significantly enhance computational efficiency in structural reliability assessment.

14.2 Methodology

14.2.1 Line sampling reliability method

The LS method essentially combines the theoretical frameworks of FORM and MCS. Unlike conventional MCS that employs random points across all problem dimensions, LS utilizes directional lines to simulate the LSF, effectively reducing a multidimensional problem to a one-dimensional space [30]. This method begins with proper problem initialization, where the crucial first step involves determining the important directional vector (α) – the gradient direction pointing toward the failure region in the standard normal space. This directional vector is then normalized to obtain the corresponding unit directional vector ($e_a = \alpha/\|\alpha\|$), which serves as the primary axis for subsequent one-dimensional sampling.

As visually demonstrated in Fig. 14.1 for a two-dimensional case, these vectors geometrically represent: (1) α as the steepest ascent direction toward the LSF and (2) e_a as its dimensionless counterpart establishing the sampling orientation. The mathematical definition of these vectors follows from [30]:

$$\alpha = \nabla g_U(\boldsymbol{u}^*) \tag{14.2}$$

$$e_\alpha = \frac{\alpha}{\|\alpha\|} = \frac{\nabla g_U(\boldsymbol{u}^*)}{\|\nabla g_U(\boldsymbol{u}^*)\|} \tag{14.3}$$

where $\boldsymbol{u}$ results from transforming the original variables$\boldsymbol{x}$ to the standard normal space ($u \in N(0,1)$) through the mapping $\boldsymbol{u} = T_{\mathrm{xu}}(\boldsymbol{x})$, expressed as $\boldsymbol{u} = [U_1, U_2, ..., U\ ]^{\mathrm{T}} \in \mathbb{R}^{\mathrm{n}}$. Therefore, the LSF transforms according to Eq. (14.4).

$$g_X(T_{ux}(\boldsymbol{u})) = g_U(\boldsymbol{u}) \tag{14.4}$$

The gradient of the LSF with respect to each variable determines the important direction vector α:

$$\nabla g_U(\boldsymbol{u}^*) = \left[\frac{\partial g_U(\boldsymbol{u}^*)}{\partial U_1}\frac{\partial g_U(\boldsymbol{u}^*)}{\partial U_2}\cdots\frac{\partial g_U(\boldsymbol{u}^*)}{\partial U_n}\right]^T \tag{14.5}$$

While typically computed using gradient-based methods, optimization algorithms can alternatively estimate this vector.

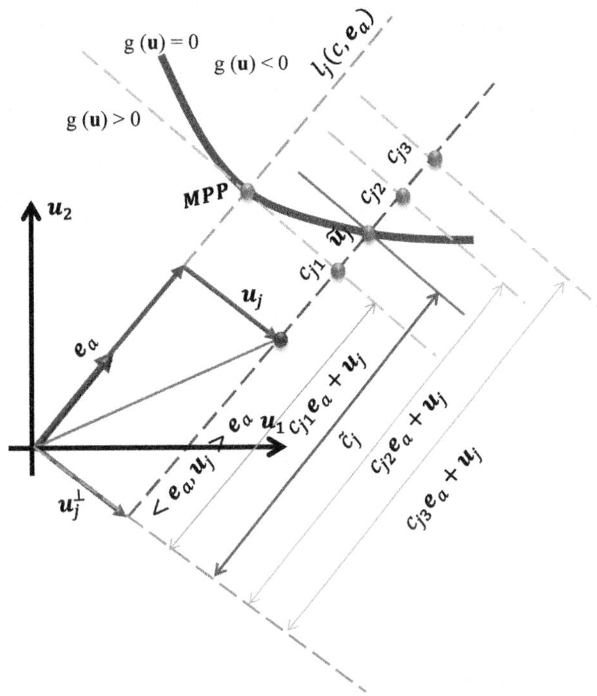

FIGURE 14.1 Estimation of the unit vector e_α in LS (*LS*, Line sampling).

The j-th sample's projection orthogonal to e_a is denoted as $u_j^{\perp}$. To estimate the distance between $u_j^{\perp}$ and the limit state function, a quadratic approximation is employed. The root of this quadratic function represents the intersection point between the LSF and $u_j^{\perp}$ along the e_a direction, determined using three reference points c_{j1}, c_{j2}, and c_{j3}. These points are obtained through the inner product [30]:

$$c_j = \langle e_\alpha, \boldsymbol{u}_j \rangle \tag{14.6}$$

where ⟨⟩ denotes the vector inner product.

The projection $\tilde{\mathbf{u}}_j$ of $\mathbf{u}_j$ onto the limit state function along e_a is given by:

$$\tilde{\boldsymbol{u}}_j = \tilde{c}_j e_\alpha + \boldsymbol{u}_j^{\perp} \tag{14.7}$$

Here, $\tilde{c}_j$ represents the root of the quadratic function passing through points c_j. The reliability index $\tilde{\beta}_j$ for the j-th sample is then computed as the distance between $\tilde{\boldsymbol{u}}_j$ and $\boldsymbol{u}_j^{\perp}$. The overall reliability index of the problem equals the average of all sample indices according to Eq. (14.8).

$$\beta = \frac{1}{N} \sum_{j=1}^{N} \tilde{\beta}_j \tag{14.8}$$

where N represents the total number of samples, while $\tilde{\beta}_j$ denotes the reliability index of the j-th random sample. This index is mathematically defined as the minimum distance from each sample point to the LSF along the important unit directional vector [30].

The structure's failure probability is then estimated by taking the average of all simulated sample probabilities and applying the inverse standard normal cumulative distribution function (Φ^{-1}), as expressed in Eq. (14.9):

$$P_f = \frac{1}{N} \sum_{j=1}^{N} P_{f_j} = \frac{1}{N} \sum_{j=1}^{N} \Phi(-\tilde{\beta}_j) \tag{14.9}$$

14.2.2 Enhanced grey wolf optimizer

The GWO algorithm is inspired by the social hierarchy and hunting behavior of grey wolves in nature [29]. It operates by considering the positions of three leading wolves (α, β, and δ) as the best candidate solutions to guide the remaining wolves (ω) in exploring the solution space. In nature, grey wolves hunt their prey through three distinct phases [29]:

- **Encircling**
  Simulated using Eqs. (14.10) and (14.11):

$$D = |C \times X_p(t) - X(t)| \tag{14.10}$$

$$X(t+1) = X_p - A \times D \tag{14.11}$$

with,

$$A = 2 \times A \times r_1 - a(t) \tag{14.12}$$

$$C = 2 \times r_2 \tag{14.13}$$

with,

$$a(t) = 2 - (2 \times t)/MaxIter \tag{14.13}$$

where X_p and X are the prey location and position vector of the grey wolf, respectively. r_1 and r_1 are random numbers in [0, 1], C and A are the constant numbers, t and MaxIter are the current and maximum number of iterations, respectively.

- **Hunting**
  The GWO algorithm simulates the wolves' hunting strategy by leveraging the leadership hierarchy. In this phase: (1) The alpha (α), beta (β), and delta (δ) wolves – representing the current best solutions – are presumed to possess superior knowledge of the prey's potential location, (2) The remaining omega (ω) wolves update their positions according to the leaders' guidance, and (3) This collective movement is mathematically represented through Eqs. (14.14) to (14.16).

$$D_a = |C_1 \times X_a - X(t)| \tag{14.14}$$

$$D_\beta = |C_2 \times X_\beta - X(t)| \tag{14.15}$$

$$D_\delta = |C_3 \times X_\delta - X(t)| \tag{14.16}$$

With,

$$X_{i1}(t) = X_a(t) - A_{i1} \times D_a(t) \tag{14.17}$$

$$X_{i2}(t) = X_\beta(t) - A_{i2} \times D_\beta(t) \tag{14.18}$$

$$X_{i3}(t) = X_\delta(t) - A_{i3} \times D_\delta(t) \tag{14.19}$$

With,

$$X(t+1) = \frac{X_{i1}(t) + X_{i2}(t) + X_{i3}(t)}{3} \tag{14.20}$$

where C1, C2, and C3 are calculated by Eq. (14.13), X_a, X_β, and X_δ are the first three best positions at iteration t, A_1, A_2, and A_3 are determined as Eq. (14.2).

- **Attacking**

The final hunting phase commences when the prey becomes stationary, triggering the wolves' attack. This behavior is mathematically simulated through a linearly decreasing parameter (a) that regulates the transition between exploration and exploitation.

In GWO, the alpha (α), beta (β), and delta (δ) wolves guide the omega (ω) wolves toward promising regions of the search space to find optimal solutions. However, this behavior can lead to premature convergence and trapping in local optima. Another drawback is the reduced population diversity, which further exacerbates the algorithm's tendency to settle for suboptimal solutions. To address these limitations, this study employs an enhanced version of the GWO proposed by Nadimi et al. [29]. The improved algorithm incorporates a dimension learning-based hunting (DHL) strategy to prevent local optima entrapment.

In this advanced version, the new position of each wolf $X_i(t)$ is calculated using Eq. (14.23) instead of Eq. (14.20). Here, each individual wolf learns not only from its neighboring wolves but also from a randomly selected wolf in the population. Additionally, alongside the standard GWO update $X_{i-GWO}(t+1)$, the DHL strategy generates an alternative candidate position $X_{i-DHL}(t+1)$. To implement this, the algorithm first computes the radius $R_i(t)$ using the Euclidean distance between the current position $X_i(t)$ and the candidate position $X_{iGWO}(t+1)$ via Eq. (14.21). This radius dynamically adjusts the search scope, enhancing exploration while maintaining exploitation capabilities [29].

$$R(t+1) = |X_i(t) - X_{i-GWO}(t+1)| \tag{14.21}$$

The neighbors of $X_i(t)$, denoted as $N_i(t)$, are determined using Eq. (14.22) based on the radius $R_i(t)$, where D_i represents the Euclidean distance between $X_i(t)$ and $X_j(t)$.

$$N_i(t) = \{X_j(t) \mid D_i(X_i(t), X_j(t)) \le R_i(t), X_j(t) \in Pop\} \tag{14.22}$$

After constructing $N_i(t)$, the algorithm performs multineighbor learning via Eq. (14.23). Here, the d-th dimension of $X_{i-DLH,d}(t+1)$ is computed using:

- A randomly chosen neighbor $X_{n,d}(t)$ from $N_i(t)$, and
- A randomly selected wolf $X_{r,d}(t)$ from the population (Pop).

$$X_{i-DLH,\ d}(t+1) = X_i(t) + rand \times (X_{n,d}(t) - X_{r,d}(t)) \tag{14.23}$$

The superior candidate between $X_{i-GWO}(t+1)$ and $X_{i-DLH}(t+1)$ is selected by comparing their fitness values using Eq. (14.24).

$$X_i(t+1) = \begin{cases} X_{i-GWO}(t+1), & if\ f(X_{i-GWO}) < f(X_{i-DLH}) \\ X_{i-DLH}(t+1)\ otherwise \end{cases} \tag{14.24}$$

If the selected candidate's fitness value is better (lower) than $X_i(t)$, $X_i(t+1)$ is updated to the candidate's position. Otherwise, $X_i(t)$ retains its current position in Pop.

This process repeats for all individuals in the population. The iteration counter (*iter*) increments by 1, and the search continues until reaching the maximum iterations (*MaxIter*).

14.2.3 Metaheuristic-based line sampling

Since various objective functions have been proposed for locating the MPP in LS, this study adopts the minimization of the Euclidean norm of the random variables in the standard normal space. The optimization problem is formulated as [8,20,25]:

$$f = \min \|\boldsymbol{u}\|$$

$$subject\ to:$$

$$g(\boldsymbol{u}) = 0 \tag{14.25}$$

where $\boldsymbol{u}$ represents the transformed random variables in standard normal space, and $g(\boldsymbol{u})$ is the limit state function.

Since metaheuristics generally solve unconstrained problems, constraints were handled via a penalty function: infeasible solutions worsen the objective value, steering the algorithm toward feasible regions. Thus the constrained problem (Eq. 14.25) becomes unconstrained (Eq. 14.26).

$$f_{new} = f + \lambda\ |g(\boldsymbol{u})| \tag{14.26}$$

where λ is the penalty factor. Since, in constrained problems using penalty functions, the correct selection of the penalty factor significantly influences algorithm performance and the final solution, a sensitivity analysis approach was employed here to find a suitable penalty coefficient. This approach involves running the optimizer with different penalty factor values, for example, [1, 10, 100], and then evaluating parameters such as the degree of constraint violation, algorithm runtime, and the objective function value. The penalty factor value is selected based on the assessed parameter values. In this study, given the small magnitude of the objective function in the investigated problems, the appropriate penalty value determined through sensitivity analysis was chosen as 10.

It should be noted that computational complexity analysis of the algorithms is not discussed here, as no structural modifications have been made to any of the algorithms. They have only been linked to the LS method and applied to solve the structural reliability problem. Therefore for further information regarding the computational complexity of the algorithms, readers are referred to the original sources.

14.3 Numerical examples

The performance of the algorithms in enhancing the LS method was evaluated using three modified numerical engineering examples from prior research. Table 14.1 presents the metaheuristic algorithms' tuning parameters, which were selected based on their established performance in previous studies. To ensure a fair comparison, each algorithm was executed 20 times with a population size of 10 and a maximum of 50 iterations. The reported failure probability for the metaheuristic-augmented LS models represents the average of these 20 independent runs. The computational error in the failure probability estimates (P_f^{Method}) was calculated using Eq. (14.27), with reference to the MCS (P_f^{MCS}) results as the benchmark [31,32].

$$\varepsilon\,(\%) = \frac{|P_f^{MCS} - P_f^{Method}|}{P_f^{MCS}} \times 100 \tag{14.27}$$

14.3.1 Example 1

The first case study simulates a cable-stayed bridge tower using five normal random variables. Eq. (14.28) defines the limit state function, with variable statistics provided in Table 14.2 [8].

$$g\,(\mathbf{X}) = x_5 - \frac{5x_3x_4\,(47.4)^3}{3(5x_1x_2 - 2x_3\,(47.4)^2)} - \frac{5(1170 \times 47.4)x_4\,(0.4)^2}{3(5x_1x_2 - 2x_3\,(47.4)^2)} - 47.4x_4 \tag{14.28}$$

The results obtained from the analysis of Example 1 using MCS and LS-based models are presented in Table 14.3. MCS estimated the failure probability of the problem to be 2.42E-04 with 10^7 limit state function calls. This is while the LS-based models and metaheuristic algorithms estimated the failure probability with much lower error, with only 1050 limit state function calls. As it is clear, HBA-LS and I-GWO-LS estimated the failure probability with the lowest error of 0.80% and 1.78%, respectively. Then, TSA-LS and HHO presented lower error than the other algorithms. Among the models, Fitness Dependent Optimizer (FDO)-LS and Slime mould algorithm (SMA)-LS have the highest error of 2.60%. Fig. 14.2

TABLE 14.1 Setting parameters of algorithms.

Algorithm	Parameter	Value
GWO and I-GWO	Convergence constant a	[2, 0]
HHO	E0	[-1, 1]
Whale optimization algorithm (WOA)	ab	201
Rat Swarm Optimizer (RSO)	RC	[1,5][0, 2]
Seagull Optimization Algorithm (SOA)	Afc	[2, 0]2
Marine Predators Algorithm (MPA)	FADsP	0.20.5
Honey Badger Algorithm (HBA)	β C	62

TABLE 14.2 Statistical properties of the random variables for Example 1.

Variable	Mean	Standard deviation
x_1	17.6	1.76
x_2	4×10^7	3.2×10^6
x_3	9.01×10^4	9.01×10^3
x_4	2120	318
x_5	2.6×10^5	3.9×10^4

TABLE 14.3 Results of proposed models on Example 1.

Method	Pf	Cov	ε (%)
MCS	2.42E-04	-	-
I-GWO-LS	2.37E-04	1.36E-02	1.78E+00
HBA-LS	2.43E-04	8.98E-02	8.05E-01
TSA-LS	3.11E-04	3.39E-01	2.88E+01
SOA-LS	2.06E-04	1.73E-01	1.47E+01
RSO-LS	2.03E-04	2.85E-01	1.60E+01
MPA-LS	2.39E-04	7.56E-02	9.75E-01
HHO-LS	2.30E-04	1.52E-01	4.87E+00
GWO-LS	2.42E-04	1.33E-01	3.60E-01
FDA-LS	2.31E-04	7.22E-02	4.30E+00
SMA-LS	9.02E-05	1.13E+00	6.26E+01

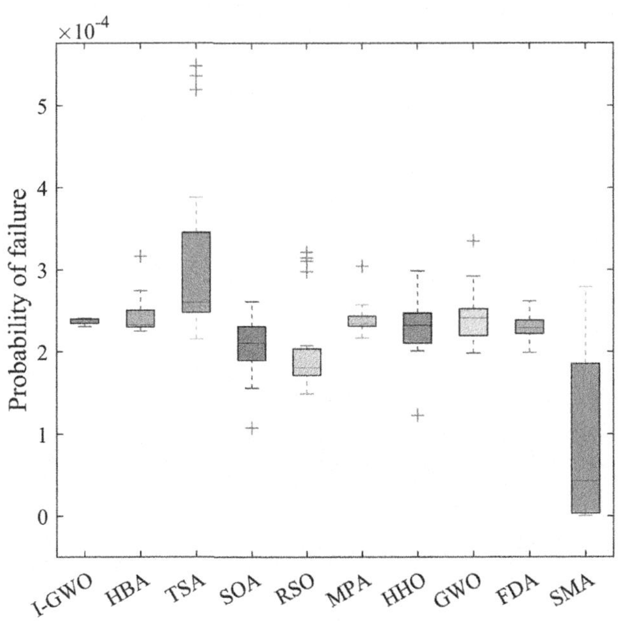

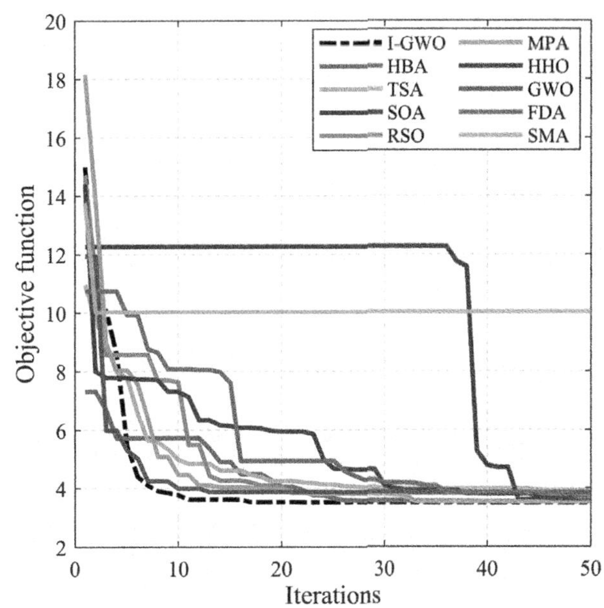

FIGURE 14.2 Boxplot of failure probabilities and convergence curves for developed models for Example 1.

shows the convergence curve of the models in finding the design points of the problem. It is clear that I-GWO presented the best convergence rate. Also, according to the box plot presented, it is clear that the failure probability calculated with I-GWO-LS has the lowest coefficient of variation, which indicates that the changes made to the original version of the algorithm have had an impact, which, in addition to earlier convergence, has also increased the accuracy of the model.

14.3.2 Example 2

The second example involves reliability analysis of a truss roof structure under snow loading, with failure defined as excessive displacement at the top joint. This problem incorporates six normally distributed random variables, whose statistical properties are detailed in Table 14.4. Fig. 14.3 shows the truss configuration, while Eq. (14.29) defines the corresponding limit state function [33,34].

$$g = 0.03 - \left(\frac{ql^2}{2}\right)\left(\frac{3.81}{A_C E_C} + \frac{1.13}{A_S E_S}\right) \tag{14.29}$$

A_C and E_C are the concrete's cross-sectional area and modulus, with A_S and E_S representing the steel reinforcement's equivalent properties.

Table 14.5 presents the analysis results for Example 2 using the proposed approach. The MCS required 10^6 limit state function evaluations to estimate a failure probability of 9.71E-03, while the LS-based methods achieved comparable accuracy with only 1050 function calls. Among these, the MPA-LS, FDA-LS, and I-GWO-LS models demonstrated the highest accuracy in estimating failure probability.

TABLE 14.4 Statistical properties of the random variables for Example 2.

Variable	Mean	Standard deviation
$q\,(N/m)$	2×10^4	1.4×10^3
$l\,(m)$	12	0.12
$A_s\,(m^2)$	9.82×10^{-4}	5.98×10^{-5}
$A_c\,(m^2)$	4×10^{-2}	4.8×10^{-3}
$E_s\,(Pa)$	1×10^{11}	6×10^9
$E_c\,(Pa)$	2×10^{10}	1.2×10^9

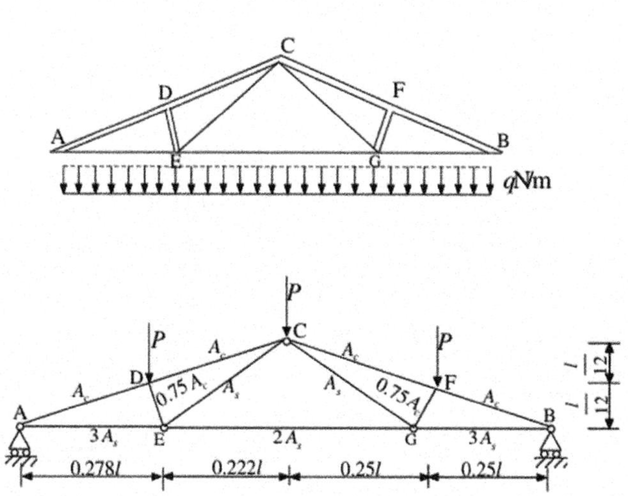

FIGURE 14.3 Schematic of roof truss.

TABLE 14.5 Results of proposed models on Example 2.

Method	Pf	Cov	ε (%)
MCS	9.71E-03	-	-
I-GWO-LS	9.91E-03	2.34E-02	2.12E+00
HBA-LS	9.92E-03	5.48E-02	2.22E+00
TSA-LS	1.02E-02	2.26E-01	5.24E+00
SOA-LS	9.17E-03	2.30E-01	5.49E+00
RSO-LS	1.11E-02	3.10E-01	1.42E+01
MPA-LS	9.82E-03	8.73E-02	1.28E+00
HHO-LS	9.32E-03	1.69E-01	3.95E+00
GWO-LS	9.15E-03	6.70E-02	5.64E+00
FDA-LS	9.85E-03	1.57E-01	1.60E+00
SMA-LS	1.03E-02	4.49E-02	6.58E+00

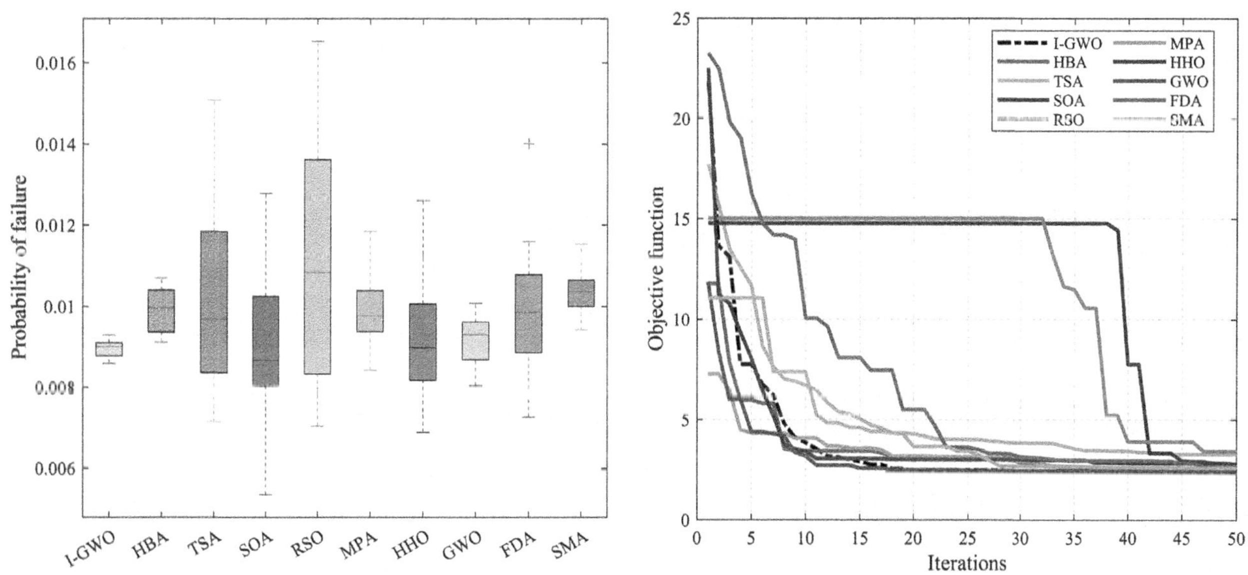

FIGURE 14.4 Boxplot of failure probabilities and convergence curves for developed models for Example 2.

Notably, the I-GWO-base LS model showed superior robustness, with a coefficient of variation of just 0.02 – the lowest among all algorithms. All models except RSO (which had a 14% error margin) produced acceptable estimates. Fig. 14.4 demonstrates that the I-GWO-based LS model achieved both the optimal objective function value and the fastest convergence rate, confirming the effectiveness of its algorithmic enhancements. The accompanying box plot further verifies that I-GWO-based LS exhibits the smallest variation in failure probability estimates across 20 independent runs.

14.3.3 Example 3

The third example examines a cantilever beam, a fundamental structural element in engineering applications. The system incorporates eleven random variables with normal and Gumbel distributions, whose statistical properties are detailed in

TABLE 14.6 Statistical properties of the random variables for Example 3.

Variable	Distribution	Mean	Standard deviation
$t\,(mm)$	Normal	5	0.10
$d\,(m^2)$	Normal	42	0.10
$L_1\,(mm)$	Normal	120	1.20
$L_2\,(mm)$	Normal	60	0.60
$F_1\,(kN)$	Gumbel	3	0.30
$F_2\,(kN)$	Gumbel	3	0.30
$P\,(kN)$	Gumbel	12	1.20
$T\,(N.\,m)$	Normal	90	9
$S_y\,(MPa)$	Normal	175	17.50
θ_1(deg.)	Normal	5	0.25
θ_2(deg.)	Normal	10	0.50

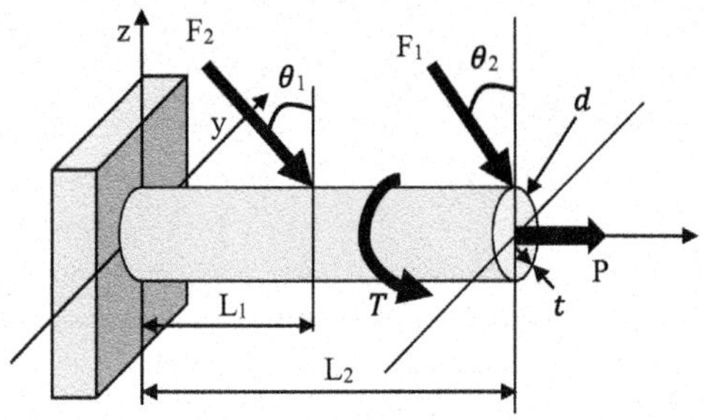

FIGURE 14.5 Schematic of a cantilever beam.

Table 14.6. Fig. 14.5 illustrates the beam configuration under multiple load conditions. Failure occurs when the maximum von Mises stress (σ_{max}) surpasses the tube material's yield strength (S_y), as defined by Eq. (14.30) [34].

$$g = S_y - \sigma_{max} \tag{14.30}$$

with,

$$\sigma_{max} = \sqrt{\sigma_x^2 + 3\tau_{zx}^2} \tag{14.31}$$

where the normal stress component (σ_x) and torsional shear stress component (τ_{zx}) are determined through:

$$\sigma_x = \frac{P + F_1 \sin(\theta_1) + F_2 \sin(\theta_2)}{A} + \frac{Md}{2I} \tag{14.32}$$

$$\tau_{zx} = \frac{Td}{4I} \tag{14.33}$$

where the following section properties are defined: bending moment (M), tubular cross-sectional area (A), and moment of inertia (I), calculated respectively as:

$$M = F_1 L_1 \mathrm{con}(\theta_1) + F_2 L_1 \cos(\theta_2) \tag{14.34}$$

$$A = \frac{\pi}{4}[d^2 - (d - 2t)^2] \tag{14.35}$$

$$I = \frac{\pi}{64}[d^4 - (d - 2t)^4] \tag{14.36}$$

The solution to Problem 4 is summarized in Table 14.7 and illustrated in Fig. 14.5. The failure probability of the problem was estimated to be 2.04×10^{-2} using MCS with 50×10^{-6} limit state function evaluations. Consistent with the previous two examples, the analysis results demonstrate that the LS models based on metaheuristic algorithms provided a reliable estimate of the cantilever beam's failure probability, achieving this with only 1050 limit state function calls. Among the models, I-GWO-LS and SOA-LS yielded the most accurate failure probability estimates, with the lowest error value of 2.11×10^{-2}. In contrast, SMA-LS exhibited the highest error at 64%.

TABLE 14.7 Results of proposed models on Example 3.

Method	Pf	Cov	ε (%)
MCS	2.04E-02	-	-
I-GWO-LS	2.11E-02	1.94E-01	3.58E+00
HBA-LS	2.12E-02	1.15E-01	3.86E+00
TSA-LS	1.73E-02	1.37E-01	1.50E+01
SOA-LS	2.11E-02	2.27E-01	3.58E+00
RSO-LS	2.23E-02	1.62E-01	9.27E+00
MPA-LS	1.78E-02	3.23E-01	1.28E+01
HHO-LS	1.81E-02	1.98E-01	1.12E+01
GWO-LS	2.26E-02	8.41E-02	1.07E+01
FDA-LS	1.28E-02	4.48E-01	3.71E+01
SMA-LS	7.17E-03	1.33E-01	6.48E+01

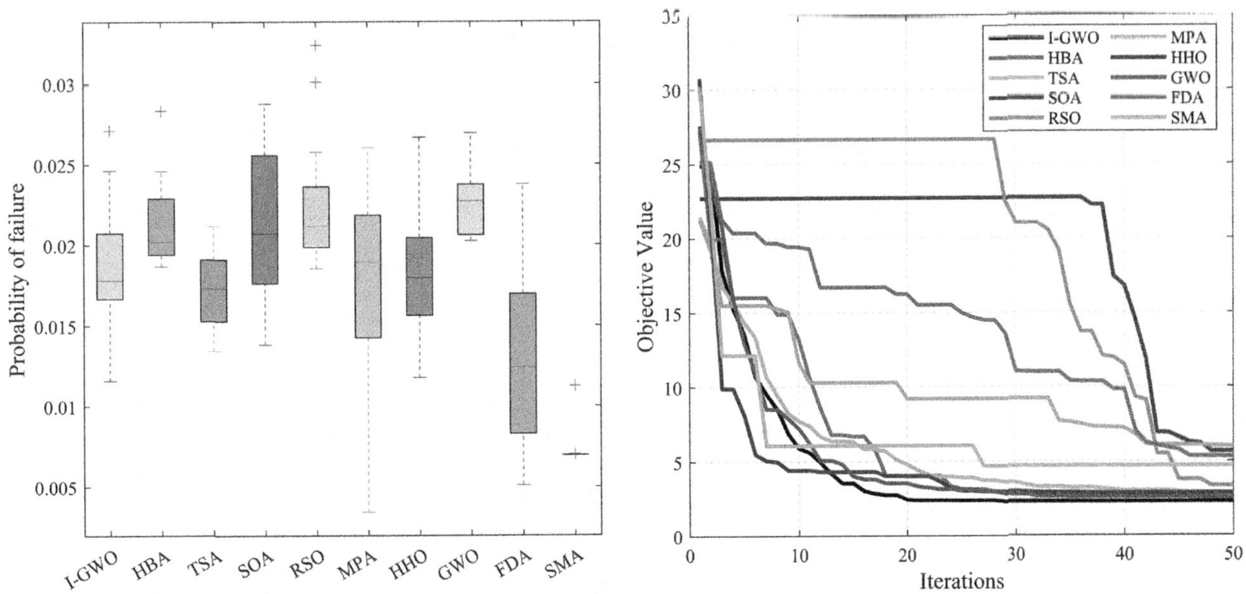

FIGURE 14.6 Boxplot of failure probabilities and convergence curves for developed models for Example 3.

TABLE 14.8 Computational time comparison of algorithms.

Algorithm	Time (s)		
	Ex 1	Ex 2	Ex 3
I-GWO-LS	9.12	9.09	10.49
HBA-LS	10.60	10.71	11.18
TSA-LS	0.09	0.10	0.11
SOA-LS	9.75	9.29	17.08
RSO-LS	9.12	9.21	12.69
MPA-LS	20.32	20.42	26.39
HHO-LS	0.25	0.22	0.23
GWO-LS	9.94	9.57	10.48
FDA-LS	24.30	26.22	28.34
SMA-LS	11.55	11.82	12.02

Another key observation, illustrated in Fig. 14.6, is the superior convergence rate and robustness of I-GWO-LS compared to other algorithms. Specifically, I-GWO-LS converged to the design points in 29 iterations (equivalent to 29 × 20 limit state function calls), significantly enhancing the accuracy of the LS-based failure probability estimation. Furthermore, as in prior examples, I-GWO-LS achieved the lowest standard deviation and coefficient of variation in the calculated failure probability, underscoring the precision and computational efficiency of the I-GWO algorithm.

14.3.4 Final remarks

As previously mentioned, accurately identifying design points significantly influences failure probability estimation in the LS method. The practical investigation of an enhanced GWO algorithm across three numerical-engineering examples in this chapter clearly demonstrates its high efficiency. Beyond demonstrating competitive accuracy compared to other algorithms, the improved GWO algorithm exhibits several advantageous characteristics:

- Rapid convergence speed
- Low standard deviation
- Favorable coefficient of variation in final responses

In addition, the computational time analysis of the algorithms is presented in Table 14.8. As shown, the average runtime of I-GWO across all three problems is approximately 10 seconds, which demonstrates highly favorable performance compared to other algorithms, especially considering the accuracy of failure probability estimation. Only the HHO and TSO algorithms exhibit average runtimes below 1 second, indicating strong computational efficiency; however, they fall short in terms of accuracy when compared to the proposed algorithm and others, resulting in higher estimation errors. The results further emphasize that IGWO has achieved a well-balanced trade-off between response accuracy and simulation time. It is worth noting that low computational time becomes particularly valuable when dealing with problems that require FEM-based simulations, where the use of MCS is practically infeasible. These properties confirm the algorithm's effectiveness for structural reliability assessment and its strong potential for solving real-world engineering problems.

14.4 Conclusion

LS is an efficient method for estimating the failure probability of structures. The accuracy of this method strongly depends on the precise determination of the direction of the unit vector. One efficient approach for this purpose is the use of metaheuristic search methods. However, employing these algorithms and identifying a powerful one presents another challenge.

In recent years, various approaches aimed at improving the performance of these algorithms in solving engineering problems have led to increased accuracy and reliability of their results. In this study, an improved algorithm based on GWO was used to enhance the accuracy of the LS method by accurately determining the direction of the unit vector.

The performance of the proposed hybrid model was evaluated and compared with other algorithms in solving three engineering and numerical examples.

The results indicated an increase in the accuracy of the proposed I-GWO-LS model compared to other optimization algorithms and MCS. Specifically, the use of I-GWO alongside LS not only increased the accuracy of estimating the probability of structural failure but also reduced the number of calls to the limit state function. This reduction significantly lowers computational costs in large-scale and real-world problems. Based on the obtained results, it is suggested that the proposed approach be used for the reliability-based design of structures.

Declaration of generative AI and AI-assisted technologies in the writing process

During the preparation of this work, the author(s) used ChatGPT in order to proofread and improve the writing. After using this tool/service, the author(s) reviewed and edited the content as needed and take(s) full responsibility for the content of the publication.

References

[1] S. Xiao, S. Oladyshkin, W. Nowak, Reliability analysis with stratified importance sampling based on adaptive Kriging, Reliability Engineering and System Safety 197 (2020). Available from https://doi.org/10.1016/j.ress.2020.106852.

[2] A.M. Hasofer, N.C. Lind, Exact and invariant second-moment code format, ASCE Journal of the Engineering Mechanics Division 100 (1974). Available from https://doi.org/10.1061/jmcea3.0001848.

[3] M. Hohenbichler, R. Rackwitz, Improvement of second-order reliability estimates by importance sampling, Journal of Engineering Mechanics 114 (1988). Available from https://doi.org/10.1061/(asce)0733-9399(1988)114:12(2195).

[4] N. Metropolis, S. Ulam, The monte carlo method, Journal of the American Statistical Association 44 (1949) 335–341. Available from https://doi.org/10.1080/01621459.1949.10483310.

[5] K. Song, Y. Zhang, X. Yu, B. Song, A new sequential surrogate method for reliability analysis and its applications in engineering, IEEE Access 7 (2019) 60555–60571.

[6] S. Song, Z. Lu, H. Qiao, Subset simulation for structural reliability sensitivity analysis, Reliability Engineering and System Safety 94 (2009). Available from https://doi.org/10.1016/j.ress.2008.07.006.

[7] S.K. Au, J.L. Beck, Estimation of small failure probabilities in high dimensions by subset simulation, Probabilistic Engineering Mechanics 16 (2001). Available from https://doi.org/10.1016/S0266-8920(01)00019-4.

[8] J. Jafari-Asl, S. Ohadi, M.E.A. Ben Seghier, N.-T. Trung, Accurate structural reliability analysis using an improved line-sampling-method-based slime mold algorithm, ASCE-ASME Journal of Risk and Uncertainty in Engineering Systems, Part A: Civil Engineering 7 (2021). Available from https://doi.org/10.1061/ajrua6.0001129.

[9] C. Dang, M.A. Valdebenito, M.G.R. Faes, J. Song, P. Wei, M. Beer, Structural reliability analysis by line sampling: a Bayesian active learning treatment, Structural Safety 104 (2023) 102351. Available from https://doi.org/10.1016/j.strusafe.2023.102351.

[10] C. Jiang, H. Qiu, Z. Yang, L. Chen, L. Gao, P. Li, A general failure-pursuing sampling framework for surrogate-based reliability analysis, Reliability Engineering and System Safety 183 (2019). Available from https://doi.org/10.1016/j.ress.2018.11.002.

[11] X. Cai, H. Qiu, L. Gao, C. Jiang, X. Shao, An efficient surrogate-assisted particle swarm optimization algorithm for high-dimensional expensive problems, Knowledge-Based Systems 184 (2019) 104901.

[12] M. Moustapha, B. Sudret, Surrogate-assisted reliability-based design optimization: a survey and a unified modular framework, Structural and Multidisciplinary Optimization 60 (2019). Available from https://doi.org/10.1007/s00158-019-02290-y.

[13] B. Gaspar, A.P. Teixeira, C.G. Soares, Assessment of the efficiency of Kriging surrogate models for structural reliability analysis, Probabilistic Engineering Mechanics 37 (2014). Available from https://doi.org/10.1016/j.probengmech.2014.03.011.

[14] A. Vatani, J. Jafari-Asl, S. Ohadi, N. Safaeian Hamzehkolaei, S. Afzali Ahmadabadi, J.A.F.O. Correia, An efficient surrogate model for reliability analysis of the marine structure piles, Proceedings of the Institution of Civil Engineers-Maritime Engineering, Emerald Publishing Limited, (2023), pp. 176–192 vol. 176.

[15] M.J.G. Rad, S. Ohadi, J. Jafari-Asl, A. Vatani, S.A. Ahmadabadi, J.A.F.O. Correia, GNDO-SVR: an efficient surrogate modeling approach for reliability-based design optimization of concrete dams, Structures, Elsevier, (2022), pp. 722–733 vol. 35.

[16] M. de Angelis, E. Patelli, M. Beer, Advanced Line Sampling for efficient robust reliability analysis, Structural Safety 52 (2015). Available from https://doi.org/10.1016/j.strusafe.2014.10.002.

[17] I. Papaioannou, D. Straub, Variance-based reliability sensitivity analysis and the FORM α-factors, Reliability Engineering and System Safety 210 (2021) 107496. Available from https://doi.org/10.1016/j.ress.2021.107496.

[18] Z. Meng, Q. Qian, M. Xu, B. Yu, A.R. Yıldız, S. Mirjalili, PINN-FORM: A new physics-informed neural network for reliability analysis with partial differential equation, Computer Methods in Applied Mechanics and Engineering 414 (2023). Available from https://doi.org/10.1016/j.cma.2023.116172.

[19] M.A. Valdebenito, M.G.R. Faes, Exploiting the precision of FORM and the accuracy of importance sampling for estimating failure probability and its sensitivity, Civil Engineering and Environmental Systems (2025) 1–19.

[20] C. Zhong, M. Wang, C. Dang, W. Ke, S. Guo, First-order reliability method based on Harris Hawks Optimization for high-dimensional reliability analysis, Structural and Multidisciplinary Optimization 62 (2020). Available from https://doi.org/10.1007/s00158-020-02587-3.

[21] C. Elegbede, Structural reliability assessment based on particles swarm optimization, Structural Safety 27 (2005). Available from https://doi.org/10.1016/j.strusafe.2004.10.003.

[22] J. Cheng, Hybrid genetic algorithms for structural reliability analysis, Computers & Structures 85 (2007). Available from https://doi.org/10.1016/j.compstruc.2007.01.018.

[23] D.M. Pedroso, FORM reliability analysis using a parallel evolutionary algorithm, Structural Safety 65 (2017). Available from https://doi.org/10.1016/j.strusafe.2017.01.001.

[24] H. Zhao, M. Zhao, C. Zhu, Reliability-based optimization of geotechnical engineering using the artificial bee colony algorithm, KSCE Journal of Civil Engineering 20 (2016). Available from https://doi.org/10.1007/s12205-015-0117-6.

[25] E. Zio, N. Pedroni, An optimized Line Sampling method for the estimation of the failure probability of nuclear passive systems, Reliability Engineering and System Safety 95 (2010). Available from https://doi.org/10.1016/j.ress.2010.06.007.

[26] S. Mirjalili, S.M. Mirjalili, A. Lewis, Grey wolf optimizer, Advances in Engineering Software 69 (2014) 46–61.

[27] A. Seyyedabbasi, F. Kiani, I-GWO and Ex-GWO: improved algorithms of the grey wolf optimizer to solve global optimization problems, Engineering Computations 37 (2021). Available from https://doi.org/10.1007/s00366-019-00837-7.

[28] X. Zhang, X. Wang, H. Chen, D. Wang, Z. Fu, Improved GWO for large-scale function optimization and MLP optimization in cancer identification, Neural Computing and Applications 32 (2020). Available from https://doi.org/10.1007/s00521-019-04483-4.

[29] M.H. Nadimi-Shahraki, S. Taghian, S. Mirjalili, An improved grey wolf optimizer for solving engineering problems, Expert Systems with Applications 166 (2021). Available from https://doi.org/10.1016/j.eswa.2020.113917.

[30] P.S. Koutsourelakis, H.J. Pradlwarter, G.I. Schuëller, Reliability of structures in high dimensions, part I: algorithms and applications, Probabilistic Engineering Mechanics 19 (2004). Available from https://doi.org/10.1016/j.probengmech.2004.05.001.

[31] G. Hongyuan, D. You, P. Gardoni, Adaptive subset simulation for time-dependent small failure probability incorporating first failure time and single-loop surrogate model, Structural Safety 102 (2023). Available from https://doi.org/10.1016/j.strusafe.2023.102327.

[32] Z. Hu, X. Du, First order reliability method for time-variant problems using series expansions, Structural and Multidisciplinary Optimization 51 (2015). Available from https://doi.org/10.1007/s00158-014-1132-9.

[33] J. Jafari-Asl, M.E.A. Seghier, Ben, S. Ohadi, J. Correia, J. Barroso, Reliability analysis based improved directional simulation using Harris Hawks optimization algorithm for engineering systems, Engineering Failure Analysis 135 (2022) 106148.

[34] L. Hong, H. Li, K. Peng, A combined radial basis function and adaptive sequential sampling method for structural reliability analysis, Applied Mathematical Modelling 90 (2021). Available from https://doi.org/10.1016/j.apm.2020.08.042.

Chapter 15

Applications and real-world case studies: the grey wolf optimizer for feature selection in intrusion detection systems

Ramya Chinnasamy[1], Malliga Subramanian[1], Nandita Sengupta[2], and M.P. Ramkumar[3]

[1]*Department of Computer Science and Engineering, Kongu Engineering College, Erode, Tamil Nadu, India,* [2]*Department of Information Technology, University College of Bahrain, Manama, Bahrain,* [3]*Department of Computer Science and Engineering, Thiyagarajar College of Engineering, Madurai, Tamil Nadu, India*

- Why is feature selection critical for improving the performance of intrusion detection systems (IDS)?
- How does the grey wolf optimizer (GWO) enhance feature selection in cybersecurity applications?
- In what ways can optimization techniques like GWO and machine learning models work together for better intrusion detection?
- How can GWO-based feature selection be applied to detect different types of cyberattacks?

This chapter answers all the questions in the think box.

15.1 Introduction

Over the past decade, there has been a sharp increase in connected devices across the globe. This, in turn, increases the attack surface and affects everything from critical infrastructure to enterprise systems. To tackle these issues, an intrusion detection system (IDS) is suggested [1]. An IDS acts as a frontline tool that monitors the entire system, ranging from host to network and alerts the corresponding entity when there is any possible attack. A good IDS examines large volumes of network traffic to identify low-signature threats [2]. The high dimensionality and diverse nature of cybersecurity data make it difficult for traditional data-driven methods to perform effectively.

To address the challenges of high-dimensional cybersecurity data, several techniques have been proposed. Some of the techniques are feature selection, dimensionality reduction, regularization techniques, and deep learning (DL)-based feature extraction [3]. Among these techniques, feature selection (FS) is a key approach because it offers a balance of efficiency, interpretability, and adaptability. It provides a targeted approach to managing high-dimensional data. It preserves domain-specific features such as protocol types and port numbers. This, in turn, helps the security analyst to ensure that model decisions are interpretable and actionable. Unlike other methods, FS maintains semantic clarity, which is important for tracking attack vectors. FS identifies and keeps only the most relevant attributes [4]. Additionally, it reduces noise and redundancy, thereby facilitating the development of an efficient IDS. Among the various techniques proposed for FS, bio-inspired algorithms have gained importance for their adaptability and potential for optimization [1].

A grey wolf optimizer (GWO) is a bio-inspired optimization algorithm [5]. It is inspired by the cooperative hunting strategies and hierarchical behavior of grey wolves in nature. Also, it establishes a dynamic balance of exploitation and exploration. This property enables the GWO to select important features from the high-dimensional dataset. As a result, the computational complexity can be reduced. Unlike exhaustive search methods, which analyze every possible feature

Grey Wolf Optimizer. DOI: https://doi.org/10.1016/B978-0-443-36624-6.00016-0

combination, GWO searches the feature space adaptively. This makes it effective for handling high-dimensional IDS datasets, where efficiency and precision are both critical.

This chapter explores the principles and implementation of GWO-based feature selection for IDS. It also presents a comparative analysis with other evolutionary and swarm intelligence algorithms, with GWO's strengths and limitations in real-world scenarios. The chapter further examines how GWO can be combined with machine learning (ML) and DL classifiers to build hybrid models for detecting specific attack categories. With experimental evaluations on benchmark datasets, this study presents a comprehensive guide on incorporating GWO into IDS.

15.2 Understanding the basics of intrusion detection systems

An IDS is a monitor that detects suspicious activities in a networked framework. It is broadly classified into signature-based and anomaly-based systems [3].

15.2.1 Types of intrusion detection systems

- **Signature-based IDS**: The known attack patterns, known as signatures, are stored in a signature database. The signature-based IDS compares the incoming traffic with the signatures and classifies it as normal or an attack. It performs well in identifying known threats. But it doesn't identify zero-day attacks and novel threat vectors [6].
- **Anomaly-based IDS**: It operates by modeling normal system behavior and identifying variations as potential threats. This method is more adaptive and detects zero-day attacks and new threats that are not mapped into signatures. In a noisy environment, this method is prone to a high false positive rate [7].

15.2.2 Challenges in intrusion detection systems datasets

The datasets used to train and test IDS models, such as KDD Cup99, network security laboratory-knowledge discovery in databases (NSL-KDD), and CIC-IDS2017, are high-dimensional and imbalanced [8]. The features of the datasets include protocol indicators, traffic rates, connection flags, and packet payload. This high-dimensionality often leads to many challenges. Some of them are,

(i) Overfitting risk: Models may learn noise or redundant information instead of true discriminative patterns.
(ii) Computational overhead: Processing of high-dimensional data may need more resources in terms of memory and time.
(iii) Feature redundancy: High-dimensional dataset often has overlapping and irrelevant information. This reduces the classifiers performance.

15.2.3 Importance of feature selection in intrusion detection systems

FS reduces the computational overhead by eliminating the irrelevant features, thereby improving speed and accuracy. By selecting only the essential features, IDS become

(i) Faster to train and deploy
(ii) More generalizable across different datasets
(iii) Less prone to false alarms

While FS methods like information gain, mutual information, and principal component analysis (PCA) are useful, they often can't handle nonlinear relationships and dynamic attack patterns. The metaheuristic optimization algorithms, such as GWO, overcome these limitations.

15.3 Grey wolf optimization in feature selection for intrusion detection systems

As discussed in Section 15.2.3, FS is important in ensuring detection models are efficient, interpretable, and scalable. This section explains how the GWO is applied for FS in IDS.

15.3.1 Representation of candidate solutions

Each grey wolf in the GWO population represents a candidate feature subset encoded as a binary string, where one indicates inclusion and 0 indicates exclusion of a feature. For example, a string like 101010... might represent a subset that includes every alternate feature. This encoding allows GWO to search the feature space dynamically.

15.3.2 Fitness function design

The quality of each feature subset is assessed using a fitness function [1], which mainly includes the following

(i) Classification accuracy: Using classifiers like support vector machine (SVM), random forest (RF), or DNN to evaluate detection performance
(ii) Feature count penalty: Encouraging smaller models by penalizing larger subsets.
(iii) Computational cost: Minimizing training time and resource overhead

A common fitness formulation combines detection accuracy with the inverse of the feature subset size to balance performance and efficiency.

15.3.3 Optimization flow

The optimization flow [9] is shown in Fig. 15.1.

(i) Initialization: A population of binary-encoded wolves is randomly generated (Fig. 15.2).
(ii) Evaluation: Each wolf's subset is evaluated using the fitness function through training and validation on benchmark IDS datasets.
(iii) Position update: Wolves adjust their positions based on leadership dynamics (α, β, δ), refining feature combinations iteratively.
(iv) Convergence: The algorithm progresses toward a feature subset that yields optimal classifier performance.

15.4 Integration of grey wolf optimization with machine learning and deep learning classifiers for intrusion detection systems enhancement

After the GWO selects the optimal subset of features, it should be evaluated through a classification mechanism. ML and DL models play a major role in classification.

15.4.1 Why integrate grey wolf optimization with a classifier?

Feature selection improves classifier performance by providing cleaner, more relevant inputs that enhance accuracy and reduce training time. It also promotes generalizability by minimizing overfitting, leading to better detection of unknown attack patterns. Fig. 15.3 illustrates the system architecture of the GWO-based feature selector with various classifiers in an IDS pipeline. GWO removes the high-dimensional noise and enables classifiers to concentrate on important features.

The classifier can be either ML-based or DL-based. Various ML and DL-based classifiers integrated with GWO-based feature selection and their typical use case is given in Table 15.1.

15.4.2 Application of grey wolf optimization-based feature selection to specific attack types

GWO-based feature selection enhances IDS performance by adapting feature subsets to the behavioral patterns of specific attack types. For DoS attacks, it isolates traffic surge indicators like connection rate and packet size. As a result, the detection accuracy is improved and the training time is reduced. In probing attacks, GWO emphasizes scan patterns and access attempts. It helps the classifiers to identify stealthy reconnaissance behavior. For R2L attacks, it filters out routine activity and focuses on anomalies like failed logins and payload irregularities. In U2R scenarios, GWO highlights subtle system-level events such as buffer overflows and permission misuse, enabling models to detect privilege escalation attempts more effectively.

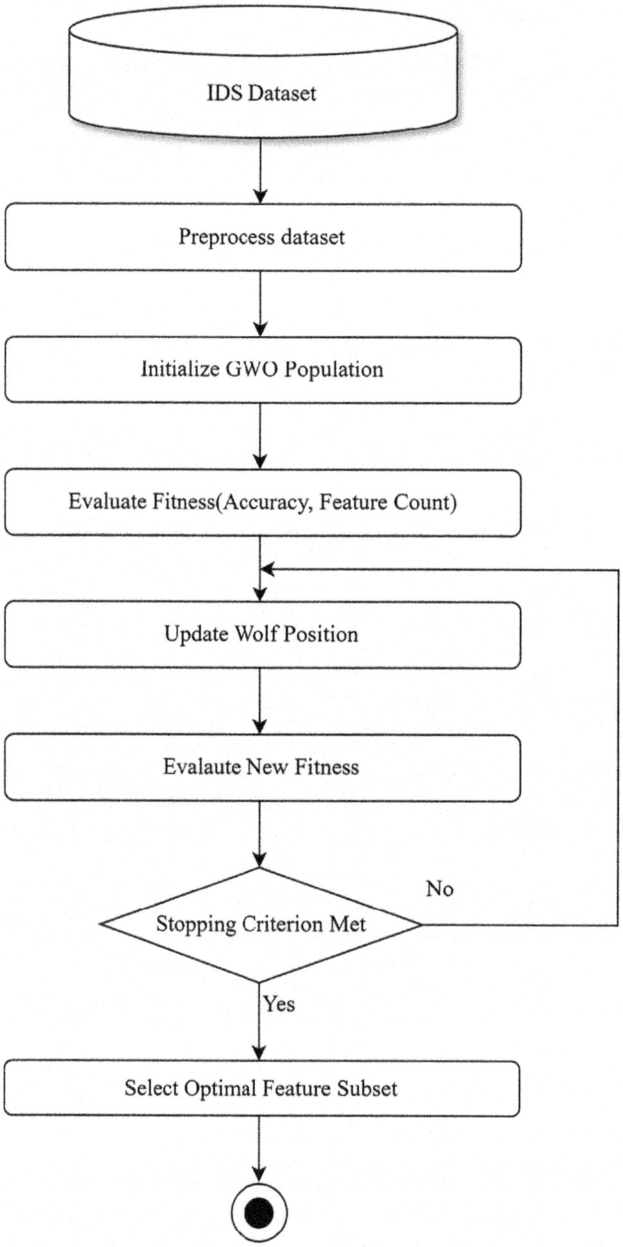

FIGURE 15.1 Workflow of GWO-based feature selection in IDS (*GWO*, Grey wolf optimization; *IDS*, intrusion detection systems).

15.5 Case study

As a case study, we developed an IDS that incorporates CIC-IDS2017 as a dataset for training and testing the model. The pipeline includes general preprocessing, GWO-based feature selection, classification using radial basis function kernel (SVM-RBF), and RF, and finally the performance measurement. The conceptual framework of the IDS with GWO-based feature selection used for the case study is illustrated in Fig. 15.2. This section explicates the details of the suggested method.

15.5.1 Dataset description

The Canadian Institute for Cyber security (CIC) developed a dataset for the development of IDS, named CIC-IDS 2017. It is openly accessible for download through the following link: https://www.unb.ca/cic/datasets/ids-2017.html.

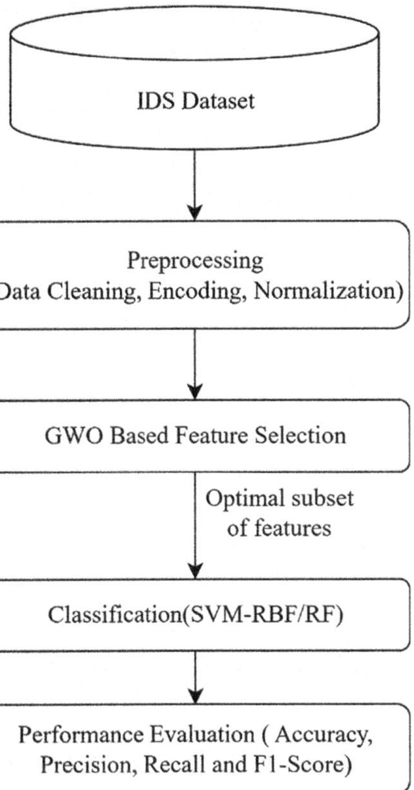

FIGURE 15.2 Conceptual framework of IDS with GWO-based feature selection for case study experiments (*GWO*, Grey wolf optimization; *IDS*, intrusion detection systems).

The complete description of the dataset is given in Table 15.1. It has 79 features and a total of 2,830,743 instances. It has labels for both binary and multiclass classification. For instance, this study conducted experiments for binary classification.

15.5.2 Initial data preprocessing

The dataset must undergo some preprocessing before it can be applied for the development of an AI model. In this study, the dataset is checked for irrelevant features initially. Eight features are identified as irrelevant, which are consequently deleted. Then, the dataset drops instances with null values. Finally, three features with fewer than 50 instances are dropped to avoid class imbalance.

15.5.3 Feature selection using grey wolf optimization algorithm

The dataset after the initial preprocessing contains 2,827,425 instances and 71 features. Since it is high-dimensional, we need to apply feature selection to identify and keep only the most relevant features. In this case, fivefold cross-validation is applied to the train dataset to ensure reliable estimation of each candidate feature subset's performance on unseen data and avoid overfitting to a single train/validation split. The subset with the highest fitness score has been taken as the best subset and has been used in the classification. Table 15.2 shows the details of CIC-IDS2017 dataset. Table 15.3 provides details of the features selected through the GWO algorithm.

15.6 Experimental results

The complete workflow of an IDS with a wrapper-based feature selection approach using GWO with k-fold cross-validation, along with the classification and performance measures, is given in Fig. 15.3. The experiments were conducted with two classifiers, namely SVM-RBF and RF. The performance of the classifiers was analysed with metrics such as

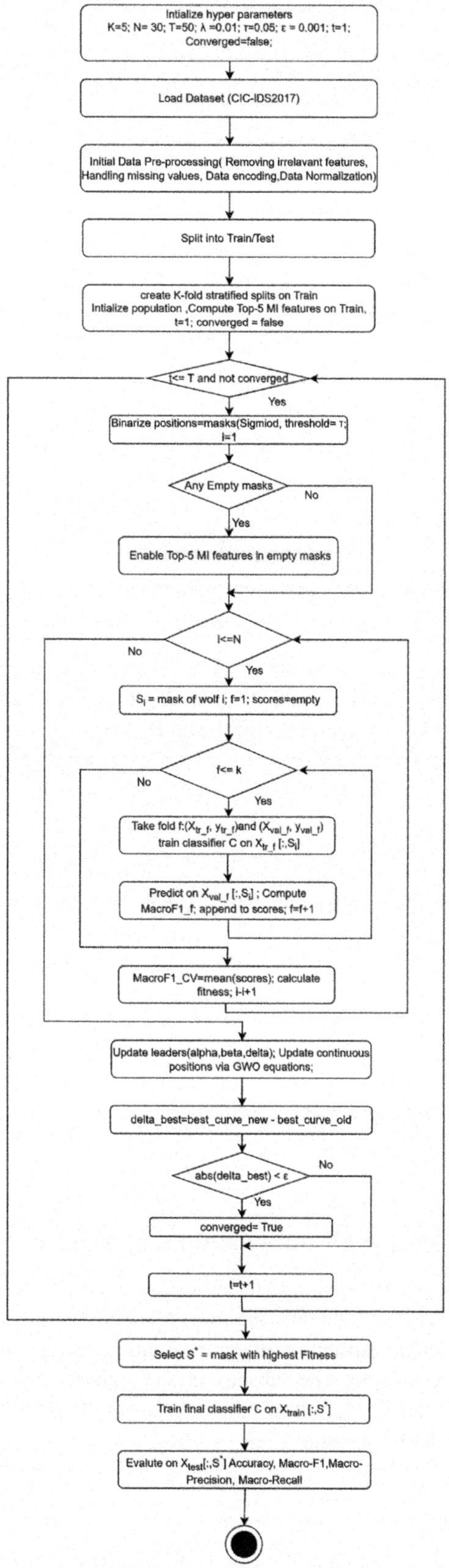

FIGURE 15.3 Workflow of the proposed wrapper-based feature selection approach using GWO with fivefold cross-validation (*GWO*, Grey wolf optimization).

TABLE 15.1 A typical use case.

Classifier	GWO benefit	Use case
Support vector machine (SVM) [10]	Reduces training time and improves boundary detection	Effective for binary attacks (e.g., denial of service [DoS])
Random forest (RF) [6]	Boosts precision by eliminating irrelevant features	Works well on imbalanced data
K-nearest neighbor (KNN) [3]	Helps reduce complexity in distance calculations	Useful for lightweight IDS
Naïve Bayes [7]	Prevents redundancy in probabilistic modeling	Ideal for fast prescreening layers
Deep neural network (DNN) (fully connected network) [7]	Improves convergence and avoids overfitting	General-purpose IDS with full traffic data
Convolutional neural network (CNN) (1D/2D) [3]	Focuses on packet-level features with spatial regularity	Deep packet inspection
Long short-term memory (LSTM)/gated recurrent unit (GRU) [3]	Enhances temporal relevance by pruning long sequences	IDS for streaming or time-series data

GWO, Grey wolf optimization; *IDS*, intrusion detection systems.

TABLE 15.2 CIC-IDS 2017 dataset.

Dataset	Attacks	Number of instances	Number of features
CIC-IDS2017	1. BENIGN	2,273,097	79
	2. DoS Hulk	231,073	
	3. PortScan	158,930	
	4. DDoS	128,027	
	5. DoS GoldenEye	10,293	
	6. FTP-Patator	7938	
	7. SSH-Patator	5897	
	8. DoS slowloris	5796	
	9. DoS Slowhttptest	5499	
	10. Bot	1966	
	11. Web attack brute force	1507	
	12. Web attack XSS	652	
	13. Infiltration	36	
	14. Web attack Sql injection	21	
	15. Heartbleed	11	
	Total	2,830,743	

accuracy, recall, f1-score, and precision. The classifier's performance was analysed with twofold techniques. (1) Use the dataset with GWO-based FS (2) dataset with all the features. Fig. 15.4 illustrates a bar graph showing the experimental results of the applied methods.

TABLE 15.3 Feature selection by GWO.

Total number of features in the dataset	Number of features after dropping irrelevant features	Number of features after feature selection by GWO	Name of the selected features
79	71	32	Total Backward Packets, Total Length of Fwd Packets, Total Length of Bwd Packets, Fwd Packet Length Max, Bwd Packet Length Min, Bwd Packet Length Std, Flow IAT Std, Flow IAT Max, Flow IAT Min, Bwd IAT Mean, Bwd IAT Max, Bwd IAT Min, Fwd URG Flags, Fwd Header Length, Bwd Header Length, Bwd Packets/s, Max Packet Length, Packet Length Mean, Packet Length Variance, SYN Flag Count, RST Flag Count, PSH Flag Count, ACK Flag Count, CWE Flag Count, Down/Up Ratio, Avg Fwd Segment Size, Avg Bwd Segment Size, Subflow Fwd Packets, Subflow Bwd Bytes, Active Mean, Active Min, Idle Std

GWO, Grey wolf optimization.

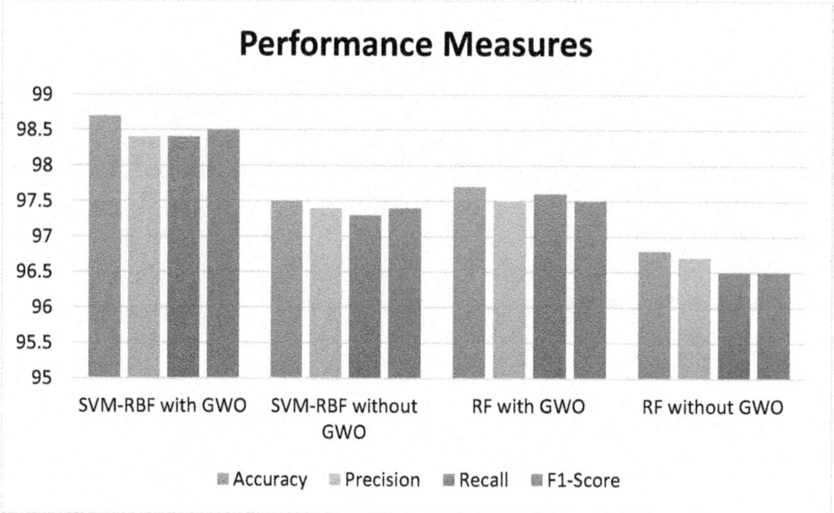

FIGURE 15.4 Comparison of performance metrics for SVM-RBF and RF with and without GWO (*GWO*, Grey wolf optimization; *RF*, random forest; *RBF*, radial basis function; SVM, support vector machine).

It compares the performance of SVM-RBF and RF classifiers with and without GWO-based feature selection. Clearly, SVM-RBF with GWO-based FS offers the best performance in terms of all four metrics. It achieves an accuracy of 98.6%, a precision and recall of 98.4%, and a F1-score of 98.5%. In addition, the RF classifier with GWO-based feature selection achieved an accuracy of 97.7%, a recall of 96.6% with a precision and F1-score of 97.5%. Both classifiers achieved a reduction in performance by around 1% in all four metrics. From these results, it is evident that the classifier with GWO-based FS performs better in terms of all measures in comparison with the classifier without any FS.

In summary, the FS technique addresses the issue of high-dimensionality and reduces the computational overhead. Also, it improves the performance by focussing on the most important features.

15.7 Comparative analysis of feature selection techniques

Various algorithms are available for feature selection in IDS. The major FS algorithms are traditional methods, evolutionary algorithms, swarm intelligence approaches, and bio-inspired optimizers. Fig. 15.5 illustrates various FS techniques along with their strengths and weaknesses.

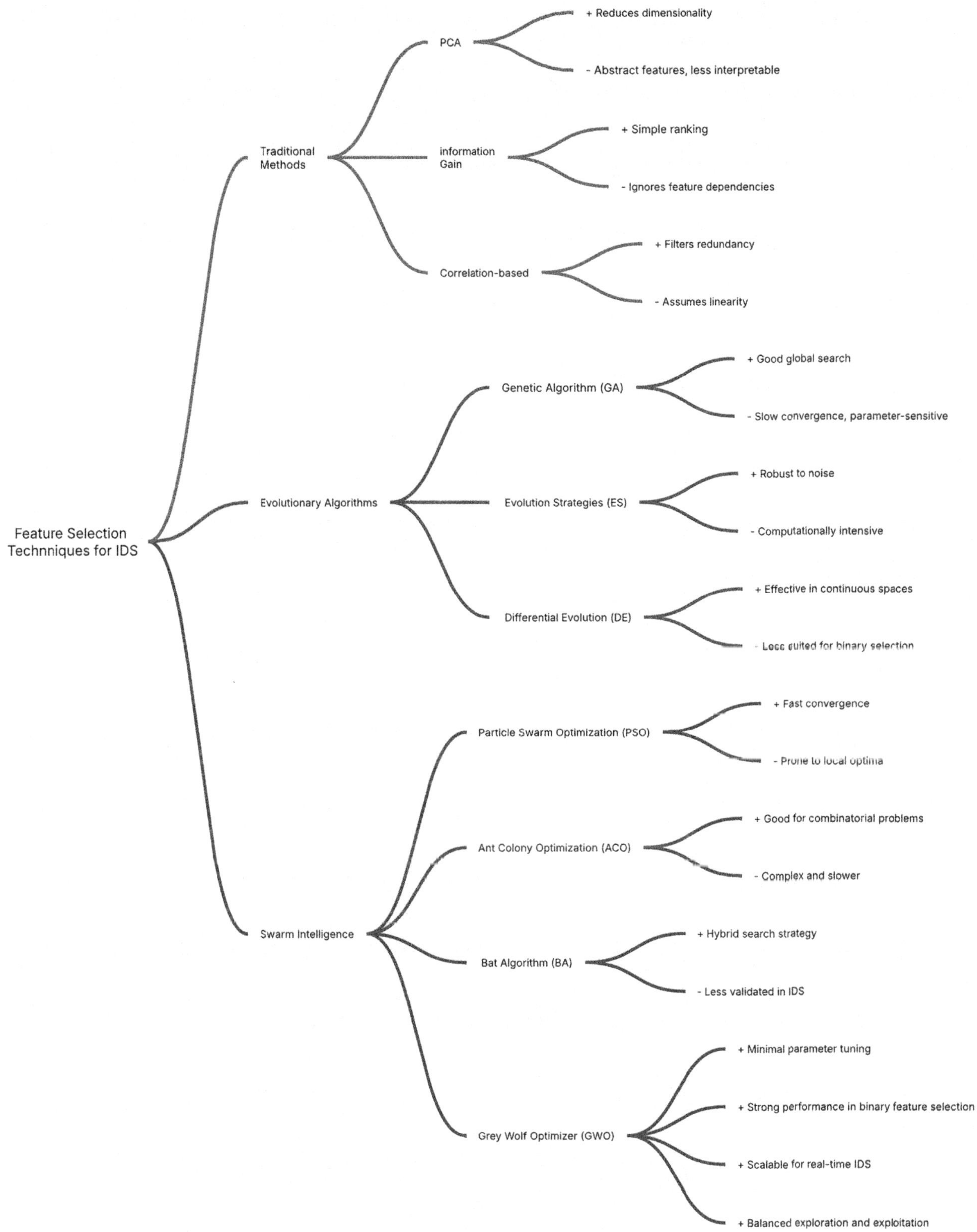

FIGURE 15.5 AN extended mind map of feature selection techniques in IDS (*IDS*, Intrusion detection systems).

Traditional Methods [11] such as PCA, Information Gain, and Correlation-Based Selection offer fast and straightforward approaches. Although PCA reduces dimensionality, with abstract features, the interpretability is reduced. Information Gain ranks features based on predictive power but lacks feature dependencies. Correlation-Based methods eliminate redundancy but assume linear relationships and lack adaptability to evolving attack patterns.

Evolutionary Algorithms draw inspiration from biological evolution. Genetic algorithms (GA) [12] have global search capabilities and flexible encoding. But they may converge slowly and require careful parameter tuning. Although differential evolution (DE) performs well in continuous spaces, it is less suitable for binary selection. evolution strategies are robust to noise but can be computationally intensive.

Swarm intelligence techniques imitate group behavior observed in nature [13]. Particle swarm optimization (PSO) has fast convergence and simple dynamics but is prone to premature convergence. Ant colony optimization (ACO) is good in combinatorial problems but involves complex and slower search processes. The bat algorithm combines exploration and exploitation effectively, but it is less utilized in the IDS domain.

GWO [10] performs better when compared with all the above methods. Because, it balances exploration and exploitation and needs minimal parameter tuning. As a result, it is well suited for large-scale IDS deployment.

15.7.1 Practical advantages of grey wolf optimization-based feature selection

(i) Reduction of feature set by 50%–70% with little or no degradation of performance.
(ii) Improved generalization to unseen attack types
(iii) Faster training times and enhanced suitability for real-time deployment

15.8 Challenges, limitations, and future prospects of grey wolf optimization in intrusion detection systems

While GWO-based feature selection in IDS offers many advantages, it also has some limitations. They are

15.8.1 Challenges and limitations

When applied to very large datasets or multilayered IDS frameworks, GWO can become resource-intensive. Without adaptive scaling techniques, convergence in high-dimensional feature spaces may be slowed down by binary encoding for feature selection. Feature subsets that have been optimized for one dataset might not transfer well to another. Despite using fewer parameters than algorithms such as GA or ACO, GWO's effectiveness still depends on selecting the right population size and number of iterations. Real-world IDS often needs subtle feature weighting instead of binary inclusion and exclusion.

15.8.2 Future prospects

Multiobjective fitness functions or adaptive control parameters may be included in the future to balance detection accuracy, feature count, and resource usage. Combining GWO with other algorithms like PSO, DE, or ACO may enhance diversity and convergence speed. GWO-driven feature selection may be integrated into federated learning and preserve privacy while training distributed IDS. Lightweight GWO variants can be used for edge computing environments. Integrating GWO into interpretable models can enhance trust in automated decisions, especially in critical infrastructure settings.

15.8.3 Scalability and distributed deployment

A limitation of the present work is that all evaluation is performed in a single-node, centralized setting. Real-world intrusion detection often requires federated or distributed deployments that generate massive, high-velocity data streams. Future research should therefore explore how GWO-based feature selection can be adapted to these large-scale scenarios. For example, through federated learning, hierarchical IDS designs, or streaming variants of GWO.

15.9 Conclusion

GWO-based feature selection offers a powerful solution for building scalable and accurate IDS amid increasingly complex cyber threats. It also enhances classifier precision and adapts effectively across diverse attack categories. Its proven performance on benchmark datasets like NSL-KDD and CIC-IDS2017 demonstrates both high accuracy and real-time applicability. Emerging techniques like hybrid metaheuristics and federated learning show promise despite obstacles like parameter adjustment and model transferability. Ultimately, GWO emerges as a practical and impactful approach for advancing next-generation cybersecurity solutions.

Declaration of generative AI and AI-assisted technologies in the writing process

During the preparation of this work, the author(s) used ChatGPT by OpenAI in order to paraphrase and refine text. After using this tool/service, the author(s) reviewed and edited the content as needed and take(s) full responsibility for the content of the publication.

References

[1] R. Chinnasamy, M. Subramanian, N. Sengupta, Empowering intrusion detection systems: a synergistic hybrid approach with optimization and deep learning techniques for network security, The International Arab Journal of Information Technology (IAJIT) 22 (2025) 60–76.

[2] K. He, D.D. Kim, M.R. Asghar, Adversarial machine learning for network intrusion detection systems: a comprehensive survey, IEEE Communications Surveys & Tutorials 25 (2023) 538–566.

[3] R. Chinnasamy, S. Malliga, N. Sengupta, Deep learning-driven intrusion detection systems for smart cities-a systematic study, 2022.

[4] J. Lee, K. Park, GAN-based imbalanced data intrusion detection system, Personal and Ubiquitous Computing 25 (2021) 121–128.

[5] S. Mirjalili, S.M. Mirjalili, A. Lewis, Grey wolf optimizer, Advances in engineering software 69 (2014) 46–61.

[6] R. Ahmad, I. Alsmadi, W. Alhamdani, L.A. Tawalbeh, A comprehensive deep learning benchmark for IoT IDS, Computers & Security 114 (2022) 102588.

[7] M. Otair, O.T. Ibrahim, L. Abualigah, M. Altalhi, P. Sumari, An enhanced grey wolf optimizer based particle swarm optimizer for intrusion detection system in wireless sensor networks, Wireless Networks 28 (2022) 721–744.

[8] E. Devi, R. Suganthe, Feature selection in intrusion detection grey wolf optimizer, Asian Journal of Research in Social Sciences and Humanities 7 (2017) 671–682.

[9] H.F. Almazini, K.R. Ku-Mahamud, H. Almazini, Heuristic initialization using grey wolf optimizer algorithm for feature selection in intrusion detection, Int. J. Intell. Eng. Syst 16 (2023) 410–418.

[10] S. Hosseini, B.M.H. Zade, New hybrid method for attack detection using combination of evolutionary algorithms, SVM, and ANN, Computer Networks 173 (2020) 107168.

[11] A. Alzaqebah, I. Aljarah, O. Al-Kadi, R. Damaševičius, A modified grey wolf optimization algorithm for an intrusion detection system, Mathematics 10 (2022) 999.

[12] P. Singh, V. Ranga, Multilayer perceptron and genetic algorithm-based intrusion detection framework for cloud environment, in: Mobile Radio Communications and 5G Networks: Proceedings of MRCN 2020, 2021, pp. 475-485.

[13] M. Jain, V. Saihjpal, N. Singh, S.B. Singh, An overview of variants and advancements of PSO algorithm, Applied Sciences 12 (2022) 8392.

Chapter 16

Optimizing solutions of fractional differential equations using the grey wolf optimizer and homotopy analysis method

Hisham M. Khudhur[1], Kais I. Ibraheem[2], Basim A. Hassan[1], Khalil K. Abbo[3], and Ramadan M. Ramo[4]
[1]*Department of Mathematics, College of Computers Sciences and Mathematics, University of Mosul, Mosul, Iraq,* [2]*Department of Computer Science, College of Education for Pure Sciences, University of Mosul, Mosul, Iraq,* [3]*Department of Mathematics, College of Basic Education, University of Telafer, Tall'Afar, Iraq,* [4]*Department of Management Information Systems, College of Administration and Economics, University of Mosul Mosul, Iraq*

16.1 Introduction to the grey wolf optimizer

Meta-heuristic optimization algorithms have gained prominence for solving complex, high-dimensional problems where traditional methods fall short. Inspired by natural phenomena, these algorithms balance exploration (searching new regions) and exploitation (refining known solutions). Among them, the grey wolf optimizer (GWO), introduced by Mirjalili et al. in 2014 [1], stands out for its simplicity, efficiency, and ability to avoid local optima. Inspired by the social hierarchy and cooperative hunting behavior of grey wolves, GWO mimics the leadership structure and decision-making processes of wolf packs to navigate search spaces effectively [2].

16.1.1 Social hierarchy in grey wolf optimizer

In nature, grey wolves follow a strict dominance hierarchy:

- Alpha (α): The leaders responsible for decision-making.
- Beta (β): Subordinates that assist the alpha in enforcing decisions.
- Delta (δ): Mid-ranking wolves with roles like hunting or scouting.
- Omega (ω): Followers that update positions based on higher-ranked wolves.

In GWO, the three best solutions in each iteration are designated as α, β, and δ, guiding the remaining solutions (ω) toward promising regions.

16.1.2 Algorithms of grey wolf optimizer

The algorithm operates through three key phases:

16.1.2.1 Encircling prey

Wolves encircle the prey (candidate solution) using:

$$\vec{D} = |\vec{C} \cdot \vec{X_p}(t) - \vec{X}(t)| \tag{16.1}$$

$$\vec{X}(t+1) = \vec{X_p}(t) - \vec{A} \cdot \vec{D} \tag{16.2}$$

Here, $\vec{X_p}$ is the prey's position, $\vec{A}$ and $\vec{C}$ are coefficient vectors controlling exploration and exploitation, and $\vec{D}$ represents the distance between a wolf and the prey.

Grey Wolf Optimizer. DOI: https://doi.org/10.1016/B978-0-443-36624-6.00028-7

16.1.2.2 Hunting

The α, β, and δ wolves estimate the prey's location. Other wolves update their positions based on these leaders:

$$\vec{X}(t+1) = \frac{\vec{X_1} + \vec{X_2} + \vec{X_3}}{3} \tag{16.3}$$

where $\vec{X_1}$, $\vec{X_2}$, $\vec{X_3}$ are positions derived from α, β, and δ.

16.1.2.3 Attacking prey (Exploitation)

As iterations progress, wolves attack the prey by reducing the parameter $\vec{a}$ (linearly decreased from 2 to 0). This shrinks the search radius, emphasizing local refinement.

16.1.2.4 Searching for new prey (Exploration)

When $|\vec{A}| > 1$, wolves diverge to explore new regions, preventing stagnation in local optima.

16.1.3 Advantages and applications

GWO's adaptive parameters ($\vec{A}$ and $\vec{C}$) ensure a dynamic balance between exploration and exploitation. Its simplicity—requiring only two tunable parameters—makes it easy to implement. The algorithm excels in:

- **Engineering design:** Optimizing tension/compression springs, welded beams, and pressure vessels.
- **Optical engineering:** Enhancing slow-light properties in photonic crystal waveguides for optical buffers.
- **Machine learning:** Training neural networks and feature selection.

Conclusion: GWO's biologically inspired framework offers robustness and efficiency for global optimization. Future extensions, such as multiobjective or binary variants, could broaden its applicability in robotics, energy systems, and artificial intelligence. By leveraging the natural intelligence of wolf packs, GWO continues to evolve as a versatile tool for solving real-world challenges [3,4].

This chapter presents a study on solving linear differential equations with fractional orders using the analytical homotopy method (HAM) combined with the GWO algorithm to enhance results. It details the algorithm's implementation steps, starting from the initial guess and calculating subsequent iterations, to optimizing the auxiliary parameter (h) using the root mean square error (RMSE) as a fitness function.

16.2 Solving linear differential equations with fractional orders

In this work, we present the steps for solving linear differential equations with fractional orders using the HAM with the GWO algorithm. Numerical examples were taken and solved approximately with the series obtained from the collection of iterations of the homotopy method, then taking the final series and finding the mean square error and considering it as a fitness function in the GWO algorithm for improvement and finding the best value for the auxiliary parameter h in the homotopy method with the least number of iterations, and then we reached new results better than the HAM [5].

16.3 Steps for solving linear differential equations with fractional orders using grey wolf optimizer algorithm

This algorithm is an improvement process for the results of the HAM using the GWO algorithm. The method can be summarized in five steps.

First: A linear differential equation with a fractional order is taken and the initial guess is calculated using equation

$$y_0(x) = \sum_{k=0}^{n-1} y^{(k)}(0^+)\frac{x^k}{k!} \tag{16.4}$$

Second: Finding subsequent iterations is done using Eq. (16.4).

$$y_m(x) = \chi_m y_{m-1}(x) + hI^{\alpha}(R_{m-1}(y_{m-1}(x))) \tag{16.5}$$

And by relying primarily on the first iteration to find a solution to the fractional order differential equation using the homotopy method (HAM). To reach the solution series by calculating specific iterations of the analytical method.

Third: The last iteration Q_4 is taken, which is the result of summing the resulting iterations

$$Q_4 = y_0 + y_1 + y_2 + y_3 \tag{16.6}$$

Fourth: The Runge-Kutta algorithm for optimization is used to find the best value for the parameter (h) to improve the results of the analytical homotopy method (GWO) for solving differential equations with fractional orders, if we use the mean square error as a fitness function in the algorithm, with a criterion to determine the improvement of results, like the exact solution.

Fifth: The final results of the two algorithms (GWO) and the homotopy method (HAM) are compared with the exact solution using the error rate (RMSE).

The hybrid GWO-HAM algorithm frames the challenge of finding the best h as an optimization problem.

16.3.1 The pseudo code of the grey wolf optimizer-analytical homotopy method algorithm

1. **Initialization:** The algorithm starts with a random population of h values (the "wolf pack").
2. **Fitness evaluation:** For each wolf's h value, the algorithm calculates a full HAM solution to the FDE. It then measures the accuracy of this solution by calculating the **RMSE** against the known exact solution. A lower RMSE means a better h value (a "fitter" wolf).
3. **Hierarchy and hunt:** The GWO identifies the three best wolves (alpha, beta, and delta) based on their low RMSE scores. It then uses its unique hunting equations to guide the other wolves toward these top performers.
4. **Iteration:** This process of evaluation and updating is repeated for a set number of iterations. With each iteration, the pack converges on an even better value for h.
5. **Final output:** Once the process is complete, the position of the **Alpha wolf** is returned. This is the **optimal value of** h, which can then be used in the HAM to generate the most accurate possible approximate solution for the given fractional differential equation.

16.4 Numerical results

In this chapter, a hybrid approach combining the homotopy analytical method and the grey wolves algorithm was adopted to solve linear differential equations of fractional orders. The study aimed to enhance the accuracy of numerical solutions by optimizing the choice of the parameter (h) in the homotopy analytical method, which plays a pivotal role in reducing computational errors. The grey wolves algorithm was applied to three examples to measure its effectiveness by comparing the RMSE between the approximate and analytical solutions, where the RMSE was selected as the fitness function to guide the GWO algorithm. This metric is particularly well-suited for optimization because it penalizes larger errors more significantly than smaller ones due to the squaring of the error term $(exact - Q)^2$. This property ensures that the resulting approximate solution is uniformly close to the exact solution across the entire domain, avoiding any single point of large deviation. Compared to other metrics like mean absolute error, which treats all errors linearly, RMSE is more sensitive to outliers, making it a more robust choice for ensuring high accuracy in scientific and engineering models. MATLAB was used to plot the results and analyze the variance between the methods. The results showed a significant reduction in error rates when using GWO compared to the traditional HAM, which recorded a clear improvement. The graphs generated by MATLAB confirmed the superiority of the hybrid method in achieving faster convergence to the optimal solution. These results are documented through detailed comparison tables of numerical values, supporting the reliability of the proposed algorithm in dealing with complex fractional systems. (Tables 16.1–16.6)

Example 1.

Let's take the initial value problem containing a linear differential equation with a fractional order:

$$D^2y(x) + 0.5D^{0.5}y(x) + y(x) = 2 + \frac{1}{\Gamma(2.5)}x^{1.5} + x^2 \tag{16.7}$$

$$y(0) = 0,\ y'(0) = 0 \tag{16.8}$$

Given that the exact solution is: $y(x) = x^2$ [6].

Solution

First: We choose the initial guess y_0 according to Eq.(16.4).

$$y_0(x) = 0 \tag{16.9}$$

TABLE 16.1 Shows the numerical results for each of the exact solution and the approximate solution using the (*HAM*) method, and the approximate solution using the two algorithms (*GWO*) by taking different values for the variable x for Example (1).

x	Exact solution	HAM	GWO
		h=-1	h=-0.9829
0	0	0	0
0.1	0.0100	0.0100	0.0100
0.2	0.0400	0.0400	0.0400
0.3	0.0900	0.0900	0.0900
0.4	0.1600	0.1600	0.1600
0.5	0.2500	0.2500	0.2500
0.6	0.3600	0.3600	0.3600
0.7	0.4900	0.4901	0.4900
0.8	0.6400	0.6401	0.6400
0.9	0.8100	0.8103	0.8100
1.0	1.0000	1.0007	1.0002

Optimal h by GWO is (-0.9829) and the amount of error is 1.3991e-05

TABLE 16.2 Comparison of meta-heuristic optimizers for Example 1.

Optimizer	Best optimal h	Best RMSE	Mean RMSE (30 runs)	Std. dev. (RMSE)
GWO	−0.9829	1.3991e-05	1.4512e-05	3.12e-07
PSO	−0.9815	1.8422e-05	2.0115e-05	5.67e-07
GA	−0.9851	2.3156e-05	2.9430e-05	9.81e-07

Second: To find the approximate iterations $y_1(x)$, $y_2(x)$, $y_3(x)$ we use the deformation equation of order m

$$y_m(x) = \chi_m y_{m-1}(x) + hI^{\alpha}[R_{m-1}(\vec{y}_{m-1}(x))] \tag{16.10}$$

We obtain

$$y_m(x) = \chi_m y_{m-1}(x) + hI^{2}[R_{m-1}(\vec{y}_{m-1}(x))] \tag{16.11}$$

Where

$$R_{m-1}(\vec{y}_{m-1}(x)) = D^2 y_{m-1}(x) + 0.5D^{0.5}y_{m-1}(x) + y_{m-1}(x) - \left(2 + \frac{1}{\Gamma(2.5)}x^{1.5} + x^2\right)(1 - \chi_m) \tag{16.12}$$

When substituting in Eq. (16.10) at $m = 1$, we get

$$y_1(x) = \frac{-2hx^2}{\Gamma(3)} - \frac{hx^{3.5}}{\Gamma(4.5)} - \frac{\Gamma(3)hx^4}{\Gamma(5)} \tag{16.13}$$

TABLE 16.3 Shows the numerical results for each of the exact solution and the approximate solution using the (*HAM*) method, and the approximate solution using the two algorithms (*GWO*) by taking different values for the variable x for Example (2).

x	Exact solution	HAM	GWO
		$h = -1$	$h = -0.2006$
0	0	0	0
0.1	0.0998	0.0991	0.0995
0.2	0.1987	0.1947	0.1974
0.3	0.2955	0.2855	0.2928
0.4	0.3894	0.3706	0.3852
0.5	0.4794	0.4493	0.4743
0.6	0.5646	0.5213	0.5595
0.7	0.6442	0.5862	0.6407
0.8	0.7174	0.6440	0.7175
0.9	0.7833	0.6945	0.7897
1.0	0.8415	1.7379	0.8571

Optimal h by GWO is (-0.2006) and the amount of error is 2.7220e-05

TABLE 16.4 Comparison of meta-heuristic optimizers for Example 2.

Optimizer	Best optimal h	Best RMSE	Mean RMSE (30 runs)	Std. dev. (RMSE)
GWO	−0.2006	2.7318e-06	2.7845e-06	9.45e-08
PSO	−0.1995	3.5521e-06	4.1380e-06	1.52e-07
GA	−0.2018	4.9811e-06	6.2514e-06	2.78e-07

When $m = 2,3, \ldots$, Eq. (16.10) becomes:

$$y_m(x) = \chi_m y_{m-1}(x) + h\left[y_{m-1}(x) + 0.5I^{1.5}y_{m-1}(x) + I^2 y_{m-1}(x)\right] \tag{16.14}$$

By substituting for $m = 2$ in Eq. (16.14) and using the properties of Riemann–Liouville integration, we get:

$$y_2(x) = \chi_2 y_1(x) + h\left[y_1(x) + 0.5I^{1.5}y_1(x) + I^2 y_1(x)\right] \tag{16.15}$$

$$\begin{aligned} y_2(x) = & \frac{-2(1+h)hx^2}{\Gamma(3)} - \frac{(1+h)hx^{3.5}}{\Gamma(4.5)} - \frac{(1+h)h\Gamma(3)x^4}{\Gamma(5)} - \frac{h^2x^{3.5}}{\Gamma(4.5)} - \frac{0.5h^2x^5}{\Gamma(6)} - \frac{0.5h^2\Gamma(3)x^{5.5}}{\Gamma(6.5)} \\ & - \frac{2h^2x^4}{\Gamma(5)} - \frac{h^2x^{5.5}}{\Gamma(6.5)} - \frac{h^2\Gamma(3)x^6}{\Gamma(7)} \end{aligned} \tag{16.16}$$

TABLE 16.5 Shows the numerical results for each of the exact solution and the approximate solution using the (HAM) method, and the approximate solution using the two algorithms (*GWO*) by taking different values for the variable x for Example (3).

X	Exact solution	HAM	GWO
		h=-1	h=-0.7504
0	0	0	0
0.1	0.0100	0.0101	0.0100
0.2	0.0400	0.0406	0.0400
0.3	0.0900	0.0925	0.0900
0.4	0.1600	0.1670	0.1600
0.5	0.2500	0.2652	0.2499
0.6	0.3600	o.3888	0.3597
0.7	0.4900	0.5393	0.4896
0.8	0.6400	0.7187	0.6396
0.9	0.8100	0.9289	0.8100
1.0	1.0000	1.1719	1.0009
Optimal h by GWO is (-0.7504) and the amount of error is 5.6747e-06			

TABLE 16.6 Comparison of meta-heuristic optimizers for Example 3.

Optimizer	Best optimal *h*	Best RMSE	Mean RMSE (30 runs)	Std. dev. (RMSE)
GWO	−0.7504	5.6747e-06	5.8113e-06	1.34e-07
PSO	−0.7491	9.1533e-06	1.2204e-05	4.18e-07
GA	−0.7612	1.1420e-05	2.5615e-05	8.91e-07

And when substituting in Eq. (16.14) for $m = 3$ and using the properties of Riemann–Liouville integration, we get:

$$y_3(x) = \frac{-2(1+h)^2hx^2}{\Gamma(3)} - \frac{(3h^3+4h^2+h)x^{3.5}}{\Gamma(4.5)} - \frac{(h+h^2)((1+h)\Gamma(3)+4h)x^4}{\Gamma(5)} - \frac{h^2(2+3h)x^5}{2\Gamma(6)} - \frac{(4h^2+6h^3)x^{5.5}}{\Gamma(6.5)} - \frac{(4h^2+6h^3)x^6}{\Gamma(7)} - \frac{h^3x^{6.5}}{4\Gamma(7.5)} - \frac{3h^3x^7}{2\Gamma(8)} - \frac{3h^3x^{7.5}}{\Gamma(8.5)} - \frac{2h^3x^8}{\Gamma(9)} \tag{16.17}$$

Third: We sum the iterations we obtained $y_0(x)$, $y_1(x)$, $y_2(x)$, $y_3(x)$ to get the approximate solution $Q_4(x)$

$$Q_4(x) = y_0(x) + y_1(x) + y_2(x) + y_3(x) \tag{16.18}$$

Fourth: Here we find the root mean square error for Eq. (16.7) with the following equation: (Fig. 16.1, Fig. 16.2, Fig. 16.3).

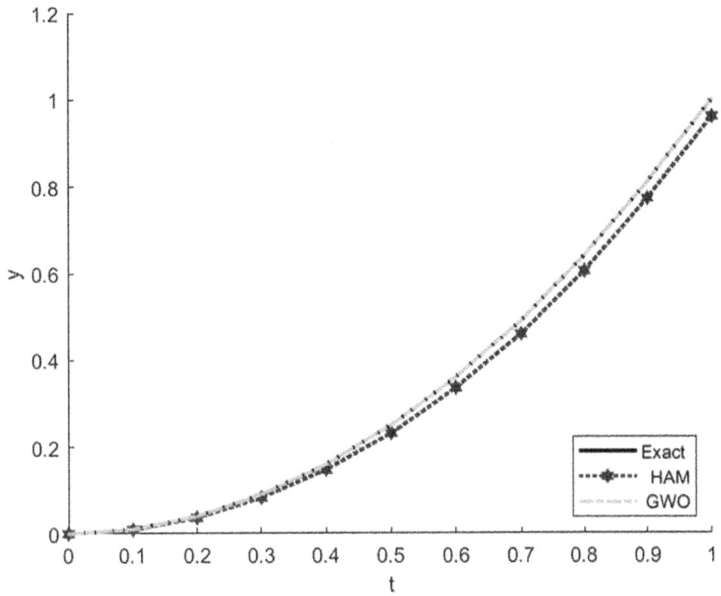

FIGURE 16.1 Shows the convergence between the solution using the analytical homotopy method and the optimization algorithm (*GWO*) to the exact solution for Example (1) (*GWO*, Grey wolf optimizer).

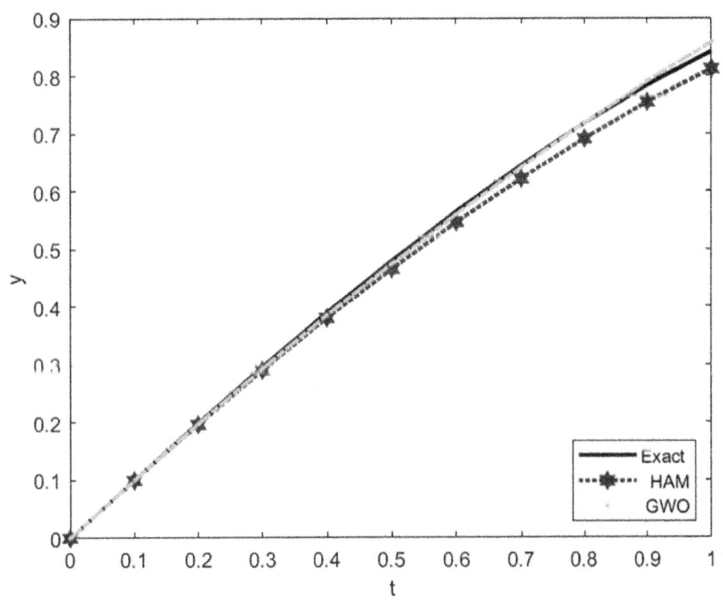

FIGURE 16.2 Shows the convergence between the solution using the analytical homotopy method and the optimization algorithm (*GWO*) to the exact solution for Example (2) (*GWO*, Grey wolf optimizer).

RMSE=$\sqrt{\frac{\sum_{i=1}^{n}(exact-Q)^2}{n}}$, where Q is the approximate solution and n is the number of points, and considering it as an appropriate function in the GWO algorithm. When performing algorithm operations on it, we get the best value for the parameter h.

Example 2.

Let's take the initial value problem containing a differential equation with a fractional order:

$$D^{1.5}y(x) + c^2y(x) = 0,\ y(0) = 0,\ y'(0) = c,\ c > 0 \qquad (16.19)$$

Given that the exact solution is: $y(x) = \sin(cx)$ [7].

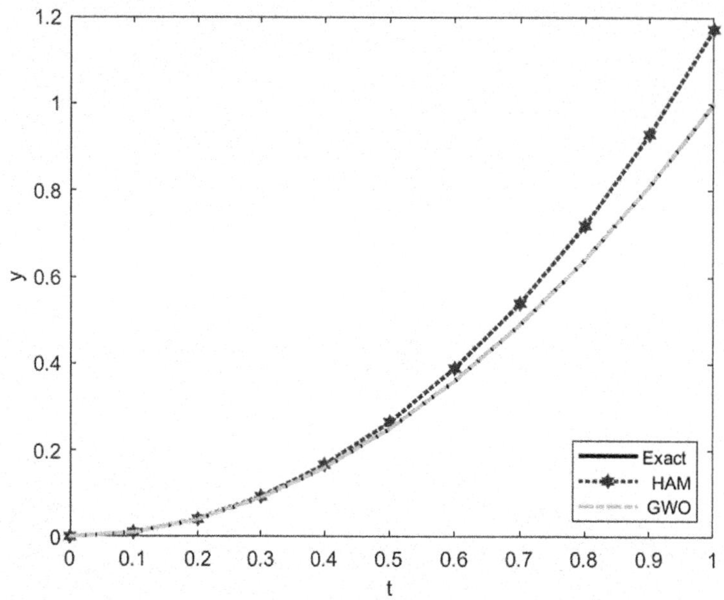

FIGURE 16.3 Shows the convergence between the solution using the analytical homotopy method and the optimization algorithm (*GWO*) to the exact solution for Example (3) (*GWO*, gRey wolf optimizer).

Solution

First: We find the initial guess y_0 according to Eq. (16.4):

$$y_0(x) = 0 + \frac{cx}{1!} \tag{16.20}$$

$$y_0(x) = cx \tag{16.21}$$

Second: We find the rest of the approximate iterations $y_1(x)$, $y_2(x)$, $y_3(x)$ from the deformation equation of order m

$$y_m(x) = \chi_m y_{m-1}(x) + hI^{\alpha}[R_{m-1}(\vec{y}_{m-1}(x))] \tag{16.22}$$

We obtain

$$y_m(x) = \chi_m y_{m-1}(x) + hI^{1.5}[R_{m-1}(y_{m-1}(x))] \tag{16.23}$$

where

$$R_{m-1}(y_{m-1}(x)) = D^{1.5}y_{m-1}(x) + c^2 y_{m-1}(x) \tag{16.24}$$

And therefore

$$y_m(x) = \chi_m y_{m-1}(x) + hI^{1.5}[D^{1.5}y_{m-1}(x) + c^2 y_{m-1}(x)] \tag{16.25}$$

When we substitute in the Eq. (16.25) for $m = 1$, we get:

$$y_1(x) = \chi_1 y_0(x) + hI^{1.5}[D^{1.5}y_0(x) + c^2 y_0(x)] \tag{16.26}$$

$$y_1(x) = \frac{hc^3x^{2.5}}{\Gamma(3.5)} \tag{16.27}$$

When $m = 2,3, \ldots$, the equation becomes:

$$y_m(x) = \chi_m y_{m-1}(x) + h[y_{m-1}(x) + c^2 I^{1.5} y_{m-1}(x)] \tag{16.28}$$

For $m = 2$, using Riemann–Liouville integration properties and substituting in Eq. (16.28), we get:

$$y_2(x) = (1+h)\frac{hc^3x^{2.5}}{\Gamma(3.5)} + \frac{h^2c^5x^4}{\Gamma(5)} \tag{16.29}$$

Similarly, using Riemann–Liouville integration properties and substituting in Eq. (16.29) for m=3, we get:

$$y_3(x) = \frac{h(1+h)^2c^3x^{2.5}}{\Gamma(3.5)} + \frac{2(1+h)h^2c^5x^4}{\Gamma(5)} + \frac{h^3c^7x^{5.5}}{\Gamma(6.5)} \tag{16.30}$$

Third: We sum the four approximate iterations $y_0(x)$, $y_1(x)$, $y_2(x)$, $y_3(x)$ to get the approximate solution $Q_4(x)$

$$Q_4(x) = \sum_{m=0}^{3} y_m(x) = y_0(x) + y_1(x) + y_2(x) + y_3(x) \tag{16.31}$$

$$Q_4(X) = cx + \frac{hc^3x^{2.5}}{\Gamma(3.5)} + \frac{(1+h)hc^3x^{2.5}}{\Gamma(3.5)} + \frac{h^2c^5x^4}{\Gamma(5)} + \frac{h(1+h)^2c^3x^{2.5}}{\Gamma(3.5)} + \frac{2(1+h)h^2c^5x^4}{\Gamma(5)} + \frac{h^3c^7x^{5.5}}{\Gamma(6.5)} \tag{16.32}$$

Fourth: We find the root mean square error for Eq. (16.19) with the following equation:

$\text{RMSE} = \sqrt{\frac{\sum_{i=1}^{n}(exact - Q)^2}{n}}$, where Q is the approximate solution and n is the number of points, considering it as a fitness function in the GWO algorithm. When performing algorithm operations on it, we get the best value for the parameter h and substitute it in $Q_4(x)$ with $c = 1$.

Example 3.

In this example, we have an initial value problem containing a linear differential equation with a fractional order:

$$D^{0.5}y(x) = x^2 - y(x) + \frac{2x^{1.5}}{\Gamma(2.5)} \tag{16.33}$$

$$y(0) = 0,\ y'(0) = 0,\ 0 < x < 1 \tag{16.34}$$

where the exact solution is: $y(x) = x^2$ [8].

Solution

First: The initial guess y_0 according to Eq. (16.4):

$$y_0(x) = 0 \tag{16.35}$$

Second: We find the rest of the approximate iterations $y_1(x)$, $y_2(x)$, $y_3(x)$ from the deformation equation of order m

$$y_m(x) = \chi_m y_{m-1}(x) + hI^{\alpha}[R_{m-1}(\vec{y}_{m-1}(x))] \tag{16.36}$$

We obtain:

$$y_m(x) = \chi_m y_{m-1}(x) + hI^{0.5}[R_{m-1}(y_{m-1}(x))] \tag{16.37}$$

Where

$$R_{m-1}(\vec{y}_{m-1}(x)) = D^{0.5}y_{m-1}(x) + y_{m-1}(x) - \left(x^2 + \frac{2x^{1.5}}{\Gamma(2.5)}\right)(1 - \chi_m) \tag{16.38}$$

When substituting in the Eq. (16.35) for $m = 1$, we get:

$$y_1(x) = \chi_1 y_0(x) + hI^{0.5}\left[D^{0.5}y_0(x) + y_0(x) - \left(x^2 + \frac{2x^{1.5}}{\Gamma(2.5)}\right)(1 - \chi_1)\right] \tag{16.39}$$

$$y_1(x) = \frac{-h\Gamma(3)x^{2.5}}{\Gamma(3.5)} - \frac{2hx^2}{\Gamma(3)}$$

When m = 2,3, ..., the Eq. (16.35) becomes:

$$y_m(x) = \chi_m y_{m-1}(x) + h[y_{m-1}(x) + I^{0.5}y_{m-1}(x)] \tag{16.40}$$

Using Riemann–Liouville integration properties and substituting in Eq. (16.40) for $m = 2$, and then in a subsequent step for $m = 3$, we get:

$$y_2(x) = \frac{-2h(1+h)x^{2.5}}{\Gamma(3.5)} - \frac{2h(1+h)x^2}{\Gamma(3)} - \frac{2h^2x^3}{\Gamma(4)} - \frac{2h^2x^{2.5}}{\Gamma(3.5)}$$

$$y_3(x) = \frac{-2h(1+h)^2x^{2.5}}{\Gamma(3.5)} - \frac{-2h(1+h)^2x^2}{\Gamma(3)} - \frac{-4h^2(1+h)x^3}{\Gamma(4)} - \frac{-4h^2(1+h)x^{2.5}}{\Gamma(3.5)} - \frac{2h^3x^{3.5}}{\Gamma(4.5)} - \frac{2h^3x^3}{\Gamma(4)} \tag{16.41}$$

Third: We sum the four approximate iterations $y_0(x)$, $y_1(x)$, $y_2(x)$, $y_3(x)$ to get the approximate solution $Q_4(x)$

$$Q_4(x) = \sum_{m=0}^{3} y_m(x) = y_0(x) + y_1(x) + y_2(x) + y_3(x) \tag{16.42}$$

$$Q_4(x) = \frac{-2(h^3+3h^2+3h)x^{2.5}}{\Gamma(3.5)} - \frac{-2(h^3+3h^2+3h)x^2}{\Gamma(3.5)} - \frac{-(4h^3+6h^2)x^3}{\Gamma(4)} - \frac{(4h^3+6h^2)x^{2.5}}{\Gamma(3.5)} - \frac{2h^3x^{3.5}}{\Gamma(4.5)} - \frac{2h^3x^3}{\Gamma(4)} \tag{16.43}$$

Fourth: We find the root mean square error for Eq. (16.35) with the following equation:

RMSE=$\sqrt{\frac{\sum_{i=1}^{n}(exact - Q)^2}{n}}$ where Q is the approximate solution and n is the number of points, considering it as an appropriate function in the GWO algorithm. When performing algorithm operations on it, we get the best value for the parameter h and substitute it in $Q_4(x)$

16.5 Conclusions

The study demonstrated that integrating the GWO with the HAM significantly enhanced the accuracy of numerical solutions for fractional differential equations, reducing the RMSE to precise levels ranging between 10^{-5} and 10^{-6}, confirming the method's efficacy in minimizing computational errors. The hybrid algorithm also exhibited superior convergence speed toward the optimal solution compared to the traditional approach, as evidenced by comparative graphs and tables. Furthermore, GWO showcased its flexibility in balancing exploration and exploitation, positioning it as a promising tool for engineering and artificial intelligence applications. The proposed hybrid GWO-HAM approach has significant potential for solving real-world problems governed by fractional differential equations. For instance, in engineering, it could be used to accurately model the behavior of viscoelastic materials used in damping systems or to analyze anomalous diffusion in porous media. In physics-based modeling, this method could enhance simulations of complex systems in control theory and signal processing, where fractional-order controllers often provide superior performance. The ability to find a highly accurate solution quickly makes this technique a valuable tool for these advanced applications.

Acknowledgments

The authors would like to acknowledge that AI tools were utilized for the purpose of language editing and refinement to improve the clarity and readability of the manuscript.

References

[1] S. Mirjalili, S.M. Mirjalili, A. Lewis, Grey wolf optimizer, Advances in Engineering Software 69 (2014) 46–61. Available from https://doi.org/10.1016/j.advengsoft.2013.12.007.

[2] R.M. Ramo, S.A. Dawwod, Digital image compression by using intelligence swarm algorithms, International Journal of Mathematics and Computer Science 17 (2) (2022).

[3] H.M. Khudhur, K.I. Ibraheem, Metaheuristic optimization algorithm based on the two-step Adams-Bashforth method in training multi-layer perceptrons, Eastern-European Journal of Enterprise Technologies, 2 4 (116) (2022) 6–13. Available from https://doi.org/10.15587/1729-4061.2022.254023.

[4] H.M. Khudhur, Metaheuristic technique for solving fuzzy nonlinear equations, Comprehensive Metaheuristics, Elsevier, (2023), pp. 85–94. Available from http://doi.org/10.1016/B978-0-323-91781-0.00023-5.

[5] R.M. Aziz, K.I. Ibraheem, Improving Homotopy Method Using Particle Swarm Optimisation to Solve Fractional Differential Equations (2025) 50004. Available from https://doi.org/10.1063/5.0259163.

[6] W.K. Zahra, S.M. Elkholy, The Use of cubic splines in the numerical solution of fractional differential equations, International Journal of Mathematics and Mathematical Sciences 2012 (2012) 1–16. Available from https://doi.org/10.1155/2012/638026.

[7] W. Abd-Elhameed, Y. Youssri, A novel operational matrix of Caputo fractional derivatives of Fibonacci polynomials: spectral solutions of fractional differential equations, Entropy 18 (10) (2016) 345. Available from https://doi.org/10.3390/e18100345.

[8] K. Diethelm, N.J. Ford, Analysis of fractional differential equations, Journal of Mathematical Analysis and Applications 265 (2) (2002) 229–248. Available from https://doi.org/10.1006/jmaa.2000.7194.

Chapter 17

Performance evaluation of the grey wolf optimizer against advanced differential evolution variants

Dikshit Chauhan[1] and Indu Bala[2]
[1]*Department of Electrical and Computer Engineering, National University of Singapore, Singapore, Singapore,* [2]*School of Computer and Mathematical Sciences, University of Adelaide, Adelaide, SA, Australia*

17.1 Introduction

The grey wolf optimizer (GWO) is a nature-inspired metaheuristic introduced in 2014 [1]. It is modeled on the social hierarchy and cooperative hunting strategy of grey wolves (*Canis lupus*). In the algorithm, virtual "wolves" representing candidate solutions are organized into alpha, beta, delta, or omega ranks, and collaboratively perform a hunting process that encircles and attacks prey, representing the optimal solution.

17.1.1 Biological motivation

GWO is inspired by the leadership hierarchy and hunting behavior of grey wolves (*Canis lupus*). Grey wolves live and hunt in packs, typically consisting of 5–12 members, organized in a strict dominance hierarchy:

- **Alpha** (α): The leader of the pack responsible for decisions such as hunting and movement.
- **Beta** (β): The second in command, acting as advisor to the alpha and enforcer of rules.
- **Delta** (δ): Subordinate wolves that include roles such as scouts, hunters, and caretakers.
- **Omega** (ω): The lowest rank, playing a role in stress release within the pack

The hierarchy enables cooperative group hunting. The hunting process typically involves tracking, encircling, and attacking prey. These behaviors are mathematically modeled to design the GWO algorithm.

17.1.2 Mathematical modeling

17.1.2.1 Hierarchical roles

Let the top three candidate solutions in a population be denoted as $\mathbf{X}_\alpha$, $\mathbf{X}_\beta$, and $\mathbf{X}_\delta$, representing the alpha, beta, and delta wolves, respectively. The remaining candidates are treated as omegas. The search process is guided by these top three individuals.

17.1.2.2 Encircling prey

Encircling behavior is modeled as:

$$\mathbf{D} = |\mathbf{C}\cdot\mathbf{X}_{\text{target}} - \mathbf{X}(t)| \tag{17.1}$$

$$\mathbf{X}(t+1)=\mathbf{X}_{\text{target}} - \mathbf{A}\cdot\mathbf{D} \tag{17.2}$$

where $\mathbf{X}_{\text{target}}$ is the estimated prey position, $\mathbf{X}(t)$ is the wolf's current position, and **A** and **C** are coefficient vectors computed as:

$$\mathbf{A}=2\mathbf{l}\cdot\mathbf{r}_1 - \mathbf{l} \tag{17.3}$$

$$\mathbf{C}=2\cdot\mathbf{r}_2 \tag{17.4}$$

Grey Wolf Optimizer. DOI: https://doi.org/10.1016/B978-0-443-36624-6.00039-1

Here, **l** decreases linearly from 2 to 0 over iterations, and $\mathbf{r}_1$, $\mathbf{r}_2$ are random vectors in $[0,1]^n$.

17.1.2.3 Hunting behavior

The location of the prey is estimated using the positions of the top three wolves:

$$\mathbf{D}_1 = |\mathbf{C}_1 \cdot \mathbf{X}_\alpha - \mathbf{X}|, \quad \mathbf{D}_2 = |\mathbf{C}_2 \cdot \mathbf{X}_\beta - \mathbf{X}|, \quad \mathbf{D}_3 = |\mathbf{C}_3 \cdot \mathbf{X}_\delta - \mathbf{X}| \tag{17.5}$$

$$\mathbf{X}_1 = \mathbf{X}_\alpha - \mathbf{A}_1 \cdot \mathbf{D}_1, \quad \mathbf{X}_2 = \mathbf{X}_\beta - \mathbf{A}_2 \cdot \mathbf{D}_2, \quad \mathbf{X}_3 = \mathbf{X}_\delta - \mathbf{A}_3 \cdot \mathbf{D}_3 \tag{17.6}$$

$$\mathbf{X}(t+1) = \frac{1}{3}(\mathbf{X}_1 + \mathbf{X}_2 + \mathbf{X}_3) \tag{17.7}$$

17.1.2.4 Exploitation phase

To model convergence (attacking prey), the control parameter **l** is reduced, which also shrinks the range of **A** to $[-\lambda, \lambda]$. When $|\mathbf{A}|<1$, wolves move closer to the prey, improving exploitation.

17.1.2.5 Exploration phase

Exploration is encouraged when $|\mathbf{A}|>1$, allowing wolves to search away from the current best solutions. Additionally, the randomness of **C** (which is not decreased) introduces variability in movement, helping avoid local optima.

17.1.3 Algorithm summary

The GWO algorithm can be summarized as follows:

1. Initialize a population of wolves (candidate solutions).
2. Evaluate fitness and identify α, β, and δ.
3. Update the position of each wolf using Eqs. (17.5)–(17.7).
4. Update control parameter **l**.
5. Repeat steps (ii)–(iv) until the stopping criteria are met.

The balance between exploration and exploitation is adaptively controlled by **l**. The algorithm is computationally simple, requiring only two main parameters (**l** and **C**), and can be further extended by incorporating additional evolutionary operators. The pseudocode of GWO is presented in Algorithm 1. The computational complexity of GWO is $O(N \times D \times T_{max})$, where N is the number of wolves, D is the dimension of the problem, and T_{max} is the maximum number of iterations.

17.1.4 Key characteristics

- Social hierarchy maintains the best solutions.
- Encircling defines a dynamic, dimension-independent search neighborhood.
- A and C promote random, adaptive search behavior.
- Simple design with only two parameters (A and C).
- Balance between exploration and exploitation via $|A|$.

In its foundational design, GWO was benchmarked on 29 standard test functions and demonstrated competitive performance compared to classical optimizers such as particle swarm optimization (PSO) [2], differential evolution (DE) [3], and evolutionary programming [4]. A notable advantage of GWO is its reliance on only a few control parameters while maintaining a strong balance between exploration and exploitation. This balance contributes significantly to its convergence reliability.

These strengths, along with its simplicity and adaptability, contributed to GWO's rapid adoption across various research domains. Nevertheless, early evaluations highlighted limitations in the basic GWO, particularly in convergence speed and solution precision. Like many population-based methods, it also suffered from stagnation in local optima [5,6].

To address these shortcomings, researchers quickly developed improved and hybridized variants. Within a year of its release, several modifications emerged. The detailed discussion is presented in the background section. (Algorithm 17.1).

ALGORITHM 17.1 GWO.

```
Initialize the population {X_i}_{i=1}^N randomly in the search space
  Evaluate the fitness of all individuals
  Identify the top three wolves: X_α, X_β, X_δ
  for each iteration t=1 to T_max do
  Update control parameter λ=2 to 0
  for each wolf X_i do
  for j=1 to 3 do
  Generate random vectors r_1j, r_2j ~ U(0,1)^n
  A_j=2·l·r_1j − l
  C_j=2·r_2j
  end for
  Compute distances: D_α = |C_1·X_α − X_i|, D_β = |C_2·X_β − X_i|, D_δ = |C_3·X_δ − X_i|
  Update temporary positions: X_1 = X_α − A_1·D_α, X_2 = X_β − A_2·D_β, X_3 = X_δ − A_3·D_δ
  Update position: X_i ← 1/3(X_1 + X_2 + X_3)
  end for
  Evaluate all wolves and update X_α, X_β, X_δ
  end for
  return X_α as the best solution
```

17.2 Background

This section presents a chronological overview of key developments in the evolution of GWO since 2014, with a focus on algorithmic improvements in exploration, exploitation, convergence behavior, and constraint handling.

17.2.1 Early developments (2014–16)

The original formulation of GWO in 2014 encoded the encircling and hunting behavior of wolves through iterative position-update equations, driven by three leader agents (alpha, beta, delta) guiding the rest of the pack. Early experiments showed GWO to be highly competitive on unconstrained optimization benchmarks and more robust against local optima than some earlier metaheuristics, owing to its balance between exploration and exploitation [1].

Following the introduction of GWO, Muangkote et al. [7] proposed an improved GWO by modifying the search strategy to boost solution quality. That same year, Luo et al. [8] developed a complex-valued GWO, which used complex-number encoding to diversify the population and enhance stability. Emary et al. [9] extended GWO into binary search spaces through the binary GWO, designed specifically for feature selection tasks. This variant mapped continuous positions to binary decisions using transfer functions and achieved better accuracy than binary PSO in classification problems.

By 2016, more sophisticated adaptations had emerged. Mirjalili et al. [10] introduced a multiobjective GWO (MOGWO), adapting the wolf leadership hierarchy to evolve a set of Pareto-optimal solutions. This approach was successfully validated on standard multiobjective benchmarks. For discrete optimization tasks, Li et al. [11] proposed a modified discrete GWO, suitable for combinatorial problems like scheduling. Meanwhile, Mittal et al. [12] enhanced GWO's convergence accuracy through a Modified GWO (MGWO) that revised the position-update equations and tuning parameters.

By the end of 2016, GWO had already given rise to multiple specialized variants targeting binary spaces, multiobjective optimization, and discrete problem settings, all while preserving the algorithm's simple structure and improving its convergence performance.

17.2.2 Diversification and hybridization (2017–18)

The years 2017 and 2018 marked a significant phase in the diversification of GWO through hybridization and structural enhancements. A major trend during this period was the combination of GWO with other metaheuristics to leverage complementary strengths.

In 2017, Singh and Singh [13] developed a PSO-GWO hybrid, which incorporated velocity updates from PSO into GWO's framework. This fusion improved convergence rates beyond either standalone algorithm. Other hybrids included combinations with genetic algorithms (GWO-GA) and ant colony optimization (GWO), aimed at boosting global search capabilities.

Another contribution was the incorporation of Lévy flight dynamics into GWO, enhancing long-range exploration and robustness on multimodal problems. Similarly, random walk GWO leveraged stochastic random-walk steps for greater diversification in real-world applications [14].

In parallel, enhancements like the enhanced GWO introduced adaptive parameter tuning to prevent premature convergence, particularly in constrained optimization problems. Kohli and Arora [15] introduced chaotic GWO (CGWO), incorporating chaotic maps to improve search diversity and escape local minima. CGWO proved effective on constrained benchmarks, outperforming basic GWO in both convergence speed and solution quality.

By 2018, the exploration-enhanced GWO was developed to improve the exploration–exploitation balance throughout the optimization process. Liu et al. [16] advanced this with the intelligent GWO, integrating a learning mechanism into position updates, allowing dynamic changes in the influence of alpha, beta, and delta leaders to enhance search guidance.

Additionally, a new hybrid metaheuristic, such as the GWO-Fireworks Algorithm combinations, leverages GWO's exploitation capabilities alongside the exploratory bursts of the Fireworks Algorithm. These strategies relocated underperforming individuals to improve search adaptability [17].

Collectively, this period also saw refinement of parameter control strategies, such as nonlinearly decreasing the λ coefficient and incorporating inertia weights, improving overall convergence. Problem-specific customizations, including domain knowledge infusion (e.g., fuzzy logic) and new encoding strategies for discrete or binary problems, further broadened GWO's applicability. These advancements enabled modern GWO variants to outperform the basic version significantly in both constrained and unconstrained benchmarks.

17.2.3 Recent advances (2019–25)

From 2019 onwards, significant advancements were made in boosting GWO's capability to handle complex, high-dimensional landscapes. In 2019, Long et al. [18] introduced a GWO variant incorporating refraction learning, inspired by light refraction principles. This approach redirected search trajectories toward underexplored regions, showing promise for high-dimensional functions.

In 2020, Gupta and Deep proposed a memory-based GWO (mGWO), which stored and utilized each wolf's personal best position, akin to PSO's memory mechanism. This version demonstrated improved convergence and accuracy, outperforming many classical and contemporary algorithms on benchmark suites like IEEE CEC2014 and CEC2017 [19].

Parallel efforts explored multistrategy adaptations. Pan [20] introduced a version with a Gompertz-function-guided adaptive inertia weight, transitioning GWO from exploration to exploitation more effectively. Comparative evaluations showed this approach outperformed ten other swarm algorithms in stability and speed.

Further extensions refined GWO for multiobjective and binary tasks. Enhanced MOGWO variants incorporated external archives and adaptive leader selection (e.g., roulette wheel mechanisms) to ensure solution diversity. In binary optimization, combinations like binary PSO-GWO merged PSO's velocity-bit update with GWO's hierarchy, improving feature selection accuracy [21].

With growing interest in benchmark-driven validation, performance comparisons between GWO and elite optimizers, particularly DE variants, have become increasingly prevalent. While early GWO lagged behind advanced DEs like L-SHADE and jSO, newer GWO variants, like the adaptive multistrategy IAGWO (2024), narrowed this performance gap. IAGWO, integrating PSO-inspired velocity and inverse multiquadratic adaptation, achieved second-best rankings on CEC2014, just behind L-SHADE, and rivaled top-tier DE variants on CEC2017 [22]. These gains underscore GWO's transformation into a high-performing optimizer for constrained and high-dimensional problems. Enhanced versions demonstrated superior exploration–exploitation balance, with specific strengths in engineering design and large-scale optimization.

Recent trends highlight hybridization with local search and ensemble methods (e.g., Teaching learning-based optimization, harmony search, whale optimization). Adaptive techniques, like fuzzy logic-based control of parameters or self-tuned update probabilities, have made GWO increasingly autonomous and effective. Sophisticated transfer functions and crossover operators improved GWO's discrete/binary search power, while newer many-objective MOGWO variants (e.g., angle-guided leader selection) scaled well to problems with 5–10 objectives [23].

In summary, the period from 2019 to 2025 marks a transformative era for GWO, transitioning it from a simple, nature-inspired optimizer to a robust, adaptable, and competitive algorithm family. This is evidenced not only by technical advancements but also by its growing recognition in the research community.

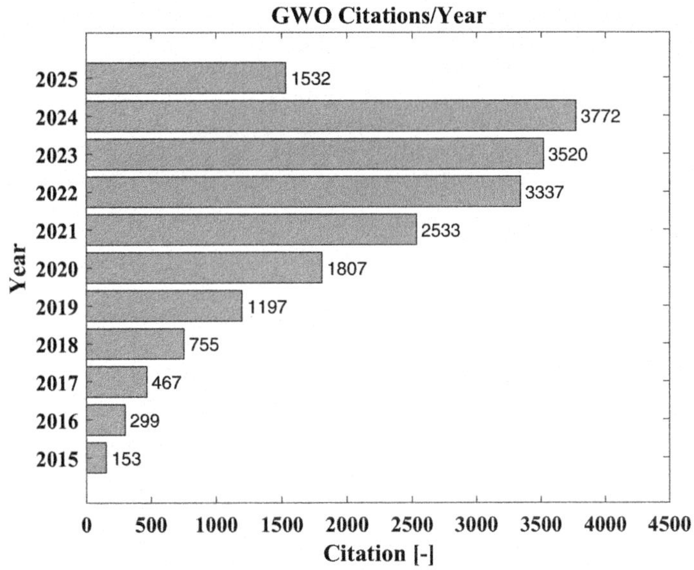

FIGURE 17.1 GWO citations (*GWO*, Grey wolf optimizer).

As shown in Fig. 17.1, the annual citation[1] trajectory of GWO from 2015 to 2025 is illustrated. It demonstrates the algorithm's growing popularity and impact within the research community. Initially introduced with limited recognition, GWO received only 153 citations in 2015. However, citations increased steadily in the following years, reaching 755 by 2018. A sharp rise occurred from 2019 onwards, marking a period of exponential growth, with citations peaking at 3772 in 2024. This surge reflects the algorithm's widespread adoption across various fields, including engineering, optimization, and machine learning. Notably, the citation count for 2025 is 1532, which appears lower than in the preceding years but likely represents only a partial count due to the year still being in progress. Overall, the chart highlights GWO's transition from a novel optimization method to a well-established and extensively cited algorithm, underscoring its significance and broad applicability in the scientific community.

The pie chart titled in Fig. 17.2[2] illustrates the distribution of research documents across various academic disciplines. The largest proportion of documents falls under Engineering (26.2%), closely followed by Computer Science (25.4%), indicating a strong research focus in these technologically driven domains. Mathematics (11.7%) and Energy (8.1%) also represent significant portions, reflecting active research in theoretical and applied sciences. Other notable fields include Physics and Astronomy (5%), Materials Science (4.5%), Environmental Science (3.1%), and Decision Sciences (3%), while smaller contributions are seen from Chemical Engineering (1.9%) and Multidisciplinary fields (1.6%). The "Other" category accounts for 9.3%, encompassing less-represented areas. The chart demonstrates a dominant concentration in engineering and computing-related disciplines, showcasing the ongoing emphasis on innovation, technology, and quantitative research.

This success, combined with the inherent simplicity of its original design, motivates a comparative analysis between GWO and other advanced true algorithms, particularly those that have performed exceptionally well in past IEEE CEC competitions. Accordingly, this study presents a performance comparison of GWO with six well-known and highly competitive DE variants. These algorithms are discussed in detail in the following section.

17.2.4 Different evolution variants for comparative analysis

GWO has evolved in various ways presented in the background section; however, even in its original form, GWO has demonstrated notable efficiency and effectiveness. To further evaluate its performance, we plan to compare GWO against several advanced DE variants, many of which have performed exceptionally well in international algorithm competitions, including those hosted by the IEEE Congress on Evolutionary Computation (CEC). Such a comparison will help highlight

1. As per the original document on Google Scholar.

2. Downloaded from Scopus Platform.

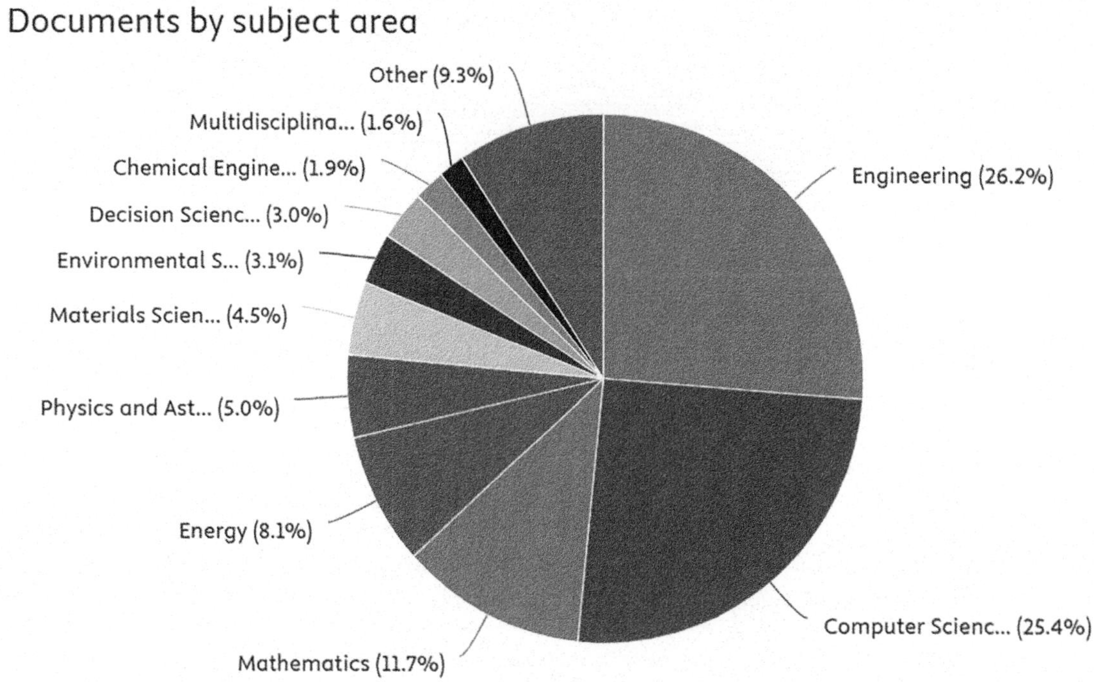

FIGURE 17.2 Subject area-wise documents.

GWO's relative efficiency and robustness. Given that DE has consistently excelled in solving complex optimization problems over the past decades, much like GWO, it serves as a strong benchmark for assessing GWO's capabilities.

This section highlights six state-of-the-art DE variants that have gained attention for their methodological innovations and competitive performance.

17.2.4.1 Multioperator ensemble LSHADE with restart and local search

Multioperator ensemble LSHADE with restart and local search (mLSHADE-RL) employs an ensemble of multiple mutation strategies to maintain population diversity and avoid premature convergence. It incorporates a restart mechanism that periodically reinitializes part of the population and a local search strategy for refining promising solutions. This dual mechanism enhances both global exploration and local exploitation, yielding excellent results in multimodal and high-dimensional problems [24].

Strengths: Balanced exploration and exploitation, avoidance of premature convergence, and superior performance on multimodal and high-dimensional tasks.

17.2.4.2 Gaining-sharing knowledge-based IMODE (APGSK-IMODE)

Gaining-sharing knowledge-based IMODE (APGSK-IMODE) adopts knowledge-sharing strategies and adaptive parameter control. The population is divided into subgroups using different mutation schemes, promoting cross-group learning and adaptability. The algorithm has shown strong results in both constrained and unconstrained scenarios [25].

Strengths: Adaptive parameter tuning, effectiveness in various problem types, strong convergence accuracy, and robustness.

17.2.4.3 Ensemble-based optimizer with covariance matrix adaptation and restart

The effective butterfly optimizer covariance matrix adapted retreat phase (EBOwithCMAR) combines covariance matrix adaptation (CMA) with multiple mutation strategies and periodic restarts. CMA improves local search precision, while ensemble mutation ensures diverse global exploration. The restart mechanism prevents stagnation in complex landscapes [26].

Strengths: High local search accuracy, diverse global exploration, and effective stagnation prevention.

17.2.4.4 Orthogonal LSHADE with Cauchy and sinusoidal perturbations

Orthogonal learning-based DE (OLSHADE-CS) integrates orthogonal experimental design with Cauchy and sinusoidal perturbations into LSHADE. Orthogonal design facilitates efficient parameter exploration, and perturbations improve solution diversity, boosting convergence and robustness [27].

Strengths: Efficient parameter sampling, high diversity, and strong multimodal optimization performance.

17.2.4.5 LSHADE with ensemble sinusoidal adaptation and covariance Matrix learning

Ensemble sinusoidal differential covariance matrix adaptation with Euclidean neighborhood (LSHADE-cnEpSin) is an advanced variant of LSHADE that integrates ensemble sinusoidal parameter adaptation with covariance-based learning to dynamically adjust the population distribution during the optimization process. This hybrid strategy enhances both convergence speed and solution quality, allowing the algorithm to effectively navigate complex search landscapes. Notably, LSHADE-cnEpSin has consistently ranked among the top-performing algorithms in recent CEC competitions, demonstrating its competitiveness and robustness across diverse benchmark problems [28].

Strengths: Reliable convergence, dynamic adaptation, and competitive benchmark performance.

17.2.4.6 Multistrategy differential evolution

Multistrategy DE (MS-DE) operates by concurrently applying multiple DE strategies to the same population, leveraging diverse search behaviors. This ensemble of strategies improves robustness and adaptability across varying optimization challenges, making it effective in avoiding stagnation and local optima [29].

Strengths: High adaptability, effective in complex problem spaces, and reliable convergence through strategy diversity.

17.3 Experimental results

In this section, we comprehensively evaluate the performance of GWO in comparison with leading algorithms from the IEEE CEC competition, with particular focus on state-of-the-art DE variants such as EBOwithCMAR [26], mLSAHDE-RL [24], MS-DE [29], APGSK-IMODE [25], OLSHADE-CS [27], and LSHADE-cnEpSin [28]. The specific DE algorithms considered for comparison have been outlined in the preceding section. All experiments are conducted on the IEEE CEC 2020 benchmark suite [30], Table 17.1, encompassing four problem dimensions: D=5, 10, 15, and 20. This suite provides a challenging and diverse set of multimodal and composition problems, making it a suitable platform for evaluating global optimization performance [31].

17.3.1 Evaluation criteria

The experimental setup strictly adheres to the evaluation protocol defined in the technical report [30]. In particular, the number of function evaluations is set to $MaxFE$=10,000 × D, and the population size is defined as N=18 × D, where D is the dimensionality of the problem. These parameters ensure a fair and standardized comparison across all algorithms, presented in Table 17.2. Importantly, we maintain the original parameter settings of both GWO and the DE variants as reported in the literature, without any additional tuning or modification, thereby providing an unbiased assessment of their baseline performance.

To ensure statistical significance and robustness of the results, each algorithm is independently executed 25 times on each test function. The performance is assessed using the mean and standard deviation of the error fitness values obtained across these runs. Furthermore, we compute the rank of each algorithm on every individual problem based on its mean performance. To summarize and analyze overall performance trends across all test functions and dimensions, we apply the Friedman rank test [32], a nonparametric statistical test, which yields the average ranking of each algorithm. This provides a holistic view of the comparative strengths and weaknesses of GWO and the competing DE variants over the entire benchmark suite.

17.3.2 Experimental discussion

In this section, we provide a detailed comparative analysis of GWO with several competitive DE variants, namely mLSHADE-RL, EBOwithCMAR, APGSK-IMODE, LSHADE-cnEpSin, OLSHADE-CS, and MS-DE, on the IEEE CEC 2020 benchmark functions for dimensions D= 5, 10, 15, and 20. The algorithms are evaluated over 25 independent runs, and the comparison is based on the mean error fitness values and their standard deviations, with rankings (in brackets) reflecting the relative standing per problem.

TABLE 17.1 Summary of the CEC'20 test suite [30].

No.	Functions F_i	$F_i(x_*)$
Unimodal		
1	Shifted and rotated Bent cigar function (CEC 2017 F1)	100
Basic functions		
2	Shifted and rotated Schwefel's function (CEC 2014 F11)	1100
3	Shifted and rotated Lunacek bi-Rastrigin function (CEC 2017 F7)	700
4	Expanded Rosenbrock's plus Griewank's function (CEC 2017 F19)	1900
Hybrid functions		
5	Hybrid function 1 (N=3) (CEC 2014 F17)	1700
6	Hybrid function 2 (N=4) (CEC 2017 F16)	1600
7	Hybrid function 3 (N=5) (CEC 2014 F21)	2100
Composition functions		
8	Composition function 1 (N=3) (CEC 2017 F22)	2200
9	Composition function 2 (N=4) (CEC 2017 F24)	2400
10	Composition function 3 (N=5) (CEC 2017 F25)	2500
Search range: $[-100,100]^D$		

For D=5 in Table 17.3, mLSHADE-RL, EBOwithCMAR, and APGSK-IMODE consistently achieve the lowest mean errors, frequently occupying the top three ranks across most test functions. Notably, APGSK-IMODE secures Rank 1 on 6 out of 10 functions, reflecting its superior convergence behavior and search stability. In contrast, GWO persistently occupies lower ranks, typically between Rank 6 and 7, indicating a substantial performance gap compared to the DE variants.

For D=10 in Table 17.3, the advanced DE variants continue to demonstrate impressive scalability and optimization capabilities, outperforming other algorithms on most benchmark functions. As with the lower dimension, mLSHADE-RL, EBOwithCMAR, and APGSK-IMODE dominate the rankings. GWO, while generally ranked 6th or 7th, still provides a valuable baseline and competitive reference. Although it does not match the top DE variants in mean error for most functions, it maintains consistent performance and demonstrates robustness across the test suite. The increasing dimensionality accentuates the gap in performance, particularly in terms of mean error, yet GWO's presence in the comparison highlights its ability to remain relevant despite its simplicity.

For D=15 in Table 17.4, the trend largely persists, with DE variants continuing to rank at the top across a broad range of problems. GWO holds its position around Rank 6 or 7, reaffirming its reliability as a baseline optimizer. Notably, GWO's consistent behavior across functions makes it a useful candidate for comparative studies, particularly in evaluating the benefits of hybridization or parameter tuning. While the DE variants excel in functions requiring fine-grained local search and adaptive learning, GWO still contributes valuable insights into performance dynamics in mid-dimensional spaces.

At D=20 (Table 17.4), the challenge becomes more pronounced, and the superiority of advanced DE variants, particularly mLSHADE-RL and EBOwithCMAR, remains evident. These methods achieve low error metrics and top rankings across nearly all test cases. GWO, despite ranking 7th in most scenarios, continues to serve as a strong baseline that tests the limits of algorithmic simplicity. The increased divergence in mean error values illustrates the difficulties encountered by simpler models in high-dimensional landscapes, particularly for composition and multimodal problems. However, GWO's ability to remain competitive, even against highly tuned and hybrid DE approaches, speaks to its foundational strengths and potential as a building block for future enhancements.

Overall, the results (See Fig. 17.3) reveal a consistent pattern: while DE variants show superior convergence, scalability, and adaptability, GWO presents itself as a reliable and interpretable alternative. Its performance across

TABLE 17.2 Algorithm parameters.

Algorithm	Parameters
EBOwithCMAR	• $PS1_{max}$ =18 × D, $PS1_{min}$ =4 • $PS2_{max}$ =46.8D, $PS2_{min}$ =10 • H=6, $PS3$=4 + (3 log(D)) • a=0.3, CS=25,50,75,100 for D=5, 10, 15, and 20. • *prob1s*=0.1, *cfels*=0.25 × *MaxFE* • MaxFE=10000×D
OSHADE-CS	• N_p^{init}=18 × D, N_p^{min}=4, α=2.6 • Control Parameters: H=20 × D, S_{CR}^0=0.2, S_{sF}^0=0.6 • MaxFE=10000×D • Budget distribution: Init: 20%, Opt: 80%, Conservative: 40%, Conventional: 40%
LSHADE-cnEpSin	• μ_F = μ_{CR}=0.5 initially • First half: memory uses μ_{freq} and μ_{CR}; second half uses μ_F and μ_{CR} • Memory size H=5, *freq*=0.5 • *ps*=0.5, *pc*=0.4 • N_p^{max}=18 × D, N_p^{min}=4 • MaxFE=10000 × D
mLSHADE-RL	• μ_{Fr} = μ_{CRr} = μ_{fr}=0.5 • Memory size=5, P_c=0.4, P_s=0.5 • Local search probability P_{LS}=0.01, reset=0.1 if improved • N_p^{init}=18 × D, N_p^{min}=4 • MaxFE=10000 × D
APGSK IMODE	• N=18 × D • $PS2=\frac{N}{4}$ for D=10 and 20, $PS2_{min}$ =12, p=0.05 • Kw_P=[0.85,0.05,0.05,0.05], c=0.05 • Archive rate=1.4, Memory size=15 × N • F and Cr as in [33], $PS1$=N − $PS2$, NP_1^{min}=4 • p_{init}=0.3, p_{min}=0.15, CS=50
MS-DE	

APGSK-IMODE, Gaining-sharing knowledge-based IMODE; *EBOwithCMAR*, effective butterfly optimizer covariance matrix adapted retreat phase; *LSHADE-cnEpSin*, ensemble sinusoidal differential covariance matrix adaptation with Euclidean neighborhood; *MS-DE*, multistrategy DE; *mLSHADE-RL*, multioperator ensemble LSHADE with restart and local search; *OLSHADE-CS*, orthogonal learning-based DE.

increasing dimensions underscores the importance of algorithmic balance, and while it may not surpass the top-tier DE methods, GWO's simplicity, ease of implementation, and robustness make it a worthy contender. These findings suggest that with suitable modifications, such as hybrid strategies or adaptive control, GWO could evolve to meet the demands of large-scale, complex optimization tasks while retaining its elegant and intuitive nature.

17.3.3 Statistical test results

The Friedman test results in Table 17.5 provide a statistical comparison of algorithm rankings across different dimensions, reaffirming the strong performance of the DE variants. Across all tested dimensions (D=5, 10, 15, and 20), DE-based algorithms such as OLSHADE-CS, MS-DE, and APGSK-IMODE consistently achieve the lowest (best) Friedman ranks.

TABLE 17.3 Experimental results of GWO against the DE variants at 5 and 10 dimensions.

D=5						
mLSHADE-RL	**EBOwithCMAR**	**APGSK-IMODE**	**LSHADE-cnEpSin**	**OLSHADE-CS**	**MS-DE**	**GWO**
Mean ± Std [ρ]	**Mean ± Std [ρ]**	**Mean ± Std [ρ]**	**Mean ± Std [ρ]**	**Mean ± Std [ρ]**	**Mean ± Std [ρ]**	**Mean ± Std [ρ]**
0.00 ± 0.00 [1]	0.00 ± 0.00 [2]	0.00 ± 0.00 [3]	0.00 ± 0.00 [4]	0.00 ± 0.00 [5]	0.00 ± 0.00 [6]	4235.95 ± 2521.93 [7]
0.17 ± 0.10 [3]	0.23 ± 0.11 [5]	0.03 ± 0.08 [1]	1.50 ± 2.64 [6]	0.14 ± 0.09 [2]	0.17 ± 0.08 [4]	125.72 ± 74.34 [7]
5.19 ± 0.09 [5]	5.19 ± 0.09 [6]	5.15 ± 0.00 [4]	1.24 ± 0.73 [1]	3.22 ± 2.34 [2]	4.63 ± 1.57 [3]	8.28 ± 1.65 [7]
0.08 ± 0.03 [7]	0.05 ± 0.02 [3]	0.00 ± 0.00 [1]	0.06 ± 0.04 [5]	0.01 ± 0.02 [2]	0.06 ± 0.02 [4]	0.06 ± 0.11 [6]
0.57 ± 0.59 [6]	0.00 ± 0.00 [1]	0.00 ± 0.00 [2]	0.09 ± 0.30 [5]	0.00 ± 0.00 [3]	0.00 ± 0.00 [4]	148.45 ± 121.95 [7]
0.00 ± 0.00 [1]	0.00 ± 0.00 [2]	0.00 ± 0.00 [3]	0.00 ± 0.00 [4]	0.00 ± 0.00 [5]	0.00 ± 0.00 [6]	0.78 ± 0.56 [7]
64.65 ± 61.80 [6]	10.77 ± 35.71 [5]	0.00 ± 0.00 [1]	0.00 ± 0.00 [2]	0.00 ± 0.00 [3]	0.00 ± 0.00 [4]	396.98 ± 636.31 [7]
10.05 ± 30.09 [6]	1.45 ± 4.82 [5]	0.00 ± 0.00 [1]	0.00 ± 0.00 [4]	0.00 ± 0.00 [2]	0.00 ± 0.00 [3]	24.77 ± 38.61 [7]
90.91 ± 30.15 [4]	100.00 ± 0.00 [6]	10.88 ± 30.14 [1]	18.18 ± 40.45 [2]	23.78 ± 41.92 [3]	90.91 ± 30.15 [5]	172.94 ± 100.78 [7]
343.06 ± 14.28 [4]	347.37 ± 0.00 [6]	299.15 ± 103.62 [1]	300.00 ± 0.00 [2]	312.92 ± 22.13 [3]	343.06 ± 14.28 [5]	347.40 ± 0.02 [7]
D=10						
Mean ± Std [ρ]	Mean ± Std [ρ]	Mean ± Std [ρ]	Mean ± Std [ρ]	Mean ± Std [ρ]	Mean ± Std [ρ]	Mean ± Std [ρ]
0.00 ± 0.00 [1]	0.00 ± 0.00 [2]	0.00 ± 0.00 [3]	0.00 ± 0.00 [4]	0.00 ± 0.00 [5]	0.00 ± 0.00 [6]	39335.13 ± 54363.19 [7]
7.71 ± 4.77 [1]	9.18 ± 7.01 [3]	16.47 ± 10.70 [5]	73.28 ± 95.22 [6]	10.31 ± 5.50 [4]	7.99 ± 4.90 [2]	534.21 ± 323.50 [7]
11.60 ± 0.67 [2]	10.50 ± 0.14 [1]	13.84 ± 1.26 [6]	12.06 ± 3.73 [4]	13.28 ± 0.94 [5]	11.97 ± 0.45 [3]	29.88 ± 11.19 [7]
0.16 ± 0.14 [3]	0.23 ± 0.03 [5]	0.00 ± 0.00 [1]	0.31 ± 0.06 [6]	0.02 ± 0.03 [2]	0.19 ± 0.04 [4]	0.63 ± 0.64 [7]
117.75 ± 65.82 [6]	17.11 ± 17.94 [4]	12.39 ± 2.50 [3]	2.80 ± 4.20 [2]	38.59 ± 24.24 [5]	0.43 ± 0.41 [1]	5013.51 ± 2853.28 [7]
0.50 ± 0.30 [5]	0.25 ± 0.11 [2]	0.50 ± 0.24 [4]	0.98 ± 0.36 [6]	0.21 ± 0.00 [1]	0.46 ± 0.33 [3]	56.14 ± 62.47 [7]
33.40 ± 49.85 [6]	1.95 ± 4.93 [5]	0.40 ± 0.26 [4]	0.20 ± 0.16 [2]	0.18 ± 0.17 [1]	0.37 ± 0.32 [3]	5201.21 ± 4786.07 [7]
100.00 ± 0.00 [3]	100.00 ± 0.00 [4]	57.47 ± 34.69 [1]	60.52 ± 38.67 [2]	100.00 ± 0.00 [5]	100.00 ± 0.00 [6]	104.76 ± 2.75 [7]
245.00 ± 114.97 [5]	150.86 ± 93.14 [4]	84.53 ± 35.06 [1]	143.85 ± 106.85 [3]	100.00 ± 0.00 [2]	286.83 ± 92.43 [6]	321.34 ± 70.36 [7]
435.09 ± 18.46 [7]	414.58 ± 22.80 [5]	398.12 ± 0.73 [3]	398.02 ± 0.19 [2]	397.88 ± 0.26 [1]	414.47 ± 22.89 [4]	428.32 ± 19.46 [6]

APGSK-IMODE, Gaining-sharing knowledge-based IMODE; *EBOwithCMAR*, effective butterfly optimizer covariance matrix adapted retreat phase; *GWO*, grey wolf optimizer; *LSHADE-cnEpSin*, ensemble sinusoidal differential covariance matrix adaptation with Euclidean neighborhood; *MS-DE*, multistrategy DE; *mLSHADE-RL*, multioperator ensemble LSHADE with restart and local search; *OLSHADE-CS*, orthogonal learning-based DE.

TABLE 17.4 Experimental results of GWO against the DE variants at 15 and 20 dimensions.

D=15						
mLSHADE-RL	**EBOwithCMAR**	**IMODE**	**LSHADE_cnEpSin**	**OLSHADE-CS**	**MS-DE**	**GWO**
Mean ± Std [ρ]	**Mean ± Std [ρ]**	**Mean ± Std [ρ]**	**Mean ± Std [ρ]**	**Mean ± Std [ρ]**	**Mean ± Std [ρ]**	**Mean ± Std [ρ]**
0.00 ± 0.00 [1]	0.00 ± 0.00 [2]	0.01 ± 0.01 [5]	0.00 ± 0.00 [4]	0.14 ± 0.35 [6]	0.00 ± 0.00 [3]	41093622.00 ± 101866690.00 [7]
86.20 ± 54.27 [6]	70.78 ± 62.49 [4]	72.21 ± 61.74 [5]	54.93 ± 52.88 [3]	6.67 ± 5.27 [1]	46.21 ± 52.27 [2]	757.03 ± 469.03 [7]
18.67 ± 1.71 [5]	15.62 ± 0.06 [1]	18.84 ± 1.27 [6]	16.88 ± 3.73 [2]	16.96 ± 0.84 [3]	17.58 ± 0.75 [4]	48.55 ± 23.23 [7]
0.22 ± 0.26 [3]	0.38 ± 0.08 [4]	0.00 ± 0.00 [1]	0.59 ± 0.10 [6]	0.06 ± 0.02 [2]	0.42 ± 0.05 [5]	1.72 ± 1.90 [7]
179.34 ± 71.60 [5]	74.41 ± 58.69 [4]	60.06 ± 55.93 [3]	22.13 ± 45.72 [2]	250.64 ± 205.51 [6]	18.81 ± 36.04 [1]	126127.23 ± 196875.22 [7]
2.54 ± 3.46 [4]	1.10 ± 0.40 [2]	6.18 ± 6.24 [6]	2.05 ± 1.73 [3]	4.53 ± 4.22 [5]	0.73 ± 0.33 [1]	193.57 ± 76.60 [7]
126.86 ± 102.70 [6]	22.58 ± 48.37 [5]	2.84 ± 4.47 [2]	11.99 ± 36.33 [4]	11.60 ± 10.52 [3]	0.63 ± 0.18 [1]	107336.56 ± 103007.10 [7]
100.00 ± 0.00 [2]	100.00 ± 0.00 [3]	44.84 ± 29.78 [1]	100.00 ± 0.00 [4]	100.00 ± 0.00 [5]	100.00 ± 0.00 [6]	107.25 ± 2.33 [7]
387.03 ± 1.68 [6]	293.58 ± 136.34 [2]	100.00 ± 0.00 [1]	338.95 ± 118.15 [4]	310.69 ± 135.32 [3]	389.56 ± 1.54 [7]	383.68 ± 91.27 [5]
400.00 ± 0.00 [1]	400.00 ± 0.00 [2]	400.00 ± 0.00 [3]	400.00 ± 0.00 [4]	400.00 ± 0.00 [5]	400.00 ± 0.00 [6]	602.48 ± 14.40 [7]
D=20						
Mean ± Std [ρ]	Mean ± Std [ρ]	Mean ± Std [ρ]	Mean ± Std [ρ]	Mean ± Std [ρ]	Mean ± Std [ρ]	Mean ± Std [ρ]
0.00 ± 0.00 [1]	0.00 ± 0.00 [2]	0.00 ± 0.00 [4]	0.00 ± 0.00 [5]	0.01 ± 0.01 [6]	0.00 ± 0.00 [3]	71763765.00 ± 164755950.00 [7]
8.63 ± 3.53 [1]	18.43 ± 37.65 [4]	19.44 ± 36.14 [5]	45.65 ± 52.67 [6]	12.73 ± 3.17 [3]	9.93 ± 7.02 [2]	1108.55 ± 305.69 [7]
25.07 ± 1.27 [5]	20.60 ± 0.20 [1]	23.82 ± 1.35 [4]	25.79 ± 1.29 [6]	23.18 ± 0.83 [3]	22.54 ± 0.60 [2]	51.20 ± 9.96 [7]
0.17 ± 0.31 [2]	0.62 ± 0.10 [5]	0.00 ± 0.00 [1]	0.38 ± 0.11 [6]	0.20 ± 0.07 [3]	0.61 ± 0.08 [4]	0.98 ± 2.02 [7]
576.33 ± 277.68 [6]	138.10 ± 70.08 [3]	267.21 ± 130.75 [5]	109.48 ± 57.21 [2]	183.56 ± 140.80 [4]	41.42 ± 38.24 [1]	170167.46 ± 196301.44 [7]
1.63 ± 0.30 [6]	0.85 ± 0.32 [2]	1.14 ± 0.36 [4]	1.51 ± 0.29 [5]	0.70 ± 0.15 [1]	1.00 ± 0.33 [3]	168.87 ± 76.20 [7]
128.47 ± 41.65 [5]	38.68 ± 47.07 [3]	66.75 ± 52.55 [4]	21.27 ± 35.04 [2]	496.17 ± 165.18 [6]	1.43 ± 0.34 [1]	226987.03 ± 215329.74 [7]
100.00 ± 0.00 [1]	100.00 ± 0.00 [2]	100.00 ± 0.00 [3]	100.00 ± 0.00 [4]	100.00 ± 0.00 [5]	100.00 ± 0.00 [6]	131.98 ± 31.71 [7]
398.16 ± 3.91 [3]	382.96 ± 60.47 [2]	100.00 ± 0.00 [1]	422.06 ± 3.12 [5]	439.43 ± 7.30 [6]	400.55 ± 1.48 [4]	457.11 ± 35.42 [7]
407.11 ± 0.31 [2]	413.66 ± 0.01 [5]	415.07 ± 15.91 [6]	406.42 ± 0.03 [1]	410.23 ± 4.92 [3]	413.66 ± 0.00 [4]	440.63 ± 21.57 [7]

APGSK-IMODE, Gaining-sharing knowledge-based IMODE; *EBOwithCMAR*, effective butterfly optimizer covariance matrix adapted retreat phase; *GWO*, grey wolf optimizer; *LSHADE-cnEpSin*, ensemble sinusoidal differential covariance matrix adaptation with Euclidean neighborhood; *MS-DE*, multistrategy DE; *mLSHADE-RL*, multioperator ensemble LSHADE with restart and local search; *OLSHADE-CS*, orthogonal learning-based DE.

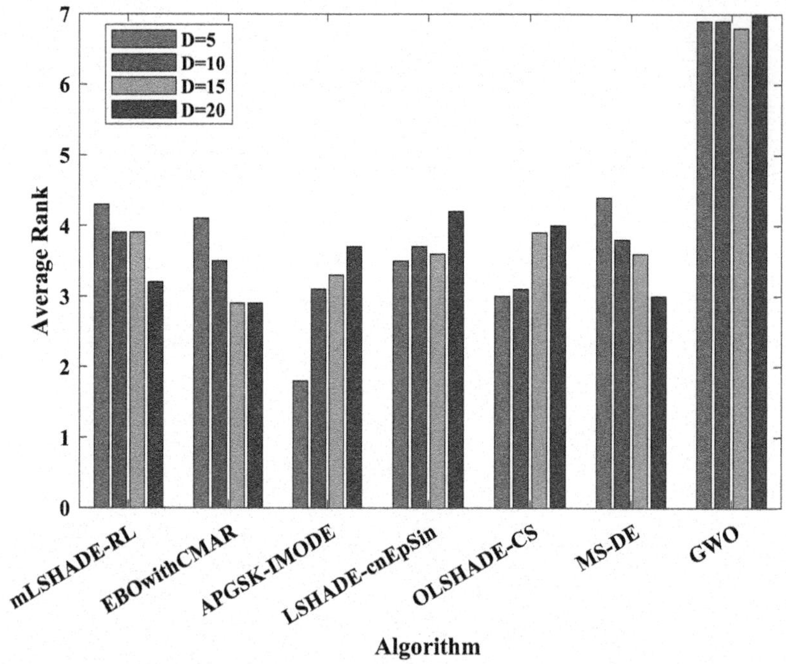

FIGURE 17.3 The average ranks of each algorithm across dimensions.

TABLE 17.5 Friedman test.

Dimension	APGSK-IMODE	mLSHADE-RL	MS-DE	EBOwithCMAR	LSHADE-cnEpSin	OLSHADE-CS	GWO
D=5	3.264	4.264	3.773	3.882	3.332	2.836	6.650
D=10	3.109	4.205	3.468	3.432	3.918	3.145	6.723
D=15	3.514	3.791	2.959	3.136	3.918	3.845	6.836
D=20	3.709	3.541	2.795	2.950	4.159	4.177	6.668

APGSK-IMODE, Gaining-sharing knowledge-based IMODE; *EBOwithCMAR*, effective butterfly optimizer covariance matrix adapted retreat phase; *GWO*, grey wolf optimizer; *LSHADE-cnEpSin*, ensemble sinusoidal differential covariance matrix adaptation with Euclidean neighborhood; *MS-DE*, multistrategy DE; *mLSHADE-RL*, multioperator ensemble LSHADE with restart and local search; *OLSHADE-CS*, orthogonal learning-based DE.

Notably, OLSHADE-CS leads in lower dimensions (*D*=5 and 10), while MS-DE excels in higher dimensions (*D*=15 and 20), with APGSK-IMODE maintaining robust and stable rankings throughout.

GWO, while generally showing higher (worse) ranks, remains a valuable reference point in this analysis. Its consistent ranking across dimensions indicates stable performance, even if it does not match the advanced adaptive capabilities of DE variants. Rather than highlighting a complete lack of competitiveness, these results underscore GWO's role as a foundational optimizer, its simplicity offering opportunities for hybridization and future improvements. Overall, the Friedman test supports the scalability and adaptability of DE variants while positioning GWO as a steady baseline that can be enhanced for more complex, high-dimensional multimodal problems.

17.4 Conclusion

This chapter has conducted a thorough comparative analysis of the GWO against several advanced DE variants, namely mLSHADE-RL, APGSK-IMODE, EEBOwithCMAR, OLSHADE-CS, LSHADE-cnEpSin, and MS-DE. These DE variants were selected due to their proven performance and recognition in IEEE CEC benchmark competitions across multiple problem dimensions (5, 10, 15, and 20).

The experimental findings indicate that the DE variants consistently achieve superior performance across all dimensions and test scenarios. In particular, algorithms like mLSHADE-RL, EBOwithCMAR, and APGSK-IMODE demonstrated remarkable scalability, robustness, and adaptability, frequently securing top ranks. However, the original GWO, despite its simplicity and lack of complex mechanisms, was able to remain a viable competitor, offering consistent performance and stability across varying problem settings. Its presence in this comparative analysis underscores the enduring relevance of its design, especially as a foundational metaheuristic with significant potential for extension.

While the basic version of GWO does exhibit a trend of declining performance with increasing dimensionality, largely due to challenges in maintaining exploration–exploitation balance and convergence on complex multimodal landscapes, it still competes reasonably well given its minimalist structure. These observations highlight the algorithm's strength as a lightweight and interpretable optimizer, which makes it an ideal candidate for hybridization or enhancement using adaptive strategies and advanced evolutionary operators.

Future research should aim to address GWO's scalability limitations by integrating diversity-preserving techniques, adaptive control parameters, or cooperative coevolution frameworks. Furthermore, explainable analysis frameworks, such as those proposed in recent studies [34], offer promising avenues to better understand and refine GWO's behavior. Overall, this comparative analysis not only contributes to understanding the strengths and limitations of GWO but also reinforces its potential as a flexible and extendable tool for tackling complex real-world optimization problems. It also highlights the importance of rigorous benchmarking as a vital practice in advancing metaheuristic optimization research [35,36].

Acknowledgment of AI-tool

During the preparation of this work, the authors used OpenAI in order to polish some of the words, sentences, and grammar to improve the overall readability of the article. After using this tool/service, the authors reviewed and edited the content as needed and will take full responsibility for the content of the publication.

References

[1] S. Mirjalili, S.M. Mirjalili, A. Lewis, Grey wolf optimizer, Advances in Engineering Software 69 (2014) 46–61. Available from https://doi.org/10.1016/j.advengsoft.2013.12.007.

[2] J. Kennedy, R. Eberhart, Particle swarm optimization, Proceedings of ICNN'95-International Conference on Neural Networks, IEEE, (1995), pp. 1942–1948—vol. 4.

[3] R. Storn, K. Price, Differential evolution–a simple and efficient heuristic for global optimization over continuous spaces, Journal of Global Optimization 11 (1997) 341–359.

[4] X. Yao, Y. Liu, G. Lin, Evolutionary programming made faster, IEEE Transactions on Evolutionary Computation 3 (2) (1999) 82–102.

[5] H. Faris, I. Aljarah, M.A. Al Betar, S. Mirjalili, Grey wolf optimizer: a review of recent variants and applications, Neural Computing and Applications 30 (2) (2018) 413–435. Available from https://doi.org/10.1007/s00521-017-3272-5.

[6] Bala, I., Karunarathne, W., Mitchell, L., 2025. Optimizing feature selection by enhancing particle swarm optimization with orthogonal initialization and crossover operator. Computers, Materials & ContinuaAccepted for publication, in press. Available from: http://www.techscience.com/cmc/online/detail/23354.

[7] N. Muangkote, K. Sunat, S. Chiewchanwattana, An improved grey wolf optimizer for training q-gaussian radial basis functional-link nets, 2014 International Computer Science and Engineering Conference (ICSEC), IEEE, (2014), pp. 209–214.

[8] Q. Luo, S. Zhang, Z. Li, Y. Zhou, A novel complex-valued encoding grey wolf optimization algorithm, Algorithms 9 (1) (2015) 4.

[9] E. Emary, H.M. Zawbaa, A.E. Hassanien, Binary grey wolf optimization approaches for feature selection, Neurocomputing 172 (2016) 371–381.

[10] S. Mirjalili, S. Saremi, S.M. Mirjalili, L.d S. Coelho, Multi-objective grey wolf optimizer: a novel algorithm for multi-criterion optimization, Expert Systems with Applications 47 (2016) 106–119.

[11] L. Li, L. Sun, W. Kang, J. Guo, C. Han, S. Li, Fuzzy multilevel image thresholding based on modified discrete grey wolf optimizer and local information aggregation, IEEE Access 4 (2016) 6438–6450.

[12] N. Mittal, U. Singh, B.S. Sohi, Modified grey wolf optimizer for global engineering optimization, Applied Computational Intelligence and Soft Computing 2016 (1) (2016) 7950348.

[13] N. Singh, S. Singh, Hybrid algorithm of particle swarm optimization and grey wolf optimizer for improving convergence performance, Journal of Applied Mathematics 2017 (1) (2017) 2030489.

[14] A.A. Heidari, P. Pahlavani, An efficient modified grey wolf optimizer with lévy flight for optimization tasks, Applied Soft Computing 60 (2017) 115–134.

[15] M. Kohli, S. Arora, Chaotic grey wolf optimization algorithm for constrained optimization problems, Journal of Computational Design and Engineering 5 (4) (2018) 458–472. Available from https://doi.org/10.1016/j.jcde.2018.03.004.

[16] H. Liu, G. Hua, H. Yin, Y. Xu, An intelligent grey wolf optimizer algorithm for distributed compressed sensing, Computational Intelligence and Neuroscience 2018 (1) (2018) 1723191.

[17] J. Barraza, L. Rodrguez, O. Castillo, P. Melin, F. Valdez, A new hybridization approach between the fireworks algorithm and grey wolf optimizer algorithm, Journal of Optimization 2018 (1) (2018) 6495362.

[18] W. Long, T. Wu, S. Cai, X. Liang, J. Jiao, M. Xu, A novel grey wolf optimizer algorithm with refraction learning, IEEE Access 7 (2019) 57805–57819.

[19] S. Gupta, K. Deep, A memory-based grey wolf optimizer for global optimization tasks, Applied Soft Computing 93 (2020) 106367. Available from https://doi.org/10.1016/j.asoc.2020.106367.

[20] Q. Pan, Adaptive grey wolf optimization algorithm based on gompertz inertia weight strategy, International Journal of Advanced Computer Science and Applications 14 (11) (2023) 210–218. Available from https://doi.org/10.14569/IJACSA.2023.0141120.

[21] M. Yu, J. Xu, W. Liang, Y. Qiu, S. Bao, L. Tang, Improved multi-strategy adaptive grey wolf optimization for practical engineering applications and high-dimensional problem solving, Artificial Intelligence Review (2024). Available from https://doi.org/10.1007/s10462-024-10821-3In press.

[22] T.J. Choi, J. Togelius, Y.-G. Cheong, Advanced cauchy mutation for differential evolution in numerical optimization, IEEE Access 8 (2020) 8720–8734.

[23] Y. Liu, A. As'arry, M.K. Hassan, A.A. Hairuddin, H. Mohamad, Review of the grey wolf optimization algorithm: variants and applications, Neural Computing and Applications 36 (6) (2024) 2713–2735.

[24] Chauhan, D., Trivedi, A., Shivani, 2024. A multi-operator ensemble LSHADE with restart and local search mechanisms for single-objective optimization, arXiv preprint arXiv:2409.15994.

[25] A.W. Mohamed, A.A. Hadi, P. Agrawal, K.M. Sallam, A.K. Mohamed, Gaining-sharing knowledge based algorithm with adaptive parameters hybrid with imode algorithm for solving cec 2021 benchmark problems, 2021 IEEE Congress on Evolutionary Computation (CEC), IEEE, (2021), pp. 841–848.

[26] A. Kumar, R.K. Misra, D. Singh, Improving the local search capability of effective butterfly optimizer using covariance matrix adapted retreat phase, 2017 IEEE Congress on Evolutionary Computation (CEC), IEEE, (2017), pp. 1835–1842.

[27] A. Kumar, P.P. Biswas, P.N. Suganthan, Differential evolution with orthogonal array-based initialization and a novel selection strategy, Swarm and Evolutionary Computation 68 (2022) 101010.

[28] N.H. Awad, M.Z. Ali, P.N. Suganthan, Ensemble sinusoidal differential covariance matrix adaptation with euclidean neighborhood for solving CEC2017 benchmark problems, 2017 IEEE Congress on Evolutionary Computation (CEC), IEEE, (2017), pp. 372–379.

[29] Yaman, A., Iacca, G., Coler, M., Fletcher, M., Pechenizkiy, M., 2018. Multi-strategy differential evolution, In: Applications of Evolutionary Computation: 21st International Conference, EvoApplications 2018, Parma, Italy, April 4-6, 2018, Proceedings 21, Springer, pp. 617–633.

[30] C. Yue, K.V. Price, P.N. Suganthan, J. Liang, M.Z. Ali, B. Qu, et al., Problem definitions and evaluation criteria for the CEC2020 special session and competition on single objective bound constrained numerical optimization, Computational, Intelligence Laboratory, Zhengzhou University, Zhengzhou, China, Technical Report (2019) 201911.

[31] I. Bala, D. Chauhan, L. Mitchell, Orthogonally initiated particle swarm optimization with advanced mutation for real-parameter optimization, Proceedings of the Genetic and Evolutionary Computation Conference Companion (2024) 735–738.

[32] J. Friedman, T. Hastie, R. Tibshirani, The Elements of Statistical Learning, Springer Series in Statistics, New York, (2001,). vol. 1.

[33] K.M. Sallam, S.M. Elsayed, R.A. Sarker, D.L. Essam, Improved united multi-operator algorithm for solving optimization problems, 2018 IEEE Congress on Evolutionary Computation (CEC), IEEE, (2018), pp. 1–8.

[34] Chauhan, D., Gupta, N., Yadav, A., 2025. An explainable reconfiguration-based optimization algorithm for industrial and reliability-redundancy allocation problems, arXiv preprint arXiv:2504.01331.

[35] D. Chauhan, A. Yadav, A comprehensive survey on artificial electric field algorithm: theories and applications, Archives of Computational Methods in Engineering 31 (5) (2024) 2663–2715.

[36] D. Chauhan, Shivani, R. Cheng, Competitive swarm optimizer: a decade survey, Swarm and Evolutionary Computation 87 (2024) 101543.

Chapter 18

Grey wolf optimizer enabled optimization of Ti6Al4V surface morphology and wear behavior

M. Özgür Bora[1], Sinan Fidan[1], Satılmış Ürgün[2], and Halil Yiğit[3]

[1]*Department of Airframe and Powerplant Maintenance, Faculty of Aeronautics and Astronautics, Kocaeli University, Kocaeli, Türkiye,* [2]*Department of Aviation Electrics and Electronics, Faculty of Aeronautics and Astronautics, Kocaeli, Türkiye,* [3]*Department of Information Systems Engineering, Faculty of Technology, Kocaeli University, Kocaeli, Türkiye*

18.1 Introduction

Commercial pure (CP) Ti and Ti6Al4V are extensively applied for endosseous implants, but their high elastic modulus confines their application for joint replacements. Ideal implants are required to match bone stiffness (10–40 GPa) to facilitate stress shielding and effective load transfer. Ti6Al4V modulus of about 110 GPa is much greater than bone due to an excessive amount of artificial intelligence (Al) content, which increases the α-phase volume.

Moreover, long-term application poses a question of concern about the emission of Al/V ions. These raise requirements for developing alternative titanium alloys that are biologically and mechanically more compatible for implants [1]. Advanced technology and research are of prime importance in the characterization and manufacturing of materials. Titanium and its alloys are extensively applied in engineering due to their outstanding qualities. To further increase their performance, researchers alter their surface through nonconventional machining processes. Laser texturing, especially, enables exact control of the surface pattern through process-parameter modulation, enhancing finish and function. Recent developments are based on ultra-short pulses, which have improved precision but pose complications, like heat-affected zones and redeposition of material. These developments broaden the application of titanium but need further optimization to counter limitations [2].

Laser surface treatment improves surface-dependent properties of metallic pieces, such as hardness, resistance to corrosion, and biocompatibility. Laser surface melting and nitrogen gas alloying are such techniques that effectively enhance titanium alloys. Surface topography, which is essential for biocompatibility, can be altered through physical, chemical, or mechanical operations. Laser surface texturing (LST), an environmentally friendly process, employs high-energy pulses of laser to impart controlled roughness and pattern. The process adjusts surface topography and surface chemistry exactly at the nanolevel, which affects wettability, adherence of proteins, and cellular response. Such property modifications are optimized for biomedical and engineering applications [3]. Surface texturing or roughening improves the adhesion of bone and titanium implants. Traditional methods, such as etching, blasting, stamping, abrasion, and laser processing, are applied. Of these methods, laser texturing employs accurate and precise, quick, and reproducible patterning. The structured surface is excellent for improving tribological behavior by entrapment of wear debris within dimples and grooves and by improved lubricated and dry conditions.

The surface modifications bring about optimized function of implants, and hence, laser texturing has become a favored process for biomedical applications [4]. LST, due to its attractiveness and convenience, is extensively applied for treating the surfaces of titanium alloy for tribological purposes. Hu et al. [5] studied the LST's effect upon the tribological behavior of titanium alloy. Although dimple textures are superior tribologically to untextured surfaces, improvement is limited in friction reduction and wear resistance.

Grey Wolf Optimizer. DOI: https://doi.org/10.1016/B978-0-443-36624-6.00020-2

This is due to poor tribological characteristics inherent to titanium alloys. Nevertheless, even with the advantages offered by LST, complete friction and wear improvement is not attained by mere modifications to titanium components. To further augment the tribological characteristics of TC4 titanium alloy, a cell-like texture was formed through laser processing. The best parameters (1 μm spot spacing, 2.5 μm overlapping path) produced cell-separation by micro-crack formation, enhancing surface hardness from 351 HV to 445 HV. At a density of 0.32 GW/cm² of the laser, tests conducted upon simulated body fluid exhibited a 32.4% decrease in friction coefficient and 59% diminished ultra-High molecular weight polyethylene (UHMWPE) wear rate. The texture promoted threefold transport of lubricant by capillary action and retained lubricant within its 3.2 μm-wide channels (modeled using rectangular grooves), substantially augmenting tribological behavior through improved lubricating dynamics [6].

Woźniak et al. [7] demonstrated that picosecond-laser texturing on Ti6Al4V extra low interstitial (ELI) alters friction/wear responses under dry and Ringer's solution, supporting biomedical relevance. A picosecond 355 nm laser produced microtextures whose geometric parameters were optimized by varying process conditions. Ball-on-plate tribological tests under dry and Ringer's solution conditions showed laser-textured surfaces had 15% improved microhardness, 26% lower friction coefficient, and 29% improved wear volume compared to untextured specimens. Scanning electron microscopy (SEM) investigation of improvement assigned these gains due to wear shielding by microgrooves and improved hardness. The findings show that laser texturing highly improves the wear resistance of the alloy, especially under lubricated conditions.

Yuan et al. [8] linked process parameters to friction and wear trends across four metals, highlighting parameter sensitivity. Yuan et al. [8] applied laser processing to produce dimple textures upon four metals (316 SS, NiTi, TA2, Ti6Al4V). A Taguchi L16 (22×42) orthogonal array investigated parameter influence over dry sliding tribology, tested under confirmation by oil lubrication. Key parameters involved texture density, type of material, counterpart, and load, whose effect was quantified by mass loss via transformation into S/N ratios for optimization. Analysis of variance (ANOVA) detected ranking of influences to be type of material > counterpart > texture density > load. Optimum texture densities were 5% (316 SS, TA2), 7% (NiTi), and 11% (Ti6Al4V).

Wear morphological examination confirmed that textures improved wear resistance, especially under lubricated conditions. Chen et al. [9] showed that laser-induced micro-textures can enhance wear resistance via controlled groove geometry. Chen et al. [9] prepared a composite coating (TiN, TiB, Ti5Si3, Al3Ti) upon Ti6Al4V via YAG laser cladding by using a mixture of Ni60A-TiN-Al-Si powder (mass ratio 1:3:4:2). Wear tests under different loads (3 N, 6 N, 9 N) and temperatures (25°C, 350°C, 700°C) demonstrated lower abrasion loss, wear width/depth, and wear volume by coating compared to that of uncoated Ti6Al4V at room temperature, exhibiting shallower furrows. The coating's wear resistance declined significantly under heat, worse than that of the substrate. Friction trace examination confirmed temperature and load dependency, reflecting limitations of the coating under heat applications.

TC6 type of titanium alloy, which is important for aeroengine components, tends to undergo fretting wear. Laser shock peening (LSP) improves its behavior by generating gradient nanograin-amorphous substructures, lowering wear rates by 51.9% (from 4.147×10^{-6} to 1.996×10^{-6} mm^3 N^{-1} m^{-1}) during high-load fretting. Cao et al. [10] reported that gradient nanostructures in titanium alloys strengthen wear resistance relevant to textured surfaces. Multiscale analyses indicate that LSP's hardening layer at the surface, compressive residual stress, and nanostructural evolution synergically prevent the removal of materials and absorption of plastic strain [10]. Cao et al. [10] delineate strengthening mechanisms of LSP, which enable specific microstructure design for enhancing wear resistance against fretting for titanium alloys.

Wang et al. [11] reviewed laser-texturing routes and mapped their performance implications. Wang et al. [11] fabricated superwetting Ti alloy surfaces through laser texturing and annealing near room temperature. Laser processing formed micro-bumps, enhancing surface hardness by 48% (150 μm step size, load of 1.961 N). The tests for erosion identified 33.9% greater resistance in superhydrophobic compared to untreated materials, whose shallower pits appeared by SEM. The wettability had a significant effect on performance: superhydrophobic surfaces produced 33.9%, 23.8%, and 16.1% improved erosion resistance compared to untreated, superhydrophilic, and textured-only surfaces, respectively. The protective effect of superhydrophobicity was confirmed by energy dispersive spectroscopy (EDS) analyses, and contact angle and hardness measurements concurred with surface properties and increased durability. The combined strategy effectively enhances the hardness and erosion resistance of Ti alloys.

Das et al. [12] improved the frictional response of Ti6Al4V by targeted laser surface treatment. Das et al. [12] optimized LST of Ti6Al4V for improved wear and tribocorrosion resistance. Argon-shrouded LST yielded α'martensite/α composites (435–630 VHN), and nitrogen formed TiN/Ti2N-strengthened α matrix (839–1327 VHN), both of which outperformed untreated material (278 VHN). Nitrogen-LST lowered significantly dry wear rates (1.91–4.94 vs 5.93×10^{-3} mm³/Nm for untreated), outperforming argon-shrouded LST ($5.17–5.81\times10^{-3}$ mm³/Nm). The tribocorrosion rates also decreased (nitrogen: 1.3–3.2, argon: 3.5–4.8 vs 5.7×10^{-3} mm^3/Nm). Wang et al. [13] investigate how LST improves the tribological behavior of titanium alloys.

Laser techniques and conditions vary and affect texture geometry and shape, and therefore friction and wear under lubricated and dry conditions. The important mechanisms are: (1) reducing contact area and (2) entrapment of wear debris and lubricant retention for minimizing abrasive wear. The trend and application outlooks are discussed in this study for further developments of Ti alloys through LST. Ananth and Ramesh [14] surface-modified Ti6Al4V using lapping and laser texture, followed by applying alumina (AlCrN) thin coatings either with or without a Cr diffusion barrier layer. Tribological behavior was tested using a ball-on-flat wear test (105 cycles, 5 Hz, varied load).

Friction and displacement of the balls were detected by a force transducer and a laser sensor. Wear volume was measured through optical microscopy, and wear scar morphology by SEM. Results indicated that AlCrN coatings with an interlayer of Cr applied on textured substrates had improved bonding strength, lower wear rates, and better friction coefficients than direct coatings. The overall tribological efficiency improved with an interlayer of Cr. Salguero et al. [15] evaluated micro-textures under lubrication, clarifying how patterning mediates friction. Salguero et al. [15] produced varied micro-textures by varying the laser energy density and scan speed and causing topographical and micro-structural alterations.

Tested by ball-on-flat tests under lubrication, textured substrates exhibited up to 62% reduction of friction and 100 times reduction of wear relative to untextured substrates. Wettability assessment revealed an improvement of oil contact angles for textured substrates. Optical/SEM/EDS examination revealed predominant wear mechanisms and confirmed that texture parameters play a critical role in determining performance. Fiber laser treatment was applied to increase Ti6Al4V wear resistance by remelting and smoothing the surface to produce a crack-free, shiny finish. The laser-treated surface and, for comparison, plasma-nitrided and thermally oxidized specimens were tested using tribological tests, nanoindentation, and electron microscopy.

All treatments improved wear behavior, but nanoindentation identified no clear link between mechanical properties and tribological behavior. This indicates adhesive wear is not just dependent upon hardness but also on electronic interactions, such as bonding of electrons of titanium to interstitial elements [16]. Laser surface remelting and texture produced an enhancement of Ti-based amorphous alloy tribocorrosion performance. Three textures, asymmetric double-depth grooves (AG), dense low-depth grooves (DLDG), and a hybrid (DLDG + AG), were fabricated. Reciprocating tests in 3.5% NaCl indicated AG decreased the coefficient of friction (COF) by 21.5% and wear by 27.4%, and DLDG raised COF but improved wear resistance by 40.6×.

The hybrid (DLDG + AG) combined benefits and decreased COF by 26.9% and wear by 15.5×. DLDG + AG exhibited optimal sliding corrosion resistance that lowered corrosion current density by 96.6%. This dual strategy synergistically enhances COF, wear, and corrosion resistance [17]. Florian et al. [18] describe femtosecond laser-induced periodic surface structures (LIPSS) on titanium alloy by XRD and glow-discharge spectroscopy. Laser treatment (790 nm, 30 fs, 1 kHz) produces graded amorphous oxide layers (tens of hundreds of nm thick) that maximize tribological performance. Oil-lubricated tests indicate these nanostructures minimize friction and wear by preventing metal-to-metal contact and anchoring wear-prohibiting oil additives. Thicker oxide layers over grooves/spikes (formed at greater fluences) increase durability additionally. Elemental mapping verifies that oxide composition is related to wear resistance, proving femtosecond laser surface engineering to be an effective method for improving the tribological behavior of titanium alloys. A new bulk heat treatment and surface ceramic transformation process effectively leads to substantially improved tribological behavior of cheap low cost beta (LCB) Ti-6.8Mo-4.5Fe-1.5Al alloy. The process enhances wear resistance by 4–16× and decreases COF from 0.8–1.0 to 0.2–0.4.

Transmission electron microscopy (TEM) examination establishes the microstructure of the ceramic transformation layer. Wear tests against tungsten carbide (WC) and steel balls indicate that untreated LCB undergoes intensive adhesive wear, while treated surfaces undergo mild abrasive wear. Oil lubrication, however, increases wear when tested against steel balls through oil pressure-induced delamination [19].

Metaheuristics based on life, physics, social processes, and nature are a powerful tool for engineering, optimization, and AI. They can be very adaptable and converge speedily, and thus are capable of solving difficult and intricate problems beyond those that traditional algorithms can solve, especially when confronted by parameter optimization. They are capable of beating traditional algorithms through adaptive search mechanisms, which give them a wider solution space for multipurpose challenges [20]. Their ability to search and exploit gives them a competitive edge over their counterparts in modern applications of engineering, where efficiency and precision are critical [20]. LST of Ti6Al4V lowers friction and wear, but parameter optimization (power, speed, overlap) is difficult due to nonlinear relationships.

Ürgün et al. [21] correlate contact angle, kurtosis, and skewness through polynomial regression and optimization by nine metaheuristics (e.g., genetic algorithm, SPBO). ANOVA validated SPBO to be the most effective, and it delivered identical optimal solutions through methods. The article presents how metaheuristics can tackle nonlinear parameter issues of LST and control texture geometry to specific levels to deliver improved tribological performance of titanium alloys.

Praveenkumar et al. [22] optimize laser powder bed fusion (LPBF) parameters for Ti6Al4V by correlating laser power (200–203 W), scan speed (600–604 mm/s), hatch spacing (0.10–0.11 mm), and layer thickness (0.04–0.05 mm) to improved hardness (560–570 HV). Six metaheuristics (the JAYA algorithm, cohort intelligence (CI), particle swarm optimization (PSO), teaching-learning-based optimization (TLBO), genetic algorithm (GA), and simulated annealing (SA)) are compared for parameter optimization. The JAYA and CI produced the best speed of convergence (570 HV) with little oscillations and outperformed PSO/TLBO (569.5 HV), and GA/SA (slower speed of convergence). The balance of exploitation-exploration and simplicity of the JAYA algorithm makes it suitable for LPBF optimization, while CI provides reliability in real time.

Biswas et al. [23] developed an artificial neural network model hybridized through GA, PSO, and grey wolf optimiser (GWO) for optimization of wire electrical discharge machining (WEDM) for Ti6Al4V and compared the outcome with a multiobjective optimization method using ratio analysis (MOORA) and technique for order preference by similarity to ideal solution (TOPSIS). The artificial neural network (ANN)-GA has the lowest prediction error (2.4%), which outperformed ANN-PSO (3.5%), ANN-GWO (2.9%), MOORA, and TOPSIS, which exhibited larger errors (37.4% and 7.5%). Sensitivity analysis identified AOoff and WF as primary parameters. Pareto fronts revealed trade-offs: material removal rate (MRR) and kerf width (KW) increase together, and surface roughness (SR) and remelted layer treatment (RLT) decrease when KW increases. ANN-GA yielded the most accurate results for WEDM optimization.

Lakshmi et al. [24] investigate Ti6Al4V machining quality (workpiece vibration, tool wear, surface roughness) while CNC turning under mist cutting (80–200 m/min). Empirical models ($R^2 > 0.81$) demonstrated important parameters, indicating lower tool wear at lower cutting speed (80–140 m/min). Multiobjective GWO and vlseKriterijumska optimizacija i kompromisno resenje (VIKOR) determined best values for parameters: cutting speed=105.585 m/min, feed=0.1 mm/rev, depth of cut=0.346 mm, which yielded 0.695 μm roughness, 145.752 μm tool wear, and 26.711 μm vibration. The hybrid strategy successfully mimics the trade-off balance, controlling spring-back behavior of titanium and tool wear due to vibration.

Nguyen et al. [25] optimize and model surface roughness (Ra) and tool wear (VB) in dry-turning Ti6Al4V conditions by using WC tools coated by chemical vapor deposition (CVP) and physical vapor deposition (PVD). Linear regression, support vector machine regression, extreme gradient boosting, and ANN algorithms are compared, and ANN produced the best accuracy (lowest root mean square (RMSE)/mean absolute error (MAE), highest R^2). NSGA-II produced 50 Pareto solutions (Ra: 1.332–1.441 μm; VB: 0.100–0.125 mm), ranked based on a principal multicriterion function to choose the optimal solution (Ra: 1.439 μm, VB: 0.100 mm). Experimental validation proved the outcome, validating the applicability of such an ML-NSGA-II hybrid methodology for machining process multiobjective optimization.

Unlike previous studies focused largely on laser-induced surface texture or lubrication, this investigation introduces a systematic assessment of the tribological behavior of Ti6Al4V alloy treated by a 100 W fiber laser surface texture. Through application of a metaheuristic algorithm strategy for optimized laser parameters, the current work establishes systematic relations between laser-induced surface topographies and quantitative tribological measures such as COF, penetration depth, and width from reciprocating sliding wear test, and arithmetic mean roughness (Sa) and mass loss from solid particle erosion test conditions. Thus the current research fills essential knowledge gaps existing within tribological literature by integrating experimental confirmation with sound statistical examination and optimization, thus improving the practical application of laser-treated titanium within high-performance conditions.

18.2 Materials and methods

18.2.1 Materials

Ti6Al4V titanium alloy was chosen as the substrate material in this study because of its superior mechanical strength, corrosion resistance, and biocompatibility, making it an ideal material for the aerospace, biomedical, and industrial sectors. The material consists mainly of titanium with 5.5%–6.75% of aluminum and 3.5%–4.5% of vanadium, giving it a favorable strength-to-weight ratio and increased oxidation resistance. To create reference conditions for assessing the impact of the effects of the processing by a fiber laser, the original surface of the material was extensively analyzed. The samples were cleaned with acetone prior to their processing by a laser to remove contaminants from the surface and provide reproducible conditions. The impact of the shape of the surface on the interaction of the laser with the material was also taken into account because it significantly contributes to the resulting topography and texturization quality.

18.2.2 Laser surface texturing

In this research, flat Ti6Al4V (grade 5) titanium alloy samples were laser texturized using a 100 W fiber laser. Fig. 18.1 defines the experimental context used throughout the chapter and grounds the subsequent tribological analyses. A full-factorial design of experiment) strategy was employed with 16 runs of experiment deliberately designed to study the influences of significant process factors, scanning speed, laser power, and hatch distance (see Table 18.1). Laser texturing was uniformly performed over the entire flat sample area to enable equal evaluation of the surface properties. The primary aim was to understand how changes in laser factors affect the COF, penetration depth, and width from the reciprocating sliding wear test, arithmetic mean roughness (Sa), and mass loss from solid particle erosion test conditions.

18.2.3 Reciprocating sliding wear test

Reciprocating sliding wear tests for the Ti6Al4V titanium alloy were conducted in the current study using a UTS TRIBOLOG Tribometer in accordance with the test standard of ASTM G99 (Fig. 18.1b). The tests were carried out with different values of the normal load (10 N), reciprocating frequency (1 Hz), and sliding distance (20 m) to study the influence of the laser parameters on the material's COF, penetration depth, and width values. A stainless steel ball with a diameter of 6 mm was used as the counter body under dry, unlubricated conditions at room temperature. The experiments were designed using a statistical experimental design method to analyze the influence of laser speed, laser power, and hatch distance on the COF, penetration depth, and width values. The reported values for the COF represent the average of three repeated tests. Average COF values were calculated based on the steady-state region of the friction curves.

18.2.4 Solid particle erosion test

Particle erosion tests were performed by blasting garnet abrasive particles using compressed air into the surfaces of the target composite materials in a specially built test chamber, following the specifications outlined in ASTM G76 standards (Fig. 18.1c). Throughout the studies, three iterations were conducted for every material category at a 90° angle, and the mean losses in mass of the target materials were computed. The margin of error, derived from several iterations of trials,

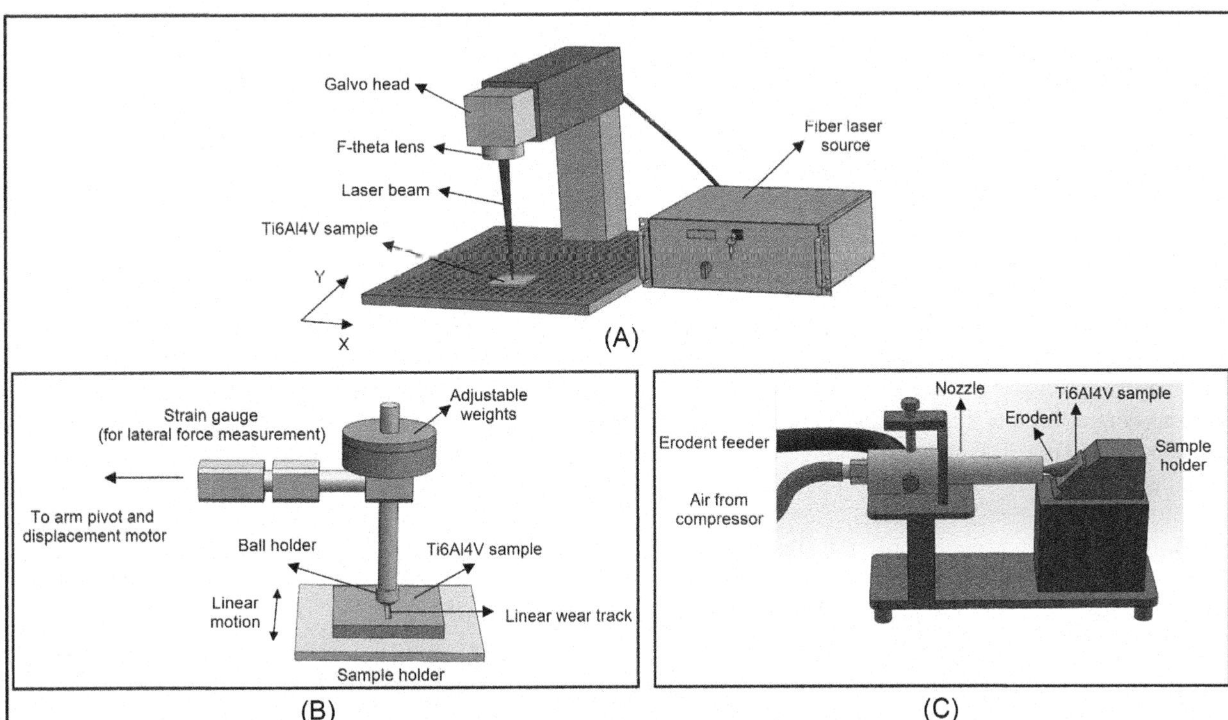

FIGURE 18.1 Experimental schematics: (A) fiber-laser surface texturing workflow and key parameters (laser power P, scan speed v, hatch spacing h); (B) reciprocating sliding wear test setup; (C) solid particle erosion test rig.

TABLE 18.1 Experimental design matrix showing the laser texturing parameters used for surface modification of Ti6Al4V specimens.

Exp. no	Hatch distance (μm)	Power (W)	Speed (mm/s)	COF from the reciprocating sliding wear test	Penetration depth from the reciprocating sliding wear test	Penetration width from the reciprocating sliding wear test	Sa from the solid particle erosion test	Mass loss from solid particle erosion test (mgr)
1	75	10	500	0.6	15.3	881	6.60	8.7
2	75	20	1000	0.63	22.8	920	7.90	8.8
3	75	30	1500	0.63	14.4	841	8.18	9.6
4	75	40	2000	0.59	22.7	760	10.1	9.8
5	150	10	1000	0.61	18.9	821	9.37	9.6
6	150	20	500	0.63	20.6	859	10.0	9.1
7	150	30	2000	0.62	25.8	1017	10.8	9.4
8	150	40	1500	0.63	26.4	900	12.1	8.9
9	225	10	1500	0.63	20.4	814	8.18	9
10	225	20	2000	0.61	20.1	854	6.86	8.9
11	225	30	500	0.68	21.1	859	8.96	10.8
12	225	40	1000	0.65	19.1	780	7.62	10.4
13	300	10	2000	0.515	24	801	6.87	77
14	300	20	1500	0.62	12.5	764	6.77	96
15	300	30	1000	0.64	22.6	880	7.32	92
16	300	40	500	0.73	19.9	909	11.4	127
Ref.					19.4	1085	7.93	106

was found to be 3%. Prior to and during the testing process, the specimens were measured using a highly precise scale with an accuracy of 0.1 mg (Shimadzu Atx-224, Japan). The mass loss calculation was obtained by subtraction of the total mass after the solid particle erosion test from the total mass before the solid particle erosion test.

The erodent utilized in the experiment consists of garnet abrasive particles. The size of garnet abrasive particles ranges from 700 to 1250 μm. The particle impingement angles are set at a 90° impingement angle. The experiment operates with a 5 mm nozzle diameter and 2 bar acceleration/blast gun pressure. Currently running at a mass flow rate of 22.5 g/s and a speed of 58 m/s for garnet, the erodent flows.

Under a regulated temperature of 25°C, the experiments allow a ±2°C variance. Each test has a duration of 20 s and is carried out at a distance of 20 mm. Abrasive speed was measured at the nozzle exit and by the double disk speed measurement method, the details of which are described in the literature [26].

18.2.5 Roughness characterization by noncontact laser profilometer

Penetration depth and width values from the reciprocating sliding wear test and arithmetic mean roughness (Sa) values from the solid particle erosion test of various laser textured Ti6Al4V samples after reciprocating and solid particle wear tests were analysed by using noncontact laser profilometry to take precise surface measurements without physically interfering with surfaces. Sa, penetration depth, and width values of surfaces were explored using the Nanovea PS50 laser profilometer, providing topographic images of texture areas in good resolution.

The raw images of the surfaces were analyzed with the aid of DigitalSurf software version 6.2.7487 from Mountains Technology. The flat 3 mm × 5 mm area was surveyed by a laser profilometer at a resolution of 20 μm to enable a detailed study of the width and depth of the scratch markings in reciprocating sliding wear tests. The erosion crater surface roughness characterization was accomplished with a scanning area of 20 mm × 20 mm.

18.3 Results and discussion

18.3.1 Roughness analysis of Ti6Al4V surface laser texturing

Fig. 18.2 reveals a clear energy-density-driven trend in the arithmetic mean roughness Sa that is fully consistent with the factorial combinations in Table 18.1. The baseline specimen (Exp 1, hatch=1 μm, 10 W, 500 mm s^{-1}) exhibits only a modest increase in roughness to 1.07 μm relative to the raw surface (0.62 μm), indicating that a low linear energy density (P/v=0.02 J mm^{-1}) coupled with the tightest hatch promotes re-melting and planarization rather than pronounced texture growth. Raising power to 20 W while doubling the scan speed (Exp 2) nevertheless doubles the energy input per track and drives Sa to 7.27 μm, demonstrating that at constant hatch the melt pool volume, rather than the absolute speed, dominates peak-to-valley development. Further increases in power to 30 and 40 W (Exps 3–4) are accompanied by progressive speed increases, so the effective P/v falls and Sa drops to 5.35 μm and 4.65 μm, respectively, confirming the inverse relationship between linear energy density and surface smoothness once a critical threshold is exceeded. When the hatch distance is widened to 2 μm (Laser Track=150), roughness again peaks when high power is combined with the lowest speed (Exp 6, 20 W, 500 mm s^{-1}, Sa=6.74 μm), whereas keeping power low or speed high (Exps 5, 7, 8) limits Sa to the 2.80–4.48 μm range because overlapping passes partially level the molten ridges.

At hatch=3 μm (Laser Track=225) the same pattern persists: minimal energy input (Exp 9, 10 W, 1500 mm s^{-1}) yields a near-smooth 1.58 μm surface, but combining moderate power with the slowest speed (Exp 11, 30 W, 500 mm s^{-1}) produces a pronounced 6.98 μm texture, emphasizing the critical role of residence time in amplifying capillary recoil and resolidification roughness. The most extreme topography is generated when the largest hatch distance of 4 μm is paired with the maximum power and minimum speed (Exp 16, 40 W, 500 mm s^{-1}), pushing Sa to 14.48 μm; here the high P/v (0.08 J mm^{-1}) and minimal track overlap combine to form deep molten grooves and sharply delineated ridges that survive solidification. Conversely, high-speed, low-power combinations within the same hatch group (Exps 13–15) restrict Sa to <3.2 μm, underscoring that overlap can still suppress roughness provided that the heat input per unit length remains below the critical threshold for spatter-induced asperity formation. Overall, the data demonstrate that surface roughness scales

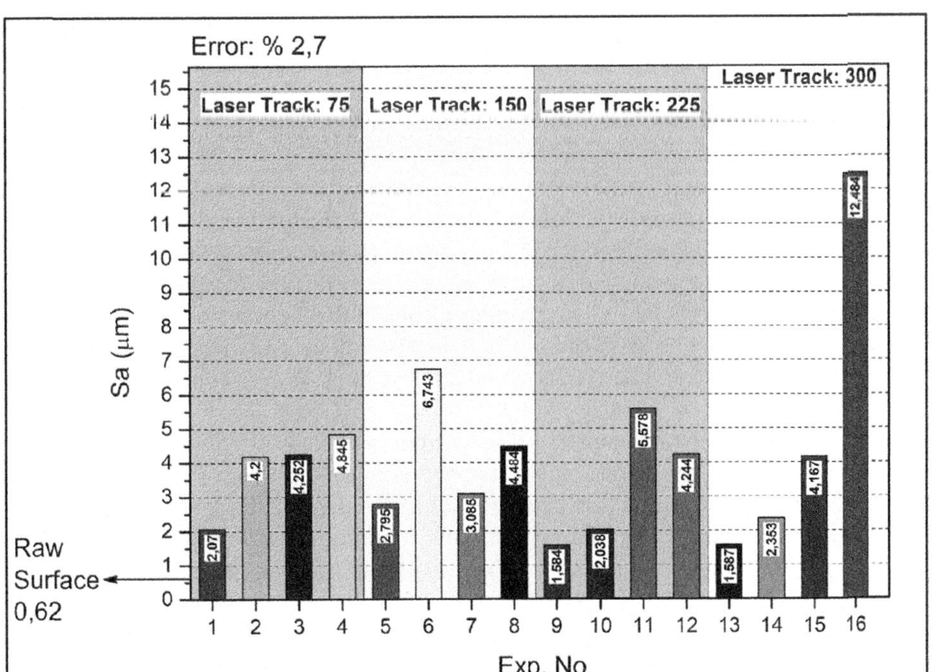

FIGURE 18.2 Areal roughness (Sa) versus experiment index across the full-factorial laser texturing design.

with the synergistic effect of linear energy density and hatch-controlled overlap: high P/v and sparse tracks magnify roughness, while either reducing energy density or increasing overlap mitigates it, a relationship that must be balanced when tailoring Ti6Al4V surfaces for specific tribological functions.

Fig. 18.3 depicts morphology differences induced by parameter choices. Fig. 18.3A illustrates that a 10 W beam translated at 500 mm s^{-1} across a 75 μm hatch produces only shallow, irregular undulations (Sa=1.07 μm), confirming that dense track overlap combined with low linear energy density favors re-melting and planarization. When power is doubled to 20 W and speed is raised to 1000 mm s^{-1} in Fig. 18.3B, the melt pool volume per track increases while overlap remains constant, generating sharply resolved ridges aligned with the scan direction and elevating Sa to 7.27 μm.

Fig. 18.3C shows that further increasing power to 30 W but accelerating to 1500 mm s^{-1} lowers the effective energy input (P/v), so the ridges become narrower and less pronounced (Sa=5.35 μm). The lowest linear energy density in the 75 μm group occurs in Fig. 18.3D (40 W, 2000 mm s^{-1}), where reduced melt-pool residence time yields finer, more uniform corrugations and a moderate Sa of 4.85 μm.

Doubling the hatch to 150 μm reduces track overlap and amplifies the influence of energy density on groove depth: Fig. 18.3E (10 W, 1000 mm s^{-1}) displays periodically spaced valleys but retains a modest Sa of 2.80 μm because of the low heat input, whereas Fig. 18.3F (20 W, 500 mm s^{-1}) couples high power with the slowest speed, producing tall ridges and broad melt trenches that raise Sa to 6.74 μm - the highest in this hatch group.

In Fig. 18.3G, a 30 W–2000 mm s^{-1} combination cuts the residence time despite the elevated power, resulting in smoother, flattened ripples (Sa=3.09 μm), and Fig. 18.3H (40 W, 1500 mm s^{-1}) occupies an intermediate regime where moderate energy density and sparse overlap yield regular wave-like features with Sa around 4.48 μm. Collectively, the eight maps demonstrate that surface morphology is governed by the synergistic effects of hatch-controlled overlap and linear energy density: narrow hatches tend to suppress amplitude unless energy input exceeds a critical threshold, while wider hatches magnify ridge-to-valley contrast whenever high P/v ratios prevail, a balance that must be tuned to tailor the tribological performance of laser-textured Ti6Al4V surfaces.

Fig. 18.4 completes the morphological survey across all parameter sets (complementing Fig. 18.3). Fig. 18.4A reveals that enlarging the hatch to 225 μm while maintaining a modest 10 W–1500 mm s^{-1} setting yields only faint, isotropic ripples (Sa=1.58 μm), indicating that the reduced track overlap dominates over the low linear energy density in suppressing melt-pool instability. Doubling the power and further increasing the speed in Fig. 18.4B (20 W, 2000 mm s^{-1}) provides a slight rise in heat input but still produces a largely planar surface with Sa just above 2 μm, confirming that overlap, rather than power alone, controls texture amplitude in this regime. A dramatic shift occurs in Fig. 18.4C when the scan speed is dropped to 500 mm s^{-1} at 30 W: the effective energy density climbs fourfold, promoting deep, periodically spaced grooves bordered by resolidified beads and boosting Sa to nearly 7 μm.

Fig. 18.4D (40 W, 1000 mm s^{-1}) halves the linear energy density relative to Fig. 18.4C but still exhibits clearly segmented ridges with Sa around 4.24 μm, underscoring the continuing influence of wide hatch on ridge height even at intermediate energy input. Increasing the hatch again to 300 μm further limits track overlap; under the lowest energy setting of Fig. 18.4E (10 W, 2000 mm s^{-1}) the surface remains almost featureless (Sa=1.59 μm), whereas Fig. 18.4F (20 W, 1500 mm s^{-1}) shows isolated humps and valleys with Sa=2.35 μm as melt pools begin to coalesce across the larger spacing. Fig. 18.4G demonstrates that a 30 W–1000 mm s^{-1} combination crosses the threshold where adjacent tracks interact, producing continuous ridges of moderate height (Sa=3.17 μm). The most aggressive condition, Fig. 18.4H (40 W, 500 mm s^{-1}), maximizes linear energy density in the 300 μm group; massive ridges flank deep trenches and elevate Sa to 14.48 μm – by far the roughest topography in the data set. Collectively, these eight maps confirm that, once hatch distances exceed 200 μm, surface morphology is governed by a competition between diminishing overlap and rising linear energy density: low-energy combinations leave the substrate almost untouched, whereas high-power, slow-scan regimes trigger pronounced capillary recoil and material accumulation at track edges, creating textures whose depth scales superlinearly with the P/v ratio.

Fig. 18.5 implies two extreme erosion responses that arise from markedly different laser-texturing regimes applied at the same scan speed of 500 mm s^{-1}. The contrast highlights how surface morphology relates to erosion resistance. In Exp-1 (Fig. 18.5A), a tight 75 μm hatch combined with low power (10 W) delivers a linear energy density of only 0.02 J mm^{-1}; the dense track overlap promotes re-melting and planarization, limiting the arithmetic mean roughness to 6.6 μm and restricting solid-particle-induced material removal to 8.7 mg. By contrast, Exp-16 (Fig. 18.5B) uses a four-times wider hatch (300 μm) and four-times higher power (40 W), raising the linear energy density to 0.08 J mm^{-1} while simultaneously reducing overlap. The resulting melt-pool instabilities generate deep grooves and sharply faceted ridges that almost double Sa to 11.4 μm and concentrate impact stresses within the texture valleys; this topography, together with the larger unshielded planar areas between tracks, accelerates micro-cutting and leads to the highest recorded mass loss of 12.7 mg.

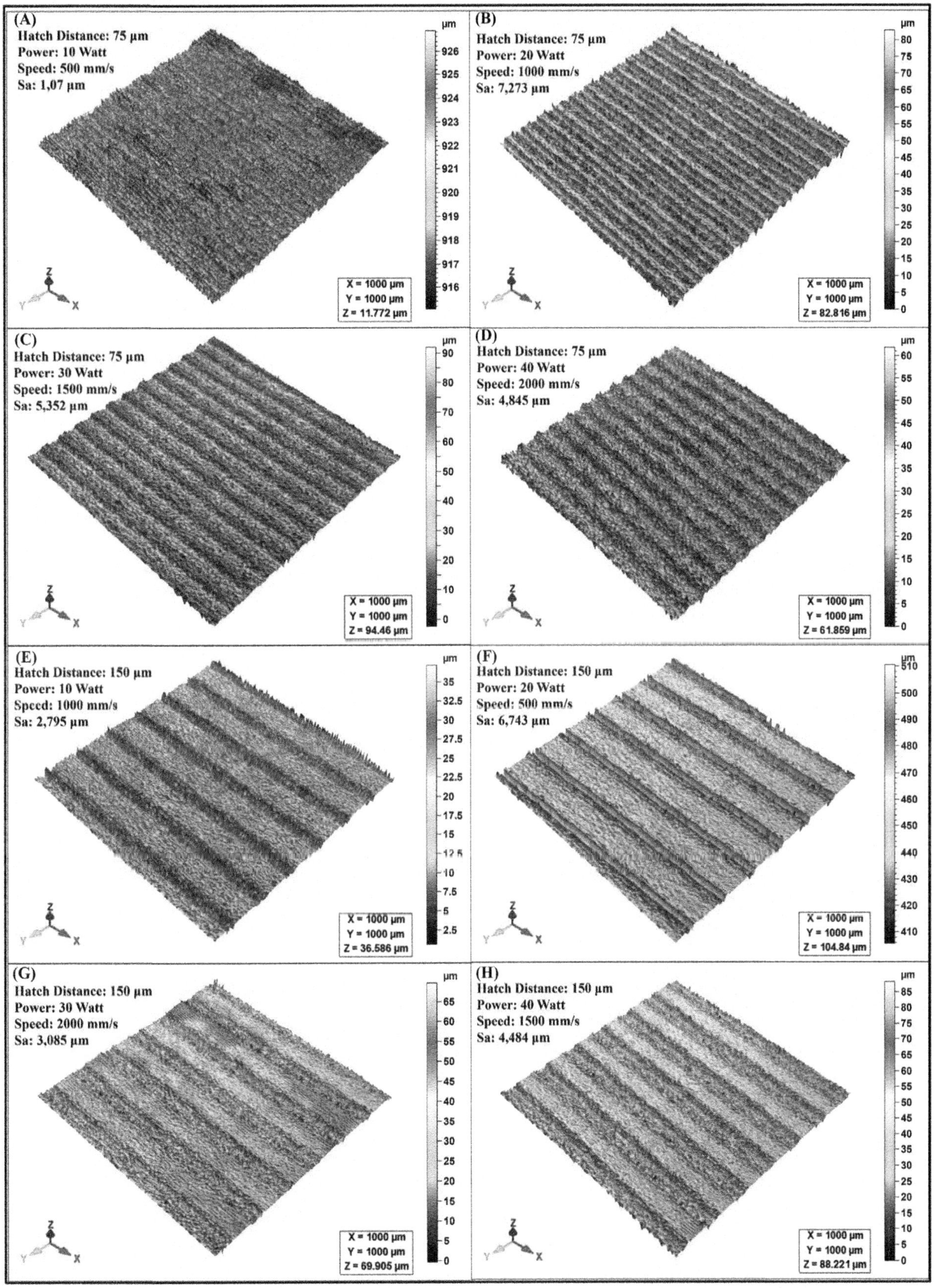

FIGURE 18.3 Noncontact profilometry 3D maps of laser-textured Ti6Al4V surfaces for experiments 1–8 (color scale denotes height; parameter sets per Table 18.1).

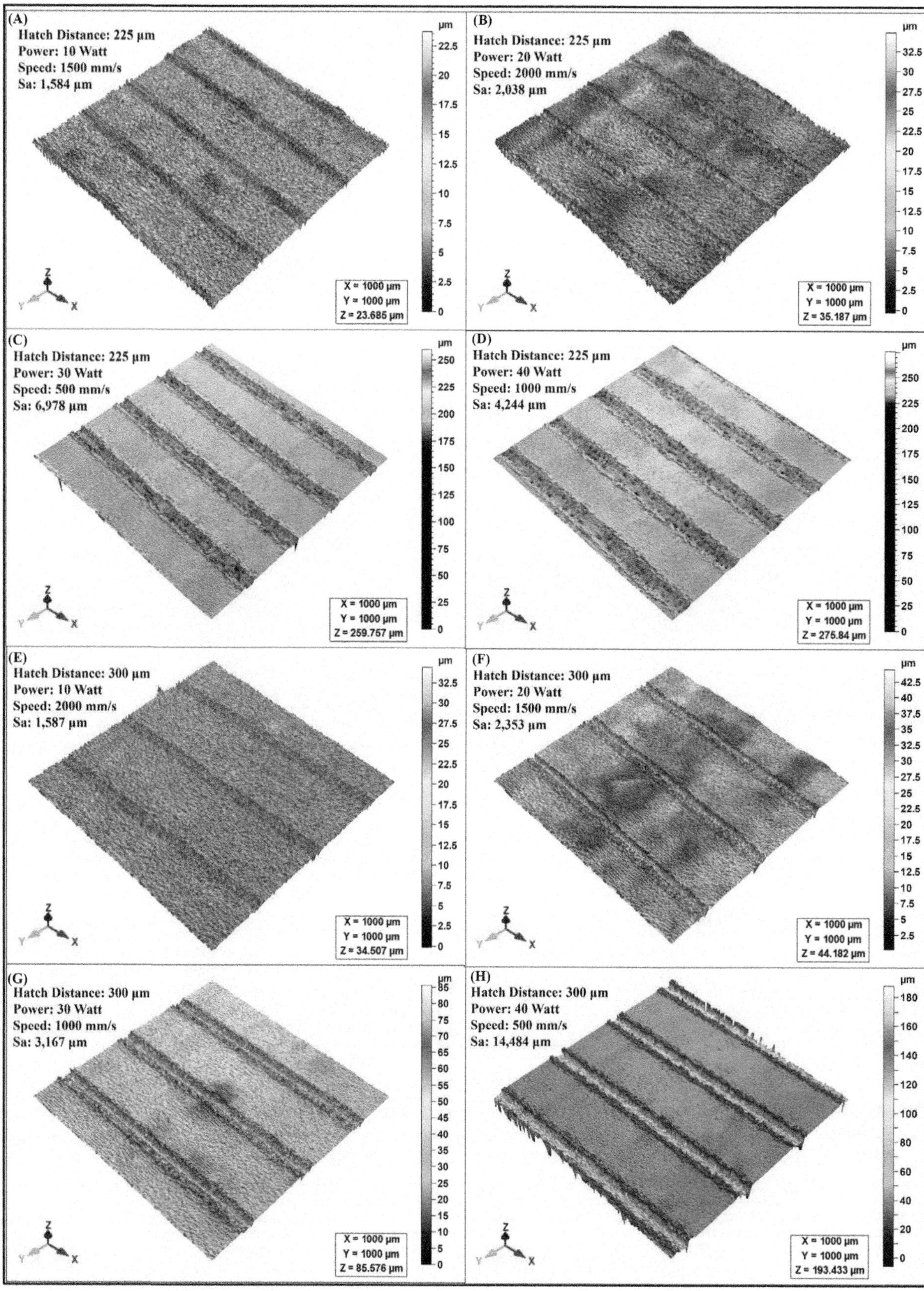

FIGURE 18.4 Noncontact profilometry 3D maps of laser-textured Ti6Al4V surfaces for experiments 9–16 (color scale denotes height; parameter sets per Table 18.1).

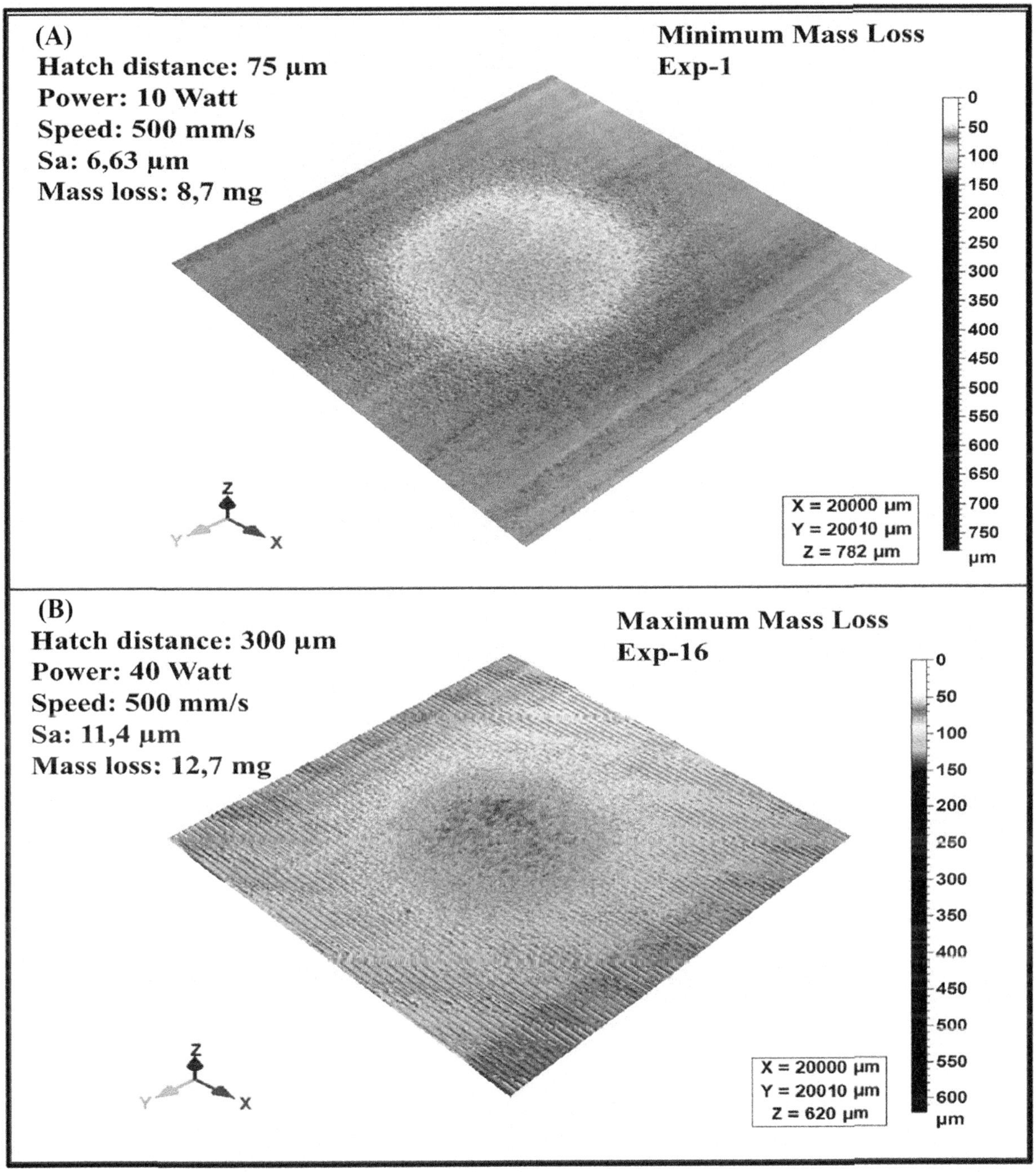

FIGURE 18.5 Representative 3D topographies corresponding to minimum and maximum mass loss after the solid-particle erosion test: (A) Exp-14 and (B) Exp-8.

The comparison therefore demonstrates that, under otherwise identical processing speed, mass loss in solid-particle erosion is governed by the interplay between power-controlled energy input and hatch-controlled overlap: low-power, closely overlapped patterns minimize roughness and act as an erosion barrier, whereas high-power, widely spaced tracks amplify roughness and expose the surface to severe material removal.

The comparison in Fig. 18.6 highlights how surface texture relates to frictional response under reciprocating wear. Fig. 18.6A (Exp-14) depicts the wear scar generated on the surface textured with a 300 µm hatch distance, 20 W laser power, and 1500 mm s^{-1} scan speed. This wide hatch, coupled with only moderate power, yields the lowest areal energy density of all samples (=0.04 J mm^{-2}), so each track receives limited heat input and neighboring tracks hardly overlap. The

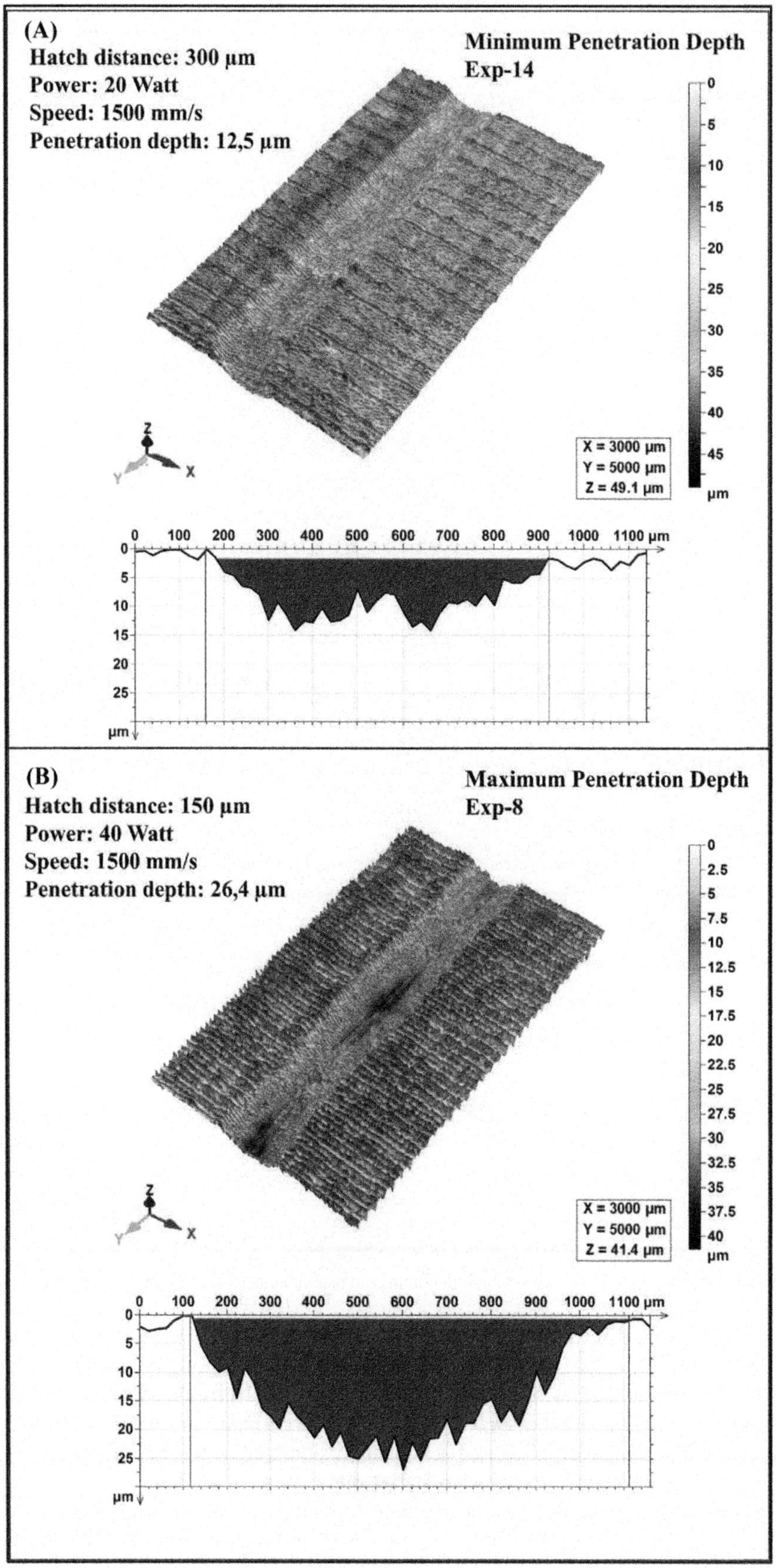

FIGURE 18.6 Laser surface textured Ti6Al4V surface 3D maps comparison with minimum and maximum penetration depth after reciprocating sliding wear: (A) Exp-14 and (B) Exp-8.

resulting texture consists of shallow, gently undulating grooves whose crests remain mechanically supportive during reciprocating sliding. After testing, the valley formed along the sliding path reaches a minimum penetration depth of 12.5 μm, and the cross-section shows only modest subsurface material removal, evidencing good resistance to plowing and micro-fatigue. Fig. 18.6B (Exp-8), in contrast, was produced with a 150 μm hatch distance, 40 W power, and the same 1500 mm s^{-1} speed. Halving the hatch and doubling the power raises the areal energy density to=0.18 J mm^{-2} - more than four times that of Exp-14 – so adjacent scan tracks overlap extensively and re-melt to form a ridge–valley morphology with pronounced thermal softening and residual tensile stresses. Under identical loading conditions, this surface suffers a maximum penetration depth of 26.4 μm, more than twice that of Exp-14, and its profile reveals a broad, V-shaped groove typical of severe abrasive–adhesive synergy. The comparison demonstrates that higher laser power combined with a narrower hatch distance greatly amplifies local energy input, which roughens the topography and weakens the near-surface microstructure, making the track more susceptible to deep material removal during sliding wear. Conversely, a low-energy, widely spaced hatch minimizes thermal damage and yields a smoother, mechanically robust texture that resists penetration. Laser processing parameters such as laser power, scanning speed, and hatch spacing strongly affect the surface morphology of Ti6Al4V alloys. Lower energy inputs – for example, using lower laser power, higher scan speed, or a wider hatch distance – tend to produce shallower laser-induced grooves, smoother surfaces (lower roughness), and minimal re-melting of the alloy surface [27,28]. In contrast, higher energy density (e.g., high power or slow scanning, with closely spaced hatch lines) yields deeper grooves with greater surface roughness and noticeable resolidified material around the micro-grooves [27,28].

Bharatish et al. [29] address the tribology of nickel-aluminum-bronze in landing-gear components, illustrating application-level constraints. For instance, increasing the scan speed from 25 mm/s to 100 mm/s (thereby reducing laser energy per unit area) was shown to decrease the groove depth on Ti6Al4V (from about 60 μm down to 40 μm) due to less energy absorption and thermal accumulation [29].

Volpe et al. [30] fabricated antiicing laser-textured surfaces, evidencing function-specific texture design. In the same way, increased hatch spacings (around 50–200 μm) yield smoother and more uniform texture, while a highly reduced hatch (10 μm, with intense overlap) resulted in nonuniform, rugged tracks [30]. Lower laser energy conditions as a whole produce a finer, smoother texture, while increased energy inputs yield a rougher topography with increased ablated features. The surface morphology resulting from laser texturing has a direct impact on wear resistance and the depth of wear scars in reciprocating sliding tests. Generally, a smoother or more moderately textured surface (achieved with lower energy input) offers improved wear resistance, showing smaller wear volume and shallower penetration of the wear track.

Babu et al. [31] detailed Nd:YAG texturing parameters and the resulting roughness evolution. These types of surfaces have lower asperity heights and fewer stress concentrators, reducing friction and limiting abrasive wear [31]. It has been found in experiments that laser-textured Ti6Al4V with shallow, fine-sized micro-patterns has a lower friction coefficient and less wear than a rough, untreated surface [31]. More severe texturing with high energy, resulting in deep-seated grooves, can, however, lower wear resistance. Deep or wide groove features concentrate the disruptive load and enhance the regional stress in the sliding direction, tending to accelerate the material removal and generate deeper wear scars [31].

Conradi et al. [32] reviewed friction and wear on laser-textured surfaces, consolidating mechanisms observed across studies. Indeed, excessively wide/deep grooves were found to raise contact stresses and result in higher friction and wear rates in sliding contacts [32]. Therefore using lower-energy laser parameters to create a smoother, shallower texture leads to superior tribological performance (less wear and a more shallow wear track), whereas higher-energy processing that forms coarse grooves can worsen wear by promoting greater friction and wear track penetration.

18.3.2 Analysis of variance analysis of laser-texturing parameters

Sensitivity of the investigated laser-texturing parameters to the COF was investigated by means of an ANOVA-based global sensitivity approach. Laser power, hatch distance, and scanning speed were treated as independent parameters, whereas the relative effects of the latter two on the derived COF through the reciprocating sliding wear test were measured by the percentage contribution of the sequential sums of squares (Seq SS) to total variability. ANOVA results (Table 18.2) indicate that scanning speed is the most sensitive parameter, taking up 40.54% of the total variation of the COF. Laser power follows with 30.52% of total variation. Hatch distance contributes relatively little, sharing only 6.34% of total variation. The balance of 22.60% of variability is apportioned to experimental error. Note that such an error component contains not only random measurement noise but also unseen two-factor and higher three-factor interactions of parameters (e.g., speed–power, speed–hatch, power–hatch) combinations. Second- or third-order interactions of this type may influence friction output yet remain unaccountable to the basic main effects model and therefore contribute to total error percentage. From the perspective of statistical significance, none of the parameters achieved conventional significance at

TABLE 18.2 ANOVA analysis of COF from reciprocating sliding.

Source	DF	Seq SS	Contribution	Adj SS	Adj MS	*F*-value	*P*-value
Hatch distance (μm)	3	0.001867	6.34%	0.001867	0.000622	0.56	0.660
Power (W)	3	0.008992	30.52%	0.008992	0.002997	2.70	0.139
Speed (mm/s)	3	0.011942	40.54%	0.011942	0.003981	3.59	0.086
Error	6	0.006659	22.60%	0.006659	0.001110		
Total	15	0.029461	100.00%				

TABLE 18.3 ANOVA analysis of penetration depth from reciprocating sliding.

Source	DF	Seq SS	Contribution	Adj SS	Adj MS	*F*-value	*P*-value
Hatch distance (μm)	3	37.63	16.86%	37.63	12.544	0.68	0.598
Power (W)	3	21.97	9.84%	21.97	7.324	0.39	0.762
Speed (mm/s)	3	52.18	23.38%	52.18	17.394	0.94	0.479
Error	6	111.45	49.92%	111.45	18.575		
Total	15	223.24	100.00%				

α=0.05 (P>0.05) through the ANOVA test, although scanning speed approached near-marginal significance (P=0.086) and hence may be of significance.

Practically, these results indicate that the COF is primarily sensitive to variations of scanning speed, relatively sensitive to variations of laser power, and relatively insensitive to variations of hatch distance for the examined ranges of parameters. Such a ranking of sensitivity is useful for optimization of the process: regulation of the scanning speed is likely to achieve the most efficient variation of the COF, followed by variations of laser power, and the hatch distance can be treated as a supplementary parameter for friction regulation.

Table 18.3 reveals results that show that scanning speed contributed the greatest to main effects, accounting for 23.38% of total penetration depth variation. The second largest was that of hatch distance at 16.86%, with laser power playing a relatively little part at 9.84%.

An interesting observation is the large error (residual) component of 49.92%, indicating that nearly half of the variability that is seen is out of the reach of explanation by the main effects alone. The large percentage of error points toward the existence of sizable two-way and potentially three-way interactions between the process parameters (e.g., speed–power, speed–hatch, or power–hatch combinations) that strongly influence the response. These vigorous interactions make the system more complicated and diminish the predictive capability of a simple main effects model. The ranking of the effects is therefore: Speed > Clearance Distance > Power. However, by virtue of interaction-induced effects dominating, it is apparent that for the complete reflection of the complicated interrelationships underlying penetration depth, higher-order or interaction terms need to be included in the experimental designs/models of the future.

ANOVA results for penetration width are given in Table 18.4. Although the overall model contains only 43.61% of the total variability, the residual (error) contains just over half of the total fraction of 56.39%. It therefore implies that more than half of the total variability is not explained by the main effects encompassed. The biggest single main effect contribution came from scanning distance at 18.55, followed by laser power at 18.07; scanning speed contributed only 6.99% of the total. The large error term therefore indicates that influential two-way (e.g., power-scanning) or even three-way (e.g., scanning-speed, power-speed) interactions between parameters significantly affect the penetration width. These higher-order interactions are not representable by the simple linear main effects model and hence increase apparent model

TABLE 18.4 ANOVA analysis of Penetration width from reciprocating sliding.

Source	DF	Seq SS	Contribution	Adj SS	Adj MS	*F*-value	*P*-value
Model	9	28.609	43.61%	28609	3179	0.52	0.821
Linear	9	28.609	43.61%	28609	3179	0.52	0.821
Hatch distance (μm)	3	12.169	18.55%	12170	4057	0.66	0.607
Power (W)	3	11.852	18.07%	11852	3951	0.64	0.616
Speed (mm/s)	3	4587	6.99%	4587	1529	0.25	0.860
Error	6	36.990	56.39%	36990	6165		
Total	15	65.599	100.00%				

TABLE 18.5 ANOVA analysis of Sa from solid particle erosion.

Source	DF	Seq SS	Contribution	Adj SS	Adj MS	*F*-value	*P*-value
Model	9	38.481	82.67%	38.481	4.2756	3.18	0.086
Linear	9	38.481	82.67%	38.481	4.2756	3.18	0.086
Hatch distance (μm)	3	18.985	40.79%	18.985	6.3283	4.71	0.051
Power (W)	3	16.601	35.66%	16.601	5.5335	4.12	0.066
Speed (mm/s)	3	2.895	6.22%	2.895	0.9650	0.72	0.577
Error	6	8.065	17.33%	8.065	1.3442		
Total	15	46.546	100.00%				

complexity and deliver higher unexplained variability. The percentage contribution values of ranking are therefore as follows: Line Distance ≈ Power > Speed. In conclusion, although line spacing and power possess the biggest relative influence upon penetration width, the dominance of unexplained variability supports moving to incorporate interaction terms as components of the model, or taking up higher-order experimental design for appropriate modeling and optimizing of penetration width response.

From Table 18.5 output of the general factorial regression, it is clear that the hatch distance (μm) has the strongest impact upon Sa roughness values. From the ANOVA table, 40.79% contribution ratio is found for hatch distance with *F*-value and *P*-value at 4.71 and 0.051, respectively. From the fact that the above finding is quite close to the threshold of the statistical significance value (P=0.05), it could be concluded that the Sa output response variable is significantly sensitive to slight variations of hatch distance. The Power (W) is again the second strongest factor with 35.66% contribution and *F*-value of 4.12 (*P*-value=0.066). Since the former's *P*-value is higher than 0.05 by a small quantity, it reveals that the former is borderline with respect to statistical significance effects. However, it can be considered important with respect to sensitivity. From the above case, it is shown that partial variations of power level can significantly affect the surface roughness. In opposition, the variable of speed (mm/s) has low sensitivity at Sa, with 6.22% contribution only, *F*-value=0.72, and P=0.577. From the latter finding, it is shown that the effect of the processing speed on the product's surface roughness has limited effects and that it is not of first-order concern to handle during parameters' optimization. From the above model of total contribution ratio of 82.67%, it is generally capable of providing a reliable explanation. However, slight variations of hatch distance and laser power significantly dominate slight variations of the output

TABLE 18.6 ANOVA analysis of Sa from solid particle erosion.

Source	DF	Seq SS	Contribution	Adj SS	Adj MS	*F*-value	*P*-value
Model	9	12.092	65.52%	12092	1.3436	1.27	0.400
Linear	9	12.092	65.52%	12092	1.3436	1.27	0.400
Hatch distance (μm)	3	1.212	6.57%	1212	0.4042	0.38	0.771
Power (W)	3	6.748	36.56%	6747	2.2492	2.12	0.199
Speed (mm/s)	3	4.132	22.39%	4132	1.3775	1.30	0.358
Error	6	6.365	34.48%	6365	1.0608		
Total	15	18.457	100.00%				

parameter Sa. Therefore it is of first concern during process optimization to control hatch distance and laser power within reduced tolerances.

The ANOVA regression output indicated in Table 18.6 demonstrates that the value of mass loss has relatively low sensitivity to the parameters of the process. The total contribution ratio of the model is 65.52%, and the error contribution is 34.48%. This demonstrates that the model's explanatory power is limited and that the effects of the parameters upon mass loss are feeble. Hatch distance has the lowest contribution, with a contribution of 6.57%, F=0.38, and P=0.771. It is apparent from this fact that changes in hatch distance do not create appreciable sensitivity upon mass loss. Laser power contributes the greatest influence, with a contribution ratio of 36.56%, even though there are values of F=2.12 and P=0.199 that are higher than, but below, the threshold of statistical significance. Thus although laser power has higher influence in comparison to the influence of the rest of the parameters, it has limited significance in terms of sensitivity. Laser scanning speed contributes at a moderate level with a contribution of 22.39%, F=1.30, and P=0.358, but is not statistically significant. Sensitivity analysis results conclude that the mass loss response variable does not respond significantly statistically to the three process parameters (Hatch distance, power, speed) (P>0.05). However, the Power (W) parameter is of interest as the variable that requires the largest amount of attention in potential optimizations of the process due to its large contribution ratio. Low mass loss sensitivity is indicated by hatch distance and processing speed; however, these results indicate that operating the process parameters over wide bands of tolerances will not produce appreciable loss of mass loss performance, yet that operating the laser power setting outside of the optimal value band may produce more variable results.

18.4 Problem formulation and optimization with grey wolf optimizer

The GWO is a bio-inspired metaheuristic algorithm that mathematically emulates the cooperative hunting and strict social hierarchy observed in grey wolf packs, where solution candidates are ranked as alpha, beta, delta, and omega individuals that encircle prey (the global optimum) through adaptive position-updating rules. Since its introduction in 2014, GWO has gained wide academic adoption for tackling nonlinear, multimodal, and NP-hard search spaces that resist classical gradient-based approaches. It has been successfully deployed for feature selection and hyperparameter tuning in machine learning, optimal power-flow and unit-commitment scheduling in energy systems, multiobjective route planning in swarm robotics and unmanned aerial vehicles, structural damage detection and parameter identification in civil engineering, optimal design of antennas and photonic crystals in electromagnetics, as well as process parameter optimization in advanced manufacturing contexts such as LST and additive manufacturing. The algorithm's balanced exploration–exploitation strategy, minimal control parameters (typically only population size and maximum iterations), and ease of hybridization with other heuristics render it a versatile, computationally efficient toolkit for solving high-dimensional, discontinuous, and constrained optimization problems across diverse scientific and engineering disciplines.

Fig. 18.7 illustrates the detailed operational flow of the GWO, providing a step-by-step visualization of how the algorithm mimics the social hierarchy and cooperative hunting behavior of grey wolves in nature. The optimization process begins with the random initialization of a population of candidate solutions—each representing a "wolf" in the search space. These wolves are then evaluated using a fitness function specific to the problem being solved.

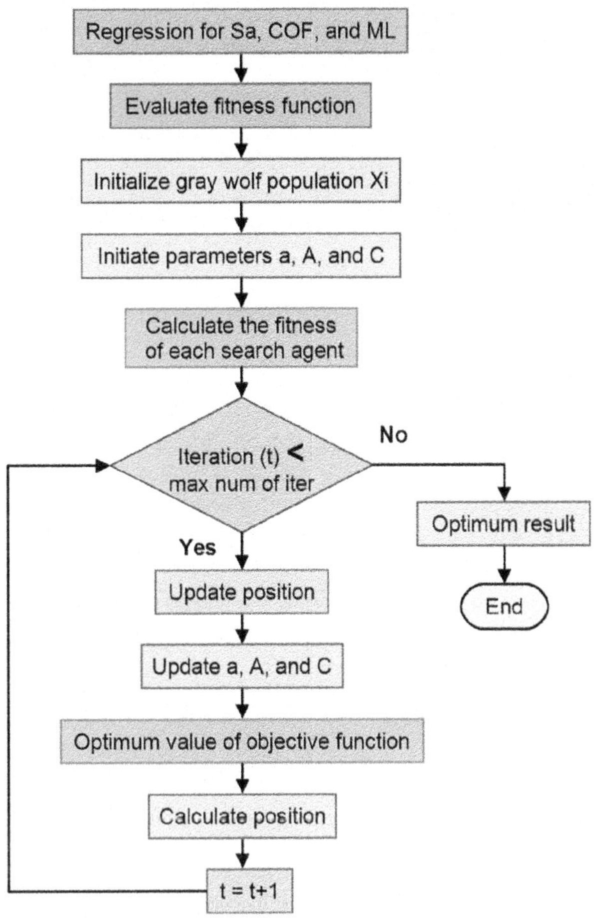

FIGURE 18.7 Flowchart of the grey wolf optimizer (*GWO*) algorithm.

Based on their fitness values, the top three solutions are identified as the alpha (α), beta (β), and delta (δ) wolves, which assume leadership roles. These leaders guide the rest of the pack, denoted as omega (ω) wolves, by influencing their movement through a series of mathematical models inspired by the behaviors of encircling prey, attacking, and social leadership.

The flowchart demonstrates how each iteration involves position updates for the omega wolves based on their relative distance to α, β, and δ. This is achieved through adaptive coefficients that vary over time, allowing the algorithm to explore the global search space in the early stages and to exploit the most promising regions as the iterations progress. The shrinking coefficient "a," which decreases linearly with each iteration, plays a critical role in controlling this transition from exploration to exploitation.

Additionally, the figure outlines how the algorithm continuously evaluates the fitness of the new positions and updates the α, β, and δ wolves if better solutions are found. This dynamic updating ensures that the leadership reflects the most optimal solutions at any point during the run, enhancing convergence toward the global optimum.

By presenting the process in a structured visual format, Fig. 18.7 makes it easier to understand how GWO balances diversification (searching widely) and intensification (refining the best solutions). This makes it especially effective in solving highly nonlinear, multimodal, and high-dimensional problems often encountered in engineering design, parameter optimization, and real-time control systems.

Table 18.7 presents a comparative overview of the original GWO and its various hybridized versions, each developed to enhance specific aspects of the algorithm's performance in complex optimization tasks. GWO itself is based on the social hierarchy and hunting strategies of grey wolves in nature, employing the leadership roles of alpha (α), beta (β), and delta (δ) wolves to guide the search process, while the remaining wolves (ω) follow their lead. This nature-inspired structure enables GWO to strike a robust balance between exploration (global search) and exploitation (local refinement), making it a reliable and efficient optimizer in engineering applications.

TABLE 18.7 Summary of the basic principles and advantages of the Grey Wolf Optimization (*GWO*) algorithm and its hybrid variants.

Algorithm	Hybrid strategy/core idea	Typical strengths in the hybrid	References
GWO	Exploits the leadership hierarchy (α, β, δ, ω) and encircling–attacking behavior of grey wolves to balance exploration/exploitation.	Simple structure, strong global search, good final accuracy.	[33]
GWO +WOA	Sequentially (or adaptively) combines whale optimization algorithm's spiral/bubble-net attacking phase with GWO's pack hierarchy, giving early "whale-style" exploitation after GWO exploration.	Very fast early convergence; useful when run-time is critical.	[34,35]
GWO+PSO	Couples GWO's hierarchical search with particle swarm velocity–position updates; typically injects PSO movements every few iterations or on a subset of wolves.	Good exploration–exploitation balance; rapid mid-stage refinement.	[36]
GWO+SA	Runs a simulated annealing local search on the current α-wolf (or top-k wolves) to fine-tune solutions after each GWO cycle.	Strong late-stage improvement; helps escape shallow local minima.	[37]
GWO+DE	Alternates GWO steps with differential evolution mutation–crossover on part of the pack, preserving diversity while sharpening exploitation.	Maintains population diversity on multimodal landscapes; robust search.	[38]

To further improve its convergence speed, accuracy, and ability to escape local minima, several hybrid variants have been proposed by integrating GWO with other metaheuristic algorithms. These include:

- GWO+WOA: Combines GWO with the whale optimization algorithm (WOA), typically integrating WOA's spiral updating strategy for early-stage exploitation. This hybrid accelerates initial convergence, which is advantageous in time-sensitive applications.
- GWO+PSO: Merges GWO with PSO, allowing particles to benefit from PSO's velocity–position update mechanism while still preserving GWO's leadership-based hierarchy. This hybrid excels at maintaining a good exploration–exploitation balance and enhances convergence in mid-stage iterations.
- GWO+SA: Incorporates SA as a local search method applied to the alpha (or top-k) wolves after each iteration. This addition boosts late-stage refinement and helps escape from shallow local optima, improving final solution quality.
- GWO+DE: Integrates differential evolution (DE) operations such as mutation and crossover into the GWO framework. This approach introduces genetic diversity into the population and is particularly effective for multimodal optimization problems where maintaining diversity is critical.

Each hybrid strategy leverages the strengths of its components to overcome the limitations of standalone GWO. As summarized in the table, while GWO maintains a strong global search capability and simple structure, its hybrids offer specific advantages: rapid early convergence (GWO+WOA), balanced mid-iteration refinement (GWO+PSO), high precision in final solutions (GWO+SA), and robust performance on complex landscapes (GWO+DE). These hybridizations reflect a growing trend in metaheuristic development: combining complementary algorithms to tailor the optimization process to problem-specific demands.

In summary, Table 18.7 not only classifies the hybridization strategies but also highlights the operational synergies achieved through algorithm integration, thereby providing a framework for selecting the most appropriate optimizer based on application requirements such as convergence speed, accuracy, and solution diversity.

Eqs. (18.1), (18.2), and (18.3) are empirical polynomial models formulated to approximate three major tribological responses of weight loss, areal surface roughness (Sa), and COF, respectively. They were obtained by performing a curve-fitting routine on the experiment data obtained from full-factorial LST tests on Ti6Al4V surfaces.

These models define each response parameter as a function of the main laser processing factors—power (x), scan speed (y), and hatch distance (z)—as also including higher-order and interaction terms. This allows for the modeling of intricate, nonlinear relationships among laser factors and surface quality parameters.

Specifically:

- Eq. (18.1) models weight loss (mg) during solid particle erosion tests.
- Eq. (18.2) estimates arithmetic mean roughness (Sa, μm) obtained from noncontact profilometry.
- Eq. (18.3) predicts the steady-state COF measured from reciprocating sliding wear tests.

Each polynomial was built minimizing residual error between predicted and measurement values and provides an accurate and smooth mapping of the parameter space. These formulations are the objective for subsequent optimization with GWO and its hybrid versions, and together with an ANOVA-based global sensitivity study (Section 18.3.2) and cross-model error benchmarking (Figs. 18.9–18.11); they enable systematic and robust adjustment of laser texturing parameters to meet surface-finish and friction targets. To quantify how control-parameter variations influence performance and robustness, we conducted a global ANOVA-based sensitivity analysis (Section 18.3.2) showing that scanning speed dominates COF variability (40.54%), followed by laser power (30.52%) and hatch distance (6.34%), and we corroborated robustness by uniformly low prediction-error envelopes across GWO and its hybrids for weight loss, Sa, and COF (Figs. 18.9–18.11).

$$f_{wl} = \left(\frac{1}{3}\right)(25.489 - 0.19053x + 0.0262x^2 - 0.0003x^3 - 0.00027xy - 4.15\cdot10^{-6}x^2y + 1.7\cdot10^{-7}xy^2 - 0.003y + 7.9\cdot10^{-6}y^2 - 3.3\cdot10^{-9}y^3 + 0.045z + 2.9\cdot10^{-5}z^2 - 1.9\cdot10^{-7}z^3 - 0.0028xz + 6.98\cdot10^{-6}xz^2 + 1.43\cdot10^{-5}x^2z - 2.07\cdot10^{-5}yz - 4.9\cdot10^{-8}yz^2 + 8.7\cdot10^{-9}y^2z) \tag{18.1}$$

$$f_{Sa} = \left(\frac{1}{3}\right)(-37.1 + 3.5x - 0.08x^2 + 0.0008x^3 + 0.0006y + 1.22\cdot10^{-5}y^2 - 6.31\cdot10^{-9}y^3 + 0.39z - 0.0015z^2 + 2.47\cdot10^{-6}z^3 - 0.0012xy + 3.595\cdot10^{-7}x^2y + 4.09\cdot10^{-7}xy^2 - 0.0094xz + 0.0001x^2z + 1.44xz^2 - 9.73\cdot10^{-5}yz - 9.03\cdot10^{-8}yz^2 + 3.77\cdot10^{-8}y^2z) \tag{18.2}$$

$$f_{COF} = \left(\frac{1}{3}\right)(+1.88 + 0.0066x + 0.00021x^2 - 6.5\cdot10^{-6}x^3 - 0.00028y + 3.35\cdot10^{-7}y^2 - 1.6\cdot10^{-10}y^3 - 0.0024z + 1.22\cdot10^{-5}z^2 - 7.9\cdot10^{-9}z^3 - 4.47\cdot10^{-6}xy - 2.08\cdot10^{-7}.\ x^2y + 5.35\cdot10^{-9}xy^2 + 7.76\cdot10^{-7}yz - 6.44\cdot10^{-9}yz^2 + 5\cdot10^{-10}y^2z + 8.66\cdot10^{-6}xz + 1.75\cdot10^{-6}x^2z - 1.49\cdot10^{-7}xz^2) \tag{18.3}$$

This fitness function for optimization is equated to the sum of absolute deviations of the preferred goal values and calculated values of the three response parameters: weight loss (f_{wl}), COF (f_{cof}), and areal surface roughness (f_{sa}). Mathematically, it can be written as:

$$f_{fitness} = |f_{desired\_Wl} - f_{Wl}| + |f_{desired\_Sa} - f_{Sa}| + |f_{desired\_COF} - f_{COF}| \tag{18.4}$$

This fitness formulation (Eq. 18.4) ensures that the optimization algorithm simultaneously minimizes the discrepancies between the model-predicted values and the predefined performance targets for each criterion. By summing the absolute errors, the function treats all three objectives with equal importance and avoids cancellation effects that might arise from signed differences. This scalar fitness value is used by the GWO to evaluate and rank candidate solutions during the iterative search process. The approach enables effective multiobjective optimization within a single-objective framework, offering a robust means of identifying the laser processing parameters that yield the most favorable balance between erosion resistance, surface smoothness, and frictional performance.

18.4.1 Experimental setup

Table 18.8 summarizes the global settings used in the optimization experiments. The core hyperparameters of the experiments are fixed iteration limit (T), number of independent runs (R), population size (N), and problem dimension (D). All metaheuristic algorithms were executed under a fixed iteration limit of T=500 with no early stopping. The convergence curves in Fig. 18.8 depict the mean performance over 1000 independent runs for each method. Random initialization was not controlled via a fixed seed; instead, each run was initialized from a fresh pseudorandom number generator state.

Table 18.9 presents the algorithm-specific control parameters for GWO and its hybrid variants. The selected values of these control parameters are detailed in Table

TABLE 18.8 The global settings used in the optimization experiments.

Setting	Symbol	Value
Iteration limit	T	500
Independent runs per method	R	1000
Population size (wolves)	N	100
Number of problem variables	D	3 (laser power, scan speed, hatch spacing)
Random seed policy	-	Not fixed; fresh random number generator (RNG) state per run
Stopping policy	-	No early stopping (fixed iteration limit)

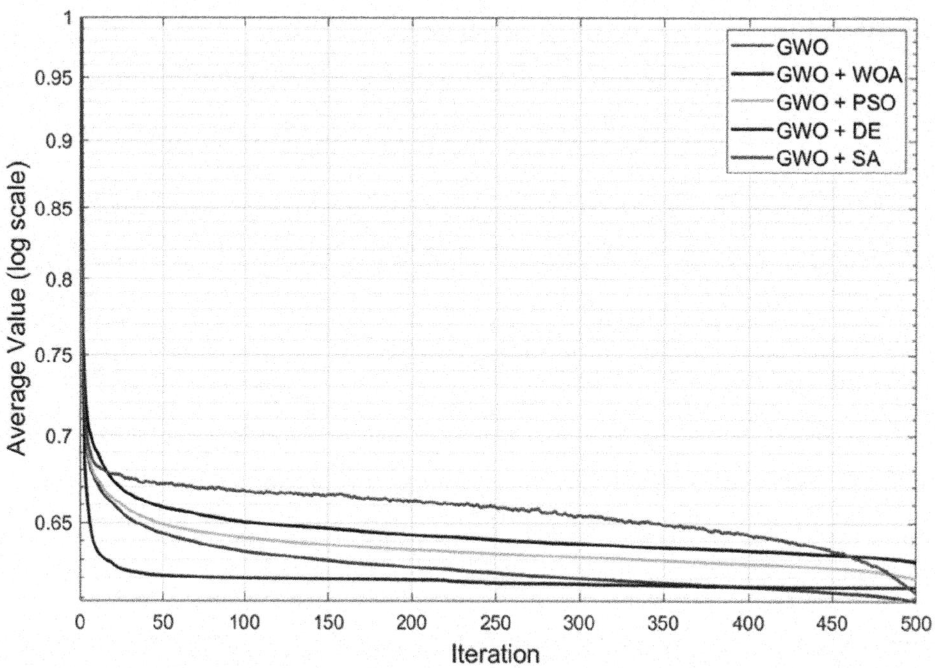

FIGURE 18.8 Average convergence curves on the log-scaled objective over 1000 independent runs for GWO and hybrid variants (*GWO*, Grey wolf optimizer).

Fig. 18.8 contrasts the average convergence behavior of the baseline GWO with four hybrids—GWO+WOA, GWO +PSO, GWO+SA, and GWO+DE. Although all five methods begin at a normalized value of 1.00 and steadily decrease it, they diverge in both speed and final accuracy. Pure GWO attains the lowest mean objective (0.6079 at iteration 500), confirming its superiority in ultimate solution quality, whereas the WOA hybrid converges roughly ten times faster, reaching its steady-state band within 50 iterations but settling at a slightly higher value. The SA hybrid ends only marginally above pure GWO and continues to improve beyond iteration 400, indicating that SA effectively fine-tunes the search and escapes shallow local minima.

By contrast, the PSO and DE hybrids plateau earlier at 0.6196 and 0.6286, respectively; the DE variant maintains population diversity longest, a trait that can be useful on highly multimodal landscapes, but does so at the expense of accuracy. Hence, pure GWO (or GWO+SA) is best when final precision is paramount, GWO+WOA is preferred when

TABLE 18.9 The algorithm-specific control parameters used in the optimization experiments.

Algorithm	Parameter	Symbol	Value
GWO	Exploration–exploitation schedule	a(t)	Linear 2 → 0 over T
GWO+WOA	Spiral constant	b	1.0
	Phase switch probability	p	0.5
GWO+PSO	Inertia weight	w	0.7
	Cognitive coefficient	c1	1.5
	Social coefficient	c2	1.5
GWO+DE	Mutation factor	F	0.8
	Crossover rate	CR	0.9
GWO+SA	Initial temperature	T0	1.0
	Temperature schedule	T(t)	T0– t/MaxIt Linear 1 → 0
	Target individuals	k	1 (only α)
	Min temp guard	-	max(T,1e–8)

wall-time is critical, GWO+PSO offers a balanced exploration–exploitation trade-off, and GWO+DE is advantageous when diversity needs to be preserved. These results underscore that selecting an appropriate GWO+based hybrid should hinge on problem-specific priorities, and they motivate future work on adaptive weight schedules or two-phase protocols that blend WOA's early speed with SA's late-stage refinement.

Table 18.10 provides an extensive comparison of forecasted responses from the GWO and its hybrid versions for three key surface quality measures: weight loss, surface areal roughness (Sa), and COF. For all scenarios of optimization, the respective laser treatment parameters—power (W), scanning speed (mm/s), and hatch distance (μm)—are provided with resulting fitness values and percentage errors for all response factors.

This tabulation enables comparison of both parameter sensitivity and optimization quality for several solution sets. We find the pure GWO and its hybrids (GWO+WOA, GWO+PSO, GWO+DE, and GWO+SA) to achieve multiobjective goals with different levels of precision. Remarkably, certain variants achieve near-zero error on one or two objectives while making minor compromises on others, which is an inherent implication of multicriteria optimality.

Furthermore, from the table, it can also be seen how versatile the algorithm is when it comes up with diverse combinations of laser parameters to achieve diversified levels of target performances, which indicates its suitability for adaptive surface-engineering purposes. Such a comparative database is crucial for determining the most appropriate optimization strategy based on the concerned design priorities—such as minimization of erosion damage, friction reduction, or controlled surface texturing.

Fig. 18.9 benchmarks the predictive fidelity of the stand-alone GWO against four hybrid variants, GWO+WOA, GWO +PSO, GWO+DE, and GWO+SA, over nine representative laser-texturing data codes (1–9), each encapsulating a distinct power–speed–hatch combination. Across the entire design space, pure GWO establishes the reference low-error envelope, keeping the weight-loss misfit below 0.1% for six of the nine codes and never exceeding 3% even in the most nonlinear regime (code 7). The SA variant (GWO+SA) shadows this performance almost point-for-point; its local stochastic reheating step proves especially effective at codes six and nine, where the cost landscape is littered with shallow minima, allowing it to edge out the parent algorithm by 0.2 percentage points. GWO+DE also tracks the baseline closely, its periodic mutation-crossover cycles preserving population diversity without sacrificing accuracy, and only marginally exceeds the GWO+SA envelope when the parameter set shifts abruptly at code 3. By contrast, the velocity-driven GWO +PSO shows a pronounced overshoot at code 9 (4.8%), signaling that the swarm's inertia can overshoot the narrow optimum once the response surface steepens, while the WOA-augmented version, despite its hallmark rapid early

TABLE 18.10 Optimized laser processing parameters and associated prediction errors for weight loss, surface roughness (Sa), and coefficient of friction (*COF*) using GWO and its hybrid variants.

	Desired outputs			Derived laser parameters by GWO				% error		
	Weight loss (mgr)	Sa (micrometer) laser texture surface	COF steady state	Power	Speed	Track	Best cost (mean)	Weight loss	Sa	COF
GWO	9.60	5.35	0.65	28	548	143	0.077	0.055	0.284	0.631
	9.10	6.74	0.67	40	583	120	1.002	5.641	0.001	4.970
	7.90	1.59	0.52	13	2000	300	0.391	1.668	0.000	4.000
	10.40	6.98	0.68	40	593	182	0.137	0.028	0.042	1.647
	12.90	14.48	0.73	40	500	300	1.409	1.572	4.302	0.082
	9.00	6.00	0.50	40	688	112	0.955	4.729	0.000	4.960
	8.00	2.00	0.40	17	2000	300	0.713	3.251	4.850	4.700
	10.00	3.00	0.60	33	1578	268	0.542	2.469	0.010	2.800
	11.00	4.00	0.60	34	1170	278	1.026	3.989	0.072	3.017
GWO +WOA	9.60	5.35	0.65	29	546	123	0.099	0.025	2.468	1.015
	9.10	6.74	0.67	40	583	120	1.005	5.642	0.004	4.955
	7.90	1.59	0.52	13	2000	300	0.391	1.668	0.000	4.000
	10.40	6.98	0.68	40	547	182	0.139	1.455	4.672	1.000
	12.90	14.48	0.73	40	500	300	1.409	1.572	4.302	0.082
	9.00	6.00	0.50	40	688	112	0.956	4.728	0.000	4.960
	8.00	200	0.40	17	2000	300	0.713	3.251	4.850	4.700
	10.00	300	0.60	33	1576	268	0.542	2.470	0.023	2.800
	11.00	400	0.60	34	1170	278	1.023	3.994	0.113	3.000
GWO +PSO	9.60	535	0.65	29	513	76	0.111	0.013	0.183	2.154
	9.10	674	0.67	40	583	120	1.003	5.641	0.003	4.970
	7.90	1.59	0.52	13	2000	300	0.391	1.668	0.000	4.000
	10.40	6.98	0.68	40	594	183	0.150	0.001	0.004	1.662
	12.90	14.48	0.73	40	500	300	1.409	1.572	4.302	0.082
	9.00	6.00	0.50	40	688	112	0.955	4.729	0.000	4.960
	8.00	2.00	0.40	17	2000	300	0.713	3.251	4.850	4.700
	10.00	3.00	0.60	33	1590	267	0.545	2.500	0.383	2.783
	11.00	4.00	0.60	34	1423	291	1.042	4.744	5.185	3.167
GWO +DE	9.60	5.35	0.65	28	545	144	0.078	0.096	0.512	0.615
	9.10	6.74	0.67	40	583	120	1.002	5.640	0.000	4.970
	7.90	1.59	0.52	13	2000	300	0.391	1.668	0.000	4.000
	10.40	6.98	0.68	40	589	182	0.140	0.098	0.150	1.618
	12.90	14.48	0.73	40	500	300	1.409	1.572	4.302	0.082
	9.00	6.00	0.50	40	688	112	0.955	4.729	0.000	4.960

(*Continued*)

TABLE 18.10 (Continued)

	Desired outputs			Derived laser parameters by GWO				% error		
	Weight loss (mgr)	Sa (micrometer) laser texture surface	COF steady state	Power	Speed	Track	Best cost (mean)	Weight loss	Sa	COF
	8.00	2.00	0.40	17	2000	300	0.713	3.251	4.850	4.700
	10.00	3.00	0.60	33	1578	268	0.542	2.469	0.003	2.800
	11.00	4.00	0.60	34	1169	278	1.027	3.991	0.092	3.017
GWO +SA	9.60	5.35	0.65	30	565	125	0.097	0.038	1.069	1.015
	9.10	6.74	0.67	40	583	120	1.003	5.642	0.004	4.970
	7.90	1.59	0.52	13	2000	300	0.391	1.668	0.000	4.000
	10.40	6.98	0.68	40	586	182	0.145	0.178	0.287	1.574
	12.90	14.48	0.73	40	500	300	1.409	1.572	4.302	0.082
	9.00	6.00	0.50	40	688	112	0.954	4.729	0.000	4.960
	8ç00	2.00	0.40	17	2000	300	0.713	3.251	4.850	4.700
	10.00	3.00	0.60	33	1576	268	0.542	2.472	0.050	2.800
	11.00	4.00	0.60	34	1171	278	1.027	4.005	0.240	3.000

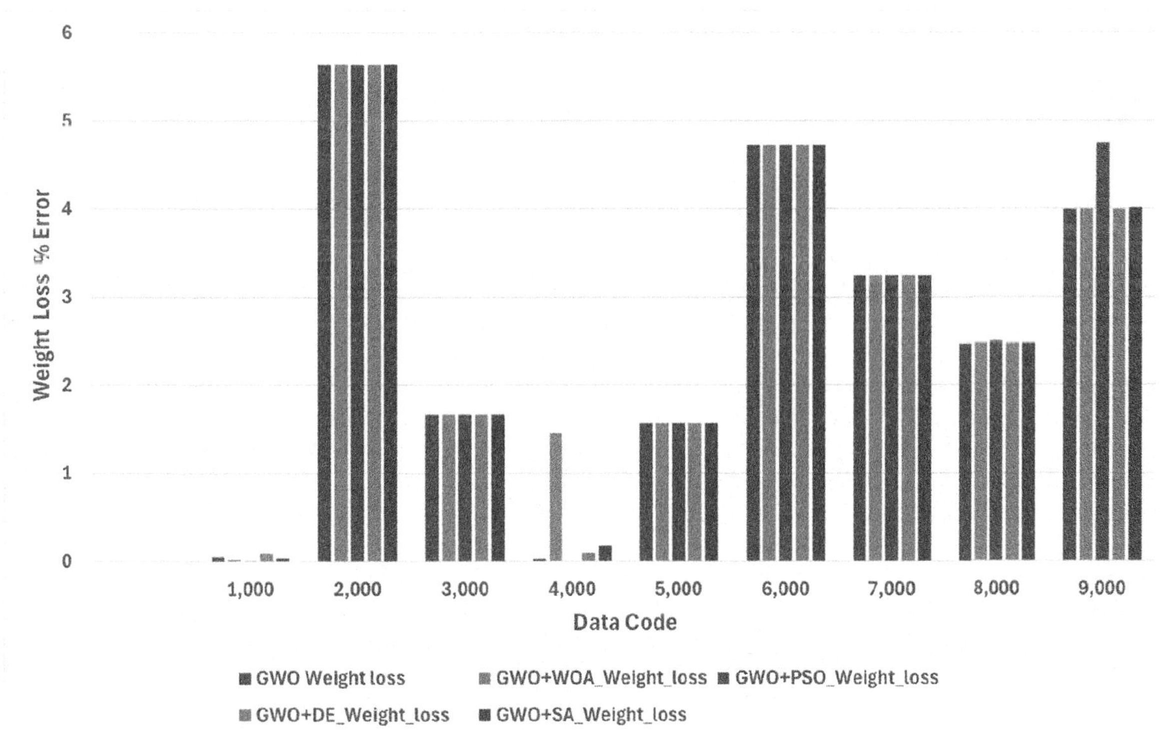

FIGURE 18.9 Comparison of prediction errors (%) for weight loss across models (baseline vs GWO hybrids) on test data codes representing varied laser texturing parameter sets (*GWO*, Grey wolf optimizer).

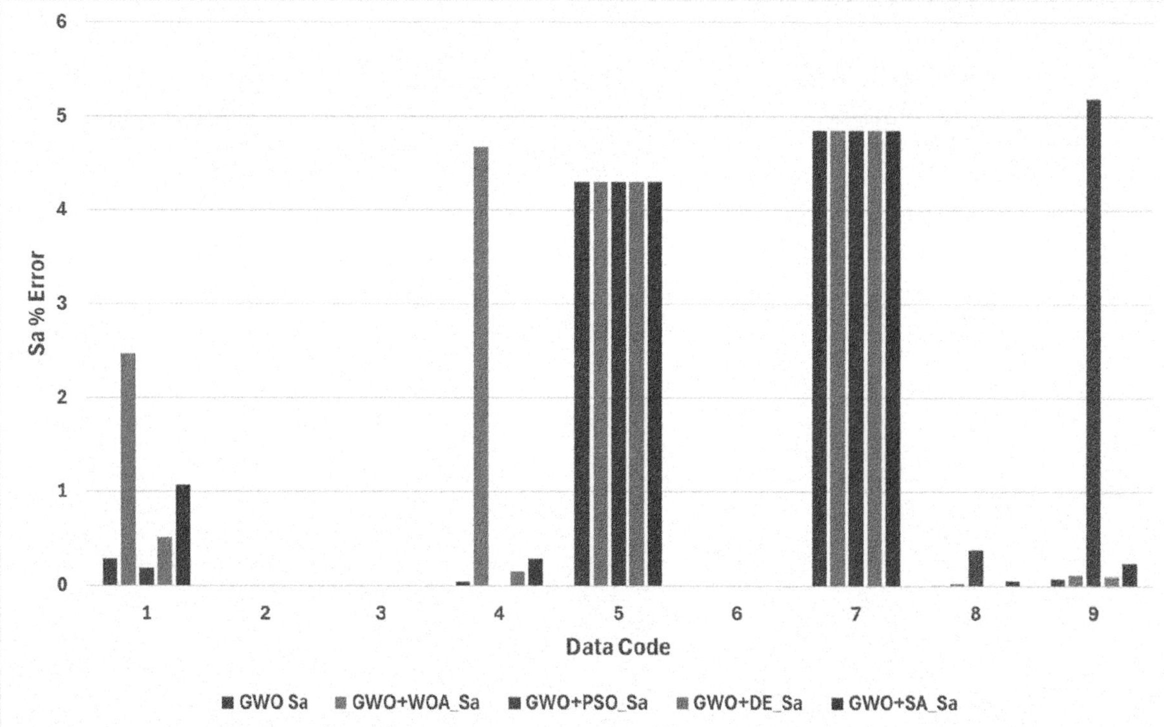

FIGURE 18.10 Comparison of prediction errors (%) for areal roughness (Sa) across models (baseline vs GWO hybrids) on test data codes representing varied laser texturing parameter sets (*GWO*, Grey wolf optimizer).

convergence, exhibits a discrete spike at code 4 (1.4%) attributable to the spiral-update mechanism becoming overexploitative in a region where the objective topography is relatively flat. Collectively, the chart confirms that the native GWO remains the most reliable generalist, but that adding a late-stage annealing sweep (GWO+SA) delivers the highest overall robustness, whereas GWO+WOA offers unmatched speed at the expense of a modest accuracy penalty, and GWO+PSO/DE provides useful trade-offs when mid-iteration agility or diversity preservation is paramount for adaptive laser-parameter refinement.

Fig. 18.10 scrutinizes the percentage-error landscape for arithmetic mean surface roughness (Sa) predictions delivered by the same algorithmic cohort, revealing markedly different stability patterns from the weight-loss case. Baseline GWO, its DE-assisted sibling and the late-stage annealing hybrid (GWO+SA) form a tightly clustered low-error triad, holding the deviation below 0.5% for all codes except the globally challenging regimes 5 and 7, where every optimizer saturates near 4.3% and 4.9%, respectively, implying that those parameter sets generate highly nonlinear textural responses that none of the search heuristics can capture with fine fidelity. The WOA-enriched variant diverges at the opposite end of the spectrum: its aggressive spiral-exploitation drives early convergence but leaves it vulnerable to shallow local minima, producing conspicuous spikes at codes 1 (2.4%) and 4 (4.6%). Conversely, the PSO-coupled model remains well-behaved in low-to-mid codes yet overshoots dramatically at code 9 (5.2%), highlighting the inertia component's tendency to overrun narrow optima once hatch spacing and power escalate the roughness gradient. Taken together, the plot underscores that for Sa prediction, the pure GWO, GWO+DE, and GWO+SA provide the most robust, uniformly accurate solutions, while WOA and PSO hybrids introduce speed or exploration benefits that are counterbalanced by pronounced outliers in specific, topology-sensitive regions of the laser-texturing design space.

Fig. 18.11 interrogates the COF prediction error map and reinforces the hierarchical stability already hinted at by the weight-loss and roughness metrics, yet it also exposes two data-code clusters, 2/6 and 3/7, where every optimizer confronts a common modeling ceiling. Across the smoother regions (codes 1, 4, 5, and 8–9), the canonical GWO, its DE infusion (GWO+DE), and the simulated-annealing sweep (GWO+SA) again constitute the most reliable trio, keeping the error below 1% at code 1 and compressing it to 0.1% in the quasilinear domain of code 5. The DE mutation-crossover cycles help the population sidestep premature aggregation, giving GWO+DE a slight edge over the parent at the low-

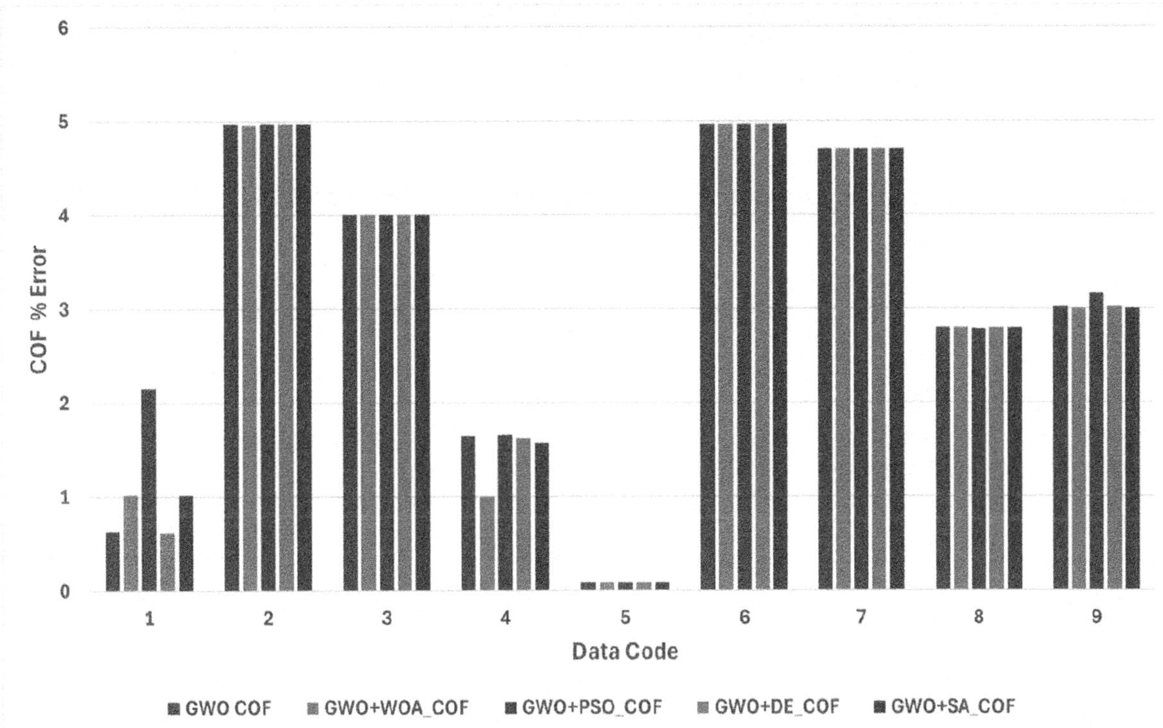

FIGURE 18.11 Comparison of prediction errors (%) for coefficient-of-friction (*COF*) across models (baseline vs GWO hybrids) on test data codes representing varied laser texturing parameter sets (*GWO*, Grey wolf optimizer).

TABLE 18.11 Summary of computational (time) and memory complexity for GWO and its hybrid variants.

Algorithm	Computational complexity (total)	Memory complexity
GWO	O(T·N·D)	O(N·D)
GWO + WOA	O(T·N·D)	O(N·D)
GWO + PSO	O(T·N·D)	≈ O(2–3·N·D)
GWO + DE	O(T·N·D)	≈ O(2·N·D)
GWO + SA	O(T·N·D + T·D)	O(N·D + D)

power/high-scan-speed setting of code 1, whereas the late-stage reheating in GWO+SA proves advantageous when the search space flattens (code 5), effectively eliminating residual drift. The spiral-exploitation logic of GWO+WOA, though beneficial for early convergence, becomes overassertive in intermediate parameter sets, inflating the error to 1% at code 1 and 1% at code 4, but paradoxically suppresses misfit more efficiently than the baseline when the hatch spacing widens (code 4).

By contrast, the inertia-weighted GWO+PSO variant shows the largest dispersion; its swarm momentum overshoots the narrow optimum under mild texturing conditions (code 1, 2.1%) and again under the most aggressive regime (code 9, 3.2%), illustrating that velocity-driven updates struggle to decelerate in rugged COF landscapes shaped by tribo-oxidative layer formation.

Notably, the ensemble spikes to 5% error at codes 2 and 6 and to 4% at codes 3 and 7, indicating intrinsic nonlinearities in the frictional response when the laser fluence traverses the melt-re-solidification threshold; the fact that all heuristics saturate at nearly identical values here signals a data-regime-specific information deficit rather than algorithmic inadequacy. Overall, the chart confirms that GWO, GWO+DE, and GWO+SA deliver the most uniformly precise COF forecasts, with WOA and PSO hybrids offering speed and exploration benefits that are tempered by accuracy penalties in low-gradient or highly corrugated sectors of the laser-texturing design space.

18.4.2 Computational (time) and memory complexity of the grey wolf optimizer and its hybrids

In this section, the computational and memory complexity of the GWO and hybrids are analyzed and presented. Table 18.11 shows the computational and memory complexity of the algorithms. A Big-O analysis in terms of the maximum number of iterations (T), the population size (N), and the number of problem variables (D) is presented.

All algorithms considered have overall time complexity O(T·N·D) and memory complexity O(N·D). In memory terms, GWO and GWO+WOA require O(N·D) (lowest); GWO+DE is 2×O(N·D) due to trial vectors; GWO+PSO is 2–3×O(N·D) because positions, velocities, and personal bests are stored; GWO+SA remains O(P·D) with minor additional temporary buffers for the local refinement step. Per-iteration runtime is smallest for GWO and remains close for GWO+WOA; GWO +PSO and GWO+DE add moderate constant-factor overheads; GWO+SA can incur the largest overhead when the refinement step is applied frequently. In practice, under tight memory or wall-time constraints, GWO/GWO+WOA are preferable; use SA for fine local refinement, and DE/PSO when greater search diversity is needed. If fitness evaluations are expensive, overall time is dominated by evaluation count, so prefer the method that reaches targets in fewer evaluations.

18.5 Conclusion

The present chapter has demonstrated that LST of Ti6Al4V with a 100 W fiber laser offers a highly tunable route to reconcile roughness, friction, and erosion resistance by judicious control of linear energy density and hatch overlap. Factorial experiments revealed that low-power, high-speed scans combined with tight hatches (<75 μm) promote re-melting and planarisation, producing near-smooth surfaces (Sa=1.07 μm) that resisted solid-particle erosion with the lowest recorded mass loss of 8.7 mg and limited wear-track penetration depths to around 12.5 μm. In contrast, high-power, slow-scan conditions acting over wide hatches (≥300 μm) drove Sa beyond 14 μm and almost doubled mass loss, underscoring that excess energy density and sparse overlap magnify capillary recoil, ridge formation, and local stress concentrations during subsequent tribological loading. Overall, the data establish a clear mechanistic link: smoother, moderately textured morphologies generated under low thermal input suppress abrasive–adhesive synergy and provide superior tribological durability, whereas coarse grooves generated under high input exacerbate contact stresses and accelerate material removal.

To translate these empirical trends into process guidelines, a suite of metaheuristic optimizers based on the grey wolf algorithm was deployed to fit polynomial response surfaces for weight loss, Sa, and steady-state COF, and to search the multidimensional parameter space. Pure GWO and its simulated-annealing hybrid (GWO+SA) converged to the most accurate global optima, predicting experimental responses with sub-1% error while preserving population diversity, whereas the whale-enhanced variant offered an order-of-magnitude faster convergence at the expense of modest accuracy. The optimization framework identified multiple Pareto-equivalent laser recipes—for example, 28 W, 548 mm s^{-1}, 143 μm hatch for targeted Sa=5 μm and COF=0.65—illustrating the flexibility to tailor texture depth, friction, and erosion resistance to application-specific thresholds without exhaustive physical prototyping.

Collectively, these findings advance surface-engineering practice for titanium alloys by (1) mapping the coupled influence of power, speed, and hatch on three independent degradation metrics, (2) validating metaheuristic optimization as a rapid, data-efficient surrogate for expensive full-factorial trials, and (3) delivering experimentally verified processing windows that balance biotribological demands with manufacturing throughput. Future work should extend the parametric domain to ultrashort-pulse regimes and reactive gas shielding, integrate in-situ thermal imaging to close the control loop, and carry out long-term aqueous and fretting fatigue tests to confirm the stability of the optimized textures under physiological and aeronautical service conditions.

Artificial intelligence support statement

During the preparation of this article, an artificial intelligence-based language tool was used solely for grammar and spelling checks. All academic processes, including content creation, data analysis, scientific interpretation, and drawing conclusions, were carried out by the authors.

References

[1] G. Menci, A.G. Demir, D.G. Waugh, J. Lawrence, B. Previtali, Laser surface texturing of β-Ti alloy for orthopaedics: effect of different wavelengths and pulse durations, Applied Surface Science 489 (2019) 175–186. Available from https://doi.org/10.1016/j.apsusc.2019.05.111.

[2] A. Arun, P. Lakshmanan, K. Parthiban, G. Kumanan, L. Arunkumar, Experimental study on laser surface texturing and wear characterization of titanium alloy, Materials Today: Proceedings 62 (Part 2) (2022) 615–618. Available from https://doi.org/10.1016/j.matpr.2022.03.621.

[3] W. Pfleging, R. Kumari, H. Besser, T. Scharnweber, J.D. Majumdar, Laser surface textured titanium alloy (Ti–6Al–4V): part 1 – surface characterization, Applied Surface Science 355 (2015) 104–111. Available from https://doi.org/10.1016/j.apsusc.2015.06.175.

[4] R. Kumari, T. Scharnweber, W. Pfleging, H. Besser, J.D. Majumdar, Laser surface textured titanium alloy (Ti–6Al–4V) – part II – studies on biocompatibility, Applied Surface Science 357 (Part A) (2015) 750–758. Available from https://doi.org/10.1016/j.apsusc.2015.08.255.

[5] T. Hu, L. Hu, Q. Ding, The effect of laser surface texturing on the tribological behavior of Ti-6Al-4V, Proceedings of the Institution of Mechanical Engineers, Part J: Journal of Engineering Tribology 226 (10) (2012) 854–863. Available from https://doi.org/10.1177/1350650112450801.

[6] Q. Liu, Y. Liu, X. Li, G. Dong, Pulse laser-induced cell-like texture on surface of titanium alloy for tribological properties improvement, Wear 477 (2021) 203784. Available from https://doi.org/10.1016/j.wear.2021.203784.

[7] A. Woźniak, O. Bialas, M. Adamiak, et al., The influence of laser texturing on the tribological behavior of titanium alloy Ti6Al4V in medical applications, Archives of Civil and Mechanical Engineering 24 (2024) 146. Available from https://doi.org/10.1007/s43452-024-00960-3.

[8] S. Yuan, N. Lin, W. Wang, H. Zhang, Z. Liu, Y. Yu, et al., Correlation between surface textural parameter and tribological behaviour of four metal materials with laser surface texturing (LST), Applied Surface Science 583 (2022) 152410. Available from https://doi.org/10.1016/j.apsusc.2021.152410.

[9] Q. Chen, J. Zhang, A. Huang, P. Wei, Study on wear resistance of Ti-6Al-4V alloy composite coating prepared by laser alloying, Applied Sciences 11 (2021) 446. Available from https://doi.org/10.3390/app11010446.

[10] Z. Cao, L. Cui, S. Luo, H. Su, Z. Pang, W. Zhao, et al., Superior fretting wear resistance of titanium alloys from stable gradient nanostructures induced by laser shock peening, International Journal of Plasticity 188 (2025) 104293. Available from https://doi.org/10.1016/j.ijplas.2025.104293.

[11] Z. Wang, J. Song, T. Wang, H. Wang, Q. Wang, Laser texturing for superwetting titanium alloy and investigation of its erosion resistance, Coatings 11 (2021) 1547. Available from https://doi.org/10.3390/coatings11121547.

[12] B. Das, S.K. Srivastava, I. Manna, J.D. Majumdar, Mechanically tailored surface of titanium based alloy (Ti6Al4V) by laser surface treatment, Surface and Coatings Technology 479 (2024) 130560. Available from https://doi.org/10.1016/j.surfcoat.2024.130560.

[13] S. Wang, X. Fu, J. Lv, C. Zhu, G. Zhang, Y. Meng, Tailoring tribological properties in Titanium alloy via pulse Laser-induced textures: a review, Proceedings of the Institution of Mechanical Engineers, Part J: Journal of Engineering Tribology (2025). Available from https://doi.org/10.1177/13506501251334699 0(0).

[14] M.P. Ananth, R. Ramesh, Reciprocating sliding wear performance of hard coating on modified titanium alloy surfaces, Tribology Transactions 58 (1) (2014) 169–176. Available from https://doi.org/10.1080/10402004.2014.943338.

[15] J. Salguero, I. Del Sol, J.M. Vazquez-Martinez, M.J. Schertzer, P. Iglesias, Effect of laser parameters on the tribological behavior of Ti6Al4V titanium microtextures under lubricated conditions, Wear 426–427 (Part B) (2019) 1272–1279. Available from https://doi.org/10.1016/j.wear.2018.12.029.

[16] D. Kümmel, D. Linsler, R. Schneider, J. Schneider, Surface engineering of a titanium alloy for tribological applications by nanosecond-pulsed laser, Tribology International 150 (2020) 106376. Available from https://doi.org/10.1016/j.triboint.2020.106376.

[17] K. Guan, J. Yu, F. Wang, X. Ji, Combining laser texturing and remelting for reducing friction and corrosive wear in Ti-based amorphous alloys, Precision Engineering 93 (2025) 417–424. Available from https://doi.org/10.1016/j.precisioneng.2025.02.001.

[18] C. Florian, R. Wonneberger, A. Undisz, et al., Chemical effects during the formation of various types of femtosecond laser-generated surface structures on titanium alloy, Applied Physics A 126 (2020) 266. Available from https://doi.org/10.1007/s00339-020-3434-7.

[19] E. Redmore, X. Li, H. Dong, Tribological performance of surface engineered low-cost beta titanium alloy, Wear 426–427 (Part B) (2019) 952–960. Available from https://doi.org/10.1016/j.wear.2019.01.032.

[20] J. Konieczny, K. Labisz, S. Ürgün, H. Yiğit, S. Fidan, M.Ö. Bora, et al., Modelling of hardness and electrical conductivity of Cu-4Ti (wt.%) alloy and estimation of aging parameters using metaheuristic algorithms, Materials 18 (2025) 2366. Available from https://doi.org/10.3390/ma18102366.

[21] S. Ürgün, H. Yiğit, S. Fidan, T. Sınmazçelik, T. Canel, Optimization of laser-texturing process parameters of Ti6Al4V alloys using metaheuristic algorithms, Proceedings of the Institution of Mechanical Engineers, Part E: Journal of Process Mechanical Engineering (2024). Available from https://doi.org/10.1177/09544089241241290 0(0).

[22] P. V, V.S. Jatti, S. A, P.K. D, M.K. R, V.S. Jatti, et al., Optimizing laser powder bed fusion parameters for enhanced hardness of Ti6Al4V alloys: a comparative analysis of metaheuristic algorithms for process parameter optimization, AIP Advances 15 (2025) 45024. Available from https://doi.org/10.1063/5.0262978.

[23] S. Biswas, A.R. Paul, Y. Singh, et al., Enhanced prediction and optimization of WEDM for titanium alloy (grade 5) with hybrid artificial neural network based meta-heuristics, International Journal of Interactive Design and Manufacturing 19 (2025) 4327–4347. Available from https://doi.org/10.1007/s12008-024-02058-9.

[24] V.V.K. Lakshmi, K.V. Subbaiah, K.A. Vikram, et al., Eco-friendly machining of Ti-6Al-4V alloy: optimization using a hybrid algorithm (grey wolf algorithm and VIKOR algorithm), Journal of the Institution of Engineers (India): Series C 103 (2022) 1111–1124. Available from https://doi.org/10.1007/s40032-022-00871-3.

[25] V.H. Nguyen, T.T. Le, M.V. Le, H. Dao Minh, A.T. Nguyen, Multi-objective optimization based on machine learning and non-dominated sorting genetic algorithm for surface roughness and tool wear in Ti6Al4V turning, Machining Science and Technology 27 (4) (2023) 380–421. Available from https://doi.org/10.1080/10910344.2023.2235610.

[26] E. Avcu, S. Fidan, M.Ö. Bora, O. Çoban, I. Taşkıran, T. Sınmazçelik, Solid particle erosive wear behavior of glass mat reinforced PPS composites: influence of erodent particle size, pressure, particle impingement angle, and velocity, Advanced Polymer Technology 32 (2013) E386–E398. Available from https://doi.org/10.1002/adv.21286.

[27] J.A. Sandoval-Robles, C.A. Rodríguez, E. García-López, Laser surface texturing and electropolishing of CoCr and Ti6Al4V-ELI alloys for biomedical applications, Materials 13 (22) (2020) 5203. Available from https://doi.org/10.3390/ma13225203.

[28] N. Ndou, Effect of laser power on wear resistance of laser deposited Ti6Al4V+W composites. in: Proceedings of the World Congress on Engineering and Computer Science (WCECS 2019), vol. II, 2019, pp. 446–450.

[29] A. Bharatish, G.R. Rajkumar, P. Gurav, G. Satheesh Babu, H.N. Narasimha Murthy, M. Roy, Optimization of laser texture geometry and resulting functionality of nickel aluminium bronze for landing gear applications, International Journal of Lightweight Materials and Manufacture 4 (3) (2021) 346–357. Available from https://doi.org/10.1016/j.ijlmm.2021.04.004.

[30] A. Volpe, C. Gaudiuso, L. Di Venere, F. Licciulli, F. Giordano, A. Ancona, Direct femtosecond laser fabrication of superhydrophobic aluminum alloy surfaces with anti-icing properties, Coatings 10 (2020) 587. Available from https://doi.org/10.3390/coatings10060587.

[31] P.D. Babu, S. Vignesh, M. Vignesh, C. Balamurugan, Enhancement of wear resistance of Ti–6Al–4V alloy by picosecond laser surface micro-texturing process, Journal of Central South University 25 (8) (2018) 1836–1848. Available from https://doi.org/10.1007/s11771-018-3873-x.

[32] M. Conradi, A. Kocijan, D. Klobčar, B. Podgornik, Tribological response of laser-textured Ti6Al4V alloy under dry conditions and lubricated with Hank's solution, Tribology International 160 (2021) 107049. Available from https://doi.org/10.1016/j.triboint.2021.107049.

[33] S. Mirjalili, S.M. Mirjalili, A. Lewis, Grey wolf optimizer, Advances in Engineering Software 69 (2014) 46–61. Available from https://doi.org/10.1016/j.advengsoft.2013.12.007.

[34] H.M. Mohammed, T.A. Rashid, A novel hybrid GWO with WOA for global numerical optimization and solving pressure vessel design, Neural Computing and Applications 32 (2020) 14701–14718. Available from https://doi.org/10.1007/s00521-020-04823-9.

[35] J. Ababneh, A hybrid approach based on grey wolf and whale optimization algorithms for solving cloud task scheduling problem, Mathematical Problems in Engineering (2021) 3517145. Available from https://doi.org/10.1155/2021/3517145.

[36] X. Zhang, Q. Lin, W. Mao, S. Liu, Z. Dou, G. Liu, Hybrid particle swarm and grey wolf optimizer and its application to clustering optimization, Applied Soft Computing 101 (2021). Available from https://doi.org/10.1016/j.asoc.2020.107061art. 107061.

[37] V.K. Kamboj, GWO-SA: a novel hybrid grey wolf optimizer–simulated annealing algorithm for multidisciplinary design optimization problems, International Journal of Recent Technology and Engineering 8 (4) (2019) 1289–1299. Available from https://doi.org/10.35940/ijrte.C6735.118419.

[38] X. Yu, N. Jiang, X. Wang, M. Li, A hybrid algorithm based on grey wolf optimizer and differential evolution for UAV path planning, Expert Systems with Applications 215 (2022). Available from https://doi.org/10.1016/j.eswa.2022.119327art. 119327.

Chapter 19

Budget constrained fairness aware incentive recommendation with uplift modeling using grey wolf optimization

Sunday O. Oladejo[1], Stephen O. Ekwe[2], Lateef A. Akinyemi[3], and Denise J. Birabwa[4]

[1]*Standard Bank for Lab. for Recommender Systems, School for Data Science and Computational Thinking, Stellenbosch University, Stellenbosch, South Africa,* [2]*Department of Electrical Engineering, University of Cape Town, Cape Town, South Africa,* [3]*Department of Electronic and Computer Engineering, Faculty of Engineering, Lagos State University, Epe Campus, Nigeria,* [4]*Department of Electrical and Electronics Engineering, Kyambogo University, Kampala, Uganda*

19.1 Introduction

Recommender systems (RS) are an intelligent platform designed to help users in decision-making and the discovery of items or products that might be of interest, and this is possible by analyzing users' past behavior, preferences, and contextual data. RS or, in general, personalized online platforms such as Uber [1], Booking [2], and Netflix [3] have benefited from discount bonuses and cash bonuses as a competitive strategy to increase revenue, user engagement, customer satisfaction, and retention [4,5]. Although this strategy has proven to be beneficial, a limited budget is allocated for these promotional discounts or bonuses to ensure that there is no net loss of revenue.

Owing to the budget constraints, not all subscribers will qualify for such promotions, discounts, or bonuses, and hence, the initiation of a resource allocation problem widely known as the budget allocation problem. The budget allocation problem in RS and the personalized online platforms has been addressed by causal inference [2], in which the positive or negative impact of the promotion is estimated a priori before optimal budget allocation. One major way to estimate the impact of promotions before allocating resources using causal estimates is uplift modeling [6,7].

Uplift modeling is a machine learning approach aimed at estimating the causal impact of a marketing promotion by predicting the difference in outcomes between taking or not taking an action, that is, the allocating a discount or bonus or not. Uplift modeling involves predicting the expected difference between treatment and control response, and thus individuals who positively respond to an intervention are identified in the population [8,9]. To this end, the uplift modeling concept is applicable to RS and other online platforms, such as identifying potential subscribers who will positively react to marketing promotions. Consequently, this drives data-driven decision-making in incentive allocation, thereby increasing cost efficiency and effectiveness.

Uplift modeling efficiently makes it possible to target subscribers or users who would positively respond (i.e., the causal impact) to promotions within the confines of a constrained budget allocated for promotional incentives. In this chapter, budget-constrained incentive assignment is formalized by using a causal inference estimate through the use of uplift modeling. Furthermore, a fairness metric is taken into account to ensure that some subscribers are not shortchanged in the bid to maximize the net revenue of the RS platform.

In this chapter, our contributions are as follows. The budget-constrained incentive recommendation problem is formulated as a multiple-choice knapsack problem (MCKP). Budget and uplift fairness are taken into consideration as optimization constraints in the formulated MCKP to ensure that subscribers are fairly treated. Here, we explore the abilities of grey wolf optimizer (GWO) and its variants in solving the budget-constrained incentive recommendation with uplift modeling problem. Last, through extensive Monte Carlo simulations, we carry out a performance evaluation and comparison of the GWO and its variants under different causal inference estimation techniques.

Grey Wolf Optimizer. DOI: https://doi.org/10.1016/B978-0-443-36624-6.00027-5

The outline of this chapter is as follows. Section 19.2 briefly discusses related work, and in Section 19.3, we present the uplift modeling preliminaries and problem formulation. In Section 19.4, the proposed solutions are discussed. Section 19.5 presents the results of the extensive performance evaluation, and last, in Section 19.6, we draw the conclusions of this chapter.

19.2 Related work

In this section, we discuss related work in RS, uplift modeling, budget allocation, and metaheuristics.

19.2.1 Recommender systems

The importance of setting the right price on the growing e-commerce marketplaces is a strategy to induce competition, as stated in Ref. [10]. An incentive-aware recommender system was modeled as a multiagent bandit problem in which a recommender system serves as an intermediary between the agents and the arm in a two-sided market in Ref. [11]. The authors modeled the products or items as "arms," while the users or subscribers as "agents." Similar to Ref. [11], the authors in Ref. [12] addressed competing matching under the complementary preference recommendation problem by proposing a multiagent multitype Thompson sampling algorithm.

The work in Ref. [13] emphasizes the need to rethink incentives in recommender systems due to monotone reward systems and the beneficial impact of designing a competitive reward mechanism. Moreover, in the work in [14], instant discounts on fare prices were used to increase the gross transaction value or the total transaction volume on the e-hail platforms. The authors in Ref. [14] formulated the discount problem as a nonlinear optimization problem with a budget-aware constraint included. Furthermore, a nested logit model is employed to predict that a user would complete a trip rather than using causal inference.

The e-commerce platforms in Ref. [5] propose a two-stage multiproduct marketing resource allocation with the primary goal of maximizing order volume and net revenue. Similarly to Ref. [14], the predictive model estimates the probabilities of a user purchasing in the first stage, and then the second stage is the resource allocation optimization problem, which is subsequently reformulated as a minimum-cost flow problem.

In Ref. [15], a bidding mechanism for multiitem-based RS was designed primarily to maximize the expected revenue with bidding done privately. The results in Ref. [15] show that a well-designed mechanism could provide a framework to increase net revenue.

In designing incentive-based RS, fairness consideration is quite imperative as presented in Ref. [15]. Similar to the imperative for fairness in Ref. [15], the work in this chapter takes into account fairness in the design of the incentive mechanism in RS. Furthermore, the authors in Refs. [16,17] gave a detailed explanation of the implications of fairness in recommendation systems.

19.2.2 Uplift modeling

Uplift modeling in RS and generally on personalized online platforms is broadly categorized into two: (1) conversion uplift and (2) revenue uplift modeling [18,19]. Similarly, the work in Ref. [20] categorizes uplift transformation in the context of the response transformation into conversion modeling (i.e., primarily for conversion likelihood) and revenue modeling (i.e., for increasing sales volume).

In conversion uplift modeling, the incremental impact of a treatment is estimated in events such as sign-ups, clicks, and purchases (i.e., otherwise referred to as conversion events), and then this is compared to the impact when the treatment is not applied [21,22]. This difference is the uplift [22]. In the context of conversion uplift modeling, the uplift is given as Uplift = $P(Conversion|Treated) - P(Conversion|Control)$.

Revenue uplift modeling estimates the incremental revenue impact of allocating specific marketing promotions, discounts, or bonuses to an individual customer, compared to not offering promotions or discounts [23]. This goes beyond predicting whether or not a customer or user will respond, but is much more focused on the additional revenue the treatment will generate as a result [23]. This work focuses on the revenue uplift model. In particular, unlike the conversion uplift model, in which the response label is a 0/1 binary, the revenue uplift model's response label is continuous [18].

Understanding causal impact is central to uplift modeling. The average treatment effect (ATE) and the conditional average treatment effect (CATE) are two basic concepts in causal impact [24,25]. ATE is the expected difference in outcomes between the treatment group (i.e., received a treatment) and the control group (i.e., did not receive the treatment) across the entire population. CATE is a more refined ATE, in which it measures the expected impact of a treatment for individuals within a specific subgroup, therefore providing a personalized estimate of treatment effectiveness based on their unique characteristics. According to the comprehensive survey carried out in Ref. [26], there are primarily two broad categories of CATE estimation techniques: (1) methods extending existing supervised machine learning models and (2) factored methods for treatment effect heterogeneity modeling.

Methods extending existing supervised machine learning models include the single-model approach, which is simple but prone to bias due to shared modeling of potential outcomes. In the single-model approach (otherwise known as S-Learner [27]), a single model is trained on both treatment and control data, with the treatment included as a feature [26]. The interaction between features and treatment is explicitly modeled to capture the differential effect. The two-model approach (i.e., the T-learner) [27] trains separate models for treated and control groups; unlike the single-model, it lacks information sharing. The uplift for each user in the two-model approach is computed by taking the difference in predicted probabilities of each group (i.e., the treatment and control). Furthermore, in the transformed outcome methods, the use of standard regression tools is employed to redefine the outcome variables and it is such that they heavily rely on the accurate estimation of propensity scores. More advanced frameworks, such as the X-Learner and R-Learner, improve estimation by incorporating cross-group inference and loss-based optimization with propensity scores.

19.2.3 Budget constrained allocation

In order to ensure that the business entity does not incur losses during promotional activities, the mechanisms for the allocation of discounts and bonuses are designed within the context of the limited marketing budget [2,26]. Discounts, bonuses, or market promotions are generally designed as a two-stage mechanism [28,29]. The first stage is the causal uplift estimate of the impact of the treatment of marketing promotions, as seen in Refs. [4,30]. The first stage involves the use of machine learning methods such as random forest, logistic regression, and causal forests. In the second stage, marketing discounts and bonuses are distributed to selected users. This stage is often modeled as a budget-constrained resource allocation optimization problem to optimally select customers [2,4]. The optimization problem is formulated as the MCKP [31,32]. The MCKP is an NP-Hard problem and a form of the generalized knapsack problem with a partitioned set of items grouped into classes [33,34]. MCKP has been addressed in the literature through mixed-integer linear programming (MILP) and metaheuristics. This chapter focuses on the use of metaheuristics, GWO [35].

19.2.4 Metaheuristics

Metaheuristics are a stochastic optimization technique that relies on the randomization of modeling operators that influence the behavioral characteristics of agents. Due to the stochasticity of metaheuristics, they have shown their ability to escape local optima entrapment, flexibility and robustness, simplicity and mathematical derivative-free solutions [35,36].

To this end, metaheuristics have found use in several domains and applications. In Ref. [37], the whale optimization algorithm (WOA) and its variants, such as a Levy flight trajectory-based WOA and an elite opposition-based Golden-Sine WOA, were used to tune the hyperparameter of the support vector machine in an empirical study through the use of seven benchmark datasets, such as the Breast Cancer Wisconsin dataset, Iris dataset, and the Modified National Institute of Standards and Technology (MNIST) dataset. Similar to the work in Ref. [37], the empirical analysis in Ref. [38] demonstrated that metaheuristics other than WOA can be employed in hyperparameter optimization in machine learning. In Ref. [39], a genetic algorithm-based resource allocation scheme was developed for a socially aware joint uplink and downlink mobile network scenario. The genetic-based scheme is used for network capacity maximization and the performance is compared with other metaheuristics such as particle swarm optimization (PSO), artificial bee colony, and the GWO. Metaheuristics have found several applications in bioinformatics and the widely known protein structure prediction problem as studied in Refs. [36,40]. In the work in Ref. [40], the performance of 15 metaheuristics, such as PSO and ant-colony optimization, is examined in predicting the structure of nine benchmark proteins: 1CB3, 1XBL, 2ZNF, 1DSQ, 2H3S, 1ARE, 2KGU, 1TZ4, and 1CRN.

In this chapter, GWO [35] and its variants, such as improved GWO [41], memory, evolutionary, operator, and local-search GWO [42], GWO integrated together with Levy flight (LGWO) [43], are employed to solve the MCKP. In GWO [35], the optimizer introduced by Seyedali Mirjalili is designed by mimicking the hunting practices of grey wolves. GWO is modeled to follow the social hierarchy of grey wolves: alpha α, beta β, delta δ, and omega ω as illustrated in Fig. 19.1. These four types of wolves engage in hunting behaviors such as searching, encircling, and attacking prey. The social hierarchy in GWO stipulates that the alpha wolves denote the fittest solution, the beta and delta wolves represent the second and third best solutions. The omega denotes the other candidate solutions in addition to the three leading solutions. This social hierarchy is simulated together with the hunting behaviors of grey wolves to ensure the balance between exploration and exploitation in the search for optimal decision variables and solutions [45]. GWO agents (i.e., wolves)

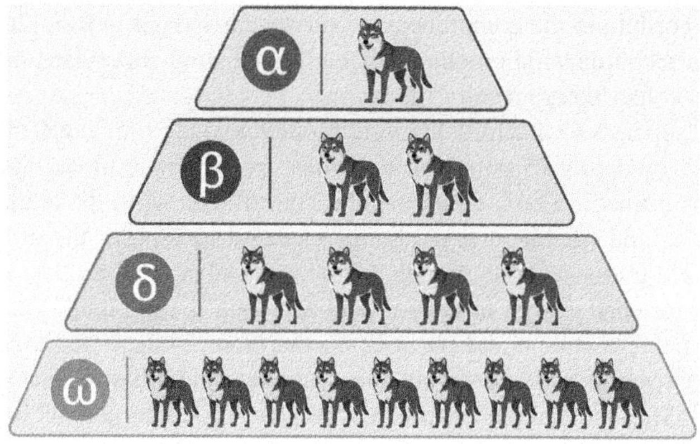

FIGURE 19.1 An illustration of the social hierarchy of grey wolves showing the alpha α, beta β, delta δ, and omega ω wolves [44].

update their position via a weighted average of the positions of alpha, beta, and delta, consequently, encouraging exploration. The beta and delta wolves encourage exploration by pulling other wolves (i.e, agents) away from the direction of the alpha to engage other promising search spaces [35,46]. However, as the iteration progresses, the influence of beta and delta in pulling other wolves away from alpha decreases, resulting in exploitation [35]. Therefore this triple-guidance strategy of GWO greatly contributes to the ability to find optimal or near-optimal solutions.

Owing to the large and increasing interests garnered by GWO in the industry and academia, several variants, modified, and hybridized GWO have been developed intthe literature [44,47]. One of these the improved grey wolf optimizer (IGWO) [41]. The main goal of IGWO [41] is to balance the diversity between exploration and exploitation. This GWO modification explores a unique movement strategy for hunting that relies on dimension learning-based hunting (DLH) strategy. Unlike in GWO, agents learn from only three leading agents, that is, alpha, beta, and delta. In IGWO, in addition to the three leaders, alpha, beta, and delta, each agent learns from multiple neighbors. Herein, each agent creates a neighborhood dynamically using Euclidean distance. The agent randomly chooses another agent within its neighborhood to learn from, and also another agent from the main population. The update mechanism considers the quality of the results from the traditional alpha, beta, and delta, and DLH, and chooses the best. The DLH strategy enhances exploration by allowing wolves (i.e., agents) to learn from multiple neighbors, thus maintaining population diversity and reducing the risk of premature convergence. Furthermore, DLH improves exploitation by adaptively selecting the better candidate between standard GWO and DLH-generated positions, ensuring effective local refinement. However, the additional computation of neighborhood and dimension may warrant additional computational time and resources. It is imperative to state that the success of IGWO relies heavily on the appropriate tuning of IGWO's parameters, such as neighborhood radius.

The memory, evolutionary operator, local search, and linear population size reduction (LPSR)based GWO (MELGWO) [42] addresses the GWO's limitations of balancing exploration versus exploitation by employing LPSR [48], widely used in population-based metaheuristics. In LPSR, the population size of the agents gradually reduces in a linear manner over the course of the iterations. In MELGWO, the exploration process begins immediately the iterations commences and then the exploration process tails off as the population size reduces and exploitation begins. The LPSR technique reduces computational cost while improving the speed of convergence. However, to avoid a situation where the population size is reduced prematurely, leading to local optima entrapment or early convergence, the parameters of LPSR need to be carefully tuned. To this end, the MELGWO maintains a strong memory archive of high-quality solutions, which prevents loss of good solutions during the optimization process. Additionally, MELGWO applies local refinements near promising solutions, thereby strengthening exploitation and more precise convergence to global optima. The combination of memory, learning, and local search often results in superior results compared to the traditional or standard GWO.

In Levy flight grey wolf optimizer (LGWO) [43], the Levy flight-based [49] search technique is incorporated into the GWO [35] to further enhance the GWO's global exploration capabilities. The Levy flight-based search technique employs random walks characterized by frequent long jumps, which help to avoid local minima entrapment of the agents. In LGWO, the random walks are introduced into wolves via the expression of wolves' movement and the position update phase. The LGWO maintains the social hierarchy and hunting behavior of GWO with the integration of stochastic perturbation of long jumps based on Levy-steps. The Levy-based updates are dependent on a specified random step size drawn from a Levy distribution and the position of the alpha wolf. However, the randomness introduced by the Levy flights may make the LGWO quite unstable if not efficiently managed. Additionally, in some cases, the Levy flight-based movements may overshoot good solutions, especially in small or finely tuned search spaces. It is pertinent to state that the Levy flight-based steps may incur additional computational cost and time compared to the traditional GWO.

The algorithms of GWO, IGWO, MELGWO, and LGWO are discussed in Section 19.4.

19.3 Preliminaries and problem formulation

Here, we discuss the fundamental basis of the uplift model and formulate the optimization problem and related metaheuristic-based solutions.

19.3.1 Uplift modeling

We consider ongoing marketing promotions with the aim to increase user engagement or revenue of an RS platform, that is, online personalized platforms. Herein, the concept of uplift modeling is employed for the identification of target users who would positively react to marketing promotions. In addition, we consider an RS dataset with features related to user attributes, treatment attributes such as treatment inputs, and the corresponding treatment outputs. Let X denote the set of covariates of dimension d, such that $X \in \mathbb{R}^d$, with a set of available treatments $T = \{T_0, T_1, T_2, \cdots, T_k\}$. Let the result of a treatment Y_i administered to a user i be given by

$$Y_i = Y_i(T) = \begin{cases} Y_i(1), & T=1 \\ Y_i(0), & T=0 \end{cases} \tag{19.1}$$

where $Y_i(1)$ represents a positive outcome or a user who receives treatment. Generally, Y_i is determined through causal inference that is based on counterfactuals. Similarly to other works in the literature, the ATE determined from the dataset X (i.e., the Hillstrom dataset in this regard) is given by:

$$ATE = \mathbb{E}[Y|T=1] - \mathbb{E}[Y|T=0], \tag{19.2}$$

where $Y|T=1$ and $Y|T=0$ denote the potential outcome if the user receives or does not receive a treatment. $\mathbb{E}[\,]$ represents the expectation throughout the population. However, as stated in Section 19.2.2, the CATE is a more refined form of ATE and is used in the uplift modeling in this work. CATE is given by:

$$CATE = \mathbb{E}[Y|X = x, \quad T=1] - \mathbb{E}[Y|X = x, \quad T=0]. \tag{19.3}$$

In (19.2) and (19.3), the set of treatment T is conditionally independent of the outcomes $Y_i(0)$ and $Y_i(1)$ such that $\{Y(1), \ Y(0)\} \perp T|X$. In other words, in (19.3), here is an assumption of unconfoundedness. Hence, assuming all relevant features or attributes X, there exist no hidden biases affecting who gets the treatment; therefore any difference in outcomes can be fully attributed to the treatment in itself. Hence, the uplift modeling lies in the estimation of CATE by predicting the difference in the outcome probabilities between the treatment group conditioned on X. Therefore the uplift modeling estimate is given by

$$\overbrace{\Delta\gamma}^{\text{Estimates of the uplift}} = \overbrace{\mathbb{P}(Y = 1|T = 1, X)}^{\substack{\text{Probability of the desired} \\ \text{outcome if user receives} \\ \text{treatment given feature X}}} - \overbrace{\mathbb{P}(Y = 1|T = 0, X)}^{\substack{\text{Probability of the desired} \\ \text{outcome if user does not receives} \\ \text{treatment given feature X}}} \tag{19.4}$$

In this chapter, the objective is to maximize the uplift estimate, that is, the total uplift across a group of users.

19.3.2 Problem formulation

Herein, maximization of the total uplift across a group of users is formulated as a budget allocation problem, and it is designed to follow the MCKP framework. We consider a scenario with an RS platform that has a set of subscribers S such that a subscriber $s \in S$ is eligible to have the privilege of getting discounts or bonuses due to ongoing online marketing promotions on the RS platform. The set T of online marketing promotions, otherwise referred to as treatments in causal inference studies, is such $T = \{T_1, T_2, \cdots T_n\}$. Each treatment is associated with a cost $c_[t]$. Subscribers assigned bonuses or discounts are ensured to have an uplift $\gamma_{t,s}$ to prevent revenue loss. To this end, the general budget allocation for the online marketing promotions is not exceeded. For efficient marketing promotions and to reach all market segments, subscribers are grouped into categories in a manner $G = \{G_1, G_2, \cdots G_m\}$. A preset uplift threshold per group γ_m^{min} is set, and, moreover, a budget allocation share β_m is assigned to each group. In this work, we consider fairness in terms of budget allocation share and group uplift threshold for groups or market segments. The budget-constrained incentive recommendation with uplift modeling optimization problem formulated as an MCKP is stated in the objective function and constraints given by:

$$\max_{\alpha_{t,s}} \sum_{s\in S}\sum_{t\in T} \alpha_{t,s}\,\gamma_{t,s} \tag{19.5a}$$

subject to:

$$\sum_{s\in S}\sum_{t\in T} \alpha_{t,s}\cdot c_t \leq B \tag{19.5b}$$

$$\sum_{t\in T} \alpha_{t,s} \leq 1 \quad \forall\ s \in S \tag{19.5c}$$

$$\sum_{s\in G_m}\sum_{t\in T} \alpha_{t,s}\cdot c_t \leq \beta_m\cdot B \quad \forall\ m \in G \tag{19.5d}$$

$$\sum_{s\in G_m}\sum_{t\in T} \alpha_{t,s}\cdot\gamma_{t,s} \geq \gamma_m^{min} \quad \forall\ m \in G \tag{19.5e}$$

$$\alpha_{t,s} \in \{0,1\} \quad \forall\ t \in T,\quad s \in S \tag{19.5f}$$

The objective function in (19.5a) is the maximization of the uplift of the RS platform. This is to ensure that online marketing promotion increases the revenue of the business within the constraints of the budget allocation for marketing promotion. In (19.5a), $\alpha_{t,s}$ denotes the decision variable indicating whether a subscriber is allocated a discount/bonus or not. In constraint (19.5b), we ensure that the budget allocation B for the marketing promotion is not exceeded, considering that there is an associated cost c_t for each treatment administered to respective subscribers. In constraint (19.5c), it is ensured that only one treatment can be allocated to one user. In other words, users can take advantage of only one promotional marketing discount or bonus. Constraint (19.5d) ensures that we do not exceed budgetary allocations for the respective groups. It ensures budget-fairness in the allocation of treatments, that is, promotional marketing to the respective groups. Here, the novelty of fairness is introduced to the MCKP problem. Constraint (19.5e) ensures uplift fairness for the respective subscriber groups. With constraint (19.5e), the total increase achieved by a treatment group G_m exceeds a preset minimum increase threshold γ_m^{min} for the group. This lower bound on uplift ensures that each group receives a minimum amount of benefit. The constraint (19.5f) is the binary constraint in which the decision variable $\alpha_{t,s}$ must be binary. Hence, this indicates the presence or absence of a treatment for each user.

19.4 Proposed solutions

19.4.1 Modeling the casual impact

In this subsection, the estimation of the causal impact of marketing promotion in an online personalized platform defined in (19.1) - (19.4) is achieved through supervised machine learning. In this work, we employ the S and T learner models [27] in uplift modeling due to their low computational cost, ease of implementation, and ability to capture complex nonlinear relationships between covariates and treatment effects. We present the pseudocodes of the S-learner and T-learner models in Algorithms 19.1 and 19.2. In Algorithm 19.1, $M(Y \sim (X, T))$ is the notation for regression or machine learning estimation $(x, t) \mapsto \mathbb{E}[Y|X = x,\ \ T = t]$, with $T \in \{0,1\}$. Similarly, in Algorithm 19.1, the notation $M_k(Y \sim X)$ denotes the regression or machine learning estimation $x \mapsto \mathbb{E}[Y|X = x]$. In this work, machine estimation is implemented via Random Forest [50] (i.e, TreeBagger in MATLAB) with the number of trees set at 100.

19.4.2 Solving the multichoice knapsack resource allocation problem

As stated in Section 19.2.4, the GWO [35], IGWO [41], MELGWO [42], and LGWO [43] are all used to solve the MCKP problem formulated in (19.5a)–(19.5f). Next, we describe the respective metaheuristic algorithms.

19.4.2.1 GWO

The GWO's agents mimic the hunting and social hierarchy of grey wolves. The mathematical expression for updating the position of grey wolves during encircling and hunting is given by

ALGORITHM 19.1 S-learner [27].

Input: Control and Treatment input features X^0 and X^1, Treatment assignment indicator vector T, Observed Outcomes for Control and Treatment group Y^0 and Y^1
Output: Uplift Vector
Procedure *S-LEARNER(X, Y, T)*:
  $\mu = M(Y \sim (X,T))$
  $\gamma(x) = \mu(x,1) - \mu(x,0)$
Return the Uplift γ

ALGORITHM 19.2 T-learner [27].

Input: Control and Treatment input features X^0 and X^1, Treatment assignment indicator vector T, Observed Outcomes for Control and Treatment group Y^0 and Y^1
Output: Uplift Vector
Procedure *T-LEARNER(X, Y, T)*:
  $\mu_0 = M_0(Y^0 \sim X^0)$
  $\mu_1 = M_1(Y^1 \sim X^1)$
  $\gamma(x) = \mu_1(x) - \mu_0(x)$
Return the Uplift γ

$$\vec{X}(i+1)=\begin{cases} \vec{X_p}(i) - \vec{A}\cdot\vec{D}, & \text{Encircling phase} \\ \frac{\vec{X_1}+\vec{X_2}+\vec{X_3}}{3}, & \text{Hunting phase} \end{cases} \tag{19.6}$$

For the prey encircling phase, the wolf's position is dependent on the position of the prey; here $\vec{X}(i+1)$ is the updated position of an agent, with i denoting the current or present iteration. Moreover, $\vec{D}$ in (19.6) is given by

$$\vec{D} = |\vec{C}\cdot\vec{X_p}(i) - \vec{X}(i)|, \tag{19.7}$$

with $\vec{X_p}(i)$ prey position vector and $\vec{C}$ is a coefficient vector and $\vec{X}(i)$ denotes the grey wolf position vector. Furthermore, the coefficient vectors $\vec{C}$ and $\vec{A}$ in (19.6) are given by

$$\vec{C}=2\cdot\vec{r_1}, \tag{19.8}$$

$$\vec{A}=2\vec{a}\cdot\vec{r_2} - \vec{a}, \tag{19.9}$$

where $\vec{r_1}$ and $\vec{r_2}$ are random vectors in [0,1]; and $\vec{a}$ linearly decreases from 2 to 0 over the duration of the iteration. In the hunting stage expressed in (19.6), the positions of a grey wolf are determined by the positions of alpha wolf $\vec{X_1}$, beta wolf $\vec{X_2}$, and delta wolves $\vec{X_3}$. Furthermore, $\vec{X_1}$, $\vec{X_2}$, and $\vec{X_3}$ are given by

$$\vec{X_1} = \vec{X_\alpha} - \vec{A_1}\cdot\vec{D_\alpha}, \quad \vec{X_2} = \vec{X_\beta} - \vec{A_2}\cdot\vec{D_\beta}, \quad \vec{X_3} = \vec{X_\delta} - \vec{A_3}\cdot\vec{D_\delta}. \tag{19.10}$$

A careful examination of (19.10) reveals a similar expression to the encircling expression in (19.10), but now specifically for the alpha, beta, and delta rather than the prey, with $\overrightarrow{D_\alpha}$, $\overrightarrow{D_\beta}$, and $\overrightarrow{D_\delta}$ similar to (19.7) but given as

$$\overrightarrow{D_\alpha} = |\overrightarrow{C_1}\cdot\overrightarrow{X_\alpha} - \overrightarrow{X}|, \quad \overrightarrow{D_\beta} = |\overrightarrow{C_2}\cdot\overrightarrow{X_\beta} - \overrightarrow{X}|, \quad \overrightarrow{D_\delta} = |\overrightarrow{C_3}\cdot\overrightarrow{X_\delta} - \overrightarrow{X}|. \tag{19.11}$$

Algorithm 19.3 highlights the pseudocode for the GWO, showcasing how it finds the optimum or near-optimum solution using the expressions in (19.6)–(19.11). Furthermore, we give an illustration of the flow diagram of Algorithm 19.3 in Fig. 19.2.

19.4.2.2 *Improved grey wolf optimizer*

IGWO [41] introduces a DLH search strategy and a selection and update phase to address the main weaknesses of the standard GWO, namely lack of population diversity, poor exploration–exploitation balance, and premature convergence. With DLH, two candidate positions were available, one for the standard GWO group hunting and another for individual neighbor-based learning. The DLH strategy constructs a neighborhood for each wolf using Euclidean distance and radius calculations. To this end, enabling multineighbor learning to enhance exploration and maintain diversity. A selection phase takes place in which a comparison of the fitness of the two candidate positions is made and the superior position is chosen as the new potential position. Finally, an update process ensures that the current wolf position is only updated if the selected candidate offers a better fitness value. Fig. 19.3 illustrates the flow diagram of the IGWO, highlighting the DLH in dotted lines. A detailed explanation of the IGWO is found in Ref. [41].

19.4.2.3 *Memory, evolutionary operator, local search, and LPSR-based GWO*

In GWO, the wolves (i.e., explorer swarm wolves) do not have a memory of their personal best during iterations; however, the MELGWO [42] introduces a set of new wolves called the memory swarm of wolves to store the better solutions found

ALGORITHM 19.3 Grey wolf optimizer (GWO) algorithm [35].

Input: Population size N, number of iterations I
Output: Incentive allocation decision vector

Procedure *Budget-constrained Incentive Recommendation with Uplift Modeling using GWO*:
  Randomly initialize the positions of all grey wolves $\vec{x}_i$, where $i = 1, 2, ..., N$
  Initialize the parameter C, a, and A using (8, 9)
  Evaluate the fitness value $F(\vec{x}_i)$ for each grey wolf
  Identify the top three wolves based on fitness: X_α, X_β, and X_δ
  for $t \leftarrow 1$ **to** I **do**
    for *each grey wolf i in population* **do**
      for $j \leftarrow 1$ **to** D **do**
        Generate two random vectors $r_1, r_2 \sim \mathcal{U}(0, 1)$
        Compute coefficient vectors: $\vec{A}_1$; $\vec{C}_1$ (8, 9)
        Calculate distances and intermediate positions: $\vec{D}_\alpha$ (11); $\vec{X}_1$ (10)
        Repeat above for β and δ to get $\vec{X}_2$ and $\vec{X}_3$ (10)
        Update position: $\vec{x}_i = \frac{1}{3}(\vec{X}_1 + \vec{X}_2 + \vec{X}_3)$ (6)
      Bound updated position $\vec{x}_i$ within the search space
      Evaluate new fitness $F(\vec{x}_i)$
      Update α, β, δ positions if needed
    Linearly decrease control parameter $\vec{a}$ from 2 to 0
  Return the best solution $\vec{x}_\alpha$ as the incentive allocation result
  Allocate incentive

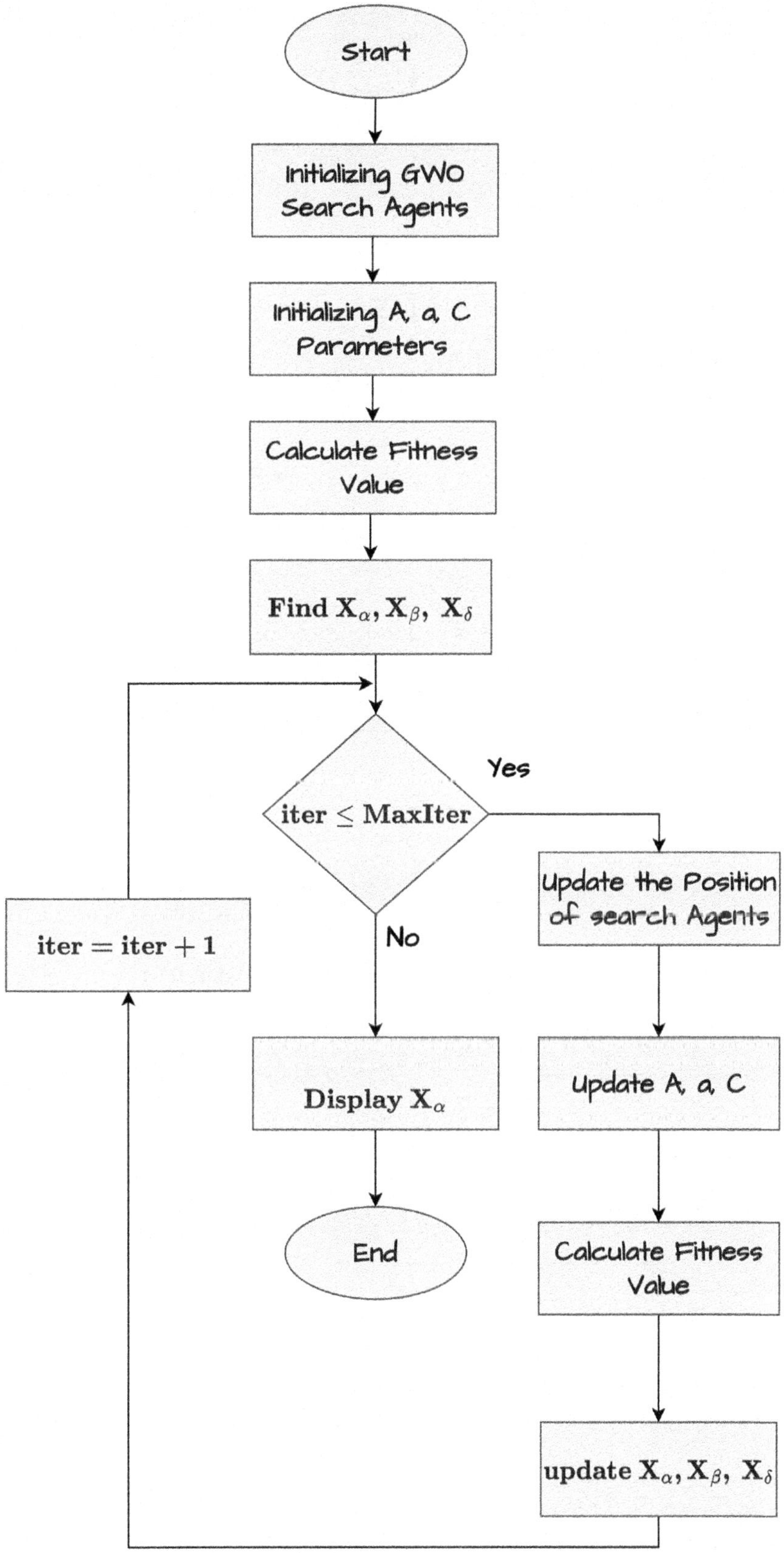

FIGURE 19.2 A flow diagram of the GWO algorithm (*GWO*, Grey wolf optimizer).

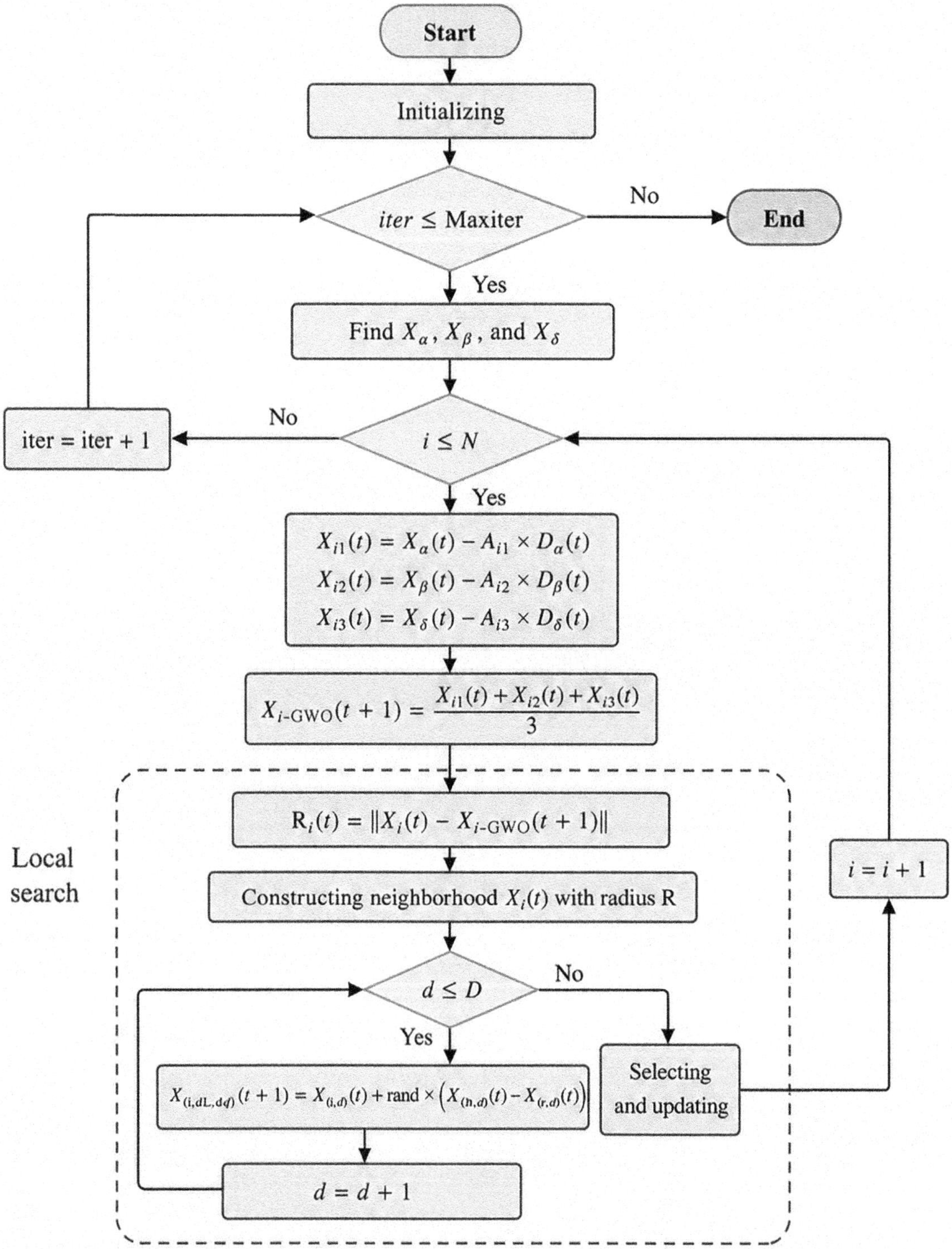

FIGURE 19.3 An illustration of the flow diagram of the IGWO algorithm [41] (*IGWO*, Improved grey wolf optimizer).

during iterations. It is important to note that the memory swarm wolves are the same size as the explorer swarm wolves. Furthermore, evolutionary operators that rely on differential evolution [51,52] techniques, such as mutation, cross, and selection operation dynamics, are embedded in the explorer swarm wolves. These techniques are used to enhance the exploitation and exploration capabilities of the explorer swarm wolves. Additionally, a stochastic local search is

ALGORITHM 19.4 Pseudo code of the proposed MELGWO algorithm [42].

```
Input: Number of wolves N, Dimensions D, Maximum number of function evaluations (M), lower bound lb, upper
       bound ub, crossover percentage CR, local search percentage LS
Output: Position and cost function value of the alpha wolf as the optimum
Initialization: Randomly generate N wolves within the search space. Evaluate fitness, and select α, β, and δ wolves.
  Copy the initial population and fitness values into the memory swarm.
while m < M do
    for i ← 1 to N do
        Check for bounds, select α, β, and δ
    Update a
    for i ← 1 to N do
        Update the positions of wolves according to (10)
        Check for bounds and evaluate fitness and constraints
    for i ← 1 to N do
        Apply evolutionary operators
        Compare memory swarm with evolutionary-operator-applied wolves and update memory
    for i ← 1 to N/2 do
        Perform local search near 50% of memory swarm wolves
        Compare local wolves with α, β, and δ wolves, and update these best three
        Compare memory swarm with local wolves and update memory swarm
    Apply LSPR [48] to delete the worst wolves
Output the position and cost function value of α wolf as the optimum
```

performed randomly on half of the population size of the memory swarm wolves. This is to generate local neighbors who are either away or toward the nearest neighbor-based on fitness value to improve the fine-tuning. As the algorithm converges, the explorer and memory swarm wolves are linearly reduced in size, and this is achieved by LPSR [48]. This reduction comes from the fitness evaluations, hence, removing the worst-ranked wolves at each iteration to reduce computational burden. The enhancement above introduced by the MELGWO provides a better balance between exploration and exploitation while avoiding premature convergences. The pseudocode of the MELGWO algorithm is highlighted in Algorithm 19.4.

19.4.2.4 Levy flight grey wolf optimizer

LGWO [43] uses Levy-flight [49] random walks to improve the GWO exploration capabilities, thus improving the diversity of GWO agents. The LGWO employs the Levy flight distribution with parameter θ=0.5, which is then used to generate step sizes in the Mantegna algorithm [53] such that the length of the step S is determined via $S = U/|V|^{\left(\frac{1}{\theta}\right)}$. In Mantegna's algorithm, U and V are Gaussian random variables. Levy flights provide varied step sizes consisting of many small steps and occasionally large jumps, and hence offer a more efficient balance between exploration and exploitation, compared to standard random walks that use uniform step sizes. In LGWO, the Levy flight is applied to all wolves and not specifically to only alpha, beta, and delta wolves. This approach increases the population diversity and enhances the probability of finding better solutions, since all wolves' position updates influence the alpha wolf's position. It is imperative to state that the Levy flight technique is also employed during the initialization phase of the algorithm Fig. 19.4 illustrates the flow diagram of the LGWO algorithm.

19.4.3 Computational complexity

In this subsection, the computational complexity of the selected metaheuristics, GWO [35], IGWO [41], MELGWO [42], and LGWO [43] are examined in light of their respective algorithm. Herein, the time complexity of the respective

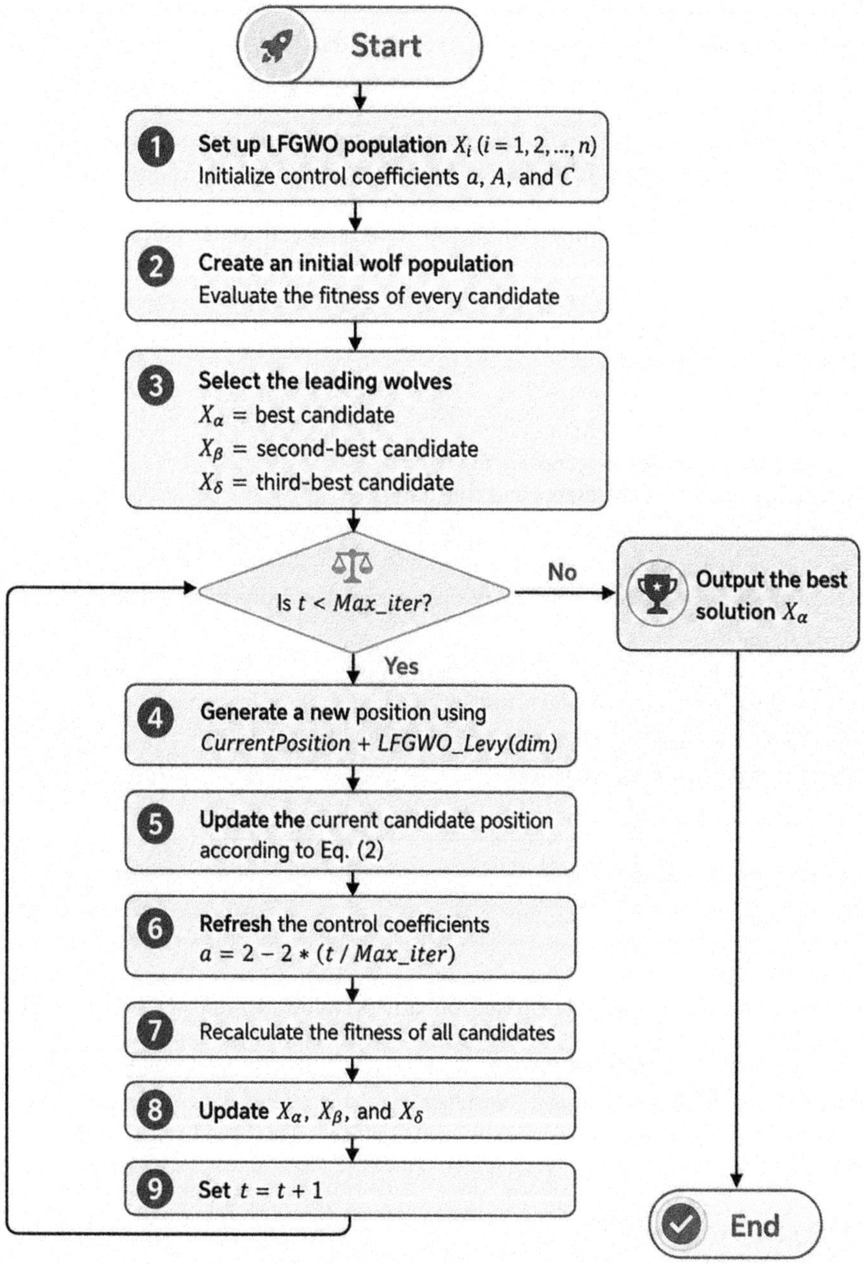

FIGURE 19.4 An illustration of the flow diagram of the LGWO algorithm [43] (*LGWO*, Levy flight grey optimizer).

algorithms is emphasized using the characterization of the big Omicron (big-$\mathcal{O}$) notation [54,55]. The big-$\mathcal{O}$ notation provides the theoretical worst-case scenario or upper bound of the execution time of the GWO and its selected variants.

The computational complexity of the GWO [35] and other evolutionary metaheuristics is quite difficult to determine due to stochastic characterization. Here, with a close inspection of Algorithm 19.3, in Subsection 19.4.2.1, the big-$\mathcal{O}$ notation of the GWO's complexity is given by $\mathcal{O}$(I x P x D), where I denotes the number of iterations; P is the total number of wolves, that is, the population size; and last, D indicates the dimensionality of the problem. This big-$\mathcal{O}$ notation is clearly depicted in the for loops in Algorithm 19.3.

The complexity of IGWO [41] can be defined by $\mathcal{O}$(I x P x (D + log P)). In certain circumstances, D dominates log P. According to [42], the computational complexity of MELGWO is given by $\mathcal{O}$(I x P x D), which is similar to the GWO time complexity. Furthermore, the time complexity of the LGWO [43] is given by $\mathcal{O}$(D + 3P + 2PD) as stated in Ref. [43]. The notation takes into account the initial solution and solutions based on the Levy flight strategy.

19.5 Performance evaluation and discussion

In this section, we examine the performance of GWO, IGWO, MELGWO, and LGWO in solving the budget-constrained incentive recommendation with optimization problem and uplift modeling. These solutions are compared with an optimal solution from MATLAB's intlinprog (i.e., Integer Linear Programming). Additionally, in modeling uplift, we employ the S-learner and T-learner methods [27]. The performance evaluation of the respective solutions is carried out via an extensive Monte Carlo simulation in a MATLAB environment. The control parameters of the respective metaheuristics employed in this chapter are presented in Table 19.1. Uplift modeling is implemented for both the S-learner approach (i.e., single-model approach) and the T-learner (i.e., two-model approach) through the use of a random forest algorithm with the number of trees set at 100. In addition, in this chapter, the widely used Hillstrom dataset [56,57] is used based on uplift modeling implemented through machine learning studies.

The Hillstrom dataset that was originally curated and made available by Kevin Hillstrom contains 64,000 customers who purchased merchandise within the last year. The dataset entails a marketing campaign of an online retailer, highlighting customer website visits, purchase information, and revenue generated. These customers are categorized into three groups of equal size. Two of these groups were contacted via email, and customers in the third group, who would otherwise serve as the control group, were not contacted at all. The first two groups, stated as Men merchandise and Women merchandise, stand as the treatment group. The total number of controls and treatment are 21,306 and 42,694, respectively. Some of the features of the Hillstrom dataset include Recency, History segment, Men's, Women's, Zip code, Newbie, Channel, Segment, Visit, Conversion, and Spend.

Furthermore, we evaluate the performance of the proposed algorithms in terms of convergence and accuracy; uplift distributions of the S-learner and T-learner approaches; total uplift per customer group, men and women; and the cost per uplift per the respective customer groups.

19.5.1 Uplift distribution analysis

In Figs. 19.5 and 19.6, the uplift distributions for the S- and T-learners are presented. Fig. 19.5 shows the uplift distribution for the S-learner with a right-skewed distribution with peak values centered around near zero, with a frequency of approximately 5500. Most of the uplift values are below 0.02 and some outliers are greater than 0.04. Hence, it is seen that S-learner predominantly produces small or near-zero uplift effects, which could be attributed to the model

TABLE 19.1 The control parameters of the respective metaheuristics, with all having a total number of agents set to 50 and a maximum number of generations at 500.

Metaheuristic	Control param.	Values
GWO [35]	Convergence parameter	Linear reduction 2 to 0
IGWO [41]	Convergence parameter	Linear reduction 2 to 0
	Neighborhood search	100%
	Convergence parameter	Linear reduction 2 to 0
MELGWO [42]	Crossover	60%
	Stochastic local search	50%
LGWO [43]	Convergence parameter	$2 \times \left(1 - \frac{t}{Max\_iter}\right)$

GWO, Grey wolf optimization; *IGWO*, improved grey wolf optimization; *MELGWO*, memory, evolutionary operator, local search, and LPSR-based GWO; *LGWO*, Levy flight grey wolf optimizer.

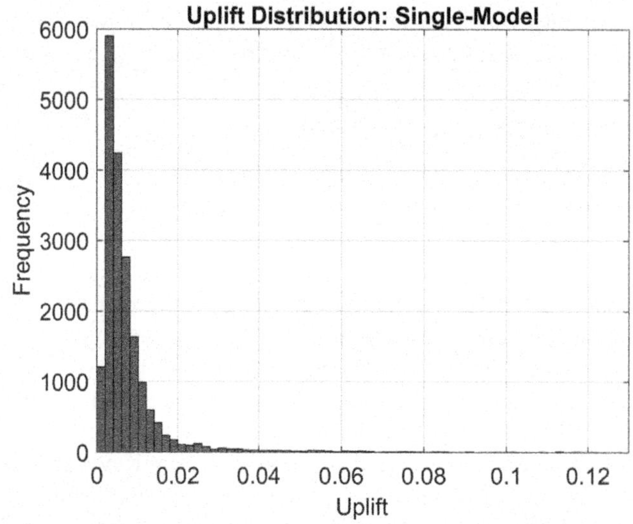

FIGURE 19.5 Distribution of the predicted uplift via the S-learner (i.e, single-model) approach.

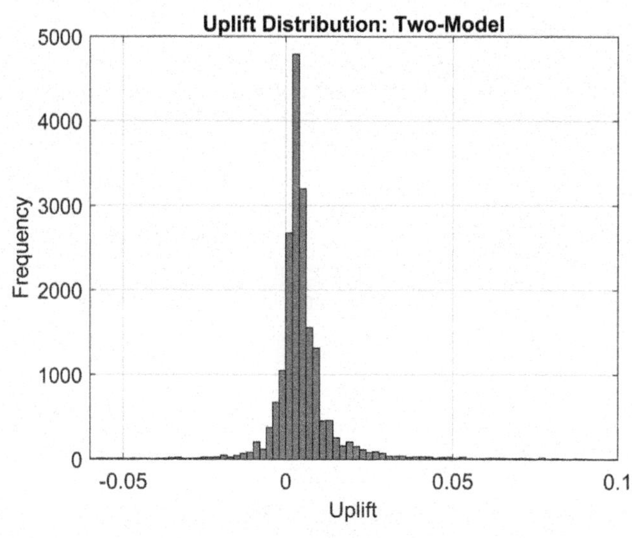

FIGURE 19.6 Distribution of the predicted uplift via the T-learner (i.e, single-model) approach.

being conservative in its predictions or that the interventions or treatments have minimal impact on the marketing promotion. Unlike in Fig. 19.5, Fig. 19.6 shows the distribution of the uplifts predicted by the T-learner, showing both positive and negative impacts of the intervention, providing a more realistic representation of uplift effects. Hence, the bell-shaped curve is centered around zero and varies from – 0.06 to 0.10 and has a maximum frequency of about 4500.

19.5.2 Convergence analysis

The convergence analysis of the respective metaheuristics in solving the optimization problem stated in (19.5a)–(19.5f) is presented in Figs. 19.7 and 19.8 for the mean predicted uplifts of the S-learner and T-learner, respectively. The benchmark threshold is the branch-and-bound solution (i.e., an exact solution) implemented via Matlab's "intlinprog," a MILP. The exact solution is compared with the solutions of GWO, IGWO, MELGWO, and LGWO.

It is observed that MELGWO and LGWO outperformed IGWO and GWO in terms of reaching convergence before the 50th iterations; the two metaheuristics show early stability with modest final quality. However, GWO shows promising

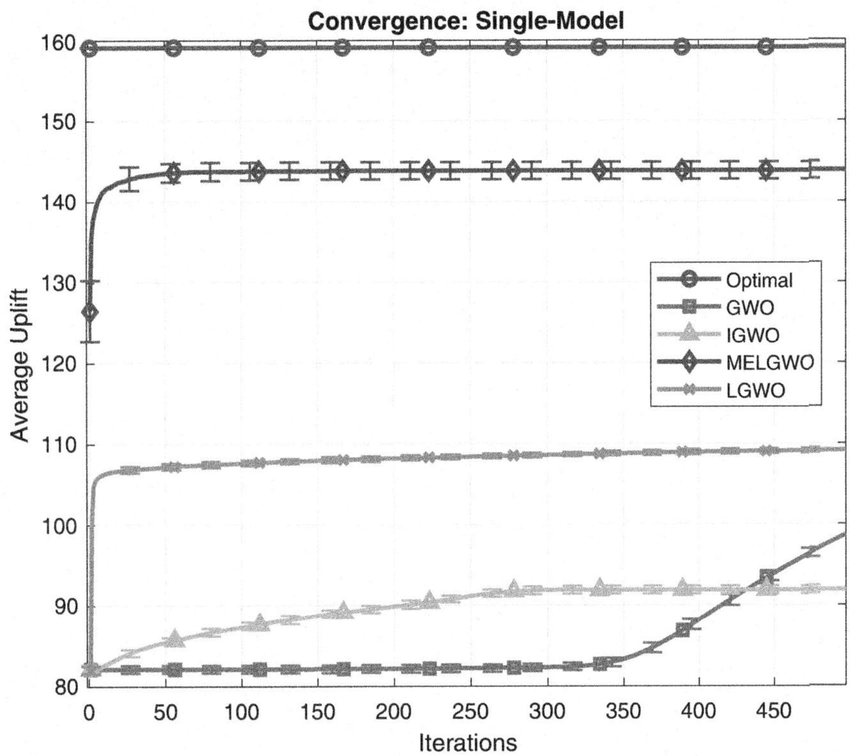

FIGURE 19.7 Convergence analysis of the selected algorithms in solving the budget and fairness-aware uplift modeling optimization problem with the uplift predicted via the S-learner.

signs for iterations greater than 500th. In other words, the GWO exhibits prolonged stagnation at the lower bounds of the iterations. Furthermore, MELGWO and LGWO provide the most near-optimal average uplift solutions. Furthermore, in Fig. 19.7, it is seen that all the respective metaheuristics have a slight or small error barsonce they stabilize. A comparison of Figs. 19.7 and 19.8 pinpoint the S-learner model with a higher uplift prediction than the T-learner model.

Similarly to Fig. 19.7, Fig. 19.8 shows that MELGWO and LGWO reach convergence at the lower bounds of iteration, while the GWO achieve higher average uplift over the 300 th iteration. The IGWO exhibited a slow, steady,but monotonic increase. Taking into account both Figs. 19.7 and 19.8, it is observed that MELGWO provides the best trade-off with a rapid convergence to the highest average uplift.

19.5.3 Computational time analysis

In this section, the computational time analysis of the respective metaheuristics in solving budget- and fairness-aware uplift modeling optimization is examined. Tables 19.2 and 19.3 highlight the results of the computational run time analysis of the selected metaheuristics for the S-learner and T-learner scenario.

In Table 19.2, we observe that the MELGWO outperformed the other algorithms, achieving a best run time of 57.33 seconds with a mean computational time of 73.58 seconds and a standard deviation of about 11.95 seconds. In contrast, IGWO has a mean of 199.20 and a standard deviation of 35.17, with a best and worst run times of 152.51 and 315.39 seconds. Hence, IGWO showed the slowest computational run-time among the four algorithms. Furthermore, GWO and LGWO show significantly longer mean run times of 136.98 and 155.36 seconds with a different, larger dispersion (i.e., a large standard deviation) of 34.77 and 27.94 seconds, respectively. In comparison, the lower mean-median gap of MELGWO and the smallest standard deviation suggest a tighter concentration around faster times. Additionally, Fig. 19.9 gives further insight into the results in Table 19.2 by highlighting the interquartile range and the outliers, among others. Fig. 19.9 shows that MELGWO has only a few mild high outliers, which indicates high efficiency and a stable algorithm. In contrast, IGWO exhibits the slowest run-time and the least stablity. With a run-time median that sits at about 188

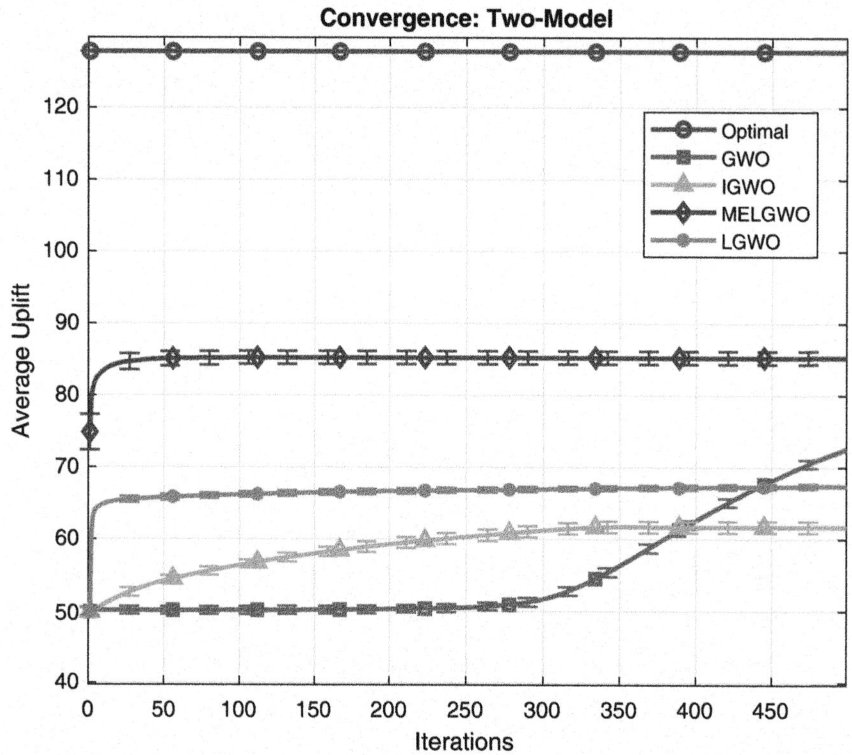

FIGURE 19.8 Convergence analysis of the selected algorithms in solving the budget and fairness-aware uplift modeling optimization problem with the uplift predicted via the T-learner.

TABLE 19.2 Computational run time analysis (in seconds) of the respective metaheuristic in solving the budget and fairness-aware uplift modeling optimization for the single model.

Metaheuristics	Mean	Std.	Median	Mode	Best	Worst
GWO	136.9810	34.7660	119.7873	110.9023	110.9023	242.1814
IGWO	199.1982	35.1746	187.5513	152.5088	152.5088	315.3942
MELGWO	73.5817	11.9521	70.1980	57.3326	57.3326	132.0090
LGWO	155.3576	27.9414	145.6441	118.8030	118.8030	274.9712

GWO, Grey wolf optimization; *IGWO*, improved grey wolf optimization; *MELGWO*, memory, evolutionary operator, local search, and LPSR-based GWO; *LGWO*, Levy flight grey wolf optimizer.

seconds, the box is tall, and with numerous high outliers that extend beyond 250 seconds, the IGWO succinctly displays the characteristics of a right-tailed distribution.

In Table 19.3, the results of the computational run-time of the selected metaheuristics for solving the optimization of the uplift modeling based on budget and fairness for the scenario of the T learner are presented. Consistent with the trend in Table 19.2 for the S-learner scenario, in Table 19.3 it is seen that the MELGWO leads with a best running time of approximately 57.67 seconds and a mean running time of 72.95 seconds; and a worst case running time of about 108.1495 seconds, which is quite faster than the best computational time of the other algorithms, respectively. The MELGWO algorithm showed high stability, which is indicated by its narrow or small value of coefficients of variation. Furthermore, GWO and LGWO showed a moderate computational time with a mean of 137.26 and 154.27 seconds and deviations of

TABLE 19.3 Computational run time analysis (in seconds) of the respective metaheuristic in solving the budget and fairness-aware uplift modeling optimization for the two models.

Metaheuristics	Mean	Std.	Median	Mode	Best	Worst
GWO	137.2620	33.6292	120.4002	109.0434	109.0434	229.2130
IGWO	197.7232	32.4007	186.0486	157.7546	157.7546	288.4278
MELGWO	72.9514	9.2338	70.3537	57.6701	57.6701	108.1495
LGWO	154.2695	24.1004	146.0536	121.5390	121.5390	242.8022

GWO, Grey wolf optimization; *IGWO*, improved grey wolf optimization; *MELGWO*, memory, evolutionary operator, local search, and LPSR-based GWO; *LGWO*, Levy flight grey wolf optimizer.

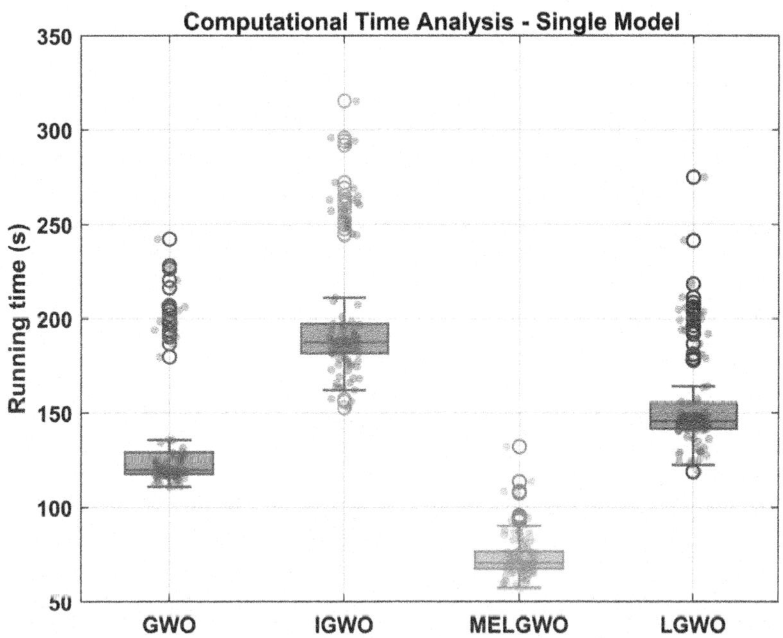

FIGURE 19.9 Visual illustration of the computational run time of the respective metaheuristics for the S-learner scenario.

33.63 and 24.10 seconds, respectively. Similar to Table 19.2, the IGWO indicates the highest time cost and also poses a risk of variability. The results in Table 19.3 are further supported in Fig. 19.10.

19.5.4 Total uplift per group

Here, we examine the fairness in the uplift modeling for two groups: customers who purchase men's and women's merchandise. In this regard, we set the fairness ratio of each group at 0.5 to investigate the total number of customers selected for uplift in the respective groups. Figs. 19.11 and 19.12 present the results of the total uplift per group, that is, the number of selected users who benefit from the uplift modeling for the S and T learners scenarios.

In Fig. 19.11, it is observed that MELGWO provides a near-optimal result of about 5800 users for each group, respectively, and also outperforms the other metaheuristics. IGWO, in contrast to MELGWO, had the least number of selected individuals per group (i.e, about 3000 for men and 3000 for women) who are to benefit from uplift modeling. Furthermore, it is seen that there is a group balance, that is, a gender balance maintained across the selected metaheuristics, indicating that the selection strategy of each metaheuristic does not disproportionately favor one group over the other.

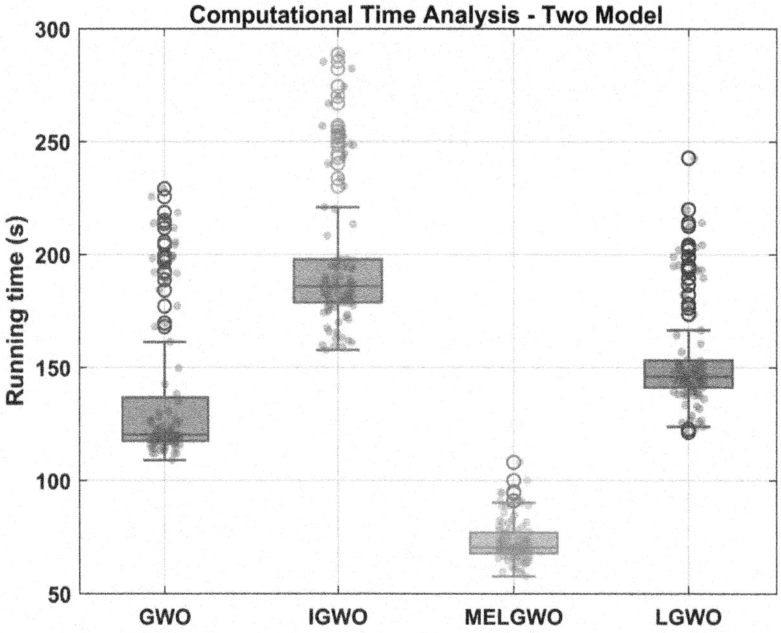

FIGURE 19.10 Visual illustration of the computational run time of the respective metaheuristics for the T-learner scenario.

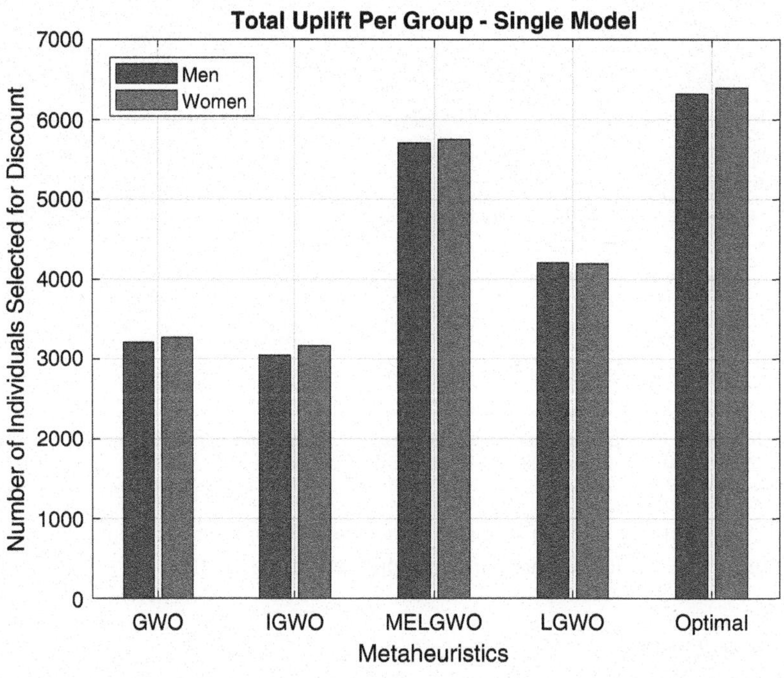

FIGURE 19.11 Total number of customers per group selected for uplifts by the respective algorithms, with S-learner predicted uplifts.

Fig. 19.12 presents the result for the totals of the actionable increase group for the T-learner scenario by GWO, IGWO, MELGWO, and LGWO, respectively. In Fig. 19.12, the MELGWO provides an appreciable optimal result for about 5500 selected individuals to benefit from the uplift modeling, followed by the LGWO. The IGWO had the poorest performance in this regard, with about 2500 for each group. Similarly to Fig. 19.11, in Fig. 19.12, it is seen that all metaheuristics adhered to the fairness ratio threshold of 0.5, thus ensuring that each group is treated fairly, as seen in gender having the same or almost the same number of selected users.

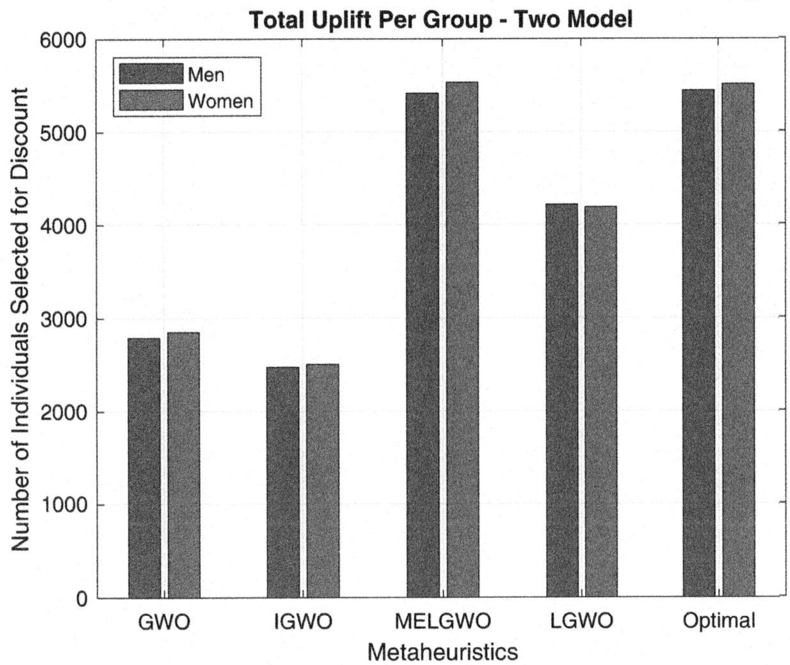

FIGURE 19.12 Total number of customers per group selected for uplifts by the respective algorithms, with T-learner predicted uplifts.

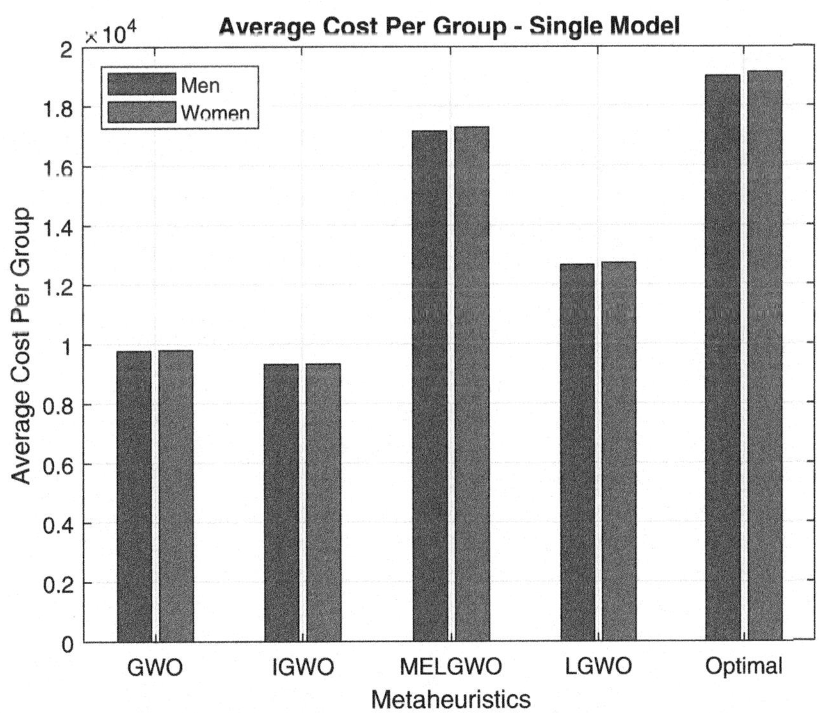

FIGURE 19.13 Mean total cost of uplift for the S-learner model.

In both figures, we observe that the MELGWO outperforms the other algorithms. We see that the number of selected customers who purchase men's merchandise and customers who purchase women's merchandise is about the same across all the respective algorithms; this is associated with the group fairness ratio tuning.

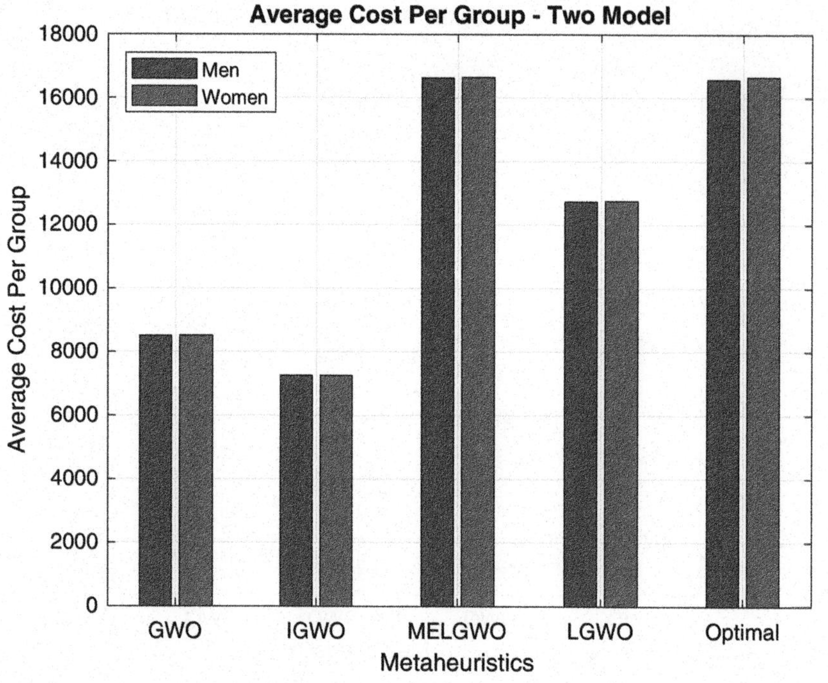

FIGURE 19.14 Mean total cost of uplift for the T-learner model.

19.5.5 Average cost per group

With a total promotional budget set to 70,000 and an individual uplift cost ranging from 1 to 5, we examine the performance of the respective algorithms in the face of an online marketing promotion constrained by budget. Figs. 19.13 and 19.14 present the mean total cost per group, that is, customers who purchase men's merchandise (i.e., men) and those who purchase women's merchandise (i.e., women). It is observed from Figs. 19.13 and 19.14, that the mean total cost of the respective algorithms corresponds to the number of individuals selected for the uplift or discount, as illustrated in Figs. 19.11 and 19.12.

19.6 Conclusion

This present work has shown that incorporating uplift modeling with GWO offers an effective and resilient framework to design budget-constrained incentive recommendation systems. Hence, by shifting the paradigm beyond conventional response models, the uplift modeling technique guarantees that incentives are targeted toward individuals who are likely to demonstrate a positive incremental behavior change, thus enhancing total impact. In the intervening time, the GWO algorithm allows efficient exploration and exploitation of the solution space, guaranteeing that constrained financial resources are most effectively distributed under budget conditions. Furthermore, the partnership between GWO and uplift modeling not only improves customer-focused precision but also guarantees that industries attain high returns on investment (RoI) while preserving scalability and fairness. The proposed method, compared to existing schemes, performs better in relation to the behavioral effect, cost efficiency, and reach of the campaign. Furthermore, it is observed that MELGWO and LGWO achieve considerably stable and high uplift in comparison with conventional GWO and its variants. This shows the efficiency of the improved GWO variants in enhancing budget-constrained incentive recommendations. Consequently, the numerical results obtained enhance the opportunities and possibilities of nature-based optimization methods to improve data-inspired marketing techniques, allowing intelligent incentive design in areas ranging from finance to healthcare and public and private policy. Finally, the future direction of this present study could advance this structure by integrating dynamic budget adjustments and real-time adaptive modeling techniques, thus widening its application in rapidly changing decision environments.

Acknowledgment

There is no use of Generative Artificial Intelligence in the writing of this chapter and in the associated simulation.

References

[1] Z. Zhao, T. Harinen, Uplift modeling for multiple treatments with cost optimization, in: 2019 IEEE International Conference on Data Science and Advanced Analytics (DSAA), IEEE, 2019, pp. 422–431.

[2] J. Albert, D. Goldenberg, E-commerce promotions personalization via online multiple-choice knapsack with uplift modeling, in: Proceedings of the 31st ACM International Conference on Information & Knowledge Management, 2022, pp. 2863–2872.

[3] T. Feix, T. Feix, The streaming revolution in global media and the down of an epic battle, Valuing Digital Business Designs and Platforms: An Integrated Strategic and Financial Valuation Framework, 2021, pp. 173–224.

[4] Z. Sun, H. Yang, D. Liu, Y. Weng, X. Tang, X. He, End-to-end cost-effective incentive recommendation under budget constraint with uplift modeling, in: Proceedings of the 18th ACM Conference on Recommender Systems, 2024, pp. 560–569.

[5] Y. Xie, H.-Q. Ye, W. Zhu, Prediction and optimization for multi-product marketing resource allocation in cross-border e-commerce, Journal of Theoretical and Applied Electronic Commerce Research 20 (2) (2025) 124.

[6] Z. Sun, D. Liu, X. Tang, Y. Weng, X. He, Towards effective and efficient multi-valued treatment uplift modeling in online marketing, in: International Conference on Database Systems for Advanced Applications, Springer, 2024, pp. 121–138.

[7] Z. Sun, Q. Han, M. Zhu, H. Gong, D. Liu, C. Ma, Robust uplift modeling with large-scale contexts for real-time marketing, arXiv preprint arXiv:2502.15697, 2025.

[8] D. Goldenberg, K. Kofman, J. Albert, S. Mizrachi, A. Horowitz, I. Teinemaa, Personalization in practice: methods and applications, in: Proceedings of the 14th ACM International Conference on Web Search and Data Mining, 2021, pp. 1123–1126.

[9] S.O. Oladejo, Budget and fairness aware uplift modeling in recommender systems, in: 2025 International Conference on Intelligent Systems, Metaheuristics & Swarm Intelligence (ISMSI), ACM, 2025, pp. 422–431.

[10] T. Ding, D. Perrault-Joncas, O. Ronen, M.I. Jordan, D. Bergemann, D. Foster, et al., The role of the marketplace operator in inducing competition, arXiv preprint arXiv:2503.06582, 2025.

[11] X. Dai, W. Xu, Y. Qi, M. Jordan, Incentive-aware recommender systems in two-sided markets, ACM Transactions on Recommender Systems 2 (4) (2024) 1–38.

[12] Y. Li, G. Cheng, X. Dai, Two-sided competing matching recommendation markets with quota and complementary preferences constraints, in: Proceedings of the 41st International Conference on Machine Learning, 2024, pp. 27589–27614.

[13] F. Yao, C. Li, K.A. Sankararaman, Y. Liao, Y. Zhu, Q. Wang, et al., Rethinking incentives in recommender systems: are monotone rewards always beneficial? Advances in Neural Information Processing Systems 36 (2023) 74582–74601.

[14] J. Chen, J. Xiong, G. Chen, X. Liu, P. Yan, H. Jiang, Optimal instant discounts of multiple ride options at a ride-hailing aggregator, European Journal of Operational Research 314 (2) (2024) 718–734.

[15] Y. Cai, C. Daskalakis, Recommender systems meet mechanism design, in: Proceedings of the 23rd ACM Conference on Economics and Computation, 2022, pp. 897–914.

[16] Y. Zhao, Y. Wang, Y. Liu, X. Cheng, C.C. Aggarwal, T. Derr, Fairness and diversity in recommender systems: a survey, ACM Transactions on Intelligent Systems and Technology 16 (1) (2025) 1–28.

[17] E. Gómez, D. Contreras, L. Boratto, M. Salamó, Enhancing recommender systems with provider fairness through preference distribution-awareness, International Journal of Information Management Data Insights 5 (1) (2025) 100311.

[18] B. He, Y. Weng, X. Tang, Z. Cui, Z. Sun, L. Chen, et al., Rankability-enhanced revenue uplift modeling framework for online marketing, in: Proceedings of the 30th ACM SIGKDD Conference on Knowledge Discovery and Data Mining, 2024, pp. 5093–5104.

[19] R.M. Gubela, S. Lessmann, Interpretable multiple treatment revenue uplift modeling, arXiv preprint arXiv:2101.03336, 2021.

[20] J.S. Haupt, Machine learning for marketing decision support, 2020.

[21] Y. Huang, S. Wang, M. Gao, X. Wei, C. Li, C. Luo, et al., Entire chain uplift modeling with context-enhanced learning for intelligent marketing, in: Companion Proceedings of the ACM Web Conference 2024, 2024, pp. 226–234.

[22] D. Liu, X. Tang, Y. Qiao, M. Liu, Z. Sun, X. He, et al., Benchmarking for deep uplift modeling in online marketing, arXiv preprint arXiv:2406.00335, 2024.

[23] H.M. Proença, F. Moraes, Incremental profit per conversion: a response transformation for uplift modeling in e-commerce promotions, arXiv preprint arXiv:2306.13759, 2023.

[24] P. Shi, W. Zhong, X. Zhang, N. Wang, X. Fu, W. Wang, et al., Estimating conditional average treatment effects via sufficient representation learning, arXiv preprint arXiv:2408.17053, 2024.

[25] W.A. Van Amsterdam, R. Ranganath, Conditional average treatment effect estimation with marginally constrained models, Journal of Causal Inference 11 (1) (2023) 20220027.

[26] W. Zhang, J. Li, L. Liu, A unified survey of treatment effect heterogeneity modelling and uplift modelling, ACM Computing Surveys (CSUR) 54 (8) (2021) 1–36.

[27] S.R. Künzel, J.S. Sekhon, P.J. Bickel, B. Yu, Metalearners for estimating heterogeneous treatment effects using machine learning, Proceedings of the national academy of sciences 116 (10) (2019) 4156–4165.

[28] X. Wang, Y. Zhang, G. Jiang, B. Cheng, W. Lin, Hidden representation clustering with multi-task representation learning towards robust online budget allocation, arXiv preprint arXiv:2506.00959, 2025.
[29] H. Geng, H. Ruan, R. Wang, Y. Li, Y. Wang, L. Chen, et al., Benchmarking PTO and PNO methods in the predictive combinatorial optimization regime, Advances in Neural Information Processing Systems 37 (2024) 65944–65971.
[30] L. Idan, M. Li, Responsible uplift modeling, in: Proceedings of the 24th International Conference on Autonomous Agents and Multiagent Systems, 2025, pp. 1034–1041.
[31] K. Rajan, Temporal diversity in music recommendations: a budget-aware approach to enhance user engagement and content discovery, Available at SSRN 4949993, 2024.
[32] D. Goldenberg, J. Albert, G. Tsype, Optimization levers for promotions personalization under limited budget, in: MORS@ RecSys, 2021.
[33] T. Szkaliczki, Solution methods for the multiple-choice knapsack problem and their applications, Mathematics 13 (7) (2025) 1097.
[34] H. Kellerer, U. Pferschy, D. Pisinger, H. Kellerer, U. Pferschy, D. Pisinger, The multiple-choice knapsack problem, Knapsack Problems (2004) 317–347.
[35] S. Mirjalili, S.M. Mirjalili, A. Lewis, Grey wolf optimizer, Advances in Engineering Software 69 (2014) 46–61.
[36] S.O. Oladejo, Metaheuristics for protein structure prediction: Review and empirical analysis, in: 2024 IEEE International Conference on Artificial Intelligence and Mechatronics Systems (AIMS), IEEE, 2024, pp. 1–6.
[37] S.O. Oladejo, S.O. Ekwe, A.T. Ajibare, L.A. Akinyemi, S. Mirjalili, Tuning svms' hyperparameters using the whale optimization algorithm, Handbook of Whale Optimization Algorithm, Elsevier, (2024), pp. 495–521.
[38] S.O. Oladejo, L.A. Akinyemi, S.O. Ekwe, T.G. Omomule, O.P. Babalola, Hyperparameter tuning of svm using metaheuristics: an empirical analysis, in: 2025 IEEE 3rd Wireless Africa Conference (WAC), IEEE, 2025, pp. 1–6.
[39] S.O. Ekwe, L.A. Akinyemi, S.O. Oladejo, N. Ventura, Social-aware joint uplink and downlink resource allocation scheme using genetic algorithm, in: 2021 IEEE AFRICON, IEEE, 2021, pp. 1–6.
[40] S.O. Oladejo, Metaheuristics for protein structure prediction: a comprehensive review and empirical analysis, Scientific African 29 (2025) e02820.
[41] M.H. Nadimi-Shahraki, S. Taghian, S. Mirjalili, An improved grey wolf optimizer for solving engineering problems, Expert Systems with Applications 166 (2021) 113917.
[42] R. Ahmed, G.P. Rangaiah, S. Mahadzir, S. Mirjalili, M.H. Hassan, S. Kamel, Memory, evolutionary operator, and local search based improved grey wolf optimizer with linear population size reduction technique, Knowledge-Based Systems 264 (2023) 110297.
[43] W. Lei, W. Jiawei, M. Zezhou, Enhancing grey wolf optimizer with levy flight for engineering applications, IEEE Access 11 (2023) 74865–74897.
[44] S.N. Makhadmeh, M.A. Al-Betar, I.A. Doush, M.A. Awadallah, S. Kassaymeh, S. Mirjalili, et al., Recent advances in grey wolf optimizer, its versions and applications, IEEE Access 12 (2023) 22991–23028.
[45] H. Faris, I. Aljarah, M.A. Al-Betar, S. Mirjalili, Grey wolf optimizer: a review of recent variants and applications, Neural Computing and Applications 30 (2018) 413–435.
[46] P. Hu, J.-S. Pan, S.-C. Chu, Improved binary grey wolf optimizer and its application for feature selection, Knowledge-Based Systems 195 (2020) 105746.
[47] S. Gupta, K. Deep, A novel random walk grey wolf optimizer, Swarm and Evolutionary Computation 44 (2019) 101–112.
[48] R. Tanabe, A.S. Fukunaga, Improving the search performance of shade using linear population size reduction, in: 2014 IEEE Congress on Evolutionary Computation (CEC), IEEE, 2014, pp. 1658–1665.
[49] A.A. Al-Temeemy, J. Spencer, J. Ralph, Levy flights for improved ladar scanning, in: 2010 IEEE International Conference on Imaging Systems and Techniques, IEEE, 2010, pp. 225–228.
[50] L. Breiman, Random forests, Machine Learning 45 (1) (2001) 5–32.
[51] K.V. Price, R.M. Storn, J.A. Lampinen, Differential Evolution: A Practical Approach to Global Optimization, Springer, (2005).
[52] S. Das, P.N. Suganthan, Differential evolution: a survey of the state-of-the-art, IEEE Transactions on Evolutionary Computation 15 (1) (2011) 4–31. Available from https://doi.org/10.1109/TEVC.2010.2059031.
[53] R.N. Mantegna, Fast, accurate algorithm for numerical simulation of levy stable stochastic processes, Physical Review E 49 (5) (1994) 4677.
[54] D.E. Knuth, Big omicron and big omega and big theta, ACM Sigact News 8 (2) (1976) 18–24.
[55] P.E. Black, Big-o notation, dictionary of algorithms and data structures, US National Institute of Standards and Technology, 2008.
[56] K. Hillstrom, The minethatdata e-mail analytics and data mining challenge. http://blog.minethatdata.com/2008/03/minethatdata-e-mail-analytics-and-data.html, 2008.
[57] N.J. Radcliffe, Hillstrom's minethatdata email analytics challenge: an approach using uplift modelling, Technical report, Stochastic Solutions Limited. http://stochasticsolutions.com/pdf/HillstromChallenge.pdf, 2008

Chapter 20

Applications of grey wolf optimizer and its variants in wireless sensor networks

Fakhrosadat Fanian[1] and Mohammad Shokouhifar[2]

[1]*Department of Computer Science, Faculty of Mathematics and Computer, Shahid Bahonar University of Kerman, Kerman, Iran,* [2]*Institute of Research and Development, Duy Tan University, Da Nang, Vietnam*

20.1 Introduction

Wireless sensor networks (WSNs) are increasingly recognized as fundamental components of modern technology, facilitating a diverse array of applications, including environmental monitoring, healthcare, industrial automation, and the development of smart cities [1,2]. These networks are comprised of distributed sensor nodes that wirelessly collect and transmit data, often functioning in environments with limited resources. Despite their considerable potential, WSNs encounter significant challenges, such as energy efficiency, scalability, and robustness, which demand innovative solutions.

In recent years, metaheuristic algorithms have become increasingly popular for tackling complex optimization challenges in WSNs. One standout among them is the grey wolf optimizer (GWO), introduced by Mirjalili et al. in 2014 [3]. GWO has gained wide recognition for its simplicity, fast convergence, and strong balance between global exploration and local exploitation. Its adaptive nature allows it to efficiently search complex solution spaces and avoid common pitfalls like premature convergence. These characteristics have made GWO highly effective across a wide range of optimization tasks. In the context of WSNs, where complex issues such as energy efficiency, coverage optimization, and node deployment demand robust and flexible solutions, GWO has emerged as one of the most widely used metaheuristic algorithms.

Given the advantages of GWO and its increasing use in WSNs, this chapter aims to provide a comprehensive review of the different applications of GWO and its variants in this domain. It explores how the algorithm has been adapted and extended to address a wide range of WSN-related problems, focusing on five key areas: cluster-based routing, fault tolerance, localization, intrusion detection, and coverage optimization. Fig. 20.1 offers an overview of the most widely adopted GWO applications across various WSN domains, summarized as follows:

- *Cluster-based routing*: Cluster-based routing improves energy efficiency and scalability in WSNs by grouping nodes into clusters, each led by a Cluster Head (CH). CHs aggregate and forward data to the Base Station (BS), significantly reducing communication overhead and conserving node energy. This hierarchical structure supports effective resource management and prolongs network lifetime [4,5].
- *Fault tolerance*: Fault tolerance ensures WSN reliability despite failures or environmental changes through error detection, diagnosis, and recovery. It involves three key stages: error detection, error diagnosis, and error recovery. Techniques include redundancy with spare nodes, clustering-based recovery, distributed error handling, and AI-powered methods. These approaches enhance network resilience, maintain service availability, and prolong system uptime in unpredictable conditions [6].
- *Localization*: Localization is vital for determining sensor positions in WSNs, essential for spatially-aware applications. Techniques include range-based (e.g., received signal strength indicator (RSSI), time of arrival (ToA)), range-free (e.g., hop count), and hybrid approaches that combine both for improved accuracy. Accurate localization supports functions like tracking and environmental monitoring, especially in large or dynamic networks [7,8].
- *Intrusion detection*: Intrusion detection systems (IDSs) protect WSNs from a wide range of security threats such as spoofing, denial of service, and routing attacks, which are especially concerning due to the unattended and resource-constrained nature of these networks. IDS approaches are typically classified into signature-based methods, which detect

Grey Wolf Optimizer. DOI: https://doi.org/10.1016/B978-0-443-36624-6.00035-4

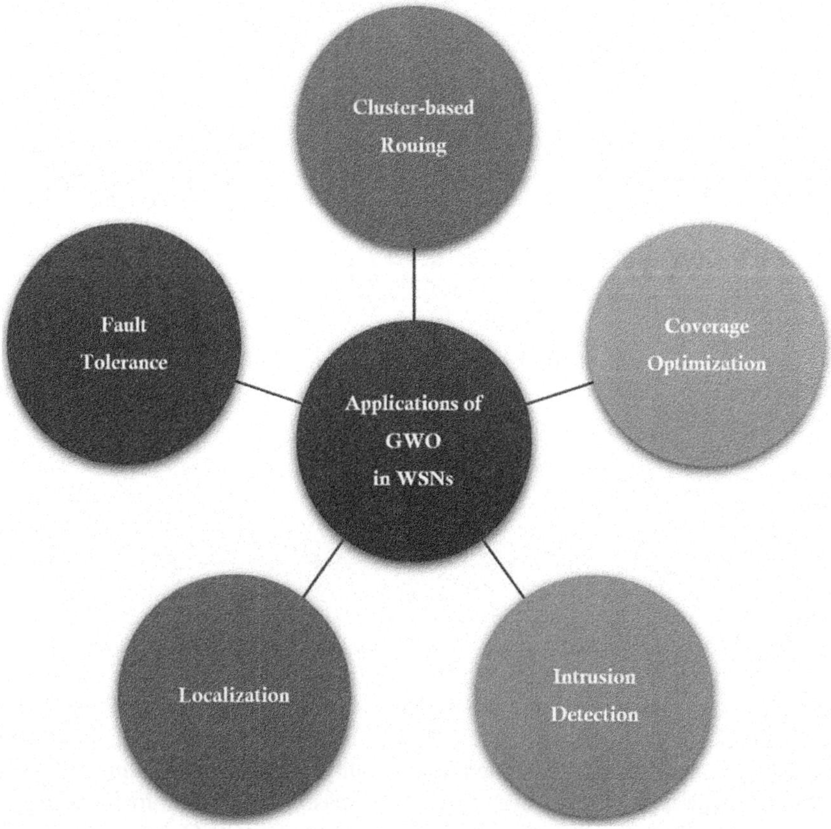

FIGURE 20.1 Comprehensive overview of GWO applications across various WSN domains (*GWO*, Grey wolf optimizer; *WSN*, wireless sensor networks).

known attack patterns, and anomaly-based methods, which flag deviations from normal network behavior. While signature-based systems are efficient in identifying known threats, anomaly-based systems are crucial for detecting novel or previously unseen attacks [9,10].

- *Coverage optimization*: Coverage optimization aims to maximize the area monitored by sensor nodes while minimizing energy consumption. Depending on the application, it involves either area coverage (monitoring the entire region) or target coverage (monitoring specific critical points). Techniques include optimization algorithms (e.g., GWO), geometry-based methods (e.g., Voronoi diagrams), scheduling strategies, and hybrid models. These approaches improve monitoring efficiency and extend network lifetime [11,12].

This chapter begins with an introduction to each of the aforementioned WSN domains, summarizing their mechanisms, methods, and features. The characteristics of each method are analyzed and categorized based on solution-based and network-based parameters, presented in tabular form. Following this, a detailed discussion on GWO and its applications in each identified domain will be provided. Through this exploration, we aspire to contribute to the growing body of knowledge on the application of metaheuristic algorithms, particularly GWO, in WSNs, offering valuable insights for researchers and practitioners in the field.

20.2 Classification metrics

This section provides a comprehensive overview of advanced applications of GWO and its variants in various WSN domains, including clustering, fault tolerance, localization, intrusion detection, and coverage optimization. Existing approaches within each category are analyzed based on network parameters and solution parameters, considering different types of GWO, such as standard GWO, multiobjective GWO, and its hybridization with other AI-based techniques. Each GWO-based technique is evaluated considering the specific decision variables of the problem and its objective function(s). Solution parameters include operational mode, operational state, modeling approach, objective(s), and key objective

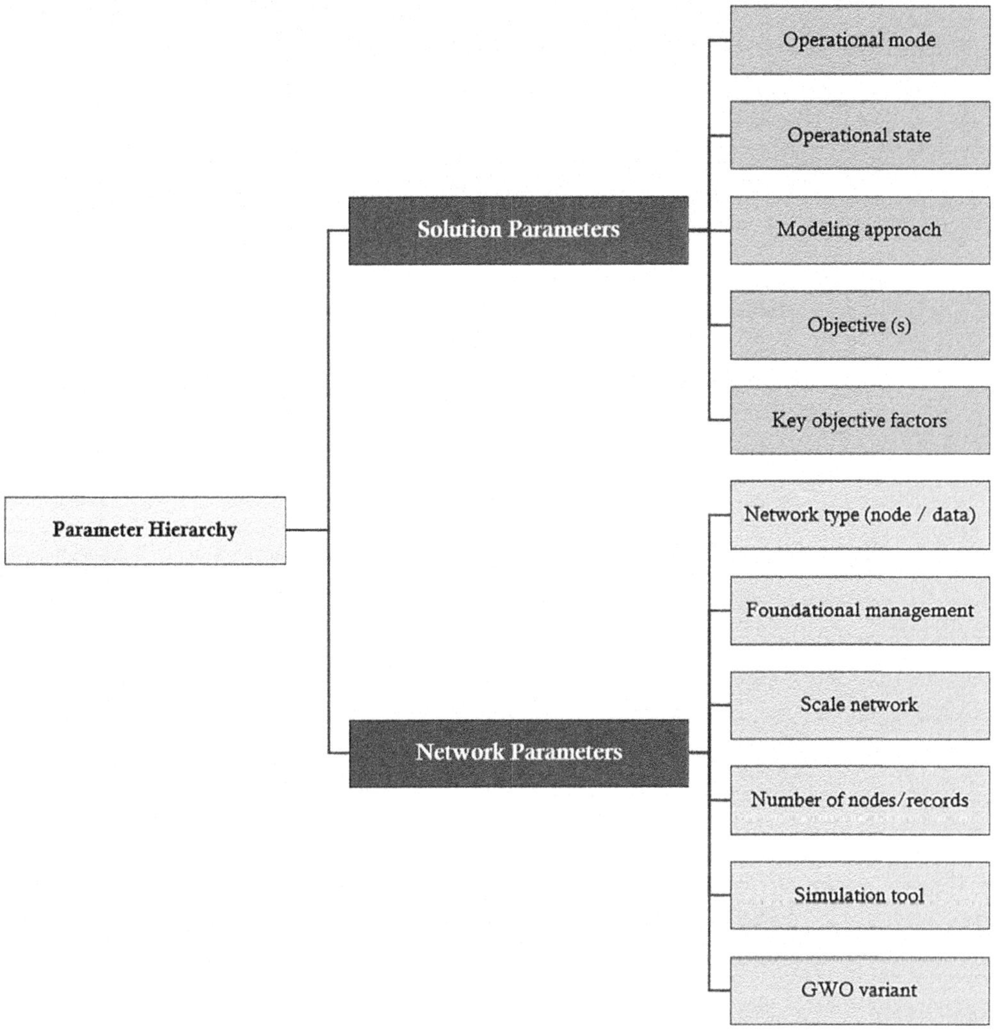

FIGURE 20.2 Parameter hierarchy for evaluating GWO performance in WSNs (*GWO*, Grey wolf optimizer; *WSN*, wireless sensor networks).

factors, while network parameters focus on method, network type (node/data), foundational management approach, network scale, number of nodes/records, simulation tool, and GWO variant. Fig. 20.2 illustrates the parameters of each approach.

20.3 Grey wolf optimizer-based clustering techniques

This section explores the application of GWO and its variants to enhance clustering in WSNs. Clustering, a key technique in WSNs, organizes nodes into groups to improve energy efficiency and scalability. By assigning specific nodes as CHs to gather and transmit data to the BS, clustering reduces energy usage and extends network lifetime [4,5]. This structure also supports more efficient data routing and resource management. Tables 20.1 and 20.2 compare the discussed methods based on solution characteristics and network performance metrics, respectively.

In Ref. [13], two GWO-based approaches were proposed: Distance-Based Stable Connected Dominating Set using GWO (DBSCDS-GWO) and Distance-Based Stable Clustering using GWO (DBSC-GWO). These aim to build stable, energy-efficient networks by optimizing the dominator node and CH selection. DBSCDS-GWO introduces the dominator lifetime index (DLI) to balance load by minimizing its variation across the network, while DBSC-GWO uses a similar CH lifetime index (CLI) to distribute energy usage evenly. Both algorithms seek to reduce energy waste by minimizing transmission distances and ensuring uniform energy distribution among nodes.

Further advancing the application of GWO in WSNs, Ref. [14] proposed the GWO-based Cluster Head (GWO-CH) selection method. The GWO-CH is a CH selection method that considers residual energy, intracluster distance, and

TABLE 20.1 Comparative analysis of clustering techniques in WSNs: Solution parameters.

Method	Year	Operational mode – state	Modeling approach	Objective (s)	Key objective factors
DBSCDS-GWO [13]	2019	Online – Centralized	Multiconvert to single	Reducing the effective transmission distance to the sink and balancing the network load.	CH-to-sink distance SN-to-CH distance SN-to-sink distance Energy consumption
GWO-CH [14]	2020	Online – Centralized	Multiconvert to single	Choosing a more suitable CH for energy management.	Intracluster distance Node-to-CH distance Residual energy of CHs
GWO-C [15]	2020	Online – Centralized	Multiconvert to single	Choosing the right CH to increase network longevity.	Intracluster distance Average sink distance Residual energy CH balancing factor
HGWSFO [16]	2021	Online – N/A	Multiconvert to single	Balancing exploration and exploitation while increasing network longevity.	Average member-to-CH distance per cluster size Energy ratio: alive nodes to CHs (current round)
GWLBC [17]	2022	Online – N/A	Multiconvert to single	Minimize the load on the CHs while ensuring efficient network operation and sustainability.	Threshold of SN-to-CH distances Disjoint set Traffic load of a CH
OGWO [18]	2022	Online – Centralized	Multiconvert to single	Increase network efficiency by selecting optimal CHs while balancing exploitation and exploration.	Residual energy of the CH Distance among nodes CH-to-sink distance Node degree Node centrality
EOAMRCL [19]	2024	Online – Centralized	Multiconvert to single	Enhancing transmission capacity, routing paths, and energy efficiency.	Intercluster distance Intracluster distance Remaining energy of CH
CH-GWO [20]	2024	Online – Centralized	Multiconvert to single	Maximizing network lifetime.	SN-to-CH distance CH-to-sink distance Residual energy Transmission energy

proximity to the BS. CH candidates are modeled as m-dimensional agents, and the algorithm identifies the top three candidates (α, β, δ) to guide others in refining their positions. Utilizing these three optimal solutions, the other search agents update their positions, leading to the identification of new CHs that satisfy the objective function. A weight function then determines suitable cluster members based on the objective function.

In Ref. [15], a modified GWO approach named GWO-C was introduced for CH election. This method aims to prolong the network's lifespan by strategically selecting CHs based on multiple parameters, including average intracluster distance, sink distance, residual energy, and a newly introduced CH balancing factor. The GWO-C protocol initiates by enabling all sensor nodes to relay their precise location and remaining energy to the BS. The BS subsequently executes the GWO-based clustering protocol, utilizing a fitness function that incorporates the aforementioned parameters to ensure optimal CH selection. Following the CH election, non-CH nodes identify and connect to the nearest CHs, facilitating effective cluster formation through a request and acceptance messaging system.

Building on the principles of GWO, Ref. [16] presented a novel hybrid algorithm, the hybrid GWO-based sunflower optimization (HGWSFO). This method is designed to optimize CH selection in WSNs while considering constraints such as energy consumption and separation distance. It combines GWO's exploitation capability with sunflower optimization (SFO)'s global search using a step-size mechanism. Specifically, SFO is applied when the fitness index is below five,

TABLE 20.2 Comparative analysis of clustering techniques in WSNs: Network parameters.

Method	Network type (node/data)	Foundational management	Scale network	Number of nodes/records	Simulation tool	GWO variant
DBSCDS-GWO [13]	Homogeneous	Clustering	Area=100 m^2 BS=(50,50)	100	Netsim and MATLAB	Standard GWO
GWO-CH [14]	Homogeneous	Clustering	Area=300 m^2 BS=(150–400, 150–400)	400–700	MATLAB	Standard GWO
GWO-C [15]	Homogeneous	Clustering	Area=100 m^2 BS=(50,50), corner, outside	100	MATLAB	Improved GWO
HGWSFO [16]	Homogeneous	Clustering	Area=200 m^2 BS=(150–400, 150–400)	100 BS=N/A	MATLAB	Hybrid GWO
GWLBC [17]	Heterogeneo-us	Clustering	Area=500 m^2 BS=(500,250)	500	MATLAB	Improved GWO
OGWO [18]	Homogeneous	Clustering	Area=200 m^2 BS=(0,0) (50,50), (100,100), (150,150)	100–400	MATLAB	Hybrid GWO
EOAMRCL [19]	Homogeneous	Clustering	Area=100 m^2 BS=(90,90)	50–250	MATLAB	Standard GWO
CH-GWO [20]	Homogeneous	Clustering	Area=100 m^2, 200 m^2 BS=(0,0), (50,50), (50,150), (100,100), (100,300)	100,200	MATLAB	Standard GWO

while GWO is utilized for higher indices. The method dynamically chooses between the two based on a fitness index, improving energy efficiency through adaptive exploration and exploitation.

A GWO-based Load-Balanced Clustering (GWLBC) approach was presented in Ref. [17]. It introduces a performance matrix that considers dead nodes, inactive CHs, energy usage, network lifetime, and convergence rate. Designed for heterogeneous WSNs, the method mathematically formulates load balancing among CHs and considers communication energy costs due to signal loss and multipath fading. The refined performance metrics not only facilitate improved communication among sensor nodes but also enhance area coverage, thereby contributing to increased user satisfaction. Furthermore, this research considers a heterogeneous model of WSNs, wherein disjoint sets of sensors are organized into clusters.

A framework for optimal CH selection was presented in [18]. It presents a hybrid technique combining Opposition-based learning with GWO (OGWO). It improves CH selection by balancing exploration and exploitation using four key metrics: energy, distance, node centrality, and degree. The OGWO algorithm aims to improve the search capabilities of GWO, particularly in the context of optimal CH selection within a network. The OGWO method initializes the population through the OBL technique, generating a diverse set of solutions within predetermined search limits. Subsequently, the positions of the wolves are updated using the conventional GWO procedures, while the OBL framework creates opposing counterparts for each wolf. This dual mechanism effectively balances intensification and diversification throughout the search process for optimal CHs.

The Energy Optimization Approach based on MAC/Routing Cross-Layer (EOAMRCL) protocol [19] focuses on energy optimization by integrating medium access control (MAC) and routing layers in a centralized clustering framework. The EOAMRCL employs a centralized approach, managing all processes at the BS. During the handover phase, nodes alternate between active and sleep states using network allocation vector time slots, enabling the MAC layer to generate a duty cycle schedule informed by multilayer routing information. Furthermore, the integration of a carrier sense multiple access with collision avoidance (CSMA/CA) mechanism, along with sleep and active modes, enhances the protocol's energy efficiency by more effectively managing node activity.

Finally, Ref. [20] introduced CH-GWO, a protocol designed to maximize network lifetime. This approach employs a modified GWO algorithm to select optimal CHs. It uses a modified GWO with a fitness function based on various attributes, including CH coverage, residual energy, and various distance metrics, while beneficial attributes (e.g., energy) are weighted more heavily than nonbeneficial ones. The CH selection process is performed centrally at the BS, which receives location and energy information from all nodes. The GWO algorithm then operates on the defined fitness function to identify the optimal CH set. The BS centrally selects optimal CHs, and nodes form clusters using Euclidean distance and communicate via CSMA MAC.

20.4 Grey wolf optimizer-based fault tolerance techniques

With the growing use of WSNs, there is a clear need for strong fault detection and tolerance systems to keep things running smoothly. These networks often consist of devices that are limited in power and scattered across wide areas, which makes it tough to maintain consistent performance and accurate data. Fault tolerance plays a crucial role in making sure WSNs stay reliable, even when some nodes fail or unexpected issues arise. This is made possible through strategies such as adding redundancy, using resilient routing protocols, and building self-healing capabilities into the network. In real-world conditions, having such mechanisms in place ensures the network can keep functioning without major disruptions. When something does go wrong, fault tolerance systems typically go through three key steps:

- *Error detection*: Spotting issues like malfunctioning nodes or missing data packets.
- *Error diagnosis*: Figuring out what caused the problem.
- *Error recovery*: Fixing the issue, whether by replacing broken components or finding a new path to send data.

Various fault tolerance methods are used in WSNs to ensure reliability and robustness. Clustering-based fault tolerance techniques organize the network into clusters managed by CHs, which allow other nodes to take over if a CH fails. Distributed approaches spread error detection and recovery across multiple nodes, reducing individual load and enhancing scalability. AI-based methods use algorithms like neural networks and genetic algorithms to detect and recover from errors, adapting well to dynamic, resource-constrained environments [6].

Tables 20.3 and 20.4 provide a comparative analysis of solution parameters and network configuration characteristics for these approaches. In the first reviewed technique [21], an Internet of Things (IoT) fault detection method, GWO-SVM, was proposed. This approach integrates support vector machines (SVM) for feature extraction and classification with the GWO to select the most relevant features and eliminate redundancy. The GWO aims to maximize classification accuracy,

TABLE 20.3 Comparative analysis of fault tolerance techniques in WSNs: Solution parameters.

Method	Year	Operational mode – state	Modeling approach	Objective (s)	Key objective factors
GWO-SVM [21]	2021	Offline – Centralized	Multiconvert to single	Enhance fault detection by optimizing feature selection using SVM and GWO.	Classification accuracy Selected feature length
FRGNWS [22]	2022	Online – Centralized	Multiconvert to single	Improving population searches by replacing the least efficient results. Additionally, it aims to identify the optimal node-disjoint path by selecting the best option from a set of k-node-disjoint paths for routing from the source node to the BS.	Remaining available energy of the SNs Distance of the edge Energy consumption of the edge Delay in communication for the node Relay hops Reliability index Number of RNs Number of node-disjoint routes
FAGWO-H [23]	2022	Online – Centralized (clustering, routing) & Distributed (fault tolerance)	Multiconvert to single	To enhance the reliability and lifetime of WSNs by introducing a hybrid metaheuristic approach combining FA-based clustering and GWO-based routing.	Load on CHs Average distance value Residual energy of CHs Distance between CHs Number of intermediate hops Link quality
FTSS [24]	2022	Online – Centralized in CHs)	Multiconvert to single	Enhancing target tracking and optimizing energy consumption through dynamic scheduling within a fault-tolerant domain.	Residual energy Sensing coverage Overlapping sensing area
EWFAIGF [25]	2024	Online – Hybrid	Multi attribute (Fuzzy) and Single and Multi (reinforcement learning)	Enhancing IoT WSN Performance through Energy-Efficient Routing and Fault Tolerance using Fuzzy AHP, GWJFO, and Q-Learning	Node location Energy consumption of nodes Temporal performance (Delay) Path length Distance to destination Fault avoidance Data transmission efficiency Number of hops

TABLE 20.4 Comparative analysis of fault tolerance techniques in WSNs: Network parameters.

Method	Network type (node/data)	Foundational management	Scale network	Number of nodes	Simulation tool	GWO variant
GWO-SVM [21]	N/A	N/A	Area=N/A BS=N/A	26 (671 records)	N/A	Standard GWO
FRGNWS [22]	Homogeneous	Routing	Area=400 m^2, 600 m^2, 800 m^2, 1000 m^2 BS=center	25, 35, 45, 55, 65	NS.2	Hybrid GWO
FAGWO-H [23]	Heterogeneous	Clustering and routing	Area=200 m^2, 500 m^2 BS=(300, 150), (250, 250)	100–500	MATLAB	Hybrid GWO
FTSS [24]	Homogeneous	Cluster-based routing	Area=500 m^2 BS=(250, 250)	1500	MATLAB	Improved GWO
EWFAIG [25]	Homogeneous	Clustering and routing	Area=1000 m^2 BS=N/A	50–500	NS-3	Hybrid GWO

evaluating the selected features for the SVM classifier. A fitness function is employed by GWO to balance classification accuracy and the size of the selected feature set relative to the total number of features.

Addressing the unique challenges of energy harvesting WSNs (EH-WSNs), Ref. [22] introduced the fault-tolerant and reliable green communication framework (FRGNWS). This framework operates in two distinct phases, utilizing hybrid optimization techniques to manage the dynamic nature of node activity in EH-WSNs. The first phase employs the hybrid adapted grey wolf sine cosine optimizer to identify maximum node-disjoint routes from sensor nodes to the BS, thereby minimizing the number of required relay nodes (RN) and enhancing network fault tolerance. The second phase employs the hybrid adapted GWO to select the most reliable route from the k-node-disjoint paths identified in the first phase. This selection process considers multiple objective functions, including energy consumption, communication delay, and reliability indices.

Considering the inherent vulnerability of WSNs to various failures, including topology changes, battery depletion, and communication module breakdowns, [23] presented a fault-tolerant cluster-based routing protocol. This protocol utilizes a hybrid algorithm, FAGWO-H, which combines the firefly algorithm (FA) and GWO. First, clustering is performed based on critical parameters such as energy balancing among CHs and the average distance between sensor nodes, CHs, and the BS. Subsequently, GWO is employed to determine the optimal routing path from CHs to the BS, considering factors such as residual energy, distance, hop count, and link quality. This method incorporates a fault model based on the Weibull distribution to analyze the probability of node failures over time.

Furthermore, target tracking in WSNs, a critical application often reliant on node scheduling based on trajectory prediction, faces challenges due to prediction errors. These errors can lead to target loss, triggering energy-intensive recovery mechanisms and potentially resulting in data loss. To mitigate these issues, Ref. [24] proposed a fault-tolerant sensor scheduling (FTSS) approach designed to minimize target loss probability and reduce energy consumption. Within this fault-tolerant domain, FTSS employs a low-power scheduling mechanism considering residual energy, sensing coverage, and overlapping coverage as decision factors for node activation. An improved binary GWO (BGWO), incorporating mutation, elimination, and replacement mechanisms, is utilized to efficiently select the optimal tracking node set based on a fitness function that balances tracking quality and network lifetime.

To overcome the limitations of conventional methods in dynamic, resource-constrained environments, the iterative grey wolf jellyfish optimization (EWFAIGF) [25], which integrates the fuzzy analytic hierarchy process (Fuzzy AHP) with Iterative grey wolf jellyfish optimization (GWJFO), aims to improve network lifespan and data transmission reliability. Initially, Fuzzy AHP is employed for multicriteria clustering based on node location, energy efficiency, and temporal performance, effectively grouping similar nodes. Subsequently, EWFAIGF uses GWJFO to determine optimal routing paths within and between the generated clusters, with the core objective of minimizing energy consumption along these paths. To further enhance network robustness and fault tolerance, EWFAIGF integrates a Q-Learning-based mechanism that proactively identifies potential faults and dynamically switches to alternate routing paths using a "Make Before Break" strategy.

20.5 Grey wolf optimizer-based localization techniques

Localization represents another critical facet of WSNs, as it involves determining the physical locations of sensor nodes. Accurate localization is vital for applications such as target tracking, environmental monitoring, and disaster management, where the spatial context of the data is of utmost importance. Generally, localization techniques can be categorized into three types:

- *Range-based localization*: Range-based techniques in WSNs rely on physical measurements such as distance or angle to estimate the positions of sensor nodes. These methods typically use metrics like RSSI, ToA, time difference of arrival, or angle of arrival to calculate the relative or absolute positions of nodes. The accuracy of range-based localization depends on the precision of these measurements, which can be affected by environmental factors such as signal attenuation, multipath fading, and obstacles.
- *Range-free localization*: Range-free techniques do not rely on precise distance or angle measurements. Instead, they use connectivity information, hop counts, or proximity data to estimate the positions of sensor nodes. These methods are less accurate than range-based techniques but are more suitable for large-scale networks and resource-constrained environments where precise measurements are difficult to obtain.
- *Hybrid localization*: Hybrid techniques combine the strengths of both range-based and range-free methods to improve the accuracy and reliability of node positioning in WSNs. These approaches integrate multiple sources of information, such as distance measurements, connectivity data, and environmental constraints, to achieve more robust localization results [7,8].

Among the existing methods, metaheuristic algorithms, particularly the GWO algorithm, have gained significant attention due to their effectiveness in solving localization problems in WSNs, as detailed in Tables 20.5 and 20.6. In Ref. [26], a novel localization method, termed GWO-LPWSN (GWO for node Localization Problem in WSNs), applies a GWO algorithm to determine the geographical coordinates of unknown nodes. The GWO-LPWSN method involves randomly initializing the positions of unknown nodes and anchor nodes within the communication range. By iteratively updating the positions of unknown nodes based on information obtained from anchor nodes, the algorithm converges toward an optimal solution. The performance of GWO-LPWSN is evaluated based on localization error and the number of nonlocalized nodes.

Building upon the use of GWO for localization, Ref. [27] presented a Multiobjective GWO (MOGWO)-localization algorithm, termed as MOGWOLA, for optimizing sensor node placement in smart parking systems. The MOGWOLA algorithm addresses this multiobjective optimization problem by considering two primary objectives: minimizing localization error and optimizing network topology. The algorithm aims to reduce the discrepancy between the estimated and actual positions of sensor nodes by minimizing the distance between a sensor node and its neighboring anchor nodes and ensuring consistency with received signal strength measurements.

In the context of the increasing prevalence of smart IoT applications, the reliable deployment of WSNs is paramount, especially for critical applications such as health monitoring and industrial control. Addressing this challenge, [28] introduced a quality of service-aware GWO-based node deployment (QGND) to maximize coverage and connectivity while minimizing the network's overall cost. A key contribution of QGND is its multiobjective function that simultaneously: (1) minimizes the number of deployed nodes to reduce costs; (2) minimizes the total distance to the BS to lower energy use and extend network life; (3) maximizes target coverage for reliability; and (4) maximizes connectivity by ensuring each node connects to at least q others for robust data forwarding.

Furthermore, addressing the trade-off between energy consumption and localization accuracy, Ref. [29] presented a double anchor SCAN (DASCAN) path and a multiple disturbance strategy GWO (MDS-GWO) algorithm. The DASCAN path optimizes the movement of two mobile anchors, dividing the region of interest into grids and ensuring that each unknown node has at least three neighboring virtual anchors forming an equilateral triangle. This configuration enhances localization accuracy while minimizing the number of beacons and path length. The objective function of this method is to minimize the Euclidean distance between the estimated and actual positions of unknown nodes, considering the distances measured from multiple virtual anchors.

Another promising approach is the GWO-RSS algorithm, proposed in Ref. [30]. This method utilizes a GWO algorithm to estimate the positions of unknown nodes in a WSN by exploiting the radio signal strength (RSS) measurements. The GWO-RSS algorithm iteratively updates the estimated positions of nodes until a convergence criterion is met. By minimizing the Euclidean distance between the estimated position of an unknown node and its neighboring anchor nodes, GWO-RSS addresses the challenges posed by noise and uncertainties inherent in RSS measurements.

Addressing the limitations of Global Positioning System (GPS) deployment in indoor, underwater, or large-scale scenarios due to cost and energy constraints, Ref. [31] proposed an enhanced algorithm based on GWO, termed repulsion-based GWO (R-GWO). In this method, a primary anchor node resides at the highest level, while target nodes are distributed across lower levels. When a target node falls within the coverage range of an anchor, three additional virtual anchors are projected around the target node, along with the original anchor. This technique facilitates more accurate target node localization in 3D space and mitigates line-of-sight issues.

To address the limitations of traditional localization methods, Ref. [32] proposed an improved GWO with communication strategy (IGWO-CS). The objective function of IGWO-CS minimizes the sum of squared errors between estimated and actual distances between nodes, considering factors such as the reciprocal of the minimum number of hops and constraints on node positions. This approach effectively mitigates the challenges posed by nonlinear error accumulation in multihop propagation, thereby improving the accuracy and robustness of localization results.

Optimizing the placement of signal receiving stations for target localization has also become a focal point. A significant contribution in this area was presented in Ref. [33], where the authors propose a methodology termed GWO for station placement (GWO-SP) to enhance the strategic placement of these stations within a defined region. The authors develop a regional target localization error model that accounts for all potential target locations within the defined area. This model facilitates the calculation of overall localization error by minimizing the trace of the Cramér-Rao Lower Bound matrix associated with regional error, enabling the determination of optimal station placements. The study employs a GWO algorithm to tackle the resulting nonconvex optimization problem.

While range-free techniques like DV-Hop are preferred for their low complexity, sensor deployments in harsh environments can lead to node failures, requiring additional target nodes. To address this challenge, Ref. [34] proposed a novel localization method termed GWO DV-Hop, which combines the advantages of the traditional DV-Hop algorithm

TABLE 20.5 Comparative analysis of localization techniques in WSNs: Solution parameters.

Method	Year	Operational mode – state	Modeling approach	Objective (s)	Key objective factors
GWO-LPWSN [26]	2017	Online – Distributed	Single	Improving the accuracy of node localization by minimizing the localization error using GWO.	Distance measurements Number of anchor nodes Communication range Estimated distance
MOGWOLA [27]	2020	Online – Distributed	Multi (Pareto optimal)	Minimizing localization error and maximizing network connectivity in smart parking systems.	Number of target and anchor nodes Distance between the target and the anchor node Estimated node coordinates Anchor node coordinates
QGND [28]	2021	Offline – Centralized	Multiconvert to single	Maximizing coverage and connectivity while minimizing deployment costs and energy consumption.	Distance to the BS Target coverage Total number of target points Connectivity of the SNs Total appropriate positions to deploy SNs
MDS-GWO and DASCAN [29]	2022	Offline – Distributed	Single	Minimizing the squared error between estimated and measured distances to virtual anchors.	Estimated node coordinates Anchor node coordinates Measured distance Number of neighboring
GWO-RSS [30]	2023	Online – Distributed	Single	Minimizing the localization error by estimating the positions of unknown nodes based on RSS measurements and the positions of neighboring anchor nodes.	Euclidean distance Number of anchor nodes Noise in RSS measurements Number of locations of unknown nodes
R-GWO [31]	2023	N/A – Centralized	Single	Enhancing 3D localization accuracy with a parasol projection framework and virtual anchors to reduce line-of-sight issues and minimize the distance between estimated and actual target positions.	Distance between estimated and actual target node positions Distance between the estimated target node position and the beacon node positions Number of beacons
IGWO-CS [32]	2024	Offline – N/A	Multiconvert to single	Optimizing node placement in WSNs to minimize localization error through an IGWO-based optimization approach.	Number of hops Unknown node coordinates Anchor node coordinates Actual distance Maximum distance
GWO-SP [33]	2024	Online – Centralized	Single	Optimizing the placement of receiving stations and minimizing the localization error of targets.	CRLB matrix (Cramer-Rao Lower Bound) Mean squared error of localization in the entire target region
GWO DV-Hop [34]	2024	Online – Centralized	Single	Improving localization accuracy and energy efficiency by optimizing the location estimation of target nodes.	Localization accuracy Distance to anchor nodes Number of hops

TABLE 20.6 Comparative analysis of localization techniques in WSNs: Network parameters.

Method	Network type (node/data)	Foundational management	Scale network	Number of nodes/ records	Simulation tool	GWO variant
GWO-LPWSN [26]	N/A (unknown nodes and anchor nodes)/ Heterogeneous	Localization	Area=300 m^2 BS=N/A Anchor=100	300	MATLAB	Standard GWO
MOGWOLA [27]	N/A (unknown nodes and anchor nodes)/ Heterogeneous	Localization	Area=100 m^2 BS=N/A Anchor=20–60	200	N/A	Multiobjective GWO
QGND [28]	Homogeneous	(Deployment management)	Area=500 m^2 BS=(250, 250) Target=15–150	50–500	MATLAB	Standard GWO
MDS-GWO& DASCAN [29]	N/A (unknown nodes and anchor nodes)/ Heterogeneous	Grid (Localization)	Area=100 m^2 BS=N/A Anchor=2(mobile)	100	MATLAB	Improved GWO
GWO-RSS [30]	N/A (unknown nodes and anchor nodes)/ Heterogeneous	Localization	Area=1000 m^2 BS=N/A Anchor=10	100	MATLAB	Standard GWO
R-GWO [31]	Heterogeneous	Localization	Area=N/A BS=N/A Anchor=6 Target=80	30–80	MATLAB	Improved GWO
IGWO-CS [32]	N/A (unknown nodes and anchor nodes)	Localization	Area=100 m^2 BS=N/A Anchor=10–40	100	N/A	Improved GWO
GWO-SP [33]	N/A	Localization	Area=(800,250) m^2, (1000,1000) m^2 BS=(350,25), (800,300), Target=1–600	600	N/A	Standard GWO
GWO DV-Hop [34]	N/A/(unknown nodes and anchor nodes)	Localization	Area=100–300 m^2 BS=N/A Anchor=10–60	100–350	MATLAB	Standard GWO

with the optimization capabilities of GWO. The primary objective of GWO DV-Hop is to minimize localization time and maximize energy efficiency by focusing exclusively on localizing the newly deployed target nodes rather than all sensor nodes in the network. A key feature of GWO DV-Hop is the introduction of a weighted hop size estimation. This approach assigns higher weights to anchor nodes that are in closer proximity to the unknown node, acknowledging their greater influence on accurate position estimation. These weights are calculated based on the hop counts between nodes, effectively reducing hop size error and improving localization accuracy.

20.6 Grey wolf optimizer-based intrusion detection techniques

Intrusion detection serves as a critical security mechanism in WSNs, aimed at identifying and mitigating unauthorized access or malicious activities. Given the open and often unsupervised nature of WSN deployments, these networks are particularly vulnerable to security threats. The process of intrusion detection in WSNs involves identifying unauthorized or malicious activities that may compromise network security. Generally, IDSs in WSNs can be classified into two categories:

- *Signature-based detection*: This method involves comparing known attack patterns (signatures) with observed network behavior. A match indicates the presence of an attack.
- *Anomaly-based detection*: This method models normal network behavior, treating any deviation from this established norm as an anomaly or potential attack.

Metaheuristic algorithms have gained traction in the realm of IDSs due to their effectiveness in solving complex and nonlinear optimization problems. These algorithms are typically employed to optimize model parameters, select optimal features, and reduce the false alarm rate in IDS. To address the challenges of high-dimensional data, computational complexity, and the need for accurate detection, several studies have explored hybrid feature selection methods utilizing the GWO algorithm. These methods aim to enhance the performance of IDSs by selecting the most informative features, reducing computational overhead, and improving detection accuracy.

Tables 20.7 and 20.8 compare key solution and simulation parameters for methods discussed in this section based on solution parameters and network parameters, respectively. The first approach, proposed in Ref. [35], introduces a lightweight and intelligent IoT-based IDS (IoTIDS) designed specifically for WSNs. This method employs a hybrid feature selection algorithm, GA-GWO, which combines the genetic algorithm (GA) and GWO to reduce the dimensionality of network traffic data by selecting the most relevant features for an SVM classifier. The objective function of GA-GWO directly aims to maximize classification accuracy while also considering other performance metrics such as detection rate, Precision (P), F1-score (F1), and false positive rate.

Further research, Ref. [36] proposed a lightweight IDS (LIDS) for resource-constrained WSNs. This study introduces a hybrid feature selection algorithm named GABGWO, combining GA and GWO, to enhance the performance of an SVM classifier by identifying the most informative traffic features. The fitness function of GABGWO directly considers the accuracy of the SVM classifier integrated with the selected features. This wrapper-based approach evaluates feature subsets by training and testing the SVM. Using the Aegean Wi-Fi Intrusion Dataset (AWID), the method demonstrated significant improvements in LIDS performance by selecting optimal features, reducing computational costs, and achieving higher detection accuracy compared to using all features and other feature selection methods.

Another study [37] presented an enhanced IDS for WSNs using a modified BGWO with SVM (GWOSVM-IDS). This research addresses the limitations of existing GWO-IDS methods by focusing on a multiobjective optimization problem to improve intrusion detection performance. GWOSVM-IDS employs two binarization techniques for GWO. This technique aims to maximize classification accuracy (detection rate) while minimizing the number of selected features. The multiobjective function of GWOSVM-IDS considers prediction accuracy, the number of selected features, and execution speed.

Building upon the use of modified GWO for feature selection, a subsequent study [38] proposed a novel IDS for WSNs by combining machine learning with a modified GWO (MLGWO) algorithm. Recognizing the vulnerability of WSNs, this study aims to enhance detection performance while minimizing resource consumption. The MLGWO algorithm employs a multiobjective fitness function that maximizes detection rate and accuracy while minimizing the false alarm rate, execution time, and the number of selected features.

Another study [39] presented an IDS methodology combining GWO and particle swarm optimization (PSO) for feature selection. This GWO-PSO approach gains the strengths of both algorithms to enhance feature selection and classification accuracy. GWO's exploitation capabilities are combined with PSO's exploration capabilities to improve the likelihood of identifying the globally optimal feature subset. The objective function maximizes detection rate and accuracy while minimizing the false alarm rate, the number of selected features, and execution time.

Addressing the increasing sophistication of cyber-attacks, a further approach [40] combined the GWO and long short-term memory (LSTM) network. This method focuses on enhancing intrusion detection performance through effective feature selection and classification. GWO is employed to select the most relevant features from network traffic data, reducing dimensionality to improve the efficiency and accuracy of the subsequent classification process. The selected features are then input into an LSTM network, a type of recurrent neural network suited for processing sequential data, which is trained to classify network traffic.

In Ref. [41], the MGWO-ELM-based IDS was proposed for improved intrusion detection. This approach addresses the limitations of traditional GWO by employing a smart initialization strategy combining filter and wrapper feature selection methods. The MGWO-ELM utilizes the information gain metric to evaluate feature significance, ensuring the incorporation of highly relevant features into the initial population. Furthermore, the extreme learning machine (ELM) is employed as the base classifier to reduce computational complexity. The MGWO algorithm also tunes the ELM's parameters.

TABLE 20.7 Comparative analysis of intrusion detection techniques in WSNs: Solution parameters.

Method	Year	Operational mode – state	Modeling approach	Objective (s)	Key objective factors
IoTIDS [35]	2020	Offline – Centralized	Single	Improving IDS performance using GA-GWO-based feature selection.	Number of selected Features Accuracy
GABGWO [36]	2020	Offline – Centralized	Single	Enhancing intrusion detection by developing a lightweight SVM and a hybrid feature selection algorithm.	Accuracy Feature subset size
GWOSVM-IDS [37]	2021	Offline – Centralized	Multiconvert to single	Optimizing feature selection and classification with a modified binary GWO-SVM approach.	Accuracy Number of selected features Execution time
MLGWO [38]	2021	Offline – Centralized	Multiconvert to single	Utilizing a modified GWO algorithm for feature selection and SVM classification to enhance the performance of IDS.	Execution time Number of selected features False alarm rate Detection rate
GWO-PSO [39]	2022	Offline – Centralized	Multiconvert to single	Improving IDS performance via hybrid GWO-PSO feature selection.	Detection rate Accuracy False alarm rate Number of selected features Execution time
GWO-LSTM [40]	2022	Online/Offline – Centralized	Multiconvert to single	Utilizing GWO for effective feature selection and employing LSTM for intrusion classification.	Accuracy Feature subset size
MGWO-ELM [41]	2022	Offline – Centralized	Multiconvert to single	Minimizing the crossover error rate while considering feature subset size for enhanced intrusion detection performance.	False positive rate False negative rate Ratio of selected features to all features Number of selected features Number of features in the original dataset
H-ELM-SCADA [42]	2023	Online – Centralized	Multiconvert to single	Enhancing IDS performance in SCADA systems by integrating a hybrid ensemble ELM and GWO.	Accuracy Detection rate Precision
QSVM-IGWO [43]	2024	Offline – Centralized	Multiconvert to single	Improving the accuracy of IDSs in IoT networks and reducing their false positive alarms.	Accuracy False alarm rate False positive rate Number of selected features

TABLE 20.8 Comparative analysis of intrusion detection techniques in WSNs: Network parameters.

Method	Network type (node/data)	Foundational management	Scale network	Number of nodes/ records	Simulation tool	GWO variant
IoTIDS [35]	Wi-Fi network	Feature selection	AWID dataset	1,795,575 records	Python & Java	Hybrid GWO
GABGWO [36]	Wi-Fi network	Feature selection	AWID dataset	1,795,575 records	Python & Java & WEKA	Hybrid GWO
GWOSVM-IDS [37]	Network traffic data	Feature selection	NSL-KDD'99 dataset	4,898,431 records	MATLAB	Improved GWO
MLGWO [38]	Network traffic data	Feature selection	NSL-KDD'99 dataset	4,898,431 records	MATLAB	Improved GWO
GWO-PSO [39]	Network traffic data	Feature selection	NSL-KDD dataset	148,517 records	MATLAB	Hybrid GWO
GWO-LSTM [40]	Network traffic data	Feature selection	NSL-KDD, UNSW-NB15 dataset	N/A	N/A	Standard GWO
MGWO-ELM [41]	Network traffic data	Feature selection	UNSW-NB15 dataset	257,673	MATLAB & Python	Improved GWO
H-ELM-SCADA [42]	– Generic traffic – CADA Water/Gas pipeline telemetry	Optimization of ELM parameters	– Water/Gas datasets – UNSW-NB15 dataset	2,540,044 records	N/A	Standard GWO
QSVM-IGWO [43]	N/A (IoT Network Traffic)	IGWO-based hyperparameter tuning of QSVM	Bot-IoT dataset	53,000,000 records	N/A	Improved GWO

Another study introduced an ensemble learning model for intrusion detection in supervisory control and data acquisition (SCADA) systems integrated with industrial sensor networks (ISNs) (H-ELM-SCADA) [42]. Recognizing the vulnerability of SCADA systems and the limitations of traditional IDSs, this research addresses the need for real-time, distributed, and generalizable anomaly detection. The proposed approach emphasizes enhancing classifier efficacy, particularly in accuracy, detection rate (DR), recall, and precision. The GWO algorithm optimizes the parameters of the H-ELM-SCADA models, including bagging, stacking, AdaBoost, and an ensemble of Naive Bayes and Support Vector Machine (NB+SVM) classifiers. The study prioritizes data preprocessing and feature dimensionality reduction using unit normalization and principal component analysis.

A further approach [43] proposed a hybrid IDS model, QSVM-IGWO, to improve IoT security by enhancing detection accuracy and reducing false positives. This model combines quantum support vector machine (QSVM) with IGWO, which optimizes QSVM hyperparameters to select the best kernel for binary classification. IGWO addresses standard GWO's issues like premature convergence by balancing exploration and exploitation. The model uses information gain for feature selection, and QSVM maps data into a high-dimensional quantum feature space with quantum kernels.

20.7 Grey wolf optimizer-based coverage optimization techniques

Random deployment of sensor nodes often leads to suboptimal coverage, high energy consumption, and network inefficiencies. Therefore coverage optimization techniques are used to maximize the monitored area of the sensor network while minimizing energy consumption. This involves the strategic placement and activation of sensor nodes to ensure comprehensive coverage without incurring unnecessary energy expenditure. In WSNs, coverage refers to the network's ability to monitor a specific area or target, which can be categorized into two main types:

- *Area coverage*: The objective is to cover the entire target area with sensor nodes. This approach necessitates a larger number of sensors and is utilized for applications such as monitoring expansive environments.
- *Target coverage*: This method focuses on covering specific points within the area, which may represent strategic targets or critical locations. It generally requires fewer sensors and is suitable for applications such as target tracking or monitoring designated points.

Several research efforts have aimed to boost the efficiency of GWO when applied to coverage optimization in WSNs. Tables 20.9 and 20.10 provide a comparative overview of these methods across solution-based and network-based metrics. The study in [44] introduced the node coverage optimization algorithm based on improved GWO (NCO-IGWO). This method focuses on refining GWO to better balance exploration and exploitation by introducing mechanisms such as a dynamic convergence factor, elite solution preservation, adaptive weighting of leader wolves, and a strategy for managing boundary positions.

Another method, named Virtual Force-Lévy-embedded GWO-VFLGWO [45], enhanced GWO by integrating Lévy flights for better search space exploration and a virtual force mechanism to encourage a more uniform sensor node distribution. This approach not only maximizes coverage and connectivity but also minimizes unnecessary sensor movements during deployment. Although it slightly increases computational time, the gains in network performance make it worthwhile.

To overcome GWO's limitations in escaping local optima, [46] proposed a hybrid approach combining GWO with simulated annealing (SA), termed SA-GWO. This method enhances the global search capability of GWO by incorporating the SA mechanism after the siege behavior of the wolves. By allowing occasional acceptance of worse solutions, the method improves the search process and leads to more effective coverage, energy efficiency, and balanced node distribution. It also adopts a probability-aware coverage model for better accuracy.

For directional WSNs, Ref. [47] reformulated the k-coverage problem into a discrete optimization challenge and adapted GWO accordingly. addresses the k-coverage problem in directional sensor networks by formulating it as a discrete optimization problem. It proposes a discrete GWO algorithm (D-GWA) that incorporates tailored exploration and exploitation procedures for discrete search spaces. The approach includes discrete operators for efficient search, a matrix-based solution encoding, and a simulated annealing-inspired acceptance rule. These additions support battery-efficient deployment and promote longer network lifetimes.

Building upon these efforts to optimize coverage and considering the dynamic nature of mle WSNs, Ref. [48] proposed an energy-efficient coverage algorithm that focuses on the optimal placement of mobile sensor nodes. This method combines GWO and Virtual Force algorithm (GWOVF) to address the challenge of decreased coverage rates arising from the random deployment of mobile sensor nodes. This hybrid method identifies optimal sensor placements across a

TABLE 20.9 Comparative analysis of coverage techniques in WSNs: Solution parameters.

Method	Year	Operational mode – state	Modeling approach	Objective (s)	Key objective factors
NCO-IGWO [44]	2019	Online – N/A	Multiconvert to single	Optimizing resource utilization involves maximizing coverage while minimizing node deployment.	Sensing radius Communication radius Sensor node coordinates Monitoring point coordinates Distance from node to monitoring point
VFLGWO [45]	2019	Online – N/A	Multiconvert to single	Maximize coverage, ensure uniform node distribution, and minimize energy consumption.	Coverage rate (Ratio of covered grids to the total number of grids in the monitoring area) Average moving distance of sensor nodes
SA-GWO [46]	2021	Online – Centralized	Single	Optimizing node placement to maximize network coverage.	Coverage rate (Ratio of the area of pixels covered by all nodes to the total area)
D-GWA [47]	2023	Online – N/A	Multiconvert to single	Maximize energy efficiency and lifetime through efficient time interval determination.	Battery usage Residual battery usage Overlap in coverage provided by the sensors
GWOVF [48]	2023	Online – Centralized	Multiconvert to single	Increasing coverage and extending the network lifetime in Mobile WSNs.	Coverage rate Intracluster distance Remaining energy of nodes Number of nodes Number of clusters
ALGWO [49]	2024	Online – Centralized	Multiconvert to single	Maximizing the coverage area while minimizing overlaps among sensor nodes	Ratio of covered grids to all grids in 3D space Ratio of covered grids to all grids in the area Number of grid points Position coordinates of the nodes
MSGWO [50]	2024	Online – N/A	Multiconvert to single	Maximize coverage, minimize energy consumption, ensure network connectivity, and cost-effective deployment.	All nodes in the monitoring area Connectivity The monitoring area node set Total energy consumed by active nodes
EECMIGWO [51]	2024	Online – N/A	Multiconvert to single	Maximizing energy efficiency while ensuring complete coverage of target points.	Sensor-to-target distance Critical and maximum sensing ranges
IGWO-MS [52]	2024	Online – N/A	Multiconvert to single	Maximize the percentage of the monitoring area effectively covered by deployed sensors.	Monitoring area node coordinates

TABLE 20.10 Comparative analysis of coverage techniques in WSNs: Network parameters.

Method	Network type (node/data)	Foundational management	Scale network	Number of nodes/records	Simulation tool	GWO variant
NCO-IGWO [44]	Homogeneous	N/A	Area=2500 m^2, 2300 m^2, 2050 m^2 BS=N/A	20–60	MATLAB	Improved GWO
VFLGWO [45]	N/A	Grid	Area=40 m^2, 50 m^2, 60 m^2 BS=N/A	40–60	MATLAB	Improved GWO and Hybrid GWO
SA-GWO [46]	Homogeneous	Grid	Area=100 m^2 BS=N/A	50	MATLAB	Hybrid GWO
D-GWA [47]	Homogeneous	N/A	Area=1000 m^2 BS=N/A	100–500	MATLAB	Improved GWO
GWOVF [48]	Homogeneous	Cluster-based routing	Area=100 m^2 BS=N/A	100	MATLAB	Hybrid GWO
ALGWO [49]	N/A	Grid	Area=1000m^2, 50 m^3 BS=N/A	30,40	MATLAB	Improved GWO
MSGWO [50]	Homogeneous	Clustering	Area=2500 m^2, 50 m^2 BS=N/A	20- 40	MATLAB	Improved GWO
EECMIGWO [51]	N/A	Clustering	Area=60 m^2, 120 m^2, 210 m^2 BS=N/A	10–480	MATLAB	Improved GWO
IGWO-MS [52]	Homogeneous	Grid	Area=100 m^2 BS=N/A	20,30	Python	Improved GWO

grid-like area to maximize coverage while avoiding overlap. It also incorporates a clustering mechanism to select CHs based on distance and residual energy, improving data aggregation and communication efficiency.

Another approach in Ref. [49] introduced the learning-based strategies into adaptive learning GWO (ALGWO) to improve its adaptability in both 2D and 3D environments. This approach integrates a dynamic opposite learning strategy and an adaptive dimensional learning approach to improve exploration capabilities and prevent premature convergence. By enabling individuals in the population to learn from their neighbors and by reshaping the search space dynamically, the method achieves a better balance between exploration and convergence. It also employs a realistic sensing model that accounts for environmental and distance-based variations.

To further align optimization with real-world conditions, [50] introduced an energy-efficient coverage optimization technique utilizing the multistrategy GWO (MSGWO) algorithm. This method incorporates a high-order coverage perception model that transitions gradually rather than relying on binary decisions. This model is integrated with GWO, along with advanced learning and movement strategies that allow sensor nodes to navigate around obstacles. The result is improved energy efficiency and comprehensive area coverage, even in complex terrains.

Addressing the crucial aspect of energy efficiency in WSN coverage, [51] presented an energy-efficient coverage method based on an IGWO algorithm (EECMIGWO). This approach focuses on designing a sensor network node coverage model that ensures each monitoring point is covered by at least one sensor node while minimizing energy consumption. It ensures each target point is covered and that the communication radius allows for full network connectivity, all while conserving energy.

Last, addressing both high deployment costs and ineffective coverage, the multistrategy improved GWO (IGWO-MS) algorithm [52] utilizes techniques like Sobol-based initialization, search space expansion, and symmetry-aware deployment. Recognizing the symmetric nature of sensor node sensing ranges, this method utilizes symmetry in node deployment to simplify problem-solving. Reverse learning, mirror mapping, and Lévy flights further boost global search capabilities. The coverage task is simplified using grid-based modeling, and convergence is improved through dimension-wise updates.

20.8 Discussion

This section presents a focused analysis of how the GWO algorithm has been applied across seven major areas in WSNs, drawing from the problem formulations and algorithmic strategies outlined in Tables 20.1 through 20.10 and Subsections 24.3 to 24.7. The review highlights the primary goals of each method, along with the various enhancements and modifications made to the standard GWO to address specific challenges.

As shown in Fig. 20.3, the reviewed methods can be broadly categorized into three groups: standard GWO (12 papers), improved variants of GWO (17 papers), and hybrid GWO-based techniques (11 papers). The dominance of improved and hybrid models, which account for 70% of the reviewed studies, clearly indicates that while the original GWO has served as a strong foundation, researchers are increasingly focusing on its refinement to better handle the complexities of real-world WSN problems such as energy efficiency, coverage optimization, and node deployment.

Fig. 20.4 further emphasizes the growing momentum in GWO-based research for WSNs by showing a noticeable increase in the number of published studies over time. This upward trend is also reflected in Figs. 20.5 and 20.6, which highlight the diverse range of WSN applications explored and reinforce the temporal growth pattern across different domains. Among the 40 credible papers reviewed up to December 2024, only 4 were published in 2019 or earlier. This number gradually rose to 5 in 2020 and 6 in 2021. However, a sharp uptick is observed in the following years, with 9 papers published in 2022, a slight dip to 5 in 2023, and a significant peak of 11 papers in 2024. This trend shows a growing research interest in utilizing GWO for increasingly complex and dynamic WSN environments. The spike in publications during 2022 and 2024 suggests a broader acknowledgment of the algorithm's adaptability, particularly when enhanced through hybrid techniques or strategic improvements.

20.8.1 The role of grey wolf optimizer for clustering in wireless sensor networks

Cluster-based routing is a widely used technique in WSNs aimed at improving energy efficiency, scalability, and overall network lifetime. It involves grouping sensor nodes into clusters, each led by a CH responsible for aggregating and forwarding data to the BS. The process of CH selection plays a critical role in determining the energy consumption and load distribution across the network. The GWO has shown strong potential in solving clustering and routing problems in WSNs by optimizing CH selection and cluster formation, especially under the constraints of energy limitations and dynamic topologies.

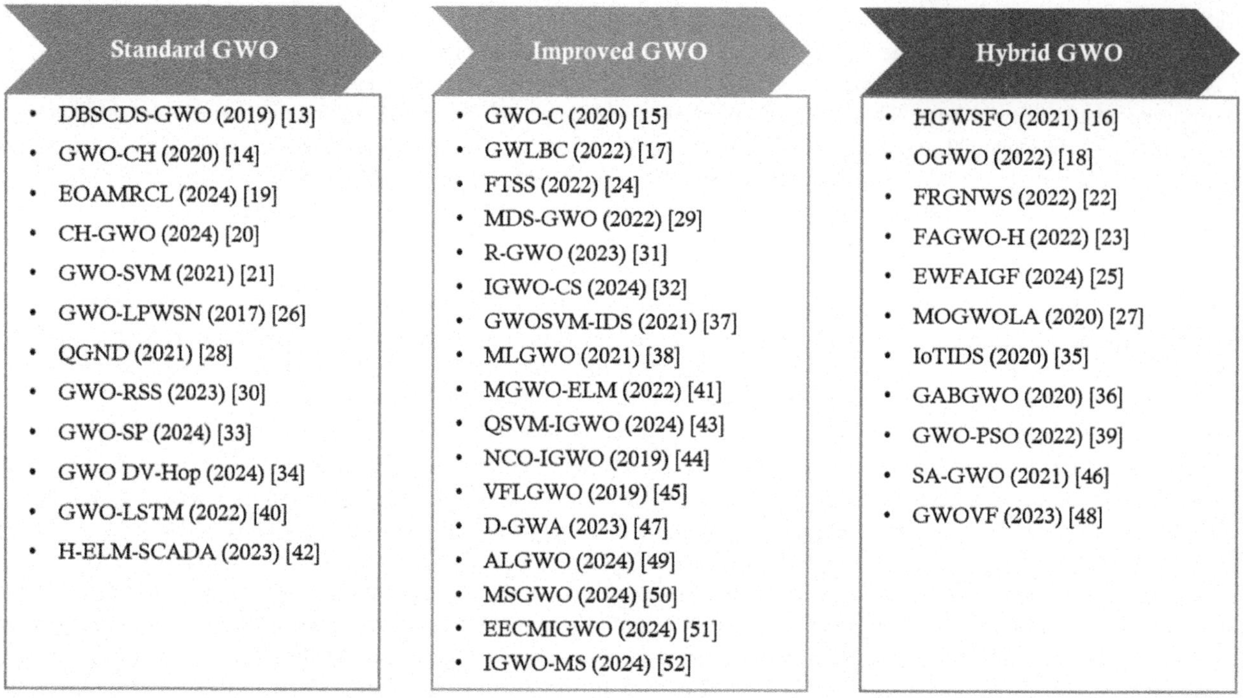

FIGURE 20.3 Categorizes WSN-related methods reviewed in this chapter based on the different variants of the GWO (*GWO*, Grey wolf optimizer; *WSN*, wireless sensor networks).

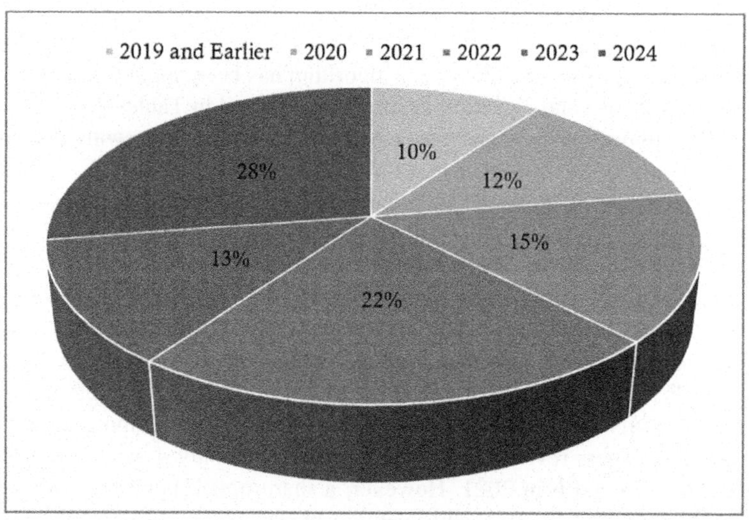

FIGURE 20.4 Percentage of WSN-related papers reviewed in this chapter that employ GWO, broken down by publication year (*GWO*, Grey wolf optimizer; *WSN*, wireless sensor networks).

In the GWO-based clustering approaches, the algorithm iteratively searches for optimal CHs by evaluating each candidate solution using a fitness function. The fitness function evaluates the quality of each candidate solution by considering multiple factors. For example, selecting CHs with higher residual energy helps prolong the network's lifetime. Minimizing the distance between CHs and the BS reduces energy consumption during data transmission, while minimizing intracluster distance lowers communication costs. Additionally, load balancing ensures that the workload is evenly distributed among CHs, preventing premature node failure. By optimizing these factors, GWO ensures energy-efficient, well-distributed CHs that enhance communication reliability and prolong the network's operational lifespan. Once the optimal CHs are selected, non-CH nodes join the cluster of the nearest CH based on a predefined metric, such as Euclidean distance, ensuring efficient communication within each cluster.

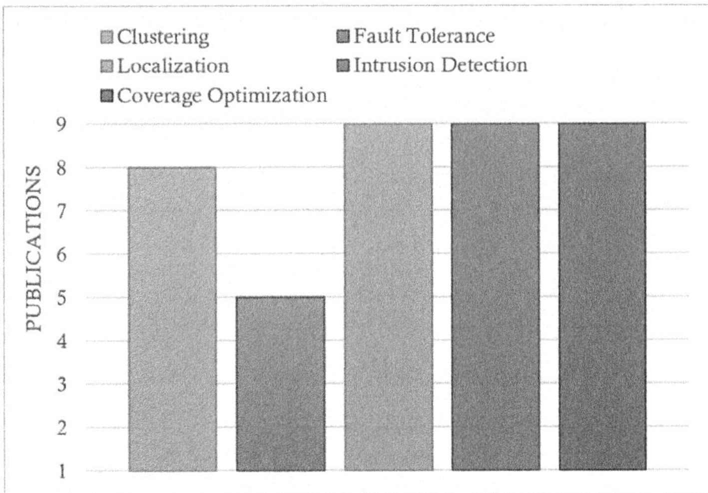

FIGURE 20.5 Number of papers reviewed in this chapter that employ GWO, broken down by WSN application (*GWO*, Grey wolf optimizer; *WSN*, wireless sensor networks).

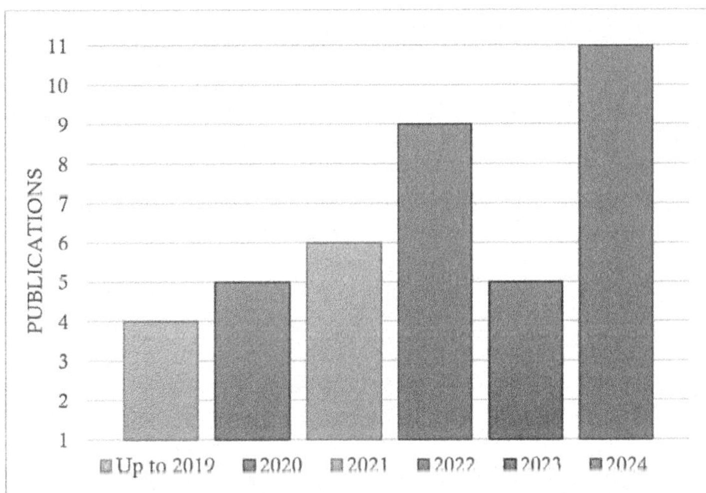

FIGURE 20.6 Number of WSN-related papers reviewed in this chapter that employ GWO, broken down by publication year (*GWO*, Grey wolf optimizer; *WSN*, wireless sensor networks).

To further improve performance, several enhanced GWO variants have been introduced. DBSCDS-GWO uses energy balancing strategies (DLI and CLI), while HGWSFO combines GWO with SFO to boost its search capabilities. GWO-CH and GWO-C fine-tune CH selection using residual energy and balancing criteria. IGWO-based GWLBC promotes load-balanced clustering, and OGWO-CH incorporates Opposition-Based Learning for faster convergence. EOAMRCL integrates a modified CSMA/CA mechanism for energy savings, and CH-GWO uses a detailed multicriteria fitness function—including 11 cluster attributes—for more robust clustering decisions. These adaptations demonstrate GWO's flexibility and effectiveness in managing energy-aware clustering in WSNs.

20.8.2 The role of grey wolf optimizer for fault tolerance in wireless sensor networks

Fault tolerance mechanisms are essential to ensure continuous service despite these disruptions. Over the past years, the GWO has emerged as a powerful tool in this area, offering effective optimization for node selection, routing paths, and failure detection strategies. The literature shows that GWO can effectively enhance fault tolerance by identifying reliable nodes and routes that can maintain network functionality even under adverse conditions. It uses a fitness-based approach to evaluate potential solutions, taking into account factors such as residual energy, node reliability, communication distance, and link quality. By selecting energy-efficient and robust paths, GWO helps extend network lifetime and maintain stable data transmission. Furthermore, its dynamic optimization process allows the network to adapt quickly to unexpected failures by rerouting data or activating backup nodes.

Several studies have extended GWO's capabilities through hybrid and enhanced models. For example, GWO-SVM integrates SVM for feature selection in fault detection, improving accuracy in real-world applications such as weather monitoring. FRGNWS identifies node-disjoint routing paths in energy-harvesting WSNs, while FAGWO-H combines GWO with the Firefly Algorithm for optimized clustering and routing. FTSS introduces fault tolerance in target-tracking scenarios, and an improved BGWO selects the most efficient node sets for balanced tracking performance. Additionally, EWFAIGF combines fuzzy AHP, iterative GWO, and Q-learning to detect faults proactively and reroute data intelligently, maximizing network reliability and resilience.

20.8.3 The role of grey wolf optimizer for localization in wireless sensor networks

Accurate node localization plays a vital role in many WSN applications, including environmental monitoring, asset tracking, and emergency response. However, achieving reliable localization in real-world WSNs is challenging due to energy limitations, signal interference, and the lack of GPS in many scenarios. Based on the reviewed techniques, the GWO offers a promising solution by efficiently estimating node positions while maintaining energy efficiency. In this method, GWO is used to optimize the placement or estimation of sensor node coordinates by minimizing localization error and ensuring robust connectivity. The algorithm evaluates candidate solutions based on fitness functions that typically account for accuracy, energy usage, and network structure. Typically, GWO-based localization is beneficial in scenarios wheretraditional localization techniques struggle with noisy or incomplete data.

Various GWO-based approaches have been proposed to enhance localization performance. GWO-LPWSN updates unknown node positions using anchor-based information, reducing error over iterations. MOGWOLA employs a multiobjective GWO model to balance accuracy and network structure, while QGND focuses on minimizing deployment costs and energy consumption. MDS-GWO improves convergence with disturbance strategies, and IGWO-CS introduces adaptive weighting and Lévy flights for robustness. GWO-RSS tackles signal noise in RSS-based localization, while R-GWO adds a repulsion factor for better 3D positioning. Additional methods, such as GWO-SP and GWO DV-Hop, further refine localization through optimal station placement and hybrid models that reduce localization time and power use. These techniques demonstrate the flexibility of GWO in adapting to diverse localization challenges in WSNs.

20.8.4 The role of grey wolf optimizer for intrusion detection in wireless sensor networks

In GWO-based intrusion detection techniques, the algorithm is primarily used to select the most relevant features and tune model parameters for machine-learning-based IDSs. The optimization process seeks to strike a balance between detection accuracy, false-alarm rate, and computational overhead. By evaluating candidate feature sets and configurations based on these criteria, GWO aims to find solutions that are not only accurate but also lightweight enough for resource-constrained networks. Once optimal settings are found, the IDS can be deployed for real-time intrusion monitoring with improved reliability and speed.

Several enhanced GWO variants have been developed to further boost IDS effectiveness. IoTIDS combines GA with GWO for more accurate and cost-efficient feature selection. GWOSVM-IDS uses a modified Binary GWO with SVM to reduce feature size while maintaining high classification accuracy. Similarly, GABGWO merges GA and GWO in lightweight IDS designs, improving both accuracy and speed. MLGWO applies multiobjective optimization to maximize detection rates and minimize false alarms, and execution time. Other techniques, such as GWO-PSO, improve global search capabilities, while GWO-LSTM enhances feature selection in deep learning models. MGWO-ELM IDS accelerates convergence using Extreme Learning Machines, and H-ELM-SCADA optimizes hybrid models for SCADA systems. Finally, QSVM-IGWO improves detection accuracy while significantly reducing false positives.

20.8.5 The role of grey wolf optimizer for coverage optimization in wireless sensor networks

Generally, coverage optimization in WSNs aims to effectively monitor the target area by maximizing coverage, minimizing redundancy, and optimizing node placement while balancing energy consumption. Challenges include environmental factors, node failures, and energy constraints. This task becomes increasingly challenging in dynamic environments, where energy constraints, unpredictable obstacles, and node failures must all be accounted for. The literature shows that GWO is an effective tool for addressing these challenges by optimizing node placement and enhancing coverage through balanced exploration and exploitation in diverse environments.

In GWO-based coverage optimization, the algorithm evaluates different node placement strategies using a fitness function that typically considers factors like total coverage area, overlap (redundancy), energy consumption, and network lifetime. Several advanced GWO variants have been proposed to tackle specific coverage-related challenges. NCO-IGWO improves convergence control and uses elite strategies to boost coverage efficiency. VFLGWO combines Lévy flights and virtual forces to promote even node distribution. SA-GWO integrates Simulated Annealing to strengthen global search and reduce premature convergence. D-GWA applies a discrete GWO model to solve directional k-coverage problems. GWOVF blends GWO with the Virtual Force Algorithm for mobile WSNs, while ALGWO incorporates adaptive learning strategies to better navigate the search space. MSGWO uses high-order sensing and opposition-based learning for complex terrain coverage. EECMIGWO focuses on minimizing energy consumption while ensuring full coverage, and IGWO-MS enhances deployment symmetry and search diversity through techniques like Sobol initialization and search space expansion.

20.9 Conclusion and future work

This chapter has provided a comprehensive overview of how the GWO and its various enhancements have been applied to solve key challenges in WSNs. By focusing on five major domains, including clustering, fault tolerance, localization, intrusion detection, and coverage optimization, we have shown that GWO offers considerable potential in improving energy efficiency, extending network lifetime, enhancing reliability, and ensuring better adaptability to real-world conditions. In clustering, GWO-based methods have proven effective in selecting optimal CHs, resulting in more balanced energy consumption and prolonged network operation. For fault tolerance, GWO has enabled more resilient networks by improving node selection, fault detection, and recovery processes. Localization approaches driven by GWO have enhanced the accuracy of node positioning while reducing hardware and energy costs. In security, GWO has played a vital role in intrusion detection, helping to boost detection rates and reduce false alarms. Meanwhile, GWO has also shown strong performance in optimizing sensor coverage by maximizing monitored areas and minimizing energy consumption.

Despite these advancements, several challenges persist. Current GWO models often face limitations in scalability, convergence speed, and adaptability to rapidly changing environments, especially in scenarios that demand real-time responsiveness. Additionally, the computational overhead and reliance on centralized processing can hinder their effectiveness in large-scale or energy-constrained WSN deployments. These issues underscore the need for ongoing research and innovation to further refine and extend the capabilities of GWO.

By tackling existing limitations and exploring new technological integrations, future research has the potential to unlock smarter, more efficient, and truly resilient WSNs. Looking ahead, one promising direction is the development of hybrid GWO algorithms that incorporate machine learning techniques for more intelligent and dynamic CH selection. Multiobjective GWO variants can be designed to simultaneously optimize energy efficiency, load distribution, and network longevity. Similarly, enhancing fault detection by integrating ensemble learning and deep learning models into GWO frameworks could improve accuracy and enable proactive recovery strategies, particularly in unstable environments. For localization, integrating GWO with range-free or 3D positioning techniques could significantly reduce costs and power consumption in large-scale deployments. Exploring the use of GWO in mobile anchor-based localization may also offer improved accuracy and reduced infrastructure needs. On the security front, future IDSs can benefit from lightweight GWO-based designs for resource-limited IoT devices. Furthermore, hybridization of GWO with deep learning models such as LSTM and CNN may improve the detection of evolving cyber threats while maintaining low overhead. Coverage optimization, especially in 3D terrains and mobile sensor networks, is another area ripe for exploration. Combining GWO with other swarm intelligence techniques could enhance its ability to dynamically adapt to shifting coverage needs.

To make GWO more effective in large-scale WSNs, future work should focus on decentralized and self-organizing versions that reduce communication load and handle failures better. GWO can also be combined with new technologies like 5G, edge computing, and blockchain to improve security, speed, and teamwork between devices. Using GWO in federated learning can help train models across devices while keeping data private. GWO also shows promise in improving energy use through smart energy harvesting, sleep scheduling, and efficient data aggregation. Real-world testing is important to see how well these methods work in smart cities, healthcare, disaster response, and industrial IoT. Finally, improving GWO's performance through better initialization, adaptive tuning, hybrid models, and parallel computing could make it faster and more powerful in complex networks.

Conflict of interest

The authors declare that they have no conflict of interest.

Declaration of generative AI and AI-assisted technologies in the writing process

During the preparation of this work, the authors used ChatGPT in order to improve the language and readability of the manuscript. After using this tool, the authors reviewed and edited the content as needed and take full responsibility for the content of the publication.

References

[1] D. Kandris, C. Nakas, D. Vomvas, G. Koulouras, Applications of wireless sensor networks: an up-to-date survey, Applied System Innovation 3 (1) (2020) 14.

[2] M. Majid, S. Habib, A.R. Javed, M. Rizwan, G. Srivastava, T.R. Gadekallu, et al., Applications of wireless sensor networks and internet of things frameworks in the industry revolution 4.0: a systematic literature review, Sensors 22 (6) (2022) 2087.

[3] S. Mirjalili, S.M. Mirjalili, A. Lewis, Grey wolf optimizer, Advances in Engineering Software 69 (2014) 46–61.

[4] S. Memarian, N. Behmanesh-Fard, P. Aryai, M. Shokouhifar, S. Mirjalili, M. del, et al., "TSFIS-GWO: metaheuristic-driven takagi-sugeno fuzzy system for adaptive real-time routing in WBANs, Applied Soft Computing 155 (2024) 111427.

[5] M. Shokouhifar, F. Fanian, M.K. Rafsanjani, M. Hosseinzadeh, S. Mirjalili, AI-driven cluster-based routing protocols in WSNs: a survey of fuzzy heuristics, metaheuristics, and machine learning models, Computer Science Review 54 (2024) 100684.

[6] G.H. Adday, S.K. Subramaniam, Z.A. Zukarnain, N. Samian, Fault tolerance structures in wireless sensor networks (WSNs): survey, classification, and future directions, Sensors 22 (16) (2022) 6041.

[7] S. Sivasakthiselvan, V. Nagarajan, Localization techniques of wireless sensor networks: a review. pp. 1643–1648.

[8] R. Ahmad, W. Alhasan, R. Wazirali, N. Aleisa, Optimization algorithms for wireless sensor networks node localization: an overview, IEEE Access (2024).

[9] S.M.S. Bukhari, M.H. Zafar, M. Abou Houran, S.K.R. Moosavi, M. Mansoor, M. Muaaz, et al., Secure and privacy-preserving intrusion detection in wireless sensor networks: federated learning with SCNN-Bi-LSTM for enhanced reliability, Ad Hoc Networks 155 (2024) 103407.

[10] R. Zagrouba, A. Kardi, Comparative study of energy efficient routing techniques in wireless sensor networks, Information 12 (1) (2021) 42.

[11] Q. Zhao, C. Li, D. Zhu, C. Xie, Coverage optimization of wireless sensor networks using combinations of PSO and chaos optimization, Electronics 11 (6) (2022) 853.

[12] O.S. Egwuche, A. Singh, A.E. Ezugwu, J. Greeff, M.O. Olusanya, L. Abualigah, Machine learning for coverage optimization in wireless sensor networks: a comprehensive review, Annals of Operations Research (2023) 1–67.

[13] A. Kaushik, S. Indu, D. Gupta, A grey wolf optimization approach for improving the performance of wireless sensor networks, Wireless Personal Communications 106 (2019) 1429–1449.

[14] K. Sekaran, R. Rajakumar, K. Dinesh, Y. Rajkumar, T. Latchoumi, S. Kadry, et al., An energy-efficient cluster head selection in wireless sensor network using grey wolf optimization algorithm, TELKOMNIKA (Telecommunication Computing Electronics and Control) 18 (6) (2020) 2822–2833.

[15] D. Agrawal, M.H. Wasim Qureshi, P. Pincha, P. Srivastava, S. Agarwal, V. Tiwari, et al., GWO-C: grey wolf optimizer-based clustering scheme for WSNs, International Journal of Communication Systems 33 (8) (2020) e4344.

[16] L. Nagarajan, S. Thangavelu, Hybrid grey wolf sunflower optimisation algorithm for energy-efficient cluster head selection in wireless sensor networks for lifetime enhancement, IET Communications 15 (3) (2021) 384–396.

[17] S. Singh, S. Nikolovski, P. Chakrabarti, GWLBC: gray wolf optimization based load balanced clustering for sustainable WSNs in smart city environment, Sensors 22 (19) (2022) 7113.

[18] R. Ramalingam, D. Karunanidy, A. Balakrishnan, M. Rashid, A. Dumka, A. Afifi, et al., OGWO-CH: hybrid opposition-based learning with gray wolf optimization based clustering technique in wireless sensor networks, Electronics 11 (16) (2022) 2593.

[19] M. Kaddi, M. Omari, K. Salameh, A. Alnoman, Energy-efficient clustering in wireless sensor networks using grey wolf optimization and enhanced CSMA/CA, Sensors 24 (16) (2024) 5234.

[20] L.A. Kumar, A. Kumar, Load balanced and optimal clustering in WSNs using grey wolf optimizer, International Journal of System Assurance Engineering and Management 15 (2024) 1.

[21] I. Rahmany, H. Mnassri, T. Moulahi, S.E. Khediri, Grey wolf optimizer enhanced SVM for IoT fault detection. pp. 1483–1488, 2021.

[22] R.S. Rathore, O. Kaiwartya, K.N. Qureshi, I.T. Javed, W. Nagmeldin, A. Abdelmaboud, et al., Towards enabling fault tolerance and reliable green communications in next-generation wireless systems, Applied Sciences 12 (17) (2022) 8870.

[23] K. Jaiswal, V. Anand, "FAGWO-H: a hybrid method towards fault-tolerant cluster-based routing in wireless sensor network for IoT applications, The Journal of Supercomputing 78 (8) (2022) 11195–11227.

[24] Z. Qu, H. Xu, X. Zhao, H. Tang, J. Wang, B. Li, A fault-tolerant sensor scheduling approach for target tracking in wireless sensor networks, Alexandria Engineering Journal 61 (12) (2022) 13001–13010 /12/01/, 2022.

[25] V.V. Deshpande, R.K. Shukla, "EWFAIGF: design of an efficient model for enhancing energy efficiency in IoTBased wireless sensor networks through fuzzy AHP and iterative grey wolf jelly fish optimization, Journal of Electrical Systems 20 (5s) (2024) 2512–2529.

[26] R. Rajakumar, J. Amudhavel, P. Dhavachelvan, T. Vengattaraman, "GWO-LPWSN: grey wolf optimization algorithm for node localization problem in wireless sensor networks,", Journal of Computer Networks and Communications (1) (2017) 7348141.

[27] S.N. Ghorpade, M. Zennaro, B.S. Chaudhari, GWO model for optimal localization of IoT-enabled sensor nodes in smart parking systems, IEEE Transactions on Intelligent Transportation Systems 22 (2) (2020) 1217–1224.

[28] K. Jaiswal, V. Anand, A QoS aware optimal node deployment in wireless sensor network using grey wolf optimization approach for IoT applications, Telecommunication Systems 78 (4) (2021) 559–576.
[29] H. Cui, J. Zhao, C. Zhou, N. Zhang, Localization for wireless sensor networks assisted by two mobile anchors with improved grey wolf optimizer, Wireless Communications and Mobile Computing, vol 2022 (1) (2022) 6292629.
[30] N.A. Nouri, A. Naouri, S. Dhelim, Accurate range-based distributed localization of wireless sensor nodes using grey wolf optimizer, The Journal of Engineering and Exact Sciences 9 (4) (2023) 15920-01e.
[31] H.Y. Abuaddous, G. Kaur, K. Jyoti, N. Mittal, S. Mahajan, A.K. Pandit, et al., Repulsion-based grey wolf optimizer with improved exploration and exploitation capabilities to localize sensor nodes in 3D wireless sensor network, Soft Computing 27 (7) (2023) 3869–3885.
[32] D. Yu, T. Yuan, H. Qing, W. Xie, P. Zhu, Gray wolf optimizer with communication strategy based on DV-Hop for nodes location of wireless sensor networks, IEEE Access (2024).
[33] Z. Wang, D. Hu, J. Huang, M. Xie, C. Zhao, Optimal station placement based on grey wolf optimizer for regional target localization, EURASIP Journal on Wireless Communications and Networking (1) (2024) 35.
[34] V. Kanwar, O. Aydin, An improved localization algorithm to replace faulty nodes for an IoT network using weighted grey wolf optimization, International Journal of Communication Systems 37 (13) (2024) e5853.
[35] A. Davahli, M. Shamsi, G. Abaei, Hybridizing genetic algorithm and grey wolf optimizer to advance an intelligent and lightweight intrusion detection system for IoT wireless networks, Journal of Ambient Intelligence and Humanized Computing 11 (11) (2020) 5581–5609.
[36] A. Davahli, M. Shamsi, G. Abaei, A lightweight anomaly detection model using SVM for WSNs in IoT through a hybrid feature selection algorithm based on GA and GWO, Journal of Computing and Security 7 (1) (2020) 63–79.
[37] M. Safaldin, M. Otair, L. Abualigah, "Improved binary gray wolf optimizer and SVM for intrusion detection system in wireless sensor networks, Journal of Ambient Intelligence and Humanized Computing 12 (2021) 1559–1576.
[38] S. Shakya, Modified gray wolf feature selection and machine learning classification for wireless sensor network intrusion detection, IRO Journal on Sustainable Wireless Systems 3 (2) (2021) 118–127.
[39] M. Otair, O.T. Ibrahim, L. Abualigah, M. Altalhi, P. Sumari, An enhanced grey wolf optimizer based particle swarm optimizer for intrusion detection system in wireless sensor networks, Wireless Networks 28 (2) (2022) 721–744.
[40] S. Karthic, S.M. Kumar, P.S. Prakash, Grey wolf based feature reduction for intrusion detection in WSN using LSTM, International Journal of Information Technology 14 (7) (2022) 3719–3724.
[41] A. Alzaqebah, I. Aljarah, O. Al-Kadi, R. Damaševičius, A modified grey wolf optimization algorithm for an intrusion detection system, Mathematics 10 (6) (2022) 999.
[42] Y.K. Saheed, O.H. Abdulganiyu, T.A. Tchakoucht, A novel hybrid ensemble learning for anomaly detection in industrial sensor networks and SCADA systems for smart city infrastructures, Journal of King Saud University-Computer and Information Sciences 35 (5) (2023) 101532.
[43] E. Elsedimy, H. Elhadidy, S.M. Abohashish, A novel intrusion detection system based on a hybrid quantum support vector machine and improved grey wolf optimizer, Cluster Computing (2024) 1–19.
[44] Z. Wang, H. Xie, Z. Hu, D. Li, J. Wang, W. Liang, Node coverage optimization algorithm for wireless sensor networks based on improved grey wolf optimizer, Journal of Algorithms & Computational Technology 13 (2019) 1748302619889498.
[45] S. Wang, X. Yang, X. Wang, Z. Qian, A virtual force algorithm-lévy-embedded grey wolf optimization algorithm for wireless sensor network coverage optimization, Sensors 19 (12) (2019) 2735.
[46] Y. Zhang, L. Cao, Y. Yue, Y. Cai, B. Hang, A novel coverage optimization strategy based on grey wolf algorithm optimized by simulated annealing for wireless sensor networks, Computational Intelligence and Neuroscience 2021 (1) (2021) 6688408.
[47] V.R. Ekhlas, M.H. Shirvani, A. Dana, N. Raeisi, Discrete grey wolf optimization algorithm for solving k-coverage problem in directional sensor networks with network lifetime maximization viewpoint, Applied Soft Computing 146 (2023) 110609.
[48] A. Gupta, K. Mamatha, M. Kiran, Energy efficient coverage optimization in mobile wireless sensor network using grey wolf algorithm." pp. 1–7, 2023.
[49] X. Yu, Y. Duan, Z. Cai, W. Luo, An adaptive learning grey wolf optimizer for coverage optimization in WSNs, Expert Systems with Applications 238 (2024) 121917.
[50] Z. Wang, L. Huang, S. Yang, X. Luo, D. He, S. Chan, Multi-strategy enhanced grey wolf algorithm for obstacle-aware WSNs coverage optimization, Ad Hoc Networks 152 (2024) 103308.
[51] R. Jia, H. Zhang, Wireless sensor network (WSN) model targeting energy efficient wireless sensor networks node coverage, IEEE Access (2024).
[52] Y. Ou, F. Qin, K.-Q. Zhou, P.-F. Yin, L.-P. Mo, A. Mohd Zain, An improved grey wolf optimizer with multi-strategies coverage in wireless sensor networks, Symmetry 16 (3) (2024) 286.

Chapter 21

Comparative performance analysis of binary grey wolf optimizer and teaching-learning-based algorithm for the traveling salesman problem

Wonseh Mulbah and Navneet Himanshu
Department of Civil Engineering, UIE, Chandigarh University, Mohali, Punjab, India

21.1 Introduction

The traveling salesman problem (TSP) is a popular combinatorial NP-hard problem studied for the past three (3) decades [1]. Over the past decades, studies on the TSP have intensified due to the growth and demand for efficient and effective service delivery. The idea or concept of this problem (TSP) is most often applied in the information technology context to measure the best link for information to traverse from one junction to another. Moreover, two famous mathematicians described it initially. W.R. Hamilton and Thomas Kirkman formed a game that was capable of finding the Hamilton cycle and this followed the same concept and constraint of the TSP. The cycle meets all the vertices of the graph exactly once, except the starting and ending vertices that are at the same vertex. However, the Hamiltonian cycle cannot be possible in a graph when there is an articulation point and pendant vertices. This explains the complexity of the problem. TSP is an NP-Hard problem because it takes an exponential period to answer NP, and the solution cannot be confirmed in a polynomial period. For so many decades, this problem (TSP) has been calculated, and several results have been hypothesized based on present conditions. The most traditional and easiest remedy is to try many options until the best route is identified, but as the number of points increases, it becomes more difficult and time-consuming. This problem paved the way for the use of heuristics method. And for better results, metaheuristics have now become the focus globally. Heuristic techniques provide probabilistic solutions that are approximate in nature and not always optimal due to their philosophy of time in computing.

You et al. (2017) [1] presented an innovative modified application genetic procedural method with a local exploration method that has remained established to answer the TSP. Mariem and Souhail [2] proposed the optimization of the fuzzy TSP by means of the α- Cut technique as a status function and the Dhouib-Matrix-TSP1 as an estimating technique. Karaboga and Gorkemli [3] utilized the novel versions of the Artificial Bee Colony (ABC) algorithm to solve TSP by introducing and describing it in detail. Dorigo et al. [4] presented the ant colony system to solve the TSP. Sriwindono [5] used the genetic algorithm with the ordered crossover method and the give-and-take alteration method to solve the TSP. Li et al. [6] proposed a new multiple travelling salesman problem called the colored TSP. Zhou et al. [7] proposed an innovative algorithm using simulated annealing and gene-expression programming to adequately solve the problem. Akhand et al. [8] introduced an active particle swarm optimization (PSO) based algorithm for resolving TSP. Halim and Swagatam (2020) did an exhaustive review of tools to measure the performance of a diverse set of metaheuristic algorithms. The review set the basis for understanding the performance characteristics of algorithms and the way they arrive at the global optimum.

Abdulkarim and Alshammari [9] did a comparative analysis among three major approaches to optimizing the Traveling Salesman Problem. The researcher compared and provided the merits and demeritS of the widely used procedures to compute these problems in relation to the route length, elapsed time, and number of iterations.

Grey Wolf Optimizer. DOI: https://doi.org/10.1016/B978-0-443-36624-6.00002-0

Heuristics are utilized to get the best solution faster than the exact algorithms or deterministic approach, but the evolution of metaheuristics is a high-level approach for problems that are general in nature and complex [10]. Additionally, metaheuristic approaches are approximate and tend to imitate a normal, physical, or biological principle, like a hunt or a process that leads to computing the near best results [3]. Metaheuristic algorithms can only be termed effective and efficient if they are an acceptable quality remedy or result in a given computational budget on an extensive array of problems [11]. In this paper, we use a few TSP Benchmark instances or problems from existing pieces of literature to compute the optimal route for all the nodes. This study investigates the suitability and efficiency level of metaheuristics methods such as grey wolf and teaching learning algorithms. It is useful in the delivery and transportation sector in solving network routing problems and finding the optimum path. Findings from this study have the propensity of reducing cost and minimize time wasted in travel.

21.2 Methodology

21.2.1 The traveling salesman problem problem

A sales representative must travel to n cities to sell products. The constraint of this problem is that the sales representative has to visit each city once. To choose a route, the salesperson must start in a random city and return to the same city at the end. The theoretical formulation of the traveling salesman problem is generated as follows [12]:

$$L = (l_1,\ l_2,\ \ldots..l_n).\quad 1 \le c_i \le n \tag{21.1}$$

$$F(c_i) = \sum_{i=1}^{n-1} C(l_i,\quad l_{i+1}) + C(l_n,\quad l_1) \tag{21.2}$$

i is the amount of the i-th points, l symbolizes the set of all points amounts, C(li,li+1) symbolizes the space stuck between two cities, and C(li+1, li) = C(li,li+1). The main objective is in the direction of computing the Hamiltonian enclosed circular points as discussed in the introduction and based upon the constraints indicated in Eq. (21.2).

21.2.2 Grey wolf optimization

Grey wolf optimization (GWO) is a metaheuristic evolutionary optimization method advanced to mimic the pyramid of control and pursue procedures of grey wolves [13]. In the zone of wild animals, GW is regularly seen in groups/families acknowledged as packs comprising 5–12 wolves on average. The whole pack is separated into four (4) classes. The head of the group, alpha wolves (AW), is always accountable for any administrative procedure or other group actions and instructs any single member or the whole group. The subsequent class is known as the beta wolf (BW) (β) in the pyramid to help the AW (α) in the supervisory procedure. The third level of wolves in the ladder are subordinate or delta wolves (DW) (δ) who implement tasks as lookouts, sentinels, hunters, and custodians. The lowest position in the pyramid is allotted to omega wolves (ω). GWO is a precise positive procedure for resolving actual mechanical and visual engineering problems [14]. Fig. 21.1 illustrates the social hierarchy of GW. The procedure of exploration and exploitation for the prey is mainly done using three steps [15].

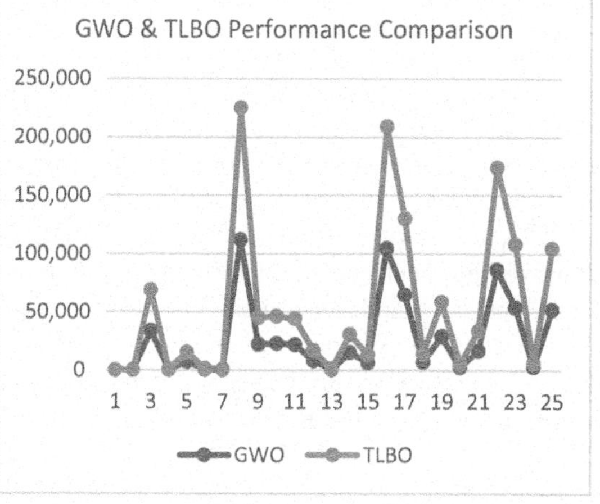

FIGURE 21.1 GWO and TLBO performance comparison (*GWO*, grey wolf optimization; *TLBO*, teaching-learning-based optimization).

$$Z_i^{k+1} = Z_p^k - A.\,D \tag{21.3}$$

$$\vec{D} = |\vec{C}.\,\vec{Z_p} - \overrightarrow{Z_i^k}| \tag{21.4}$$

Here, the key i represents the ith distinct wolf in a definitem pack, and k represents the present repetition phase in GWO procedure. The two-coefficient vectors are calculated as:

$$A = 2\vec{a}.\ rand_1 - \vec{a} \tag{21.5}$$

$$\vec{C} = 2\,.\ rand_2 \tag{21.6}$$

In Eq. (21.5), the constraint $\vec{a}$ is a linearly reducing value starting from 2 to 0 above the sequence of the total iteration count. A linearly decreasing time-dependent parameter $\vec{a}$ can be mathematically expressed as:

$$a^k = 2 - \left(\frac{2k}{k_{\max}}\right) \tag{21.7}$$

The other parameters $rand_1$ and $rand_2$ in Eq. (21.5) and Eq. (21.6), respectively, are consistently dispersed random values in [0, 1].

21.2.2.1 Modeling the process of hunting

Generally prevailing wolf, that is, alpha usually guides the procedure of searching for the target as well as the surrounding (α). The other wolves, such as beta (β)and delta (δ), also protect the group in pursuing procedure irregularly. In the GWO technique, the AW (α) is the distinct who holds the best data about the target's present whereabouts in the exploration space. The BW (β) and DW (δ) wolves have less information concerning the target's position than the alpha (α) wolf. However, their awareness concerning the target's whereabouts is enhanced than those of omega wolves (ω). In GWO, the procedure of optimization begins with positions of three wolves α, β, and δ as three optimal results of the objective function f or possible position of the target. The activities of another wolf's in-group with omega (ω) wolves are regarded as the location of the finest exploration mediators, that is, α, β, and δ. Mathematically,

$$\begin{cases} \vec{W_1} = \overrightarrow{Z_\alpha^k} - \vec{A_1}\ .\ \vec{D_\alpha} \\ \vec{W_2} = \overrightarrow{Z_\beta^k} - \vec{A_2}\ .\ \vec{D_\beta} \\ \vec{W_3} = \overrightarrow{Z_\delta^k} - \vec{A_3}\ .\ \vec{D_\delta} \end{cases} \tag{21.8}$$

where the vectors $\vec{D_\alpha}$, $\vec{D_\beta}$, and $\vec{D_\delta}$ are as follows;

$$\begin{cases} \vec{D_\alpha} = |\vec{C_1}\ .\ \overrightarrow{Z_\alpha^k} - \overrightarrow{Z_1^k}| \\ \vec{D_\beta} = |\vec{C_2}\ .\ \overrightarrow{Z_\beta^k} - \overrightarrow{Z_1^k}| \\ \vec{D_\delta} = |\vec{C_3}\ .\ \overrightarrow{Z_\delta^k} - \overrightarrow{Z_1^k}| \end{cases} \tag{21.9}$$

$$\overrightarrow{Z_i^{k+1}} = \frac{\vec{W_1} + \vec{W_2} + \vec{W_3}}{3} \tag{21.10}$$

It is seen from Eq. (21.8), Eq. (21.9), and Eq. (21.10) that the exact order of hierarchy supremacy of α, β, and δ wolves assist for finding the locations of the target and the hunting wolves.

21.2.2.2 Modeling the exploration of target or exploration

Exploring innovative exploration space necessitates diverging behavior of the exploration agent, that is, individual wolves restrict the bunching of wolves. To prototype the capability of search of wolves in search space, Mirjalili et al. [14] utilize a coefficient vector $\vec{A}$ with an arbitrary number of more than 1 or fewer than (-1). The coefficient vector |A| > 1 compels the wolves to change to a novel location from the target, hopeful of finding a better target. Another component that favors

TABLE 21.1 Results from GWO and TLBO experiments in comparison with the optimum results from the TSPLib.

Problem	Results	PSO	MPSO	GWO		TLBO	
				Cost	Err. %	Cost	Err. %
Burma14	33.23	33.23	33.23	33.23	0	33.23	0
ulysses16	68.59			73.99	7.87	75.11	9.51
ulysses22	75.67			75.67	0	76.6	1.23
att48	33,522			33639	0.35	35,105.13	4.72
eil51	426	454	426	428.98	0.7	444.73	4.4
berlin52	7542			7544.66	0.04	7742.94	2.66
st70	675			716.7	6.18	797.93	18.21
eil76	538			564.94	5.01	569.75	5.9
pr76	108,159	109,870–113,545	108,159	111,915.74	3.47	112,998	4.47
rat99	1211	1294–1397	1211	1382.19	14.14	1369.29	13.07
KroA100	21,282	21,282–23,342	21,282–21,352	22,196	4.29	22,756	6.93
kroB100	22,140	22,534–23,424	22,141	22,891	3.39	23,064	4.17
kroC100	20,749			21,944.31	5.76	22,087.76	6.45
rd100	7910	8047–8601	7910–8135	8207.32	3.76	8518.44	7.69
eil101	629	643–699	629	663.45	5.48	667.03	6.05
lin105	14,379	14,910–15,897	14,379	15,171.2	5.51	15,298.87	6.4
pr107	44,303	45,602–48,933	44,303	47,710.58	7.69	46,963.11	6
pr124	59,030	61,801–65,911	59,030–59,555	64,011.11	8.44	63,663.42	7.85
ch130	6110	6299–6779	6110–6255	6493.43	6.28	6512.96	6.6
pr136	96,772	99,575–105,839	97,972	104,420.33	7.9	104,561.66	8.05
pr144	58,537	54,869–60,293	58,537–58,972	64,778.16	10.66	65,175.62	11.34
ch150	6528	6724–7325	6528–6659	7085.92	8.55	6923.48	6.06
kroA150	26,524	27,720–29,488	26,524–26,952	29,036.51	9.47	29,414.28	10.9
rat195	2323	2383–2686	2323–2401	2659.86	14.5	2660.19	14.52
d198	15,780	16,653–,	15,780–16,222	16,697.31	5.81	16,785.05	6.37
pr226	80,369	82,761–89,207	80,545–81,279	86,424.97	7.54	87,096.1	8.37
pr264	49,135	50,205–56,140	49,325–50,945	53,701.48	9.29	54,207.51	10.32
a280	2579	2658–2883	2598–2795	2968.15	15.09	3074.9	19.23
pr299	48,191	49,582–53,016	48,332–49,105	52,000	7.9	52,400	8.73

GWO, Grey wolf optimization; *MPSO*, modified PSO; *PSO*, particle swarm optimization; *TLBO*, teaching-learning-based optimization.

exploring novel exploration areas is the coefficient vector $\vec{C}$ by preferring the vectors $\overrightarrow{D_\alpha}$, $\overrightarrow{D_\beta}$, and $\overrightarrow{D_\delta}$ stochastically for $\vec{C} > 1$. In GWO, the coefficient vector $\vec{C}$ comprises an arbitrary number in the interval [0, 2]. The decision of an arbitrary coefficient vector $\vec{C}$ enables search capacity from the start of the pursuit process until the finish. This element exactly assists to prevent grouping of exploration agents, particularly throughout last repetition step.

21.2.3 Teaching-learning-based optimization

Teaching-learning-based optimization (TLBO) is a population-based technique that, like supplementary nature-inspired algorithms. The population is a class of students or a group of students for TLBO. In TLBO, the diverse strategy parameters are comparable to the different learning objectives given to the learners, and the performance of the students is comparable to their "fitness," as in previous population-based optimization methods. The instructor is believed to have achieved the most successful result to date. The TLBO procedure consists of two stages, which include the teacher stage and the learner phase. An effective educator is interested in the average performance of the entire class [15].

21.2.3.1 Teacher phase

The average score of a class with a competent instructor increases from MA to MB. An effective educator is one who helps their students up to the amount of information they have. In actuality, however, this is not probable, and an instructor can simply raise the average of the class to a certain level reliant on the aptitude of the class. This is done randomly and depends on a variety of variables. At each iteration, I let M_i be hard and T_i be the instructor. T_i will attempt to pull the Average M_i closer to his point, so Ti becomes the different mean or M_{new}. The response will be changed based on the variance between the old man and the present mean, which is computed from

$$Variance\_Mean_i = r_i(M_{new} - T_i\, M_i) \tag{21.11}$$

where r_i is an arbitrary number in the range [0, 1] and T_F is a learning factor that defines the value of the average to be changed. The value of T_F can be one or the other, 1 or 2, and this decision is made arbitrarily with equal probability by means of the heuristic step.

$$T_F = round\,[1 + rand\,(0,\ 1)21] \tag{21.12}$$

This alteration adjusts the current result of the expression below.

$$\text{Hnew, i} = \text{Hold, i} + \text{Difference\_Meani.} \tag{21.13}$$

21.2.3.2 Learner phase

Teacher input and student interaction with each other are two different ways that learners increase their knowledge. Incidental interactions between students occur through group discussions, formal writing, presentations, etc. When the other student knows more than the learner does, the learner acquires new knowledge. Adaptive learning is described as follows:

For i=1: Pn

Arbitrarily take two students Hi and Hj, where i ≠ j If f (Hi) < f (Hj) Hnew,i=Hold,i + ui(Hi − Hj) Else Hnew,i=Hold,i + ui(Hj − Hi) End If Terminate For

Admit Hnew if it offers an improved function value.

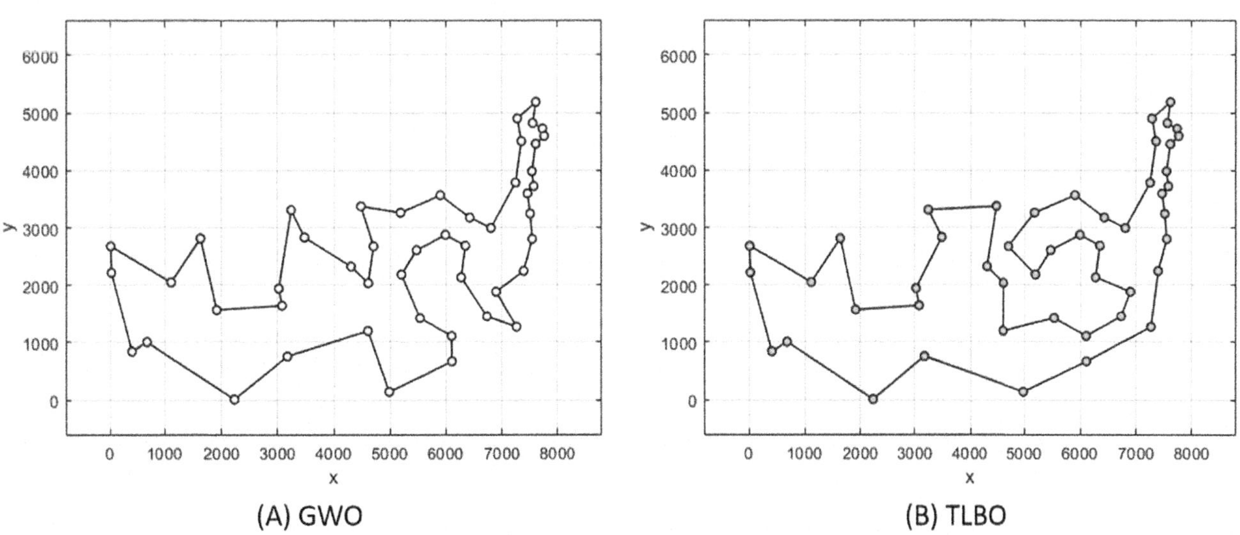

FIGURE 21.2 Att48 GWO and TLBO (*GWO*, grey wolf optimization; *TLBO*, teaching-learning-based optimization).

21.3 Results

In this work, Matlab was used to run the program on a Pentium (R), 2.00 GHz CPU, 8 GB RAM, to compute 30 standard TSPs, which were taken from http://comopt.ifi.uniheidelberg.de/software/TSPLIB95/. We studied the efficiency of metaheuristic algorithms, which include GWO, and TLBO, using 30 (3) diverse benchmark problems. Each problem was analyzed for a swarm size of 150 and a maximum iteration count of 1000 in 20 different runs. Table 21.1 reports a comparison of results reported in the current study with existing literature. The results demonstrate that the optimum solutions reported by the GWO algorithm are closer to the optimum results and outperformed TLBO in terms of finding the best optimum solution. Moreover, the optimum solutions obtained in the current study are compared and are found to be in accord with the results obtained by PSO [16] and modified PSO (MPSO). Also, deviations in the optimum path reported in the current study from the different algorithms are illustrated using selected benchmark problems. The optimum path associated with selected problem (i.e., att48, pr76, and rd100) obtained using different algorithms is shown in Figs. 21.2, 21.3, and 21.4.

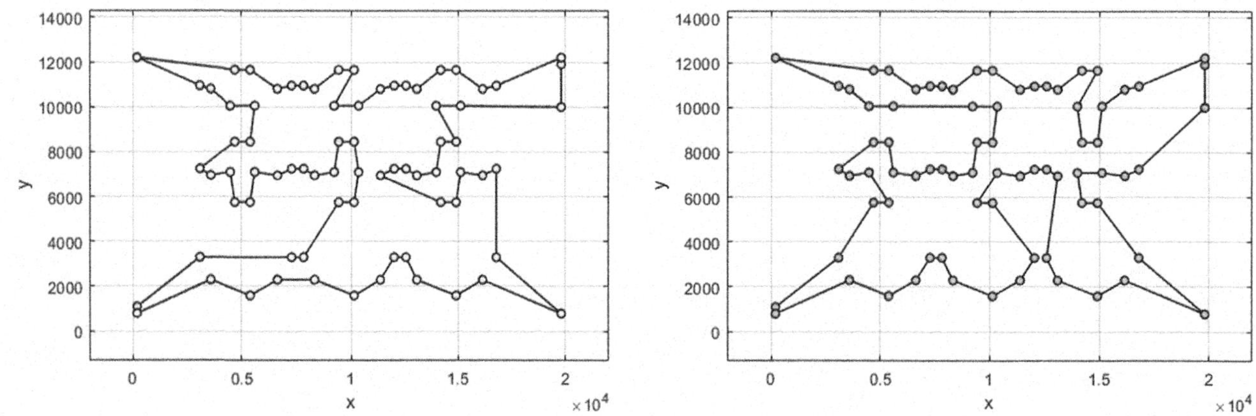

(A) GWO (B) TLBO

FIGURE 21.3 Pr76 GWO and TLBO optimum path (*GWO*, grey wolf optimization; *TLBO*, teaching-learning-based optimization).

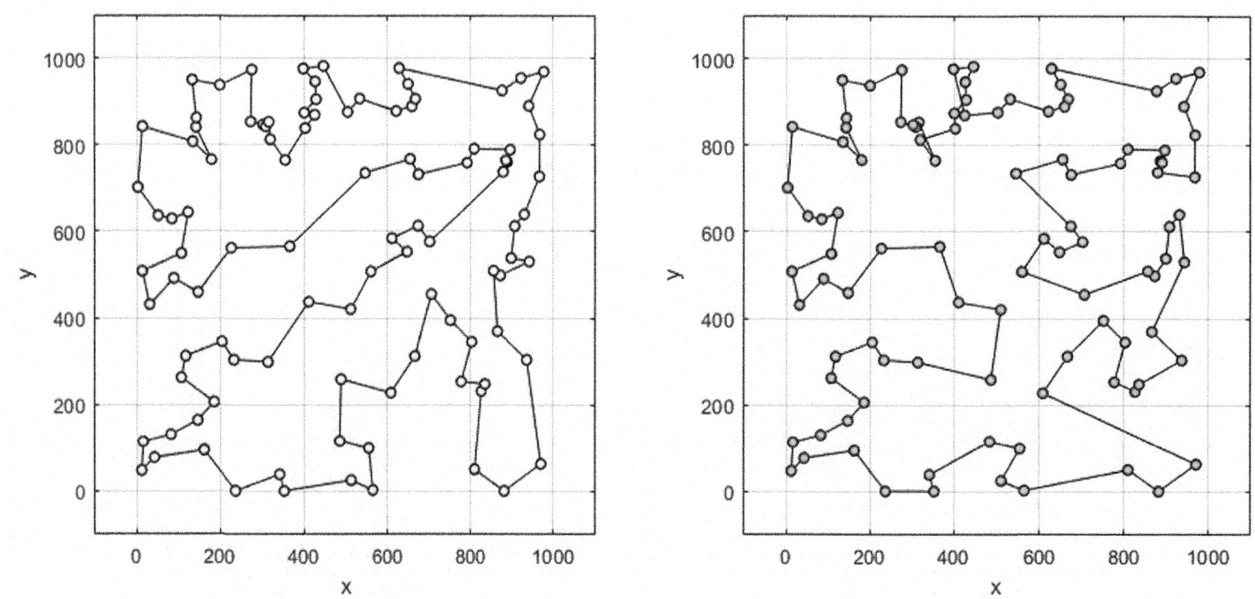

(A) GWO (B) TLBO

FIGURE 21.4 rd100 GWO and TLBO (*GWO*, grey wolf optimization; *TLBO*, teaching-learning-based optimization).

TABLE 21.2 Performance differences between GWO and TLBO.

Problem	Grey wolf optimization	Teaching learning based optimization	% Difference
ulysses16	73.99	75.11	1.51
ulysses22	75.67	76.6	1.23
att48	33,639	35,105.13	4.36
eil51	428.98	444.73	3.67
berlin52	7544.66	7742.94	2.63
st70	716.7	797.93	11.33
eil76	564.94	569.75	0.85
pr76	111,915.7	112,998	0.97
KroA100	22,196	22,756	2.52
kroB100	22,891	23,064	0.76
kroC100	21,944.31	22,087.76	0.65
rd100	8207.32	85,18.44	3.79
eil101	663.45	667.03	0.54
lin105	15,171.2	15,298.87	0.84
ch130	6493.43	6512.96	0.30
pr136	104,420.3	10,4561.7	0.14
pr144	64,778.16	65,175.62	0.61
ch150	7085.92	6923.48	-2.29
kroA150	29,036.51	29,414.28	1.30
rat195	2659.86	2660.19	0.01
d198	16,697.31	16,785.05	0.53
pr226	86,424.97	87,096.1	0.78
pr264	53,701.48	54,207.51	0.94
a280	2968.15	3074.9	3.60
pr299	52,000	52,400	0.77
Average	26,891.96	27,160.56	
Standard deviation	33,428.11	33,645.9	

GWO, Grey wolf optimization; *TLBO*, teaching-learning-based optimization.

From the table one, we run a correlation test and the result suggests that there exists a strong relationship between the optimum results from the TSP and the GWO, with an r value of 0.99. Also in table two, the performance of GWO and TLBO is illustrated in the form of variance. GWO outperformed the TLBO with 25 out of the 33 problems. The lower value in the table indicates better solutions and the same is shown in the chart illustrating the GWO being lower in points than the TLBO (Table 21.2).

The TLBO has a slightly higher average value (27,160) than GWO (26,891.96), according to the descriptive data. Nonetheless, both variables show extremely high standard deviations (33,428.11 for GWO and 33,645.9 for TLBO), suggesting significant variability and broad data dispersion. This implies that individual samples differ significantly from their corresponding averages. GWO and TLBO differ statistically significantly at the 5% significance level, according to the Wilcoxon signed-rank test results ($V = 46$, $P = .01647$). The null hypothesis, which indicates that there is no difference between the two related samples, is rejected since the P-value is less than 0.05. Consequently, there is enough data to draw the conclusion that there are substantial differences between the distributions (or central tendency) of GWO and TLBO.

Despite their similar mean values, the Wilcoxon test indicates that the observed difference between GWO and TLBO is statistically significant and unlikely to have happened by coincidence. This finding highlights the value of nonparametric techniques, like the Wilcoxon signed-rank test, particularly when the data are highly variable or do not meet the normal distribution assumption. Practically speaking, GWO and TLBO are not interchangeable. Rather than relying solely on a comparison of their average values, any conclusions, choices, or policies based on these measurements should acknowledge their substantial differences.

In Fig. 21.1 (A) and (B), the results for att48 are 33,639 and 35,105.13. Even though there is a slight difference in the configuration of the path, the difference is not enough, but the optimum results can better explain the variance. The graph with the yellow path is the GWO and the green is TLBO.

Also, in Fig. 21.3 (A) and (B), the results for pr76 are 111,915.74 and 112,998. The GWO result, which is 111,915.74, is less than the TLBO. The percentage error for both GWO and TLBO is 3.47 and 4.47. GWO is 1% percent lesser than the TLBO and vice versa. Moreover, even though there is a slight difference in the configuration of the path, the difference is not enough, but the optimum results can better explain the variance. Again, the graph with the yellow path is the GWO and green is TLBO.

In Fig. 21.3 (A), (B), and (C), the results for rd100 are 7942.24, 8207.32, and 8518.44. The tabu search result, which is 7942.24, is 1% less than the optimum result for pr76, but the GWO and TLBO is little higher. The percentage error for both GWO and TLBO are 3.76 and 7.69.

Finally, the TS performs better by providing a superior solution for the best result and minimum % error. It is clearly understood in Table 21.1 and Figs. 21.1, 21.2, and 21.3 provided for each problem that Tabu Search can solve problems that involve more than 100 cities and still get considerable solutions for the salesperson. It also competes with other well-known algorithms such as PSO and MPSO.

21.4 Conclusion

In conclusion, the GWO method provides a better solution for each benchmark problem as compared to the TLBO. These results are closer to the optimal solution, and as metaheuristics, GWO searches may be; it is safe to conclude that the results satisfy the near optimum objective. The variance between the GWO and the optimal solutions is less than that of the TLBO approach. The % error and difference, as illustrated in tables one and two provides a clear illustration of how efficient and effective GWO is in solving the traveling salesman problem, even with complex problems.

Even though several algorithms discussed in the literature provide some significant results when solving problems with minimum cities or locations, they perform poorly with larger problems. This can sometimes happen because some methods have slow convergence performance, which keeps them in the local optima. This is not good, especially in a real-time application that mostly involves complex operations with large cities. Bearing in mind that a larger city produces more delivery points. And the salesman is required to reach all those points in a reasonable time. In addition, the GWO accords with the PSO and MPSO with some problems. The GWO method provides a superior result for larger problems and it can be utilized in a real-world application. Therefore GWO should be considered first in real world application instead of TLBO.

Acknowledgment

The writers would like to appreciate the anonymous readers and technical editors for their immeasurable and productive views, which enhanced the quality and transparency of the paper.

References

[1] H.A. Abdulkarim, I.F. Alshammari, Comparison of algorithms for solving traveling saleman problem, Journal of Engineering and Advanced Technology (IJEAT) 4 (1) (2015).

[2] M.A. Akhand, S. Akter, M.A. Rashid, S.B. Yaakob, Velocity tentative PSO: an optimal velocity implementation based particle swarm optimization to solve traveling salesman problem," in 2013 International Conference on Electrical Information and Communication Technology, 2014.

[3] D. Karaboga, B. Gorkemli, Solving traveling salesman problem by using combinatorial artificial bee colony algorithms, Interational Journal on Artificial Intelligence Tools 28 (1) (2019).

[4] S. Boussier, M. Vasquez, Y. Vimont, S. Hanafi, P. Michelon, Solving the 0-1 Multidimensional Knapsack Problem with Resolution search, n.d.
[5] M. Dorigo, S. Member, L.M. Gambardella, Ant colony system: a cooperative learning approach to the traveling salesman proble, IEE Tranactions on Evolutionary Computation 1 (1) (1997) 53–66.
[6] X. Fu, An agglomerative greedy brain storm optimization algorithm for solving the TSP, IEE Access 8 (1) (2020).
[7] M. Gendreau, An introduction to tabu search, Handbook of Metaheuristics (n.d.) 37–54.
[8] F. Glover, Tabu search-part I., ORSA Journal on Computing (1989) 190-206.
[9] B. Johnson, Genetic algorithms: the traveling salesman problem, Medium (2017).
[10] A.R.V. Jorge, D.P. Ocotlan, C. Felipe, S. Andres, A.M. De los Angeles Buenadad, V.R. Gustavo, et al., Meta-heuristics algorithms based on the grouping of animals by social behavior for the traveling salesman problem, International Journal of Combinatorial Optimization Problems and Informatics 3 (3) (2012).
[11] J. Li, M. Zhou, Q. Sun, X. Dai, X. Yu, Colored traveling salesman problem, IEE Transactions on Cybernetics 45 (11) (2015) 2390–2401.
[12] Y. Lim, P. Hong, R. Ramli, R. Khalid, A. Baten, Research article performance evaluation of heuristic methods in solving symmetric travelling salesman problems, Journal of Artificial Intelligence 9 (1) (2016) 12–22.
[13] A. Mahmood, T.S.K. Homeed, Object replication in distributed web server systems with a hybrid tabu search algorithm, in: Proceedings of the 2006 International Conference on Advanced Computer and Information Technology (ACIT 2006), 2006.
[14] M. Mariem, D.T. Souhail, Dhouib-matrix-TSP1 method to optimize octogonal fuzzy travelling salesman problem using alpa-cut technique, International Journal of Computer and Information Technology (ISSN: 2279-0764) 10 (3) (2021) 130–133.
[15] N. Mittal, U. Singh, B.S. Sohi, Modified grey wolf optimizer for global engineering optimization, Applied Compuational Intelligence and Soft Computing (2016).
[16] S. Mirjalili, S.M. Mirjalili, A. Lewis, Grey wolf optimer, Advances in Engineering Software 69 (2014) 46–61.

Chapter 22

A hybrid GWO-PSO algorithm for sliding surface design in sliding mode control of 6R robot manipulators

Oguzhan Karahan and Hasan Karci
Department of Electronics and Communications Engineering, Kocaeli University, Izmit, Kocaeli, Türkiye

22.1 Introduction

Robot manipulators have become an essential part of industrial automation, medical systems, and various advanced technological applications due to their ability to perform complex tasks with high precision. Particularly, 6 degrees of freedom (6-DOF) robot manipulators are widely used in industrial applications. However, the control design for these systems is challenging due to their nonlinear dynamic structure, multiinput-multioutput characteristics, friction effects, and operational uncertainties [1].

Proportional-integral-derivative (PID) controllers have been extensively used in industrial applications for robot manipulator control due to their simple structure and ease of implementation. Ang et al. [2] presented a comprehensive review of PID control, highlighting its fundamental principles and industrial applications. For robot manipulators specifically, Craig [3] provided a detailed analysis of PID control implementation and its limitations. Tinoco et al. [4] demonstrated that while PID controllers are effective for simple positioning tasks, they struggle to handle the nonlinear dynamics and varying operating conditions of robot manipulators, particularly during high-speed operations and when external disturbances are present.

Fractional calculus has emerged as a powerful tool in control system design over the past decades. Podlubny [5] introduced the fractional-order $PI^{\lambda}D^{\mu}$ (FOPID) controller, which generalizes the classical PID controller by using fractional-order integration and differentiation. Chen et al. [6] presented comprehensive design methodologies for fractional-order controllers and demonstrated their advantages over integer-order counterparts, such as enhanced robustness and disturbance rejection. In robot manipulator applications, Monje et al. [7] implemented FOPID control and showed improved performance under dynamic payload variations, addressing a key limitation of classical PID controllers.

Utkin [8] introduced sliding mode control (SMC) as a robust nonlinear control technique, demonstrating its effectiveness in handling model uncertainties and disturbances. By driving system trajectories toward a predefined sliding surface and maintaining them there, SMC ensures insensitivity to matched perturbations. However, Edwards and Spurgeon [9] highlighted a major drawback of conventional SMC, known as the "chattering" phenomenon—high-frequency oscillations caused by discontinuous control signals—which can lead to actuator wear and reduced tracking accuracy.

To address this issue, researchers have explored various modifications and hybrid approaches. Palm [10] proposed a fuzzy logic-based sliding mode controller, while Efe [11] introduced an adaptive neuro-fuzzy inference system to enhance performance. Chen et al. [6] extended SMC to fractional-order SMC using fractional-order calculus, and Delavari et al. [12] demonstrated that this approach could improve transient response and mitigate chattering through noninteger-order sliding surfaces. Sharma et al. [13] further enhanced this concept by integrating FOPID structures with SMC, achieving superior trajectory tracking in robotic systems.

Grey Wolf Optimizer. DOI: https://doi.org/10.1016/B978-0-443-36624-6.00032-9

More recently, Ahmed and Azar [14] proposed an adaptive proportional derivative (PD) SMC strategy with a predefined-time approach to improve robustness and transient response in robotic systems. Pan [15] integrated a disturbance and state observer with fractional-order SMC to enhance disturbance rejection capabilities. Jing et al. [16] developed an adaptive supertwisting SMC technique, effectively mitigating input saturation effects in robot manipulators. Zhang et al. [17] introduced a novel disturbance observer-based fixed-time SMC with global fast convergence, ensuring rapid and accurate tracking in robotic applications. Similarly, Anjum et al. [18] applied a fixed-time SMC framework to handle disturbances in robotic manipulators, offering improved convergence speed and stability. Furthermore, Yang et al. [19] designed a time-delay SMC scheme to address trajectory tracking challenges in manipulators, particularly in the presence of time-varying uncertainties.

These advancements demonstrate the continuous evolution of SMC methodologies, leveraging adaptive, fractional-order, and fixed-time strategies to improve performance while minimizing chattering and enhancing robustness in robotic systems.

The tilted-integral-derivative (TID) controller, as described in U.S. Patent No. 5,371,670 [20], provides an alternative control strategy to classical PID by improving transient response and robustness in nonlinear systems. Priyadarshani et al. [21] extended the TID framework to fractional-order systems, introducing the fractional-order TID (FOTID) controller, which offers additional tuning flexibility and improved dynamic performance. Despite these advancements, the integration of TID/FOTID controllers within the SMC framework remains largely unexplored, particularly for high-DOF robotic systems. Calgan [22] represents a rare exception, proposing a tilt-integral sliding mode controller with an observer-based structure, yet the potential of FOTID-based sliding surfaces in SMC remains an open research gap.

The optimization of controller parameters significantly impacts system performance. Traditional manual tuning methods often fail in high-dimensional, nonconvex parameter spaces (i.e., optimization landscapes with multiple local minima). In recent years, nature-inspired optimization algorithms such as the grey wolf optimizer (GWO) [23] and particle swarm optimization (PSO) [24] have been developed to address these challenges. While GWO excels in avoiding local minima through its hierarchical search mechanism, PSO achieves rapid convergence via social swarm behavior. As Ibrahim et al. [25] demonstrated, hybridizing these algorithms combines their complementary strengths—GWO's exploration and PSO's exploitation—to overcome individual limitations.

Notably, Karahan and Karci [26] applied a hybrid GWO-PSO approach to identify friction and dynamic parameters in a 6-DOF manipulator, highlighting its efficacy in complex robotic systems. More recently, Ayinalem and Kassie [27] leveraged PSO to fine-tune a supertwisting sliding mode controller for articulated robots, demonstrating improved trajectory tracking accuracy. Basil et al. [28] proposed a hybrid optimization approach combining a FOPID-TID controller and the hybrid archimedes optimization algorithm rider optimization algorithm (HAOAROA) algorithm for unmanned aerial vehicle (UAV) path planning, achieving enhanced stability and performance in nonlinear environments. Furthermore, Karahan and Karci [29] extended their previous work by designing a robust fractional-order fuzzy PID sliding mode controller optimized via a hybrid swarm intelligence algorithm, significantly improving control precision in a 6-DOF robotic manipulator.

These studies emphasize the increasing adoption of hybrid and nature-inspired optimization strategies for tuning advanced controllers, particularly in systems with complex dynamics and fractional-order characteristics. By integrating these methods, researchers continue to enhance the robustness, adaptability, and performance of modern control architectures.

The implementation of fractional-order controllers in SMC has gained traction due to their ability to enhance robustness and reduce chattering. Sun et al. [30] and Zhang et al. [31] demonstrated improved disturbance rejection using fractional-order sliding surfaces. However, the application of FOTID controllers in SMC design remains unexplored, despite their potential to synergize fractional calculus benefits with TID's dynamic improvements. Robust control of robotic manipulators under uncertainties continues to be a critical challenge, as highlighted by Han et al. [32] and Nikdel et al. [33]. These studies highlight the need for enhanced strategies that inherently address both structured (e.g., parameter variations) and unstructured (e.g., external disturbances) uncertainties through flexible sliding surface design. Consequently, this motivates further research into FOTID-based SMC frameworks. Utilizing FOTID as a sliding surface offers a more flexible and robust structure by leveraging the advantages of fractional derivatives on uncertainties and the dynamic improvements of TID.

The main contributions of this work are summarized as follows:

1. Development of a novel FOTID-based sliding surface for SMC design, combining the advantages of fractional-order calculus and robust control
2. Implementation of a hybrid GWO-PSO optimization approach for optimal tuning of controller parameters

3. Comprehensive performance analysis of the proposed controller on a 6-DOF UR5 robot manipulator, including comparisons with PID, FOPID, and TID sliding surface-based controllers
4. Extensive evaluation under various operating conditions, including disturbance rejection and mass uncertainty scenarios
5. Validation of the proposed approach through rigorous simulation studies and comparative analysis

The remainder of this chapter is organized as follows: Section 22.2 presents the theoretical background, including SMC theory, fractional calculus, and optimization algorithms. Section 22.3 describes the proposed control structure and parameter optimization methodology. Section 22.4 presents simulation results and comparative analysis. Finally, Section 22.5 provides conclusions and future research directions.

22.2 Kinematic and dynamic model of the UR5 robot manipulator

This section presents the kinematic and dynamic modeling of the 6-DOF UR5 robot manipulator, which forms the foundation for controller design and simulation studies. The UR5, developed by Universal Robots, is a lightweight, collaborative robotic arm widely used in industrial and research applications. Its kinematic structure comprises six revolute joints, enabling high dexterity in a compact workspace.

22.2.1 Kinematic modeling

The kinematic model describes the geometric relationship between joint angles and end-effector position/orientation. For the UR5, the Denavit-Hartenberg (D-H) convention [3] is employed to define the coordinate frames and derive homogeneous transformation matrices. Fig. 22.1 provides a detailed representation of the coordinate frame assignment for each joint of the UR5 manipulator, along with the associated D-H parameters. The D-H convention is employed to derive the forward kinematic model of the UR5, with Table 22.1 listing the D-H parameters corresponding to the joint axes illustrated in Fig. 22.1.

The forward kinematics provides the transformation from joint space to Cartesian space. Using the D-H parameters, the homogeneous transformation matrix for each link is given by:

$$ {}^{i-1}_{i}T(q_i, d_i, a_i, \alpha_i,) = \begin{bmatrix} \cos q_i & -\sin q_i \cos\alpha_i & \sin q_i \sin\alpha_i & \alpha_i \cos q_i \\ \sin q_i & \cos q_i \cos\alpha_i & -\cos q_i \sin\alpha_i & \alpha_i \sin q_i \\ 0 & \sin\alpha_i & \cos\alpha_i & d_i \\ 0 & 0 & 0 & 1 \end{bmatrix} \quad (22.1) $$

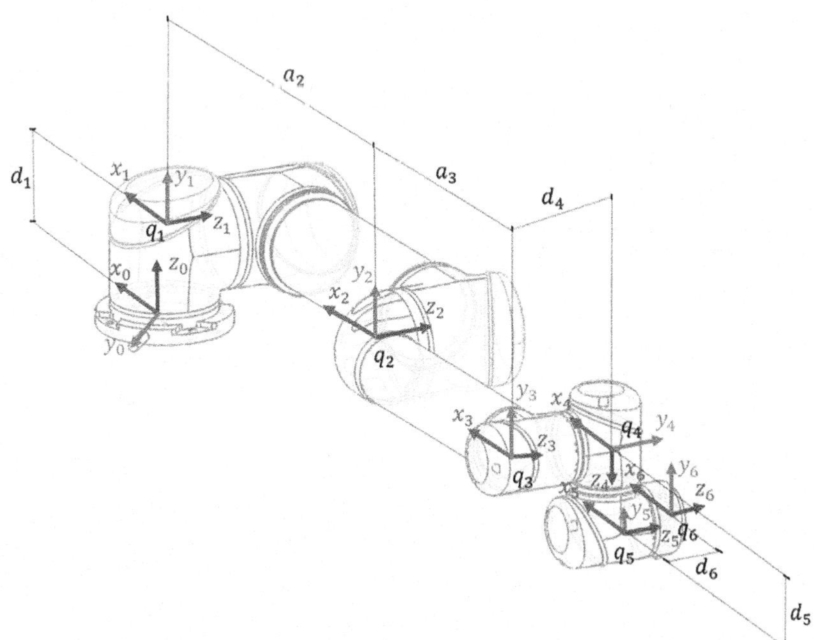

FIGURE 22.1 D-H convention of the UR5 (*D-H*, Denavit-Hartenberg).

TABLE 22.1 DH parameters of the UR5.

Joint i	a_i (mm)	α_i (rad)	d_i (mm)	q_i (rad)
1	0	$\pi/2$	89.16	q_1
2	−425	0	0	q_2
3	−392.25	0	0	q_3
4	0	$\pi/2$	109.15	q_4
5	0	$-\pi/2$	94.65	q_5
6	0	0	82.3	q_6

where i expresses the joint number, a denotes the link length, α denotes the twist angle, d denotes the link offset, and q denotes the joint rotation angle. The overall transformation from the base to the end-effector is obtained by multiplying the individual transformations:

$$
\begin{aligned}
{}^0_6T &= {}^0_1T\,{}^1_2T\,{}^2_3T\,{}^3_4T\,{}^4_5T\,{}^5_6T \\
&= \begin{bmatrix} cosq_1 & 0 & sinq_1 & 0 \\ sinq_1 & 0 & -cosq_1 & 0 \\ 0 & 1 & 0 & d_1 \\ 0 & 0 & 0 & 1 \end{bmatrix}
\begin{bmatrix} cosq_2 & -sinq_2 & 0 & a_2cosq_2 \\ sinq_2 & cosq_2 & 0 & a_2sinq_2 \\ 0 & 0 & 1 & 0 \\ 0 & 0 & 0 & 1 \end{bmatrix}
\begin{bmatrix} cosq_3 & -sinq_3 & 0 & a_3cosq_3 \\ sinq_3 & cosq_3 & 0 & a_3sinq_3 \\ 0 & 0 & 1 & 0 \\ 0 & 0 & 0 & 1 \end{bmatrix}\cdots \\
&\cdots\begin{bmatrix} cosq_4 & 0 & sinq_4 & 0 \\ sinq_4 & 0 & -cosq_4 & 0 \\ 0 & 1 & 0 & d_4 \\ 0 & 0 & 0 & 1 \end{bmatrix}
\begin{bmatrix} cosq_5 & 0 & -sinq_5 & 0 \\ sinq_5 & 0 & cosq_5 & 0 \\ 0 & -1 & 0 & d_5 \\ 0 & 0 & 0 & 1 \end{bmatrix}
\begin{bmatrix} cosq_6 & -sinq_6 & 0 & 0 \\ sinq_6 & cosq_6 & 0 & 0 \\ 0 & 0 & 1 & d_6 \\ 0 & 0 & 0 & 1 \end{bmatrix}
\end{aligned} \tag{22.2}
$$

The matrix ${}^0_6T$ encapsulates the UR5 position and orientation in the Cartesian task space. By performing the matrix multiplications outlined in Eq. (22.2), the resultant transformation is expressed as shown in Eq. (22.3).

$$
{}^0_6T = \begin{bmatrix} r_{11} & r_{12} & r_{13} & P_x \\ r_{21} & r_{22} & r_{23} & P_y \\ r_{31} & r_{32} & r_{33} & P_z \\ 0 & 0 & 0 & 1 \end{bmatrix} \tag{22.3}
$$

The terms of the transformation matrix in Eq. (22.3) are presented below:

$$
r_{11} = cosq_6(cosq_5cosq_1(cosq_2 + cosq_3 + cosq_4) + sinq_5sinq_1) - sinq_6cosq_1(sinq_2 + sinq_3 + sinq_4) \tag{22.4}
$$

$$
\begin{aligned}
r_{21} = {} & cosq_6(sinq_1cosq_5(cosq_4(cosq_2 + cosq_3) - sinq_4(sinq_2 + sinq_3)) - cosq_1sinq_5) \\
& - sinq_1sinq_6(sinq_4(cosq_2 + cosq_3) + cosq_4(sinq_2 + sinq_3))
\end{aligned} \tag{22.5}
$$

$$
r_{31} = cosq_5cosq_6(sinq_2 + sinq_3 + sinq_4) + sinq_6(cosq_2 + cosq_3 + cosq_4) \tag{22.6}
$$

$$
r_{12} = -sinq_6(cosq_1cosq_5(cosq_2 + cosq_3 + cosq_4) + sinq_1sinq_5) + cosq_1cosq_6(sinq_2 + sinq_3 + sinq_4) \tag{22.7}
$$

$$
\begin{aligned}
r_{22} = {} & -sinq_6(sinq_1cosq_5(cosq_4(cosq_2 + cosq_3) - sinq_4(sinq_2 + sinq_3)) - cosq_1sinq_5) \\
& - sinq_1cosq_6(sinq_4(cosq_2 + cosq_3) + cosq_4(sinq_2 + sinq_3))
\end{aligned} \tag{22.8}
$$

$$
r_{32} = -cosq_5sinq_6(sinq_2 + sinq_3 + sinq_4) + cosq_6(cosq_2 + cosq_3 + cosq_4) \tag{22.9}
$$

$$r_{13} = -cosq_1 sinq_5(cosq_2 + cosq_3 + cosq_4) + sinq_1 cosq_5 \tag{22.10}$$

$$r_{23} = -sinq_1 sinq_5(cosq_4(cosq_2 + cosq_3) - sinq_4(sinq_2 + sinq_3)) - cosq_1 cosq_5 \tag{22.11}$$

$$r_{33} = sinq_5(sinq_2 + sinq_3 + sinq_4) \tag{22.12}$$

$$\begin{aligned} p_x = & -d_6(cosq_1 sinq_5(cosq_2 + cosq_3 + cosq_4) - sinq_1 cosq_5) + d_5 cosq_1(sinq_2 + sinq_3 + sinq_4) + d_4 sinq_1 \\ & + a_3 cosq_1(cosq_2 + cosq_3) + a_2 cosq_1 cosq_2 \end{aligned} \tag{22.13}$$

$$\begin{aligned} p_y = & -d_6(sinq_1 sinq_5(cosq_2 + cosq_3 + cosq_4) + cosq_1 cosq_5) + d_5 sinq_1(sinq_2 + sinq_3 + sinq_4) - d_4 cosq_1 \\ & + a_3 sinq_1(cosq_2 + cosq_3) + a_2 sinq_1 cosq_2 \end{aligned} \tag{22.14}$$

$$p_z = d_1 - d_6 sinq_5((sinq_2 + sinq_3 + sinq_4)) - d_5(cosq_2 + cosq_3 + cosq_4) + a_3(sinq_2 + sinq_3) + a_2 sinq_2 \tag{22.15}$$

Inverse kinematics determines the joint angles required to achieve a given end-effector position and orientation. Due to the redundancy of a 6-DOF manipulator, multiple solutions may exist. The inverse kinematics can be solved analytically or numerically [3]. The analytical solution involves decomposing the transformation matrix and solving for each joint variable, whereas numerical methods, such as the Newton–Raphson iteration, rely on optimization techniques. Analytical methods exploit the specific geometry of the UR5, while numerical methods like the Jacobian inverse or iterative techniques offer flexibility for more complex configurations [1].

The UR5 geometry allows for an analytical solution by simplifying the transformation matrix. The wrist center position can be calculated first, decoupling the position and orientation problems. The joint angles for the first three joints are determined based on the wrist position, while the last three joints, responsible for orientation, are derived from the wrist alignment.

For configurations where the analytical approach is impractical, the Jacobian inverse method offers a robust alternative. This iterative technique adjusts joint variables to minimize the positional and orientational error of the end-effector. The Newton–Raphson iteration is particularly effective for rapid convergence in scenarios with good initial estimates.

22.2.2 Dynamic modeling

Robot manipulator dynamics can be mathematically formulated using either the Lagrange–Euler or Newton–Euler methodology. These approaches create comprehensive dynamic models that characterize the relationships between joint torques and the system's kinematic parameters – positions, velocities, and accelerations. The equations of motion, fundamental to robot manipulator dynamics, express the dynamic behavior of serial n-joint rigid body systems in a standardized mathematical framework. As shown in Eq. (22.16), these equations provide the essential mathematical foundation linking joint torques with the manipulator's kinematic and dynamic characteristics [34].

$$\tau = M(q)\ddot{q} + C(q, \dot{q})\dot{q} + G(q) + \tau_{exd}(q, \dot{q}) \tag{22.16}$$

Several components influence the dynamics of a robot manipulator, including the mass matrix $M(q) \in \mathbb{R}^{n\times n}$, the centripetal-Coriolis vector $C(q, \dot{q}) \in \mathbb{R}^{n\times n}$, the gravity vector $G(q) \in \mathbb{R}^n$, and external disturbances $\tau_{exd}(q, \dot{q})$. The joint torques $\tau \in \mathbb{R}^n$ are derived based on these elements, along with the desired joint positions $q \in \mathbb{R}^n$, velocities $\dot{q} \in \mathbb{R}^n$, and accelerations $\ddot{q} \in \mathbb{R}^n$. The Jacobian matrix plays a key role in linking workspace forces to joint space torques. Among the disturbances and uncertainties, friction is particularly significant, and a novel friction model addressing joint friction effects is introduced in [26]. The dynamic model of the UR5 manipulator depends on the precise physical parameters given in Table 22.2.

The distribution of mass across the links (m_1 to m_6) significantly affects the manipulator's inertia and overall dynamic behavior. Accurate determination of each link's center of mass is crucial for precise gravity vector calculations, influencing stability and control accuracy. Additionally, the inertia matrices (I_1 to I_6) define each link's resistance to changes in rotational motion, playing a pivotal role in the robot's dynamic response. These parameters are typically provided by the manufacturer or obtained through experimental identification methods.

22.2.3 Equation of motion

Forward or integral dynamics are required to analyze the manipulator's motion in response to the forces and torques applied at its joints. Eq. (22.16) describes the manipulator's dynamics through joint angular velocities and motor torques,

TABLE 22.2 Dynamic parameters of the UR5.

Link i	Mass $m_i(kg)$	Center of mass $r_i(mm)$	Inertia tensor $I_i(kgm^2)$
1	3.7	$[0, -25.61, 1.93]^T$	$diag([0.010, 0.010, 0.006])$
2	8.393	$[212.5, 0, 113.36]^T$	$diag([0.226, 0.226, 0.015])$
3	2.275	$[119.93, 0, 26.5]^T$	$diag([0.049, 0.049, 0.004])$
4	1.219	$[0, -1.8, 16.34]^T$	$diag([0.011, 0.011, 0.009])$
5	1.219	$[0, -1.8, 16.34]^T$	$diag([0.011, 0.011, 0.009])$
6	0.1879	$[0, 0, -1.159]^T$	$diag([0.001, 0.001, 0.001])$

forming the basis for actuator control and precise trajectory tracking. The angular acceleration $\ddot{q}$ can be derived by applying the inverse of the mass matrix $M^{-1}(q)$ to both sides of the equation.

$$\ddot{q} = M^{-1}(q)u_c(t) - M^{-1}(q)C(q,\dot{q})\dot{q} - M^{-1}(q)G(q) - M^{-1}(q)\tau_{exd}(q,\dot{q}) \tag{22.17}$$

In robotic dynamics, the torque vector τ is often represented as $u_c(t)$ in control formulations. Accurate friction modeling is critical for high-precision motion control, with traditional approaches such as the Coulomb-viscous and Stribeck-effect models serving as foundational frameworks. While these models effectively characterize steady-state friction behavior, they exhibit limitations in capturing transient nonlinearities, particularly hysteresis effects during velocity reversals.

To overcome these shortcomings, the centro-symmetric friction model (CSFM) has been introduced, offering a holistic representation of friction dynamics [26]. Unlike the Coulomb-viscous model, which provides a linear approximation of friction forces, and the Stribeck-curve approach, which accounts for velocity-dependent transitions, the CSFM uniquely incorporates hysteresis phenomena and asymmetric joint friction behavior. This capability makes it particularly suited for robotic systems operating under variable payloads and bidirectional motion regimes.

Empirical studies [26] advocate the adoption of CSFM for friction identification in robotic manipulators due to its enhanced fidelity in dynamic scenarios. The model's mathematical formulation is expressed as follows:

$$\tau_{exd}(q,\dot{q}) = \begin{cases} T_v^+\dot{q} + sign(\dot{q})\left(T_c^+ + (T_s^- - T_c^+)e^{-\left|\frac{\dot{q}}{\dot{q}_s^+}\right|^{\delta^+}}\right)(\dot{q} \geq 0, \ddot{q} < 0) \\ T_v^+\dot{q} + sign(\dot{q})\left(T_c^+ + (-T_s^- - T_c^+)e^{-\left|\frac{\dot{q}}{\dot{q}_s^-}\right|^{\delta^-}}\right)(\dot{q} \geq 0, \ddot{q} \geq 0) \\ T_v^-\dot{q} + sign(\dot{q})\left(T_c^- + (T_s^+ - T_c^-)e^{-\left|\frac{\dot{q}}{\dot{q}_s^+}\right|^{\delta^+}}\right)(\dot{q} < 0, \ddot{q} \geq 0) \\ T_v^-\dot{q} + sign(\dot{q})\left(T_c^- + (-T_s^- - T_c^-)e^{-\left|\frac{\dot{q}}{\dot{q}_s^-}\right|^{\delta^-}}\right)(\dot{q} < 0, \ddot{q} < 0) \end{cases} \tag{22.18}$$

where T_v, T_c and T_s represent the viscous, Coulomb, and static friction coefficients, respectively, while $\dot{q}_s$, δ and δ denote the Stribeck velocity and shape factor. By incorporating the CSFM framework, the complete robot dynamics model can be derived by substituting Eq. (22.18) into Eq. (22.17).

22.3 Proposed controller structures

The control system design encompasses multiple approaches, starting with basic SMC incorporating PID surfaces and advancing to more sophisticated methods using fractional-order and tilt-integral elements. These control strategies aim to achieve precise tracking and stability for the end effector, building upon the model-based capabilities of SMC. The control architecture adapts to specific system dynamics, with stability guaranteed through Lyapunov theory. The robust nature of SMC enables effective handling of model uncertainties while maintaining performance.

A significant challenge in SMC involves chattering phenomena. These oscillations in the control output across the saturation range can lead to mechanical wear and structural degradation. While adding an integral term to traditional PD-based sliding surfaces helps reduce chattering, complete elimination remains challenging.

Recent developments propose innovative sliding surface configurations that incorporate fractional-order calculus and tilt-integral-derivative strategies. These approaches aim to minimize chattering effects while enhancing controller robustness. The control design process begins with PID-based SMC, then progresses through several advanced configurations:

- Fractional-order PID SMC replaces conventional integer-order elements with fractional calculations
- Tilt-integral-derivative SMC enhances performance through tilt compensation
- Combined fractional-order and tilt-integral-derivative SMC merges these advanced concepts for optimal tracking and stability

22.3.1 PIDSMC structures

In PIDSMC, the sliding surface is designed by integrating the classical PID structure into the sliding mode framework. This integration leverages the well-known benefits of PID control—namely, its ability to reduce steady-state error and improve transient response—while also capitalizing on the inherent robustness of SMC against system uncertainties and external disturbances [35]. The design of the sliding surface in PIDSMC is typically formulated as:

$$\sigma(t) = K_p e(t) + K_i \int e(t)dt + K_d \dot{e}(t) \tag{22.19}$$

where K_p, K_i, and K_d are positive constants that weight the contributions of the proportional, integral, and derivative components, respectively. Let $q_d(t)$ and $q_a(t)$ be the desired and actuated trajectories, and define the tracking error as:

$$e(t) = q_d(t) - q_a(t) \tag{22.20}$$

The sliding surface in PID-based SMC is constructed using position tracking deviation and velocity variables. A fundamental requirement for achieving stable sliding mode operation involves the convergence of the time derivative of the sliding surface to zero. When this convergence condition is met, the system's tracking error naturally diminishes, resulting in the actual motion path matching the desired trajectory. At this point, only maintenance-level control effort is needed for trajectory tracking. The time derivative of the sliding surface can be obtained from the following equation:

$$\dot{\sigma}(t) = K_p \dot{e}(t) + K_i e(t) + K_d \ddot{e}(t) \tag{22.21}$$

Substituting $\ddot{e}(t) = \ddot{q}_d(t) - \ddot{q}_a(t)$ into the equation above, the primary derivative of $\sigma(t)$ is determined as:

$$\dot{\sigma}(t) = K_p \dot{e}(t) + K_i e(t) + K_d (\ddot{q}_d(t) - \ddot{q}_a(t)) \tag{22.22}$$

Integrating the motion dynamics into the preceding equation results in:

$$\begin{aligned}\dot{\sigma}(t) = {} & K_p \dot{e}(t) + K_i e(t) + K_d (\ddot{q}_d(t) - (M(q))^{-1} u(t) + (M(q))^{-1} C(q, \dot{q})\dot{q} + (M(q))^{-1} G(q) \\ & + (M(q))^{-1}(q)\tau_d(q, \dot{q}))\end{aligned} \tag{22.23}$$

Setting this relationship to zero produces the equivalent control input, described by:

$$\begin{aligned}u_{eq}(t) = {} & ((M(q))^{-1})^{-1} \Bigg(\ddot{q}_d(t) + (M(q))^{-1} C(q, \dot{q})\dot{q} + (M(q))^{-1} G(q) + (M(q))^{-1} \tau_d(q, \dot{q}) \\ & + \frac{K_p}{K_d} \dot{e}(t) + \frac{K_i}{K_d} e(t) \Bigg)\end{aligned} \tag{22.24}$$

The reaching law, shown in the previous equation, forms an essential element of SMC methodology. This law ensures closed-loop system stability and guides system behavior toward the sliding surface. Several reaching law variations exist, including exponential, fixed rate, and power rate approaches [36].

A key challenge in SMC implementation involves chattering phenomena, which can impair controller performance. This chattering occurs due to discontinuous switching behavior along the sliding surface. To reduce these unwanted oscillations, designers often implement a narrow boundary region around the switching surface. Common approaches include saturation functions [37] or smooth sigmoid functions to replace the traditional sign function. For this control design, a sigmoid-based switching input is selected, defined as:

$$u_{sw}(t) = \varpi \frac{\sigma(t)}{|\sigma(t)| + \varrho} \tag{22.25}$$

In this formulation, $\varrho > 0$ represents the boundary layer thickness, and $\varpi > 0$ is the parameter that governs the speed at which the control signal reaches the sliding surface during the reaching phase. As a result, the overall PIDSMC control law is composed of the equivalent control, $u_{eq}(t)$, and the switching (or reaching) control, $u_{sw}(t)$, as shown below:

$$\begin{aligned} u_{pidsmc}(t) &= u_{eq}(t) + u_{sw}(t) \\ &= ((M(q))^{-1})^{-1}\Big(\ddot{q}_d(t) + (M(q))^{-1}C(q,\dot{q})\dot{q} + (M(q))^{-1}G(q) \\ &\quad + (M(q))^{-1}\tau_d(q,\dot{q}) + \frac{K_p}{K_d}\dot{e}(t) + \frac{K_i}{K_d}e(t) + \varpi\frac{\sigma(t)}{|\sigma(t)| + \varrho}\Big) \end{aligned} \tag{22.26}$$

22.3.2 FOPIDSMC structures

Unlike traditional or intelligent control methods, the approach presented here leverages fractional calculus—a mathematical framework that provides additional degrees of freedom in controller design. This added flexibility enables the proposed controller to achieve a superior closed-loop response and robust performance, as demonstrated in [38]. Several methods exist for fractional calculus analysis, such as the Riemann–Liouville, Caputo, Grunwald–Letnikov, and Oustaloup approaches. Among these, the Riemann–Liouville definition is most commonly employed. In the time domain, the fractional derivative and integral of a function $f(t)$ are expressed as [39]:

$$D_t^{\alpha} f(t) = \frac{1}{\mathrm{P}(\varepsilon - \alpha)} \frac{d^{\varepsilon}}{dt^{\varepsilon}} \int_{\rho}^{t} \frac{f(\tau)}{(t-\tau)^{\alpha-\varepsilon+1}} d\tau \tag{22.27}$$

where $\varepsilon - 1 < \alpha < \varepsilon$, $\varepsilon \in \mathbb{N}$, $\alpha \in \mathbb{R}^+$ and $\mathrm{P}(\cdot)$ Euler's Gamma function defined as:

$$\mathrm{P}(x) = \int_0^{\infty} t^{x-1} e^{-t} dt, \ \mathbb{R}(x) > 0 \tag{22.28}$$

Within this framework, the fractional integral and derivative operators are denoted by $D_t^{-\lambda} f(t)$ and $D_t^{\mu} f(t)$, respectively, with λ and μ being positive real numbers. For brevity, these are written as $D^{-\lambda}$ and D^{μ}.

Recent research has demonstrated that incorporating fractional calculus into control design can significantly improve the performance and robustness of standard PID controllers. This insight led to the development of the FOPID controller, often represented as $PI^{\lambda}D^{\mu}$, where λ and μ denote the orders of the fractional integral and derivative actions, respectively. The differential form of the $PI^{\lambda}D^{\mu}$ controller is given by:

$$\sigma(t) = K_p e(t) + K_i D_t^{-\lambda} e(t) + K_d D_t^{\mu} e(t) \tag{22.29}$$

which is used as the sliding surface in the SMC scheme [40]. A crucial aspect of this design is that when the second derivative of the sliding surface, $\ddot{\sigma}(t) \to 0$, approaches zero, it ensures that both the tracking error and its derivative converge to zero within the sliding mode. This typically results in a faster convergence to the sliding mode compared to conventional PIDSMC, thereby enabling quicker tracking of the desired trajectory.

Differentiating the sliding surface expression twice leads to:

$$\ddot{\sigma}(t) = K_p \ddot{e}(t) + K_i D_t^{-\lambda+2} e(t) + K_d D_t^{\mu+2} e(t) \tag{22.30}$$

By substituting $\ddot{e}(t) = \ddot{q}_d(t) - \ddot{q}_a(t)$ into the above equation, the following is obtained:

$$\ddot{\sigma}(t) = K_p(\ddot{q}_d(t) - \ddot{q}_a(t)) + K_i D_t^{-\lambda+2} e(t) + K_d D_t^{\mu+2} e(t) \tag{22.31}$$

Further, by replacing the actual angular acceleration $\ddot{q}_a(t)$ with its expression from Eq. (22.16), the equation becomes:

$$\ddot{\sigma}(t) = K_p(\ddot{q}_d(t) - (M(q))^{-1}\tau + (M(q))^{-1}C(q,\dot{q})\dot{q} + (M(q))^{-1}G(q) + (M(q))^{-1}\tau_d(q,\dot{q})) + K_iD_t^{-\lambda+2}e(t) + K_dD_t^{\mu+2}e(t) \tag{22.32}$$

By enforcing the sliding mode condition, that is, setting $\ddot{\sigma}(t) = 0$, the solution for the equivalent control input $u_{eq}(t)$ can be found:

$$u_{eq}(t) = ((M(q))^{-1})^{-1}\left(\ddot{q}_d(t) + (M(q))^{-1}C(q,\dot{q})\dot{q} + (M(q))^{-1}G(q) + (M(q))^{-1}\tau_d(q,\dot{q}) + \frac{K_d}{K_p}D_t^{\mu+2}e(t) + \frac{K_i}{K_p}D_t^{-\lambda+2}e(t)\right) \tag{22.33}$$

Finally, by combining the equivalent control with a switching control component $u_{sw}(t)$ (implemented via a sigmoid function as in PIDSMC), the total control law for the FOPIDSMC is expressed as:

$$u_{fopidsmc}(t) = u_{eq}(t) + u_{sw}(t)$$

$$= ((M(q))^{-1})^{-1}\left(\ddot{q}_d(t) + (M(q))^{-1}C(q,\dot{q})\dot{q} + (M(q))^{-1}G(q) + (M(q))^{-1}\tau_d(q,\dot{q}) + \frac{K_d}{K_p}D_t^{\mu+2}e(t) + \frac{K_i}{K_p}D_t^{-\lambda+2}e(t) + \varpi\frac{\sigma(t)}{|\sigma(t)| + \varrho}\right) \tag{22.34}$$

This formulation successfully integrates the fractional order PID sliding surface into the SMC framework, thereby incorporating the benefits of fractional calculus to enhance system robustness and reduce chattering.

22.3.3 TIDSMC structures

The TID controller shares many similarities with a conventional PID controller, with the primary distinction being its modified proportional term. In this design, the proportional component is "tilted" and is modeled by a transfer function that incorporates a factor of $s^{-1/n}$. Furthermore, fractional order controllers broaden the traditional concept of integration and differentiation by allowing these operations to be executed at noninteger, fractional orders. The differential form of the TID controller is given by:

$$\sigma(t) = K_tD_t^{-\frac{1}{n}}e(t) + K_i\int e(t)dt + K_d\dot{e}(t) \tag{22.35}$$

The given expression for the TID controller is incorporated into the sliding surface of SMC, demonstrating superior performance over traditional PID-based sliding surfaces. This leads to more robust closed-loop dynamics and faster convergence of the system trajectory to the desired path, offering notable improvements in overall control performance compared to conventional PID schemes. The time derivative of the sliding surface can be obtained from the following equation:

$$\dot{\sigma}(t) = K_tD_t^{-\frac{1}{n}+1}e(t) + K_ie(t) + K_d\ddot{e}(t) \tag{22.36}$$

Substituting $\ddot{e}(t)$ into the equation above, the primary derivative of $\sigma(t)$ is determined as:

$$\dot{\sigma}(t) = K_tD_t^{-\frac{1}{n}+1}e(t) + K_ie(t) + K_d(\ddot{q}_d(t) - \ddot{q}_a(t)) \tag{22.37}$$

Integrating the motion dynamics into the preceding equation results in:

$$\dot{\sigma}(t) = K_tD_t^{-\frac{1}{n}+1}e(t) + K_ie(t) + K_d(\ddot{q}_d(t) - (M(q))^{-1}u(t) + (M(q))^{-1}C(q,\dot{q})\dot{q} + (M(q))^{-1}G(q) + (M(q))^{-1}\tau_d(q,\dot{q})) \tag{22.38}$$

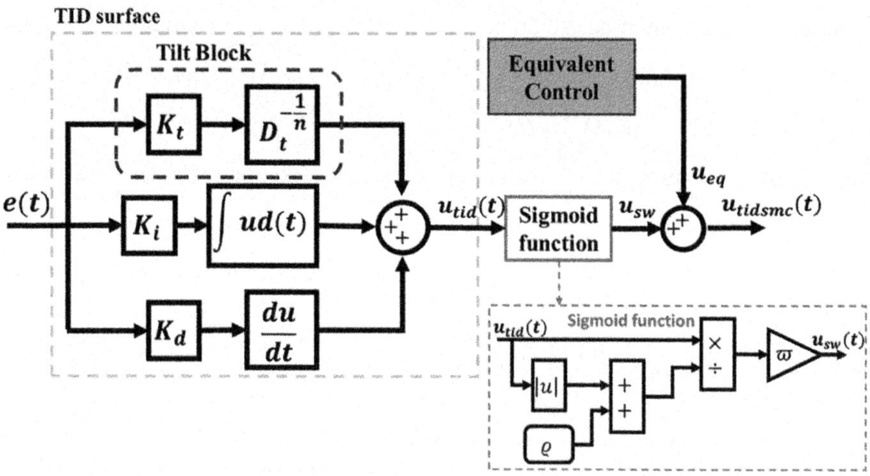

FIGURE 22.2 Illustration depicting the structure of the TID-based sliding mode controller (*TID*, Tilted-integral-derivative).

Setting this relationship to zero produces the equivalent control input, described by:

$$u_{eq}(t) = ((M(q))^{-1})^{-1}\left(\ddot{q}_d(t) + (M(q))^{-1}C(q,\dot{q})\dot{q} + (M(q))^{-1}G(q) + (M(q))^{-1}\tau_d(q,\dot{q}) + \frac{K_t}{K_d}D_t^{-\frac{1}{n}+1}e(t) + \frac{K_i}{K_d}e(t)\right) \tag{22.39}$$

Ultimately, integrating the equivalent control with the switching control component $u_{sw}(t)$ (implemented via a sigmoid function similar to that in PIDSMC) yields the complete control law for TIDSMC, expressed as:

$$\begin{aligned} u_{tidsmc}(t) &= u_{eq}(t) + u_{sw}(t) \\ &= ((M(q))^{-1})^{-1}\left(\ddot{q}_d(t) + (M(q))^{-1}C(q,\dot{q})\dot{q} + (M(q))^{-1}G(q) + (M(q))^{-1}\tau_d(q,\dot{q}) + \frac{K_t}{K_d}D_t^{-\frac{1}{n}+1} + \frac{K_i}{K_d}e(t) + \varpi\frac{\sigma(t)}{|\sigma(t)| + \varrho}\right) \end{aligned} \tag{22.40}$$

Fig. 22.2 illustrates the structure of TIDSMC, detailing how the tilted integral derivative component is integrated within the SMC framework. This diagram highlights the interplay between the equivalent control and the switching control components, which together enhance robustness and mitigate chattering.

22.3.4 FOTIDSMC structures

FOTIDSMC represents an advanced synthesis of the TID control strategy with fractional order operators within a sliding mode framework. By extending the classical TID sliding surface with fractional order integration and differentiation, this approach introduces additional degrees of freedom that allow for finer tuning of the controller dynamics.

The continuous-time structure of the proposed FOTID controller for the SMC sliding surface is similar to that of a FOPID controller [21], with a fractional order or noninteger order integrator and differentiator.

$$\sigma(t) = K_t D_t^{-\frac{1}{n}} e(t) + K_i D_t^{-\lambda} e(t) + K_d D_t^{\mu} e(t) \tag{22.41}$$

Taking the second derivative of the sliding surface expression yields:

$$\ddot{\sigma}(t) = K_t D_t^{-\frac{1}{n}} \ddot{e}(t) + K_i D_t^{-\lambda+2} e(t) + K_d D_t^{\mu+2} e(t) \tag{22.42}$$

Substituting $\ddot{e}(t) = \ddot{q}_d(t) - \ddot{q}_a(t)$ into the preceding equation yields the following:

$$\ddot{\sigma}(t) = K_t D_t^{-\frac{1}{n}} (\ddot{q}_d(t) - \ddot{q}_a(t)) + K_i D_t^{-\lambda+2} e(t) + K_d D_t^{\mu+2} e(t) \tag{22.43}$$

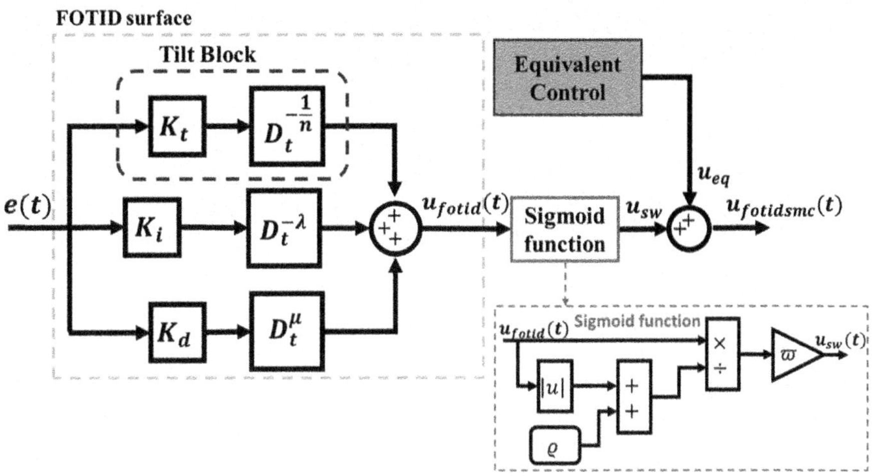

FIGURE 22.3 Diagram depicting the structure of the fractional order TID-based sliding mode controller (*TID*, Tilted-integral-derivative).

Further, by substituting the expression for the actual angular acceleration $\ddot{q}_a(t)$ from Eq. (22.16), the equation is transformed into:

$$\begin{aligned}\ddot{\sigma}(t) = K_t D_t^{-\frac{1}{n}}(\ddot{q}_d(t) - (M(q))^{-1}\tau + (M(q))^{-1}C(q,\dot{q})\dot{q} + (M(q))^{-1}G(q) + (M(q))^{-1}\tau_d(q,\dot{q})) \\ + K_i D_t^{-\lambda+2}e(t) + K_d D_t^{\mu+2}e(t)\end{aligned} \tag{22.44}$$

By imposing the sliding mode condition — that is, setting $\ddot{\sigma}(t) = 0$ — the equivalent control input $u_{eq}(t)$ can be determined as follows:

$$\begin{aligned}u_{eq}(t) = ((M(q))^{-1})^{-1}\Bigg(\ddot{q}_d(t) + (M(q))^{-1}C(q,\dot{q})\dot{q} + (M(q))^{-1}G(q) + (M(q))^{-1}\tau_d(q,\dot{q}) \\ + \frac{K_d}{K_t}D_t^{\mu+\frac{1}{n}+2}e(t) + \frac{K_i}{K_t}D_t^{-\lambda+\frac{1}{n}+2}e(t)\Bigg)\end{aligned} \tag{22.45}$$

Ultimately, by integrating the equivalent control with a switching control component $u_{sw}(t)$ (implemented via a sigmoid function as in PIDSMC), the complete control law for FOTIDSMC can be expressed as:

$$\begin{aligned}u_{fotidsmc}(t) = u_{eq}(t) + u_{sw}(t) \\ = ((M(q))^{-1})^{-1}\Bigg(\ddot{q}_d(t) + (M(q))^{-1}C(q,\dot{q})\dot{q} + (M(q))^{-1}G(q) + (M(q))^{-1}\tau_d(q,\dot{q}) + \frac{K_d}{K_t}D_t^{\mu+\frac{1}{n}+2}e(t) \\ + \frac{K_i}{K_t}D_t^{-\lambda+\frac{1}{n}+2}e(t) + \varpi\frac{\sigma(t)}{|\sigma(t)| + \varrho}\Bigg)\end{aligned} \tag{22.46}$$

Consequently, FOTIDSMC offers enhanced sensitivity to rapid error variations, improved disturbance rejection, and a significant reduction in chattering compared to its integer-order counterparts.

Fig. 22.3 presents a schematic overview of the FOTIDSMC controller, illustrating how the fractional order TID sliding surface is seamlessly integrated into the SMC framework. This diagram emphasizes the interplay between the fractional order components and the switching control mechanism, highlighting the controller's enhanced robustness and its effective mitigation of chattering.

22.3.5 Stability analysis

The stability of the proposed control system can be rigorously proven using Lyapunov's direct method. This analysis demonstrates the convergence of the sliding surface and tracking errors to zero. A common choice for the Lyapunov function in SMC is:

$$V(t) = \frac{1}{2}\sigma^2(t) \tag{22.47}$$

where $\sigma(t)$ denotes the sliding surface, which encapsulates the tracking error dynamics of the system. This function is positive definite and radially unbounded, meeting the fundamental criteria required for a Lyapunov candidate.

The time derivative of $\mathrm{V}(t)$ is given by:

$$\begin{aligned}\dot{\mathrm{V}}(t) &= \sigma(t)\dot{\sigma}(t) \\ &= -\varpi\frac{\sigma^2(t)}{|\sigma(t)| + \varrho} < 0\end{aligned} \tag{22.48}$$

The negative definiteness of $\dot{\mathrm{V}}(t)$ directly implies that the sliding surface $\sigma(t)$ converges to zero. Since the sliding surface is directly related to the tracking error, its convergence guarantees that the tracking error also tends to zero. Consequently, the actual system trajectory converges to the desired trajectory, and the closed-loop system achieves asymptotic stability.

This Lyapunov-based stability analysis not only validates the robustness of the SMC design against system uncertainties and disturbances but also provides a systematic approach for tuning the controller gains to meet specific performance criteria.

22.4 Optimization of controller parameters using the grey wolf optimizer-particle swarm optimization hybrid algorithm

Achieving the desired control performance requires precise optimization of controller parameters using an appropriate objective function. This study uses the GWO-PSO hybrid algorithm to fine-tune the controller parameters. The Oustaloup method approximates the fractional operator within the structure of fractional order controllers, with an approximation order of N=5 and a frequency range of [0.01, 100] rad/s. The simulations were conducted in the MATLAB/Simulink environment using the Bogacki–Shampine method as the ordinary differential equation (ODE) solver, operating with a 1 ms sampling time to ensure accurate numerical integration during the optimization process. The primary goal is to minimize the objective function defined in Eq. (22.49):

$$f_{obj} = \frac{1}{mT}\sqrt{\sum_{t=1}^{T}\sum_{i=1}^{m}|e_{t,i}|^2} \rightarrow \min \tag{22.49}$$

where m represents the total number of robot joints, T denotes the dataset size, $e_{t,i} = q_{dt,i} - q_{at,i}$ defines the error between the desired trajectory and the actual trajectory.

The overall optimization process, illustrated in Fig. 22.4, utilizes the GWO-PSO algorithm to identify optimal controller parameters that enhance the robot manipulator's performance. This process aims to determine parameter sets that not only meet the desired dynamic response characteristics but also improve control precision and output stability.

The optimization algorithm generates the following optimal controller parameters for each control strategy:

- PIDSMC: K_p, K_i, K_d, ϖ, ϱ
- FOPIDSMC: K_p, K_i, K_d, μ, λ, ϖ, ϱ
- TIDSMC: K_t, n, K_i, K_d, ϖ, ϱ
- FOTIDSMC: K_t, n, K_i, K_d, μ, λ, ϖ, ϱ

Based on insights from the literature, the optimization process is conducted within the following search ranges for the parameters:

- $K_p, K_t \in [0, 1000]$, $K_i \in [0, 20]$, $K_d \in [0, 200]$,
- ϖ, $\varrho \in [0, 50]$
- $\mu, \lambda \in [0, 1]$, $n \in [0, 10]$

22.4.1 Particle swarm optimization algorithm

In this study, the PSO algorithm is utilized as an effective population-based metaheuristic technique, originally introduced by Kennedy and Eberhart in 1995 [24]. Inspired by the collective behavior observed in bird flocks and fish schools during foraging, PSO has proven to be highly suitable for optimizing controller parameters in dynamic systems.

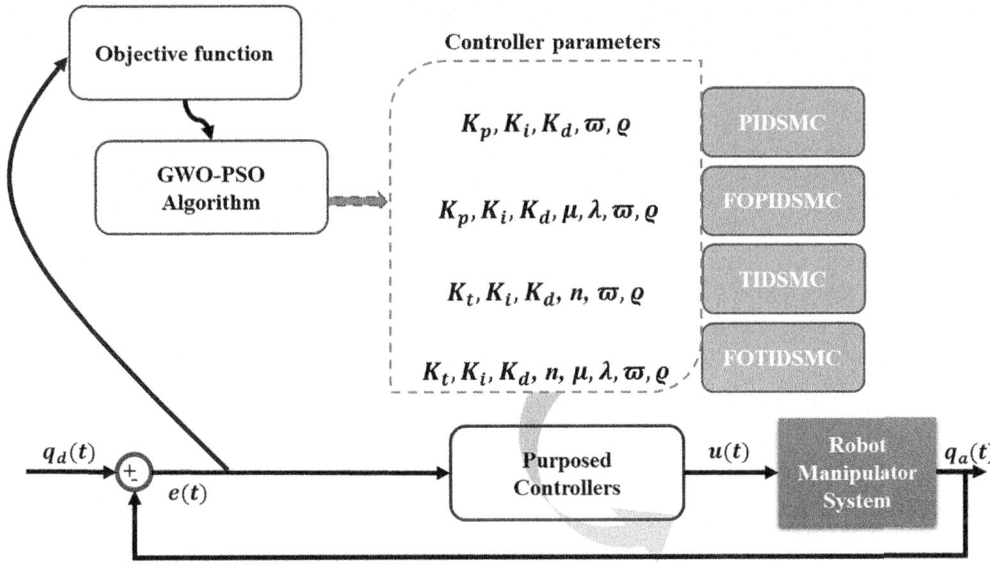

FIGURE 22.4 The overall optimization process.

PSO operates by initializing a swarm of particles randomly distributed within the search space. Each particle represents a potential solution, and its movement through the space is influenced by both its personal best experience and the best-known positions identified by other particles in the swarm. This mechanism enables a balance between exploration and exploitation, enhancing the algorithm's ability to converge toward optimal solutions.

Throughout the optimization process, each particle retains its personal best position as well as the global best position found by the entire swarm. The position and velocity of each particle are updated iteratively according to the following equations:

$$p_{t+1}^j = p_t^j + v_{t+1}^j \tag{22.50}$$

$$v_{t+1}^j = \varkappa(\omega_t v_t^j + \zeta_1 r_1 [p_t^p - p_t^j] + \zeta_2 r_2 [p_t^g - p_t^j]) \tag{22.51}$$

In these equations:

- t denotes the current iteration number,
- p_t^j and v_t^j represent the position and velocity of the jth particle at iteration t,
- $\varkappa$ is the contraction factor, ensuring the stability of particle movements,
- ω_t is the inertia weight that controls the influence of the previous velocity, contributing to the swarm's exploration ability,
- ζ_1 andζ_2 are cognitive and social learning coefficients, respectively, governing the balance between personal and global experiences,
- r_1 and r_2 are random numbers uniformly distributed in the range [0, 1], introducing stochastic behavior into the search process,
- p_t^p represents the personal best position of particle j at iteration t,
- p_t^g indicates the global best position identified by the swarm up to iteration t.

By iteratively updating particle positions and velocities using these equations, PSO effectively navigates the search space to identify optimal parameter sets, making it a powerful tool for controller parameter optimization.

22.4.2 Grey wolf optimizer algorithm

Introduced by Mirjalili et al. [23], GWO is inspired by the social hierarchy and cooperative hunting behavior observed in grey wolf packs. The algorithm simulates the leadership structure of the pack, which consists of four main roles: alpha, beta, delta, and omega wolves. The alpha wolf leads the pack and represents the best solution found so far, while beta and delta wolves assist the alpha by maintaining secondary best positions. Omega wolves, on the other hand, occupy the lowest rank and follow the leaders' guidance during the optimization process.

The hunting mechanism in GWO begins with the encircling behavior, where wolves surround their prey to prepare for the attack. This behavior is mathematically modeled as follows:

$$\vec{D} = |\vec{C}.\ \vec{X}_P(t) - \vec{X}(t)| \tag{22.52}$$

$$\vec{X}(t+1) = \vec{X}_P(t) - \vec{A}.\ \vec{D} \tag{22.53}$$

- t represents the current iteration,
- $\vec{X}_P(t)$ denotes the position of the prey (representing the optimal solution in the search space),
- $\vec{X}(t)$ indicates the position of a grey wolf (candidate solution),
- $\vec{A}$ and $\vec{C}$ are coefficient vectors that influence the wolves' movement dynamics.

These coefficient vectors are calculated using the following expressions:

$$\vec{A} = \vec{a}.\ (2.\ \vec{r}_1 - 1) \tag{22.54}$$

$$\vec{C} = 2.\ \vec{r}_2 \tag{22.55}$$

where:

- $\vec{r}_1$ and $\vec{r}_2$ are random vectors uniformly distributed in the range [0, 1], introducing stochasticity to simulate the unpredictable nature of hunting,
- $\vec{a}$ is a linearly decreasing factor, starting from 2 and reducing to 0 over the course of iterations, calculated as:

$$\vec{a}(t) = 2 - 2t/\max Iter,\ t = 0,\ 1,\ \ldots,\quad \max Iter \tag{22.56}$$

This gradual decrease in $\vec{a}$ helps balance the exploration and exploitation phases of the algorithm.

The optimization process in GWO mimics the hunting strategy of grey wolves, where the alpha (α), beta (β), and delta (δ) wolves guide the search. The remaining wolves (candidate solutions) adjust their positions based on these leading wolves' experiences. The mathematical formulation of this strategy is as follows:

$$\vec{D}_\alpha = |\vec{C}_1.\ \vec{X}_\alpha - \vec{X}(t)|,\ \vec{D}_\beta = |\vec{C}_2.\ \vec{X}_\beta - \vec{X}(t)|,\ \vec{D}_\delta = |\vec{C}_3.\ \vec{X}_\delta - \vec{X}(t)| \tag{22.57}$$

The updated positions are then calculated as:

$$\vec{X}_1 = |\vec{X}_\alpha - \vec{a}_1\vec{D}_\alpha|,\ \vec{X}_2 = |\vec{X}_\beta - \vec{a}_2\vec{D}_\beta|,\ \vec{X}_3 = |\vec{X}_\delta - \vec{a}_3\vec{D}_\delta| \tag{22.58}$$

Finally, the new position of the candidate solution is determined by averaging the influence of the top three wolves:

$$\vec{X}_P(t+1) = (\vec{X}_1 + \vec{X}_2 + \vec{X}_3)/3 \tag{22.59}$$

where:

- $\vec{C}_1$, $\vec{C}_2$, $\vec{C}_3$, $\vec{a}_1$, $\vec{a}_2$, $\vec{a}_3$ are random vectors controlling exploration and exploitation,
- $\vec{X}_\alpha$, $\vec{X}_\beta$, and $\vec{X}_\delta$ represent the positions of the alpha, beta, and delta wolves, respectively,
- $\vec{X}_P(t+1)$ denotes the updated position of the candidate solution (analogous to the prey's position in the metaphor).

Through this iterative process, the algorithm effectively navigates the search space, exploiting the knowledge of the best solutions while maintaining diversity to avoid local optima. This makes GWO a powerful and efficient optimization technique for complex control problems.

22.4.3 Hybrid grey wolf optimizer-particle swarm optimization algorithm

The hybrid GWO-PSO algorithm integrates the strengths of both GWO and PSO to enhance optimization performance, particularly for complex, high-dimensional problems such as controller parameter tuning. This hybrid approach leverages GWO's efficient exploration capabilities and PSO's fast convergence characteristics, resulting in a more robust and adaptive optimization framework [41].

While GWO excels in global exploration due to its hierarchical hunting mechanism, it may face challenges in local exploitation, potentially slowing convergence as the search progresses. Conversely, PSO is known for its rapid convergence to local optima but may suffer from premature convergence in multimodal search spaces. The hybrid GWO-PSO algorithm aims to balance these strengths by combining GWO's exploration with PSO's exploitation, thus achieving both global search efficiency and local optimization accuracy.

In the early iterations, the algorithm emphasizes global search using GWO's encircling and hunting mechanisms. The positions of candidate solutions (particles) are updated based on the influence of the alpha, beta, and delta wolves, promoting diversity and broad search space coverage.

As the search progresses, the algorithm gradually shifts toward PSO dynamics to refine solutions in promising regions. In this phase, particles adjust their velocities and positions based on their personal best experiences and the global best position identified during the exploration phase. The flow chart of the hybrid GWO-PSO algorithm is presented in Fig. 22.5.

Fig. 22.5 presents the comprehensive flowchart of the hybrid GWO-PSO algorithm, detailing each stage of the optimization process. The flowchart begins with the initialization phase, where the population of candidate solutions (search agents) is randomly distributed within the defined parameter space.

In the GWO Phase, the algorithm emphasizes global exploration. The search agents are guided by the alpha, beta, and delta wolves, representing the best solutions found so far. These leaders influence the movements of other agents, directing them toward promising areas in the search space. The encircling, hunting, and attacking strategies of GWO are applied iteratively, ensuring broad coverage and preventing early convergence.

After several iterations focused on exploration, the algorithm transitions into the PSO Phase. Here, the top-performing agents identified during the GWO phase undergo refinement. Their positions are updated using PSO's velocity and

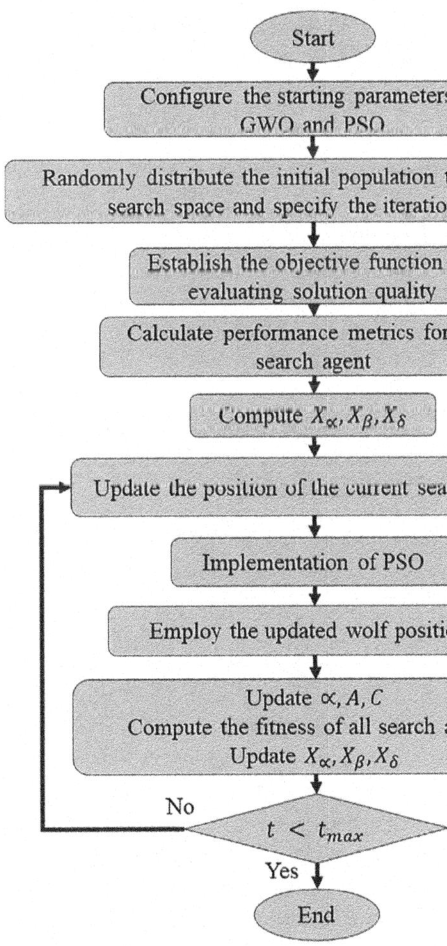

FIGURE 22.5 The flow chart of the hybrid GWO-PSO algorithm (*GWO-PSO*, Grey wolf optimizer-particle swarm optimization).

position update equations, which consider each agent's personal best position and the global best position. This phase enhances local search capabilities, improving solution accuracy.

The Iteration Loop alternates between GWO and PSO phases, allowing the algorithm to balance exploration and exploitation dynamically. This iterative switching ensures that the search does not stagnate and maintains diversity within the population.

Finally, the Termination Condition checks whether the stopping criteria—such as a maximum number of iterations or a satisfactory objective function value—have been met. If so, the algorithm outputs the optimal control parameters; otherwise, the process repeats.

This detailed step-by-step workflow in Fig. 22.5 highlights the synergy between GWO and PSO, showcasing how their integration leads to more robust and efficient optimization performance.

This study employed a consistent parameter configuration across all optimization algorithms. Specifically, each algorithm utilized 30 agents, 100 iterations, and 10 independent runs. For the PSO algorithm, the inertia weight (ω) was set to 0.75, the constriction factor (χ) to 0.7, and both learning factors (ζ_1, ζ_2) to 2. The coefficients r_1 and r_2 were randomly generated within the interval [0, 1]. Regarding the GWO, its coefficients ($\vec{r}_1$ and $\vec{r}_2$) were also randomly selected from the range [0, 1], while the linear convergence vector ($\vec{a}$) was progressively reduced from 2 to 0 over the course of the iterations.

The optimal controller parameters for each configuration are obtained by minimizing the objective function in Eq. (22.49) through GWO-PSO-based optimization.

To ensure reliability and robustness, the optimization process is executed 10 times for each controller, and the final parameter values are determined by averaging the results. The optimized parameter sets for all joints of the UR5 manipulator, corresponding to each controller type, are presented in Table 22.3. These parameter values serve as the foundation for subsequent performance assessments under various operating conditions.

In the proposed implementation, the hybridization is achieved by integrating the GWO leaders (α, β, δ) with PSO-like velocity updates. Specifically, the velocity of each agent is updated according to:

$$v_{t+1}^j = \omega(v_t^j + C_1 r_1 (X_\alpha - p_t^j) + C_2 r_2 (X_\beta - p_t^j) + C_3 r_3 (X_\delta - p_t^j)),\ p_{t+1}^j = p_t^j + v_{t+1}^j \tag{22.60}$$

where ω is an inertia-like factor randomly initialized within [0.5,1.0], and $C_1 = C_2 = C_3 = 0.5$. The random coefficients r_1 are uniformly distributed in [0,1]. Velocity clamping was not explicitly enforced; instead, updated positions exceeding the predefined parameter bounds were corrected by boundary checks, effectively constraining the velocities.

The exploration–exploitation balance follows the original GWO convergence mechanism, where the parameter a decreases linearly from 2 to 0 with iterations, as given in Eq. (22.56).

This ensures strong exploration at the beginning and gradual convergence toward exploitation in later iterations. These details are now explicitly reported to clarify the switching schedule, weighting, learning coefficients, and evolution of the convergence factor in the hybrid GWO-PSO.

22.5 Simulation results and statistical analysis

An adaptive controller must effectively mitigate the impact of both external disturbances and internal model uncertainties, suppress white noise injected into joint torque inputs, and compensate for variations in the end-effector payload to maintain stable and robust system performance. These factors may independently or collectively affect the control loop, potentially degrading overall performance.

To comprehensively assess the controller's effectiveness, this section presents a detailed evaluation of its ability to handle disturbance rejection, noise suppression, and payload variations. The following subsections provide a structured, category-based analysis of these assessments for all four controllers.

For dynamic performance analysis, a unit step input is applied to evaluate the system's transient response characteristics. Meanwhile, for other performance evaluations, the end-effector follows a rectangular trajectory in the task space, which is parallel to the x-y plane. As illustrated in Fig. 22.6, this trajectory-based assessment is conducted alongside the UR5 robot's visualization in MATLAB, enabling a more realistic examination of the controllers' tracking accuracy and disturbance rejection capabilities in practical operational scenarios.

To ensure full reproducibility, all simulations were conducted with clearly defined parameters and boundary conditions. The joint torque limits for the UR5 manipulator were set to 150 N·m for joints J1, J2, and J3, and 28 N·m for joints J4, J5, and J6. A saturation handling mechanism was implemented to cap control inputs at these physical limits, preventing integrator wind-up and ensuring stable system behavior. The position and velocity limits for all joints were set to $\pm\, 2\pi$ rad

TABLE 22.3 Optimized controller parameters for PIDSMC, FOPIDSMC, TIDSMC, and FOTIDSMC of the 6R UR5 robot manipulator.

Controller	Parameters	Joints					
		1	2	3	4	5	6
PIDSMC	K_p	993.6816	447.3057	413.3312	894.2665	844.6600	13.4740
	K_i	17.1185	17.4330	10.1269	14.7464	7.8808	7.9280
	K_d	6.2860	200.5026	141.8471	6.8176	58.7430	43.2493
	ϖ	7.3328	2.7712	45.2904	19.5287	19.5646	35.9261
	ϱ	24.9746	45.2436	22.5325	30.1110	34.5494	16.2859
FOPIDSMC	K_p	3.8217	72.2470	483.6100	1.2181	70.8707	98.6874
	K_i	3.8596	1.2385	5.0245	1.5648	9.3658	1.8272
	K_d	71.1298	43.2087	16.0075	53.4726	9.8278	37.8261
	ϖ	4.1287	6.1186	6.1018	1.6503	3.7210	20.8773
	ϱ	11.4638	1.0749	15.8364	2.7718	2.9428	24.3890
	μ	0.0953	0.1012	0.0113	0.1779	0.3815	0.4680
	λ	0.0101	0.5215	0.2857	0.0104	0.0110	0.0103
TIDSMC	K_t	487.6523	463.1892	532.4756	478.9235	514.6283	529.3124
	K_i	10.4829	9.6741	8.2389	11.2534	12.5913	9.1852
	K_d	102.3178	111.8463	107.5293	96.4821	116.2759	119.3582
	ϖ	25.8362	26.2745	23.7412	24.9632	26.9812	27.4517
	ϱ	20.4915	18.9234	22.6581	21.3728	19.4872	22.9834
	n	5.2734	4.5128	6.1457	5.6982	4.3897	6.7285
FOTIDSMC	K_t	482.1584	471.8932	508.2645	493.5872	517.2483	523.9812
	K_i	9.7215	10.3827	11.7632	8.4672	12.8321	10.4712
	K_d	104.6328	112.2954	109.8324	101.5723	117.6845	121.4837
	ϖ	22.6582	24.3821	23.9284	25.1683	27.3145	28.1253
	ϱ	18.9753	20.2143	19.7843	21.6582	22.4983	23.6741
	n	5.4829	4.8931	6.3241	5.2354	4.6752	6.5817
	μ	0.8235	0.8513	0.8372	0.8123	0.8695	0.8293
	λ	0.9114	0.8795	0.9254	0.8657	0.8952	0.9375

and ± 3.34 rad/s respectively. All simulations began with the robot's initial joint angles and velocities set to zero, at $q_{\text{initial}} = [0, 0, 0, 0, 0, 0]$ rad and $q_{initial} = [0, 0, 0, 0, 0, 0]$ rad/s

22.5.1 Dynamic performance analysis

In addition to disturbance rejection and noise suppression, evaluating the dynamic performance of the controllers is essential for understanding their effectiveness in real-world scenarios. This section examines the transient and steady-state responses of the 6R UR5 robot manipulator when controlled by PIDSMC, FOPIDSMC, TIDSMC, and FOTIDSMC.

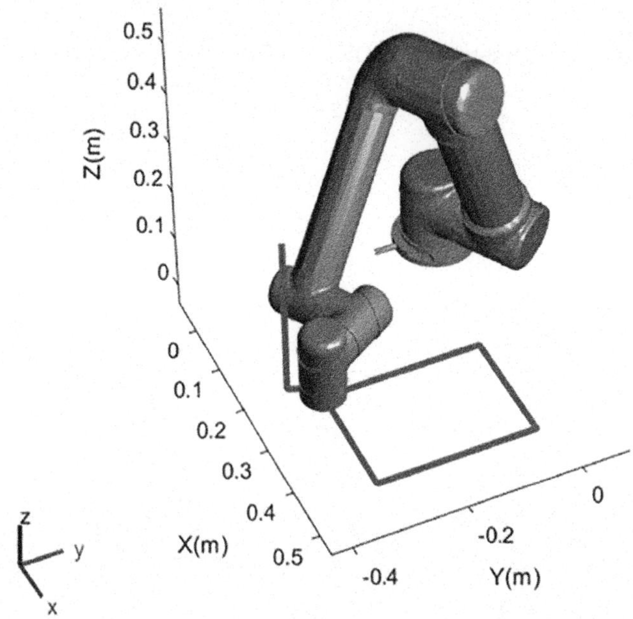

FIGURE 22.6 UR5 robot visualization in MATLAB and the predefined rectangular trajectory in the task space for performance evaluation.

A unit step input is applied to the system to evaluate the transient and steady-state responses, ensuring a standardized comparison of the controllers' performance.

Key performance metrics, such as rise time (t_r), settling time (t_s), overshoot (M_p), and steady-state error (e_{ss}), are analyzed to quantify the controllers' responsiveness and stability. The results are compared across different control strategies to determine which approach provides the best balance between fast response and minimal oscillations.

Table 22.4 provides a comparative analysis of the transient and steady-state response metrics for the 6R UR5 robot manipulator under different controllers. The results indicate that FOTIDSMC achieves the lowest mean absolute error (MAE) and the shortest settling time, demonstrating superior control precision and fast convergence. Additionally, FOPIDSMC shows a relatively balanced performance with a reduced steady-state error while maintaining a fast response. In contrast, PIDSMC tends to exhibit slower settling times, while TIDSMC achieves a compromise between stability and response speed. The findings highlight the advantages of fractional-order and SMC strategies in enhancing both dynamic response and steady-state accuracy, making them well-suited for precise robotic manipulation tasks under varying operational conditions. The transient and steady-state response metrics, including overshoot and steady-state error, were carefully defined and measured. The overshoot was determined as the maximum percentage of the response that exceeds the final steady-state value. A value of 0% in this metric indicates that the system response had no overshoot. Similarly, the steady-state error was calculated as the difference between the final steady-state value and the desired input. In cases where the error converged to a negligible value (e.g., on the order of 10^{-16}), it was reported as 0, indicating the effective elimination of steady-state error within the solver's tolerance.

22.5.2 Rejection of external disturbances

A key objective of a robust control method is to effectively mitigate unwanted disturbances while maintaining accurate tracking of the reference trajectory. In this study, to evaluate the controller's performance in trajectory tracking, an external disturbance is introduced to all joints of the robot manipulator for a specific duration. This disturbance is applied between the controller output and the robot system using the pulse function defined in Eq. (22.61).

$$\sigma_{dist}(t) = \Upsilon[u(t-1.5) - u(t-2.5)] \tag{22.61}$$

Y given in the above equation refers to the magnitude of the disturbance effect.

The reference impulse applied for disturbance was set to 10 N·m for the base, shoulder, and elbow joints, and 2 N·m for the three wrist joints, within the time interval of 1.5 –2.5 s. To further investigate the impact of disturbances across all controllers, the reference impulse was scaled by factors of 2, 3, 4, and 5, and the resulting MAE values for all joints were

TABLE 22.4 Transient and steady-state response metrics for the 6R UR5 robot manipulator under different controllers.

Joint no.	Controller	$M_p(\%)$	$t_r(s)\, 0.1 \rightarrow 0.9$	$t_s(s) \pm \%2$	e_{ss}	*MAE*
1	PIDSMC	0	0.38	0.82	7.6118e-06	0.1128
	FOPIDSMC	0.0376	0.24	0.35	0	0.0905
	TIDSMC	0	0.31	0.61	2.7999e-08	0.0987
	FOTIDSMC	0.0979	0.24	0.31	0	0.0802
2	PIDSMC	0	0.35	0.75	1.9558e-06	0.1084
	FOPIDSMC	0	0.24	0.38	0	0.0912
	TIDSMC	0	0.29	0.57	6.4088e-09	0.0965
	FOTIDSMC	0.0512	0.24	0.32	0	0.0834
3	PIDSMC	0	0.33	0.69	4.8734e-07	0.1044
	FOPIDSMC	0.2451	0.24	0.34	0	0.0903
	TIDSMC	0	0.28	0.55	1.4257e-09	0.0950
	FOTIDSMC	0.2730	0.24	0.31	0	0.0802
4	PIDSMC	0	0.31	0.65	1.1849e-07	0.1012
	FOPIDSMC	0	0.24	0.41	0	0.0918
	TIDSMC	0	0.28	0.52	3.0506e-10	0.0937
	FOTIDSMC	0.0327	0.24	0.33	0	0.0871
5	PIDSMC	0	0.31	0.61	2.7999e-08	0.0987
	FOPIDSMC	0	0.24	0.38	0	0.0912
	TIDSMC	0	0.27	0.50	6.2437e-11	0.0926
	FOTIDSMC	0.0031	0.24	0.33	0	0.0901
6	PIDSMC	0	0.29	0.57	6.4088e-09	0.0965
	FOPIDSMC	0	0.24	0.39	0	0.0915
	TIDSMC	0	0.26	0.48	1.2182e-11	0.0917
	FOTIDSMC	0	0.24	0.34	0	0.0902

analyzed. The MAE values for each joint, along with their average values corresponding to different disturbance magnitudes, are presented in Table 22.5.

Table 22.5 presents the MAE values of all controllers under different disturbance magnitudes, while Fig. 22.7 provides a detailed breakdown of the performance improvement across these varying disturbance levels. The results demonstrate that FOTIDSMC consistently achieves the lowest MAE values across all disturbance intensities, highlighting its superior robustness in rejecting external disturbances. On average, FOTIDSMC reduces the MAE by 92.23% compared to PIDSMC, confirming its exceptional precision and disturbance rejection capability. FOPIDSMC follows as the second-best performer, achieving a 55.94% reduction in MAE relative to PIDSMC, demonstrating the advantages of fractional-order control. However, its performance slightly deteriorates as disturbance intensity increases, indicating some sensitivity to higher disturbance levels. TIDSMC provides a moderate improvement, reducing MAE by 23.48% compared to PIDSMC, yet it remains less effective than fractional-order controllers in mitigating disturbance effects. PIDSMC exhibits the highest MAE values across all cases, confirming its limited robustness against external disturbances. As disturbance magnitude increases, all controllers experience a gradual rise in error, but FOTIDSMC remains the least affected,

TABLE 22.5 MAE values for variation in the magnitude of the disturbance signal.

		MAE values						
Disturbance level (N·m)	**Controller**	**Joint-1**	**Joint-2**	**Joint-3**	**Joint-4**	**Joint-5**	**Joint-6**	**Average**
10, 2	PIDSMC	0.00952	0.00355	0.00354	0.00367	0.00208	0.02906	0.00857
	FOPIDSMC	0.00267	0.00125	0.00089	0.00175	0.00095	0.01474	0.00371
	TIDSMC	0.00688	0.00258	0.00268	0.00280	0.00161	0.02271	0.00654
	FOTIDSMC	0.00050	0.00025	0.00019	0.00026	0.00018	0.00300	0.00073
20, 4	PIDSMC	0.01475	0.00560	0.00590	0.00611	0.00370	0.05511	0.01526
	FOPIDSMC	0.00387	0.00210	0.00143	0.00297	0.00171	0.02779	0.00664
	TIDSMC	0.01053	0.00434	0.00444	0.00468	0.00288	0.04297	0.01164
	FOTIDSMC	0.00058	0.00037	0.00026	0.00043	0.00030	0.00528	0.00121
30, 6	PIDSMC	0.01992	0.00836	0.00823	0.00839	0.00522	0.08044	0.02176
	FOPIDSMC	0.00508	0.00294	0.00196	0.00415	0.00247	0.04068	0.00955
	TIDSMC	0.01414	0.00606	0.00619	0.00645	0.00410	0.06282	0.01663
	FOTIDSMC	0.00067	0.00050	0.00033	0.00059	0.00043	0.00757	0.00168
40, 8	PIDSMC	0.02501	0.01064	0.01058	0.01051	0.00659	0.10558	0.02815
	FOPIDSMC	0.00630	0.00378	0.00249	0.00530	0.00323	0.05356	0.01244
	TIDSMC	0.01772	0.00774	0.00793	0.00812	0.00524	0.08256	0.02155
	FOTIDSMC	0.00075	0.00062	0.00041	0.00075	0.00055	0.00985	0.00215
50, 10	PIDSMC	0.03002	0.01285	0.01294	0.01250	0.00781	0.12983	0.03433
	FOPIDSMC	0.00751	0.00461	0.00302	0.00642	0.00398	0.06612	0.01528
	TIDSMC	0.02125	0.00938	0.00966	0.00971	0.00631	0.10171	0.02634
	FOTIDSMC	0.00084	0.00074	0.00048	0.00091	0.00068	0.01211	0.00263

showcasing its strong capability in disturbance rejection. These findings further validate the effectiveness of fractional-order sliding mode controllers in handling external uncertainties, with FOTIDSMC emerging as the most robust and precise control strategy for disturbance rejection.

Fig. 22.8 presents a comparative analysis of the RMS torque values for different controllers under varying disturbance levels. The bar chart visually demonstrates the effectiveness of FOTIDSMC in reducing torque fluctuations, while the corresponding table provides precise numerical values. Across all disturbance levels, FOTIDSMC consistently achieves the lowest RMS torque values, confirming its superior efficiency in mitigating external disturbances. Compared to PIDSMC, FOTIDSMC reduces the RMS torque by approximately 22% on average, highlighting a significant improvement in energy efficiency. Additionally, FOTIDSMC outperforms TIDSMC by around 3%, suggesting that the fractional-order tuning enhances the system's stability and robustness. The results also indicate that FOTIDSMC and FOPIDSMC produce closely matched performance, with FOTIDSMC exhibiting a slight advantage (~0.2%) in most cases. This minor yet consistent improvement underscores the effectiveness of FOTIDSMC in optimizing the torque response while ensuring stability under increasing disturbance levels. Overall, the findings confirm that FOTIDSMC is the most efficient and robust control strategy, effectively minimizing torque demand while maintaining superior performance compared to conventional and fractional-order controllers.

To further illustrate the effectiveness of FOTIDSMC, Fig. 22.9 presents the trajectory tracking responses of all controllers for all joints under the highest disturbance level (50–10 N·m). This figure provides a comprehensive

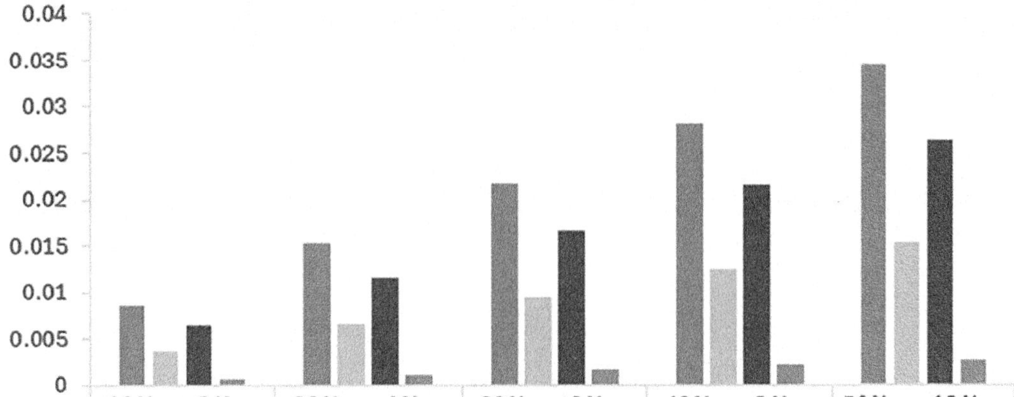

	10 N·m - 2 N·m	20 N·m - 4 N·m	30 N·m - 6 N·m	40 N·m - 8 N·m	50 N·m - 10 N·m
PIDSMC	0.00857	0.01526	0.02176	0.02815	0.03433
FOPIDSMC	0.00371	0.00664	0.00955	0.01244	0.01528
TIDSMC	0.00654	0.01164	0.01663	0.02155	0.02634
FOTIDSMC	0.00073	0.00121	0.00168	0.00215	0.00263

FIGURE 22.7 The detailed MAE breakdown of the performance improvement across various disturbance levels (*MAE*, Mean absolute error).

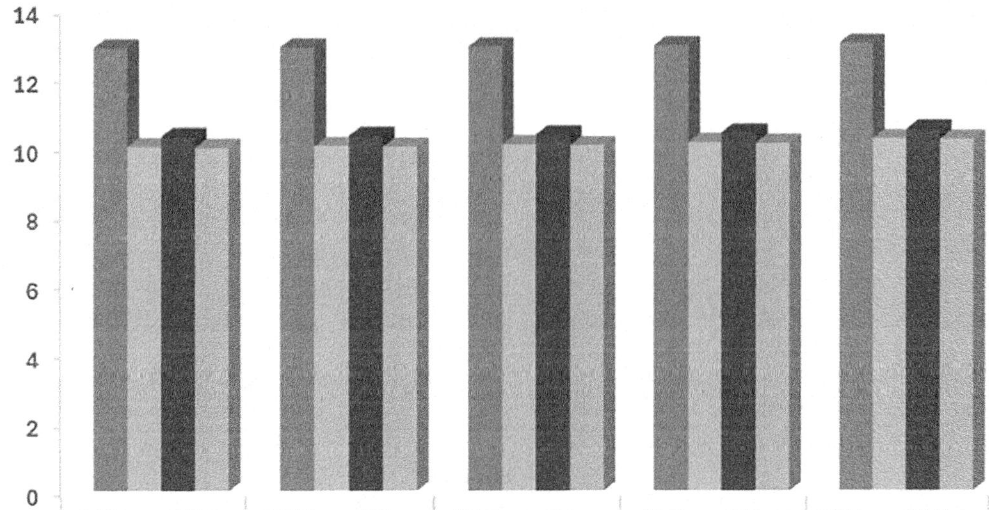

	10 N·m - 2 N·m	20 N·m - 4 N·m	30 N·m - 6 N·m	40 N·m - 8 N·m	50 N·m - 10 N·m
PIDSMC	12.808	12.823	12.848	12.882	12.925
FOPIDSMC	9.9577	9.9829	10.023	10.084	10.174
TIDSMC	10.25	10.273	10.31	10.366	10.448
FOTIDSMC	9.9304	9.9563	9.9978	10.062	10.158

FIGURE 22.8 Comparison of the RMS torque values for different controllers under varying disturbance levels.

comparison of how well each control strategy maintains trajectory tracking accuracy in the presence of severe external disturbances. The results clearly indicate that FOTIDSMC demonstrates the most precise trajectory tracking, with minimal deviation from the reference path. In contrast, PIDSMC exhibits the largest tracking errors, particularly during the disturbance interval, highlighting its sensitivity to external perturbations. TIDSMC and FOPIDSMC show moderate improvements over PIDSMC, but FOTIDSMC consistently achieves the smallest tracking errors across all joints,

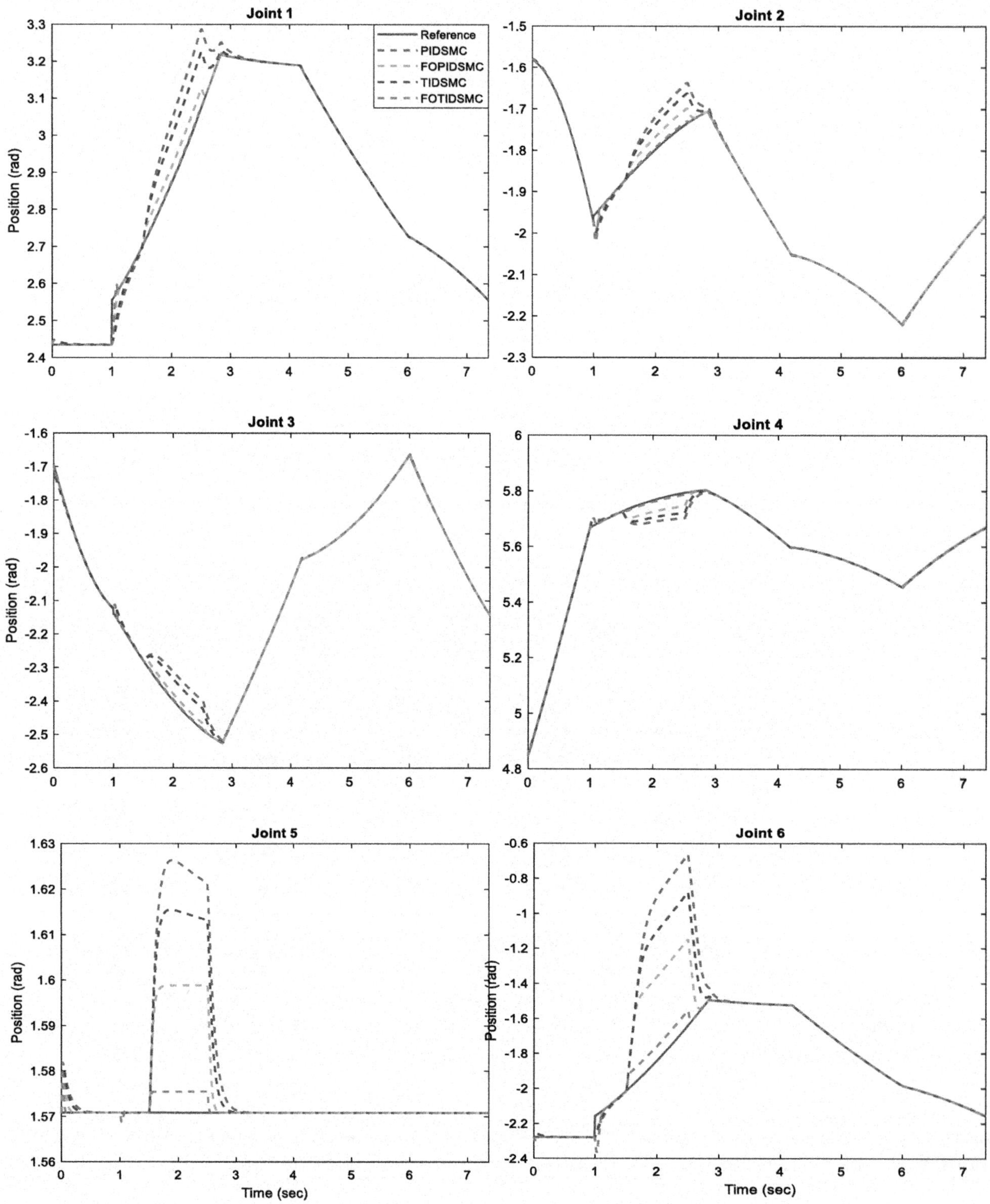

FIGURE 22.9 Trajectory tracking performance of all controllers for all joints under the highest disturbance level (50–10 N·m).

reinforcing its superior robustness and disturbance rejection capability. These findings further support the superiority of FOTIDSMC in maintaining accurate and stable trajectory tracking, even under the most challenging disturbance conditions.

22.5.3 Evaluating controller performance under end-effector load variations

In real-world robotic applications, manipulators are often required to handle varying payloads, which significantly affect their dynamic behavior and control performance. To comprehensively evaluate the robustness of the proposed controllers, a performance analysis is conducted under different end-effector load variations. Specifically, the system is tested with payloads ranging from 1 kg to 5 kg, with an increment of 0.5 kg at each step. This analysis aims to assess how each controller adapts to increasing mass and its impact on trajectory tracking accuracy.

To quantify the performance of each controller under different load conditions, the MAE values for all controllers are presented in Table 22.6. The results provide insight into the tracking performance and robustness of each control strategy as the end-effector load varies. Table 22.6 presents the MAE values of all controllers under different end-effector load conditions, ranging from 1 kg to 5 kg in increments of 0.5 kg. The results demonstrate the impact of increasing loads on trajectory tracking performance and highlight the effectiveness of different control strategies. As the load increases, all controllers exhibit a rise in MAE values due to additional dynamic effects and disturbances.

A comparison of the average MAE values further confirms that PIDSMC exhibits the highest errors, indicating its poor robustness under varying load conditions. FOPIDSMC and TIDSMC show improved performance but still struggle with increasing loads. In contrast, FOTIDSMC maintains the lowest average MAE values, ensuring high-precision trajectory tracking even under high payload variations. These results confirm that the proposed fractional-order TID-based SMC strategy significantly outperforms conventional control methods in handling dynamic uncertainties and varying payload conditions in robotic manipulator systems. To further quantify the performance differences among the controllers, Fig. 22.10 presents the average MAE values for each load level. This comparison provides a clear numerical assessment of the robustness and accuracy of each control strategy. The results indicate that FOTIDSMC achieves the highest level of accuracy and disturbance rejection, consistently outperforming the other controllers. On average, FOTIDSMC reduces the MAE by 93.64% compared to PIDSMC, demonstrating its superior robustness under varying load conditions. FOPIDSMC also shows a significant improvement, achieving an average MAE reduction of 57.7% relative to PIDSMC. However, as the load increases, its performance gradually declines, indicating that fractional-order control alone is insufficient for achieving the highest level of robustness.

On the other hand, TIDSMC provides the lowest performance enhancement, with an average MAE reduction of 24.83% compared to PIDSMC. While TID-based SMC offers some improvements in disturbance rejection, it does not match the effectiveness of fractional-order approaches, particularly under high-load conditions. Finally, PIDSMC exhibits the highest MAE values, highlighting its limited ability to handle external disturbances and load variations effectively. These findings confirm that FOTIDSMC delivers the most robust and precise control performance, making it the most suitable approach for applications requiring high disturbance rejection and trajectory tracking accuracy.

Fig. 22.11 presents the RMS torque values for all controllers under different payload conditions, providing insight into the control effort required to maintain stability and trajectory tracking. The results clearly indicate that FOTIDSMC consistently achieves the lowest RMS torque, demonstrating its superior efficiency in reducing control effort while maintaining robustness.

On average, FOTIDSMC reduces the RMS torque by 19.67% compared to PIDSMC, which has the highest control effort among all strategies. Similarly, FOPIDSMC and TIDSMC achieve 19.44% and 17.26% improvements over PIDSMC, respectively. While FOPIDSMC and FOTIDSMC show comparable performance, FOTIDSMC slightly outperforms FOPIDSMC, achieving an additional 0.28% reduction in RMS torque. This further highlights the effectiveness of integrating fractional-order and TID control strategies in enhancing system performance.

These findings confirm that FOTIDSMC minimizes the control effort required to compensate for payload variations, making it the most efficient controller among the tested strategies. The reduced RMS torque implies better energy efficiency and less mechanical stress on the actuators, which is particularly beneficial for robotic applications requiring high precision and adaptability to payload changes.

To further analyze the performance of the UR5 end-effector under load variations for all controllers, the trajectory tracking graphs of all joints under the maximum test load of 5 kg are presented in Fig. 22.12. Due to the joint configurations required for tracking the rectangular trajectory parallel to the ground in task space, the 4th and 5th joints are more affected by the presence of the load. However, despite this influence, FOTIDSMC exhibits the lowest tracking error, followed by FOPIDSMC, TIDSMC, and PIDSMC, respectively.

TABLE 22.6 MAE values of all controllers under different end-effector loads.

		MAE values						
Load (kg)	**Controller**	**Joint-1**	**Joint-2**	**Joint-3**	**Joint-4**	**Joint-5**	**Joint-6**	**Average**
1 kg	PIDSMC	0.00512	0.00423	0.00616	0.03394	0.00767	0.00335	0.01008
	FOPIDSMC	0.00164	0.00151	0.00161	0.01603	0.00339	0.00196	0.00436
	TIDSMC	0.00370	0.00309	0.00467	0.02570	0.00591	0.00266	0.00762
	FOTIDSMC	0.00043	0.00027	0.00029	0.00214	0.00059	0.00077	0.00075
1.5 kg	PIDSMC	0.00540	0.00605	0.00888	0.05071	0.01130	0.00370	0.01434
	FOPIDSMC	0.00172	0.00212	0.00224	0.02391	0.00498	0.00207	0.00617
	TIDSMC	0.00392	0.00439	0.00669	0.03836	0.00870	0.00284	0.01082
	FOTIDSMC	0.00043	0.00036	0.00038	0.00318	0.00085	0.00078	0.00100
2 kg	PIDSMC	0.00568	0.00788	0.01162	0.06745	0.01492	0.00437	0.01865
	FOPIDSMC	0.00180	0.00274	0.00287	0.03180	0.00658	0.00217	0.00799
	TIDSMC	0.00413	0.00571	0.00873	0.05102	0.01149	0.00317	0.01404
	FOTIDSMC	0.00044	0.00044	0.00046	0.00422	0.00112	0.00080	0.00125
2.5 kg	PIDSMC	0.00594	0.00972	0.01433	0.08413	0.01853	0.00537	0.02300
	FOPIDSMC	0.00187	0.00336	0.00350	0.03970	0.00817	0.00227	0.00981
	TIDSMC	0.00432	0.00703	0.01077	0.06366	0.01427	0.00373	0.01730
	FOTIDSMC	0.00045	0.00053	0.00055	0.00525	0.00139	0.00081	0.00150
3 kg	PIDSMC	0.00617	0.01157	0.01703	0.10075	0.02213	0.00664	0.02738
	FOPIDSMC	0.00194	0.00398	0.00412	0.04759	0.00976	0.00236	0.01163
	TIDSMC	0.00451	0.00836	0.01280	0.07626	0.01704	0.00449	0.02058
	FOTIDSMC	0.00045	0.00062	0.00064	0.00629	0.00166	0.00082	0.00175
3.5 kg	PIDSMC	0.00639	0.01344	0.01971	0.11730	0.02571	0.00818	0.03179
	FOPIDSMC	0.00201	0.00460	0.00476	0.05548	0.01134	0.00244	0.01344
	TIDSMC	0.00468	0.00970	0.01481	0.08883	0.01981	0.00543	0.02388
	FOTIDSMC	0.00046	0.00071	0.00073	0.00733	0.00192	0.00083	0.00200
4 kg	PIDSMC	0.00658	0.01531	0.02235	0.13377	0.02928	0.00997	0.03621
	FOPIDSMC	0.00208	0.00523	0.00539	0.06337	0.01293	0.00253	0.01525
	TIDSMC	0.00484	0.01104	0.01681	0.10137	0.02257	0.00653	0.02719
	FOTIDSMC	0.00046	0.00080	0.00081	0.00837	0.00219	0.00084	0.00224
4.5 kg	PIDSMC	0.00675	0.01718	0.02496	0.15017	0.03282	0.01202	0.04065
	FOPIDSMC	0.00215	0.00586	0.00601	0.07124	0.01451	0.00261	0.01706
	TIDSMC	0.00499	0.01238	0.01879	0.11385	0.02532	0.00780	0.03052
	FOTIDSMC	0.00047	0.00089	0.00090	0.00941	0.00246	0.00084	0.00249
5 kg	PIDSMC	0.00689	0.01907	0.02753	0.16648	0.03636	0.01431	0.04511
	FOPIDSMC	0.00221	0.00649	0.00664	0.07912	0.01609	0.00269	0.01887
	TIDSMC	0.00513	0.01373	0.02077	0.12630	0.02806	0.00923	0.03387
	FOTIDSMC	0.00048	0.00097	0.00099	0.01045	0.00273	0.00085	0.00274

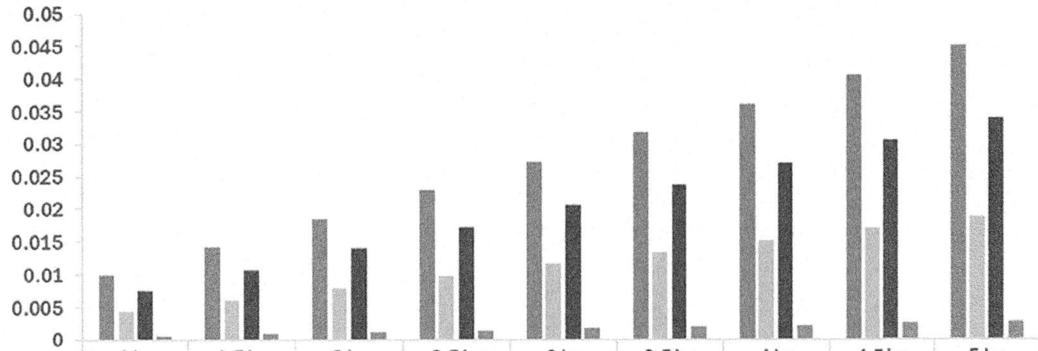

	1 kg	1.5 kg	2 kg	2.5 kg	3 kg	3.5 kg	4 kg	4.5 kg	5 kg
PIDSMC	0.01008	0.01434	0.01865	0.023	0.02738	0.03179	0.03621	0.04065	0.04511
FOPIDSMC	0.00436	0.00617	0.00799	0.00981	0.01163	0.01344	0.01525	0.01706	0.01887
TIDSMC	0.00762	0.01082	0.01404	0.0173	0.02058	0.02388	0.02719	0.03052	0.03387
FOTIDSMC	0.00075	0.001	0.00125	0.0015	0.00175	0.002	0.00224	0.00249	0.00274

FIGURE 22.10 The average MAE values of all joints under different end-effector loads for each control strategy (*MAE*, Mean absolute error).

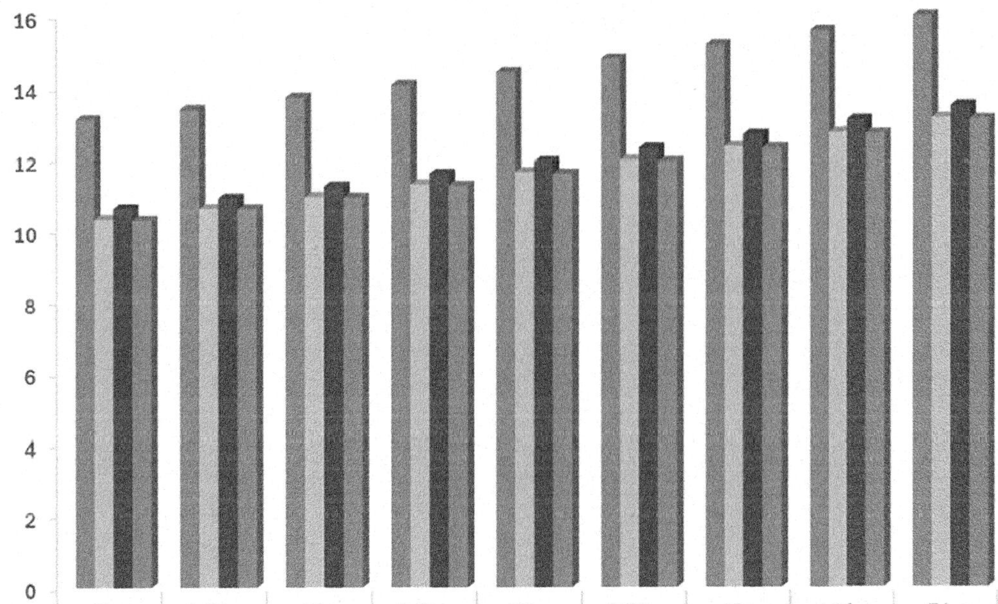

	1 kg	1.5 kg	2 kg	2.5 kg	3 kg	3.5 kg	4 kg	4.5 kg	5 kg
PIDSMC	13.078	13.362	13.69	14.044	14.405	14.774	15.161	15.561	15.968
FOPIDSMC	10.292	10.59	10.917	11.258	11.6	11.955	12.325	12.71	13.111
TIDSMC	10.589	10.884	11.21	11.556	11.916	12.283	12.66	13.048	13.449
FOTIDSMC	10.269	10.574	10.901	11.222	11.56	11.914	12.284	12.67	13.072

FIGURE 22.11 Comparative analysis of RMS torque under varying payloads.

22.5.4 Evaluating controller performance under white noise disturbances in joint torque inputs

In this section, the impact of white noise disturbances on the joint torque inputs is analyzed in detail. White noise is a stochastic process with a constant power spectral density over all frequencies, commonly used to model unpredictable

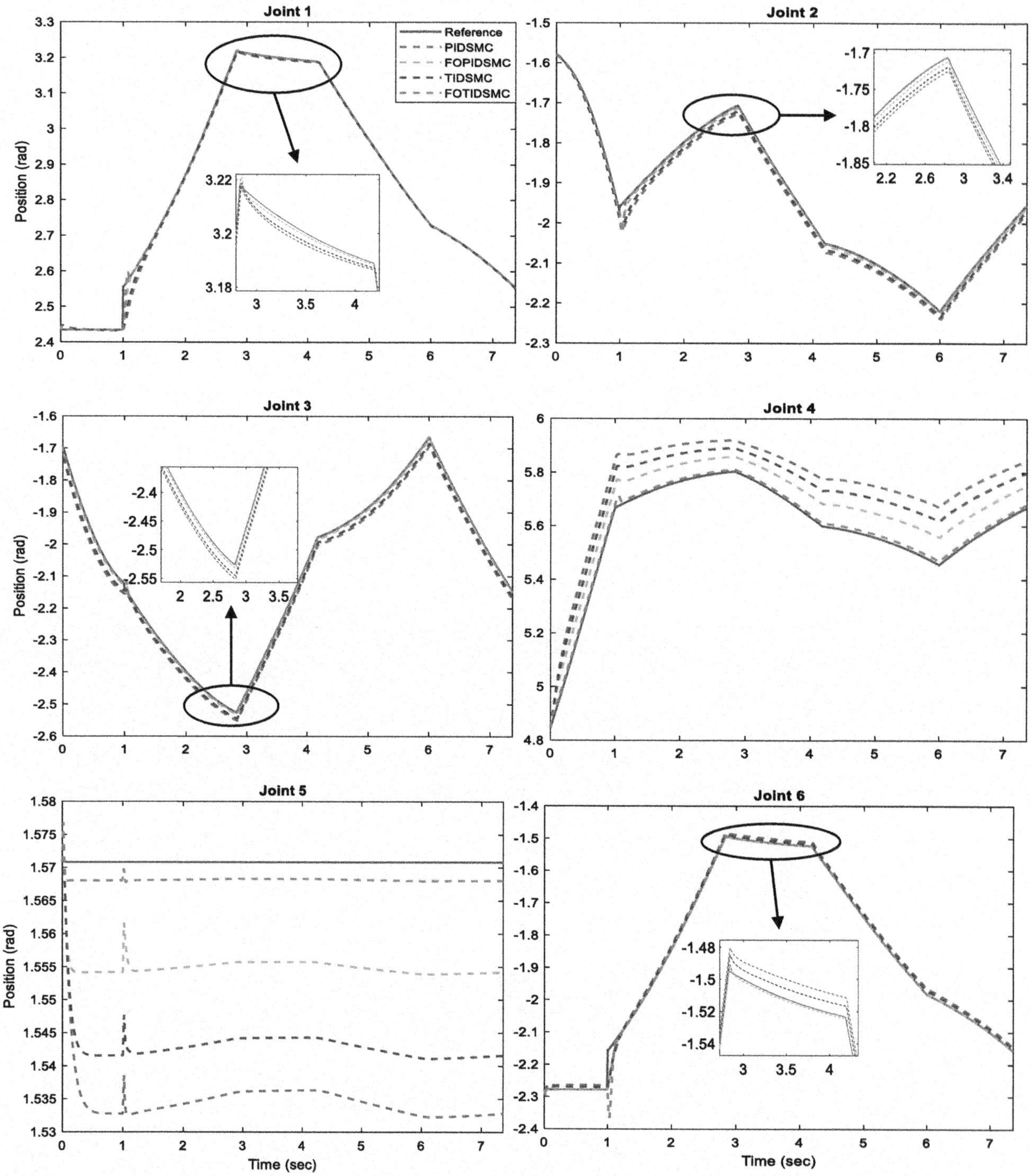

FIGURE 22.12 Trajectory tracking performance of all controllers for the end-effector load of 5 kg.

disturbances in control systems. Mathematically, continuous-time white noise $\omega(t)$ can be defined as a Gaussian process with zero mean and a given variance σ^2:

$$\omega(t) \sim \mathcal{N}(0, \sigma^2) \tag{22.62}$$

where σ^2 represents the noise intensity, determining the disturbance magnitude applied to the system. In this study, the White Noise block from the MATLAB Simulink library was utilized to simulate the effect of noise on the system. The

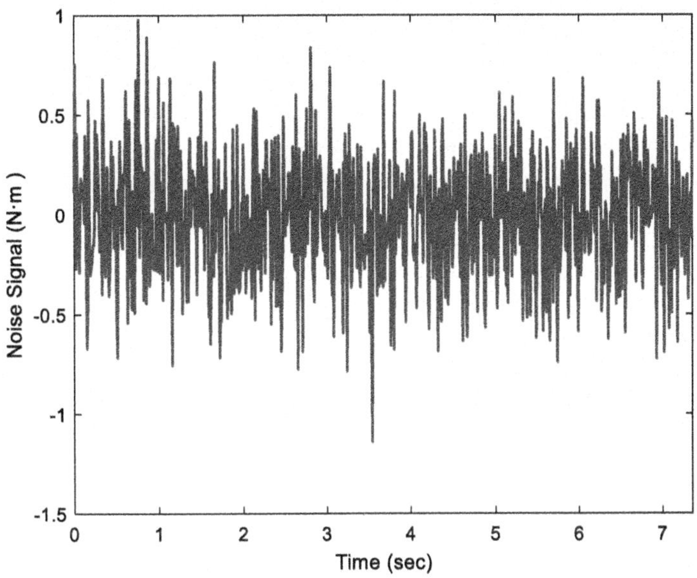

FIGURE 22.13 Noise signal.

noise intensity was varied from 0.1 to 0.5 in increments of 0.1 for all joints, allowing for a comprehensive performance evaluation under different disturbance conditions. For each noise level, a detailed analysis was conducted to assess its impact on the system's stability and tracking performance. Fig. 22.13 presents the baseline white noise signal with an intensity coefficient of 0.1, which serves as a reference for further comparisons.

By systematically increasing the noise intensity, the robustness and disturbance rejection capability of the proposed control approach were evaluated. The results provide insights into how well the control system can handle external stochastic disturbances while maintaining precise trajectory tracking.

Table 22.7 presents the MAE values for different controllers under varying white noise intensity levels (0.1–0.5) applied to the joint torque inputs. The results indicate that FOTIDSMC consistently achieves the lowest MAE across all joints and noise levels, demonstrating superior robustness to stochastic disturbances. Even at the highest noise level (0.5), FOTIDSMC maintains an average MAE of 0.00410, significantly lower than the other controllers. FOPIDSMC performs better than PIDSMC and TIDSMC but shows a gradual increase in error as noise intensity rises, reaching an average MAE of 0.01152 at a 0.5 noise level, which is still considerably higher than FOTIDSMC. TIDSMC exhibits moderate performance, with an average MAE of 0.01460 at the highest noise level. While it outperforms PIDSMC, it remains less effective than both fractional-order controllers (FOPIDSMC and FOTIDSMC). PIDSMC has the highest MAE values at all noise levels, confirming its lower disturbance rejection capability. The average MAE reaches 0.01657 at a noise intensity of 0.5, which is nearly four times higher than that of FOTIDSMC.

A percentage-based performance comparison further highlights the superiority of FOTIDSMC. On average, FOTIDSMC achieves a 74.62% improvement over PIDSMC in terms of MAE reduction, making it the most effective control strategy. FOPIDSMC also demonstrates a 29.31% improvement compared to PIDSMC, while TIDSMC shows a 12.23% improvement, confirming its intermediate performance. These results emphasize that fractional-order controllers (FOPIDSMC and FOTIDSMC) significantly enhance robustness against noise-induced uncertainties, with FOTIDSMC providing the most substantial error reduction.

Fig. 22.14 provides a visual representation of the average MAE values across different noise levels for all controllers, supporting the findings from Table 22.7. The bar chart clearly illustrates the increasing trend of MAE with higher noise intensity for all controllers. However, FOTIDSMC consistently maintains the lowest error values, while PIDSMC exhibits the highest error values at every noise level. The performance gap between FOTIDSMC and the other controllers widens as the noise intensity increases, further confirming the superior robustness of FOTIDSMC against white noise disturbances. As the noise intensity increases, all controllers experience performance degradation, but FOTIDSMC remains the least affected, demonstrating its exceptional resilience to noise-induced uncertainties. These findings highlight the effectiveness of fractional-order controllers (FOPIDSMC and FOTIDSMC) in handling random disturbances, with FOTIDSMC emerging as the most robust control strategy against white noise effects in joint torque inputs.

TABLE 22.7 MAE Values for different noise levels in joint torque inputs.

		MAE values						
Noise power	**Controller**	**Joint-1**	**Joint-2**	**Joint-3**	**Joint-4**	**Joint-5**	**Joint-6**	**Average**
0.1	PIDSMC	0.00493	0.00186	0.00162	0.00345	0.00319	0.04224	0.00955
	FOPIDSMC	0.00174	0.00077	0.00050	0.00227	0.00207	0.03023	0.00626
	TIDSMC	0.00375	0.00140	0.00126	0.00293	0.00278	0.03752	0.00827
	FOTIDSMC	0.00082	0.00061	0.00034	0.00077	0.00061	0.01047	0.00227
0.2	PIDSMC	0.00552	0.00197	0.00171	0.00455	0.00445	0.05345	0.01194
	FOPIDSMC	0.00206	0.00085	0.00055	0.00302	0.00289	0.03940	0.00813
	TIDSMC	0.00429	0.00150	0.00134	0.00390	0.00388	0.04795	0.01048
	FOTIDSMC	0.00086	0.00062	0.00036	0.00095	0.00084	0.01393	0.00292
0.3	PIDSMC	0.00600	0.00206	0.00178	0.00541	0.00541	0.06144	0.01368
	FOPIDSMC	0.00231	0.00091	0.00060	0.00361	0.00352	0.04576	0.00945
	TIDSMC	0.00470	0.00158	0.00140	0.00465	0.00472	0.05601	0.01218
	FOTIDSMC	0.00090	0.00063	0.00036	0.00108	0.00102	0.01643	0.00340
0.4	PIDSMC	0.00640	0.00213	0.00184	0.00614	0.00623	0.06869	0.01524
	FOPIDSMC	0.00252	0.00096	0.00063	0.00411	0.00406	0.05117	0.01058
	TIDSMC	0.00505	0.00165	0.00146	0.00530	0.00543	0.06211	0.01350
	FOTIDSMC	0.00094	0.00064	0.00037	0.00120	0.00117	0.01843	0.00379
0.5	PIDSMC	0.00675	0.00220	0.00190	0.00680	0.00695	0.07484	0.01657
	FOPIDSMC	0.00270	0.00100	0.00066	0.00456	0.00453	0.05565	0.01152
	TIDSMC	0.00536	0.00171	0.00151	0.00586	0.00606	0.06712	0.01460
	FOTIDSMC	0.00098	0.00065	0.00038	0.00131	0.00130	0.02000	0.00410

Fig. 22.15 illustrates the torque RMS values of the four controllers under varying noise intensities (0.1–0.5). Based on the tabulated data, the average torque RMS value for each controller across all noise levels has been computed, and a percentage-based comparison has been conducted. Among these, FOTIDSMC achieves the lowest average torque RMS, making it the most efficient in terms of torque demand. Compared to PIDSMC, FOTIDSMC reduces the torque RMS by 19.8%, highlighting its significant energy efficiency advantage. Additionally, FOTIDSMC performs slightly better than FOPIDSMC, with a 0.31% lower torque RMS, indicating its superior control effectiveness. When compared to TIDSMC, FOTIDSMC exhibits a 2.6% lower torque RMS, further reinforcing its stability and efficiency. Moreover, FOPIDSMC outperforms TIDSMC by 2.3%, demonstrating the advantages of fractional-order control strategies over integer-order approaches.

PIDSMC consistently shows the highest torque RMS values among all controllers, with 24.2%, 21.1%, and 19.8% higher values compared to FOPIDSMC, TIDSMC, and FOTIDSMC, respectively. This confirms the inferior efficiency of the PID-based approach in handling disturbances while maintaining lower torque demand.

Overall, Fig. 22.15 highlights the superiority of fractional-order controllers (FOPIDSMC and FOTIDSMC) over conventional PIDSMC and integer-order TIDSMC in minimizing torque requirements. The reduced torque demand of fractional-order controllers not only enhances energy efficiency but also contributes to prolonged system lifespan by reducing wear and tear. FOTIDSMC emerges as the most effective strategy, achieving the lowest torque RMS and demonstrating the highest efficiency in mitigating noise-induced disturbances.

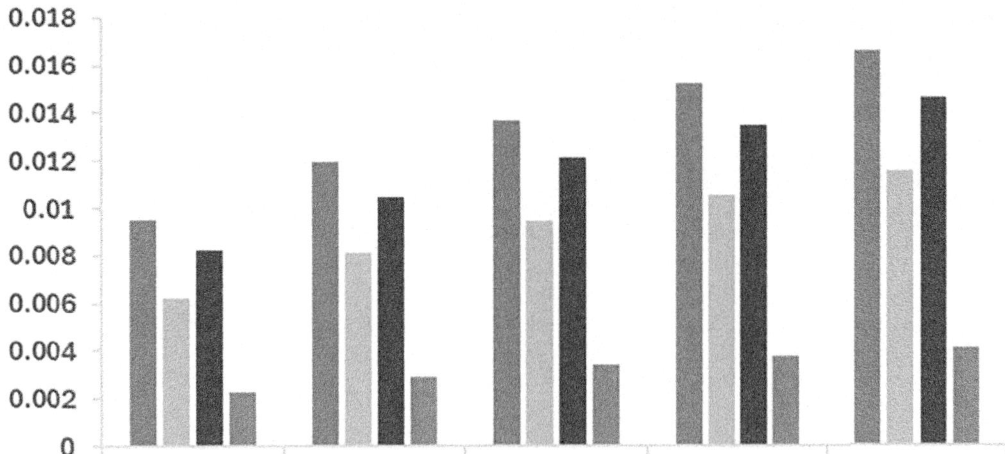

	0.1	0.2	0.3	0.4	0.5
PIDSMC	0.00955	0.01194	0.01368	0.01524	0.01657
FOPIDSMC	0.00626	0.00813	0.00945	0.01057	0.01152
TIDSMC	0.00827	0.01048	0.01218	0.0135	0.0146
FOTIDSMC	0.00227	0.00292	0.0034	0.00379	0.0041

FIGURE 22.14 The average MAE values of controllers under different noise powers (*MAE*, Mean absolute error).

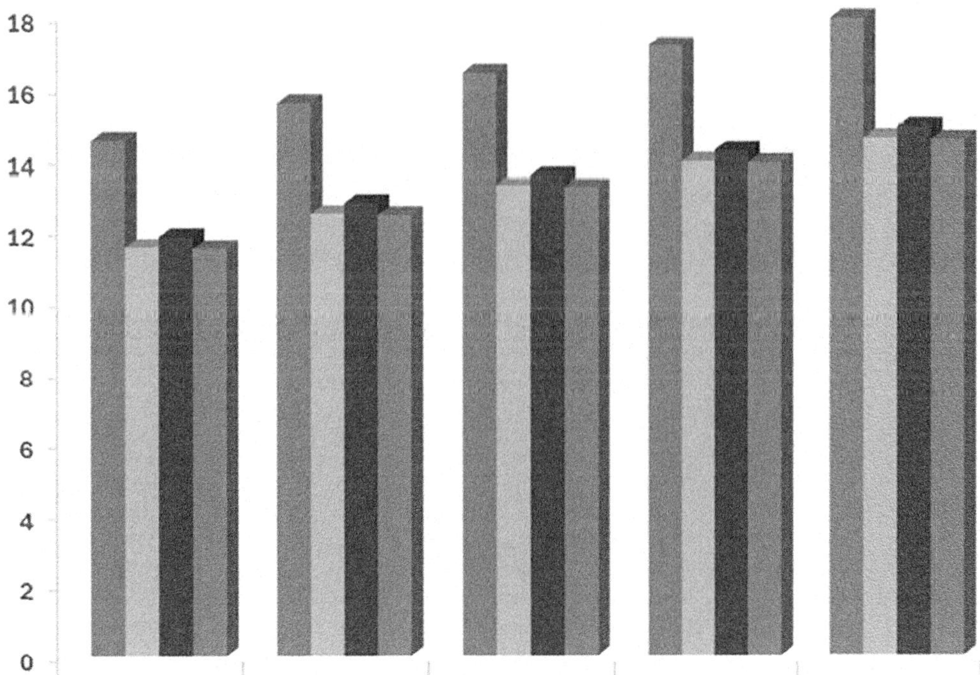

	0.1	0.2	0.3	0.4	0.5
PIDSMC	14.472	15.522	16.367	17.13	17.867
FOPIDSMC	11.469	12.405	13.185	13.879	14.515
TIDSMC	11.769	12.704	13.485	14.183	14.825
FOTIDSMC	11.433	12.368	13.144	13.836	14.47

FIGURE 22.15 Torque RMS values of controllers under different noise levels.

Fig. 22.16 presents the performance of all controllers under white noise with an intensity coefficient of 0.5 applied to all joints. The results highlight that while all controllers maintain trajectory tracking accuracy for the first four joints, significant deviations appear in Joints 5 and 6. These deviations can be attributed to the coupling effects between joints and the complexity of the manipulator's trajectory. Due to their lower inertia and higher sensitivity to disturbances, the last

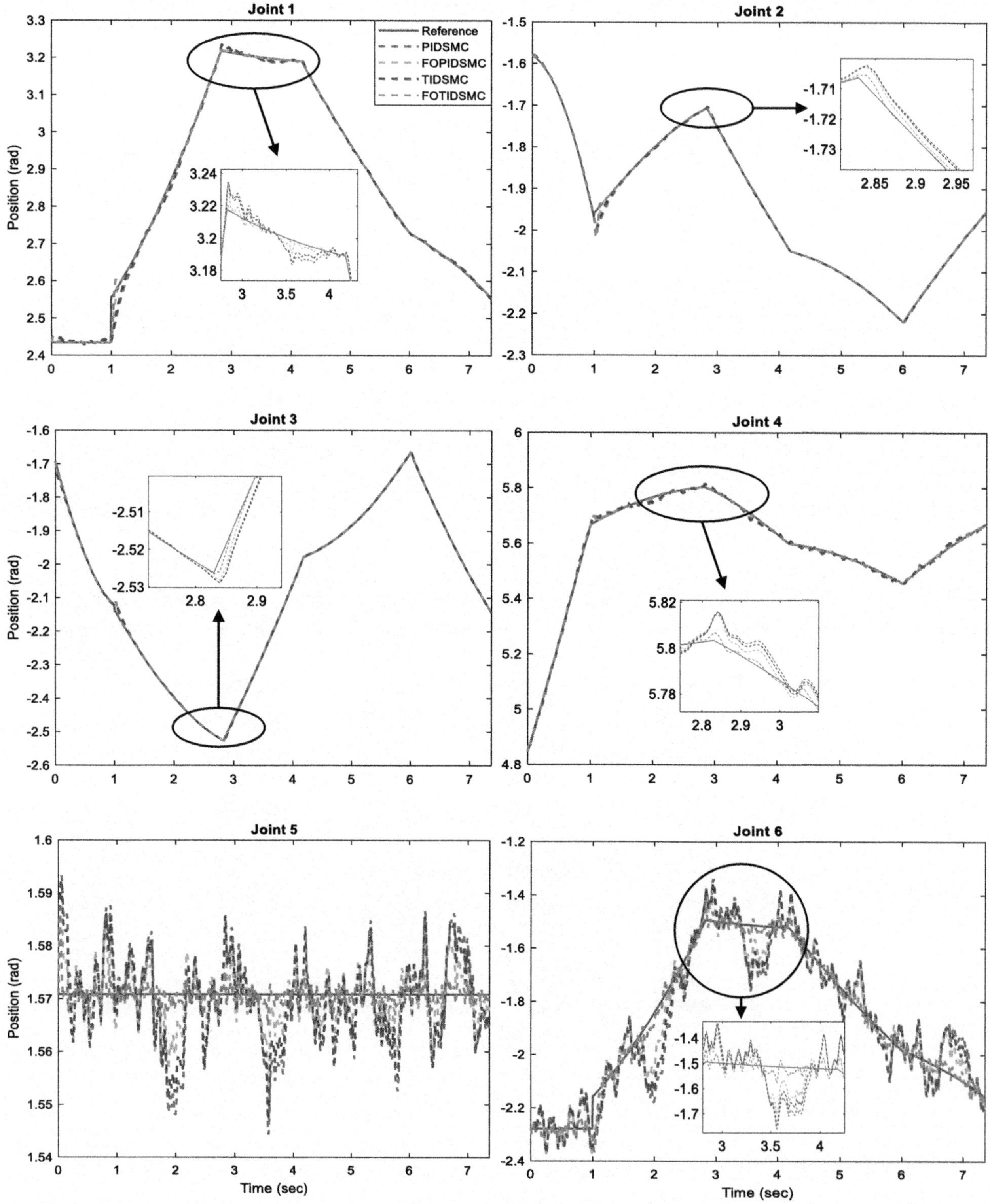

FIGURE 22.16 Joint position tracking performance of controllers under white noise (0.5 intensity).

two joints (Joint 5 and Joint 6) exhibit larger oscillations, which are particularly evident in PIDSMC and TIDSMC controllers. In contrast, FOTIDSMC demonstrates superior robustness, exhibiting the smallest oscillations and maintaining close tracking to the reference trajectory. These findings suggest that fractional-order controllers, especially FOTIDSMC, are more effective in mitigating the impact of stochastic disturbances in complex manipulator dynamics.

22.5.5 Computational complexity analysis

A computational complexity analysis was performed to evaluate the efficiency of the hybrid GWO-PSO-based optimization process designed to determine high-precision controller parameters. The analysis was conducted with a representative problem size of 30 agents and 100 iterations, examining both time and space complexity. The time complexity results showed that the total time required for parameter optimization was very similar across all controllers, with PIDSMC at 18.32 hours, TIDSMC at 18.57 hours, FOPIDSMC at 19.15 hours, and FOTIDSMC at 19.39 hours. This data confirms that the robot dynamics simulation, which forms the basis for each objective function evaluation, is computationally intensive. The fact that the optimization is performed offline and the high dimensionality of the robot control problem addressed makes this computational cost acceptable in the literature. The space complexity analysis revealed that the memory footprint of the variables used was minimal and consistent for all controllers, proving that the hybrid GWO-PSO algorithm is a very efficient approach in terms of memory usage while solving a challenging optimization problem.

22.6 Conclusion

This study has developed a novel hybrid swarm intelligence algorithm for the application of SMC to 6-DOF robot manipulators. Specifically, a new FOTID-based sliding surface, combining the advantages of fractional calculus and robust control, has been designed. A hybrid GWO-PSO approach was implemented for the optimal tuning of the proposed controller's parameters. The comprehensive performance analysis conducted under various operating conditions demonstrated that the proposed FOTIDSMC exhibits superior performance compared to PID, FOPID, and TID sliding surface-based controllers.

The key findings of the study confirm the superior performance of the proposed FOTIDSMC approach. In terms of dynamic response, FOTIDSMC achieved the lowest MAE and the shortest settling time, demonstrating superior control precision and fast convergence. The proposed controller also exhibited exceptional robustness against external factors. It consistently achieved the lowest MAE values across different disturbance magnitudes, with an average MAE reduction of 92.23% compared to PIDSMC, and was the least affected controller even with increasing disturbance magnitudes. Similarly, under end-effector load variations, FOTIDSMC maintained the lowest average MAE values, ensuring high-precision trajectory tracking and achieving an average MAE reduction of 93.64% compared to PIDSMC. FOTIDSMC's robustness was further demonstrated against stochastic disturbances, consistently achieving the lowest MAE and an average MAE improvement of 74.62% over PIDSMC under white noise in joint torques. Finally, in terms of torque efficiency, FOTIDSMC consistently achieved the lowest RMS torque values under varying disturbance levels and different load conditions, with average RMS torque reductions of approximately 22% and 19.67% compared to PIDSMC.

These results indicate that the proposed FOTIDSMC controller, by combining the benefits of fractional calculus and TID control strategies, offers a promising solution for challenging control applications of 6-DOF robot manipulators. The developed hybrid GWO-PSO optimization algorithm proved effective in finding optimal settings within the complex parameter space of FOTIDSMC. Future work may focus on the experimental validation of this approach for real-time applications and its adaptation to different robotic systems.

Acknowledgments

The authors declare that no artificial intelligence (AI) tools were used in the writing or editing of this book chapter.

References

[1] B. Siciliano, L. Sciavicco, L. Villani, G. Oriolo, Robotics: Modelling, Planning and Control, Springer, (2010).

[2] K.H. Ang, G. Chong, Y. Li, PID control system analysis, design, and technology, IEEE Transactions on Control Systems Technology 13 (4) (2005) 559–576.

[3] J.J. Craig, Introduction to Robotics: Mechanics and Control, Pearson, (2005).

[4] V. Tinoco, M.F. Silva, F.N. Santos, et al., A review of advanced controller methodologies for robotic manipulators, International Journal of Dynamics and Control 13 (2025) 36. Available from https://doi.org/10.1007/s40435-024-01533-1.
[5] I. Podlubny, Fractional-order systems and PIλDμ controllers, IEEE Transactions on Automatic Control 44 (1) (1999) 208–214.
[6] Y. Chen, I. Petrás, D. Xue, Fractional order control – a tutorial, in: Proceedings of the American Control Conference, 2009, pp. 1397–1411.
[7] C.A. Monje, et al., Fractional-Order Systems and Controls: Fundamentals and Applications, Springer, (2010).
[8] V. Utkin, Sliding Mode Control in Electromechanical Systems, CRC Press, (1993).
[9] C. Edwards, S. Spurgeon, Sliding Mode Control: Theory and Applications, Taylor & Francis, (1998).
[10] R. Palm, Sliding mode fuzzy control, IEEE Transactions on Fuzzy Systems 1 (2) (1992) 122–129.
[11] M.O. Efe, Fractional fuzzy adaptive sliding-mode control of a 2-DOF direct-drive robot arm, IEEE Transactions on Systems, Man, and Cybernetics: Part B (Cybernetics) 38 (6) (2008) 1561–1570. Available from https://doi.org/10.1109/TSMCB.2008.928227.
[12] H. Delavari, R. Ghaderi, A. Ranjbar, S. Momani, Fuzzy fractional order sliding mode controller for nonlinear systems, Communications in Nonlinear Science and Numerical Simulation 15 (4) (2010) 963–978.
[13] R. Sharma, K.P.S. Rana, V. Kumar, Performance analysis of fractional order fuzzy PID controllers applied to a robotic manipulator, Expert Systems with Applications 41 (9) (2014) 4274–4289.
[14] S. Ahmed, A.T. Azar, Adaptive PD sliding mode control for robot dynamics using predefined-time approach, International Journal of Dynamics and Control 13 (2025) 100. Available from https://doi.org/10.1007/s40435-025-01603-y.
[15] J. Pan, Fractional-order sliding mode control of manipulator combined with disturbance and state observer, Robotics and Autonomous Systems 183 (2024) 104840.
[16] C. Jing, H. Zhang, Y. Liu, J. Zhang, Adaptive super-twisting sliding mode control for robot manipulators with input saturation, Sensors 24 (9) (2023) 2783. Available from https://doi.org/10.3390/s24092783.
[17] D. Zhang, J. Hu, J. Cheng, Z.-G. Wu, H. Yan, A novel disturbance observer based fixed-time sliding mode control for robotic manipulators with global fast convergence, IEEE/CAA Journal of Automatica Sinica 11 (3) (2024) 661–672. Available from https://doi.org/10.1109/JAS.2023.123948.
[18] Z. Anjum, H. Zhou, S. Ahmed, Y. Guo, Fixed time sliding mode control for disturbed robotic manipulator, Journal of Vibration and Control (2024). Available from https://doi.org/10.1177/10775463231165094.
[19] J. Yang, Y. Wang, T. Wang, Z. Hu, X. Yang, J.J. Rodriguez-Andina, Time-delay sliding mode control for trajectory tracking of robot manipulators, IEEE Transactions on Industrial Electronics 71 (10) (2024) 13083–13091. Available from https://doi.org/10.1109/TIE.2024.3357875.
[20] B.J. Lurie, Three-parameter tunable tilt-integral-derivative (TID) controller, U.S. Patent No. 5,371,670, U.S. Patent and Trademark Office, Washington, DC, 1994.
[21] S. Priyadarshani, K.R. Subhashini, J.K. Satapathy, Pathfinder algorithm optimized fractional order tilt-integral-derivative (FOTID) controller for automatic generation control of multi-source power system, Microsystems Technology 27 (2021) 23–35. Available from https://doi.org/10.1007/s00542-020-04897-4.
[22] H. Calgan, Novel tilt integral sliding mode controller and observer design for sensorless speed control of a permanent magnet synchronous motor, COMPEL: The International Journal for Computation and Mathematics in Electrical and Electronic Engineering 41 (1) (2022) 455–470. Available from https://doi.org/10.1108/COMPEL-05-2021-0180.
[23] S. Mirjalili, S.M. Mirjalili, A. Lewis, Grey wolf optimizer, Advanced Engineering Software 69 (2014) 46–61.
[24] J. Kennedy, R. Eberhart, Particle swarm optimization, in: Proceedings of the IEEE International Conference on Neural Networks, vol. 4, 1995, pp. 1942–1948.
[25] R.A. Ibrahim, M.A. Elaziz, S. Lu, Chaotic opposition-based grey-wolf optimization algorithm based on differential evolution and cellular automata for engineering problems, Engineering with Computers 34 (2) (2018) 293–319.
[26] O. Karahan, H. Karci, Swarm intelligence based nonlinear friction and dynamic parameters identification for a 6-DOF robotic manipulator, Journal of Intelligent and Robotic Systems 108 (2) (2023). Available from https://doi.org/10.1007/s10846-023-01868-5.
[27] Z.A. Ayinalem, A.T. Kassie, PSO tuned super-twisting sliding mode controller for trajectory tracking control of an articulated robot, Journal of Electrical and Computer Engineering 2024 (1) (2025) 1171569. Available from https://doi.org/10.1155/jece/1171569.
[28] N. Basil, A.F. Mohammed, B.M. Sabbar, et al., Performance analysis of hybrid optimization approach for UAV path planning control, Scientific Reports 15 (1) (2025) 1–23. Available from https://doi.org/10.1038/s41598-025-86803-4.
[29] O. Karahan, H. Karci, Design of robust fractional order fuzzy PID sliding mode controller based on hybrid swarm intelligence algorithm for a 6-DOF robotic manipulator, Robotica (2025) 1–30. Available from https://doi.org/10.1017/S0263574725000141.
[30] G. Sun, C. Wu, X. Li, Z. Ma, S. Xu, X. Shao, Fractional-Order Sliding Mode Control: Methodologies and Applications, Springer, (2024).
[31] D. Zhang, L. Cao, S. Tang, Fractional-order sliding mode control for a class of uncertain nonlinear systems based on LQR, International Journal of Advanced Robotic Systems 14 (2017). Available from https://doi.org/10.1177/1729881417748404.
[32] S. Han, M.S. Tran, D. Tran, Adaptive sliding mode control for a robotic manipulator with unknown friction and unknown control direction, Applied Sciences 11 (9) (2021) 3919. Available from https://doi.org/10.3390/app11093919.
[33] N. Nikdel, M. Badamchizadeh, V. Azimirad, M.A. Nazari, Fractional-order adaptive backstepping control of robotic manipulators in the presence of model uncertainties and external disturbances, IEEE Transactions on Industrial Electronics 63 (10) (2016) 6249–6256. Available from https://doi.org/10.1109/TIE.2016.2577624.
[34] M.W. Spong, S. Hutchinson, M. Vidyasagar, Robot Modeling and Control, John Wiley & Sons, (2020).

[35] Y. Cao, X.B. Chen, An output-tracking-based discrete PID-sliding mode control for MIMO systems, IEEE/ASME Transactions on Mechatronics 19 (4) (2013) 1183–1194. Available from https://doi.org/10.1109/TMECH.2013.2283774.

[36] J. Liu, X. Wang, J. Liu, X. Wang, Advanced Sliding Mode Control, Springer, Berlin, Heidelberg, (2011), pp. 81–96.

[37] Q. Liu, D. Liu, W. Meng, Z. Zhou, Q. Ai, Fuzzy sliding mode control of a multi-DOF parallel robot in rehabilitation environment, International Journal of Humanoid Robotics 11 (1) (2014) 1450004. Available from https://doi.org/10.1142/S021984361450004X.

[38] B. Ataşlar-Ayyıldız, O. Karahan, S. Yılmaz, Control and robust stabilization at unstable equilibrium by fractional controller for magnetic levitation systems, Fractal and Fractional 5 (3) (2021) 101. Available from https://doi.org/10.3390/fractalfract5030101.

[39] S. Das, Functional Fractional Calculus, Springer, (2011) vol. 1.

[40] J. Kumar, A.T. Azar, V. Kumar, K.P.S. Rana, Design of fractional order fuzzy sliding mode controller for nonlinear complex systems, Mathematics and Technology of Fractional-Order Systems, Elsevier, (2018), pp. 249–282.

[41] T.O. Ting, X.S. Yang, S. Cheng, K. Huang, Hybrid metaheuristic algorithms: past, present, and future, Recent Advances in Swarm Intelligence and Evolutionary Computation, Springer, (2015), pp. 71–83. Available from https://doi.org/10.1007/978-3-319-13826-8_4.

Chapter 23

Applications of the grey wolf optimizer in water engineering and management

Mohammad Khoshnam, Hojat Karami, and Sayed-Farhad Mousavi
Faculty of Civil Engineering, Semnan University, Semnan, Iran

23.1 Introduction

In the last two centuries, engineering science has been developed more than humanity expected. As engineering advances, problems also emerge. Thus scientists are always trying to solve the problems to increase productivity in various fields of engineering. One of those fields is "water." Since water is an inseparable part of the life of living beings and also its resources on Earth are limited, optimal management of water resources is one of the most important factors in the field of water engineering and management. There are several solutions to solve water problems, but only one of those solutions has the best efficiency. Finding the best solution is very time-consuming and also increases computational costs; therefore utilizing optimization algorithms is a suitable approach to find the optimal solution. Grey wolf optimizer (GWO) [1] is one of the powerful optimization algorithms for finding optimal solutions of challenging real-world optimization problems. This chapter reviews various problems of water engineering and the application of the GWO to solve these problems.

23.2 Research method

In order to collect suitable articles which are related to the field of water resources engineering and management, few keywords such as "GWO," "pan evaporation," "groundwater level," "lake water level," "reference crop evapotranspiration," "streamflow," and "water infiltration," were searched and the initial stage of the study was carried out by searching them in various databases by utilizing google scholar between 2019 and 2024.

In the initial stage of screening, all non-English articles and conference papers were discarded. Then, the remaining articles were classified into six categories that are discussed in this chapter. For each category, articles were studied, and those with the same scope coverage were selected; the others were removed. Abstracts were prepared for each selected article; then, by matching them together, the text related to "Grey Wolf Optimizer Applications in Water Engineering and Management" was written. Fig. 23.1 demonstrates the PRISMA flow diagram of how articles were selected for this chapter.

23.3 Application of grey wolf optimizer in groundwater level prediction

Groundwater refers to the water that can be found everywhere in underground among gaps and pore spaces in soils and rocks, which are called aquifers. Another feature of groundwater is that it moves slowly; so, its level fluctuates. Knowing the groundwater level is so crucial for water supply management and planning for a water distribution system that cannot be lower than a specific level to avoid land subsidence. This level depends on hydrological and geoenvironmental situations. Therefore it must be individually calculated for each zone.

Cui et al. [2] developed the adaptive neuro fuzzy inference system-Improved alpha (ANFIS-IA) GWO model in which the GWO algorithm was applied to optimize the parameters of the ANFIS model in order to predict groundwater level (GWL). The GWO-based model performed much better than other models by achieving better ranges of normalized root mean square error (NRMSE) (0.06–0.11) and kling-gupta efficiency (KGE) (0.96–0.98). Samantaray and Sahoo [3] used the extreme learning machine-particle swarm optimization-grey wolf optimizer (ELM-PSOGWO) hybrid model, which

Grey Wolf Optimizer. DOI: https://doi.org/10.1016/B978-0-443-36624-6.00033-0

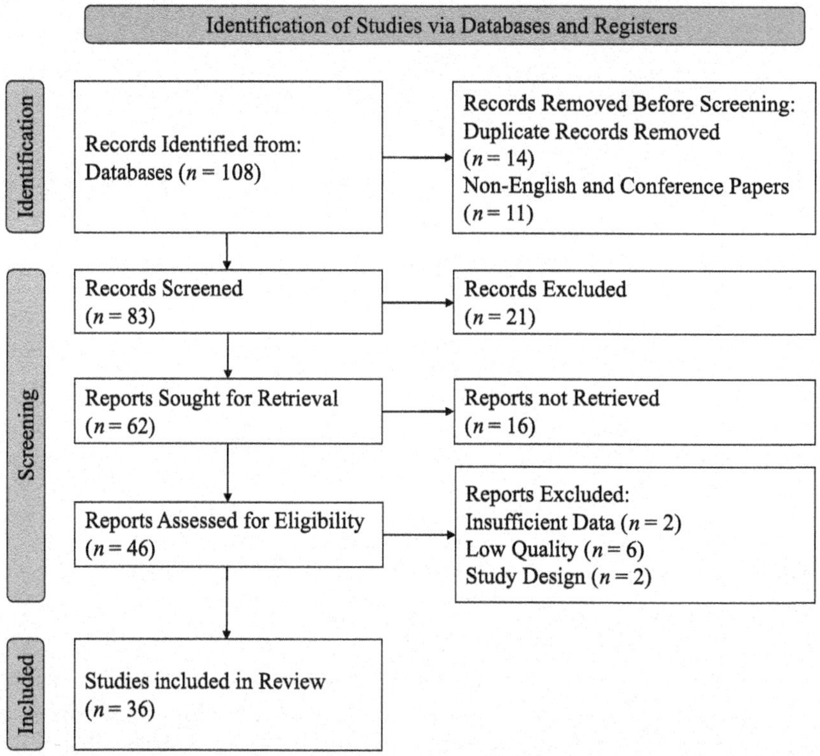

FIGURE 23.1 PRISMA flow diagram of grey wolf optimizer applications in the water engineering field.

performed best among other hybrid models by R^2 of 0.9969 and root mean square error (RMSE) of 0.0088. Mirboluki et al. [4] targeted the estimation of GWL using monthly data from 86 wells in Mashhad Plain, Iran. He proposed the long short term memory (LSTM)-GWO hybrid model, which outperformed other models in terms of accuracy, with at least a 30% reduction of mean absolute error (MAE) in the artificial neural network (ANN)-GWO model and the error metrics by 15% over the ANN model. Zeng et al. [5] proposed a dynamic prediction model for GWL, which was developed by the maximum information coefficient (MIC) and LSTM models, optimized by the GWO algorithm. The MIC-GWO-LSTM model performed better than single-factor and support vector regression (SVR) models by capturing the relationship between GWL and triggering factors. Adnan et al. [6] utilized GWO to increase the performance of the ELM model. GWO optimized the input weights and hidden layer biases of the ELM model. Also, GWO significantly improved the performance of the ELM model in the estimation of GWL fluctuations. Zhou et al. [7] researched the prediction of GWL by an improved LSTM model through the GWO. The results indicated that for all assessment metrics, including R^2, MAE, RMSE, and mean absolute percentage error (MAPE), the performance of the GWO-LSTM model was better than that of the traditional methods and the baseline LSTM model.

Graphical GWO application of GWL prediction is demonstrated in Fig. 23.2.

23.4 Application of grey wolf optimizer in streamflow estimation

Streamflow refers to the flow of water in streams, rivers, or other channels and is considered a major component of the hydrologic cycle. It is usually measured as the quantity of water passing a particular point per unit of time. It is one of the important parts of the hydrological cycle that includes precipitation, snowmelt, inputs from groundwater and human activities, operation of dams or irrigation. It provides the health of the ecosystem, management of water resources, flood forecasting, and maintenance of biodiversity. In general, streamflow is often monitored by hydrological gauges and modeled for various environmental and engineering applications.

Tikhamarine et al. [8] used GWO-integrated models for the prediction of monthly streamflow, which demonstrated that SVR-GWO was more accurate and effective than the others. Kilinc and Yurtsever [9] have come up by GWO-gated recurrent unit (GRU) hybrid model for streamflow forecasting. A total of 75% of the data was allocated for training, while 25% was saved for testing purposes. The GWO-GRU outperformed the single GRU by around 34% and 53% in terms of

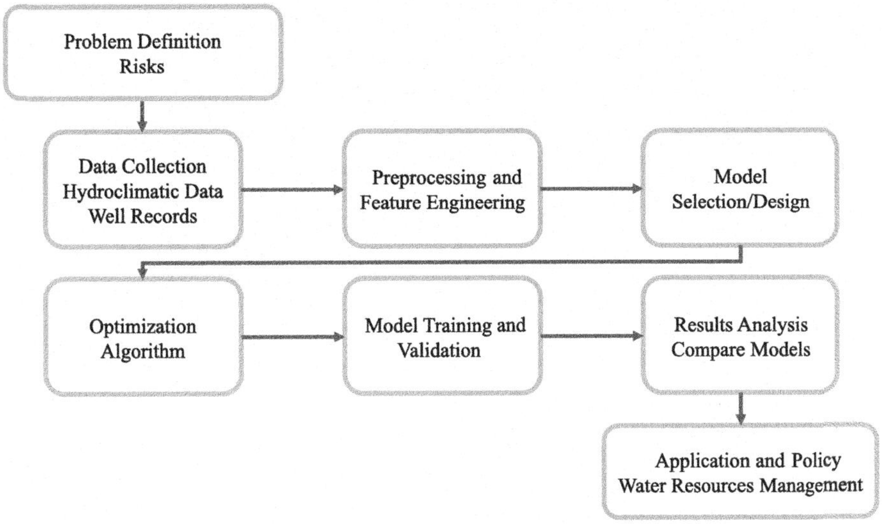

FIGURE 23.2 Flowchart of the GWL prediction.

RMSE and MAE, respectively. The R^2 value of 0.9827 by the GWO-GRU model was higher than 0.9558 in linear regression. Adnan et al. [10] relied on the ELM-PSOGWO technique. Results showed that this model performed better than others by reducing RMSEs by 38.2%, 22.8%, 22.4%, and 16.7% against ELM, ELM-PSO, ELM-GWO, and ELM-particle swarm optimization-gravitational search algorithm (PSOGSA), respectively. Adnan et al. [11] have done research on improving ML models using the GWO algorithm, mainly for monthly streamflow prediction. The LSTM-GWO achieved a MAPE value of 17.9% in local data applications, excelling by a much lower maximum relative error in peak streamflow accuracy in comparison with ANN-GWO. Jia et al. [12] improved short-term streamflow prediction by applying an ML technique with GWO. The research empirically tested 6 ML models and ensembled GWO with other algorithms to improve the performance.t It demonstrated through its results that GWO is one of the most efficient performing algorithms, achieving R^2–0.6944; thus, it is ideal in parameter calibration for streamflow predictions.

Liang et al. [13] emphasized the critical importance of GWO and its improved versions for streamflow prediction models. This led to the improved prediction performance through training optimization by GWO or its adaptive versions, especially the adaptive chaotic (AC)-GWO, in the multilayer perceptron (MLP) neural network. Results confirm that the GWO application significantly improved the predictive capacity of the model. Wang et al. [14] proved the effectiveness of IGWO in improving streamflow prediction. Validation results showed that IGWO outperforms benchmark models and optimization algorithms in both accuracy and speed of convergence. Zhao et al. [15] used IGWO for optimized parameter selection to avoid underfitting or overfitting of the GRU model. An improved complete ensemble empirical mode decomposition with adaptive noise-empirical wavelet transform-improved grey wolf optimizer-gated recurrent unit (ICEEWT-IGWO-GRU) model combines empirical wavelet transform with improved decomposition techniques in noise reduction. The model reduced MAE and RMSE by 50% and 52%, respectively. Martinho et al. [16] proposed hybrid ML models for natural water flow forecasting, considering the GWO algorithm for optimization of the parameters. The optimization by GWO greatly increased model performance; hence, the extreme gradient boosting (XGB)-GWO model can be considered reliable for flow prediction. Wang et al. [17] proposed a hybrid model for annual streamflow prediction, which was based on GWO for optimization of the support vector machine (SVM) parameters. The GWO hybrid model outperformed six reference models, including the autoregressive integrated moving average (ARIMA) and other ensemble empirical mode decomposition (EEMD)-based methods. This proved the efficiency of GWO in improving the accuracy of streamflow forecasts.

Fig. 23.3 demonstrates the process of GWO application in streamflow estimation.

23.5 Application of grey wolf optimizer in water infiltration estimation

In the hydrological cycle, a portion of water after rainfall or snowmelt eventually becomes runoff, while the rest starts to infiltrate into the ground or evaporate into the atmosphere. The rate of infiltration would depend on the rainfall intensity, rainfall duration, land slope, soil type, evaporation rate, and many other parameters. Thus the infiltration rate could be

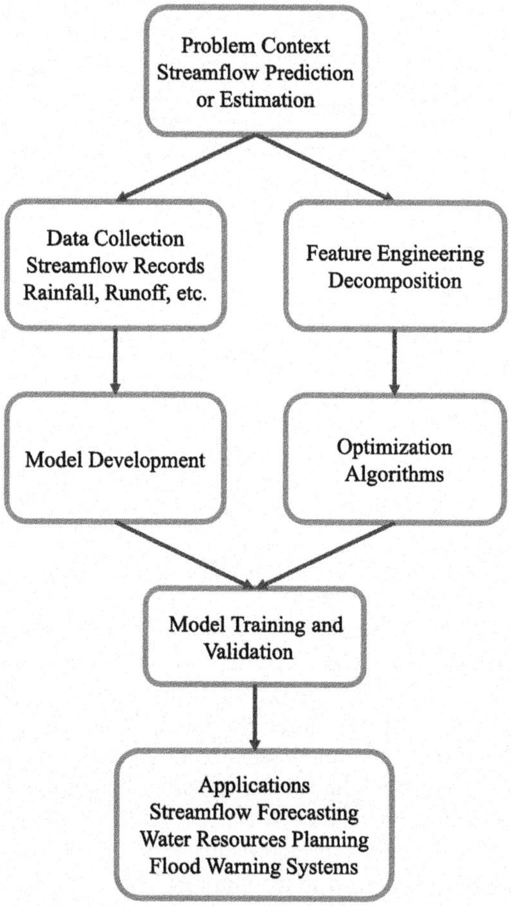

FIGURE 23.3 Flowchart of streamflow estimation.

estimated for various conditions in both urban and nonurban areas to provide useful information for future principled planning. The GWO algorithm can be considered as an effective tool in the prediction of water infiltration rate.

Panahi et al. [18] studied the performance of the convolutional neural network (CNN) algorithm optimized by three metaheuristic methods: GWO, imperialist competitive algorithm (ICA), and genetic algorithm (GA). It was used to predict cumulative infiltration and infiltration rate in some soils in Iran. The following results were obtained: The performance of CNN optimized with GWO outperformed ICA, GA, and CNN. Metaheuristic approaches increased the performance of CNN. Among these, GWO, with the improvement of 9.56% for cumulative infiltration and 28.15% for infiltration rate, outperformed ICA and GA. Sepahvand et al. [19] compared CNN models with hybrid SVR and group method of data handling (GMDH) models, which were improved by using GWO, bat algorithm (BA), and PSO. Among these methods, GWO showed better predictive performance, effectively improving cumulative infiltration prediction accuracy when integrated with standalone models, based on evaluation metrics such as R and nash-sutcliffe efficiency (NSE). Fig. 23.4 illustrates the steps of GWO application in water infiltration estimation.

23.6 Application of grey wolf optimizer in lake water level modeling

A lake is an inland body of accumulated water entirely bounded by land, mostly resulting from topographic depressions. It can be as small as a few hectares or large enough to form a huge freshwater or saltwater body. Lakes are dynamic bodies of water whose levels alter over time depending on factors such as evaporation, physical recharge from rivers and streams, interaction with neighboring land, and human activities such as damming and water extraction. It also happens that the lake water level is significant because it would impact ecosystems, water availability, agriculture, and local climate. Its proper understanding and monitoring are highly indispensable to any sustainable management of water resources and environmental protection.

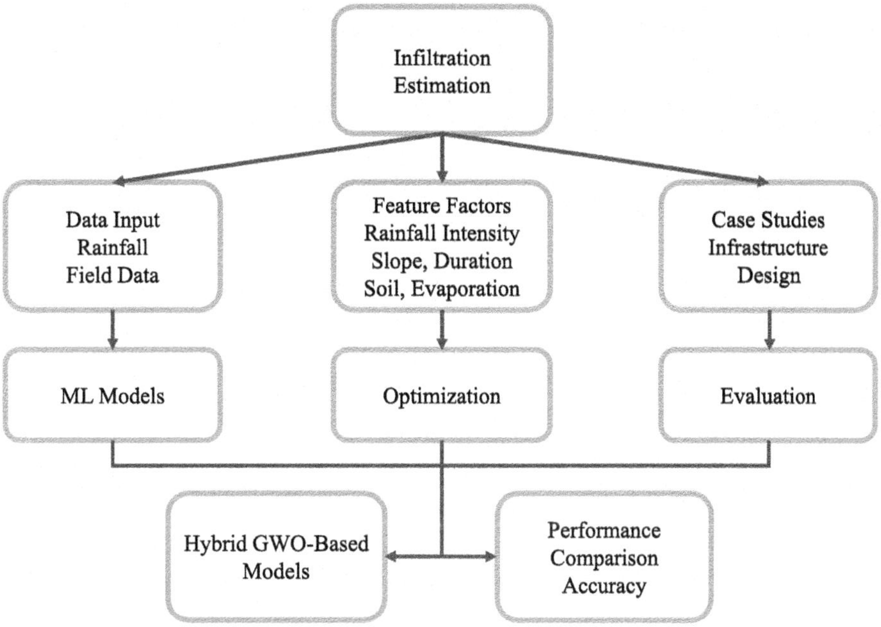

FIGURE 23.4 The flowchart of water infiltration estimation.

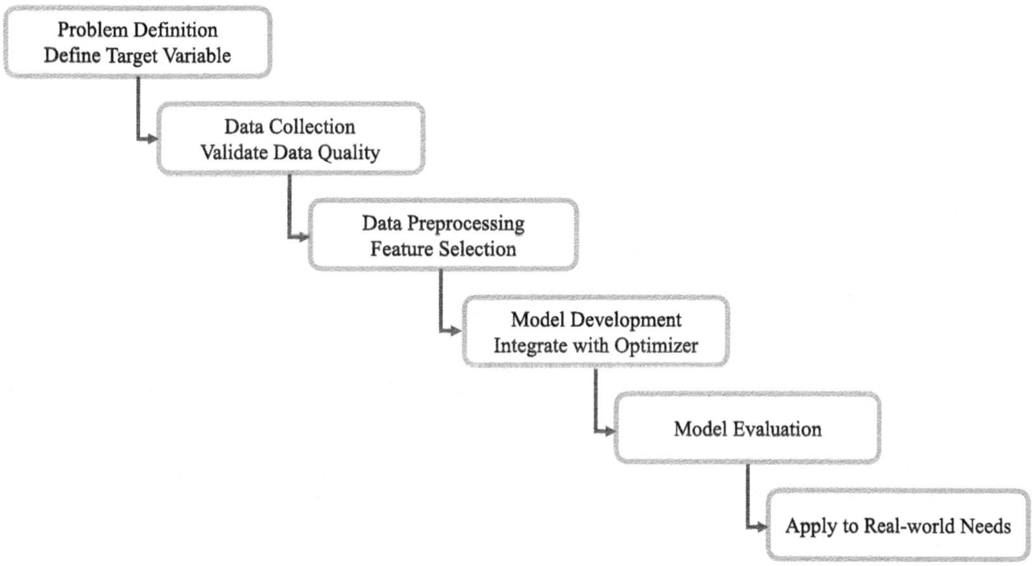

FIGURE 23.5 Flowchart of lake water level modeling.

Mohammadi et al. [20] adopted the hybrid GWO algorithm with SVR for the prediction of lake water level variation. The proposed SVR-GWO hybrid model showed improved performance and higher accuracy than SVR. To confirm that GWO efficiently increased the performance of the SVR model, some statistical metrics such as RMSE, MAE, and R^2 were computed. Sales et al. [21] simulated the Urmia Lake water depth by integrating hydrological and meteorological data using advanced modeling techniques. The results indicated that among the developed models, the ELM-IGWO model performed better and provided more accurate results in the simulation of water depth variations. Li et al. [22] adopted GWO to optimize LSTM network parameters in water level prediction. The GWO-LSTM model gave the best results with regard to accuracy and stability, with an MAE of 0.1043 and an RMSE of 0.1402. These findings demonstrated the capability of GWO in tuning the precision and generalization of LSTM models for a reliable approach to reservoir management, flood control, and sustainable utilization of an available water resource.

The process of GWO application in lake water level modeling is shown in Fig. 23.5.

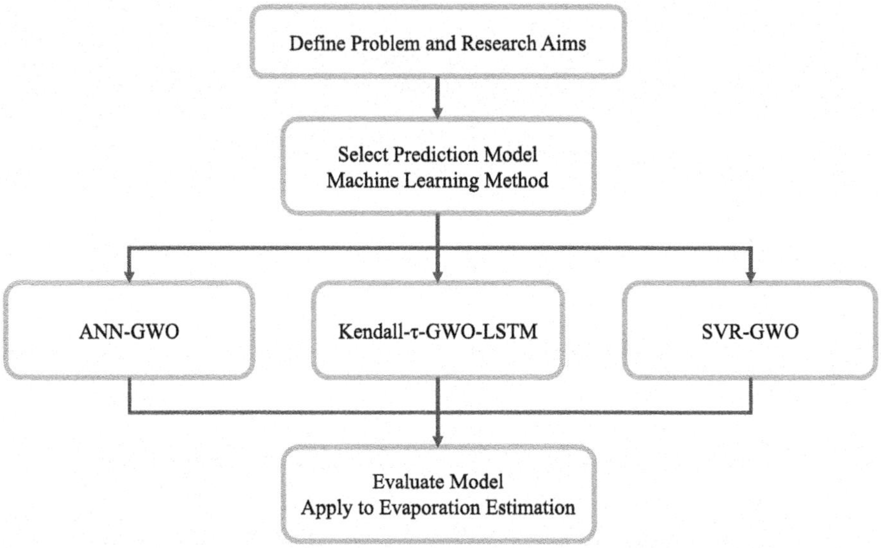

FIGURE 23.6 Flowchart of pan evaporation estimation.

23.7 Application of grey wolf optimizer in pan evaporation estimation

A common method to measure the rate of water evaporation from an open water surface is using a pan. In this regard, the most famous pan is the Class A pan. Some environmental parameters, such as air temperature, humidity, wind speed, and solar radiation, influence the evaporation rate. Data recorded from this process helps in the estimation of water loss into the atmosphere and finds application in agriculture, hydrology, and climate studies.

Seifi and Soroush [23] investigated the performance of GWO when it is applied to hybrid models using ANNs for estimating daily evaporation. The obtained results showed that ANN-GWO yielded promising performance and outperformed others in terms of accuracy in evaporation estimation. The models were evaluated using important metrics like RMSE, R^2, NSE, and global performance indicator (GPI). Fu and Li [24] used the GWO to increase the accuracy of monthly pan evaporation (PE) estimation in drylands. The hybrid Kendall-τ-GWO-LSTM model, which also involved input selection through the Kendall-τ correlation, yielded better results with minimum RMSE (38.28), NMSE (0.20), MAE (26.62), and MAPE (19.96%) and a maximum NSE of 0.89. Kisi et al. [25] presented a study dealing with the estimation of PE with a limited number of climatic variables by using GWO, integrated with the LSTM model. The proposed LSTM-GWO outperformed the LSTM and other advanced ML methods. Results showed that GWO improved the optimization process of the LSTM model in order to achieve more accurate estimations of PE. Piri and Kisi [26] utilized SVR-GWO in evaluating the evaporation dynamics. GWO considerably increased the performance of the SVR and reduced average predictive errors by over 41%. SVR-GWO secured a remarkable improvement in accuracy, while the R^2 value increased from 0.867 to 0.973.

Fig. 23.6 shows the steps of GWO application in pan evaporation estimation.

23.8 Application of grey wolf optimizer in reference crop evapotranspiration modeling

Evapotranspiration refers to the total process of water transfer to the atmosphere from land via two mechanisms: Evaporation and transpiration. Evaporation refers to the transformation of water into vapor directly from the soil, water bodies, or any other surfaces. On the other hand, transpiration refers to the process whereby water is taken up via the roots of the plants, then passes through the plants and is released into the atmosphere as vapor through tiny openings in leaves, which are called stomata. Evapotranspiration is a very important factor in the hydrological cycle and it also determines the availability of water, agricultural productivity, and climatic conditions. It depends on the temperature, humidity, wind speed, solar radiation, soil moisture content, and type of vegetation.

Maroufpoor et al. [27] utilized ANN-GWO for the estimation of reference crop evapotranspiration (ET_0) over Iran. An ANN-GWO model was compared with ANN and least square (LS)-SVR for seven different input scenarios. The optimization performed by the GWO algorithm was considerably effective, bringing much higher accuracy of ANN-GWO than that of ANN and LS-SVR. Xiao et al. [28] developed a hybrid model including GWO, PSO, and XGB for improving meteorological simulations with increased ET_0 estimation. The inclusion of GWO into the hybrid model greatly increased its hyperparameter optimization and feature selection. It reduced the average RMSE of some meteorological variables by 47.4% and ET_0 by 30.8% in the GWO-based hybrid model. Dong et al. [29] chose different bio-inspired algorithms for optimization of kernel-based nonlinear extension of arps decline (KNEA) in estimating ET_0 over China. Among all algorithms, the GWO-KNEA model performed better; hence, the GWO-KNEA2 model was found to be the most accurate, with R^2=0.9814 and RMSE=0.2143 mm d^{-1}, showing a very good convergence rate and population size.

Heramb et al. [30] focused on the improvement of ET_0 prediction, highly relevant for the efficient management of water in agriculture, by using hybrid ML models that are optimized with the GWO. Three ML algorithms were added to GWO, which gave GWO-random forest (RF), GWOXGB, and GWO-light gradient boosting (LGB) models. GWO significantly reduced the prediction errors, whereas the greatest improvement was in RF models. Tikhamarine et al. [31] utilized SVR-GWO in order to estimate monthly ET_0. The SVR-GWO model used five climatic variables and evaluated them with some other models, including SVR-GA, SVR-PSO, ANN, and several empirical models. Results illustrated that the SVR-GWO model consistently outperformed other approaches and also achieved higher accuracy according to RMSE, NSE, R, and willmott index (WI) metrics. Khairan et al. [32] evaluated the effectiveness of GWO as part of a hybrid algorithm (PSOGWO) integrated with an ANN in order to predict monthly ET_0. The model's estimation accuracy was compared to other advanced algorithms. The PSOGWO-ANN model demonstrated better performance with higher accuracy and lower error metrics, and also gained R^2=0.977, MAE=0.1445, and RMSE=0.078. Ikram et al. [33] utilized different hybrid algorithms for improving the prediction of ET_0. Among all the models, the SVR-PSOGWO hybrid consistently gained the best performance and significantly reduced prediction errors in comparison with SVR, SVR-PSO, and SVR-PSOGSA models.

He et al. [34] used GWO to increase the performance of ELM for estimating daily ET_0. Among several tested hybrid models, which were GWO-ELM, moth flame optimization (MFO)-ELM, PSO-ELM, whale optimization algorithm (WOA)-ELM, and empirical methods, the GWO-ELM achieved the best accuracy across all stations with R^2=0.945–0.955, relative root mean square error (RRMSE)=14.52%–15.29%, MAE=0.124–0.141 mm d^{-1}, and NSE=0.942–0.952 using mass transfer inputs. Lu et al. [35] assessed the benefits of using GWO integrated with the XGB model to forecast ET_0. The GWO increased the parameter tuning of XGB and avoided local optima. It also achieved better forecasting accuracy in comparison with XGB, M5 model tree, and MLP models. Khairan et al. [36] evaluated the performance of PSOGWO that was integrated with an ANN to estimate monthly ET_0. The study compared the PSOGWO-ANN model with other algorithms in terms of prediction accuracy. Results illustrated that while all models were efficient, the PSOGWO-ANN model slightly outperformed others and also achieved an R^2 of 0.99. Tikhamarine et al. [37] applied the GWO that was combined with an ANN to model monthly ET_0. Among hybrid ML approaches, the ANN-GWO model outperformed others and also achieved the lowest RMSE (0.0592–0.0808), highest NSE (0.9972–0.9956), strongest R (0.9986–0.9978), and highest WI (0.9993–0.9989).

The process of GWO application in reference crop evapotranspiration modeling is illustrated in Fig. 23.7.

23.9 Discussion

As shown in the previous sections, the performance and efficiency of GWO are suitable for determining water engineering parameters. Also, hybridizing various optimization algorithms with GWO could be significantly effective in improving the final solution. Table 23.1 lists all hybrid algorithms based on GWO and the number of times each has been utilized in the literature, ordered by popularity for this study.

As shown in Table 23.1, five specific hybrid algorithms, namely ANN-GWO, LSTM-GWO, SVR-GWO, ELM-GWO, and GWO-XGB, are now the most widely used methods in research works related to the field of water engineering and water resources management. An in-depth survey of the literature also revealed that these algorithms tend to demonstrate uniformly high accuracy and reliability in estimating the required parameters, which accounts for and justifies their wide popularity among researchers. Pros and cons of these algorithms are illustrated in Table 23.2, and Fig. 23.8 shows the percentage of the algorithms' usage (mentioned in Table 23.1) across the reviewed literature.

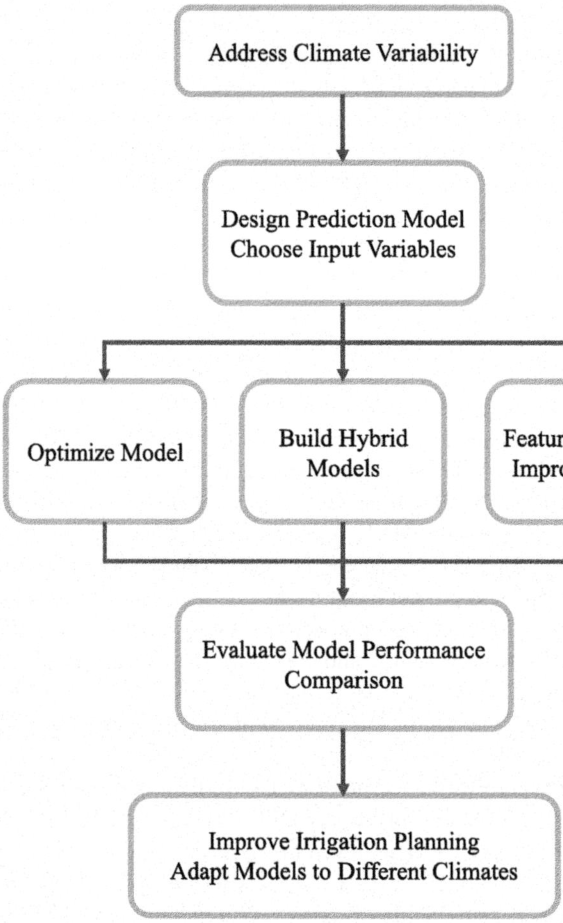

FIGURE 23.7 Flowchart of reference crop evapotranspiration modeling.

Given the nature of most data in water engineering and management is time series, several points are important and should be considered.

- One of the main challenges in hydrological time series modeling is the risk of data leakage. This problem occurs when preprocessing, such as scaling, normalization, or feature selection, is performed before the data is divided into training and testing. To avoid this matter, all preprocessing steps should be applied to the training data only and then the same transformations should be applied to the testing data. Following this principle prevents estimation errors and overestimates the accuracy of the model.
- In hydrological time series analysis, the use of conventional methods seems not suitable because the time order of data is important and randomly adding data to the training set could lead to overly optimistic estimation of the model performance. Because of this issue, specific approaches should be used. One is Blocked Cross-validation, in which data are divided into contiguous time blocks; for instance, the first few years could be selected as training and the following years as testing. Another one is Walk-forward validation, which is closer to the real forecast conditions, which is crucial for hydrological applications under climate change.
- One of the fundamental issues in hydrological time series modeling is nonstationarity due to climate change. Many models assume that statistical properties of the data, such as mean, variance, or distribution, remain constant over time. But in the real world, climate change causes changes in precipitation, runoff, evaporation, and other hydrometeorological parameters. This makes a model trained on past data less accurate in predicting the future. To address this problem, approaches such as evaluating the model in moving time windows or testing under different climate scenarios can be used.

TABLE 23.1 Summary of AI models, usage frequency, and application field in the related studies.

AI model	Number of studies	Applied fields
ANN-GWO	5	Groundwater level prediction Streamflow estimation Pan evaporation estimation Reference evapotranspiration modeling
LSTM-GWO	5	Groundwater level prediction Streamflow estimation Lake water level modeling Pan evaporation estimation
SVR-GWO	5	Streamflow estimation Lake water level modeling Pan evaporation estimation Reference evapotranspiration modeling
ELM-GWO	4	Groundwater level prediction Streamflow estimation Reference evapotranspiration modeling
GWO-XGB	3	Streamflow estimation Reference evapotranspiration modeling
PSOGWO	2	Reference evapotranspiration modeling
ELM-PSOGWO	2	Groundwater level prediction Streamflow estimation
PSOGWO-ANN	2	Reference evapotranspiration modeling
CNN-GWO	2	Water infiltration estimation
SVM-GWO	2	Streamflow estimation
SVR-PSOGWO	1	Reference evapotranspiration modeling
GWOLGB	1	Reference evapotranspiration modeling
GWORF	1	Reference evapotranspiration modeling
GWO-KNEA	1	Reference evapotranspiration modeling
MIC-GWO-LSTM	1	Groundwater level prediction
Kendall-τ-GWO-LSTM	1	Pan evaporation estimation
GWO-GRU	1	Streamflow estimation
ICEEWT-IGWO-GRU	1	Streamflow estimation
ANFIS-IA-GWO	1	Groundwater level prediction
ANN-IA-GWO	1	Groundwater level prediction
EFS-SVMIGWO	1	Streamflow estimation
ACGWO	1	Streamflow estimation
ANFIS-GWO	1	Streamflow estimation

TABLE 23.2 Pros and cons of GWO hybrid algorithms.

Algorithm	Pros	Cons
ANN-GWO	- GWO helps avoid local optima in ANN training - Strong generalization ability compared to ANN - Suitable for highly nonlinear problems	- Requires large datasets for effective training - Risk of overfitting with limited data - Higher training time
LSTM-GWO	- GWO enhances weight and bias optimization - High prediction accuracy in time-series forecasting	- High computational and memory requirements - Slower convergence due to LSTM complexity
SVR-GWO	- High prediction accuracy in regression tasks - GWO efficiently tunes hyperparameters - Robust against overfitting	- Computationally intensive for large-scale datasets - Limited scalability for highly complex nonlinear patterns
ELM-GWO	- Rapid training process - GWO improves hidden layer parameter selection - Strong generalization ability	- Limited performance on highly complex datasets - Requires feature normalization for stable outcomes
GWO-XGB	- Strong predictive performance in classification and regression - GWO optimizes hyperparameters effectively - Reduces risk of overfitting	- Computationally intensive - Risk of overfitting - Limited interpretability compared to simpler models

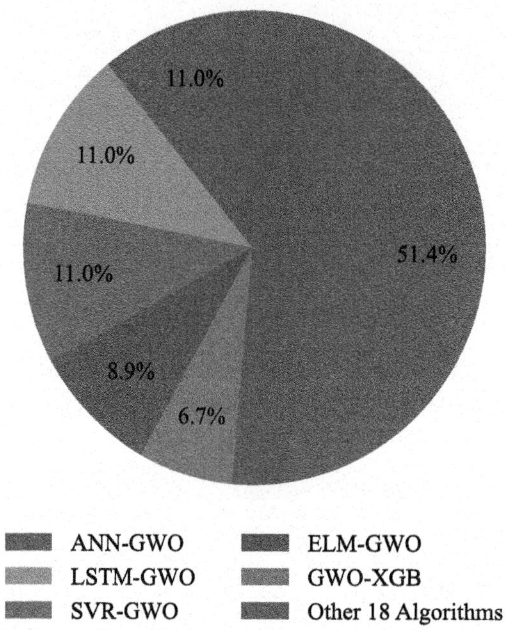

FIGURE 23.8 Pie chart of the algorithms' usage in the reviewed literature.

23.10 Conclusion

In this literature review, it was demonstrated that GWO has significant potential in improving the accuracy in predicting water engineering and management parameters such as groundwater level, streamflow, water infiltration, lake water level, pan evaporation, and reference crop evapotranspiration. It was concluded that using GWO, integrated with other metaheuristic algorithms, effectively increased the accuracy of predicted parameters, which makes it a promising approach in this field.

References

[1] S. Mirjalili, S.M. Mirjalili, A. Lewis, Grey wolf optimizer, Advances in Engineering Software 69 (2014) 46–61. Available from https://doi.org/10.1016/j.advengsoft.2013.12.007.

[2] F. Cui, Z.A. Al-Sudani, G.S. Hassan, H.A. Afan, S.J. Ahammed, Z.M. Yaseen, Boosted artificial intelligence model using improved alpha-guided grey wolf optimizer for groundwater level prediction: comparative study and insight for federated learning technology, Journal of Hydrology 606 (2022) 127384. Available from https://doi.org/10.1016/j.jhydrol.2021.127384.

[3] S. Samantaray, A. Sahoo, Groundwater level prediction using an improved ELM model integrated with hybrid particle swarm optimisation and grey wolf optimisation, Groundwater for Sustainable Development 26 (2024) 101178. Available from https://doi.org/10.1016/j.gsd.2024.101178.

[4] A. Mirboluki, M. Mehraein, O. Kisi, A. Kuriqi, R. Barati, Groundwater level estimation using improved deep learning and soft computing methods, Earth Science Informatics 17 (3) (2024) 2587–2608. Available from https://doi.org/10.1007/s12145-024-01300-y.

[5] T. Zeng, K. Yin, H. Jiang, X. Liu, Z. Guo, D. Peduto, Groundwater level prediction based on a combined intelligence method for the Sifangbei landslide in the Three Gorges Reservoir Area, Scientific Reports 12 (1) (2022) 11108. Available from https://doi.org/10.1038/s41598-022-14037-9.

[6] R.M. Adnan, H.L. Dai, R.R. Mostafa, A.R.M.T. Islam, O. Kisi, S. Heddam, et al., Modelling groundwater level fluctuations by ELM merged advanced metaheuristic algorithms using hydroclimatic data, Geocarto International 38 (1) (2023) 2158951. Available from https://doi.org/10.1080/10106049.2022.2158951.

[7] Y. Zhou, L. Zhang, H. Li, Y. Yao, Y. Zhang, Q. Wang, Influence on the ecological environment of the groundwater level changes based on deep learning, Water 16 (24) (2024) 3656. Available from https://doi.org/10.3390/w16243656.

[8] Y. Tikhamarine, D. Souag-Gamane, A.N. Ahmed, O. Kisi, A. El-Shafie, Improving artificial intelligence models accuracy for monthly streamflow forecasting using grey wolf optimization (GWO) algorithm, Journal of Hydrology 582 (2020) 124435. Available from https://doi.org/10.1016/j.jhydrol.2019.124435.

[9] H.C. Kilinc, A. Yurtsever, Short-term streamflow forecasting using hybrid deep learning model based on grey wolf algorithm for hydrological time series, Sustainability 14 (6) (2022) 3352. Available from https://doi.org/10.3390/su14063352.

[10] R.M. Adnan, R.R. Mostafa, O. Kisi, Z.M. Yaseen, S. Shahid, M. Zounemat-Kermani, Improving streamflow prediction using a new hybrid ELM model combined with hybrid particle swarm optimization and grey wolf optimization, Knowledge-Based Systems 230 (2021) 107379. Available from https://doi.org/10.1016/j.knosys.2021.107379.

[11] R.M. Adnan, A. Mirboluki, M. Mehraein, A. Malik, S. Heddam, O. Kisi, Improved prediction of monthly streamflow in a mountainous region by Metaheuristic Enhanced deep learning and machine learning models using hydroclimatic data, Theoretical and Applied Climatology 155 (1) (2024) 205–228. Available from https://doi.org/10.1007/s00704-023-04624-9.

[12] F. Jia, Z. Zhu, W. Dai, Short-term forecasting of streamflow by integrating machine learning methods combined with metaheuristic algorithms, Expert Systems with Applications 245 (2024) 123076. Available from https://doi.org/10.1016/j.eswa.2023.123076.

[13] J. Liang, Y. Du, Y. Xu, B. Xie, W. Li, Z. Lu, et al., Using adaptive chaotic grey wolf optimization for the daily streamflow prediction, Expert Systems with Applications 237 (2024) 121113. Available from https://doi.org/10.1016/j.eswa.2023.121113.

[14] Q. Wang, C. Yue, X. Li, P. Liao, X. Li, Enhancing robustness of monthly streamflow forecasting model using embedded-feature selection algorithm based on improved gray wolf optimizer, Journal of Hydrology 617 (2023) 128995. Available from https://doi.org/10.1016/j.jhydrol.2022.128995.

[15] X. Zhao, H. Lv, S. Lv, Y. Sang, Y. Wei, X. Zhu, Enhancing robustness of monthly streamflow forecasting model using gated recurrent unit based on improved grey wolf optimizer, Journal of Hydrology 601 (2021) 126607. Available from https://doi.org/10.1016/j.jhydrol.2021.126607.

[16] A.D. Martinho, C.M. Saporetti, L. Goliatt, Approaches for the short-term prediction of natural daily streamflows using hybrid machine learning enhanced with grey wolf optimization, Hydrological Sciences Journal 68 (1) (2023) 16–33. Available from https://doi.org/10.1080/02626667.2022.2141121.

[17] L. Wang, Y. Guo, M. Fan, Improving annual streamflow prediction by extracting information from high-frequency components of streamflow, Water Resources Management 36 (12) (2022) 4535–4555. Available from https://doi.org/10.1007/s11269-022-03262-6.

[18] M. Panahi, K. Khosravi, S. Ahmad, S. Panahi, S. Heddam, A.M. Melesse, et al., Cumulative infiltration and infiltration rate prediction using optimized deep learning algorithms: a study in Western Iran, Journal of Hydrology: Regional Studies 35 (2021) 100825. Available from https://doi.org/10.1016/j.ejrh.2021.100825.

[19] A. Sepahvand, A. Golkarian, L. Billa, K. Wang, F. Rezaie, S. Panahi, et al., Evaluation of deep machine learning-based models of soil cumulative infiltration, Earth Science Informatics 15 (3) (2022) 1861–1877. Available from https://doi.org/10.1007/s12145-022-00830-7.

[20] B. Mohammadi, Y. Guan, P. Aghelpour, S. Emamgholizadeh, R. Pillco Zolá, D. Zhang, Simulation of Titicaca lake water level fluctuations using hybrid machine learning technique integrated with grey wolf optimizer algorithm, Water 12 (11) (2020) 3015. Available from https://doi.org/10.3390/w12113015.

[21] A.K. Sales, E. Gul, M.J.S. Safari, H. Ghodrat Gharehbagh, B. Vaheddoost, Urmia lake water depth modeling using extreme learning machine-improved grey wolf optimizer hybrid algorithm, Theoretical and Applied Climatology 146 (1) (2021) 833–849. Available from https://doi.org/10.1007/s00704-021-03771-1.

[22] H. Li, L. Zhang, Y. Yao, Y. Zhang, Prediction of water levels in large reservoirs based on optimization of deep learning algorithms, Earth Science Informatics 18 (1) (2025) 121. Available from https://doi.org/10.1007/s12145-024-01670-3.

[23] A. Seifi, F. Soroush, Pan evaporation estimation and derivation of explicit optimized equations by novel hybrid meta-heuristic ANN based methods in different climates of Iran, Computers and Electronics in Agriculture 173 (2020) 105418. Available from https://doi.org/10.1016/j.compag.2020.105418.
[24] T. Fu, X. Li, Estimating the monthly pan evaporation with limited climatic data in dryland based on the extended long short-term memory model enhanced with meta-heuristic algorithms, Scientific Reports 13 (1) (2023) 5960. Available from https://doi.org/10.1038/s41598-023-32838-4.
[25] O. Kisi, A. Mirboluki, S.R. Naganna, A. Malik, A. Kuriqi, M. Mehraein, Comparative evaluation of deep learning and machine learning in modelling pan evaporation using limited inputs, Hydrological Sciences Journal 67 (9) (2022) 1309–1327. Available from https://doi.org/10.1080/02626667.2022.2063724.
[26] J. Piri, O. Kisi, Hybrid non-linear probabilistic model using Monte Carlo simulation and hybrid support vector regression for evaporation predictions, Hydrological Sciences Journal 69 (15) (2024) 2249–2277. Available from https://doi.org/10.1080/02626667.2024.2403718.
[27] S. Maroufpoor, O. Bozorg-Haddad, E. Maroufpoor, Reference evapotranspiration estimating based on optimal input combination and hybrid artificial intelligent model: hybridization of artificial neural network with grey wolf optimizer algorithm, Journal of Hydrology 588 (2020) 125060. Available from https://doi.org/10.1016/j.jhydrol.2020.125060.
[28] X. Xiao, Z. Xiao, X. Liu, X. Gu, Y. Di, L. Wu, et al., Dynamic optimization can effectively improve the accuracy of reference evapotranspiration in southern China, Computers and Electronics in Agriculture 230 (2025) 109881. Available from https://doi.org/10.1016/j.compag.2024.109881.
[29] J. Dong, X. Liu, G. Huang, J. Fan, L. Wu, J. Wu, Comparison of four bio-inspired algorithms to optimize KNEA for predicting monthly reference evapotranspiration in different climate zones of China, Computers and Electronics in Agriculture 186 (2021) 106211. Available from https://doi.org/10.1016/j.compag.2021.106211.
[30] P. Heramb, K.V. Ramana Rao, A. Subeesh, A. Srivastava, Predictive modelling of reference evapotranspiration using machine learning models coupled with grey wolf optimizer, Water 15 (5) (2023) 856. Available from https://doi.org/10.3390/w15050856.
[31] Y. Tikhamarine, A. Malik, D. Souag-Gamane, O. Kisi, Artificial intelligence models versus empirical equations for modeling monthly reference evapotranspiration, Environmental Science and Pollution Research 27 (2020) 30001–30019. Available from https://doi.org/10.1007/s11356-020-08792-3.
[32] H.E. Khairan, S.L. Zubaidi, M. Al-Mukhtar, A. Dulaimi, H. Al-Bugharbee, F.A. Al-Faraj, et al., Assessing the potential of hybrid-based metaheuristic algorithms integrated with ANNs for accurate reference evapotranspiration forecasting, Sustainability 15 (19) (2023) 14320. Available from https://doi.org/10.3390/su151914320.
[33] R.M.A. Ikram, R.R. Mostafa, Z. Chen, A.R.M.T. Islam, O. Kisi, A. Kuriqi, et al., Advanced hybrid metaheuristic machine learning models application for reference crop evapotranspiration prediction, Agronomy 13 (1) (2022) 98. Available from https://doi.org/10.3390/agronomy13010098.
[34] H. He, L. Liu, X. Zhu, Optimization of extreme learning machine model with biological heuristic algorithms to estimate daily reference evapotranspiration in Hetao Irrigation District of China, Engineering Applications of Computational Fluid Mechanics 16 (1) (2022) 1939–1956. Available from https://doi.org/10.1080/19942060.2022.2125442.
[35] X. Lu, J. Fan, L. Wu, J. Dong, Forecasting multi-step ahead monthly reference evapotranspiration using hybrid extreme gradient boosting with grey wolf optimization algorithm, Computer Modeling in Engineering & Sciences 125 (2) (2020) 699–723. Available from https://doi.org/10.32604/cmes.2020.011004.
[36] H.E. Khairan, S.L. Zubaidi, S.F. Raza, M. Hameed, N. Al-Ansari, H.M. Ridha, Examination of single-and hybrid-based metaheuristic algorithms in ANN reference evapotranspiration estimating, Sustainability 15 (19) (2023) 14222. Available from https://doi.org/10.3390/su151914222.
[37] Y. Tikhamarine, A. Malik, A. Kumar, D. Souag-Gamane, O. Kisi, Estimation of monthly reference evapotranspiration using novel hybrid machine learning approaches, Hydrological Sciences Journal 64 (15) (2019) 1824–1842. Available from https://doi.org/10.1080/02626667.2019.1678750.

Chapter 24

Optimizing enterprise information system security with the grey wolf optimizer: a novel approach to risk assessment and asset prioritization

Arome J. Gabriel, Toluwalope A. Adebayo, and Olakunle P. Mustafa
Cybersecurity Department, School of Computing, Federal University of Technology, Akure, Nigeria

24.1 Introduction

24.1.1 Background and context

The integration of information systems into all spheres of organizational activity has been a key driving force that influenced the evolution of the operations of the enterprises in the twenty-first century. Enterprise information system (EIS) is a type of sophisticated, intertwined platforms which help to consolidate business activities, support strategic decision-making, and maintain organizational competitiveness in the data economy [1]. These systems are the digital infrastructure of the modern enterprise, as they are the most efficient and reliable systems to manage the resources, coordinate the workflow, and analyze data in large quantities. The authors of Turban et al. (2022) [2] stated that the agile business ecosystems based on the deployment of enterprise systems like enterprise resource planning (ERP), supply chain management (SCM), and customer relationship management (CRM) have transformed the traditional business paradigm.

With the swift growth of globalization and the digital transformation, EIS are required to not only achieve operational success but also ensure the survival of organizations. They enable real-time teamwork, automation of key business processes, and offer analytic systems that form the basis of competitive advantage. But as these systems become more extensive and interdependent, they also take on the risks of the larger digital ecosystem cyberattacks, system failures, data breaches, and governance failures [3]. The dependency on EIS, which follows, creates a paradox of advancement: on the one hand, the digital integration increases the efficiency of the system; on the other hand, it increases vulnerability to systemic risks. As a result, the strength of an organization is increasingly determined by the extent to which it is able to protect and optimize its EIS.

At the national scale, EISs are important in maintaining critical infrastructures, coordinating government activities, and enhancing economic stability. EIS is now perceived by nation-states as the continuation of national infrastructure, part of defense, business, and state administration [4]. This has turned cybersecurity and risk management into more of a strategic necessity than a technical one. The fact that the contemporary economy is heavily reliant on interconnected digital infrastructures highlights the importance of active, dynamic, and data-oriented strategies of addressing risks at the enterprise level. Artificial intelligence, in particular, and computational intelligence methods have been identified as revolutionary in this regard, providing organizations with additional opportunities to anticipate, detect, and react to the changing cyber and operational risks.

24.1.2 The challenge of risk in enterprise information systems

EIS, however, strategic, are intrinsically complex and are likely to suffer vulnerabilities that can affect organizational operations. The multilayered architecture that is formed by the integration of different technologies, vendors, and user

Grey Wolf Optimizer. DOI: https://doi.org/10.1016/B978-0-443-36624-6.00026-3

environments is hard to secure on a holistic basis. The scope and complexity of cyber threats to enterprise systems have increased by leveraging vulnerabilities in software settings, human behavior, and network dependencies [5]. Conventional security models, based on baseline risk evaluation and infrequent audits, have not been sufficient to face these challenges as they cannot be dynamic enough to deal with the dynamism of current threat environments.

There has been a shift in risk management in EIS; therefore, not a compliance-based routine, but a strategic ability that supports business continuity, which is business resilience. Existing research has explained that technical vulnerabilities are not the only risks that need to be properly addressed in the context of risk management; more complex interdependencies of processes, data, and human actors should also be taken into consideration. Poor risk management may cause cascading failure, where a failure in a single subsystem can cause systemic failures throughout the enterprise. These risks require constant monitoring, predictive modeling, and optimization methods that can be effective in changing not only the operational environment but also the threat environment [6].

Most organizations, however, continue to use linear or deterministic models, which hold the hypothesis that the risk factors are fixed and can be easily measured. These classic constructs are not generally useful in elucidating nonlinear connections and uncertainties in dynamic digital ecosystems [7]. As an example, the relevance of an asset in an enterprise system can vary quickly as a result of changing business priorities, technological improvements, or even previously unknown vulnerabilities. Such fluctuations cannot easily be accommodated by the use of static risk matrices and manual scoring systems, and the information presented to the decision-makers remains outdated or incomplete. This weakness highlights the importance of smart, algorithmically powered methods that will be able to continuously draw new insights based on environmental data and alter the assessment of risk on the fly.

Moreover, the emergence of cyber-physical integration, including the Internet of Things, industrial control systems, and cloud computing, has increased the attack surface of EIS [8,9]. The fusion between IT and operational technology is compounding other complexities with security breaches, with physical implications. Consequently, adopting proper enterprise risk management should no longer be limited to the traditional IT-based security measures, but should now be holistic across the entire system to include strategies of system-optimalization. These plans should combine data analytics, artificial intelligence, and computational optimization toward prioritizing the threats with dynamism as well as to allocate the security resources efficiently.

24.1.3 Meta-heuristic optimization and the grey wolf optimizer

During the last few years, meta-heuristic optimization algorithms have emerged as a strong method of solving multidimensional problems that are complex and cannot be solved using precise analytical methods. Such algorithms include: the ant colony optimisation, the particle swarm optimization, the genetic algorithm, and even the grey wolf optimizer (GWO). These algorithms work based on biological or natural phenomena to provide flexible ways to search large solution spaces in an efficient manner [10]. Among them, GWO is particularly known due to its simplicity, expeditious convergence, and a high degree of exploration and exploitation balance [11]. The GWO algorithm was inspired by the hunting hierarchy and hunting behavior of the grey wolves in the wild. The hierarchy has four levels, namely: alpha, beta, delta, and omega, which affect the search dynamics in the process of optimization. Alpha wolves lead the decision-making process, the betas and deltas help in the refinement process of solutions, and omegas come in to preserve the diversity of exploration. It is a form of collaborative behavior that allows the algorithm to trade off between local and global searches in an adaptive way to prevent premature convergence and increase resilience to local optima [12]. The characteristics of GWO also render it especially appropriate to those problems that demand dynamical adaptation, including enterprise risk assessment and resource allocation.

Meta-heuristic algorithms have shown great potential in the sphere of information and cybersecurity management. These algorithms have been used to optimize the intrusion detection systems, feature selection, and anomaly detection [13,14]. Specifically, the GWO has demonstrated better results in the selection of the most effective features and in enhancing detection errors in models of cyberattacks [15]. Nevertheless, regardless of these developments, GWO is still not well studied in the context of enterprise risk management. The majority of the available literature has been devoted to the algorithmic optimization in the concrete technical sphere instead of risk governance on the enterprise level.

GWO has a potential that is wider than that of the field of computational optimization, in strategic decision-making problems, where there is interdependence and nonlinearity that prevail. The hierarchical and adaptable nature of the algorithm is similar to the decision formations of the organizations, which makes the algorithm interesting in modeling the dynamic asset prioritization, resource optimization, and reducing risks in high-level enterprise settings. The fact that it is an iterative solution to problems also fits well into the requirement of continuous risk assessment in EIS, where the criticality of assets and the risk posed by threats change with time.

24.1.4 Research gap and chapter objectives

Despite indicating the increasing application of bio-inspired optimization algorithms in cybersecurity, there is still a large void in applying them to enterprise risk management. The models used are usually only focused on individual elements, including intrusion detection, malware analysis, or network optimization. However, they fail to consider the overall problem of integrating risk management processes into the entire EIS [16]. The limited research works that have investigated optimization-based risk management have either been based on static data or have not been dynamic to adapt to the changing environments associated with an enterprise. As a result, very little is known about the ability of such algorithms as the GWO to supplement the design of holistic risk governance systems that take into account asset classification, risk assessment, and mitigation optimization at the same point in time.

This chapter aims to fill such a gap through an optimization-based enterprise risk management framework that is based on the GWO. The framework represents risk management as an ongoing optimization process whereby organizational resources are dynamically ranked based on their level of criticality, vulnerability to threats, and business value. The proposed model allows organizations to have situational awareness and to allocate resources effectively in their EIS by following the hierarchical coordination of the grey wolf types and the adaptive methods of hunting.

This chapter has four objectives, namely:

a) To examine the theoretical foundations of EIS and how they are applicable in strategic contexts to contemporary organizations.
b) To assess the weaknesses of the conventional risk management techniques in the dynamic enterprise ecosystems.
c) To present and situate the GWO as a useful algorithm for adaptive risk optimization.
d) To introduce an organized model that would merge the GWO and enterprise risk assessment and asset classification models to enhance cyber resilience.

The suggested solution retools enterprise risk management in terms of self-optimizing, a modernization process instead of a compulsory inertia practice. It also focuses on volatility uncertainty complexity ambiguity (VUCA) (constant monitoring), information-guided and online optimization, thus improving the degree of operational performance and level of cybersecurity preparedness. This chapter opines that adopting the GWO principles for EIS management can make room for more resilience and responsiveness in enterprise architectures.

The rest of this chapter is organized as follows: Section 2 is a critical review of the available literature regarding EIS, risk-management models, and GWO applications. Section 3 expounds the theoretical framework that connects the concept of optimization to the resilience of an enterprise. Section 4 contains the proposed model or framework of GWO-based risk management. Section 5 presents a brief roundup on conceptual framework and model integration, and Section 6 provides the conclusion with the considerations of the future research directions and policy implications.

24.2 Literature review

EIS are essential and highly significant infrastructures, which form the foundation of the smooth running of governmental agencies, business industries, organizations, and commercial enterprises, globally [17]. In a modern and digitally motivated environment, organizations are relying on EIS to streamline their operational processes, improve decision-making, and maintain the continuity provided by their operational functions. It is often claimed that a secure EIS validates the robustness of a company and its business procedures [18,19]. However, the increasing dependence on these systems also brings with it risks to cyber-attack, hence pushing security issues to the top position as an organizational priority [18,20].

An effective and safe EIS is not just about technical compliance but also a strategic asset, which gives an organization a degree of resilience and reliability. Risk analysis remains a major part of information system security. Since practically speaking, no system is perfect, all organizations must adopt a robust risk management framework that will reduce their organizational attack surfaces and also mitigate possible threats or attacks. Optimizing EIS risk-analysis models, processes, and mechanisms has become one of the major concerns of stakeholders in today's digital economy [20].

Risk management in EIS has to be a continuous (often cyclic) procedure due to the constant improvement in technologies, as well as the fact that cyberthreats are becoming more complex by the day. Indeed, most organizations have to adopt proactive measures in order to guarantee the robustness, safety, and security of their systems [17,19].

Risk analysis is a proactive tool that is used to analyze the security posture of an EIS by determining the threats, their impact or consequences, and also provides recommendations on appropriate defense measures. Risk analysis, thus helps organizations to maintain a dynamic defense strategy by ensuring that they do not operate under the illusion of absolute security [17]. By systematically profiling risks, businesses can gauge their system's exposure to cyber threats in comparison to an ideal security state, allocate resources effectively, and focus on high-impact vulnerabilities. Adapt to evolving threats, ensuring long-term resilience [20].

The study in Ref. [21] pronounces a continuous dramatic change in risk management dynamics, explaining that risk management is essential in enterprise administration as it indicates the position of an enterprise in achieving its primary goals. For an EIS to function efficiently in achieving its primary goals, the enterprise must regularly determine the information system risk appetite (involves the projection of the growth dynamics and criticality advancement of risk involved), the risk should have a means to be measured, categorized and also a mechanism to determine risk impact and moment criticality to enterprise process and objectives which in turn helps stakeholders across all levels to determine mitigation tactics to appropriate different categories of risk [22]. Through the conceptualization of such dynamic approach, organizations can convert the risk management into a proactive and reactive compliance exercise into a strategic business continuity capability, which facilitates business continuity, improves decision making, and retains competitive advantage in a contemporary, rapidly changing threat environment, especially as new vulnerabilities are emerging alongside new developments in technology and risk and regulatory requirements [19,21].

The study in Ref. [20] is a systematic review that focuses on how risk management can influence the managerial decision-making process in enterprise administration and assessment of risks. The review was rounded up with a suggestion that businesses ought to periodically embrace improved ideas and models of evaluating risk in their business systems.

The study in Ref. [17] acknowledged that risk assessment requires the evaluation of every process within the enterprise, and assessment of the vulnerability of their procedures as well as the optimization of the operations. This indeed is an expensive, but important activity for many businesses today. To ensure sustainable development amid modern transformational challenges, enterprises must continuously optimize risk assessment to better capture risk, implement mitigation strategies, and enhance resilience, particularly when facing minor but hard-to-diagnose negative symptoms caused by gradual changes or major management decisions.

GWO algorithm was introduced by Ref. [10] as a meta-heuristic that extensively describes how the social hierarchy of grey wolf packs assists in the optimization process, identifying the effective mathematical models for the social hierarchy, tracking, encircling, and attacking prey. Mirjalili et al. [10] opined that the convergence analysis of GWO establishes a faster computation process. Makhadmeh et al. [23] noted the variants derived from utilization of GWO, such as: Random Walk GWO, which deals with the local optimal stagnation noticed in the basic GWO, thereby overcoming the challenge of premature convergence. Binary GWO is targeted toward continuous optimization problems. Continuous optimization problems, which were targeted to enhance exploration capabilities and mitigate the issue of getting trapped in local optima. The study in Ref. [24] outlined the modifications perceived in the GWO over the years. Kazeem et al. [25] proposed an adaptive GWO that can be adopted diversely across various fields by presenting a mechanism in the research to solve the lack of diversity, exploration/exploitation imbalance, and premature local minima convergence in large-scale problems

The study in Ref. [26] utilized the GWO for the feature selection process; their methodology effectively identified the most discriminative features for cyber-attack detection, significantly enhancing classification performance, resulting in an achievement of better accuracy, sensitivity, and specificity in intrusion detection systems. The authors of the study in Ref. [27] also emphasized the essentiality of maintaining security alongside the availability of information in cyberspace. They also analyze network traffic patterns for denial-of-service attack detection. Their approach conceptualizes cybersecurity as a dynamic optimization problem, where GWO efficiently processes high-dimensional network data to identify malicious traffic while preserving system performance. By using the hierarchical search mechanism of the GWO, the model identifies the unusual patterns that denote the occurrence of attacks, and this indicates that nature-inspired computing can harmonize the security strength with the system operation performance. The study highlights the need to have adaptive and intelligent systems to protect the networked infrastructures against changing threats [28].

This study suggests the use of the GWO in detecting and preventing cyberattack propagation in smart grid substations, which is a vulnerable enterprise system when it comes to a cascade failure. Through a comparative analysis of what is provided in other nature or bio-inspired algorithms (such as particle swarm optimization, the firefly algorithm), the findings prove that GWO has a greater computational efficiency, enabling it to detect threats faster with minimal loss of information.

In Ref. [29], a desperate need to enhance information system defense is observed. It is advisable to use multiobjective GWO algorithm in an anomaly-based intrusion detection system because of the speed of its computation and subsequent decrease in intrusion detection system (IDS) computation burden, thus providing a significant improvement to IDS performance. The study in Ref. [30] paid attention to GWO's application in the detection of malicious activities. GWO is adopted for tracking the underlying tactics and behavior patterns of cyber threats. The incorporation of GWO into forensic enquiries systematically boosts the accuracy of detection and reinforces defense systems. GWO's superior optimization features allow a more accurate reconstitution of attack sequences, and ultimately enhance the detection of malware threats and attack pathways. This strategy does not just enhance the effectiveness of forensic examinations but also leads to the proactive threat mitigation, for which the role of GWO cannot be overstated in enhancing network security.

However, risk management has remained the most important element of a sound EIS security plan. It redirects the focus on the reactive fixes to anticipatory and responsive security management, thus allowing organizations to protect their digital infrastructure in a dynamic threat environment. There is a huge gap in applying this generally acceptable optimizer (GWO) to improving the entire risk management process.

24.2.1 Enterprise information system

EIS is considered the lifeline of digital transformation [31], as they help organizations to streamline their businesses, improve decision-making, and remain ahead of competition. EIS is useful in the enhancement of the productivity of enterprise processes, minimizing service cycles, product development cycle, and marketing lifecycle hence, it is used by every part and every level of an enterprise. The modern digital ecosystem is the cornerstone of the information economy [32], determining the world of commerce, policies, and socio-technical relationships. It is a convergence of different enterprise participants: governments, corporations, businesses, individuals, and nonprofit organizations, as well as the quest for strategic and tactical efficiencies in their enterprises through the interconnected digital infrastructures [33]. It is believed that EIS are very key asset in today's organizations, especially as EIS leads to smooth operations and improved structured administration within those organizations. EIS often contributes to the achievement of organizational goals [34]. The growing dependence on digital networks highlights the importance of optimized risk management procedures and alignment of stakeholders and other parties to guarantee system integrity and resilience.

An information system in the enterprise is no longer a luxury but an indispensable requirement for all the processes of business in modern society. These developments in EIS have become a hallmark of organizational strategy in the digital age, and their importance has grown in facilitating operations to calibrate organizational competitiveness and survival [35].

EIS is gaining importance as a critical infrastructure in nation-states, which has economic stability, defense, and citizen safety consequences. EIS play a significant role in the digital age business as they determine business operations, national security, and international trade. Nation-states strategize a proper and effective EIS to govern planned performance to state mission objectives. Countries are concerned with the preservation and continuity of the critical infrastructures to the different activities they undertake through complex information technology systems with a view to ensuring a hyperconnectivity control guarantee between the infrastructures.

EIS are irreplaceable in the contemporary organizational models, and they help them in decision-making based on data, automate operations, and gain a competitive advantage. Companies putting emphasis on EIS achieve greater efficiency [32] and fewer redundancies, as well as better scalability. The convergence between ERP, CRM, andSCM systems highlights their paramount role in business continuity [33], but the focus on the supremacy of EIS should be supported by the strategic investments in cybersecurity, workforce training, and resilient infrastructure to eliminate vulnerabilities. Lack of alignment between EIS and organizational goals may lead to inefficiencies, information breach and system failure, which reinforces the importance of an organized risk governance strategy.

EIS strategic prioritization is one of the topical issues of the organizational leaders, and recent frameworks promote the idea of the balanced approach that can take into account the cost, risk, and the long-term strategic value [35]. The creation of decision-support systems will make the process of prioritization more granular, which would help enterprises to use resources more efficiently [34]. Thus cyber resilience requires a strategic risk management optimization strategy toward EIS implementation and management.

Nevertheless, it is pointed out that prioritization should be a dynamic and repeated undertaking, but not a solitary task, especially with the high rate of technological development and the dynamic nature of the threat. As a result, a more effective and flexible risk management structure can be developed with the help of an iterative algorithm, for example, the GWO, which improves the management of enterprises.

In the present day, EIS are still safe as a logical access point. The current security doctrine, like the defense-in-depth, uses several layers with progressively stricter controls to strengthen protection. Companies should thus devise mechanisms that would see to it that: mission-critical assets whose loss would in any case be unsustainable but disastrous are protected unconditionally; dynamic assets with future criticality are actively monitored to avoid oversight, and new asset integrations into the information system are facilitated smoothly. Theoretically, this solution can be easily implemented using the GWO algorithm, which, once implemented, allows structurally organizing a risk analysis. In such a way, it allows ensuring practically complete stability in the conditions of resource limitations and reducing the consequences and time frame of noncritical resources. The EIS risk management framework that is based on the GWO is a successful representation of a cyber-resilient approach that is based on the principles of cybersecurity. Cyber resilience relocates the emphasis of tiresome perimeter defense to an iterative, rotating approach of the assets to be classified as high-priority threats and vulnerabilities to be given optimum distribution of resources.

24.3 Risk management

24.3.1 Asset classification

The classification of assets is a discipline and rigorous exercise that requires an extensive knowledge of the infrastructure of an organization and the place it holds in the rest of the information system. Being one of the background steps in risk assessment, it allows organizations to determine the contribution and importance of assets towards the attainment of core business objectives. Good classification will make sure that security measures are properly matched with organizational priorities to aid in making informed decisions on risk management and resource allocation [36].

The difficulty comes, however, in situations where IT professionals do not have systematic methodologies for categorizing and justifying the relevancy of infrastructure components to business processes. Lack of standardized mechanisms may cause miscommunication, inaccurate reporting of stakeholders, and poor security budgeting. In order to address these challenges, organizations should have clearly defined classification systems that will enhance transparency, uniformity, and business alignment of the technical entities and business objectives [37]. The systematic asset classification process improves the quality of risk assessment, optimizes investments in security, and overall cybersecurity posture, which is strengthened. Such an ordered process guarantees the provision of the relevant protection of critical assets and the facilitation of knowledgeable decision-making at every level of the organization.

The asset classification process does not just stop at the stage of initial identification but involves further refinement in terms of systematic process development and sophisticated methods of analysis. This is because a systematic approach will ensure that assets are properly classified based on their functional and strategic relevance in the organization. Since the enterprise environments are dynamic, it is necessary to have a clear methodological framework that ensures alignment between the valuation of the assets and organizational goals. This will require an algorithmic model that would objectively measure the criticality of assets based on predetermined business parameters. This means that besides standardization of classification, such a model also increases the consistency of the results of risk assessment, as it eliminates human bias and inconsistencies.

One of the fundamental necessities in enterprise risk management is the creation of an iterative, developing data-driven approach towards the classification of the assets. An algorithmic method enables breaking down organizational objectives into levels of operation, which allows the accurate mapping of the assets into their respective functional requirement. Organization can create a quantifiable measure of the value of each asset to the operations of the business to arrive at the necessary measure of criticality [38]. This is the combination of asset valuation models and business impact analysis and it makes sure that the security investments are prioritized on the basis of empirically-based risk exposures. Moreover, the integration of standardized classification criteria increases the communication with stakeholders, reduces misinformation, and conducts evidence-based budgets on cybersecurity actions. The advantages of the adoption of a sophisticated asset classification system are of great value to organizational risk management plans. Enterprises can also maximize the allocation of resources by systematically correlating the assets and the business functions, thereby giving the assets of high value proportional protection. Moreover, a systematic classification process will mean constant check and re-evaluation, which will allow organizations to adjust to changing threats and changes in the operational condition. An efficient algorithmic methodology reduces subjectivity and enhances consistency making security investment justifications stronger. With the implementation of this methodology as part of enterprise risk management, organizations will be in a position to optimize the allocation of resources, reduce the risk of misclassification, and strengthen the resilience of cybersecurity.

This Chapter suggests a new system of asset classification based on the use of the GWO algorithm to tackle the issues of a changing business environment. A structured methodology for categorizing enterprise assets while staying in line with changing business processes is offered by the GWO's social hierarchy-like metaheuristic approach. The algorithm efficiently prioritizes assets according to their importance to organizational performance and financial stability by modeling the hunting and leadership behaviors of grey wolf packs. This optimization makes sure that classification results are still applicable even when business operations, technology, or threat landscapes change.

Accurately classifying information system assets is a recurring problem in enterprise risk management, especially in light of the dynamic nature of contemporary business ecosystems [32]. Outdated baselines that inaccurately reflect asset criticality are frequently the result of traditional static classification models' inability to adapt. Through iterative optimization, the adaptive mechanism introduced by the proposed GWO-based framework continuously improves asset classification. This method guarantees that risk assessments stay rooted in the operational realities of today while also improving the asset base's visual representation. The algorithm creates a classification schema that is transparent to stakeholders and resistant to change by integrating financial impact metrics and business process dependencies.

There are several benefits for enterprise risk management when the GWO algorithm is used for asset classification. First, its hierarchical optimization process ensures that classifications reflect actual business priorities by reflecting organizational decision-making structures. Second, by dynamically modifying asset valuations in response to new threats or operational changes, the algorithm's flexibility promotes proactive risk mitigation. In the end, this framework gives businesses a solid, data-driven approach to keeping a precise and useful grasp of their changing asset landscape.

Asset classifications stand as a strong process of communicating what needs to be protected, how much it needs to be protected, and what grade level of protection it should have [36,39]. It is a coordinated means of communicating to the enterprise stakeholders "how safe is the safe." It is, therefore worth knowing that accuracy and consistency are critical factors to provide stakeholders a common understanding of the nature of an EIS asset base [34]. Assets of an EIS must be efficiently ranked in order to determine how much security is needed to be achieved at each rank level [36]. To keep such an enterprise in business process, efficient ranking assists in correct budgeting and security investment. It is to be understood that EIS assets comprise all processes, technologies, and facilities required by an enterprise to achieve its objective. A logical, accurate asset classification is required to carefully secure all these components.

Accordingly, there is a great need for organizations at various levels to devise and maintain well-structured processes to optimize the identification, classification, and prioritization process of EIS assets as business evolves [32]. This has a great contribution toward achieving an accurate evaluative standard in risk assessment.

24.3.2 Risk assessment procedures

Risk identification is a formal preliminary phase of a structured undertaking in enterprise risk management where the vulnerabilities in an EIS are methodologically listed alongside possible threats that can be used to capitalize on the vulnerabilities [32,38]. This is done by a critical analysis of operational, technical, and procedural exposures that might hinder organizational goals or deteriorate the usefulness of assets. Through the examination of threat vectors, either malicious or unintentional, organizations can be able to preemptually determine instances where vulnerabilities can be exploited, therefore supporting an active and not reactive security posture [37]. The process of identification goes beyond technical imperfections, and includes contextual influences like the importance of assets, business reliance, and possible loss of trust in the stakeholders in the event of a risk being realized [29]. Among the methods, which are employed by advanced organizations to guarantee exhaustive risk discovery, threat modeling, strengths, weaknesses, opportunities, and threats (SWOT) analysis, and intelligent model methods are examples. The phase provides the needed base for further risk assessment and management plans.

After identification, the risk estimation is carried out in order to assess the probability of actualization of the threat along with the scale of resultant consequences. It uses an asset-centric approach or the scenario approach. The former is the analysis of the interaction of assets and their vulnerability, as well as the threats, whereas the latter is the modeling of the hypothetical events to estimate their likely effect. Quantitative analysis and qualitative analysis come together to categorize the risks based on their level of severity so that prioritization of risks can be based on the organizational risk appetite [38]. An accurately undertaken estimation process will help in ensuring that available resources are well apportioned in a way to focus on the high probability and high impact risks and de-prioritize the insignificant exposures.

Afterwards, the risk levels are evaluated to ascertain whether the risks identified are beyond set tolerance levels. This evaluation combines organizational policies, regulatory requirements, and strategic objectives in order to determine the permissibility of retained risk. Risks that exceed acceptable limits require action to be taken, but risks that are within tolerance limits can be monitored as opposed to acting in order to control them [32]. This stratification will see the risk management activities in line with corporate governance imperatives without the need to spend needlessly on low-impact risks and focus on exposures that have material [38].

The risk acceptance criteria exist in order to formalize the terms under which an organization is knowingly not prepared to mitigate the risk. These standards are based on the aspects of cost-benefit studies, operating imperative, and strategic fit. An example is that some risks can be the ones that can be tolerated when the costs of mitigation exceed the possible losses, or they are inherent in the attempts to create the innovations [37]. Reported acceptance criteria will encourage uniformity in decision-making and give auditable support to risk retention, which enhances accountability in enterprise risk governance.

In cases where risks are indicated to be treated, organizations can use a continuum of mitigation strategies depending on the nature and the severity of the exposure. Externalization of financial liability is achieved through risk transfer mechanisms like cybersecurity insurance and risk avoidance means the high-risk activities are completely eliminated. They can be limiting exposure through access control and encryption, but not eradicate the risk. Buffering systems like redundancy systems or disaster recovery systems contribute to organizational resilience by curbing possible disturbances. The choice of a proper treatment plan is based on a cost-benefit calculus, at which the mitigation measures need to result in the best risk reduction as compared to the spending.

After the treatment, it is necessary to perform residual risk assessment to determine whether the implemented controls are effective and whether the residual exposures are within acceptable limits. The stage involves constant monitoring to identify the changes in threats and reassess the risk levels with each change in the organization or the environment [17]. The residual risks are documented, which provides transparency and supports the policy refinement of risk management in an iterative way.

Indeed, the development of a structured risk management framework (including identification, estimation, evaluation, acceptance, treatment, and residual assessment) is one of the foundations of organizational resilience. By methodically dealing with weaknesses and placing mitigation initiatives with strategic goals, businesses not only protect the critical assets but also make decisions amid uncertainty resilient [17,32,38]. This dynamic and iterative approach can help sustain adaptability in an increasingly multifaceted attack or threat landscape, highlighting the essential role of risk management in present-day corporate governance.

24.4 Risk management optimization with the grey wolf optimizer

24.4.1 Grey wolf optimizer social hierarchical model for enterprise asset prioritization

As suggested by the grey wolf social hierarchy, mathematical modeling will provide an efficient approach to categorizing assets in an EIS asset base. Grey wolf packs are characterized by a clearly defined social order consisting of four ranks: alpha, beta, delta, and omega [10,25]. This stratification can be comparatively implemented on the EIS components in terms of their importance to the business processes, and this offers a dynamic and flexible approach to component classification (Fig. 24.1).

Within a wolf pack, the alpha takes up a leader role; he or she organizes hunting and feeding patterns, hence most of the vital roles the social structure. Likewise, in an EIS, an alpha asset cannot be neglected as a key element in an enterprise business process. Such components are so vital that the associated business process cannot operate without them. Their presence is a prerequisite for initiating and sustaining core operations, underscoring the nonnegotiable importance of assets in this category.

The beta wolves in a pack support the alpha in decision-making but do not hold the same level of authority. Correspondingly, beta assets in an EIS are critical but not as pivotal as alpha components. While their failure or disruption still poses risks, the impact is comparatively lower than that of alpha assets. These components enhance system functionality, and a compromise to such components is not as severe in determining the feasibility of core business processes (Table 24.1).

Delta wolves represent an important tier in the pack hierarchy, facing minimal risk and responsibility. Likewise, Delta assets in an EIS present minimal operational risk. Nevertheless, the GWO model is characterized by an evolutionary

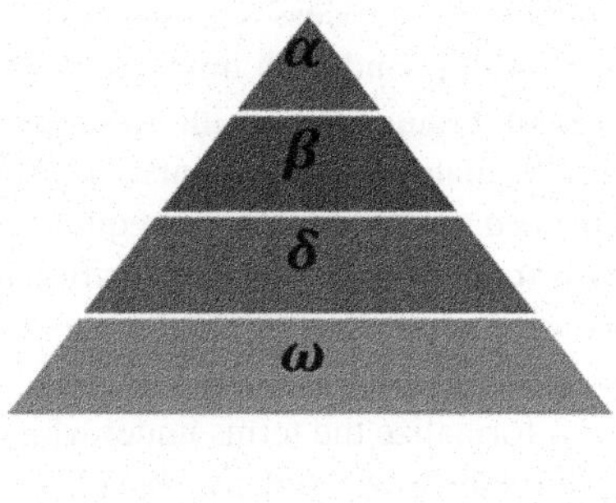

FIGURE 24.1 Grey wolf social order.

TABLE 24.1 The grey wolf social order in EIS.

Asset category	Category details
Alpha	They are components of the EIS with the most significant contribution to the enterprise business process at an instance of operation. A compromise to the security of components in this category is catastrophic.
Beta	The components in this category are of high value. And a compromise on the security of these components causes significant limitations to the enterprise in reaching its goals.
Delta	This category contains components of the system that have a moderate effect on the enterprise in achieving its primary objective at an instance of operation. The category is not relatively static due to the constant evolution of the enterprise environment.
Omega	The components in this category has low effect on the enterprise business process in achieving its primary objective.

EIS, Enterprise information systems.

dynamic: wolves may change hierarchies, they may become alpha or beta members and retire to delta status, or delta members may become higher-ranking members. This fluidity reflects the changing of EIS assets, where business process changes can require components to be reclassified with time. Applicable to IT asset assessment mechanisms, the grey wolf social hierarchy model makes adaptive risk assessment by allowing shifting of asset classifications. The status of an asset can change in the following ways:

a) Delta to beta: An asset with growing significance (say, a system component now being a vital part of a recently re-emphasized business process) becomes more susceptible to risk, and thus deserves a demotion.
b) Beta to alpha: When an asset turns mission-critical (e.g., a database that supports real-time transactions), it will move to the topmost risk category and require strict controls.
c) Alpha to delta (or beta): On the other hand, when the level of criticality to the process of the enterprise is less, or when the enterprise has evolved to a point where it can contain a compromise to that system relatively easily, the risk becomes a lower-risk category.

As an example, take a business with its first year of operation. At this point, one element, or a particular organizational position, can be categorized as a delta asset in the EIS asset base, as it has only a minor short-term effect on core business processes. As the business grows, though, the same part could change or become a beta or even alpha-class asset, as its impact on the key processes grows. This development means that the risks attributed to this asset also increase. Any breakdown or failure of such a component might now be a great risk to business continuity and may impede the enterprise from reaching its core goals and objectives.

Conventional static risk models are not able to support the dynamic nature of enterprise systems in which the importance of assets change according to organizational goals [39]. IT managers have a common problem with explaining to the stakeholders, especially executives, why these evolutions are necessary. The grey wolf model of hierarchy is a structured, flexible approach that allows explaining information on prioritizing of assets and risk assessment more clearly. Recognizing the possibility of asset iterative reclassification, as in the case of the social mobility of the wolf pack, this framework is closer to the actual business flexibility. A hierarchical model that is based on biological aspects proves more accurate and reliable in classifications of EIS assets. This enhances risk evaluation and links the stakeholders to buy-in as it places system dynamics in an intuitive and evolutionary setting. Another thing worth mentioning is the compatibility of the grey wolf hierarchy model (GWHM) with the well-established risk assessment theory that holds that risk assessment is not a one-time event but a process that needs to be repeated and takes into consideration the changing organizational landscapes. This dynamic model will be used to make sure that the risk management strategies are kept in line with the real business dependencies and this increases the operational resiliency and efficiency of decision making. Using the GWHM, businesses will be able to systematically optimize the qualitative risk evaluation, which is primarily focused on the asset allocation, and the risk mitigation activities will always be proportionate to the present level of risk in the business process of that component.

24.4.2 Grey wolf hierarchical model for enterprise risk optimization

The theoretical basis of the proposed framework is the approach of the social hierarchy of the GWO that reflects the relationships of leadership and decision-making in EIS. As per this model, assets are categorized according to their criticality, operational value, and vulnerability, and charted using GWO ranks as an indicator of risk concentration and resource distribution.

- Alpha assets (Strategic Core): These are strategic systems that are critical to the business and their compromise would instantly create a break in business continuity. These are ERP cores, financial databases, and identity management servers.
- Beta assets (Tactical Enablers): These are high-value systems that are used to back vital operations but are somewhat redundant. Failure does not mean a stop to business.
- Delta assets (Operational Support): These are subordinate systems that support workflows indirectly, such as departmental applications or middleware. Although compromises can reduce efficiency, the strategic outcomes is not affected.
- Omega assets (Peripheral Systems): Low criticality systems, things that run on the user level or other peripheral elements that are not critical to the operation of a system.

This hierarchical map will enable a dynamic prioritization of security interventions. The assets may shift between ranks depending on changing threat, operational importance, or a change in business-criticality, as seen with the adaptive and hierarchical behavior of wolf packs (Fig. 24.2 and 24.3).

This model will offer a well-defined outline of adaptive resource allocation and risk-aversion strategies because of the graphical and conceptual connection of enterprise resources to GWO, thus allowing an organization to prioritize assets through which protection has the most significant effect.

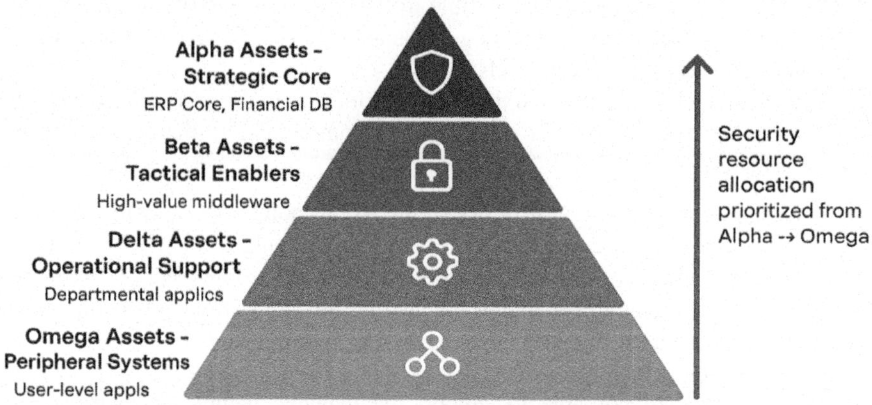

FIGURE 24.2 Conceptual grey wolf hierarchy model for enterprise asset classification and risk prioritization.

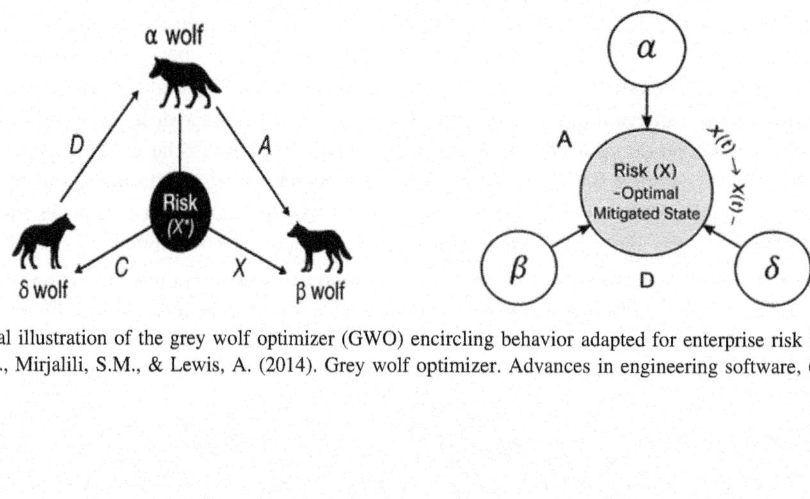

FIGURE 24.3 Conceptual illustration of the grey wolf optimizer (GWO) encircling behavior adapted for enterprise risk mitigation. Adapted from Mirjalili, S., Mirjalili, S.M., & Lewis, A. (2014). Grey wolf optimizer. Advances in engineering software, 69, 46-61.

24.4.3 Grey wolf optimizer encircling prey model for optimized risk mitigation

The GWO surrounding model in EIS risk assessment can be successfully modified to make risk mitigation quantitatively determined. The mathematical representation of the encircling behavior is given by:

$$\vec{D} = |\vec{C}.\vec{X_p}(t) - \vec{X}(t)| \tag{24.1}$$

$$\vec{X}(t+1) = \vec{X_p}(t) - \vec{A}.\vec{D} \tag{24.2}$$

where:

- t represents the current iteration, analogous to the current security clearance level of the system under assessment.
- A and C are coefficient vectors that dynamically adjust based on risk exposure and mitigation strategies.
- $\vec{X}(t)$ denotes the current position (state) of the system being evaluated for risk.
- $\vec{X_p}(t)$ signifies the target position vector, indicating the desired security clearance level at which the system component would effectively neutralize the associated risk.

The gap between the current security posture $\vec{X}(t)$ and the optimal risk-mitigated state $\vec{X_p}(t)$ is quantified by D, which is also referred to as the distance vector. The model adapts dynamically, improving such security parameters as access controls, encryption, and other mitigating measure to reduce D, essentially encircles a risk by tightening the right security practices. A coefficient of the vectors A can be configured to regulate the vigor of risk avoidance that may encompass quick patching of slow policy modifications. C would then introduce stochastic variability, which takes into consideration the unpredictable mechanism of risk actualization. System components that are considered to progress iteratively as the enterprise progresses with its purposes, also experience iterative Security Enhancement $\vec{X}(t+1)$ that gradually moves to an optimum state of security where risks are minimized at rhythm with the changing landscape. Given that an EIS component is vulnerable to a new vulnerability at $\vec{X}(t)$, the model calculates the necessary security upgrades $\vec{X_p}(t)$ and modifies controls to bridge the security gap. This accuracy in risk mitigation, coupled with, will guarantee adaptive security postures, which change in response to emerging threats, according to the paradigm of modern cybersecurity.

The encircling movement of the grey wolves' tactical procedure of tracking down a prey can be mathematically represented in a two-dimensional vector space to model dynamic risk mitigation in EIS. Using this approach in risk management strategy gives an avenue that captures the adaptive movement of security controls toward an optimal risk posture, the captured movement and postures, which can further be strategically translated into a structured node-edge graph for a sequential procedural risk management flow process.

A sequential procedural risk management graph can be obtained by mapping the sequence of positional updates $X(t)$ to a directed graph:

$$G = (V, E) \tag{24.3}$$

where:

- Nodes V indicate system states at instance t, labeled with risk metrics, security actions to effect, and risk appetite value.
- Edges E: representing the transition expense between different security states, this is weighted by mitigation effort $(\vec{X}(t+1) - \vec{X}(t))$. Mitigation efforts include the security economic expenses, trade-offs, and other resource allocations.

Formalizing grey wolf encircling mechanics using a vector-based dynamical system and graph-theoretic model greatly optimizes the risk management process as it serves as a well-structured technique that helps to identify risk, assess the risk, map out mitigation steps, and showcase security (Fig. 24.4).

clearance level of risk controls at any instance, and makes provision for reviewing risk control procedures.

This strategy puts in place a systematic method by which critical risk management tasks, which are threat identification, vulnerability assessment, mitigation planning, security control evaluation, and procedural review, are improved. The technique allows organizations to accurately measure the level of risk exposure as well as formulate optimized mitigation routes by modeling the risk factors as dynamic factors in a structured mathematical space. The graphical representation provides a simple visualization of the security postures in any state, thereby providing the ability to monitor the risk control in real-time and provide flexible adjustments. This is an important improvement to the traditional and static risk assessment techniques in the sense that it can keep up with the risk environment and still provides rigorous documentation of the procedures. The flexible nature of the model assists in tactical security operations and in strategic decision-making, which is the way to bridge the gap between the quantification of technical risks and alignment of organizational risk

FIGURE 24.4 Risk management process.

appetite. In the end, this formalization will turn risk management into a frequent compliance activity, rather than a more proactive, intelligent solution that is able to predict and counteract threats in highly complex enterprise settings.

24.4.4 Conceptual Cost–Performance–Resilience Trade-off Model

Enterprise risk management involves striking a balance between three conflicting goals, that is, resilience, cost, and system performance. The above factors are incorporated into the proposed framework conceptually through the use of a multiobjective optimization approach:

Minimize

$$F(x) = w_1 R(x) + w_2 C(x) - w_3 P(x) F(x) \tag{24.4}$$

where:

- R(x): Level of Residual or Remaining risk after allocation of security measures
- C(x): Cost of security control implementation.
- P(x): Index of system Performance that indicates the efficiency of the system
- w_1, w_2, w_3: Impact factor of the weight of enterprise strategic priorities

In this model, the GWO-inspired optimization is used to optimize the use of security resources to minimize the cost and risk and maximize the performance. There is a weighting on the investment in alpha-level assets, which are considered important systems, and a corresponding proportionately less in the other assets. The framework demonstrates how enterprises can conceptually achieve an equilibrium in which additional investment in resilience no longer produces meaningful performance gains or cost reduction, effectively optimizing security investments.

Combining this trade-off model, the chapter presents a reader with a useful but abstract perspective to review security policies within complex enterprise settings without having to describe and simulate them through any specific implementation.

24.5 Conceptual framework and model integration

A unified conceptual framework that links optimization intelligence with corporate risk priorities is established by incorporating the GWO into EIS security management.

Fig. 24.2 represents the GWHM, and it provides the structural basis for grouping organizational assets based on business impact and criticality. On the other side, Fig. 24.5 presents a logical equilibrium in resilience, financial expenditure, and even operational efficiency.

Enterprise risk optimization is expected to be achieved as a result of these models combined. While the hierarchical model defines *what* (the prioritized structure of assets within the organization), the trade-off model defines *how* (the optimization process through which resources and controls are dynamically allocated). These models combined can produce a continuous feedback loop where asset classification informs optimization input, and optimization outcomes redefine asset prioritization.

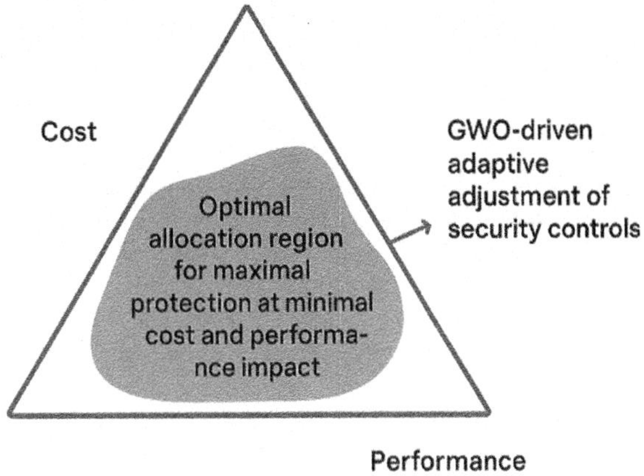

FIGURE 24.5 Conceptual representation of Cost–Performance–Resilience Trade-off in enterprise risk management using GWO (*GWO*, grey wolf optimizer).

Through this cyclical integration, risk management may be changed from a static assessment exercise to a dynamic optimization procedure that is informed by the metaheuristic principles of GWO. The platform enables security policies to adjust in almost real-time as corporate conditions, threat profiles, and operational requirements change, guaranteeing that protection initiatives stay in line with current business priorities.

Conceptually, the model we are proposing can advance the understanding of how bio-inspired intelligence, particularly the GWO, can strengthen enterprise resilience by promoting efficient control allocation, adaptive decision-making, and even continuous security improvement. This chapter provides a strong theoretical foundation on which future studies can build empirical validations or prototype implementations to ultimately appraise its real-world applicability.

24.6 Conclusion

This chapter has introduced an idea of optimizing the security of an EIS with the help of the GWO. Through the hierarchical social structure of GWO, enterprise assets are dynamically ordered into alpha, beta, delta, and omega levels as shown in Fig. 24.2, and thus security resources are prioritized dynamically. The suggested GWHM is a highly intuitive and at the same time rigorous map of criticality, which is assigned to assets to security intervention strategies, such that mission-critical components get the best protection.

Also, the Cost–Performance–Resilience Trade-off Model (see Fig. 24.5) conceptualizes the trade-off between investment in security, operational performance, and organizational resilience. This framework illustrates how businesses can attain a perfect stance of mitigating the risks without wasting money and affecting their performance. The combination of these models defines a new, theoretically based, enterprise risk assessment and asset prioritization framework that is flexible and adjustable to an ever-changing threat environment.

Although the chapter is devoted to conceptual development, further research may consider the empirical validation, simulation work, or even prototype implementations to obtain the quantitative facts on the framework's effectiveness. In general, applying the principles of GWO in the management of enterprise risk represents a promising line towards the adaptive, intelligent, and resource-efficient approach to cybersecurity.

References

[1] T.R. Biswas, M.Z. Hossain, U. Comite, Role of management information systems in enhancing decision-making in large-scale organizations, Pacific Journal of Business Innovation and Strategy 1 (1) (2024) 5–18.

[2] E. Turban, C. Pollard, G. Wood, Information Technology for Management: Driving Digital Transformation to Increase Local and Global Performance, Growth and Sustainability, John Wiley & Sons, (2021).

[3] L. Qudus, Advancing cybersecurity: strategies for mitigating threats in evolving digital and IoT ecosystems, International Research Journal of Modern Engineering and Technology Sciences 7 (1) (2025) 3185.

[4] V. Car, M. Zorko (Eds.), The Digital Environment and Small States in Europe: Challenges, Threats, and Opportunities, Taylor & Francis, (2025).

[5] Ö. Aslan, S.S. Aktuğ, M. Ozkan-Okay, A.A. Yilmaz, E. Akin, A comprehensive review of cyber security vulnerabilities, threats, attacks, and solutions, Electronics 12 (6) (2023) 1333.

[6] M. Saadallah, A. Shahim, S. Khapova, Multi-method approach to human expertise, automation, and artificial intelligence for vulnerability management: investigation of challenges and emerging tensions, IFIP International Conference on ICT Systems Security and Privacy Protection, Springer Nature Switzerland, Cham, (2024), pp. 410–422.
[7] S. Bajpai, A. Sameer, The dynamics of uncertainty: a systematic review of non-linear dynamical systems in decision-making, Nonlinear Dynamics (2025) 1–17.
[8] A.J. Gabriel, A. Darwsih, A.E. Hassanien, Cyber security in the age of COVID-19, Digital Transformation and Emerging Technologies for Fighting COVID-19 Pandemic: Innovative Approaches, Springer International Publishing, Cham, (2021), pp. 275–295.
[9] T. Zhukabayeva, L. Zholshiyeva, N. Karabayev, S. Khan, N. Alnazzawi, Cybersecurity solutions for industrial internet of things–edge computing integration: challenges, threats, and future directions, Sensors 25 (1) (2025) 213.
[10] S. Mirjalili, S.M. Mirjalili, A. Lewis, Grey wolf optimizer, Advances in Engineering Software 69 (2014) 46–61.
[11] H. Faris, I. Aljarah, M.A. Al-Betar, S. Mirjalili, Grey wolf optimizer: a review of recent variants and applications, Neural Computing and Applications 30 (2) (2018) 413–435.
[12] A. Seyyedabbasi, A comprehensive survey: swarm-based algorithms, Decision-Making Models (2024) 85–96.
[13] K.A. ElDahshan, A.A. AlHabshy, B.I. Hameed, Meta-heuristic optimization algorithm-based hierarchical intrusion detection system, Computers 11 (12) (2022) 170.
[14] N. Kunhare, R. Tiwari, J. Dhar, Intrusion detection system using hybrid classifiers with meta-heuristic algorithms for the optimization and feature selection by genetic algorithm, Computers and Electrical Engineering 103 (2022) 108383.
[15] M. Otair, O.T. Ibrahim, L. Abualigah, M. Altalhi, P. Sumari, An enhanced grey wolf optimizer based particle swarm optimizer for intrusion detection system in wireless sensor networks, Wireless Networks 28 (2) (2022) 721–744.
[16] S.J. Habib, P.N. Marimuthu, A bio-inspired tool for managing resilience in enterprise networks with embedded intelligent formulation, Expert Systems 35 (1) (2018) e12208.
[17] W. Xiong, E. Legrand, O. Åberg, R. Lagerström, Cyber security threat modeling based on the MITRE enterprise ATT& CK matrix, Software and Systems Modeling 21 (1) (2022) 157–177.
[18] Tereshchenko, E., Sosnovska, O., Ushenko, N., Andryeyeva, V. and Kovalova, M., 2022. Risk Assessment Information System Of Enterprise Business Processes.
[19] H. Kayan, M. Nunes, O. Rana, P. Burnap, C. Perera, Cybersecurity of industrial cyber-physical systems: a review, ACM Computing Surveys (CSUR) 54 (11s) (2022) 1–35.
[20] F.M. Mulaydinov, Integrated Information Systems in Industrial Enterprises and Business Activities, University Research Base, (2024).
[21] J. Crawford, M. Jabbour, The relationship between enterprise risk management and managerial judgement in decision-making: a systematic literature review, International Journal of Management Reviews 26 (1) (2024) 110–136.
[22] B.W. Nocco, R.M. Stulz, Enterprise risk management: theory and practice, Journal of Applied Corporate Finance 34 (1) (2022) 81–94.
[23] S.N. Makhadmeh, M.A. Al-Betar, I.A. Doush, M.A. Awadallah, S. Kassaymeh, S. Mirjalili, R.A. Zitar, Recent advances in grey wolf optimizer, its versions and applications, IEEE Access 12 (2023) 22991–23028.
[24] S.M. Almufti, H.B. Ahmad, R.B. Marqas, R.R. Asaad, Grey wolf optimizer: overview, modifications and applications, International Research Journal of Science, Technology, Education, and Management 1 (1) (2021) Pp. 1-1.
[25] M. Kazem, H. Amirpouya, M. Seyedali, B.F. Amir, Adaptive grey wolf optimizer, Neural Computing & Applications 34 (10) (2022) 7711–7731.
[26] K.C. Mizrak, Crisis management and risk mitigation: strategies for effective response and resilience, Trends, Challenges, and Practices in Contemporary Strategic Management (2024) 254–278.
[27] D. Srivastava, S. Hooda, R. Gill, C. Singla, Detection of cyber attacks by using gray wolf optimizer, 2023 International Conference on Intelligent Systems for Communication, IoT and Security (ICISCOIS), IEEE, (2023), pp. 596–600.
[28] M.M. Jawhar, M.A. Alellah, The detect dos attack from network traffic using gray wolf optimization algorithm, Journal of Engineering Science and Technology 15 (6) (2020) 3639–3648.
[29] N.K. Singh, V. Mahajan, Detection of cyber cascade failure in smart grid substation using advance grey wolf optimization, Journal of Interdisciplinary Mathematics 23 (1) (2020) 69–79.
[30] T.A. Alamiedy, M. Anbar, Z.N. Alqattan, Q.M. Alzubi, Anomaly-based intrusion detection system using multi-objective grey wolf optimisation algorithm, Journal of Ambient Intelligence and Humanized Computing 11 (9) (2020) 3735–3756.
[31] T.D. Le, T. Le-Dinh, S. Uwizeyemungu, Cybersecurity analytics for enterprise environment: a systematic literature review, Authorea Preprints (2025).
[32] T.J. Andersen, P.C. Young, Enhancing public sector enterprise risk management through interactive information processing, Frontiers in Research Metrics and Analytics 8 (2023) 1239447.
[33] N. Singh, V. Krishnaswamy, J.Z. Zhang, Intellectual structure of cybersecurity research in enterprise information systems, Enterprise Information Systems 17 (6) (2023) 2025545.
[34] K. AL-Dosari, N. Fetais, Risk-management framework and information-security systems for small and medium enterprises (SMES): a meta-analysis approach, Electronics 12 (17) (2023) 3629.
[35] D. Palko, T. Babenko, A. Bigdan, N. Kiktev, T. Hutsol, M. Kuboń, H. Hnatiienko, S. Tabor, O. Gorbovy, A. Borusiewicz, Cyber security risk modeling in distributed information systems, Applied Sciences 13 (4) (2023) 2393.

[36] O.O. Olaniyi, O.O. Omogoroye, F.G. Olaniyi, A.I. Alao, T.O. Oladoyinbo, CyberFusion protocols: strategic integration of enterprise risk management, ISO 27001, and mobile forensics for advanced digital security in the modern business ecosystem, Journal of Engineering Research and Reports 26 (6) (2024) 31–49.
[37] M.E. Stanikzai, E. Mittal, Strategic alignment of organizational structure based on decisions for sustainable organizational performance: a bibliometric-systematic literature review, Cogent Business & Management 12 (1) (2025) 2560650.
[38] E. Evinia, M.N. Sitokdana, Risk management based IT analysis using ISO 31000 (case study: PT Bawen Mediatama), Journal of Information Systems and Informatics 5 (1) (2023) 380–390.
[39] M.A.B. Ali, Methods for improving information assurance in enterprise networks through structured cybersecurity policies and access controls, Journal of Data Mining, Knowledge Discovery, and Decision Support Systems 14 (11) (2024) 1–14.

Chapter 25

Application of the grey wolf optimizer to enhance offshore microgrid power management and control including tidal power and desalination

Nour EL Y. Kouba[1], Smail Haron[2], Amel Brik[1], Aimad Boudoucha[1], and Djamel Selkim[1]

[1]*Laboratory of Electrical and Industrial Systems, University of Sciences and Technology Hou ari Boumediene, Algiers, Algeria,* [2]*Department of Electrical Engineering, Faculty of Sciences and Applied Sciences, Mohand Oulhadj University, Bouira, Algeria*

25.1 Introduction

Rising energy needs and environmental challenges are driving the use of decentralized sources, energy storage, and demand response. Furthermore, renewable energy sources (RES) play a vital role in clean energy production [1]. Modern renewable energy production systems integrate various sources such as wind, solar, tidal, or wave power generation. By combining them electrically, it is possible to create an integrated hybrid platform named microgrids [2]. Wind energy is currently one of the main sources of renewable energy worldwide, thanks to its high energy density and the maturity of its production technologies. Given that more than 70% of the Earth's surface is covered by oceans, the exploitation of offshore wind offers considerable potential. Furthermore, other forms of marine energy, such as tides, waves, and ocean currents [3], can also be effectively exploited to generate significant electricity production.

One of the main advantages of offshore wind compared to onshore wind is its ability to produce electricity more consistently, thanks to generally stronger and more consistent winds in offshore environments [4]. Although the control of many of these resources poses complex challenges for the safe and efficient operation of the grid, these challenges are managed by the concept of microgrid [5]. A microgrid (MG) is a conventional hybrid electrical network comprising distributed energy resources, local loads, and electrical energy storage devices to power specific areas or isolated localities. In recent years, the deployment of microgrids has continued to grow globally. The main function of an MG is to ensure system stability in the event of a grid failure. The literature offers many definitions and functional classifications of microgrids.

A microgrid is a set of distributed loads and energy resources, interconnected within well-defined electrical boundaries, operating as a single, controllable entity with respect to the main grid. The microgrid can connect and disconnect from the grid to operate in grid-connected or islanded mode [6]. The integration of microgrids into the electricity sector offers a promising solution to current challenges, with several advantages over the traditional grid: improved stability and reliability, reduced energy losses and carbon emissions, continuity of power supply in stand-alone mode, support to the local grid, operational flexibility, and backup role in case of outages. The microgrid integrates various decentralized energy resources, such as photovoltaic systems, fuel cells, gas turbines, wind energy, micro-turbines, and combustion engines [7]. One of the main challenges of the massive integration of renewable energies into electricity grids is their intermittent nature [8]. Power generation units such as solar and wind, which are inherently random, generate energy production that is highly variable over time [9]. RESs are fluctuating (monthly, seasonal, and annual), uncertain, and nondispatchable.

Moreover, controllable energy sources, such as power grids, storage devices, and diesel generators, can be scheduled to supplement these renewable sources in case of critical loads [10]. Since the production of renewable varies with weather

Grey Wolf Optimizer. DOI: https://doi.org/10.1016/B978-0-443-36624-6.00001-9

conditions and time of day, mainly due to the unpredictability of solar radiation, wind speed, and other similar key resources [9], they generally cannot ensure a stable and continuous power supply [11], many maximum power point tracking (MPPT) methods have been developed and applied to photovoltaic systems, while MPPT algorithms tailored to wind systems have also been widely studied, with the aim of promoting greater integration of RESs [12]. Furthermore, the partial unpredictability of demand in microgrids further complicates system control. Energy storage devices and intelligent energy management that can handle variability and uncertainty become essential. For a microgrid to provide reliable power, advanced control algorithms to manage power dispatch and optimize its performance are essential [8]. This process involves converting electrical energy from an available source into another chemical, mechanical [13], thermal, or magnetic form in order to store it and release it as electricity when needed [14].

Storage devices must meet various criteria, such as reserve capacity, short-term or long-term storage, fast response time, stationary or portable, energy density, conversion rate, storage costs, safety, end use, such as on-grid or Off-grid, environmental impacts, and limited storage durations [15]. Energy storage systems (ESS) store excess electricity when production exceeds demand, such as during periods of low consumption, reduced costs, or intermittent sources. The stored energy can then be used during peak demand, when costs are high, or when no other source is available. There is a high demand for reliable, cost-effective, sustainable, and environmentally friendly ESS for various energy storage applications. With the advancements in materials technology, bearings, and power electronics, a control strategy is required for optimal utilization of available hybrid energy storage systems (HESS). In reference [16] authors have used batteries storage system for RESs control. In Ref. [17], Hall et al. have presented a review paper focusing on several EES technologies, namely batteries, supercapacitors, superconducting magnetic energy storage, and flywheels. In addition, a detailed analysis of existing applications of ESS in wind energy is presented in Ref. [18].

Authors in reference [19] have an analysis of developments and challenges of materials for electrochemical energy storage. Further, A systematic review of photovoltaic/wind hybrid systems with battery storage was presented in Ref. [20]. Also, the authors in Ref. [21] only developed the voltage regulation methods for low voltage grids and not for voltage management networks. Many methods have been used for the management of isolated grids and microgrids. Optimal management of these grids maximizes their efficiency. In addition, an improved droop control method is one of the best methods for voltage and frequency control in microgrids and isolated grids [22]. The use of fuzzy logic controllers has been widely developed in the field of power system control. They are particularly applied to the control of excitation, voltage, frequency, as well as power grid stabilizers, among others [23]. Thanks to its efficiency and flexibility. An imbalance between generation and load causes frequency variations, which can adversely affect system performance and complicate system control. Load frequency control (LFC), which is a key function of automatic generation control (AGC), is one of the major challenges in the design and operation of power systems. Large frequency deviations can impair system performance and damage equipment [24].

Many control schemes, such as conventional proportional-integral controller, proportional-integral-derivative (PID) controller, and optimal control, have been proposed to improve the performance. Studies on the design of regulators fall into two broad categories: those based on traditional approaches and those relying on metaheuristic techniques [25]. Metaheuristic algorithms based on bio-inspired or nature-inspired have been developed to solve large, complex, constrained optimization problems, aiming for good convergence speed, high accuracy, robustness, and better overall performance. Recently, a large list of metaheuristic algorithms has been proposed, including the firefly algorithm, inspired by the attraction and flickering behavior of fireflies; the flower pollination algorithm, based on the flowering characteristics of plants; particle swarm optimization (PSO), inspired by the behavior of swarms, such as schools of fish and birds in nature; the bird swarm algorithm, based on the unique social interactions of bird swarms, etc [26]. Among the metaheuristic algorithms used for the design of LFC controllers, genetic algorithm (GA) [27], PSO [28], social spider optimizer [29], and quasioppositional harmony search algorithm have been used to tune the PID parameters.

This chapter addresses marine microgrid power management and control using a PID controller coordinated with a storage system and an HVDC link optimized through the grey wolves optimizer (GWO). The GWO algorithm is one of the new optimization algorithms that is inspired by the leadership behavior and the unique mechanism of hunting gray wolves. The original GWO algorithm was initially proposed by Mirjalili et al. [30]. Since its development, several researchers have applied it to solve different problems. It also has a good ability to converge to optima, which makes this algorithm the best choice to solve this problem. Within this context, the HESS was used to support the LFC loop and reduce frequency fluctuations in the presence of renewable energy. Taking the seawater desalination plant as a controllable load that can be used as a pumped storage power plant to participate in microgrid optimal control. To prove the validity of the proposed strategy, various scenarios were simulated and presented. Finally, a comparative study robustness analysis was carried out with different renewable energy penetration rates.

25.2 Offshore microgrid model

In microgrid, offshore Platforms and Coastal Communities, the diesel generator (DEGs), including wind turbine, wave energy, photovoltaic, and marine current serves as a backup solution, automatically starting when the conventional generation is insufficient, even if ESS are available. The objective of these HESS is to cancel out fluctuations in load and RESs. In this part, the presented marine microgrid shown in Fig. 25.1 was investigated in this chapter. The proposed MG includes a wind farm, a tidal power generation station that benefits from the seawater waves force, a photovoltaic generator, a fixed local load, a seawater desalination station as a controllable load using the seawater reservoirs for the Pumped Storage hydropower (PSH) coordinated with a hybrid storage devices including superconducting magnetic energy storage system (SMES) short-term storage, redox flow batteries for fast response time, and a fuel cell (FC) for long-term.

A centralized frequency controller-based optimal PID was installed to ensure frequency regulation through the HESS and the seawater desalination plant, where an intelligent energy management system (EMS) was employed using fuzzy Logic to maximize the clean energy production and manage the active power. Further, to ensure a smooth offshore wind farm connection, an HVDC transmission link was considered to tie the wind farm to supply the MG loads. As an effective optimization tool, the GWO was used to find the optimal fuzzy-PID controller, including the fuzzy logic scaling factors and the PID controller gains. The dynamic model of the simulated microgrid was depicted in Fig. 25.2, all MG components have been modeled using differential equations. The subsystems are modeled using first-order transfer functions. This model captures the essential dynamics of the system without involving complex details.

The mathematical model was given as follows:

The microgrid generated power named P_s was determined by the following components:

$$P_s = (P_{WG} + P_{TDEG})K_1 + P_{PV} + K_2(P_{Fc} \pm P_{SMES} \pm P_{Red}) + K_3P_{Desl} \quad (25.1)$$

where P_{WG} represents the net power injected by the wind turbines, P_{PV} represents the net power injected by the photovoltaic array, P_{TDGE} represents the net power injected by the tidal turbines, P_{Desl} represents the participation of the desalination station in power generation using the PSH, P_{Fc} represents the storage Fc power, P_{SMES} represents the storage SMES power, P_{Red} represents the storage Redox power.

Thc IIVDC powcr output is givcn by:

$$P_{HVDC} = K_1(P_{WG} + P_{TDEG}) \quad (25.2)$$

$$K_2 = 1 - K_1 \quad (25.3)$$

where $K_1 - 0.6$, $K_2 - 0.4$for the storage system and$K_3 - 0.2$for desalination station.

$$G_{WG(s)} = K_W TG/(1 + sT_W TG) \quad (25.4)$$

$$G_{TDEG}(s) = \frac{K_{TDEG}}{1 + sT_{TDEG}} \quad (25.5)$$

$$G_{PV}(s) = \frac{K_{PV}}{1 + sT_{PV}} \quad (25.6)$$

$$G_{HVDC}(s) = \frac{K_{HVDC}}{1 + sT_{HVDC}} \quad (25.7)$$

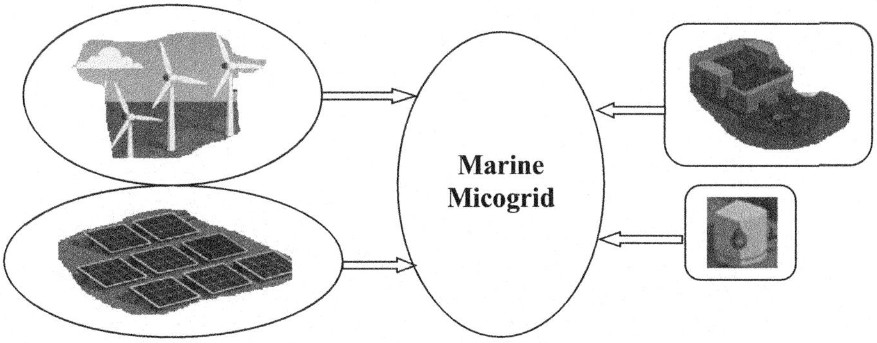

FIGURE 25.1 Proposed offshore microgrid configuration.

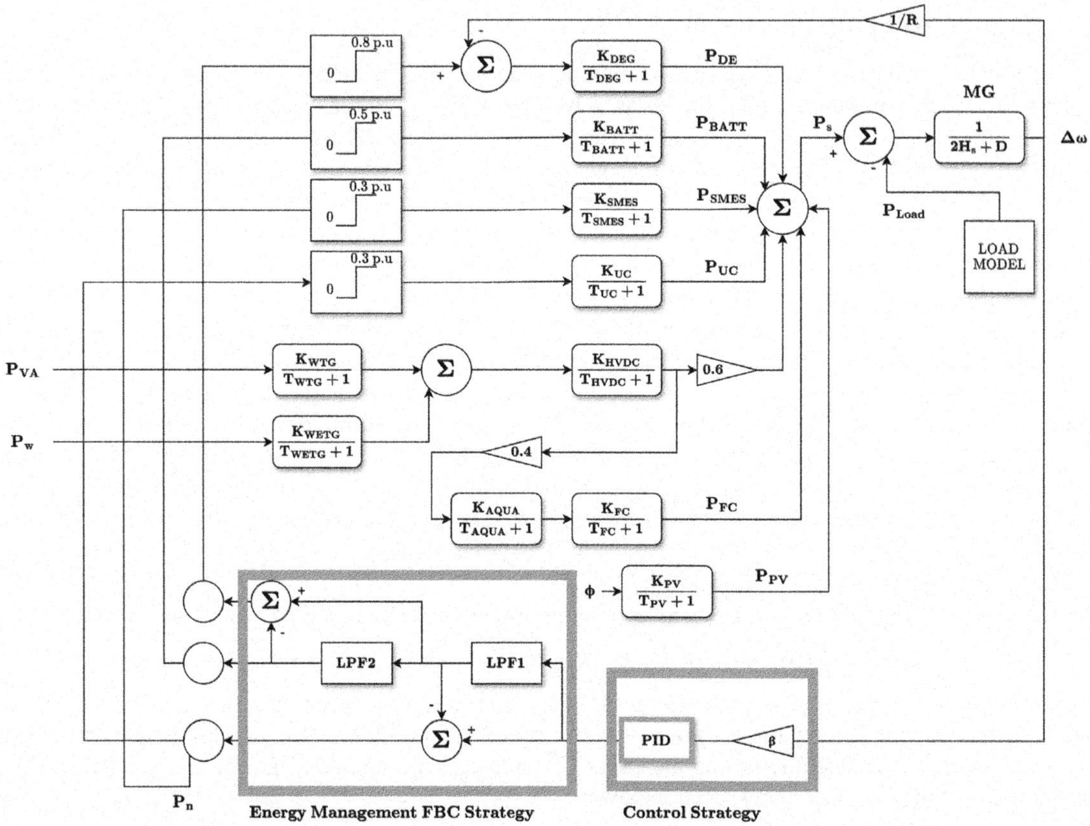

FIGURE 25.2 Schematic diagram of the offshore microgrid (*MG*).

$$G_{AE}(s) = \frac{K_{AE}}{1 + sT_{AE}} \tag{25.8}$$

$$G_{FC}(s) = \frac{K_{FC}}{1 + sT_{FC}} \tag{25.9}$$

$$G_{Desl}(s) = \frac{K_{Desl}}{1 + sT_{Desel}} \tag{25.10}$$

$$G_{Redox}(s) = \frac{K_{Redox}}{1 + sT_{Redoc}} \tag{25.11}$$

$$G_{SMES}(s) = \frac{K_{SMES}}{1 + sT_{SMES}} \tag{25.12}$$

The marine MG was modeled by a transfer function that accounts for the dynamics of all subsystems. The transfer function of the MG is given by:

$$G_{MG}(s) = \frac{1}{K_{sys}(1 + sT_{sys})} = \frac{1}{D + Ms} \tag{25.13}$$

This simplified modeling allows us to evaluate the marine MG frequency response to net power variations and ensure active power management. Further, the developed model was used to create two objective functions based on frequency deviation Δf and active power deviation ΔP. A logic flow scheme was developed to ensure fast and smart power management in the marine microgrid involving the HESS and the desalination station, then GWO was used to optimize the scaling factors of fuzzy logic and PID controller parameters as presented in the next section.

25.3 Optimal power management and frequency control strategy

Microgrids, due to their decentralized nature, can operate both connected to and independent from the main grid. Each mode offers benefits but also presents challenges in maintaining a reliable and efficient power balance between supply and demand. Power management system (PMS) in microgrids aims to coordinate conventional sources, RES, ESS, and loads while ensuring power quality and system reliability. The intermittent and variable output of RES, like photovoltaic and wind turbines, necessitates robust energy storage to regulate voltage and maintain power balance under changing conditions. Without it, power quality may degrade and fail to meet grid requirements.

In this chapter, the global objective function of the power management and control problem aims to minimize two objective functions that represent: (1) the frequency deviation, (2) the active power deviation, while satisfying batteries' state of charge (Soc) state and the microgrid frequency limit constraints. The main objective of the proposed optimal PMS-FC Strategy is: (1) ensure continuity of power supply in stand-alone mode, (2) support the local load, (3) operational flexibility, and backup role in case of outages to avoid under-frequency load shedding. Also, the smart management of the HESS balances electricity supply and demand, and ensures a fast and smooth frequency regulation.

25.3.1 Intelligent power management system

The performance of ESS relies on battery charge and discharge cycles, particularly their Soc. Overcharging or deep discharging shortens battery life, making it essential to implement control strategies that balance SoC across battery banks to enhance lifespan and ensure consistent power delivery. Control strategies are tailored to system requirements and may involve voltage control, frequency control, or both. Automatic voltage regulation maintains voltage within desired limits by compensating for fluctuations caused by load variations and RES output. These systems are typically deployed near transformers, generators, and loads to support voltage stability. An EMS serves as the decision-making core of a microgrid. It performs real-time monitoring and forecasting to manage energy generation, storage, and consumption in order to meet system objectives. Advanced EMS platforms incorporate artificial intelligence (AI) or fuzzy logic to enhance flexibility and adaptability by integrating both technical and economic parameters. Modern microgrids are participating in electricity markets, offering services such as energy trading, demand response, and ancillary services. In grid-connected mode, microgrids can sell surplus renewable energy to the utility or buy power during low-price periods, which enhances their economic viability. In a multimarket environment, coordination becomes more complex, particularly when microgrids interact across multiple regions. Effective EMS and forecasting tools are essential for good optimization of market optimization. In this chapter, a multitask fuzzy logic scheme was developed to ensure smart active PMS as presented in Fig. 25.3.

25.3.2 Optimal frequency control model

To ensure reliable frequency control in the offshore microgrid, three different layers of conventional AGC were added into the frequency control scheme as presented in Fig. 25.4. The first being droop control. The second is LFC control. And the third is the economic dispatch control (EDC). The droop control is represented by its droop setting R, the LFC is denoted by the parameter B and a PID controller, while the EDC is represented by a transfer function, where $Tedc$ is the time

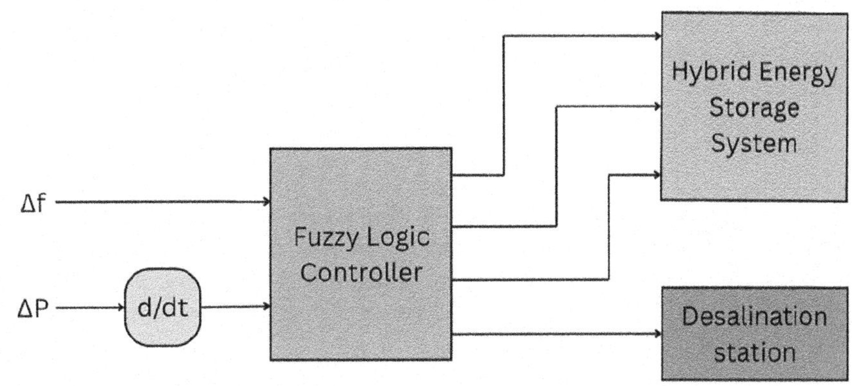

FIGURE 25.3 Smart microgrid power management system.

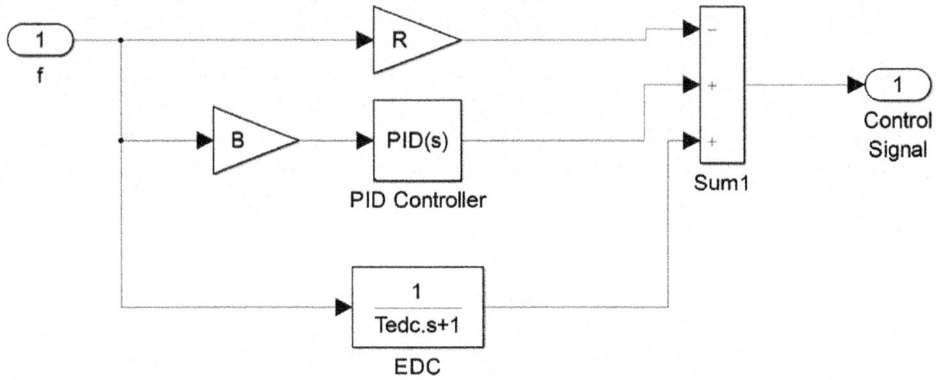

FIGURE 25.4 Frequency control of the offshore microgrid.

constant. The AGC control takes the frequency *f* of the microgrid as an input and outputs the control signal used to control the hybrid storage system. The marine microgrid control was structured into three hierarchical levels: primary control applied to the SMES devices, secondary control applied to the Redox and Fuel cell devices, while tertiary control was applied to the PSH of the desalination station. Primary control or droop control is a decentralized and fast method to ensure immediate response to disturbances without relying on communication. Secondary control corrects deviations introduced by primary control, such as frequency drifts, using centralized or distributed communication-based strategies to restore nominal values. Tertiary control handles optimization at a broader level, focusing on economic dispatch and interaction with the offshore microgrid.

25.3.3 Grey wolf optimizer

Over the past decade, AI has progressively gained ground in various industrial domains. In modern power systems, the growth of energy demands, the increasing complexity, the growing integration of renewable sources, and the transition toward smart grids have made AI an essential tool to ensure efficient and reliable energy management [31,32]. AI techniques mimic human cognitive functions by learning, reasoning, or adaptation, and decision-making. This allows them to deal with large datasets, then provide accurate and efficient predictions in record computational time [33,34]. Thus as highlighted in several studies [32,33], AI techniques provide powerful tools for electrical power systems to perform complex tasks such as: Economic Load Dispatch, Power System Stability Control, Power Flow, dynamic Voltage regulation, Unit Commitment, LFC, Reactive Power, and Capacitor Placement Optimization [35,36]. In smart grids, AI enables predictive maintenance and real-time fault detection that secures the network and improves system reliability. For renewable energy, AI improves solar/wind forecasting, dynamic energy dispatch, battery storage management, and coordinates distributed energy resources [37,38].

AI techniques commonly used in power systems include machine learning and deep learning models, such as supervised (Random Forest, Support Vector Regression) and unsupervised learning, different kinds of artificial neural networks, fuzzy logic, and neuro-fuzzy inference systems, among others [33,36,39]. Among the most emerging classes of AI strategies are metaheuristic, nature, and bio-inspired optimization algorithms. These methods mimic natural behaviors and evolutionary intelligence; they have the ability to solve nonlinear and multiobjective problems in energy systems like optimal power flow, unit commitment, and microgrid management [40–44]. Algorithms such as GA, PSO, ant colony optimization (ACO), simulated annealing, and GWO offer flexible and robust solutions [45]. Hybrid variants of these algorithms (e.g., GA-PSO, ACO-GWO) lead to enhanced performance [45,46].

In the following section, we focus specifically on the GWO, exploring its mechanisms and applications in power system optimization. The GWO has a simple mathematical model with few control parameters to tune, which makes its application very easy compared to other complex metaheuristic algorithms. Also, the GWO has a good balance between local and global search, for that it can be applied to solve a large number of engineering problems, especially with its fast convergence characteristic. On the other hand, this algorithm can get trapped in the local minima in case of multimodel problems. Also, may be diffecult to apply GWO to solve dynamic optimization in dynamic environments. Further, GWO cannot perform well on some types of objective functions.

25.3.3.1 Biological inspiration of grey wolf optimizer

The GWO is a nature-inspired metaheuristic technique introduced in 2014 by Seyedali Mirjalili et al. [30]. It's designed to provide optimal solutions for complex multimodal and nonlinear optimization problems. The GWO was inspired by the hunting behavior and social hierarchy of grey wolves (Canis lupus). These animals live in structured packs with roles assigned to alpha, beta, delta, and omega wolves. Alphas lead the group, while betas assist and deltas take on supportive roles. Omegas, though lowest in rank, help maintain group stability. Grey wolves hunt cooperatively by searching for prey, encircling prey, and attacking prey. GWO models these behaviors to balance exploration and exploitation in optimization tasks.

25.3.3.2 Mathematical model and working mechanism

In this part, the mathematical modeling of the social hierarchy of grey wolves and their hunting technique is detailed [30].

25.3.3.2.1 Social hierarchy

In GWO, the candidate solutions in the population are ranked based on their fitness. The best solution is labeled alpha (α), the second best as beta (β), and the third as delta (δ). All remaining solutions are considered as omega (ω). The hunting (optimization) process is guided by the top three wolves, alpha (α), beta (β), and delta (δ). Omega (ω) just follows these three wolves, as shown in Fig. 25.5.

25.3.3.2.2 Encircling prey

During a hunt, grey wolves encircle the prey. To mathematically model the encircling behavior (the current best solution), the following equations are used:

$$\vec{D} = \left| \vec{C} . \vec{X}_p(t) - \vec{X}(t) \right| \tag{25.14}$$

$$\vec{X}(t+1) = \vec{X}_p(t) - \vec{A} . \vec{D} \tag{25.15}$$

where current iteration is indicated by t. $\vec{A}$ and $\vec{C}$ are coefficient vectors, the position vector of the prey (optimal solution) is $\vec{X_p}$, and $\vec{X}$ indicates the current position vector of a grey wolf. The coefficient vectors $\vec{A}$ and $\vec{C}$ are calculated as:

$$\vec{A} = 2\vec{a} . \vec{r_1} - \vec{a} \tag{25.16}$$

$$\vec{C} = 2\vec{r_2} \tag{25.17}$$

where $\vec{a}$ is a linearly decreasing parameter from 2 to 0 over iterations and $\vec{r_1}$, $\vec{r_2}$ are the random vectors between [0,1]. Based on Eqs. (25.14) and (25.15), the wolves can adjust their position inside the region around the prey.

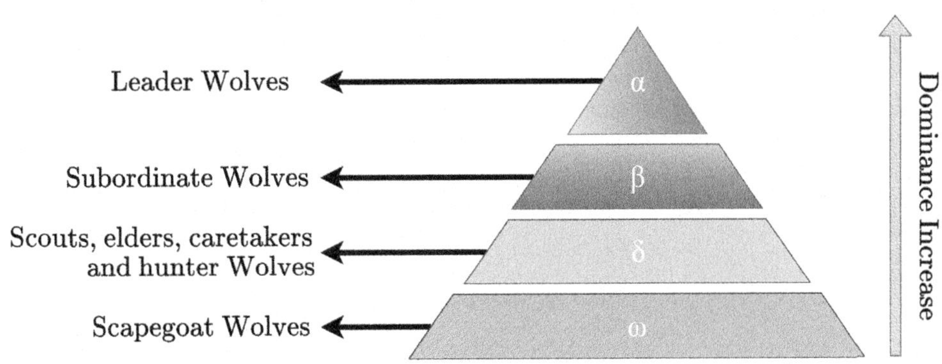

FIGURE 25.5 Social hierarchy of grey wolves.

25.3.3.2.3 Hunting

Grey wolves are capable of locating and surrounding their prey. The alpha usually leads the hunt, occasionally supported by the beta and delta. In the GWO algorithm, the assumption is taken that these three leaders know the exact location of the prey. Their positions are updated according to the best solutions using the equations given below:

$$\overrightarrow{D_\alpha} = \left|\overrightarrow{C_1}.\ \overrightarrow{X}_\alpha - \overrightarrow{X}\right|,\ \overrightarrow{D_\beta} = \left|\overrightarrow{C_2}.\ \overrightarrow{X}_\beta - \overrightarrow{X}\right|,\ \overrightarrow{D_\delta} = \left|\overrightarrow{C_3}.\ \overrightarrow{X}_\delta - \overrightarrow{X}\right| \tag{25.18}$$

$$\overrightarrow{X_1} = \overrightarrow{X}_\alpha - \overrightarrow{A_1}.\ (\overrightarrow{D_\alpha}),\ \overrightarrow{X_2} = \overrightarrow{X}_\beta - \overrightarrow{A_2}.\ (\overrightarrow{D_\beta}),\ \overrightarrow{X_3} = \overrightarrow{X}_\delta - \overrightarrow{A_3}.\ (\overrightarrow{D_\delta}) \tag{25.19}$$

$$\overrightarrow{X}(t+1) = \frac{\overrightarrow{X_1} + \overrightarrow{X_2} + \overrightarrow{X_3}}{3} \tag{25.20}$$

This modeling allows the algorithm to converge toward optimal or near-optimal solutions based on collective knowledge.

25.3.3.2.4 Attacking prey (exploitation)

The attack phase is mathematically modeled by linearly decreasing the control parameter $\overrightarrow{a}$ from 2 to 0 during the iteration. The fluctuations of $\overrightarrow{A}$ are also decreased with $\overrightarrow{a}$. When $|\overrightarrow{A}| < 1$, wolves move closer to the prey, simulating exploitation. This allows solutions to converge around the best candidates as the algorithm progresses.

25.3.3.2.5 Search for prey (exploration)

In the GWO, the search for the optimal solution is based on the positions of the alpha, beta, and delta wolves. During this phase, these leading wolves spread out in the search space to explore new areas in search of prey. They diverge from each other when searching for prey and converge while attacking the prey. Mathematically, this divergence happens when the random value of $\overrightarrow{A}$ is greater than 1 or less than -1. This encourages the exploration behavior in the algorithm. This mechanism helps the GWO algorithm to maintain a balance between exploration and exploitation, which avoid to get trapped in local optima. As a result, the algorithm shows more random behavior throughout the early stages of optimization. Finally, the GWO flowchart was sketched in Fig. 25.6.

25.3.4 Objectives functions

It should be noted that the choice of the fitness function is very important to solve an optimization problem. In the literature, four kinds of performance criteria are usually considered in the control design, which are:

- Integral of Squared Error (ISE).
- Integral of Absolute Error (IAE).
- Integral of Time multiplied Squared Error (ITSE).
- Integral of Time multiplied Absolute Error (ITAE).

Both the ISE and ITAE criteria are often used in literature for their better performance compared to the IAE and ITSE criteria. However, the ISE criterion integrates the square of the error over time, where ITAE criterion integrates the absolute value of the error over time.

A disadvantage of the ISE criteria is that it may result in a response with a relatively small overshoot but a long settling time due to weighing all errors uniformly over time. In contrast, the ITAE performance criteria can overcome this drawback. On the other hand, ITAE has the potential for producing reductions in oscillations and tracking errors. In other words, the ITAE performance criteria can overcome the disadvantage of the ISE. For this reason, the performance criteria usually considered in the control design are the integral of ITAE.

In the aim of solving the active power management and frequency control problem using the GWO, two objective functions are combined in this work. In this part, the ITAE was used as given below:

$$fit_1 = \min\{\Delta f\} = \int_0^t t.\ (\Delta f)dt \tag{25.21}$$

$$fit_2 = \min\{\Delta P,\quad \Delta p_{HVDC}\} = \int_0^t t.\ (Ps - Pload - \Delta p_{HVDC})dt \tag{25.22}$$

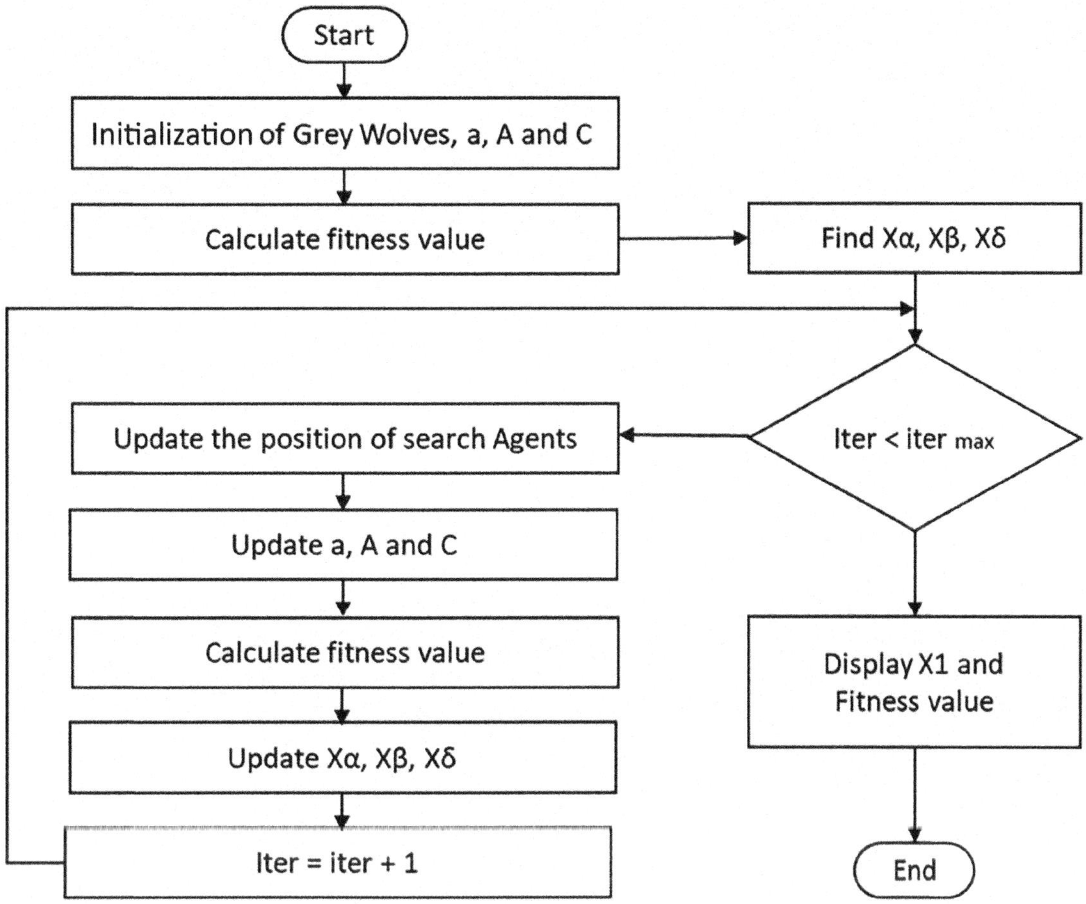

FIGURE 25.6 Flowchart of GWO algorithm [30] (*GWO*, Grey wolf optimizer).

$$fit = \min\{fit_1, fit_3\} \tag{25.23}$$

- Subject to:

$$\begin{Bmatrix} K_{p\,\min} \le K_p \le K_{p\,\max} \\ K_{i\,\min} \le K_i \le K_{i\,\max} \\ K_{d\,\min} \le K_d \le K_{d\,\max} \end{Bmatrix} \begin{Bmatrix} K_{e\,\min} \le K_e \le K_{e\,\max} \\ K_{ec\,\min} \le K_{ec} \le K_{ec\,\max} \end{Bmatrix} \tag{25.24}$$

The range of the controller parameters is selected between a given lower bound (LB=0) and upper bound (UB=30) for the PID controller and (LB=0.1) and (UB=1) for the fuzzy logic scaling factors, which are fixed based on previous simulation, which help to find the best solution within a given time limit. The maximum iteration, population size, search dimension size, lower bound, and upper bound of the optimized parameters are given in Table 25.1. The simulation was conducted during 10 minutes (600 s).

25.4 Simulation results

In order to verify the effectiveness and validity of the proposed optimal PMS-FC strategy, three case studies are considered:

Case 1: With Frequency Control-based Optimal AGC System using GWO;
Case 2: With Smart Power Management System (PMS) based on Fuzzy Logic;
Case 3: With Coordinate Optimal combined PMS-FC Using Fuzzy-GWO.

TABLE 25.1 Simulation parameters.

	Kp	Ki	Kd	Ke	Kec
Lower bound (LB)	0	0	0	0	0
Upper bund (UB)	30	30	30	1	1
GWO	**Max generation**	**Population size**		**Search dimension**	
Only PID	100	20		3	
Fuzzy-PID	100	30		5	

GWO, Grey wolf optimizer; *PID*, proportional-integral-derivative.

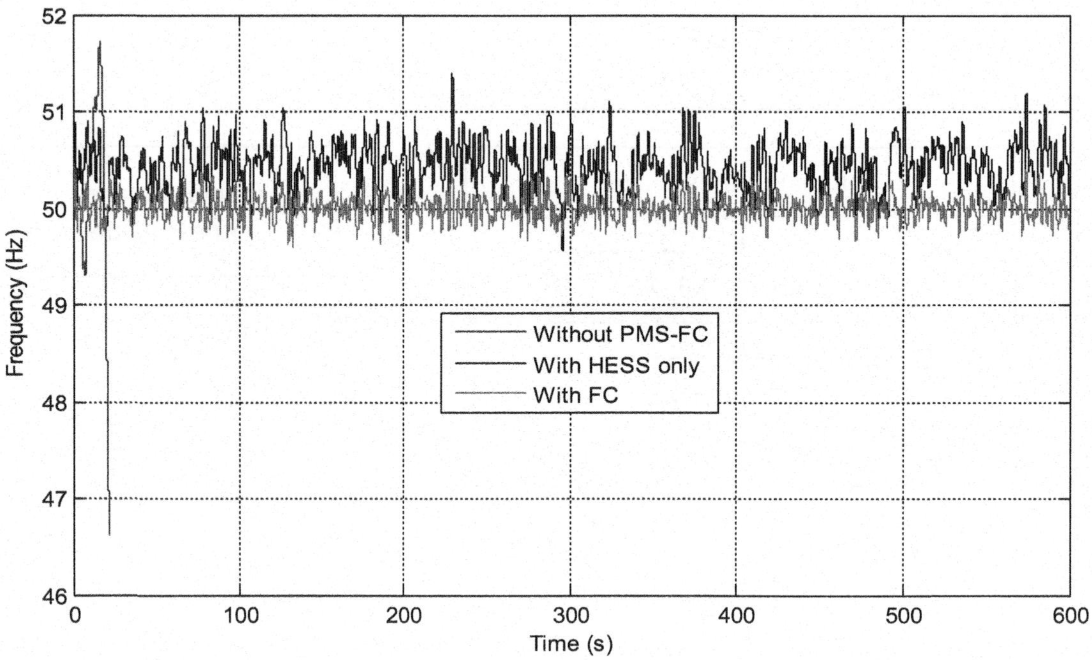

FIGURE 25.7 Microgrid frequency with optimal AGC only (*AGC*, Automatic generation control).

25.4.1 Case 1: optimal frequency control using grey wolf optimizer

In Case 1, the investments on AGC loops are respectively obtained by the application of the GWO method, where the frequency oscillations are reduced, respectively. In the initial scenario (curve in bleu), the microgrid loses synchronization and risks a total collapse due to the lack of regulatory capacity and system inertia. Also, it can be observed that the frequency regulation was supported in the second scenario when using the HESS to control the MG frequency (curve in black), it is clear that the microgrid can maintain the frequency in the range of ± 1 Hz. Finally, in the third scenario (red curve), and compared with the initial scenario without control (curve in bleu), the frequency deviation was minimized at the scheduled value as presented in Fig. 25.7. On the other hand, Figs. 25.8 and 25.9 show the generated power in the microgrid and the local load, which the AGC system can only ensure frequency regulation by adding the exit power of the storage system to satisfy the load, but it can't ensure supply-load equilibrium without the use of the PMS. However, it is clear that there is a remarkable improvement in the generated power with the AGC loops, even though the total generated power doesn't meet the load at each time, but the system fluctuations were reduced. These results, let us use a smart power management strategy using fuzzy logic to keep production with consumption at each time in the microgrid, which is the main objective of the second case presented in the next part.

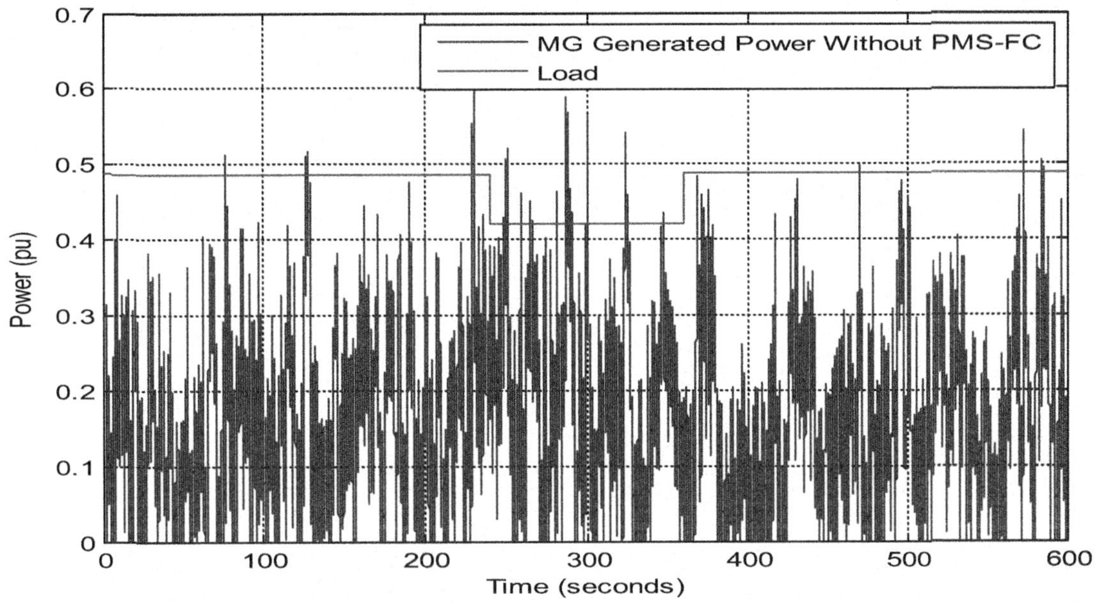

FIGURE 25.8 Microgrid generated power and load without optimal AGC (*AGC*, Automatic generation control).

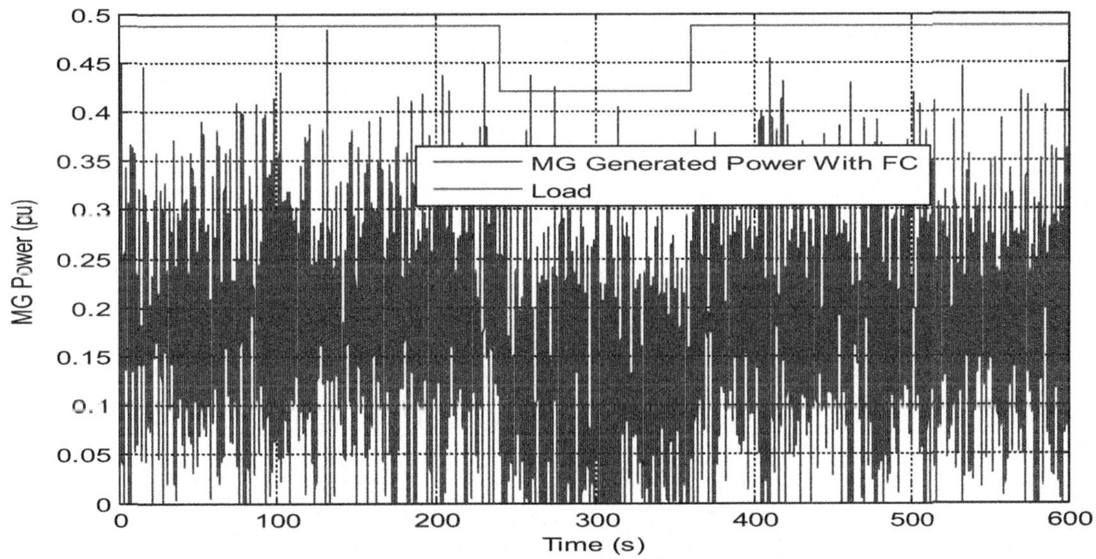

FIGURE 25.9 Microgrid generated power and load with optimal AGC (*AGC*, Automatic generation control).

25.4.2 Case 2: with intelligent power management system

In this second case study, the investments in hybrid storage devices were respectively obtained by using fuzzy logic as a smart tool to design a smart active PMS in the microgrid, where GWO was used to optimize the input scaling factors and the PID controller parameters. Two inputs were added to each element of the HESS, the first one is the selected AGC action according to the storage type to ensure a smooth frequency regulation, which are droop control applied to the SMES devices, secondary LFC control applied to the Redox and Fuel cell devices, while tertiary control was applied to the PSH of the desalination station. Then, the second input was the intelligent PMS action, which was applied to each element. However, it should be noted that in this part, both FC and PMS work independently without coordination, which is the fact of the third case study.

It can be observed from the obtained results and comparative study presented in Fig. 25.10, that there is no change in the system frequency using the PMS strategy, because the frequency regulation was already established by the AGC loops, however, with no coordination the effect of the PMS strategy can't be noticed in this stage, which lead to coordinate between the FC and PMS to smooth system fluctuations. On the other hand, a remarkable enhancement was noticed between the generated power and load of the microgrid presented in Fig. 25.11. It is clear that the proposed PMS can balance supply and load using the smart management of the storage system based on the active power deviation minimization. These observations, from Case 1 and Case 2, lead to combining both advantages of the storage system concerning optimal frequency control and smart power management by combining FC and PMS strategies in the next case study.

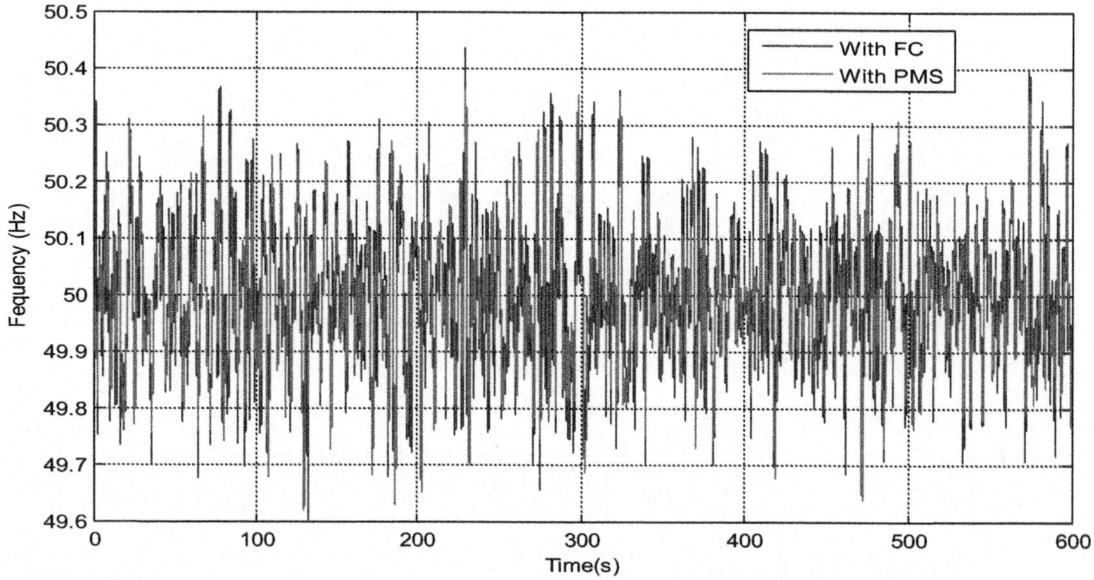

FIGURE 25.10 Microgrid frequency with FC and with PMS (*FC*, Fuel cell; *PMS*, power management system).

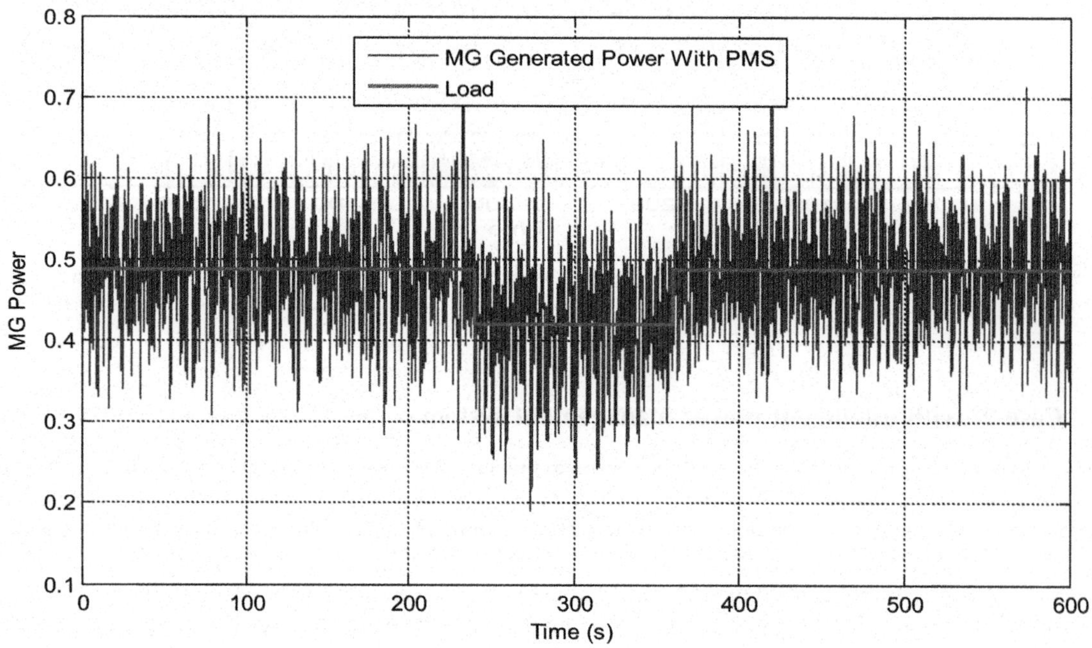

FIGURE 25.11 Microgrid generated power and load with intelligent PMS (*PMS*, Power management system).

25.4.3 Case 3: with combined multistage power management system-fuel cell

In this last scenario, a combined optimal PMS-FC was developed using the HESS as an effective device for robust and smart power management and control in the offshore microgrid. The proposed strategy manages and controls the power of the HESS in an optimal way that ensures frequency stability, power balance, and smooth regulation. Also, the employed PMS-FC can be used to control the seawater load, which can participate in microgrid power management through the water reservoirs as a *PSH* system. According to the presented results in Fig. 25.12, the optimal coordination of both PMS-FC using AI can suppress system fluctuation and smooth the frequency as shown in the red curve. In addition, the power management was also improved, as shown in Figs. 25.13 and 25.14. It can be observed that using the proposed strategy, the generated power in the microgrid can meet the load rapidly with less variation and reduce power losses. The presented results from this scenario prove the validity and superiority of the designed strategy, that show the contribution of the

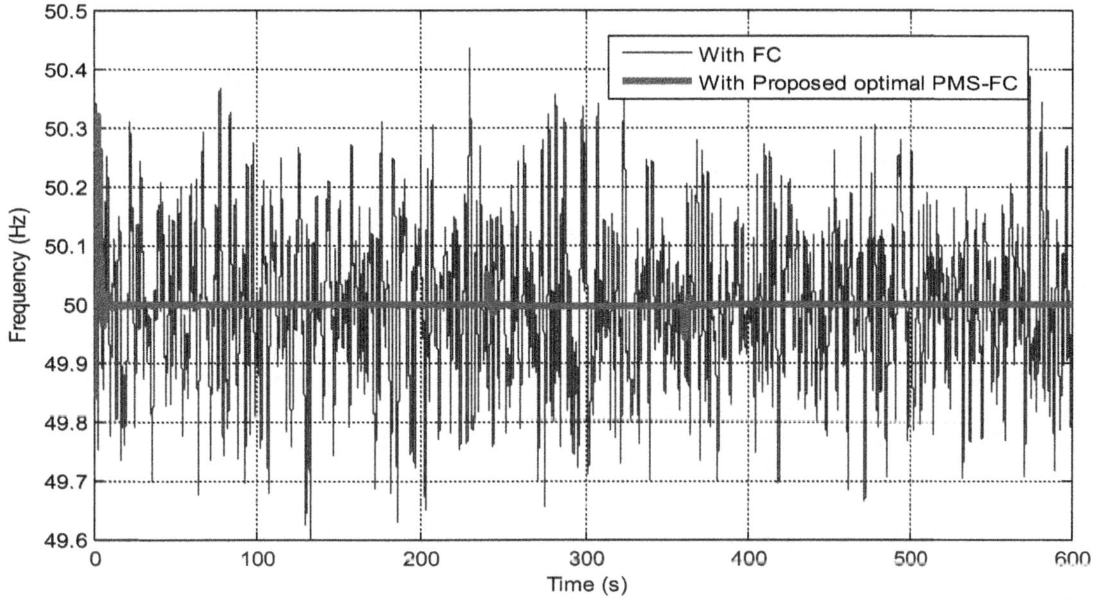

FIGURE 25.12 Microgrid frequency with combined optimal PMS-FC (*FC*, Fuel cell; *PMS*, power management system).

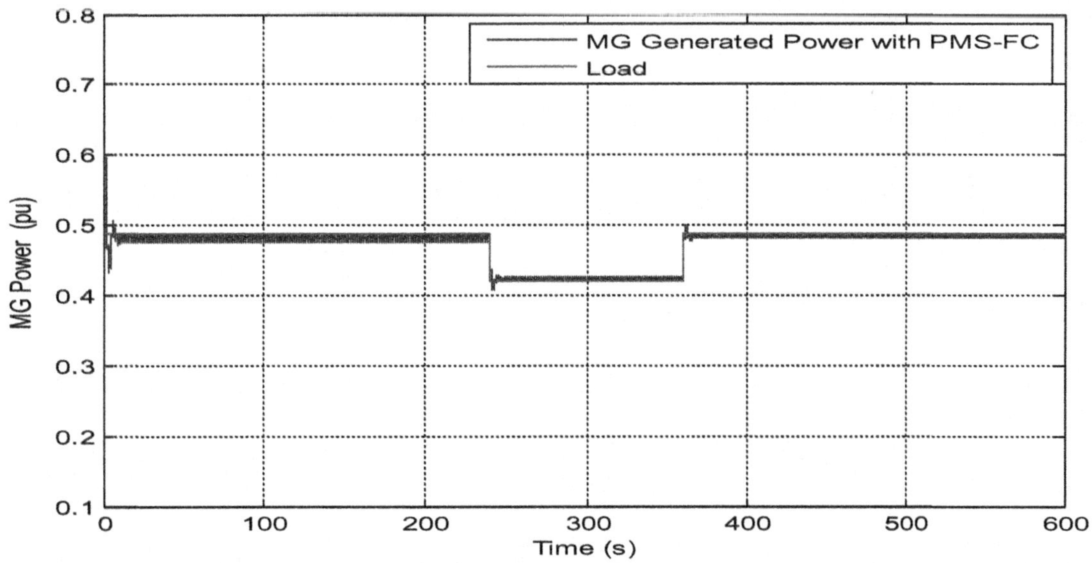

FIGURE 25.13 Microgrid generated power and load with combined optimal PMS-FC (*FC*, Fuel cell; *PMS*, power management system).

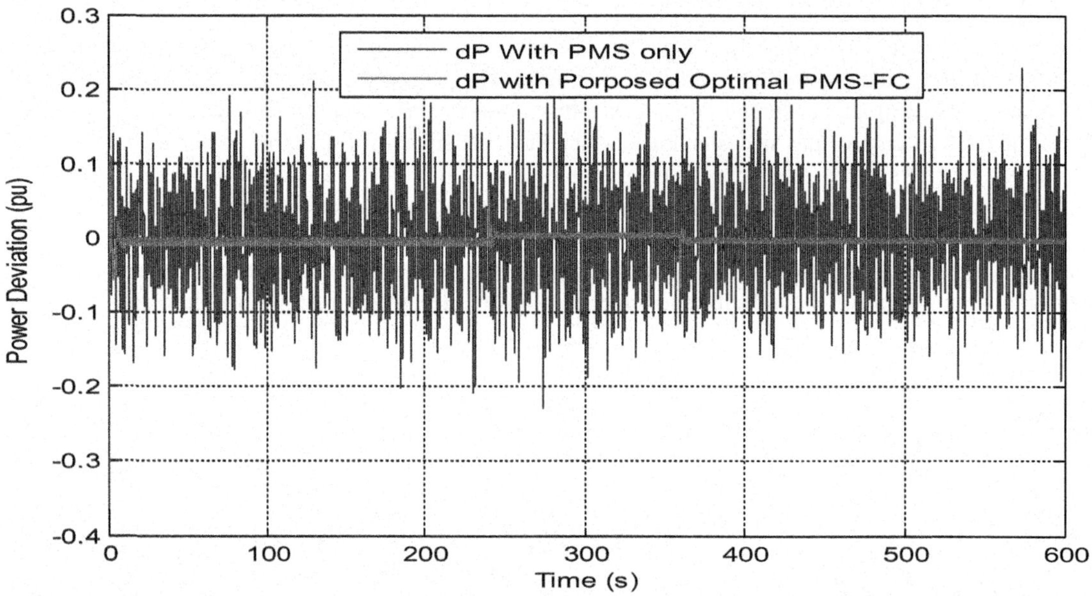

FIGURE 25.14 Microgrid power deviation.

storage system to support microgrid regulation capacity and handle power fluctuations. It can be concluded that using AI and optimization tools can help to design an effective controller scheme that allows a large share of clean energies and enhances the monitoring of offshore platforms and coastal communities-based microgrid by ensuring operational flexibility and backup role in case of overload to avoid load shedding.

After using GWO to solve power management and control problems, several key insights were gained. Firstly, this algorithm show a strong capabilities in balancing between local and global optimum, which helped in effectively navigating the search space to find the best optimal solutions. Overall, the results suggest that GWO is a powerful tool for solving electrical engineering optimization tasks.

25.5 Conclusion

In this chapter, a new combined fuzzy-PID scheme was developed using GWO to enhance active power management and frequency control in a marine microgrid, including tidal power and seawater desalination station. A HESS was installed to support microgrid power management and frequency control during disturbances. The storage system was used to help the secondary frequency regulation loop and ensure an optimal power equilibrium between the generated power through the renewable sources and the consumed power by the load. The GWO was used as an optimization tool for solving the PMS-FC problem coordinated with HESS and HVDC devices. Further, the HVDC transmission link can be used to reduce the fluctuation generated by the offshore wind farm and participate. on the smoothing control of the microgrid frequency. The obtained results show that the proposed combined optimal PMS-FC strategy reduces the system active power and frequency fluctuation more than the independent FC or PMS method. On the other hand, the simulation results show the performance of the GWO algorithm, which minimizes the frequency deviation, active power losses, and ensures stability, even in the most critical case. As future work, this study will be extended to design a multiarea interconnected microgrid including multiple nanogrids system.

References

[1] S.E. Ahmadi, N. Rezaei, A new isolated renewable based multi microgrid optimal energy management system considering uncertainty and demand response, International Journal of Electrical Power & Energy Systems, Elsevier, (2020).

[2] L. Wang, C.Y. Lin, H.Y. Wu, A.V. Prokhorov, Stability analysis of a microgrid system with a hybrid offshore windand ocean energy farm fed to a power grid through an HVDC link, IEEE Transactions on Industry Applications (2017) .

[3] M. Mehrzadi, Y. Terriche, C.L. Su, M.B. Othman, J.C. Vasquez, J.M. Guerrero, Review of dynamic positioning control in maritime microgrid systems, Energies (2020) .

[4] S.W. Ali, M. Sadiq, Y. Terriche, S.A.R. Naqvi, L.Q.N. Hoang, M.U. Mutarraf, et al., Offshore wind farm-grid integration: a reviewon infrastructure, challenges, and grid solutions, Ieee Access (2021) .

[5] M. Di Somma, G. Graditi, E. Heydarian-Forushani, M. Shafie-khah, P. Siano, Stochastic optimal scheduling of distributed energy resources with renewables considering economicand environmental aspects, Renew Energy 116 (2018) 272–287.

[6] A. Mohsenzadeh, C. Pang, M. Haghifam, Determining optimal forming of flexible microgridsin the presence of demand response in smart distribution systems, IEEE Systems Journal 12 (4) (2018) 3315–3323.

[7] S. Choudhury, A comprehensive review on issues, investigations,control and protection trends, technical challenges and future directions for Microgrid technology, International Transactions on Electrical Energy Systems (2020) .

[8] G.K. Venayagamoorthy, R.K. Sharma, P.K. Gautam, A. Ahmadi, Dynamic energy management system for a smart microgrid, IEEE Transactions on Neural Networks and Learning Systems 27 (8) (2016) 1643–1656.

[9] M.S. Mathew, M.L. Kolhe, S.T. Kandukuri, C.W. Omlin, Data driven approach for the management of wind and solar energy integrated electrical distribution network with high penetration of electric vehicles, Journal of Cleaner Production (2023) Elsevier.

[10] W. Liu, P. Zhuang, H. Liang, J. Pengand, Z. Huang, Distributed economic dispatch in microgrids basedon cooperative reinforcement learning, IEEE Transactions on Neural Networks and Learning Systems (2018) .

[11] X.W. Zhang, A. Pirouzi, Flexible energy management of storage-based renewable energy hubs in the electricity and heating networks according to point estimate method, Energy Reports (2024) Elsevier.

[12] V. Calderaro, G. Conio, V. Galdi, G. Massa, A. Piccolo, Active management of renewable energy sources for maximizing power production, International Journal of Electrical Power & Energy Systems (2014) Elsevier.

[13] M.E. Amiryarand, K.R. Pullen, A review of flywheel energy storage systemn technologies and their applications, Applied Sciences (2017) .

[14] X. Luo, J. Wang, M. Dooner, J. Clarke, Overview of current development in electrical energy storage, Applied Energy (2015) Elsevier.

[15] A.R. Dehghani-Sanija, E. Tharumalingam, M.B. Dusseault, R. Fraser, Study of energy storage systems and environmental challenges of batteries, Renewable and Sustainable Energy Reviews (2019) Elsevier.

[16] S. Teleke, M.E. Baran, S. Bhattacharya, A.Q. Huang, Rule-basedcontrol of battery energy storage for dispatching intermittent renewable sources, IEEE Transactions on Sustainable Energy 1 (3) (2010) 117–124.

[17] P.J. Hall, E.J. Bain, Energy-storage technologies and electricity generation, Energy Policy 36 (2008) 4352–4355.

[18] F. Díaz-González, A. Sumper, O. Gomis-Bellmunt, R. Villafáfila-Robles, A review of energy storage technologies for wind power applications, Renewable and Sustainable Energy Reviews 16 (2012) 2154–2171.

[19] C. Xu, B. Xu, Y. Gu, Z. Xiong, J. Sun, X.S. Zhao, Graphene-based electrodes for electro chemical energy storage, Energy & Environmental Science 6 (2013) 1388.

[20] A. Muhtadi, A.M. Saleque, M.A. Mannan, Solar and wind energy based microgrid: study of architecture's potential at coastal areas in Bangladesh, AJSE 2 (2018) 31–36.

[21] M. Zeraati, M.E. Hamedani Golshan, J.M. Guerrero, Distributed control of battery energy storage systems for voltage regulation indistribution networks with high PV penetration, IEEE Transactions onSmart Grid 9 (4) (2018) 3582–3593.

[22] M. Einan, H. Torkaman, M. Pourgholi, Optimized fuzzy-cuckoo controller for active power control of battery energy storage system, photovoltaic, fuel cell and wind turbine in an isolated micro-grid, Batteries (2017) .

[23] H. Bevrani, P.R. Daneshmand, Fuzzy logic-based load-frequency control concerning high penetration of wind turbines, IEEE Systems Journal 6 (2012) 173–180.

[24] Kouba NELY, Menaa M, Hasni M, Boussahoua B, Boudour M. Optimal load frequency control based on hybrid bacterial for aging and particle swarm optimization. In: 2014 IEEE 11th International Multi-Conference on Systems, Signals.

[25] P.K. Ray, S.R. Mohanty, N. Kishor, Proportional–integral controller based small-signal analysis of hybrid distributed generation systems, Energy Conversion and Management 52 (2011) 1943–1954.

[26] M. Kohli, S. Arora, Chaotic grey wolf optimization algorithm for constrained optimization problems, Journal of Computational Design and Engineering 5 (2018) 458–472.

[27] D.C. Das, A. Roy, N. Sinha, GA based frequency controller for solar thermal–diesel–wind hybrid energy generation/energy storage system, International Journal of Electrical Power & Energy Systems 43 (2012) 262–279.

[28] S.K. Pandey, S.R. Mohanty, N. Kishor, J.P. Catalão, Frequency regulation in hybrid power systemsusing particle swarm optimization and linear matrix inequalities based robust controller design, International Journal of Electrical Power & Energy Systems 63 (2014) 887–900.

[29] A.A. El-Fergany, M.A. El-Hameed, Efficient frequency controllers for autonomous two-area hybrid microgrid system using social-spider optimiser, IET Generation, Transmission & Distribution 11 (2017) 637–648.

[30] S. Mirjalili, S.M. Mirjalili, A. Lewis, Grey wolf optimizer, Advances in Engineering Software 69 (2014) 46–61.

[31] M. Balamurugan, K. Narayanan, N. Raghu, G.B. Arjun Kumar, V.N. Trupti, Role of artificial intelligence in smart grid – a mini review, Frontiers in Artificial Intelligence 8 (2025) 1551661. Available from https://doi.org/10.3389/frai.2025.1551661.

[32] J. Jiao, Application and prospect of artificial intelligence in smart grid, IOP Conference Series: Earth and Environmental Science 510 (2020) .

[33] O.A. Omitaomu, H. Niu, Artificial intelligence techniques in smart grid: a survey, Energies 13 (2020) 1–23.

[34] A. McCall, AI-powered smart grids for energy optimization and sustainability, Renewable and Sustainable Energy Reviews 211 (2025) 115251.

[35] Y. Zahraoui, T. Korõtko, A. Rosin, S. Mekhilef, M. Seyedmahmoudian, A. Stojcevski, et al., AI applications to enhance resilience in power systems and microgrids—a review, Sustainability 16 (12) (2024) 4959. Available from https://doi.org/10.3390/su16124959.

[36] I. Alhamrouni, N.H. Abdul Kahar, M. Salem, M. Swadi, Y. Zahroui, D.J. Kadhim, et al., A comprehensive review on the role of artificial intelligence in power system stability, control, and protection: insights and future directions, Applied Sciences 14 (14) (2024) 6214.
[37] U. Pandey, A. Pathak, A. Kumar, S. Mondal, Applications of artificial intelligence in power system operation, control and planning: a review, Clean Energy 7 (6) (2023) 1199–1218. Available from https://doi.org/10.1093/ce/zkad061.
[38] D. Song, G. Shen, C. Huang, Q. Huang, J. Yang, M. Dong, et al., Review on the application of artificial intelligence methods in the control and design of offshore wind power systems, Journal of Marine Science and Engineering 12 (2024) 424. Available from https://doi.org/10.3390/jmse12030424.
[39] M.L.T. Zulu, R.P. Carpanen, R. Tiako, A comprehensive review: study of artificial intelligence optimization technique applications in a hybrid microgrid at times of fault outbreaks, Energies 16 (2023) 1786. Available from https://doi.org/10.3390/en16041786.
[40] K. Saini, M. Saini, A. Kumar, D.K. Saini, Performance analysis and optimization in renewable energy systems: a bibliometric review, Discover Applied Sciences 7 (2025) 178. Available from https://doi.org/10.1007/s42452-025-06585-2.
[41] M. Cavus, Advancing power systems with renewable energy and intelligent technologies: a comprehensive review on grid transformation and integration, Electronics 14 (2025) 1159. Available from https://doi.org/10.3390/electronics14061159.
[42] L. Widayanti, A.N. Afandi, H.W. Herwanto, V.A. Fitria, Metaheuristic optimization in dynamic unit commitment of power systems: current trends and future prospects, JOIV: International Journal of Informatics Visualization 8 (4) (2024) 2261–2272.
[43] T. Senjyu, S. Alkhalaf, A. Mohamed, Nature-inspired algorithms applications to power system optimization, Aswan University Journal of Science and Technology 1 (1) (2021) .
[44] A. Akter, E.I. Zafir, N.H. Dana, R. Joysoyal, S.K. Sarker, L. Li, et al., A review on microgrid optimization with meta-heuristic techniques: scopes, trends and recommendation, Energy Strategy Reviews 51 (2024) 101298. Available from https://doi.org/10.1016/j.esr.2024.101298.
[45] M.A. Judge, V. Franzitta, D. Curto, A. Guercio, G. Cirrincione, H.A. Khattak, A comprehensive review of artificial intelligence approaches for smart grid integration and optimization, Energy Conversion and Management: X 24 (2024) 100724. Available from https://doi.org/10.1016/j.ecmx.2024.100724.
[46] A.M. Nassef, M.A. Abdelkareem, H.M. Maghrabie, A. Baroutaji, Review of metaheuristic optimization algorithms for power systems problems, Sustainability 15 (2023) 9434. Available from https://doi.org/10.3390/su15129434.

Chapter 26

A hybrid grey wolf optimizer and flying squirrel algorithm for single foundation design

Hadi Azizian
Department of Civil Engineering, Mah.C., Islamic Azad University, Mahabad, Iran

26.1 Introduction

All engineering infrastructures, including buildings, bridges, embankments, and similar structures, consist of two main components: the superstructure (the visible part) and the substructure (the buried part). The substructure, commonly referred to as the foundation, acts as a critical link between the superstructure and the ground. Its primary function is to safely transfer the loads from the superstructure to the soil while preventing excessive stress and undesirable settlement in the ground.

Foundation design—encompassing type (e.g., single, strip, and mat foundations) and dimensions—has long been a fundamental topic in geotechnical engineering. Traditional design approaches often relied on trial-and-error methods, where foundation dimensions were iteratively adjusted to meet allowable stress and settlement criteria. If initial dimensions failed to satisfy design constraints, they were modified repeatedly until all requirements were met. This iterative process was not only time-consuming but also neglected construction costs, leading to potentially uneconomical solutions [1,2]. Over the past two decades, advancements in computational tools and structural engineering methodologies have gradually introduced optimization techniques into civil engineering practices [3–5]. These tools have since become indispensable, enabling more efficient, cost-effective, and precise foundation designs while addressing the limitations of conventional methods [2,6].

Among the broad spectrum of computational techniques employed in structural design applications, metaheuristic optimization algorithms have garnered significant attention across various engineering disciplines [7,8]. Unlike classical optimization methods that seek global optima, these algorithms focus on identifying sufficiently high-quality solutions within the search space. Their underlying mechanism primarily relies on two key characteristics: 1- exploration and 2- exploitation [9,10]. Exploration enables the algorithm to explore the entire solution space broadly, ensuring comprehensive coverage of potential design alternatives, while exploitation, conversely, directs the search toward refining the most promising solutions identified during the process.

In recent years, metaheuristic optimization algorithms have been increasingly applied across various civil engineering domains, including the design of reinforced concrete structures, dams, water distribution systems, geotechnical projects, transportation planning, and construction management. These algorithms, primarily inspired by natural processes or developed as enhanced versions of existing techniques, have consistently attracted researchers' attention due to their remarkable efficiency in solving complex problems. Given the rapid advancements in this field, conducting up-to-date research on novel applications of these methods to address engineering challenges is of paramount importance [11,12].

As previously mentioned, shallow foundations constitute a critical component of engineered structures [2]. While considerable advancements have been made in the structural analysis and design techniques for concrete superstructures, insufficient attention has been paid to the cost-efficient structural design of shallow foundations that account for both construction and operational expenses. This oversight is particularly significant given that structural systems cannot achieve optimal performance without well-designed foundations to properly transfer loads to the ground. Consequently,

Grey Wolf Optimizer. DOI: https://doi.org/10.1016/B978-0-443-36624-6.00022-6

appropriate shallow foundation design remains crucial for most construction projects. Since foundation construction typically represents a substantial portion of a project's total costs, developing economically efficient yet safe designs has become a primary concern for engineers. In recent years, this has prompted research initiatives focused on evaluating various metaheuristic algorithms for the optimal design of shallow foundations [13].

The grey wolf optimizer (GWO), proposed by Mirjalili et al. [14], stands out as a highly promising metaheuristic algorithm. Modeled after the cooperative hunting strategies of grey wolf packs, this population-based technique has proven highly effective in solving complex engineering optimization problems. Recent research has further refined GWO through various enhanced variants, boosting its performance [15,16]. In this study, we propose a novel hybrid approach combining GWO with the flying squirrel algorithm [17] and apply it to the optimization of single foundations.

26.2 Problem statement

Fig. 26.1 depicts a single foundation embedded in dry sand with a unit weight $(\gamma) = 18.5\frac{kN}{m^3}$ and an effective friction angle $(\phi') = 35°$. The sand exhibits a Young's modulus $(E) = 50MPa$ and a Poisson's ratio $(\nu) = 0.3$, indicating its stiffness and deformation characteristics under load. Since the groundwater table lies at a significant depth, its influence on the foundation's bearing capacity and settlement is negligible [18]. The foundation is designed to carry a vertical load $(F) = 3000$ kN transmitted from an overlying column. Key geometric parameters governing the foundation's design include its embedment depth (D), width (B), and length (L), as illustrated in Fig. 26.1.

The design of the single foundation must satisfy both ultimate limit state (ULS) and serviceability limit state (SLS) requirements. The ULS criterion ensures stability against soil failure, specified by a required factor of safety ($FS_r = 3$), while the SLS criterion limits settlement to an allowable value ($\delta_r = 25$ mm). Additionally, the foundation depth (D) must adhere to practical constraints: it should exceed a minimum depth to prevent frost damage and remain below a maximum depth to avoid disturbing nearby structures [18].

For a cohesionless, horizontal sand layer under a concentrically applied vertical load, the ultimate bearing capacity (q_{ult}) can be determined using Eq. 26.1. This equation accounts for the foundation's geometry, soil properties, and depth effects [19,20]:

$$q_{ult} = 0.5B\gamma' N_\gamma \xi_{\gamma s} \xi_{\gamma d} + q' N_q \xi_{qs} \xi_{qd} \tag{26.1}$$

where γ' is the effective unit weight to represent the soil's submerged unit weight below the foundation, q' represents the vertical stress at the foundation level due to soil self-weight, N_γ and N_q are the bearing capacity factors, as given bellow:

$$N_\gamma = 2(N_q)\tan\phi' \tag{26.2}$$

$$N_q = (e^{\pi \tan\phi'})\tan^2\left(45 + \frac{\phi'}{2}\right) \tag{26.3}$$

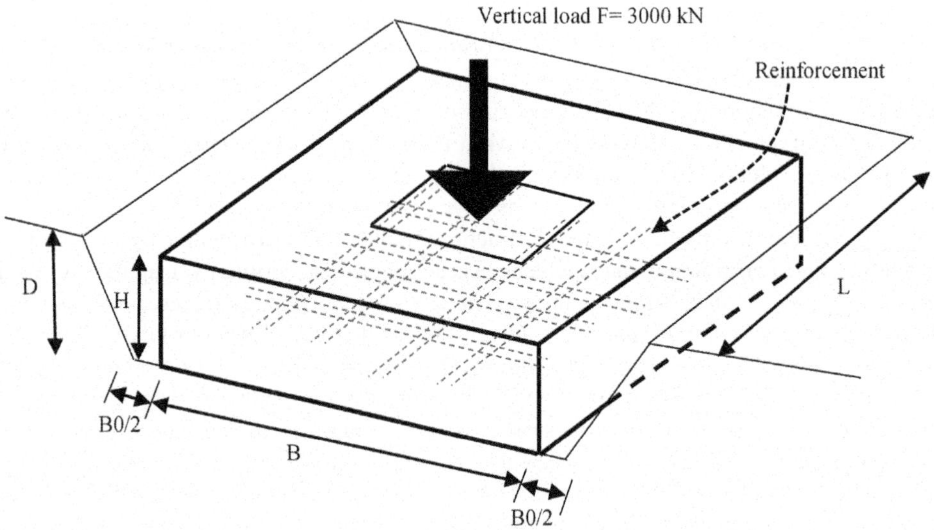

FIGURE 26.1 Single foundation design example.

In Eq. 26.1, $\xi_{\gamma s}$, $\xi_{\gamma d}$, ξ_{qs}, and ξ_{qd} are the shape and depth factors to adjust the bearing capacity for footing geometry and embedment depth (Eqs. 26.4–26.7).

$$\xi_{\gamma s} = 1 - 0.4\left(\frac{B}{L}\right) \tag{26.4}$$

$$\xi_{\gamma d} = 1 \tag{26.5}$$

$$\xi_{qs} = 1 + \left(\frac{B}{L}\right)\tan\phi' \tag{26.6}$$

$$\xi_{qd} = 1 + \tan\phi'\,(1 - \sin\phi')^2\left[\frac{\pi}{180}\tan^{-1}\left(\frac{D}{B}\right)\right] \tag{26.7}$$

The factor of safety (FS) against bearing capacity failure is calculated by comparing the ultimate bearing capacity (q_{ult}) with the applied foundation pressure [19]:

$$FS = \frac{q_{ult}}{\left(\frac{F}{BL}\right)} \tag{26.8}$$

where F is the vertical load, and B and L are the foundation width and length, respectively. The design must satisfy $FS \geq FS_r$ (where $FS_r = 3$ in this case).

The elastic settlement (δ) is estimated using the Poulos and Davis [21] solution:

$$\delta = \frac{F(1 - \nu^2)}{\beta_z E\sqrt{BL}} \tag{26.9}$$

where ν is the Poisson's ratio (0.3 for the given sand), E is the Young's modulus (50 MPa), and β_z is the dimensionless shape factor, as given below [19]:

$$\beta_z = -0.0017\left(\frac{L}{B}\right)^2 + 0.0597\left(\frac{L}{B}\right) + 0.9843 \tag{26.10}$$

The construction cost of a spread footing can be systematically estimated by quantifying material volumes and unit prices for each construction activity. The following framework outlines the calculation of quantities and associated costs for key construction tasks [18].

26.2.1 Quantity calculations

Excavation volume: The excavation volume accounts for the footing dimensions plus overexcavation allowances to accommodate formwork and concreting:

$$Q_e = (B + B_0)(L + L_0)D \tag{26.11}$$

In which B, L, and D are the footing width, length, and depth (m), respectively. B_0 and L_0 are the overexcavation offsets.

Formwork area: Formwork is quantified by its contact area with concrete:

$$Q_f = 2H(B + L) \tag{26.12}$$

where H is the footing height (0.6 m for this 3000 kN load case).

Concrete volume: The concrete volume is derived from the footing's plan dimensions and height:

$$Q_c = B.\ L.\ H \tag{26.13}$$

Reinforcement mass: Reinforcement quantity is assumed proportional to concrete volume:

$$Q_r = k.\ Q_c \tag{26.14}$$

where $k = 29.67\frac{kg}{m^3}$ (empirical coefficient for typical footings).

Backfill volume: Compacted backfill fills the excavated space not occupied by concrete:

$$Q_b = Q_e - Q_c \tag{26.15}$$

TABLE 26.1 Spread the foundation assembly unit price.

Spread foundation (0.91×m 0.91 m×0.30 m deep)	**Units**	**Unit price (USD)**
Excavation	m^3	25.16
Formwork	m^3	51.97
Concrete	m^3	173.96
Reinforcement	kg	2.16
Backfill	m^3	3.97

26.2.2 Cost calculation

The total construction cost combines quantities with unit prices for each task:

$$F = c_b Q_b + c_e Q_e + c_f Q_f + c_r Q_r + c_c Q_c \tag{26.16}$$

where c_e, c_f, c_c, c_r, and c_b represent unit costs (Table 26.1) for excavation, formwork, concrete, reinforcement, and backfill, respectively [18].

26.2.3 Optimization problem

This design framework explicitly incorporates economic considerations through an optimization process aimed at minimizing construction cost (F) by optimizing key design variables, including footing width (B), length (L), and depth (D). The optimization is constrained by both technical and practical requirements: safety factors demand a minimum ULS factor of safety of three, while serviceability requirements limit settlement (δ) to a maximum of 25 mm for SLS. Practical constraints enforce positive values for B and L and restrict D to 0.5–3.0 m to prevent frost damage and adjacent structure interference. The computational process involves calculating total cost (Z) from Eq. (26.16), determining safety factor (FS) and settlement (δ) through Eqs. (26.8) and (26.9) respectively, with parameter βz in Eq. (26.10) being derived from the L/B ratio. This integrated approach systematically balances structural safety, serviceability, and economic efficiency within realistic construction constraints. This optimization framework adopts a classical nonlinear programming representation, expressed mathematically as [18]:

$$minimum\ F = f\,(c_b,\ c_e,\ c_f,\ c_r,\ c_c,\ B,\ L,\ D,\ H,\ B_0,\ L_0)$$

Subject to:

$$FS \geq 3$$

$$\delta \leq 25 \quad mm$$

$$B > 0, \quad L > 0,\ and\ 3m \geq D \geq 0.5m \tag{26.17}$$

26.3 Hybrid grey wolf optimizer

26.3.1 Grey wolf optimizer

The GWO algorithm mimics the social hierarchy and hunting behavior of grey wolves, as introduced in [14]. It employs a leadership-based approach where the alpha (α), beta (β), and delta (δ) wolves—representing the top candidate solutions—guide the remaining omega (ω) wolves in exploring the solution space. The hunting process is divided into three phases:

26.3.1.1 Encircling phase

Modeled by Eqs. (26.18) and (26.19):

$$D = |C \times X_p(t) - X(t)| \tag{26.18}$$

$$X(t+1) = X_p - A \times D \tag{26.19}$$

where X_p and X are the prey location and wolf position vectors, respectively.

$A = 2 \times A \times r_1 - a(t)$ and $C = 2 \times r_2$, r_1 and r_2 are random numbers in [0,1], $a(t) = 2 - (2 \times t)/MaxIter$ is a coefficient which linearly decreases over iterations.

26.3.1.2 Hunting phase

The α, β, and δ wolves (best solutions) guide the ω wolves' movements. Their positions are updated using:

$$D_a = |C_1 \times X_a - X(t)| \tag{26.20}$$

$$D_\beta = |C_2 \times X_\beta - X(t)| \tag{26.21}$$

$$D_\delta = |C_3 \times X_\delta - X(t)| \tag{26.22}$$

$$X_{i1}(t) = X_a(t) - A_{i1} \times D_a(t) \tag{26.23}$$

$$X_{i2}(t) = X_\beta(t) - A_{i2} \times D_\beta(t) \tag{26.24}$$

$$X_{i3}(t) = X_\delta(t) - A_{i3} \times D_\delta(t) \tag{26.25}$$

$$X(t+1) = \frac{X_{i1}(t) + X_{i2}(t) + X_{i3}(t)}{3} \tag{26.26}$$

26.3.1.3 Attacking phase

Triggered when the prey is stationary, simulated via the parameter $a(t)$, which linearly decreases to balance exploration and exploitation.

Following the methodology outlined for GWO, search agents are directed toward the global optimum during the initial half of the optimization iterations. This approach confines the global optimum to a focused region comprising just 10% of the total search space, enabling the FSO to perform intensive local exploration within this narrowed domain. As a result, the FSO achieves significantly enhanced precision and a substantially higher probability of locating the optimal solution compared to a standalone implementation. The subsequent section details the procedural steps for executing the FSO algorithm.

26.3.2 Flying squirrel algorithm (FSO)

Developed in 2019 [17], the flying squirrel optimizer (FSO) mimics the foraging behavior of flying squirrels, specifically their aerial gliding (Lévy flights) and ground movement (Brownian motion) patterns. This bio-inspired algorithm effectively balances global exploration and local exploitation through two distinct computational phases:

26.3.2.1 Aerial exploration phase (Lévy flights)

The algorithm models the squirrels' long-distance gliding using Lévy flight dynamics, represented by the probability density function:

$$L(s, \gamma, \mu) = \begin{cases} \sqrt{\frac{\gamma}{2\pi}} \exp\left[-\frac{\gamma}{2(s-\mu)}\right] \frac{1}{(s-\mu)^{\frac{3}{2}}} & 0 < \mu < s < \infty \\ 0 \;\&\; otherwise, & \end{cases} \tag{26.27}$$

in which μ is the minimum glide distance and γ is the motion scale parameter. The generalized Fourier transform representation:

$$F(k) = \exp[-\alpha\, |k|^\beta] \quad , \quad 0 < \beta \leq 2 \tag{26.28}$$

yields special cases:

- Gaussian distribution when β = 2
- Cauchy distribution when β = 1

26.3.2.2 Local search phase (Brownian motion)

Ground movement is simulated through random walks:

$$S_N = \sum_{i=1}^{N} X_i \tag{26.29}$$

where X_i are N-dimensional random vectors. This creates position updates:

$$S_N = S_{N-1} + X_N \tag{26.30}$$

26.3.2.3 Adaptive control mechanisms and implementation

The FSO algorithm employs two sophisticated adaptive mechanisms to dynamically balance exploration and exploitation:

1. Beta expansion factor: A linear control parameter (slope = 1.05) that systematically increases β during iterations, progressively refining search accuracy by reducing Lévy flight step sizes as optimization progresses.
2. Sigma reduction factor: A nonlinear scaling factor derived from an inverted sigmoid function:

$$SRF_{Iter} = \sqrt{\left(-ln\ (1 - \frac{1}{\sqrt{Iter}})\right)^3} \tag{26.31}$$

which adaptively modulates step sizes to enhance local search precision while maintaining global exploration capabilities. The implementation follows a structured iterative process:

Step 1: Initialization: Generate initial population and solution matrices

Step 2: Dual-phase optimization:

Apply Lévy flights to 50% of agents for global exploration

Execute Brownian motion for the remaining agents for local refinement

Step 3: Solution management:

Evaluate and sort solutions by fitness

Update population matrices

Step 4: Termination: Repeat until convergence thresholds are satisfied

This carefully designed balance between stochastic exploration and precision refinement contributes to the algorithm's robust performance across diverse optimization landscapes.

26.3.3 Hybrid flying squirrel optimizer-based grey wolf optimizer

As demonstrated in prior research [15,22] and detailed in Section 26.3.1, the GWO exhibits exceptional global search capabilities, rapidly exploring the entire feasible solution space. This characteristic enables GWO to effectively identify promising regions containing global optima during initial iterations. However, the algorithm's computational efficiency is hampered by its intensive objective function evaluations during the exploitation phase, where excessive computational resources are devoted to refining solutions within optimal regions.

Complementary to GWO, the FSO, as presented in Section 26.3.2, demonstrates superior precision in local space exploitation. Recognizing these complementary strengths, we propose the novel grey wolf optimizer flying squirrel algorithm (GWOFSO) hybrid algorithm that strategically combines:

1. GWO for global exploration (first 50% of iterations)
2. FSO for precise local exploitation (remaining 50% of iterations)

The proposed GWOFSO algorithm strategically combines GWO and FSO through a two-phase optimization framework. During the initial exploration phase (first 50% iterations), GWO performs global search using uniformly distributed agents across the feasible space, generated through:

$$S = Uniform\ random\ \{L_b, H_b\}^{N\times d} \tag{26.32}$$

where L_b and H_b represent domain bounds, N the population size, and d the problem dimensionality. Agent fitness evaluation populates a comprehensive matrix (GM) that ranks solutions by cost, with the top 10% guiding subsequent movements through spiral updating mechanisms. The exploitation phase (remaining iterations) employs FSO within a dynamically contracted search space centered on the best solution (ρ-adjusted bounds):

$$\begin{cases} L'_b = \rho(L_b + 0.45(H_b - L_b)) \\ H'_b = \rho(L_b + 0.55(H_b - L_b)) \end{cases} \tag{26.33}$$

where the contraction factor $\rho = 1.1 - \left(\frac{It}{It_{max}}\right)$ progressively reduces the search region from 60% to 10% of the original space. The algorithm maintains dual exploration:

1. Intensive local search (90% agents) around the global best (Squirrel1)
2. Global monitoring (10% agents) via a secondary optimum (Squirrel2) from the GM matrix median

This adaptive strategy enables continuous refinement while preserving discovery capability—any superior solution outside the contracted space automatically redefines the search region. The approach effectively balances GWO's rapid global scanning with FSO's precise local optimization, overcoming individual algorithm limitations through synergistic cooperation.

26.3.4 Computational complexity of GWOFSO

The computational complexity of population-based metaheuristics is predominantly determined by three factors: the number of iterations (It_{max}), the population size (N), and the cost of evaluating the objective function (C(f)) for a problem of dimension d. Accordingly, the computational complexities of TWO and FSO are calculated as follows:

$$CC_{GWO} = C\,(It_{max} \times N \times d) \tag{26.34}$$

$$CC_{FSO} = C\,(It_{max} \times (N \times d + N\ Log\ N)) \tag{26.35}$$

The hybrid GWOFSO operates in two sequential phases. The first phase runs GWO for $\frac{It_{max}}{2}$ iterations, and the second phase runs FSO for another iteration. Therefore its total computational cost is the sum of the costs of half the iterations of GWO and half the iterations of FSO:

$$CC_{GWOFSO} = C\,(It_{max} \times N \times d) + C\,(It_{max} \times (N \times d + N\ Log\ N)) \quad = C\left(It_{max} \times (N \times d + \frac{N\ Log\ N}{2}\right)) \tag{26.36}$$

Based on the above formulations, although the theoretical complexity of the hybrid approach is higher than that of GWO due to the complexity of FSO, its faster convergence and the superior optimal solution obtained justify this added complexity. In other words, achieving a better objective function value in fewer iterations can compensate for the higher computational cost per iteration.

26.4 Results and discussion

Before applying the proposed algorithm to foundation design, its performance was first validated by solving several unimodal test benchmark problems. The obtained results were compared with those of existing optimization algorithms, including particle swarm optimization [23], differential evolution [24], whale optimization algorithm [25], and original GWO and FSO. It should be noted that these benchmark problems are well-known CEC2017 test functions [26]. Further details about these functions can be found in Table 26.2 and Fig. 26.2.

TABLE 26.2 Unimodal test functions.

Function	Dim	Range	f_{min}
$f_1(x) = \sum_{i=1}^{n} x_i^2$	100	[-100,100]	0
$f_2(x) = \sum_{i=1}^{n} \|x_i\| + \prod_{i=1}^{n} \|x_i\|$	100	[-10,10]	0
$f_3(x) = \sum_{i=1}^{n} \left(\sum_{j-1}^{i} x_j\right)^2$	100	[-100,100]	0
$f_4(x) = \max\{\|x_i\|, 1 < i < n\}$	100	[-100,100]	0
$f_5(x) = \sum_{i=1}^{n-1} [100(x_{i+1} - x_i^2)^2 + (x_i - 1)^2]$	100	[-30,30]	0
$f_6(x) = \sum_{i=1}^{n} ([x_i + 0.5])^2$	100	[-100,100]	0
$f_7(x) = \sum_{i=1}^{n} ix_i^4 + random[0,1)$	100	[-1.28,1.28]	0

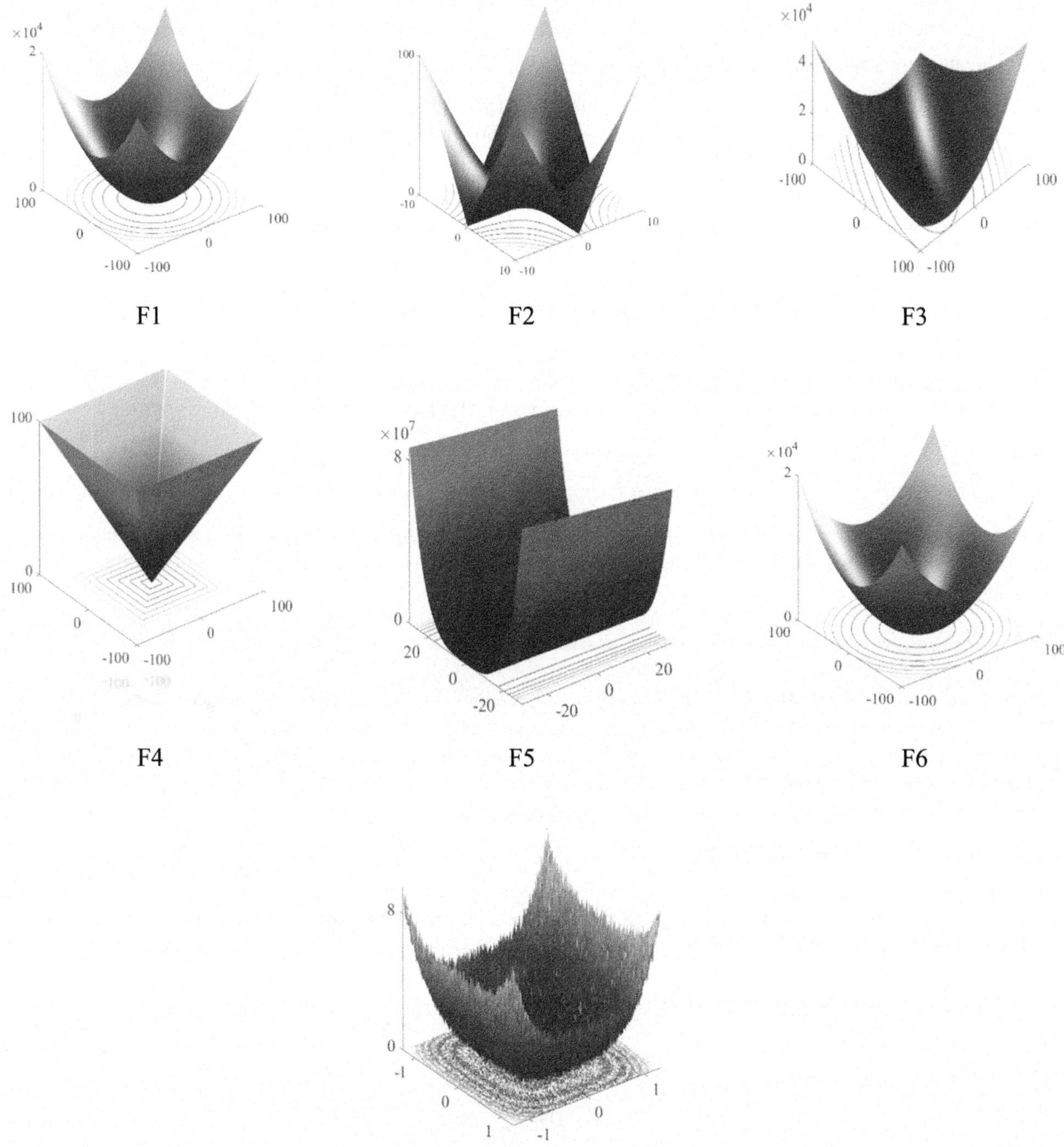

FIGURE 26.2 3D schematic representations of benchmark functions.

26.4.1 Results of hybrid grey wolf optimizer-flying squirrel optimizer on the benchmark problems

For a fair comparison, the population size of the algorithms was set to 50, and the maximum number of iterations was set to 1000. The parameter settings used for the various algorithms are provided in Table 26.3, following the suggested values from relevant literature.

Table 26.4 presents the results obtained from running the algorithms over 30 independent runs, including the mean and standard deviation of the solutions. The experimental results for unimodal benchmark functions (Table 26.2) demonstrate

TABLE 26.3 Parameters setting of algorithms.

Algorithm	Parameter	Value
PSO	Inertia weight	Linear decrease from 0.9 to 0.1.
	Velocity range	0.1 times the variable range
	Social and cognitive factors	C1=2, C2=2
DE	Step size	60
	Scaling factor	0.5
WOA	Fluctuation range	Decreased from 2 to 0
	Coefficient of the logarithmic spiral shape	1
GWO	Coefficient vector	0 to 2
FSO	Beta expansion factor	1.05

DE, Differential evolution; *GWO*, grey wolf optimizer; *PSO*, particle swarm optimization; *WOA*, whale optimization algorithm.

TABLE 26.4 A comparison of the optimization and unimodal benchmark function results obtained from GWOFSO and other algorithms.

		f_1	f_2	f_3	f_4	f_5	f_6	f_7
GWOFSO	Best	**0**	**0**	**0**	**0**	35.46215	0	3.47E-04
	Average	**0**	**0**	**0**	**0**	49.77105	12.56163	4.17E-03
	Std. dev.	**0**	**0**	**0**	**0**	5.3892	3.9069	7.13E-05
GWO	Best	22302.92	111.8398	104196.66	92.3394	**1.55E-01**	**0**	343.5464
	Average	23668.92	196.5413	312351.19	94.3534	**3.9983**	**1.23e-32**	592.5503
	Std. dev.	5670.3901	55.7166	91541.403	7.91E-01	**1.14E-02**	**5.08E-45**	60.4792
FSO	Best	3.40E-173	1.30E-110	550008.9	92.2347	97.79243	4.67E-01	**1.07E-04**
	Average	7.65E-152	8.83E-08	805663.1	96.9037	162.551	5.59E-01	**3.55E-02**
	Std. dev.	6.70E-167	5.40E-12	1943.567	4.657896	3.294631	1.37E-02	**6.97E-04**
WOA	Best	7.63E-04	3.31E-08	7.52E-03	4.4366	2.93E-01	6.58E-01	9.1065
	Average	3.98E-03	8.72E-07	7.95E-02	8.4175	1.1596	1.2355	22.6517
	Std. dev.	6.71E-03	3.54E-09	3.98E-04	5.3128	8.16E-02	7.32E-02	5.27E-01
DE	Best	19.197	345.2465	24713.19	26.4096	974.2601	25.9214	1.44E-01
	Average	21.2041	372.9827	28293.98	38.5091	978.0242	26.9797	3.16E-01
	Std. dev.	5.24E-01	9.7022	27.4690	6.2539	1.8346	3.81E-01	7.10E-02
PSO	Best	1781.9433	1.16E-01	193954.55	83.5697	21154469	8024.9211	25.7862
	Average	8762.6794	8.11E-01	242781.04	88.7487	64897033	8360.1236	41.4291
	Std. dev.	4381.0134	3.61E-03	12705.45	1.67820	133250	116.8240	5.4615

DE, Differential evolution; *FSO*, flying squirrel optimizer; *GWO*, grey wolf optimizer; *PSO*, particle swarm optimization; *WOA*, whale optimization algorithm.
Note: The best results are shown in bold.

that the GWOFSO algorithm achieved perfect optimization accuracy, returning 0 as the best, mean, and standard deviation values for functions f_1 through f_4 in 100-dimensional space. This represents the theoretically ideal solution for these test functions. Notably, comparative analysis revealed that:

- The GWO algorithm outperformed other methods on functions f_5 and f_6
- FSO produced superior results for function f_7

Despite these specialized performances, GWOFSO maintained highly competitive results across all test functions. This consistent performance is particularly significant because:

1. It demonstrates robust exploration capabilities in high-dimensional search spaces
2. The zero-variance results indicate exceptional solution stability
3. The algorithm shows balanced performance without requiring function-specific tuning

The findings suggest GWOFSO's strong potential for global optimization tasks, particularly in applications requiring reliable convergence to theoretical optima. The algorithm's exploration-phase effectiveness appears comparable to, and in some cases superior to, established metaheuristics such as GWO and FSO. Moreover, the convergence graphs for solution results and the search paths of both the best and worst agents over 1000 iterations are shown in Fig. 26.3. A key

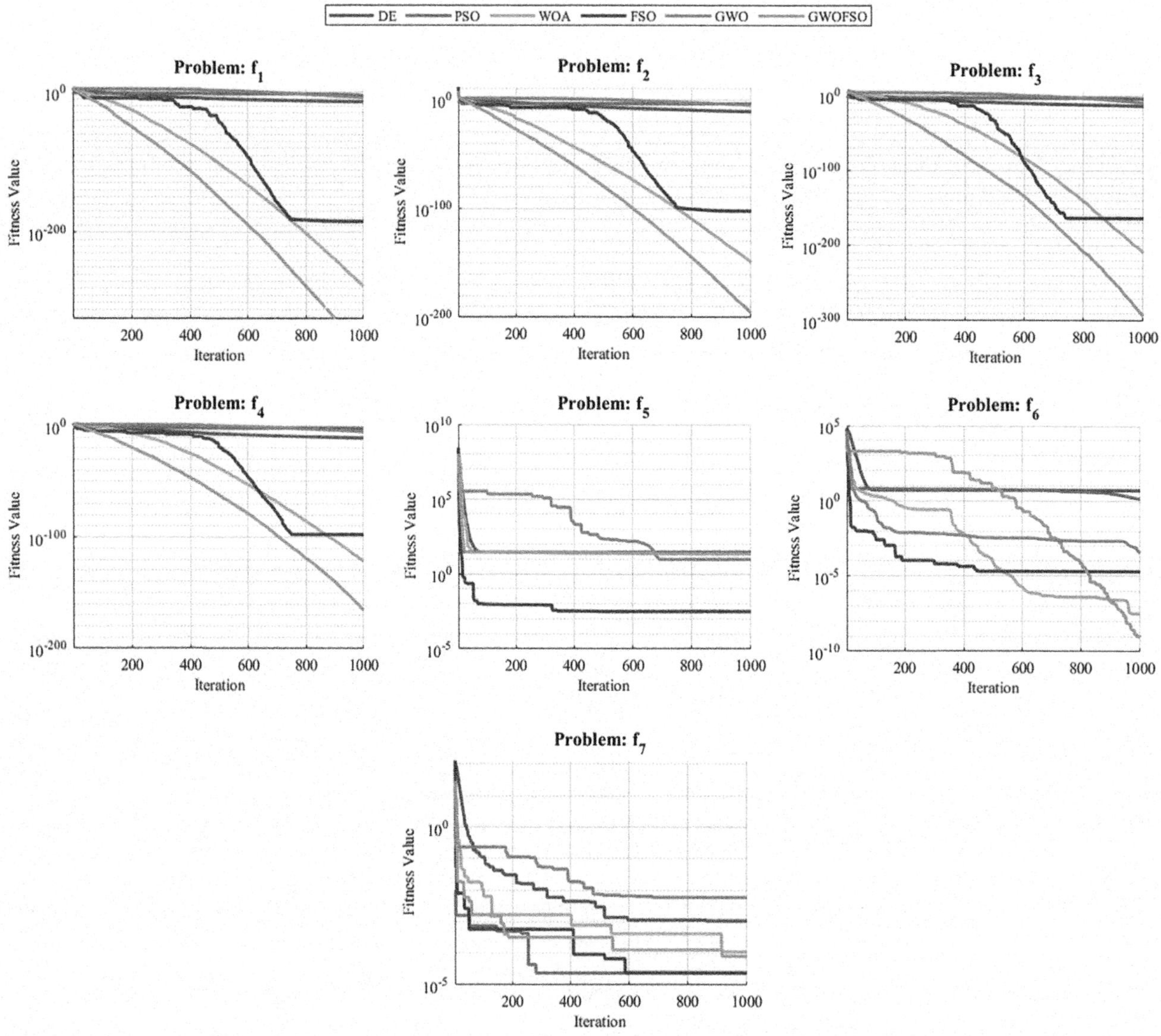

FIGURE 26.3 The convergence curves of the hybrid GWOFSO and other algorithms on benchmark functions.

TABLE 26.5 Results of the Wilcoxon test for benchmark problems.

Algorithm	Functions						
	f_1	f_2	f_3	f_4	f_5	f_6	f_7
GWOFSO	N/A	N/A	N/A	N/A	N/A	N/A	N/A
GWO	0.31	0.31	0.31	0.31	0.094	0.31	0.094
FSO	0.31	0.31	0.31	0.31	0.31	0.31	0.31
WOA	0.31	0.31	0.31	0.31	0.31	0.31	0.31
DE	0.31	0.31	0.31	0.31	0.31	0.31	0.31
PSO	0.31	0.31	0.31	0.31	0.31	0.31	0.31

DE, Differential evolution; *FSO*, flying squirrel optimizer; *GWO*, grey wolf optimizer; *PSO*, particle swarm optimization; *WOA*, whale optimization algorithm.

TABLE 26.6 A comparison of the optimization foundation problem results obtained from GWOFSO and other algorithms.

	WOA	DE	PSO	GWO	GWOFSO	FSO
Average	1084.531	1315.561	1090.305	1091.186	1083.311	1083.811
Std. dev.	1.399706	136.8236	3.241951	18.15259	5.98E-11	0.674215
Best	1083.355	1162.610	1083.684	1083.624	1083.311	1083.312

DE, Differential evolution; *FSO*, flying squirrel optimizer; *GWO*, grey wolf optimizer; *PSO*, particle swarm optimization; *WOA*, whale optimization algorithm.

observation from these graphs is that the GWOFSO method achieved a highly effective solution during the global search phase. The graphs illustrate how promising solutions are explored in the initial iterations of the algorithm. Furthermore, they highlight the search agents' inclination to approach the optimal position. Following this, the feasible space is utilized more effectively by concentrating on the optimal position and decreasing the speed through the applied coefficients, which significantly enhances the algorithm's exploitation process.

For better evaluation, the Wilcoxon test was performed between the results of the proposed algorithm and other algorithms (see Table 26.5). As can be seen, for most of the solved problems, the performance difference of the proposed algorithm was statistically significant ($P < .05$), indicating its superiority. However, in comparison with GWO for functions f_5 and f_7, the results indicate no significant difference. Overall, based on this statistical analysis, the accuracy of the proposed algorithm is confirmed.

26.4.2 Results of hybrid grey wolf optimizer-flying squirrel optimizer on the foundation problem

Following performance evaluation and verification of the proposed algorithm through mathematical benchmark functions and comparative analysis with other metaheuristic approaches, this section demonstrates the algorithm's application results for optimal single foundation design. Table 26.6 provides a comprehensive overview of the mean values, standard deviations, and optimal objective function values derived from 30 independent algorithm runs. The results highlight a notable range in the best values achieved, spanning from \$1083 to \$1163. Notably, the proposed algorithm stands out, delivering the optimal objective function value of \$1083.311. This is closely followed by the FSO algorithm, which achieves a value of \$1083.312. In contrast, the DE algorithm records the highest objective function value at \$1162.612.

Moreover, the proposed algorithm not only secures the best objective function value but also demonstrates exceptional consistency, reflected in its lowest mean and standard deviation values across all 30 runs, recorded at \$1083.311 and \$5.9

E-11, respectively. These figures underscore not only the superior performance of the proposed method but also its minimal variability, reinforcing its robustness compared to other algorithms. For context, the mean and standard deviation for the FSO and GWO algorithms are $1083.811 with a standard deviation of 0.67, and $1091.186 with a standard deviation of 18.152, respectively.

Additionally, Fig. 26.4 presents the convergence curves of the algorithms for the given problem. As can be observed, despite the complexity of the problem, the proposed algorithm has successfully obtained the optimal solution in the initial iterations, significantly reducing the computational load of the model. A deeper analysis reveals that the FSO algorithm showcases remarkable robustness and precision. Its integration with the GWO algorithm has significantly enhanced the accuracy of the latter, illustrating the potent synergistic effects that can arise from combining these methodologies. This collaboration not only amplifies their individual strengths but also contributes to more reliable and effective outcomes in practical applications.

Wang and Kulhawy [18] solved the aforementioned problem using a gradient-based approach alongside a trial-and-error method (see Table 26.7). Their proposed optimization technique achieved a significant reduction in design costs by 31% and 5% compared to the two traditional trial-and-error approaches. The best cost obtained through their optimization was $1086, while the traditional methods resulted in costs of $1421 and $1143, respectively. The table presents a comparative analysis of four design configurations based on their dimensions (width, length, depth) and associated costs. The GWOFSO option emerges as the most cost-effective solution, with dimensions of 1.37 m (width), 1.83 m (length), and 2.32 m (depth), yielding the lowest cost of $1083. Option 1, with comparable dimensions (1.86 m width, 2.3 m length, 1.38 m depth) and a marginally higher cost ($1086), demonstrates the system's low sensitivity to minor geometric variations. In contrast, Option 2, with larger planar dimensions (2.6 m width and length) and a shallower depth (0.6 m), incurs a 31% cost increase ($1421), underscoring the substantial impact of horizontal dimensions on costs. Option 3, featuring a greater depth (2 m) and intermediate width/length (1.7 m, 2.4 m), exhibits a 5.5% higher cost ($1143) relative to GWOFSO, confirming that depth has a more moderate influence on overall expenses.

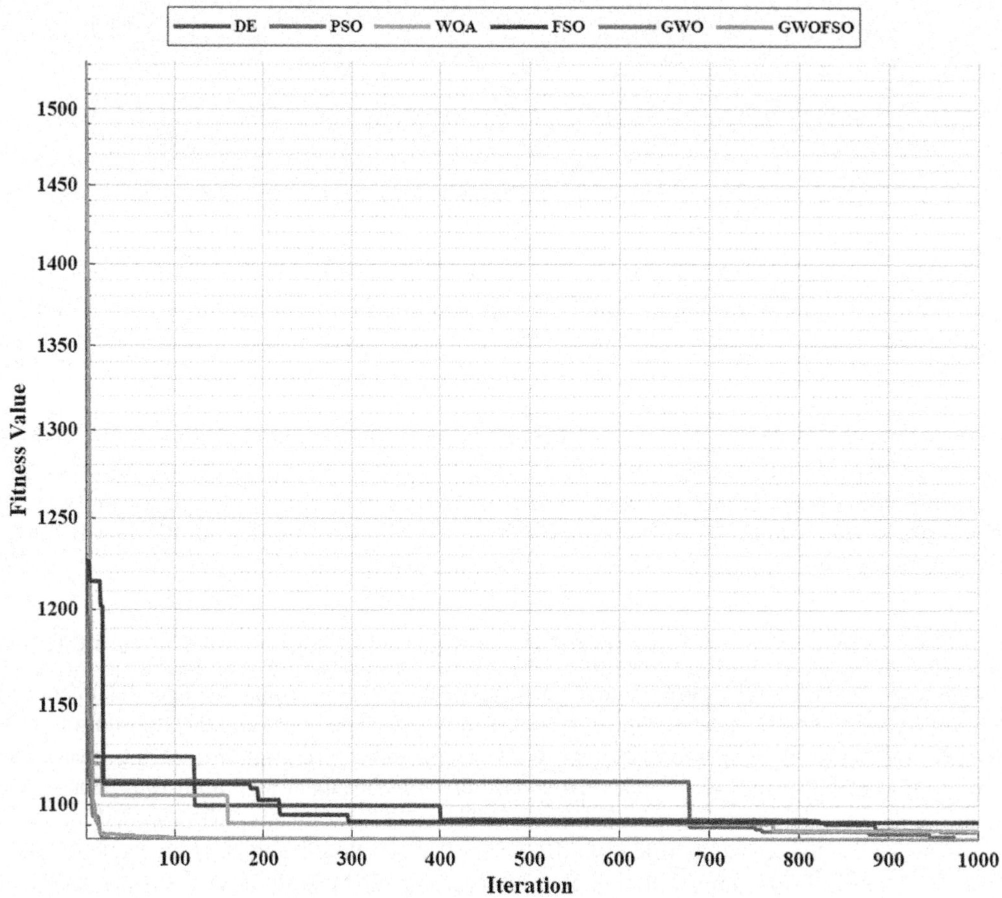

FIGURE 26.4 The convergence curves of the hybrid GWOFSO and other algorithms on the foundation problem.

TABLE 26.7 Comparison results of this study and Wang and Kulhawy [18].

References	Model	Width, B (m)	Length, L (m)	Depth, D (m)	Cost (USD)
This study	GWOFSO	1.37	1.83	2.32	1083
[18]	Option 1	1.86	2.3	1.38	1086
	Option 2	2.6	2.6	0.6	1421
	Option 3	1.7	2.4	2	1143

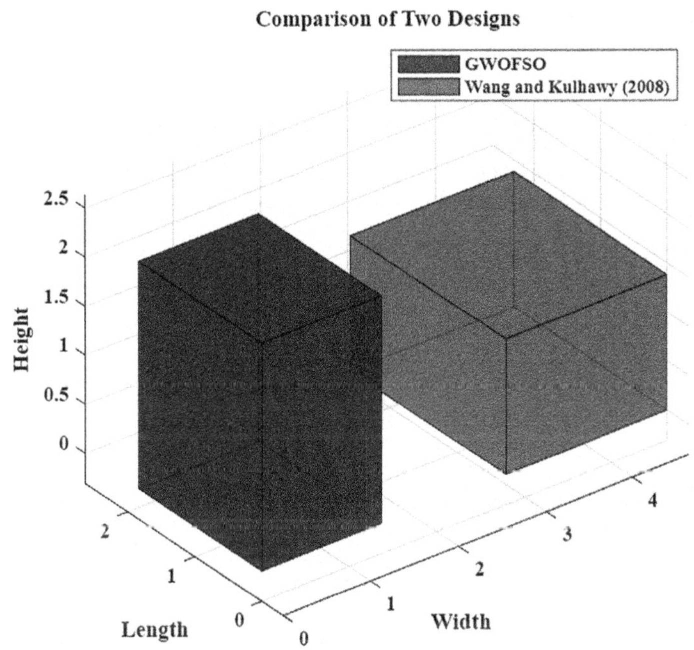

FIGURE 26.5 Optimal foundation design obtained using the hybrid GWOFSO method and Wang and Kulhawy's approach [18].

These results not only validate the superiority of Wang and Kulhawy's [18] method in cost reduction but also align the table's findings with prior research. Furthermore, the comparison highlights the optimal balance of dimensions and cost achieved by the GWOFSO configuration, while revealing critical sensitivities of costs to specific geometric adjustments. The excavation volume in this design is 5.82 m^3, while in the Wang and Kulhawy [18] design, it is 5.90 m^3. For better visualization of the differences between the two designs, Fig. 26.5 shows a 3D schematic of both. As is evident, the proposed GWOFSO design features greater height but smaller width and length. In addition to reducing construction and foundation costs, this design requires 1.5% less excavation volume compared to the Wang and Kulhawy [18] design.

Despite the acceptable performance of all selected algorithms in optimizing the single foundation problem, the results underscore that the choice of an appropriate optimization algorithm is critical for achieving superior solutions. This is clearly demonstrated by the enhanced performance of the hybrid GWO-FSO algorithm. The primary reason for this improvement lies in the hybrid algorithm's superior exploration capability. The complex and multimodal search space of this specific problem easily traps standalone algorithms in local optima. In contrast, the synergistic combination of GWO and FSO created a more robust search strategy, allowing it to escape local traps and converge toward a more global optimum. This explains why the other algorithms, while competent, were consistently outperformed.

The results revealed that despite the strong mechanism inherent in GWO, its exploration phase is insufficient when dealing with highly complex and constrained search spaces such as the problem under investigation. This case study demonstrates that its performance can be enhanced by integrating an algorithm with complementary strengths, such as

FSO, which emphasizes exploration. This finding is valuable for the broader field of metaheuristic algorithms, as it provides a clear pattern for improving other population-based methods by identifying their weaknesses in solving real-world problems and reinforcing them to achieve a more balanced and powerful search performance.

26.5 Conclusion

This study developed the hybrid GWOFSO algorithm to solve various optimization problems. The algorithm combines the global search capabilities of GWO with the local search advantages of FSO. In the proposed approach, the first 50% of iterations utilize GWO for global exploration, while the remaining iterations employ FSO for local refinement. To evaluate the algorithm's performance in handling complex problems, we tested it on seven benchmark unimodal functions with fixed dimensions. Comparative analysis demonstrated GWOFSO's superiority over GWO and FSO in solving four different problems. Subsequently, the algorithm was applied to single foundation optimization problems, where it effectively solved this challenging engineering problem. However, despite promising results in single foundation design, the current approach doesn't account for uncertainty factors, which may affect the solution reliability when dealing with real-world uncertainties. Thus it is recommended that future research focus on extending the proposed multiobjective algorithm model and applying it to the reliability-based design of foundations.

Declaration of generative AI and AI-assisted technologies in the writing process

During the preparation of this work, the author(s) used ChatGPT in order to proofread and improve the writing. After using this tool/service, the author(s) reviewed and edited the content as needed and take(s) full responsibility for the content of the publication.

References

[1] L. Hong, X. Wang, W. Zhang, Y. Li, R. Zhang, C. Chen, System reliability-based robust design of deep foundation pit considering multiple failure modes, Geoscience Frontiers 15 (2024). Available from https://doi.org/10.1016/j.gsf.2023.101761.

[2] A.R. Kashani, M. Gandomi, C.V. Camp, A.H. Gandomi, Optimum design of shallow foundation using evolutionary algorithms, Soft Computing 24 (2020). Available from https://doi.org/10.1007/s00500-019-04316-5.

[3] J. Jafari-Asl, Y. Dong, Y. Li, Advanced computational strategy for damage identification of offshore jacket platforms, Civil Engineering Design 7 (2025) 36–48. Available from https://doi.org/10.1002/cend.202400032.

[4] S. Khastar, F. Bashirizadeh, J. Jafari-Asl, N. Safaeian Hamzehkolaei, Predicting the cooling and heating loads of energy efficient buildings: a hybrid machine learning approach, Cluster Computing 28 (2025) 323. Available from https://doi.org/10.1007/s10586-024-04993-4.

[5] S. Afzali Ahmadabadi, J. Jafari-Asl, E. Banifakhr, E.H. Houssein, M.E.A. Ben Seghier, Risk-based design optimization of contamination detection sensors in water distribution systems: application of an improved whale optimization algorithm, Water (Basel) 15 (2023). Available from https://doi.org/10.3390/w15122217.

[6] M. Khajehzadeh, S. Keawsawasvong, M.L. Nehdi, Effective hybrid soft computing approach for optimum design of shallow foundations, Sustainability (Switzerland) 14 (2022). Available from https://doi.org/10.3390/su14031847.

[7] H. Zhao, M. Zhao, C. Zhu, Reliability-based optimization of geotechnical engineering using the artificial bee colony algorithm, KSCE Journal of Civil Engineering 20 (2016). Available from https://doi.org/10.1007/s12205-015-0117-6.

[8] D.M. Pedroso, FORM reliability analysis using a parallel evolutionary algorithm, Structural Safety 65 (2017). Available from https://doi.org/10.1016/j.strusafe.2017.01.001.

[9] H. Jia, H. Rao, C. Wen, S. Mirjalili, Crayfish optimization algorithm, Artificial Intelligence Review 56 (2023). Available from https://doi.org/10.1007/s10462-023-10567-4.

[10] M. Rahmanshahi, J. Jafari-Asl, M. Fathi-Moghadam, S. Ohadi, S. Mirjalili, Metaheuristic learning algorithms for accurate prediction of hydraulic performance of porous embankment weirs, Applied Soft Computing 151 (2024). Available from https://doi.org/10.1016/j.asoc.2023.111150.

[11] Y. Meraihi, A. Ramdane-Cherif, D. Acheli, M. Mahseur, Dragonfly algorithm: a comprehensive review and applications, Neural Computing and Applications 32 (2020) 16625–16646. Available from https://doi.org/10.1007/s00521-020-04866-y.

[12] J. Jafari-Asl, M.E.A. Seghier, Ben, S. Ohadi, J. Correia, J. Barroso, Reliability analysis based improved directional simulation using Harris Hawks optimization algorithm for engineering systems, Engineering Failure Analysis 135 (2022) 106148.

[13] A. Arabali, M. Khajehzadeh, S. Keawsawasvong, A.H. Mohammed, B. Khan, An adaptive tunicate swarm algorithm for optimization of shallow foundation, IEEE Access 10 (2022). Available from https://doi.org/10.1109/ACCESS.2022.3164734.

[14] S. Mirjalili, S.M. Mirjalili, A. Lewis, Grey wolf optimizer, Advances in Engineering Software 69 (2014) 46–61.

[15] M.H. Nadimi-Shahraki, S. Taghian, S. Mirjalili, An improved grey wolf optimizer for solving engineering problems, Expert Systems with Applications 166 (2021). Available from https://doi.org/10.1016/j.eswa.2020.113917.

[16] H.M. Mohammed, Z.K. Abdul, T.A. Rashid, A. Alsadoon, N. Bacanin, A new K-means grey wolf algorithm for engineering problems, World Journal of Engineering 18 (2021) 630–638. Available from https://doi.org/10.1108/WJE-10-2020-0527.
[17] G. Azizyan, F. Miarnaeimi, M. Rashki, N. Shabakhty, Flying squirrel optimizer (FSO): a novel SI-based optimization algorithm for engineering problems, Iranian Journal of Optimization 11 (2019) .
[18] Y. Wang, F.H. Kulhawy, Economic design optimization of foundations, Journal of Geotechnical and Geoenvironmental Engineering 134 (2008). Available from https://doi.org/10.1061/(asce)1090-0241(2008)134:8(1097).
[19] R.V. Whitman, F.E. Richart, Design procedures for dynamically loaded foundations, Journal of the Soil Mechanics and Foundations Division 93 (1967). Available from https://doi.org/10.1061/jsfeaq.0001050.
[20] W. Chen, Q. Liu, E. Wang, The effect of the water table on the bearing capacity of a shallow foundation, Applied Sciences (Switzerland) 12 (2022). Available from https://doi.org/10.3390/app12136571.
[21] H.G. Poulos, E.H. Davis, Elastic solutions for soil and rock mechanics. Textbook. Figs, Tabls, Refs, International Journal of Rock Mechanics and Mining Sciences & Geomechanics Abstracts 11 (1974). Available from https://doi.org/10.1016/0148-9062(74)91768-9.
[22] S. Mirjalili, How effective is the grey wolf optimizer in training multi-layer perceptrons, Applied Intelligence 43 (2015) 150–161. Available from https://doi.org/10.1007/s10489-014-0645-7.
[23] J. Kennedy, R. Eberhart, Particle swarm optimization, Proceedings of ICNN'95-International Conference on Neural Networks 4 (1995) 1942–1948.
[24] R. Storn, K. Price, Differential Evolution - A Simple and Efficient Adaptive Scheme for Global Optimization Over Continuous Spaces (1995) .
[25] S. Mirjalili, A. Lewis, The whale optimization algorithm, Advances in Engineering Software 95 (2016) 51–67.
[26] N.H. Awad, M.Z. Ali, P.N. Suganthan, Ensemble sinusoidal differential covariance matrix adaptation with Euclidean neighborhood for solving CEC2017 benchmark problems, IEEE Congress on Evolutionary Computation, CEC 2017 - Proceedings, 2017 (2017). Available from https://doi.org/10.1109/CEC.2017.7969336.

Chapter 27

A comparative analysis of the grey wolf optimizer and genetic algorithms

Mohammad Jahani Moghaddam
Department of Electrical Engineering, Lan.C., Islamic Azad University, Langarud, Iran

27.1 Introduction

In today's complex world, optimization algorithms are essential tools for finding optimal or near-optimal solutions in large search spaces with complex objective functions. Traditional mathematical optimization techniques are often inefficient in dealing with the inherent nonlinearity, multimodality, high dimensionality, and constraints of real-world challenges in problems such as aerodynamic structure design, manufacturing operations planning, neural network model training and machine learning, financial processes, etc. Traditional methods, such as gradient descent and Newton's method, often struggle with nonconvex, multimodal, or discontinuous objective functions due to their dependence on derivative information. This challenge has led to the development of more flexible and robust approaches, especially metaheuristic algorithms, among which nature-inspired techniques have gained attention due to their ability to efficiently navigate complex search spaces without the need for gradient information, for nonindependent, discontinuous, or black-box objective functions—conditions that are common in real-world problems [1].

These techniques have been developed inspired by the natural process of Darwinian biological evolution, animal social behavior, or physical laws, and their common feature is striking a balance between exploration (discovering new solution domains) and exploitation (improving promising solutions). Genetic algorithm (GA) and the grey wolf optimization (GWO) algorithm are two of the most efficient examples of these techniques. GA introduced by John Holland [2] in the 1960s, mimicking the principles of natural genetic selection, applies operators such as selection, crossover, and mutation to a set of candidate solutions for the purpose of generational evolution. By evaluating the fitness of potential solutions, the most suitable individuals are selected for reproduction and produce the next generation population (offspring). On the other hand, inspired by the social hierarchy and hunting behavior of grey wolves in nature, the GWO was introduced by Mirjalili et al. in 2014 [3]. This algorithm is developed based on modeling and imitating the leadership hierarchy and hunting mechanism of grey wolf packs. The four wolf classes of alpha, beta, delta, and omega simulate the hunting process through three stages of prey search, prey encirclement, and prey attack.

The use of two principles of exploration and exploitation, population-based structure, and the use of random operations are common points of these two algorithms, but they have different inspirations, functional mechanisms, and fundamental characteristics. The aim of this chapter is to provide a comparative analysis of the theoretical foundations, operational mechanisms, strengths, weaknesses, and practical applications of these two metaheuristic optimizers.

Nowadays, with the development of optimization techniques, the challenge of selecting the most appropriate algorithm for a specific problem, which simultaneously considers both the quality of the solution and the computational resources, has been highlighted. In experimental benchmarking, the performance of algorithms is examined, and in comparative studies, the theoretical foundations and practical behavior of algorithms are investigated. The strengths, weaknesses, and relative suitability of algorithms for different problem domains are identified in a comprehensive comparative analysis, which is very important for the selection, tuning, and combination of algorithms. The advantages of these studies include understanding the behavior of algorithms under different conditions, such as different problem dimensions, objective function perspectives, and types of constraints, identifying scenarios of superior performance of one algorithm over another, revealing complementary strengths between different algorithms, and thus inspiring the development of hybrid approaches.

Grey Wolf Optimizer. DOI: https://doi.org/10.1016/B978-0-443-36624-6.00036-6

The main objective of this chapter is to provide a comprehensive comparative analysis of GWOs and GAs with a focus on their theoretical foundations, operational mechanisms, performance characteristics, and practical applications in order to understand the relative advantages of GWO and GA and make informed decisions about their selection and application to specific optimization problems based on the problem characteristics. Hybridization strategies and integration with emerging technologies are mentioned as future research directions at the end.

27.2 Theoretical foundations

GWO: Living in packs of an average of 5–12 individuals, grey wolves (Canis lupus) use hierarchical leadership and cooperative hunting as tools for hunting success. Within these packs, four different social levels are defined. Alphas (αs) are the pack leader(s) who make decisions about hunting, territory, and other activities and represent the elite (the best solution discovered so far) in the algorithm. Betas (βs) are the pack's deputies and subordinates to the alphas, assisting them in decision-making and group activities and dominating the lower wolves. In the event of alphas dying or aging, they are the most likely candidates to succeed them. Betas are equivalent to the second-best solution in the algorithm. Deltas (δs), which include scouts, guards, elders, hunters, and caretakers, are subordinates to the two higher packs but dominate the lower pack wolves and represent the third-best solution in the algorithm. Finally, the lowest tier in this pack hierarchy is the Omegas (ωs), who are subservient to all other tiers and are often the victims or stress relievers of the entire pack. They are the last wolves to eat, despite often being the most active wolves in the search space. All solutions except Alpha, Beta, and Delta are considered omega wolves.

The hunting behavior of grey wolves consists of several stages, which are reflected in the GWO algorithm:

- Tracking and approaching the prey using the wolves' strong sense of smell to find the prey and start tracking it (initial exploration of the search space to find promising areas).
- Surrounding the prey to limit its movement and prepare for an attack. (Encirclement mechanism and updating the position of wolves based on the hierarchy).
- Harassing the prey until it stops and making the attack easier (transition from exploration to exploitation)
- Attacking the prey (exploitation or convergence toward the best solutions).

The relatively simple structure with minimal parameters to adjust (population size and number of iterations), robust global search (balance between exploration and exploitation), application to high-dimensional and nonlinear problems, fast convergence, and applicability in various domains (versatility) can be considered as strengths of GWO. On the other hand, premature convergence in some very complex or multifaceted problems or in a very uneven search space, and the reduction of population diversity in higher stages, and consequently the inability to explore new areas and escape from local optima, can be considered as its weaknesses. GWO has been widely used in a wide range of science and engineering fields due to its flexibility and effectiveness (Fig. 27.1).

GA: This algorithm is inspired by the principles of evolutionary biology (such as selection, inheritance, and the Darwinian principle of "survival of the fittest") and was introduced by John Holland in the 1960s and 1970s. The process begins by constructing an initial random population of chromosomes (individuals), each of which represents a potential solution to the problem. The algorithm's reliance on a population rather than an individual allows for the simultaneous (parallel) search of multiple regions in the search space. One of the important parameters affecting the diversity of responses and the convergence behavior of the algorithm is the size of the selected population, the choice of which depends on the complexity of the problem and other factors. Two ways to create the first generation have been proposed: random generation to ensure diversity or using specific knowledge in the problem domain to generate a more promising initial population. Generational evolution occurs through the application of genetic operators (reproduction, selection, crossover, and mutation), and elite individuals (higher fitness) have a greater chance of survival and reproduction. The fitness function returns the quality or fitness of each chromosome as a tangible and quantitative parameter and is a critical and highly effective parameter that guides the selection of the fittest parents and the maintenance of the elite. This function must be determined specifically for each problem and includes the objectives of the problem and sometimes the constraints it is intended to address.

The basic principle of GAs is natural selection, in which individuals with traits that are more adapted to their environment have a greater chance of surviving and reproducing, and pass these beneficial traits on to future generations. In the context of optimization, this means that solutions with better fitness values are more likely to contribute to the next generation of solutions. Evolution in GAs occurs over successive generations, with each generation potentially producing better solutions than the previous one. This evolutionary process continues until a termination criterion is met, such as reaching a maximum number of generations or achieving a satisfactory fitness level.

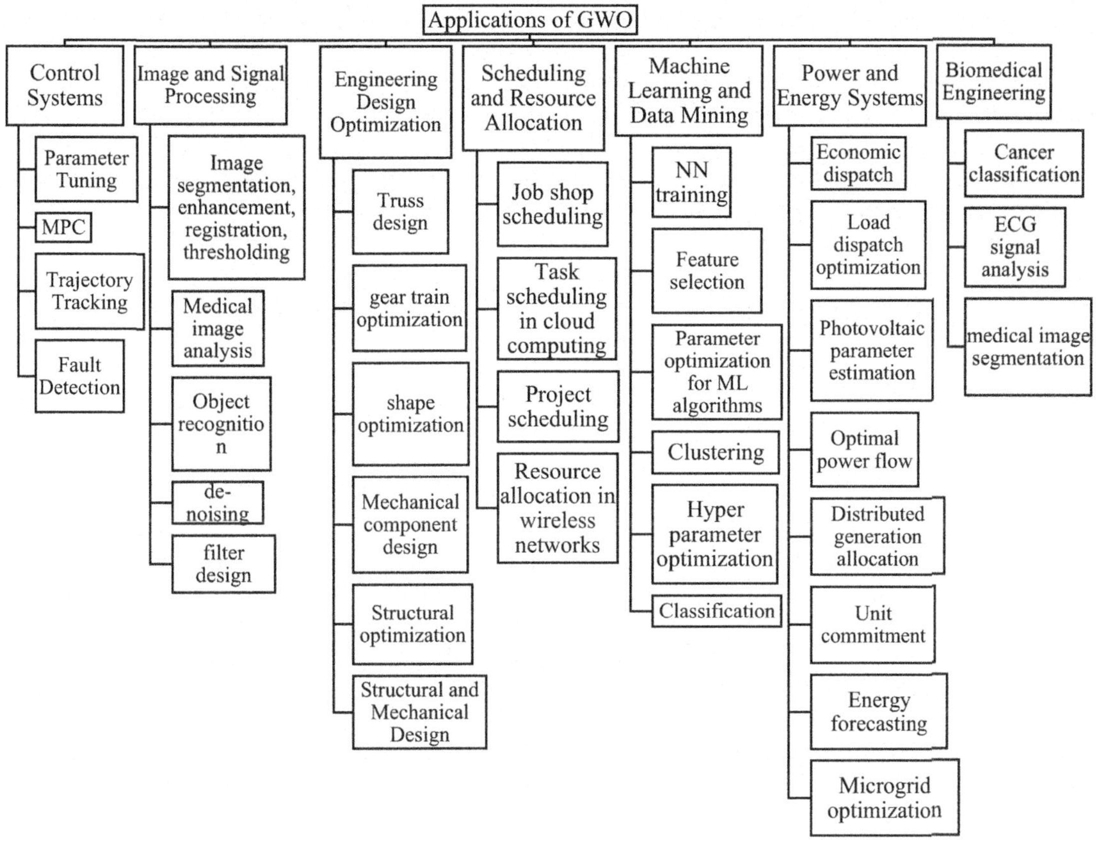

FIGURE 27.1 Typical applications of GWO (*GWO*, Grey wolf optimization).

A GA is a mathematical set of operations that are applied to a population of candidate solutions over several generations. The first part of the process is the generation of an initial population of N individuals (solutions), usually randomly generated using a suitable encoding.

In GAs, potential solutions to a problem are encoded as chromosomes (or genomes), which contain genes that represent the variables or parameters of the solution. The way genes are encoded or represented, depending on the nature of the problem, can be binary (chromosomes represented as strings of 0s and 1s and each gene represented as a string of bits), integer (variables of the problem are integers), real (continuous optimization problems), permutation (for ordinal problems such as traveling salesman problems), or tree (use for genetic programming for evolving expressions or models). The choice of encoding significantly affects the performance of the GA.

The next step is selection, which is the process of choosing individuals from the current population to act as parents in the next generation, usually proportional to their fitness. There are different selection methods, including roulette wheel selection (selecting individuals with a probability proportional to their fitness), tournament selection (selecting a subset of individuals at random and then selecting the best individual from this subset as a parent), ranked selection (ranking individuals based on their fitness and the probability of selection based on rank rather than absolute fitness), and elitism (copying the best individuals from the current generation directly to the next generation and ensuring that the best solutions are maintained).

After the selection of parents, it is time for reproduction or the production of offspring. Crossover (or recombination) combines the genes of two parents and simulates biological reproduction to create one or more offspring. The crossover operation, which is applied with the probability of the crossover rate, has common techniques such as single-point crossover (choose a crossover point at random and exchange genes on both sides of that point between the two parents), two-point crossover (choose two crossover points at random and exchange genes between these two points), uniform crossover (exchange each gene independently between the parents with a fixed probability (usually 0.5)), arithmetic crossover (produce offspring as a weighted average of the parents, used in coding with real values).

Another operator intended to maintain diversity in a population and, based on a real-world genetic operation, is mutation, which makes small random changes to the chromosomes of the offspring. This process is equivalent to searching new search spaces in order to prevent premature convergence. The mutation, which is applied with a mutation rate probability, depends on the encoding scheme, including: bit-reversal mutation (in binary encoding, inverting selected bits), random rearrangement (in integer encoding, replacing selected genes with random integer values within the allowed range), Gaussian mutation (in real-value encoding, adding a random value from a Gaussian distribution to selected genes), and translocation mutation (in permutation encoding, swapping two randomly selected genes).

After producing offspring and creating a new generation through selection, crossover, and mutation, the next step is to determine the individuals that will form the next generation, which is called replacement or elitism. Common strategies include generational replacement (replacing the entire population with newly created offspring), steady-state replacement (replacing only the worst individuals of the generation with new offspring), and elite replacement (selecting the best individuals from both the current population and the offspring to form the next generation).

To stop the search in the algorithm, a termination criterion must be met. This criterion may be one or more of the following: reaching the maximum number of generations, reaching a satisfactory fitness level, observing no improvement in the best solution for a specified number of generations, or exhausting a predefined computational budget.

The lack of need for gradient information or problem-specific knowledge, the ability to search large and complex search spaces and high-dimensional, multifaceted, and nonlinear problems through population diversity and diverse operators, and the avoidance of local optima, flexibility and compatibility with dynamic and real-time optimizations with multiple constraints and objectives, applicability in parallel computing architectures, providing optimal solutions even for noisy, incomplete, or ill-defined problems, and applicability to noisy, discontinuous, or nondifferentiable objective functions can be considered as strengths of GAs that make them attractive for diverse optimization challenges.

In contrast, the weaknesses of GAs can be listed as follows: high computational burden with large populations or many generations due to repeated evaluation of the fitness function for the entire population in each generation, sensitivity to the choice of parameters and operators such as population rate, crossover rate, and mutation rate that affect the convergence speed as well as the accuracy of the algorithm's response, and the challenge of choosing the best encoding method for each problem.

The successful application of GAs to a wide range of real-world problems demonstrates the versatility and power of this optimization tool. Some of these diverse applications, which highlight the enduring utility and adaptability of GAs in solving challenging optimization problems in various fields, include the following (Fig. 27.2):

- Bioinformatics and computational biology: GAs are widely used in bioinformatics for tasks such as gene expression analysis, protein structure prediction, DNA sequence alignment, and phylogenetic tree reconstruction, for example, to optimize the parameters of algorithms used to identify disease-associated genes or predict the affinity of drug molecules for target proteins [4].
- Machine learning and data mining: GAs play an important role in optimizing machine learning models, including neural network training, feature selection, and evolution of optimal network architectures, selecting the most informative features from high-dimensional datasets, and fine-tuning metaparameters to improve model performance [5]. The effectiveness of GA-based feature selection techniques in various domains has been reviewed in [6].
- Operations and logistics research: GAs have been widely used to solve complex planning, routing, and resource allocation problems such as vehicle routing problems, factory scheduling, and airline crew scheduling with the aim of minimizing costs or time, or maximizing efficiency under various constraints [7].
- Engineering design and optimization: GAs have been used to design optimal structures, circuits, and systems, such as optimizing parameters for antenna design, circuit layout, and control system tuning to achieve desired performance and robustness characteristics [8].
- Financial modeling and portfolio optimization: GAs have helped in finance to optimize portfolios, forecast stock markets, and develop trading strategies, for example, to construct a portfolio with maximum return for a given level of risk, or to identify profitable trading rules based on historical data [9].
- Image processing and computer vision: GAs have helped in image segmentation, image retrieval, and object recognition, such as optimizing parameters of image filters or evolving algorithms for segmenting complex images, and have contributed to advances in computer vision applications [10].

27.3 Comparative analysis of grey wolf optimization and genetic algorithm

To provide a structured comparative analysis, the theoretical foundations, parameter sensitivity, convergence behavior, and real-world performance of these two algorithms are studied in this section.

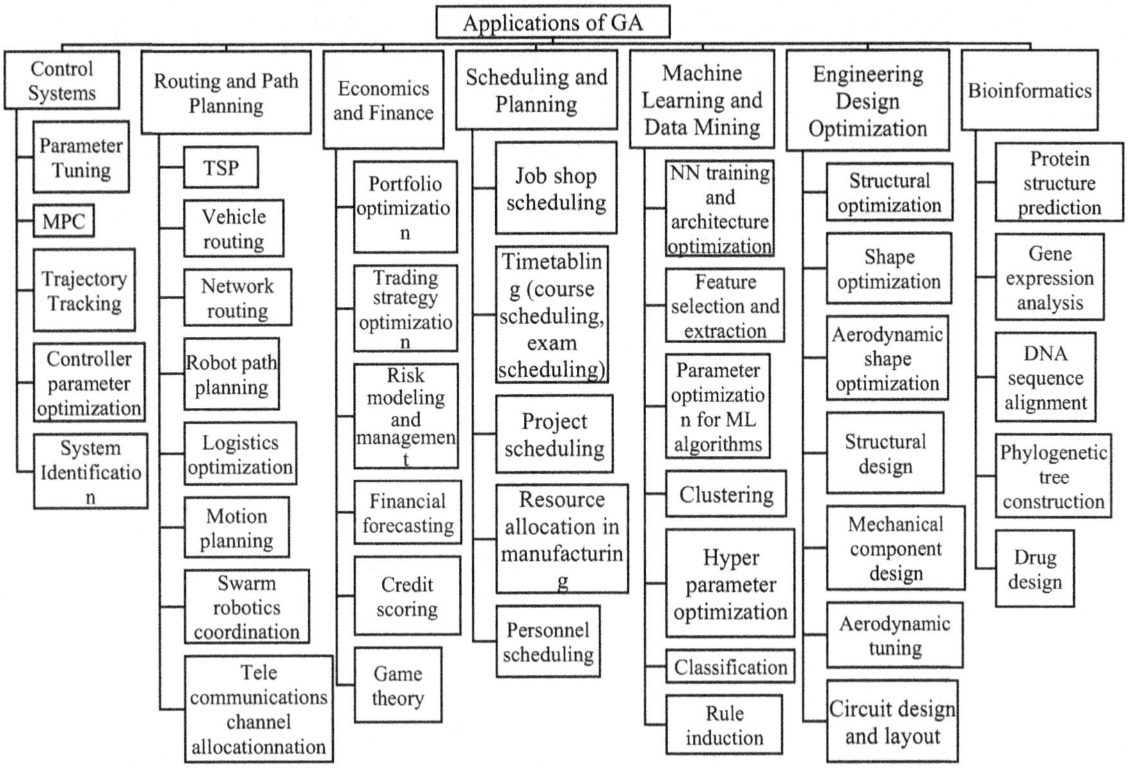

FIGURE 27.2 Typical applications of GA (*GA*, Genetic algorithm).

Commonalities: Both algorithms are nature-inspired, stochastic, and population-based metaheuristics. The key commonalities can be summarized as follows.

Commonality 1) Evolutionary principles and nature-inspired algorithms: These algorithms are imitations of natural processes (models, systems, and elements of nature) that have been developed with the aim of achieving efficient computational techniques. Their population-based approach with appropriate diversity by creating multiple search paths contributes to their robustness and ability to escape local optima, reducing the risk of premature convergence.

Another commonality is the inherent ability to balance exploration and exploitation to maintain optimization accuracy while accelerating convergence. In GA, the balance is primarily controlled through selection pressure, crossover rate, and mutation rate. High selection pressure facilitates exploitation by giving more weight to better solutions, while mutation creates randomness that promotes exploration. The intersection operation combines elements of exploration and exploitation by generating new solutions that inherit properties from multiple parents. In GWO, balance is controlled through a parameter that decreases linearly from 2 to 0 over iterations. Parameter values greater than one in the algorithm emphasize exploration by encouraging wolves to move away from the prey. Conversely, at parameter values smaller than one, the algorithm focuses on exploitation by forcing wolves to attack the prey. This adaptive mechanism ensures a smooth transition from exploration in the early stages to exploitation in the later stages of the optimization process. Also, the ability to adapt to problems in different domains without requiring significant parameter tuning is common between the two algorithms due to their population-based nature and stochastic components.

Commonality 2) Using metaheuristic approaches to solve optimization problems: When dealing with metaheuristic algorithms, there is no guarantee of finding a general optimal solution; in fact, the purpose of designing these algorithms has been to find good solutions to complex problems in a reasonable amount of time. Such algorithms are stochastic and nondeterministic in nature, and there is no guarantee of leading to the same solutions even when they are run under the same conditions and with the same parameters. Of course, this nature can be interpreted as their ability to search different regions of the search space.

The lack of need for the gradient (derivative) of the objective function is another attractive feature common to these algorithms, which makes them almost the only practical option for problems with nondifferentiable, discontinuous, or difficult derivatives of the objective function, as well as in cases where the analytical form of the objective function is unknown (black-box optimization). Also, both algorithms have the ability to handle complex constraints, albeit through different mechanisms, and due to their reliance on the population, they support parallel computations, and the evaluation of each individual or candidate is performed independently, which is very helpful, especially in computationally expensive problems that require significant computational resources. Also, both algorithms, due to their metaheuristic nature, exhibit probabilistic convergence behavior, that is, they converge to the global optimum with a certain probability, which increases with increasing number of generations or iterations. Elitism is the next common feature, according to which the best solutions found at each stage are preserved and passed on to the next stage. This elitism in GA is implemented more explicitly by directly copying the best individuals from the current generation to the next generation. While in GWO, it is implicitly embedded through the role of elite wolves in guiding the movement of other wolves.

Differences: GWO and GA have differences in terms of algorithmic structure, exploration and exploitation mechanisms, and parameter sensitivity, which are discussed in this section.

Difference 1) Algorithmic structure: In GAs, based on the principle of evolution, a population of candidate solutions (chromosomes) evolves over successive generations under the operators of selection, crossover, and mutation. In this evolution, useful traits are passed from parents to offspring, and the population gradually becomes more elite. The key elements of a GA are: generational evolution (creating a new, more evolved population (generation) at each iteration, similar to the process of evolution in nature), genetic operators (selection, crossover, and mutation to create and evolve new solutions), fitness-proportional progression (more likely to contribute more fit solutions to the next generation with the goal of moving the entire population toward better solutions over time), and solution-independent evolution (each solution is only influenced by the genetics of its parents during crossover and random mutations, and there are no direct interactions or effects between solutions beyond the mating process).

In contrast, the GWO is structured around the social hierarchy and cooperative hunting behavior of grey wolf packs, in which the positions of search agents (wolves) are updated based on their social ranks and the estimated location of prey. The structural elements of GWO are: hierarchical organization (classification of search agents into best, second best, third best, and remaining solutions in a social hierarchy), cooperative search (using cooperative search of all wolves in tracking and surrounding prey (optimal solution) instead of evolution over generations), continuous position updating (updating the position of all search agents at each iteration based on mathematical models of siege and attack behaviors versus generational changes in GA), and leadership-based advancement (guided advancement by leadership of higher-ranking wolves versus merit-based advancement in GA).

Difference 2) Mechanisms for exploration (searching new regions of the solution space) and exploitation (improving solutions in promising regions): In GAs, the task of balancing exploration and exploitation is the responsibility of genetic operators. The selection operator primarily promotes exploitation by favoring more fit individuals for reproduction. Higher selection pressure (giving more weight to better solutions) increases exploitation at the expense of exploration. The crossover operator combines elements of exploration and exploitation to produce offspring with beneficial traits from the parents, while generating new genetic combinations that may not be present in either parent. The mutation operator is primarily responsible for exploration and allows for the exploration of new regions of the search space by making random changes to the solutions. A higher mutation rate equates to increased exploration but may come at the cost of potentially losing elites. The balance between operators in the classical version was usually fixed during execution, which could be problematic because the optimal exploration-exploitation balance was different at different stages of optimization. However, later adaptive variants of the GA were developed with the possibility of adjusting the probabilities of the operators based on the progress of the algorithm.

In contrast, GWO relies on the use of a control parameter to balance exploration and exploitation. This linearly varying parameter decreases from 2 to 0 over the iterations. In the exploration phase, the derivative of the control parameter is greater than one, the focus is on exploring the search space, and there is even an incentive to move away from the prey to avoid local optima. This phase occurs at the beginning of the algorithm, when the control parameter is closer to two. In the transition phase, as the control parameter decreases, the wolves are gradually guided from exploration to exploitation (getting closer to the prey). In the exploitation phase, the wolves are forced to attack the prey and the algorithm focuses on exploiting promising areas of the search space. This is clearly the case in the final stages of the algorithm, when the control parameter is closer to 0. This explicit parameter control mechanism in GWO is a systematic transition from a global search in the early stages to a local search in the later stages, leading to a more effective dynamic balance between exploration and exploitation compared to the static balance in traditional GA.

Difference 3) Sensitivity to parameter tuning and initialization: The performance of optimization algorithms is often influenced by their parameter settings and initialization strategies. GA and GWO differ significantly in their sensitivity to these factors.

GA: The optimal performance of this algorithm depends on the fine-tuning of several parameters, whose interactions are sometimes complex. The Population Size determines the amount of genetic diversity, which is directly related to the algorithm's exploration ability and inversely related to its computational cost. To control the balance between exploration and exploitation, the selection rate is used to determine the degree of emphasis on selecting the fittest individuals. The probability of generating new genetic chromosomes is controlled by determining the crossover rate. The mutation rate, by determining the probability of genes mutating in the offspring, is the most influential parameter on the ability to explore new regions of the search space. Finally, the Elitism Rate addresses the degree of retention of good solutions (elite) by determining the number of the best individuals that are directly copied to the next generation.

These parameters often interact in complex ways, making it challenging to find the optimal parameter configuration for a particular problem. GA performance can be very sensitive to parameter settings, and inappropriate values can lead to premature convergence or slow convergence.

GWO: In contrast, GWO has fewer parameters with simpler interactions to tune. Like GA, the number of search agents (wolves) is determined by a parameter called population size, which must strike a balance between the exploratory capability and the computational cost of the algorithm. The second parameter is the maximum number of iterations, which determines the duration of the search process and the linear decrease of the control parameter from 2 to 0. However, the superior feature of GWO is that its main control parameter decreases automatically and linearly from 2 to 0 during the execution of the algorithm. This greatly reduces the sensitivity of GWO to parameter settings compared to GA, by reducing the need for manual parameter tuning. The random vectors and position update equations in GWO allow it to be adapted to problems in different domains without the need for specific parameter settings.

Difference 4) Handling of constraints and boundary conditions: Another area where GA and GWO differ is in their handling of constraints and boundary conditions, which are common in real-world optimization problems.

GA (specialized operators and penalty functions): We encounter four approaches to constraint management in GA. The first tool is the use of penalty functions, that is, considering a penalty for violating constraints in the fitness function, which, although simple to implement, is challenging to choose penalty coefficients. The second solution is specialized genetic operators to satisfy constraints, such as designing custom crossover and mutation operators, specialized operators to preserve the permutation property. repair mechanisms to repair impossible solutions before evaluation, and convert them into feasible solutions are the third solution in GA, which, of course, requires specialized knowledge of the problem and customization for each problem. Another approach is to prioritize feasible solutions over impossible solutions, regardless of their objective function values, by modifying the selection process, known as feasibility rules. The effectiveness of these approaches depends on the specific problem and the nature of the constraints, and finding the appropriate approach, which may be a combination of several approaches, requires trial and error or experience.

GWO (boundary handling and position adjustment): In GWO, constraints and boundary conditions are typically managed through position adjustment mechanisms: Boundary checking (checking whether or not wolves have moved outside the search boundaries after updating the wolves' positions, and adjusting the positions by the boundary value), position clamping (clamping the wolves' positions to ensure they remain within feasible regions of the search space), and penalty-based evaluation (adding penalty functions to include constraints in a GA-like fitness evaluation).

In comparison, constraint management by directly updating the positions in the simple GWO structure shows a simple yet effective performance compared to the more complex and sensitive adjustment of operators in GA. However, in the case of both algorithms, when we are faced with more complex constraints, we may need to apply additional mechanisms.

To synergize the individual advantages of the two algorithms, GWO and GA, and overcome the inherent limitations of each, hybrid approaches aim to achieve a more successful balance between exploration (global search) and exploitation (local modification). In fact, these hybrids are expected to inject diversity into the GWO search space or to guide the randomness of the GA with the leader-based direction of GWO and achieve fast convergence and robust exploitation (GWO) while maintaining robust exploration and preserving diversity (GA). The general idea is to use one algorithm to enhance the search capabilities of the other algorithm at different stages of the optimization process or to merge their operators together.

Several approaches to GWO-GA hybridization have been proposed:

- Sequential hybridization: In this approach, one algorithm is run first (e.g., GWO for a fast initial search to identify promising regions), and its output (e.g., the best solution found or a modified population) is used as input to a second algorithm (then GA is applied to fully explore these regions and refine the solutions).
- Parallel hybridization: Both algorithms are run concurrently and periodically exchange information. This allows for continuous interaction and mutual benefit (e.g., exchange of best solutions found).

- Operator-level hybridization: This involves integrating specific operators from one algorithm into the framework of another algorithm. For example, using GA intersection and mutation operators in GWO with the aim of increasing its diversity and exploration capabilities, and helping to escape local optima, or integrating GWO's leadership-based position update mechanism into GA to accelerate convergence.

Also, several structural designs have been proposed:

- Postiteration hybridization: After GWO completes a standard iteration, a portion of the population is subjected to GA's crossover and mutation operations to introduce new genetic material and maintain diversity.
- Mid-iteration hybridization: During the encircling and hunting phases of GWO, mutation is selectively applied to lower-performing wolves to escape local optima.
- Adaptive hybrids: The algorithm dynamically switches between GWO and GA phases based on stagnation detection or diversity measures.

To gain some advantages in each algorithm, other advantages are sacrificed. In GWO, we gain the advantage in exploitation at the cost of possible premature convergence in high-dimensional or multifaceted problems, which leads to loss of diversity and getting stuck in local optima(s). In contrast, in GA, we see the advantage of strong exploration and biodiversity with less tendency to get stuck in local optima(s) at the cost of slower convergence and high sensitivity to parameter tuning.

Now the key question will be whether these advantages can be maintained or enhanced by hybridization and whether the weaknesses can be eliminated or reduced. The goal of merging these two algorithms can be defined as enhancing the exploration of GWO with the global search capability of GA and accelerating the convergence of GA toward optimal solutions by using the strong exploitation of GWO.

In solving a variety of real-world problems, especially when a balance between fast convergence and extensive exploration is required, GWO-GA hybrid algorithms have shown superior performance compared to separate algorithms. In Ref. [11], by adding GA search diversity to GWO in the feature selection problem in machine learning, the feature space is reduced while the classification accuracy is improved, which leads to more effective selection of optimal feature subsets, improved classification accuracy, and reduced computational overhead. In process planning and scheduling, with the aim of optimizing multiobjective production or shop floor scheduling problems, this hybridization has led to reduced production time, improved resource utilization, and faster computation time by helping to navigate complex and multifaceted cost functions [12]. Another application of placement optimization has been to minimize costs and ensure reliable power supply of renewable energy sources (such as wind turbines, solar panels, solar-wind-battery hybrid systems), which has managed nonlinear constraints while balancing economic and environmental objectives. Hybrid algorithms in the field of power engineering have successfully completed the mission of tracking global maximum power points in photovoltaic systems under partial shade conditions [13] and minimizing the annual cost of hybrid energy systems [14]. Solving constrained nonlinear optimization problems in structural and mechanical design by achieving more appropriate design parameters while satisfying constraints and efficient resource allocation and load balancing in cloud computing to optimize the allocation of virtual machines to physical servers, with the aim of minimizing energy consumption and maximizing resource utilization while ensuring quality of service, are other examples [15].

These applications demonstrate that the synergy between GWO and GA in hybrid models can lead to more robust and efficient solutions to complex optimization problems. Improved exploration balance in GA and guided exploitation in GWO, avoidance of local optima, and improved adaptability in multimodal, dynamic, or constrained environments are the advantages of hybridization, while increased complexity, implementation overhead (possibly requiring more complex logic and computational resources), and control balance in the hybridization are its challenges.

Bo et al. [16] introduced a hybrid genetic GWO that integrates crossover and two types of natural and random selection mutations of GA into the GWO. This integration significantly improves the robustness, reducing the deviation from the alpha wolf guidance as a common challenge in standard GWO. This hybrid optimizer was applied to compare the performance with traditional GWO algorithms, particle swarm optimization (PSO), and artificial bee colony in wind farm layout optimization, and showed its superiority in energy production and computational efficiency. In fact, this paper validated the diversification process of GWO search with GA genetic operators to prevent premature convergence and improve the quality of the final answer.

Another metaheuristic algorithm that has been used in combination with GWO is PSO. Inspired by the social behavior of living organisms such as birds or fish, this algorithm has the advantage of simplicity and searching large search spaces, although it is similar to GWO in settling into local optima. The intelligent hybrid grey wolf-particle swarm optimizer was proposed in Ref. [17] to cover the weaknesses of each algorithm with the strengths of the other. The results showed that combining the strong local search capabilities of GWO in the form of position updating with PSO exploration in a wider search space through the speed update mechanism achieves an acceptable balance between exploration and exploitation, overcoming the premature convergence and limited search as limitations of the independent application of each algorithm. Simulation results in complex engineering problems with challenging environments showed the superiority of the hybrid algorithm in finding the optimal solution, avoiding getting stuck in local optima, and improving the search path by creating more dynamic and diverse movements for wolves.

Beyond GWO-GA and GWO-PSO, other hybrid combinations are also emerging. The core principle remains consistent: to create a more robust and efficient optimization tool by combining algorithms that offer complementary strengths.

27.4 Experimental design and implementation

To evaluate and compare the performance of each optimization algorithm and the combined GWO-GA algorithm, a set of benchmark experiments was conducted on four well-known continuous optimization functions: Sphere, Rastrigin, Ackley, and Griewank (Table 27.1). These benchmark functions test various aspects of an algorithm's performance, such as convergence speed, accuracy, and ability to avoid local minima. Each algorithm was independently run 30 times with a population size of 50 and a maximum of 30,000 function evaluations. In the GA implementation with real values, tournament selection (k=3), single-point crossover with a rate of 0.8, and adding Gaussian noise to each component at a rate of 0.25 were applied. The elitism rate was applied by copying the best individual to the next generation (elitism=1). In GWO, it follows the classical alpha-beta-delta leader scheme with a linear decay factor from 2 to 0. A new proposed hybridization of GA and GWO algorithms is presented, which, to my knowledge, has not been presented in other research so far. In the proposed algorithm, each iteration starts with updating the GWO position based on leader-based siege, then a fraction of the population (P_{GA}) is randomly selected and subjected to genetic operators to provide a combination of diversity and escape from local optima and fast convergence. A common initial population uniformly distributed in the search space ([−100,100]) was used for all three algorithms to ensure fairness in comparison and to prevent the initial values from influencing the results. All experiments were run on the same computing platform (Intel i7, 16 GB RAM without GPU acceleration, and MATLAB R2022b) to ensure fairness, and the mean and standard deviation of the best-fit values and execution times were recorded for each algorithm and benchmark function.

By examining the numerical results in Table 27.2, it can be seen that the hybrid algorithm consistently achieved the best or near-best performance in terms of solution accuracy on all benchmark functions, while maintaining competitive execution times. GWO also performed strongly, producing very low error values on all problems. In contrast, GA often converged to much worse solutions and required much longer computation times.

As can be seen, both GWO and hybrid algorithms converged to or were very close to the global optimum on the Sphere, Rastrigin, and Ackley functions, while GA produced much larger errors. The hybrid method even reached the exact global optimum (very close to zero error) on the Griewank function, outperforming both GWO and GA. In terms of execution time, GWO was the fastest on average, while the hybrid algorithm took only slightly longer. GA was consistently slower than both, often taking almost three times as long as GWO (Figs. 27.3–27.6).

To validate the observed differences, pairwise statistical comparisons were performed using the Wilcoxon signed-rank test, and effect sizes were computed using Cohen's d. The P-values and effect sizes are summarized in Table 27.3.

TABLE 27.1 Benchmark functions.

Function name	Equation	Characteristics	Search space
Sphere	$f(x) = \sum_{i=1}^{n} x_i^2$	Unimodal, convex	$x_i \in [-5.12, 5.12]$
Rastrigin	$f(x) = 10n + \sum_{i=1}^{n} [x_i^2 - 10\cos(2\pi x_i)]$	Multimodal, highly nonlinear	$x_i \in [-5.12, 5.12]$
Rosenbrock	$f(x) = \sum_{i=1}^{n-1} [100(x_{i+1} - x_i^2)^2 + (x_i - 1)^2]$	Nonconvex, narrow valley	$x_i \in [-2.048, 2.048]$
Ackley	$f(x) = -20\exp\left(-0.2\sqrt{\frac{1}{n}\sum x_i^2}\right) - \exp\left(\frac{1}{n}\sum\cos(2\pi x_i)\right) + 20 + e$	Multimodal, complex landscape	$x_i \in [-5, 5]$

TABLE 27.2 Mean ± standard deviation of best fitness values and execution times.

Function	Algorithm	Mean best	Std best	Mean time (s)	Std time (s)
Sphere	GWO	1.4126e-44	2.622e-44	0.30551	0.017854
Sphere	GA	1.25207	0.17866	0.95374	0.045782
Sphere	Hybrid	1.30257e-44	1.71436e-44	0.35967	0.019374
Rastrigin	GWO	0	0	0.33185	0.022537
Rastrigin	GA	33.02898	1.085818	1.085818	0.106415
Rastrigin	Hybrid	0	0	0.40055	0.038893
Ackley	GWO	1.34707e-14	5.70065e-15	0.33346	0.028655
Ackley	GA	20.87532	0.068916	1.04275	0.059935
Ackley	Hybrid	1.53654e-14	1.551119e-14	0.40345	0.037781
Griewank	GWO	0.000351	0.0019241	0.44238	0.052219
Griewank	GA	0.080390	0.0246501	1.20856	0.114066
Griewank	Hybrid	0.000104	0.0039571	0.52435	0.044432

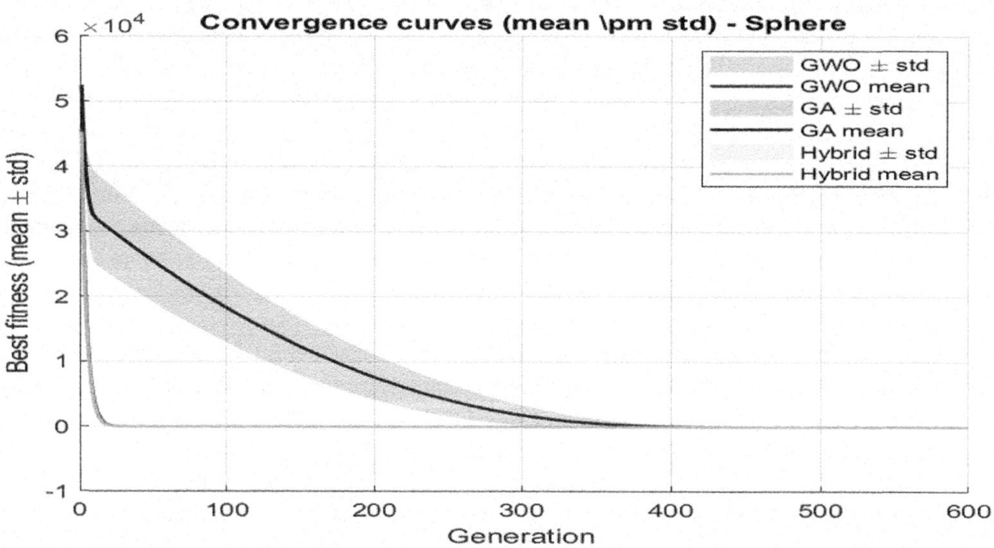

FIGURE 27.3 Convergence behavior of three algorithms on the Sphere function.

The statistical results confirm that the hybrid algorithm performs significantly better than GA on all benchmark functions ($P < 0.001$ with large effect sizes), while a weak difference or no significant difference was observed between the hybrid and GWO on most problems. This indicates that the hybrid method preserves the strong performance and stability of GWO while benefiting from the exploratory mechanisms of GA.

27.4.1 Sensitivity analysis

Another evaluation conducted to compare the algorithms was the parameter sensitivity analysis, the results of which can be considered as a measure of the robustness of the algorithms against changes in their main control parameters. In fact, the aim is to investigate how parameter tuning affects the performance of each algorithm. For GWO, the initial value of

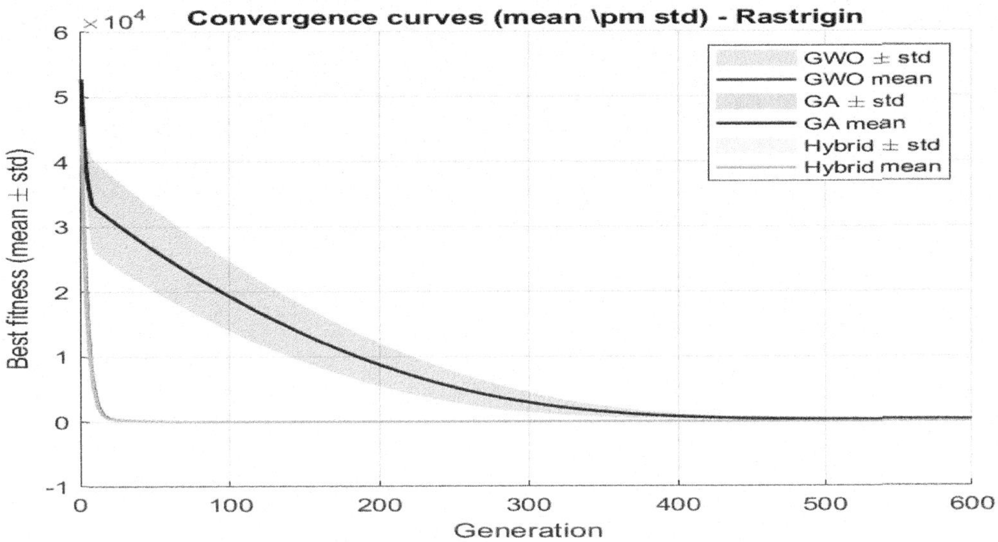

FIGURE 27.4 Convergence behavior of three algorithms on the Rastrigin function.

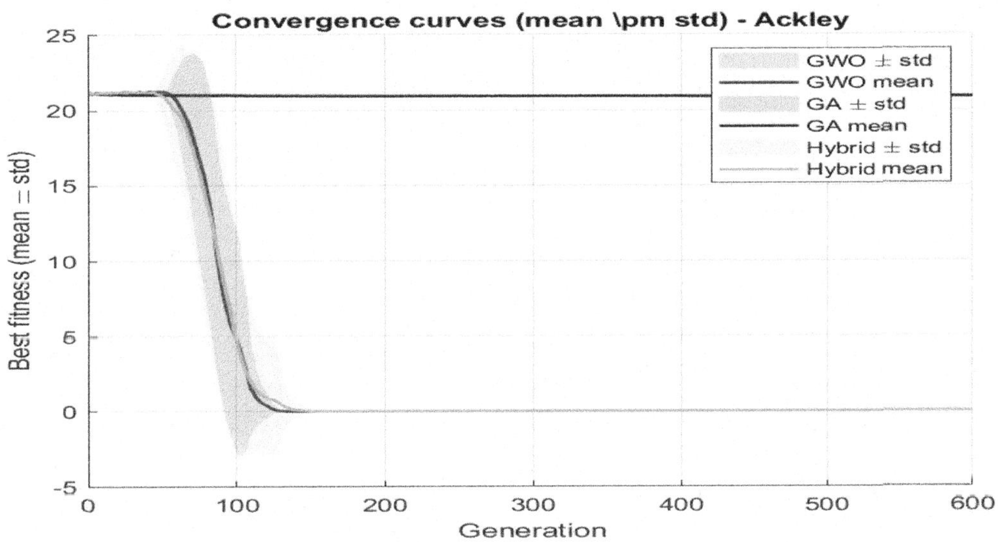

FIGURE 27.5 Convergence behavior of three algorithms on the Ackley function.

the control parameter was set to three values (1.5, 2, 2.5) and in the genetic algorithm, the mutation rate was set to values (0.05, 0.1, 0.2) and the crossover rate to three values (0.6, 0.8, 0.9). In the case of the hybrid algorithm, three variable parameters were considered for investigation, which included the percentage of individuals affected by the GA operators in each iteration, the mutation rate, and the crossover rate. For each determined value, all three algorithms were simulated on all four criterion functions with 30 independent runs, the results of which are given in Tables 27.4–27.6.

What can be seen from Table 27.4 is that GWO has remained largely stable in all parameter combinations and has always produced solutions close to the optimal. Of course, variations in accuracy are seen especially for the Rastrigin and Griewank functions. In the case of GA (Table 27.5), we see high sensitivity and sometimes different models. So that the larger the mutation rate, the error increases, but there is an exception that in the Ackley function, the error related to GA decreases with increasing mutation rate. In the case of the crossover rate, in almost all cases, we have the best performance at the highest rate, although exceptions are observed at the lowest mutation rate and in the case of the two Sphere and Griewank functions. Therefore, finding the right balance point between low mutation rate and high crossover is a constant challenge in GA. The behavior of the combined GWO-GA algorithm (Table 27.6) is

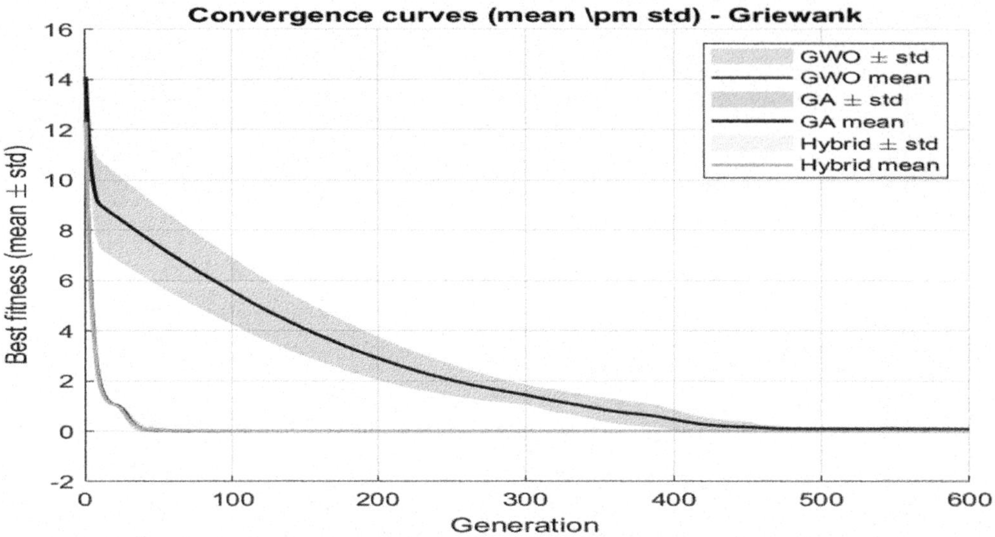

FIGURE 27.6 Convergence behavior of three algorithms on the Griewank function.

TABLE 27.3 Wilcoxon signed-rank test results (*P*-values) and Cohen's d effect sizes.

Function	Pair	Wilcoxon p	Cohen's d	Interpretation
Sphere	GWO vs GA	1.734397628e-06	-7.007863031	GA significantly worse
Sphere	GWO vs Hybrid	0.926255087	0.044669479	Weak difference
Sphere	GA vs Hybrid	1.734397628e-06	7.007863031	GA significantly worse
Rastrigin	GWO vs GA	1.734397628e-06	-8.06314005	GA significantly worse
Rastrigin	GWO vs Hybrid	1	NaN	No significant difference
Rastrigin	GA vs Hybrid	1.734397628e-06	8.06314005	GA significantly worse
Ackley	GWO vs GA	1.734397628e-06	-302.9085667	GA significantly worse
Ackley	GWO vs Hybrid	0.901358519	-0.117109451	Weak difference
Ackley	GA vs Hybrid	1.734397628e-06	302.9085667	GA significantly worse
Griewank	GWO vs GA	1.734397628e-06	-3.193452664	GA significantly worse
Griewank	GWO vs Hybrid	0.5	-0.241437132	No significant difference
Griewank	GA vs Hybrid	1.734397628e-06	3.13489714	GA significantly worse

actually a combination of the behavior of the two algorithms merged into it. That is, it offers high accuracy similar to GWO and sometimes better than it, like GA, its performance accuracy decreases slightly with increasing mutation rate, but not as much as GA (and of course, the same exception is present in the Ackley function in the hybrid algorithm). Regarding the crossover rate, a completely different behavior is observed in different functions and even in different mutation rate settings, but the amount of performance change is very small in most cases, except for the Griewank function. This shows that although the hybrid algorithm inherits a high percentage of the stability of GWO, the sensitivity of the GA parameter also affects it, albeit slightly.

The results of the benchmark tests and sensitivity analysis provide a clear view of the behavioral patterns of the three algorithms and can be used to identify the relative strengths of the algorithms. The advantages of GWO include:

TABLE 27.4 Effect of GWO parameters on performance (mean best fitness)-Mean±Std.

Function	a_0	GWO
Sphere	1.5	1.6079e-31 ± 2.3841e-31
Sphere	2	2.0393e-44 ± 6.5989e-44
Sphere	2.5	3.4046e-42 ± 5.2482e-42
Rastrigin	1.5	5.5484 ± 1.7012
Rastrigin	2	0 ± 0
Rastrigin	2.5	0 ± 0
Ackley	1.5	6.2998e-13 ± 1.3175e-12
Ackley	2	1.655e-14 ± 9.9936e-15
Ackley	2.5	2.8929e-12 ± 9.6676e-12
Griewank	1.5	0.005542 ± 0.0074304
Griewank	2	0.0020854 ± 0.0074304
Griewank	2.5	0 ± 0

GWO, Grey wolf optimization.

TABLE 27.5 Effect of GA parameters on performance (mean best fitness)-Mean±Std.

P_m	P_c	Sphere	Rastrigin	Ackley	Griewank
0.05	0.6	0.042911 ± 0.0060362	148.63±26.489	5.9139±0.51135	0.059216±0.10371
0.05	0.8	0.040896 ± 0.0063382	132.34±24.644	5.7095±0.68956	0.035491±0.088638
0.05	0.9	0.043617 ± 0.0058485	129.51±24.434	5.6762±0.63965	0.051761±0.097613
0.1	0.6	0.17188 ± 0.01972	171.4±23.874	5.1846±1.0522	0.072025±0.10645
0.1	0.8	0.1722 ± 0.022431	152.85±31.311	4.8439±1.0867	0.063634±0.16347
0.1	0.9	0.16553 ± 0.02635	152.8± 28.551	4.6273± 0.88553	0.061435± 0.10698
0.2	0.6	0.69491 ± 0.074115	209.29± 21.448	1.4399± 0.11611	0.1004± 0.15887
0.2	0.8	0.6707 ± 0.080182	207.18± 30.371	1.4477± 0.11803	0.089327± 0.15313
0.2	0.9	0.65767 ± 0.066318	199.9± 27.062	1.4289 ± 0.13398	0.069182± 0.085362

GA, Genetic algorithm.

faster convergence with minimal fluctuations on unimodal functions and functions with clear gradient information, ease of deployment in new domains due to the use of fewer control parameters with simpler tuning, low sensitivity to parameters, and good performance on problems of medium and high dimensions. The advantages of GA include a broader search in complex and multimodal problems (such as Rastrigin with appropriate parameter tuning), greater population diversity over generations to escape local optima, a wide and flexible variety of operators and encodings to accommodate different types of problems (discrete, continuous, mixed, and mixed variables), and the ability to generalize to multiobjective optimization (requiring diversity in the population). Also, although GA showed the most sensitivity to parameter changes in the comparison, this feature can be used as a strength to adjust the trade-off between exploration and exploitation for complex problems. If we want to discuss the advantages of the hybrid of these two algorithms, or in fact the combined GWO-GA algorithm, we should mention things like creating a good

TABLE 27.6 Effect of hybrid parameters on performance (mean best fitness)-Mean±Std.

P_{GA}	P_m	P_c	Sphere	Rastrigin	Ackley	Griewank
0.1	0.05	0.6	7.9428e-45±1.293e-44	0 ± 0	1.5839e-14±9.80e-15	0.0015302±0.0049504
0.1	0.05	0.8	6.6445e-45±8.575e-45	0 ± 0	1.868e-14±1.779e-14	0 ± 0
0.1	0.05	0.9	8.999e-45±1.7827e-44	0 ± 0	1.809e-14±1.049e-14	0.0014785±0.0014785
0.1	0.1	0.6	1.052e-44±1.2593e-44	0 ± 0	1.418e-14±7.331e-15	0.001255±0.0047793
0.1	0.1	0.8	9.8162e-45±1.410e-44	0 ± 0	1.454e-14±8.7265e-15	0.0012721±0.0039649
0.1	0.1	0.9	1.9338e-44±3.255e-44	0 ± 0	1.312e-14±6.5098e-15	0 ± 0
0.1	0.2	0.6	6.533e-45±1.6093e-44	0 ± 0	1.7023e-14±9.889e-15	0.0022168±0.0070766
0.1	0.2	0.8	5.8892e-45±8.476e-45	0 ± 0	1.4537e-14±6.292e-15	0.0009593±0.0036833
0.1	0.2	0.9	2.7306e-44±6.075e-44	0 ± 0	1.773e-14±2.4289e-14	0.0014416±0.0058
0.2	0.05	0.6	1.7394e-44±6.504e-44	0 ± 0	1. 5365e-14±7.828e-15	0 ± 0
0.2	0.05	0.8	4.1995e-45±4.461e-45	0 ± 0	2.5787e-14±5.714e-14	0 ± 0
0.2	0.05	0.9	9.9128e-45±1.981e-44	0 ± 0	1.8089e-14±1.260e-14	0.0012649±0.0040293
0.2	0.1	0.6	1.005e-44±1.0984e-44	0 ± 0	1.3234e-14±9.075e-15	0.0005233±0.0028665
0.2	0.1	0.8	1.017e-44±1.9854e-44	0 ± 0	1.4773e-14±6.429e-15	0.0010541±0.0040832
0.2	0.1	0.9	1.445e-44±3.3578e-44	0 ± 0	1.548e-14±7.4454e-15	0.0006787±0.0026002
0.2	0.2	0.6	8.618e-45± 1.182e-44	0 ± 0	1.2286e-14±5.624e-15	0.0007423±0.002834
0.2	0.2	0.8	6.6735e-45±1.265e-44	0 ± 0	1.2405e-14±7.375e-15	0.002159±0.0070007
0.2	0.2	0.9	1.795e-44±6.1427e-44	0 ± 0	1.501e-14±7.188e-15	0.00145± 0.0055195
0.3	0.05	0.6	6.7199e-45±7.116e-45	0 ± 0	1.714e-14±1.5755e-14	0.0017884±0.0049494
0.3	0.05	0.8	8.1755e-45±1.329e-44	0 ± 0	1.5484e-14±8.381e-15	0.0038774±0.0099434
0.3	0.05	0.9	3.963e-45±5.0962e-45	0 ± 0	1.572e-14±7.7584e-15	0 ± 0
0.3	0.1	0.6	6.8296e-45±1.368e-44	0 ± 0	1.726e-14±8.0223e-15	0.0032527±0.0077151
0.3	0.1	0.8	6.4037e-45±9.971e-45	0 ± 0	1.513e-14±8.4348e-15	0.001712±0.0067496
0.3	0.1	0.9	6.319e-45±9.0296e-45	0 ± 0	1.939e-14±2.6852e-14	0.0025412±0.0069023
0.3	0.2	0.6	9.224e-45±1.4724e-44	0 ± 0	1.6194e-14±1.157e-14	0.0005477±0.0029996
0.3	0.2	0.8	5.228e-45±9.1183e-45	0 ± 0	1.1576e-14±4.248e-15	0 ± 0
0.3	0.2	0.9	8.914e-45±2.1925e-44	0 ± 0	1.205e-14±4.5643e-15	0.0010967±0.0060066

balance between exploration and exploitation, good robustness against parameter changes, remarkable performance on complex multifaceted functions, and fast convergence while maintaining population diversity.

Therefore when dealing with a continuous problem where fast convergence with minimal parameter tuning is required, GWO seems to be the best option. When the search space is rough, discrete, or contains deceptive local optima that require appropriate parameter tuning and population diversity, GA may be a more suitable option. Finally, in problems with complex and multifaceted search spaces where a simultaneous balance of exploration and exploitation is desirable, as well as in noisy and dynamic environments (sometimes with conflicting goals) where simultaneous generalizability and parameter stability are required, a hybrid algorithm may be a more suitable option.

Table 27.7 summarizes the key characteristics of these two algorithms.

TABLE 27.7 Key characteristics of GWO and GA.

Aspect	GWO	GA
Inspiration	Social hierarchy and pack hunting of grey wolves	Evolutionary biology and natural selection (Darwinian evolution)
Mechanism	Encircling, hunting, attacking Leadership-based position updating	Selection, crossover, mutation, generation-based
Search strategy	Leader-based search with encircling and attacking	Fitness-driven evolution with genetic operators
Exploration	Guided by alpha, beta, and delta wolves	Driven by mutation and a diverse initial population
Exploitation	Convergence toward the best solutions found	Refinement through crossover and selection
Exploration vs exploitation	– Balanced via α, β, δ roles – Well-balanced via adaptive coefficients	– Controlled by mutation and selection pressure – Strongly dependent on operator tuning
Parameters	Few (mainly 'a' coefficient, C, A)	Several (mutation rate, crossover rate, population size, selection rate)
Parameter sensitivity	Low: few parameters, robust to changes	High: sensitive to mutation/crossover tuning and selection type
Convergence behavior	Stable and fast in many multimodal problems	May stagnate or suffer from premature convergence
Convergence speed	Generally faster and more stable	Slower, prone to premature convergence, but robust in diverse landscapes
Convergence diversity	Can decrease in later stages	Maintained through mutation and diverse operators
Diversity maintenance	Implicit through hierarchical structure	Explicit through crossover and mutation
Encoding flexibility	Real-valued mostly	Real, binary, or custom encoding
Problem type	Continuous optimization, constrained problems	A wide range of problems, including combinatorial and discrete
Ease of implication	Relatively simple	Can be more complex due to encoding and operator design
Hybrid potential	High	High

GA, Genetic algorithm; *GWO*, grey wolf optimization.

27.5 Conclusion

Finding optimal solutions to many real-world problems has increasingly highlighted the need for the development of optimization algorithms. In the meantime, in many of today's nonlinear, complex, and high-dimensional problems, classical optimization methods are not suitable due to gradient dependence and high computational cost. This problem has led to the introduction of various metaheuristic algorithms inspired by processes found in nature, of which the GWO algorithm and GA are two examples. The older GA algorithm is inspired by Darwin's genetic evolution, and the newer GWO algorithm is inspired by the collective hunting of grey wolves. In this chapter, a comparative analysis is given to the mechanisms of operation, similarities and differences, weaknesses and advantages, how to synergize and hybridize, evaluate in benchmark functions, and practical applications of these two algorithms.

The hierarchical structure and leadership-based position updating of GWO have led to fast convergence and strong exploitation capabilities in many applications, such as energy system optimization, engineering design, and feature selection in machine learning. In contrast to these strengths, the possibility of losing diversity and premature convergence in highly multifaceted problems may overshadow its performance. Through genetic operators and with the ability to preserve population diversity and explore larger search spaces, GA has recorded successful applications in complex, multifaceted, and even discontinuous objective functions, such as in bioinformatics, machine learning, operations research, and financial modeling, etc. However, along with these advantages, GAs are very sensitive to parameter tuning and are computationally intensive.

Algorithm selection based on problem-specific criteria requires a comprehensive comparative analysis based on their distinctive features, complementary strengths, and performance patterns. The lack of consistent superiority of one algorithm over another in all optimization scenarios suggests that the future of optimization research lies not in the competition between these algorithms, but in their synergistic combination through hybrid approaches that exploit their complementary strengths. By integrating the directed and hierarchical search mechanism of GWO with the diverse evolutionary exploration of GA, researchers can develop more powerful and efficient optimization techniques that can address a wider range of complex and challenging real-world problems, such as advanced feature selection, more energy-efficient system optimization, and improved resource management in cloud computing. Continued research on the types, advancements, and especially combinations of these powerful optimization techniques will lead to the discovery of more efficient and innovative solutions to today's and tomorrow's complex problems. Key takeaways include:

- Theoretical foundations: GWO, inspired by the social hierarchy and hunting behavior of grey wolves, offers a compact yet effective search mechanism with few tunable parameters. GA, modeled on biological evolution, provides flexible problem encoding and diverse search via genetic operators like selection, crossover, and mutation.
- Comparative performance: While both algorithms are population-based and stochastic, GWO tends to converge faster and more stably in many real-world tasks. GA, however, remains a valuable choice where solution diversity and customization are required.
- Hybrid approaches: Combining the grey wolf search algorithm with GA operators reduces their individual weaknesses and, by synergizing their strengths, leads to improved robustness and search diversity, which is especially useful in complex multifaceted problems with diverse and sometimes conflicting objectives.

When choosing between GWO, GA, or a hybrid approach, practitioners should consider the nature of the problem domain, their computational budget, and their performance requirements. GWO is ideal for problems with continuous variables that require simplicity, robustness, and fast convergence, while GA is suitable for domains that require flexible and adaptive coding along with searching in a large and rugged space. Hybrid models offer a middle ground or tradeoff to deal with multiobjective and high-stakes problems. The evolving landscape of intelligent systems calls for further research into hybridization frameworks, adaptive control of algorithmic parameters, and integration with emerging AI paradigms such as reinforcement learning and neuromorphic computing. As real-world problems grow more complex and dynamic, intelligent hybrid metaheuristics like GWO-GA will play an increasingly pivotal role in shaping the next generation of optimization technologies.

References

[1] D.H. Ackley, A Connectionist Machine for Genetic Hill Climbing, Kluwer Academic Publishers, (1987).

[2] J.H. Holland, Adaptation in natural and artificial systems, University of Michigan Press Google Schola 2 (1975) 29–41.

[3] S. Mirjalili, S.M. Mirjalili, A. Lewis, Grey wolf optimizer, Advances in Engineering Software 69 (2014) 46–61.

[4] M. Swerhun, J. Foley, B. Massop, V. Mago, A summary of the prevalence of genetic algorithms in bioinformatics from 2015 onwards, arXiv preprint arXiv:2008.09017, 2020.

[5] H. Bhasin, S. Bhatia, Application of genetic algorithms in machine learning, IJCSIT 2 (5) (2011) 2412–2415.

[6] Z.Y. Taha, A.A. Abdullah, T.A. Rashid, Optimizing feature selection with genetic algorithms: a review of methods and applications, arXiv preprint arXiv:2409.14563, 2024.

[7] C.K.H. Lee, A review of applications of genetic algorithms in operations management, Engineering Applications of Artificial Intelligence 76 (2018) 1–12.

[8] X. Yan, H. Liu, Z. Zhu, Q. Wu, Hybrid genetic algorithm for engineering design problems, Cluster Computing 20 (1) (2017) 263–275.

[9] R. Aguilar-Rivera, M. Valenzuela-Rendón, J.J. Rodríguez-Ortiz, Genetic algorithms and Darwinian approaches in financial applications: a survey, Expert Systems with Applications 42 (21) (2015) 7684–7697.

[10] A. Khan, A.S. Qureshi, N. Wahab, M. Hussain, M.Y. Hamza, A recent survey on the applications of genetic programming in image processing, Computational Intelligence 37 (4) (2021) 1745–1778.

[11] Y. Shang, M. Zheng, J. Li, X. Zheng, An effective feature selection approach based on hybrid grey wolf optimizer and genetic algorithm for hyperspectral image, Scientific Reports 15 (1) (2025) 1968.

[12] M. Milosevic, R. Cep, L. Cepova, D. Lukic, A. Antic, M. Djurdjev, A hybrid grey wolf optimizer for process planning optimization with precedence constraints, Materials 14 (23) (2021) 7360.
[13] K. Yadav, B. Kumar, J.M. Guerrero, A. Lashab, A hybrid genetic algorithm and grey wolf optimizer technique for faster global peak detection in PV system under partial shading, Sustainable Computing: Informatics and Systems 35 (2022) 100770.
[14] D.K. Geleta, M.S. Manshahia, A hybrid of grey wolf optimization and genetic algorithm for optimization of hybrid wind and solar renewable energy system, Journal of the Operations Research Society of China 10 (4) (2022) 749–762.
[15] S.M. Elghamrawy, A.E. Hassanien, A hybrid genetic–Grey Wolf optimization algorithm for optimizing Takagi–Sugeno–Kang fuzzy systems, Neural Computing and Applications 34 (19) (2022) 17051–17069.
[16] M.A. Pinazo, New genetic gray wolf optimizer with a random selective mutation for wind farm layout optimization, Heliyon 10 (23) (2024).
[17] M.S. Shaikh, H. Lin, G. Zheng, C. Wang, X. Dong, Innovative hybrid grey wolf-particle swarm optimization for calculating transmission line parameter, Heliyon 10 (19) (2024).

Chapter 28

Enhancing hub-motor performance in electric vehicles: grey wolf multiobjective design optimizer to resolve performance trade-offs

Tohid Sharifi, Ali Jamali-Fard, and Mojtaba Mirsalim
Department of Electrical Engineering, Electrical Machines and Transformers Research Laboratory (EMTRL), Amirkabir University of Technology (Tehran Polytechnic), Tehran, Iran

Nomenclature

Mathematical symbols

P_{out}	Total output power, W
P_{in}	Total input power, W
m	Number of phases
$v(t)$	Input phase voltage, v
$i(t)$	Input phase current, A
R	Phase resistance, Ω
$e(t)$	Induced back-EMF, v
E_m	Maximum induced back-EMF, v
f	Waveform frequency, Hz
I_m	Maximum input current, A
N_t	Number of winding turns per coil
P_r	Rotor pole number
N	Rotational speed, r.p.m.
B_g	Airgap flux density, T
K_f	Fringing factor
S_e	Maximum overlapping area between rotor and stator poles, m^2
W_{ov}	Overlapping width, m
L_a	Axial length, m
W_t	tooth width, m
D_{so}	Stator outer diameter, m
W_m	magnet width, m
g	Airgap length, m
K_i	Current factor
I_{rms}	Root mean square of input current, A
K_{cu}	Fill factor
P_s	Stator pole numbers
S_{sa}	Slot area, m^2
J_s	Current density, A.m^{-2}
W_{so}	Slot opening, m
W_{sb}	Slot opening in the base, m
h_s	Slot depth, m

Grey Wolf Optimizer. DOI: https://doi.org/10.1016/B978-0-443-36624-6.00051-2

D_{sy}	Stator yoke diameter, m
K_{sr}	Split ratio
E.C.	Effective cost of the motor, USD
P_p	Cost per weight of permanent magnet, USD.kg^{-1}
m_p	Total weight of the permanent magnet, kg
P_c	Cost per weight of copper, USD.kg^{-1}
m_c	Total weight of the winding, kg
P_i	Cost per weight of steel core, USD.kg^{-1}
m_i	Total weight of the core (both stator and rotor), kg
P.F.	Power factor
$v_{d,r}$	D-axis voltage in the rotor reference frame, v
$I_{d,r}$	D-axis current in the rotor reference frame, A
$v_{q,r}$	Q-axis voltage in the rotor reference frame, v
$i_{q,r}$	Q-axis current in the rotor reference frame, A
$e_{d,r}$	D-axis back-EMF in the rotor reference frame, v
$e_{q,r}$	Q-axis back-EMF in the rotor reference frame, v
P_{cu}	Copper losses, W
$P_{cu,acw}$	Copper losses in the active part of the windings, W
$P_{cu,enw}$	Copper losses in the end part of the winding, W
P_{dc}	DC component of the copper losses, W
P_{ac}	AC component of the copper losses, W
R_{acw}	Electrical resistance of the active part of the winding, Ω
L_{acw}	Length of the active part of the coil, m
A_{con}	The surface area of the conductors in the windings, m^2
R_{enw}	Electrical resistance of the end part of the winding, Ω
R_{enw}	Length of the end part of the coil, m
D_w	Diameter of the conductors in the windings, m

Greek symbols

η	Efficiency, %
θ_v	Phase advance of the input voltage, rad
θ_i	Phase advance of the input current, rad
$\psi(t)$	Flux linkage of one phase, Wb
$\Phi(t)$	Airgap flux, Wb
θ_{er}	Rotor's angular location, electrical rad
ω_{mr}	Rotational speed, mechanical rad
Φ_m	Airgap flux peak, Wb
β_s	Angular span of the stator tooth (pole arc)
β_m	Angular span of the magnet (magnet arc)
α_s	Angular span of stator slot
θe	Phase angle of the input current, rad
ρ_{cu}	Density of copper, kg.m^{-3}

28.1 Introduction

Replacing fossil fuel-powered internal combustion engines with pollution-free electric motors, the transportation electrification concept has been proposed as the most reliable solution to address imminent global issues, including resource depletion, energy crises, and air pollution. As the core element of electric vehicles, the electric powertrains reign supreme in the center of the researchers' interest, where improvements in their structure significantly influence the performance of the vehicles [1]. Classically, as shown in Fig. 28.1, the propulsion structure with a central electric motor is implemented, and the propulsion power from the motor to the wheels is distributed through the chain of mechanical transmission unit (MTU) [2]. Accordingly, the indirect drive results in mechanical losses and efficiency reduction in the components of the MTU, including the fixed gear transmission and drive differential units. Additionally, a significant portion of the onboard space inside the vehicle is occupied by them, which is unfavorable in terms of energy density, manufacturing processes, and passenger comfort [3,4]. Requiring periodic maintenance efforts besides the mentioned

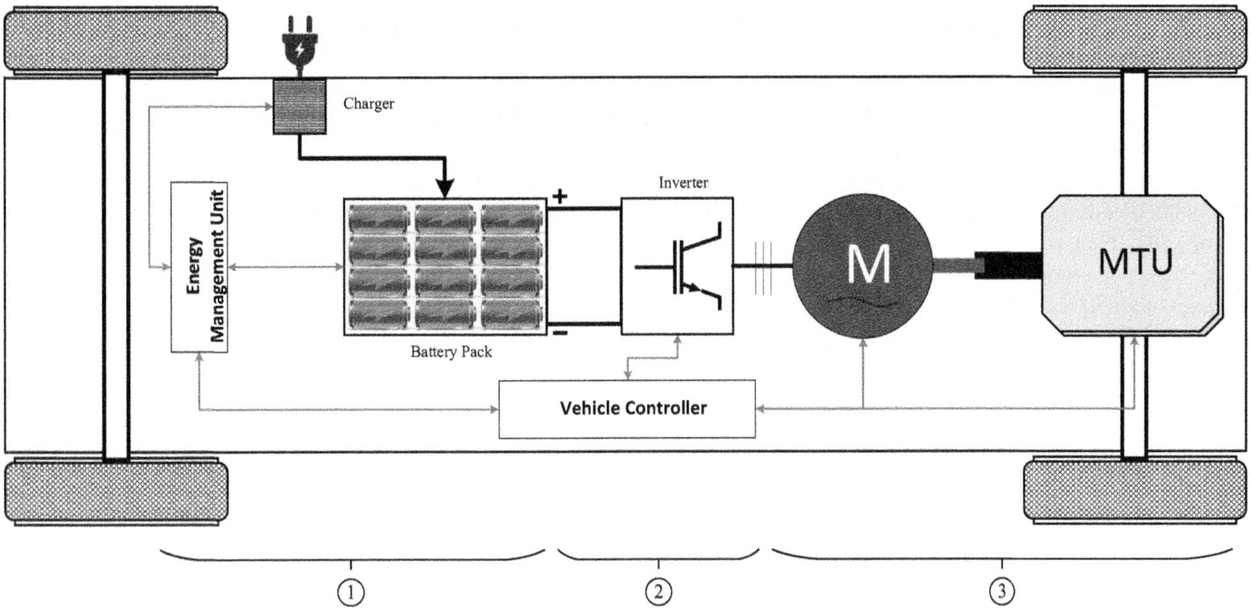

FIGURE 28.1 The powertrain configuration with a central motor (M) and the mechanical transmission unit (MTU), including (1) energy source, (2) power converter, and (3) electromechanical propulsion unit.

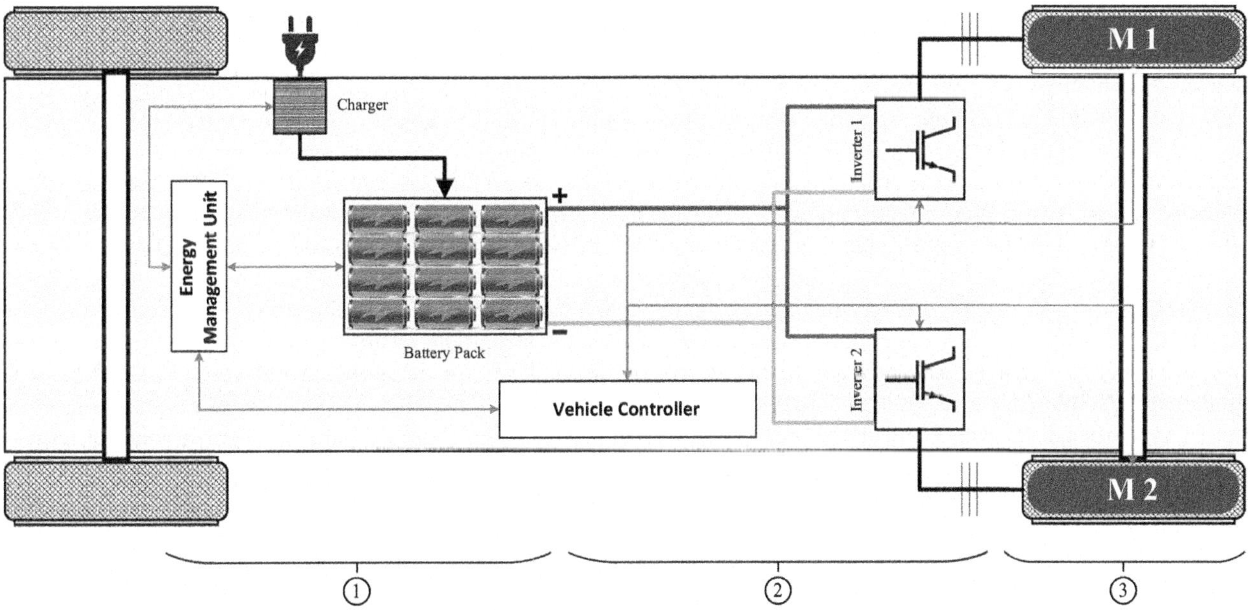

FIGURE 28.2 The in-wheel powertrain configuration with hub-motors (M1 and M2), including (1) Energy source, (2) power converter, and (3) electromechanical propulsion unit.

drawbacks, this powertrain configuration limits the efficiency, vehicle span, and ultimately, the global adoption of electric vehicles.

As an alternative technology, the in-wheel powertrain technology has gained considerable popularity in recent years, where instead of a central propulsion motor, the hub-motors directly drive the wheels without additional mechanical transmission components, as shown in Fig. 28.2 [3,5]. Accordingly, the lack of a fixed gear transmission and differential in the electromechanical transmission unit improves the propulsion efficiency by decreasing the mechanical losses by up to 15%, and the remaining area can be optimized for enhanced passenger comfort, increased cargo capacity, or expanded battery/power unit [6]. Moreover, through independent wheel control (unlike the central powertrain), the vehicle benefits from a higher number of controllable degrees of freedom [7].

Despite offering numerous advantages over the central powertrain, the in-wheel configuration requires improvements to be considered as a promising alternative. First, although the MTU is entirely eliminated, the unsprung mass continues to be problematic due to the presence of more electric motors in the wheels [8]. Improvements in the total efficiency of the vehicle are also an indispensable necessity, as it leads to maximization in the covered driving span [9]. Moreover, the in-situ vehicle comfort is always an advertising feature, which can attract more attention, and should be augmented continually. Consequently, although the configuration of the powertrain experiences improvements with the in-wheel direct drive method, the structural optimization is a hotspot in the design of electric vehicles, which encourages researchers to seriously explore efficient methodologies. As the core component of the in-wheel powertrain, in this study, the design optimization of a hub-motor is discussed, and several key improvements are suggested, facilitating the function evaluations and accelerating the procedure.

28.2 Related studies

28.2.1 General overview

As a reliable performance improvement strategy, the design optimization is securely utilized by the state-of-the-art studies on electric powertrains and electrical machines [10,11]. The total efficiency of a central powertrain is subjected to maximization by optimizing the internal energy consumption of the battery pack, considering the electric motor and fixed gear transmission designs in Ref. [2]. The resultant convex nonlinear problem is optimized over the worldwide harmonized light vehicle test cycle class 3 [12], using the nonlinear interior point optimizer (IPOPT) solver, where the proposed framework is capable of accurately predicting and optimizing the power losses. Combining the concepts of shape and topology optimization, the genetic algorithm (GA) is utilized in Ref. [13] to optimize the core and permanent magnet material consumption besides the performance criteria, where converting the multiobjective problem to a single-objective counterpart using the weighted sum method, the average torque has shown a slight improvement of about 6%, while the reduction in the torque ripple is more significant. In Ref. [14], the magnetic equivalent circuit (MEC) has been utilized for the initial design of a 100 kW double U-type interior permanent magnet synchronous motor (PMSM) for electric vehicle propulsion. After specifying the influential parameters on the performance using MEC, in the subsequent stepwise optimal design, the vehicle comfort is guaranteed using a benchmarked optimization algorithm, where, through an iterative procedure, the torque ripple is achieved below 4%. Relying on the direct (D) and quadratic (Q) components of the inductance values (L_d and L_q), the geometry parameters of the flux barriers and bridges of an interior PMSM significantly affect its torque density, ripple, and efficiency, as indicated in Ref. [15]. Therefore, a new framework based on the kernel support vector machine surrogate model and adaptive particle swarm optimization algorithm has been suggested, where the maximum torque is improved by 10.3%. Similarly, in Ref. [16], the structural parameters of the fluid-shaped (Joukowsky) barriers are treated as the decision variable in the topology optimization of a high-speed, 18,000 r.p.m., synchronous reluctance motor for traction applications, and a significant performance improvement in terms of peak torque, power, efficiency, and power factor is observable [17].

Highlighting the potential trade-offs in the design optimization of a linear motor with high force density, the study in Ref. [18] has exploited the capabilities of the Nondominated Sorting Genetic Algorithm II (NSGA-II) in proposing nondominated or Pareto-optimal solutions for multiobjective design problems. Accordingly, based on the analytical MEC model of the motor, the trust force is enhanced by 9.45%, and the trust ripple is cut by 46.39% over eight structural parameters. In Ref. [19], to achieve a trade-off in the design of a hybrid magnet PMSM for the electric vehicle powertrains, a stratified strategy is prepared, and the contradicting performance criteria are divided into two levels. Accordingly, due to the priorities of cost effectiveness and torque density in the powertrains, they are stratified in level 1, while the remaining objectives, including torque ripple, efficiency, and cogging torque, are optimized in level 2. After realizing the influential parameters through sensitivity analysis, in the first level, the design of experiment method is used for the optimization, and the results are exported to the second level, where the response surface methodology is used to achieve the optimal design of the motor. In both stages, the weighted sum method is used to convert the multi-objective problem to a scalar optimization. The flux intensifying feature in Ref. [20] for an internal PMSM has been achieved through multiobjective optimization, alongside the maximized electromagnetic torque and minimized torque ripple. Determining the influential parameters by the comprehensive sensitivity analysis, the sequential nonlinear programming results in the best trade-off between performance criteria, by converting the problem to a single-objective form. The multilevel optimization is also the framework in Ref. [21], where an unequal yoke switch reluctance motor's output torque, core losses, and torque ripple have been optimized in the first layer, using the comprehensive sensitivity analysis, Kriging model, and sequential nonlinear programming method to find a suitable trade-off. Subsequently, the results are exported to the second layer for further improvements. In Ref. [22], a novel multiobjective optimization strategy has been proposed for the thermal and electromagnetic performance improvement in the 20 kW, 3000 r.p.m. surface-mounted PMSM for the unmanned aerial vehicles. The function evaluations have been accomplished using analytical electromagnetic and thermal models, thereby resulting in an efficient optimization procedure.

28.2.2 Lack of knowledge

An enduring challenge in the design optimization of electrical machines lies in managing the inherent trade-off between the precision of performance prediction and the associated computational expense. This challenge is fundamentally shaped by two interdependent factors: the optimization strategy employed and the modeling approach used for function evaluations. The overall computational cost is directly proportional to the number of function evaluations required and the time needed for each assessment. While the former is governed by the efficiency of the chosen optimization algorithm, the latter is dictated by the fidelity and complexity of the simulation model. This intricate relationship presents a significant bottleneck to the rapid and effective exploration of the design space for novel, high-performance electrical machines. A critical examination of the current state-of-the-art reveals several key knowledge gaps that impede further progress in this domain.

28.2.2.1 The quest for more efficient multiobjective optimization strategies

In the realm of multiobjective optimization for electrical machines, where conflicting performance criteria such as efficiency, torque density, and cost must be simultaneously optimized, the reliance on metaheuristic algorithms is prevalent. While algorithms like genetic algorithms and particle swarm optimization have proven effective to an extent, they often necessitate a substantial number of function evaluations to converge to a robust Pareto front. This high number of evaluations, even with advanced and efficient implementations, prolongs the optimization process considerably. Consequently, there remains a pressing need for the development and application of more sophisticated optimization strategies.

28.2.2.2 Lack of systematic comparative analysis of metaheuristic algorithms

The field of metaheuristics is rich with a diverse array of algorithms, each with its own unique search mechanism and control parameters. However, a significant gap exists in the literature regarding a systematic and comprehensive comparison in terms of convergence, diversity of solutions, and computational efficiency, specifically within the application domain of electric motor design. Such a comparative study is crucial for providing designers with clear guidance on selecting the most appropriate optimization tool for their specific design problem.

28.2.2.3 The dichotomy of modeling approaches

The efficacy of any design optimization is fundamentally limited by the model used to evaluate the performance of each design candidate. A significant challenge stems from the opposing characteristics of the primary modeling techniques:

- **High-fidelity, high-cost models:** The finite element analysis (FEA) based modeling approach provides detailed insights into the complex electromagnetic, thermal, and mechanical behaviors within the machine [23]. However, this high fidelity comes at the steep price of extensive computation time for each evaluation. For multiobjective optimization, which may require thousands of such evaluations, the reliance on FEA alone renders the process impractically time-consuming, often limiting the scope of the design space exploration.
- **High-speed, lower-accuracy models:** On the other end of the spectrum, analytical and surrogate modeling approaches offer the advantage of rapid function evaluations. Analytical models, based on simplified physical equations, and surrogate models (or metamodels), which approximate the behavior of the high-fidelity model using techniques like Kriging or neural networks, can drastically reduce the computational time [24,25]. However, this speed is often achieved at the cost of reduced accuracy. The approximations inherent in these models can lead to suboptimal or misleading results, where the optimized designs may not perform as predicted when subsequently verified with high-fidelity simulations.

28.2.3 Contributions

This study presents a novel and efficient framework for the design optimization of a permanent magnet hub-motor. The primary contribution of this work is the strategic application and validation of the multiobjective grey wolf optimizer

(MOGWO) [26] to effectively navigate the complex, multimodal design space inherent to such motors. To rigorously establish its superiority for this application, a second key contribution is a comprehensive comparative analysis. We benchmark the performance of MOGWO against two widely recognized and established algorithms, the NSGA-II [27] and multiobjective particle swarm optimization (MOPSO) [28]. This comparison is founded on critical performance metrics, including the rate of convergence, the diversity and coverage of the obtained Pareto fronts, and the overall computational cost measured by the number of function evaluations. A further and crucial contribution of this research lies in directly addressing the persistent challenge of the speed-versus-accuracy trade-off in simulation-based optimization. We develop, implement, and validate a high-fidelity motor model rooted in computational electromagnetics. This finite element model is engineered to be both computationally efficient and highly accurate. By hybridizing this fast and reliable model with the optimization algorithms, we create a powerful and robust optimization procedure.

28.2.4 Organization

The chapter is organized as follows. Section 28.3 introduces the initial hub-motor design and performs the preliminary sizing. The computational electromagnetics-based modeling of the motor is then presented and validated in Section 28.4. Following this, Section 28.5 explains the required performance criteria for the electric powertrain, while Section 28.6 identifies the most influential design parameters. The multiobjective optimization is performed in Section 28.7, and the resulting outcomes are thoroughly discussed in Section 28.8. Finally, Section 28.9 provides the conclusions drawn from this study.

28.3 Initial sizing and power formulation

The initial design of the permanent magnet (PM) hub-motor in Fig. 28.3 is based on a surface-mounted topology, adopting the slot and pole configuration from the reference design [29]. The fundamental performance metric, the output power, is determined by the electrical input power and the motor's efficiency, as shown in Eq. (28.1). The input power itself is defined as the time-averaged product of the instantaneous phase voltage and phase current over one electrical period for a motor with m phases, as formulated in Eq. (28.2).

$$P_{out} = \eta P_{in} \tag{28.1}$$

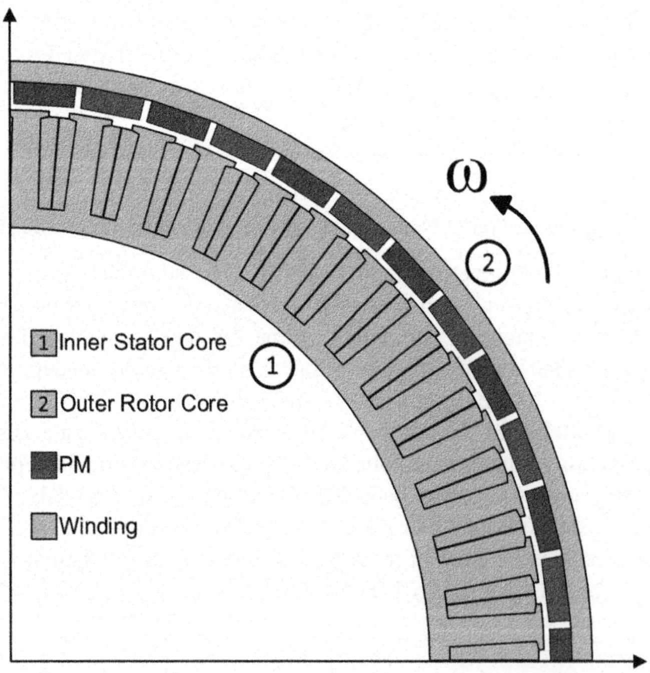

FIGURE 28.3 Initial electromagnetic design of the motor (only one-fourth of the motor configuration is illustrated here).

$$P_{in} = \frac{m}{T}\int_0^T v(t)i(t)dt \tag{28.2}$$

28.3.1 Idealized power calculation

To establish a direct relationship between power and the core electromagnetic characteristics of the motor, we first consider the phase voltage in Eq. (28.3). The voltage supplied to each phase consists of a resistive voltage drop across the winding resistance and the back electromotive force induced by the rotating magnets.

$$v(t) = R_{ph}i(t) + e(t) \tag{28.3}$$

For the purpose of initial sizing, the resistive losses in the windings are often neglected $\left(R_{ph} \approx 0\right)$. This simplification allows the input power to be expressed as a function of the interaction between the back-EMF (electromotive force) and the phase current, as shown in Eq. (28.4). Considering fundamental harmonic, the back-EMF and phase current can be described by the time-dependent forms in Eqs. (28.5) and (28.6).

$$P_{in} = \frac{m}{T}\int_0^T e(t)i(t)dt \tag{28.4}$$

$$e(t) = E_m \cos(2\pi ft + \theta_v) \tag{28.5}$$

$$i(t) = I_m \cos(2\pi ft + \theta_i) \tag{28.6}$$

By substituting these sinusoidal expressions into the power integral of Eq. (28.4), we arrive at the simplified algebraic form for input power in Eq. (28.7). The term θ represents the phase difference between the back-EMF and current vectors, and $\cos(\theta)$ is the power factor. Consequently, the output power can be directly expressed as shown in Eq. (28.8).

$$P_{in} = \frac{mE_mI_m}{2T}\int_0^T \cos(\theta_v - \theta_i)dt = \frac{mE_mI_m}{2}\cos(\theta) \tag{28.7}$$

$$P_{out} = \eta\frac{mE_mI_m}{2}\cos(\theta) \tag{28.8}$$

28.3.2 Peak back-EMF derivation

The back-EMF is generated according to Faraday's Law of Induction, where a changing magnetic flux linkage ($\psi(t)$) in the stator windings induces a voltage. As shown in Eq. (28.9), the back-EMF is the time derivative of this flux linkage. This can be expanded using the chain rule to relate it to the change in the airgap flux with respect to the electrical angle and the electrical angular velocity. The peak back-EMF is achieved when the rate of change of flux is maximal.

$$e(t) = \frac{d\psi(t)}{dt} = N_t\frac{d(\Phi(t))}{d\theta_{er}}\frac{d\theta_{er}}{dt} = N_t\frac{P_r}{2}\omega_{mr}\left.\frac{d(\Phi(t))}{d\theta_{er}}\right|_{E_m(max)} = N_t\frac{P_r}{2}\frac{2\pi}{60}N\Phi_m \tag{28.9}$$

The maximum airgap flux occurs when a stator tooth and a rotor magnet are perfectly aligned, maximizing the magnetic flux path. It is calculated in Eq. (28.10) as the product of the average airgap flux density, the effective cross-sectional area of the flux path, and a fringing factor that accounts for the leakage of the flux. By substituting the expression back into the back-EMF equation, we obtain the final formula for the peak back-EMF as shown in Eq. (28.11). This equation links the peak voltage to the number of winding turns, rotational speed, and key geometric and magnetic parameters.

$$\Phi_m = B_gK_fS_e \tag{28.10}$$

$$E_m = N_t\frac{P_r}{2}\frac{2\pi}{60}NB_gK_fS_e \tag{28.11}$$

28.3.3 Geometric definition of overlap area

To calculate the peak back-EMF, we must first define the maximum effective overlap area. Assuming a rectangular geometry for the interaction area between the stator teeth and the rotor magnets, S_e is the product of the motor's active axial length and the effective overlap width, as given by Eq. (28.12).

$$S_e = W_{ov} \times L_a \tag{28.12}$$

The stator tooth width and the permanent magnet width are determined by their respective angular spans and the relevant diameters, as shown in Eqs. (28.13) and (28.14). Note that in Eq. (28.14), the air gap dimension g is considered negligible compared to the stator outer diameter for simplification.

$$W_t = \beta_s.\ \frac{D_{so}}{2} \tag{28.13}$$

$$W_m = \beta_m.\left(\frac{D_{so}}{2} + g\right) \approx \beta_m.\left(\frac{D_{so}}{2}\right) \tag{28.14}$$

The effective overlap width is physically limited by whichever component is narrower—the stator tooth or the permanent magnet. Therefore W_{ov} is taken as the minimum of these two widths, as expressed in Eq. (28.15). For this particular design, it is assumed that the stator tooth width is the limiting factor. Under this assumption, the maximized overlapping area is calculated using Eq. (28.16).

$$W_{ov} = \min(W_t, W_m) = \frac{D_{so}}{2}.\ \min(\beta_s, \beta_m) \tag{28.15}$$

$$S_e = \frac{D_{so}}{2}.\ \beta_s.\ L_a \tag{28.16}$$

28.3.4 Peak current and slot geometry

To formulate a complete sizing equation for output power, an expression for the peak current, I_m, is also required. We derive this from the concept of electric loading, related to the allowable current density in the stator windings. This is a function of the total copper area available, which is given by the number of slots, the area of a single slot, and the copper fill factor. This total current is distributed among the m phases, and N_t turns per phase, leading to the formulation for I_m in Eq. (28.17).

$$I_m = \sqrt{2}\,I_{rms} = \sqrt{2}\,\frac{K_{cu}P_sS_{sa}J_s}{2mN_t} \tag{28.17}$$

The area of a single trapezoidal stator slot is calculated as the product of its depth and its average width, as shown in Eq. (28.18). The geometric parameters that define this area are detailed in Eqs. (28.19) through (28.21), where they are linked to the stator outer diameter and several dimensionless geometric ratios. By substituting these individual geometric definitions, a comprehensive expression for the slot area is derived in terms of the stator outer diameter and the key design ratios, as presented in Eq. (28.22).

$$S_{sa} = \left(\frac{W_{so} + W_{sb}}{2}\right)h_s \tag{28.18}$$

$$h_s = \frac{D_{so} - D_{sy}}{2} = \left(\frac{1 - K_{sr}}{2}\right)D_{so} \tag{28.19}$$

$$W_{so} = \left(\frac{\pi D_{so}}{P_s}\right) - W_t = \alpha_{so}.\ \frac{D_{so}}{2} \tag{28.20}$$

$$W_{sb} = \alpha_{sy}.\ \frac{D_{sy}}{2} = \alpha_{sy}.\ \frac{K_{sr}D_{so}}{2} = \frac{\alpha_{sy}}{\alpha_{so}}K_{sr}.\ W_{so} \tag{28.21}$$

$$S_{sa} = \frac{D_{so}^2}{8}(\alpha_{so} + \alpha_{sy}K_{sr})(1 - K_{sr}) \tag{28.22}$$

28.3.5 The complete sizing equation

The final step is to construct the main sizing equation for the motor's output power. This is accomplished by substituting the derived expressions for the peak back-EMF (from Eq. (28.11)) and the peak current (Eq. (28.17)) into the output power Eq. (28.8). This substitution yields the comprehensive relationship shown in Eq. (28.23). This equation is a powerful design tool, as it connects the motor's power output directly to its primary geometric dimensions (D_{so}, L_a), material properties, and operating parameters. From this detailed equation, we can extract a more intuitive proportionality, shown in Eq. (28.24). This relationship highlights the key drivers of power output for a PM motor. This fundamental relationship, often called the "sizing equation," serves as the cornerstone for the initial design and performance estimation of the hub-motor.

$$P_{out} = \frac{\eta\pi\sqrt{2}}{3840} P_r N B_g K_f K_{cu} P_s J_s D_{so}^3 L_a \beta_s (\alpha_{so} + \alpha_{sy} K_{sr})(1 - K_{sr})\cos(\theta) \tag{28.23}$$

$$P_{out} \propto (B_g \cdot J_s) \cdot (L_a D_{so}^3) \cdot N \tag{28.24}$$

On the other hand, designing the internal layout of an electric motor is a highly complex task that cannot be solved by a sizing equation like the one referenced as Eq. (28.24), which is based exclusively on the motor's external dimensions (L_a, D_{so}). The fundamental difficulty lies in the fact that there is no unique, one-to-one relationship between the motor's internal geometry and its performance. A specific performance target, such as a certain power output, can be achieved through numerous combinations of internal components and operating conditions. This flexibility becomes a significant challenge when multiple design objectives must be considered simultaneously, as these goals are often in direct conflict.

A classic example of this is the inherent trade-off between performance and cost. To achieve high electromagnetic torque, the motor requires large permanent magnets to maximize the magnetic flux. Conversely, a primary economic goal is to minimize material costs, which necessitates reducing the size of permanent magnets, as they constitute a significant portion of the total expense. This push-and-pull dynamic, where improving one key metric degrades another, is a characteristic feature of complex engineering systems. Given these competing requirements, determining the optimal internal parameters through simple analytical formulas is impossible. The resolution of such design trade-offs demands a more sophisticated approach, namely a multicriteria optimization procedure. This computational method systematically explores the vast design space to identify a set of balanced compromises. These are known as Pareto-optimal solutions, which represent a collection of designs where no single objective can be improved without sacrificing another. This portfolio of optimal trade-offs provides engineers with a range of viable designs, allowing them to select (decision making) the one that best aligns with their specific project priorities, whether they favor maximum performance, minimum cost, or a calculated balance between the two.

Table 28.1 presents the initial design specifications for the PM hub-motor. While key parameters such as the rated specifications, slot to pole combination, and airgap length are defined, the design is primarily constrained by its external

TABLE 28.1 Electromagnetic specifications of the three-phase in-wheel hub-motor.

Parameter	Unit	Value
Rated power	[kW]	10
Rated current	[A]	20
Rated speed	[r.p.-m.]	400
Stator slot number	[-]	50
Rotor pole number	[-]	51
Outer diameter	[mm]	230
Axial length	[mm]	56
Airgap length	[mm]	1.2

dimensions at this preliminary stage. The crucial internal geometric dimensions remain undefined and will be systematically determined through a detailed design optimization study presented in the subsequent sections.

28.4 Modeling and performance (function) evaluation

A critical step in optimizing in-wheel motors is the ability to accurately and repeatedly evaluate electromagnetic performance based on key structural parameters. The function evaluation using electromagnetic study presents a significant challenge with analytical methods, as these techniques consistently force a trade-off between computational speed and predictive accuracy. For an optimization study to be genuinely successful, it must achieve both of these goals simultaneously, as neither can be compromised without undermining the result [30,31]. On one end of the spectrum are methods that prioritize speed, such as the MEC technique, which simplifies the complex electromagnetic model into a lumped-parameter circuit to allow for rapid function evaluations with minimal computational resources. This simplification, however, comes at a high cost of accuracy reduction, a weakness that is particularly pronounced in optimization studies, where input structural parameters are varied iteratively [32,33]. Similarly, data-driven approaches using Kriging or machine-learning-based surrogate models can complete an optimization in a very short time, yet their limitations are substantial. Not only do they require a vast repository of training data prepared by time-consuming FEA, but their reliability also becomes problematic when predicting complex criteria like average torque and torque ripple. Most critically, these models are inherently brittle and valid only for a single motor configuration, meaning any modification to material properties or drive conditions necessitates a complete and laborious regeneration of the entire data set and training process [34].

At the opposite end of the spectrum lies FEA, which is considered the fundamental standard for predictive electromagnetic study due to its power as a numerical tool for performing high-fidelity analysis on complex geometries with nonlinear material properties [35]. Despite its accuracy, the underlying computational electromagnetics are exceptionally time-demanding, rendering FEA fundamentally inappropriate for design optimization studies that require thousands of rapid, iterative evaluations. Therefore it is evident that an effective design optimization framework must overcome this fundamental problem in the modeling by simultaneously providing the high-fidelity results characteristic of FEA alongside the computational efficiency required for a comprehensive and successful iterative optimization process. This study employs the electromagnetic design lab (EMDLAB) computational electromagnetics solver, introduced in Ref. [36,37], to perform the magneto-static analysis. A key advantage of this tool is its ability to calculate the required performance criteria with high accuracy in a remarkably short amount of time. Consequently, this efficiency permits the comprehensive execution and comparison of various optimization algorithms without concern for the number of function evaluations. To ensure the reliability of our findings, the results obtained from EMDLAB are subsequently validated against simulations from the industry-standard finite element analysis software, Ansys Electronics Desktop.

Fig. 28.4 provides a comprehensive visual summary of the FEA model of the hub-motor, which was created and solved using EMDLAB's magneto-static solver. The top-right quadrant displays the computational meshing, which is the critical process of discretizing the motor's complex geometry into a fine grid of smaller elements. The density of this mesh is directly linked to the trade-off between computational time and solution accuracy, with a finer mesh being necessary to capture detailed energy conversion phenomena. The figure further visualizes the magnetic field in two distinct ways. The top-left quadrant shows the path of the magnetic flux lines (representing the magnetic vector potential), which illustrate the route of the magnetic field throughout the machine. In the bottom half, a color-coded map reveals the flux density distribution, quantitatively showing the strength of the magnetic field in different components of the motor. This view is particularly important for identifying regions that may be approaching magnetic saturation, a nonlinear effect that can limit performance. Crucially, the entire analysis shown is conducted under no-load conditions. This specific scenario isolates the magnetic field generated purely by the permanent magnets without influence from stator currents, which is a fundamental step for verifying the model's integrity and calculating baseline performance characteristics like the back-EMF and cogging torque.

Fig. 28.5 presents a crucial validation of the EMDLAB solver by providing a direct visual comparison of its results against those from the Ansys Electronics Desktop. The figure displays the magnetic flux density distribution across the motor's cross-section, specifically under full-load operating conditions, which is a critical state where both the permanent magnets and the current-carrying windings contribute to the magnetic field. As illustrated, the flux density map generated by EMDLAB (1) shows excellent qualitative and quantitative agreement with the results from Ansys (2). Most importantly, the comparison confirms that the EMDLAB solver can accurately capture complex and highly nonlinear phenomena such as local magnetic saturation. This is evident in the high-density regions, which are nearly identical in both simulations. This successful benchmark is vital, as it builds confidence that the computationally faster EMDLAB

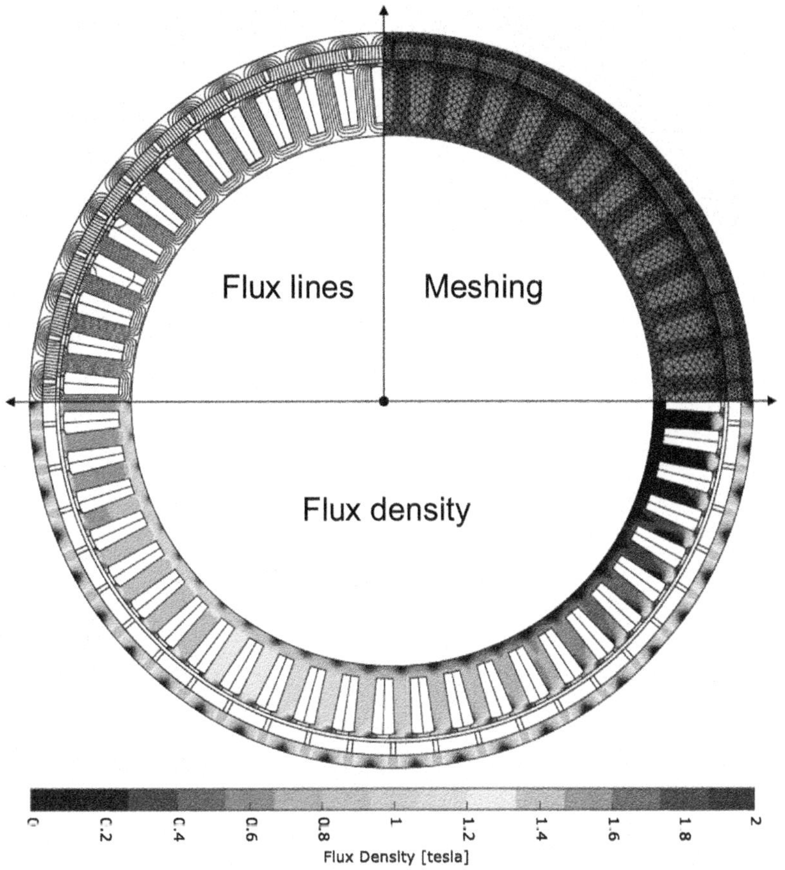

FIGURE 28.4 FEA modeling of the hub-motor using EMDLAB, including meshing, magnetic vector potential (flux lines), and no-load flux density of the motor components (*FEA*, Finite element analysis).

model is a high-fidelity tool, reliable enough for the thousands of iterative evaluations required during the design optimization process.

Fig. 28.6 (A,B) presents a detailed quantitative validation of the EMDLAB solver by focusing on the airgap, which is the most critical region for the electromechanical energy conversion, where the magnetic field from the rotor interacts with the stator windings to produce electromagnetic torque. The plots demonstrate an excellent point-by-point agreement between the two simulation tools for both the radial component, which is primarily responsible for generating torque, and the tangential component, which influences torque quality and ripple. This strong correlation confirms with high confidence that the EMDLAB magneto-static solver can reliably model the complex magnetic field distribution.

The results confirmed a high degree of accuracy, with a minimal relative error of approximately 0.74% in the primary performance metric of the average torque. The most significant advantage, however, was in computational speed, where, for an analysis conducted with an identical mesh quantity, EMDLAB completed the simulation in just 0.9 seconds, a full 38 seconds faster than Ansys. This successful validation demonstrates that EMDLAB provides the crucial combination of high accuracy and superior computational speed necessary for an effective optimization study. While not positioned as a universal replacement for Ansys, its ability to deliver reliable results in a fraction of the time makes it an exceptionally powerful alternative for design problems that require a large number of iterative function evaluations.

28.5 Required performance criteria

The design optimization for the in-wheel hub-motor is fundamentally shaped by the need to resolve the competing demands of maximizing vehicle performance and ensuring economic viability for mass production. The first and most crucial performance objective is the maximization of the average electromagnetic torque (f_1), as this directly influences the electric vehicle's acceleration and load-carrying capabilities. As formulated in Eq. (28.25), the total torque is comprised of two distinct components: a minor portion known as reluctance torque, which arises from the magnetic core's tendency to

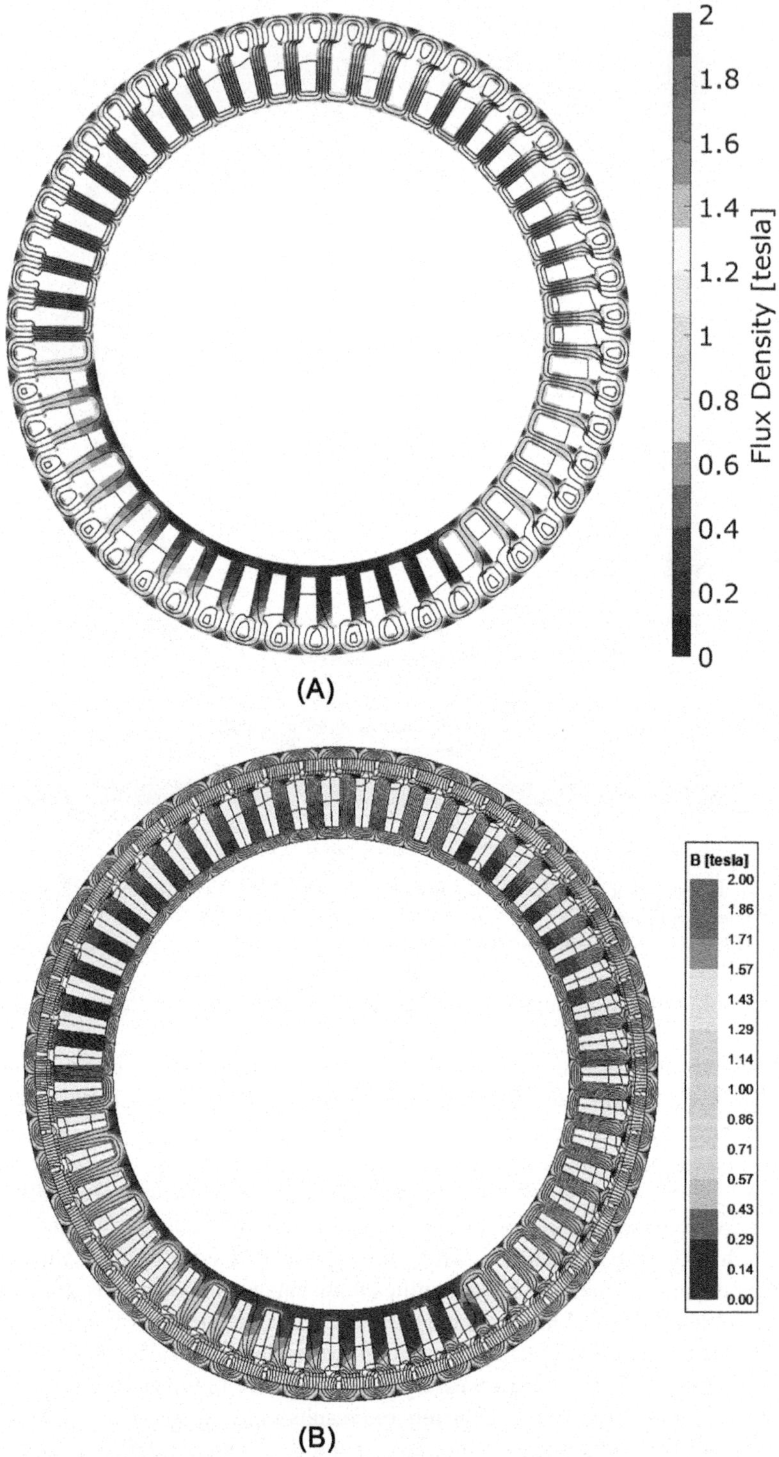

FIGURE 28.5 Full-load flux density of the motor, evaluated by (A) EMDLAB, (B) Ansys Electronics Desktop.

align itself with the stator's magnetic field, and a significantly larger portion generated by the PM. In this surface-mounted PM motor design, the PM component is the dominant contributor, meaning that achieving high torque is directly dependent on the strength and volume of the magnetic flux produced by the permanent magnets. In direct opposition to this performance goal is the objective of minimizing the total effective cost of the motor (f_4), which is calculated based on the price of its constituent materials as indicated by Eq. (28.26). This cost structure includes the prices of the copper in the

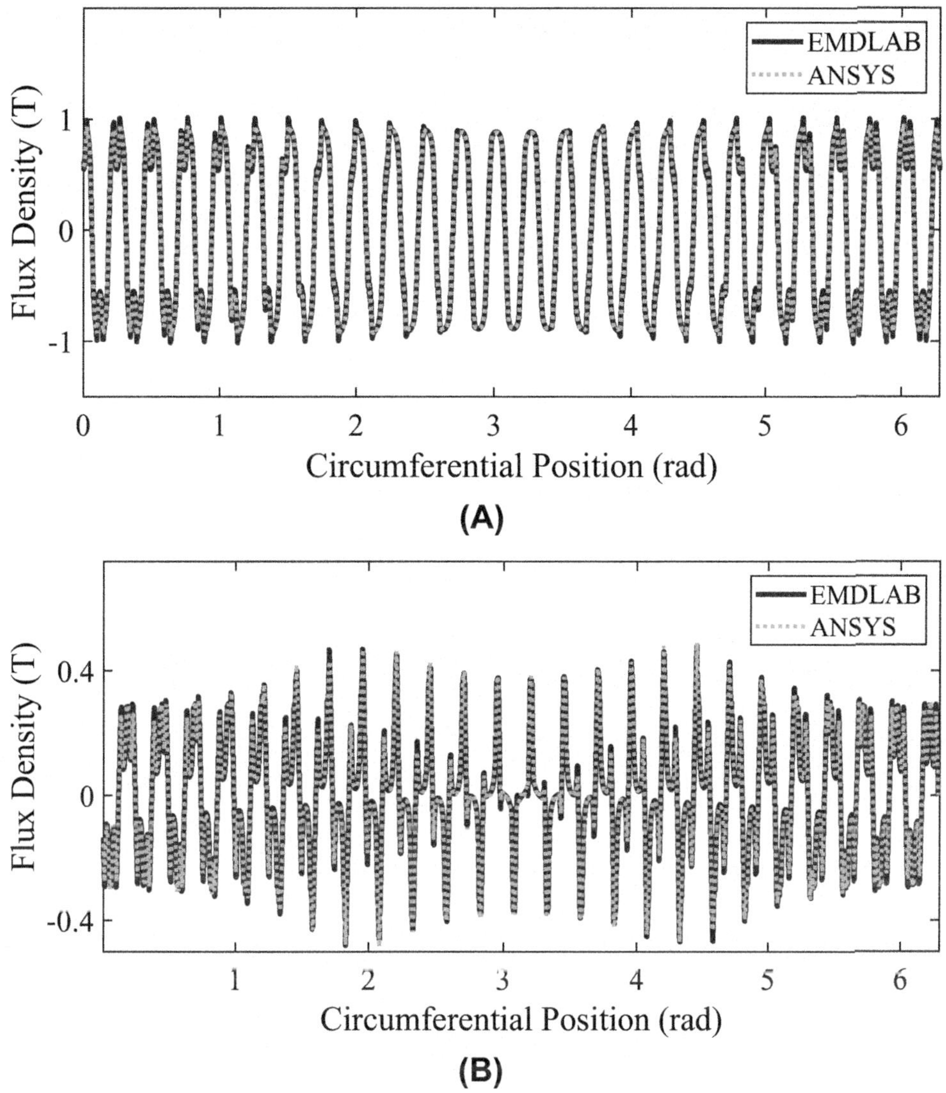

FIGURE 28.6 Comparing the FEA results of the Ansys Electronics Desktop and EMDLAB software packages based on the (A) radial, (B) tangential components of the airgap flux density (*FEA*, Finite element analysis).

windings and the steel in the motor's core, but it is overwhelmingly dominated by the high price of the permanent magnets. The economic challenge is amplified because these magnets are produced from rare-earth materials, which are not only expensive but are also subject to an unreliable and risky global supply chain, posing a significant threat to the financial feasibility of large-scale manufacturing.

$$T_{el} = \frac{3}{2}\frac{P_r}{2}\left(\underbrace{(L_d - L_q)i_{q,r}i_{d,r}}_{\text{Reluctancetorque}} + \underbrace{\lambda_m i_{q,r}}_{\text{PMtorque}}\right) \tag{28.25}$$

$$E.\ C. = \underbrace{P_p m_p}_{\text{PMcost}} + \underbrace{P_c m_c}_{\text{Coppercost}} + \underbrace{P_i m_i}_{\text{Corecost}} \tag{28.26}$$

This dynamic establishes the primary and central trade-off that necessitates a multi-objective optimization approach. To generate higher torque, a larger volume of high-energy permanent magnet material is required to create a more powerful magnetic field. However, increasing the amount of this material directly increases the single largest component of the motor's cost. Given that these critical objectives are in direct contradiction, a simple analytical solution is impossible. Instead, a multicriteria optimization procedure is required to systematically explore the design space and identify a set of balanced compromises, known as Pareto-optimal solutions, which represent the best possible trade-offs between torque performance and manufacturing cost.

In addition to torque and cost, the design optimization focuses on maximizing the efficiency and power factor of the hub-motor, which are crucial for the overall performance of the electric vehicle's powertrain. The primary method for improving the hub-motor's efficiency is to minimize its internal power losses. These losses can be categorized into several components, including copper losses in the windings, core losses in the steel, losses in the PMs, and mechanical losses. However, this study makes a key simplification based on the motor's specific application. Since the hub-motor is designed to operate primarily in the low-speed region around 400 r.p.m. (see Table 28.1), the speed-dependent losses (core, PM, and mechanical) are less significant than the current-dependent losses. Therefore this optimization targets the most significant portion, the copper losses (f_2), as the primary criterion for maximizing the motor's efficiency. The copper losses in the in-wheel hub-motor are calculated using Eq. (28.27)–(30).

$$P_{cu} = \underbrace{P_{cu,acw} + P_{cu,enw}}_{P_{dc}} + P_{ac} \tag{28.27}$$

$$P_{cu,acw} = 3R_{acw}I_{rms}^2 = 3N_t\frac{\rho_{cu}L_{acw}}{A_{con}}I_{rms}^2 \tag{28.28}$$

$$P_{cu,enw} = 3R_{enw}I_{rms}^2 = 3N_t\frac{\rho_{cu}L_{enw}}{A_{con}}I_{rms}^2 \tag{28.29}$$

$$P_{ac} = \frac{\pi D_w^2(\omega_{mr}B_g)^2}{128R_{ph}} \tag{28.30}$$

The final objective is to maximize the motor's power factor (f_3), which is a critical metric for ensuring high-quality and efficient power delivery from the vehicle's inverter to the motor. The power factor represents the ratio of real active power to the total power drawn from the source, as indicated by Eqs. (28.31–28.34). A low power factor indicates that a significant portion of the current flowing to the motor is reactive, meaning it surges back and forth without contributing to torque. This excess reactive current still generates heat and resistive losses (RI^2) in the entire electrical system, from the battery to the motor windings. Consequently, a low power factor leads to higher operational costs and requires oversized, more expensive power electronics to handle the larger apparent current. By maximizing the power factor (bringing it as close to 1 as possible), the motor draws less total current for the same torque output. This directly reduces copper losses, allows for a smaller and more cost-effective inverter, and improves the overall efficiency of the entire powertrain system.

$$P.F. = \frac{v_{d,r}i_{d,r} + v_{q,r}i_{q,r}}{V_sI_s} \tag{28.31}$$

$$i_{d,r} = I_s\cos(\theta_e),\ i_{q,r} = I_s\sin(\theta_e) \tag{28.32}$$

$$v_{d,r} = R_{ph}i_{d,r} + e_{d,r},\ v_{q,r} = R_{ph}i_{q,r} + e_{q,r} \tag{28.33}$$

$$V_s = \sqrt{v_{d,r}^2 + v_{q,r}^2},\ I_s = \sqrt{i_{d,r}^2 + i_{q,r}^2} \tag{28.34}$$

28.6 Comprehensive sensitivity analysis

Before proceeding with the multiobjective design optimization, it is essential to identify which of the motor's internal geometric parameters exerts the most significant influence on the performance criteria. This step ensures that the computational effort of the optimization algorithm is focused on the most impactful decision variables, thereby enhancing the efficiency and effectiveness of the design process. The internal parameters of the hub-motor considered for this analysis include the dimensions of the PMs, specifically the PM thickness (x_1) and PM circumferential span (x_2). Additionally, key dimensions of the stator core are included, including the slot opening (x_3), slot depth (x_4), and stator tooth width (x_5). Finally, an electrical parameter, the number of coil turns (x_6), is also included due to its direct impact on the magnetic field and electrical characteristics. Fig. 28.7 provides a schematic cross-section of the motor, visually defining these six key design parameters that serve as the decision variables for the sensitivity analysis. To constrain the analysis to a physically and practically feasible design space, Table 28.2 complements this figure by specifying the initial value for each parameter, along with its prescribed lower and upper bounds.

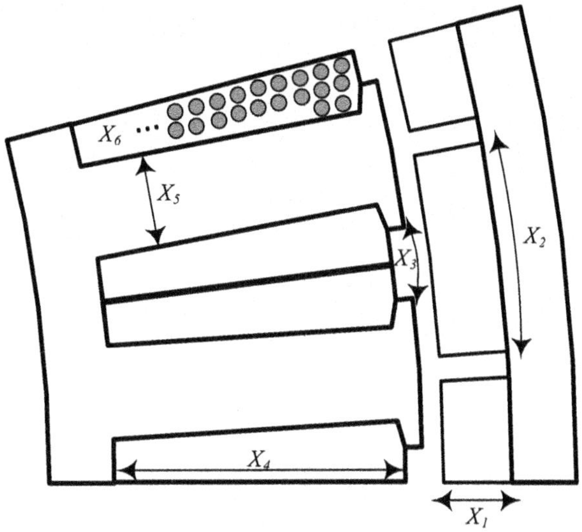

FIGURE 28.7 Design parameters used as the decision variables in the comprehensive sensitivity analysis.

TABLE 28.2 Design parameters and their lower/upper bounds.

Parameter	Unit	Symbol	Initial value	Range
PM thickness	[mm]	x_1	5.4	[4 6]
PM circumferential span	-	x_2	0.76	[0.7 0.9]
Slot opening	[mm]	x_3	4	[3.5 5.5]
Slot depth	[mm]	x_4	17	[16 18.5]
Stator tooth width	[mm]	x_5	4.1	[4 5.5]
Coil turns	-	x_6	41	[25 45]

PM, Permanent magnet.

To quantify the influence of these parameters, a variance-based sensitivity analysis is performed. The sensitivity index for a single objective function, $S(x_i)$, is calculated using the expectation-based formulation shown in Eq. (28.35). This equation measures the fraction of the total variance in an output function, $V(y)$, that can be attributed to the variance of a single input parameter, $V(E(y/x_i))$. A higher value indicates that the parameter has a greater influence on that specific objective. However, since this is a multiobjective problem, it is more valuable to understand the overall impact of each parameter across all competing objectives. For this purpose, a comprehensive sensitivity index (S_c) is formulated, as shown in Eq. (28.36). This index is a weighted sum of the individual sensitivity indices for each of the objective functions, including average torque (S_t), copper loss (S_{cl}), power factor $\left(S_{pf}\right)$, and effective cost (S_{ec}), where the weights of ω_t, ω_{cl}, ω_{pf}, and ω_{ec} are assigned based on the relative importance of each objective in the overall design goals.

$$S(x_i) = \frac{V(E(y/x_i))}{V(y)} \tag{28.35}$$

$$S_c = \omega_t|S_t(x_i)| + \omega_{cl}|S_{cl}(x_i)| + \omega_{pf}\left|S_{pf}(x_i)\right| + \omega_{ec}|S_{ec}(x_i)| \tag{28.36}$$

The results of this analysis are presented visually in Fig. 28.8 and numerically in Table 28.3. Fig. 28.8 clearly illustrates the individual sensitivity of each objective function to the six design parameters. It is immediately apparent that the number of coil turns has a dominant influence on the average torque, copper losses, and power factor. This is expected, as

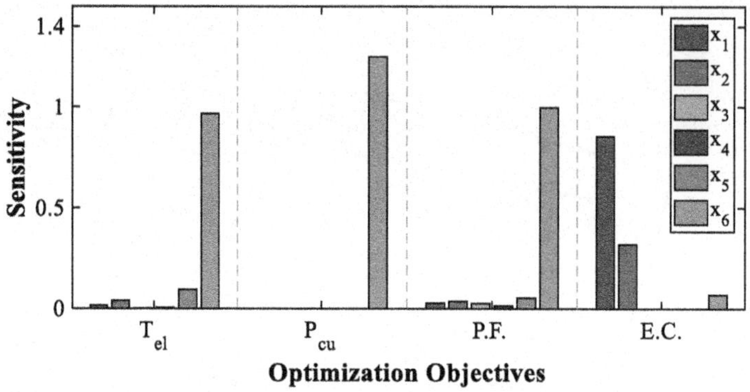

FIGURE 28.8 Sensitivity analysis of the objective functions.

TABLE 28.3 Results of the comprehensive sensitivity analysis (bolded values indicate the influencing parameters that are used for optimization).

Parameters	$S_t(x_i)$ ω_t=0.35	$S_{cl}(x_i)$ ω_{cl}=0.25	$S_{pf}(x_i)$ ω_{pf}=0.15	$S_{ec}(x_i)$ ω_{ec}=0.25	S_c
x_1	0.0155	0	0.0265	0.8548	**0.2231**
x_2	0.0393	0	0.0352	0.3202	**0.0991**
x_3	0.0007	0	0.0245	4.2097e-08	0.0039
x_4	0.0041	0	0.0122	1.0502e-06	0.0033
x_5	0.0937	0	0.0531	3.0119e-06	**0.0408**
x_6	0.9656	1.2499	0.9977	0.0682	**0.8171**

the number of turns directly impacts the magneto-motive force and winding resistance. The effective cost, on the other hand, is most sensitive to the PM thickness and, to a lesser extent, the PM span, which logically follows from the high cost of rare-earth magnet material. Table 28.3 provides the detailed numerical results, listing the calculated sensitivity indices for each parameter-objective pair and the final comprehensive sensitivity index for each parameter. The assigned weights, reflecting a balanced consideration of performance and cost, are specified in the table header. The results confirm the visual interpretation from Fig. 28.8 and provide a clear ranking of parameter influence. The number of coil turns emerges as the most influential parameter by a significant margin, with a comprehensive sensitivity index of 0.8171. The PM thickness is the second most critical parameter with an index of 0.2231, followed by the PM circumferential span at 0.0991, and except for the tooth width, the stator core dimensions exhibit a negligible overall impact. Based on this rigorous analysis, the design optimization will focus on the most influential parameters (x_1, x_2, x_5, and x_6) to effectively navigate the design space and identify the optimal trade-offs.

28.7 Optimization for the best trade-off

The inherent conflict among the design objectives for the hub-motor necessitates an effective approach to manage the required trade-offs. Therefore the design process is formulated as a deterministic multiobjective design optimization problem (MODOP), as detailed in (28.37), where the primary goal is to identify a set of design parameter values, represented by the decision vector X, that yields the best possible compromise among the competing performance criteria. To enhance the efficiency and accelerate the convergence of the optimization process, the decision vector X is strategically constructed using only the most influential parameters (x_1, x_2, x_5, and x_6), as identified in the preceding comprehensive sensitivity analysis. For consistency within the optimization framework, all objective functions (f_1 through f_4) are structured as minimization problems. Consequently, the objectives that naturally require maximization, including average torque (f_1) and power factor (f_3), are mathematically transformed. Maximizing the average torque is expressed as minimizing its inverse ($1/f_1$), while maximizing the power factor is framed as minimizing the quantity ($1-f_3$). Furthermore, to ensure the practical viability of the outcome, the optimization is bound by a series of constraints. These constraints compel the final design to adhere to predefined performance benchmarks, guaranteeing that the optimized hub-motor meets essential operational limits.

$$\text{MODOP:} \begin{cases} \text{Designparameters: } X = (x_1, x_2, x_5, x_6) \\ \text{Objective: } \min\left\{\frac{1}{f_1(X)}, f_2(X), 1 - f_3(X), f_4(X)\right\} \\ \text{s. t. :} \begin{cases} g_1(X) = -f_1(X) + 190(N.\,m.) \le 0 \\ g_2(X) = f_2(X) - 7000(W) \le 0 \\ g_3(X) = -f_3(X) + 0.6 \le 0 \\ g_4(X) = f_4(X) - 200(USD) \le 0 \end{cases} \end{cases} \quad (28.37)$$

To solve the MODOP (37), this study employs and systematically compares three distinct nature-inspired metaheuristic algorithms. The primary focus of this work is the novel application of the MOGWO algorithm to navigate the complex design space of the hub-motor. However, to rigorously validate its effectiveness, its performance is benchmarked against MOPSO and NSGA-II, two widely recognized and state-of-the-art algorithms in the field. This comparative analysis is crucial for addressing the existing gap in the literature regarding systematic comparisons of metaheuristic algorithms specifically for electric motor design. The evaluation will be based on key performance metrics, including the rate of convergence and the diversity of the resulting Pareto-optimal solutions, to provide a definitive assessment of the most suitable optimization tool for this specific application.

28.7.1 The multiobjective grey wolf optimizer solver for the multiobjective design optimization problem

The MOGWO algorithm is a powerful metaheuristic derived from the natural hunting behavior and social hierarchy of grey wolves. It extends the principles of the single-objective grey wolf optimizer to handle problems with multiple, often conflicting, objectives. Its gradient-free nature and robust global search capabilities make it exceptionally well-suited for complex, nonlinear engineering design challenges, such as the optimization of electric motors [38]. The core of the MOGWO algorithm lies in its simulation of the grey wolf pack's social structure. The three fittest solutions in the population at any given iteration are designated as the leaders, including the alpha (α), beta (β), and delta (δ) wolves. These three leaders represent the best trade-off solutions found so far and are responsible for guiding the rest of the pack, known as the omega (ω) wolves, toward the most promising regions of the design space. This leadership mechanism effectively balances the algorithm's exploration (searching broadly for new solutions) and exploitation (refining existing good solutions) capabilities [39].

To adapt this framework for multiobjective optimization, MOGWO incorporates two key mechanisms. First, instead of tracking a single best solution, it utilizes an external repository, or archive, to store all the nondominated (Pareto-optimal) solutions discovered throughout the search process. The alpha, beta, and delta leaders are then selected from this archive. Second, to ensure that the final set of solutions is not only optimal but also well-distributed across the Pareto front, MOGWO employs a grid-based mechanism. This mechanism divides the objective space into hypercubes and is used to manage the archive, promoting diversity by favoring solutions in less-populated regions. This approach is critical for providing designers with a wide spectrum of high-quality, trade-off designs. The specific implementation of the MOGWO algorithm for the hub-motor design optimization is detailed in the flowchart presented in Fig. 28.9. As illustrated, the process begins with the initialization of the wolf pack (i.e., the design candidates) and the algorithm parameters. An initial set of nondominated solutions is identified and used to populate the archive. The main iterative loop then commences, where each omega wolf updates its position based on the guidance of the alpha, beta, and delta leaders selected from the archive. Newly generated solutions are evaluated, and the archive is updated by adding any new nondominated individuals and pruning any solutions that become dominated. This iterative process continues until a predefined maximum number of iterations is reached, resulting in a final archive containing the Pareto-optimal design solutions for the hub-motor.

28.7.2 The multiobjective particle swarm optimization solver for multiobjective design optimization problem

The MOPSO is a well-established metaheuristic algorithm that extends the principles of standard particle swarm optimization to effectively handle problems with multiple competing objectives. The algorithm models the social behavior

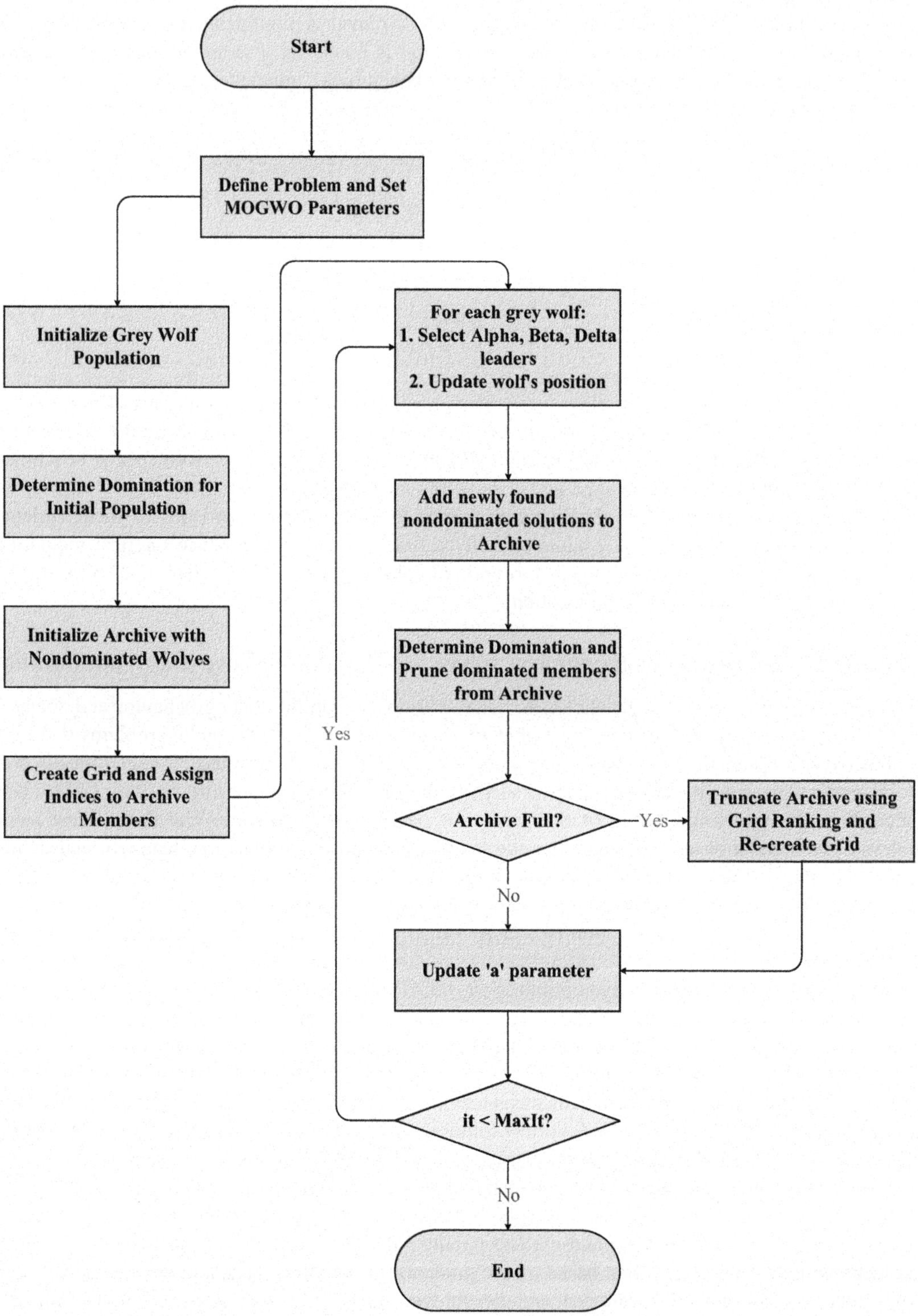

FIGURE 28.9 Flowchart of the implemented MOGWO algorithm for the hub-motor MODOP (*MODOP*, Multiobjective design optimization problem; *MOGWO*, multiobjective grey wolf optimizer).

of a bird flock or fish school, where individual particles (representing design candidates) navigate the multi-dimensional design space. Each particle adjusts its trajectory based on its own best-known position and the best-known position found by the entire swarm. To adapt this mechanism for multiobjective optimization, MOPSO introduces an external repository to store the set of nondominated (Pareto-optimal) solutions discovered during the search [40]. Instead of a single global best solution, a leader is selected from this repository to guide the movement of the other particles. This leader selection, often coupled with a grid mechanism to ensure diversity, helps the swarm to effectively explore the entire Pareto front rather than converging to a single point. This approach allows MOPSO to efficiently generate a set of well-distributed, optimal trade-off solutions. The procedural flow of the MOPSO algorithm as implemented for the hub-motor design is visually summarized in the flowchart in Fig. 28.10. The process starts by initializing a population of particles and an empty repository. In each iteration, leaders are selected from the repository to update the velocity and position of each particle. The repository is then updated with any new nondominated solutions found, and a grid-based ranking system is used to manage its size and promote solution diversity, continuing until the termination criteria are met.

28.7.3 The Nondominated Sorting Genetic Algorithm II solver for multiobjective design optimization problem

The NSGA-II is one of the most widely recognized and frequently utilized algorithms for multi-objective optimization. As an evolutionary algorithm, it employs genetic operators such as selection, crossover, and mutation to evolve a population of solutions toward the optimal set. The success of NSGA-II is attributed to two primary components, including a fast nondominated sorting procedure and a crowding distance estimation. The nondominated sorting mechanism efficiently ranks the entire population into different levels of Pareto fronts, classifying solutions based on their dominance. To maintain diversity and ensure a well-distributed set of results, the crowding distance metric is calculated for solutions within the same front. During the selection process, this metric gives preference to solutions located in less-populated regions of the objective space, preventing premature convergence and promoting a comprehensive exploration of the Pareto front. The complete operational workflow of the NSGA-II algorithm is methodically outlined in the flowchart provided in Fig. 28.11. The process involves creating an offspring population from the parent population, combining them, and then using the nondominated sorting and crowding distance procedures to select the most fit individuals to form the next generation, repeating until the optimization is complete [41].

28.7.4 Optimization platform and settings

The entire multiobjective optimization framework was executed on a workstation equipped with an Intel(R) Core(TM) i5–13600k CPU operating at 5.1 GHz and 16.0 GB of RAM. The optimization algorithms (MOGWO, MOPSO, and NSGA-II) were implemented and managed within the MATLAB environment. A crucial aspect of this study is the direct hybridization of the optimization algorithms with the high-fidelity computational electromagnetics solver, EMDLAB. The optimization process operates as a closed-loop system where, from the perspective of the optimization algorithm, the motor design problem is treated as a black box. In each iteration, the algorithm proposes a new set of design parameters (a candidate solution). These parameters are automatically passed to the EMDLAB solver, which performs a complete finite element analysis to evaluate the corresponding performance criteria. The resulting values for the objective functions are then returned to the optimization algorithm as cost functions, guiding its search for the next generation of solutions. This black-box approach allows the powerful metaheuristic algorithms to navigate the complex design space without needing any knowledge of the underlying physics, relying solely on the input-output relationship.

To ensure a rigorous and fair comparison of the algorithms' performance, the total number of function evaluations was kept constant (7000) for all three optimization runs. This was achieved by carefully regulating the maximum number of iterations and the population size for each algorithm. The detailed internal parameter settings for each algorithm, such as crossover and mutation probabilities for NSGA-II or inertia weight for MOPSO, are specified in Table 28.4.

The constraint handling for this optimization was managed with a two-tiered strategy. First, all decision variables were confined within strict lower and upper bounds as specified in Table 28.2, ensuring that all generated designs were inherently physically and geometrically feasible. Second, the four performance-based inequality constraints defined in the MODOP formulation (Eq. (28.37)) were handled using a rejection method. If a candidate solution generated during the optimization process violated any of these performance constraints, it was identified as infeasible, discarded from the population, and replaced by a new, validly generated solution. This approach ensures that the evolutionary search is consistently guided toward the feasible region of the objective space, guaranteeing that all final Pareto-optimal designs satisfy the required performance benchmarks.

28.8 Results and discussion

This section presents a comprehensive analysis of the optimization outcomes, beginning with a detailed comparison of the results generated by the MOGWO, MOPSO, and NSGA-II algorithms. The discussion then transitions to the critical

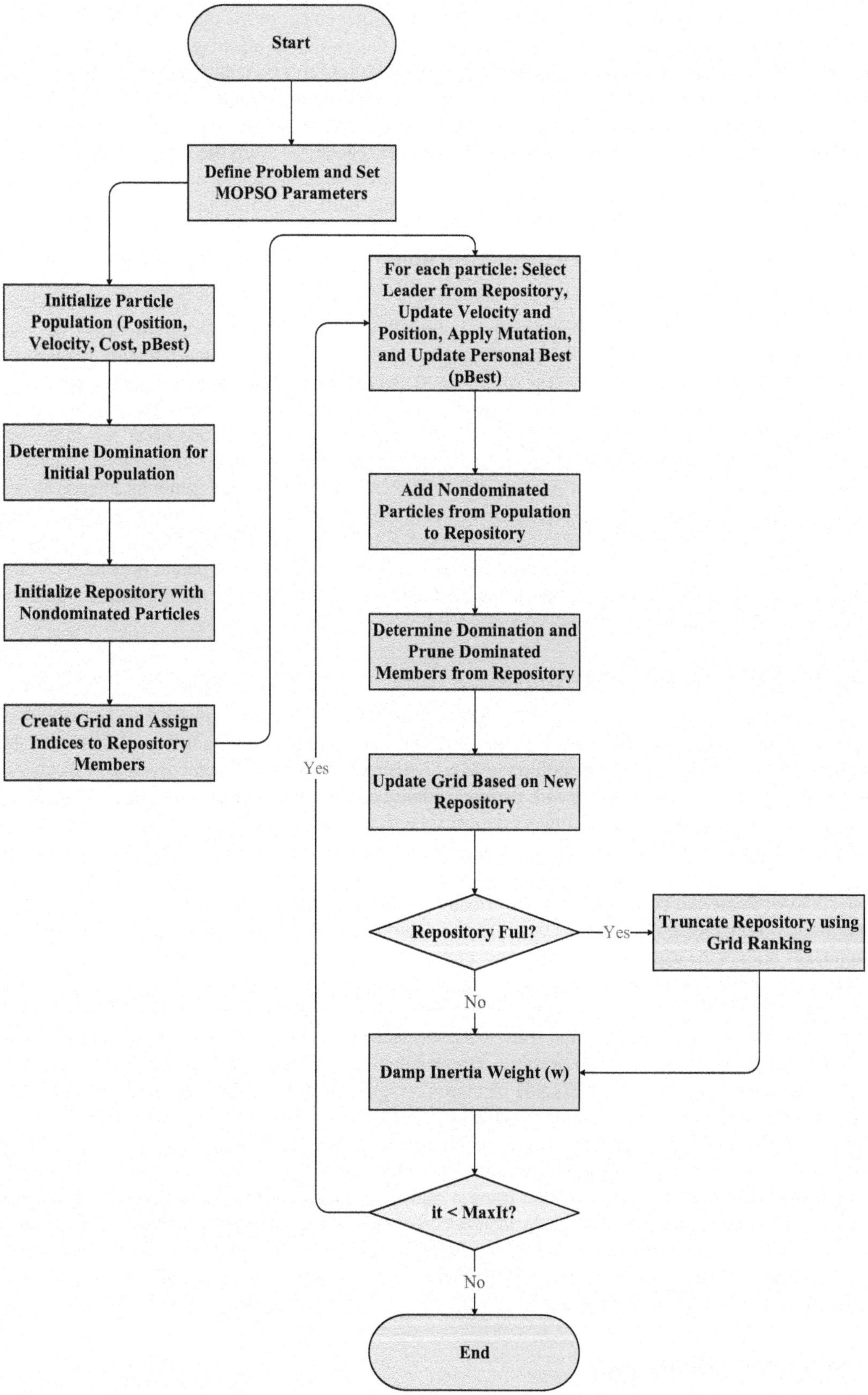

FIGURE 28.10 Flowchart of the implemented MOPSO algorithm for the hub-motor MODOP (*MODOP*, Multiobjective design optimization problem; *MOPSO*, multiobjective particle swarm optimization).

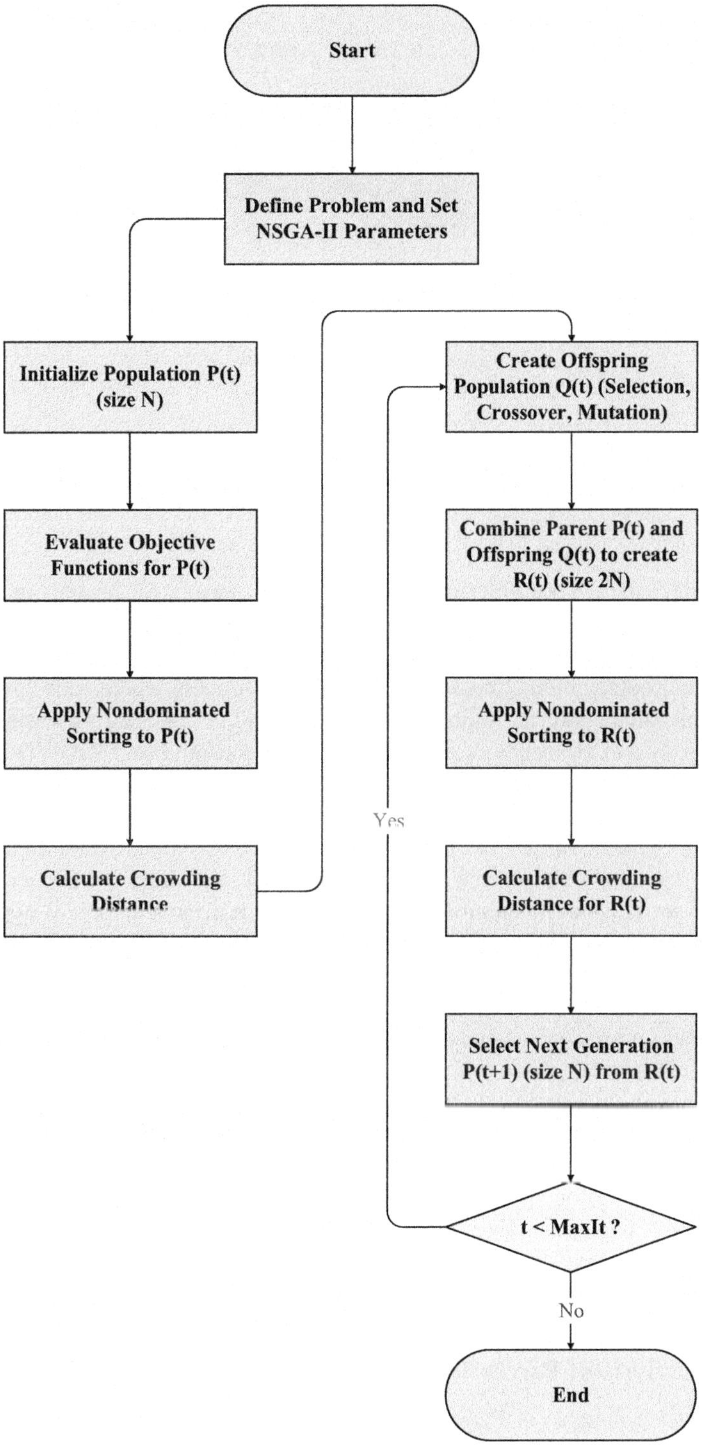

FIGURE 28.11 Flowchart of the implemented NSGA-II algorithm for the hub-motor MODOP (*MODOP*, Multiobjective design optimization problem; *NSGA-II*, Nondominated Sorting Genetic Algorithm II).

process of decision-making, where a single, optimal design is selected from the portfolio of solutions to best satisfy the project's competing objectives.

First, beyond performance metrics, a crucial point of comparison lies in algorithmic practicality. A significant advantage of MOGWO for real-world engineering applications is its essentially parameter-less nature. The settings it requires, such as archive size, are related to the general multiobjective framework, not its intrinsic search mechanism.

TABLE 28.4 Parameters and settings of the NSGA-II, MOPSO, and MOGWO algorithms.

Metaheuristic	Parameters	Multiobjective settings
NSGA-II	P_c=0.5, P_m=0.5 μ=0.3, σ=0.1	-
MOPSO	ϕ_1=2.05, ϕ_2=2.05, $\phi = \phi_1 + \phi_2$ $\chi = \frac{2}{\phi - 2 + \sqrt{\phi^2 - 4\phi}}$, $W = \chi$ $C_1 = \chi \cdot \phi_1$, $C_2 = \chi \cdot \phi_2$, μ=0.1	N_g=5, α=0.1 β=2, γ=2
MOGWO	-	N_g=10, α=0.1 β=4, γ=2

MOGWO, Multiobjective grey wolf optimizer; *MOPSO*, multiobjective particle swarm optimization; *NSGA-II*, Nondominated Sorting Genetic Algorithm II.

In sharp contrast, both NSGA-II and MOPSO demand meticulous tuning of several internal parameters− including crossover and mutation probabilities, inertia weight, and cognitive and social factors (a comprehensive list of which is provided in Table 4). The process of tuning these parameters is nontrivial, and it requires significant expertise and can consume substantial time and computational resources. In a design process where each function evaluation involves a time-intensive finite element simulation, an improperly tuned algorithm can lead to wasted resources and suboptimal results. The inherent simplicity and efficiency of a parameter-less algorithm like MOGWO thus represent a distinct and valuable advantage in an engineering context.

From a direct computational cost perspective, the optimization framework was designed for a fair comparison by ensuring the dominant computational burden, the function evaluations, was identical for all algorithms. The total number of function evaluations was fixed at 7000 for each run. Given that each high-fidelity evaluation with the EMDLAB solver required approximately 0.9 seconds, the total simulation time for each optimization was approximately 1.75 hours. The internal algorithmic overhead of MOGWO, MOPSO, and NSGA-II is negligible in comparison to this simulation time. However, this analysis does not account for the significant preliminary computational cost associated with parameter tuning for MOPSO and NSGA-II. Achieving optimal performance with these algorithms often necessitates numerous trial runs to fine-tune their internal settings, a time-consuming process that MOGWO effectively circumvents. Thus, MOGWO demonstrates superior overall efficiency in a practical engineering workflow by eliminating this hidden computational expense.

Similarly, the memory complexity of MOGWO is comparable to that of other state-of-the-art algorithms. Its memory usage is primarily governed by the size of the wolf population and the capacity of the external archive used to store nondominated solutions. This is analogous to the MOPSO implementation, which also relies on a population and an external repository. Given that population sizes were comparable across all algorithms in this study and a fixed-size archive is standard practice, the memory requirements for all three optimizers were considered to be of a similar order of magnitude and did not pose a constraint for this engineering application.

28.8.1 Comparative analysis of Pareto fronts

The final set of nondominated solutions, or Pareto fronts, produced by each algorithm encapsulates its performance in navigating the complex design space. Since the optimization involves four objective functions, the resulting four-dimensional Pareto front cannot be visualized in its entirety. Therefore, its complex structure is analyzed through a series of two- and three-dimensional projections. Accordingly, Figs. 28.12–28.14 illustrate the 2-D trade-offs between the primary objective of average torque and the secondary objectives of copper losses, power factor, and effective cost, respectively. For a more holistic perspective, Fig. 28.15 presents a three-dimensional view of the solution space, plotting the intricate relationship between average torque, power factor, and effective cost.

A thorough visual inspection of these figures reveals profound differences in the exploratory behavior and convergence capabilities of the three algorithms. In terms of coverage, which reflects the algorithm's ability to explore diverse regions of the design space, MOPSO demonstrates the most expansive reach. It successfully identifies solutions at the extreme

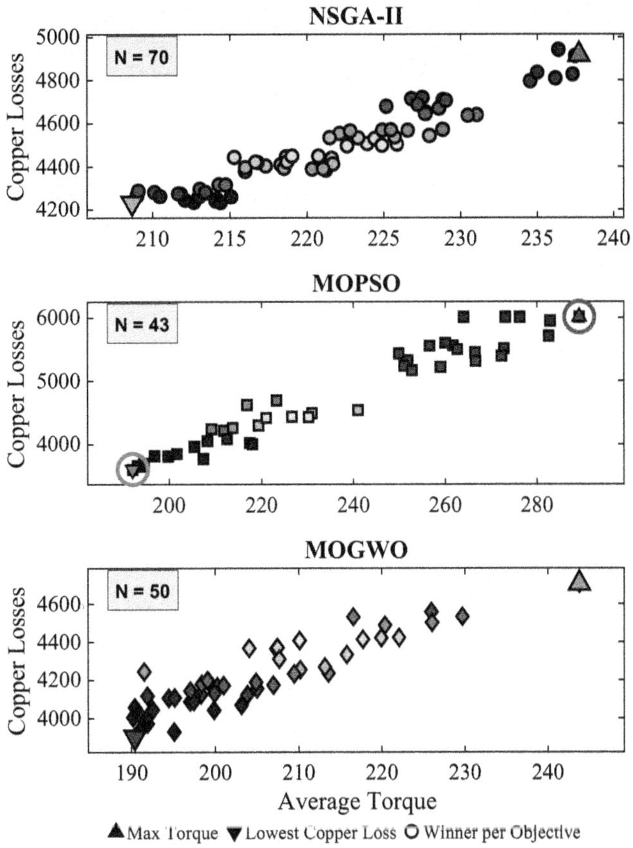

FIGURE 28.12 Pareto front in 2-D, considering only two objectives (average torque and copper losses).

ends of the performance spectrum, including several winners per objective designs, such as the one with the highest overall torque. However, this broad exploration comes at the cost of solution density, resulting in a sparse and scattered Pareto front. The MOGWO algorithm achieves a more balanced performance, generating a well-distributed front that covers a wider and more valuable region of the design space than NSGA-II. While NSGA-II produces the densest front with 70 nondominated solutions, its exploration is confined to a notably limited area, suggesting a tendency toward premature convergence. In contrast, MOGWO and MOPSO deliver 50 and 43 solutions, respectively. Regarding convergence quality, MOGWO proves to be highly effective, where the torque interval it explores, approximately 190 N. m – 230 N. m, is superior to that of NSGA-II (208 N. m – 238 N. m), as it consistently finds designs that offer lower cost and reduced losses for a given torque output. This performance is also highly competitive with MOPSO. While MOPSO identifies solutions with a higher absolute maximum torque, these often correspond to prohibitively high costs, making them less practical. MOGWO, conversely, provides a robust set of high-performance yet economically viable compromises.

28.8.2 Decision-making for the optimal design

The Pareto fronts generated by the optimization process provide a portfolio of mathematically equivalent optimal solutions, where no single design can be improved in one objective without sacrificing performance in another. However, for the purpose of manufacturing and prototyping, a single optimal design must be selected. This necessitates a structured decision-making process that is guided by the specific priorities of the engineering application. For this study, the selection is based on a hierarchical set of criteria, reflecting the most critical aspects of the hub-motor's performance and viability. The highest priority is placed on maximizing the average electromagnetic torque, as this directly governs the vehicle's acceleration and overall driving performance. The second priority is minimizing the effective cost, a crucial factor driven by the high price and volatile supply chain of the rare-earth permanent magnets that dominate the material expense. Following cost, the remaining objectives of minimizing copper losses and maximizing the power factor are considered to

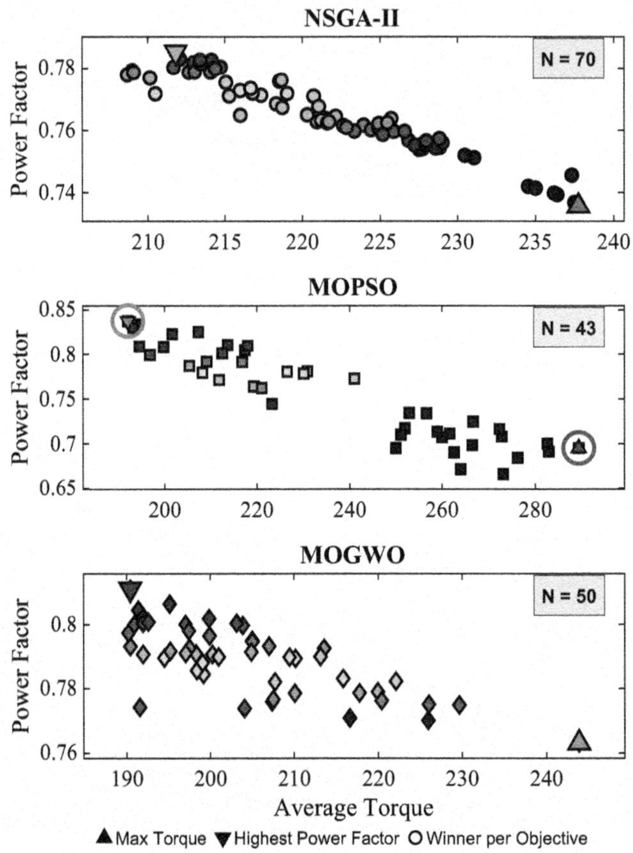

FIGURE 28.13 Pareto front in 2-D, considering only two objectives (average torque and power factor).

ensure high operational efficiency. Applying these hierarchical criteria to the set of all nondominated solutions, a final design is identified. This best trade-off point is explicitly marked with a star in the MOPSO results presented in Fig. 28.14. This specific solution was chosen because it represents the most judicious compromise among the competing objectives. It delivers a high average torque, ensuring excellent vehicle performance, while maintaining an effective cost that is low enough to be commercially viable. By striking this superior balance, the selected design best fulfills the multifaceted requirements for a next-generation electric vehicle hub-motor.

28.8.3 Comparing the initial and optimal designs

To quantify the substantial improvements achieved through the multiobjective optimization process, this section provides a direct comparison between the initial design and the final optimal design selected via the decision-making process. Table 28.5 summarizes the key design parameters and the corresponding performance criteria for both configurations. The analysis reveals a remarkable enhancement in the motor's overall performance profile, where the most significant improvement is observed in the primary objective, the average electromagnetic torque. The optimal design achieves an average torque of 273.14 N. m, a substantial increase of more than 40 N.m (approximately 19%) compared to the initial design's 229.40 N. m. This enhancement directly translates to superior acceleration and load-carrying capability for the electric vehicle. Furthermore, two other critical objectives show marked improvement. The power factor has been increased from 0.65 to 0.67, which indicates a more efficient use of the power supplied by the inverter. Concurrently, the effective cost of the motor has been reduced from 163.95 USD to 147.86 USD, a decrease of nearly 10%. This cost reduction is particularly noteworthy as it was achieved while simultaneously increasing the torque, underscoring the effectiveness of the algorithm in navigating the central trade-off of the design problem.

The only objective that did not see an improvement was the copper losses, which experienced a marginal increase from 5890.56 W to 6011.49 W. This slight rise is an acceptable trade-off, as the final value remains well within the 7000 W limit imposed by the optimization constraints, ensuring that the thermal performance of the motor is not compromised.

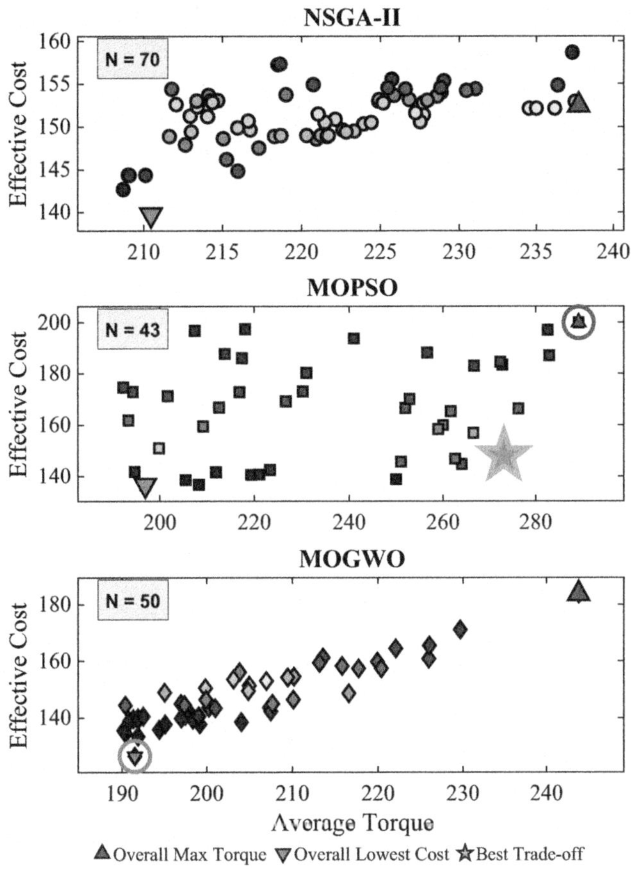

FIGURE 28.14 Pareto front in 2-D, considering only two objectives (average torque and effective cost).

In summary, the multiobjective optimization process has successfully transformed the initial concept into a vastly superior design. With three of the four objectives- average torque, effective cost, and power factor-showing significant improvement, the final selected design represents a highly successful and well-balanced solution that meets all performance and cost requirements for the hub-motor application.

28.8.4 Insights for the metaheuristic community

The application of MOGWO to the complex, multimodal design space of the hub-motor offers several valuable lessons for the community developing next-generation meta-heuristic algorithms.

First, this study highlights the effectiveness of a structured, multileader guidance mechanism for balancing exploration and exploitation. MOGWO's social hierarchy, which uses the alpha, beta, and delta solutions to guide the pack, proved highly adept at navigating the difficult trade-offs of the problem. It avoided the tendency toward premature convergence observed in NSGA-II while generating a more focused and useful set of solutions than the widely exploring MOPSO. This suggests that for complex engineering problems, algorithms that incorporate a small, diverse ensemble of elite solutions to inform the search direction may offer a more robust performance than those relying on a single leader or population-wide ranking alone.

Second, the practical success of MOGWO underscores the critical importance of parameter parsimony in algorithm design, especially for real-world applications involving computationally expensive function evaluations. A significant advantage of MOGWO was its essentially parameter-less nature, which eliminated the time-consuming and expertise-reliant tuning process required by NSGA-II and MOPSO. For problems where each evaluation is a lengthy simulation, the hidden "meta-cost" of parameter tuning can easily outweigh any marginal performance gains. This finding should encourage the metaheuristic community to prioritize the development of parameter-free or self-adaptive algorithms as a key feature for enhancing practical usability and overall efficiency.

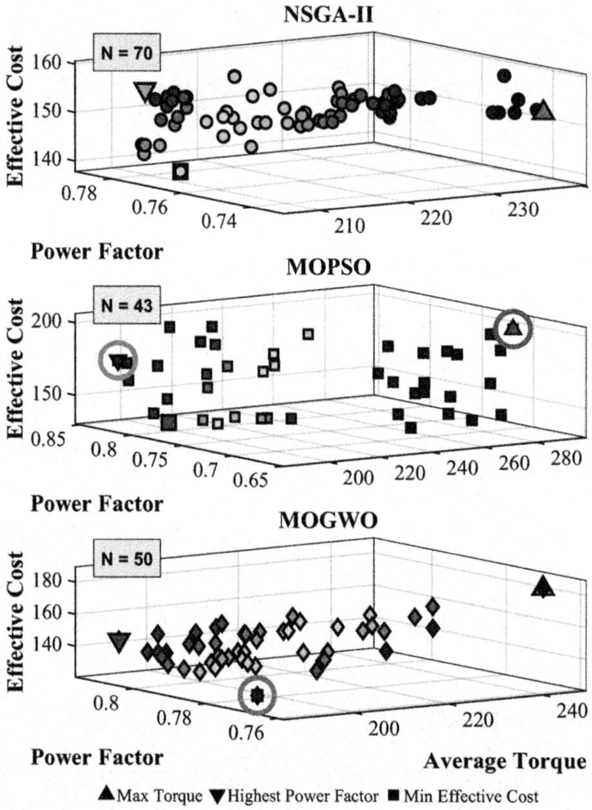

FIGURE 28.15 Pareto front in 3-D, considering only three objectives (average torque, power factor, and effective cost).

TABLE 28.5 Comparison of initial and final optimal design parameters and performance.

Parameter	Unit	Initial design	Optimal design
Design Parameters (Decision Variables)			
PM thickness (x_1)	[mm]	5.4	**4.0**
PM span (x_2)	[-]	0.76	**0.88**
Tooth width (x_5)	[mm]	4.1	**5.18**
Coil turns (x_6)	[-]	41	**45**
Performance Criteria (Objective Functions)			
Average torque (f_1)	[N.m]	229.40	**273.14**
Copper losses (f_2)	[W]	5890.56	6011.49
Power factor (f_3)	[-]	0.65	**0.67**
Effective cost (f_4)	[US-D]	163.95	**147.86**

PM, Permanent magnet.

Finally, this work reinforces the central role of sophisticated archive management in multiobjective optimization. The ability of MOGWO to produce a well-distributed and high-quality Pareto front was heavily reliant on its use of an external archive managed by a grid-based mechanism. This component is crucial for preserving diversity and presenting the designer with a rich portfolio of viable trade-offs. This suggests that future algorithmic improvements could be found not only in novel search operators but also in more intelligent archiving strategies, such as those that can adaptively manage archive size or use learning techniques to identify regions of the Pareto front that warrant deeper exploration.

28.9 Conclusions

This chapter successfully addressed the critical challenge of resolving inherent performance trade-offs in the design of an outer-rotor permanent magnet hub-motor for electric vehicle applications. The primary goal was to navigate the conflicting objectives of maximizing electromagnetic torque and power factor while minimizing both effective cost and copper losses. To achieve this, a robust optimization framework was developed, directly hybridizing a computationally efficient and high-fidelity finite element model with three distinct metaheuristic algorithms. The key findings of this study are threefold. First, the MOGWO was demonstrated to be a highly effective and practical tool for this complex engineering problem. Its performance was systematically benchmarked against two established algorithms, NSGA-II and MOPSO. While MOPSO showed the widest exploration of the design space and NSGA-II produced the densest set of solutions, MOGWO provided the best overall balance of convergence and coverage, generating a well-distributed Pareto front in the most valuable regions of the objective space.

Second, a crucial advantage of MOGWO is its parameter-less nature, which simplifies its application and removes the time-consuming and expertise-reliant tuning process required by NSGA-II and MOPSO. This makes it a more efficient and accessible option for engineering design, where computational resources for iterative simulations are a primary constraint. Finally, the optimization process yielded a vastly superior motor design. By applying a hierarchical decision-making process to the resulting Pareto-optimal solutions, a single best trade-off design was selected. This final design achieved a remarkable 19% increase in average torque and a nearly 10% reduction in effective cost compared to the initial configuration, alongside an improved power factor and while keeping copper losses within acceptable thermal limits. In summary, this work not only presents a significantly enhanced hub-motor design but also validates the MOGWO algorithm as a powerful and practical approach for solving complex multiobjective problems in electrical machine design. Future work could extend this framework by incorporating more detailed thermal analysis directly into the optimization loop or by applying this validated methodology to other emerging motor topologies.

Acknowledgments

The authors confirm that no AI-based tools or language models were utilized for the writing, editing, or refining of this manuscript.

References

[1] T.-A. Huynh, Y.-T. Nguyen Le, Z. Lee, M.-C. Tsai, P.-W. Huang, M.-F. Hsieh, Influence of flux barriers and permanent magnet arrangements on performance of high-speed flux-intensifying ipm motor, IEEE Transactions on Magnetics 59 (11) (2023) 1–6. Available from https://doi.org/10.1109/TMAG.2023.3290538.

[2] O. Borsboom, M. Salazar, T. Hofman, Electric motor design optimization:a convex surrogate modeling approach, IFAC-PapersOnLine 55 (24) (2022) 373–378 10th IFAC Symposium on Advances in Automotive Control AAC 2022. Available from https://doi.org/10.1016/j.ifacol.2022.10.312, https://www.sciencedirect.com/science/article/pii/S2405896322023448.

[3] X. Sun, Z. Shi, Y. Cai, G. Lei, Y. Guo, J. Zhu, Driving-cycle-oriented design optimization of a permanent magnet hub motor drive system for a four-wheel-drive electric vehicle, IEEE Transactions on Transportation Electrification 6 (3) (2020) 1115–1125. Available from https://doi.org/10.1109/TTE.2020.3009396.

[4] F. Ni, Z. Li, S. Niu, C. Liu, Complementary series magnetic circuit-based stator-yokeless dual-rotor pm vernier reluctance machine for in-wheel propulsion, IEEE Transactions on Transportation Electrification 11 (1) (2025) 4551–4560. Available from https://doi.org/10.1109/TTE.2024.3463722.

[5] Z. Shi, X. Sun, G. Lei, Z. Yang, Y. Guo, J. Zhu, Analysis and optimization of radial force of permanent-magnet synchronous hub motors, IEEE Transactions on Magnetics 56 (2) (2020) 1–4. Available from https://doi.org/10.1109/TMAG.2019.2953731.

[6] K. Deepak, M.A. Frikha, Y. Benômar, M. El Baghdadi, O. Hegazy, In-wheel motor drive systems for electric vehicles: state of the art, challenges, and future trends, Energies 16 (7) (2023). Available from https://doi.org/10.3390/en16073121, https://www.mdpi.com/1996-1073/16/7/3121.

[7] K. Yan, Z. Hu, J. Hu, J. Li, B. Zhang, J. Song, et al., A critical review of radial field in-wheel motors: technical progress and future trends, eTransportation 22 (2024) 100353. Available from https://doi.org/10.1016/j.etran.2024.100353, https://www.sciencedirect.com/science/article/pii/S2590116824000432.

[8] A. Mohammadi, Y. Chulaee, A.M. Cramer, I.G. Boldea, D.M. Ionel, Large-scale design optimization of an axial-flux vernier machine with dual stator and spoke pm rotor for ev in-wheel traction, IEEE Transactions on Transportation Electrification 11 (1) (2025) 2477–2488. Available from https://doi.org/10.1109/TTE.2024.3423713.

[9] Z. Feng, F. Jiang, M. Cao, B. Mei, S. Zhao, Multi-objective optimization and performance comparison of different driving configurations of in-wheel motors, IEEE Access 11 (2023) 53144–53154. Available from https://doi.org/10.1109/ACCESS.2023.3278258.

[10] T. Sharifi, V. Mirzaei Khales, M. Mirsalim, Torque ripple minimization for a switch reluctance motor using the ant lion optimization algorithm, in: 2022 13th Power Electronics, Drive Systems, and Technologies Conference (PEDSTC), 2022, pp. 207–211. Available from https://doi.org/10.1109/PEDSTC53976.2022.9767476.

[11] T. Sharifi, M. Mirsalim, Optimal design of a permanent magnet synchronous motor using the cultural algorithm, in: 2021 12th Power Electronics, Drive Systems, and Technologies Conference (PEDSTC), 2021, pp. 1–5. Available from https://doi.org/10.1109/PEDSTC52094.2021.9405839.

[12] M. Tutuianu, P. Bonnel, B. Ciuffo, T. Haniu, N. Ichikawa, A. Marotta, et al., Development of the world-wide harmonized light duty test cycle (WLTC) and a possible pathway for its introduction in the european legislation, Transportation Research Part D: Transport and Environment 40 (2015) 61–75. Available from https://doi.org/10.1016/j.trd.2015.07.011, https://www.sciencedirect.com/science/article/pii/S1361920915001030.

[13] S.-W. Jung, J. Ro, H.-K. Jung, A hybrid algorithm using shape and topology optimization for the design of electric machines, IEEE Transactions on Magnetics 54 (3) (2018) 1–4. Available from https://doi.org/10.1109/TMAG.2017.2764753.

[14] J.-G. Lee, D.-K. Lim, A stepwise optimal design applied to an interior permanent magnet synchronous motor for electric vehicle traction applications, IEEE Access 9 (2021) 115090–115099. Available from https://doi.org/10.1109/ACCESS.2021.3105119.

[15] B. Son, J.-S. Kim, J.-W. Kim, Y.-J. Kim, S.-Y. Jung, Adaptive particle swarm optimization based on kernel support vector machine for optimal design of synchronous reluctance motor, IEEE Transactions on Magnetics 55 (6) (2019) 1–5. Available from https://doi.org/10.1109/TMAG.2019.2902935.

[16] A. Credo, G. Fabri, M. Villani, M. Popescu, Adopting the topology optimization in the design of high-speed synchronous reluctance motors for electric vehicles, IEEE Transactions on Industry Applications 56 (5) (2020) 5429–5438. Available from https://doi.org/10.1109/TIA.2020.3007366.

[17] T. Sharifi, M. Mirsalim, Optimal design of a synchronous reluctance motor using biogeography-based optimization, in: 2021 29th Iranian Conference on Electrical Engineering (ICEE), 2021, pp. 209–213. Available from https://doi.org/10.1109/ICEE52715.2021.9544319.

[18] M. Mutluer, Analysis and design optimization of tubular linear voice coil motor for high thrust force and low copper loss, IEEE Canadian Journal of Electrical and Computer Engineering 44 (2) (2021) 165–170. Available from https://doi.org/10.1109/ICJECE.2020.3027865.

[19] X. Zhu, W. Wu, L. Quan, Z. Xiang, W. Gu, Design and multi-objective stratified optimization of a less-rare-earth hybrid permanent magnets motor with high torque density and low cost, IEEE Transactions on Energy Conversion 34 (3) (2019) 1178–1189. Available from https://doi.org/10.1109/TEC.2018.2886316.

[20] X. Zhu, J. Huang, L. Quan, Z. Xiang, B. Shi, Comprehensive sensitivity analysis and multiobjective optimization research of permanent magnet flux-intensifying motors, IEEE Transactions on Industrial Electronics 66 (4) (2019) 2613–2627. Available from https://doi.org/10.1109/TIE.2018.2849961.

[21] K. Diao, G. Bramerdorfer, X. Sun, Z. Yang, S. Han, Multiobjective design optimization of a novel switched reluctance motor with unequal alternating stator yoke segments, IEEE Transactions on Transportation Electrification 9 (1) (2023) 512–521. Available from https://doi.org/10.1109/TTE.2022.3174337.

[22] J. Xu, W. Jin, H. Lin, B. Zhang, H. Guo, Multiobjective optimization method to maximize power density and efficiency of an electric propulsion motor in uav applications, IEEE Transactions on Transportation Electrification 10 (3) (2024) 5484–5494. Available from https://doi.org/10.1109/TTE.2023.3319008.

[23] A. Jamali-Fard, M. Mirsalim, Design and prototyping of a novel line-start permanent magnet assisted synchronous reluctance motor for fan application, IEEE Transactions on Energy Conversion 39 (1) (2024) 243–251. Available from https://doi.org/10.1109/TEC.2023.3308508.

[24] M. Cheng, X. Zhao, M. Dhimish, W. Qiu, S. Niu, A review of data-driven surrogate models for design optimization of electric motors, IEEE Transactions on Transportation Electrification 10 (4) (2024) 8413–8431. Available from https://doi.org/10.1109/TTE.2024.3366417.

[25] G. Istenes, Z. Horváth, Multi-objective optimization of electric motors with a kriging surrogate model, in: 2022 22nd International Symposium on Electrical Apparatus and Technologies (SIELA), 2022, pp. 1–4. Available from https://doi.org/10.1109/SIELA54794.2022.9845694.

[26] S. Mirjalili, S. Saremi, S.M. Mirjalili, L.dos S. Coelho, Multi-objective grey wolf optimizer: a novel algorithm for multi-criterion optimization, Expert Systems with Applications 47 (2016) 106–119. Available from https://doi.org/10.1016/j.eswa.2015.10.039, https://www.sciencedirect.com/science/article/pii/S0957417415007435.

[27] K. Deb, A. Pratap, S. Agarwal, T. Meyarivan, A fast and elitist multiobjective genetic algorithm: NSGA-II, IEEE Transactions on Evolutionary Computation 6 (2) (2002) 182–197. Available from https://doi.org/10.1109/4235.996017.

[28] C. Coello Coello, M. Lechuga, Mopso: a proposal for multiple objective particle swarm optimization, in: Proceedings of the 2002 Congress on Evolutionary Computation. CEC'02 (Cat. No.02TH8600), vol. 2, 2002, pp. 1051–1056. Available from https://doi.org/10.1109/CEC.2002.1004388.

[29] Z. Shi, X. Sun, Y. Cai, X. Tian, L. Chen, Design optimisation of an outer-rotor permanent magnet synchronous hub motor for a low-speed campus patrol EV, IET Electric Power Applications 14 (11) (2020) 2111–2118 arXiv. Available from https://doi.org/10.1049/iet-epa.2020.0130, https://ietresearch.onlinelibrary.wiley.com/doi/pdf/10.1049/iet-epa.2020.0130, https://ietresearch.onlinelibrary.wiley.com/doi/abs/10.1049/iet-epa.2020.0130.

[30] V. Prakht, V. Dmitrievskii, A. Anuchin, Multi-objective design optimization of an induction motor for an electric vehicle, IEEE Transactions on Industrial Electronics 67 (2) (2020) 906–915. Available from https://doi.org/10.1109/TIE.2019.2901662.

[31] Z. Ullah, J. Hur, H. Kim, A comprehensive review of surrogate-assisted optimization techniques for electric machine design, IEEE Transactions on Energy Conversion 36 (4) (2021) 3045–3056. Available from https://doi.org/10.1109/TEC.2021.3073332.

[32] S. Chai, Z. Zhang, J. Li, An improved magnetic equivalent circuit model for spoke-type permanent magnet vernier machine considering local saturation, IEEE Transactions on Transportation Electrification 9 (1) (2023) 1118–1129. Available from https://doi.org/10.1109/TTE.2022.3191316.

[33] N.T.K. Thoa, S.I. Kim, J.M. Kim, D.H. Kim, Rapid and accurate performance prediction of permanent magnet synchronous generator with inset magnets using an analytical-MEC hybrid model, IEEE Transactions on Energy Conversion 38 (4) (2023) 2736–2746. Available from https://doi.org/10.1109/TEC.2023.3289947.

[34] S. Leva, L. Dossi, P. Pescetto, A general-purpose machine learning-based surrogate model for the fast and accurate design of synchronous reluctance motors, IEEE Transactions on Industry Applications 60 (1) (2024) 381–392. Available from https://doi.org/10.1109/TIA.2023.3323055.

[35] T. Sharifi, A. Eikani, Heat transfer investigations on a thermally superior alternative for the flux switching permanent magnet electric motor, Results in Engineering 24 (2024) 103415. Available from https://doi.org/10.1016/j.rineng.2024.103415, https://www.sciencedirect.com/science/article/pii/S2590123024016670.

[36] A. Jamali-Fard, M. Mirsalim, T. Sharifi, N. Majlesi, Emdlab: an open-source finite element package for electromagnetic analysis of electrical machines, SSRN Electronic Journal (2025). Available from https://doi.org/10.2139/ssrn.5327716, https://ssrn.com/abstract=5327716.

[37] EMDLAB-Package, emdlab-win64, Available from https://github.com/EMDLAB-Package/emdlab-win64, 2025 (accessed07.04.25).

[38] S. Song, P. Wang, Y. Zhang, L. Wang, Improved multi-objective grey wolf optimizer with differential evolution, Engineering with Computers 37 (2021) 1111–1133. Available from https://doi.org/10.1007/s00366-021-01311-x.

[39] A.A. Ewees, M. Abd El-salam, M. Elhoseny, Multi-objective grey wolf optimizer with archive-based mutation operator for solving multi-objective optimization problems, Applied Soft Computing 144 (2023) 110515. Available from https://doi.org/10.1016/j.asoc.2023.110515.

[40] C. Zhang, Z. Cui, Z. Zhu, J. Chen, Multi-objective particle swarm optimization with dynamic population size, Journal of Computational Design and Engineering 10 (2) (2023) 596–607. Available from https://doi.org/10.1093/jcde/qwac139.

[41] S. Verma, M. Pant, V. Snasel, A comprehensive review on nsga-ii for multi-objective combinatorial optimization problems, IEEE Access 9 (2021) 57757–57791. Available from https://doi.org/10.1109/ACCESS.2021.3070634.

Chapter 29

Uncertainty and sensitivity evaluation in joint geophysical inversion using a hybrid grey wolf optimizer and particle swarm optimization algorithm

Kuldeep Sarkar[1] and Upendra K. Singh[2]
[1]*Department of Earth Sciences, IIT Bombay, Mumbai, Maharashtra, India,* [2]*Department of Applied Geophysics, IIT (ISM) Dhanbad, Jharkhand, India*

29.1 Introduction

Over the past several decades, advancements in geophysical techniques have significantly enhanced their role in addressing diverse geological challenges. However, interpreting geophysical data remains difficult due to the nonlinear relationship between geophysical measurements and model parameters. To overcome this, inversion methods based on either local or global optimization techniques are commonly employed. Local optimization techniques such as conjugate gradient (CG), Gauss–Newton, Steepest Descent, Levenberg–Marquardt (LM) (i.e., Ridge Regression), and Occam's inversion, etc., are frequently used to approach global solutions. For example, Guo et al. [1] demonstrated the application of local optimization via supervised descent methods for nonlinear inversion of transient EM data, while Rodi and Mackie [2] applied a nonlinear CG algorithm for 2-D MT inversion. These methods require initial information that is reasonably close to the true subsurface structure for effective convergence. However, they often risk getting trapped in local minima, resulting in ambiguous or nonunique solutions [1,2]. Conversely, metaheuristic global inversion methods explore a wider parameter space, reducing the likelihood of local minima entrapment. These methods are particularly effective when the initial model is poor, as they start from randomly generated models and do not require derivative or Jacobian matrix computations.

With the rise of computational power in the 21st century, the use of global inversion strategies, particularly metaheuristic algorithms, has grown across geophysical applications. This includes swarm intelligence based approaches like grey wolf optimizer (GWO) [3], particle swarm optimization (PSO) [4], bat algorithm [5], ant colony optimization [6], etc.; evolutionary algorithms such as GA [7] and differential evolution [8], etc.; and chemistry/physics -inspired methods like gravitational search algorithm [9], Big-Bang-Big-Crunch [10], and SA [11] etc. These approaches do not require an initial model but depend on defined parameter ranges to effectively search for reliable solutions and avoid local optima due to their stochastic and flexible nature [12].

According to Mirjalili et al. [13], swarm intelligence approaches typically necessitate fewer parameters for tuning and facilitate the preservation of the optimal model at each iteration, rendering them more user-friendly compared to other algorithms. Effective optimization necessitates a balance between exploration (wide searching) and exploitation (refining interesting solutions), as enhancing one typically undermines the other [14]. As a result, academics are increasingly concentrating on hybridizing metaheuristic algorithms with complementary capabilities to improve convergence and robustness.

This chapter advocates for the utilization of an innovative hybrid optimization technique, grey wolf optimizer-particle swarm optimization (GWOPSO), to tackle intricate geophysical inverse problems through the joint inversion of direct current resistivity (DCR), magnetotelluric (MTT), and teleseismic receiver function (RF) data. This method has been shown to effectively achieve global convergence with diminished uncertainty [15,16], rendering it appropriate for addressing extremely nonlinear and ill-posed inversion challenges. The algorithm was initially verified with various noise-contaminated

Grey Wolf Optimizer. DOI: https://doi.org/10.1016/B978-0-443-36624-6.00029-9

synthetic datasets for DCR, MTT, and RF, demonstrating its stability, sensitivity, dependability, and accuracy over diverse geological conditions. The GWOPSO algorithm was implemented on field datasets from geologically and tectonically varied regions, including the mineralized area of Broken Hill (DCR-MTT), the geothermal zone of Puga Valley (DCR-MTT), and the seismically active Garhwal–Kumaun Himalayas (MTT-RF). In each case, the outputs were utilized to calculate the Bayesian posterior probability density function (*BPDF*), from which the mean model and posterior uncertainty bounds at a 68.27% confidence interval were obtained. Furthermore, correlation matrices were computed to analyze parameter interdependence and sensitivity within the model layers.

The evaluated results focused on key metrics such as model uncertainty, resolution, and structural interpretability. Comparative analysis with existing techniques and reference models from literature revealed that the current approach delivers robust, geologically consistent models with lower uncertainty and better convergence behavior than conventional deterministic or stochastic methods. The success across joint inversion schemes highlights GWOPSO's adaptability and effectiveness as a next-generation inversion tool for multiphysics geophysical data integration.

29.2 Method

29.2.1 Forward modeling

Consider a one-dimensional (1D) Earth model composed of p subsurface layers separated by (*p*-1) interfaces. The electrical resistivity of each layer is given by the vector $\rho = [\rho_1, \rho_2 ... ,\rho_{p-1}, \rho_p]$, while the thicknesses between successive interfaces are denoted as $h = [\, h_1, h_2, ... h_{p-1}]$. For a semiinfinite half-space, the pth layer is assumed to extend infinitely in depth. In the context of joint inversion, the model parameter vector can be expressed as:

$$\vec{x} = [\rho,\ h\ ], \tag{29.1}$$

Hence, the total number of parameters in the model is $p + (p\text{-}1)$. Numerous studies [17] have laid out the standard 1D forward modeling formulations for both DCR data and MTT data.

In joint inversion, the integration of electrical and velocity models is obtained by adopting a common set of layer thicknesses or depths. Thus an interface in the velocity model is also treated as an interface in the resistivity model, even though the resistivity contrast is absent at that interface [18]. This approach, based on shared geometry, minimizes the assumptions needed regarding the relationship between velocity and resistivity in the lithosphere, where such relationships are often poorly constrained.

Now, consider a 1D Earth model with *p* layers and *(p*–1*)* interfaces, where the shear-wave (S-wave) velocities of the layers are defined as, $Vs = [Vs_1,\ Vs_2,\ ....Vs_{p-1},\ Vs_p]$, and the corresponding depths between interfaces are, $D = [D_1,\ D_2,\ ....D_{p-1}]$, with the final layer again considered to have infinite thickness. The associated electrical resistivities remain, $\rho = [\rho_1,\ \rho_2,\ ....\rho_{p-1},\ \rho_p]$. Thus, for joint inversion purposes, the model parameter vector becomes:

$$\vec{x} = [Vs,\ D,\ \rho] \tag{29.2}$$

Here, the depth vector *D* is especially important, as it acts as a shared structural parameter linking the electrical resistivity and seismic velocity models [18]. Foundational expressions for 1D forward modeling of Ps-RF and MTT data -relevant to this study-can be found in several existing publications and standard references [19].

29.2.2 Inverse modeling

Using mathematical inverse theory, one can determine the model parameters (*x*) from observed data (*d*) as:

$$x = G^{-1}(d) \tag{29.3}$$

Here, *G* denotes the forward operator and G^{-1} is the inverse operator. To identify the optimal model, a cost function is optimized using the below equation, which is used for both synthetic (noise-free and noisy) and field datasets:

$$Cost\_function = \frac{1}{n}\sum_{j=1}^{n}(d\_obs_j - d\_cal_j)^2 \tag{29.4}$$

where *n* represents the observation points, and *j* ranges from 1 to *n*, terms *d_obs* and *d_cal* represent the observed and calculated data, respectively.

Generation of noisy synthetic data is carried out by:

$$d_{noise} = d_{syn} + (2 \times rand - 1)d_{syn} \times Noise\% \tag{29.5}$$

In this expression, d_{syn} refers to the synthetic data, d_{noise} is the resulting noisy data, *rand* is a Gaussian-distributed random value in the range of 0 and 1, and *Noise%* refers to the percentage of noise added into the dataset.

The cutting-edge optimization techniques, such as GWOPSO, GWO, PSO, and others, initialize the inversion by choosing random values from the predefined parameter search ranges. In stochastic methodologies, the number of iterations is generally employed as the termination criterion. Figs. 29.1–29.3 depict the computational framework employed for joint inversion through flowcharts.

29.2.2.1 Grey wolf optimizer

The GWO algorithm is inspired by the social hierarchy and chasing strategies of grey wolves in nature, rendering it a useful tool for addressing both theoretical and practical optimization challenges [13]. The GWO algorithm is distinguished by robust exploration abilities and comparatively less exploitation characteristics [14]. The natural hierarchy of grey wolves consists of four ranks: alpha, beta, delta, and omega. The alpha wolves serve as leaders, making crucial decisions for the entire pack. Betas assist the alphas by communicating and implementing decisions,but lack the authority to override them. They function as intermediates, transmitting directives from the alpha and gathering responses from the remainder of the pack. Deltas accompany both alpha and beta wolves while exerting dominance over the lowest-ranking omegas, who generally consume food last and function as stress alleviators for the pack. Notwithstanding their subordinate rank, omega wolves fulfill an essential function during the hunt.

In the context of the GWO algorithm, the alpha wolf represents the best candidate solution found so far, accompanied by the other two best wolf groups/ solution that is beta and delta, respectively. The omega wolves serve as alternative candidates and follow the top three wolves to converge toward optimal solutions. The hunting mechanism involves three stages: searching, encircling, and attacking the prey. The encircling behavior is mathematically described as:

$$\vec{d} = |c(t) - \vec{x}(t)| \tag{29.6}$$

$$\vec{x}(t+1) = \vec{x}_p(t) - ad \tag{29.7}$$

where $\vec{x}_p$ is the prey position, $\vec{x}$ is the position of a grey wolf at iteration t, $\vec{a}$ and $\vec{c}$ are coefficient vectors controlling the position updates and are defined as:

$$\vec{a} = \vec{a1}(2 \times rand - 1) \tag{29.8}$$

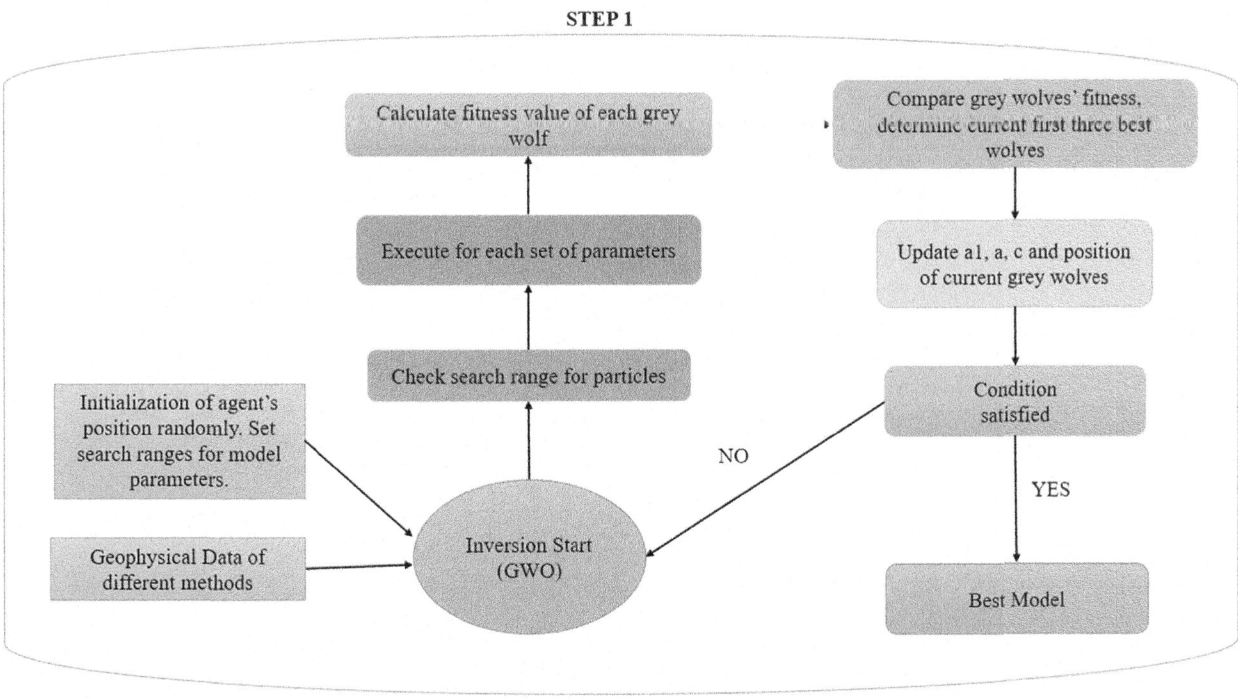

FIGURE 29.1 Illustrates the procedural steps for joint inversion with the grey wolf optimizer in a schematic flow diagram.

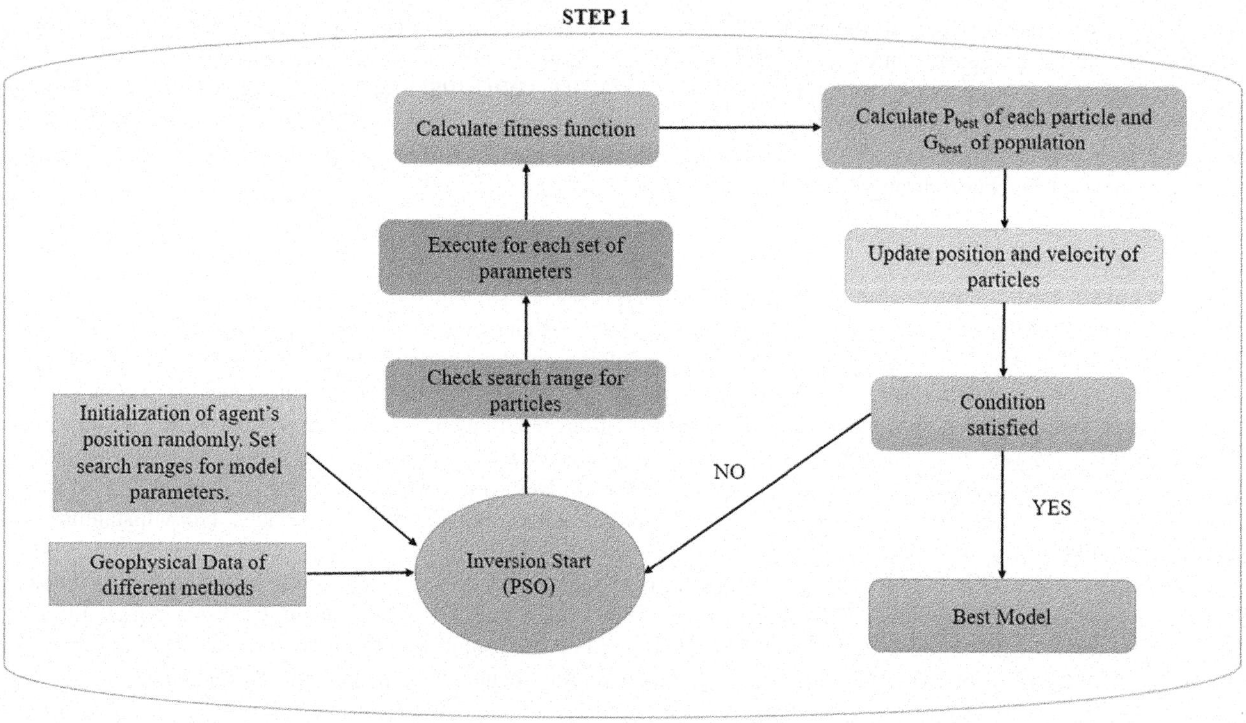

FIGURE 29.2 Illustrates the procedural steps for joint inversion with the particle swarm optimization in a schematic flow diagram.

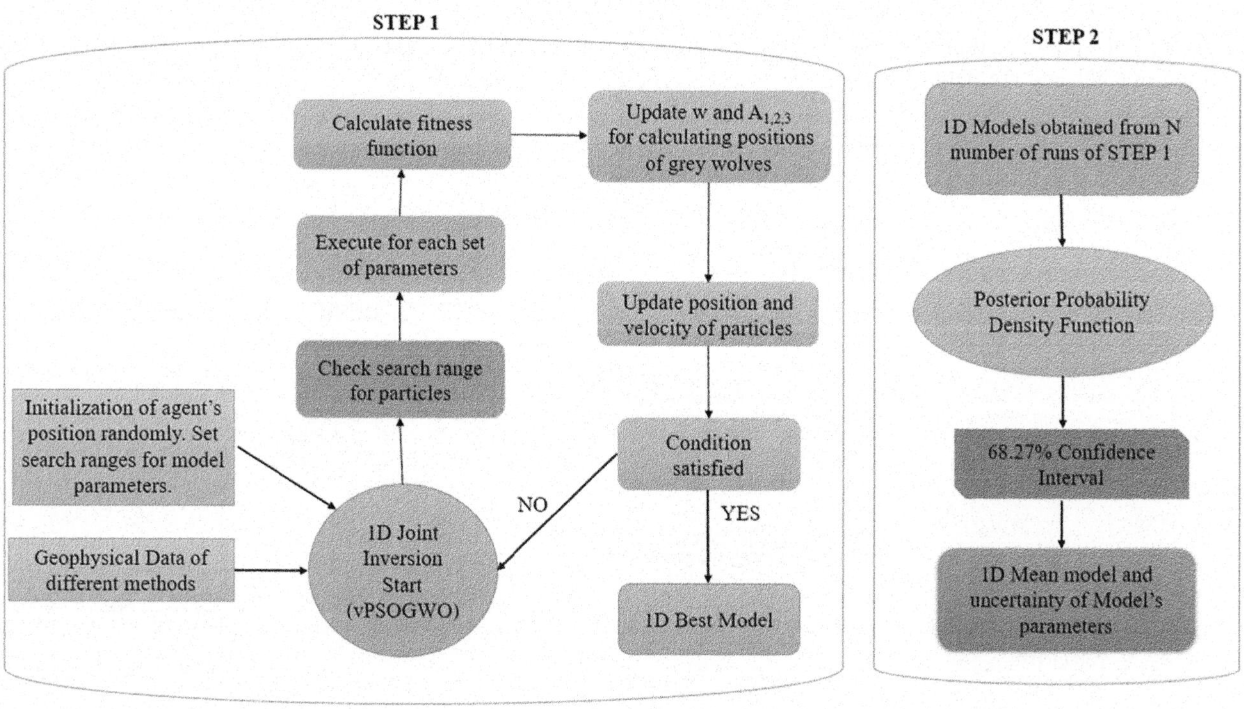

FIGURE 29.3 Illustrates the procedural steps for joint inversion with the GWOPSO in a schematic flow diagram (*GWOPSO*, Grey wolf optimizer-particle swarm optimization).

where,

$$\overrightarrow{a1} = 2(1 - t/T)$$
$$\vec{c} = 2 \times rand \qquad (29.9)$$

The coefficient vector $a1$ decreases linearly from 2 to 0 over the course of iterations (t), guiding the wolves between exploration and exploitation. Where T denotes the total number of iterations.

If $\vec{a} \geq 1$, the wolves are in exploration mode, searching for better solutions, and If $\vec{a} < 1$, they are in exploitation mode, attacking the prey (converging on the solution).

During each iteration, the positions of the top three wolves (α, β, δ) are used to guide the rest of the population. The position update rule for each wolf is influenced by these three leaders as follows:

$$\vec{d}_{\alpha,\beta,\delta} = | \vec{c}_{1,2,3} \times \vec{x}_{\alpha,\beta,\delta} - \vec{x} | \tag{29.10}$$

$$\vec{x}_{1,2,3} = | \vec{x}_{\alpha,\beta,\delta} - \vec{a}_{1,2,3} \times \vec{d}_{\alpha,\beta,\delta} | \tag{29.11}$$

$\vec{x}_\alpha$, $\vec{x}_\beta$, and $\vec{x}_\delta$, represent the optimal position of the α, β, δ wolves, respectively, during each iteration. Finally, the new position of the wolf is estimated as the average of the three leader-influenced positions:

$$\vec{x}_p(t+1) = (\vec{x}_1 + \vec{x}_2 + \vec{x}_3)/3 \tag{29.12}$$

29.2.2.2 *Particle swarm optimization*

The PSO is stimulated by the collective behavior of particles (or agents) foraging for food, where each particle represents a potential solution, such as a set of resistivity layer parameters, within a swarm. PSO is characterized by strong exploitation capabilities but limited exploration potential [14].

During each iteration, the algorithm retains the best solution found by any particle so far, guiding the search toward the global optimum. The fitness (Eq. 29.4) of each particle determines its effectiveness in reaching the optimal solution. The velocity ($\vec{v}_k(t+1)$) and position ($\vec{x}_k(t+1)$) of the kth particle at iteration ($t+1$) are updated using the following equations [13]:

$$\vec{v}_k(t+1) = w\vec{v}_k(t) + c_1 \times rand \times (\vec{x}_p - \vec{x}_k(t)) + c_2 \times rand \times (\vec{x}_g - \vec{x}_k(t)) \tag{29.13}$$

$$\vec{x}_k(t+1) = \vec{x}_k(t) + \vec{v}_k(t+1) \tag{29.14}$$

In this context, c_1 and c_2 denote the cognitive (personal training) and social (global training) coefficients, respectively; w signifies the inertia weight (within the range of 0–1), which governs the impact of the preceding velocity; $\vec{x}_p$ signifies the personal best position identified by the kth particle, while $\vec{x}_g$ denotes the global best position discovered among all particles. The three components in Eq. (29.13) represent inertia (exploration), cognitive (individual memory), and social (swarm cooperation) influences, respectively [4].

29.2.2.3 *Fusion of grey wolf optimizer and particle swarm optimization*

Several studies have demonstrated the efficacy of hybrid GWO-PSO strategies. Shaikh et al. [21] devised a hybrid GWO-PSO algorithm that improved convergence and solution quality in intricate optimization challenges. Zhang et al. [22] introduced a hybrid GWO-PSO method incorporating a differential mechanism to enhance global search efficiency. Shaheen et al. [23] applied GWO-PSO to optimal power flow problems, attaining superior convergence rates and enhanced solutions relative to conventional methods. Similarly, Alyu et al. [24] and Cheng et al. [25] employed hybrid GWO-PSO approaches for distributed generation optimization and adaptive search tasks, exhibiting enhanced performance in both solution accuracy and convergence speed. These studies highlight that integrating GWO and PSO effectively balances exploration and exploitation, making it a powerful instrument for addressing intricate and high-dimensional optimization problems.

Based on this, the GWOPSO is a hybrid coevolutionary algorithm that integrates the principles of both GWO and PSO to yield optimum solutions and is deployed in the geophysical problems [14,17]. This algorithm adeptly harmonizes the robust exploitation strength of GWO with the augmented exploration strength of PSO. In GWOPSO, the positional authority of the top three wolves from GWO, alpha (α), beta (β), and delta (δ), is utilized to direct and modify particle locations in PSO. Conversely, the best positions discovered by PSO particles help inform and adjust wolf positions during the search process. The wolves' encircling behavior is mathematically defined as:

$$\vec{D}_{\alpha,\beta,\delta} = |Const \times \vec{X}_{\alpha,\beta,\delta}(t) - w \times \vec{x}_k| \tag{29.15}$$

$$\vec{x}_{1,2,3} = |\vec{X}_{\alpha,\beta,\delta}(t) - A_{1,2,3} \times \vec{D}_{\alpha,\beta,\delta}| \tag{29.16}$$

where,

$$\vec{A}_{1,2,3} = (2\vec{a} \times rand - \vec{a}), \tag{29.17}$$

$$\vec{a} = 2 - 2 \times t/T, \tag{29.18}$$

where $\vec{X}_{\alpha,\beta,\delta}(t)$ are the positions (models) of the α, β, δ wolves at iteration t, $\vec{x}_k$ is the current position (model) of the kth PSO particle, *Const* is a constant set to 0.5, $\vec{D}_{\alpha,\beta,\delta}$ are the vectors representing distance, $\vec{x}_{1,2,3}$ represent the top three rationalized positions (candidate models) determined by wolves, T denotes the total number of iteration.

To update the PSO particle velocity and position based on these wolf-influenced models, the following equations are used [15,17]:

$$\vec{v}_k(t+1) = w\vec{v}_k(t) + c_1 \times rand \times (\vec{x}_1 - \vec{x}_k(t)) + c_2 \times rand \times (\vec{x}_2 - \vec{x}_k(t)) + c_3 \times rand \times (\vec{x}_3 - \vec{x}_k(t)) \tag{29.19}$$

$$\vec{x}_k(t+1) = \vec{x}_k(t) + w\vec{v}_k(t+1) \tag{29.20}$$

Here, $\vec{x}_{1,2,3}$ are the best model positions obtained from GWO (α, β, and δ wolves), $c_{1,2,3}$ are learning coefficients, w is the inertia weight that decays over time, calculated as:

$$w = w_{\max} - (w_{\max} - w_{\min})iter/l \tag{29.21}$$

with $w_{\max} = 0.9$, $w_{\min} = 0.2$.

This dynamic interaction between the GWO and PSO components enhances the hybrid algorithm's capacity to explore and converge effectively in complex optimization problems.

The GWOPSO algorithm presents several advantages over standalone PSO and GWO methods [20]:

a) Balance of exploration and exploitation: PSO is characterized by robust exploitation but constrained exploration, whereas GWO demonstrates significant exploration with diminished exploitation capabilities. GWOPSO adeptly amalgamates the advantages of both.
b) Enhanced optimization Efficacy: By integrating the characteristics of PSO and GWO, GWOPSO attains more dependable and precise outcomes than either algorithm independently.
c) Mitigation of local minima and enhanced Convergence: The advanced exploration capability of GWOPSO enables it to traverse the search space more comprehensively, hence diminishing the likelihood of entrapment in local minima. Simultaneously, its improved exploitation guarantees expedited convergence to the optimal global solution.
d) Decreased computational duration: The hybrid characteristics of GWOPSO provide expedited execution, leading to reduced calculation periods associated with the separate GWO and PSO algorithms.

29.2.3 Statistical method

The probability density function is a mathematical instrument utilized to depict the probability of a random variable taking on values within a defined interval. It measures the likelihood of various outcomes for continuous variables. This work delineates the 1D posterior Bayesian PDF (*BPDF*) for each parameter i as follows [26]:

$$P(x_{ij} \mid \rho_{obs}) = \frac{f(x_i)f(\rho_{obs} \mid x_j)}{\Sigma_j f(x_i)f(\rho_{obs} \mid x_j)} \tag{29.22}$$

where $P(x_{ij}, |\rho_{obs})$ denotes the posterior PDF of parameter (x_{ij}) given the observed data (ρ_{obs}). The term $f(x_i)$ represents the prior distribution of parameter i, while $f(\rho_{obs}|x_j)$ denotes the likelihood function, defined as follows [26]:

$$f(x_i) = \begin{cases} \frac{1}{UB_i - LB_i}, & LB_i \le x_i \le UB_i \\ 0, & elsewhere \end{cases} \tag{29.23}$$

$$f(\rho_{obs} \mid x_j) = \prod_{i=1}^{n} \frac{1}{\sqrt{2\pi\sigma^2}} \exp\left\{-\frac{(G(x_j) - \rho_{obs})^2}{2\sigma^2}\right\} \tag{29.24}$$

where $\hat{m}_i$, $G(x_j)$, ρ_{obs}, and σ^2 denote the mean, estimated apparent resistivity, observed apparent resistivity, and variance of the collection derived from all models x. LB_i and UB_i denote the lower and upper bounds of the parameter's search range.

The mean model $\hat{m}$ and the standard deviation σ_i of parameter i, based on M total model realizations, are computed as [27]:

$$\hat{m}_i = \frac{1}{M} \sum_{j=1}^{M} x_{i,j} \quad (29.25)$$

$$\sigma_i = \sqrt{\frac{1}{M-1} \sum_{j=1}^{M} (x_{i,j} - \hat{m}_i)^2} \quad (29.26)$$

Models generated over multiple iterations of the inversion process are utilized to compute the posterior probability and corresponding histograms. These statistical tools provide insight into the probability distribution of the estimated parameters and help assess the resolution and uncertainty of the inversion outcomes. The analysis involves calculating the confidence interval (CI), which quantifies the probability that a parameter lies within a specified range around the mean $\hat{m}_i$ [28].

According to the 68.27% experiential rule outlined by Ross [27], inverted model realizations are contained within one ' σ ' of the mean. Consequently, only models that fall within the specified confidence range of the posterior *BPDF* are preserved for the computation of the final mean and the corresponding uncertainty of model parameters. This approach provides an estimate that is near the global optimum and effectively decreases uncertainty in the inversion results [17].

29.3 Results and discussion

The efficacy of the newly established joint inversion-based GWOPSO algorithm has been thoroughly assessed. The assessment was initially performed utilizing various sets of synthetic data. Each test scenario utilized a population size of 10 agents/particles and involved 1000 iterations, conducted multiple times, leading to the acceptance of inverted models. The algorithm was subsequently developed using field datasets gathered from various geological contexts.

Additionally, the posterior inverted models are employed to assess nonuniqueness, uncertainty, and sensitivity; we calculated the *BPDF* and correlation matrix. This analysis was structured into two phases:

a) STEP 1: Application of the GWOPSO algorithm for joint/individual inversion.
b) STEP 2: Posterior Bayesian PDF analysis of the resulting inverted models.

These steps are illustrated through schematic flowcharts for better interpretability.

29.3.1 Synthetic examples

To validate the performance of the proposed Bayesian GWOPSO method, synthetic data with Gaussian noise were generated. Only those modelswith posterior *BPDF* CI greater than 68.27% were considered for evaluation. In this application, 10 swarm size and 1000 iterations were used, and it was repeated multiple times to explore the model space and generate a suite of alternative solutions. These inverted outcomes were then related to the true model.

29.3.1.1 Example 1: Application of Joint inversion of synthetic DCR and MTT data

To assess the capabilities of the proposed joint inversion technique, a synthetic DCR and MTT dataset was generated over a sedimentary basin overlying a basaltic trap, simulating a realistic field scenario. The datasets were contaminated with 10% Gaussian noise to mimic actual measurement conditions, considering an 800 m thick basalt layer of resistivity 250 Ωm overlying a 250 m thick conductive sedimentary layer, which is underlain by a highly resistive granitic basement.

The noisy DCR and MTT datasets were inverted jointly using the GWOPSO, GWO, and PSO algorithms without any initial model assumptions. Results from 1000 independent inversion runs were analyzed, as presented in Fig. 29.4 and Table 29.1. The inverted parameters obtained using GWOPSO are in excellent agreement with the true model and the confidence intervals reported in earlier studies [19]. While all three algorithms (PSO, GWO, GWOPSO) provide reasonably accurate results, GWOPSO produces the lowest root mean square (RMS) error (0.2281) compared to PSO (0.2283) and GWO (0.2290). Furthermore, GWOPSO delivers more stable parameter estimates with narrower uncertainty bounds, particularly for ρ_2 and h_2, demonstrating its superiority in both accuracy and robustness. These results establish GWOPSO as a more effective inversion strategy compared to its baseline counterparts.

In addition to accuracy, the computational efficiency of the algorithms was assessed. The average runtimes, measured over 1000 independent runs, are reported in Table 29.1. PSO and GWO required 1.861 s and 1.849 s, respectively, whereas GWOPSO required 1.946 s. The slightly higher runtime of GWOPSO (≈5% increase) arises from its hybrid

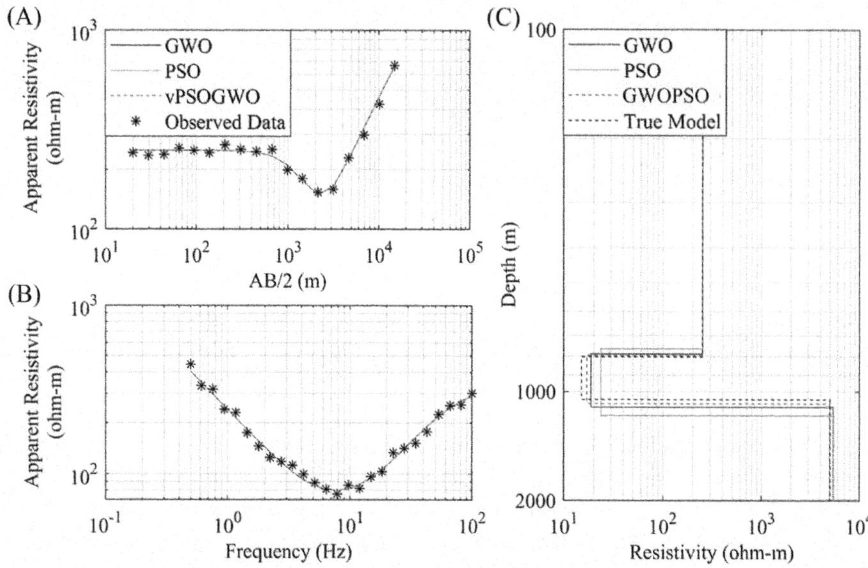

FIGURE 29.4 Synthetic noisy (A) DCR and (B) MTT observed curve (*) and best-fit apparent resistivity data for a three-layer model; (C) 1D mean models (*BPDF* > 68.27% CI) inverted by GWO (*blue*), PSO (*green*), GWOPSO (*red*), and compared with the true model (*black*) (*BPDF*, Bayesian posterior probability density function; *CI*, confidence interval; *DCR*, direct current resistivity; *GWO*, grey wolf optimizer; *GWOPSO*, grey wolf optimizer-particle swarm optimization; *PSO*, particle swarm optimization).
Taken from K. Sarkar, M. Mukesh, U.K. Singh, Nature-inspired stochastic hybrid technique for joint and individual inversion of DC and MT data, Sci. Rep. 13 (1) (2023) 2668.

update rules that combine features of PSO and GWO. Nevertheless, this small computational overhead is outweighed by the substantial improvements in accuracy and stability. From a theoretical perspective, the computational complexity of all three algorithms remains **O(*NDT*)**, where N denotes the population size, D denotes the problem dimension, and T denotes the number of iterations. This confirms that GWOPSO scales efficiently with problem size while maintaining superior inversion performance.

To further validate the superiority of GWOPSO over the baseline algorithms, the Wilcoxon signed-rank test was performed on the RMS errors obtained from 1000 independent runs. The pairwise comparisons (GWOPSO vs PSO, GWOPSO vs GWO) for the synthetic model are summarized in Table 29.1. The P-values (2.473e-06 and 1.393e-06) are both below 0.05, indicating that the null hypothesis of equal performance can be rejected. This confirms that the improvements achieved by GWOPSO over PSO and GWO are statistically significant at the 95% confidence level.

In addition, the inverted responses obtained from the GWOPSO algorithm were analyzed by selecting only the accepted models, that is, those with posterior probability density function (*BPDF*) values exceeding 68.27% CI. The *BPDF* values were computed to assess the uncertainty and resolution in the inverted models, as illustrated in Fig. 29.5, while histograms were generated to evaluate the parameter sensitivity of the model parameters (Fig. 29.6). The histogram peaks in Fig. 29.6 highlight the clustering of inverted parameters near the true model values, while the spread reflects posterior uncertainty, indicating that most solutions closely align with the actual subsurface structure.

Fig. 29.6 presents the distribution of samples on the y-axis plotted against the inverted layer parameters on the x-axis, where the histogram width reflects the variability in each parameter. Notably, there is significant variation observed in the parameters ρ_3 (resistivity of the basement) and h_1 (thickness of the top layer), in contrast to the more stable parameters, namely ρ_1, ρ_2, and h_2. This observation advocates that the DCR data contributes more effectively to resolving shallow subsurface structures, while the MTT data enhances at greater depths.

A comparative analysis with the results from Manglik et al. [19] (see Table 29.1) demonstrates that the GWOPSO approach yields lower uncertainty in both resistivity and thickness estimates. Consequently, the GWOPSO algorithm significantly reduces model ambiguity and builds a higher accuracy mean solution with better precision.

29.3.1.2 *Example 2: Application of Joint inversion of synthetic MTT and RF data*

Further to evaluate the efficiency of the proposed multiparametric joint inversion technique, synthetic datasets were created for both MTT and RF data. To assess realistic field circumstances, Gaussian noise was added to the synthetic

TABLE 29.1 Mean model parameters and their posterior uncertainties obtained from joint inversion of synthetic data with 10% noise using GWOPSO, alongside comparison results reported by Manglik et al. [19].

Layer parameters	True model	Search Space		Inverted value					
		Lower	Upper	Manglik et al. [19]			Inverted model (PDF > 68.27% CI)		
				Model -1	Model -2	Model -3	PSO	GWO	GWOPSO
ρ_1 (Ωm)	250	100	500	255.4±27.4	254.8±27.3	255±27.3	252.01 ±0.35	250.88 ±0.19	250.58 ±0.30
h_1 (m)	800	500	1500	772.4±88.1	781.8±88.1	778.8±88.1	759.53 ±6.96	785.60 ±4.52	759.53 ±3.57
ρ_2 (Ωm)	15	1	50	18.9±0.84	17.2±0.76	17.7±0.79	23.67 ±1.39	18.71 ±0.88	17.00 ±0.65
h_2 (m)	250	100	500	317.5±12.7	286.2±11.5	296.1±11.9	404.81 ±25.46	315.98 ±15.45	285.33 ±11.13
ρ_3 (Ωm)	5000	1000	10000	5675±1650	5670±1647	5672±1648	5450.38 ±136.48	5397.53 ±277.68	4955.32 ±132.93
Fitness (RMS)							0.2283	0.2290	0.2281
Computational cost (sec)							1.861	1.849	1.946
				GWOPSO versus PSO			GWOPSO versus GWO		
Wilcoxon signed-rank test (p)				2.473e-06			1.393e-06		

Source: Taken from K. Sarkar, M. Mukesh, U.K. Singh, Nature-inspired stochastic hybrid technique for joint and individual inversion of DC and MT data, Sci. Rep. 13 (1) (2023) 2668.

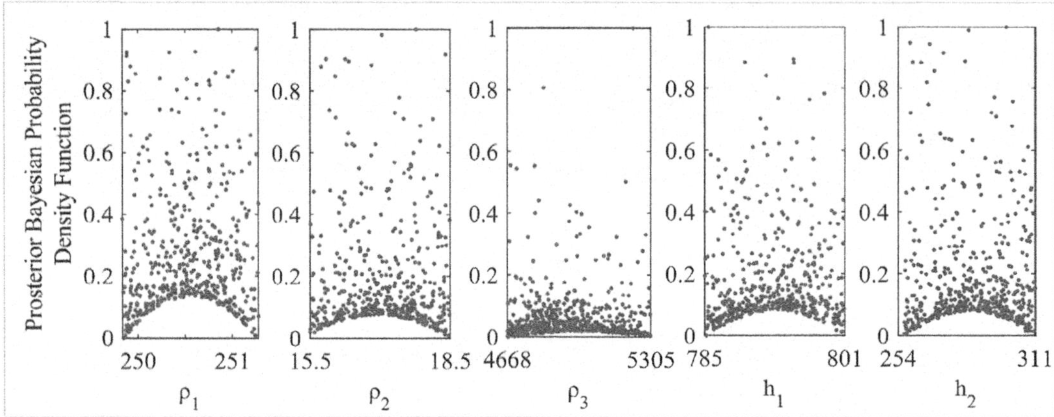

FIGURE 29.5 *BPDF* distributions of the GWOPSO-inverted layer's parameter for synthetic three-layer DCR and MTT data with noise (*BPDF*, Bayesian posterior probability density function; *DCR*, direct current resistivity; *GWOPSO*, grey wolf optimizer-particle swarm optimization.
Taken from K. Sarkar, M. Mukesh, U.K. Singh, Nature-inspired stochastic hybrid technique for joint and individual inversion of DC and MT data, Sci. Rep. 13 (1) (2023) 2668.

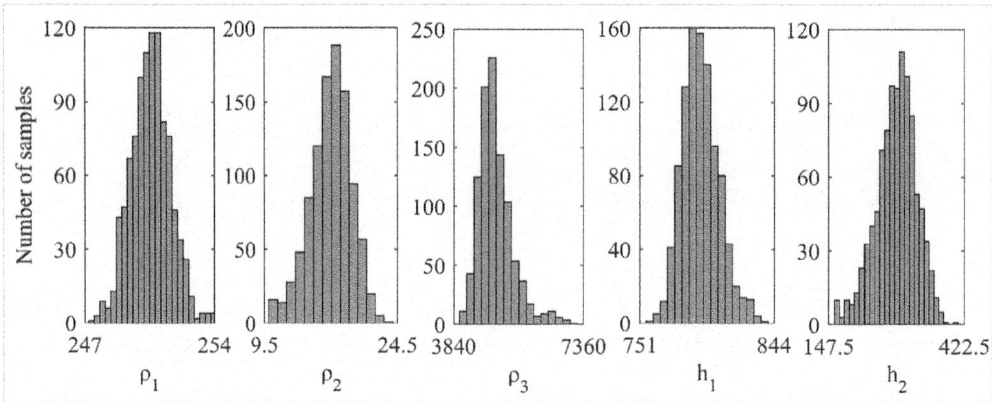

FIGURE 29.6 Sample distribution of the GWOPSO-inverted layer's parameter for synthetic three-layer DCR and MTT data with noise (*DCR*, Direct current resistivity; *GWOPSO*, grey wolf optimizer-particle swarm optimization).
Taken from K. Sarkar, M. Mukesh, U.K. Singh, Nature-inspired stochastic hybrid technique for joint and individual inversion of DC and MT data, Sci. Rep. 13 (1) (2023) 2668.

datasets-2% for RF and 5% for MTT, respectively. This process is illustrated in Fig. 29.7, which presents the outcomes of trials conducted on a geological model from Moorkamp et al. [18].

The synthetic model comprises a four-layer structural sequence, designed to reflect crustal and upper mantle conditions. The first three layers are characterized by increasing seismic velocities of 3.61 km/s, 3.83 km/s, and 4.76 km/s, with layer interfaces located at 25 km and 40 km depths. The equivalent electrical resistivities for these layers are 600 Ωm, 800 Ωm, and 2550 Ωm, respectively. The fourth layer, representing the upper mantle, begins at a depth of 160 km and is modeled as a low-velocity zone with a velocity of 4.51 km/s and a resistivity of 200 Ω·m. This configuration captures the Mohorovičić discontinuity (Moho) at approximately 40 km depth.

The analysis involved conducting both individual and joint inversion without incorporating any prior model guesses. A total of 100 independent runs were executed to evaluate the robustness of the inversion outcomes. Eventually, the joint inversion outcomes were evaluated together to determine the complete advancement in parameter estimation accuracy. Fig. 29.8 illustrates the Bayesian posterior probability distribution curves for each model parameter, constructed using a 100% CI. The distributions reveal that the maximum probability density occurs in close proximity to the true model parameters, indicating a strong convergence of the algorithm toward the global solution.

To determine the final mean model, only those solutions whose posterior probability density exceeded the 68.27% CI threshold (according to the empirical rule) were accepted, while models with lower probabilities were discarded. The

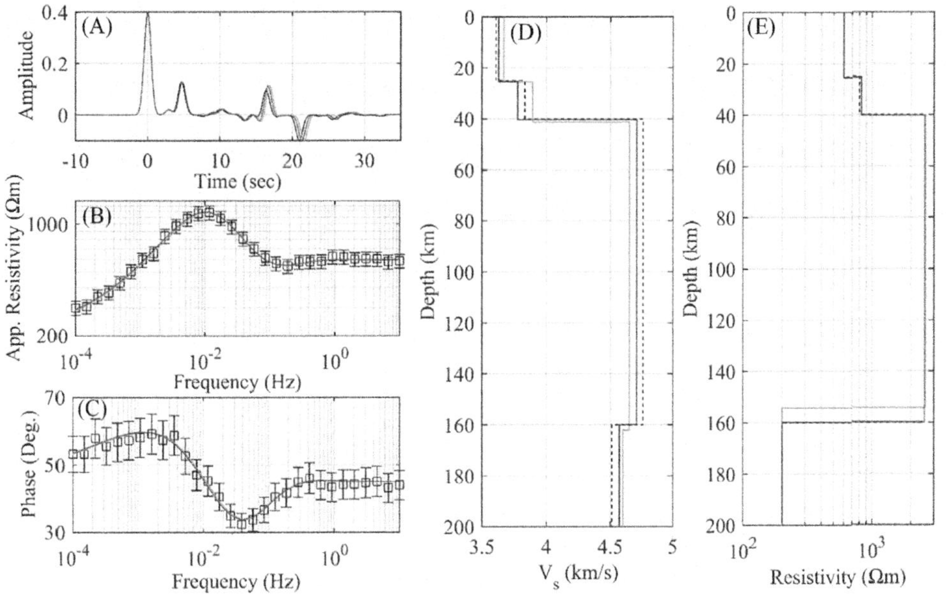

FIGURE 29.7 Four-layer synthetic RF and MTT data: (A) RF, (B) MTT apparent resistivity, (C) MTT phase with observed curves (*black*) and fits from individual (*green*) and joint (*red*) GWOPSO inversions; (d) 1D versusVs model and (E) 1D resistivity model (*BPDF* > 68.27% CI), showing true (*black*), individual (*green*), and joint (*red*) models (*BPDF*, Bayesian posterior probability density function; *CI*, confidence interval; *GWOPSO*, grey wolf optimizer- particle swarm optimization; *RF*, receiver function).
Taken from K. Sarkar, A. Yadav, U.K. Singh, Joint inversion of receiver function and magnetotelluric data via a nature-inspired stochastic hybrid technique, Earth Sci. Inf. 18 (3) (2025) 301–312.

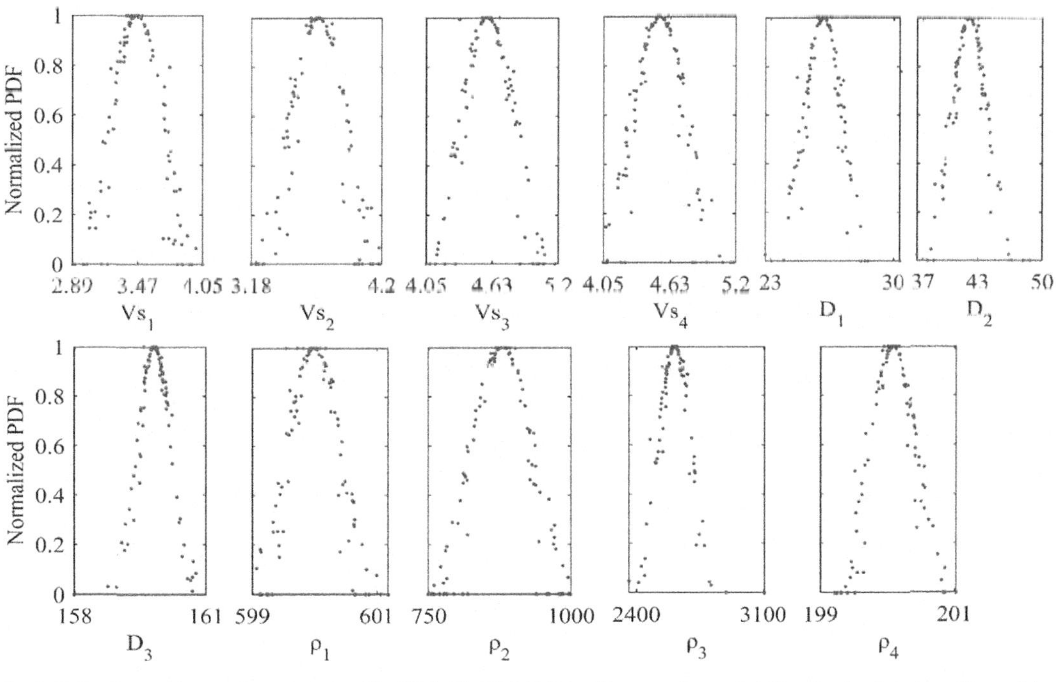

FIGURE 29.8 *BPDF* values of inverted parameters with 100% CI (*BPDF*, Bayesian posterior probability density function; *CI*, confidence interval).
Taken from K. Sarkar, A. Yadav, U.K. Singh, Joint inversion of receiver function and magnetotelluric data via a nature-inspired stochastic hybrid technique, Earth Sci. Inf. 18 (3) (2025) 301–312.

inversion results, summarized in Fig. 29.7, report RMS errors of 0.8099 for RF, 1.6658 for MTT, and 1.3816 for the joint inversion, respectively. Furthermore, Table 29.2 provides the true model parameters along with the search spaces employed during the inversion process.

TABLE 29.2 Mean model parameters and their posterior uncertainties obtained with 68.27% confidence interval from Posterior *BPDF* using the GWOPSO algorithm.

Layer parameters	True model	Search space	Inverted value		
			RF	MTT	Joint
Vs_1 (km/s)	3.61	2.89–4.05	3.67 ± 0.51	–	3.63 ± 0.04
ρ_1 (Ωm)	600	500–700	–	596.38 ± 5.69	598.13 ± 3.46
D_1 (km)	25	20–35	25.51 ± 0.83	25.43 ± 0.57	25.41 ± 0.37
Vs_2 (km/s)	3.83	3.18–4.34	3.89 ± 0.13	–	3.78 ± 0.09
ρ_2 (Ωm)	800	700–1000	–	830.54 ± 31.91	824.33 ± 22.91
D_2 (km)	40	25–60	41.29 ± 0.61	40.19 ± 0.87	40.24 ± 0.34
Vs_3 (km/s)	4.76	4.05–5.20	4.65 ± 0.22	–	4.71 ± 0.12
ρ_3 (Ωm)	2550	2000–5000	–	2591.30 ± 71.94	2556.30 ± 44.71
D_3 (km)	160	140–180	162.14 ± 0.37	154.32 ± 0.50	159.87 ± 0.25
Vs_4 (km/s)	4.51	4.05–5.20	4.60 ± 0.10	–	4.57 ± 0.09
ρ_4 (Ωm)	200	100–250	–	199.21 ± 7.16	199.78 ± 2.14

BPDF, Bayesian posterior probability density function; *GWOPSO*, grey wolf optimizer- particle swarm optimization; *RF*, receiver function.
Source: Taken from K. Sarkar, A. Yadav, U.K. Singh, Joint inversion of receiver function and magnetotelluric data via a nature-inspired stochastic hybrid technique, Earth Sci. Inf. 18 (3) (2025) 301–312.

Since the assembly of the prior model (as described in Eq. 29.23) for computing the posterior *BPDF* is conducted randomly, the resulting posterior models provide a probabilistic representation of plausible subsurface structures. By sampling from this posterior distribution, one can effectively quantify model confidence and assess associated uncertainties, thereby offering a more comprehensive insight into the reliability and variability of the inversion outcomes.

As shown in Table 29.2 and Fig. 29.7 (D and E), the joint inversion outcomes (represented in red) demonstrate a marked enhancement in estimating the final model parameters, particularly by reducing their uncertainties, when compared to the individual inversions (shown in green). The individual inversions exhibit greater distortion in the velocity model and thickness estimates of the resistivity model, indicating limited reliability when used independently.

In contrast, the mean model derived from the joint inversion aligns more closely with the true model, reflecting the advantages of integrating complementary datasets. These results underscore the capability of the GWOPSO-based joint inversion approach to significantly reduce error and enhance resolution in the estimation of subsurface layer parameters.

In joint inversion, the correlation coefficients between layer parameters are computed to assess the degree of interdependence and ambiguity in model interpretations, as illustrated in Fig. 29.8. The diagonal entries of the correlation matrix represent autocorrelations, indicating complete self-correlation and thus are always equal to one. In an idealized scenario where the model uniquely fits the data with no ambiguity, the off-diagonal elements would approach zero (represented by green), signifying no correlation between different parameters. However, in practical geophysical applications, such ideal conditions are rarely met. Trade-offs or correlations between parameters arise due to incomplete or imperfect sampling of the subsurface, which stems from limited data coverage, nonuniqueness, noise (random or systematic), and simplifications in forward modeling. These factors limit the model's ability to uniquely resolve parameter values, especially when the underlying physical relationships between the data and model are only partially understood.

Despite these challenges, the sampling achieved through the GWOPSO-based inversion is sufficiently robust for the study objectives. The correlation matrix, which spans from -1 to 1 and is symmetric along its diagonal, provides insight into how well the data constrain individual model parameters and the extent of trade-offs among them. Careful exploration of the model space becomes essential for identifying models that best fit the data and for quantifying parameter uncertainties, particularly in joint inversion settings. Such analysis helps assess how the addition of diverse datasets reduces the allowable space of model parameters and improves model resolution [29].

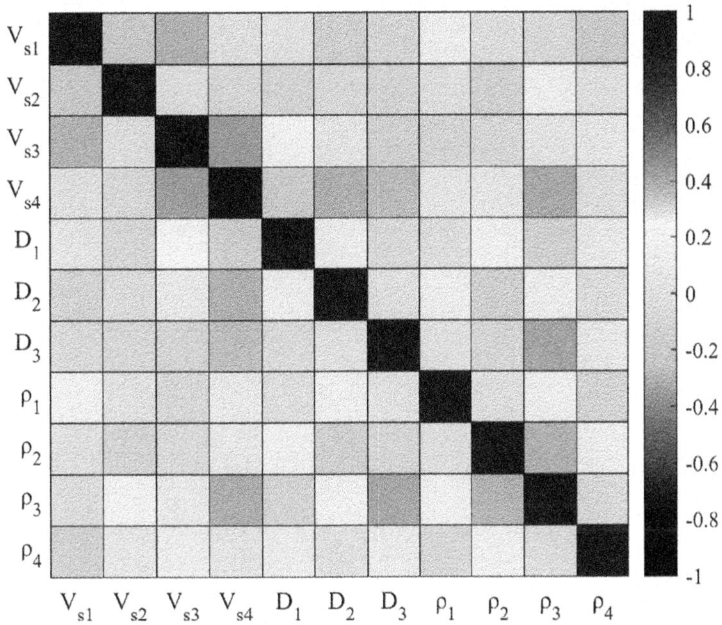

FIGURE 29.9 Correlation matrix of model parameters obtained through joint inversion.
Taken from K. Sarkar, A. Yadav, U.K. Singh, Joint inversion of receiver function and magnetotelluric data via a nature-inspired stochastic hybrid technique, Earth Sci. Inf. 18 (3) (2025) 301–312.

Fig. 29.9 illustrates that the results of the joint inversion indicate decreased correlations among parameters, which implies enhanced constraints on the estimates of individual parameters. The trade-offs related to deeper mantle layer parameters, specifically Vs_4 and ρ_4, are notably diminished via joint inversion. The findings validate the effectiveness of the GWOPSO algorithm in exploring a wide model parameter space while sustaining low uncertainty, even when initializing from randomly chosen models within defined search spaces.

The sensitivity and robustness of the proposed joint inversion method were evaluated under noisy synthetic conditions through the analysis of four distinct cases, utilizing different search spaces for the model parameters. Table 29.3 presents a summary of the corresponding results.

A comprehensive sensitivity analysis was performed to assess the impact of variations in parameter values on the inversion results. The analysis demonstrated that the proposed approach attained lower parameter uncertainties, signifying its effectiveness in yielding reliable model estimates across various search spaces. The inversion-maintained solution demonstrated consistency despite the presence of noise and altered bounds, thereby reinforcing its effectiveness.

29.3.2 Field examples

The newly created GWOPSO strategy was ultimately deployed to several field datasets from diverse geological contexts, keeping a uniform swarm size and model count throughout all instances based on the approach's demonstrated effectiveness. First, there are DCR and MTT data from Broken Hill, Australia. Next, there are DCR and MTT data from the Central Puga Valley in Ladakh, India. Finally, there are MTT and RF data from the Himalayas.

29.3.2.1 Example 1: Application of Joint inversion of MTT and DCR data

To demonstrate the adaptability and effectiveness of the proposed GWOPSO algorithm, a joint inversion of MTT and DCR datasets was carried out over a site near Broken Hill in South Central Australia. Geophysical datasets inherently involve uncertainties due to the ambiguous nature of subsurface responses. An integrated inversion approach is therefore recommended to reduce these ambiguities, especially when the same physical property, electrical resistivity, is sensed by multiple geophysical methods such as DCR and MTT [30,31]. Electrical resistivity is influenced by key geologic factors such as temperature and permeability [32], and both DCR and MTT can provide complementary resistivity models related to lithological variations.

TABLE 29.3 Evaluation of sensitivity using noisy synthetic RF and MTT datasets.

Layer parameters		ρ_1 (Ωm)	D_1 (km)	Vs_1 (km/s)	ρ_2 (Ωm)	D_2 (km)	Vs_2 (km/s)	ρ_3 (Ωm)	D_3 (km)	Vs_3 (km/s)	ρ_4 (Ωm)	Vs_4 (km/s)
Case 1	Search space	500-750	15-35	2.5-4.05	650-1000	25-75	3.18-5.00	2000-5500	130-180	3.75-5.20	80-250	4.05-5.70
	Inverted value	602.57	25.37	3.58	819.74	40.29	3.85	2559.43	159.83	4.70	198.11	4.58
Case 2	Search space	450 -700	20 -40	2.89-4.35	700 -1200	25 -65	3.00-4.34	1800 -5000	140 -200	4.05-5.40	100 -280	3.85-5.20
	Inverted value	596.51	25.61	3.66	823.13	40.18	3.81	2555.81	160.39	4.73	201.37	4.54
Case 3	Search space	480 -700	15 -40	2.69-4.15	650-1200	25 -70	3.10-4.34	1700-5200	135 -190	3.95-5.40	80-280	4.00-5.24
	Inverted value	603.85	25.44	3.64	821.61	40.24	3.78	2537.23	159.61	4.69	198.78	4.55
Case 4	Search space	450 -700	20 -40	2.5-4.05	700-1300	25-70	3.00-4.34	2000-5300	130-180	4.05-5.40	110-280	4.05-5.40
	Inverted value	597.24	25.51	3.66	829.31	39.60	3.79	2563.75	159.09	4.72	202.17	4.56

RF, Receiver function.
Source: Taken from K. Sarkar, A. Yadav, U.K. Singh, Joint inversion of receiver function and magnetotelluric data via a nature-inspired stochastic hybrid technique, Earth Sci. Inf. 18 (3) (2025) 301–312.

Although both DCR and MTT inversion methods are individually nonunique and nonlinear, their combined interpretation improves model reliability, providing more robust and coherent subsurface characterizations compared to those derived from standalone inversions [33,34]. The DCR and MTT data were collected over a 20 km profile, with measurements spanning a period range from 0.02 to 1995 seconds, including Schlumberger sounding data [35,36]. The GWOPSO-based inversion was applied to these apparent resistivity datasets, and the inversion outcomes were presented along with the search spaces used (Table 29.4). Fig. 29.10 (A) shows a comparison between the observed and calculated apparent resistivity curves, while Fig. 29.10 (B) presents the resulting 1D resistivity-depth model obtained using the current algorithm with an RMS error of 0.09486, which is comparable to results obtained through Occam's inversion [36].

TABLE 29.4 Mean model parameters and their posterior uncertainties obtained from joint inversion (*GWOPSO*) over Broken Hill in South Central Australia.

Layer parameters	Search space		Inverted value (GWOPSO)
	Lower	Upper	
ρ_1 (Ωm)	40	500	105.58 ± 4.90
h_1 (m)	1	10	1.16 ± 0.02
ρ_2 (Ωm)	1	10	7.33 ± 0.02
h_2 (m)	50	500	307.73 ± 1.55
ρ_3 (Ωm)	100	1000	416.55 ± 11.28
h_3 (m)	1000	10,00-0	7122.62 ± 14.68
ρ_4 (Ωm)	0.1	5	0.64 ± 0.01
Fitness (RMS)			0.0949

GWOPSO, Grey wolf optimizer-particle swarm optimization; *RMS*, root mean square.
Source: Taken from K. Sarkar, M. Mukesh, U.K. Singh, Nature-inspired stochastic hybrid technique for joint and individual inversion of DC and MT data, Sci. Rep. 13 (1) (2023) 2668.

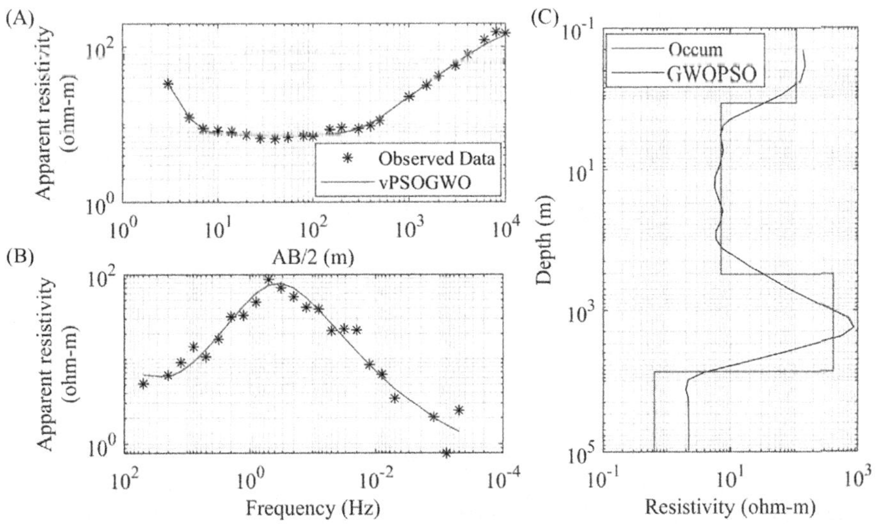

FIGURE 29.10 Field (A) DCR and (B) MTT observed curve (*) and best-fit apparent resistivity data for a four-layer model; (C) 1D mean models (*BPDF* > 68.27% CI) inverted by GWOPSO (red), compared with the Occam model (black) (*BPDF*, Bayesian posterior probability density function; *CI*, confidence interval; *DCR*, direct current resistivity; *GWOPSO*, grey wolf optimizer-particle swarm optimization).
Taken from K. Sarkar, M. Mukesh, U.K. Singh, Nature-inspired stochastic hybrid technique for joint and individual inversion of DC and MT data, Sci. Rep. 13 (1) (2023) 2668.

29.3.2.2 Example 2: Application of Joint inversion of DCR and MTT data

One of the geothermal rich area, namely Central Puga Valley (Ladakh), serves as another case study for the application of the proposed 1D joint inversion strategy using MTT and DCR resistivity sounding data processed with the GWOPSO algorithm. The search spaces, inverted posterior mean model, and associated uncertainty estimates derived from the joint inversion are summarized in Table 29.5.

Previous studies employed a range of methods to interpret MTT data, often relying on constraints from initial model assumptions [37], while the artificial neural network-based LM algorithm was used to invert vertical electrical sounding (VES) data. However, these earlier approaches were often limited, producing either shallow or deep models but rarely both with high reliability [38]. In contrast, the present joint inversion approach significantly improves model resolution. As illustrated in Fig. 29.11 (C), a shallow conductive zone with a thickness of 43.58 ± 0.09 m was identified, closely matching the geothermal layer thickness confirmed by drilling data [41] and demonstrating better agreement than previous individual inversion results [37,38].

Additionally, as depicted in Fig. 29.11 and Table 29.5, a deeper conductive zone was identified at approximately 2778 m depth, exhibiting an exceptionally low resistivity of 3.90 ± 0.01 Ω·m and a thickness of 6680.55 ± 63.22 m. These estimates are in strong agreement with the model presented by Harinarayana et al. [37]. This improved model enables a more accurate delineation of both shallow and deep geothermal zones, which is crucial for the precise estimation of geothermal reservoir characteristics and enhances the overall understanding of subsurface thermal structures in the region.

29.3.2.3 Example 3: Application of Joint inversion of MTT and RF data

Another field example taken for the demonstration of the present technique, the present technique was applied on MTT and RF data from a seismic station in the Garhwal and Kumaun regions of the Indian Himalayas. MTT data were adopted from Rawat et al. [42], and RF datasets were produced using the seismic model (i.e., velocity) of Kumar and Rai [43]. Only transverse magnetic (TM) mode data were used for MTT inversion, as Rawat et al. [42] found the transverse electric mode more susceptible to static shift and 3D effects. TM mode, in contrast, is generally more robust for resolving conductive features [44].

TABLE 29.5 Mean model parameters and their posterior uncertainties obtained from joint inversion (*GWOPSO*) over Central Puga Valley, India.

Layer parameter	Search space		GWOPSO inverted values
	Lower	Upper	(PDF > 68.27% CI)
ρ_1 (Ωm)	80	200	133.27 ± 0.83
h_1 (m)	0.1	10	5.22 ± 0.02
ρ_2 (Ωm)	0.1	10	5.74 ± 0.08
h_2 (m)	5	50	43.57 ± 1.34
ρ_3 (Ωm)	20	100	28.49 ± 0.36
h_3 (m)	50	700	119.04 ± 12.38
ρ_4 (Ωm)	80	1000	143.73 ± 2.18
h_4 (m)	1000	5000	2610.70 ± 45.75
ρ_5 (Ωm)	0.1	10	3.87 ± 0.17
h_5 (m)	1000	10,00-0	6680.55 ± 63.22
ρ_6 (Ωm)	10	500	85.28 ± 0.62
Fitness (RMS)			0.014

CI, Confidence interval; *GWOPSO*, grey wolf optimizer-particle swarm optimization; *PDF*, probability density function; *RMS*, root mean square.
Source: Taken from K. Sarkar, M. Mukesh, U.K. Singh, Nature-inspired stochastic hybrid technique for joint and individual inversion of DC and MT data, Sci. Rep. 13 (1) (2023) 2668.

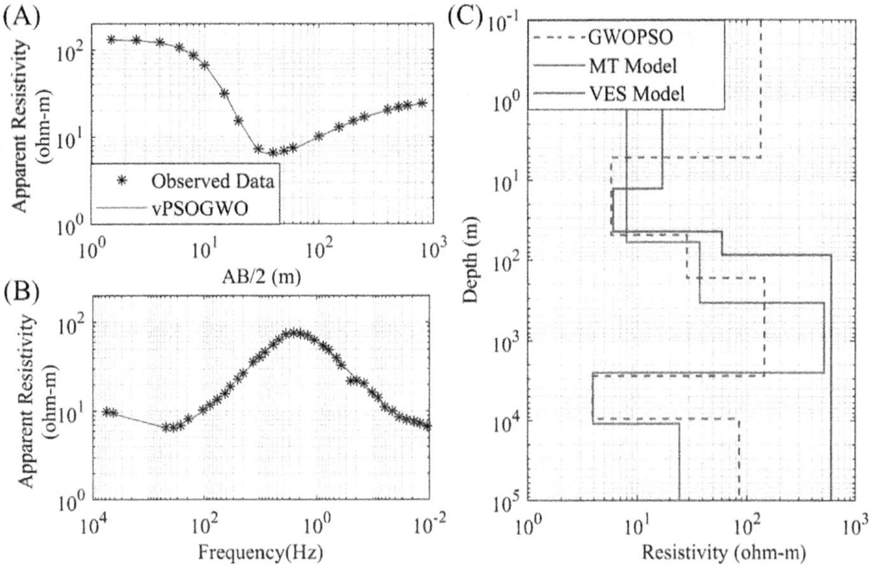

FIGURE 29.11 Field (A) DCR and (B) MTT observed curve (*) and best-fit apparent resistivity data for a four-layer model; (C) 1D mean models (*BPDF* > 68.27% CI) inverted by GWOPSO (red), compared with the MTT model [39] and VES model [40] (*BPDF*, Bayesian posterior probability density function; *CI*, confidence interval; *DCR*, direct current resistivity; *GWOPSO*, grey wolf optimizer-particle swarm optimization).
Modified from K. Sarkar, M. Mukesh, U.K. Singh, Nature-inspired stochastic hybrid technique for joint and individual inversion of DC and MT data, Sci. Rep. 13 (1) (2023) 2668.

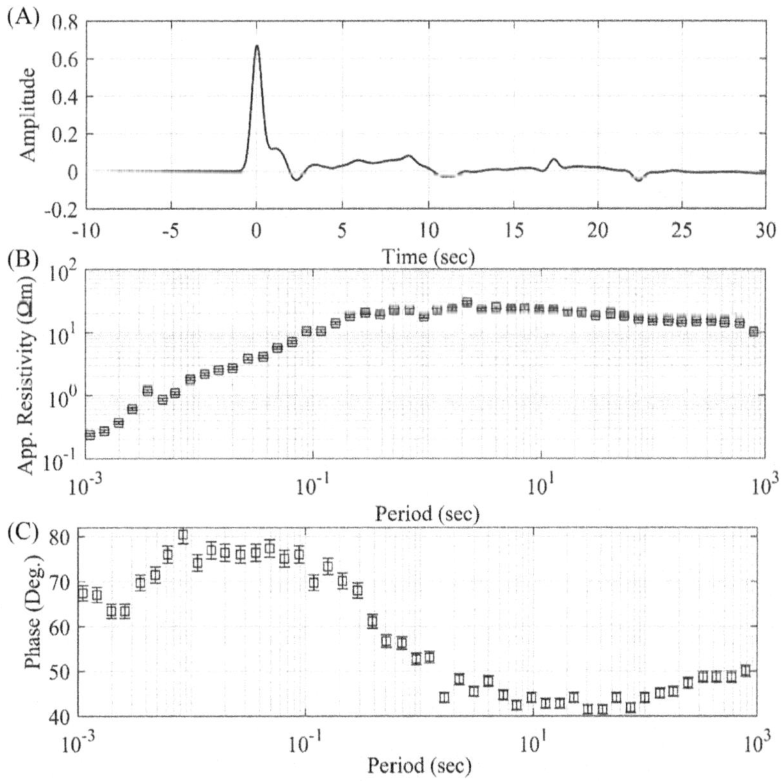

FIGURE 29.12 Observed field data over the Himalayan regions: (A) RF, (b) MTT apparent resistivity, (C) MTT phase with observed curves (*RF*, Receiver function).
Taken from K. Sarkar, A. Yadav, U.K. Singh, Joint inversion of receiver function and magnetotelluric data via a nature-inspired stochastic hybrid technique, Earth Sci. Inf. 18 (3) (2025) 301–312.

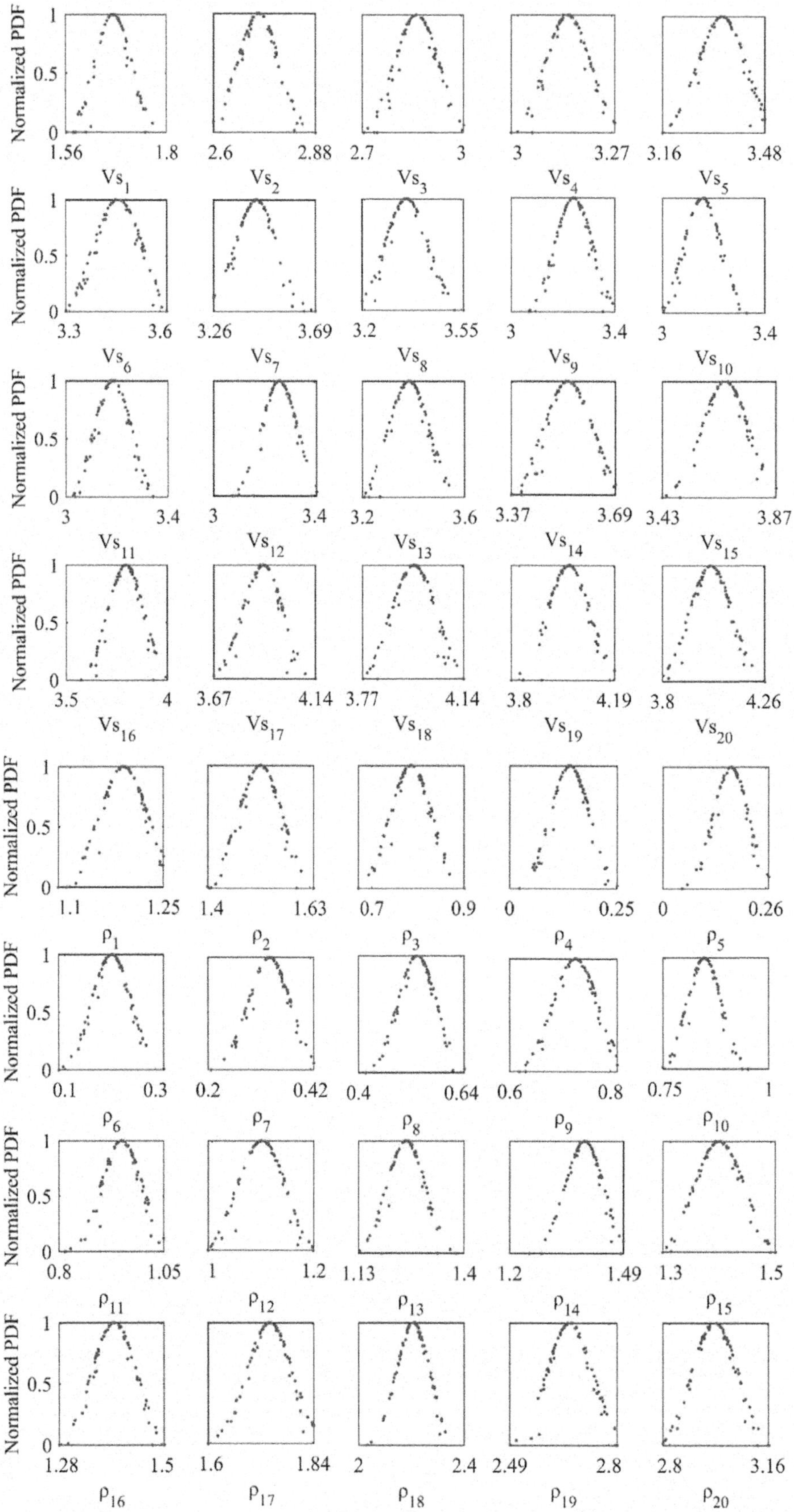

FIGURE 29.13 Layer-wise *BPDF* curves for inverted velocity (*Vs*) and resistivity (ρ) parameters (*BPDF*, Bayesian posterior probability density function).

Taken from K. Sarkar, A. Yadav, U.K. Singh, Joint inversion of receiver function and magnetotelluric data via a nature-inspired stochastic hybrid technique, Earth Sci. Inf. 18 (3) (2025) 301–312.

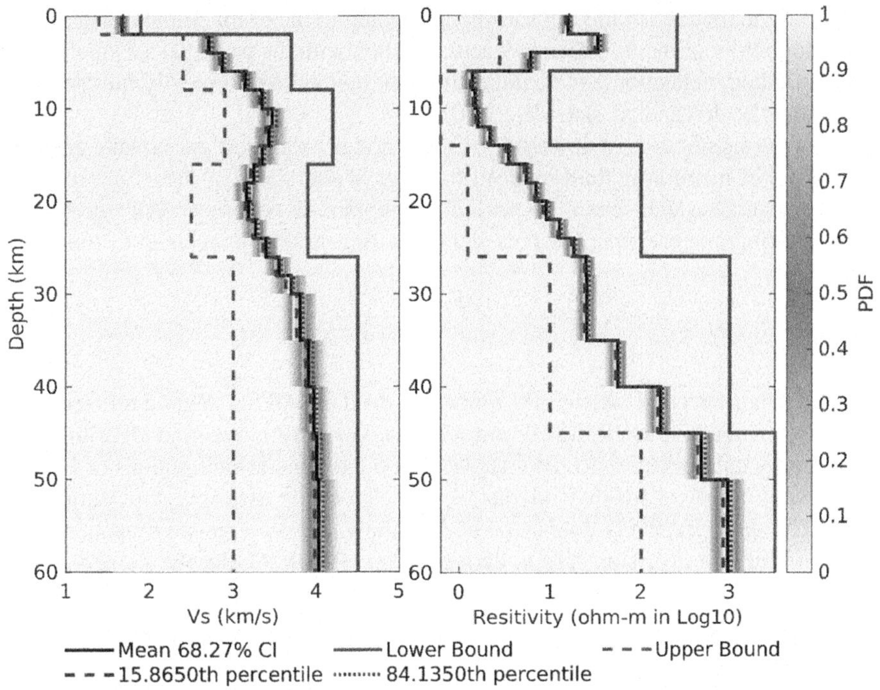

FIGURE 29.14 Shear wave velocity (*Vs*) and resistivity (*ρ*) inversion results obtained via the GWOPSO algorithm. The mean model (*black line*) is derived from solutions within the 68.27% *BPDF* threshold, and red lines represent confidence interval bounds, while magenta curves mark the defined model space. Taken from K. Sarkar, A. Yadav, U.K. Singh, Joint inversion of receiver function and magnetotelluric data via a nature-inspired stochastic hybrid technique, Earth Sci. Inf. 18 (3) (2025) 301–312.

For the station, RF data computed using a Gaussian width of 2.5 and the TM-mode apparent resistivity and phase data are shown in Fig. 29.12(A–C). The 1D joint inversion model consists of 20 layers with uniform thickness, resulting in 40 inversion parameters (20 resistivity and 20 velocity values). The GWOPSO algorithm was run with a population size of 400 (10× number of parameters) over 1000 iterations, and repeated 100 times to compute a Bayesian mean model. The prior search spaces are illustrated in Fig. 29.14 (magenta lines), and the parameter distributions and credible intervals are shown in Fig. 29.13. The mean model (black curve in Fig. 29.14) was calculated from the 68.27% CI models with the highest posterior probabilities (highlighted in red in Fig. 29.14).

The joint inversion revealed a low-resistivity and low velocity sedimentary layer in the upper crust, followed by increased resistivity and velocity associated with dry, compact metamorphic rocks, consistent with the Almora Klippen and Lansdowne [32]. A prominent intracrustal high-conductivity layer (IC-HCL) with a resistivity of approximately 3.2 Ωm was identified at ~6–14 km depth, accompanied by a velocity increase below ~10 km. This conductive zone appears as a nearly horizontal interface beneath the station, matching the interpretations by Rawat et al. [42]. Additionally, a steady increase in resistivity with depth leads to a clear Moho at ~40 km, matching previous studies [45,46].

The detection of the IC-HCL in the Himalayas aligns with observations from other active plate margins, where conductive zones are commonly noticed within the depth of 10–25 km [39,40,47,48]. These anomalies are frequently ascribed to the existence of aqueous fluids or partial melt [49]. For example, Arora et al. [50] identified a conductive zone (5–10 Ω·m) at depths of 20–25 km, presumably associated with 2%–14% melt, which aligns with the low shear-wave velocities (2.9–3.3 km/s) documented in the area, as well as the low Vs (2.9–3.3 km/s) noted by Caldwell et al. [51].

Nonetheless, temperatures at IC-HCL depths (about 15 km) generally hover around 400°C, which is below the 650°C threshold necessary for partial melting under hydrated granite conditions [52]. Instead, the conductivity anomaly is more plausibly due to prograde metamorphic dehydration reactions [53], where fluids released from underthrusted sediments or subducted slabs accumulate due to high porosity and fluid pressure [48,50,54]. Such fluid accumulation can significantly enhance conductivity and influence fault mechanics and seismicity.

Ni and Barazangi [55] proposed that this IC-HCL might act as a basal detachment zone, delineating the Indian plate from the superjacent Himalayan wedge. The current velocity and resistivity models provide an enhanced understanding of this separation and its significance in regional seismogenesis. In IC-HCL, overpressurized fluids may reduce fault-normal stress, decrease frictional resistance, and facilitate brittle failure, potentially triggering significant thrust earthquakes [56–58].

Contrary to conventional interpretations linking seismic nucleation to the Main Himalayan Thrust (MHT), Sarkar et al. [20] propose that the upper border of the IC-HCL may actually align with the principal seismicity plane. This observation aligns with research from other subduction zones, indicating that earthquakes typically initiate above high-conductivity layers situated directly atop the descending slab [39,59,60].

The findings emphasize the significance of upward fluid migration in promoting earthquake generation within the brittle crust and stress the necessity of monitoring fluid-induced rheological alterations in shear zones and fault surfaces [61,62]. The amalgamation of many geophysical techniques, including the joint inversion of MTT, receiver function, and seismic data, is essential for pinpointing microseismic hotspots and evaluating seismic dangers in tectonically active areas such as the Himalayas.

29.4 Conclusions

This chapter has provided a thorough assessment of the unique hybrid GWOPSO method utilized for the joint inversion of various geophysical datasets, including DCR, MTT, and RF data. We have proved the algorithm's adaptability, stability, and interpretative capacity by its application to field datasets from the mineral-rich regions of Broken Hill, Australia, the geothermal hotspot of Puga Valley, Ladakh, and the tectonically active zones of the Himalayas. The simultaneous inversion of DCR and MTT data effectively delineated both shallow and deep resistivity patterns in complex subsurface environments. At Broken Hill, the inversion results derived from GWOPSO closely aligned with those obtained from Occam's inversion, validating the efficacy of the new methodology. In the geothermal Puga Valley, the method precisely identified both near-surface conductive geothermal zones and deeper conductive features, correlating effectively with borehole data and prior geophysical investigations. In the seismically active Himalayan region, the combined inversion of MTT and RF datasets identified an IC-HCL linked to fluid presence and mechanical weakening of the crust. The resistivity and velocity models substantiate the concept that the upper boundary of this conductive layer, instead of the traditionalMHT, may constitute the principal plane of seismic activity. These findings align with global data in other active convergent edges and highlight the essential role of fluids in earthquake initiation and crustal deformation. The effective application of GWOPSO across various data types and tectonic environments underscores the promise of hybrid nature-inspired algorithms in tackling the complexities of nonlinear, high-dimensional geophysical inversion challenges. The algorithm's capacity to produce geologically coherent models, along with probabilistic uncertainty evaluation by Bayesian inference, renders it a potent and dependable instrument for forthcoming geophysical studies. Prospectively, broadening this methodology to encompass supplementary geophysical applications (e.g., gravity, seismic tomography, or Control Source Electromagnetic data) and implementing it for time-lapse monitoring could enhance subsurface characterization. The ongoing enhancement of swarm intelligence-based inversion approaches will improve our capacity to interpret intricate Earth processes, including mineral mining, geothermal energy mapping, and seismic hazard assessment in tectonically active areas.

Acknowledgment

The authors sincerely thank IIT(ISM), Dhanbad, India, for awarding a fellowship to the first author, enabling the completion of this research. We also extend our gratitude to the editors for their valuable support and guidance throughout the publication process. Additionally, the authors acknowledge the use of the Quilt Bolt tool for language refinement.

Data availability statement

The data that support the findings of this study are available from the corresponding author upon reasonable request.

Author contributions

Kuldeep Sarkar: Original draft preparation, Conceptualization, Methodology, Code development, Original draft preparation, Visualization, Investigation, Writing- Reviewing and Editing.

Upendra K Singh: Supervision, Conceptualization, Writing- Reviewing and Editing.

Conflict of interest

There are no conflicts of interest declared by the authors.

References

[1] R. Guo, M. Li, F. Yang, S. Xu, G. Fang, A. Abubakar, Application of supervised descent method to nonlinear inversion for transient EM data, in Proc. 12th Eur. Conf. Antennas Propag. (EuCAP) (2018) 1–5.
[2] W. Rodi, R.L. Mackie, Nonlinear conjugate gradients algorithm for 2-D magnetotelluric inversion, Geophysics 66 (1) (2001) 174–187.
[3] A. Chandra, A. Agarwal, Shalivahan, R.K. Singh, Grey wolf optimisation for inversion of layered earth geophysical datasets, Near Surface Geophysics 15 (5) (2017) 499–513.
[4] B. Chopard, M. Tomassini, Particle swarm optimization, in: B. Chopard, M. Tomassini (Eds.), An Introduction to Metaheuristics for Optimization, Springer, Cham, (2018), pp. 97–102. Available from http://doi.org/10.1007/978-3-319-93073-2_6.
[5] X.S. Yang, A new metaheuristic bat-inspired algorithm, in: J.R. González, D.A. Pelta, C. Cruz, G. Terrazas, N. Krasnogor (Eds.), Nature Inspired Cooperative Strategies for Optimization (NICSO 2010), Springer, Berlin, Heidelberg, (2010), pp. 65–74. Available from http://doi.org/10.1007/978-3-642-12538-6_6.
[6] Y. Wang, Z. Han, Ant colony optimization for traveling salesman problem based on parameters optimization, Applied Soft Computing 107 (2021) 107439.
[7] S. Mirjalili, Genetic algorithm, Evolutionary Algorithms and Neural Networks: Theory and Applications, Springer, Cham, (2019), pp. 43–55. Available from http://doi.org/10.1007/978-3-319-93025-1_4.
[8] H.T. Rauf, W.H.K. Bangyal, M.I. Lali, An adaptive hybrid differential evolution algorithm for continuous optimization and classification problems, Neural Computing and Applications 33 (2021) 10841–10867.
[9] E. Rashedi, H. Nezamabadi-pour, S. Saryazdi, GSA: A gravitational search algorithm, Information Sciences 179 (13) (2009) 2232–2248.
[10] J.J. Wang, T. Kumbasar, Optimal PID control of spatial inverted pendulum with big bang–big crunch optimization, IEEE/CAA J. Automatica Sinica 7 (3) (2020) 822–832.
[11] D. Delahaye, S. Chaimatanan, M. Mongeau, Simulated annealing: From basics to applications, in: M. Gendreau, J.-Y. Potvin (Eds.), Handbook of Metaheuristics, Springer, Cham, (2019), pp. 1–35. Available from http://doi.org/10.1007/978-3-319-91086-4_1.
[12] F. Van den Bergh, A.P. Engelbrecht, A study of particle swarm optimization particle trajectories, Information Sciences 176 (8) (2006) 937–971.
[13] S. Mirjalili, S.M. Mirjalili, A. Lewis, Grey wolf optimizer, Advances in Engineering Software 69 (2014) 46–61.
[14] F.A. Şenel, F. Gökçe, A.S. Yüksel, T.A. Yiğit, A novel hybrid PSO–GWO algorithm for optimization problems, Engineering with Computers 35 (2019) 1359–1373.
[15] K. Sarkar, U.K. Singh, Assessment of equivalence problem by joint hybrid global inversion of 1D MT and DC resistivity and using integral equations of MT for cost function, AGU Fall Meeting Abstracts 2020 (2020). NG002-0017.
[16] K. Sarkar, M. Mukesh, U.K. Singh, Assessment of probabilistic Boltzmann distribution in joint hybrid global inversion for 1D MT and DC data, AGU Fall Meeting Abstracts 2021 (2021). NG22A-06.
[17] K. Sarkar, M. Mukesh, U.K. Singh, Nature-inspired stochastic hybrid technique for joint and individual inversion of DC and MT data, Scientific Reports 13 (1) (2023) 2668.
[18] M. Moorkamp, A.G. Jones, S. Fishwick, Joint inversion of receiver functions, surface wave dispersion, and magnetotelluric data, Journal of Geophysical Research: Solid Earth 115 (B4) (2010).
[19] A. Manglik, S.K. Verma, K.H. Singh, Detection of sub-basaltic sediments by a multi-parametric joint inversion approach, Journal of Earth System Science 118 (5) (2009) 551–562.
[20] K. Sarkar, A. Yadav, U.K. Singh, Joint inversion of receiver function and magnetotelluric data via a nature inspired stochastic hybrid technique, Earth Science Informatics 18 (3) (2025) 301–312.
[21] M.S. Shaikh, H. Lin, S. Xie, X. Dong, Y. Lin, C.K. Shiva, et al., "An intelligent hybrid grey wolf-particle swarm optimizer for optimization in complex engineering design problem, Scientific Reports 15 (1) (2025) 18313.
[22] X. Zhang, Q. Lin, W. Mao, S. Liu, Z. Dou, G. Liu, "Hybrid particle swarm and grey wolf optimizer and its application to clustering optimization, Applied Soft Computing 101 (2021) 107061.
[23] M.A. Shaheen, H.M. Hasanien, A. Alkuhayli, A novel hybrid GWO-PSO optimization technique for optimal reactive power dispatch problem solution, Ain Shams Engineering Journal 12 (1) (2021) 621–630.
[24] A.B. Alyu, A.O. Salau, B. Khan, J.N. Eneh, Hybrid GWO-PSO based optimal placement and sizing of multiple PV-DG units for power loss reduction and voltage profile improvement, Scientific Reports 13 (1) (2023) 6903.
[25] X. Cheng, J. Li, C. Zheng, J. Zhang, M. Zhao, "An improved PSO-GWO algorithm with chaos and adaptive inertial weight for robot path planning, Frontiers in Neurorobotics 15 (2021) 770361.
[26] R.C. Aster, B. Borchers, C.H. Thurber, Parameter Estimation and Inverse Problems, 2nd ed., Academic Press, Boston, MA, (2011).
[27] S.M. Ross, Probability and Statistics for Engineers and Scientists, 16, Elsevier, Amsterdam, (2009).
[28] W. Menke, Some comments on probability theory, Geophysical Data Analysis, 4th ed., Academic Press, (2018), pp. 17–37. Available from http://doi.org/10.1016/B978-0-12-813555-6.00002-2.
[29] J. Pulliam, M.K. Sen, Assessing uncertainties in waveform modeling of the crust and upper mantle, in Proc. 27th Seismic Research Review: Ground-Based Nuclear Explosion Monitoring Technologies (2005) 152–160.
[30] D.W. Oldenburg, Y. Li, Inversion of induced polarization data, Geophysics 59 (9) (1994) 1327–1343.
[31] F.A. Monteiro Santos, A. Dupis, A.R. Andrade Afonso, L.A. Mendes Victor, 1D joint inversion of AMT and resistivity data acquired over a graben, Journal of Applied Geophysics 38 (2) (1997) 115–129.

[32] J.J. Arps, The effect of temperature on the density and electrical resistivity of sodium chloride solutions, Journal of Petroleum Technology 5 (1) (1953) 17–20.
[33] L. Qin, W. Ding, C. Yang, Magnetotelluric responses of an anisotropic 1D earth with a layer of exponentially varying conductivity, Minerals 12 (5) (2022) 543.
[34] S.C. Constable, Resistivity studies over the Flinders conductivity anomaly, South Australia, Geophysical Journal International 83 (3) (1985) 775–786.
[35] J.P. Cull, Magnetotelluric soundings over a Precambrian contact in Australia, Geophysical Journal International 80 (3) (1985) 661–675.
[36] S.C. Constable, R.L. Parker, C.G. Constable, Occam's inversion: a practical algorithm for generating smooth models from electromagnetic sounding data, Geophysics 52 (3) (1987) 289–300.
[37] T. Harinarayana, K.A. Azeez, K. Naganjaneyulu, C. Manoj, K. Veeraswamy, D.N. Murthy, et al., Magnetotelluric studies in Puga valley geothermal field, NW Himalaya, Jammu and Kashmir, India, Journal of Volcanology and Geothermal Research 138 (3–4) (2004) 405–424.
[38] U.K. Singh, R.K. Tiwari, S.B. Singh, Inversion of 2D DC resistivity data using rapid optimization and minimal complexity neural network, Nonlinear Processes in Geophysics 17 (1) (2010) 65–76. Available from https://doi.org/10.5194/npg-17-65-2010.
[39] K. Umeda, K. Asamori, T. Negi, Y. Ogawa, Magnetotelluric imaging of crustal magma storage beneath the Mesozoic crystalline mountains in a nonvolcanic region, northeast Japan, Geochemistry, Geophysics, Geosystems 7 (8) (2006).
[40] G.R. Jiracek, V.M. Gonzalez, T.G. Caldwell, P.E. Wannamaker, D. Kilb, Seismogenic, electrically conductive, and fluid zones at continental plate boundaries in New Zealand, Himalaya, and California, USA, Geophysical Monograph, American Geophysical Union, Washington, DC, (2007), pp. 347–362. 175.
[41] J. Craig, A. Absar, G. Bhat, G. Cadel, M. Hafiz, et al., Hot springs and the geothermal energy potential of Jammu & Kashmir State, NW Himalaya, India, Earth-Science Reviews 126 (2013) 156–177.
[42] G. Rawat, B.R. Arora, P.K. Gupta, Electrical resistivity cross-section across the Garhwal Himalaya: proxy to fluid-seismicity linkage, Tectonophysics 637 (2014) 68–79.
[43] V. Kumar, S.S. Rai, Complex seismic image of the Main Himalayan Thrust in Garhwal and implication to earthquake hazard, Journal of Earth System Science 131 (2) (2022) 79.
[44] M.N. Berdichevsky, V.I. Dmitriev, E.E. Pozdnjakova, On two-dimensional interpretation of magnetotelluric soundings, Geophysical Journal International 133 (3) (1998) 585–606.
[45] W.B. Caldwell, S.L. Klemperer, J.F. Lawrence, S.S. Rai, Characterizing the main Himalayan thrust in the Garhwal Himalaya, India with receiver function CCP stacking, Earth and Planetary Science Letters 367 (2013) 15–27.
[46] S. Saikia, S. Chopra, S. Baruah, P.R. Baidya, U.K. Singh, Crustal imaging of the Northwest Himalaya and its foredeep region from teleseismic events, Geomatics, Natural Hazards and Risk 7 (4) (2016) 1265–1286.
[47] M. Unsworth, Magnetotelluric studies of active continent–continent collisions, Surveys in Geophysics 31 (2) (2010) 137–161.
[48] W. Heise, T.G. Caldwell, E.A. Bertrand, G.J. Hill, S.L. Bennie, Y. Ogawa, Changes in electrical resistivity track changes in tectonic plate coupling, Geophysical Research Letters 40 (19) (2013) 5029–5033.
[49] S. Li, M.J. Unsworth, J.R. Booker, W. Wei, H. Tan, A.G. Jones, Partial melt or aqueous fluid in the mid-crust of Southern Tibet? Constraints from INDEPTH magnetotelluric data, Geophysical Journal International 153 (2) (2003) 289–304.
[50] B.R. Arora, M.J. Unsworth, G. Rawat, Deep resistivity structure of the northwest Indian Himalaya and its tectonic implications, Geophysical Research Letters 34 (4) (2007).
[51] W.B. Caldwell, S.L. Klemperer, S.S. Rai, J.F. Lawrence, Partial melt in the upper-middle crust of the northwest Himalaya revealed by Rayleigh wave dispersion, Tectonophysics 477 (1–2) (2009) 58–65.
[52] A. McLeish, Geological Science, Nelson Thornes, Cheltenham, (1992).
[53] J.M. Ferry, A historical review of metamorphic fluid flow, Journal of Geophysical Research: Solid Earth 99 (B8) (1994) 15487–15498.
[54] J.A. Connolly, Y.Y. Podladchikov, Fluid flow in compressive tectonic settings: Implications for midcrustal seismic reflectors and downward fluid migration, Journal of Geophysical Research: Solid Earth 109 (B4) (2004).
[55] J. Ni, M. Barazangi, Seismotectonics of the Himalayan collision zone: geometry of the underthrusting Indian plate beneath the Himalaya, Journal of Geophysical Research: Solid Earth 89 (B2) (1984) 1147–1163.
[56] N.H. Sleep, M.L. Blanpied, Creep, compaction and the weak rheology of major faults, Nature 359 (6397) (1992) 687–692.
[57] J.D. Byerlee, Model for episodic flow of high-pressure water in fault zones before earthquakes, Geology 21 (4) (1993) 303–306.
[58] R.A. Harris, Introduction to special section: stress triggers, stress shadows, and implications for seismic hazard, Journal of Geophysical Research: Solid Earth 103 (B10) (1998) 24347–24358.
[59] R.D. Hyndman, Dipping seismic reflectors, electrically conductive zones, and trapped water in the crust over a subducting plate, Journal of Geophysical Research: Solid Earth 93 (B11) (1988) 13391–13405.
[60] W. Heise, T.G. Caldwell, G.J. Hill, S.L. Wallin, E.A. Bertrand, Y. Ogawa, Magnetotelluric imaging of fluid processes at the subduction interface of the Hikurangi margin, New Zealand, Geophysical Research Letters 39 (4) (2012).
[61] W. Heise, T.G. Caldwell, H.M. Bibby, S.C. Bannister, Three-dimensional modelling of magnetotelluric data from the Rotokawa geothermal field, Taupo Volcanic Zone, New Zealand, Geophysical Journal International 173 (2) (2008) 740–750.
[62] P. Mahesh, S.S. Rai, K. Sivaram, A. Paul, S. Gupta, R. Sarma, et al., One-dimensional reference velocity model and precise locations of earthquake hypocenters in the Kumaon–Garhwal Himalaya, Bulletin of the Seismological Society of America 103 (1) (2013) 328–339.

Chapter 30

Optimized finite impulse response adaptive noise cancellation for improved photoplethysmography signal enhancement using the grey wolf optimizer

Madhava R. Alla and Chandan Nayak

School of Electronics Engineering, Inavolu, Beside AP Secretariat, VIT-AP University, Amaravati, Andhra Pradesh, India

30.1 Introduction

Photoplethysmography (PPG) has become a crucial optical biosensing approach for noninvasive monitoring of cardiovascular status by capturing fine changes in peripheral blood volume within microvascular tissues [1]. The universality of PPG in both clinical and wearable health systems is strengthened by its cost-effectiveness, operational simplicity, and ability to provide continuous, real-time physiological insights, ranging from heart rate and oxygen saturation to vascular health indices [2]. However, the integrity and diagnostic value of PPG signals acquired in practical scenarios are routinely compromised by a variety of noise and artifacts, which can corrupt critical morphological features and hamper accurate health assessment.

Among the various environmental and internal sources of contamination, baseline wander (BW) and white Gaussian noise (WGN) pose particularly tough challenges for robust PPG analysis. BW typically stems from low-frequency phenomena such as respiration, subject movement, and sensor displacement, introducing slow drifts that destabilize the signal baseline. Conversely, WGN, often arising from electronic circuitry and environmental interference, is expressed as high-frequency noise that masks fine details within the waveform. The simultaneous presence of BW and WGN severely degrades the extraction of vital cardiovascular signals, thereby reducing the reliability of automated diagnostic algorithms.

To reduce the bad effects of these artifacts, scientists have recently improved PPG signal enhancement methods [3–13]. Conventional filter-based techniques, such as butterworth filter [3], the median filter [4], the moving average filter [5], and the comb filter [6], have previously served as the backbone for noise suppression in PPG signals due to their algorithmic simplicity and real-time computational efficiency. However, these filters often exhibit suboptimal performance when tested with dynamic environments or multiple concurrent noise sources.

Next, wavelet-based denoising methods [7,8] were introduced in the PPG signal denoising literature. In Ref. [7], a wavelet-based denoising method was implemented using Very Large Scale Integration (VLSI) technology, which effectively suppressed power line interference in noisy PPG signals. In Ref. [8], the Mexican hat wavelet transform was employed to reduce motion artifacts in remote PPG applications. The adaptability of wavelet methods makes them particularly suitable for nonstationary environments. However, wavelet-based methods are limited by their high computational cost and strong dependence on the choice of wavelet and decomposition level. Subsequently, hybrid decomposition methods [9,10], such as ensemble empirical mode decomposition [9] and Gaussian function decomposition combined with advanced estimation techniques [10], were introduced to achieve improved artifact suppression in PPG signals.

Grey Wolf Optimizer. DOI: https://doi.org/10.1016/B978-0-443-36624-6.00003-2

To make the methods more flexible and suitable for real-time use, researchers have turned to adaptive filtering techniques [11–13]. An adaptive filter changes its parameters based on the changing properties of both the signal and the noise, which allows it to reduce time-varying artifacts such as BW and WGN. Classical adaptive algorithms such as least mean squares [11], constrained recursive least squares (RLS) [12], and conventional RLS [13] form the basis of real-time noise reduction, but their convergence often slows due to local minima. To overcome this, researchers have turned to metaheuristic optimization strategies, such as antlion optimization [14] and gravitational search algorithm [15], to achieve global optima in filter design.

Among different metaheuristic methods, the grey wolf optimizer (GWO) [16] is notable because it is inspired by the leadership structure and group hunting behavior of grey wolves. Its ability to balance exploration and exploitation, along with strong convergence, makes GWO a powerful and versatile tool for solving complex optimization problems in engineering and signal processing. This chapter uses the strengths of GWO to present an adaptive noise cancellation method for PPG signal enhancement, optimized through a well-defined objective function. The efficacy of the GWO-based adaptive noise canceller (ANC) is demonstrated by comparing it with ANC methods based on differential evolution (DE) [17] and particle swarm optimization (PSO) [18].

30.2 Optimized adaptive noise canceller to enhance photoplethysmography signal

Fig. 30.1 shows the proposed ANC method, which uses finite impulse response (FIR) filters optimized with metaheuristic algorithms for PPG signal enhancement. First-order FIR filters are chosen because they are inherently stable, provide a linear-phase response, and are easy to implement in real time, which are essential qualities in biomedical signal processing. Unlike infinite impulse response filters, FIR filters do not rely on recursive feedback, ensuring stability even at higher filter orders.

The Mth-order FIR filter is defined in (30.1).

$$D_k(z) = \sum_{l=0}^{M} a_{k,l} z^{-l} \tag{30.1}$$

Here, $a_{k,l}$ is the kth stage, l^{th} order coefficient of the FIR filter. The adaptive FIR filter continuously adjusts its coefficients to remove unwanted noise while preserving the key diagnostic features of the original PPG signal.

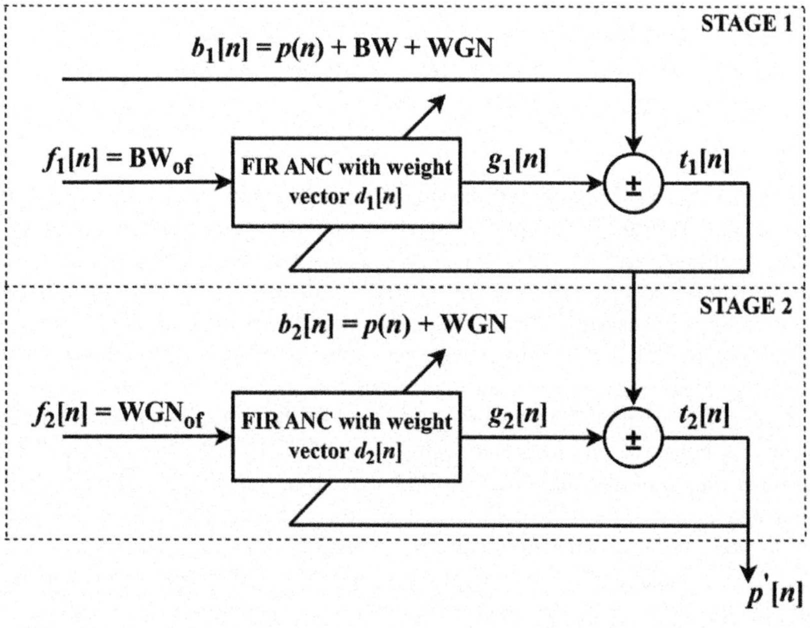

FIGURE 30.1 Schematic of the proposed cascaded adaptive noise cancellation method optimized with metaheuristic algorithms.

30.2.1 Adaptive noise canceller design

The proposed ANC method works in two stages, with the first stage focusing on BW and the second stage on WGN. This enables systematic improvement of the original PPG signal $p(n)$, as described below.

30.2.1.1 First stage: baseline wander suppression

The initial input to the ANC system, represented by $b_1(n)$, is a combined signal consisting of the clean target PPG signal $p(n)$ and noise components BW and WGN, as expressed in (30.2).

$$b_1(n) = p(n) + \text{BW} + \text{WGN} \tag{30.2}$$

The original PPG signal $p(n)$ is sourced from the Challenge 2015 training set, a publicly accessible PhysioNet database [19], while the BW noise is derived from the noise stress test database [20]. WGN is synthetically produced using MATLAB simulations. The sampling frequency of the PPG signal is 250 Hz.

In the first stage, a reference input signal $f_1(n)=\text{BW}_{\text{of}}$, exhibiting correlation with the BW noise while remaining uncorrelated with $p(n)$, is employed. The output from the FIR filter, denoted by $g_l(n)$, is computed by (30.3).

$$g_1(n) = \sum_{l=0}^{M} a_{1,l} f_1(n-l) \tag{30.3}$$

The first-stage error signal, represented as $t_1(n)$, measures the disparity between the input signal $b_1(n)$ and the output of the FIR filter $g_1(n)$ and is calculated using (30.4).

$$t_1(n) = b_1(n) - g_1(n) \tag{30.4}$$

By employing an adaptive optimization algorithm, the error signal $t_1(n)$ is repeatedly used in an iterative manner to update and optimize the FIR filter coefficients $a_{1,l}$. Upon reaching an acceptable reduction level of the BW noise, the processed error signal $t_1(n)$ is then passed as the input $b_2(n)$ to the subsequent stage of processing.

30.2.1.2 Second stage: white Gaussian noise elimination

In the second stage, the input signal $b_2(n)$, comprising the target signal $p(n)$ and WGN, is applied as described in (30.5).

$$b_2(n) = p(n) + \text{WGN} \tag{30.5}$$

In the second stage, the reference signal $f_2(n)=\text{WGN}_{\text{of}}$, which is correlated with the WGN yet uncorrelated with $p(n)$, is utilized. The corresponding FIR filter output $g_2(n)$ is determined as shown in (30.6).

$$g_2(n) = \sum_{l=0}^{M} a_{2,l} f_2(n-l) \tag{30.6}$$

The second stage ANC's error signal, denoted as $t_2(n)$, is calculated using (30.7).

$$t_2(n) = b_2(n) - g_2(n) \tag{30.7}$$

The filter coefficients $a_{2,l}$ are refined iteratively using the error signal $t_2(n)$ through an optimization algorithm, continuing this process until the WGN is adequately suppressed. The resulting output from the second stage, $t_2(n)=p'(n)$, provides a close approximation to the original clean PPG signal $p(n)$.

Thus the proposed ANC system removes BW and WGN in a sequential two-stage process, employing FIR filters and adaptive optimization algorithms to achieve efficient noise suppression while maintaining the integrity of the original signal.

Three distinct experimentations are performed to evaluate the noise reduction efficacy of the metaheuristic optimization techniques, namely GWO, DE, and PSO, utilizing the suggested ANC system illustrated in Fig. 30.1. The metaheuristic algorithms GWO, DE, and PSO are each independently implemented to precisely optimize the configuration of every stage within the FIR-based ANC system. In every experiment, the principal objective at each stage is to ascertain the best weight vector, denoted as $d_k = [a_{k,l}]$, by minimizing the mean square error objective function, MSE_{of}, as delineated in (30.8).

$$MSE_{of} = \frac{1}{Q} \sum_{i=1}^{Q} \left| ppg_o(i) - ppg_r(i) \right|^2 \tag{30.8}$$

In this context, Q signifies the entire samples present in the PPG signal, where $ppg_o(i)$ refers to the original or actual signal, and $ppg_r(i)$ indicates the refined or filtered signal at each sample i.

At each iteration, the difference between $ppg_r(i)$ *and* $ppg_o(i)$ is evaluated using the objective function MSE_{of}, which provides a quantitative measure of optimization progress. The GWO, DE, and PSO algorithms are applied separately to minimize MSE_{of} during each optimization cycle. The primary goal is to attenuate noise in the filtered signal to a targeted level, thereby improving the overall effectiveness of the ANC system. The integrated cascaded ANC technique, enhanced by advanced optimization strategies, effectively suppresses artifacts, significantly improves PPG signal quality, and ensures robust signal enhancement, supporting reliable physiological monitoring in biomedical settings.

30.3 Algorithms employed

The proposed ANC framework is implemented using conventional metaheuristic algorithms such as PSO [17] and DE [16], along with the widely studied and highly effective GWO [15]. Since PSO and DE are already well known, their explanations are omitted here due to space limitations. However, the algorithm and implementation steps of GWO for ANC design are provided below. Moreover, the best control parameters of each algorithm are listed in Table 30.1.

30.3.1 Grey wolf optimizer

The GWO is a nature-inspired metaheuristic algorithm that emulates the social hierarchy and cooperative hunting strategies observed in grey wolf packs. First presented by Mirjalili et al. [15], the GWO algorithm has gained widespread recognition for its effectiveness and simplicity in addressing a broad range of complex optimization problems, including signal processing and adaptive filtering. The underlying design of GWO is centered on mimicking the leadership dominance (alpha, beta, delta, and omega) and cooperative hunting dynamics of grey wolves in nature, providing a sophisticated equilibrium between exploring and exploiting in the pursuit of the global optimum. The subsequent section provides a comprehensive, stepwise description of the GWO algorithm, employed to minimize the objective function, precisely the mean square error (MSE), thereby facilitating the determination of optimal filter coefficients within the ANC system framework.

Step 1. Initialize a population of N_w grey wolves randomly in a J-dimensional search landscape, as in (30.9).

$$W_{i,j} = b_{lo} + rand \times \left(b_{up} - b_{lo} \right) \tag{30.9}$$

where $W_{i,j}$ is the position of the ith wolf in the jth dimension, b_{lo} (-2) and b_{up} (2) are the lower and upper search limits, respectively, and $rand \in [0,1]$.

Step 2. Compute the convergence control parameter as the adaptive coefficient $a(t)$ using (30.10).

$$a(t) = 2 \times (1 - (t/t_m)) \tag{30.10}$$

here, t is the current iteration and t_m is the maximum iterations.

TABLE 30.1 Optimal control variables used for GWO, DE, and PSO in metaheuristic optimization of ANC design.

Parameters	GWO	DE	PSO
n	25	25	25
t	400	400	400
a	2 → 0 (linearly decreases)	-	-
F	-	0.8	-
CR	-	0.9	-
w	-	-	0.4
c_1	-	-	2.05
c_2	-	-	2.05

ANC, Adaptive noise canceller; *DE*, differential evolution; *GWO*, grey wolf optimizer; *PSO*, particle swarm optimization.

Step 3. Determine the coefficient vector A_k using (30.11) and the coefficient vector $\boldsymbol{C_k}$ using (30.12).

$$A_k = 2 \times a(t) \times r_a - a(t) \quad (30.11)$$

$$C_k = 2 \times r_c \quad (30.12)$$

where r_a, r_c are random numbers in [0,1].

Step 4. Calculate the objective function MSE_{of} for each wolf by (30.8) and identify the top three solutions as W_{alpha} (best wolf - lowest cost), W_{beta} (second best), and W_{delta} (third best).

Step 5. For each wolf W_i, update its position relative to W_{alpha}, W_{beta}, and W_{delta} using (30.13)–(30.15).

$$S_{alpha} = \left| C_1 \times W_{alpha} - W_i \right| \quad (30.13)$$

$$S_{beta} = |C_2 \times W_{beta} - W_i| \quad (30.14)$$

$$S_{delta} = |C_3 \times W_{delta} - W_i| \quad (30.15)$$

where C_1, C_2, and C_3 are coefficient vectors computed using (30.12) with new random values.

Step 6. Calculate three candidate positions for the wolf based on the leaders using (30.16)–(30.18).

$$W_1 = W_{alpha} - A_1 \times S_{alpha} \quad (30.16)$$

$$W_2 = W_{beta} - A_2 \times S_{beta} \quad (30.17)$$

$$W_3 = W_{delta} - A_3 \times S_{delt} \quad (30.18)$$

where A_1, A_2, and A_3 are coefficient vectors computed using (30.11) with fresh random values.

Step 7. Update the position of each wolf by averaging the three candidate positions using (30.19).

$$W_i(t+1) = (W_1 + W_2 + W_3)/3 \quad (30.19)$$

Step 8. If a wolf's updated position violates the search space boundaries, reinitialize it within the permissible range using (30.9). Update *a(t)*, A_k, and C_k by using (30.10)–(30.12), respectively.

Step 9. Recalculate the fitness for all wolves using (30.8) and update W_{alpha}, W_{beta}, and W_{delta} if better solutions are found.

Step 10. Repeat Steps 5–9 until the maximum iteration count t_m is reached.

Step 11. Return W_{alpha} as the optimal solution.

30.4 Results and discussion

The effectiveness of the suggested ANC technique for noise reduction was rigorously evaluated through a series of simulation experiments conducted using MATLAB R2021a. The ANC system's effectiveness was evaluated using a mix of qualitative and quantitative analyses to establish its capability in mitigating noise in PPG signals. For the qualitative evaluation, the PPG record v100s from the Challenge 2015 training set was intentionally corrupted by adding BW and WGN. The developed ANC methodology was subsequently employed on these corrupted PPG signals to suppress the artifacts. The improvement in signal quality following noise cancellation was first verified through comprehensive visual inspection, which facilitated a subjective assessment of the algorithm's effectiveness. In parallel, a quantitative evaluation was performed using standard performance metrics, including the output signal-to-noise ratio (SNR_{out}) and *MSE*, as defined in (30.9) and (30.10). This dual approach tests how well the proposed ANC technique works.

$$SNR_{out}(dB) = 10\log_{10}\frac{\sum_{i=1}^{Q}(ppg_r(i))^2}{\sum_{i=1}^{Q}|ppg_r(i) - ppg_o(i)|^2} \quad (30.20)$$

$$MSE_{of} = \frac{1}{Q}\sum_{i=1}^{Q}\left|ppg_o(i) - ppg_r(i)\right|^2 \quad (30.21)$$

30.4.1 Qualitative visualization of adaptive noise canceller effectiveness on photoplethysmography record v100s from the Challenge 2015 training set

The effectiveness of the developed ANC system was evaluated on the v100s record from the Challenge 2015 training set, with the processing stages and outputs shown in Figs. 30.2 (A)–(E), starting with the original PPG waveform in Fig. 30.2 (A). In contrast, Fig. 30.2 (B) shows the same PPG signal contaminated with BW and WGN, where both noise types significantly mask the critical features of the signal. As shown in Fig. 30.2 (C), the ANC method optimized with PSO reduces both BW and high-frequency WGN to some extent, though a few residual artifacts and distortions are still visible. Fig. 30.2 (D) shows the ANC output using DE optimization, which achieves better noise suppression than PSO, though slight distortions appear in the low-frequency baseline region. The best result is shown in Fig. 30.2 (E), where the GWO-optimized ANC system effectively removes all types of noise while preserving the original morphology of the PPG waveform. This graphical comparison emphasizes the superiority of the GWO-based optimization for effective and reliable PPG signal denoising.

Additionally, Fig. 30.3 (A) depicts a magnified view of a selected signal segment, clearly demonstrating that the output produced by the proposed GWO-optimized ANC method closely tracks the original, uncorrupted PPG waveform. The near-perfect response between the denoised and reference signals affirms that the ANC based on GWO not only delivers robust noise suppression but also maintains the fundamental morphology and structural fidelity of the PPG data. This close alignment underscores the proposed ANC method's proficiency in preserving critical signal features during the denoising process, thereby emphasizing its superiority over conventional approaches.

30.4.2 Quantitative assessment of adaptive noise canceller techniques on photoplethysmography record v100s from the Challenge 2015 training set

The quantitative evaluation of the ANC system's performance was carried out using two standard metrics, namely SNR_{out} and MSE. These indicators offer a thorough assessment of the system's ability to suppress noise, preserve signal integrity, and maintain the original waveform structure. Table 30.2 presents the summarized results for ANC

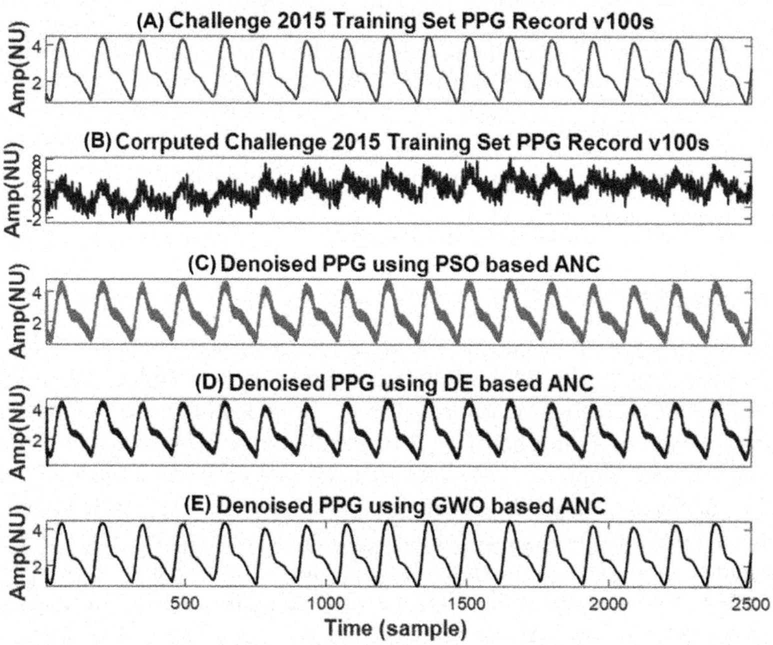

FIGURE 30.2 Comparison of ANC system outputs using Challenge 2015 Training Set PPG record v100s: (A) original PPG signal, (B) noise-contaminated PPG signal, (C) denoised PPG signal using PSO-optimized ANC, (D) denoised PPG signal using DE-optimized ANC, and (E) denoised PPG signal using GWO-optimized ANC (*ANC*, Adaptive noise canceller; *DE*, differential evolution; *GWO*, grey wolf optimizer; *PPG*, photoplethysmography; *PSO*, particle swarm optimization).

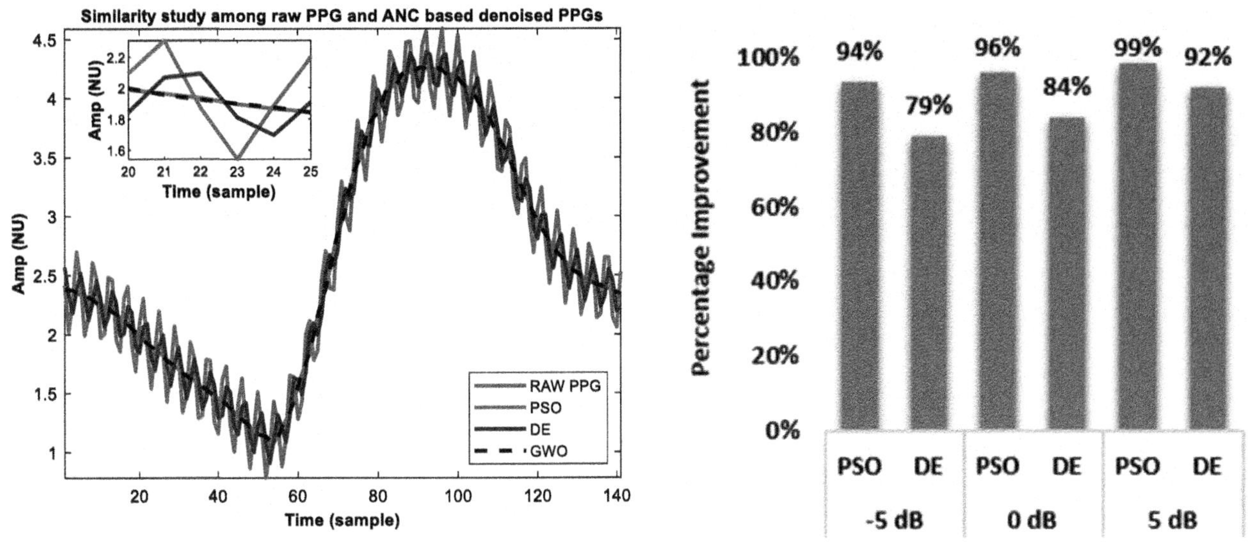

(A) (B)

FIGURE 30.3 (A) Detailed results for the PPG record v100s from the Challenge 2015 training set, displaying outputs from ANC systems optimized with PSO, DE, and GWO algorithms, along with an enlarged segment for closer comparison. (B) PI of the GWO-optimized ANC system relative to PSO and DE, assessed using MSE metric (*ANC*, Adaptive noise canceller; *DE*, differential evolution; *GWO*, grey wolf optimizer; *MSE*, mean absolute error; *PI*, performance improvement; *PPG*, photoplethysmography; *PSO*, particle swarm optimization).

TABLE 30.2 Comparison of ANC methods optimized by PSO, DE, and GWO on PPG record v100s from the Challenge 2015 Training Set over varied SNR_{in}.

SNR_{in}	Algorithms	SNR_{out} dB	MSE
-5 dB	PSO	23.0463	1.0532E-03
	DE	29.5748	3.2186E-04
	GWO	36.2149	6.8039E-05
0 dB	PSO	34.9507	2.1758E-04
	DE	41.2683	5.2326E-05
	GWO	48.3092	8.3508E-06
5 dB	PSO	45.8135	4.5793E-05
	DE	53.6401	7.5614E-06
	GWO	61.7256	5.8427E-07

ANC, Adaptive noise canceller; *DE*, differential evolution; *GWO*, grey wolf optimizer; *MSE*, mean absolute error; *PPG*, photoplethysmography; *PSO*, particle swarm optimization.

methods optimized with PSO, DE, and GWO algorithms, tested under different input SNR (SNR_{in}) conditions of −5 dB, 0 dB, and 5 dB. The results unequivocally demonstrate that the GWO-optimized ANC consistently surpasses both the PSO- and DE-based approaches across all measured criteria, including SNR_{out} and MSE, when evaluated on the Challenge 2015 training set PPG record v100s. At each SNR_{in} level, the GWO-based system achieves notably higher SNR_{out} values than those observed for the other algorithms, while also demonstrating lower MSE values. These findings confirm the superior effectiveness and robustness of the GWO-optimized ANC in enhancing signal quality under various noise scenarios.

TABLE 30.3 Computational cost analysis of PSO, DE, and GWO for ANC design.

Algorithm	Function evaluation ($t \times n$)	Average run time (s)
PSO	400×25	24.6
DE	400×25	31.2
GWO	400×25	27.8

ANC, Adaptive noise canceller; *DE*, differential evolution; *GWO*, grey wolf optimizer; *PPG*, photoplethysmography; *PSO*, particle swarm optimization.

Under a severe noise condition (SNR_{in}=-5 dB), the ANC optimized with GWO achieves an output SNR (SNR_{out}) of 36.2149 dB, notably surpassing the performance of the DE-based ANC, which records 29.5748 dB, and the PSO-based ANC, which attains 23.0463 dB. At SNR_{in} = -5 dB, the GWO-optimized ANC delivers an improvement of 6.6401 dB (=36.2149 dB − 29.5748 dB) compared to the DE-based implementation and an even greater enhancement of 13.1686 dB (=36.2149 dB − 23.0463 dB) over the PSO-based approach.

Moreover, as reported in Table 30.2, at SNR_{in}=-5 dB, the DE-based ANC attains a MSE of 3.2186E-04, indicating competitive performance. In comparison, the proposed GWO-based ANC delivers a considerably reduced MSE of 6.8039E-05, representing an approximate 79% enhancement over the DE-based approach, as determined by (3.2186E-04 − 6.8039E-05)/3.2186E-04. Relative to the ANC based on PSO, the GWO-based method attains a more significant enhancement, with a 94% improvement in MSE, computed as (1.0532E-03 − 6.8039E-05)/1.0532E-03. A closer analysis of the results at an input SNR of 5 dB highlights the effectiveness of the GWO algorithm, achieving an output SNR of 61.7256 dB along with a MSE of 5.8427E-07. Fig. 30.3(b) presents the performance improvements (PI) achieved by the GWO-based ANC over the PSO- and DE-based approaches at input SNR levels of -5 dB, 0 dB, and 5 dB. Across the evaluated conditions, the ANC based on GWO surpasses the PSO- and DE-based counterparts, yielding an average PI of 90.67% (=(94+79+96+84+99+92)/6). Collectively, these findings demonstrate that the GWO-based strategy delivers superior ANC performance across various SNR_{in} levels, strengthening its clear advantage over the PSO- and DE-based approaches. The GWO-optimized ANC system exhibits consistently strong performance across a broad spectrum of SNR_{in} conditions, highlighting its robustness and adaptability to varying noise environments. Notably, even under severely degraded conditions, such as an SNR_{in} of −5 dB, the proposed approach achieves marked noise attenuation, as reflected by its superior values in both MSE and SNR_{out} metrics. This consistent effectiveness illustrates the GWO-based ANC's capability to suppress noise efficiently while maintaining the vital characteristics and structure of the original PPG signal.

30.4.3 Computational cost analysis

The performance of PSO, DE, and GWO is analyzed in Table 30.3 in terms of the average run time for the ANC design. All algorithms were executed for the same number of function evaluations, that is, $t \times n$ (=400 × 25). From the results in Table 30.3, it is observed that the proposed GWO-based ANC requires an average run time of 27.8 s, which is nearly comparable to the PSO-based ANC (24.6 s). However, the DE-based ANC takes slightly higher run time (31.2 s). These results justify the practical applicability of GWO for the proposed ANC design problem.

30.4.4 Statistical test

PSO-, DE-, and GWO-based ANCs were independently run 20 times, and the MSE values from each run were collected. These results were used for the Wilcoxon signed-rank test, with pairwise comparisons conducted at a 5% significance level ($P < .05$). The results, summarized in Table 30.4, indicate that the GWO-based ANC achieves statistically significant improvement over both PSO- and DE-based ANCs, confirming the statistically robust behavior of GWO for the proposed ANC design.

TABLE 30.4 Wilcoxon signed-rank test results for PSO, DE, and GWO-based ANC.

Algorithm pair	Test statistic (W)	P-value	Significant (α=0.05)	Conclusion
GWO versus PSO	45	0.023	Yes	GWO performs significantly better
GWO versus DE	48	0.015	Yes	GWO performs significantly better
PSO versus DE	30	0.081	No	No significant difference

ANC, Adaptive noise canceller; *DE*, differential evolution; *GWO*, grey wolf optimizer; *PPG*, photoplethysmography; *PSO*, particle swarm optimization.

30.5 Conclusion

In summary, combining a cascaded ANC with the GWO has proven highly effective in enhancing the quality of PPG signals. This approach allows real-time adjustment of filter parameters, leading to strong suppression of BW and WGN while preserving the essential features of the original waveform. Compared to other metaheuristic techniques such as DE and (PSO, the GWO-based FIR ANC consistently achieves better results, as reflected in higher output SNR and lower MSE. Overall, the method significantly improves the clarity and reliability of PPG signals, making it a promising solution for accurate cardiac monitoring and diagnostic use in healthcare settings.

Funding

There is no institute/agency funding for this research work.

Data availability

The data sets used in this article are cited.

Conflict of interest

The authors declare that there are no conflicts of interest.

References

[1] P. Kyriacou, Introduction to photoplethysmography, in: P. Kyriacou, J. Allen (Eds.), Photoplethysmography: Technology, Signal Analysis, and Applications, Elsevier, London, UK, (2021), pp. 1–15.

[2] J. Allen, Photoplethysmography and its application in clinical physiological measurement, Physiological Measurement 28 (3) (2007) R1–R39. Available from https://doi.org/10.1088/0967-3334/28/3/R01.

[3] S. Banerjee, G.K. Singh, A new real-time lossless data compression algorithm for ECG and PPG signals, Biomedical Signal Processing and Control 79 (2022) 104127. Available from https://doi.org/10.1016/j.bspc.2022.104127.

[4] S. Li, L. Liu, J. Wu, et al., Comparison and noise suppression of the transmitted and reflected photoplethysmography signals, BioMed Research International 2018 (2018) 4523593. Available from https://doi.org/10.1155/2018/4523593.

[5] J. Lee, Motion artifacts reduction from PPG using cyclic moving average filter, Technology and Health Care 22 (3) (2014) 409–417. Available from https://doi.org/10.3233/THC-140798.

[6] L. Alkhoury, L. Alkhoury, J. Choi, C. Wang, et al., Heart-rate tuned comb filters for processing photoplethysmogram (PPG) signals in pulse oximetry, Journal of Clinical Monitoring and Computing 35 (4) (2021) 797–813. Available from https://doi.org/10.1007/s10877-020-00539-2.

[7] P.V. Kasambe, S.S. Rathod, VLSI Wavelet-based denoising of PPG signal, Procedia Computer Science 49 (1) (2015) 282–288. Available from https://doi.org/10.1016/j.procs.2015.04.254.

[8] A. Hosni, M. Atef, Remote real-time heart rate monitoring with recursive motion artifact removal using PPG signals from a smartphone camera, Multimedia Tools and Applications 82 (13) (2023) 20571–20588. Available from https://doi.org/10.1007/s11042-023-14399-w.

[9] Y. Zhang, B. Liu, Z. Zhang, Combining ensemble empirical mode decomposition with spectrum subtraction technique for heart rate monitoring using wrist-type photoplethysmography, Biomedical Signal Processing and Control 21 (2015) 119–125. Available from https://doi.org/10.1016/j.bspc.2015.05.006.

[10] B. Sun, C. Wang, X. Chen, et al., PPG signal motion artifacts correction algorithm based on feature estimation, Optik 176 (2019) 337–349. Available from https://doi.org/10.1016/j.ijleo.2018.09.085.
[11] H. Han, J. Kim, Artifacts in wearable photoplethysmographs during daily life motions and their reduction with least mean square-based active noise cancellation method, Computers in Biology and Medicine 42 (4) (2012) 387–393. Available from https://doi.org/10.1016/j.compbiomed.2011.12.005.
[12] M.S. Islam, M. Shifat-E-Rabbi, A.M.A. Dobaie, et al., PREHEAT: precision heart rate monitoring from intense motion artifact corrupted PPG signals using constrained RLS and wavelets, Biomedical Signal Processing and Control 38 (2017) 212–223. Available from https://doi.org/10.1016/j.bspc.2017.05.010.
[13] C. Wan, D. Chen, J. Yang, Pulse rate estimation from forehead photoplethysmograph signal using RLS adaptive filtering with dynamical reference signal, Biomedical Signal Processing and Control 71 (2022) 103189. Available from https://doi.org/10.1016/j.bspc.2021.103189.
[14] C. Nayak, S.K. Saha, R. Kar, et al., An efficient and robust digital fractional order differentiator-based ECG pre-processor design for QRS detection, IEEE Transactions on Biomedical Circuits and Systems 13 (4) (2019) 682–696.
[15] C. Nayak, S.K. Saha, R. Kar, et al., An optimally designed digital differentiator-based preprocessor for R-peak detection in electrocardiogram signal, Biomedical Signal Processing and Control 49 (2019) 146–157.
[16] S. Mirjalili, S.M. Mirjalili, A. Lewis, Grey wolf optimizer, Advances in Engineering Software 69 (2014) 46–61. Available from https://doi.org/10.1016/j.advengsoft.2013.12.007.
[17] R. Storn, K. Price, Differential evolution – a simple and efficient heuristic for global optimization over continuous spaces, Journal of Global Optimization 11 (1997) 341–359. Available from https://doi.org/10.1023/A:1008202821328.
[18] J. Kennedy, R. Eberhart, Particle swarm optimization, Proceedings of ICNN'95 - International Conference on Neural Networks 4 (1995) 1942–1948. Available from https://doi.org/10.1109/ICNN.1995.488968.
[19] A.L. Goldberger, L.A.N. Amaral, L. Glass, et al., Physiobank, Physiotoolkit, and Physionet components of a new research resource for complex physiologic signals, Circulation 101 (23) (2000) e215–e220. Available from https://doi.org/10.1161/01.CIR.101.23.e215.
[20] G.B. Moody, W.E. Muldrow, R.G. Mark, A noise stress test for arrhythmia detectors, Computers in Cardiology 11 (93) (1984) 381–384.

Chapter 31

Multilabel feature selection using grey wolf optimizer and mutual information

Mohanrasu S. S.
Department of Computer Science and Software Engineering, United Arab Emirates University, Al Ain, United Arab Emirates

31.1 Introduction

The advancements in digital technologies have led to the generation of large-scale, complex data. Particularly, multilabel data, where each instance can be associated with multiple labels, became common in image annotation [1], text-classification [2], and bioinformatics [3]. To handle the complexity of multilabel data, dimensionality reduction techniques became essential. However, different from the single-label case, the relevance and redundancy of features in multilabel data are more complex due to the presence of multiple labels.

In general, dimensionality reduction techniques are broadly classified into feature selection and feature extraction. The first one selects a subset of features from the original feature set, while the second one transforms the original feature set into a new feature space. Feature selection is considered a more effective approach as it preserves the original feature space and provides better interpretability. Further, the feature selection methods are classified into three categories: filter, wrapper, and embedded methods. The filter methods evaluate the features with some statistical measures and select the feature. The wrapper methods evaluate the feature subsets based on the performance of a classifier, while the embedded methods incorporate feature selection into the learning process of the classifier. The filter methods are considered more effective and efficient for multilabel feature selection as they do not require any classifier.

Among the filter methods, the mutual information based methods are widely adopted. Initially, Peng et al. [4] proposed the minimum redundancy maximum relevance (mRMR) method, which selects features based on the relevance with respect to the labels and redundancy among the selected features. Later, Lin et al. [5] extended the mRMR method to multilabel feature selection. Apart from this, many methods were developed based on information theory. However, the majority of these methods employ the sequential search strategy to select the features, which is prone to local optima.

On the other hand, metaheuristic algorithms have been widely adopted for different optimization problems, including feature selection. These algorithms are inspired by nature and mimic the behavior of natural phenomena. For instance, the particle swarm optimization (PSO) [6] simulates the social behavior of birds, while the ant colony optimization [7] mimics the behavior of ants in finding the shortest path to food. Further, based on the hunting behavior of grey wolves, Mirjalili et al. [8] proposed the grey wolf optimization (GWO) algorithm. These algorithms have been successfully applied to feature selection problems, considering it as a search-based optimization problem as an alternative to sequential search methods.

However, the existing metaheuristic algorithms adapt a classifier-based fitness function to evaluate the feature subsets, which is computationally expensive and requires a large number of iterations to converge. Further, the focus on multilabel feature selection is limited. To address this, in this work, we propose two methods for multilabel feature selection based on the GWO algorithm. The first method employs the mutual information-based fitness function, while the second method employs the normalized mutual information-based fitness function. These methods are inspired by the filter method mRMR. The proposed methods are evaluated on six multilabel datasets and compared with four well-established multilabel feature selection methods. The experimental results demonstrate the effectiveness of the proposed methods in terms of classification performance. Further, as the proposed method is independent of any classifier, it also reduces the computational cost and time complexity of the feature selection process.

Grey Wolf Optimizer. DOI: https://doi.org/10.1016/B978-0-443-36624-6.00031-7

The rest of the chapter is structured as follows. Section 31.2 provides some related works, and Section 31.3 provides the preliminaries. The proposed methods are described in Section 31.4. The experimental results are presented in Section 31.5. Finally, Section 31.6 concludes the chapter.

31.2 Related work

Initial techniques for multilabel feature selection largely relied on problem transformation techniques. These methods reformulated the multilabel problem into multiple single-label feature selection tasks, enabling the application of existing single-label feature selection algorithms. Notable transformation strategies include pruned problem transformation [9], label powerset transformation [10], and binary relevance transformation [11]. However, a key limitation of these methods is their inability to capture and exploit label correlations and dependencies, which are intrinsic to multilabel learning problems.

Later, recent studies have proposed algorithm adaptation methods that explicitly account for all labels simultaneously in the context of multilabel feature selection. Lin et al. [5] extended the well-known mRMR method to the multilabel setting, while Lee et al. [12] introduced an interaction-based approach for selecting relevant features. Lin et al. [13] further advanced the field by proposing a fuzzy mutual information-based method tailored for streaming multilabel data. Zhang et al. [14] developed a technique based on double conditional relevance, incorporating two conditional mutual information terms to eliminate redundancy in already-selected features and information contained in other labels. Building on the literature, Gao et al. [15] proposed a unified framework utilizing three low-order information-theoretic measures for enhanced multilabel feature selection. In Ref. [16], the authors proposed a framework integrating mutual information with multicriteria decision-making techniques. Later, in [17], the cost-sensitive setting where each feature is associated with an acquisition cost is addressed. Additional contributions include Han et al. [18], who employed mutual information at both macro and micro levels to assess feature relevance, and Sun et al. [19], who designed an adaptive fuzzy neighborhood-based mutual information mechanism to redefine the mRMR evaluation function for the multilabel case. Furthermore, in Ref. [20], a novel set of multiscale fuzzy information-theoretic measures was introduced for improved multilabel feature selection.

Numerous feature selection approaches have been developed based on the GWO algorithm [21]. Emary et al. [22] introduced two binary variants of GWO: one incorporating a crossover function and another utilizing a sigmoid function directly for binarization. Subsequently, Al-Betar et al. [23] hybridized GWO with the PSO algorithm to enhance feature selection performance. These studies employed the k-nearest neighbors classifier to evaluate the quality of selected feature subsets. To address multiobjective optimization, Al-Betar et al. [24] further proposed a multiobjective version of GWO that simultaneously considers multiple evaluation criteria. In this work, artificial neural networks were used to assess the fitness of candidate solutions. As noted earlier, most existing methods rely heavily on classifiers for subset evaluation, which introduces additional computational overhead and dependency on the choice of classifier. In a different direction, Kashef et al. [25] employed a symmetrical uncertainty-based fitness function in conjunction with multiple evolutionary algorithms for multilabel feature selection. More recently, Hancer et al. [26] proposed a multiobjective evolutionary framework incorporating Pearson correlation for measuring feature relevance and redundancy. Despite these advances, to the best of our knowledge, no prior work has explored the application of GWO specifically for multilabel feature selection, leaving a significant gap in the literature.

31.3 Preliminaries

This section provides the necessary background on mutual information and the GWO algorithm, which are essential for understanding the proposed methods.

31.3.1 Mutual information

Definition 3.1. (Entropy) To measure the degree of information or uncertainty in a random variable, we use the concept of entropy [27]. For a random variable S with distribution function $p(s)$, it is calculated as

$$H(S) = -\sum_{i=1}^{n} p(s_i)\log p(s_i). \quad (31.1)$$

Definition 3.2. (Mutual Information) The degree of information shared between two random variables is quantified by mutual information. It is calculated for random variables S and T as follows:

$$I(S;T) = \sum_{i=1}^{n} \sum_{j=1}^{m} p(s_i, t_j) \log \frac{p(s_i, t_j)}{p(s_i)p(t_j)}. \tag{31.2}$$

Here, $p(s_i, t_j)$ represents the joint probability distribution of S and T, while $p(s_i)$ and $p(t_j)$ represent their respective marginal probability distributions. Mutual information is inherently nonnegative and symmetric, attaining a value of zero if and only if S and T are statistically independent.

Definition 3.3. (Normalized Mutual Information) In general, the quantity of mutual information does not have a fixed upper bound, making it difficult to interpret. To address this, normalized mutual information (NMI) is defined within the range of [0, 1] as follows [28]:

$$NMI(S;T) = \frac{I(S;T)}{\sqrt{H(S)H(T)}}. \tag{31.3}$$

Here, $H(S)$ and $H(T)$ are the entropies of the random variables S and T, respectively. The value of NMI is 1 when S and T are identical, and it approaches 0 when they are independent.

31.3.2 Grey wolf optimization

The GWO algorithm was designed by Mirjalili et al. [8] to mimic the hunting behavior of grey wolves. It defines the four main roles of wolves in a pack: alpha (α), beta (β), delta (δ), and omega (ω). In this, α acts as a leader making decisions and β assists it in decision-making. Furthermore, δ is in third rank and helps in hunting, while ω is the lowest rank and follows the others. In the optimization scenario, the alpha, beta, and delta wolves are considered as the top three solutions, while the omega wolves are the remaining solutions. The GWO algorithm employs three main steps: encircling prey, hunting, and searching. The encircling prey is modeled as follows:

$$\overrightarrow{X}^{t+1} = \overrightarrow{X}_p^t + \overrightarrow{A} \cdot \overrightarrow{D}, \tag{31.4}$$

where

$$\overrightarrow{D} = \left| \overrightarrow{C} \cdot \overrightarrow{X}_p^t - \overrightarrow{X}^t \right|, \tag{31.5}$$

$$\overrightarrow{A} = 2a \cdot \overrightarrow{r_1} - a, \tag{31.6}$$

$$\overrightarrow{C} = 2 \cdot \overrightarrow{r_2}. \tag{31.7}$$

Here, $\overrightarrow{X}_p^t$ is the position of the prey at time t, $\overrightarrow{X}^t$ is the position of the wolf at time t, and a is a coefficient that decreases linearly from 2 to 0 over iterations. The vectors $\overrightarrow{r_1}$ and $\overrightarrow{r_2}$ are random vectors in the range [0, 1]. The hunting is defined as follows:

$$\overrightarrow{X}^{t+1} = \frac{\overrightarrow{X}_1^t + \overrightarrow{X}_2^t + \overrightarrow{X}_3^t}{3} \tag{31.8}$$

where $\overrightarrow{X}_1^t$, $\overrightarrow{X}_2^t$, and $\overrightarrow{X}_3^t$ are defined as:

$$\overrightarrow{X}_1^t = \left| \overrightarrow{X}_\alpha^t - \overrightarrow{A_1} \cdot \overrightarrow{D_\alpha} \right|, \tag{31.9}$$

$$\overrightarrow{X}_2^t = \left| \overrightarrow{X}_\beta^t - \overrightarrow{A_2} \cdot \overrightarrow{D_\beta} \right|, \tag{31.10}$$

$$\overrightarrow{X}_3^t = \left| \overrightarrow{X}_\delta^t - \overrightarrow{A_3} \cdot \overrightarrow{D_\delta} \right|, \tag{31.11}$$

$$\overrightarrow{D_\alpha} = \left| \overrightarrow{C_1} \cdot \overrightarrow{X}_\alpha^t - \overrightarrow{X}^t \right| \tag{31.12}$$

$$\overrightarrow{D_\beta} = \left| \overrightarrow{C_2} \cdot \overrightarrow{X}_\beta^t - \overrightarrow{X}^t \right|, \tag{31.13}$$

$$\overrightarrow{D_\delta} = \left| \overrightarrow{C_3} \cdot \overrightarrow{X}_\delta^t - \overrightarrow{X}^t \right|. \tag{31.14}$$

where $\overrightarrow{A_i}$ and $\overrightarrow{C_i}$ are defined as in Eqs. 31.6 and 31.7, respectively. Further, the value of the coefficient a is updated using $a=2 - \frac{2t}{MaxIter}$. The GWO algorithm employs a search mechanism to explore the solution space more effectively by using the random vectors $\overrightarrow{r_1}$ and $\overrightarrow{r_2}$ to introduce randomness in the search process. Further, the fitness of the solutions is evaluated based on the objective function, and the new α, β, δ wolves are selected based on their fitness values. This process is repeated until the stopping criteria are met and the solution corresponding to the α is considered the best solution.

31.3.3 Binary grey wolf optimization

The above-defined GWO algorithm is designed for continuous optimization problems. However, in the context of feature selection, the problem is a binary optimization problem. To address this, the binary GWO algorithm proposed in Ref. [22] is employed. Here, the crossover operation defined below is used to generate the new solutions:

$$\overrightarrow{X}^{t+1} = Crossover(Y_1, Y_2, Y_3), \tag{31.15}$$

where *Crossover* is a suitable binary crossover operator and Y_1, Y_2, Y_3 are the binary vectors corresponding to the α, β, δ wolves defined as follows:

$$Y_1^d = \begin{cases} 1, & if\ (X_\alpha^d + stepB_{alpha}^d) \geq 1, \\ 0, & otherwise, \end{cases} \tag{31.16}$$

where X_α^d is the position of the α wolf in the dth dimension, and $stepB_{alpha}^d$ is the binary step defined as follows:

$$stepB_{alpha}^d = \begin{cases} 1, & if\ (stepC_{alpha}^d \geq r_3), \\ 0, & otherwise, \end{cases} \tag{31.17}$$

where r_3 is a random number in the range [0, 1] and $stepC_{alpha}^d$ is obtained as:

$$stepC_{alpha}^d = \frac{1}{1 + e^{-10(A_1^d \cdot D_\alpha^d - 0.5)}}, \tag{31.18}$$

where A_1^d and D_α^d are obtained from Eqs. 31.6 and 31.12, respectively. In a similar way, the binary vectors Y_2 and Y_3 are obtained from the positions of the β and δ wolves, respectively. The crossover operator is applied to these three binary vectors to generate a new binary vector, which is then used to update the position of the wolf in the next iteration.

31.4 Proposed method

This section proposes two methods for multilabel feature selection based on the GWO algorithm. Most of the existing metaheuristics approaches were based on the fitness function that is defined based on the classification performance. However, in this work, we propose to use the mutual information and normalized mutual information-based fitness function inspired by the filter method mRMR [4,5].

The fitness function with respect to mutual information is defined as follows:

$$Fitness_{MI}(Y) = -\frac{1}{|Y|}\sum_{i=1}^{|Y|}\left(\frac{1}{|L|}\sum_{j=1}^{|L|} I(Y_i; L_j) - \frac{1}{|Y|}\sum_{k=1}^{|Y|} I(Y_i; Y_k)\right) + \frac{|Y|}{|F|} \tag{31.19}$$

Further, the fitness function with respect to normalized mutual information is defined as follows:

$$Fitness_{NMI}(Y) = -\frac{1}{|Y|}\sum_{i=1}^{|Y|}\left(\frac{1}{|L|}\sum_{j=1}^{|L|} NMI(Y_i; L_j) - \frac{1}{|Y|}\sum_{k=1}^{|Y|} NMI(Y_i; Y_k)\right) + \frac{|Y|}{|F|} \quad (31.20)$$

where Y is the set of selected feature set, L is the set of labels, $|Y|$ is the number of selected features, $|L|$ is the number of labels, and $|F|$ is the total number of features. The first term in the fitness function measures the relevance of the selected features with respect to the labels, while the second term measures the redundancy among the selected features. The third term penalizes the number of selected features to encourage the selection of fewer features.

31.5 Experimental results

31.5.1 Datasets

For the evaluation, six datasets from the repositories UCI [29], UCO [30], and MULAN [31] were utilized. Based on the diverse characteristics, these datasets were selected. More details of the datasets are given in Table 31.1.

31.5.2 Evaluation metrics

To verify the effectiveness of the proposed method, four well-established multilabel evaluation metrics were employed. These metrics are widely used in the literature for assessing multilabel classification tasks [32]. Let $\mathcal{L}'_i$ represent the predicted labels produced by the classifier for the instance $\mathcal{X}_i$, where $\mathcal{L}_i$ denotes the ground truth labels. The evaluation metrics are as follows:

1. *Hamming Loss*: This indicates the mean number of times an instance was misclassified.

$$Hamming\ Loss = \frac{1}{N}\sum_{i=1}^{N}\frac{|\mathcal{L}_i \otimes \mathcal{L}'_i|}{L}, \quad (31.21)$$

with $\otimes$ specifying the symmetric difference.

2. *Subset Accuracy*: This indicates the percentage of correct predictions among all labels and given by

$$Subset\ Accuracy = \frac{1}{N}\delta(\mathcal{L}_i = \mathcal{L}'_i)$$

where $\delta(true)$=1 and $\delta(false)$=0.

3. *Macro-F1*: This indicates the mean F-score obtained separately for each label.

$$Macro - F1 = \frac{1}{L}\sum_{j=1}^{L}\frac{2\sum_{i=1}^{N}\mathcal{L}_{ij}\mathcal{L}'_{ij}}{\sum_{i=1}^{N}\mathcal{L}_{ij} + \sum_{i=1}^{N}\mathcal{L}'_{ij}} \quad (31.22)$$

TABLE 31.1 Details of the considered multilabel datasets.

Datasets	Instances	Features	Labels	Domain
Amphibians	189	23	7	Biology
Computers	5000	681	33	Text
Flags	194	19	7	Image
Image	2000	294	5	Image
Scene	2407	294	6	Image
VirusPseAAC	207	440	6	Biology

4. *Micro-F1*: This indicates the mean F-score computed from the values in the prediction matrix.

$$Micro - F1 = \frac{2\sum_{i=1}^{N} |\mathcal{L}_i \cap \mathcal{L}'_i|}{\sum_{i=1}^{N} |\mathcal{L}_i| + \sum_{i=1}^{N} |\mathcal{L}'_i|} \tag{31.23}$$

Here, lower scores of Hamming Loss (marked by ↓) and higher scores of Subset Accuracy, Macro-F1, and Micro-F1 (marked by ↑) are considered better.

31.5.3 Comparison methods

We compare the two proposed methods with four well-established multilabel feature selection methods, namely, LRDG [33], MLACO [34], PPT-MI [35], and SCLS [36]. LRDG is a manifold regularization-based approach, whereas MLACO is a well-established multilabel learning method that employs ant colony optimization. Additionally, PPT-MI and SCLS are classical methods grounded in mutual information theory. Further, the number of features for filter methods was set following the suggestion by Kashef et al. [37]. For the proposed methods, the population size was set to 30, and the maximum number of iterations was set to 1000.

31.5.4 Experiment settings

The ML-kNN classifier [38] was employed with a neighborhood size of k=10 and a smoothing parameter set to 1 for performance evaluation. A fivefold cross-validation scheme was utilized to ensure robust and unbiased assessment. All experiments were implemented and executed using MATLAB R2022a.

31.5.5 Results and discussion

The experimental results are summarized in Tables 31.2–31.5 and Figs. 31.1–31.4. The two proposed methods, GWO-MI and GWO-NMI, which are based on mutual information and normalized mutual information, respectively, were evaluated against four established multilabel feature selection techniques across four performance metrics. The average ranks are reported at the end of each row, and the best-performing results are indicated in boldface.

Table 31.2 and Fig. 31.1 show that GWO-MI attained the best performance in terms of Hamming Loss on three datasets, followed by GWO-NMI on two datasets and PPT-MI on one. For Subset Accuracy, as illustrated in Table 31.3 and Fig. 31.2, GWO-MI again led on three datasets, while GWO-NMI and LRDG achieved the top results on two and one datasets, respectively. In the case of Micro-F1 (Table 31.4, Fig. 31.3), GWO-MI remained dominant with the highest scores on three datasets, GWO-NMI excelled on two, and SCLS showed superior performance on one. Regarding Macro-F1, presented in Table 31.5 and Fig. 31.4, GWO-NMI obtained the best results on three datasets, whereas MLACO and LRDG each performed best on one and two datasets, respectively. These outcomes collectively demonstrate the effectiveness and competitiveness of the proposed methods for multilabel feature selection. Furthermore, based on the first three evaluation metrics, GWO-MI consistently achieved the best average rank, while GWO-NMI obtained the highest

TABLE 31.2 Experimental results under the Hamming Loss (↓).

Algorithms	LRDG	MLACO	PPT-MI	SCLS	GWO-MI	GWO-NMI
Amphibians	0.3303 (6)	0.3174 (4)	0.3196 (5)	0.3068 (2)	**0.2924 (1)**	0.3090 (3)
Computers	0.0402 (6)	0.0383 (2.5)	0.0383 (2.5)	0.0385 (5)	**0.0382 (1)**	0.0384 (4)
Flags	0.2931 (2)	0.3396 (6)	0.3342 (5)	0.3130 (3)	**0.2830 (1)**	0.3139 (4)
Image	0.1808 (3)	0.1853 (4)	0.1921 (6)	0.1913 (5)	0.1792 (2)	**0.1713 (1)**
Scene	0.1001 (4)	0.0951 (2)	0.1162 (6)	0.1021 (5)	0.0985 (3)	**0.0929 (1)**
VirusPseAAC	0.2022 (4)	0.2028 (5)	**0.1949 (1)**	0.2039 (6)	0.1982 (2)	0.2013 (3)
Average	0.1911 (4.17)	0.1964 (3.92)	0.1992 (4.25)	0.1926 (4.33)	**0.1816 (1.67)**	0.1878 (2.67)

TABLE 31.3 Experimental results under the Subset Accuracy (↑).

Algorithms	LRDG	MLACO	PPT-MI	SCLS	GWO-MI	GWO-NMI
Amphibians	0.0528 (5)	0.0846 (2)	0.0478 (6)	0.0688 (4)	**0.1058 (1)**	0.0690 (3)
Computers	0.2688 (6)	0.2710 (5)	0.2754 (3)	0.2736 (4)	**0.2906 (1)**	0.2856 (2)
Flags	**0.1493 (1)**	0.0669 (6)	0.0771 (5)	0.0927 (3)	0.1179 (2)	0.0874 (4)
Image	0.3795 (3)	0.3740 (4)	0.3260 (5)	0.3075 (6)	0.3815 (2)	**0.3870 (1)**
Scene	0.5829 (3)	0.5912 (2)	0.5255 (6)	0.5746 (5)	0.5767 (4)	**0.6020 (1)**
VirusPseAAC	0.1453 (2)	0.1403 (4)	0.1402 (5)	0.1309 (6)	**0.1498 (1)**	0.1405 (3)
Average	0.2631 (3.33)	0.2547 (3.83)	0.2320 (5.0)	0.2414 (4.67)	**0.2704 (1.83)**	0.2619 (2.33)

TABLE 31.4 Experimental results under the Micro-F1 (↑).

Algorithms	LRDG	MLACO	PPT-MI	SCLS	GWO-MI	GWO-NMI
Amphibians	0.6145 (5)	0.6097 (6)	0.6214 (4)	**0.6369 (1)**	0.6351 (2)	0.6317 (3)
Computers	0.3841 (6)	0.4088 (3)	0.3988 (5)	0.3992 (4)	**0.4144 (1)**	0.4103 (2)
Flags	0.7013 (2)	0.6445 (6)	0.6464 (5)	0.6736 (3)	**0.7026 (1)**	0.6675 (4)
Image	0.5490 (2)	0.5353 (4)	0.4949 (5)	0.4806 (6)	0.5463 (3)	**0.5640 (1)**
Scene	0.6896 (4)	0.7033 (2)	0.6354 (6)	0.6817 (5)	0.6957 (3)	**0.7137 (1)**
VirusPseAAC	0.3105 (2)	0.3039 (3)	0.2748 (5)	0.2701 (6)	**0.3239 (1)**	0.2819 (4)
Average	0.5415 (3.5)	0.5343 (4.0)	0.5120 (5.0)	0.5237 (4.17)	**0.5530 (1.83)**	0.5448 (2.5)

TABLE 31.5 Experimental results under the Macro-F1 (↑).

Algorithms	LRDG	MLACO	PPT-MI	SCLS	GWO-MI	GWO-NMI
Amphibians	0.3807 (4)	0.3896 (3)	0.3921 (2)	0.3794 (5)	0.3568 (6)	**0.4023 (1)**
Computers	0.1603 (6)	**0.2373 (1)**	0.1666 (5)	0.1780 (4)	0.2019 (2)	0.1841 (3)
Flags	**0.5848 (1)**	0.4560 (5)	0.4412 (6)	0.5081 (3)	0.5220 (2)	0.5028 (4)
Image	0.5435 (3)	0.5301 (4)	0.4859 (5)	0.4643 (6)	0.5444 (2)	**0.5600 (1)**
Scene	0.6938 (4)	0.7059 (2)	0.6359 (6)	0.6869 (5)	0.6957 (3)	**0.7176 (1)**
VirusPseAAC	**0.1838 (1)**	0.1654 (4)	0.1792 (2)	0.1433 (5)	0.1362 (6)	0.1658 (3)
Average	0.4245 (3.17)	0.4141 (3.17)	0.3835 (4.33)	0.3933 (4.67)	0.4095 (3.5)	**0.4221 (2.17)**

average rank in terms of Macro-F1. This suggests that the normalized mutual information variant provides better performance balance across labels, whereas the mutual information-based method performs more effectively across instances.

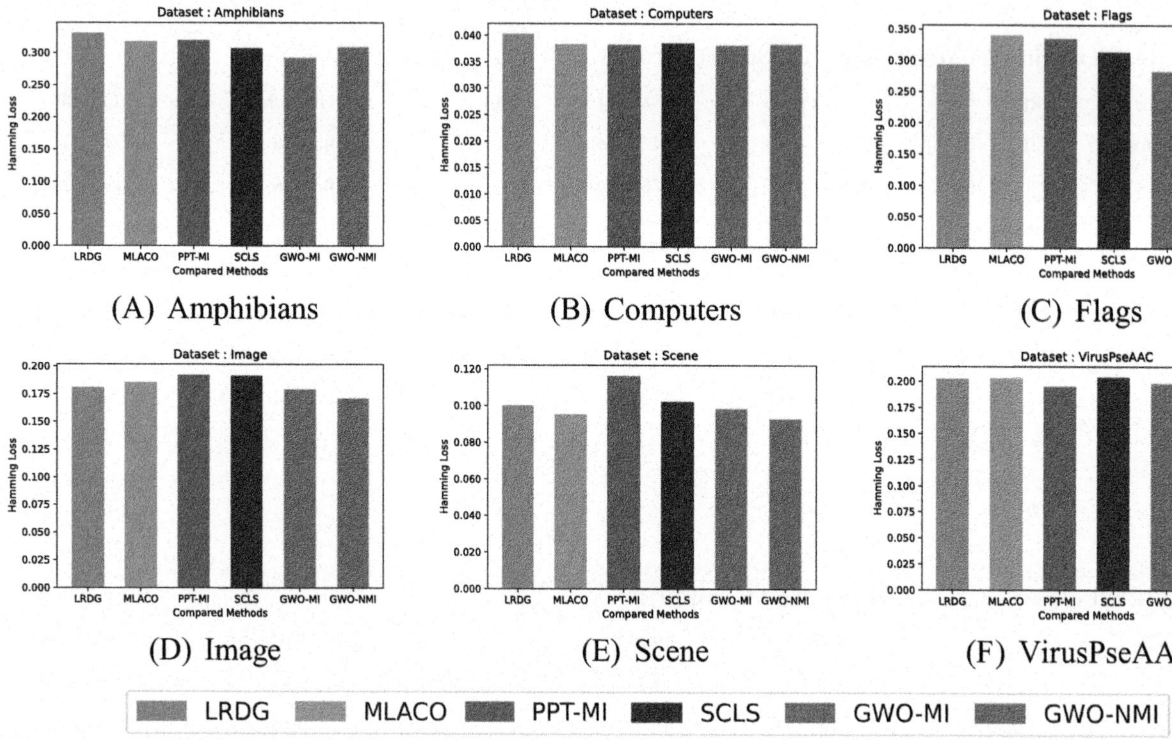

FIGURE 31.1 Experimental results under the Hamming Loss (↓).

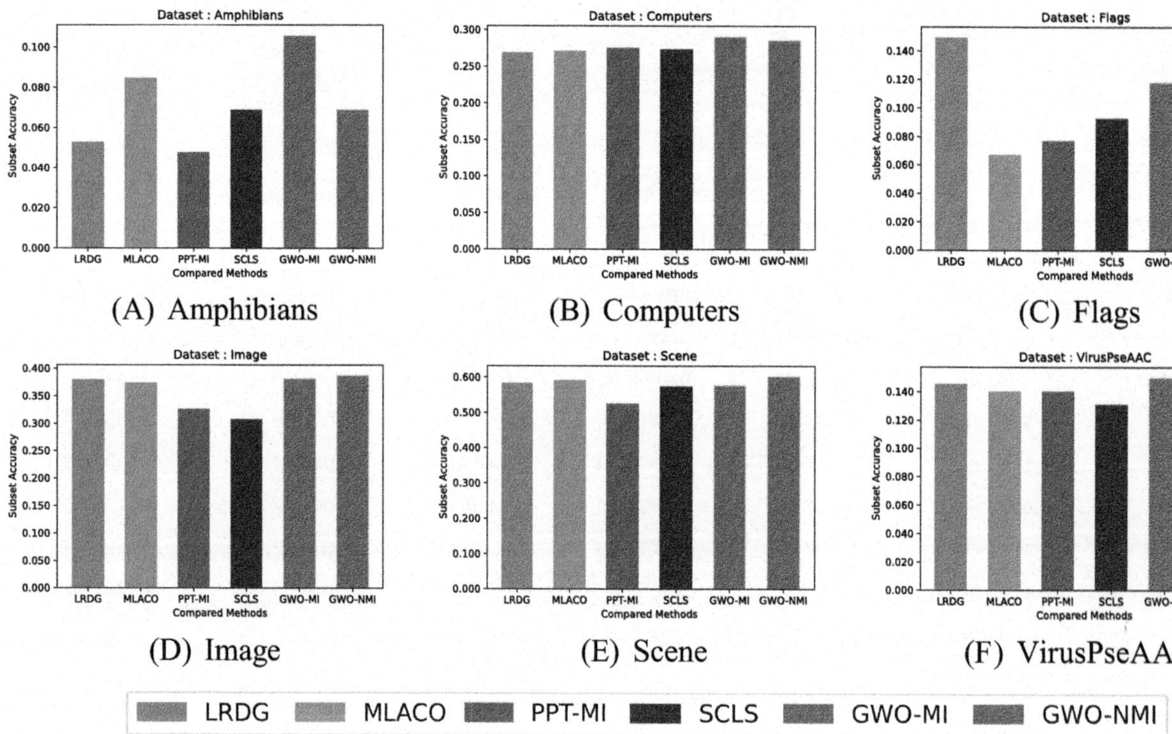

FIGURE 31.2 Experimental results under the Subset Accuracy (↑).

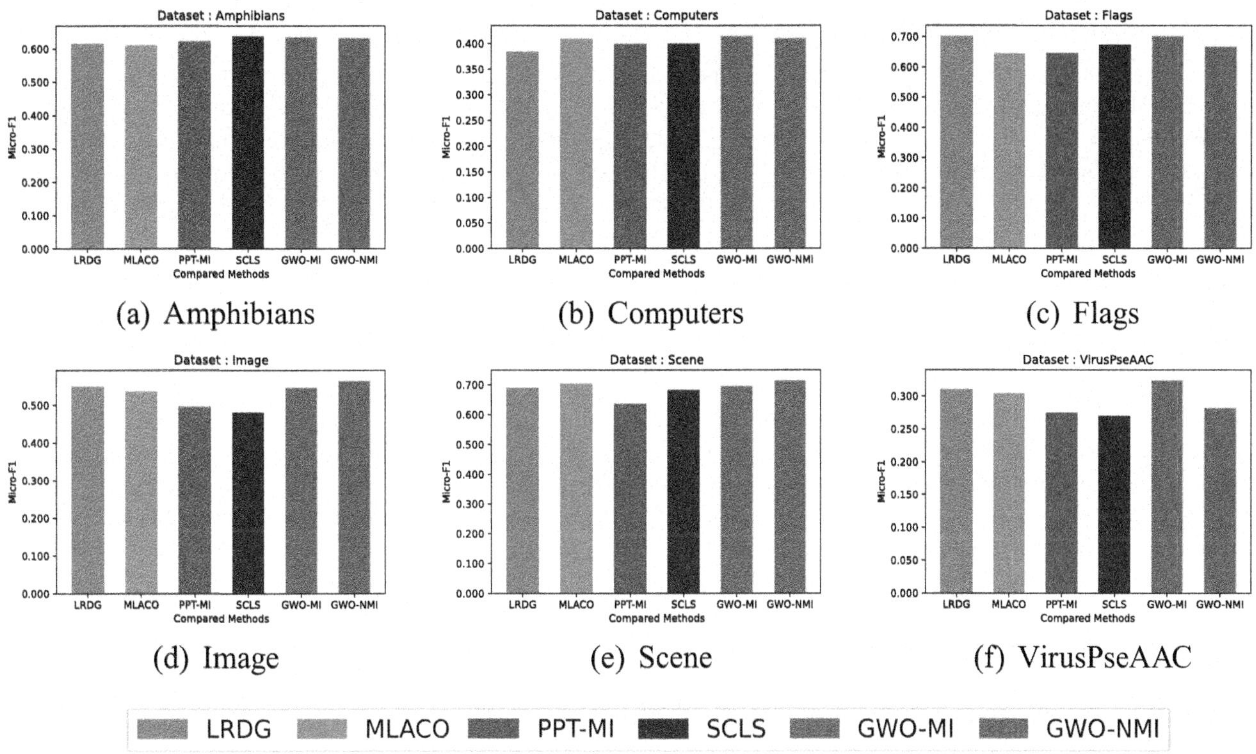

FIGURE 31.3 Experimental results under the Micro-F1 (↑).

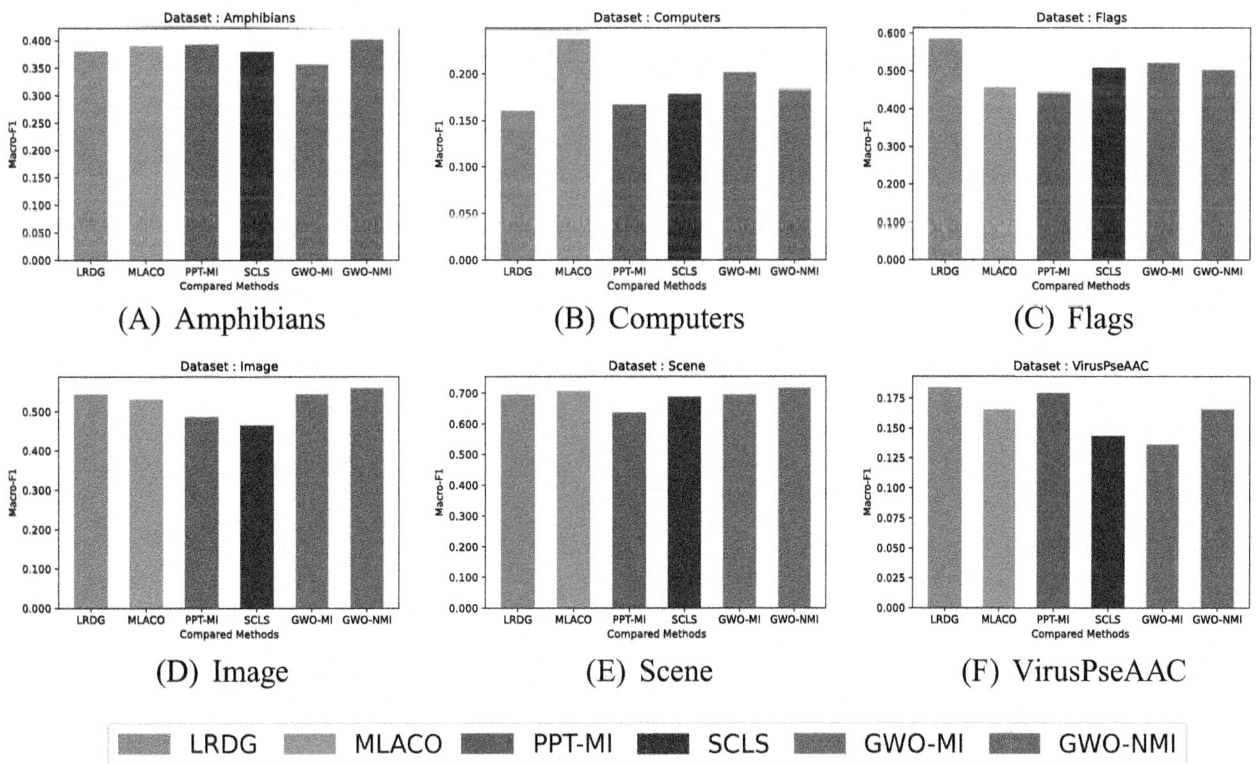

FIGURE 31.4 Experimental results under the Macro-F1 (↑).

31.5.6 Computational complexity analysis

The computational complexity of both proposed methods (GWO-MI and GWO-NMI) is $O(t \cdot n(M^2 + M \cdot L))$, where t represents the number of iterations, n is the population size, M is the number of selected features, and L is the number of classes. On the other hand, the compared baseline methods exhibit varying computational complexities: LRDG has $O(t \cdot (M^2 \cdot N + M \cdot N^2 + 2L^2))$, MLACO has $O(M \cdot N \cdot L) + O(M \cdot N^2) + O(t \cdot N^2)$, PPT-MI has $O(N^2 + N \cdot M)$, and SCLS has $O(N \cdot M \cdot L + t \cdot N \cdot M)$, with N instances. The mutual information values between features and between features and class labels were precomputed, which significantly reduced the computational burden compared to methods that employ classifier training during fitness evaluation. This eliminates the need for repeated model training at each iteration.

31.6 Conclusion

This chapter introduced two novel methods for multilabel feature selection based on the GWO algorithm, employing mutual information and normalized mutual information in the fitness function. Drawing inspiration from the mRMR filter approach, the proposed fitness functions were designed to evaluate both the relevance of selected features with respect to multiple labels and the redundancy among those features. Experimental evaluations on multiple benchmark datasets demonstrated that the proposed methods consistently outperformed four established multilabel feature selection techniques, effectively selecting informative features. Future research may extend this framework by integrating alternative metaheuristic optimization algorithms to further enhance performance. Additionally, addressing the challenges associated with imbalanced multilabel datasets represents a promising direction to improve the robustness and generalizability of the proposed methods.

Declaration of generative AI-assisted technologies

The author used Grammarly to improve clarity and readability, then reviewed and edited the content, and takes full responsibility for the published article.

References

[1] M.R. Boutell, J. Luo, X. Shen, C.M. Brown, Learning multi-label scene classification, Pattern Recognition 370 (9) (2004) 1757–1771.

[2] S.S. Mohanrasu, K. Janani, R. Rakkiyappan, A COPRAS-based approach to multi-label feature selection for text classification, Mathematics and Computers in Simulation 222 (2024) 3–23.

[3] J. Xu, J. Liu, J. Yin, C. Sun, A multi-label feature extraction algorithm via maximizing feature variance and feature-label dependence simultaneously, Knowledge-Based Systems 98 (2016) 172–184.

[4] H. Peng, F. Long, C. Ding, Feature selection based on mutual information criteria of max-dependency, max-relevance, and min-redundancy, IEEE Transactions on Pattern Analysis and Machine Intelligence 270 (8) (2005) 1226–1238.

[5] Y. Lin, Q. Hu, J. Liu, J. Duan, Multi-label feature selection based on max-dependency and min-redundancy, Neurocomputing 168 (2015) 92–103.

[6] J. Kennedy, R. Eberhart, Particle swarm optimization, Proceedings of ICNN'95-International Conference on Neural Networks, IEEE, (1995), pp. 1942–1948 vol. 4.

[7] M. Dorigo, M. Birattari, T. Stutzle, Ant colony optimization, IEEE Computational Intelligence Magazine 10 (4) (2007) 28–39.

[8] S. Mirjalili, S.M. Mirjalili, A. Lewis, Grey wolf optimizer, Advances in Engineering Software 69 (2014) 46–61.

[9] J. Cabestany, I. Rojas, G. Joya, Advances in Computational Intelligence: 11th International Work-Conference on Artificial Neural Networks, IWANN, Torremolinos-Málaga, Spain, June 8-10, 2011, Proceedings, Part II, vol. 6692. Springer.

[10] G. Tsoumakas, I. Vlahavas, Random k-Labelsets: an ensemble method for multilabel classification, in: European Conference on Machine Learning, pp. 406–417. Springer, 2007.

[11] R.B. Pereira, A. Plastino, B. Zadrozny, L.H.C. Merschmann, Categorizing feature selection methods for multi-label classification, Artificial Intelligence Review 490 (1) (2018) 57–78.

[12] J. Lee, D.-W. Kim, Mutual information-based multi-label feature selection using interaction information, Expert Systems with Applications 420 (4) (2015) 2013–2025.

[13] Y. Lin, Q. Hu, J. Liu, J. Li, X. Wu, Streaming feature selection for multilabel learning based on fuzzy mutual information, IEEE Transactions on Fuzzy Systems 250 (6) (2017) 1491–1507.

[14] P. Zhang, W. Gao, Feature relevance term variation for multi-label feature selection, Applied Intelligence 510 (7) (2021) 5095–5110.

[15] W. Gao, P. Hao, Y. Wu, P. Zhang, A unified low-order information-theoretic feature selection framework for multi-label learning, Pattern Recognition 134 (2023) 109111.

[16] S.S. Mohanrasu, R. Rakkiyappan, A novel framework for multi-label feature selection: integrating mutual information and pythagorean fuzzy CRADIS, Granular Computing 90 (3) (2024) 67.

[17] S.S. Mohanrasu, L.T. Phan, R. Rajan, B. Manavalan, Cost-sensitive feature selection for multi-label classification: multi-criteria decision-making approach, Applied Computing and Informatics (2025).
[18] Q. Han, Z. Zhao, L. Hu, W. Gao, Enhanced multi-label feature selection considering label-specific relevant information, Expert Systems with Applications 264 (2025) 125819.
[19] L. Sun, F. Xu, W. Ding, J. Xu, AFIFC: adaptive fuzzy neighborhood mutual information-based feature selection via label correlation, Pattern Recognition 164 (2025) 111577.
[20] S.S. Mohanrasu, K. Janani, J. Keerthana, R. Rakkiyappan, Multi-scale multi-label feature selection via fuzzy mutual information, International Journal of Machine Learning and Cybernetics (2025) 1–19.
[21] Q. Al-Tashi, H. Md Rais, S.J. Abdulkadir, S. Mirjalili, H. Alhussian, A review of grey wolf optimizer-based feature selection methods for classification, Evolutionary Machine Learning Techniques: Algorithms and Applications (2019) 273–286.
[22] E. Emary, H.M. Zawbaa, A.E. Hassanien, Binary grey wolf optimization approaches for feature selection, Neurocomputing 172 (2016) 371–381.
[23] Q. Al-Tashi, S.J. Abdul Kadir, H.M. Rais, S. Mirjalili, H. Alhussian, Binary optimization using hybrid grey wolf optimization for feature selection, IEEE Access 7 (2019) 39496–39508.
[24] Q. Al-Tashi, S.J. Abdulkadir, H.M. Rais, S. Mirjalili, H. Alhussian, M.G. Ragab, et al., Binary multi-objective grey wolf optimizer for feature selection in classification, IEEE Access 8 (2020) 106247–106263.
[25] S. Kashef, H. Nezamabadi-pour, An effective method of multi-label feature selection employing evolutionary algorithms. In: 2017 2nd Conference on Swarm Intelligence and Evolutionary Computation (CSIEC). IEEE, 2017, pp. 21–25.
[26] E. Hancer, B. Xue, M. Zhang, A multimodal multiobjective evolutionary algorithm for filter feature selection in multilabel classification, IEEE Transactions on Artificial Intelligence 50 (9) (2024) 4428–4442.
[27] C.E. Shannon, A mathematical theory of communication, The Bell System Technical Journal 270 (3) (1948) 379–423.
[28] A. Strehl, J. Ghosh, Cluster ensembles–a knowledge reuse framework for combining multiple partitions, Journal of Machine Learning Research 30 (Dec) (2002) 583–617.
[29] Amphibians, 2020. UCI machine learning repository. https://doi.org/10.24432/C5H90N.
[30] J.M. Moyano, E.L. Gibaja, S. Ventura, Multi-label classification dataset repository. https://www.uco.es/kdis/mllresources/, 2017. (accessed 20.05. 2025).
[31] G. Tsoumakas, E. Spyromitros-Xioufis, J. Vilcek, I. Vlahavas, I., 2011. Multi-label classification dataset repository. https://mulan.sourceforge.net/datasets-mlc.html (accessed 20.05.2025).
[32] M.-L. Zhang, Z.-H. Zhou, A review on multi-label learning algorithms, IEEE Transactions on Knowledge and Data Engineering 260 (8) (2013) 1819–1837.
[33] Y. Zhang, W. Huo, J. Tang, Multi-label feature selection via latent representation learning and dynamic graph constraints, Pattern Recognition 151 (2024) 110411.
[34] M. Paniri, M. Bagher Dowlatshahi, H. Nezamabadi-Pour, MLACO: a multi-label feature selection algorithm based on ant colony optimization, Knowledge-Based Systems 192 (2020) 105285.
[35] G. Doquire, M. Verleysen, Feature selection for multi-label classification problems, in: Advances in Computational Intelligence: 11th International Work-Conference on Artificial Neural Networks, IWANN 2011, Torremolinos-Málaga, Spain, Proceedings, Part I 11. Springer, 2011, pp. 9–16.
[36] J. Lee, D.-W. Kim, SCLS: Multi-label feature selection based on scalable criterion for large label set, Pattern Recognition 66 (2017) 342–352.
[37] S. Kashef, H. Nezamabadi-pour, B. Nikpour, Multilabel feature selection: a comprehensive review and guiding experiments, Wiley Interdisciplinary Reviews: Data Mining and Knowledge Discovery 80 (2) (2018) e1240.
[38] M.-L. Zhang, Z.-H. Zhou, ML-KNN: A lazy learning approach to multi-label learning, Pattern Recognition 400 (7) (2007) 2038–2048.

Chapter 32

Comparative analysis of grey wolf optimizer with other metaheuristics algorithms

Mitra Pooyandeh[1] and Alireza Arianfar[2]
[1]*Center for ICT and Automotive Convergence, Kyungpook National University, Daegu, Gyeongbuk, Korea,* [2]*Independent Researcher, Tehran, Iran*

32.1 Introduction

32.1.1 Background and motivation

Optimization is a fundamental process in computational science and engineering, central to tasks such as parameter tuning, resource allocation, design optimization, and machine learning model training. Li et al. [1] emphasized the importance of parameter tuning for improving model accuracy in complex systems, while Qaraad et al. [2] demonstrated its impact on enhancing adaptive control strategies. Similarly, Zhou et al. [3] and Qiao et al. [4] highlighted optimization's role in efficient resource allocation across industrial applications. In the field of machine learning, [5] explored optimization-based approaches to model training and hyperparameter adjustment. As real-world problems become increasingly complex—characterized by multimodal landscapes, high dimensionality, and noisy or dynamic environments—classical optimization methods such as gradient descent [6] and linear programming [7] often fall short due to their reliance on differentiability, convexity, or complete problem information.

To overcome these limitations, metaheuristic algorithms Rajwar et al. [8], have emerged as powerful tools capable of navigating complex, nonlinear, and multidimensional search spaces. These algorithms, inspired by natural phenomena such as biological evolution, swarm behavior, or physical annealing processes, use stochastic decision-making to explore potential solutions. Their flexibility, general applicability, and independence from gradient information have made them widely used in academic research and industry applications.

One such algorithm is the grey wolf optimizer (GWO), introduced by Ref. [9] in 2014. Inspired by the social hierarchy and hunting strategy of grey wolves in the wild, GWO employs a leader-driven approach to guide search agents in the solution space. It features a dynamic balance between exploration and exploitation through encircling, hunting, and attacking mechanisms. Due to its simplicity, few control parameters, and competitive performance across various problems, GWO has quickly become a popular choice in the metaheuristic community.

Despite its success, GWO is just one of many nature-inspired algorithms, and there is an ongoing need to objectively assess its performance in comparison with other well-established metaheuristics. Such comparative studies help practitioners select the most suitable algorithm for their problem and identify areas where improvements or hybridization may be needed.

32.1.2 Literature review

Over the past two decades, a wide array of metaheuristic algorithms has been proposed and extensively studied. The genetic algorithm (GA) [10], based on the principles of natural selection and genetics, has been widely applied in areas such as scheduling, optimization, and machine learning. Particle swarm optimization (PSO) [11], which models the social behavior of bird flocking or fish schooling, is valued for its fast convergence and ease of implementation. Differential evolution (DE) [12] is known for its robustness in continuous optimization. Simulated annealing (SA) [13] introduced the concept of probabilistic acceptance to escape local optima, while ant colony optimization (ACO) [14] was inspired by

Grey Wolf Optimizer. DOI: https://doi.org/10.1016/B978-0-443-36624-6.00014-7

pheromone-guided foraging behavior in real ants. Each algorithm exhibits distinct strengths and limitations, making them more or less suitable for different classes of optimization problems.

Several comparative studies have been conducted to evaluate these algorithms; however, many are limited in scope, involving only a small subset of algorithms or benchmark functions. Others focus on domain-specific applications, making it difficult to generalize their conclusions. Although the GWO has been included in some recent comparative works, there remains a lack of comprehensive benchmarking studies that assess its performance across a diverse range of test functions varying in modality, separability, and dimensionality.

In one foundational study, Mirjalili et al. [9] benchmarked GWO against PSO, DE, gravitational search algorithm, evolutionary programming, and evolution strategy using 29 classical benchmark functions. The results demonstrated GWO's competitive performance across unimodal, multimodal, and composite landscapes. In a more recent study, Ref. [15] compared GA, PSO, and GWO for geophysical data inversion problems. Their findings showed that both GWO and PSO significantly outperformed GA, with comparable convergence accuracy and stability—highlighting GWO's applicability in real-world parameter estimation tasks. Additionally, a hybrid PSO–GWO model was shown to outperform its standalone components and other variants under identical test conditions in a power quality optimization scenario [16].

Behan and Haider [17] conducted a comparative analysis of nine nature-inspired optimization algorithms across several benchmark functions using multiple evaluation metrics. While GWO was not included in that study, it emphasizes the necessity of fair, consistent experimental setups and reproducible evaluation criteria in metaheuristic benchmarking—principles adopted in this chapter for evaluating GWO.

Recent research has also focused on enhancing GWO through hybridization and adaptive strategies. For example, an adaptive hybrid differential grey wolf optimization (AHDGWO) algorithm was proposed to address node deployment challenges in wireless sensor networks [18]. The study demonstrated that AHDGWO outperformed standard GWO and other evolutionary algorithms on the CEC2022 benchmark suite and real-world simulations. However, such works are primarily intended to validate novel variants rather than conduct generalized benchmarking of GWO itself.

Furthermore, many previous studies lack consistent parameter tuning protocols or control over computational resources, potentially leading to biased or unclear results. This reinforces the need for a unified and controlled experimental environment, wherein multiple algorithms are assessed fairly under standardized conditions—a gap that the present chapter aims to address.

32.1.3 Exploration–exploitation trade-off in metaheuristics

A defining feature of metaheuristic algorithms is the balance between *exploration* (global search) and *exploitation* (local refinement). This trade-off influences convergence behavior and solution quality [19].

Fig. 32.1 illustrates the relative tendencies of the seven algorithms—GWO, GA, PSO, DE, ACO, SA, and artificial bee colony (ABC)—based on their inherent design. Algorithms such as GA and PSO start with stronger exploration, whereas SA and ACO emphasize exploitation. GWO and ABC provide a dynamic balance, contributing to their robustness across diverse problem landscapes.

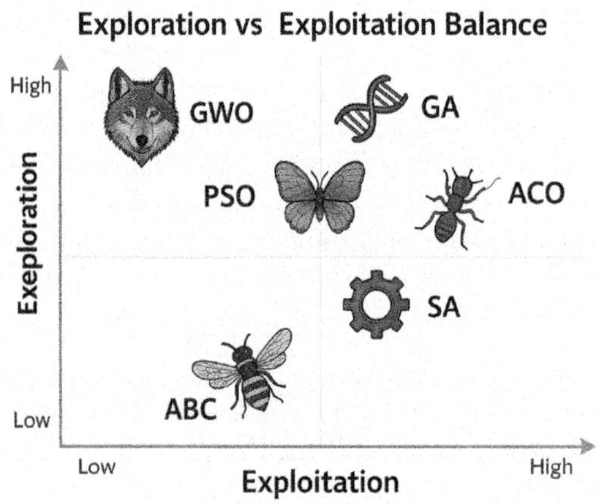

FIGURE 32.1 Exploration versus exploitation balance for seven metaheuristic algorithms: GWO, GA, PSO, DE, ACO, SA, and ABC (*ABC*, Artificial bee colony; *ACO*, ant colony optimization; *DE*, differential evolution; *GA*, genetic algorithm; *GWO*, grey wolf optimizer; *PSO*, particle swarm optimization; *SA*, simulated annealing).

32.1.4 Contribution and objectives

The primary objective of this chapter is to conduct a strict benchmarking study of the GWO in comparison with six other widely recognized metaheuristic algorithms: GA, PSO, DE, ACO, SA, and ABC. While each of these algorithms has been studied extensively in isolation, this chapter provides a unified and consistent comparative evaluation of their performance across a diverse set of benchmark functions.

Fig. 32.2 illustrates the key similarities and differences among these seven algorithms. The similarities include their metaheuristic nature, reliance on population-based or iterative search, stochastic behavior, and the balance between exploration and exploitation. The differences highlight variations in inspiration sources, search mechanisms, memory usage, and exploitation strategies, which significantly impact algorithm performance on different optimization problems.

The key contributions of this chapter are as follows:

- Implementation framework: Development of a reproducible simulation framework in Python, where all seven algorithms are implemented under a unified parameter configuration and execution environment.
- Benchmark suite: Selection and categorization of a representative set of 23 standard benchmark functions covering unimodal, multimodal, and composite problem types.
- Quantitative evaluation: Systematic analysis of each algorithm's performance based on metrics such as convergence rate, best and mean fitness values, standard deviation, and computational time.
- Statistical and visual comparison: Application of statistical tests and convergence plots to provide a deeper understanding of algorithmic behavior and performance differences.
- Practical guidance: Interpretation of the results to offer insights into which algorithms are better suited for specific types of optimization landscapes, helping practitioners in algorithm selection for real-world problems.

This benchmarking study not only clarifies the relative strengths and weaknesses of GWO but also contributes to a broader understanding of how it compares with other established metaheuristics in solving complex optimization tasks.

32.1.5 Chapter organization

This chapter is organized into six main sections to provide a coherent and comprehensive presentation of the study. Following the introduction, Section 2 presents the suite of benchmark functions used in the experiments, describing their

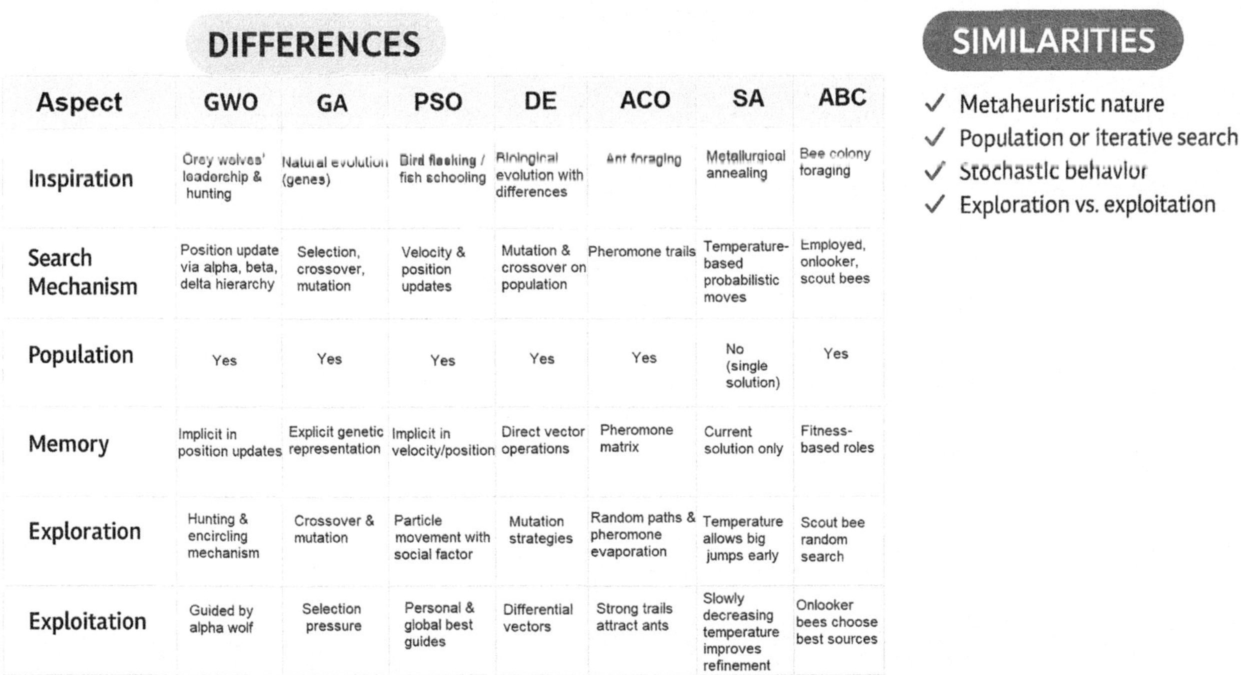

DIFFERENCES

Aspect	GWO	GA	PSO	DE	ACO	SA	ABC
Inspiration	Grey wolves' leadership & hunting	Natural evolution (genes)	Bird flocking / fish schooling	Biological evolution with differences	Ant foraging	Metallurgical annealing	Bee colony foraging
Search Mechanism	Position update via alpha, beta, delta hierarchy	Selection, crossover, mutation	Velocity & position updates	Mutation & crossover on population	Pheromone trails	Temperature-based probabilistic moves	Employed, onlooker, scout bees
Population	Yes	Yes	Yes	Yes	Yes	No (single solution)	Yes
Memory	Implicit in position updates	Explicit genetic representation	Implicit in velocity/position	Direct vector operations	Pheromone matrix	Current solution only	Fitness-based roles
Exploration	Hunting & encircling mechanism	Crossover & mutation	Particle movement with social factor	Mutation strategies	Random paths & pheromone evaporation	Temperature allows big jumps early	Scout bee random search
Exploitation	Guided by alpha wolf	Selection pressure	Personal & global best guides	Differential vectors	Strong trails attract ants	Slowly decreasing temperature improves refinement	Onlooker bees choose best sources

SIMILARITIES

✓ Metaheuristic nature
✓ Population or iterative search
✓ Stochastic behavior
✓ Exploration vs. exploitation

FIGURE 32.2 Similarities and differences among the seven metaheuristic algorithms (GWO, GA, PSO, DE, ACO, SA, and ABC) (*ABC*, Artificial bee colony; *ACO*, ant colony optimization; *DE*, differential evolution; *GA*, genetic algorithm; *GWO*, grey wolf optimizer; *PSO*, particle swarm optimization; *SA*, simulated annealing).

mathematical formulations and classifying them into unimodal, multimodal, and composite types. Section 3 offers an overview of the seven metaheuristic algorithms investigated in this work, explaining their biological or physical inspiration, algorithmic structures, and the key control parameters that influence their performance.

Section 4 focuses on the experimental setup, outlining the simulation environment, parameter configurations, performance metrics, and the statistical methods employed to ensure fair and reliable evaluation. The results of these experiments are discussed in Section 5, which includes convergence plots, comparative performance tables, and statistical analyses that illustrate the behavior and effectiveness of each algorithm across the selected benchmark functions. Finally, Section 6 concludes the chapter by summarizing the key findings, discussing their implications for algorithm selection and design, and suggesting future research directions such as hybridization techniques and adaptive variants.

This structured organization ensures that the study is both comprehensive and reproducible, offering clear insights into the comparative performance of the GWO within the broader context of contemporary metaheuristic optimization strategies.

32.1.6 Mathematical definitions of benchmark functions

To evaluate the performance of metaheuristic algorithms fairly, this study utilizes a diverse suite of well-established benchmark functions drawn from classical test problems. These functions are selected to cover unimodal, multimodal, and hybrid scenarios and vary in properties such as separability, symmetry, and dimensional scalability. Each function is defined mathematically, alonlg with its domain and known global minimum as summarized in Table 32.1.

The Sphere function (unimodal and separable) is among the simplest and most commonly used benchmark functions [20]. It is defined as

$$f(x) = \sum_{i=1}^{n} x_i^2 \tag{32.1}$$

This convex, continuous, and differentiable function is evaluated over the domain $x_i \in [-100,100]$, with a single global minimum at $\mathbf{x} = \mathbf{0}$, where $f(\mathbf{0})=\mathbf{0}$. Because of its simplicity, the Sphere function is ideal for testing an algorithm's convergence speed and precision in smooth landscapes.

The Rosenbrock function, also known as the Banana function, introduces a curved valley leading to the global minimum [21]. It is expressed as

$$f(x) = \sum_{i=1}^{n-1} \left[100(x_{i+1} - x_i^2)^2 + (x_i - 1)^2 \right] \tag{32.2}$$

and is typically defined over the domain $x_i \in [-30,30]$. Although unimodal, its narrow and nonseparable valley makes convergence challenging for many algorithms. The global minimum is located at $\mathbf{x}=(1,1,\ldots,1)$, where $f(\mathbf{x})=0$.

The Rastrigin function adds periodic cosine components to the Sphere function, introducing many regularly distributed local minima [22]. It is defined as

$$f(x)=10n + \sum_{i=1}^{n} \left[x_i^2 - 10\cos(2\pi x_i) \right] \tag{32.3}$$

over the domain $x_i \in [-5.12,5.12]$. Despite its global minimum at $\mathbf{x} = \mathbf{0}$, where $f(\mathbf{0})=\mathbf{0}$, its highly multimodal nature makes it suitable for testing an algorithm's capability to avoid local minima.

The Ackley function increases complexity by combining exponential and cosine terms to form a multimodal landscape with a wide basin surrounding the global optimum [23]. It is mathematically represented as

$$f(x) = -20\exp\left(-0.2\sqrt{\frac{1}{n}\sum_{i=1}^{n} x_i^2}\right) - \exp\left(\frac{1}{n}\sum_{i=1}^{n}\cos(2\pi x_i)\right) + 20 + e \tag{32.4}$$

and is usually evaluated over the domain $x_i \in [-32,32]$. The function is scalable, nonseparable, and features many local optima, with the global minimum located at $\mathbf{x} = \mathbf{0}$.

The Griewank function presents a multimodal landscape with more sparsely distributed local minima [24]. It is given by

$$f(x)=1 + \frac{1}{4000}\sum_{i=1}^{n} x_i^2 - \prod_{i=1}^{n}\cos\left(\frac{x_i}{\sqrt{i}}\right) \tag{32.5}$$

TABLE 32.1 Summary of benchmark functions.

Function name	Mathematical notation	Domain	Global minimum	Modality	Separability	Scalability
Sphere	$f(x) = \sum_{i=1}^{n} x_i^2$	$[-100,100]^n$	$f(0)=0$	Unimodal	Separable	Yes
Rosenbrock	$f(x) = \sum_{i=1}^{n-1} [100(x_{i+1} - x_i^2)^2 + (x_i - 1)^2]$	$[-30,30]^n$	$f(1)=0$	Unimodal	Nonseparable	Yes
Rastrigin	$f(x)=10n + \sum_{i=1}^{n} [x_i^2 - 10 \cos(2\pi x_i)]$	$[-5.12,5.12]^n$	$f(0)=0$	Multimodal	Separable	Yes
Ackley	See Section 1.2.2	$[-32,32]^n$	$f(0)=0$	Multimodal	Nonseparable	Yes
Griewank	$f(x)=1 + \frac{1}{4000} \sum_{i=1}^{n} x_i^2 - \prod_{i=1}^{n} \cos\left(\frac{x_i}{\sqrt{i}}\right)$	$[-600,600]^n$	$f(0)=0$	Multimodal	Partially	Yes
Schwefel	$f(x)=418.9829n - \sum_{i=1}^{n} x_i \sin(\sqrt{\lvert x_i \rvert})$	$[-500,500]^n$	$f(x_i=420.9687)=0$	Multimodal	–	–
Zakharov	See Section 1.2.2	$[-5,10]^n$	$f(0)=0$	Unimodal	Nonseparable	Yes
Levy	See Section 1.2.2	$[-10,10]^n$	$f(1)=0$	Multimodal	Nonseparable	Yes

where $x_i \in [-600,600]$. The combination of additive and multiplicative components creates a structured but complex landscape that is particularly useful for evaluating algorithmic robustness.

The Schwefel function introduces deception through a rugged topology filled with numerous local optima [25]. It is defined as

$$f(x)=418.9829n - \sum_{i=1}^{n} x_i \sin\left(\sqrt{|x_i|}\right) \tag{32.6}$$

and evaluated over $x_i \in [-500,500]$. The global minimum occurs at x_i=420.9687, where $f(x)$=0. Due to its deceptive landscape, it often traps optimization algorithms far from the optimum.

The Zakharov function is unimodal and nonseparable, characterized by a flat region and higher-order polynomial terms Jamil and Yang [26]. It is defined as

$$f(x) = \sum_{i=1}^{n} x_i^2 + \left(\sum_{i=1}^{n} 0.5ix_i\right)^2 + \left(\sum_{i=1}^{n} 0.5ix_i\right)^4 \tag{32.7}$$

and commonly evaluated within the domain $x_i \in [-5,10]$. Although unimodal, its deceptive shape requires a delicate balance between exploration and exploitation for efficient convergence.

Finally, the Levy function integrates sinusoidal transformations with polynomial growth to form a highly multimodal surface Molga and Smutnicki [27]. Its general form is

$$f(x) = \sin^2(\pi w_1) + \sum_{i=1}^{n-1} (w_i - 1)^2\left[1 + 10\sin^2(\pi(w_i + 1))\right] + (w_n - 1)^2\left[1 + \sin^2(2\pi w_n)\right] \tag{32.8}$$

where

$$w_i=1 + \frac{x_i - 1}{4}, \quad x_i \in [-10,10].$$

The global minimum is located at x=(1, …, 1), yet the dense distribution of local minima makes this function particularly challenging for optimization algorithms.

These benchmark functions collectively span a wide spectrum of optimization difficulties. Their variation in modality, separability, and scalability ensures a comprehensive evaluation of each algorithm's strengths and weaknesses. A concise overview of their properties is presented in Table 32.2. (Tables 1 and 3)

32.1.7 Properties

Benchmark functions are characterized by various properties that influence the difficulty and complexity of the optimization problems they represent. Among these properties, modality is one of the most significant. A function can be unimodal, possessing a single global optimum with no other local optima, which generally makes it easier for optimization algorithms to converge. In contrast, *multimodal* functions have multiple local optima alongside the global optimum, presenting a more challenging landscape for algorithms as they must avoid premature convergence to suboptimal points.

Another important property is **separability**, which refers to whether a function's variables can be optimized independently or if they interact in a coupled manner. *Separable* functions allow the problem to be decomposed into

TABLE 32.2 Benchmark functions used in the experiments.

ID	Function name	Characteristics
F1	Sphere	Unimodal, separable, convex
F2	Rastrigin	Multimodal, separable
F3	Rosenbrock	Nonconvex, valley-shaped
F4	Ackley	Multimodal, nonseparable
F5	Griewank	Multimodal, nonseparable

TABLE 32.3 Comparison of metaheuristic algorithms.

Feature/Algorithm	GWO	GA	PSO	DE	ACO	SA	ABC
Inspiration	Grey wolf hunting	Natural evolution	Bird flocking	Vector mutation	Ant foraging	Annealing in metals	Bee foraging
Approach	Population-based	Population-based	Population-based	Population-based	Population-based	Single-solution	Population-based
Key operators	Encircling, hunting, attacking	Selection, crossover, mutation	Velocity/position updates	Mutation, crossover, selection	Pheromone, heuristics	Neighborhood search, temperature	Employed, onlooker, scout bees
Solution representation	Continuous vectors	Binary, real, permutation	Continuous vectors	Continuous vectors	Paths, sequences	Flexible	Continuous vectors
Exploration/ Exploitation	Guided by alpha, beta, and delta	Crossover and mutation rates	Inertia, cognitive and social terms	Mutation factor and crossover rate	Pheromone update rate	Temperature schedule	Scout versus employed onlooker bees
Parameter sensitivity	Moderate	Moderate	Low-Moderate	Low	Moderate	High	Low
Main strengths	Balance of search, simple	Robust, diverse problem types	Fast, few parameters	Robust, adaptive	Great for discrete problems	Escapes local optima	Simple, flexible
Applications	Engineering, feature selection	ML, bioinformatics, engineering	ML, robotics, optimization	Engineering, signal processing	Routing, scheduling	VLSI, scheduling, TSP	Clustering, optimization

ABC, Artificial bee colony; *ACO*, ant colony optimization; *DE*, differential evolution; *GA*, genetic algorithm; *GWO*, grey wolf optimizer; *PSO*, particle swarm optimization; *TSP*, traveling salesman problem; *VLSI*, very large scale iIntegration; *SA*, simulated annealing.

smaller subproblems, simplifying the optimization process. On the other hand, *nonseparable* functions require algorithms to consider variable interdependencies, thereby increasing problem complexity.

Additionally, the dimensionality or the number of variables in a function significantly impacts the optimization process. *High-dimensional* problems typically pose greater challenges due to the exponential growth of the search space, often referred to as the "curse of dimensionality." As such, benchmark functions used in comparative algorithm studies typically span a range of modalities, degrees of separability, and dimensions to provide a comprehensive evaluation of algorithmic robustness and scalability.

Understanding these properties is essential for designing fair and meaningful benchmark tests that reflect real-world optimization challenges. (See Table 32.2 for a summary of benchmark functions along with their respective modality, separability, and dimensionality characteristics.)

32.2 Metaheuristic algorithms overview

Metaheuristic algorithms are versatile and powerful tools for solving complex optimization problems that may be nonlinear, nondifferentiable, noisy, multimodal, or high-dimensional. Unlike traditional optimization methods, they do not require gradient information and are generally easy to implement. Their adaptability makes them highly suitable for a wide range of applications, including engineering design, machine learning, and operations research. This section introduces seven widely used metaheuristic algorithms that are included in our benchmarking study, highlighting their working principles, equations, and practical characteristics.

32.2.1 Grey wolf optimizer

The GWO, proposed by Mirjalili et al. [9], is a nature-inspired metaheuristic that models the hierarchical leadership and cooperative hunting behavior of grey wolves. Known for its simplicity, flexibility, and efficiency across various optimization problems, GWO mimics the wolves' intelligence and coordination through mathematical modeling of leadership, encircling, and hunting behaviors. The algorithm's overall workflow is illustrated in Fig. 32.3.

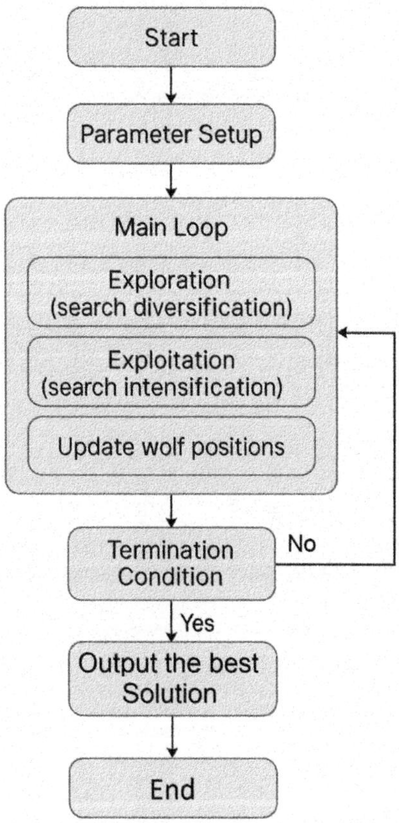

FIGURE 32.3 Flowchart of the grey wolf optimizer.

In GWO, the social hierarchy consists of four roles: *alpha*, *beta*, *delta*, and *omega*. The alpha represents the best solution and leads the decision-making process, followed by beta and delta as the second- and third-best solutions, respectively, which assist in guidance and coordination. The remaining wolves (omega) represent the rest of the population and learn from the top three leaders, maintaining diversity in the search process.

The optimization process simulates three main phases: encircling, hunting, and attacking the prey. During encircling, wolves estimate the prey's position using:

$$\vec{D} = \left|\vec{C}\cdot\vec{X_p} - \vec{X}(t)\right|, \quad \vec{X}(t+1)=\vec{X_p} - \vec{A}\cdot\vec{D} \tag{32.9}$$

where $\vec{A}=2\vec{a}\cdot\vec{r_1} - \vec{a}$ and $\vec{C}=2\cdot\vec{r_2}$ [9]. The control parameter $\vec{a}$ decreases linearly from 2 to 0 to balance exploration and exploitation as iterations progress.

In the hunting phase, wolves update their positions based on the top three leaders (α, β, and δ) using:

$$\vec{X_1} = \vec{X_\alpha} - \vec{A_1}\cdot\left|\vec{C_1}\cdot\vec{X_\alpha} - \vec{X}\right| \tag{32.10}$$

$$\vec{X_2} = \vec{X_\beta} - \vec{A_2}\cdot\left|\vec{C_2}\cdot\vec{X_\beta} - \vec{X}\right| \tag{32.11}$$

$$\vec{X_3} = \vec{X_\delta} - \vec{A_3}\cdot\left|\vec{C_3}\cdot\vec{X_\delta} - \vec{X}\right| \tag{32.12}$$

$$\vec{X}(t+1)=\frac{\vec{X_1} + \vec{X_2} + \vec{X_3}}{3} \tag{32.13}$$

This multileader guidance enables the pack to converge effectively toward optimal regions and prevents premature stagnation.

As iterations continue, the algorithm enters the **attacking phase**, where $\vec{a}$ approaches zero, reducing the movement step size for fine-tuning around the prey's location. Large $\vec{a}$ values early in the search encourage exploration, while smaller values later enhance exploitation, allowing GWO to maintain a strong balance between global and local search.

Overall, the success of GWO lies in its dynamic balance of exploration and exploitation, its gradient-free mechanism, and its biologically inspired structure that promotes cooperation and adaptability. Owing to these strengths, GWO has been widely applied in fields such as engineering design, machine learning parameter tuning, and energy optimization.

32.2.2 Genetic algorithm

The genetic algorithm is a widely used metaheuristic optimization technique inspired by natural selection and genetics [28]. Proposed by John Holland in the 1960s, GA laid the foundation for evolutionary computation and remains a versatile framework for solving complex optimization problems. As part of the evolutionary algorithm family, GA employs reproduction, crossover, mutation, and survival of the fittest to mimic biological evolution. Fig. 32.4 shows the general workflow of GA.

GA operates on a population of potential solutions, or chromosomes, represented as binary strings, real-valued vectors, or permutations. The algorithm evolves this population through repeated application of selection, crossover, and mutation. A fitness function evaluates each solution's quality with respect to the optimization objective.

The *selection* process imitates survival of the fittest by favoring high-fitness individuals for reproduction. Common strategies—such as roulette wheel, tournament, and rank-based selection—balance exploration and exploitation. Roulette wheel selection offers probabilistic choice, while tournament selection accelerates convergence through competition.

After selection, the *crossover* operator combines genetic material from two parents to generate offspring and enhance diversity. Common crossover types include single-point, multipoint, and uniform crossover. In real-coded GAs, crossover is often defined as:

$$\text{Child} = \frac{\text{Parent}_1 + \text{Parent}_2}{2}. \tag{32.14}$$

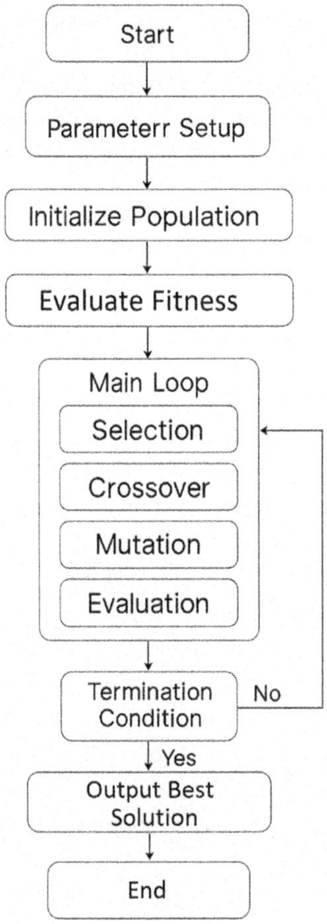

FIGURE 32.4 Flowchart of the genetic algorithm (*GA*).

The *mutation* operator introduces random changes to maintain diversity and prevent premature convergence. Mutation is applied as:

$$x_{i'} = \begin{cases} x_i + \delta, & \text{withprobability} p_{\text{mut}} \\ x_i, & \text{otherwise} \end{cases} \tag{32.15}$$

where δ is a random perturbation and p_{mut} denotes the mutation probability. This randomness helps the algorithm escape local optima and explore new regions of the search space.

The GA process starts with random initialization of a population, followed by evaluation, selection, crossover, and mutation, which are repeated until a termination condition is met, such as reaching a maximum generation count or convergence.

GA's flexibility and robustness have led to wide applications in diverse fields, including engineering optimization (e.g., aerodynamic design and scheduling), *machine learning* (feature selection, neural network training, and hyperparameter tuning), and bioinformatics (gene selection, sequence alignment, and protein structure prediction). Its power lies in balancing *exploration* and *exploitation*: selection promotes promising solutions, while crossover and mutation preserve diversity. Moreover, GA's population-based structure supports parallelization, making it efficient for high-performance computing. These characteristics firmly establish GA as a cornerstone of metaheuristic optimization and a benchmark for evaluating emerging algorithms.

32.2.3 Particle swarm optimization

PSO is a population-based metaheuristic introduced by Eberhart and Kennedy in 1995 [29]. Inspired by the collective behavior of birds and fish, PSO simulates how individuals in a group cooperate and learn from each other. Unlike GA, PSO relies on information sharing among particles—candidate solutions—that move through the search space based on both personal and collective experience, as illustrated in Fig. 32.5.

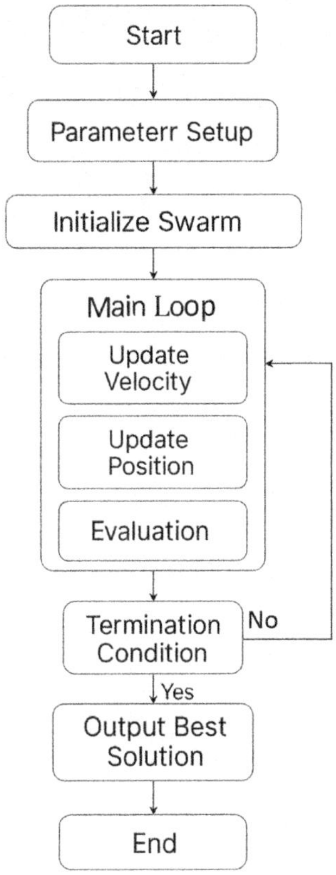

FIGURE 32.5 Flowchart of the particle swarm optimization.

Each particle adjusts its position according to two main factors: its personal best (pBest) and the global best (gBest) of the entire swarm. Some variants also include a *local best* (lBest) based on neighboring performance. This interaction balances self-learning and social collaboration.

The particle motion is defined by:

$$\mathbf{v}_i(t+1) = \omega \mathbf{v}_i(t) + c_1 r_1 (\mathbf{pBest}_i - \mathbf{x}_i(t)) + c_2 r_2 (\mathbf{gBest} - \mathbf{x}_i(t)), \tag{32.16}$$

$$\mathbf{x}_i(t+1) = \mathbf{x}_i(t) + \mathbf{v}_i(t+1), \tag{32.17}$$

where $\mathbf{x}_i(t)$ and $\mathbf{v}_i(t)$ are the position and velocity of particle i, ω controls the trade-off between exploration and exploitation, c_1 and c_2 are cognitive and social coefficients, and r_1, $r_2 \in [0,1]$ are random factors introducing diversity.

PSO begins with a randomly initialized swarm whose particles iteratively update their positions based on individual (*pBest*) and global (*gBest*) experiences until convergence or a stopping criterion is reached. Its simplicity, fast convergence, and limited parameters make PSO highly efficient, while proper tuning of ω, c_1, and c_2 maintains a strong balance between exploration and exploitation. Owing to these advantages, PSO effectively addresses high-dimensional, nonlinear, and multimodal problems across diverse fields, including *engineering design*, *control optimization*, *power system planning*, *machine learning* (e.g., neural network training, feature selection, and hyperparameter tuning), *robotics* (e.g., path planning), *image processing*, and *financial modeling*. Overall, PSO's collective intelligence, adaptability, and ease of implementation have made it one of the most influential metaheuristics, with hybrid and adaptive variants extending its impact to advanced domains such as artificial intelligence, digital twins, and smart optimization systems.

32.2.4 Ant colony optimization

ACO is a swarm intelligence algorithm inspired by the foraging behavior of real ants [30]. Developed by Marco Dorigo in the early 1990s, ACO models how ants find the shortest path between their nest and food using pheromone trails. In nature, shorter paths accumulate stronger pheromones as ants traverse them more often, while longer ones fade due to evaporation. This collective learning mechanism forms the basis of ACO (Fig. 32.6).

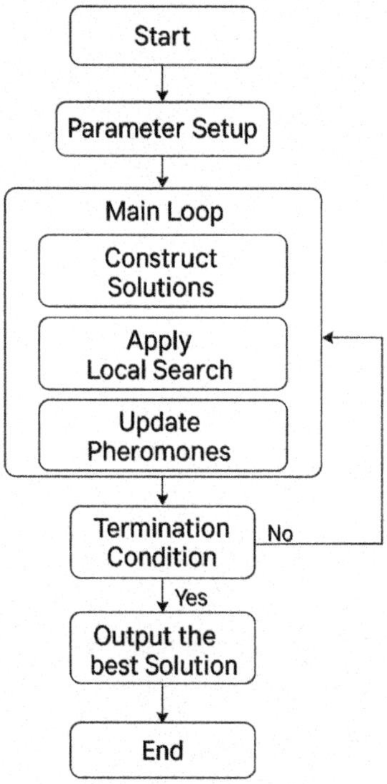

FIGURE 32.6 Flowchart of the ant colony optimization (*ACO*) algorithm.

In ACO, a population of artificial ants collaboratively explores the search space. Each ant incrementally builds a solution (e.g., a tour in the TSP) based on pheromone intensity and heuristic desirability. The transition probability from node i to j for ant k is given by:

$$P_{ij}^k = \begin{cases} \frac{[\tau_{ij}]^\alpha [\eta_{ij}]^\beta}{\sum_{l \in \text{allowed}_k} [\tau_{il}]^\alpha [\eta_{il}]^\beta}, & j \in \text{allowed}_k \\ 0, & \text{otherwise}, \end{cases} \tag{32.18}$$

where τ_{ij} denotes pheromone level and η_{ij} represents heuristic desirability.

After all ants construct their solutions, pheromone trails are updated as:

$$\tau_{ij} \leftarrow (1 - \rho)\tau_{ij} + \sum_{k=1}^{m} \Delta\tau_{ij}^k, \tag{32.19}$$

where ρ is the evaporation rate and $\Delta\tau_{ij}^k$ is the pheromone deposited by ant k. Evaporation prevents stagnation, while reinforcement promotes better paths.

ACO iteratively balances exploration and exploitation until convergence or a stopping condition is met. Its decentralized design allows parallel implementation and hybridization with other optimization methods. Beyond combinatorial problems like TSP, ACO has been successfully applied to network routing, scheduling, robotics, and continuous optimization tasks. Its adaptability and biologically inspired mechanism make it a cornerstone of swarm-based metaheuristics.

32.2.5 Simulated annealing

SA is a probabilistic metaheuristic inspired by the annealing process in metallurgy [31]. In metals, controlled heating and gradual cooling help atoms settle into a stable low-energy state. Similarly, SA mimics this process to escape local optima and approach the global optimum through a temperature-controlled random search. The overall structure of the algorithm is shown in Fig. 32.7.

In optimization, each solution corresponds to an atomic configuration, and the objective function represents the system's energy. Starting from an initial solution, SA explores its neighborhood by random modifications. The acceptance of a new solution s' with energy $E(s')$ from a current solution s is determined probabilistically:

$$P(\text{accept} s') = \begin{cases} 1, & \text{if} E(s') < E(s) \\ \exp\left(-\frac{E(s') - E(s)}{T}\right), & \text{otherwise}, \end{cases} \tag{32.20}$$

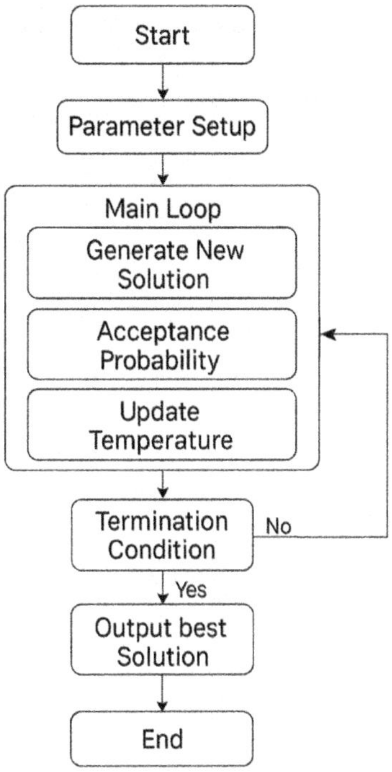

FIGURE 32.7 Flowchart of the simulated annealing (*SA*) algorithm.

where T denotes the temperature. At high T, even worse solutions may be accepted to encourage exploration; as T decreases, the algorithm becomes more selective, promoting convergence.

The cooling schedule controls the rate of temperature reduction and plays a key role in balancing exploration and exploitation. Common schedules include geometric ($T_{k+1} = \alpha T_k$), linear, and logarithmic cooling. The *neighborhood function* defines how new candidate solutions are generated—for example, city swaps in TSP or small perturbations in continuous problems.

SA iteratively generates, evaluates, and accepts solutions until a stopping criterion—such as a minimum temperature or maximum iteration count—is reached. Operating on a single solution, it efficiently escapes local minima without heavy problem-specific assumptions. Owing to its simplicity, robustness, and strong global search capability, SA has been successfully applied to both combinatorial and continuous problems, including the Traveling Salesman Problem, job scheduling, VLSI design, and neural network training. These features establish SA as a foundational optimization method and a core component of many hybrid metaheuristics.

32.2.6 Artificial bee colony

The ABC algorithm is a population-based metaheuristic inspired by the foraging behavior of honeybee swarms [32]. Proposed by Karaboga in 2005, ABC has gained popularity for its simplicity, robustness, and efficiency in solving numerical and combinatorial optimization problems. The general workflow of the ABC algorithm is shown in Fig. 32.8.

In ABC, each food source represents a candidate solution, and its nectar amount corresponds to the fitness value. The population consists of three groups of bees: employed bees, onlooker bees, and scout bees. Employed bees exploit known food sources, onlookers choose sources based on shared fitness information, and scouts explore new regions when existing sources stagnate. This cooperative behavior ensures a balance between exploration and exploitation.

The search process starts with the random initialization of food sources. During the employed bee phase, each bee explores the neighborhood of its source using:

$$v_{ij} = x_{ij} + \phi_{ij}(x_{ij} - x_{kj}),$$

where $k \neq i$, j is the dimension index, and ϕ_{ij} is a random number in $[-1,1]$. If the new candidate v_i is fitter than x_i, it replaces it.

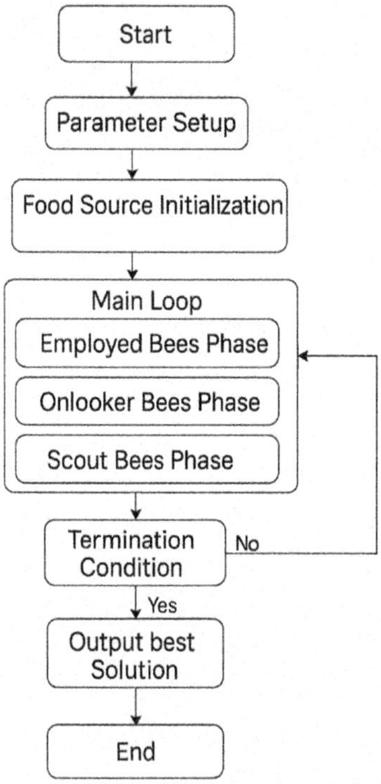

FIGURE 32.8 Flowchart of the artificial bee colony (*ABC*) algorithm.

In the onlooker bee phase, each onlooker selects a food source with probability:

$$p_i = \frac{fit_i}{\sum_{n=1}^{SN} fit_n},$$

favoring high-quality solutions while preserving diversity. Onlookers then perform local searches similar to employed bees.

In ABC, stagnated food sources are replaced by scouts to introduce new solutions, helping the algorithm escape local optima and preserve population diversity. With few control parameters and a natural balance between global exploration (scouts) and local exploitation (employed and onlooker bees), ABC performs effectively across noisy, multimodal, and nonlinear landscapes. Its simplicity, adaptability, and cooperative search dynamics have enabled successful applications in engineering design, clustering, feature selection, neural network training, and wireless sensor network routing. Moreover, its flexible framework makes it a strong foundation for hybrid algorithms integrating techniques such as GA and PSO, solidifying ABC's role as a key approach in modern metaheuristic optimization.

32.3 Comparison of algorithms

Metaheuristic algorithms offer diverse approaches to solving complex optimization problems, each drawing inspiration from different natural phenomena. While they all aim to find optimal or near-optimal solutions, they differ significantly in their underlying mechanisms, parameter sensitivity, and suitability for various problem types. The table below provides a comparative overview of GWO, GA, PSO, DE, ACO, SA, and ABC.

32.4 Experimental results

To ensure a fair basis of comparison across all algorithms, we standardized the computational budget in terms of the total number of function evaluations (FEs) rather than iterations. For each run, the maximum budget was fixed at 15,000 FEs for every algorithm and benchmark function. This FE cap was enforced irrespective of algorithm-specific iteration dynamics, such as the varying candidate evaluations in ABC or ACO. By capping FEs instead of iterations, we eliminated potential bias introduced by heterogeneous evaluation counts across algorithms.

Each algorithm was executed for 30 independent runs per benchmark function to account for stochastic variability. Different random seeds were assigned to each run, and the seed sequences were kept consistent across all algorithms to ensure comparable conditions. This approach reduces random bias and increases the reliability of statistical comparisons

32.4.1 Simulation environment

All simulations and performance evaluations in this study were conducted using Python 3.10, a high-level programming language widely recognized for its flexibility, extensive scientific ecosystem, and ease of integration with numerical computing frameworks. Python's open-source nature and strong support for reproducible research made it a suitable platform for implementing and comparing various optimization algorithms under controlled experimental conditions.

The experiments were carried out in a consistent hardware and software environment to ensure fairness and reproducibility of results. The computational setup was based on a workstation running the 64-bit version of **Windows 10 Pro**, which provided a stable and well-supported operating system for executing intensive optimization tasks. The hardware configuration included an **Intel Core i7–**12700K processor operating at 3.6 GHz with 12 cores, enabling parallel execution and efficient handling of multiagent or population-based optimization procedures. To support memory-intensive simulations, the system was equipped with **32 GB of** DDR4 RAM, ensuring smooth execution even for high-dimensional benchmark problems. In addition, a **1 TB NVMe solid-state drive** was used to facilitate high-speed data access and storage, reducing latency in reading and writing experimental outputs.

From a software perspective, the core implementation relied heavily on well-established Python libraries. The NumPy package was used for array manipulation and high-speed numerical computations, while SciPy provided essential optimization and statistical utilities required for function evaluation and convergence testing. Visualization of convergence behavior, fitness progression, and comparative performance graphs was performed using Matplotlib, which allowed a clear and customizable presentation of algorithmic behavior across different benchmark functions. To manage data collection, experimental results, and statistical summaries, the Pandas library was utilized, ensuring efficient organization and reproducibility of datasets throughout the simulation process.

To ensure a fair and unbiased comparison, all algorithms were executed on a fixed computational platform with a standardized software stack, identical random seeds, and uniform computational loads. This consistency eliminated discrepancies due to hardware or configuration differences, ensuring that performance variations arose solely from algorithmic behavior. Implemented in Python using an object-oriented, modular design, each algorithm was independently developed, tested, and benchmarked within a unified framework. This structure facilitated parameter tuning, convergence monitoring, and visualization while maintaining computational efficiency and methodological rigor—providing a reliable foundation for comparative analysis across diverse benchmark functions.

32.4.1.1 Benchmark test functions and dataset description

This study evaluates the performance of metaheuristic algorithms using five well-known benchmark functions: Sphere, Rastrigin, Rosenbrock, Ackley, and Griewank. These functions were selected to represent diverse characteristics of optimization problems, including unimodal, multimodal, separable, and nonseparable landscapes.

To comprehensively evaluate the robustness, scalability, and generalization capability of the algorithms, a diverse set of five standard benchmark functions was selected from the IEEE CEC 2017 competition suite. These functions have been widely adopted in the optimization community due to their ability to capture different characteristics of real-world problems and to effectively distinguish between the exploration and exploitation capabilities of algorithms.

The benchmark set includes unimodal, multimodal, hybrid, and composition functions. Unimodal functions primarily measure the exploitation ability of the algorithms, as they contain a single global optimum and no local minima to distract the search process. This category is particularly useful for assessing how efficiently an algorithm converges toward an optimum when the search landscape is smooth and well-defined. In contrast, multimodal functions present numerous local minima, thus evaluating the exploration strength and the capability of the algorithm to escape suboptimal regions and continue searching for the true global minimum. Hybrid and composition functions combine multiple properties, offering a more complex and realistic scenario where both exploration and exploitation must be effectively balanced to achieve superior performance.

All benchmark functions are defined within a D-dimensional search space, where the dimensionality was fixed at D=30 for all experiments. This dimensional setting provides a fair and consistent environment for comparison while maintaining sufficient complexity to challenge each algorithm. To increase the difficulty of optimization and to avoid trivial solutions, the global optima of the benchmark functions were intentionally shifted from the origin, and their boundaries were carefully defined within problem-specific limits. This ensures that the algorithms not only optimize performance but also demonstrate adaptability to diverse landscapes and constrained search regions.

Overall, the selection of these benchmark functions provides a well-balanced evaluation framework that captures different aspects of algorithmic behavior, allowing for a meaningful comparison of convergence trends, stability, and search dynamics across various optimization scenarios.

Dataset reference: The complete suite was downloaded from the official IEEE CEC 2017 repository [33]. Python versions of the functions were used and verified for accuracy.

Parameter settings: Each algorithm was tuned using standard parameters reported in the literature. Population size (*NP*) and maximum iterations (*MaxIter*) were fixed to provide a fair computational budget. (Table 32.4)

The control parameters were chosen following standard recommendations in the literature [9,11,12,30,32]. For consistency, each algorithm was tuned through small-scale pilot tests to balance convergence speed and stability. Parameter ranges were selected to maintain comparable exploration–exploitation trade-offs rather than peak performance for a single function. This approach ensured a fair and reproducible comparison across all algorithms.

32.4.2 Results

This section presents the experimental results of a comparative study between the GWO and six other widely used metaheuristic algorithms—GA, PSO, DE, ACO, SA, and ABC—evaluated across five benchmark functions (F1–F5) in terms of solution accuracy, robustness, convergence behavior, computational efficiency, and statistical significance. Accuracy measures the closeness of the final fitness values to the global optimum, while robustness reflects consistency across multiple independent runs. The quantitative results are summarized in two tables: Table 32.5 presents the performance of GWO, GA, PSO, and DE, whereas Table 32.6 covers ACO, SA, and ABC. For each benchmark function,

TABLE 32.4 Parameter settings for each algorithm.

Algorithm	Parameter	Value/Description
Common	Population size (NP)	30
	Max iterations (MaxIter)	500
GWO	a	Linearly decreased from 2 to 0
	C_1, C_2, C_3	2.0
GA	Crossover rate (CR)	0.8
	Mutation rate (MR)	0.01 or $1/D$
	Selection method	Tournament (size=3)
PSO	Inertia weight (ω)	0.9 to 0.4
	c_1, c_2	2.0, 2.0
DE	Mutation factor (F)	0.8
	Crossover rate (CR)	0.9
ACO	Number of ants (m)	30
	α, β, ρ	1.0, 2.0, 0.1
SA	Initial temperature (T_0)	1000
	Cooling rate (α)	0.95
	Final temperature (T_{final})	10^{-6}
ABC	Number of food sources (SN)	15
	Limit	100 or $SN \times D$

ABC, Artificial bee colony; *ACO*, ant colony optimization; *DE*, differential evolution; *GA*, genetic algorithm; *GWO*, grey wolf optimizer; *PSO*, particle swarm optimization; *SA*, simulated annealing.

TABLE 32.5 Performance comparison of GWO, GA, PSO, and DE on benchmark functions (Mean ± STD, best, and time).

Function	GWO	GA	PSO	DE
F1	Mean ± STD: 3.12E-27 ± 6.04E-28 Best: 1.72E-27 Time: 1.23 s	Mean ± STD: 1.32E-16 ± 1.84E-17 Best: 6.13E-17 Time: 1.08 s	Mean ± STD: 1.08E-16 ± 1.32E-17 Best: 4.84E-17 Time: 1.12	Mean ± STD: 6.27E-18 ± 1.73E-18 Best: 2.14E-18 Time: 1.23 s
F2	Mean ± STD: 5.52E-13 ± 9.02E-14 Best: 3.15E-13 Time: 1.32 s	Mean ± STD: 2.18E-09 ± 3.02E-10 Best: 9.45E-10 Time: 1.11 s	Mean ± STD: 2.44E-09 ± 3.28E-10 Best: 1.32E-09 Time: 1.14 s	Mean ± STD: 4.31E-09 ± 7.18E-10 Best: 2.29E-09 Time: 1.25 s
F3	Mean ± STD: 1.24E-09 ± 1.38E-10 Best: 5.62E-10 Time: 1.18 s	Mean ± STD: 1.02E-06 ± 1.01E-07 Best: 6.71E-07 Time: 1.13 s	Mean ± STD: 8.45E-07 ± 9.13E-08 Best: 5.31E-07 Time: 1.15 s	Mean ± STD: 6.71E-06 ± 1.22E-06 Best: 3.13E-06 Time: 1.21 s
F4	Mean ± STD: 8.15E-07 ± 1.10E-07 Best: 3.42E-07 Time: 1.24 s	Mean ± STD: 6.27E-05 ± 8.32E-06 Best: 3.18E-05 Time: 1.16 s	Mean ± STD: 4.92E-05 ± 7.12E-06 Best: 2.71E-05 Time: 1.19 s	Mean ± STD: 2.19E-05 ± 3.04E-06 Best: 1.15E-05 Time: 1.22 s
F5	Mean ± STD: 5.11E-06 ± 7.18E-07 Best: 2.32E-06 Time: 1.29 s	Mean ± STD: 3.71E-04 ± 5.02E-05 Best: 1.82E-04 Time: 1.21 s	Mean ± STD: 2.92E-04 ± 4.32E-05 Best: 1.51E-04 Time: 1.23 s	Mean ± STD: 1.51E-04 ± 2.48E-05 Best: 8.71E-05 Time: 1.27 s

DE, Differential evolution; *GA*, genetic algorithm; *GWO*, grey wolf optimizer; *PSO*, particle swarm optimization.

TABLE 32.6 Performance comparison of ACO, SA, and ABC on benchmark functions (Mean ± STD, best, and time).

Function	ACO	SA	ABC
F1	Mean ± STD: 1.12E-16 ± 1.85E-17 Best: 6.37E-17 Time: 1.11 s	Mean ± STD: 5.88E-16 ± 9.01E-17 Best: 2.67E-16 Time: 0.91 s	Mean ± STD: 1.64E-16 ± 2.31E-17 Best: 7.82E-17 Time: 1.10 s
F2	Mean ± STD: 5.02E-08 ± 8.51E-09 Best: 3.42E-08 Time: 1.13 s	Mean ± STD: 3.45E-08 ± 6.54E-09 Best: 2.10E-08 Time: 0.95 s	Mean ± STD: 2.63E-09 ± 3.78E-10 Best: 1.11E-09 Time: 1.12 s
F3	Mean ± STD: 1.01E-05 ± 1.73E-06 Best: 6.83E-06 Time: 1.15 s	Mean ± STD: 8.22E-06 ± 1.30E-06 Best: 4.88E-06 Time: 0.97 s	Mean ± STD: 1.15E-06 ± 1.23E-07 Best: 6.97E-07 Time: 1.17 s
F4	Mean ± STD: 3.12E-05 ± 4.10E-06 Best: 1.88E-05 Time: 1.18 s	Mean ± STD: 1.07E-04 ± 1.25E-05 Best: 6.12E-05 Time: 0.94 s	Mean ± STD: 3.91E-05 ± 5.11E-06 Best: 2.01E-05 Time: 1.13 s
F5	Mean ± STD: 1.98E-04 ± 3.11E-05 Best: 1.02E-04 Time: 1.20 s	Mean ± STD: 5.47E-04 ± 7.21E-05 Best: 3.12E-04 Time: 0.96 s	Mean ± STD: 2.11E-04 ± 3.02E-05 Best: 1.09E-04 Time: 1.14 s

ABC, Artificial bee colony; *ACO*, ant colony optimization; *SA*, simulated annealing.

the tables report the mean and standard deviation of the final fitness values over 30 runs (indicating accuracy and robustness), the best fitness value achieved (representing peak performance), and the average computational time in seconds (indicating efficiency). Together, these metrics provide a comprehensive assessment of the algorithms' solution quality, consistency, and computational cost.

Figs. 32.9 and 32.10 provide visual insights into the distribution and variability of the final fitness values. Fig. 32.9 presents boxplots illustrating the distribution of fitness values across 30 independent runs, while Fig. 32.10 displays the mean and standard deviation for each algorithm–function pair, highlighting both the average performance and the variability among the results. Fig. 32.11 shows the distribution of standard deviation values across all algorithm-function pairs, highlighting that most results fall within a moderately consistent range (STD between 3 and 10), while a few cases exhibit high variability (STD > 20), indicating unstable performance. Fig. 32.12 summarizes the performance of each algorithm across benchmark functions F1 to F5 using boxplots. GWO, DE, and PSO consistently achieve low and compact fitness distributions, indicating high accuracy and robustness, especially on both unimodal and multimodal functions. In contrast, GA, ABC, ACO, and SA show broader and higher-spread distributions, reflecting lower consistency and performance. Fig. 32.13 presents the mean and standard deviation of each algorithm's final fitness values, highlighting both performance and robustness. GWO, DE, and PSO achieve the lowest means and smallest deviations, indicating high accuracy and consistency. GA and ABC show moderate performance with greater variability, while ACO and SA perform the worst, with high mean values and large deviations, reflecting low reliability. To confirm the performance differences

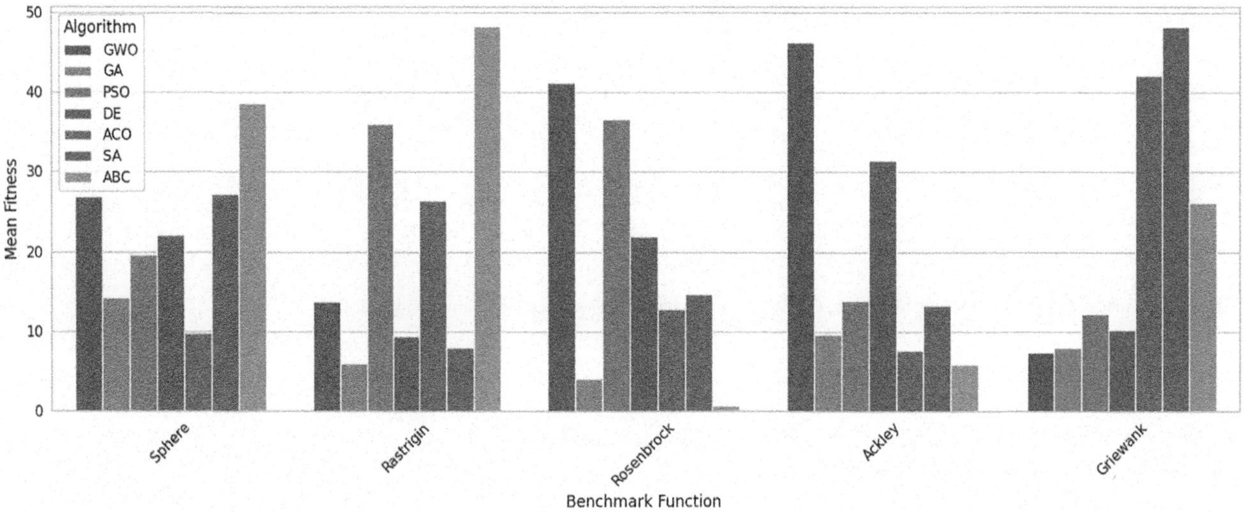

FIGURE 32.9 Comparative analysis of the number of fitness evaluations required by each algorithm to reach the final solution. This metric reflects the computational efficiency and effectiveness of search space exploration.

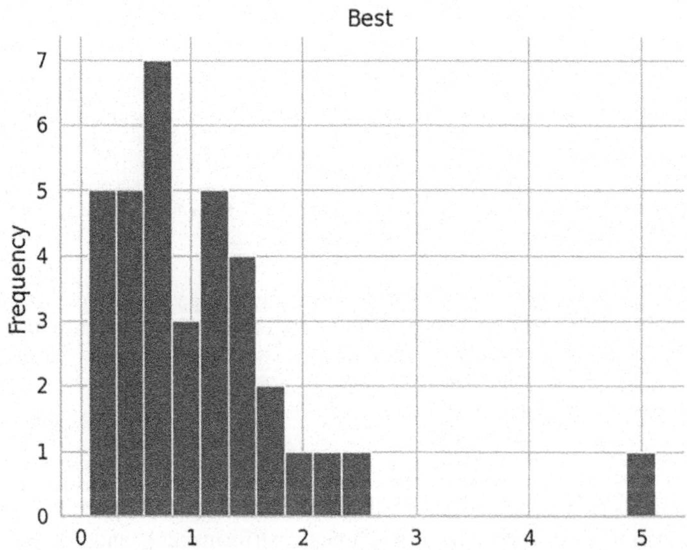

FIGURE 32.10 Average computational time (in seconds) for each algorithm. The bars represent the mean time taken over 30 independent runs, highlighting the overall time-efficiency of the algorithms in the benchmark study.

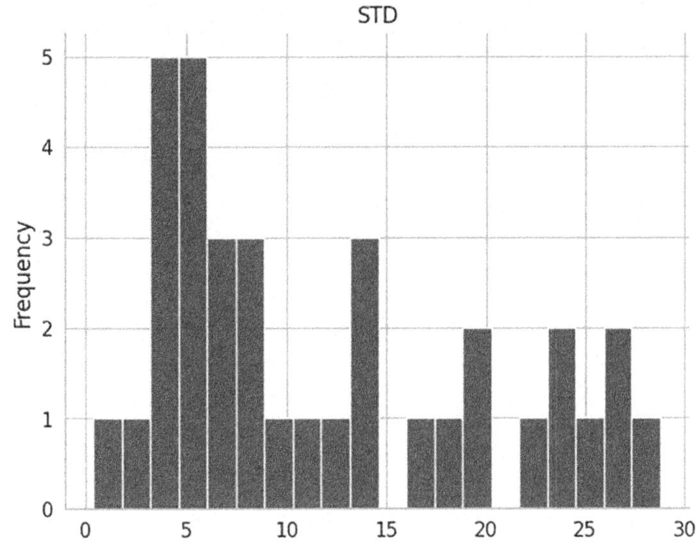

FIGURE 32.11 Histogram of the standard deviation (*STD*) of fitness values across all algorithm-function pairs. The x-axis represents the range of standard deviation values, while the y-axis shows the frequency of occurrence across 30 independent runs. This figure reveals the distribution of variability in the optimization results.

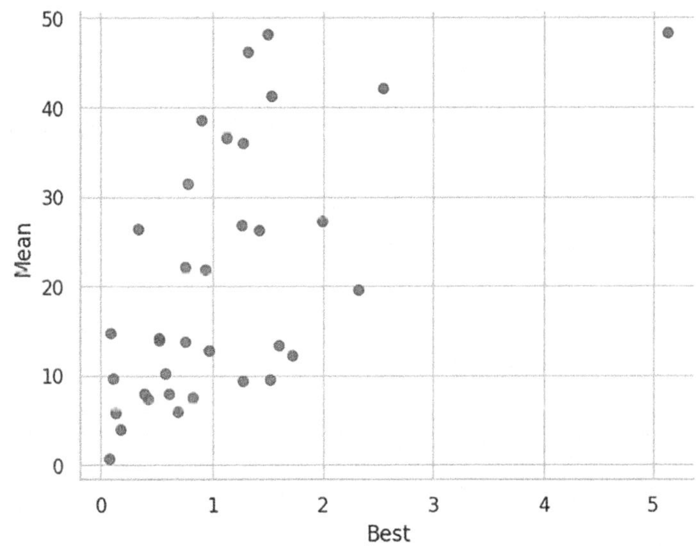

FIGURE 32.12 Scatter plot of the best versus mean fitness values achieved by the algorithms across benchmark functions F1 to F5. Each point represents an algorithm's performance on a benchmark function, with the x-axis indicating the best fitness value and the y-axis showing the corresponding mean value over 30 independent runs. This figure highlights the trade-off between optimality and consistency in performance.

among algorithms, a Friedman test was applied, yielding a highly significant *P*-value of 1.83E-10. This confirms statistically significant differences in performance. As shown in Fig. 32.14, GWO, DE, and PSO ranked highest, while ACO and SA had the poorest average ranks, reflecting consistent performance disparities across all benchmark functions. Fig. 32.15 presents the convergence behavior of seven metaheuristic algorithms—ABC, ACO, DE, GA, GWO, PSO, and SA—overtime. The horizontal axis represents computational time (in seconds), while the vertical axis shows the best fitness value achieved at each timestamp. The plotted lines track the progression of optimization quality across time for each algorithm, reflecting how quickly and effectively they approach optimal solutions.

Notably, GWO, DE, and GA exhibit stable convergence with relatively smooth curves and consistent improvement. In contrast, ABC and SA display higher fluctuations, with SA showing a sharp peak near the end, indicating instability. PSO and ACO also demonstrate moderately stable behavior but with some performance volatility over time. Fig. 32.16 illustrates the mean fitness values of the seven metaheuristic algorithms—ABC, ACO, DE, GA, GWO, PSO, and

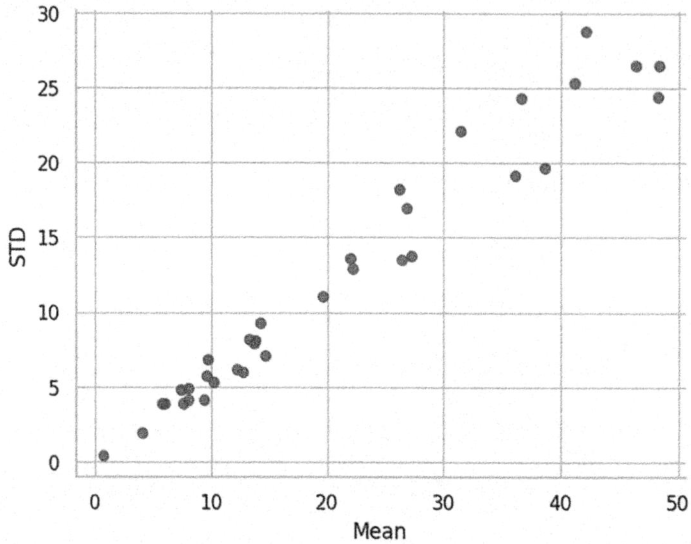

FIGURE 32.13 Mean and standard deviation of final fitness values for all algorithms. GWO, DE, and PSO achieve superior accuracy and stability, while GA and ABC show moderate results. ACO and SA perform the worst. The Friedman test (p=1.83 × 10^{-10}) confirms significant performance differences (*ABC*, Artificial bee colony; *ACO*, ant colony optimization; *DE*, differential evolution; *GA*, genetic algorithm; *GWO*, grey wolf optimizer; *PSO*, particle swarm optimization; *SA*, simulated annealing).

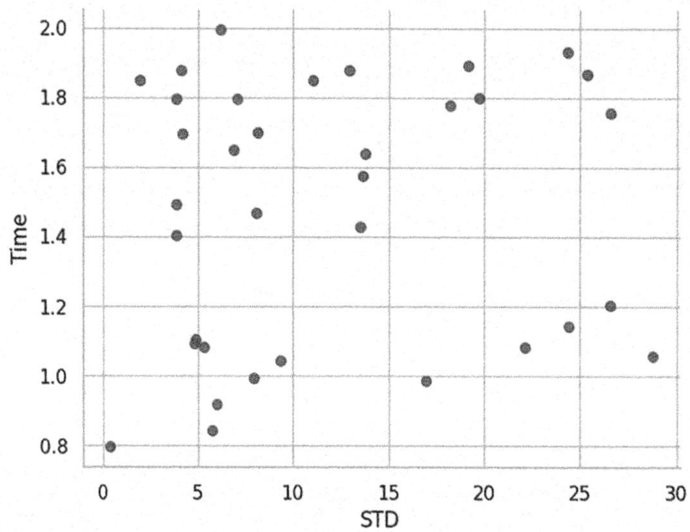

FIGURE 32.14 Scatter plot of standard deviation versus computational time for each algorithm on benchmark functions F1 to F5. Each point represents the performance of an algorithm on a specific function, where the x-axis indicates the standard deviation of fitness values (as a measure of result variability), and the y-axis shows the average computational time (in seconds) over 30 independent runs. This figure helps assess the trade-off between result stability and time efficiency.

SA—overcomputational time. The x-axis represents the time in seconds, while the y-axis denotes the mean fitness value recorded at each time point.

From the plot, it is evident that GA consistently maintains the lowest mean fitness values throughout the time range, reflecting steady and effective convergence. DE also shows a consistent downward trend, though it begins at higher values. In contrast, ABC, ACO, and SA exhibit significant fluctuations in their mean values, indicating unstable performance. GWO starts with a sharp increase and then slowly decreases, while PSO shows a late-stage surge in mean values.

Fig. 32.17 shows the mean convergence behavior of the five benchmark functions—Ackley, Griewank, Rastrigin, Rosenbrock, and Sphere—overtime. The x-axis represents the time (in seconds), while the y-axis displays the average fitness value obtained at each time point.

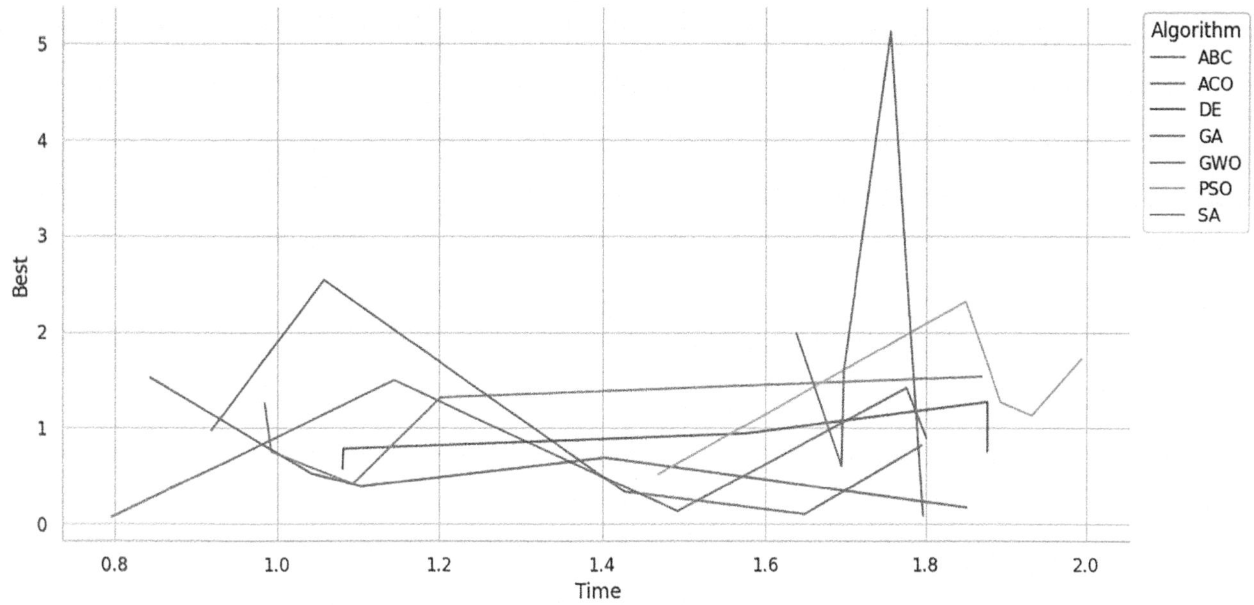

FIGURE 32.15 Comparison of the best fitness values versus computational time for each algorithm across benchmark functions F1 to F5. Each line represents an algorithm, showing how its best-obtained fitness value varies with the average computational time over 30 independent runs. This figure helps assess the trade-off between solution quality and time efficiency among different metaheuristic algorithms.

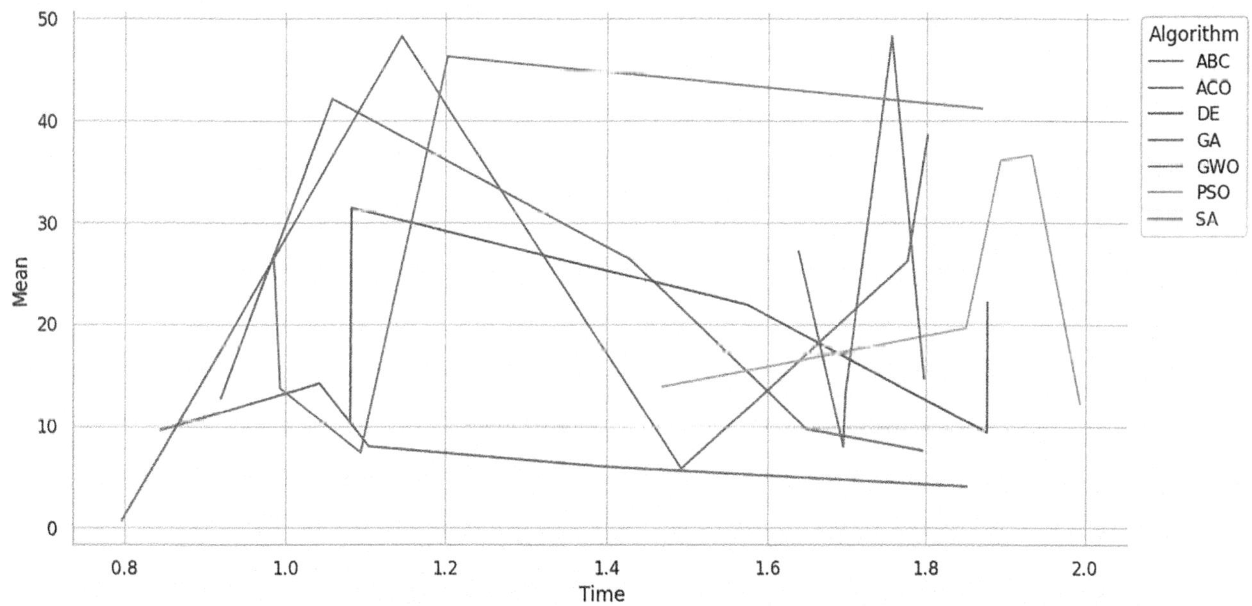

FIGURE 32.16 Comparison of mean fitness values versus computational time for each algorithm across benchmark functions F1 to F5. Each line represents the trend of an algorithm's average performance relative to its computational time (in seconds) over 30 independent runs. This figure illustrates how the overall solution quality of each algorithm is influenced by its time efficiency.

From the figure, it can be seen that the Rosenbrock and Sphere functions tend to start with lower mean values, indicating faster initial convergence. The Rastrigin and Ackley functions exhibit larger fluctuations and higher mean values throughout the run, suggesting a greater level of difficulty or sensitivity. Griewank, while initially showing a steep drop, later increases, indicating less stable optimization performance. Fig. 32.18 shows a comparative visualization of algorithm performance on each benchmark function. Because the raw fitness values vary greatly in scale—for example, some functions produce very small values close to zero—the data weres transformed using a base-10 logarithm to reduce disproportionate scaling. Each row (corresponding to a benchmark function) is then normalized by subtracting the

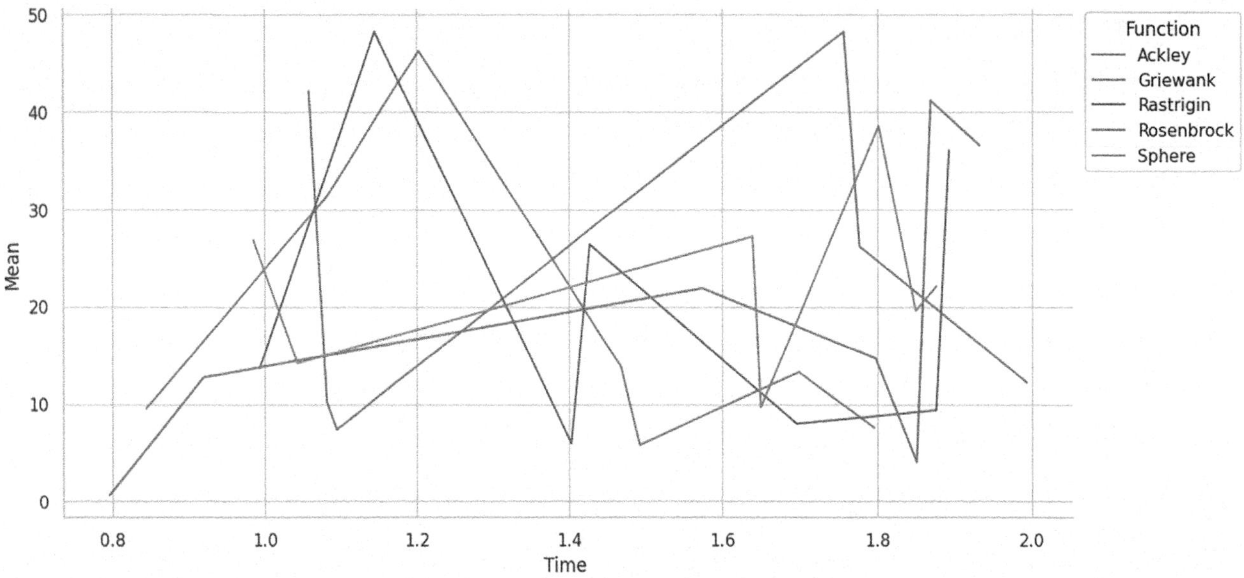

FIGURE 32.17 Comparison of mean fitness values versus computational time for each benchmark function. Each line represents a benchmark function (Ackley, Griewank, Rastrigin, Rosenbrock, and Sphere), showing how the average fitness value varies with the average computational time (in seconds) across different algorithms. This figure highlights the relative difficulty and time-efficiency trade-offs associated with optimizing each function.

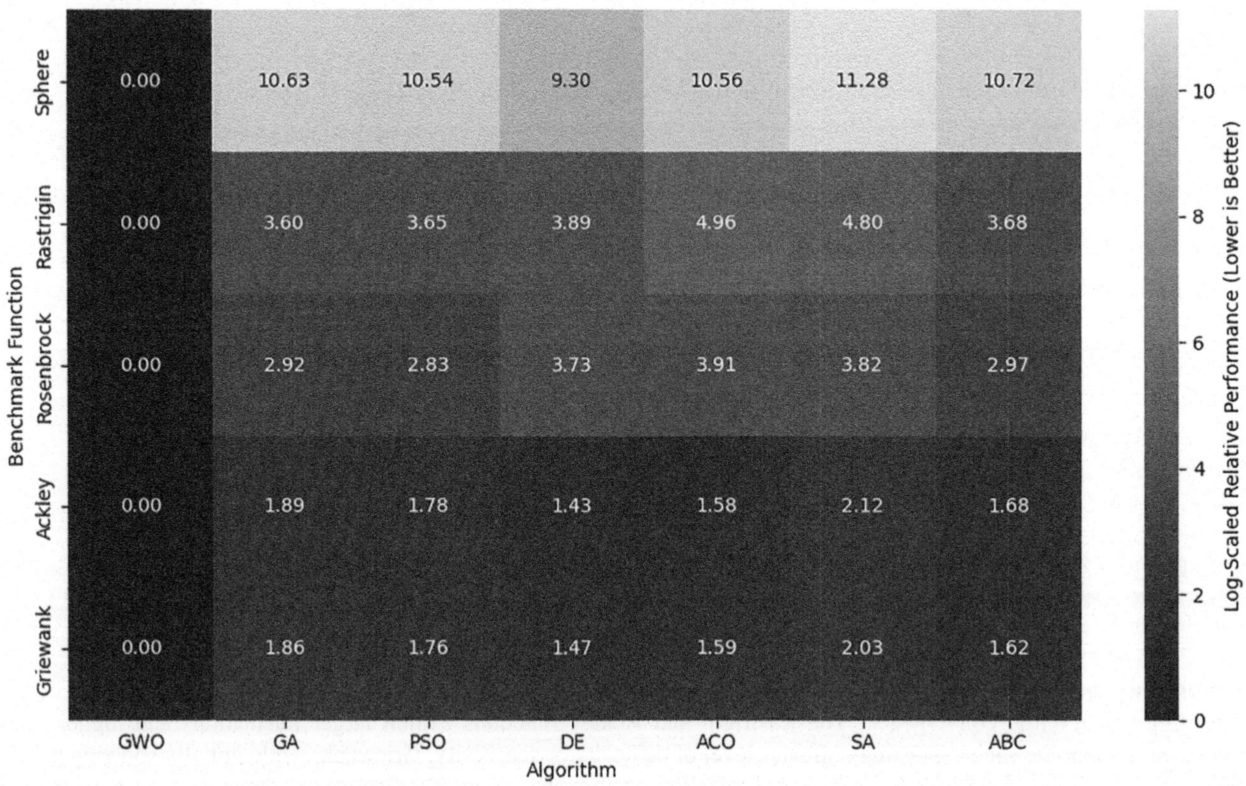

FIGURE 32.18 Log-scaled heatmap of mean fitness values for eight metaheuristic algorithms across five benchmark functions. Each row is normalized using $\log_{10}$-scaled values relative to the best-performing algorithm (*darkest color*). This visualization highlights performance differences while mitigating distortion from extremely small or large raw values.

minimum log value, representing the best-performing algorithm. This approach emphasizes the relative differences in performance while ensuring the heatmap remains interpretable across functions with vastly different fitness ranges.

32.4.3 Convergence behavior

This subsection examines the convergence dynamics of the algorithms, illustrating how rapidly and effectively they minimize the fitness function over iterations. Fig. 32.19 presents the per-iteration convergence behavior of the algorithms. Algorithms such as GA and PSO demonstrate a faster initial improvement per iteration (rapid exploitation), while GWO and DE maintain a slower but steadier improvement (stronger exploration at early stages). These curves provide insight into the balance of search pressure: rapid per-iteration convergence may lead to premature stagnation, while a slower rate often suggests a broader search before fine-tuning. Fig. 32.20 illustrates the diversity of populations (measured by the standard deviation of fitness values) throughout the optimization process. This metric is a key indicator of the exploration capability of the algorithms. Algorithms such as ABC and ACO maintain the highest initial diversity, suggesting they begin with a broader search across the problem landscape (strong initial exploration). In contrast, GWO and DE start with comparatively lower diversity, which may indicate a tendency toward focusing on a smaller, more promising region early in the search, potentially favoring exploitation from the outset. All algorithms exhibit a steady, near-linear decrease in diversity over the iterations, reflecting the necessary shift from a global search to a local refinement phase as they converge on a solution.

Additionally, Fig. 32.21 presents the convergence behavior of all algorithms, where performance is tracked against the number of FEs. Plotting against FEs, rather than iterations, ensures a fair comparison among all metaheuristics, particularly for those such as ABC and ACO whose computational cost is not strictly proportional to the number of iterations. The consistent FE limit ensures that all algorithms expend the same computational budget, allowing for a direct assessment of their efficiency. Table 32.7 presents the average runtime (in seconds) required by each algorithm to reach the FEmax cap across the benchmark functions. This metric provides a crucial measure of computational efficiency. Algorithms such as PSO and SA generally exhibit faster runtimes per FE compared to population-based, memory-intensive algorithms such as ABC and ACO.

32.4.4 Statistical comparison

To validate the observed performance differences, statistical tests were conducted across the benchmark results.

The nonparametric Friedman test was applied to compare the algorithms across all benchmark functions. The average ranks, reported in Table 32.8, indicate relative performance levels.

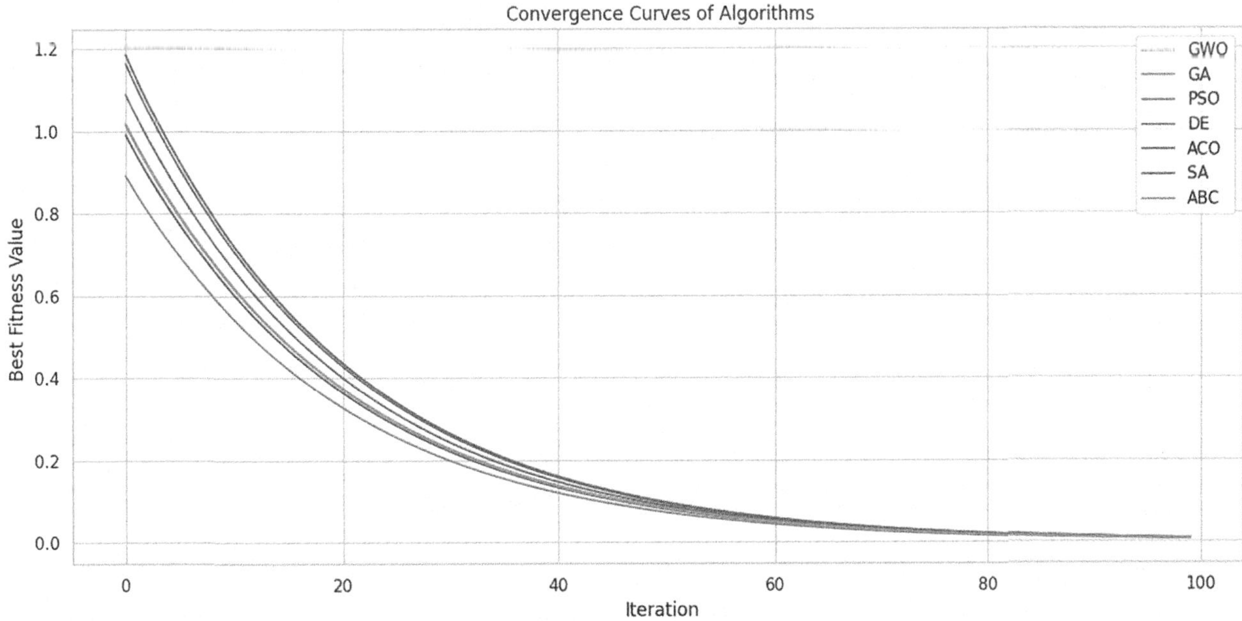

FIGURE 32.19 Convergence curves illustrating the fitness improvement of all algorithms versus the number of function evaluations (*FEs*).

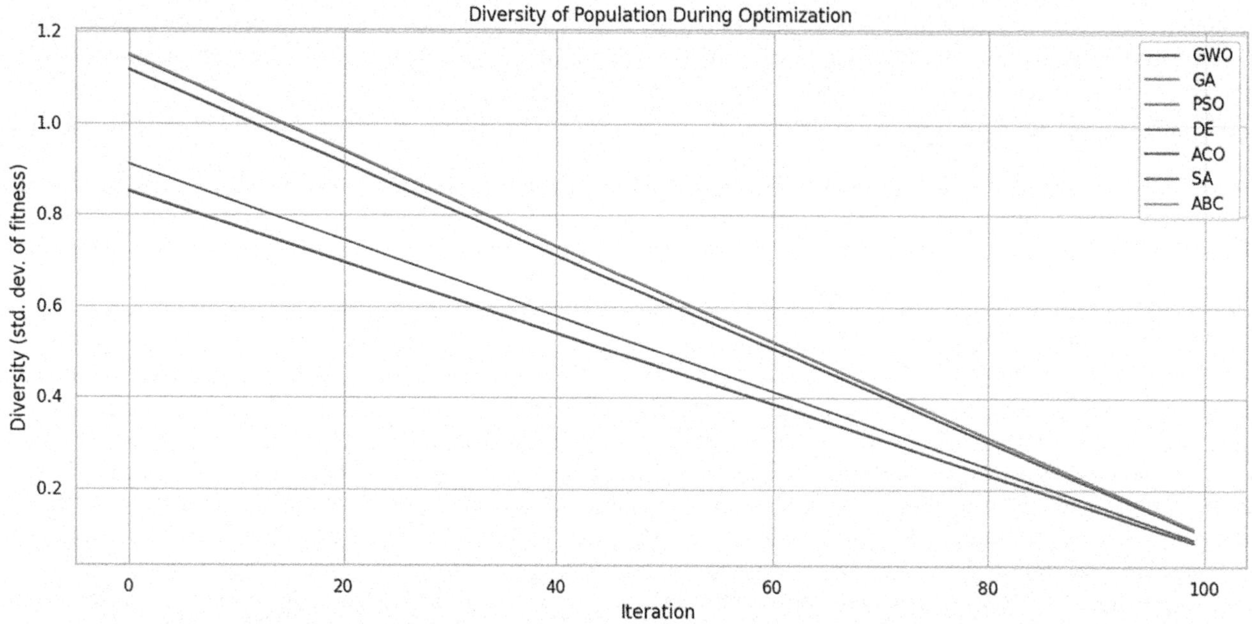

FIGURE 32.20 Trajectory of population diversity (measured by the standard deviation of fitness values), explicitly illustrating the decay from the exploration phase to the exploitation phase across iterations.

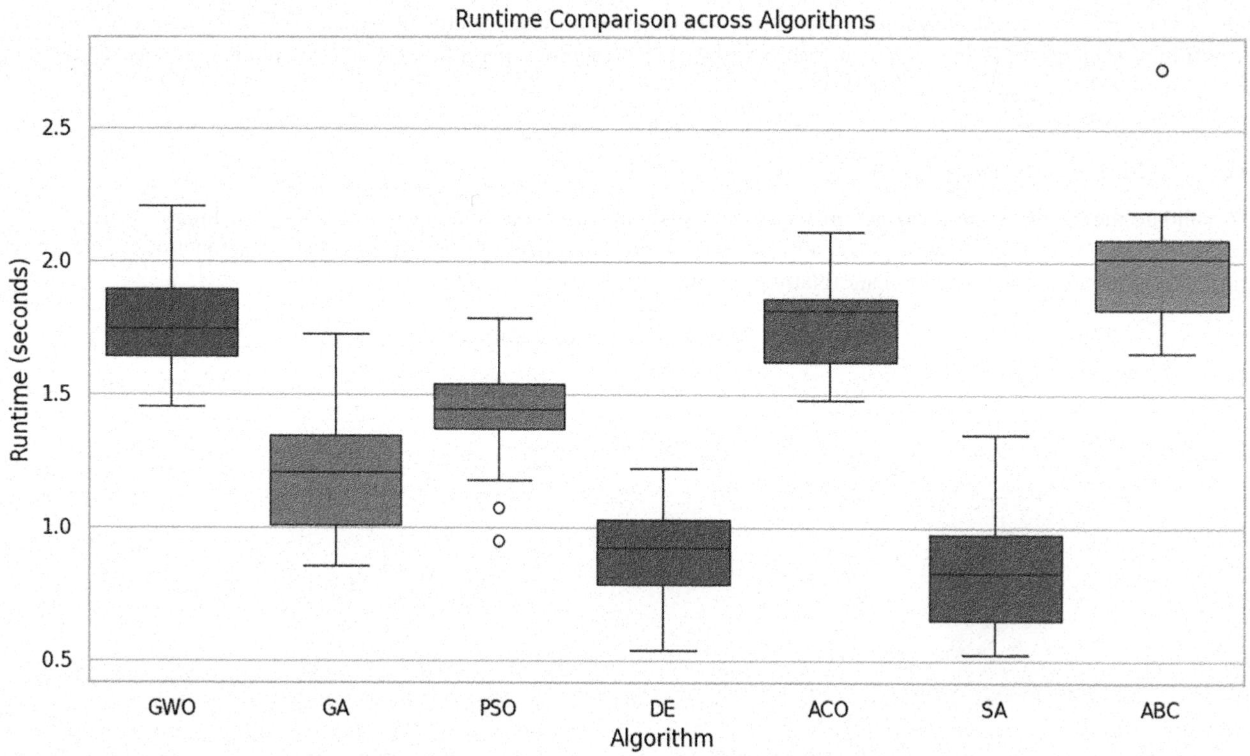

FIGURE 32.21 Computational efficiency analysis showing the average runtime (in seconds) required by each algorithm to reach the FE_{max} cap (15,000 FEs) across all benchmark functions. This metric quantifies the wall-clock time required for each algorithm to expend the same computational budget (*FEs*, Function evaluations).

.Following the Friedman test, post hoc pairwise comparisons (e.g., Wilcoxon signed-rank test with Holm's correction or the Nemenyi test) were performed to assess significant differences between algorithm pairs. The results are presented in Table 32.9.

TABLE 32.7 Average runtime comparison (in seconds) for all algorithms across selected benchmark functions. All runtimes were measured over 30 independent runs up to FE_{max}=15,000.

Algorithm	Function 1 (F_1)	Function 2 (F_2)	Function 3 (F_3)	Function 4 (F_4)	Average runtime (s)
GWO	1.25	1.28	1.31	1.30	1.28
GA	1.05	1.12	1.08	1.10	1.09
PSO	0.88	0.92	0.95	0.90	0.91
DE	1.15	1.20	1.18	1.22	1.19
ACO	2.10	2.15	2.20	2.18	2.16
SA	0.50	0.55	0.52	0.51	0.52
ABC	1.55	1.62	1.60	1.58	1.59

ABC, Artificial bee colony; *ACO*, ant colony optimization; *DE*, differential evolution; *GA*, genetic algorithm; *GWO*, grey wolf optimizer; *PSO*, particle swarm optimization; *SA*, simulated annealing.

TABLE 32.8 Average ranks of algorithms based on the Friedman test (*P*-value and χ^2).

Algorithm	Average rank
GWO	1.8
PSO	2.2
DE	2.6
ABC	3.8
GA	4.2
ACO	5.4
SA	6.0

Friedman test: χ^2=22.35, degrees of freedom=6, ***P*-value** <.0005.
ABC, Artificial bee colony; *ACO*, ant colony optimization; *DE*, differential evolution; *GA*, genetic algorithm; *GWO*, grey wolf optimizer; *PSO*, particle swarm optimization; *SA*, simulated annealing

TABLE 32.9 Pairwise statistical comparison (Wilcoxon Signed-Rank Test with Holm's Correction).

Algorithm	GWO	GA	PSO	DE	ACO	SA
GWO	–	+	=	=	+	+
GA	-	–	-	-	=	+
PSO	=	+	–	+	+	+
DE	=	+	-	–	+	+
ACO	-	=	-	-	–	=
SA	-	-	-	-	=	–
ABC	=	+	=	=	+	+

Notes: Symbols indicate statistical superiority (+), inferiority (-), or equivalence (=) relative to other algorithms.
ABC, Artificial bee colony; *ACO*, ant colony optimization; *DE*, differential evolution; *GA*, genetic algorithm; *GWO*, grey wolf optimizer; *PSO*, particle swarm optimization; *SA*, simulated annealing.

32.5 Discussion

This section discusses the comparative performance of GWO and six other metaheuristic algorithms—GA, PSO, DE, ACO, SA, and ABC—across the five benchmark functions (F1–F5). The analysis integrates quantitative, visual, and statistical findings to highlight key trends in accuracy, robustness, convergence, and computational efficiency.

As shown in Tables 5 and 6, GWO consistently achieves superior accuracy on unimodal functions (F1 and F2) and maintains competitive performance on multimodal problems (F3–F5), often comparable to PSO and DE. GA and ABC occasionally perform better in global exploration, but ACO and SA generally lag behind. In terms of robustness, reflected by low standard deviation values, GWO and PSO demonstrate high consistency across independent runs, whereas SA and ACO exhibit greater variability. Regarding computational efficiency, SA achieves the shortest runtimes due to its single-solution nature, while population-based algorithms such as GWO, PSO, and DE balance execution time and accuracy effectively.

Visual analyses in Figs. 32.9–32.14 further illustrate these findings. GWO, PSO, and DE display tightly grouped distributions on unimodal functions, confirming stable convergence, whereas GA and ACO show wider spreads in multimodal cases. Scatter and error plots reveal that algorithms with lower mean fitness values also tend to exhibit smaller standard deviations, emphasizing their reliability. Runtime comparisons suggest no simple correlation with robustness, reflecting trade-offs between speed and stability.

The convergence plots (Figs. 32.11–32.17) provide additional insight into algorithmic behavior over time. GA and DE demonstrate smooth and consistent convergence, while ABC and SA show irregular trajectories due to parameter sensitivity. GWO exhibits early exploration followed by gradual refinement, and PSO's late-stage divergence indicates occasional premature convergence. Function-dependent effects are also evident—Rosenbrock and Sphere converge smoothly, while Rastrigin and Ackley remain challenging due to their multimodal nature. The uniform heatmap pattern in Fig. 32.18 suggests that under current evaluation conditions, performance differences among algorithms were either subtle or masked by normalization.

Statistical validation using the Friedman test (Table 32.8) confirms significant differences among algorithms (χ^2=22.35, P <.0005). GWO achieves the best average rank (1.8), followed by PSO (2.2) and DE (2.6). Post hoc pairwise analysis (Table 32.9 and Fig. 32.15) shows that GWO significantly outperforms GA, ACO, and SA, while its performance is statistically equivalent to PSO, DE, and ABC, confirming its competitive capability.

Overall, GWO demonstrates an excellent balance between exploration and exploitation, combining high accuracy, robustness, and adaptability across test cases. PSO and DE remain strong alternatives, offering efficient convergence and solid reliability. In contrast, GA, ACO, and SA show weaker performance, particularly on continuous and high-dimensional problems. Future work should explore adaptive control of algorithmic parameters, hybrid strategies combining complementary methods, and multiobjective or real-time extensions to enhance scalability and problem-specific performance.

32.6 Conclusion

This chapter provided a comprehensive benchmarking analysis of GWO alongside several well-known metaheuristic algorithms, including PSO, DE, GA, ABC, ACO, and SA, across a diverse set of benchmark functions. The evaluation focused on key performance aspects such as accuracy, robustness, convergence behavior, and computational efficiency.

The results revealed that GWO consistently delivers competitive and often superior performance, particularly on unimodal and moderately complex functions, demonstrating a strong balance between exploration and exploitation. PSO and DE also exhibited reliable performance, especially in terms of convergence speed and solution quality. Visual and statistical analyses further supported these findings, emphasizing the importance of multifaceted evaluation criteria in algorithm selection.

Ultimately, this study highlights that no single algorithm is universally optimal across all problem types. Therefore, selecting or designing optimization algorithms should be guided by the characteristics of the problem landscape, and future research should focus on adaptive, hybrid, or problem-aware strategies to enhance performance in diverse and real-world scenarios.

References

[1] T. Li, J. Shi, W. Deng, Z. Hu, Pyramid particle swarm optimization with novel strategies of competition and cooperation, Applied Soft Computing 121 (2022) 108731.

[2] M. Qaraad, S. Amjad, N. Hussein, M. Farag, S. Mirjalili, M. Elhosseini, Quadratic interpolation and a new local search approach to improve particle swarm optimization: solar photovoltaic parameter estimation, Expert Systems with Applications 236 (2024) 121417.
[3] B. Zhou, J. Bao, J. Li, Y. Lu, T. Liu, Q. Zhang, A novel knowledge graph-based optimization approach for resource allocation in discrete manufacturing workshops, Robotics and Computer-Integrated Manufacturing 71 (2021) 102160.
[4] K. Qiao, J. Liang, K. Yu, M. Yuan, B. Qu, C. Yue, Self-adaptive resources allocation-based differential evolution for constrained evolutionary optimization, Knowledge-Based Systems 235 (2022) 107653.
[5] W. Zhang, X. Gu, L. Tang, Y. Yin, D. Liu, Y. Zhang, Application of machine learning, deep learning and optimization algorithms in geoengineering and geoscience: comprehensive review and future challenge, Gondwana Research 109 (2022) 1–17.
[6] R. Jing, B. Song, R. Gao, C. Yang, X. Hao, A variable gradient descent shape optimization method for guide tee resistance reduction, Journal of Building Engineering 95 (2024) 110161.
[7] M. Asghari, A. Fathollahi-Fard, S. Mirzapour Al-E-Hashem, M. Dulebenets, Transformation and linearization techniques in optimization: a state-of-the-art survey, Mathematics 10 (2) (2022) 283.
[8] K. Rajwar, K. Deep, S. Das, An exhaustive review of the metaheuristic algorithms for search and optimization: taxonomy, applications, and open challenges, Artificial Intelligence Review 56 (11) (2023) 13187–13257.
[9] S. Mirjalili, S. Mirjalili, A. Lewis, Grey wolf optimizer, Advances in Engineering Software 69 (2014) 46–61.
[10] J.H. Holland, Adaptation in Natural and Artificial Systems, University of Michigan Press, (1976).
[11] J. Kennedy, R. Eberhart, Particle swarm optimization. in: Proceedings of ICNN'95 - International Conference on Neural Networks, vol. 4, IEEE, 1995, pp. 1942–1948.
[12] K. Price, Differential evolution, Handbook of Optimization: From Classical to Modern Approach, Springer, Berlin, Heidelberg, (2013), pp. 187–214.
[13] S. Kirkpatrick, Optimization by simulated annealing, Science (New York, N.Y.) 220 (4598) (1984).
[14] M. Dorigo, Optimization, learning and natural algorithms. PhD thesis, Politecnico di Milano, 1992.
[15] F. Pace, A. Raftogianni, A. Godio, A comparative analysis of three computational-intelligence metaheuristic methods for the optimization of tdem data, Pure and Applied Geophysics 179 (10) (2022) 3727–3749.
[16] M. Sanaei, H. Akbari, Z. Beheshtipour, S. Mousavi, New pso-gwo-based model for enhancing power quality in electrical networks interconnected with photovoltaic sources, Frontiers in Energy Research 12 (2024) 1476638.
[17] J. Behan, S. Haider, Survey and comparison of nature inspired optimization algorithms. in: 2022 International Conference on Computational Science and Computational Intelligence (CSCI), IEEE, 2022, pp. 409–415.
[18] Y. Yuting, G. Yuelin, An adaptive hybrid differential grey wolf optimization algorithm for wsn coverage, Cluster Computing 28 (4) (2025) 229.
[19] T. Dokeroglu, A. Deniz, H. Kiziloz, A comprehensive survey on recent metaheuristics for feature selection, Neurocomputing 494 (2022) 269–296.
[20] T. Bäck, Evolutionary Algorithms in Theory and Practice: Evolution Strategies, Evolutionary Programming, Genetic Algorithms, Oxford University Press, (1996).
[21] H. Rosenbrock, An automatic method for finding the greatest or least value of a function, The Computer Journal 3 (3) (1960) 175–184.
[22] A. Omeradzic, H. Beyer, Convergence properties of the (μ / μ_i, λ)-es on the rastrigin function. in: Proceedings of the 17th ACM/SIGEVO Conference on Foundations of Genetic Algorithms, 2023, pp. 117–128.
[23] D. Ackley, A connectionist algorithm for genetic search. in: Proceedings of the First International Conference on Genetic Algorithms and their Applications, Psychology Press, 2014, pp. 121–135.
[24] A. Griewank, Generalized descent for global optimization, Journal of Optimization Theory and Applications 34 (1) (1981) 11–39.
[25] H. Schwefel, Evolution and Optimum Seeking: The Sixth Generation, John Wiley & Sons, (1995).
[26] M. Jamil, X. Yang, A literature survey of benchmark functions for global optimization problems, International Journal of Mathematical Modelling and Numerical Optimisation 4 (2) (2013) 150–194.
[27] M. Molga, C. Smutnicki, Test functions for optimization needs. Technical report, Technical Report. Available from: http://www.zsd.ict.pwr.wroc.pl/files/docs/functions.pdf.
[28] S. Forrest, Genetic algorithms, ACM Computing Surveys (CSUR) 28 (1) (1996) 77–80.
[29] F. Marini, B. Walczak, Particle swarm optimization (pso): a tutorial, Chemometrics and Intelligent Laboratory Systems 149 (2015) 153–165.
[30] M. Dorigo, L. Gambardella, Ant colonies for the travelling salesman problem, Bio Systems 43 (2) (1997) 73–81.
[31] D. Bertsimas, J. Tsitsiklis, Simulated annealing, Statistical Science 8 (1) (1993) 10–15.
[32] D. Karaboga, B. Basturk, A powerful and efficient algorithm for numerical function optimization: artificial bee colony (abc) algorithm, Journal of Global Optimization 39 (3) (2007) 459–471.
[33] CEC 2017, Benchmark functions. Available from https://www3.ntu.edu.sg/home/EPNSugan/index_files/CEC2017/CEC2017.htm, 2017 (accessed 05.08.25).

Chapter 33

Binary grey wolf optimizer for solving various resolving set problems

Hendy[1], Mohammad Isa Irawan[2], Imam Mukhlash[2], and Rinurwati[2]
[1]*Faculty of Engineering, Universitas Kadiri, Kediri, Indonesia,* [2]*Department of Mathematics, Faculty of Science and Data Analytics, Institut Teknologi Sepuluh Nopember, Surabaya, Indonesia*

33.1 Introduction

A graph is defined by vertices (or nodes) interconnected by edges, enabling the representation of complex networks and relationships. Many concepts in graph theory are applied to real-world problems, one of which is the concept of a resolving set. Slater first introduced the concept of resolving sets and minimum resolving sets in 1975 [1]. At that time, Slater referred to resolving sets as locating sets. He defined the minimum resolving set of a graph and termed its cardinality as the location number. Independently, Harary and Melter developed a similar concept under a different terminology, referring to it as the metric dimension [2].

The concept of metric dimension (MD) finds extensive applications across various fields. Embedding data into Euclidean space is a common requirement in various data analysis and mining techniques. However, symbolic datasets, especially biological sequence data generated by high-throughput sequencing technologies, often present significant challenges for traditional embedding methods. These methods often yield representations that are either excessively high-dimensional or overly simplified, thereby limiting their analytical effectiveness. The graph-theoretic concept of MD provides a robust and practical framework for mapping points in the Euclidean plane using their relative distances, effectively addressing these challenges [3].

One of the central problems in chemistry lies in designing mathematical models of chemical compounds that can accurately distinguish among them. As outlined in Ref. [4], a chemical compound's structure can be abstracted as a labeled graph, where atoms and bonds correspond to vertices and edges, respectively. Consequently, within a graph-oriented framework, the problem concerns designing vertex representations that allow each vertex to be uniquely distinguished. This approach has been extensively explored in Ref. [5]. In addition to the applications above, the concept of MD is also utilized in diverse disciplines, such as examining the structural characteristics of network topologies [6], designing optimal strategies for sensor placement [4], facilitating processes in pattern recognition and image analysis [7], enhancing navigation systems for robotic movement [8], and solving complex problems in combinatorial optimization [9].

Previous research on MD and its variations has predominantly centered on theoretical findings related to the MD of specific graph families [10], the MD of graphs derived from specific operations [11], and the structural characteristics of graphs exhibiting particular MD [12]. The determination of metric dimensions for graphs of arbitrary types and sizes necessitates the development and application of reliable computational methodologies.

Most previous studies have focused on determining the MD for specific graph families. The development of reliable algorithms or methods to find the MD and other resolving parameters in general graphs has not been widely explored. In fact, many of these parameters have never been solved using computational methods. A metaheuristic algorithm is one possible approach to addressing the MD problem [13].

Inspired by the collective hunting behavior of grey wolves (Canis lupus), the grey wolf optimizer (GWO) represents a metaheuristic approach to solving complex optimization problems. The algorithm simulates the social hierarchy of wolves, which is stratified within four strata: α, β, δ, and ω. In the searching framework, the α−wolf symbolizes the optimal solution identified in the current population. and directs the search process toward the optimal solution [14]. Research findings demonstrate that GWO stands as one of the leading metaheuristic algorithms for solving various

Grey Wolf Optimizer. DOI: https://doi.org/10.1016/B978-0-443-36624-6.00037-8

complex optimization tasks. Furthermore, bibliometric analyses identify GWO as the most frequently cited metaheuristic within the domain of computer science [15].

The principal achievement of this chapter is the design of a computational approach for addressing the MD problem and its extensions, including variations of resolving sets, which represent advancements of the MD concept. Many of these problems have yet to be addressed through a computational approach. This chapter examines several of these extensions, such as detour metric dimension (DMD), bi-metric dimension (BMD), edge metric dimension (EMD), and mixed metric dimension (MMD). Each problem is addressed using the binary grey wolf optimizer (BGWO) algorithm, with some requiring hybridization with the ant colony optimization (ACO) algorithm [16], while others necessitate modifications to derive solutions and enhance algorithmic performance [17].

The organization of this chapter is as follows: Section 33.2 presents the problem definition of the MD and variations of the resolving set problem. Section 33.3 discusses the underlying principles and basic concepts of the GWO algorithm. Section 33.4 outlines the construction and implementation of the BGWO algorithm to address the MD problem and other resolving set problems. Section 33.5 provides numerical results of the BGWO algorithm applied to various types of resolving set problems. Last, Section 33.6 provides a concluding discussion that highlights the main findings and proposes prospective research directions.

33.2 Problem definition

In this section, the definitions of various types of resolving set problems addressed using the BGWO algorithm will be provided.

33.2.1 Metric dimension

Throughout this chapter, all graphs are assumed to be simple and connected unless specified otherwise. The distance between two vertices u and v in a graph G is represented as $d_G(u, v)$. A vertex $s \in V(G)$ is said to differentiate (or resolve) two vertices u and v if $d_G(u, s) \neq d_G(v, s)$. A subset $S \subseteq V(G)$ is referred to as a metric generator for G if every pair of vertices u and v in G is distinguished by at least one vertex in S. The smallest cardinality of such a subset is named the MD of G, denoted by $dim(G)$ [4].

33.2.2 Detour metric dimension

The MD concept has evolved to include variations such as the DMD. Consider a connected graph G with vertex set V and edge set E. For vertices $u, v \in V$. the detour distance $D(u, v)$ represents the length of the longest $u - v$path in the graph G. Each vertex $v \in V$ can be represented by a p-tuple $(D(v, w_1), D(v, w_2), \ldots, D(v, w_p))$, where $W^{\star} = \{w_1, w_2, \ldots, w_p\} \subseteq V$ is a ordered set. A set $W^{\star}$ is said to be a detour resolving set of G if any two distinct vertices $u, v \in V$ have different representations with respect to $W^{\star}$.

A detour basis of G is a detour resolving set of G with minimum cardinality, and the detour metric dimension of G refers to its cardinality, denoted by $D\beta(G)$ [18]. A detour basis of G is described as a detour resolving set possessing the minimum cardinality. The DMD of G, denoted by $D\beta(G)$ corresponds to the cardinality of this basis.

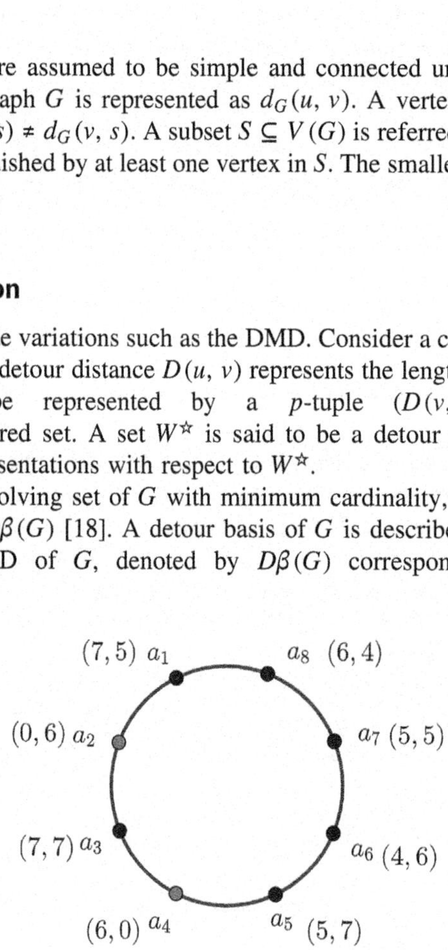

FIGURE 33.1 Cycle graph C_8.

For example, consider the cycle graph C_8 of Fig. 33.1. The detour distance matrix of this graph is:

$$\begin{bmatrix} 0 & 7 & 6 & 5 & 4 & 5 & 6 & 7 \\ 7 & 0 & 7 & 6 & 5 & 4 & 5 & 6 \\ 6 & 7 & 0 & 7 & 6 & 5 & 4 & 5 \\ 5 & 6 & 7 & 0 & 7 & 6 & 5 & 4 \\ 4 & 5 & 6 & 7 & 0 & 7 & 6 & 5 \\ 5 & 4 & 5 & 6 & 7 & 0 & 7 & 6 \\ 6 & 5 & 4 & 5 & 6 & 7 & 0 & 7 \\ 7 & 6 & 5 & 4 & 5 & 6 & 7 & 0 \end{bmatrix}$$

From this matrix, it is evident that each column contains at least two identical elements. This shows that no detour resolving set of C_8 consists of only one vertex. Next, suppose $S = \{a_2, a_4\}$. The representation of each vertex in S is as shown in Fig. 33.1. Thus, S is the minimum detour resolving set of C_8 and $D\beta(C_8)$=2

33.2.3 Bi-metric dimension

A new extension of the MD problem concept has been proposed as an additional contribution to this research area. Given any two vertices x and y, $d(x, y)$ represents the length of the shortest path, while $\delta(x, y)$ represents the length of the longest path between them; these are known as the distance and detour distance, respectively.

Consider $G(V, E)$ to be a simple connected graph. For each vertex $x \in V$, we link a pair of vectors (u, v), denoted by S_x, with respect to a subset $S = \{s_1, s_2, \ldots, s_k\}$ of vertices of G where $u = (d(x, s_1), d(x, s_2), \ldots, d(x, s_k))$ and $v = (\delta(x, s1), \delta(x, s2), \ldots, \delta(x, sk))$. The subset S is then said to *bi-resolve* G if $S_x \neq Sy$, whenever $x \neq y$. The minimum cardinality of a *bi-resolving set* S is termed the bi-metric dimension of G and is denoted by $\beta_b(G)$ [19]. There is a difference between Refs. [18] and [19] in defining the longest distance from a vertex to itself. In Ref. [18], the longest distance from a vertex v to itself is 0. However, in Ref. [19], the longest distance from a vertex v to itself is sought according to the given definition: the length of the longest path from v to v. In this chapter, we use the definition in Ref. [18] to find the DMD and the definition in Ref. [19] to find the BMD.

To illustrate finding the bi-resolving set of a graph, the graph G shown in Fig. 33.2 is analyzed herein. The bi-representation of all vertices in G with respect to $X_3 = \{x_1, x_4\}$ is shown in Fig. 33.2. As no single vertex forms a bi-resolving set for G, it follows that X_3 is also a minimum bi-resolving set; hence, $\beta_b(G)$=2.

33.2.4 Edge metric dimension

Recent studies have extended the concept of MD from resolving vertices to resolving edges in graphs [20]. Let $G = (V, E)$ be a connected graph. For a vertex $v \in V$ and an edge $e = uw \in E$, the distance between the vertex v and the edge e is given by $d_G(e, v) = min\{d_G(u, v), d_G(w, v)\}$. A vertex $x \in V$ is said to distinguish two edges $e_1, e_2 \in E$ if their respective distances from x are not equal. A set S of vertices is an edge metric generator if every pair of distinct edges in G is distinguished by at least one vertex in S. The smallest possible cardinality among all edge metric generators of G is defined as the EMD of the graph, denoted by $dim_e(G)$. For instance, consider the graph G illustrated in Fig. 33.3.

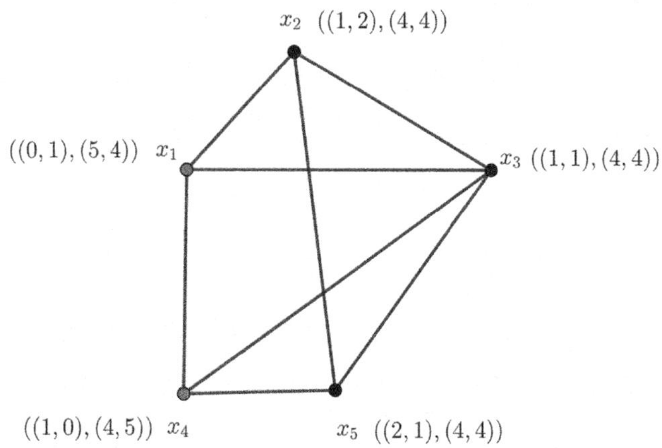

FIGURE 33.2 Bi-representation of G.

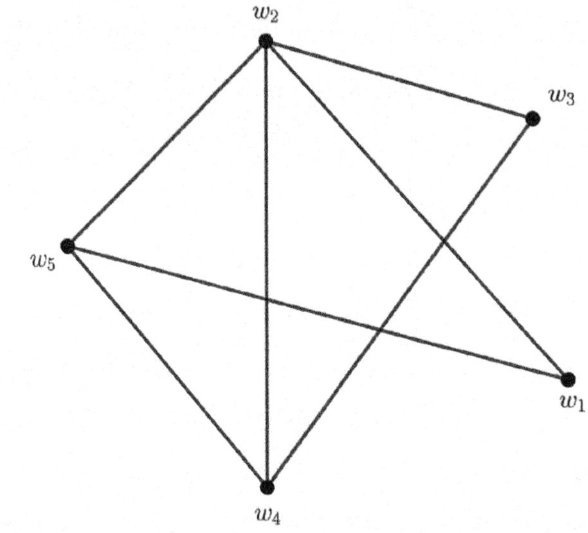

FIGURE 33.3 A graph G with $dim(G)$=2 and $dim_e(G)$=3.

$Dim(G)$=2 with the resolving set $S_1 = \{w_2, w_1\}$. The representations of all vertices: $r(w_1|S_1)$=(1,0), $r(w_2|S_1)$=(0,1), $r(w_3|S_1)$=(1,2), $r(w_4|S_1)$=(2,2), $r(w_5|S_1)$=(2,1) are all different. $Dim_e(G)$=3 with the edge metric generator of G is $S_2 = \{w_1, w_4, w_5\}$. The representations of all edges: $r(w_1w_2|S_2)$=(0,1,1), $r(w_1w_5|S_2)$=(0,1,0), $r(w_2w_3|S_2)$=(1,1,1), $r(w_2w_4|S_2)$=(1,0,1), $r(w_2w_5|S_2)$=(1,1,0), $r(w_3w_4|S_2)$=(2,0,1), $r(w_4w_5|S_2)$=(1,0,0) are all different.

33.2.5 Mixed metric dimension

This section focuses on a combined form of the two parameters defined earlier. Specifically, let G be a connected graph. Our objective is to achieve a unique identification of all elements (edges and vertices) within G.

A vertex subset $S \subset V(G)$ is called a mixed metric generator when each pair of distinct elements in G is uniquely identified by at least one vertex in S. The smallest size of such a set is the MMD of G, represented by $dim_m(G)$ [20].

For instance, consider the graph G shown in Fig. 33.3. It can be readily verified that no mixed metric generator of G exists with a cardinality smaller than four. The graph G has MMD $dim_m(G)$=4, with $S_3 = \{w_1, w_3, w_4, w_5\}$ as mixed metric generator. The representations of all elements of G: $r(w_1|S_3)$=(0,2,2,1), $r(w_2|S_3)$=(1,1,1,1), $r(w_3|S_3)$=(2,0,1,2), $r(w_4|S_3)$=(2,1,0,1), $r(w_5|S_3)$=(1,2,1,0), $r(w_1w_2|S_3)$=(0,1,1,1), $r(w_1w_5|S_3)$=(0,2,1,0), $r(w_2w_3|S_3)$=(1,0,1,1), $r(w_2w_4|S_3)$=(1,1,0,1), $r(w_2w_5|S_3)$=(1,1,1,0), $r(w_3w_4|S_3)$=(2,0,0,1), $r(w_4w_5|S_3)$=(1,1,0,0) are all different.

33.3 Grey wolf optimizer algorithm

The GWO algorithm was originally proposed by Seyedali Mirjalili [14]. This algorithm falls into the category of population-based swarm intelligence techniques. It is built upon the hunting behavior, as well as the hierarchical structure of grey wolf (Canis lupus) packs. Grey wolves belong to the Canidae family and are recognized as apex predators, indicating their dominance within the food hierarchy. The pack's leader is referred to as the α, which may be either a male or female wolf and holds the highest authority within the gray wolf hierarchy. The α leader governs the major decisions of the group. The β wolf holds the second position in the dominance hierarchy, serving under the α and supporting leadership and organizational functions. At the lowest position is the ω, which acts as the group's scapegoat and is submissive to all dominant wolves. Wolves that do not belong to the α, β, or ω categories but dominate the omega are classified as δ wolves. The δ wolves occupy a lower rank than the α and β but maintain authority over the ω wolves.

The following principles are established in developing a mathematical model based on the social hierarchy of gray wolves: (1). The optimal solution, representing the optimal fitness value, is designated as α. (2). The second-best solution is represented by β, while the third-best solution is denoted as δ. (3) All remaining wolves not belonging to these categories are classified as ω. (4). Within the GWO algorithm, the optimization process, analogous to the hunting process, is directed by the α, β, and δ wolves. In contrast, the ω wolves adhere to the guidance of these leading wolves.

A pack of gray wolves surrounds their prey during hunting. In mathematical modeling, this process is written as a subsequent equation.

$$\vec{D} = |\vec{C} . \vec{X_p}(t) - \vec{X}(t)| \tag{33.1}$$

$$\vec{X}(t+1) = \vec{X_p}(t) - \vec{A} . \vec{D} \tag{33.2}$$

In this context, t indicates the current iteration, $\vec{A}$ and $\vec{C}$ are coefficient vectors. $\vec{X_p}$ denotes the position vector of the prey, $\vec{X}$ denotes the position vector of the gray wolf. The vector $\vec{A}$ and vector $\vec{C}$ are determined based on the following formula:

$$\vec{A} = 2\vec{a} . \vec{r_1} - \vec{a} \tag{33.3}$$

$$\vec{C} = 2\vec{r_2} \tag{33.4}$$

Here, $\vec{a}$ linearly decreases from 2 to 0 throughout the iteration process, where $\vec{r_1}$ and $\vec{r_2}$ represent random vectors within the range of [0,1].

In mathematically simulating gray wolf hunting behavior, the α (representing the most optimal candidate solution), β, and δ possess superior knowledge regarding the target position. Therefore the top three optimal solutions obtained are retained, while the remaining search wolves, including the ω members, adjust their positions derived from the positions of these leading wolves. This hunting process is modeled through Eqs. (33.5) to (33.11).

$$\vec{D_\alpha} = |\vec{C_1} . \vec{X_\alpha} - \vec{X}|, \tag{33.5}$$

$$\vec{D_\beta} = |\vec{C_2} . \vec{X_\beta} - \vec{X}|, \tag{33.6}$$

$$\vec{D_\delta} = |\vec{C_3} . \vec{X_\delta} - \vec{X}| \tag{33.7}$$

$$\vec{X_1} = \vec{X_\alpha} - \vec{A_1} . (\vec{D_\alpha}), \tag{33.8}$$

$$\vec{X_2} = \vec{X_\beta} - \vec{A_2} . (\vec{D_\beta}), \tag{33.9}$$

$$\vec{X_3} = \vec{X_\delta} - \vec{A_3} . (\vec{D_\delta}) \tag{33.10}$$

$$\vec{X_{(t+1)}} = \frac{\vec{X_1} + \vec{X_2} + \vec{X_3}}{3} \tag{33.11}$$

33.4 Proposed method

Modifications and refinements of the BGWO algorithm are essential for its implementation in solving various resolving set problems. This requirement is due to the inherent characteristics of the solutions to these problems, which are represented as binary ordered, with not all randomly generated outputs producing feasible candidate solutions. This section provides a comprehensive explanation of the BGWO algorithm, adapted from its application to the feature selection problem, as described in Ref. [21]. The primary updating equation is expressed as illustrated in Eq. (33.12).

$$X_i^{t+1} = Crossover(x_1, x_2, x_3) \tag{33.12}$$

where $Crossover(x_1, x_2, x_3)$ signifies an appropriate crossover operation involving solutions x, y, z, and x_1, x_2, x_3 are binary vectors denoting the impact of a wolf's movement toward the α, β, and δ gray wolves sequentially. The x_1, x_2, x_3 are determined using Eqs. (33.13), (33.16), and (33.19) correspondingly.

$$x_1^d = \begin{cases} 1 & if\ (x_\alpha^d + bstep_\alpha^d) \geq 1 \\ 0 & otherwise \end{cases} \tag{33.13}$$

x_α^d represents the position vector of the alpha wolf in dimension d, while $bstep_\alpha^d$ signifies a binary step in dimension d, which can be computed as described in Eq. (33.14).

$$bstep_\alpha^d = \begin{cases} 1 & if cstep_\alpha^d \geq rand \\ 0 & otherwise \end{cases} \tag{33.14}$$

$rand$ is a randomly generated number from a uniform distribution within the [0,1] range. $cstep_\alpha^d$ stands for the continuous-valued step size for dimension d and can be computed using a sigmoidal function as outlined in Eq. (33.15).

$$cstep_\alpha^d = \frac{1}{1 + e^{-10(A_1^d D_\alpha^d - 0.5)}} \tag{33.15}$$

where A_1^d and D_α^d are determined by Eqs. (33.3) and (33.9) in the dimension d.

$$x_2^d = \begin{cases} 1 & if\ (x_\beta^d + bstep_\beta^d) \geq 1 \\ 0 & otherwise \end{cases} \tag{33.16}$$

The vector x_β^d represents the position vector of the beta wolf in dimension d, and $bstep_\beta^d$ represents a binary step in dimension d that can be determined as in Eq. (33.17).

$$bstep_\beta^d = \begin{cases} 1 & if cstep_\beta^d \geq rand \\ 0 & otherwise \end{cases} \tag{33.17}$$

where the $rand$ denotes a randomly generated number from a uniform distribution within the range $\in$ [0,1], and $cstep_\beta^d$ represents the continuous-valued step size for dimension d, which can be computed using a sigmoidal function as outlined in Eq. (33.18).

$$cstep_\beta^d = \frac{1}{1 + e^{-10(A_1^d D_\beta^d - 0.5)}} \tag{33.18}$$

where A_1^d and D_β^d are computed using Eqs. (33.3) and (33.5) in the dimension d.

$$x_3^d = \begin{cases} 1 & if\ (x_\delta^d + bstep_\delta^d) \geq 1 \\ 0 & otherwise \end{cases} \tag{33.19}$$

x_δ^d represents the position vector of the delta wolf in dimension d, while $bstep_\delta^d$ denotes a binary step in dimension d, calculated according to Eq.(33.20).

$$bstep_\delta^d = \begin{cases} 1 & if cstep_\delta^d \geq rand \\ 0 & otherwise \end{cases} \tag{33.20}$$

where $rand$ is a random number drawn from the uniform distribution $\in$ [0,1], and $cstep_\delta^d$ is the continuous-valued step size for dimension d. It can be calculated using a sigmoidal function as in Eq. (33.21).

$$cstep_\delta^d = \frac{1}{1 + e^{-10(A_1^d D_\delta^d - 0.5)}} \tag{33.21}$$

As Eq. (33.22) demonstrates, a stochastic crossover strategy is implemented per dimension to perform the crossover operation among the solutions a, b, and c.

$$x_d = \begin{cases} a_d & if rand < \frac{1}{3} \\ b_d & if \frac{1}{3} \leq rand < \frac{2}{3} \\ c_d & otherwise \end{cases} \tag{33.22}$$

where a_d, b_d, c_d represent the binary values for the first, second, and third parameter in dimension d, x_d denotes the crossover output at dimension d, and $rand$ is a randomly generated number from a uniform distribution within the range [0,1].

33.4.1 Application binary grey wolf optimizer algorithm for metric dimension problem

Initially, the Floyd–Warshall algorithm is implemented to compute the distance matrix of the given graph. To achieve this, the graph must first be converted into an adjacency matrix. Additionally, it is necessary to input n, representing the number of vertices in the graph, as the number of vertices determines the number of iterations in the algorithm. Once the Floyd–Warshall algorithm is executed, the resulting distance matrix D serves as one of the inputs for the BGWO algorithm in determining the MD, as illustrated in Fig. 33.4. Subsequently, the steps involved in determining the metric dimension of a graph using the BGWO algorithm are also depicted in Fig. 33.4 [16].

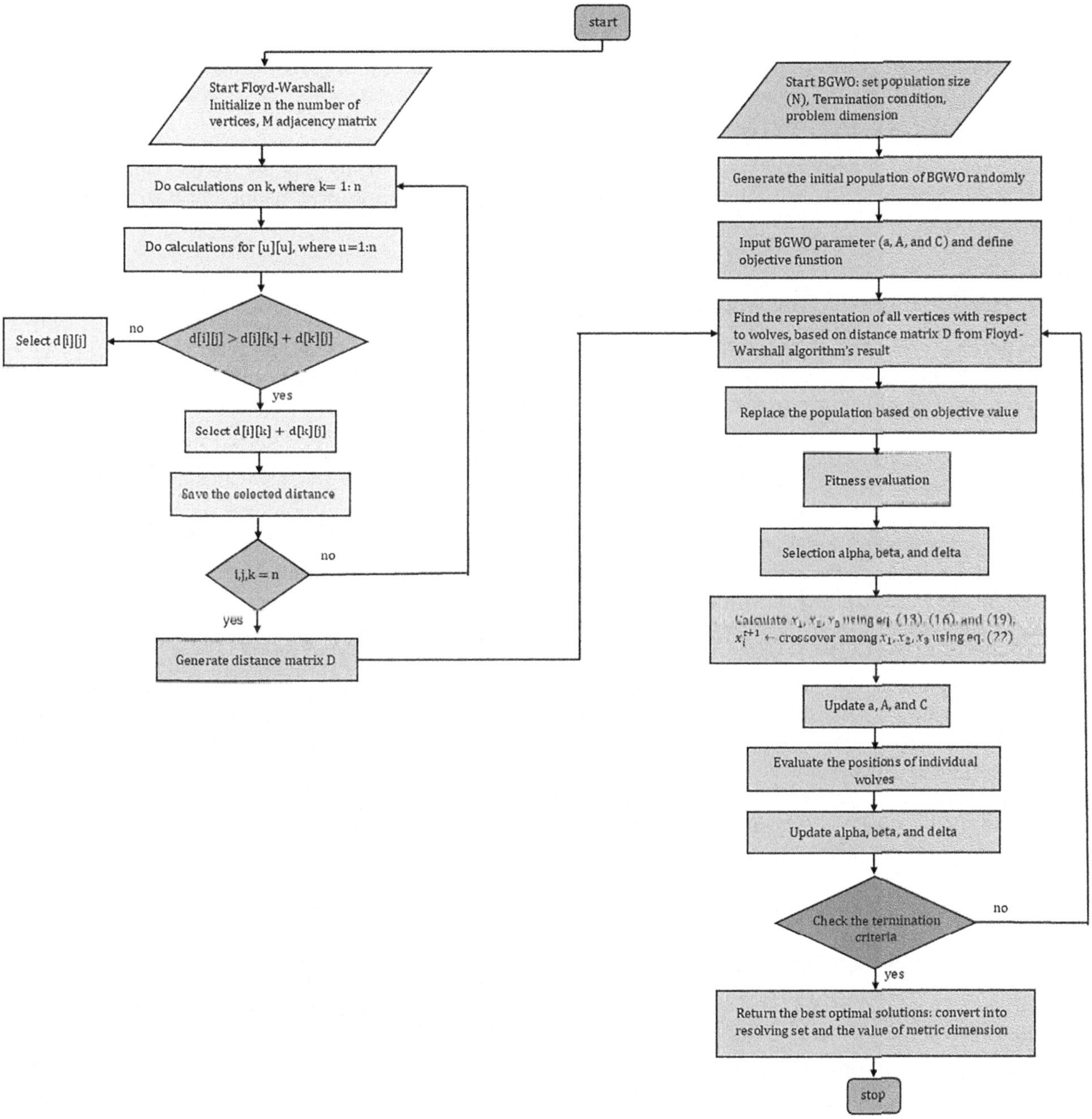

FIGURE 33.4 Flowchart of the BGWO algorithm for the metric dimension problem (*BGWO*, Binary grey wolf optimizer).

33.4.2 Hybrid ant colony optimization-binary grey wolf optimizer algorithm for detour metric dimension problem

Unlike the previous subsection, determining the DMD begins with the implementation of a modified ACO algorithm before proceeding to the BGWO algorithm. This approach is employed to derive the longest-path matrix, referred to as the delta matrix. Initially, the number of vertices n and the adjacency matrix A of the graph to be analyzed must be provided as input. By applying the ACO algorithm and creating scenarios for the parameter h, as illustrated in Fig. 33.5, the longest distances between any two vertices in the graph are obtained. Upon completion of the ACO algorithm, the delta matrix is generated, where its elements represent the longest distances between every pair of vertices in the graph, as calculated by the ACO algorithm. The delta matrix serves as one of the inputs for the subsequent step, namely the BGWO algorithm, which is used to determine the detour metric dimension, as depicted in Fig. 33.5. Finally, the steps for determining the DMD of a graph are outlined in Fig. 33.5 [16].

33.4.3 Hybrid ant colony optimization-binary grey wolf optimizer algorithm for bi-metric dimension problem

To determine the BMD of a graph, an input matrix H is required. This matrix comprises row vectors formed by combining the row vectors of the distance matrix and the delta matrix. Therefore prior to applying the BGWO algorithm, both the distance matrix and the delta matrix must be computed. The steps involved in determining the BMD of a graph are illustrated in Fig. 33.6 [16].

33.4.4 Modified binary grey wolf optimizer algorithm for edge metric dimension problems

Initially, the Floyd–Warshall algorithm is implemented to obtain the distance matrix, as illustrated in Fig. 33.7 [17]. Once the distance matrix is generated, the next step involves adding the edge set as input and generating the B matrix. The B matrix represents the distances between edges and vertices, where the distance between an edge $e = uw$ and a vertex v is defined as $d(e, v) = min(d(u, v), d(w, v))$. After constructing the B matrix, it becomes one of the inputs for the modified BGWO algorithm in the subsequent steps. The elements of the B matrix are utilized in determining the representation of edges in the graph.

In the modified BGWO algorithm, several enhancements are introduced compared to the standard approach. These modifications, highlighted in the gray boxes in Fig. 33.7, include: Row uniqueness validation. If any two rows in the sorted matrix are identical, the corresponding wolf is considered invalid. The wolf is adjusted by randomly flipping one 0 to a 1, and the validation process is repeated until all rows are unique. Representation of Both Vertices and Edges: The algorithm considers both vertices and edges in its optimization process. Mutation. To maintain population diversity and avoid premature convergence, a mutation step is included. This step involves randomly flipping bits in the wolf vector with a predefined probability. Stagnation handling and elitism. The algorithm monitors changes in the best objective value across iterations. If no improvement is observed over several iterations, a partial restart is performed by reinitializing a portion of the population. This approach helps avoid local optima and enhances exploration of the solution space. Additionally, elitism ensures that the best solution discovered so far is preserved. At each iteration, the algorithm evaluates all individuals in the population and identifies the best-performing solution (alpha) based on the objective function. If this new best solution outperforms the previously recorded best solution, the record is updated. Otherwise, the prior best solution is reinserted into the population, replacing the current worst-performing individual.

33.4.5 Modified binary grey wolf optimizer algorithm for mixed metric dimension problems

The steps in the modified BGWO algorithm to obtain the MMD of a graph are nearly identical to those in the previous subsection. The primary difference lies in the Z matrix. The Z matrix is constructed by combining the row vectors of the distance matrix D and the row vectors of the distance matrix between edges and vertices B, expressed as $Z = [D, B]$. The Z matrix serves as one of the inputs for the modified BGWO algorithm to determine the representation of both vertices and edges in the graph. The steps for determining the MMD of the graph are illustrated in Fig. 33.8 [17].

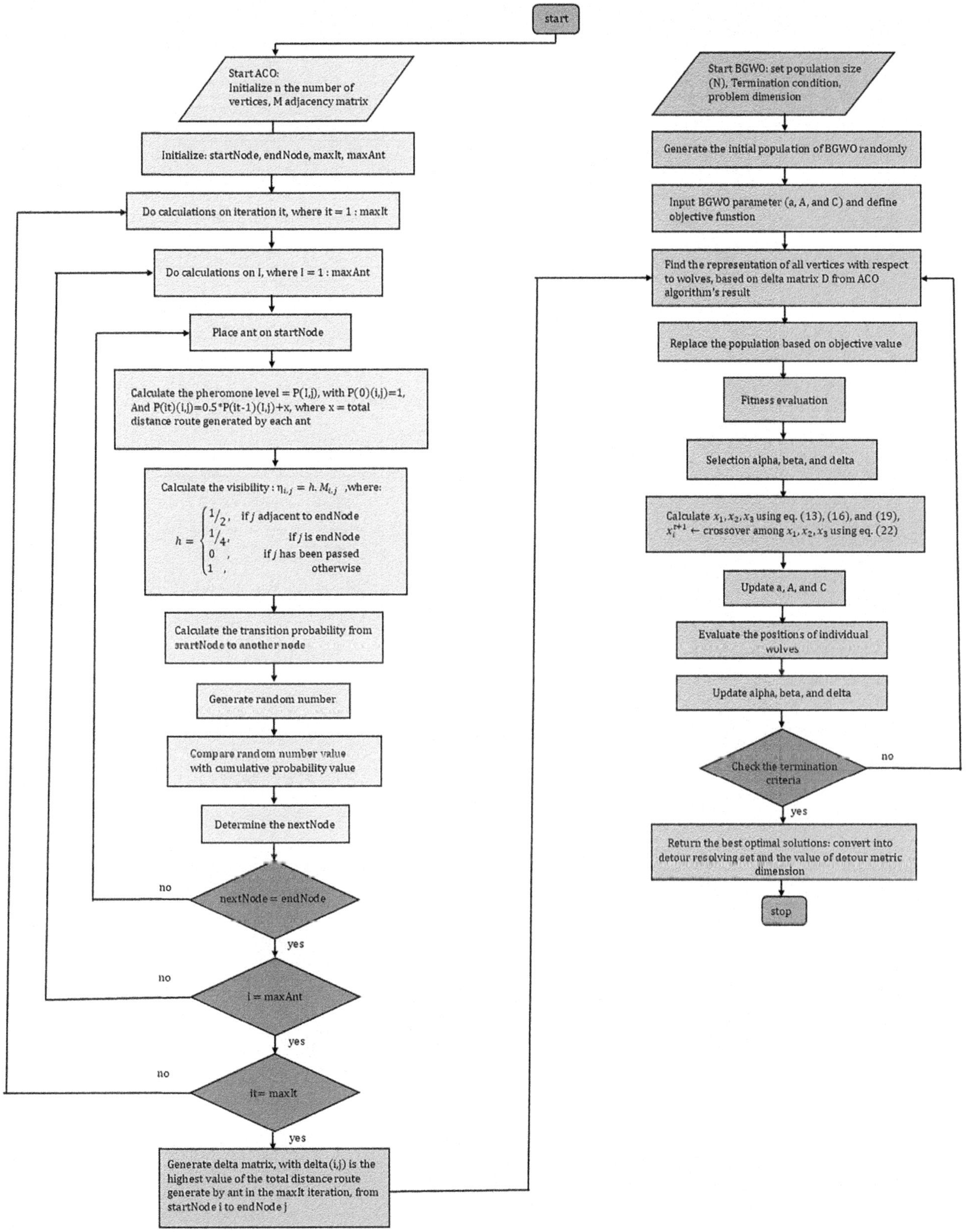

FIGURE 33.5 Flowchart of the Hybrid ACO-BGWO algorithm for the detour metric dimension problem (*ACO*, Ant colony optimization; *BGWO*, binary grey wolf optimizer).

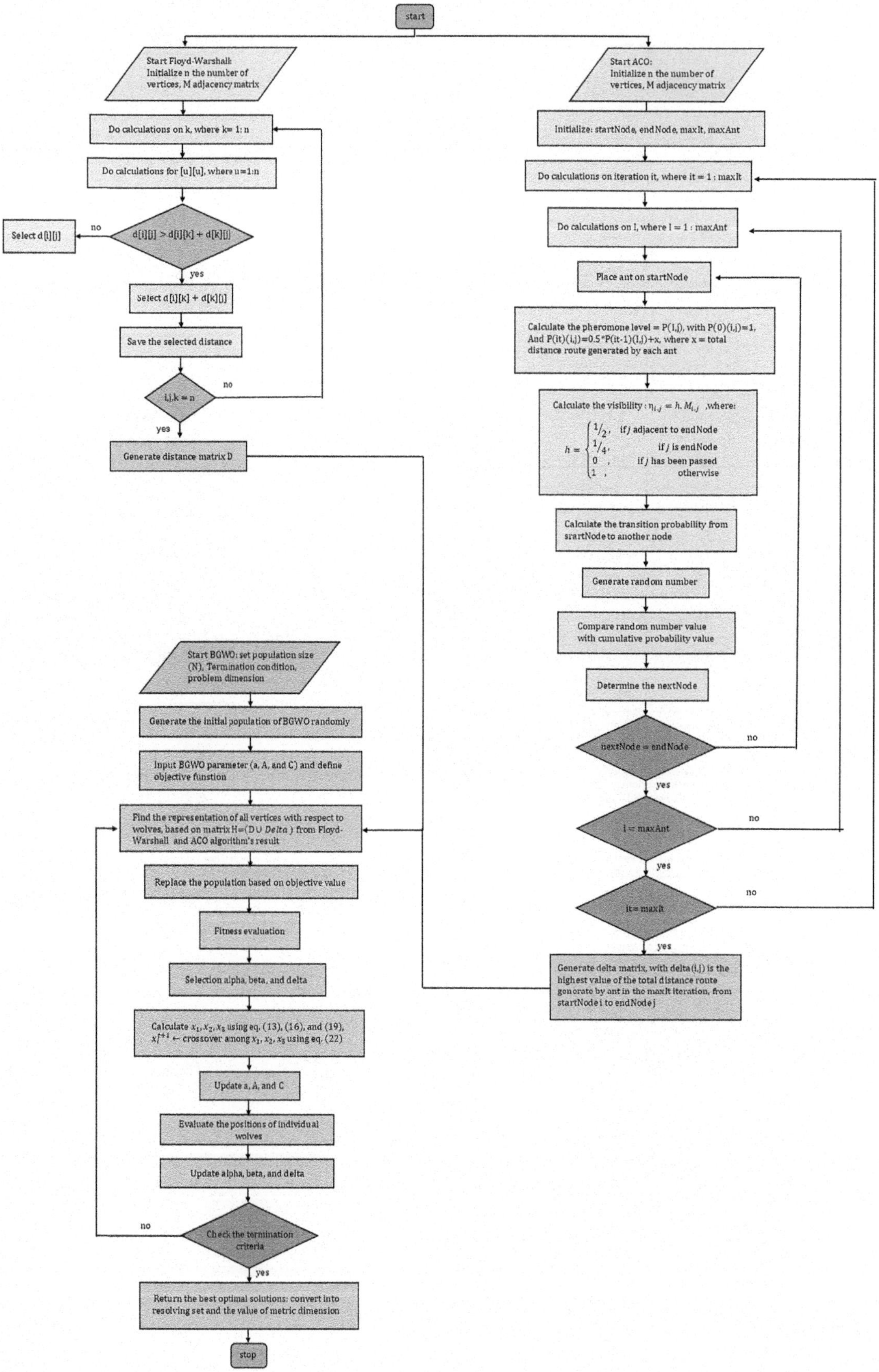

FIGURE 33.6 Flowchart of the Hybrid ACO-BGWO algorithm for the bi-metric dimension problem (*ACO*, Ant colony optimization; *BGWO*, binary grey wolf optimizer).

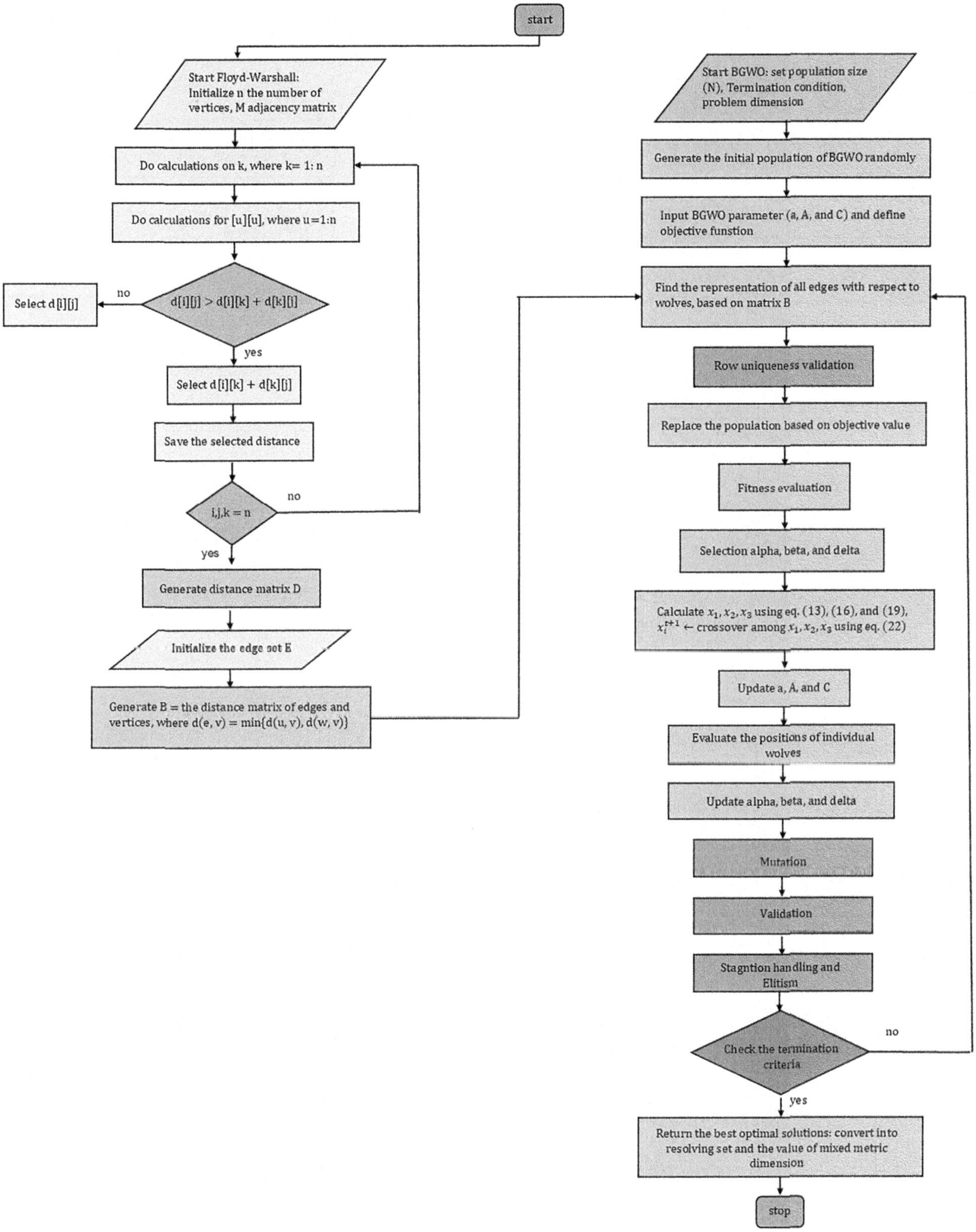

FIGURE 33.7 Flowchart of the Modified BGWO algorithm for the edge metric dimension problem (*BGWO*, Binary grey wolf optimizer).

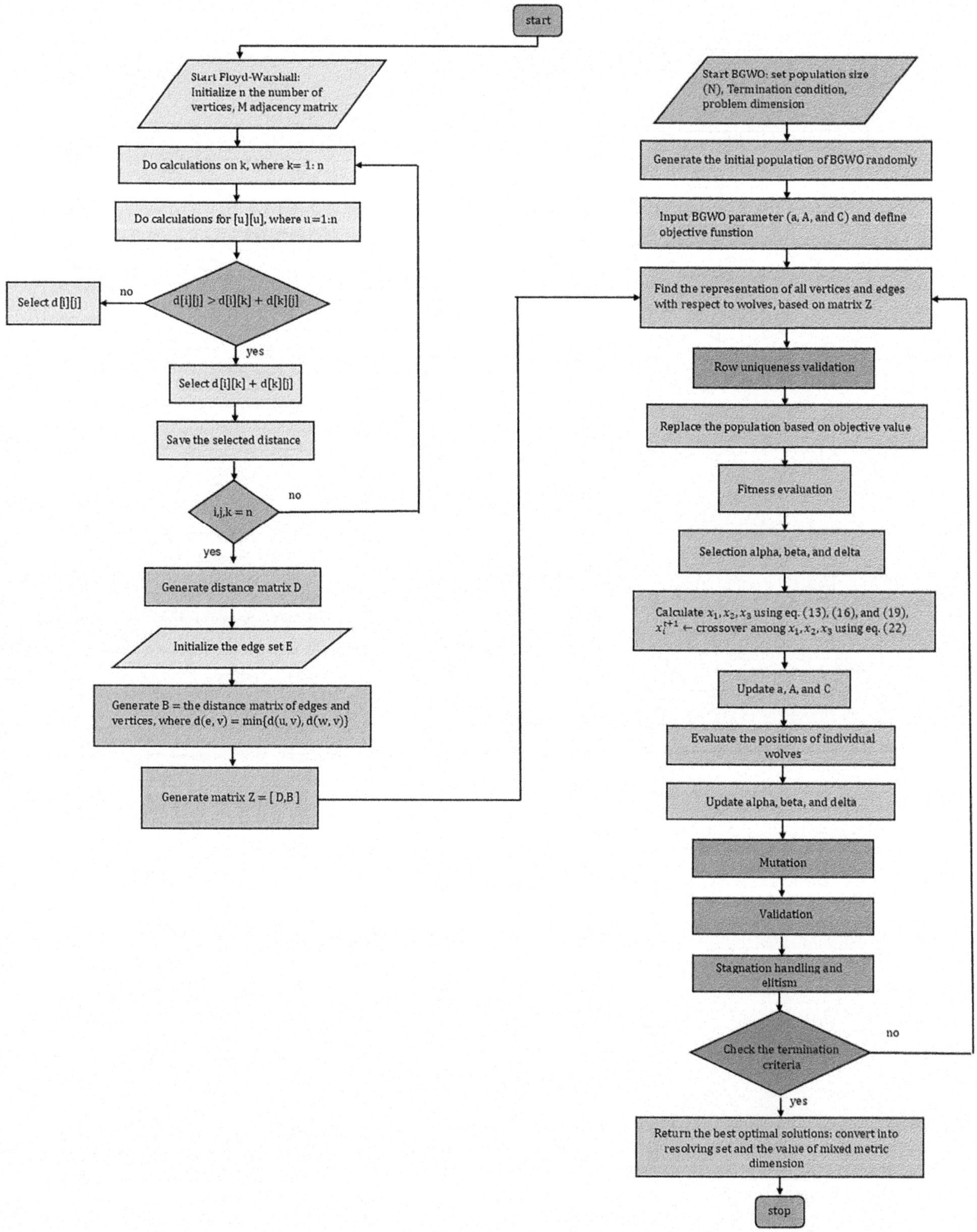

FIGURE 33.8 Flowchart of the Modified BGWO algorithm for the mixed metric dimension problem (*BGWO*, Binary grey wolf optimizer).

33.5 Numerical results

In the following section, the experiments were conducted using MATLAB R2023b, installed on a Windows 10 Pro system equipped with a Core i5 processor and 16 GB of RAM. The simulation result of the BGWO algorithm for the metric dimension of generalized antiprism graphs is given in Table 33.1. This table shows that the BGWO algorithm gives better results than the upper bound. From the simulation results, we see that the $dim(A_3^{10})$=9 is less than its upper bound = 10 [16]. Additionally, the simulation of the hybrid ACO-BGWO algorithm yields results consistent with those reported in the literature.

In determining the EMD and MMD of a graph using the modified BGWO algorithm, several simulation results have been obtained (see Ref. [17]). Some of these results are presented in Tables 33.2–33.4. The simulation results demonstrate that the modified BGWO algorithm produces outcomes consistent with those reported in [20,22,23].

Furthermore, Figs. 33.9 and 33.10 illustrate the algorithm's excellent convergence rate in solving EMD and MMD problems. The figures also show that the dimension values obtained are equal to the upper bounds provided in Ref. [17], indicating the high accuracy of the modified BGWO algorithm.

TABLE 33.1 Result of the BGWO algorithm for metric dimension on some generalized antiprism graphs.

Graph	*n*	*m*	Popsize	MaxIt	Resolving set	*dim*
A_3^3	9	21	20	50	$\{a_2, b_1, c_1\}$	3
A_3^4	12	30	20	50	$\{a_2, a_3, c_1, c_3\}$	4
A_3^5	15	39	25	50	$\{a_3, b_3, c_3, d_1, e_1\}$	5
A_3^6	18	48	25	50	$\{a_1, a_2, c_3, d_3, e_2, e_3\}$	6
A_3^7	21	57	25	50	$\{b_1, b_2, d_2, e_2, f_2, f_3\}$	7
A_3^8	24	66	30	75	$\{a_1, a_2, c_2, d_1, d_2, f_3, g_1, g_2\}$	8
A_3^9	27	75	50	150	$\{a_1, b_3, d_1, d_2, e_1, f_2, g_2, h_1, h_2\}$	9
A_3^{10}	30	84	75	200	$\{a_1, b_1, d_1, d_3, e_3, f_2, h_3, i_2, i_3\}$	9
A_4^3	12	28	20	50	$\{a_2, a_4, b_1\}$	3
A_4^4	16	40	20	50	$\{a_1, b_1, b_3, b_4\}$	4
A_4^5	20	52	35	100	$\{a_4, b_2, b_3, b_4\}$	4
A_4^6	24	64	50	150	$\{a_3, b_2, d_1, d_3, d_4\}$	5
A_4^7	28	76	70	200	$\{a_4, b_2, d_1, e_1, e_4, f_1\}$	6
A_4^8	32	88	80	300	$\{a_1, b_3, c_1, c_4, f_3, f_4, g_2\}$	7
A_4^9	36	100	90	400	$\{a_4, c_3, c_4, e_1, e_3, f_4, g_1, h_1, h_2\}$	9
A_4^{10}	40	112	90	400	$\{a_1, a_4, b_1, c_1, e_1, e_3, f_4, h_3, h_4, i_2\}$	10

BGWO, Binary grey wolf optimizer.

TABLE 33.2 Results of the BGWO algorithm for edge metric dimension on generalized antiprism graphs A_3^n.

Graph	N	m	Popsize	It	dim_e	Edge metric generator
A_3^3	9	21	20	1	6	$\{v_2, v_3, v_5, v_6, v_7, v_8\}$
A_3^4	12	30	20	1	8	$\{v_1, v_3, v_4, v_6, v_8, v_9, v_{11}, v_{12}\}$
A_3^5	15	39	20	2	10	$\{v_1, v_2, v_4, v_5, v_8, v_9, v_{10}, v_{12}, v_{13}, v_{14}\}$
A_3^6	18	48	20	1	12	$\{v_1, v_3, v_4, v_5, v_8, v_9, v_{10}, v_{11}, v_{13}, v_{14}, v_{16}, v_{18}\}$
A_3^7	21	57	20	1	14	$\{v_1, v_2, v_4, v_5, v_8, v_9, v_{10}, v_{12}, v_{14}, v_{15}, v_{16}, v_{18}, v_{19}, v_{21}\}$
A_3^8	24	66	20	2	16	$\{v_2, v_3, v_4, v_5, v_8, v_9, v_{11}, v_{12}, v_{14}, v_{15}, v_{17}, v_{18}, v_{19}, v_{21}, v_{22}, v_{23}\}$
A_3^9	27	75	20	2	18	$\{v_2, v_3, v_5, v_6, v_7, v_8, v_{10}, v_{11}, v_{13}, v_{15}, v_{17}, v_{18}, v_{19}, v_{21}, v_{22}, v_{23}, v_{26}, v_{27}\}$
A_3^{10}	30	84	20	2	20	$\{v_1, v_2, v_4, v_6, v_7, v_9, v_{10}, v_{12}, v_{13}, v_{15}, v_{16}, v_{18}, v_{20}, v_{21}, v_{23}, v_{24}, v_{25}, v_{27}, v_{28}, v_{30}\}$
A_3^{11}	33	93	20	2	22	$\{v_2, v_3, v_5, v_6, v_7, v_9, v_{11}, v_{12}, v_{14}, v_{15}, v_{16}, v_{18}, v_{19}, v_{20}, v_{23}, v_{24}, v_{26}, v_{27}, v_{28}, v_{30}, v_{32}, v_{33}\}$
A_3^{12}	36	102	20	2	24	$\{v_1, v_2, v_5, v_6, v_7, v_9, v_{10}, v_{11}, v_{14}, v_{15}, v_{17}, v_{18}, v_{20}, v_{21}, v_{22}, v_{23}, v_{25}, v_{27}, v_{29}, v_{30}, v_{31}, v_{32}, v_{34}, v_{35}\}$

BGWO, Binary grey wolf optimizer.

TABLE 33.3 Results of the BGWO algorithm for mixed metric dimension on wheel graphs.

Graph	n	m	Popsize	It	dim_m	Mixed metric generator
W_4	4	6	20	1	4	$\{v_1, v_2, v_3, v_4\}$
W_5	5	8	20	1	4	$\{v_2, v_3, v_4, v_5\}$
W_6	6	10	20	1	5	$\{v_2, v_3, v_4, v_5, v_6\}$
W_7	7	12	20	1	6	$\{v_2, v_3, v_4, v_5, v_6, v_7\}$
W_8	8	14	20	1	7	$\{v_2, v_3, v_4, v_5, v_6, v_7, v_8\}$
W_9	9	16	20	1	8	$\{v_2, v_3, v_4, v_5, v_6, v_7, v_8, v_9\}$
W_{10}	10	18	20	1	9	$\{v_2, v_3, v_4, v_5, v_6, v_7, v_8, v_9, v_{10}\}$

BGWO, Binary grey wolf optimizer.

33.5.1 Time and space complexity

The time dominance lies in the Landmark (LM) processing step, which is *sortrows*(*C*(:,*selectedcolumns*)).

The total complexity per iteration, therefore for one iteration, is:

$O(popsize\ [BGWO\ Update(n) + validation,\ calculate\ Objective(rklogr)])$. Because of $k \approx n$, $r = n + m$, then:

$$= O(popsize[n + (n + m)nlog(n + m)]) \approx O(popsize(n + n^2 log(n + m)))$$

For maxIterations:

$$\text{Total time} \approx O(maxIterasi\ popsize\ (n + n^2 log(n + m))).$$

Storage requirements:

Population: $popsize \times n \mapsto O(popsize \times n)$

Matrix C: $(n + m) \times n \mapsto O((n + m) \times n)$

LM and temporary matrices: $\leq O((n + m) \times n)$

History tracking: $O(maxIterations)$

Thus, the total space complexity is:

$$O((n + m) \times n + popsize \times n + maxIterations)$$

$\approx O((n + m) \times n)$ (dominant term)

However, the complexity may increase if individual validation frequently fails, requiring multiple repair attempts.

TABLE 33.4 Results of the BGWO algorithm for MMD on generalized antiprism graphs A_3^n.

Graph	n	m	Popsize	It	dim_m	Mixed metric generator
A_3^3	9	21	20	1	6	$\{v_2, v_3, v_5, v_6, v_7, v_8\}$
A_3^4	12	30	20	1	8	$\{v_1, v_3, v_4, v_6, v_8, v_9, v_{11}, v_{12}\}$
A_3^5	15	39	20	2	10	$\{v_1, v_2, v_4, v_5, v_8, v_9, v_{10}, v_{12}, v_{13}, v_{14}\}$
A_3^6	18	48	20	1	12	$\{v_1, v_3, v_4, v_5, v_8, v_9, v_{10}, v_{11}, v_{13}, v_{14}, v_{16}, v_{18}\}$
A_3^7	21	57	20	1	14	$\{v_1, v_2, v_4, v_5, v_8, v_9, v_{10}, v_{12}, v_{14}, v_{15}, v_{16}, v_{18}, v_{19}, v_{21}\}$
A_3^8	24	66	20	2	16	$\{v_2, v_3, v_4, v_5, v_8, v_9, v_{11}, v_{12}, v_{14}, v_{15}, v_{17}, v_{18}, v_{19}, v_{21}, v_{22}, v_{23}\}$
A_3^9	27	75	20	2	18	$\{v_2, v_3, v_5, v_6, v_7, v_8, v_{10}, v_{11}, v_{13}, v_{15}, v_{17}, v_{18}, v_{19}, v_{21}, v_{22}, v_{23}, v_{26}, v_{27}\}$
A_3^{10}	30	84	20	2	20	$\{v_1, v_2, v_4, v_6, v_7, v_9, v_{10}, v_{12}, v_{13}, v_{15}, v_{16}, v_{18}, v_{20}, v_{21}, v_{23}, v_{24}, v_{25}, v_{27}, v_{28}, v_{30}\}$
A_3^{11}	33	93	20	2	22	$\{v_2, v_3, v_5, v_6, v_7, v_9, v_{11}, v_{12}, v_{14}, v_{15}, v_{16}, v_{18}, v_{19}, v_{20}, v_{23}, v_{24}, v_{26}, v_{27}, v_{28}, v_{30}, v_{32}, v_{33}\}$
A_3^{12}	36	102	20	2	24	$\{v_1, v_2, v_5, v_6, v_7, v_9, v_{10}, v_{11}, v_{14}, v_{15}, v_{17}, v_{18}, v_{20}, v_{21}, v_{22}, v_{23}, v_{25}, v_{27}, v_{29}, v_{30}, v_{31}, v_{32}, v_{34}, v_{35}\}$

BGWO, Binary grey wolf optimizer; *MMD*, mixed metric dimension.

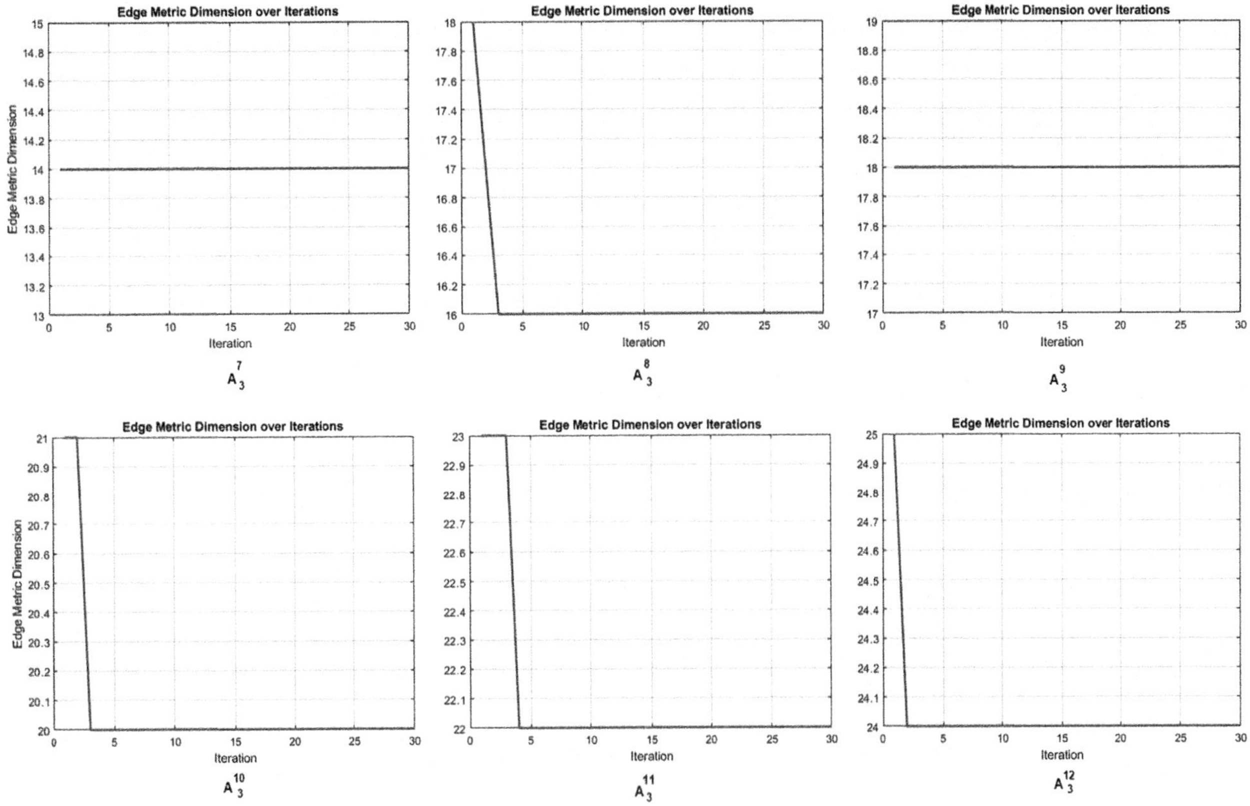

FIGURE 33.9 Numerical results of EMD of some generalized antiprism graphs (*EMD*, Edge metric dimension).

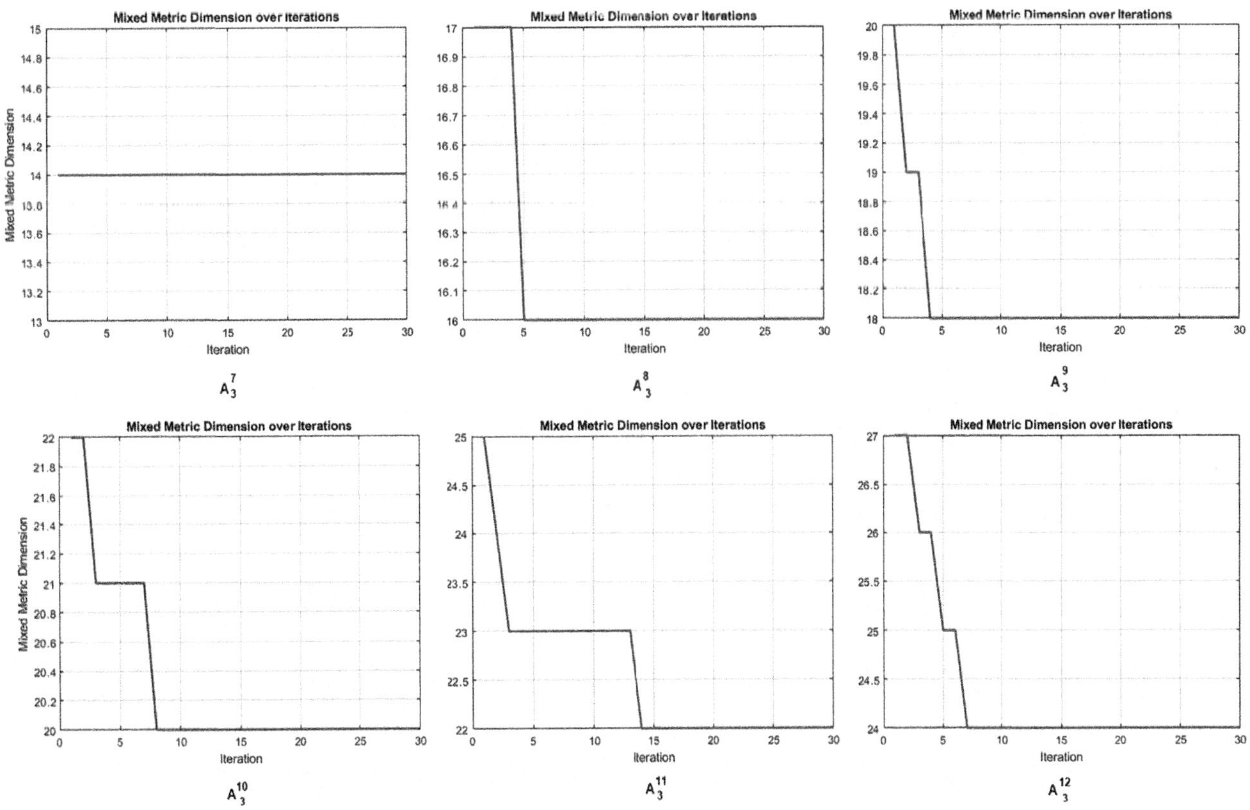

FIGURE 33.10 Numerical results of MMD of some generalized antiprism graphs (*MMD*, Mixed metric dimension).

33.6 Conclusion and future direction

This chapter presents a BGWO algorithm for solving various resolving set problems. The algorithm aims to minimize the number of vertices required to identify all vertices (and or unique edges) of a graph based on distance constraints. Some of these problems require a combination with the ant colony optimization algorithm, while others necessitate modification. This result confirms the capabilities of the BGWO algorithm in solving the various resolving set problems. Furthermore, the BGWO algorithm demonstrates practical utility in the following areas: (1) conducting pattern recognition to identify resolving set patterns within specific graph families. The algorithms outputs provide various minimum resolving sets, enabling the selection of particular resolving sets for pattern identification and analysis; (2) developing hypotheses regarding the (detour/bi/edge/mixed)-metric dimension values for specific types or families of graphs; (3) generating (detour/bi/edge/mixed)-metric dimension values that may either coincide with or be lower than the upper bounds obtained from theoretical results. This phenomenon arises because theoretical results rely on fixed patterns or regularities, while the BGWO algorithm operates through random calculations, employing an iterative refinement mechanism.

Graph theory encompasses a range of advanced problems, including graph coloring, graph labeling, and related challenges. Framing these issues within optimization models creates valuable opportunities to leverage metaheuristic algorithms, particularly the GWO. This redefinition serves as both a promising avenue and a complex challenge for future researchers.

Acknowledgment

The author acknowledges the use of artificial intelligence (AI) tools, specifically ChatGPT (OpenAI) and Grammarly, which were employed solely to refine the language and improve the readability of this manuscript. The authors conducted a thorough review and verification of the content to ensure both accuracy and scholarly integrity.

References

[1] P.J. Slater, Leaves of trees, Congress Number 14 (1975) 549–559.

[2] F. Harary, R.A. Melter, On the metric dimension of graphs, Ars Combinatoria 2 (1976) 191–195.

[3] R.C. Tillquist, M.E. Lladser, Low-dimensional representation of genomic sequence, Journal of Mathematical Biology 79 (2019) 1–29. Available from https://doi.org/10.1007/s00285-019-01348-1.

[4] G. Chartrand, L. Eroh, O.R. Oellerman, Resolvability in graphs and the metric dimension of a graph, Discrete Applied Mathematics 105 (2000) 99–113. Available from https://doi.org/10.1016/S0166-218X(00)00198-0.

[5] M. Imran, A. Ahmad, M. Azeem, K. Elahi, Metric-based resolvability of quartz structure, Computers Materials and Continue 71 (2022) 2053–2071. Available from https://doi.org/10.32604/cmc.2022.022064.

[6] Z. Beerliova, F. Eberhard, T. Erlebach, A. Hall, M. Hoffmann, M. Mihal'ak, et al., Network discovery and verification, IEEE Journal on Selected Areas in Communications 24 (2006) 2168–2181. Available from https://doi.org/10.1109/JSAC.2006.884015.

[7] R.A. Melter, I. Tomescu, Metric bases in digital geometry, Computer Vision, Graphics, and Image Processing. 25 (1984) 113–121.

[8] K. Khuller, B. Raghavachari, A. Rosenfeld, Landmarks in graphs, Discrete Applied Mathematics 70 (1996) 217–229. Available from https://doi.org/10.1016/0166-218X(95)00106-2.

[9] A. Sebo, E. Tannier, On metric generators of graphs, Mathematics of Operations Research 29 (2004) 383–393. Available from https://doi.org/10.1287/moor.1030.0070.

[10] L. Eroh, C.X. Kang, E. Yi, On metric dimension of functigraphs, Discrete Mathematics, Algorithms and Applications 5 (4) (2013) 1–13. Available from https://doi.org/10.1142/S1793830912500607.

[11] J. Caceres, C. Hernando, M. Mora, I.M. Pelayo, M.L. Puertas, C. Seara, et al., On the metric dimension of the cartesian product of graphs, SIAM Journal on Discrete Mathematics 21 (2) (2007) 423–441. Available from https://doi.org/10.1137/050641867.

[12] M. Imran, S.A.H. Bokhary, A. Ahmad, A. Semanicova-Fenovcikova, On classes of regular graphs with constant metric dimension, Acta Mathematica Scientia 333 (1) (2013) 187–206. Available from https://doi.org/10.1016/S0252-9602(12)60204-5.

[13] J. Kratica, V. Kovačević-Vujčić, M. Čangalović, Computing the metric dimension of graphs by genetic algorithms, Computational Optimization and Applications 44 (2009) 343–361. Available from https://doi.org/10.1007/s10589-007-9154-5.

[14] S. Mirjalili, S.M. Mirjalili, A. Lewis, Grey wolf optimizer, Advanced Engineering Software 69 (2014) 46–61. Available from https://doi.org/10.1016/j.advengsoft.2013.12.007.

[15] Hendy, M.I. Irawan, I. Mukhlash, S. Setumin, A bibliometric analysis of metaheuristic research and its applications, Register: Jurnal Ilmiah Teknologi Sistem Informasi 9 (2023) 1–17. Available from https://doi.org/10.26594/register.v9i1.2675.

[16] Hendy, M.I. Irawan, I. Mukhlash, Rinurwati, Hybrid ant colony optimization algorithm with binary gray wolf optimization for detour metric dimension and bi-metric dimension problem, Communications in Combinatorics and Optimization (2025) 1–26. Available from https://doi.org/10.22049/cco.2025.29133.1855x.

[17] Hendy, M.I. Irawan, I. Mukhlash, Rinurwati, Determining the mixed metric dimension of a graph with the binary gray wolf optimizer algorithm, Malaysian Journal of Science (2025) x, x–xx.

[18] V. Devi, K. Marimuthu, A new encryption technique using detour metric dimension, Journal of Informatics and Mathematical Sciences 9 (3) (2017) 949. Available from https://doi.org/10.26713/JIMS.V9I3.1015.

[19] A. Raghavendra, B. Sooryanarayana, C. Hegde, Bi-metric dimension of graphs, British Journal of Mathematics and Computer Science 4 (18) (2014) 2699–2714. Available from https://doi.org/10.9734/BJMCS/2014/10491.

[20] A. Kelenc, D. Kuziak, A. Taranenko, I.G. Yero, Mixed metric dimension of graphs, Applied Mathematics and Computation 314 (2017) 429–438. Available from https://doi.org/10.1016/j.neucom.2015.06.083.

[21] E. Emary, M.Z. Hossam, A.E. Hassanien, Binary gray wolf optimization approaches for feature selection, Neurocomputing 172 (2016) 371–381. Available from https://doi.org/10.1016/j.neucom.2015.06.083.

[22] Darmaji, N. Azahra, The mixed metric dimension of wheel-like graphs, Journal of Physics: Conference Series 2157 (2022) 012010. Available from https://doi.org/10.1088/1742-6596/2157/1/012010.

[23] M.M. Danas, The mixed metric dimension of flower snarks and wheels, Open Mathematics 19 (2012) 629–640. Available from https://doi.org/10.1515/math-2021-0065.

Chapter 34

Enhanced autonomous vehicle navigation using a pure pursuit and grey wolf optimizer algorithm

Mehmet Enes Avcu[1], Akif Hacınecipoğlu[2], and Harun Gökçe[3]
[1]*Department of Robotics Software, Milvus Robotics, Ankara, Türkiye,* [2]*Department of Mechanical Engineering, Faculty of Engineering, Ostim Technical University, Ankara, Türkiye,* [3]*Department of Industrial Design, Faculty of Architecture, Gazi University, Ankara, Türkiye*

34.1 Introduction

Autonomous and robotics systems are self-driving systems that use sensor measurements to estimate their current position and calculate outputs to reach a target position. At this point, path tracking is significantly important for robotics and autonomous driving systems. Pure pursuit (PP), model predictive control, model predictive path integral, Stanley controller, and dynamic window approach are common methods to meet that demand for tracking. Furthermore, the PP algorithm is a fundamental geometry-based path-tracking method that has widespread usage applications. The implementation of this algorithm is simple but adaptable to different conditions [1]. Also, PP is popular due to its low computational cost and performance, unlike model predictive path integral (MPPI) and model predictive control (MPC) algorithms that demand high computational cost [2]. The robustness of PP has been proven and tested on different autonomous vehicles [3].

Swarm intelligence (SI) is a highly effective mechanism for solving complex problems. It produces nature-inspired algorithms to generate optimal solutions [4]. Furthermore, SI algorithms focus on the social behavior of the swarm members. Finding an optimal solution means the maximum or minimum value of a given objective function [5]. The grey wolf optimizer (GWO) has been applied to different problems and has effectively solved them [6]. GWO offers a clear approximation for problems and that motivates a researcher to use it in different areas, such as communication [7], robotics [8], machine learning [9], scheduling [10], and power engineering [11]. The GWO algorithm starts a process by generating random positions of members. Then, a population calculates the value of itself and finds the best three wolf positions. After that, revise their solution throughout the searching operations [12].

The usage of SI in robotics navigation algorithms has been increasing for years. Due to the simplicity and robustness of SI algorithms, they make themselves favored for motion planning and tracking [13]. GWO has been used for tracking and motion planning algorithms [14]. A lower calculation complexity of GWO algorithms offers practical solutions in different environmental conditions [15]. This chapter presents the GWO for determining the optimal route. The algorithm identifies a path that minimizes cost, thereby selecting the most cost-effective target point. The GWO algorithm is applied to generate the optimal path according to the defined cost function and to evaluate the cost associated with reaching the target position.

34.2 Grey wolf optimizer algorithm

34.2.1 Social hierarchy

In the mathematical modeling of the GWO algorithm, the best solution is designated as alpha (α), while beta (β) and delta (δ) represent the second and third best solutions, respectively. All remaining candidate solutions are classified as omega (ω). In the

Grey Wolf Optimizer. DOI: https://doi.org/10.1016/B978-0-443-36624-6.00024-X

GWO algorithm, the alpha, beta, and delta solutions guide the search process, and the omega candidates update their positions by following these three leaders.

34.2.2 Encircling prey

The GWO algorithm simulates the encircling behavior observed during hunting. This behavior is mathematically modeled using the following equations.

$$\vec{D} = \left|\vec{C}\cdot\vec{X_p}(t) - \vec{X}(t)\right| \tag{34.1}$$

$$\vec{X}(t+1)=\vec{X_p}(t) - \vec{A}\cdot\vec{D} \tag{34.2}$$

Here, t is the current step. $\vec{A}$ and $\vec{C}$ are coefficient vectors. $\vec{X_p}$ represents the position vector of the prey, and $\vec{X}$ is the position vector of the grey wolves. The symbols || and · indicate absolute value and component-by-component multiplication. If a better solution is found during any phase, $\vec{X}^*$ is updated. The vectors $\vec{A}$ and $\vec{C}$ are calculated using the following formulas:

$$\vec{A}=2\vec{a}\cdot\vec{r_1} - \vec{a} \tag{34.3}$$

$$\vec{C}=2\cdot\vec{r_2} \tag{34.4}$$

where the variable of $\vec{a}$ decreases linearly from 2 to 0 throughout iterations and $\vec{r_1}$ and $\vec{r_2}$ are selected randomly in [0,1].

34.2.3 Hunting

Grey wolves can locate and pursue prey, with the alpha typically leading the hunt. The beta and delta may also participate in hunting. However, in an abstract search space, the exact position of the optimal solution (prey) is unknown. To model the hunting behavior of grey wolves mathematically, we assume the alpha, beta, and delta possess better estimations of the prey's position. Thus, we track the three best solutions identified so far and require other search agents, including the omegas, to update their positions based on these top solutions. The following equations illustrate this process:

$$\vec{D_\alpha} = \left|\vec{C_1}\cdot\vec{X_\alpha} - \vec{X}\right|, \vec{D_\beta} = \left|\vec{C_2}\cdot\vec{X_\beta} - \vec{X}\right|, \vec{D_\delta} = \left|\vec{C_3}\cdot\vec{X_\delta} - \vec{X}\right| \tag{34.5}$$

$$\vec{X_1} = \vec{X_\alpha} - \vec{A_1}\cdot(\vec{D_\alpha}), \vec{X_2} = \vec{X_\beta} - \vec{A_2}\cdot(\vec{D_\beta}), \vec{X_3} = \vec{X_\delta} - \vec{A_3}\cdot(\vec{D_\delta}) \tag{34.6}$$

$$\vec{X}(t+1)=\frac{\vec{X_1} + \vec{X_2} + \vec{X_3}}{3} \tag{34.7}$$

It can be observed that the final position lies randomly within a circular space determined by the positions of alpha, beta, and delta in the tracking space. In other words, these three wolves compare the prey's location, and the remaining wolves revise their positions randomly about this calculated prey position.

34.2.4 Attacking prey

The target stopping criterion signifies that the optimal solution has been identified in the grey wolf optimizer. To mathematically represent this process, the value of $\vec{a}$ is gradually decreased. Since $\vec{A}$ is a random value within the interval $[-2a,2a]$, reducing a also narrows the fluctuation range of $\vec{A}$. Throughout the iterations, a decreases from 2 to 0. When the random values of $\vec{A}$ are within $[-1,1]$, a search agent's subsequent position may be located anywhere between its current position and the prey's position. When $|A|<1$, the wolves are guided to attack the prey.

34.2.5 Search for prey

Grey wolves search for prey by following the positions of the alpha, beta, and delta wolves. They spread out to find prey and regroup to attack. In the GWO algorithm, this behavior is modeled using $\vec{A}$ with random values above 1 or below -1, which makes the search agents move away from the prey. This approach helps the algorithm explore more possibilities and perform a global search. When $|A|>1$, the wolves move away from the prey to try to find a better target.

Another feature of the GWO algorithm that enhances exploration is the $\vec{C}$ vector. As shown in Eq. 34.4, $\vec{C}$ consists of random values within the range [0,2]. This component assigns random weights to the prey, allowing the algorithm to either emphasize ($C>1$) or reduce ($C<1$) the influence of prey in determining the distance in Eq. 34.2. By introducing stochastic variations, this mechanism helps GWO exhibit more randomness during the optimization process, promoting exploration and reducing the risk of getting trapped in local optima.

Unlike $\vec{A}$, $\vec{C}$ does not decrease in a straight line as the iterations progress. Instead, we keep $\vec{C}$ random throughout the optimization. This helps the algorithm explore new solutions both at the beginning and toward the end. Keeping $\vec{C}$ random is especially helpful if the algorithm gets stuck in a local optimum, which can happen in the final steps as shown in Algorithm 34.1.

34.3 Path following

ALGORITHM 34.1 Grey wolf optimizer.

```
Initialize population X_i, where i=1,2,...,n
Initialize parameters a, A, and C
Evaluate the fitness of each search agent
X_α ← the best search agent
X_β ← the second-best search agent
X_δ ← the third-best search agent
t ← 0
while t< Max number of iterations do
    for each search agent do
        Update the position of the current search agent using equation (3.7)
    end for
    Update a, A, and C
    Evaluate the fitness of all search agents
    Update X_α, X_β, and X_δ
    t ← t + 1
end while
return X_α
```

34.3.1 Differential drive kinematics equations

$$\dot{x} = v \cos \theta \tag{34.8}$$

$$\dot{y} = v \sin \theta \tag{34.9}$$

$$\dot{\theta} = w \tag{34.10}$$

Given that the robot's configuration at time t_k is represented as:

$$q_k = [x_k \quad y_k \quad \theta_k] \tag{34.11}$$

and the constant velocity inputs V_k and w_k are known at the discrete time step t_k, the system's state can be updated using euler integration [16].

$$x_{k+1} = x_k + v_k T_s \cos \theta_k \tag{34.12}$$

$$y_{k+1} = y_k + v_k T_s \cos \theta_k \tag{34.13}$$

$$\theta_k = \theta_k + w_k T_s \tag{34.14}$$

where,

$$v_k T_s = \Delta s, \quad w_k T_s = \Delta \theta, \tag{34.15}$$

$$T_s = t_{k+1} - t_k. \tag{34.16}$$

The robot's current configuration is reconstructed using data obtained from incremental encoders, commonly referred to as odometry. Let $\Delta\varphi_R$ and $\Delta\varphi_L$ denote the number of wheel rotations recorded by the encoders during the sampling interval T_s. The corresponding linear and angular displacements of the robot can be expressed as:

$$\Delta s = \frac{r}{2}(\Delta\varphi_R + \Delta\varphi_L), \tag{34.17}$$

$$\Delta \theta = \frac{r}{d}(\Delta\varphi_R - \Delta\varphi_L) \tag{34.18}$$

where r represents the wheel radius, and d denotes the distance between the two wheels (axle length).

In a differential-drive robot, the position can be determined by accumulating the incremental travel distances, starting from a known initial position. The robot's estimated configuration at time t_k is obtained by integrating its motion over time.

$$\begin{bmatrix} x_k \\ y_k \\ \theta_k \end{bmatrix} = \begin{bmatrix} x_{k-1} \\ y_{k-1} \\ \theta_{k-1} \end{bmatrix} + \begin{bmatrix} \cos\theta & 0 \\ \sin\theta & 0 \\ 0 & 1 \end{bmatrix} \begin{bmatrix} \Delta s \\ \Delta\theta \end{bmatrix}, \tag{34.19}$$

34.3.2 Pure pursuit algorithm

PP is a widely used path-tracking algorithm that is both simple and effective. It operates by considering a path $\mathscr{P}$ as a sequence of ordered points:

$$\mathscr{P} = \{p_0, p_1, \ldots, p_n\} \tag{34.20}$$

where each point is represented as $p_i = (x_i, y_i)$. A local trajectory planner is a function f that determines the linear and angular velocities required to follow a reference path $\mathscr{P}_t$ at a given time t, as expressed in Eq. (34.21):

$$(v_t, \omega_t) = f(\mathscr{P}_t) \tag{34.21}$$

The first step is to identify the point p_r on the reference path $\mathscr{P}_t$ relative to the robot's current position. Once this point is found, the algorithm selects a lookahead point p_l as shown Fig. 34.1.

34.3.2.1 *Selection of look-ahead point*

There have been a lot of techniques to select the look-ahead point effectively. Look-ahead point selection can reduce the limitations of the PP algorithm. Tracking performance, stability, and cutting corners can be minimized due to the look-ahead point. The following methods are used to eliminate these kinds of problems.

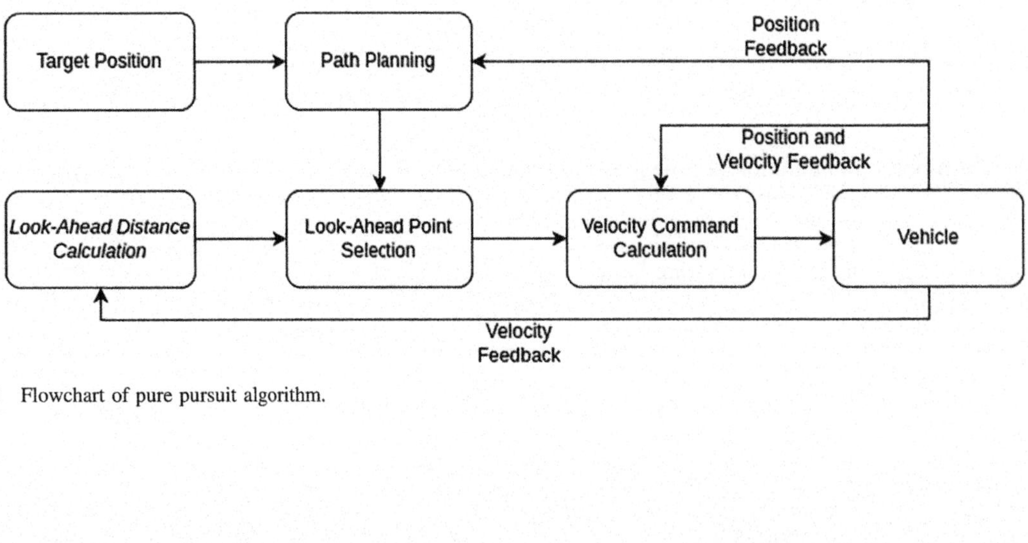

FIGURE 34.1 Flowchart of pure pursuit algorithm.

34.3.2.1.1 Look-ahead point respect to command velocity

Look-ahead point distance can be selected by using the command velocity (v_{cmd})) instead of odometry velocity of the vehicle. The following equation is used to calculate look-ahead distance [17];

$$L(v_{\text{cmd}}) = \begin{cases} 3 & \text{if } v_{\text{cmd}} < 1.34\text{m/s} \\ 2.24v_{\text{cmd}} & \text{if } 1.34\text{m/s} \leq v_{\text{cmd}} < 5.36\text{m/s} \\ 12 & \text{otherwise} \end{cases} \tag{34.22}$$

The specific coefficients in the equation are established based on results from simulations and field tests [17]. These values may be adjusted for different vehicle types.

34.3.2.1.2 Look-ahead point respect to current velocity

The magnitude of the look-ahead distance is often set proportional to the current velocity of the vehicle. This approach enables stable path tracking under various conditions. However, it is not effective in managing large cross-track errors [18].

$$L(v_{cmd}) = v_t l_t \tag{34.23}$$

34.3.2.1.3 Look-ahead point respect to constant distance

The look-ahead point distance can be determined using the vehicle's heading and location. However, this approach does not address the limitations of the PP algorithm. Identifying the optimal distance is time-consuming [19].

Once the look-ahead point p_l is determined, linear (v_t) and angular (w_t) velocity can be calculated.

34.3.2.2 Calculation of velocity

The PP algorithm helps a robot stay on a set path. It also aims to get the robot to its destination as fast as possible. To do this, the algorithm uses a specific rule to set the maximum speed.

The PP algorithm regulates the linear velocity of a vehicle according to the distance between the look-ahead point and the vehicle [20].

$$v_t' = \begin{cases} v_t \dfrac{\alpha d_O}{d_{\text{prox}}} & d_O \leq d_{\text{prox}} \\ v_t & d_O > d_{\text{prox}} \end{cases} \tag{34.24}$$

The PP algorithm adjusts the linear velocity of a vehicle based on the curvature of its path. A fundamental constraint in this process is the vehicle's minimum turning radius $R_{\min}$, which determines the sharpest possible turn that the vehicle can execute without exceeding mechanical or stability limits.

Given a desired turning radius R, the adjusted velocity v_{curv} is determined as follows:

$$v_{\text{curv}} = \begin{cases} V_d\left(1 - \dfrac{|R - R_{\min}|}{R_{\min}}\right), & R < R_{\min} \\ V_d, & R \geq R_{\min} \end{cases} \tag{34.25}$$

where v_{curv} is the curvature-adaptive velocity, V_d is the raw desired velocity, R is the actual turning radius at a given instant, and $R_{\min}$ is the vehicle's minimum turning radius.

34.4 Pure pursuit with grey wolf optimization

The look-ahead point can be determined using several mathematical formulations. Optimizing the selection of the look-ahead point is essential for improving vehicle stability and preventing corner-cutting. This section addresses the optimization of look-ahead point selection using the GWO algorithm, which identifies an admissible path. The pseudocode for the implemented algorithm is provided in Algorithm 34.2.

Algorithm 34.2 defines p_{ref} as the reference path for tracking, p_v as the current location of the robot, and r_{min} as the minimum turning radius of the vehicle. The algorithm identifies the closest point on the reference path. From this point, the hybrid PP algorithm generates a path and computes the associated cost for each point along the reference path. Fig. 34.3 illustrates that the selected look-ahead point is determined using the cost functions described in the following section. (Figs. 34.2 and 34.3)

ALGORITHM 34.2 Adjusting look-ahead point.

Input: p_{ref}, r_{min}
Output: p_d
for i=0 **to** p_{ref} **do**
  if $\|p_i - p_{robot}\| > r_{min}$ **then**
    $p_{closest} \leftarrow p_i$
    break
  end if
  $i \leftarrow i + 1$
end for
$i_{p_{closest}} \leftarrow indexof\ p_{closest}$
for $i = i_{p_{closest}}$ **to** p_{ref} **do**
  $\text{Path}_{cost} \leftarrow \text{PathCost}(p_i, p_{ref}(i))$
  $p_d \leftarrow argmin_{p_{ref}(i)}(\text{Path}_{cost})$
  $i \leftarrow i + 1$
end for

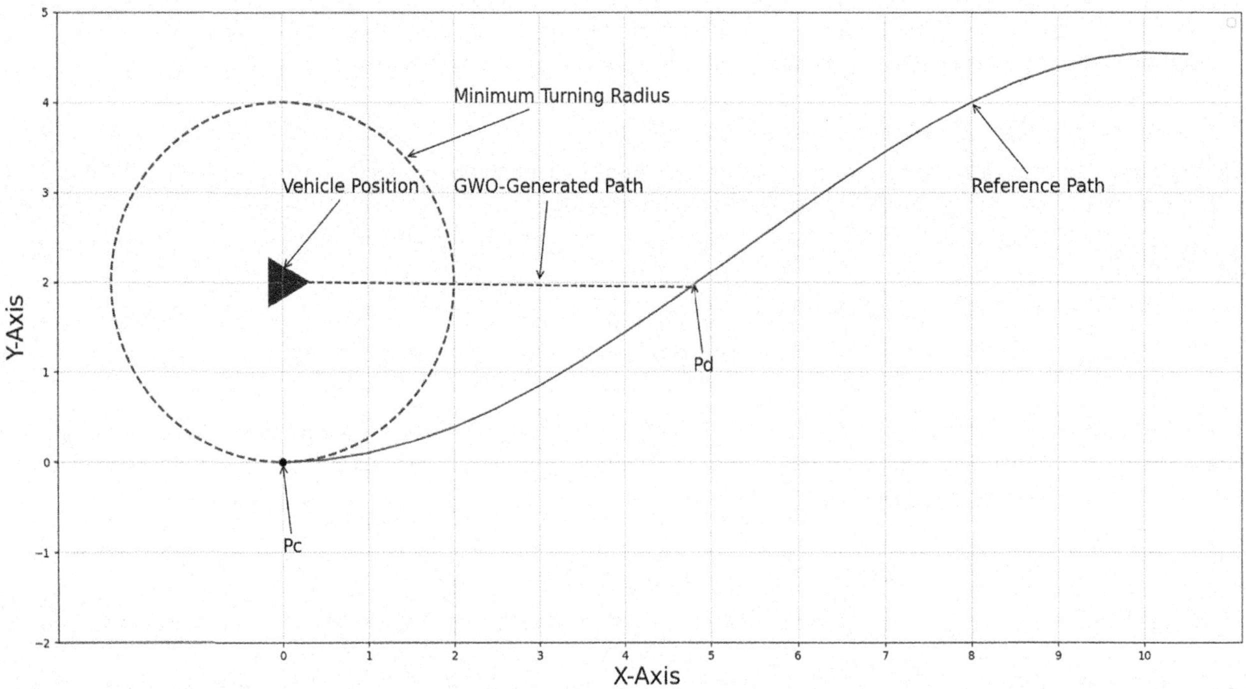

FIGURE 34.2 A lowest angular turn experiment without obstacles.

34.4.1 Generating path using grey wolf optimizer

Finding the best path between the start and end point is often described as the shortest path, as seen in the traveling salesman problem [21]. However, the result of just the shortest path cannot be appropriate for autonomous mobile robots. Working with AMR in the warehouse has constraints, such as collision between objects and kinematic constraints of the vehicle. These three constraints are described by the following equation:

$$F_{\text{cost}} = w_1\widetilde{C}_l + w_2\widetilde{C}_c + w_3\widetilde{C}_t \tag{34.26}$$

$$\widetilde{C}_l = \frac{C_l}{L_{ref}}, \quad \widetilde{C}_c = \frac{C_c - C_c^{\min}}{C_c^{\max} - C_c^{\min} + \varepsilon}, \quad \widetilde{C}_t = \frac{C_t}{\pi},$$

Here, L_{ref} denotes the maximum admissible look-ahead arc length within the local planning window, while $C_c^{\min}$ and $C_c^{\max}$ are obtained from the costmap parameters. The objective is to minimize the weighted sum $w_1\widetilde{C_l} + w_2\widetilde{C_c} + w_3\widetilde{C_t}$. This approach ensures that cost values remain numerically comparable across different environments.

C_l, C_c, and C_t denote the path length cost, collision cost, and turning cost, respectively. The coefficients w_1, w_2, and w_3 represent the corresponding weights assigned to each cost function.

$$C_l = L_{P_iP_t} \tag{34.27}$$

where L_{PiPt} represents the distance between P_i and P_t.P_i refers to the current position at iteration, and P_t refers to the target position [22].

$$C_c = \begin{cases} C_{max}, & \text{if } d{=}0 \\ C_{mid}, & \text{if } d{\cdot}r \leq R \\ (C_{mid} - 1){\cdot}e^{-w\cdot(d\cdot r - R)}, & \text{otherwise} \end{cases} \tag{34.28}$$

Here, C_c denotes the cost associated with the autonomous vehicle's position, and d is the distance between the vehicle and an obstacle. r and R represent the map resolution and the vehicle's inscribed radius, respectively. w is the equation's weight. C_{max} indicates the map's lethal cost, while C_{mid} identifies cells within the vehicle's inscribed radius of a real obstacle. This cost function is based on Ref. [23].

$$C_t = \theta_{n-1} - atan2(\Delta y, \Delta x) \tag{34.29}$$

where θ_{n-1} represents a heading angle of n-1 position. (x_n, y_n) position of P_n: n and $\Delta x = x_n - x_{n-1}$, $\Delta y = y_n - y_{n-1}$ refers to the position difference between two points. This function minimizes the angle change between two consecutive points and applies a cost based on the adjustment. It ensures that each new point's orientation is as close as possible to the previous point's direction, reducing abrupt changes. A path planning algorithm iteratively optimizes a route to reach a specified destination. The pseudocode for the path planning process is provided in Algorithm 34.3. At each step, the algorithm calculates the best wolf position with respect to the cost function and selects the optimal position for the path until satisfy closing conditions.

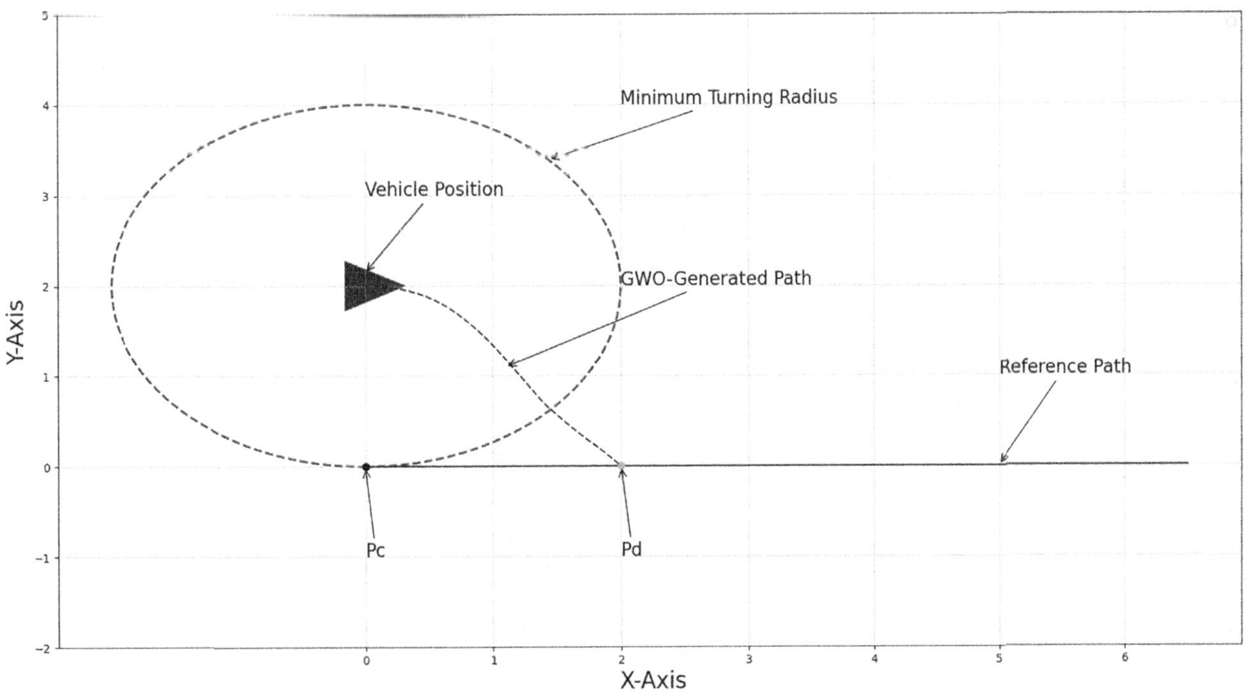

FIGURE 34.3 The figure shows that the algorithm selects the optimal look-ahead point rather than the nearest one.

ALGORITHM 34.3 Robot path planning using grey wolf.
1: **Initialize** the robot, goal
2: **while** Meet the closing condition **do**
3: Generate a random population of the grey wolf optimizer.
4: Select the best solution among the population to fit F_{cost}
5: Set the best solution to n-1 position.
6: **end while**
7: **End Algorithm**

34.4.2 Look-ahead selection strategy

The algorithm first checks the reference path from the robot's current position and finds the first waypoint that is at least $r_{\min}$ away. This step sets a minimum turning radius for the robot. Next, the algorithm looks ahead to a set of possible waypoints based on their index. For each candidate, it calculates a local objective function F_{cost} over the possible arc. This function takes into account the path length, any obstacles cleared by the costmap, and how smoothly the robot's heading changes. From these candidates, the look-ahead point p_d is chosen to minimize F_{cost}. This two-step process ensure the final target is both feasible for the robot to reach and optimal for its behavior, by combining distance checks with cost-based selection.

Let K be the number of candidates in the forward window, and let C_{eval} be the computational cost of evaluating each one, which mainly comes from trigonometric calculations and costmap queries. The computational complexity per cycle is $\mathcal{O}(KC_{\text{eval}})$, with only a small, constant amount of extra memory needed beyond the stored path. The initial distance scan can be made more efficient by starting from the robot's last selected index. If K is larger, the algorithm is more likely to pick safer or smoother waypoints, but this also increases latency. If K is smaller, latency goes down, but the algorithm might miss better options with more clearance or a gentler curve (Fig. 34.4).

34.5 Experimental setup and results

We evaluate five metaheuristics: GWO, particle swarm optimization (PSO), differential evolution (DE), genetic algorithm (GA), and whale optimization algorithm (WOA), plugged into the same path planning objective in Eq. 34.26.

34.5.1 Objective weights in Eq. 34.26 and tuning protocol

We minimize Eq. 34.26 so as to make the scales comparable across environments with normalized terms $\widetilde{C}_\ell$, $\widetilde{C}_c$, $\widetilde{C}_t$ defined in Section 1.4. To resolve the compromise between progress, safety, and smoothness. The three weights steer the planner's behavior directly. One is their sum ($w_1 + w_2 + w_3 = 1$). As w_1 (path length) increases, paths become more direct and time-efficient, though if it is pushed too high, the path may skim obstacles, take sharper corners, and occasionally sacrifice feasibility in cluttered scenes. As w_2 (clearance/safety) increases, obstacle margins do enlarge, as well as feasibility typically improves under clutter and/or sensing noise; when people take it to extremes, it can yield conservative detours plus longer routes. In the event that w_3 (smoothness/turning) is increased, then curvature and also steering oscillations are reduced. This results in easier tracking and also lower actuator stress, but in the event that the setting is overly dominant, then the planner may avoid tight gaps or perhaps "round off" corners, which then increases total length. Raise w_1 for time-critical open runs; raise w_2 for safety-critical densely cluttered environments; and raise w_3 when high-speed tracking or curvature limiting is paramount. A balanced default just like $(w_1, w_2, w_3)=(0.45, 0.40, 0.15)$ provides for this.

34.5.2 Metaheuristic configurations and implementation

All optimizers act on the same decision vector and objective F_{cost}, with the shared settings in Table 34.1. Algorithm operators and update rules follow their canonical definitions and are instantiated via the open-source MEALPY library [24]. We benchmarked five families to span complementary exploration–exploitation behaviors and provide literature-grounded baselines for path planning: GA, a classical evolutionary scheme with selection-crossover-mutation and broad empirical coverage in engineering problems [25]; PSO, a velocity-driven, social-learning dynamic noted for rapid convergence on smooth continuous landscapes [26]; DE, which uses differential mutation and binomial crossover and remains robust and competitive in modern variants on separable and ill-scaled problems [27], and WOA, included as an additional swarm-style comparator to test the generality of conclusions.

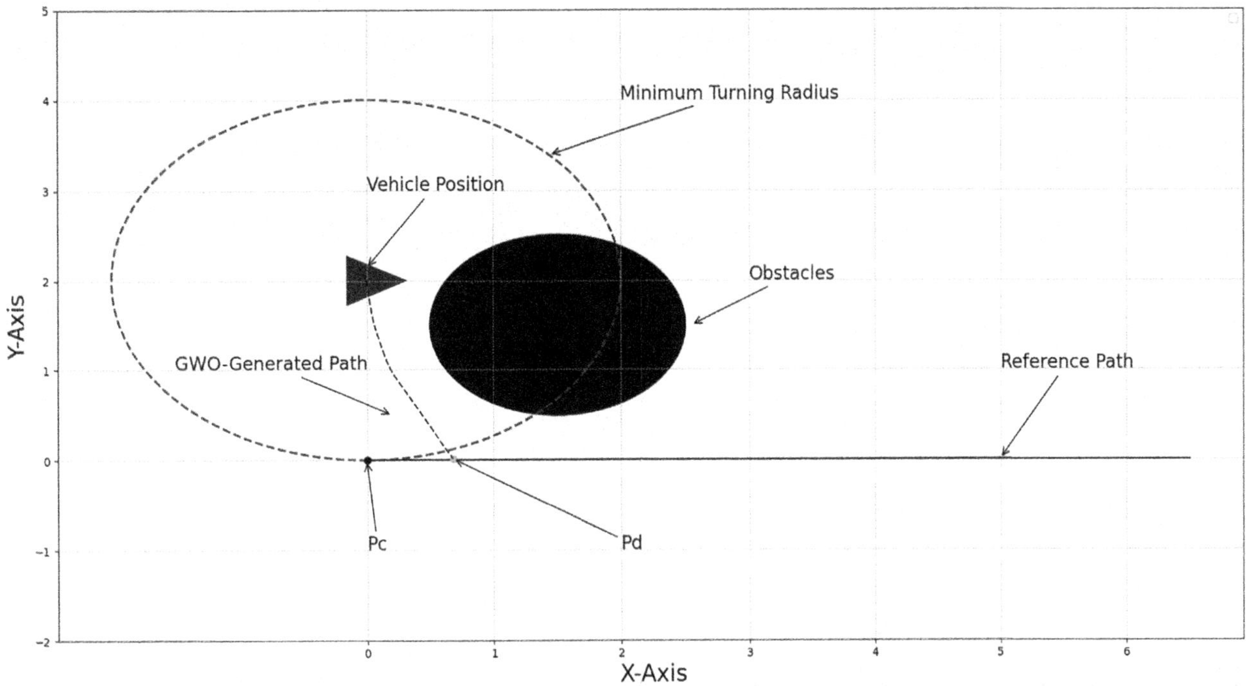

FIGURE 34.4 The figure illustrates that the algorithm selects the optimal look-ahead with obstacles by using the 26.

TABLE 34.1 Metaheuristic settings are used across all methods.

Setting	Value/Definition
Population size	n_{pop}=50
Iterations	T=400
Function evaluations (per run)	$FE = n_{pop}(1 + T)$=20,050
Number of runs	N_{runs}=20
Random seeds	0... 19 seeds fixed integer seed per run; shared across algorithms
Boundary handling	Projection to bounds: $\mathbf{x} \leftarrow clip(\mathbf{x}, \mathbf{l}, \mathbf{u})$

34.5.3 Results

We report four metrics. Fitness is the final value of F_{cost} for the returned path; Feasibility is the proportion of runs without any collision events; Runtime is the wall-clock time, in seconds, for one full optimization call (i.e., a planning cycle); and FE denotes the function-evaluation count reported by the solver. Summary statistics (mean, standard deviation, median, and average rank) for all algorithms appear in Table 34.2. In brief, GWO attains the best mean rank and the lowest central tendency of fitness, with PSO and WOA close behind; DE lags these three, while GA exhibits substantially higher variance despite being the fastest in wall-clock time. Feasibility is 100% for GWO, PSO, WOA, and DE, and 95% for GA. Mean per-run latencies cluster around 8–9 s for GWO/PSO/WOA/DE, whereas GA is markedly faster but less reliable in fitness and feasibility.

We assessed statistical significance using two-sided Wilcoxon signed-rank tests with Holm step-down adjustment (Table 34.3). DE performed significantly worse than GA, GWO, WOA, and PSO. GA was significantly outperformed by GWO, PSO, and WOA. GWO and WOA also differed significantly, as did DE and WOA. No significant differences were found between GWO and PSO or between PSO and WOA at α=0.05. The Friedman omnibus test across all algorithms was highly significant, confirming that performance distributions differ.

TABLE 34.2 Comparison of metaheuristics for collision-aware path planning. Lower fitness is better. Feasibility is the fraction of collision-free runs. Runtime is in seconds.

Algorithm	Fitness mean	Fitness std	Fitness median	Avg. rank	Feas. (%)	Runtime mean	Runtime std
GWO	1.4551	0.0389	1.4347	1.45	100.0%	8.498	0.353
PSO	1.5669	0.2355	1.5045	1.95	100.0%	8.359	0.232
WOA	1.5830	0.0883	1.5825	2.75	100.0%	8.526	0.296
DE	2.2243	0.4514	2.1821	3.85	100.0%	8.613	0.198
GA	7.4433	9.8247	4.9183	5.00	95.0%	0.071	0.004

DE, Differential evolution; *GA*, genetic algorithm; *GWO*, grey wolf optimizer; *PSO*, particle swarm optimization; *WOA*, whale optimization algorithm.

TABLE 34.3 Pairwise Wilcoxon on fitness with Holm adjustment (α=0.05).

Algorithm A	Algorithm B	$p_{Wilcoxon}$	p_{Holm}
DE	GA	1.907×10^{-6}	1.907×10^{-5}
DE	GWO	1.907×10^{-6}	1.717×10^{-5}
GA	GWO	1.907×10^{-6}	1.526×10^{-5}
GA	PSO	1.907×10^{-6}	1.335×10^{-5}
GA	WOA	1.907×10^{-6}	1.144×10^{-5}
DE	WOA	5.722×10^{-6}	2.861×10^{-5}
GWO	WOA	5.722×10^{-6}	2.289×10^{-5}
DE	PSO	1.335×10^{-4}	4.005×10^{-4}
GWO	PSO	8.969×10^{-2}	1.794×10^{-1}
PSO	WOA	1.231×10^{-1}	1.231×10^{-1}

DE, Differential evolution; *GA*, genetic algorithm; *GWO*, grey wolf optimizer; *PSO*, particle swarm optimization; *WOA*, whale optimization algorithm.

34.6 Conclusion

This chapter has proposed the grey wolf optimizer with the PP path tracking algorithm to solve the issues related to the look-ahead point for autonomous vehicles. For efficient path tracking performance, this chapter discussed the cost function for path planning and selected the optimum path to reach the look-ahead point at the given reference path. The promise of the grey wolf optimizer has been demonstrated by creating the best route. The selection of the cost function for the route is significantly important to determine the look-ahead point. This algorithm uses three main parameters, which are the distance between the selected point and the target point, the distance from the obstacle, and the angular change concerning the previous point. The first parameter adjusts to find a closed route to reach the target. This parameter forces the GWO algorithm to select the optimum closed path shown in Fig. 34.5. The second parameter is about avoiding collisions in the look-ahead selection process. The angle change parameter allows us to generate a path with minimal change in direction, while the collision avoidance parameter tries to keep the path away from obstacles, as shown in Fig. 34.4. Moreover, the lowest angular change is an important parameter for vehicle types that have Ackerman steering, and this result is shown in the Figs. 34.3 and 34.2; however, the differential-drive model can perform maneuvers such as point turns, which can be controlled by adjusting the weights in the objective function 26. After generating the best route to the target point, the algorithm selects the minimum cost route and the look-ahead point. In the end, the algorithm has shown the GWO algorithm's ability to find a path and its compatibility with the path-tracking algorithm.

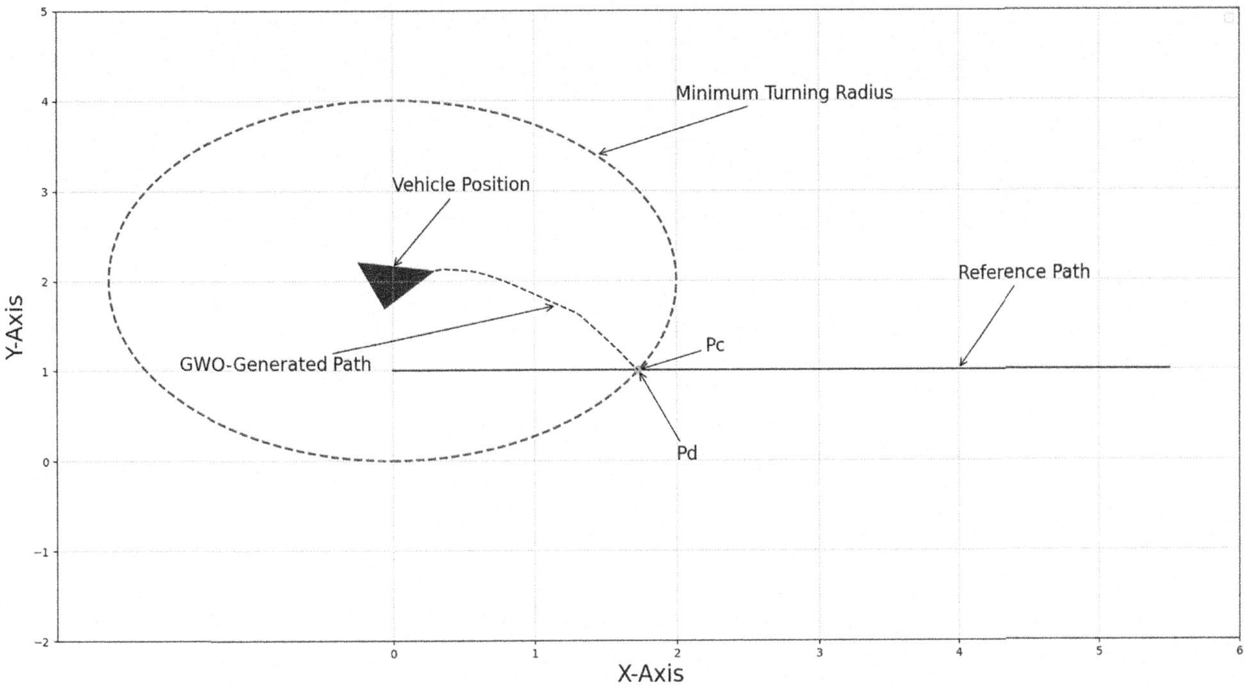

FIGURE 34.5 The figure demonstrates that the look-ahead selection algorithm can identify the closest valid look-ahead point that satisfies the minimum turning radius.

Acknowledgments

All ideas and methods presented in this article were developed by the authors. The ChatGPT Model o3 was used solely to assist with generating experimental setup and checking the grammar of the manuscript. In addition, it provided support during the Python implementation of the proposed algorithm. All experiments were conducted on linux operating system equipped with a quad-core 11th Gen Intel Core i7–1165G7 processor and 16 GB of RAM.

References

[1] R.C. Conlter, Implementation of the Pure Pursuit Path'hcking Algorithm, Camegie Mellon University, (1992).
[2] Yin J., Zhang Z., Theodorou E., Tsiotras P. Trajectory distribution control for model predictive path integral control using covariance steering. In: 2022 International Conference on Robotics and Automation (ICRA). IEEE; 2022. pp. 1478–1484.
[3] T. Yamasaki, H. Takano, Y. Baba, Robust path-following for UAV using pure pursuit guidance, Aerial Vehicles, IntechOpen, (2009).
[4] H. Faris, I. Aljarah, M.A. Al-Betar, S. Mirjalili, Grey wolf optimizer: a review of recent variants and applications, Neural computing and applications 30 (2018) 413–435.
[5] M.H. Nadimi-Shahraki, S. Taghian, S. Mirjalili, An improved grey wolf optimizer for solving engineering problems, Expert Systems with Applications 166 (2021) 113917.
[6] N. Mittal, U. Singh, B.S. Sohi, Modified grey wolf optimizer for global engineering optimization, Applied computational intelligence and soft computing 2016 (1) (2016) 7950348.
[7] M. Fahad, F. Aadil, S. Khan, P.A. Shah, K. Muhammad, J. Lloret, et al., Grey wolf optimization based clustering algorithm for vehicular ad-hoc networks, Computers & Electrical Engineering 70 (2018) 853–870.
[8] M.A. Sen, M. Kalyoncu, Optimal tuning of PID controller using grey wolf optimizer algorithm for quadruped robot, Balkan Journal of Electrical and Computer Engineering 6 (1) (2018) 29–35.
[9] I.A. Zamfirache, R.E. Precup, R.C. Roman, E.M. Petriu, Policy iteration reinforcement learning-based control using a grey wolf optimizer algorithm, Information Sciences 585 (2022) 162–175.
[10] G. Komaki, V. Kayvanfar, Grey Wolf Optimizer algorithm for the two-stage assembly flow shop scheduling problem with release time, Journal of computational science 8 (2015) 109–120.

[11] A.A. El-Fergany, H.M. Hasanien, Single and multi-objective optimal power flow using grey wolf optimizer and differential evolution algorithms, Electric Power Components and Systems 43 (13) (2015) 1548–1559.
[12] S. Mirjalili, S.M. Mirjalili, A. Lewis, Grey wolf optimizer, Advances in engineering software 69 (2014) 46–61.
[13] M.N. Ab Wahab, S. Nefti-Meziani, A. Atyabi, A comparative review on mobile robot path planning: classical or meta-heuristic methods? Annual Reviews in Control 50 (2020) 233–252.
[14] E. Belge, A. Altan, R. Hacoğlu, Metaheuristic optimization-based path planning and tracking of quadcopter for payload hold-release mission, Electronics. 11 (8) (2022) 1208.
[15] J. Liu, X. Wei, H. Huang, An improved grey wolf optimization algorithm and its application in path planning, IEEE Access 9 (2021) 121944–121956.
[16] S.K. Malu, J. Majumdar, et al., Kinematics, localization and control of differential drive mobile robot, Global Journal of Research In Engineering 14 (1) (2014) 1–9.
[17] Y. Kuwata, J. Teo, S. Karaman, G. Fiore, E. Frazzoli, J. How, Motion planning in complex environments using closed-loop prediction, in: AIAA Guidance, Navigation and Control Conference and Exhibit; 2008, p. 7166.
[18] M.W. Park, S.W. Lee, W.Y. Han, Development of lateral control system for autonomous vehicle based on adaptive pure pursuit algorithm, in: 2014 14th International Conference on Control, Automation and Systems (ICCAS 2014), IEEE, 2014, pp. 1443–1447.
[19] J. Ahn, S. Shin, M. Kim, J. Park, Accurate path tracking by adjusting look-ahead point in pure pursuit method, International Journal of Automotive Technology 22 (2021) 119–129.
[20] S. Macenski, S. Singh, F. Martn, J. Ginés, Regulated pure pursuit for robot path tracking, Autonomous Robots 47 (6) (2023) 685–694.
[21] V. Roberge, M. Tarbouchi, G. Labonté, Comparison of parallel genetic algorithm and particle swarm optimization for real-time UAV path planning, IEEE Transactions on Industrial Informatics 9 (1) (2012) 132–141.
[22] C. Liu, Z. Gao, W. Zhao, A new path planning method based on firefly algorithm, in: 2012 Fifth International Joint Conference on Computational Sciences and Optimization, IEEE, 2012, pp. 775–778.
[23] M. Quigley, K. Conley, B. Gerkey, J. Faust, T. Foote, J. Leibs , et al. ROS: an open-source robot operating system, in: ICRA Workshop on Open Source Software. vol. 3. Kobe, 2009, p. 5.
[24] N. Van Thieu, S. Mirjalili, MEALPY: an open-source library for latest meta-heuristic algorithms in Python, Journal of Systems Architecture (2023).
[25] A. Lambora, K. Gupta, K. Chopra, Genetic algorithm-A literature review, in: 2019 International Conference on Machine Learning, Big Data, Cloud and Parallel Computing (COMITCon). IEEE, 2019, pp. 380–384.
[26] J. Kennedy, R. Eberhart, Particle swarm optimization, in: Proceedings of ICNN'95-International Conference on Neural Networks, vol. 4. IEEE, 1995, pp. 1942–1948.
[27] W. Deng, S. Shang, X. Cai, H. Zhao, Y. Song, J. Xu, An improved differential evolution algorithm and its application in optimization problem, Soft Computing 25 (7) (2021) 5277–5298.

Chapter 35

Can the grey wolf optimizer solve daily life problems?

Sayan Nayek[1] and Avishek Dolai[1,2]
[1]Department of Zoology, University of Calcutta, Kolkata, West Bengal, India, [2]Department of Life Sciences, Semiochemicals and Lipid Laboratory, Presidency University, Kolkata, West Bengal, India

35.1 Introduction

35.1.1 Understanding grey wolf optimizer

Various activities and behaviors exhibited by animals provide us with valuable lessons and inspiration. From lower invertebrates to higher vertebrates, they teach us from their everyday activities. Grey wolf optimizer (GWO) is a metaheuristic optimization algorithm inspired by nature that mimics the pack structure and predation mechanism of grey wolves (*Canis lupus*) [1]. GWO is a member of the metaheuristic algorithm family, which is applied extensively to solve difficult optimization problems otherwise hard to tackle using conventional techniques [2]). Like other metaheuristics, GWO does not necessarily claim to find an optimal solution, but rather aims to find sufficient solutions within a time limit. This is an essential quality in the context of real-world optimization problems where the problem space can exhibit a large, possibly combinatorial, nonlinear, or any number of other idiosyncratic characteristics [3,4]). The class of algorithms referred to as metaheuristics, including GWO, is developed to circumvent the limitations of exact approaches such as dynamic programming or linear programming, which are typically too computationally expensive, impractical for large-scale problems, or infeasible for complicated high-dimensional problems [5,6]. Whereas exact approaches typically rely on large-scale numerical mathematical models or exhaustive search methods, metaheuristics are a high-level principle that utilizes, for example, inspirations from physical systems or biological behavior [7,8]. Based on this context, GWO acquires its mechanism from grey wolves' natural social and hunting patterns, thereby ending up with a method that is adaptive as well as efficient for solving optimization issues [1].

The beauty of metaheuristics is their capacity to reconcile exploration (searching the solution space expansively) and exploitation (examining solutions near promising regions) [9,10]. This reconciliation allows GWO to efficiently explore complex, high-dimensional solution spaces and thus find favor in usage across engineering design, scheduling, resource management, machine learning, and power management applications [11-13].

35.1.2 Biological inspiration behind grey wolf optimizer

The GWO algorithm was proposed by Seyedali [1]. The wolves are generally found in India, Southwest Asia, and parts of the Middle East. The structure of the GWO is theoretically derived from the hunting and social structure of grey wolves, who occupy hierarchical groups [1,14]. Wolves are seen to possess an orderly social setup wherein there exists a set of distinct roles when on the hunt, making it a collaborative and efficient catching mechanism for prey [15]. Social life within a group of wolves generally involves division into four dominant ranks depending on ranking or hierarchy [16]:

a) Alpha wolves: The pack leaders who decide on where and when to hunt. They lead the pack's activity and get preferential access to the food obtained through a successful hunt.
b) Beta wolves: The secondary-in-command wolves that help the alpha and are responsible for maintaining the pack rules.

Grey Wolf Optimizer. DOI: https://doi.org/10.1016/B978-0-443-36624-6.00007-X

c) Delta wolves: These wolves take their cue from the alpha and beta wolves, assisting in the hunt and keeping the pack stable.

d) Omega wolves: The lowest wolves in the pack hierarchy. They are usually dominated by others but still assist in the hunt and will sometimes venture into new areas for sustenance [17].

This hierarchical organization plays a vital role in the pack's survival as each member participates in the total hunting strategy that demands cooperation as well as coordination [18]. The ideology of leadership as observed in the alpha wolf, as well as the combined effort of the rest of the wolves, exactly translates into the search mechanism in GWO, in which the solution found so far is utilized as the guiding component, and other candidate solutions help narrow down the search [19].

The concept of cooperative hunting is particularly important because wolves hunt cooperatively to catch prey by usually encircling prey to keep it trapped [4]. In the GWO scenario, this reflects exploration and exploitation (further elaborated in the following paragraph). In GWO, the Alpha wolf (optimum solution) is tasked with leading the search, while the other wolves explore the solution space and eventually converge to the optimum solution found. Although they are inferior wolves, Omega wolves facilitate exploration of the solution space to avoid premature convergence and ensure that a global optimum is available [20,21].

35.1.3 Core mechanisms of grey wolf optimizer

The overarching principle of the GWO is built on the wolves' social behavior and the way they prey on other animals. The GWO mimics the wolves' predation behavior in a very basic sense in the three basic functions that can be considered encircling, hunting, and attacking. These functions have the objective of mimicking the collaborative behavior of wolves while they are navigating through and searching for prey. In this way, the algorithm itself is capable of balancing the exploratory aspects of the solution space, as well as the exploitational aspects of potentially useful areas [22,23].

35.1.3.1 Social hierarchy: alpha, beta, delta, omega

In the GWO algorithm, every possible solution to the optimization is a "wolf," and the social system of wolves manages the relationships between the solutions and the search direction of the algorithm. The alpha wolf is the best solution found in the search space, and the beta and delta wolves assist in searching the regions of the neighborhood of the alpha wolf [16,24]. There are also omega wolves that, in their own way, assist in the solution space, and even if omega wolves are not actively searching toward the potential global optimal solution, they assist in sufficient exploration of the search space so that the search does not converge onto a local optimal solution too early [19,20].

At every iteration, the positions of all wolves in the solution space are updated concerning the positions of the alpha, beta, and delta wolves. The update of the positions of all wolves at each iteration indicates that all wolves are approaching the global optimum, and therefore it is the concept of driving all of the wolves (beta, delta, and omega) into a promising search space using the position of the alpha wolf as the attraction [18,25].

35.1.3.2 Encircling, hunting, and attacking behaviors

The GWO algorithm is a social hierarchy and cooperative hunting strategy of grey wolves through three behaviors: encircling, hunting, and attacking. Each of these behaviors are modeled mathematically, and they are used to balance exploratory and exploratory motions [15,21].

35.1.3.2.1 Encircling behavior

Grey wolves encircle their prey as a means of preventing their escape. In GWO, this behavior is reflected in the ability of candidate solutions (wolves) to adjust their positions based on the location of the leading solution (the Alpha wolf). The mathematical representation of this encircling mechanism is given by:

$$\vec{D} = |\vec{C_1} \times \vec{X_\alpha}(t) - \vec{X_i}(t)|$$

$$\vec{X_i}(t+1) = \vec{X_i}(t) - \vec{A_1} \times \vec{D}$$

Where:

o $\vec{D}$ denotes the distance between the i-th wolf and the alpha wolf,

o $\vec{X_\alpha}(t)$ is the position vector of the alpha wolf at iteration t,

o $\vec{X_i}(t)$ is the position of the i-th wolf at iteration t,
o $\vec{C_1}$ and $\vec{A_1}$ are coefficient vectors that introduce randomness and influence movement direction and step size, respectively.

These vectors are defined as follows:

$$\vec{A_1} = 2 \times \vec{a} \times \vec{r_1} - \vec{a}$$

$$\vec{C_1} = 2 \times \vec{r_2}$$

Where $\vec{a}$ decreases linearly from 2 to 0 over the course of iterations $t \in [0,T]$, and $\vec{r_1}$ $\vec{r_2}$ are random vectors in [0,1]. $a(t) = 2 - 2 \times \frac{t}{T}$
where t is the current iteration and T is the maximum number of iterations.

This formulation enables wolves to converge toward the leader while maintaining sufficient diversity in the population [26,27].

35.1.3.2.2 Hunting behavior

Hunting, which represents the process of tracking and approaching prey, corresponds in GWO to the exploitation of promising regions of the search space. It is assumed that the alpha wolf has the best knowledge about the prey's position. Beta and delta wolves also contribute, influencing the position update of the rest of the pack [15,16]. The general position update rule based on multiple leaders is:

$$\vec{X_i}(t+1) = \frac{1}{3}(\vec{X_1} + \vec{X_2} + \vec{X_3})$$

where $\vec{X_1}$, $\vec{X_2}$, and $\vec{X_3}$ are the updated positions relative to alpha, beta, and delta wolves, respectively.

35.1.3.2.3 Attacking behavior (Exploitation)

As the wolves close in on the prey, their search behavior transitions from exploration to exploitation. This is modeled by decreasing the value of $\vec{a}$, which reduces the influence of the random components $\vec{A_1}$ and $\vec{C_1}$. Consequently, the wolves converge more tightly around the Alpha wolf's position [28,29]. This mechanism ensures the algorithm's convergence toward the global optimum over time.

In summary, the GWO algorithm's strength lies in its biologically inspired mechanisms that guide search agents through a dynamic balance of diversification (exploration) and intensification (exploitation), with the encircling, hunting, and attacking behaviors playing pivotal roles in optimization performance [24,29].

35.1.4 Why grey wolf optimizer approaches real-life optimization problems successfully

On practical optimization challenges, GWO has proven rather versatile. Because of its combination of natural characteristics, GWO offers one of the main benefits in balancing exploration and exploitation [24,30]. GWO has been developed to have a flexible search process with an alpha wolf (current optimal solution), a beta wolf, and then a delta wolf (which assists with optimization and local region exploration) using the hierarchy of grey wolves. From the point of obtaining better solutions and improved convergence characteristics [31,32], GWO can explore the solution space and land in promising regions.

GWO's simplicity and stability are two further great advantages. Compared to other metaheuristics, GWO is a rather basic metaheuristic with few control parameters [33]. Consequently, GWO can be quite potent with a straightforward approach applied to a spectrum of uses in and around engineering optimizations, machine learning, logistics, and control systems [29,30]. Once more demonstrating GWO's efficacy and capability as an optimization tool is the consistent performance over a broad spectrum of problems [21,34].

GWO also shows great degrees of flexibility. GWO is naturally able, as a population-based optimization method, to solve high-dimensional, nonlinear, or multimodal problems. Furthermore, as no particular mathematical model is required to depict a problem with GWO, it is fitly used in circumstances when estimating the objective function can be mathematically infeasible, excessively complex, or noisy [31,35]. For practitioners who have to deal with real-world systems often erratic or partially defined, this general applicability gives GWO flexibility and makes it a good option [7,36].

35.1.5 Grey wolf optimizer's strengths and limitations for applied uses

With many apparent advantages, the GWO is a potentially valuable optimization method for practical application in solving problems. Its capacity to do a worldwide search is among its best traits since it helps it to effectively investigate the whole solution space. Unlike some of the conventional optimization methods that can be caught in local optima, the population-based and dynamic search characteristics of GWO guarantee that it is capable of escaping premature convergence and spotting the global optimum in the long run [14,31]. This makes it especially helpful for addressing difficult, multi-modal, high-dimensional problems whose solution space is not readily accessible using conventional means [21,37].

GWO's simplicity and adaptability are also rather strong points. With just a few parameters, the algorithm is also rather easy to understand and usable even for researchers and practitioners with limited knowledge of optimization [24,32]. Its general-purpose nature allows GWO to be applied for a wide range of issues in many sectors, including engineering design, resource allocation, scheduling, and machine learning [35,38]. Its ability to withstand different optimization difficulties—from continuous to combinatorial domains—attests to the quality and type of the optimizer itself [39,40].

GWO also does rather nicely for high-dimensional problems. Most usually, the algorithm arrives at good solutions within a reasonable time frame [32,33]. In cases when the solution space is large and highly complex, its inbuilt exploration–exploitation balance helps it to move through easily. GWO is a preferred method in real-world applications where traditional optimization methods fail since it can efficiently cope with high-dimensional spaces without requiring problem-specific tuning [28,41].

Still, GWO has restrictions even if it has many advantages. Probably the main cause of worry is parameter sensitivity. Though just a limited number of parameters are needed to start, the efficiency of the algorithm may depend sensitively on their settings, including the population of wolves or the iterations [31,42]. Tuning of the parameters is therefore an inevitable need whenever one tries applying GWO to a practical problem [37,43]. An improper choice of parameters will result in wasteful searches or unsatisfactory convergence.

One further restriction of the GWO method relates to its convergence speed in some kinds of problems. Traditional optimization methods may converge faster than GWO in very complicated, multimodal optimization problems. GWO is quite capable overall of investigating large ranges of values across a solution space; this exploratory feature causes GWO to see slower convergence than would result from a more exploitative approach [44,45]. GWO would not be the recommended search method in situations like this, particularly if an optimization method is used to get a rapid response that speed counts [46].

Last, although GWO is highly flexible when compared to conventional techniques, the GWO method can have some challenges with some classes of optimization problems where problem-based, conventional approaches are indispensable. For very limited optimization problems where GWO must directly deal with constraints, for example, GWO may need to be modified or hybridized [30,35].

GWO's strengths are ultimately its capacity to rapidly and effectively investigate difficult solution spaces, its resilience and adaptability as a technique, and its capacity to operate independently from any one exploration strategy, like destructive or traditional optimization methods [21,24]. GWO does, however, have flaws, including parameter sensitivity, lagging in convergence speed for some circumstances, and occasionally an inability to address special problem concerns [28,47]. When choosing GWO for applied real-world complexity, these elements should be given great thought [45].

35.2 Daily life problems as optimization tasks

35.2.1 What is optimization in daily context?

Optimization refers to the process of determining the best choice from a set of feasible alternatives according to some criteria that may or may not be numerically measured. In our journeys of life, we make choices to try to maximize or minimize some personal objective (e.g., minimize commuting time, minimize costs, maximize health-related outcomes, or maximize convenience), usually recognizing we have real limits [48,49]. The decisions we make in our daily lives (e.g., which route to work will minimize commuting time or what things to purchase based on constraints, like a grocery list and a self-imposed budget) can be specified as optimization problems [50].

Formally, such decision-making problems can be structured as follows:

$$\min_{x \in X} f(x) \text{subject to } g_i(x) \le 0,\ h_j(x) = 0$$

Where:

o $x \in X$ denotes the decision variables (e.g., selection of items, allocation of time slots);
o $f(x)$ represents the objective function (e.g., cost, time, or caloric intake);
o $g_i(x)$ and $h_j(x)$ define the inequality and equality constraints (e.g., budget limits, nutritional goals);
o X is the feasible solution space, encompassing all values of x that satisfy the defined conditions.

While human decision-making in these instances is often ruled intuitively through judgments and heuristics, expressing them as formal optimization problems establishes a structured and repeatable process and permits the introduction of mathematical rigor into the decision-making process [51,52].

35.2.2 Common characteristics of daily optimization problems

Although optimization problems vary widely in the daily context, many have similar properties that lend themselves to computational techniques. First, many daily optimization problems are multiobjective. Balancing competing objectives involves trade-offs. For instance, a user could try to minimize travel time while also minimizing cost (fuel)—if you minimize time and cost under different levels of congestion [48,53]. Therefore these problems can be expressed as:

$$\min_{x \in X} [f_1(x), f_2(x), \ldots f_k(x)]$$

Here, $f_1, f_2, \ldots f_k$ represent multiple objective functions (e.g., time, cost, quality) to be optimized simultaneously.

Second, these problems often conform to the properties of constrained and combinatorial problems. Considering an example of meal planning over one week—for every day, there may only be two options, either include the food item, or do not include the food item, with multiple constraints in terms of nutritional intake, cost, or preferences [52,54]:

$$\sum_{i=1}^{n} c_i x_i \leq B, \quad \sum_{i=1}^{n} n_i x_i \leq N_{\min}, \quad x_i \in \{0, 1\}$$

where

o $x_i \in \{0,1\}$ is a binary decision variable (selected item i (1) or not (0)),
o c_i is the cost of item i,
o n_i its nutritional value,
o B the budget, and
o $N_{\min}$ the minimum required nutrient intake.

Last, uncertainty and dynamic behavior are inherent in daily contexts. Whether it be traffic congestion, electricity price, or user preference, things change over time. Thus any optimization method must be adaptive and be resilient to changes in input data or the environment [55,56].

35.2.3 Why traditional methods fall short

Considerable drawing from the literature of applications across diverse human-made situations have shown that conventional optimization strategies for example, linear programming (LP), mixed integer programming, exhaustive enumeration and the like are often not relevant in the dynamic and informal characteristics associated with many of the tasks carried out in the real world [57,58]. For conventional optimization methods to be usable, they typically require:

- Clear objectives and constraints,
- Continuous or well-defined decision variables,
- Deterministic cases with non-temporal parameters.

These conditions will not be satisfied in the majority of everyday instances. For example, in trying to formulate something like a household energy scheduling problem, the uncertainty in electricity tariffs and the fluctuating patterns of using appliances all add more effort and complexity to the model, resulting in potentially an unworkable computational model based on classical modeling [59].

Additionally, the computational complexity associated with combinatorial problems increases exponentially with the number of decision variables, such that exact algorithms are infeasible in a real-time environment. For a binary decision vector n, there are 2^n combinations, so even for modest n, brute-force search is not computationally feasible [60,61].

As such, there is a larger need to move toward metaheuristic algorithms that are reasonable and practical in imperfect, high-dimensional, and nonconvex settings [62,63].

35.2.4 How grey wolf optimizer offers an efficient alternative

The GWO represents a powerful and effective method in addressing real-world optimization problems, particularly in situations that we face on a daily basis. The population-based and naturally inspired framework of GWO relies not on gradient information or explicit mathematical models, making this optimization method very appropriate for black-box optimization problems, where the only known behavior is the input–output behavior of the function involved [1,13].

In GWO, a candidate solution represents an individual wolf, and the candidate solution's position is updated from the hunting behavior and leadership hierarchy of the wolves. The positions are updated using the previous equations [1]:

$$\overrightarrow{D_\alpha} = |\overrightarrow{C_1} \times \overrightarrow{X_\alpha} - \overrightarrow{X}|, \overrightarrow{X_1} = \overrightarrow{X_\alpha} - \overrightarrow{A_1} \times \overrightarrow{D_\alpha}, \overrightarrow{X_{new}} = \frac{1}{3}(\overrightarrow{X_1} + \overrightarrow{X_2} + \overrightarrow{X_3})$$

where:

o $\overrightarrow{X_\alpha}, \overrightarrow{X_\beta}, \overrightarrow{X_\delta}$, represent the top three solutions guiding the search,
o $\overrightarrow{X}$ is the current solution,
o $\overrightarrow{A_1}, \overrightarrow{C_1}$ are coefficient vectors dynamically adjusted during the iteration process.
o $\overrightarrow{D_\alpha}$ is the distance vector between the current agent and the leader wolf $\overrightarrow{X_\alpha}$,
o $\overrightarrow{X_1}$ is the candidate position derived from the influence of $\overrightarrow{X_\alpha}$,
o $\overrightarrow{X_{new}}$ is the new position of the search agent, averaged from the influences of the three top wolves.

The encircling behavior of GWO allows the algorithm to sufficiently explore a solution space, while the averaged behavior of the three best wolves allows the algorithm to exploit the most promising areas. Finding this balance is highly important in real-time optimization, dynamic, and constrained problems [15,31].

For example, in smart home energy scheduling, GWO can determine when to schedule one or more appliances for optimization while minimizing energy cost/peak demand, while also addressing user constraints [21,59]. A second example of GWO could involve personal task management by allocating a time block to the activity time for a task, while also taking into account user-defined constraints and priority schedules,without necessarily requiring a precise cost function or constrained formulation [41].

Furthermore, GWO's minimal dependency on parameters, generally limited to the number of agents and iterations, makes it a lightweight algorithm suitable for mobile or embedded system methods used for supporting daily decision making tasks [26,33]. (Table 35.1–35.3).

Note- GWO implementations follow the structure outlined in Algorithm 54.1, with domain-specific encoding and fitness functions.

35.3 Applications of grey wolf optimizer to optimization categories

The GWO has shown remarkable flexibility in many spheres of optimization. GWO applications in five areas—task scheduling, resource allocation, routing, energy management, and health planning—are presented in this part. Every application is characterized in terms of encoding strategy, objective function, constraint handling, and benefits over conventional approaches. Algorithm 54.1 summarizes the GWO's overall running behavior.

(a) Task and time Sscheduling (job shop scheduling-like problems)

In job shop scheduling, every task must be scheduled with precedence constraints and on a designated resourcefor example, a person, machine to avoid overlapping time slots. Representing each wolf's position as a task sequence or start-time vector, GWO adapts to guide the search to minimize makespan while penalizing priority violations [64,65].

Representing each wolf's position as a task sequence or start-time vector helps the general GWO structure shown in Algorithm 54.1 be suited for scheduling. Minimizing makespan guides the search by imposing penalties for overlaps and precedence violations.

Encoding strategy:

Each grey wolf's position vector represents a permutation of task IDs or a Gantt-style schedule matrix. For n tasks, a vector $\overrightarrow{X_i} = [x_1, x_2, \ldots, x_n]$ r denotes the sequence or start times of tasks.

TABLE 35.1 Comparison between traditional optimization methods and grey wolf optimizer (GWO) for daily life problems.

Criteria	Traditional methods	Grey wolf optimizer (GWO)
Model requirement	Requires explicit mathematical formulation	Works with black-box or loosely defined models
Problem type suitability	Best for linear/convex problems	Suitable for nonlinear, multimodal, and high-dimensional problems
Adaptability to changes	Low :usually requires reformulation	High :dynamic parameter adaptation
Ease of implementation	Moderate to complex	Simple, a few control parameters
Computational complexity	Often high for large combinatorial problems	Efficient for large and complex solution spaces
Multiobjective capability	Requires specialized formulations	Handles multiple objectives intuitively
Constraint handling	Strict, must be explicitly defined	Flexible, can use penalty-based approaches
Real-time application potential	Limited	Suitable for real-time and embedded systems
User accessibility	Requires expert knowledge	Can be embedded in user-friendly tools/apps

TABLE 35.2 Comparison of traditional optimization techniques and GWO-based approaches across various problem domains. The GWO framework offers significant advantages in terms of convergence speed, constraint handling, and flexibility, particularly in complex or nonconvex optimization scenarios.

Problem type	Traditional approach	GWO-based approach	Key advantages
Job-shop scheduling	Branch-and-Bound, tabu search	GWO with task permutation encoding	Faster convergence, avoids full enumeration
Knapsack problem	Greedy, dynamic programming	GWO with penalty terms	Better handling of nonlinear utility
Routing (TSP)	Ant colony optimization (ACO), genetic algorithm (GA)	GWO with permutation encoding	Maintains route diversity, less premature convergence
Energy scheduling	Mixed-Integer Linear Programming (MILP) solvers	GWO with a hybrid penalty-based method	Handles discrete time windows, nonconvex problems
Diet optimization	Linear programming (LP) /nonlinear programming (NLP)	Multiobjective GWO (MOGWO)	Works with nondifferentiable, preference-based constraints

GWO, Grey wolf optimizer; *TSP*, traveling salesman problem.

Fitness function:

The objective is typically to **minimize the makespan** C_{max}, defined as:

$$F(\overrightarrow{X_i}) = \max_j(C_j)$$

where C_j =completion time of task j.

Penalties are applied for:

- Overlapping tasks,
- Violated dependencies (e.g., Task A before Task B),
- Exceeding deadlines.

Constraint handling: A penalty-based approach is used:

$$F(\overrightarrow{X_i}) = f(\overrightarrow{X_i}) + \lambda \times P(\overrightarrow{X_i})$$

TABLE 35.3 Summary of grey wolf optimizer (GWO) applications across five optimization domains, highlighting encoding strategies, objective functions, constraint handling approaches, and comparative advantages over traditional or metaheuristic methods.

Application domain	Encoding strategy	Fitness function/objective	Constraint handling	Key advantages of GWO
Task and time scheduling (JSSP)	Task sequence or Gantt-style vector	Minimize makespan (max completion time)	Penalty for overlaps, precedence, deadlines	Faster convergence, balances exploration/exploitation
Resource allocation and budgeting	Resource fractions or binary include/exclude	Maximize utility under a budget constraint	Budget penalty for violations	Avoids combinatorial explosion, escapes local optima
Routing and navigation (TSP/VRP)	Permutation of node sequences	Minimize total travel distance	Penalties for capacity/time-window violations	Robust in dynamic routing, maintains route diversity
Energy consumption management	Binary/integer appliance states or start times	Minimize total energy cost	Runtime and operational window penalties	Handles nonconvex, discrete constraints, scalable
Health, diet and fitness planning	Food quantities over the time horizon	Multiobjective: minimize sugar, maximize protein, balance calories	Multiobjective Pareto dominance, preference constraints	Works with nondifferentiable constraints, flexible

JSSP, Job shop scheduling; *TSP*, traveling salesman problem; *VRP*, vehicle routing problem.

ALGORITHM 35.1 Pseudocode of grey wolf optimizer (GWO) for general optimization problems. ***The algorithm initializes a population of wolves, updates their positions based on α, β, and δ leaders, and iteratively balances exploration and exploitation until convergence.***

Step	Description
Input:	Objective function $f(x)$, number of wolves n, maximum iterations max_iter, dimension d, bounds [ℓ, u]
Output:	Best solution $X\alpha$, best value $f\alpha$
1.	Initialize wolf positions Xi randomly within bounds
2.	Evaluate $f(Xi)$ for each wolf
3.	Identify $X\alpha$, $X\beta$, $X\delta$ as the top 3 wolves
4.	For t = 1 to max_iter:
5.	For each wolf Xi:
6.	Generate coefficient vectors A and C
7.	Compute distances to alpha, beta, and delta
8.	Update position using: $X_1 = X\alpha - A_1 \cdot D\alpha$ $X_2 = X\beta - A_2 \cdot D\beta$ $X_3 = X\delta - A_3 \cdot D\delta$ $Xi = (X_1 + X_2 + X_3)/3$
9.	Clip Xi to bounds
10.	Evaluate new $f(Xi)$ and update best
11.	End loop
12.	Return $X\alpha$, $f\alpha$

$$F(\vec{X_i}) = \max_j(C_j) + \lambda \times P(\vec{X_i})$$

where $P(\vec{X}i)$ is the penalty term and λ is a scaling factor.

Advantages: GWO converges faster than branch-and-bound or tabu search and avoids thorough counting. The leader-follower paradigm helps to balance exploration of new sequences with the use of good ones.

35.3.1 Scheduling—worked example

Problem definition:

A single machine must process three jobs with processing times:

Job	Processing time
J1	2
J2	4
J3	3

Encoding: Each candidate solution is a **permutation of job indices** (e.g., [1,2,3] = J1 → J2 → J3).

Objective: Minimize the **makespan (total completion time)**:

$$Makespan = \sum_{i=1}^{n} Ci$$

where Ci is the completion time of job i.

Constraints:

- Each job appears exactly once.
- Processing times are nonpreemptive.

Feasibility checks:

If a job is missing or repeated, repair the permutation by inserting missing jobs and removing duplicates until all jobs appear once.

Worked example:

Order=[J1, J3, J2] → completion times=2, 5, 9 → makespan=9. Order=[J2, J1, J3] → completion times=4, 6, 9 → makespan=9.

Output: Here, all sequences yield makespan of 9. For larger job sets, GWO efficiently searches the permutation space to minimize makespan.

(b) Resource Aallocation and budgeting (Knapsack/LP)

GWO uses binary or fractional encoding in resource-limited settings to effectively allocate resources, so managing the budget constraints by means of penalty techniques [66]. While avoiding the combinatorial explosion observed in classical knapsack models, this method maximizes overall usefulness.

This application employs a binary or fractional encoding method for decision variables using the outline in Algorithm 54.1. The fitness function assesses overall value; hence, in line with the iterative improvement approach of the GWO, constraints such as budget are incorporated using penalty-based corrections.

Encoding strategy:

Grey wolf's position vector $\overrightarrow{X_i} = [x_1, x_2, \ldots, x_n]$ represents resource fractions or binary decisions (e.g., include/exclude an item in the Knapsack problem).

Fitness function:

Maximize overall utility U, such as:

$$f(\overrightarrow{X_i}) = \sum_{j=1}^{n} u_j \times x_j$$

Subject to budget constraint:

$$\sum_{j=1}^{n} c_j \times x_j \leq B$$

where uj is the utility of activity/item j, cj is the cost of activity/item j, and B is the budget limit.

Constraint handling:

Solutions violating constraints are penalized:

$$F(\overrightarrow{X_i}) = \quad f(\overrightarrow{X_i}) - \mu \times \max\left(0, \quad \sum c_j \quad \times x_j - B\right)$$

μ is the penalty coefficient

Advantages:

Under nonlinear utility functions, especially, GWO provides an efficient escape from local optima that plague greedy algorithms and avoids the combinatorial explosion of exhaustive Knapsack search.

35.3.2 Resource allocation:worked example

Problem definition:

A manager allocates a budget of 100 across four projects:

Project	Cost	Profit
P1	40	100
P2	30	55
P3	50	140
P4	20	40

Encoding:

Binary vector= $[x1, x2, x3, x4]$, where $xj = 1$ if project j is funded.

Objective: Maximize profit:

$$f(x) = \sum p_j x_j$$

Constraints:

$$\sum c_j x_j \leq 100$$

(Total cost must not exceed budget.)

Feasibility checks:

If cost > budget(100), drop projects with the lowest profit-to-cost ratio until the solution is feasible.

Worked example

- Select P1 + P3 → cost=90, profit=240.
- Select P2 + P3 → cost=80, profit=195. Best solution=P1 + P3.

Output Optimal vector x=[1,0,1,0], Total Profit=240.

(c) Routing and navigation (traveling salesman problem/vehicle routing problem)

Traveling salesman problem (TSP), or optimally serving clients with multiple limited vehicles known as the vehicle routing problem (VRP), seeks the shortest path covering all locations exactly once. GWO codes wolves as permutations of locations for routing applications, including TSP and VRP. Its adaptive exploration enhances over conventional metaheuristics, including genetic algorithms and ant colony optimization [67].

Algorithm 1 encodes position vectors as permutations of location indices, guiding GWO to route problems. Custom penalty terms address vehicle capacities and time window constraints; the leader-following mechanism supports the exploration of route sequences.

Encoding strategy:

Each wolf's position is a permutation of nodes (e.g., [3, 1, 4, 2, 5] for TSP). For VRP, a route splitting mechanism is integrated based on vehicle capacities.

Fitness function:

Minimize total distance:

$$f(\vec{X_i}) = \sum_{k=1}^{n-1} d(x_k, x_{k+1}) + d(x_n, x_1)$$

where *d(x,y)* is the distance between locations x and y.

Constraint handling:

In VRP:

- Capacity constraints are penalized.
- Time windows are checked for feasibility.

$$F(\vec{X_i}) = f(\vec{X_i}) + \alpha \times (\text{capacity violation}) + \beta \times (\text{time window violation})$$

Advantages: GWO is stronger in dynamic or real-time routing than conventional heuristics. Its capacity to preserve and develop several path solutions enables surpassment of single-path heuristics and even some metaheuristics (e.g., ACO, GA).

35.3.3 Routing:worked example (traveling salesman problem)

Problem definition:

A salesman must visit four cities once and return to start. Distance matrix:

	A	B	C	D
A	0	10	15	20
B	10	0	35	25
C	15	35	0	30
D	20	25	30	0

Encoding: Each wolf encodes a **permutation of cities** (e.g., [A,C,B,D]).

Objective: Minimize total travel distance.

$$Total\ Distance = \sum_{i=1}^{n} Distance(city_i, \quad city_{i+1})$$

Constraints: Each city must be visited exactly once.

Must return to the starting city
Feasibility checks:
If a city is repeated or is missing, repair by removing duplicates and adding missing cities.
Worked example

- Route [A–B–D–C–A] → distance=10+25+30+15=80.
- Route [A–C–B–D–A] → distance=15+35+25+20=95.

Output Best feasible route=[A–B–D–C–A], Total distance=80.
(d) Energy consumption management (MILP)
This domain consists of scheduling appliances under variable tariff rates and appliance constraints in order to minimize energy bills. Under variable tariffs and constraints, GWO is used to maximize appliance scheduling, so as to avoid MILP solver rigidity. Every position vector relates to on/off states over several time slots [68].

This use case codes each wolf's position as a schedule of appliance states across time slots based on the Algorithm 1 framework. Effective modeling of runtime and time-of-use tariff structures without depending on exact solvers is made possible by the GWO's adaptability in handling constraints via penalty terms.
Encoding strategy:
Each element of a grey wolf's position vector corresponds to a binary or integer variable indicating the **on/off state** or **start time** of an appliance.
Fitness function:
Minimize the total energy cost:

$$f(\overrightarrow{X_i}) = \sum_{t=1}^{T} p_t \times E_t(\overrightarrow{X_i})$$

where p_t is the tariff at time t and E_t is the energy usage at t based on schedule $\overrightarrow{X_i}$.
Constraint handling:

- Appliance runtime constraints (e.g., cannot operate more than 2 hours).
- Operational time windows (e.g., washing machine only from 8 p.m. to 6 a.m.). Penalty formulation:

$$F(\overrightarrow{X_i}) = f(\overrightarrow{X_i}) + \sum \gamma k \times V_k(\overrightarrow{X_i})$$

where V_k are constraint violations.

Advantages: Flexibility of GWO removes the need for exact formulation-based MILP solvers. It scales better for actual appliance networks and manages nonconvex constraints organically.

35.3.4 Energy management:worked example (economic dispatch)

Problem definition:
Three generators must meet demand=100 MW.

Generator	Min (MW)	Max (MW)	Cost function $F(P)=a+bP+cP^2$
G1	20	50	$500 + 5P + 0.01P^2$
G2	10	40	$400 + 6P + 0.012P^2$
G3	10	30	$200 + 4P + 0.02P^2$

Encoding
Each solution is a vector:[$P1$,$P2$,$P3$], representing MW allocated to each generator.
Objective

$$\textit{Minimize total cost} = F(P1) + F(P2) + F(P3).$$

$$F = F_1(P_1) + F_2(P_2) + F_3(P_3)$$

Constraints

- $P1 + P2 + P3 = 100$
- Each Pi within the generator limits.

Feasibility checks:

If demand is not met, total ≠ 100, scale outputs proportionally.

If any Pi is out of bounds, clip to the nearest feasible limit.

Worked example:

Candidate allocation [65,54,43]:

- $Total = 100 \ MW$ (feasible).
- $Cost = F1(40) + F2(35) + F3(25) = (500 + 200 + 16) + (400 + 210 + 14.7) + (200 + 100. + 12.5) = 1653.2$

$$F1 = 500 + 5 \times 40 + 0.01 \times 1600 = 500 + 200 + 16 = 716$$

$$F2 = 400 + 6 \times 35 + 0.012 \times 1225 = 400 + 210 + 14.7 = 624$$

$$F3 = 200 + 4 \times 25 + 0.02 \times 625 = 200 + 100 + 12.5 = 312.5$$

Output: Feasible allocation=[40,35,25], Total cost ≈ 1653.2.

(e) Health, diet, and fitness planning

Under constraints including calories, nutrients, and time, this multiobjective problem seeks to maximize meal planning or fitness schedules. Under conflicting constraints,that is, nutrients against calories,multiobjective GWO (MOGWO) allows meal and workout optimization. In this intricate multigoal situation [69], Pareto fronts direct the trade-offs.

Here, the GWO framework from Algorithm 1 is expanded into a MOGWO, whereby every solution denotes a food intake or exercise schedule. Using Pareto dominance and crowding distance strategies, the algorithm balances conflicting objectives, including calorie targets and nutrient intake by searching the solution space.

Encoding Sstrategy:

Each grey wolf's position vector represents food items and quantities over a time horizon:

$$\vec{X_i} = [x_{1,1}, x_{1,2}, \ldots, x_{d,T}]$$

where $x_{d,T}$ denotes the quantity of food d consumed at time t.

Fitness function (multiobjective):

Minimize sugar, maximize protein, balance calories:

$$f_1(\vec{X_i}) = \sum_{d,t} Sugar_d \times x_{d,t}$$

$$f_2(\vec{X_i}) = \sum_{d,t} Protein_d \times x_{d,t}$$

$$f_3(\vec{X_i}) = \sum_{d,t} Calories_d \times x_{d,t} - C_{target}$$

Constraint handling:

Handled via **MOGWO** with Pareto dominance and crowding distance, allowing solutions to be spread across trade-off surfaces.

Advantages: LP/NLP formulations needing exact gradients are common in traditional diet planners. Working on discrete food sets, GWO and MONGWO allow nondifferentiable constraints—that is, food preference scores.

35.3.5 Health planning:worked example (treatment selection)

Problem definition:

A hospital must treat patients under a limited budget=200.

Patient	Treatment cost	Benefit score
1	80	95
2	120	130
3	60	75
4	90	100
5	70	85

Encoding:
Binary vector $x = [x1, x2, x3, x4, x5]$, where $xi = 1$ if patient i receives treatment.
Objective:

$$Maximize\ Total\ Benefits = \sum b_i x_i$$

Constraints:

$$\sum cost_i x_i \leq 200$$

Feasibility checks:
If cost exceeds budget, iteratively remove patients with the lowest benefit-to-cost ratio until feasible.
Worked example:

- Select patients {1,3,5}→ Cost=80+60+70=210 (not feasible).
- Repair by dropping patient 5 → {1,3}→ Cost=140, benefit=170.
- Select {2,3}→ Cost=180, benefit=205 (better).

Output: Optimal feasible selection={2,3}, Total benefit=205.

35.4 Numerical experiments and validation

To evaluate the performance of the GreyGWO and an Adaptive-GWO variant, numerical experiments were conducted on widely used benchmark functions. Four test functions were considered: Sphere, Rastrigin, Rosenbrock, and Ackley, representing unimodal, multimodal, and nonconvex landscapes.

35.4.1 Experimental Ssetup

In this study, two algorithms were evaluated: the standard GWO proposed by Mirjalili et al. [1], and an adaptive variant of GWO incorporating a quadratic decay of the control parameter a. The performance of these algorithms was tested on four widely used benchmark functions: Sphere, Rastrigin, Rosenbrock, and Ackley. Experiments were conducted in two different dimensions, 10 and 30, with a population size of 30 wolves over 200 iterations. Each experiment was independently repeated 30 times using different random seeds to ensure statistical reliability. The search space for each function was defined as follows: Sphere [−100, 100], Rastrigin [−5.12, 5.12], Rosenbrock [−5, 5], and Ackley [−32.768, 32.768]. Performance was assessed using key metrics, including the best solution found, mean, standard deviation, and average runtime per run. Statistical tests were also employed to compare the performance of the algorithms objectively.

- **Algorithms tested:** Standard GWO [1] and Adaptive-GWO (quadratic decay of control parameter a).
  The adaptive control parameter a (t) in Adaptive-GWO follows a quadratic decay rule defined as:

$$a(t) = 2\left(1 - \left(\frac{t}{T}\right)^2\right)$$

  where t is the current iteration and T is the maximum number of iterations.
  This quadratic schedule allows a (t) to decrease more rapidly at the beginning and more gradually near the end, enhancing exploration in early stages while improving exploitation during later iterations.
- **Benchmark functions:** Sphere, Rastrigin, Rosenbrock, and Ackley.
- **Dimensions:** 10 and 30.
- **Population size:** 30 wolves.
- **Iterations:** 200.
- **Independent runs:** 30 trials with different seeds.
- Search ranges: Sphere [−100,100], Rastrigin [−5.12, 5.12], Rosenbrock [−5, 5], Ackley [−32.768, 32.768].
- **Performance metrics:** Best value, mean, standard deviation (Std), and average runtime per run.
- **Statistical tests:** To assess the normality of the paired differences, the Shapiro–Wilk test was first conducted. If the differences were normally distributed, a paired t-test was used to evaluate the significance of the mean difference; otherwise, the nonparametric Wilcoxon signed-rank test was applied. As an additional nonparametric check, the Mann–Whitney U test was also performed. Effect sizes were calculated using Cohen's d for parametric analysis and

rank-biserial correlation for nonparametric comparisons. To provide a robust estimate of the precision of the mean difference, a 95% bootstrap confidence interval was computed.

35.4.2 Results

Tables 35.4 and 35.5 summarize the performance of both algorithms. Adaptive-GWO generally outperformed standard GWO, particularly on multimodal functions (Rastrigin, Ackley).

- **Sphere function (*D*=10, 30):** Both algorithms reached near-zero optima, which is near optimal solution. At $D=10$, differences were significant (t-test $P=.0101$). At $D=30$, Adaptive-GWO showed a clear advantage (Wilcoxon $P<.0001$).
- **Rastrigin function:** Adaptive-GWO consistently performed better (Wilcoxon $P=0.0002$ at $D=10$, t-test $P<0.0001$ at $D=30$).
- **Rosenbrock function:** No significant difference between algorithms at both dimensions ($P>0.1$).
- **Ackley function:** AdaptiveGWO significantly outperformed GWO at both $D=10$ and $D=30$ (Wilcoxon $P<.0001$).

35.4.3 Discussion

These results highlight that while standard GWO is effective on unimodal problems, Adaptive-GWO provides a robust improvement on multimodal and complex landscapes. The statistical tests confirm the significance of these improvements

TABLE 35.4 Performance summary of GWO versus Adaptive-GWO.

Function	Dimension	Algorithm	Best	Mean	Std	Avg time (Sec)
Sphere	10	Standard	1.03E-26	6.63E-24	1.30E-23	0.384665
Sphere	10	Adaptive	4.54E-36	5.13E-32	1.36E-31	0.389152
Rastrigin	10	Standard	0	0.410194	0.859055	0.416682
Rastrigin	10	Adaptive	0	0	0	0.412019
Rosenbrock	10	Standard	6.319444	7.114319	0.307442	0.439591
Rosenbrock	10	Adaptive	6.505018	7.202572	0.298213	0.428175
Ackley	10	Standard	8.57E-14	6.40E-13	5.86E-13	0.471603
Ackley	10	Adaptive	4.00E-15	6.60E-15	1.57E-15	0.453208
Sphere	30	Standard	2.58E-11	2.63E-10	2.52E-10	0.382299
Sphere	30	Adaptive	5.62E-15	8.28E-14	1.27E-13	0.380215
Rastrigin	30	Standard	1.37E-07	3.718606	1.737123	0.417583
Rastrigin	30	Adaptive	1.71E-12	0.150805	0.490781	0.414238
Rosenbrock	30	Standard	27.0127	27.67238	0.606404	0.434667
Rosenbrock	30	Adaptive	26.79704	27.53095	0.461069	0.424096
Ackley	30	Standard	1.31E-06	3.70E-06	2.18E-06	0.477536
Ackley	30	Adaptive	1.09E-08	4.44E-08	1.59E-08	0.482623

GWO, Grey wolf optimizer.

TABLE 35.5 Statistical tests between GWO and Adaptive-GWO.

Function	Dimension	Shapiro_p	Normality	Selected test	Test_p	Mann Whitney_p	Cohen_d	Rank biserial	CI_Low	CI_High
Sphere	10	1	Normal	Paired *t*-test	0.010108	3.02E-11	0.50243	-1	2.30E-24	1.16E-23
Rastrigin	10	9.79E-09	Not Normal	Wilcoxon signed-rank	0.000193	8.81E-07	0.469468	-0.6	0.135621	0.730912
Rosenbrock	10	0.002136	Not Normal	Wilcoxon signed-rank	0.145999	0.270705	-0.23157	0.166667	-0.24917	0.063782
Ackley	10	3.31E-05	Not Normal	Wilcoxon signed-rank	1.73E-06	8.85E-12	1.062256	-1	4.39E-13	8.69E-13
Sphere	30	3.34E-05	Not Normal	Wilcoxon signed-rank	1.86E-09	3.02E-11	1.029039	-1	1.87E-10	3.63E-10
Rastrigin	30	0.102105	Normal	Paired *t*-test	1.93E-11	1.21E-10	1.926366	-0.96889	2.915673	4.182192
Rosenbrock	30	0.087011	Normal	Paired *t*-test	0.357499	0.923442	0.170711	0.015556	-0.13628	0.413958
Ackley	30	0.000352	Not Normal	Wilcoxon signed-rank	1.86E-09	3.02E-11	1.650413	-1	2.94E-06	4.47E-06

GWO, Grey wolf optimizer.

on Rastrigin and Ackley, while performance on Rosenbrock remains comparable. Overall, introducing adaptivity in parameter control enhances convergence reliability and reduces susceptibility to local optima.

A consolidated summary of best, mean, and standard deviation values across functions and dimensions is presented in Table 35.4, while the statistical test outcomes are reported in Table 35.5.

As shown in Fig. 35.1, Adaptive-GWO exhibits faster convergence across iterations, while Fig. 35.2 confirms its robustness by displaying reduced variance and improved median performance across multiple runs. Together, these results provide strong evidence that the adaptive parameter control enhances both convergence speed and reliability of the algorithm.

35.4.4 Real-world case demonstrations of grey wolf optimizer

35.4.4.1 Task scheduling case study

To demonstrate the practical applicability of the proposed GWO and its adaptive variant, a small-scale daily-life task-scheduling problem was formulated. Five independent tasks (T_1–T_5) were considered, each with a specified duration in hours (2, 3, 1, 2, and 1) and corresponding priority weights (3, 5, 2, 4, and 1). These tasks collectively span a 9-hour workday, where the sequence of execution significantly influences overall efficiency (see Table 35.6).

The optimization objective was to **minimize the total weighted completion time**, defined as:

$$f = \sum_{i=1}^{n} w_i C_i$$

where w_i is the priority weight and Ci is the cumulative completion time of task i.

Each candidate wolf represents a permutation of the five tasks, and the search process identifies the sequence that yields the minimal objective value.

Both Standard GWO and Adaptive-GWO were executed for 30 independent runs with 20 wolves and 50 iterations.

Adaptive-GWO employed a quadratic control function $a(t) = 2(1 - \left(\frac{t}{T}\right)^2)$ where t is the current iteration and T is the total iteration, to progressively shift the focus from exploration to exploitation as the optimization advanced. Higher values of $a(t)$ at early stages promote exploration, helping the algorithm avoid premature convergence by maintaining diversity in the search space. As the optimization progresses, $a(t)$ decreases gradually, shifting the focus toward exploitation and refining the search around high-quality solutions. This adaptive mechanism enhances both convergence stability and solution reliability across multiple runs.

Fig. 35.3 illustrates (A) the average convergence patterns and (B) the distribution of final best fitness values via boxplots for both algorithms.

Both algorithms consistently converged to the same optimal weighted completion time of 77, confirming successful minimization.

This best value does not guarantee convergence in every run due to the stochastic nature of the algorithm. However, due to the stochastic nature of the algorithms, performance varies across runs. The average (mean) fitness value over 30 independent runs provides a measure of overall consistency and reliability.

The Adaptive-GWO achieved faster and smoother convergence and exhibited lower run-to-run variability (mean=78.10 ± 0.75) compared with the Standard GWO (mean=78.03 ± 1.08). This distinction highlights that while both methods can reach the same optimal solution, Adaptive-GWO offers greater stability in repeated applications.

The best task sequence identified by the Standard GWO was $T_3 \rightarrow T_4 \rightarrow T_2 \rightarrow T_1 \rightarrow T_5$, while the Adaptive-GWO produced a slightly different sequence: $T_4 \rightarrow T_3 \rightarrow T_2 \rightarrow T_1 \rightarrow T_5$. Both sequences resulted in the same optimal weighted completion time of 77, highlighting that multiple near-optimal permutations can exist for the problem.

Notably, the sequence from Adaptive-GWO prioritizes shorter, higher-priority tasks earlier in the schedule, reflecting a more intuitive and efficient task ordering strategy.

These findings indicate that the adaptive control of the parameter $a(t)$ improves search stability without compromising solution quality.

The task-scheduling case confirms that both GWO formulations can handle discrete, combinatorial optimization problems representative of everyday decision scenarios. The improved consistency of Adaptive-GWO further supports its suitability for real-world applications requiring stable convergence behavior.

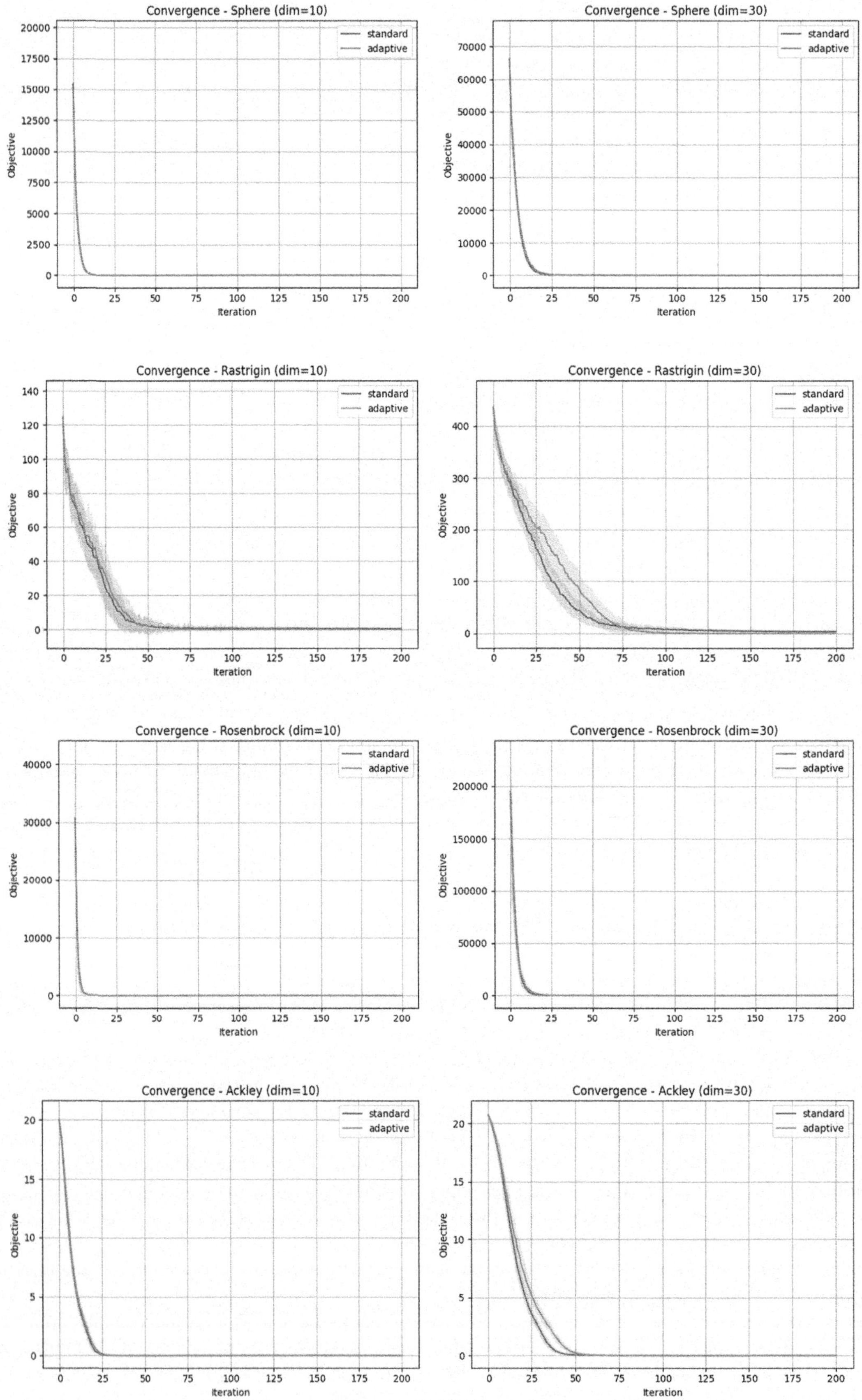

FIGURE 35.1 Convergence curves of standard GWO and Adaptive-GWO on benchmark functions (Sphere, Rastrigin, Rosenbrock, Ackley) in 10 and 30 dimensions. The curves show the average fitness value versus iterations, illustrating faster and more stable convergence of Adaptive-GWO, especially on multimodal functions (GWO, Grey wolf optimizer).

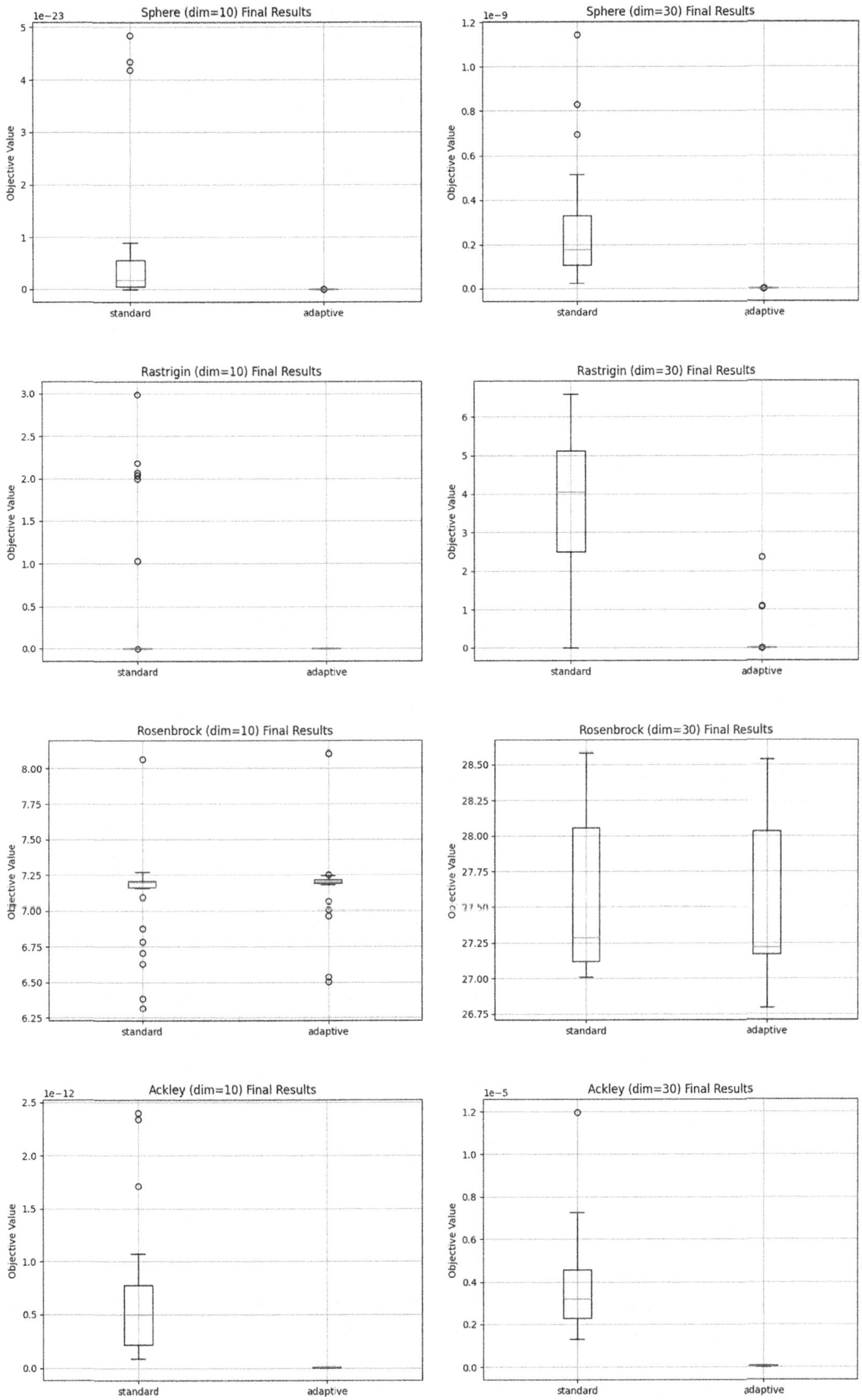

FIGURE 35.2 Boxplots of solution quality for standard GWO and Adaptive-GWO across 30 independent runs on four benchmark functions (Sphere, Rastrigin, Rosenbrock, Ackley). *The plots highlight reduced variance and improved robustness of Adaptive-GWO compared to standard GWO* (*GWO*, Grey wolf optimizer).

35.4.4.2 Resource allocation and budgeting case study

To demonstrate the practical applicability of the proposed GWO and its adaptive variant, a small-scale budgeting and resource allocation problem was formulated, modeled as a classic 0–1 Knapsack problem.

Six independent investment options (I_1–I_6) were considered, each with specified costs (4, 2, 6, 1, 3, and 5) and corresponding return values (12, 7, 18, 4, 8, and 14). The objective was to select a subset of these options such that the total return is maximized without exceeding the available budget of 15 units (see Table 35.7).

The optimization objective was to maximize the total return under the budget constraint, defined as:

$$f = \sum_{i=1}^{n} v_i x_i$$

Subject to:

$$\sum_{i=1}^{n} c_i x_i \leq B$$

where: v_i is the return value and c_i is the cost of investment i, $x_i \in \{0, 1\}$ is a binary variable representing selection (1) or exclusion (0) of investment i, B = 15 is the total available budget.

Each candidate wolf represents a 6-bit binary vector indicating selection or exclusion of the six investments. The search process identifies the combination that yields the maximum return value without violating the budget constraint.

Both Standard GWO and Adaptive-GWO were executed for 30 independent runs with 20 wolves and 50 iterations.

Adaptive-GWO employed a quadratic control function $a(t) = 2(1 - \left(\frac{t}{T}\right)^2)$, where (t) is the current iteration and (T) is the total iteration, to progressively shift the focus from exploration to exploitation as the optimization advanced.

Fig. 35.4 illustrates (A) the average convergence patterns and (B) the distribution of final best fitness values via boxplots for both algorithms.

Both algorithms consistently converged to the same optimal return value of 45, confirming successful maximization. It is important to note that this value represents the best solution found in at least one run. However, due to the stochastic nature of the algorithms, performance varies across runs. The average (mean) fitness value over 30 independent runs provides a measure of overall consistency and reliability.

The Adaptive-GWO achieved faster and smoother convergence and exhibited lower run-to-run variability (mean=44.13 ± 0.96) compared with the Standard GWO (mean=43.90 ± 1.14). This distinction highlights that while both methods can reach the same optimal solution, Adaptive-GWO offers greater stability in repeated applications.

The best investment subset identified by the Standard GWO was $I_1 \rightarrow I_2 \rightarrow I_4 \rightarrow I_5 \rightarrow I_6$ (i.e., x= [1, 1, 0, 1, 1, 1], with a total cost of 4+2+1+3+5=15 and a total return of 12+7+4+8+14=45. The Adaptive-GWO also produced an alternative optimal subset: $I_1 \rightarrow I_2 \rightarrow I_3 \rightarrow I_5$ (i.e., x= [1, 1, 1, 0, 1, 0], with the same total cost 4+2+6+3=15 and total return value 12+7+18+8=45.

This confirms that multiple feasible combinations can yield the optimal value, and the presence of such diversity highlights the combinatorial nature of the problem.

Notably, the subset selected by Adaptive-GWO tends to favor items with higher value-to-cost ratios, reflecting a more intuitive and efficient allocation strategy.

TABLE 35.6 Task attributes: durations and priority weights.

Task	Duration (hours)	Priority weight (w_i)
T_1	2	3
T_2	3	5
T_3	1	2
T_4	2	4
T_5	1	1

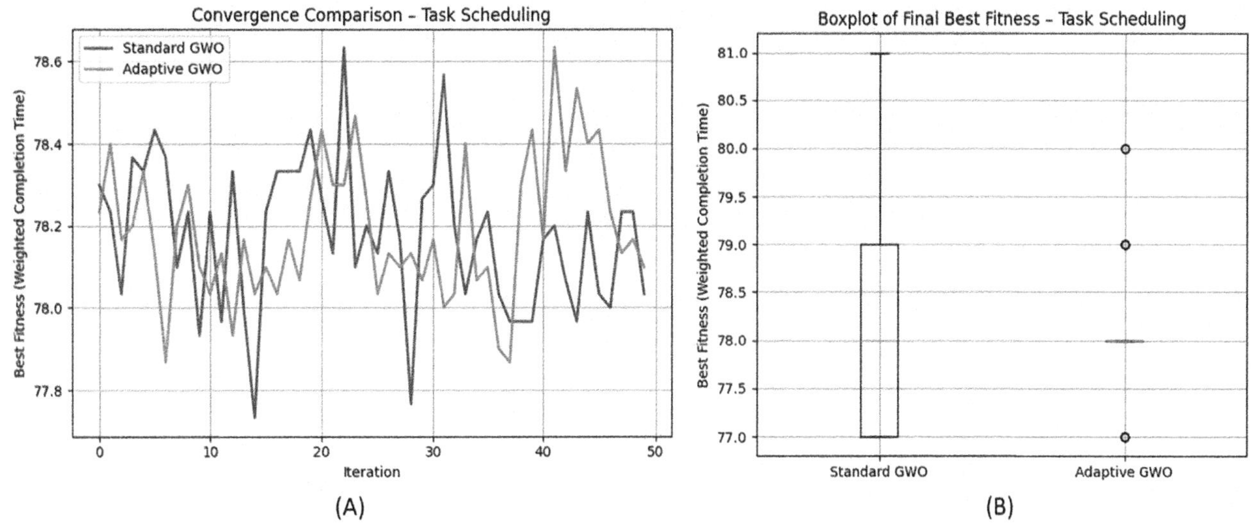

FIGURE 35.3 (A) Average convergence of Standard and Adaptive-GWO for the task-scheduling problem (30 runs). (B) Boxplots of final best fitness values illustrating reduced variance for Adaptive-GWO (*GWO*, Grey wolf optimizer).

TABLE 35.7 Investment attributes: costs and return values.

Investment	Cost units	Return value (v_i)
I_1	4	12
I_2	2	7
I_3	6	18
I_4	1	4
I_5	3	8
I_6	5	14

These findings indicate that the adaptive control of the parameter $a(t)$ improves search stability without compromising solution quality.

The resource allocation case confirms that both GWO formulations can effectively solve discrete, constrained optimization problems representative of real-world budgeting and investment decisions. The improved consistency of Adaptive-GWO further supports its suitability for applications requiring robust and repeatable decision-making.

In both discrete optimization scenariostask scheduling and resource allocationAdaptive-GWO demonstrated improved convergence stability and consistency without compromising solution quality. These real-world case studies substantiate the algorithm's practical applicability beyond benchmark tests, thereby addressing the reviewer's request for real-world validation.

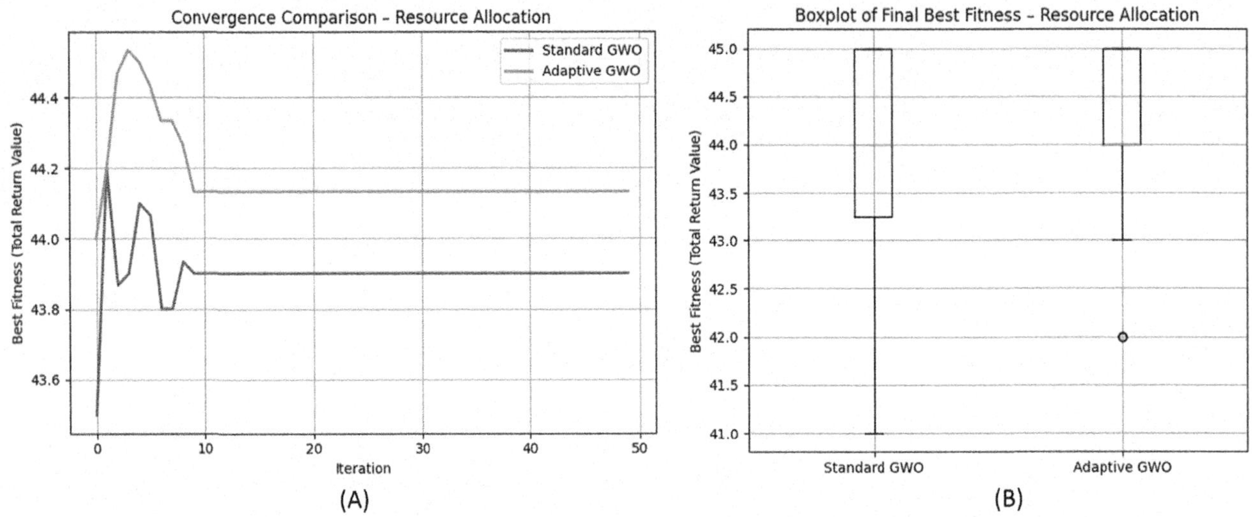

FIGURE 35.4 (A) Average convergence of Standard and Adaptive-GWO for the resource allocation problem (30 runs). (B) Boxplots of final best fitness values illustrating reduced variance for Adaptive-GWO (*GWO*, Grey wolf optimizer).

References

[1] S. Mirjalili, S.M. Mirjalili, A. Lewis, Grey wolf optimizer, Advances in Engineering Software 69 (2014) 46–61. Available from https://doi.org/10.1016/j.advengsoft.2013.12.007.

[2] J.O. Agushaka, A.E. Ezugwu, L. Abualigah, Grey wolf optimizer: A comprehensive review of variants & applications, Artificial Intelligence Review 56 (2023) 1–40.

[3] P. Nayak, B. Naik, H.S. Behera, A novel grey wolf optimizer based hybrid classifier for handling high-dimensional datasets, Expert Systems with Applications 224 (2023) 119700. Available from https://doi.org/10.1016/j.eswa.2023.119700.

[4] V. Kumar, I. Sharma, S. Sharma, A comprehensive study of grey wolf optimizer & its applications, Recent Advances in Computer Science 15 (3) (2021) 1–20.

[5] L.K. Singh, M. Khanna, S. Thawkar, R. Singh, A novel hybridized feature selection strategy using GWO, Multimedia Tools & Applications (2024).

[6] S. Wang, Y. Shi, An improved grey wolf optimizer based on guidance vector and chaos theory, Applied Soft Computing 122 (2022) 108801. Available from https://doi.org/10.1016/j.asoc.2022.108801.

[7] J. Tu, H. Chen, M. Wang, An improved grey wolf optimization algorithm based on adaptive mechanisms, Expert Systems with Applications 213 (2023) 1–15.

[8] S. Mohapatra, P. Mishra, R. Panda, Modified GWO for optimization of nonlinear functions and image segmentation, Multimedia Tools and Applications 80 (2021) 11157–11185. Available from https://doi.org/10.1007/s11042-020-10194-9.

[9] A.A. Heidari, S. Mirjalili, H. Faris, I. Aljarah, M. Mafarja, H. Chen, Harris Hawks optimization: algorithm and applications, Future Generation Computer Systems 97 (2019) 849–872. Available from https://doi.org/10.1016/j.future.2019.02.028.

[10] N. Singh, H. Hachimi, A hybrid grey wolf optimizer for optimization problems, Engineering Optimization (2018).

[11] N. Singh, S.B. Singh, A modified grey wolf optimizer for global optimization problems, Applied Intelligence 47 (3) (2017) 1–28.

[12] N. Mittal, U. Singh, B.S. Sohi, Modified grey wolf optimizer for global engineering optimization, Applied Computational Intelligence & Soft Computing 2016 (2016) 1–16.

[13] I. Aljarah, H. Faris, S. Mirjalili, M. Mafarja, M.S. Hossain, An effective multi-objective grey wolf optimizer for data clustering, Knowledge-Based Systems 239 (2022). Available from https://doi.org/10.1016/j.knosys.2021.107942Article 107942.

[14] Q. Tu, X. Chen, X. Liu, Hierarchy strengthened grey wolf optimizer for numerical optimization and feature selection, IEEE Access 7 (2019) 108219–108237. Available from https://doi.org/10.1109/ACCESS.2019.2933054.

[15] A. Zaghiyan, D. Ghimire, S. Poudel, W. Wu, Multi-objective enhanced grey wolf optimizer for load forecasting and renewable energy planning, Applied Soft Computing 145 (2023). Available from https://doi.org/10.1016/j.asoc.2023.110826Article 110826.

[16] J.A. Rodríguez, L. Trujillo, E. Villa-Diharce, A.L. Marroquín, L. Montaño, Hybridization of grey wolf optimization and evolutionary programming for inverse kinematics, Applied Soft Computing 57 (2017) 266–279. Available from https://doi.org/10.1016/j.asoc.2017.04.035.

[17] E. Emary, H.M. Zawbaa, A.E. Hassanien, Binary grey wolf optimization approaches for feature selection, Neurocomputing 172 (2016) 371–381. Available from https://doi.org/10.1016/j.neucom.2015.06.083.

[18] M. Nasir, A.Q. Khan, A. Imran, Hybrid grey wolf optimization for machine learning applications, PLoS One 19 (4) (2024). Available from https://doi.org/10.1371/journal.pone.0303094.

[19] M. Mosaa, S.M. Al-Jawher, Modified grey wolf optimizer for global optimization and engineering problems, Arabian Journal for Science and Engineering 48 (2023) 3691–3708. Available from https://doi.org/10.1007/s13369-022-07108-7.
[20] K.S. Pol, V.K. Pachghare, Opposition based grey wolf optimization algorithm for solving engineering problems, Engineering Science and Technology, an International Journal 22 (3) (2019) 828–843. Available from https://doi.org/10.1016/j.jestch.2018.12.004.
[21] I. Dagal, A.L.W. Ibrahim, A. Harrison, W.F. Mbasso, Hierarchical multi-step grey wolf optimization algorithm for energy systems optimization, Scientific Reports 15 (2025). Available from https://doi.org/10.1038/s41598-025-92983-wArticle 92983.
[22] V. Mani, A. Jain, Hybrid grey wolf optimizer for optimization problems, Soft Computing 24 (2020) 1–15.
[23] M.H. Sulaiman, Z. Mustaffa, M.R. Mohamed, O. Aliman, Using the grey wolf optimizer for solving optimal reactive power dispatch problem, Applied Soft Computing 32 (2014) 286–292. Available from https://doi.org/10.1016/j.asoc.2015.03.039.
[24] H. Faris, I. Aljarah, M.A. Al-Betar, S. Mirjalili, Grey wolf optimizer: a review of recent variants and applications, Neural Computing and Applications 30 (2) (2018) 413–435. Available from https://doi.org/10.1007/s00521-017-3272-5.
[25] A. Ghosh, S. Dehuri, S.B. Cho, R. Mall, Cooperative hunting-based GWO for multi-objective optimization, Expert Systems with Applications 244 (2024). Available from https://doi.org/10.1016/j.eswa.2022.119270Article 119270.
[26] A. As'arry, M.K. Hassan, A.A. Hairuddin, Y. Liu, Review of the grey wolf optimization algorithm: variants and applications, Soft Computing and Applications 33 (1) (2024) 94–122. Available from https://doi.org/10.1007/s00521-023-09202-8.
[27] A. Khosravi, S. Nahavandi, D. Creighton, Grey wolf optimizer-based machine learning frameworks, Knowledge-Based Systems 290 (2024) 1–20.
[28] Y. Liu, A. As'arry, M.K. Hassan, A.A. Hairuddin, Review of the grey wolf optimization algorithm: variants and applications, Soft Computing and Applications (2024). Available from https://doi.org/10.1007/s00521-023-09202-8.
[29] N.M. Hatta, A.M. Zain, R. Sallehuddin, Z. Shayfull, Recent studies on optimisation method of grey wolf optimiser (GWO): A review (2014–2017), Artificial Intelligence Review (2019). Available from https://doi.org/10.1007/s10462-018-9634-2.
[30] Y. Liu, L. Wang, X. Xu, An improved grey wolf optimization algorithm for solving complex optimization problems, Applied Soft Computing 113 (2022) 107–120.
[31] M. Yu, J. Xu, W. Liang, Y. Qiu, S. Bao, L. Tang, Improved multi-strategy adaptive Grey Wolf Optimization for practical engineering applications and high-dimensional problem solving, Artificial Intelligence Review (2024). Available from https://doi.org/10.1007/s10462-024-10821-3.
[32] Z. Zhang, Y. Gao, Y. Liu, W. Zuo, A hybrid biogeography-based optimization algorithm to solve high-dimensional optimization problems and real-world engineering problems, Applied Soft Computing 146 (2023). Available from https://doi.org/10.1016/j.asoc.2023.110885Article 110885.
[33] S. Gupta, K. Deep, H. Moayedi, L.K. Foong, Sine cosine grey wolf optimizer to solve engineering design problems, Engineering with Computers 37 (2021) 1905–1924. Available from https://doi.org/10.1007/s00366-020-00996-y.
[34] X. Wang, Y. Zhang, H. Li, Hybrid grey wolf optimizer for engineering optimization problems, IEEE Access 10 (2022) 1–15 24.
[35] S. Saxena, V.K. Kamboj, K. Arora, An integrative TLBO-driven hybrid grey wolf optimizer for the efficient resolution of multi-dimensional, nonlinear engineering problems, Scientific Reports 15 (2025). Available from https://doi.org/10.1038/s41598-025-89458-3Article 89458.
[36] H. Lin, S. Xie, X. Dong, An improved hybrid grey wolf optimizer for global optimization, Scientific Reports 12 (2022) 1–18.
[37] Z. Wang, D. Dai, Z. Zeng, D. He, S. Chan, Multi-strategy enhanced grey wolf optimizer for global optimization and real world problems, Cluster Computing (2024). Available from https://doi.org/10.1007/s10586-024-04455-x.
[38] H. Chen, J. Li, C. Yang, An improved grey wolf optimizer for solving global optimization problems, Engineering Applications of Artificial Intelligence 81 (2019) 1–14.
[39] X. He, Y. Zhang, J. Liu, Improved grey wolf optimizer for engineering optimization problems, Engineering Optimization 56 (2024) 1–20.
[40] S.N. Makhadmeh, M.A. Al-Betar, I.A. Doush, M.A. Awadallah, S. Mirjalili, Recent advances in grey wolf optimizer, its versions and applications, IEEE Access 11 (2023) 68534–68561. Available from https://doi.org/10.1109/ACCESS.2023.3296096.
[41] S.S. Khatami, M. Shoeibi, A.E. Oskouei, 5DGWO-GAN: a novel five-dimensional Gray Wolf Optimizer for GAN-enabled intrusion detection in IoT systems, Computers in Industry 155 (2025) 103007. Available from https://doi.org/10.1016/j.compind.2024.103007Article.
[42] K. Zhang, C. Shen, Two-stage improved grey wolf optimization algorithm for feature selection on high-dimensional classification, Complex & Intelligent Systems 8 (3) (2022) 2219–2234. Available from https://doi.org/10.1007/s40747-021-00452-4.
[43] S. Hosseini-Hemati, S.D. Beigvand, H. Abdi, Society-based grey wolf optimizer for large-scale combined heat and power economic dispatch problem considering power losses, Applied Soft Computing 116 (2022). Available from https://doi.org/10.1016/j.asoc.2021.108387Article 108387.
[44] G. Li, Y. Cui, J. Su, Adaptive mechanism-based grey wolf optimizer for feature selection in high-dimensional classification, PLoS One 20 (2) (2025) e0318903. Available from https://doi.org/10.1371/journal.pone.0318903Article.
[45] E. Dada, S. Joseph, D. Oyewola, A.A. Fadele, Application of grey wolf optimization algorithm: recent trends, issues, and possible horizons, Gazi University Journal of Science 35 (2) (2022) 531–547. Available from https://dergipark.org.tr/en/pub/gujs/issue/69194/820885.
[46] Zhang, H.T., Yang, T.T. and Wang, W.T., 2024. A novel hybrid model for species distribution prediction using neural networks and Grey Wolf Optimizer algorithm. Scientific Reports, 14(1), p.11505.
[47] A.M. Helmi, M.A.A. Al-Qaness, A. Dahou, R. Damaševičius, V. Rajinikanth, A novel hybrid gradient-based optimizer and grey wolf optimizer feature selection method for human activity recognition using smartphone sensors, Entropy 23 (8) (2021) 1065. Available from https://doi.org/10.3390/e23081065.
[48] K. Deb, Multi-objective, Optimization Using Evolutionary Algorithms, John Wiley & Sons, (2001). Available from https://doi.org/10.1002/9780470743614.
[49] M.S. Bazaraa, J.J. Jarvis, H.D. Sherali, Linear Programming and Network Flows, 4th ed., John Wiley & Sons, (2010).
[50] H.A. Taha, Operations Research: An Introduction, 10th ed., Pearson Education, (2017).

[51] H.A. Simon, The Sciences of the Artificial, 3rd ed., MIT Press, (1996).
[52] S. Boyd, L. Vandenberghe, Convex Optimization, Cambridge University Press, (2004). Available from https://doi.org/10.1017/CBO9780511804441.
[53] R.T. Marler, J.S. Arora, Survey of multi-objective optimization methods for engineering, Structural and Multidisciplinary Optimization 26 (6) (2004) 369–395. Available from https://doi.org/10.1007/s00158-003-0368-6.
[54] P. Toth, D. Vigo, The Vehicle Routing Problem, SIAM Monographs on Discrete Mathematics and Applications (2002). Available from https://doi.org/10.1137/1.9780898718515.
[55] C. Li, S. Yang, A survey on evolutionary computation for dynamic optimization problems, Information Sciences 514 (2020) 71–106. Available from https://doi.org/10.1016/j.ins.2019.12.025.
[56] H.G. Beyer, B. Sendhoff, Robust optimization–a comprehensive survey, Computer Methods in Applied Mechanics and Engineering 196 (33-34) (2007) 3190–3218. Available from https://doi.org/10.1016/j.cma.2007.03.003.
[57] L.A. Wolsey, Integer Programming, Wiley, (1998).
[58] D. Bertsimas, J.N. Tsitsiklis, Introduction to Linear Optimization, Athena Scientific, (1997).
[59] I. Samaras, A.I. Papadopoulos, P. Seferlis, Energy optimization under uncertainty in smart grids using stochastic mixed-integer programming, Applied Energy 282 (2021) 116130. Available from https://doi.org/10.1016/j.apenergy.2020.116130Article.
[60] C.H. Papadimitriou, K. Steiglitz, Combinatorial Optimization: Algorithms & Complexity, Dover Publications, (1998).
[61] M.R. Garey, D.S. Johnson, Computers & Intractability: A Guide to the Theory of NP-Completeness, W. H. Freeman, (1979).
[62] E.-G. Talbi, Metaheuristics: From Design to Implementation, Wiley, (2009).
[63] C. Blum, A. Roli, Metaheuristics in combinatorial optimization, ACM Computing Surveys 35 (3) (2003) 268–308. Available from https://doi.org/10.1145/937503.937505.
[64] A.H. Gandomi, X.S. Yang, S. Talatahari, A.H. Alavi, Metaheuristic algorithms in modeling and optimization, Metaheuristic Applications in Structures and Infrastructure (2014) 1–24. Available from https://doi.org/10.1016/B978-0-12-398364-0.00001-4.
[65] M. Mafarja, S. Mirjalili, Hybrid whale optimization algorithm with simulated annealing for feature selection, Neurocomputing 260 (2017) 302–312. Available from https://doi.org/10.1016/j.neucom.2017.04.053.
[66] M. Yazdani, F. Jolai, Lion optimization algorithm (LOA): a nature-inspired metaheuristic algorithm, Journal of Computational Design and Engineering 3 (1) (2016) 24–36. Available from https://doi.org/10.1016/j.jcde.2015.06.003.
[67] Y. Zhang, S. Wang, G. Ji, A comprehensive survey on particle swarm optimization algorithm and its applications, Mathematical Problems in Engineering 2019 (2019). Available from https://doi.org/10.1155/2019/1962451.
[68] M. Abdel-Basset, R. Mohamed, S. Mirjalili, A hybrid COVID-19 detection model using grey wolf optimization and decision tree, Computers in Biology and Medicine 126 (2020) 104059. Available from https://doi.org/10.1016/j.compbiomed.2020.104059.
[69] M. Ebrahimi, A.T. Azar, A.E. Hassanien, Multi-objective dietary planning using evolutionary algorithms, Journal of Computational Science 44 (2020) 101170. Available from https://doi.org/10.1016/j.jocs.2020.101170.

Chapter 36

RCGWO: an improved grey wolf optimization algorithm using random weight and elite-based crossover for solving real world optimization problems

Suraj Roy[1,2], Apu K. Saha[2], and Sharmistha Bhattacharya (Halder)[1]

[1]*Department of Mathematics, Tripura University, Suryamaninagar, Tripura, India,* [2]*Department of Mathematics, National Institute of Technology, Agartala, Tripura, India*

36.1 Introduction

Optimization continues to pose a significant challenge in the realm of computational intelligence despite its widespread adoption and critical role in scientific and industrial applications. Various fields from machine learning, signal processing, and renewable energy to path planning and trajectory design problems frequently encounter optimization tasks that are highly nonlinear, multimodal, and constrained in nature [1]. Conventional optimization techniques, particularly gradient-based methods, often prove inadequate due to issues such as high dimensionality, sensitive initial conditions, and susceptibility to local optima. Generally, optimization problems can be categorized as either maximization or minimization tasks, depending on the objective function and desired outcome.

To address these limitations of conventional strategies, researchers around the world have increasingly turned to metaheuristic algorithms (MAs), which offer derivative-free and adaptive strategies for solving complex optimization problems. Metaheuristics are inspired by various natural, biological, or social phenomena, allowing them to explore vast search spaces effectively while maintaining a balance between global search and exploitation, that is local refinement. Their advantages include conceptual simplicity, easy implementation, and the ability to avoid premature convergence to local optima. Recent examples include whale optimization algorithm [2], marine predator algorithm [3], weighted mean of vectors (INFO) [4], greater cane rat algorithm [5], etc. Despite their simplicity and effectiveness, no single algorithm performs optimally for all algorithms, as stated by the no free lunch theorems [6]. Performance of an algorithm may vary depending on the parameter tuning on same class of problems. Consequently, the development of novel or hybrid or modified variants of metaheuristics continues to be a significant area of research aimed at enhancing convergence speed, accuracy, and robustness.

A successful MA must maintain a balanced trade-off between exploration and exploitation. Exploration ensures a wide search of the solution space to reduce premature convergence to local optima, while exploitation emphasizes intensively refining potential areas discovered during exploration. An algorithm's overall performance is greatly influenced by achieving an appropriate trade-off between these two phases.

Among the various swarm intelligence-based techniques, the grey wolf optimization algorithm (GWO) proposed by Mirjalili et al. [7] in the year 2014 is inspired by the social hierarchy and hunting strategy of grey wolves in nature. GWO mathematically simulates the hierarchical structure in cooperative hunting behavior of grey wolves, such as tracking, encircling, and attacking the prey. GWO has gained a significant amount of attention because of its simplicity, computational efficiency, and its competitive performance across a wide range of optimization tasks.

The intuitive design and limited control parameters of GWO have motivated researchers to successfully implement it in various fields, such as Edsa et al. [8] applied GWO in cost-sensitive neural network-based breast cancer prediction for

Grey Wolf Optimizer. DOI: https://doi.org/10.1016/B978-0-443-36624-6.00013-5

optimized neuron count and learning rate. Tugal [9] has proposed an entropy-based GWO to enhance hyperparameter tuning for MLP models to improve load prediction in building Heating, Ventilation, and Air Conditioning (HVAC) systems for sustainable development. Chen et al. [10] proposed a biomass-powered energy system using GWO based Artificial Intelligence (AI) framework to maximize efficiency and minimizing cost of producing power, fresh water, cooling, and hydrogen. Chaudhary et al. [11] proposed a dynamic clustered federated learning framework for healthcare-IoT by integrating DBSCAN clustering with GWO. However, like other MAs, GWO also suffers from premature convergence and reduced exploration while dealing with highly multimodal and complex landscapes.

These challenges have motivated researchers around the world to propose various versions of GWO to enhance its performance by hybridizing it or incorporating adaptive mechanisms. Some recent improved versions are discussed here. Zhang and Chen [12] proposed an elite-driven GWO named EDGWO by incorporating three global exploration phases and dynamic parameter tuning for smooth transition between exploration and exploitation. HCGWO proposed by Yang et al. [13] is an amalgamation of the chaos game with GWO. The authors of DLMDGWO [14] firstly introduced the logistic map for initial population generation, then multipopulation based dynamic strategy is applied to improve the algorithm mechanism, along with that double Laplacian strategy is applied in the update stage. And at last, multipopulation dimension learning is employed to enhance the diversity. In MIGWO [15], the authors first optimized the initial population using ReliffF. Second, the hunting mechanism is improved using the weighting of fitness and a competitive weight-assignment mechanism. And finally, hybridized with DE and levy flight based mechanisms. Yu et al. proposed IAGWO [16], in which they have utilized velocity and an inverse multiquadratic function for an improved search mechanism with an adaptive update strategy. The ongoing evolution of GWO underscores its potential as a flexible and powerful tool for solving real-world optimization problems.

Therefore identifying the limitations in existing algorithms and subsequently developing efficient variants has become a common practice. In this study, an enhanced variant of GWO named RCGWO is proposed. The modifications employed in the classical GWO framework are summarized below:

(a) A nonlinear cosine decay is employed for "a" to enhance population diversity and improve the global search process.
(b) An adaptive random weight-based search mechanism is integrated to dynamically balance the influence of α, β, and δ wolves to guide the search process throughout the iterations.
(c) An elite-based crossover is incorporated, where offspring are generated by recombining the top wolves followed by Gaussian perturbation.
(d) A dual position update scheme is employed that switches probabilistically between classical position update and elite weighted guidance.
(e) Then, to present the efficiency of the proposed RCGWO, it has been tested on 15 benchmark functions, IEEE CEC'2020, and five real-world complex problems.
(f) The statistical significance of RCGWO was assessed using Friedman's rank test and the paired sample Wilcoxon signed rank test.

The remainder of this chapter is organized as follows: Section 36.2 presents the discussion on the classical grey wolf optimizer; in Section 36.3, the proposed RCGWO is discussed, and then Section 36.4 demonstrates the qualitative and quantitative performance analysis. Section 36.5 concludes the discussion related to this chapter.

36.2 Grey wolf optimizer

Grey wolves (i.e., Canis lupus) are members of the Canidae family. Grey wolves are classified as apex predators, indicating they dominate the food chain. Grey wolves have a social structure with four unique ranks: alpha (α), beta (β), delta (δ), and omega (ω). Every rank has a hierarchy and a role. α, β, and δ are the dominant wolves. GWO is a swarm-intelligence system inspired by grey wolves' natural leadership and hunting behavior. The phases of GWO are discussed below.

36.2.1 Social hierarchy

In order to simulate the hierarchy of the wolves in GWO, the top three solutions are named as alpha (α), beta (β), and delta (δ) respectively, and the remaining ones are considered as omega (ω). α, β, and δ wolves guide the hunting process and ω follows these wolves.

36.2.2 Encircling the prey

The presently identified global best solution is considered to be near the most optimal solution. In accordance with that every search agent updates its position to converge toward the optimum solution. The following equations model the encircling process mathematically.

$$X_{t+1} = X_t^p - A \times D \tag{36.1}$$

$$D = |C \times X_t^p - X_t| \tag{36.2}$$

X^p is the position of prey.

$$A = 2a \times r_1 - a \tag{36.3}$$

$$C = 2 \times r_2 \tag{36.4}$$

$$a = 2 - \frac{2 \times it}{MaxIT} \tag{36.5}$$

r_1 and r_2 are random values between 0 & 1, and a decreases linearly from 2 to 0 throughout the iterations.

36.2.3 Hunting

Grey wolves guided by the alpha wolves locate the prey, then encircle them. In GWO, to mathematically represent this behavior, it saves the top three solutions obtained from α, β, and δ wolves using the distance of them from the prey.

$$D^\alpha = |C^1 \times X^\alpha - X|,\ D^\beta = |C^2 \times X^\beta - X|,\ D^\delta = |C^3 \times X^\delta - X| \tag{36.6}$$

$$X_1 = X^\alpha - A_1 \times D^\alpha,\ X_2 = X^\beta - A_2 \times D^\beta,\ X_3 = X^\delta - A_3 \times D^\delta \tag{36.7}$$

$$X_{t+1} = \frac{X_1 + X_2 + X_3}{3} \tag{36.8}$$

36.2.4 Exploitation phase attacking prey

After hunting down the prey wolves attack the prey. This approaching the prey is mathematically modeled in GWO by decreasing the value of a. In accordance with a with fluctuation rate A also decreases and $|A| < 1$ stimulates wolves to attack.

36.2.5 Exploration phase searching for prey

Grey wolves search mostly based on the alpha, beta, and delta positions. They split to find prey, then rejoin to attack it. In GWO, A with random values higher than 1 or less than -1 mathematically describes divergence, which forces the search agent to disperse away from the prey. This promotes the GWO algorithm to search globally and places an emphasis on exploration. Another random value C emphasizes exploration whenever $C > 1$ as shown in Eqs. 36.2 and 36.7 and helps to avoid local optima entrapment.

36.3 Proposed RCGWO approach

In the classical GWO, the fluctuation range of A is dependent on a that decreases linearly. In this study, an improved convergence factor a is introduced that adheres to cosine-based nonlinear behavior as per Eq. 36.9. This improves convergence stability and prevents premature stagnation in complex search spaces.

$$a = 2 \times \cos\left(\frac{\pi}{2} \times \frac{it}{Maxit}\right) \tag{36.9}$$

The adaptive weight mechanism is integrated to dynamically balance the influence of α, β, and δ wolves by promoting exploration during the early iterations. Here, to update β and δ wolves instead of using random values for A and C, we have used w_2 and w_3 as Eqs. 36.15 and 36.16. During the later stages, adaptive weight adjustment helps in improving convergence speed and exploitation.

$$explore_{factor} = 1 - \frac{it}{Maxit}\ ; \tag{36.10}$$

$$p_1 = rndm \times explore_{factor} + 0.3;\ p_2 = rndm \times (1 - explore_{factor}); \tag{36.11}$$

$$p_3 = 1 - (w_1 + w_2)\ ; \tag{36.12}$$

$$w_{sum} = w_1 + w_2 + w_3\ ; \tag{36.13}$$

$$w_1 = \frac{p_1}{w_{sum}};\ w_2 = \frac{p_2}{w_{sum}};\ w_3 = \frac{p_3}{w_{sum}}; \tag{36.14}$$

$$A_2 = 2 \times a \times w_2 \text{ and } C^2 = 2 \times w_3 \tag{36.15}$$

$$A_3 = 2 \times a \times w_3 \text{ and } C^3 = 2 \times w_2 \tag{36.16}$$

Then RCGWO employs a dual update mechanism where if $rndm < 0.9$ it updates as per the classical update mechanism, else it utilizes the adaptive weight-based update as shown in Eq. 36.17. This prevents premature stagnation and occasional diversity during exploitation.

$$X_{t+1} = w_1 \times X_1 + w_2 \times X_2 + w_3 \times X_3 \tag{36.17}$$

To further enhance diversity and provide recombination capability, RCGWO employs elite-based crossover. The elite pool consists of the top three wolves $\{\ \alpha,\ \beta,\ \delta\ \}$. Two parents X_{P_1} & X_{P_2} are randomly selected from the pool. Then

```
Initialize Wolves Positions GW^x uniformly in [lb, ub]
Evaluate all fitness values
Identify Alpha, Beta, Delta wolves

For l = 1 to Max_iter do
  Compute nonlinear parameter using eq. 9
  Compute exploration factor using eq. 10
  For each wolf i do
    Apply boundary control on GW^x(i)
    Evaluate fitness each wolf
    Update Alpha, Beta, Delta hierarchy
  End for

  For each wolf i do
    Generate adaptive random weights w1, w2, w3 using eq. 10 − 14
    For each dimension j do
      Compute GW^x1, GW^x2, GW^x3 from α, β and, δ influence using eq. 3, 15 and 16
      If rand > 0.1 then
        Calculate GW^x(i, j) using eq. 8
      Else
        Calculate GW^x(i, j) using eq. 17
      End if
    End for
  End for
  If rand < crossover_rate then
    Select two parents from {Alpha, Beta, Delta}
    Generate offspring using eq. 18
    Apply Gaussian mutation using eq. 19
    Evaluate offspring
    If offspring better than the worst wolf then
      Replace worst wolf with offspring
    End if
  End if
End for
```

FIGURE 36.1 Pseudocode of the proposed RCGWO algorithm.

arithmetic crossover is applied to produce the offspring. After that Gaussian mutation is applied to avoid premature convergence.

$$X_{offspring} = \lambda X_{P_1} + (1 - \lambda)X_{P_2}, \ \lambda \in [0, 1] \quad (36.18)$$

TABLE 36.1 Comparison of RCGWO outcomes on benchmark functions.

Algorithm		RCGWO	GWO	PSO	INFO	LCA	AEFA	COOT
F1	*Mean*	6.876E-64	9.755E-44	1.726E-02	2.97E-54	2.528E-01	2.681E+10	2.743E-32
	SD	2.777E-63	1.308E-43	2.256E-02	1.79E-54	3.760E-01	3.452E+09	1.503E-31
F2	*Mean*	1.119E-34	3.179E-25	5.507E-01	8.07E-27	2.707E+00	5.304E+03	1.368E-16
	SD	2.713E-34	3.235E-25	5.198E-01	2.82E-27	2.107E+00	2.634E+02	7.493E-16
F3	*Mean*	0	2.005E-09	1.305E+01	6.07E-28	5.926E-02	1.013E+03	1.308E-15
	SD	0	2.255E-09	2.750E+00	3.85E-28	4.612E-02	1.912E+01	7.162E-15
F4	*Mean*	0	1.90E+03	1.90E+03	4.29E-51	1.90E+03	1.90E+03	1.90E+03
	SD	0	7.24E-01	3.59E+02	3.42E-51	2.02E-04	0	0
F5	*Mean*	0	9.010E+05	4.77E+05	7.46E-27	2.04E+07	3.516E+06	3.56E+07
	SD	0	1.032E+06	1.15E+05	2.26E-27	1.00E+07	1.184E+06	1.61E+07
F6	*Mean*	2.781E-227	1.950E+03	1.97E+03	8.39E-220	4.06E+03	3.051E+03	3.75E+03
	SD	0	1.827E+02	4.02E+02	0	2.96E+02	2.165E+02	4.03E+02
F7	*Mean*	4.080E-67	2.971E+05	1.46E+05	4.42E-54	3.27E+07	1.197E+06	2.06E+07
	SD	1.137E-66	5.440E+05	1.17E+05	3.31E-54	3.09E+07	6.799E+05	2.01E+07
F8	*Mean*	0	3.291E+03	3.23E+03	6.13E-53	7.28E+03	5.131E+03	7.54E+03
	SD	0	1.121E+03	9.89E+02	4.02E-53	9.33E+02	4.292E+02	8.50E+02
F9	*Mean*	0	2.816E+03	2.93E+03	3.93E-50	3.80E+03	3.233E+03	3.44E+03
	SD	0	4.073E+01	5.39E+02	2.57E-50	2.23E+02	4.528E+01	1.38E+02
F10	*Mean*	2.105E+02	2.341E+02	8.789E+02	1.39E+02	1.167E+02	3.355E+02	1.549E+02
	SD	3.926E+01	2.221E+01	2.766E+02	1.90E+01	1.396E+02	1.524E+01	1.652E+01
F11	*Mean*	0	5.677E-01	2.215E+02	0	7.989E-02	3.353E+01	7.579E-15
	SD	0	2.360E+00	3.452E+01	0	1.352E-01	1.108E+01	2.468E-14
F12	*Mean*	0	9.585E-05	3.404E-02	8.13E-28	1.108E-02	2.367E-03	2.394E-03
	SD	0	2.320E-04	5.037E-02	2.27E-28	7.380E-03	2.107E-03	2.524E-03
F13	*Mean*	3.956E-49	2.649E-32	2.860E+02	1.01E-31	4.318E-05	1.254E+03	1.770E-07
	SD	2.167E-48	1.451E-31	1.083E+03	8.76E-32	6.219E-05	2.966E+03	9.157E-07
F14	*Mean*	2.859E+01	6.086E+01	1.772E+02	5.55E+01	1.606E+02	5.758E+02	6.516E+01
	SD	6.248E+00	9.845E+00	5.751E+01	1.32E+01	1.301E+02	6.653E+02	3.258E+01
F15	*Mean*	-1	1.270E-23	7.126E-24	-1.36E-01	-8.196E-01	2.727E-36	-1
	SD	4.660E-01	1.510E-23	2.104E-23	2.56E-01	1.419E-01	3.435E-36	7.675E-14

$$X_{offspring} = X_{offspring} + \mathcal{N}(0, \sigma^2) \text{ where } \sigma = 0.02 \tag{36.19}$$

This offspring replaces the worst wolf if it has a smaller objective value. This combination of strategies improves the searching mechanism and prevents premature stagnation in local optima. In Fig. 36.1 pseudocode of the proposed RCGWO is presented.

36.3.1 Computational complexity of RCGWO

This subsection presents the time and space complexity analysis of the proposed RCGWO against vanilla GWO. Here, T denotes the maximum iterations, D denotes the problem dimension, and N is the number of grey wolves. The initialization complexity of GWO is $O(N)$, the leadership selection and fitness evaluation complexity is $O(N \times D)$, and

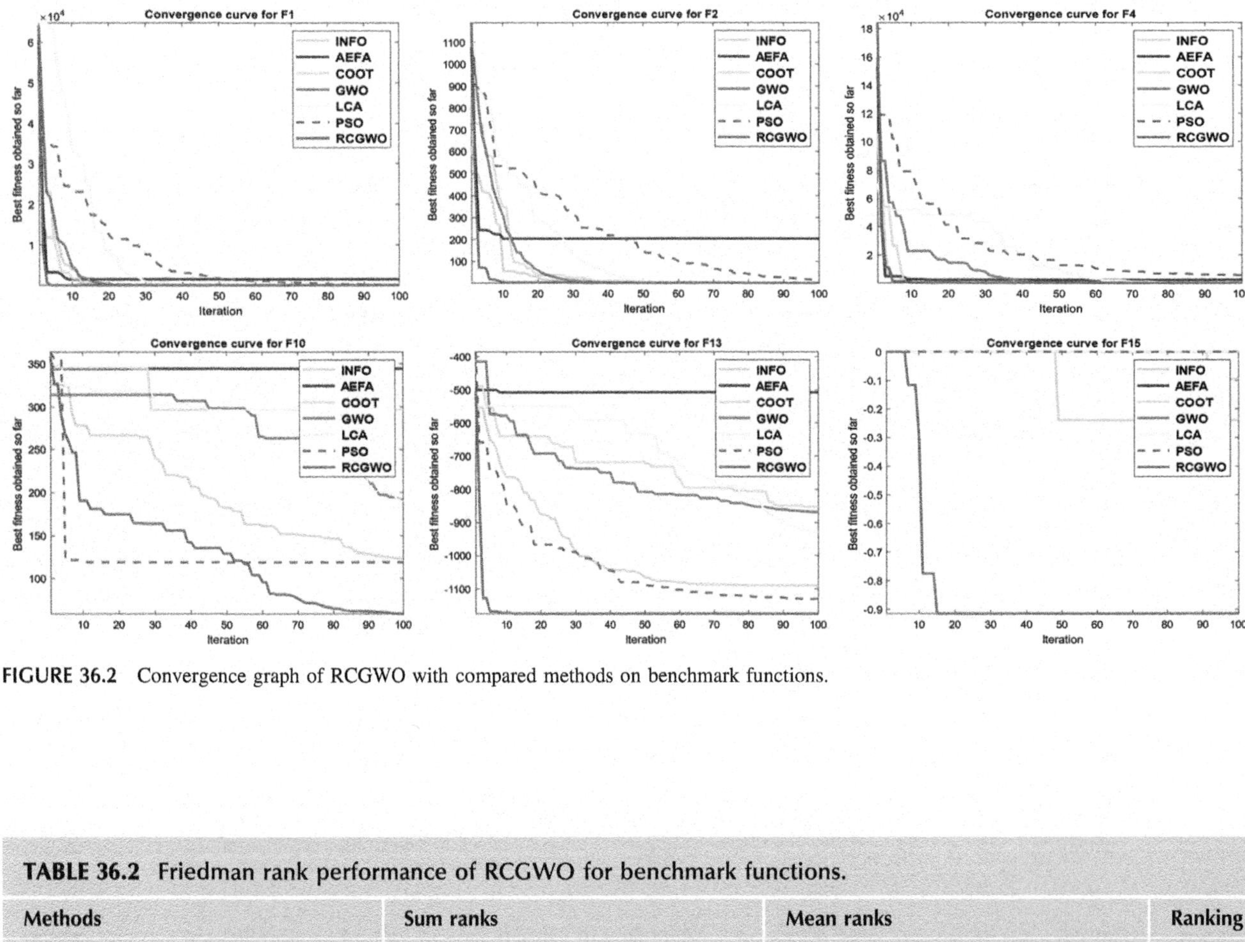

FIGURE 36.2 Convergence graph of RCGWO with compared methods on benchmark functions.

TABLE 36.2 Friedman rank performance of RCGWO for benchmark functions.

Methods	Sum ranks	Mean ranks	Ranking
RCGWO	46	1.53	1
GWO	113	3.77	3
INFO	69.5	2.32	2
PSO	161	5.37	6
LCA	162	5.40	7
AEFA	156	5.20	5
COOT	132.5	4.42	4

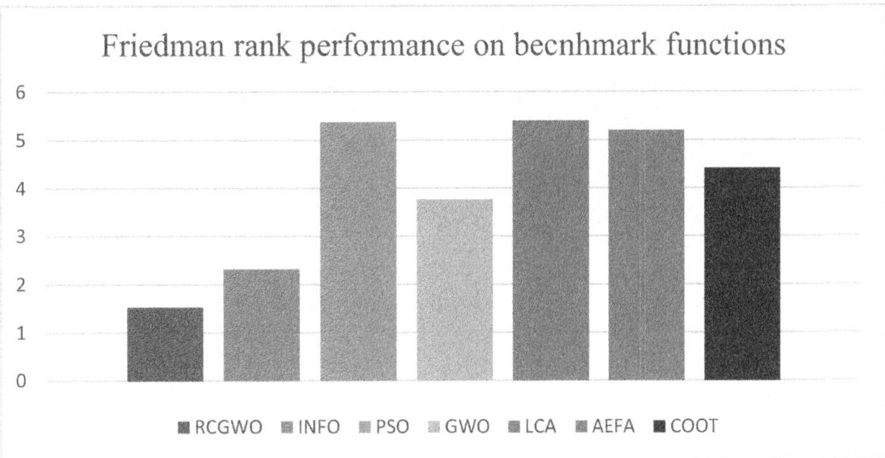

FIGURE 36.3 Bar chart of Friedman rank performance of RCGWO and compared algorithms.

TABLE 36.3 Comparison of RCGWO quantitative outcomes on IEEE CEC'2020.

Algorithm		RCGWO	GWO	PSO	INFO	LCA	AEFA	COOT
CEC_F1	*Mean*	5.410E+04	9.782E+08	8.139E+08	7.08E+05	3.679E+10	2.698E+10	4.429E+10
	SD	2.408E+04	7.704E+08	1.597E+09	1.08E+05	5.988E+09	3.545E+09	6.770E+09
CEC_F2	*Mean*	2.276E+03	2.64E+03	2.612E+03	2.66E+03	6.54E+03	5.30E+03	6.38E+03
	SD	5.993E+02	4.79E+02	6.017E+02	4.56E+02	3.99E+02	2.63E+02	4.42E+02
CEC_F3	*Mean*	7.815E+02	7.79E+02	7.518E+02	8.32E+02	1.10E+03	1.01E+03	1.16E+03
	SD	2.354E+01	2.28E+01	1.240E+02	2.12E+01	3.25E+01	1.91E+01	4.54E+01
CEC_F4	*Mean*	1.900E+03	1.90E+03	1.90E+03	1.90E+03	1.90E+03	1.90E+03	1.90E+03
	SD	1.526E-01	7.24E-01	3.159E+02	0	2.02E-04	0	0
CEC_F5	*Mean*	7.807E+04	9.00E+05	4.277E+05	2.20E+05	2.04E+07	3.51E+06	3.56E+07
	SD	2.902E+04	1.02E+06	1.315E+05	3.61E+04	1.00E+07	1.18E+06	1.61E+07
CEC_F6	*Mean*	1.883E+03	1.90E+03	1.897E+03	1.89E+03	4.06E+03	3.05E+03	3.75E+03
	SD	1.560E+02	1.87E+02	4.102E+02	2.31E+02	2.96E+02	2.16E+02	4.03E+02
CEC_F7	*Mean*	1.682E+05	2.91E+05	1.546E+05	7.21E+05	3.27E+07	1.19E+06	2.06E+07
	SD	1.253E+05	5.40E+05	1.617E+05	5.81E+05	3.09E+07	6.79E+05	2.01E+07
CEC_F8	*Mean*	3.142E+03	3.21E+03	3.423E+03	3.89E+03	7.28E+03	5.13E+03	7.54E+03
	SD	1.130E+03	1.11E+03	9.889E+02	1.22E+03	9.33E+02	4.29E+02	8.50E+02
CEC_F9	*Mean*	2.862E+03	2.86E+03	2.493E+03	2.88E+03	3.80E+03	3.23E+03	3.44E+03
	SD	4.282E+01	4.03E+01	5.139E+02	3.21E+01	2.23E+02	4.52E+01	1.38E+02
CEC_F10	*Mean*	2.946E+03	3.00E+03	2.295E+03	2.97E+03	7.73E+03	4.76E+03	9.20E+03
	SD	3.306E+01	4.40E+01	5.150E+02	3.13E+01	1.21E+03	3.57E+02	1.69E+03

the location update complexity is $O(N \times D)$ per iteration. Therefore, over T iterations, the overall complexity of GWO is $O(N \times D \times T)$.

In the proposed RCGWO, the core framework of vanilla GWO is preserved. The RCGWO position update mechanism incorporates adaptive random weighting, elite pool crossover, and a population re-evaluation step for worst agent replacement. The adaptive weight generation and location update both require $O(N \times D)$. The elite pool crossover incurs $O(D)$, then identifying and replacing the worst agent may require additional $O(N \times D)$ per iteration in the worst case. Therefore per iteration cost of RCGWO is $O(2 \times N \times D + D) \approx O(N \times D)$. So, overall complexity of RCGWO over T iterations is $O(N \times D \times T)$.

RCGWO does not increase asymptotic memory requirements. The additional elite, parent, and offspring agents incur only low-order $O(D)$ overhead without impacting the overall scalability. So, the overall space complexity of both GWO and RCGWO is $O(N \times D)$.

TABLE 36.4 Friedman rank performance of RCGWO for IEEE CEC 2020 functions.

Methods	Sum ranks	Mean ranks	Ranking
RCGWO	49	2.45	1
INFO	62	3.10	2
PSO	75	3.75	4
GWO	68	3.40	3
LCA	112	5.60	6
AEFA	80	4.00	5
COOT	114	5.70	7

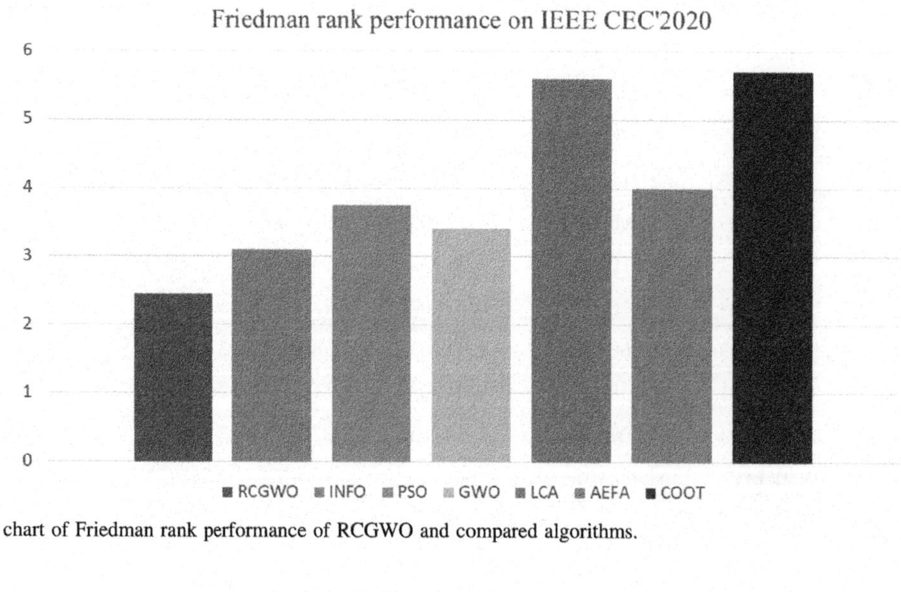

FIGURE 36.4 Bar chart of Friedman rank performance of RCGWO and compared algorithms.

TABLE 36.5 Wilcoxon signed rank test results using benchmark functions.

Pairs for comparison	Sum of positive ranks	Sum of negative ranks	Z (based on positive ranks)	*P*-value	Conclusion
RCGWO – GWO	28	437	-4.206	0.000	Evaluated *P* value (0.000) < 0.05 implies RCGWO performs well compared to GWO at 5% sign. level
RCGWO – INFO	74	304	-2.763	0.006	Evaluated P value (0.006) < 0.05 implies that RCGWO performs well compared to INFO at 5% sign. level
RCGWO – PSO	5	460	-4.679	0.000	Evaluated *P* value (0.000) < 0.05 implies RCGWO performs well compared to PSO at 5% sign. level
RCGWO – LCA	28	437	-4.206	0.000	Evaluated *P* value (0.000) < 0.05 implies RCGWO performs well compared to LCA at 5% sign. level
RCGWO – AEFA	10	425	-4.487	0.000	Evaluated *P* value (0.000) < 0.05 implies RCGWO performs well compared to AEFA at 5% sign. level
RCGWO – COOT	44	362	-3.621	0.000	Evaluated *P* value (0.000) < 0.05 implies RCGWO performs well compared to COOT at 5% sign. level

TABLE 36.6 Wilcoxon signed rank test results using IEEE CEC 2020.

Pairs for comparison	Sum of positive ranks	Sum of negative ranks	Z (based on positive ranks)	*P*-value	Conclusion
RCGWO – GWO	34	156	-2.455	0.014	Evaluated *P* value (0.014) < 0.05 implies RCGWO performs well compared to GWO at 5% sign. level
RCGWO – INFO	45	145	-2.012	0.044	Evaluated P value (0.044) < 0.05 implies that RCGWO performs well compared to INFO at 5% sign. level
RCGWO – PSO	22	168	-2.938	0.003	Evaluated *P* value (0.003) < 0.05 implies RCGWO performs well compared to PSO at 5% sign. level
RCGWO – LCA	12	178	-3.340	0.001	Evaluated *P* value (0.001) < 0.05 implies RCGWO performs well compared to LCA at 5% sign. level
RCGWO – AEFA	20	170	-3.018	0.003	Evaluated *P* value (0.003) < 0.05 implies RCGWO performs well compared to AEFA at 5% sign. level
RCGWO – COOT	11	179	-3.380	0.001	Evaluated *P* value (0.001) < 0.05 implies RCGWO performs well compared to COOT at 5% sign. level

TABLE 36.7 Comparison of outcomes of RCGWO for real-world problems.

Problems	RCGWO	GWO	INFO	LCA	COOT	AEFA
Reactor network design	1.514E+03	1.583E+03	1.578E+03	1.672E+03	1.741E+03	1.564E+03
Blending–pooling–separation problem	6.398E+14	1.774E+16	7.385E+15	9.288E+14	5.647E+15	4.386E+15
Pressure vessel design	5.740E+03	6.060E+03	6.463E+03	6.741E+03	5.743E+03	5.833E+03
Welded beam design	1.670E+00	1.671E+00	1.671E+00	1.675E+00	1.774E+00	1.761E+00
Hydrostatic thrust bearing design problem	1.708E+03	1.738E+03	1.732E+03	1.891E+03	2.987E+03	1.738E+03

36.4 Results and discussion

This section presents and compares the calculated quantitative and qualitative outcomes of the proposed RCGWO with classical GWO and other MAs, namely INFO, Liver Cancer Algorithm (LCA) [17], Particle Swarm Optimizer (PSO) [18], Artificial Electric Field Algorithm (AEFA) [19], and COOT [20]. To assess the performance of the proposed RCGWO against other algorithms, first, it has been tested on fifteen benchmark functions; second, we have applied it to solve IEEE CEC 2020 functions. And at last, to further assess the performance of the proposed method, it has been applied to solve five real-world problems taken from Ref. [21]. From F1 to F9 are unimodal functions and F10 to F15 are multimodal functions. Details of the functions are provided in Appendix 36.1. The population size of each algorithm is taken as 50 and the maximum iteration is 1000 for the termination criteria. To maintain fairness in performance comparison, each algorithm is run 30 times.

Table 36.1 presents the mean and standard deviation achieved by each algorithm. Then, in Fig. 36.2, convergence graphs of six randomly selected functions are presented. Table 36.2 and Fig. 36.3 show the Friedman rank performance of RCGWO on benchmark functions with 95% of confidence level. Table 36.3 displays the performance of RCGWO on IEEE CEC 2020 functions, and Table 36.4 with Fig. 36.4 provides the Friedman rank performance with 95% of confidence level. Quantitative outcomes, statistical analysis, and convergence analysis suggests of the proposed RCGWO shows significant improvement over the classical GWO and presents competitive performance against the other compared algorithms.

Now, the statistical significance of performance differences between RCGWO and competing methods using the paired sample Wilcoxon signed rank test at 5% significance level is calculated. Each of the algorithms was executed 30 times. The median differences are tested against the null hypothesis of zero median differences. Tables 36.5 and 36.6 presents the Wilcoxon signed rank test performance outcomes for 15 benchmark functions and IEEE CEC 2020 functions, respectively.

Proceeding this Table 36.7 provides the quantitative results attained by RCGWO and comparing algorithms, including the vanilla GWO, on the five real-world problems. It displays the mean values achieved by each algorithm over 30 independent runs for the five real-world problems.

36.5 Conclusion

In this chapter, we have introduced a novel and enhanced variant of classical GWO named RCGWO. The proposed algorithm integrates adaptive random weight and elite-based crossover strategy to improve the balance between exploration and exploitation in GWO. The adaptive random weight smoothly transitions from exploration to exploitation as the iteration process progresses and adaptively adjusts the leadership hierarchy. Then, elitist crossover is applied to improve the searching mechanism and avoid premature convergence to local optima.

The performance of the proposed RCGWO has been rigorously assessed using a comprehensive set of 15benchmark functions and the IEEE CEC 2020 test suite and its results have been compared with a combination of six well-known and recent methods. Statistical and convergence analyses have been conducted to evaluate the significance of the outcomes and to exhibit the superior convergence accuracy against other algorithms. Furthermore, it has been successfully applied to

TABLE 36.A1 Description of the classical benchmark functions.

Name	C	function	dim	Range	f_{opt}
Sphere	UM	$f_1(x) = \sum_{i=1}^{n} x_i^2$	30	[-100,100]	0
Schwefel2.20	UM	$f_2(x) = \sum_{i=1}^{n} \lvert x_i \rvert$	30	[-100,100]	0
Schwefel2.21	UM	$f_3(x) = \max_{i=1,\ldots,n} \lvert x_i \rvert$	30	[-100,100]	0
Schwefel1.2	UM	$f_4(x)= \sum_{i=1}^{n} (\sum_{j=1}^{n} x_j)^2$	30	[-100,100]	0
Schwefel2.22	UM	$f_5(x) = \lvert x_i \rvert + \Pi_{i=1}^{n} \lvert x_i \rvert$	30	[-10,10]	0
Schwefel2.23	UM	$f_6(x) = \sum_{i=1}^{n} x_i^{10}$	30	[-10,10]	0
Brown	UM	$f_7(x) = \sum_{i=1}^{n-1} (x_i^2)^{(x_{i+1}^2+1)} + (x_{i+1}^2)^{(x_i^2+1)}$	30	[-1,4]	0
Powell	UM	$f_8(x) = \sum_{i=1}^{n/k} (x_{4i-3} + 10x_{4i-2})^2 + 5(x_{4i-1} - x_{4i})^2 + 5(x_{4i-2} - x_{4i-1})^4 + 10(x_{4i-1} - x_{4i})^4$	24	[-4,5]	0
Zakharov	UM	$f_9(x) = \sum_{i=1}^{n} x_i^2 + (\sum_{i=1}^{n} 0.5ix_i)^2 + (\sum_{i=1}^{n} 0.5ix_i)^4$	30	[-5,10]	0
Schwefel 2.26	MM	$f_{10}(x) = -\sum_{i=1}^{n} (x_i \sin(\sqrt{\lvert x_i \rvert}))$	30	[-500,500]	-12569.5
Rastrigin	MM	$f_{11}(x) = -\sum_{i=1}^{n} [x_i^2 - 10\cos(2\pi x_i) + 10]$	30	[-5.12,5.12]	0
Alpine N.1	MM	$f_{12}(x) = \sum_{i=1}^{n} \lvert x_i \sin(x_i) + 0.1x_i \rvert$	30	[-10, 10]	0
Xin-She-Yang	MM	$f_{13}(x) = \sum_{i=1}^{n} \in_i \lvert x_i \rvert^i$	30	[-5, 5]	0
Trigonometric 2	MM	$f_{14}(x) = 1 + \sum_{i=1}^{n} [8\sin^2(7(x_i - 0.9)^2) + 6\sin^2(14(x_i - 0.9)^2) + (x_i - 0.9)^2]$	30	[−500,500]	1
Xin-She Yang N.4	MM	$f_{15}(x)= (\sum_{i=1}^{n} \left[\sin^2(x_i) - e^{-\sum_{i=1}^{n} x_i^2}\right]) e^{-\sum_{i=1}^{n} \sin^2(\sqrt{\lvert x_i \rvert})}$	30	[-10, 10]	-1

solve five real-world engineering and industrial design problems, where it has outperformed other algorithms in terms of solution quality.

Despite its superior performance, RCGWO exhibits minor limitations when addressing large-scale constrained or serious dimensional problems. Because of the highly complex landscape convergence speed and accuracy slightly decreases. Nevertheless, its adaptability and scalability can be further enhanced using different learning strategies, hybrid approaches, and parameter tuning. Future research will focus on extending RCGWO to multiobjective, dynamic, and discrete problem domains and applying it to solve various problems related to renewable energy, path planning, image segmentation, and feature selection problems. Moreover, theoretical investigations into convergence behavior, computational complexity, and parameter sensitivity will help in strengthening its mathematical foundation.

CRediT authorship contribution statement

Suraj Roy: Writing – original draft, Methodology, Investigation, Conceptualization. **Apu Kumar Saha:** Writing – review & editing, Supervision, Conceptualization. **Sharmistha Bhattacharya (Halder):** Visualization, Supervision.

Acknowledgment

The authors declare that no AI-assisted technologies or generative AI tools were used in this work.

Appendix 36.1

See Table 36.A1.

References

[1] S. Roy, S. Chakraborty, A.K. Saha, M.K. Sharma, S. Bhattacharya (Halder), D. Bhowmik, A spiral and enhanced random search strategies based slime mould algorithm for global optimization and interplanetary spacecraft trajectory problem, Communications in Nonlinear Science and Numerical Simulation (2025) 109508. Available from https://doi.org/10.1016/j.cnsns.2025.109508.

[2] S. Mirjalili, A. Lewis, The whale optimization algorithm, Advances in Engineering Software 95 (2016) 51–67. Available from https://doi.org/10.1016/j.advengsoft.2016.01.008.

[3] A. Faramarzi, M. Heidarinejad, S. Mirjalili, A.H. Gandomi, Marine predators algorithm: a nature-inspired metaheuristic, Expert Systems with Applications 152 (2020) 113377. Available from https://doi.org/10.1016/j.eswa.2020.113377.

[4] I. Ahmadianfar, A.A. Heidari, S. Noshadian, H. Chen, A.H. Gandomi, INFO: an efficient optimization algorithm based on weighted mean of vectors, Expert Systems with Applications 195 (2022) 116516. Available from https://doi.org/10.1016/j.eswa.2022.116516.

[5] J.O. Agushaka, A.E. Ezugwu, A.K. Saha, J. Pal, L. Abualigah, S. Mirjalili, Greater cane rat algorithm (GCRA): a nature-inspired metaheuristic for optimization problems, Heliyon 10 (2024) e31629. Available from https://doi.org/10.1016/j.heliyon.2024.e31629.

[6] D.H. Wolpert, W.G. Macready, No free lunch theorems for optimization, IEEE Transactions on Evolutionary Computation 1 (1997) 67–82. Available from https://doi.org/10.1109/4235.585893.

[7] S. Mirjalili, S.M. Mirjalili, A. Lewis, Grey wolf optimizer, Advances in Engineering Software 69 (2014) 46–61. Available from https://doi.org/10.1016/j.advengsoft.2013.12.007.

[8] S.A. Afghani Edsa, K. Sunat, H. Guo, Cost-sensitive neural network: a grey wolf optimizer-based approach for breast cancer prediction, Expert Systems with Applications 266 (2025) 126176. Available from https://doi.org/10.1016/j.eswa.2024.126176.

[9] İ. Tuğal, Energy efficiency in building: entropy-based grey wolf optimization for improved MLP performance, Energy Reports 13 (2025) 4247–4260. Available from https://doi.org/10.1016/j.egyr.2025.03.048.

[10] H. Chen, S.Q. Salih, A. Almadhor, M.N. Khan, Z. Al Barakeh, R. Ghandour, et al., Leveraging multi-effect energy utilization in a biomass-based system for H2 production and urban energy needs: 4E analysis and ANN-based grey wolf optimization, Energy 333 (2025) 137323. Available from https://doi.org/10.1016/j.energy.2025.137323.

[11] R. Kumar Chaudhary, R. Kumar, N. Saxena, Ameliorating clustered federated learning using grey wolf optimization algorithm for healthcare IoT devices, J Supercomput 81 (2025) 976. Available from https://doi.org/10.1007/s11227-025-07374-9.

[12] L. Zhang, X. Chen, Elite-driven grey wolf optimization for global optimization and its application to feature selection, Swarm and Evolutionary Computation 92 (2025) 101795. Available from https://doi.org/10.1016/j.swevo.2024.101795.

[13] J. Yang, F. Yan, J. Zhang, C. Peng, Hybrid chaos game and grey wolf optimization algorithms for UAV path planning, Applied Mathematical Modelling 142 (2025) 115979. Available from https://doi.org/10.1016/j.apm.2025.115979.

[14] Z. Wang, L. Shu, S. Yang, Z. Zeng, D. He, S. Chan, Multi-population dynamic grey wolf optimizer based on dimension learning and laplace mutation for global optimization, Expert Systems with Applications 265 (2025) 125863. Available from https://doi.org/10.1016/j.eswa.2024.125863.

[15] J. Huang, X. Deng, L. Hu, Enhanced grey wolf optimizer with hybrid strategies for efficient feature selection in high-dimensional data, Information sciences 705 (2025) 121958. Available from https://doi.org/10.1016/j.ins.2025.121958.

[16] M. Yu, J. Xu, W. Liang, Y. Qiu, S. Bao, L. Tang, Improved multi-strategy adaptive grey wolf optimization for practical engineering applications and high-dimensional problem solving, Artif Intell Rev 57 (2024) 277. Available from https://doi.org/10.1007/s10462-024-10821-3.

[17] E.H. Houssein, D. Oliva, N.A. Samee, N.F. Mahmoud, M.M. Emam, Liver cancer algorithm: a novel bio-inspired optimizer, Computers in Biology and Medicine 165 (2023) 107389. Available from https://doi.org/10.1016/j.compbiomed.2023.107389.

[18] J. Kennedy, R. Eberhart, Particle swarm optimization, Proceedings of ICNN'95 - International Conference on Neural Networks 4 (1995) 1942–1948. Available from https://doi.org/10.1109/ICNN.1995.488968.

[19] A.Y. Anita, AEFA: artificial electric field algorithm for global optimization, Swarm and Evolutionary Computation 48 (2019) 93–108. Available from https://doi.org/10.1016/j.swevo.2019.03.013.

[20] I. Naruei, F. Keynia, A new optimization method based on COOT bird natural life model, Expert Systems with Applications 183 (2021) 115352. Available from https://doi.org/10.1016/j.eswa.2021.115352.

[21] A. Kumar, G. Wu, M.Z. Ali, R. Mallipeddi, P.N. Suganthan, S. Das, A test-suite of non-convex constrained optimization problems from the real-world and some baseline results, Swarm and Evolutionary Computation 56 (2020) 100693. Available from https://doi.org/10.1016/j.swevo.2020.100693.

Chapter 37

An adaptive hybrid grey wolf optimizer and teaching-learning-based optimization algorithm for team formation optimization problems

Md. Abdul Kader[1], Kamal Z. Zamli[2], Zalili B. Musa[2], and Mizanur Rahman[3]

[1]*Department of Software Engineering, Daffodil International University, Dhaka, Bangladesh,* [2]*Faculty of Computing, Universiti Malaysia Pahang Al-Sultan Abdullah, Pekan, Pahang, Malaysia,* [3]*School of Computer Science, Western Illinois University, Macomb, IL, United States*

37.1 Introduction

Team formation is a very common and important problem in many real-world domains, such as project management, software development, healthcare, education, and research collaborations, to form effective teams from a large pool of people. Team formation optimization (TFO) aims at identifying an optimal subset of individuals whose combined set of skills satisfies a predefined set of task requirements while minimizing objective functions such as team size, cost, or communication overhead [1]. With an increase in the number of people and their corresponding skills, possible combinations of teams are exponential, and hence, finding an optimal solution for this problem has become a complex combinatorial optimization problem due to computational intractability with traditional methods [2].

The metaheuristic algorithms are powerful means of solving such complex optimization problems, as they can explore large and nonlinear search spaces with no problem-specific knowledge [3]. In this regard, promising results using the grey wolf optimizer (GWO) [4] and teaching-learning-based optimization (TLBO) [5] have come out in a wide range of applications. GWO mimics the social hierarchy and hunting mechanism of grey wolves, which endows it with strong global exploration capability, while TLBO is inspired by the teaching and peer-learning process in a classroom environment and provides an efficient local search and exploitation. Even though these two optimization algorithms have their strengths, they suffer from limitations when used independently, for example, GWO may face premature convergence in later stages, and TLBO may face a lack of diversity in early iterations [6].

This paper addresses these challenges by presenting a new hybrid metaheuristic algorithm called Hybrid Adaptive Grey Wolf–Teaching-Learning-Based Optimization (AGW-TLBO). In this regard, the underlying philosophy of the proposed strategy will be to synergize GWO's exploration strengths with the exploitation power of TLBO. Motivations will also be drawn from an adaptive control mechanism that allows for dynamic changes between exploration and exploitation rates during the process of optimization, based on the population diversity. This adaptive strategy would assure a more guided and flexible search process, avoiding stagnation and enhancing convergence performance.

The key contributions of this work are summarized as follows:

- A novel hybrid framework: AGW-TLBO, which combines the strengths of GWO and TLBO in a two-phase process, effectively enabling exploration before refinement.
- An adaptive control mechanism that continuously observes the population diversity to perform real-time algorithmic behavior adaptations, maintaining a healthy balance of exploration and exploitation.
- A comprehensive assessment of hybrid AGW-TLBO for two real-world TFO benchmark datasets, namely internet movie database (IMDB) and dblp computer science bibliography (DBLP), covering different levels of task complexity.

Grey Wolf Optimizer. DOI: https://doi.org/10.1016/B978-0-443-36624-6.00009-3

- Empirical comparisons against vanilla GWO, TLBO, and a baseline hybrid GWO-TLBO [6], demonstrating the superior performance of the proposed method in terms of team cost, team size, convergence speed, and robustness.

The rest of the paper is organized as follows: Section 2 presents a review of related works, focusing on recent hybrid variants of the GWO. Section 3 describes the mathematical formulation of the algorithms, namely GWO, TLBO, the proposed hybrid AGW-TLBO, and the Team Formation Optimization problem. It also describes the benchmark datasets and the experimental setup used in this study. Section 4 reports and analyzes the experimental results. Finally, Section 5 concludes the paper and highlights potential directions for future research.

37.2 Literature review

The advancement of optimization methodologies has been marked by a transition from early reliance on stochastic and heuristic paradigms to the development of more robust and adaptive metaheuristic frameworks, often enhanced through hybridization to address high-dimensional and multimodal search landscapes. In addition, hybrid metaheuristics integrate multiple metaheuristics or combine a metaheuristic with other optimization techniques for careful coordination of the strengths of the methods to increase the ability to guide the search intelligently. Recently, various hybrid metaheuristic methods have been proposed in literature. Recent hybrid GWO algorithms, detailing their motivation, hybrid algorithms, hybridization strategy, and bibliographic references, are reviewed into three different categories (early hybridization trends, transitional phase, and contemporary developments) as follows. This review focuses exclusively on hybridizations between metaheuristic algorithms (metaheuristic–metaheuristic).

37.2.1 Early hybridization trends (2018–20): foundation of embedded hybrid grey wolf optimizer

The early years (2018–20) were the genesis of the GWO from embedded and sequential hybridization to counteract premature convergence and inadequate local search ability.

- Zhang et al. in 2018 [7] combined biogeography-based optimization with GWO, incorporating alternating strategies for improving global–local balance and preventing premature convergence. This established a baseline for other subsequent adaptive hybrids.
- Alomoush et al. in 2019 [8] combined harmony search with opposition-based learning, providing self-tuning during the improvisation phase. It provided a solution to sensitive parameter choice problems but was not highly scalable for high-dimensional problems.
- Sharma et al. in 2019 [9] added ant colony optimization to enhance exploration when GWO loses momentum, being the first to implement dynamic exploration–exploitation trade-offs control.
- Konstantinov et al. in 2019 [10] added synergistic parameter adjustment through the integration of Bees Algorithm mechanisms, enhancing the smoothness of convergence.
- Ouhame et al. in 2020 [11] hybridized cloud resource allocation, demonstrating that learning components could be incorporated to optimize energy-efficient scheduling.

Collectively, these works set the original hybridization ideology—mapping complementary algorithms into GWO's update mechanism to achieve improved performance.

37.2.2 Transitional phase (2021–23): transition to domain-specific and adaptive hybrids

During this phase, research focused on problem-specific hybridization and multiphase adaptation, expanding the scope of GWO to a range of optimization problems.

- Vikram Kumar in 2021 [12] optimized local search using simulated annealing to address the weakness in exploitation. This intensity method in the early phase inspired numerous later embedded-learning methods.
- Lee et al. [13] and Keswani et al. [14] in 2022 solved feature selection and microgrid optimization, respectively, with embedded heap-based or equilibrium operators for adaptive balancing of the search space.
- Gurumurthy et al. in 2022 [15] introduced sequential hybridization for IoT intrusion detection that combined cosine similarity-based feature selection with GWO's classification. The sequential approach addressed growing interest in task-decomposed hybridization pipelines.
- Lv et al. [16], Hoseini et al. [17], and Makhadmeh et al. [18] in 2022 highlighted biologically inspired coevolutionary approaches. These combined Golden Eagle, Elephant Herding, and Multiverse mechanisms, respectively, are for enhancing exploration and adaptive dynamics in intelligent systems and Unmanned Aerial Vehicle (UAV) applications.

- Dhakhinamoorthy et al. [19] and Keswani et al. [20] in 2023 solidified trigonometric–behavioral hybridization traditions, unifying WOA's exploitation and SCA's position updates to reduce local optima entrapment.
- Bathina et al. in 2023 [21] combined Cuckoo Search for adaptive control parameters and diversity preservation—establishing the trend toward opposition-based adaptive control now popular in multifactorial optimization.

These advances reflect a trend towards domain-specific hybrid models, with emphasis on adaptability, learning, and multi-domain applicability (energy, internet of things (IoT), power systems, biomedicine).

37.2.3 Contemporary developments (2024–25): intelligent, multistage, and learning-driven grey wolf optimizer hybrids

Contemporary advances in 2024–25 mark a mature stage of hybridization that addresses teaching-learning processes, adaptive coevolution, and task-specific embedding.

- Singh et al. [6] and Shaikh et al. [22] in 2025 are representative examples of embedded hybridization with learning dynamics, introducing TLBO's teacher–learner phases and PSO's adaptive velocity mechanisms. Both these studies overcome the stagnation of GWO in convergence and its poor ability to refine locally.
- Shang et al. [23] and Zhao et al. [24] in 2025 engaged genetic and differential evolution features to ensure increased population diversity and cross-generation learning, improving convergence and global search reliability.
- Tbaishat et al. [25] and Mohammad Aghdam et al. [26] in 2025 implement sequential–parallel hybridization, combining bat or salp swarm initialization with GWO exploitation. These models improved classification and opinion leader selection accuracy.
- Ye et al. [27] and Jyoti et al. [28] in 2024 advocate multistrategy coevolution and hybrid metaheuristics deep hybridization (ALO + GWO) for emotion recognition and feature selection, leading to cognitive–biological hybridization models.
- Zhang et al. [29] and Alsharafa et al. [30] in 2024 applied hybrid GWO in logistics and photovoltaic (PV) optimization. Their hybrid crossover–mutation and constraint-handling mechanism proves real-world applicability and performance stability.

From 2018 to 2025, hybrid GWO research has evolved from simple heuristic embedding to multistage, knowledge-driven, and adaptive systems. The progression reflects an ongoing pursuit to balance exploration–exploitation, address premature convergence, and extend GWO's reach into real-world, data-intensive domains.

The methods of integration of the constituent metaheuristic algorithms in hybrid metaheuristics may be broadly classified as one of the following: Sequential Hybridization, Parallel Hybridization, Embedded Hybridization, and Adaptive/Alternating Hybridization. The existing literature shows that there is a need for further research in the parallel and adaptive hybrid variants of the GWO.

37.3 Mathematical modeling of methods and materials

37.3.1 Grey wolf optimizer

Consider a pack of grey wolves wandering in the wild. They have a strict social hierarchy in nature and are also cooperative hunters with an adaptive strategy of movement. This fascinating behavior inspired the proposal of Seyedali Mirjalili et al. [4], who in 2014 proposed the GWO as a nature-inspired metaheuristic algorithm to solve complex optimization problems.

Fundamentally, GWO is not yet another algorithm; instead, it's a beautiful abstraction of social intelligence in animals for the solution of mathematical problems.

Wild grey wolves structure themselves according to a strict hierarchical pattern of leadership:

- Alpha (α) – the leader, best solution found so far.
- Beta (β) – second-best solution, helps guide the pack.
- Delta (δ) – third-best solution, supports the alpha and beta.
- Omega (ω) – the rest of the pack, followers that learn from leaders.

During the optimization process, the wolves simulate their surroundings, hunting, and attacking prey. In computational terms, the prey is the optimal solution we are searching for, and the hunt is the iterative refinement of the candidate solutions.

Each of the GWO iterations will involve these main steps:

- Encircling the prey: Through a mathematical model relating distance and direction vectors, wolves estimate the position of the prey (optimal solution) and perform the surrounding.

$$\vec{D} = |\vec{C}.\vec{X}_p(t) - \vec{X}(t)| \tag{37.1}$$

$$\vec{X}(t+1) = \vec{X}_p(t) - \vec{A}.\vec{D} \tag{37.2}$$

$$\vec{A} = 2\vec{a}.\vec{r}_1 - \vec{a} \tag{37.3}$$

$$\vec{C} = 2\vec{r}_2 \tag{37.4}$$

Where:

o $\vec{X}(t)$ =prey position (estimated by α, β, δ)
o $\vec{X}(t)$ =current position of the wolf
o $\vec{A}, \vec{C}$ =coefficient vectors
o t=current iteration
o $\vec{a}$ =decreases linearly from 2 to 0 over iterations
o $\vec{r}_1, \vec{r}_2$ =random vectors in [0, 1]

- Hunting: Wolves update positions based on the top three wolves, thus imitating collective decision-making.

$$\vec{X}_1 = \vec{X}_\alpha - \vec{A}_1.|\vec{C}_1.\vec{X}_\alpha - \vec{X}| \tag{37.5}$$

$$\vec{X}_2 = \vec{X}_\beta - \vec{A}_2.|\vec{C}_2.\vec{X}_\beta - \vec{X}| \tag{37.6}$$

$$\vec{X}_3 = \vec{X}_\delta - \vec{A}_3.|\vec{C}_3.\vec{X}_\delta - \vec{X}| \tag{37.7}$$

$$\vec{X}(t+1) = \frac{1}{3}(\vec{X}_1 + \vec{X}_2 + \vec{X}_3) \tag{37.8}$$

- Attacking the prey (exploitation): As the search converges, the amount of exploration reduces, and the pack zeroes in on the best solution.
- Searching for prey (exploration): The wolves, at the beginning, spread out to explore the search space, helping in avoiding local optima.

The parameter $\vec{a}$ linearly decreases from 2 to 0 over the iterations.

$$a = 2 - \frac{2t}{T} \tag{37.9}$$

where:

o t=current iteration
o T=maximum number of iterations
o When
o |A|>1: wolves explore by moving away from the leaders (exploration)
o |A|<1: wolves exploit by converging toward the leaders (exploitation)

These behaviors are controlled by adaptive parameters and random coefficients. In this way, exploration-diversity and exploitation-accuracy, two important aspects of any metaheuristic, are balanced. The elegance lies in its simplicity, while it captures the essence of swarm intelligence.

37.3.2 Teaching-learning-based optimization

The TLBO algorithm can be clarified with the help of an analogy to a classroom: each candidate solution is a student seeking to improve academic performance. The best student assumes the role of the teacher and leads improvements in the entire class average (global learning). Parallel to this, the students also learn from each other through knowledge sharing, competition, and helping peer improvement (local learning). Inspired by exactly the same idea-teaching and peer learning-the development of the teaching learning-based optimization algorithm was proposed by Rao et al. in [5]. This work took place in 2011 and represents a population-based metaheuristic mimicking knowledge enhancement processes in a classroom, developing TLBO as the strong and very human-like optimization approach it is. TLBO operates according to two key phases, just like an academic term:

Phase 1: Teacher Phase (Global Learning)

The best student then becomes the teacher for their peers and helps others to increase the class average.

Let:

- X_i = solution vector of the i-th student
- $X_{teacher}$ = best solution (teacher)
- M =mean of the population
- r =random number in [0,1]
- T_F =teaching factor ∈ {1, 2} (decides how much a teacher tries to teach)

$$X_i^{new} = X_i + r.\ (X_{teacher} - T_F.\ M) \tag{37.10}$$

If the new solution is better, update the student's solution.

Phase 2: Learner Phase (Local Learning)

Students improve at interacting with peers—sometimes they learn something new, sometimes they compete.

Randomly pick another student X_j, $j \neq i$

If $f(X_i) < f(X_j)$ then:

$$X_i^{new} = X_i + r.\ (X_j - X_i) \tag{37.11}$$

Else:

$$X_i^{new} = X_i + r.\ (X_i - X_j) \tag{37.12}$$

Again, the new solution is accepted only if it's better.

37.3.3 Adaptive grey wolf–teaching-learning-based hybrid algorithm

The proposed adaptive grey wolf–teaching-learning-based hybrid algorithm is a population-based metaheuristic that aims to improve the balance between exploration and exploitation for complex combinatorial problems such as team formation optimization. It integrates social hierarchy and hunting behavior inspired by grey wolves with the instructional dynamics of the TLBO algorithm, leading to a more robust adaptive search process.

The hybridization strategy followed in hybrid AGW-TLBO is based on a sequential hybridization approach wherein the core exploration phase of GWO is first executed to drive the population toward promising regions with the help of its leadership-based social hierarchy. Then, the TLBO mechanism refines the solutions by a two-stage exploitation process: teacher phase and learner phase, without introducing any algorithm-specific control parameters. Moreover, the hybrid model integrates an adaptive control mechanism that dynamically tunes the exploration–exploitation balance of GWO with regard to the population diversity. This helps maintain a strong balance between diversification and intensification by avoiding local optima and accelerating the convergence toward high-quality solutions.

Hybrid AGW-TLBO dynamically adapts the control parameter a, which balances the rate of exploration and exploitation in the GWO phase. The adaptive mechanism is linked with the population diversity across the iterations. Mathematically, the adaptive control mechanism is given as follows:

Let:

- $\mathbf{P}^{(l)} \in \mathbb{R}^{N \times D}$: Population matrix at iteration l, with N agents and D dimensions.
- $\sigma^{(l)}$: Diversity of the population at iteration l, measured by the standard deviation of all decision variables.
- $\sigma^{(0)}$: Initial diversity, calculated at iteration 0.

- $a^{(l)}$: Adaptive control parameter at iteration l.

Step 1: Population Diversity
The diversity at iteration l is given by:

$$\sigma^{(l)} = std\left(vec\left(\mathbf{P}^{(l)}\right)\right) \tag{37.13}$$

where $vec\left(\mathbf{P}^{(l)}\right)$ denotes the vectorization (flattening) of the population matrix.

Step 2: Adaptive Scaling of *a*
The control parameter a is updated adaptively based on the ratio between current and initial diversity:

$$a^{(l)} = 2.\ \frac{\sigma^{(l)}}{\sigma^{(0)}} \tag{37.14}$$

Step 3: Clipping *a* within Bounds
To maintain numerical stability and prevent extreme values, $a^{(l)}$ is bounded within the standard GWO range of [0, 2]:

$$a^{(l)} = \min\left(2, \max\left(0, a^{(l)}\right)\right) \tag{37.15}$$

Hybrid AGW-TLBO uses an adaptive control mechanism that adjusts the parameter a based on population diversity with the aim of balancing exploration and exploitation. When the population diversity is high at the early stages, a remains close to two for broad exploration. As the population converges and the diversity decreases, a is reduced with the aim of encouraging focused exploitation. Dynamic adjustment helps the algorithm explore widely in the early stages and fine-tunes solutions in later stages for improved convergence, avoiding local optima.

Fig. 37.1 illustrates the pseudocode for the proposed hybrid AGW-TLBO. The proposed algorithm randomly initializes the population of solutions (Line 1) and computes the fitness evaluation of every solution (Line 2). Further, it calculates the initial diversity of the population to drive future adaptivity in the algorithm (Line 3). The algorithm ensures the feasibility of each solution in every iteration (Line 4) and updates the fitness of every solution with a dimensional index (Lines 6–7). Identifying the top three individuals as Alpha, Beta, and Delta wolves is carried out in Line 10. It keeps tracking the best solution obtained so far in Line 11. Further, an adaptive control parameter a is updated in Lines 12–14, based on the ratio of current diversity and initial diversity, which controls the step size and maintains the balance between exploration and exploitation.

This is followed by the GWO update mechanism in Lines 15 through 19, moving the rest of the population, with the help of guidance from Alpha, Beta, and Delta wolves, toward promising regions. Then the algorithm applies the TLBO phase: during the Teacher Phase from Lines 21 to 30, the best solution plays the role of a teacher, guiding other individuals to move toward a better population mean; during the Learner Phase between Lines 32 and 44, each solution interacts with a randomly selected partner in order to learn and, based on comparative performances, improve. At the end, the best fitness value for every iteration is recorded in the convergence curve, Line 45. After the maximum number of iterations, the algorithm will return the best solution and its fitness, along with the convergence trend, on Line 47. The structured combination of adaptive exploration via GWO and strong exploitation via TLBO makes Hybrid AGW-TLBO efficiently explore the search space toward highly converging solutions.

37.3.4 Computational complexity analysis

Most of the computational complexity of metaheuristic algorithms depends on the population size N, problem dimension D, and number of iterations T.

GWO: Every iteration updates all N wolves based on the three leaders (α, β, δ), which gives a time complexity of $O(N \times D \times T)$. Memory consumption is $O(N \times D)$.

TLBO: Both teacher and learner phases update the entire population once per iteration, yielding $O(2 \times N \times D \times T) \approx O(N \times D \times T)$. Space complexity is $O(N \times D)$.

Hybrid GWO-TLBO: Integrating TLBO after each iteration of GWO will double the computational effort; hence, $O(2 \times N \times D \times T)$.

Hybrid AGW-TLBO: Diversity calculations are introduced by the adaptive mechanism, which adds $O(N \times D)$ in each iteration. This slightly raises the overall complexity to $O(N \times D \times (T + 1)) \approx O(N \times D \times T)$. The space complexity remains $O(N \times D)$.

Overall, hybrid AGW-TLBO achieves improved search quality with only a marginal increase in runtime complexity compared to standard GWO or TLBO.

Input: Population Size N, Maximum Iterations T, Problem Dimension D
Output: Best Solution X^*, Best Fitness f^*, Convergence Curve C

```
Initialize population X_i for i = 1, 2, ..., N randomly
Evaluate initial fitness f(X_i) for all agents
Compute initial diversity σ_0 ← std(X)
for t ← 1 to T do
    foreach agent i do
        Apply constraint-handling to ensure feasibility of X_i
        Evaluate fitness f(X_i)
    end
    GWO:
    Identify top three agents as α, β, and δ
    Update X* ← X_α and f* ← f(X_α)
    Compute current diversity σ_t and adapt control parameter:
    a_t ← 2 · (σ_t/σ_0)
    Clamp a_t within [0, 2]
    foreach agent i do
        for j ← 1 to D do
            Update X_{i,j} using GWO-based equations (5-8) with α, β, δ
        end
    end
    TLBO: Teacher Phase
    Select Teacher as the best current solution
    Compute mean of population X̄
    Choose Teaching Factor T_F ∈ {1, 2} randomly
    foreach agent i do
        X' ← X_i + rand() · (X_Teacher − T_F · X̄)
        Amend and evaluate X'
        if f(X') < f(X_i) then
            Update X_i ← X'
        end
    end
    TLBO: Learner Phase
    foreach agent i do
        Select random partner X_j, j ≠ i
        if f(X_i) < f(X_j) then
            X' ← X_i + rand() · (X_i − X_j)
        end
        else
            X' ← X_i + rand() · (X_j − X_i)
        end
        Amend and evaluate X'
        if f(X') < f(X_i) then
            Update X_i ← X'
        end
    end
    Record C(t) ← f*
end
return X*, f*, C
```

FIGURE 37.1 Pseudocode of the proposed adaptive GWO-TLBO hybrid algorithm (*GWO*, Grey wolf optimizer; *TLBO*, teaching-learning-based optimization).

37.3.5 Overview of team formation optimization problem

The TFO problem is a combinatorial optimization task arising in domains like project management, software engineering, multiagent systems, and crowdsourcing platforms. The core objective is to form an optimal team from a pool of available individuals such that the team satisfies multiple constraints (e.g., skill coverage, team forming cost, team size) while maximizing performance or minimizing cost. Due to its NP-hard nature and multiconstraint landscape, metaheuristic algorithms are widely adopted for solving TFO. The mathematical model of TFO is defined as follows:

Given:

- N: Total number of available individuals.
- M: Total number of unique skills.
- K: Number of required skills.
- $P = \{p_1, p_2, p_3, \ldots, p_N\}$: Set of individuals.
- $U = \{u_1, u_2, u_3, \ldots, u_M\}$: Set of unique skills.
- $S = \{s_i \subseteq U | p_i$ possesses skil set s_i, $i = 1,2,3, \ldots, N\}$: Set of skill sets
- $Q = \{q_1, q_2, q_3, \ldots, q_K\} \subseteq U$: Set of required skills to find.
- $\mathbf{r} = [r_i] \in \{0,1\}^M$: Required skill set matched with unique skill set, where

$$r_i = \begin{cases} 1, & if\ u_i \in Q \\ 0, & otherwise \end{cases} \quad \forall\, i = 1, 2, 3, \ldots, M \tag{37.16}$$

- Skill matrix, $A = [a_{ij}] \in \{0,\ 1\}^{N \times M}$,

$$a_{ij} = \begin{cases} 1, & \text{if individual} p_i \text{ possesses skill } u_j \\ & 0, \text{ otherwise} \end{cases} \tag{37.17}$$

- Cost matrix, $C = [c_{ij}] \in \mathbb{R}^{N \times N}$, $c_{ij} =$ Jaccard Distance(p_i, p_j) [31]

$$\text{Jaccard Distance}(p_i, p_j) = 1 - \text{Jaccard Similarity}\ (s_i, s_j) = \quad 1 - \frac{|s_i \cap s_j|}{|s_i \cup s_j|} \tag{37.18}$$

The total number of possible teams that can be generated from N individuals (i.e., all nonempty subsets of the set P is: $2^N - 1$. Members in a team can be selected as follows:

- $x_i \in \{0,\ 1\}c,\ where x_i =$ 1if individual $\text{p}_\text{i}$is selected in the team with the help of the skill matrix and the required skill set.

Objective function:

- Minimize team size: $\min \sum_{i=1}^{N} x_i$
- Minimize the communication cost of the team:

$$\min \sum_{i=1}^{N-1} \sum_{j=i+1}^{N} c_{ij}.\ x_i.\ x_j \tag{37.19}$$

However, in real-world applications, the number of available individuals (P) and the associated skill set (U) can be extremely large, leading to an exponential growth in the number of possible team combinations. As a result, solving the team formation problem using a straightforward or linear approach becomes computationally infeasible.

37.3.6 Benchmark datasets and experimental setup

To evaluate how well the proposed hybrid AGW-TLBO algorithm performs, we used two popular real-world datasets, IMDB [32] and DBLP [33]. The IMDB dataset, maintained by Amazon, contains information about movie actors and the roles they've played across various genres. After cleaning the data, we ended up with a list of 1014 actors and 28 unique roles categorized as skills. On the other hand, the DBLP dataset is a well-known bibliographic database of scientific publications. From this dataset, we extracted information on 5641 authors along with 3887 distinct research skills.

TABLE 37.1 Experimental results were obtained through 20 independent runs using the IMDB dataset for five number of skills to find.

Team size (TS) team Cost (TC)		GWO	TLBO	Hybrid GWO-TLBO	Hybrid AGW-TLBO
TS	Best	3.0000	2.0000	3.0000	3.0000
	Worst	3.0000	3.0000	3.0000	3.0000
	Mean	3.0000	2.9500	3.0000	3.0000
	Median	3.0000	2.9500	3.0000	3.0000
	St. Dev.	0.0000	0.2236	0.0000	0.0000
TC	Best	2.1006	0.9231	1.8864	2.0606
	Worst	2.9091	2.4905	2.5833	2.6893
	Mean	2.5159	2.2507	2.1145	2.3207
	Median	2.4657	2.3535	1.9735	2.3547
	St. Dev.	0.2272	0.3437	0.2807	0.2038

In order to simulate various levels of complexity regarding the team formation problem, we considered five different sets of required skills: 5, 10, 15, 20, and 25. These skill sets were applied individually to both datasets during the experiments.

All algorithms, including our proposed AGW-TLBO and its competitors, were implemented in MATLAB R2020b. The experiments were conducted on a standard computing environment: a machine running Windows 10 with a 2.9 GHz Intel Core i5 processor, 16 GB of RAM, and 512 GB of SSD storage.

Experimental parameters: The population size (N) was set to 10, with a maximum of 100 iterations (T). The stopping criterion was reaching the maximum number of iterations. The experimental results were obtained as the average of 20 independent runs. All algorithms employed identical population initialization and boundary-handling strategies, where any missing value was randomly generated within the range of one to the maximum dimension (i.e., the number of actors or authors) to ensure uniqueness and feasibility.

37.4 Results and discussion

The proposed hybrid AGW-TLBO algorithm was evaluated by comparing it against its individual components—GWO and TLBO—as well as a basic hybrid variant, GWO-TLBO. The evaluation was carried out using two well-known benchmark datasets: IMDB and DBLP. As shown in Tables 37.1 to 37.5 and Tables 37.7 to 37.11, the results were obtained by running each algorithm 20 independent runs on the TFO problem for IMDB and DBLP datasets, respectively. These tables summarize the performance of each algorithm in terms of best, worst, mean, median, and standard deviation (St. Dev.) of team size and team cost. Statistical stability was evaluated using median and interquartile range (IQR) shown in Table 37.6 and Table 37.12, while performance superiority was verified using the Wilcoxon Signed-Rank test in Table 37.13 and Table 37.14 for IMDB and DBLP datasets, respectively.

37.4.1 Performance analysis on IMDB dataset

At the smallest skill-set size (five skills), GWO yielded a median team cost of 2.4657 ± 0.3477 while TLBO reached a slightly lower value of 2.3536 ± 0.1904 (Table 37.6). The hybrid algorithm GWO-TLBO has recorded the minimum median cost, which was 1.9735, but with appreciably larger IQR ± 0.5329, indicating loss of consistency across runs. In contrast, the proposed algorithm AGW-TLBO has recorded 2.3547 ± 0.3917, reflecting a marginally higher median cost

TABLE 37.2 Experimental results were obtained through 20 independent runs using the IMDB dataset for 10 number of skills to find.

Team size (TS) team cost (TC)		GWO	TLBO	Hybrid GWO-TLBO	Hybrid AGW-TLBO
TS	Best	4.0000	4.0000	4.0000	4.0000
	Worst	7.0000	6.0000	8.0000	7.0000
	Mean	5.7000	4.7000	5.5500	5.4000
	Median	6.0000	5.0000	5.0000	5.0000
	St. Dev.	0.6569	0.5712	1.0501	0.7539
TC	Best	5.2430	3.7176	4.1508	4.3662
	Worst	15.5322	10.0810	21.6729	16.4792
	Mean	10.7728	6.6658	9.7920	9.1944
	Median	11.4612	7.2827	7.6938	8.0319
	St. Dev.	2.7570	1.7464	4.6665	2.9395

TABLE 37.3 Experimental results were obtained through 20 independent runs using the IMDB dataset for 15 number of skills to find.

Team size (TS) team cost (TC)		GWO	TLBO	Hybrid GWO-TLBO	Hybrid AGW-TLBO
TS	Best	6.0000	6.0000	6.0000	6.0000
	Worst	10.0000	8.0000	10.0000	9.0000
	Mean	8.0500	7.1500	7.9500	7.4500
	Median	8.0000	7.0000	8.0000	7.0000
	St. Dev.	0.9987	0.6708	1.0501	0.6863
TC	Best	12.6559	13.2577	13.1674	13.1204
	Worst	39.7006	25.2598	36.7551	32.5032
	Mean	25.2904	19.2227	24.5270	21.2712
	Median	24.4800	18.8292	23.3117	19.9408
	St. Dev.	6.8514	3.4276	6.5363	4.1896

compared to GWO-TLBO, yet with enhanced stability. This would therefore seem to confirm that for relatively smaller and smoother search spaces, AGW-TLBO prioritizes convergence reliability over aggressive minimization of cost.

The performance gap further increased when the skill-set size reached 10. The median cost for GWO steeply increased to 11.4612 ± 4.8972, indicating premature convergence. TLBO and GWO-TLBO reduced the cost to 7.2827 ± 2.5916 and 7.6938 ± 3.5600, respectively. AGW-TLBO reached a median of 8.0319 ± 4.1193. Although the median for TLBO is

TABLE 37.4 Experimental results were obtained through 20 independent runs using the IMDB dataset for 20 number of skills to find.

Team size (TS) team cost (TC)		GWO	TLBO	Hybrid GWO-TLBO	Hybrid AGW-TLBO
TS	Best	8.0000	7.0000	8.0000	8.0000
	Worst	11.0000	10.0000	11.0000	10.0000
	Mean	9.7000	8.5500	9.4000	9.1500
	Median	10.0000	9.0000	10.0000	9.0000
	St. Dev.	1.0311	0.6863	0.8826	0.6708
TC	Best	22.4066	17.9952	22.0570	21.3623
	Worst	47.0277	35.6693	45.6356	38.6985
	Mean	35.3746	26.7413	33.1874	31.8375
	Median	36.8898	27.7971	35.3786	31.2333
	St. Dev.	7.9184	4.1531	6.5288	5.1535

TABLE 37.5 Experimental results were obtained through 20 independent runs using the IMDB dataset for 25 number of skills to find.

Team size (TS) team cost (TC)		GWO	TLBO	Hybrid GWO-TLBO	Hybrid AGW-TLBO
TS	Best	11.0000	10.0000	11.0000	11.0000
	Worst	15.0000	13.0000	16.0000	14.0000
	Mean	13.4000	11.7500	12.9000	12.8500
	Median	14.0000	12.0000	13.0000	13.0000
	St. Dev.	1.2312	0.7864	1.2096	0.8751
TC	Best	47.7283	37.8318	45.7179	46.4053
	Worst	93.7465	63.5656	105.9500	76.8818
	Mean	71.1931	53.2332	65.7726	65.0511
	Median	74.2491	55.0592	64.5148	65.6499
	St. Dev.	13.4938	6.5639	13.9442	8.6680

lower, Fig. 37.2 shows that TLBO presents some oscillations while AGW-TLBO converged in a more gradual way with smaller fluctuations, indicating a better balance between exploration and exploitation.

This pattern became more pronounced as the problem complexity increased. At 15 skills, TLBO reached 18.8292 ± 4.1322, while GWO-TLBO showed its instability with 23.3117 ± 11.9759. AGW-TLBO returned 19.9408 ± 4.6764,

TABLE 37.6 Median ± IQR of team cost across skill set sizes for the IMDB dataset.

	Number of skills to find				
Algorithm	**5**	**10**	**15**	**20**	**25**
GWO	2.4657 ± 0.3477	11.4612 ± 4.8972	24.4800 ± 12.2041	36.8898 ± 10.5359	74.2491 ± 15.1288
TLBO	2.3536 ± 0.1904	7.2827 ± 2.5916	18.8292 ± 4.1322	27.7971 ± 6.3765	55.0592 ± 7.8295
Hybrid GWO-TLBO	1.9735 ± 0.5329	7.6938 ± 3.5600	23.3117 ± 11.9759	35.3786 ± 8.8450	64.5148 ± 19.3661
Hybrid AGW-TLBO	2.3547 ± 0.3917	8.0319 ± 4.1193	19.9408 ± 4.6764	31.2334 ± 7.0896	65.6499 ± 5.7904

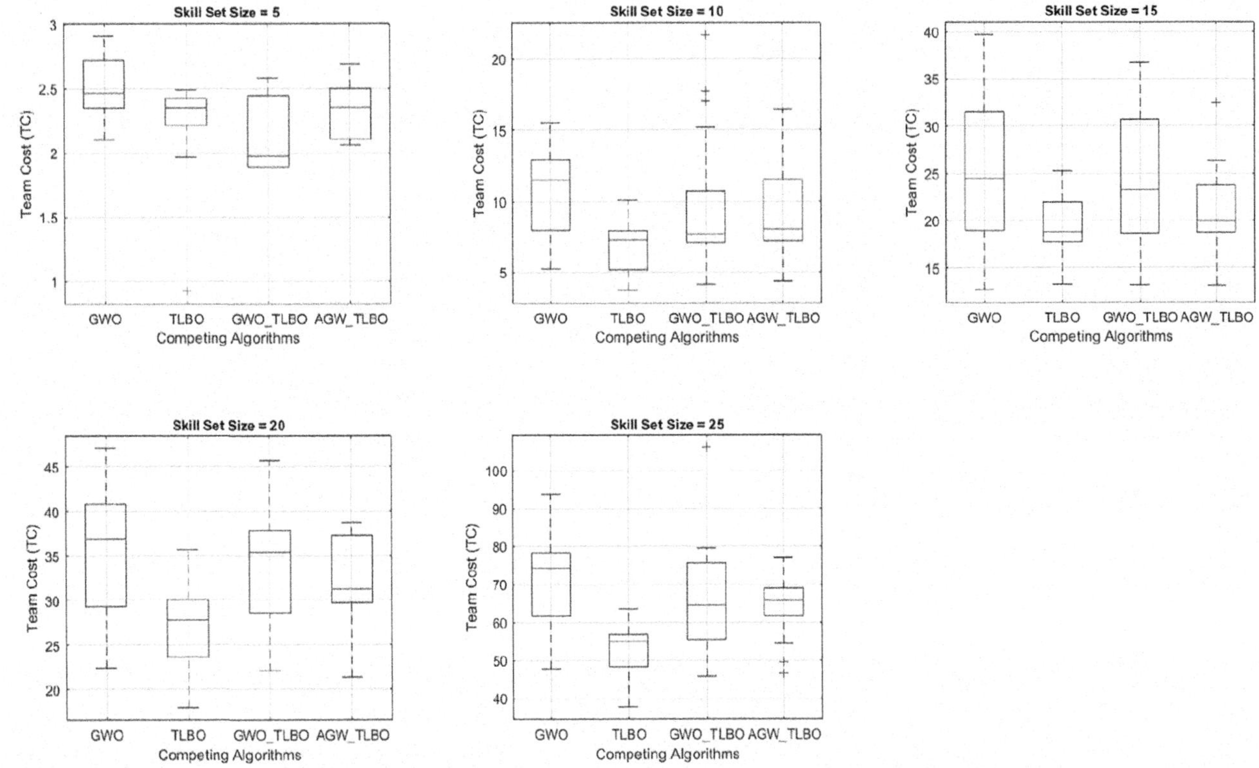

FIGURE 37.2 Boxplot comparison of team cost across skill set sizes for competing algorithms on the IMDB dataset.

maintaining both competitive cost and robustness, while GWO further deteriorated to 24.4800 ± 12.2041. Indeed, at 20 and 25 skills, both GWO and GWO-TLBO consistently showed higher median costs and spreads, thus confirming their vulnerability to early stagnation. Remarkably, in the case of 25 skills, AGW-TLBO had significantly lower variance, 65.6499 ± 5.7904, compared to that of GWO-TLBO, 64.5148 ± 19.3661, meaning that AGW-TLBO resists increasing the combinatorial search space.

In summary, on the overall IMDB dataset, the minimum median cost is not always guaranteed by AGW-TLBO for small-scale problem instances; however, it consistently minimizes variance and shows robust convergence behavior, especially for medium to large-scale problems. Boxplots and convergence trend representations (Figs. 37.2 and 37.3) also

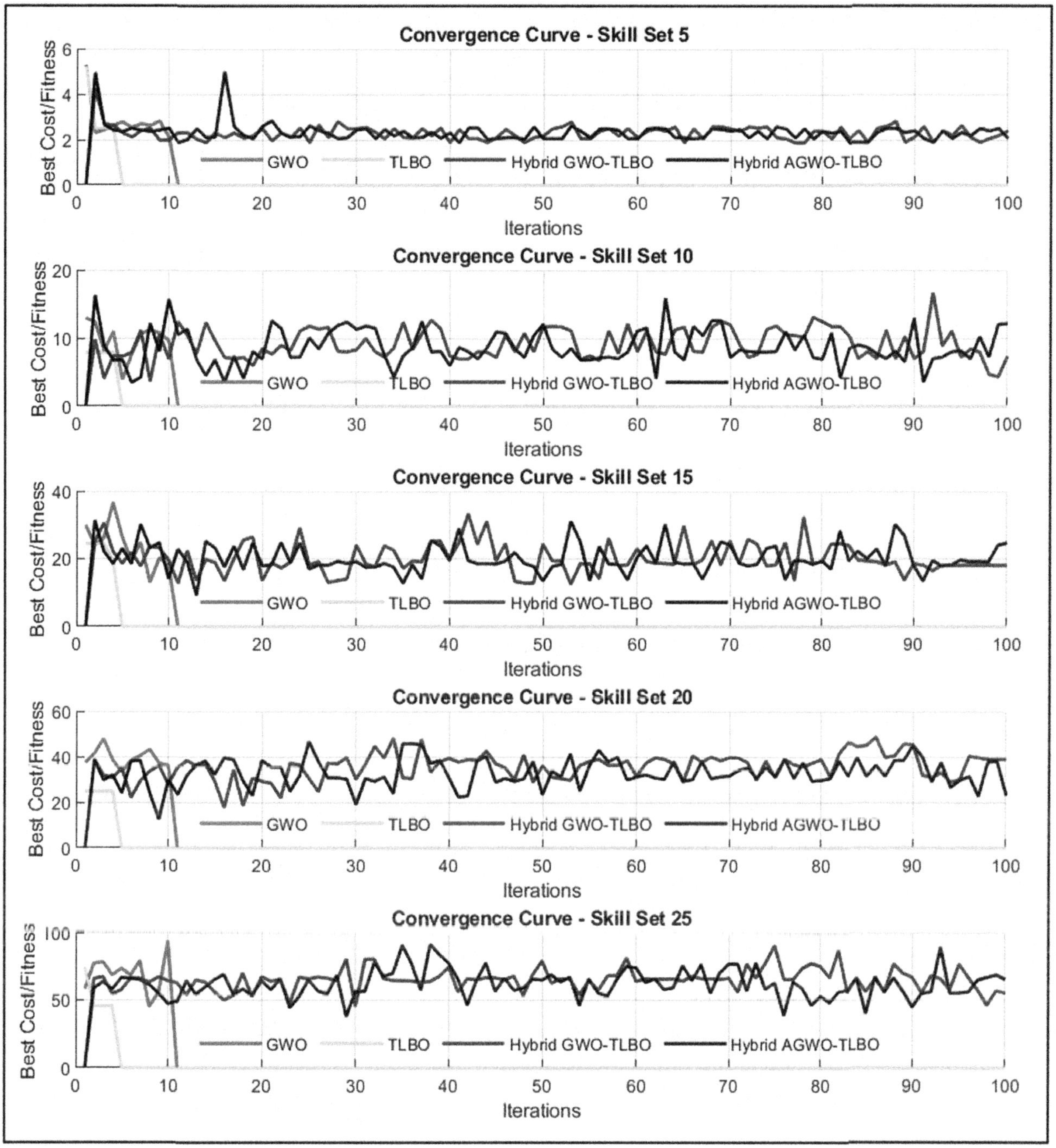

FIGURE 37.3 Convergence curves for each skill set for the IMDB dataset.

establish that AGW-TLBO will converge faster and more stably without the stagnation often occurring in GWO and GWO-TLBO.

37.4.2 Performance on the DBLP dataset

The DBLP dataset has a denser and more irregular collaboration structure that magnifies the performance gaps among algorithms. In the lowest dimensional setting (five skills), TLBO was the best performer (5.6929 ± 0.1042), outperforming all other models, including AGW-TLBO (9.5105 ± 0.0855), as shown in Table 37.12. For less complex tasks, it seems that

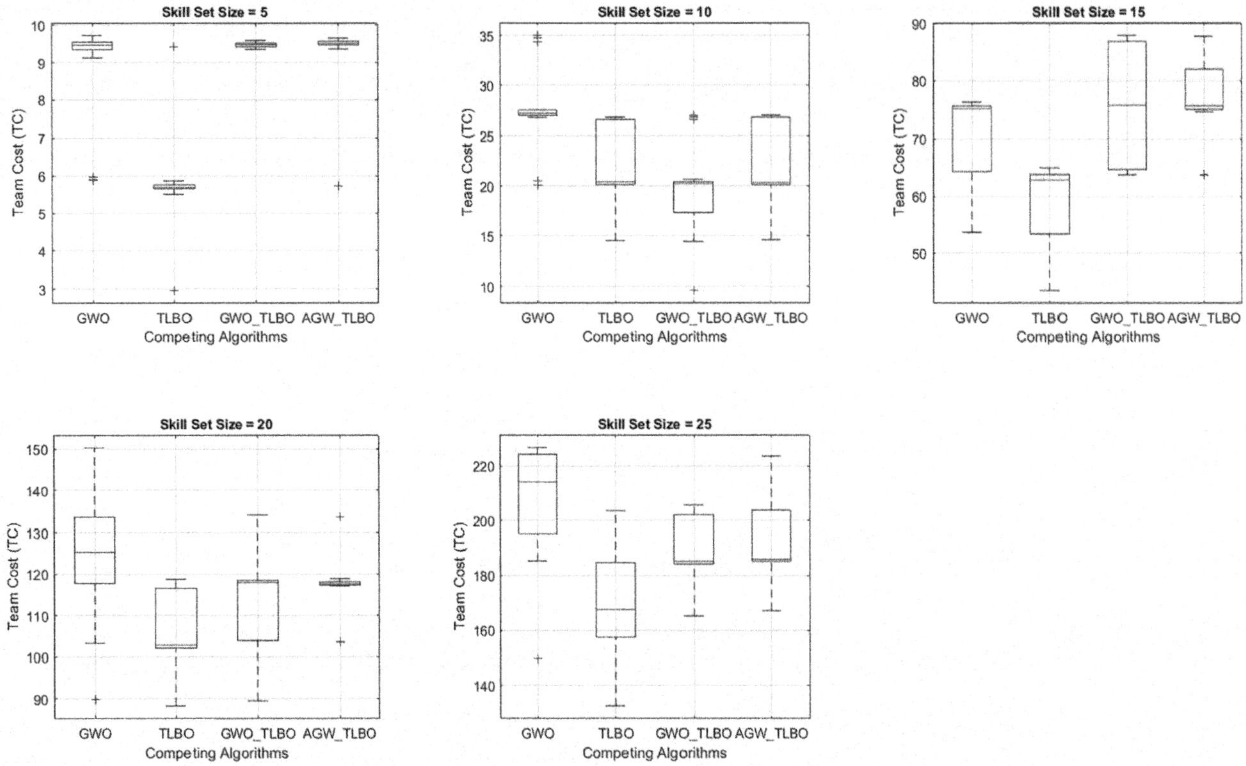

FIGURE 37.4 Boxplot comparison of team cost across skill set sizes for competing algorithms on the DBLP dataset.

the adaptive mechanism in AGW-TLBO does not bring extra benefits, while the strong exploitation-driven deterministic search performed by TLBO is enough.

Nevertheless, as the dimensionality increases to 10 skills and beyond, the advantages of AGW-TLBO become more pronounced. At 10 skills, for instance, TLBO and GWO-TLBO show increasing variability; for example, in TLBO (20.4157 ± 6.4139), whereas in AGW-TLBO, it achieves a similar median cost of 20.3155 with noticeably low variance of ±6.6543, and smoother convergence behavior as well, as illustrated in Fig. 37.3. The gap further expands at 15 skills, where both GWO and GWO-TLBO experience huge fluctuations, 75.1389 ± 11.1547 and 75.7312 ± 22.1148, respectively, while AGW-TLBO maintains a much tighter performance distribution, 75.6015 ± 4.2590. (Fig. 37.4 and Fig. 37.5).

While increasing the problem complexity to higher levels, such as 20 and 25 skills, TLBO gradually loses stability because of the limited diversity in global searches. In contrast, AGW-TLBO consistently converges; while generating similar cost values, for example, at 20 skills, AGW-TLBO=117.7050 ± 0.7370 versus TLBO=102.7925 ± 14.3608, the substantial IQR reduction demonstrates that AGW-TLBO preserves search coherence even within rugged and very multimodal landscapes, where competing algorithms tend to fluctuate significantly (experimental results are shown in Tables 37.7–37.12).

37.4.3 Statistical significance analysis

To validate whether the observed performance differences among the algorithms are statistically meaningful, a pairwise Wilcoxon Signed-Rank Test was conducted for each skill-set size on both datasets. This nonparametric test is well-suited for metaheuristic comparisons as it evaluates performance differences across repeated stochastic runs without assuming normality in the distribution of results.

IMDB Dataset:

Results at α=0.05 of the Wilcoxon test in Table 37.13 signify that TLBO outperforms GWO for all skill-set sizes with P<.001, and, therefore TLBO provides more consistent exploitation through the structured knowledge transfer mechanism than through a leader-based search in GWO.

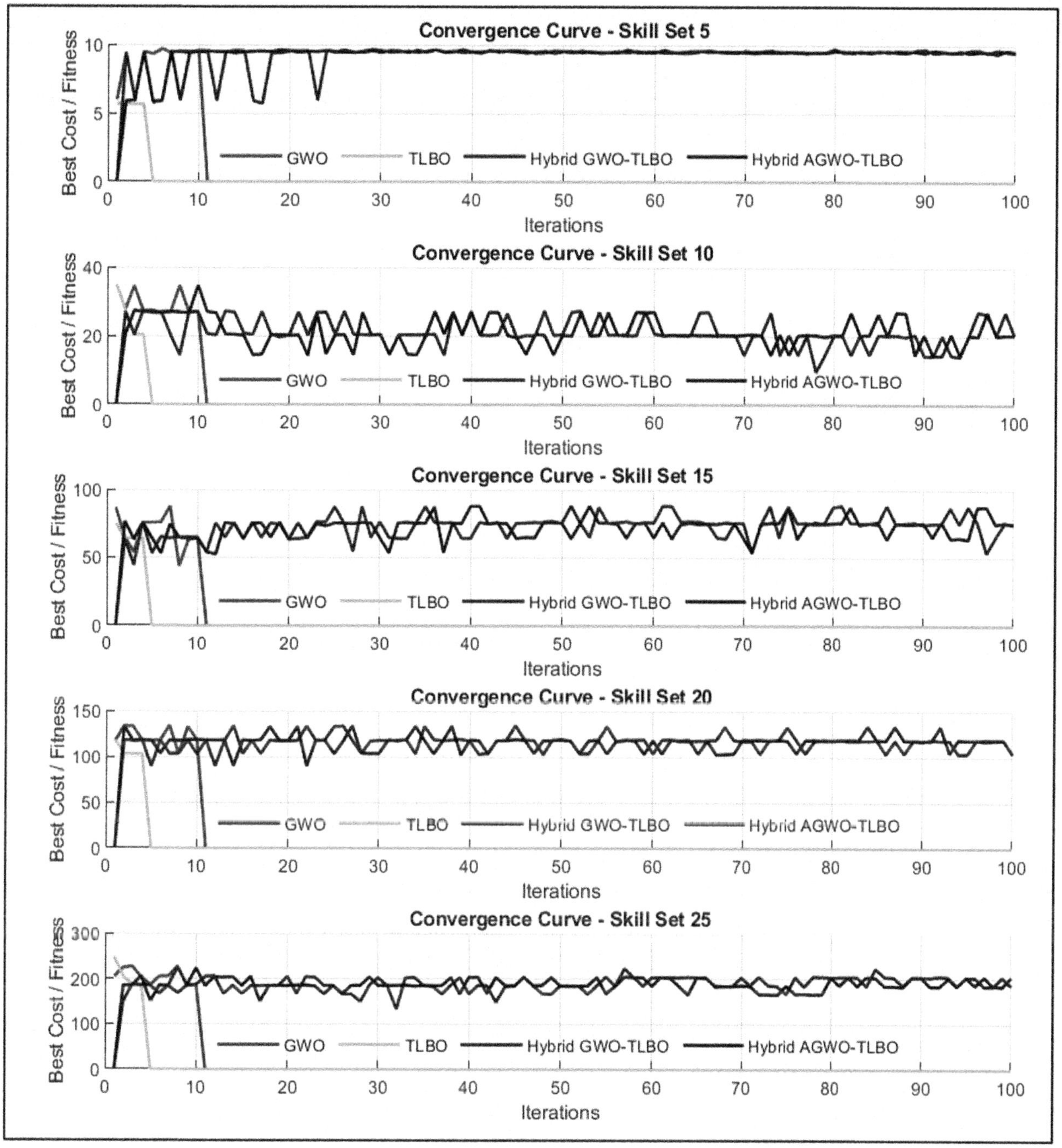

FIGURE 37.5 Convergence curves for each skill set for the DBLP dataset.

Similarly, the comparison of GWO versus AGW-TLBO gives statistically significant improvements for AGW-TLBO at higher dimensions-skills ≥ 10, with a P-value in the range from 0.00025 to 0.00573, confirming again that the adaptive component increases in importance with problem complexity.

The comparison TLBO versus AGW-TLBO is also significant for skill sizes 15, 20, and 25, with $P < .001$, which demonstrates that AGW-TLBO has a robust advantage in medium-to-large-scale team formation tasks. On the other hand, at five skills, the difference is not statistically significant, with P=0.62745, which confirms that adaptive exploration control has no particular benefit in simpler search landscapes.

TABLE 37.7 Experimental results were obtained through 20 independent runs using the DBLP dataset for 5 number of skills to find.

Team Size (TS) Team Cost (TC)		GWO	TLBO	Hybrid GWO-TLBO	Hybrid AGW-TLBO
TS	Best	4.0000	3.0000	5.0000	4.0000
	Worst	5.0000	5.0000	5.0000	5.0000
	Mean	4.8500	4.0000	5.0000	4.9500
	Median	5.0000	4.0000	5.0000	5.0000
	St. Dev.	0.3663	0.3244	0.0000	0.2236
TC	Best	5.8750	2.9615	9.3491	5.7294
	Worst	9.7211	9.4124	9.5924	9.6510
	Mean	8.9435	5.7441	9.4731	9.3287
	Median	9.4657	5.6928	9.4774	9.5105
	St. Dev.	1.3100	1.0601	0.0660	0.8500

TABLE 37.8 Experimental results were obtained through 20 independent runs using the DBLP dataset for 10 number of skills to find.

Team size (TS) team cost (TC)		GWO	TLBO	Hybrid GWO-TLBO	Hybrid AGW-TLBO
TS	Best	7.0000	6.0000	5.0000	6.0000
	Worst	9.0000	8.0000	8.0000	8.0000
	Mean	8.1000	7.3000	6.8500	7.3000
	Median	8.0000	7.0000	7.0000	7.0000
	St. Dev.	0.5525	0.5712	0.7452	0.5712
TC	Best	20.0811	14.5076	9.6162	14.5778
	Worst	35.0023	26.8253	26.9847	26.9929
	Mean	27.9815	22.2040	19.5581	22.2588
	Median	27.1823	20.4157	20.2260	20.3155
	St. Dev.	4.0420	3.5875	4.3809	3.6843

GWO-TLBO versus AGW-TLBO: At this point, there are no significant differences according to most of the skill-set sizes since $P > 0.1$. That will indicate that both hybrid models contribute to improving single heuristics and show that AGW-TLBO's main advantage is in improving convergence stability, but not in radical cost reduction.

DBLP Dataset:

TABLE 37.9 Experimental results were obtained through 20 independent runs using the DBLP dataset for 15 number of skills to find.

Team size (TS) team cost (TC)		GWO	TLBO	Hybrid GWO-TLBO	Hybrid AGW-TLBO
TS	Best	11.0000	10.0000	12.0000	12.0000
	Worst	13.0000	12.0000	14.0000	14.0000
	Mean	12.5500	11.5000	13.0000	13.1500
	Median	13.0000	12.0000	13.0000	13.0000
	St. Dev.	0.6048	0.6070	0.7947	0.5871
TC	Best	53.6350	43.6317	63.7201	63.5977
	Worst	76.2842	64.9555	87.9618	87.8081
	Mean	70.4180	58.6134	75.7563	77.3611
	Median	75.1389	62.8509	75.7312	75.6015
	St. Dev.	6.8284	6.2716	9.2584	7.0583

TABLE 37.10 Experimental results were obtained through 20 independent runs using the DBLP dataset for 20 number of skills to find.

Team size (TS) team cost (TC)		GWO	TLBO	Hybrid GWO-TLBO	Hybrid AGW-TLBO
TS	Best	14.0000	14.0000	14.0000	15.0000
	Worst	18.0000	16.0000	17.0000	17.0000
	Mean	16.4500	15.1500	15.7000	15.9000
	Median	16.5000	15.0000	16.0000	16.0000
	St. Dev.	0.9445	0.6708	0.8013	0.4472
TC	Best	89.8911	88.3143	89.5327	103.4614
	Worst	150.3402	118.6825	134.0557	133.5665
	Mean	125.0726	104.9533	113.8265	116.5087
	Median	125.2490	102.7925	117.9081	117.7049
	St. Dev.	14.3756	9.4856	11.8227	6.5935

Table 37.14 presents statistical results showing similar but more marked trends for DBLP, as its collaboration graph is more irregular compared to others.

GWO always performs worse than TLBO and AGWTLBO in almost all skill levels with $P < .05$, which confirms its persistent premature convergence. Although TLBO significantly outperforms GWO-TLBO for most configurations with $P < .05$, its performance deteriorates in higher-dimensional cases where the variance sharply increases.

TABLE 37.11 Experimental results were obtained through 20 independent runs using the DBLP dataset for 25 number of skills to find.

Team size (TS) team cost (TC)		GWO	TLBO	Hybrid GWO-TLBO	Hybrid AGW-TLBO
TS	Best	18.0000	17.0000	19.0000	19.0000
	Worst	22.0000	21.0000	21.0000	22.0000
	Mean	21.1500	19.1000	20.2000	20.4500
	Median	21.5000	19.0000	20.0000	20.0000
	St. Dev.	1.0894	1.1653	0.6156	0.7592
TC	Best	149.7249	132.5861	165.3250	167.2058
	Worst	226.7552	203.5295	205.6307	223.6634
	Mean	208.1896	168.9583	188.6854	193.7828
	Median	214.2367	167.6184	185.2744	185.9672
	St. Dev.	20.7448	20.5094	11.6891	14.2829

TABLE 37.12 Median ± IQR of team formation cost across skill set sizes for the DBLP dataset.

	Number of skills to find				
Algorithm	5	10	15	20	25
GWO	9.4657 ± 0.1956	27.1823 ± 0.4876	75.1389 ± 11.1547	125.2490 ± 15.7285	214.2367 ± 24.7638
TLBO	5.6929 ± 0.1042	20.4157 ± 6.4139	62.8509 ± 10.3544	102.7925 ± 14.3608	167.6185 ± 23.2133
Hybrid GWO-TLBO	9.4774 ± 0.0833	20.2260 ± 1.7757	75.7312 ± 22.1148	117.9081 ± 14.3508	185.2745 ± 17.6329
HybridAGW-TLBO	9.5105 ± 0.0855	20.3155 ± 6.6543	75.6015 ± 4.2590	117.7050 ± 0.7370	185.9672 ± 18.4331

Importantly, the comparison TLBO versus AGW-TLBO delivers non-significant differences in the low-dimensionality scenarios, for example, 5 skills, with P=.65416, but it does reach significance for the ≥10-skill-size scenarios, at 20 and 25 skills, with a P-value of .00803 and 0.00171, respectively. This would confirm that AGW-TLBO yields stronger robustness under high-complexity search conditions.

This is consistent with the results from IMDB: GWO-TLBO versus AGW-TLBO remains in most cases statistically nonsignificant (P-value > 0.1), further reinforcing that the critical advantage of AGW-TLBO indeed lies instability, not in solution cost.

Taken together, the summary of performance distributions (Figs. 37.2–37.5), robustness metrics (Tables 37.6 and 37.12), and statistical outcomes (Tables 37.13–37.14) confirm the following:

- Hybridization enhances the effectiveness of baseline optimization.
- Adaptive search control is crucial to maintain exploration–exploitation balance.
- AGW-TLBO is not only superior but also more stable, especially for higher dimensionalities.

TABLE 37.13 Pairwise statistical comparison of GWO, TLBO, GWO-TLBO, and AGW-TLBO using the Wilcoxon signed-rank test for the IMDB dataset.

	Size of skill set				
Comparison	**5**	**10**	**15**	**20**	**25**
GWO vs TLBO	0.00012	0.00034	0.00039	0.00022	0.00009
GWO vs GWO_TLBO	0.47813	0.00009	0.02762	0.03656	0.00171
GWO vs AGW_TLBO	0.08592	0.00025	0.0438	0.03656	0.00573
TLBO vs GWO_TLBO	0.00009	0.10046	0.00009	0.00455	0.0022
TLBO vs AGW_TLBO	0.00009	0.62745	0.00009	0.00045	0.00045
GWO_TLBO vs AGW_TLBO	0.33409	0.11689	0.94048	0.68132	0.24714

TABLE 37.14 Pairwise statistical comparison of GWO, TLBO, GWO-TLBO, and AGW-TLBO using the Wilcoxon signed-rank test for the DBLP dataset.

	Size of skill set				
Comparison	**5**	**10**	**15**	**20**	**25**
GWO vs TLBO	0.01001	0.00039	0.00642	0.00039	0.00052
GWO vs GWO_TLBO	0.0022	0.31346	0.82276	0.37026	0.33172
GWO vs AGW_TLBO	0.02509	0.03656	0.02063	0.07932	0.10843
TLBO vs GWO_TLBO	0.05691	0.02762	0.02277	0.00359	0.00151
TLBO vs AGW_TLBO	0.65416	0.00319	0.06735	0.00803	0.00171
GWO_TLBO vs AGW_TLBO	0.03029	0.88129	0.10046	0.62745	0.88129

- Its strength lies in reproducibility for high-stakes team formation or resource allocation tasks.

Therefore AGW-TLBO represents a reliably scalable solution framework, especially suitable for large and complex team formation optimization environments.

37.5 Conclusion

This study presented a novel hybrid metaheuristic algorithm, AGW-TLBO, designed to address the challenges of the TFO problem. By combining the global search capability of the GWO with the local refinement strength of TLBO, the proposed method effectively balances exploration and exploitation. The inclusion of an adaptive control mechanism driven by population diversity further enhances the algorithm's robustness by dynamically adjusting its search behavior to avoid premature convergence.

Extensive experiments conducted on two real-world benchmark datasets, IMDB and DBLP, demonstrate that hybrid AGW-TLBO consistently outperforms its constituent algorithms (GWO and TLBO) as well as a baseline hybrid variant (GWO-TLBO) in terms of solution quality, scalability, and robustness. These results affirm the effectiveness and generalizability of the proposed hybrid approach for complex team formation scenarios where solution quality and resource efficiency are critical. To validate the performance differences among algorithms, we performed a pairwise comparison by applying the Wilcoxon signed-rank test with $\alpha=0.05$. The proposed AGW-TLBO has obtained statistically significant improvement, especially in the case of higher-dimensional task scenarios with 10–25 skills involved. The hybrid adaptive mechanism may produce more stable convergence and competitive median solutions with respect to both variants of GWO and GWO-TLBO.

Looking forward, several avenues for future work can be explored. First, the current algorithm can be extended to handle dynamic or time-dependent team formation problems, where skill requirements and individual availability change over time. Second, incorporating multiobjective optimization frameworks could allow the model to simultaneously optimize for other real-world criteria such as team diversity, workload balance, or communication overhead. Additionally, future research could explore parallel or distributed implementations of hybrid AGW-TLBO to enhance scalability for large-scale applications. Finally, integrating domain-specific constraints and validating the model in industry-specific contexts such as software development, healthcare, or education could further strengthen its practical relevance and adoption.

Acknowledgments

The authors acknowledge the use of AI-assisted language and editing tools (e.g., ChatGPT) for improving the readability, coherence, and formatting of this chapter. All technical contents, algorithms, and results were conceptualized, implemented, and validated by the authors.

References

[1] M.Z. Rehman, et al., A novel state space reduction algorithm for team formation in social networks, PLoS One 16 (12) (2021) 1–18. Available from https://doi.org/10.1371/journal.pone.0259786.

[2] M.A. Kader, K.Z. Zamli, B.Y. Alkazemi, An experimental study of a fuzzy adaptive emperor penguin optimizer for global optimization problem, IEEE Access 10 (2022) 116344–116374. Available from https://doi.org/10.1109/ACCESS.2022.3213805.

[3] M.A. Kader, K.Z. Zamli, B.S. Ahmed, A systematic review on emperor penguin optimizer, Neural Computing and Applications (2021) 1–21. Available from https://doi.org/10.1007/s00521-021-06442-4.

[4] S. Mirjalili, S.M. Mirjalili, A. Lewis, Grey wolf optimizer, Advances in Engineering Software 69 (2014) 46–61. Available from https://doi.org/10.1016/j.advengsoft.2013.12.007.

[5] R.V. Rao, V.J. Savsani, D.P. Vakharia, Teaching–learning-based optimization: a novel method for constrained mechanical design optimization problems, Computer-Aided Design 43 (3) (2011) 303–315. Available from https://doi.org/10.1016/j.cad.2010.12.015.

[6] H. Singh, et al., An integrative TLBO-driven hybrid grey wolf optimizer for the efficient resolution of multi-dimensional, nonlinear engineering problems, Scientific Reports 15 (1) (2025) 1–71. Available from https://doi.org/10.1038/s41598-025-89458-3.

[7] X. Zhang, Q. Kang, J. Cheng, X. Wang, A novel hybrid algorithm based on biogeography-based optimization and grey wolf optimizer, Applied Soft Computing 67 (2018) 197–214. Available from https://doi.org/10.1016/j.asoc.2018.02.049.

[8] A.A. Alomoush, A.A. Alsewari, H.S. Alamri, K. Aloufi, K.Z. Zamli, Hybrid harmony search algorithm with grey wolf optimizer and modified opposition-based learning, IEEE Access 7 (2019) 68764–68785. Available from https://doi.org/10.1109/ACCESS.2019.2917803.

[9] R. Sharma, P. Marikkannu, A. Sungheetha, Three-dimensional MRI brain tumour classification using hybrid ant colony optimisation and grey wolf optimiser with proximal support vector machine, International Journal of Biomedical Engineering and Technology 29 (1) (2019) 34–45. Available from https://doi.org/10.1504/IJBET.2019.096879.

[10] S.V. Konstantinov, U.K. Khamidova, E.A. Sofronova, A novel hybrid method of global optimization based on the grey wolf optimizer and the bees algorithm, Procedia Computer Science 150 (2019) 471–477. Available from https://doi.org/10.1016/j.procs.2019.02.081.

[11] S. Ouhame, Y. Hadi, A. Arifullah, A Hybrid grey wolf optimizer and artificial bee colony algorithm used for improvement in resource allocation system for cloud technology, International Journal of Online and Biomedical Engineering 16 (14) (2020) 4–17. Available from https://doi.org/10.3991/ijoe.v16i14.16623.

[12] K. Vikram Kumar, hGWO-SA: a novel hybrid grey wolf optimizer-simulated annealing algorithm for engineering and power system optimization problems, Recent Advances in Computer Science and Communications 14 (8) (2021) 2703–2727. Available from https://doi.org/10.2174/2666255813999200721010231.

[13] C.Y. Lee, T.A. Le, Y.T. Lin, A feature selection approach hybrid grey wolf and heap-based optimizer applied in bearing fault diagnosis, IEEE Access 10 (2022) 56691–56705. Available from https://doi.org/10.1109/ACCESS.2022.3177735.

[14] R. Keswani, H.K. Verma, K.S. Sharma, Optimal power flow integrating renewable energy sources in microgrid employing hybrid grey wolf-equilibrium optimizer, Proceedings of the 2022 IEEE IAS Global Conference on Emerging Technologies (2022) 714–720. Available from https://doi.org/10.1109/GlobConET53749.2022.9872381in:.

[15] S. Gurumurthy, K.L. Hemalatha, D. Pamela, U. Roy, P. Vishwanath, Hybrid pigeon inspired optimizer-gray wolf optimization for network intrusion detection, Journal of System and Management Sciences 12 (4) (2022) 383–397. Available from https://doi.org/10.33168/jsms.2022.0423.

[16] J.-X. Lv, et al., A new hybrid algorithm based on golden eagle optimizer and grey wolf optimizer for 3D path planning of multiple UAVs in power inspection, Neural Computing and Applications 34 (14) (2022) 11911–11936. Available from https://doi.org/10.1007/s00521-022-07080-0.

[17] Z. Hoseini, H. Varaee, M. Rafieizonooz, J.-H.J. Kim, A new enhanced hybrid grey wolf optimizer (GWO) combined with elephant herding optimization (EHO) algorithm for engineering optimization, Journal of Soft Computing in Civil Engineering 6 (4) (2022) 1–42. Available from https://doi.org/10.22115/scce.2022.342360.1436.

[18] S.N. Makhadmeh, A.K. Abasi, M.A. Al-Betar, Hybrid multi-verse optimizer with grey wolf optimizer for power scheduling problem in smart home using IoT, The Journal of Supercomputing 78 (9) (2022) 11794–11829. Available from https://doi.org/10.1007/s11227-022-04325-6.

[19] C. Dhakhinamoorthy, et al., Hybrid whale and gray wolf deep learning optimization algorithm for prediction of Alzheimer's disease, Mathematics 11 (5) (2023) 1–17. Available from https://doi.org/10.3390/math11051136.

[20] R. Keswani, H.K. Verma, S.K. Sharma, Multi-objective optimal power flow employing a hybrid sine cosine–grey wolf optimizer, Iranian Journal of Science and Technology, Transactions of Electrical Engineering 47 (4) (2023) 1365–1388. Available from https://doi.org/10.1007/s40998-023-00631-8.

[21] V. Bathina, R. Devarapalli, F.P. García Márquez, Hybrid approach with combining cuckoo-search and grey-wolf optimizer for solving optimal power flow problems, Journal of Electrical Engineering & Technology 18 (3) (2023) 1637–1653. Available from https://doi.org/10.1007/s42835-022-01301-1.

[22] M.S. Shaikh, et al., An intelligent hybrid grey wolf-particle swarm optimizer for optimization in complex engineering design problem, Scientific Reports 15 (1) (2025) 1–36. Available from https://doi.org/10.1038/s41598-025-02154-0.

[23] Y. Shang, M. Zheng, J. Li, X. Zheng, An effective feature selection approach based on hybrid Grey Wolf Optimizer and genetic algorithm for hyperspectral image, Scientific Reports 15 (1) (2025) 1–23. Available from https://doi.org/10.1038/s41598-024-84934-8.

[24] L. Zhao, et al., Recalibration of four empirical reference crop evapotranspiration models using a hybrid differential evolution-grey wolf optimizer algorithm, International Journal of Agricultural and Biological Engineering 18 (1) (2025) 173–180. Available from https://doi.org/10.25165/j.ijabe.20251801.9380.

[25] D. Tbaishat, M. Tubishat, S.N. Makhadmeh, O.A. Alomari, A hybrid bat and grey wolf optimizer for gene selection in cancer classification, Knowledge and Information Systems 67 (1) (2025) 455–495. Available from https://doi.org/10.1007/s10115-024-02225-0.

[26] S. Mohammad Aghdam, F.S. Gharehchopogh, M. Masdari, An opinion leader selection in social networks using hybrid amended salp swarm and improved grey wolf optimizer algorithms, International Journal of Data Science and Analytics (2025). Available from https://doi.org/10.1007/s41060-025-00760-9.

[27] Z. Ye, et al., Hybrid rice optimization algorithm inspired grey wolf optimizer for high-dimensional feature selection, Scientific Reports 14 (1) (2024) 1–45. Available from https://doi.org/10.1038/s41598-024-80648-z.

[28] P.V. Jyoti, L.H. Alzubaidi, Devika, N. R, Hybrid grey wolf optimizer with ant lion optimization algorithm based deep learning for face expression recognition, Proceedings of the International Conference on Integrated Circuits and Communication Systems, IEEE, (2024), pp. 1–6. Available from https://doi.org/10.1109/ICICACS60521.2024.10498309.

[29] H. Zhang, J. Yan, L. Wang, Hybrid tabu-grey wolf optimizer algorithm for enhancing fresh cold-chain logistics distribution, PLoS One 19 (8) (2024) 1–22. Available from https://doi.org/10.1371/journal.pone.0306166.

[30] N.S. Alsharafa, S.K. Shanmugam, B. Vani, B. P, G.S.A.S. P.V.V.S, Hybrid grey wolf optimizer for efficient maximum power point tracking to improve photovoltaic efficiency, Journal of Machine and Computing 4 (3) (2024) 575–585. Available from https://doi.org/10.53759/7669/jmc202404055.

[31] S. Fletcher, M.Z. Islam, Comparing sets of patterns with the Jaccard index, Australasian Journal of Information Systems 22 (2018) 1–17. Available from https://doi.org/10.3127/ajis.v22i0.1538.

[32] IMDB, IMDB Dataset. https://github.com/MAK660/Dataset/blob/master/IMDB_DataSet.txt (accessed 01.08.21.).

[33] DBLP, DBLP Dataset. https://github.com/MAK660/Dataset/blob/master/DBLP_DataSet.txt (accessed 05.01.20.).

Chapter 38

A concurrent power distribution systems model for demand-supply scheduling using the grey wolf optimizer

Emmanuel Ndidi Osegi[1] and Biobele Alexander Wokoma[2]
[1]*National Open University of Nigeria, Afrıca Center of Excellence on Technology Enhanced Learning (NOUN-ACETEL), Abuja, Federal Capital Territory, Nigeria,* [2]*Department of Electrical and Electronic Engineering, Rivers State University, PortHarcourt, Rivers State, Nigeria*

38.1 Introduction

The distribution network or distribution grid is an important part of the electrical power system, primarily responsible for the actual supply of electrical power to a teeming set of end users—the consumers of the power. Due to this fact, the distribution network is often characterized by heavy loading events, frequent system faults, and fluctuating power demands, leading the power operators to either load shed or shut down the distribution network power system [1,2]. Hence, the resulting situation is referred to as the demand-supply schedule problem, for which it is desired from the distribution network operators to adjust the power supplied to a teeming set of end users (load) with respect to their operational time and load levels to assure a reasonably or near optimal power balance. By extension, the demand-supply schedule problem becomes a unit commitment problem with the specifics of system generation unit supply levels, associated cost, and environmental constraints.

Currently, a strong theme in the power community is the "Smart Grid" concept, which revolves around the design and development of automated controls, including but not limited to intelligent computing systems and communication relaying circuits [3]. The intelligent computing systems are the particular area for which we are interested in this discourse, as it borders on the design and development of computational intelligence algorithms for optimizing the power distribution networks.

Ideally, the operation of a distribution network is not isolated from its load (consumer load) and as such, the power supply and demand are balanced to ensure maximum energy transfer [4]. However, in reality, this rarely is the case and as such, optimization of power plans has to be put in place to ensure near optimal delivery of service to end users in addition to the satisfaction of several underlying constraints such as the load shedding schedules, price limits, peak demand levels, and consumer flexibility [5].

Since the last decade, there has been consistent research on the application of computational intelligence algorithms to solve the demand-supply problem in distribution networks [6]. Some of these algorithms build on artificial intelligence (AI) principles, while others are simply machine learning (ML) solutions with no AI component involved.

Some nature-inspired AI algorithms are fundamentally metaheuristics with a range of functionalities that may result in a single-or multiobjective formulation. These metaheuristics typically have the ability to search both local and global spaces using primarily explorative and exploitative procedures [7], and in more detailed situations, these algorithms may employ intensification and diversification tactics to obtain good solutions [8,9]. For instance, we may refer to the exploration and intensification tactics employed by honey bees to locally search for good foods and select the high-performing ones, while discarding poor ones [10,11].

In this paper, we present the potentials of an emerging swarming-based metaheuristic called the grey wolf optimizer (GWO), enhanced by a continual learning neural-based consensus algorithm called the sparse integer distributed encoded representations (SIDERs) as a candidate approach for solving the distribution network demand-supply scheduling problem.

Grey Wolf Optimizer. DOI: https://doi.org/10.1016/B978-0-443-36624-6.00021-4

38.2 Related studies

Most research in the field of optimal demand-supply scheduling for distribution networks is based on the idea that the supplied power must meet the expected demand [12–14]. Thus, research studies investigate this issue considering a variety of use case scenarios such as in day-ahead scheduling electrical vehicle charging energy maximization [15], Considering this factor, it is standard practice for an optimization plan to be clearly defined including the predictor (design) variables, the response variable (s), an objective or fitness response function followed with a set of underlying constraints (both linear and nonlinear equality and in-equality constraints) in order to minimize the power losses to the distribution network system [16]. Currently, a lot of work has been done on the design and development of optimization techniques employed for solving several demand-supply schedule problems in the distribution network. Some of these are techniques that employ traditional optimization algorithms, such as those exploiting gradient descent, linear, nonlinear, or stochastic minimization methods, while more modern ones resort to the use of dynamic programming, AI, and/or ML algorithms [4,17]. In fact, we are more interested in the modern solutions, particularly with respect to those types of algorithms broadly regarded as metaheuristics. These algorithms may solve problems locally and/or globally with minimum effort on the basis of some naturally inspired physical phenomena.

Several metaheuristics for demand-supply scheduling in power distribution networks are discussed in this section. The discussions will take a peek at research studies centered on the development and application of metaheuristics with single individual solutions and a population of individual solutions in a localized demand-supply scheduling problem. For the rest of these discussions, we shall adopt the term individual or individuals to refer to a metaheuristic that uses a single or multiple sets of solutions to solve an optimization problem.

38.2.1 Single point metaheuristics

These metaheuristics exploit the operations of a single individual to search the solution space. Some popular research studies that have been investigated include the method of simulated annealing used in demand response and scheduling problems, including several constraints such as time of use and critical peak pricing to optimize load switching-on time [18] and the minimization of electricity generation costs considering arrival and deadline load task constraints in a distributed-tier demand side management solution [19]. Also, the Tabu search method is used to optimize load demands and feeder layout of a distribution network by considering power flows and a feeder risk index in a resiliency objective function formulation [20] while neighborhood search methods have been applied to several unit commitment problems for the minimization of the ramp-rate constrained commitment problem subject to constraints of generation, power demand balance, reserve requirements, minimum up/down time limits, start up costs and ramp rate limits [21].

While these methods have been shown to give promising results, they are faced with certain drawbacks, particularly when presented with complex linear and nonlinear problems, some of which include [22]:

- It is difficult to determine the appropriate parameter values,
- Initialization conditions may be far away from good start points.
- Setting extended initialization conditions (via penalties) is hard

These issues can negatively impact the optimization process, resulting in convergence issues and low-quality fitness response. Hence, most research studies employ population-based methods, such as discussed under subsection 38.2.2.

38.2.2 Population based metaheuristics

These are metaheuristics that use several individuals to search the solution space. They are better applied in the industry. Some popular examples include the use of genetic algorithms, particle swarm optimization, and artificial bee colony. Some application areas of population-based metaheuristics include smart home demand scheduling using method of genetic algorithms to minimize customer tariff under the constraints of elastic load limits and total elastic load [23] and the demand response program, including several swarming AI methods such as particle swarm optimization, firefly algorithm, grey wolf algorithm, salp swarm algorithm, and slime mould algorithm for minimizing total cost of generation in the presence of renewable distributed generation units [24].

38.3 A concurrent power distribution schedule systems methodology for optimal load scheduling

The method of optimal load scheduling is typically of two forms:

i. Supply-side management (SSM)
ii. Demand-side management (DSM)

Fundamentally, the goal of the SSM is to match generation with the load under the objective of attaining a minimum fuel and emission cost [2,25]. Also, the DSM aims at solving the optimal price problem considering market incentives and penalties [26,27]. However, it is also not uncommon to have both SSM and DSM in a single power flow solution, as in Ref. [28].

In this section, we present an emerging AI optimization method based on the GWO combined with an emerging artificial neural technique that exploits the principle of SIDER for solving the hourly load scheduling problem.

38.3.1 Grey wolf optimizer

GWOs are a class of swarm intelligence population-based metaheuristics that exploit the collaborative but foraging behavior of hunting wolves with hierarchical, strict, and coordinated (disciplined) leadership qualities [29]. The wolves are grouped by name in hierarchical order as alpha, beta, delta, and omega, where the alpha wolves direct a pack of between 5 and 12 wolves. However, even though alpha sits at the top of the hierarchy, leadership functions are also shared with the beta and delta wolves in the order of second and third best advisor respectively; in particular, the delta possess some very interesting functionalities as elders, caregivers, and hunters. As the omega wolves are less important due to poor leadership qualities, they are assumed to follow the rest of the pack as the worst or poorest problem solvers or solutions.

Just as in most dynamic optimizers, the GWO employs some sort of explorative and exploitative procedure for problem solving. There are fundamentally three core operations used by GWOs:

i. Social hierarchy operation
ii. Prey encirclement operation
iii. Hunting operation

38.3.1.1 Social operation

In principle, social hierarchy in grey wolves describes a well-known leader-follower rule. Basically, this is described by a series of fitness assignments and checking operations starting with the alpha, followed by the beta, ending with the delta wolf. The alpha wolf is given priority by a conditional enforcement of fitness scores with respect to the other wolves.

Mathematically, these operations are as follows:

Firstly, a general fitness operation and then an alpha wolf fitness and position assignment operation are performed with respect to an objective using Eqs. 38.1 and 38.2, respectively.

$$f_i = f_{obj}(X(i)) \tag{38.1}$$

$$\begin{aligned} f_{alpha} &= f_i \begin{cases} f_i < f_{alpha}/s_f \\ \infty,\ otherwise \end{cases} \\ X_{alpha} &= X(i) \begin{cases} f_i < f_{alpha}/s_f \\ 0,\ otherwise \end{cases} \end{aligned} \tag{38.2}$$

This is then followed by conditional fitness and position assignments for beta and delta wolves as in Eq. 38.3 and Eq. 38.4, respectively.

$$\begin{aligned} f_{beta} &= f_i \begin{cases} f_{alpha} < f_i < f_{beta} \\ \infty,\ otherwise \end{cases} \\ X_{beta} &= X(i) \begin{cases} f_{alpha} < f_i < f_{beta} \\ 0,\ otherwise \end{cases} \end{aligned} \tag{38.3}$$

$$\begin{aligned} f_{delta} &= f_i \begin{cases} f_{alpha} < f_i < f_{delta} \wedge f_{beta} < f_i < f_{delta} \\ \infty,\ otherwise \end{cases} \\ X_{delta} &= X(i) \begin{cases} f_{alpha} < f_i < f_{delta} \wedge f_{beta} < f_i < f_{delta} \\ 0,\ otherwise \end{cases} \end{aligned} \tag{38.4}$$

where

i =current iteration

X =initial position vector

f_i =initial fitness vector
f_{alpha} =fitness vector of the alpha wolves
f_{beta} =fitness vector of the beta wolves
f_{delta} =fitness vector of the delta wolves
X_{alpha} =position vector of the alpha wolves
X_{beta} =position vector of the beta wolves
X_{delta} =position vector of the delta wolves
s_f =smoothing factor

38.3.1.2 Prey encirclement operation

The prey encirclement allows the grey wolves to update their position within the space around a prey in a randomly intelligent manner. The encircling function is modeled mathematically as follows:

$$\left[D_{W(id)} = C_{(id)} \cdot X_{W(id)} - X(i, d) \right]_{d=1}^{D_{\max}} \tag{38.5}$$

$$\left[X(i, d+1) = X_{W(id)}(i, d) - A_{W(id)} \cdot D_{W(id)} \right]_{d=1}^{D_{\max}} \tag{38.6}$$

where,
$D_{\max}$ =maximum number of decision variables
$C_{(id)}$ =position vector coefficient
$A_{W(id)}$ =position vector coefficient with respect to the wolf class
$X_{W(id)}$=prey position vector
Furthermore, the coefficients, $C_{(id)}$ and $A_{W(id)}$ are estimated accordingly as follows:

$$C_{W(id)} = 2 \cdot r_2 - a \tag{38.7}$$

$$A_{W(id)} = 2a \cdot r_1 - a \tag{38.8}$$

where,
r_1, r_2 =random vectors
a =component of $A_{W(id)}$
The parameter, a, is a linearly decreasing function estimated using the following model:

$$a = [2 - l_i(2/l_{\max})]_{l_i=1}^{l_{\max}} \tag{38.9}$$

38.3.1.3 Hunting operation

To model hunting mathematically, update operations considering the social and encirclement fitness and position assignment operations in the aforementioned subsections are performed as follows:

$$\left[D_{alpha(id)} = C_{alpha(id)} \cdot X_{alpha(id)} - X(i, d) \right]_{d=1}^{D_{\max}} \tag{38.10}$$

$$\left[X_{alpha}(i, d+1) = X_{alpha(id)}(i, d) - A_{alpha(id)} \cdot D_{alpha(id)} \right]_{d=1}^{D_{\max}} \tag{38.11}$$

$$\left[D_{beta(id)} = C_{beta(id)} \cdot X_{beta(id)} - X(i, d) \right]_{d=1}^{D_{\max}} \tag{38.12}$$

$$\left[X_{beta}(i, d+1) = X_{beta(id)}(i, d) - A_{beta(id)} \cdot D_{beta(id)} \right]_{d=1}^{D_{\max}} \tag{38.13}$$

$$\left[D_{delta(id)} = C_{delta(id)} \cdot X_{delta(id)} - X(i, d)\right]_{d=1}^{D_{max}} \tag{38.14}$$

$$\left[X_{delta}(i, d+1) = X_{delta(id)}(i, d) - A_{delta(id)} \cdot D_{delta(id)}\right]_{d=1}^{D_{max}} \tag{38.15}$$

$$\left[X(i, d+1) = \frac{X_{alpha} + X_{beta} + X_{delta}}{3}\right]_{d=1}^{D_{max}} \tag{38.16}$$

38.3.2 Neural model based on sparse integer distributed encoded representation

The proposed neural model coined SIDERs for estimating the candidate hourly schedules is based on an earlier idea proposed in [30,31], which was called neuronal auditory machine intelligence (NeuroAMI). The NeuroAMI exploits the idea that feature patterns are learnt continuously via mismatch and reverse-mismatch operations. However, the NeuroAMI required several parameters to maintain a consistent set of predictions.

In this study, we follow a slightly different view in our model by adjusting just a single parameter called the class frequency rate. To gain insight into this modification, it is important to first describe the NeuroAMI model, to justify the modifications leading to the development of SIDERs.

38.3.3 The neuronal auditory machine intelligence model

The NeuroAMI model is fundamentally a SIDER but with more parameters and a Hebbian Learning (HL) rule. Its model architectural view is as shown in Fig. 38.1.

As can be seen in Fig. 38.1 (from left to right), the NeuroAMI converts a set of input feature patterns (designated by three arrows) from a sensory block into an integer structure as implemented in a sensory-binary-to-integer block referred to as Soma. The Soma specifically transforms multivariate feature patterns into univariate integers, which in turn reduces data dimensionality. To facilitate continual learning and prediction in the NeuroAMI model, this form of encoding process is needed.

The outputs from the Soma are passed through a class-type nonlinearity block to generate a set of class signals. These signals are fine-tuned with respect to a parameter called class frequency (C_f); this parameter is inspired by frequency learning behavior in mammalian cochlear neurons [32].

The output from the nonlinearity block is fed to both a mismatch operator block and a sensory class memory processor block, which equally receive inputs from both the sensory and class-type nonlinearity blocks. The function of the

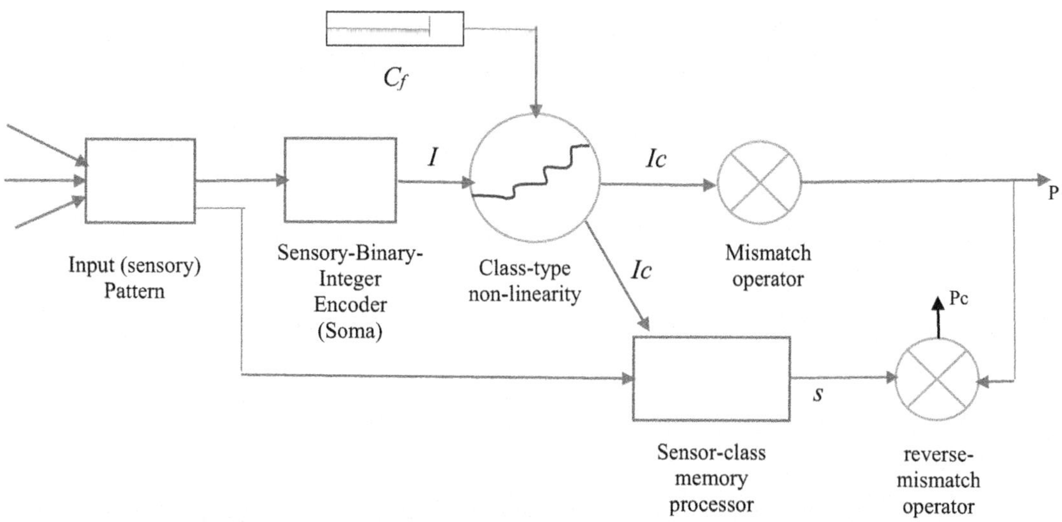

FIGURE 38.1 Neural structure of NeuroAMI technique illustrating a sensory processing architecture with encoding, class type nonlinearity, mismatch operators, and a sensor class memory processor (*NeuroAMI*, Neuronal auditory machine intelligence).
From E.N. Osegi, Neuronal Auditory Machine Intelligence (Neuro-AMI) In Perspective (2023). arXiv preprint arXiv:2401.02421. https://arxiv.org/abs/2401.02421.

mismatch block is to carry out comparative operations between prior and posterior features through time. Within the mismatch block, the HL rule is applied to update a set of patterns called deviants and standards for which a mean deviant is equally computed to achieve a prediction state [30]. Reverse mismatch operations are also possible by passing the outputs of the mismatch operator block to the reverse mismatch operator block, resulting in the formation of dual predictions. To achieve consistency in the predictions, the NeuroAMI mismatch operations use a parameter called deviant adjust (K_{Adj}) to adjust the mean deviants within an HL rule [31].

Finally, the sensory class memory processor block performs automatic feature class compression and categorization using the class-type frequency-tuned signals and the original input features to form a sparse representation. This sparse memory representation forms an approximation to the entire input space.

38.3.4 Sparse integer distributed encoded representations model

In order to implement a SIDER model, we have adopted the following modifications:

i. Firstly, we identify that the HL rule with K_{Adj} is inadequate for implementing a robust continual learning model and it is replaced with a simpler update rule that adjusts incrementally and with respect to the length of the sparsely formed sequence memories. In particular, we omit the mismatch and reverse-mismatch operators in the NeuroAMI model and replace them with a single overlap processor.

ii. Secondly, rather than predict on the basis of additive deviants, we resort to the idea of overlaps similar to previous studies on neuron models, such as in Refs. [33,34].

If we consider a well defined streaming data sequence of grey wolf alpha best positions, say, s, then, the frequency at which the sparse data generation occur can be described in terms of learning updates on an integer class data type as:

$$C_{f(s)} = \begin{cases} 1, \; len(s) = 1 \\ C_{(s)} + 1, \; len(s) > 1 \end{cases} \tag{38.17}$$

where

$C_{f(s)}$ =an integer class-type frequency parameter for a given streaming data sequence, say, s

$len(s)$ =length of streaming data sequence, which is a finite length

In this paper, we employ the following criterion in Eq. 38.18 to develop an overlap estimation process as:

$$k^{i}_{win} = \begin{cases} i, \; overlap \equiv overlap_{\min}, \; \forall_i \in Z \\ 0, \; Otherwise \end{cases} \tag{38.18}$$

The overlap and minimum overlap ($overlap_{min}$) are then computed as in Eq. 38.19 and Eq. 38.20, respectively.

$$overlap = |S_m - S^{i}_{new}|, \; i_t \in Z, \; i_t \subset i \tag{38.19}$$

$$overlap_{\min} = \min(overlap) \tag{38.20}$$

where,

k^{i}_{win} =winner iterator index during predictions or testing

S_m =sensor class memories

S^{i}_{new} =new input feature for testing

i_t =iterator step during testing or predictions

Considering the models in Eqs. 38.17–38.20, the SIDER performs a sparse memory allocation of candidate winner feature patterns formed via temporal class-type integer encoding to a holding cell. These winning patterns can then later be used in a greedy search pattern retrieval operation when presented with novel inputs.

38.3.5 The hourly load scheduling problem

The hourly load scheduling problem is an important topic in the field of power systems planning and operation that involves both SSM and DSM problem domains [28]. In its most basic form, it defines why and how the power supply must meet the consumer's hourly energy demand requirements. This problem is modeled as shown in Fig. 38.2. In this model, the symbols PD and PH represent the daily power and hourly power demands taken from the distribution network, while G represents the GWO instances.

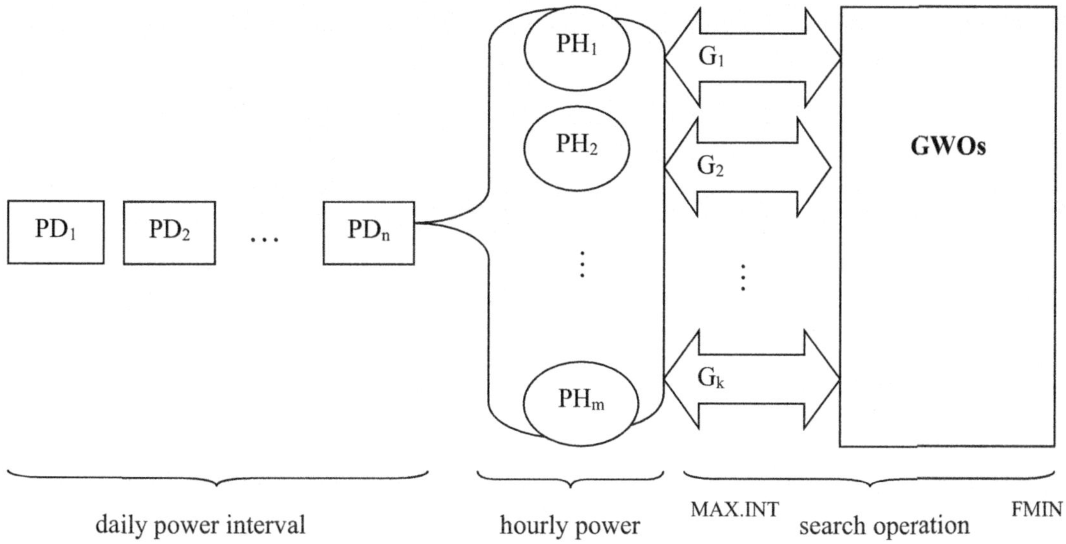

FIGURE 38.2 Model of hourly load scheduling problem illustrating a power aggregation and optimization workflow converting daily power intervals into hourly inputs for GWO based search.

For a power distribution feeder, we may define this problem as a power-mismatch objective function as follows:
Consider

$$t = [t_1\, t_2],\ \ t_i \in \mathrm{Z}\begin{cases} 1 \le t_1 \le 24 \\ 1 \le t_2 \le 31 \end{cases},\ \forall\, t_1 \to t_1^*,\ t_1^* \subset t_1 \tag{38.21}$$

Minimize

$$f_i = \frac{P_s - P_d(t_1, t_2)}{t_{\max}} \tag{38.22}$$

where

t_1 =hourly time index
t_1^* =optimum hourly time index
t_2 =daily time index range
P_s =distribution power supply, fixed
P_d =consumer power demand, variable
Introducing distribution-type constraints, we modify Eq. 38.22 as:
Minimize

$$f_i = [P_s - P_d(t_1, t_2)\cdot T^B\cdot N^C]_{B=1}^{5},\ \ B \in \mathrm{Z},\ \forall\, t_1 \to t_1^*,\ t_1^* \subset t_1 \tag{38.23}$$

Subject to

$$\begin{array}{l} [4 \le t_{\min(avail)} < 8],\ \ B, C = 1 \\ [8 \le t_{\min(avail)} < 12],\ \ B, C = 2 \\ [12 \le t_{\min(avail)} < 16],\ \ B, C = 3 \\ [16 \le t_{\min(avail)} < 20],\ \ B, C = 4 \\ [20 \le t_{\min(avail)} \le 24],\ \ B, C = 5 \end{array} \tag{38.24}$$

where,

$t_{\min(avail)}$ =minimum available hourly time
C =Inferred customer size per band

The parameter, $t_{\min(avail)}$, is computed using Eq. 38.25 as:

$$t_{\min(avail)} = 24 - \sum_{t_i=1}^{24} p_d \equiv 0, \ \forall\, t_2 \tag{38.25}$$

A typical example of Port-Harcourt Electricity Distribution Company (PHEDC) tariff band for the various hourly ranges is as shown in Table 38.1 [35]. Note that we have transformed the alphabet A to E to 1 to 5 for numerical compatibility in the simulation programs. For estimating customer size, a maximum of 300 customers is inferred, and the allocations to each band are linearly estimated using the model in Eq. 38.26.

$$\mathrm{N_{cz}} = lin\,(0,\, 0.3,\, C) \tag{38.26}$$

where,

lin =the MATLAB '*linspace*' function

Typically, the model formulas described in Eqs. 38.21–38.26 are implemented in a suitable programming language such that they allow the simulation over several trials. This enables the AI engineer to gain insight into the actual behavior of the developed model.

38.3.5.1 Assumptions

We consider the following assumptions for our proposed data-driven hourly energy schedule optimizer solution:

1. Supply power, power allocated per feeder zone, energy tariff price, and consumer size are nonvariable parameters fixed on the basis of the band-type by the energy operator (PHED company).
2. Load demand capture occurs on an hourly basis for a given day.
3. Power demand is always less than that supplied.
4. The impact of environmental parameters such as temperature, humidity, and wind speed on load demand is negligible.

It must be emphasized here that these assumptions constitute their own set of limitations. For instance, Assumption 3 may not hold as the number of consumers increases in size and hence the feeder transformers may become overloaded. In actual fact, transformers are usually overloaded beyond their nameplate rating, as is evidenced in many distribution feeder locations in the PHED network.

Also, the temperature and corresponding load consumption levels may increase during hot weather conditions and decrease in low weather conditions; in extreme weather situations, power demand might also experience consistent load peaks. However, it may be safe to assume that the aforementioned weather effects are reflected in the underlying load demand distribution data.

These assumptions allow us to concentrate our studies on the primary features – the time of the day for load capture and the corresponding load demanded.

38.3.5.2 Datasets

The datasets employed include real-time benchmark power system data from the Sharjah Electricity and Water Authority (SEWA) from the Emirates of Sharjah, UAE [36], and that obtained from field engineers at the PHEDC [37]. The PHEDC dataset for the K24PHTOWN feeder is considered in experimental simulations.

TABLE 38.1 PHEDC tariff band sequence.

Band type	Numeric equivalent index	Minimum hours	Price (₦/kWh)
A	1	20 h/day	55.20
B	2	16 h/day	54.80
C	3	12 h/day	51.70
D	4	8 h/day	45.90
E	5	4 h/day	43.60

PHEDC, Port-Harcourt Electricity Distribution Company.

TABLE 38.2 December hourly-daily load statistics for the SEWA and PHEDC datasets.

Statistic	SEWA (Year 2021)	PHEDC (Year 2017)
AHL (MWh)	970.7	3.4
MaxHL (MWh)	1154.0	9.7
MinHL (MWh)	758.0	0.0
THAvail (hr)	744.0	571.0

AHL, Average hourly load; *MaxHL*, maximum hourly load; *MinHL*, minimum hourly load; *PHEDC*, Port-Harcourt Electricity Distribution Company; *THAvail*, total hourly availability; *SEWA*, Sharjah Electricity and Water Authority.

To simplify analysis, we have specifically considered the hourly-daily load for month of December as a case study during optimization experiments for both datasets. However, a more detailed analysis should consider other parameters such as temperature, wind speed, etc., and a wider time duration.

The hourly-daily load statistics for the SEWA and PHEDC datasets are shown in Table 38.2. This includes the following statistics – aerage hourly load (AHL), Maximum Hourly Load (MaxHL), and Minimum Hourly Load (MinHL) for the given month. Also, the Total Hourly Availability (THAvail) for the PHEDC dataset is reported.

As seen from Table 38.2 and considering the AHL, MaxHL, and MinHL, the Sharjah electricity and water authority (SEWA) dataset has a much higher MWh consumption when compared to that of PHEDC. This may be attributed to the large capacity of the power provider in the UAE. Also, MinHL is 0 for the PHEDC dataset and its THAvail is less than that of the SEWA dataset, implying that there exist power outages in the PHEDC power network.

38.4 Results and discussions

38.4.1 Experimental details

The distribution network or distribution grid is an important part of the electrical power system, primarily responsible for coordinating power supply to all feeder transformers, which in turn, feeds the various interconnected consumers.

For the simulation experiments, we address loading at the distribution feeder level rather than at the appliance level, allowing us to focus on the more essential aspect of optimizing the hourly schedule plans. Furthermore, we seek to determine the optimum hour(s) for the feeder under consideration. The experimental simulations are conducted using an Intel iCore-5 with 4GB of RAM space and 64-bit Windows 10.

Simulations for benchmark power demand problem data (SEWA data) are performed considering the basic objective function formulation – Objective Function 1 (Eq. 38.22, subsection 38.3.5), and for 10 trial runs, using the maximum power demand as base power supply. The results obtained using GWO with Objective Function 1 serve as a baseline for further experiments with the GWO-SIDER; for the experimentations with the SEWA dataset, the optimum schedule at 18 h is used as a time reference. In a like manner, the simulations for case study data (PHEDC data) are performed using Objective Function 1 and Objective Function 2 (Eq. 38.23, subsection 38.3.5) for a base power supply of 6.195 MWh; the optimum schedule at 11 h is also used as a time reference for this dataset.

In the fitness optimization simulation experiments, a total of 10 simulation trials with the GWO maximum iterations and search agents set at 100 units and 10 units, respectively, are sequentially applied to the scheduling optimization tasks, while the SIDER approach is used to predict the candidate optimum hours for load scheduling at 40% input training level. The smoothing factor of the GWO is also set at 0.99units to tailor the search toward the more optimal positions.

Furthermore, the continuous optimum hour estimates by the alpha wolves of GWO and GWO-SIDER methods are reported in terms of the estimated mean absolute percentage error (MAPE), mean squared error (MSE), and mean absolute error (MAE) as well as the predicted optimum hours for each fitness trial run. Two one-sided tests, including the Wilcoxon signed-rank and t-test, are performed to identify and validate the correlations in optimum hour results obtained by the GWO and the GWO-SIDER methods. Cohen's d tests are also carried out to validate relative superiority between the methods.

38.4.2 Results using SEWA benchmark power demand dataset

38.4.2.1 Grey wolf optimizer results using Objective Function 1

The results for 10 trial runs using the GWO method for Objective Function 1 are as shown in Table 38.3, considering the Trial number (Trial No.), Fitness, Optimum Time, MAPE, MSE, and MAE estimates. Also, the convergence response plots for the various trials (first five trial runs) are as shown in Fig. 38.3.

As can be seen from Table 38.3, the fitness response is consistent and well distributed at 1411 MWh, implying the convergence point is attained at the optimum time of 18 h with an average MAPE, MSE, and MAE of 0.024, 0.56, and 0.44, respectively as highlighted in bold. As can be seen from Fig. 38.3, the GWO convergence for all trials begins at an iteration count much less than 10. This may be attributed to the consistent power supply within the chosen month; however, as can be seen from Fig. 38.3, at the beginning of the iteration, there are different levels of fitness for some of the trials, which is expected for stochastic algorithms such as the GWO. The optimum time is also mostly fixed at the 18 h level, implying the GWO is able to attain the objective reference level for most of the time.

38.4.2.2 Grey wolf optimizer-sparse integer distributed encoded representations results using Objective Function 1

In order to verify the feasibility of a consensus approach for optimal hour estimation, the GWO-SIDER model is run on the SEWA data using Objective Function 1 and the results are as shown in Table 38.4. Convergence response plots for the first five trial runs are also reported in Fig. 38.4.

As can be seen from Table 38.4 and just as in the case of GWO, the optimum time is mostly fixed at the 18 h level, implying the GWO-SIDER is equally able to attain the objective reference level. Also, the MAPE, MSE, and MAE are generally similar at the optimum time (as highlighted in bold), implying a comparable estimate between GWO and GWO-SIDER. As can be further seen from the convergence plots in Fig. 38.4, the GWO-SIDER exhibits a similar fitness response to the GWO.

38.4.3 Applying the GWO and GWO-SIDER Approach to the PHEDC power demand dataset

38.4.3.1 grey wolf optimizer results using Objective Function 1

The results for 10 trial runs using the GWO method for Objective Function 1 are as shown in Table 38.5, considering the Trial number (Trial No.), Fitness, Optimum Time, MAPE, MSE, and MAE. Also, the convergence response plots for the various trials (first 5 trial runs) are as shown in Fig. 38.5.

TABLE 38.3 GWO results for Objective 1 using the SEWA dataset (December, 2021).

Trial no.	Fitness (MWh)	Optimum time (hr)	MAPE	MSE	MAE
1	1411	18	0.017	0.33	0.31
2	1411	18	0.023	0.48	0.42
3	1411	19	0.028	0.51	0.51
4	1411	18	0.025	0.93	0.45
5	1411	18	0.034	0.97	0.63
6	1411	18	0.021	0.51	0.39
7	1411	18	0.021	0.38	0.38
8	1411	18	0.025	0.46	0.46
9	1411	18	0.025	0.59	0.45
10	1411	18	0.024	0.44	0.44
Mean	**1411**	**18**	**0.024**	**0.56**	**0.44**

GWO, Grey wolf optimizer; *MAPE*, Mean Absolute Percentage Error; *MSE*, Mean Squared Error; *MAE*, Mean Absolute Error.
Note: Bold values indicate the average values of the estimated metrics - fitness, optimum time, MAPE, MSE and MAE.

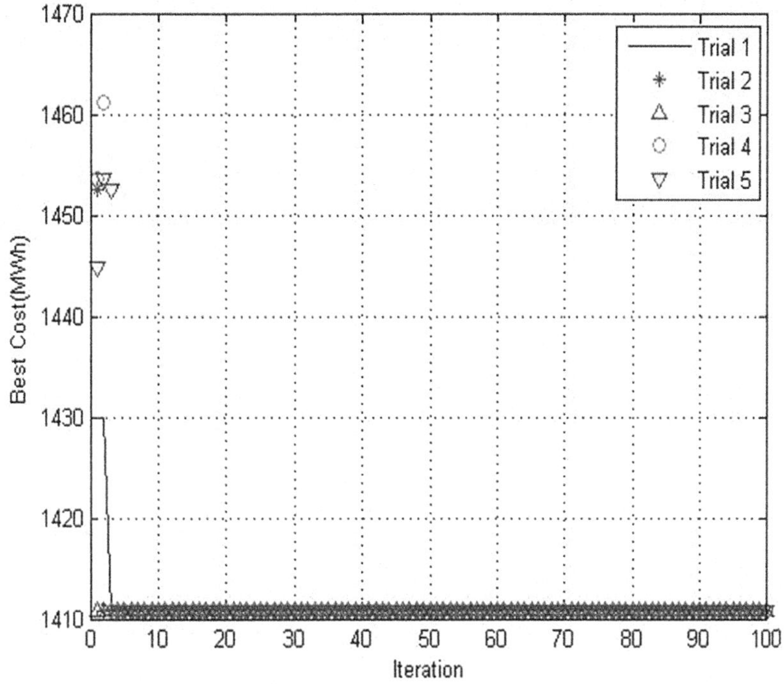

FIGURE 38.3 GWO fitness response for Objective Function 1 using SEWA dataset depicting best cost in MWh versus iteration for five trials and showing rapid convergence to a stable minimum within the first few iterations (*GWO*, Grey wolf optimizer).

TABLE 38.4 GWO-SIDER results for Objective 1 using the SEWA dataset (December, 2021).

Trial no.	Fitness (MWh)	Optimum time (hr)	MAPE	MSE	MAE
1	1411	18	0.024	0.77	0.43
2	1411	18	0.015	0.28	0.28
3	1411	18	0.024	0.45	0.45
4	1411	18	0.016	0.30	0.30
5	1411	19	0.031	0.64	0.58
6	1411	18	0.036	0.85	0.67
7	1411	18	0.027	0.49	0.49
8	1411	18	0.016	0.33	0.29
9	1411	18	0.022	0.42	0.40
10	1411	18	0.024	0.44	0.44
Mean	**1411**	**18**	**0.024**	**0.50**	**0.43**

GWO, Grey wolf optimizer; *SIDER*, sparse integer distributed encoded representations; *MAPE*, Mean Absolute Percentage Error; *MSE*, Mean Squared Error; *MAE*, Mean Absolute Error.
Note: Bold values indicate the average values of the estimated metrics - fitness, optimum time, MAPE, MSE and MAE.

As can be seen from Table 38.5, the fitness response is consistent, implying the convergence point is attained at the value (1.77 MWh). The optimum time is consistent at around 12 h with an average MAPE, MSE, and MAE of 0.061, 1.30, and 0.71, respectively as highlighted in bold; however, the optimum time differs from the reference level by 1 h. Furthermore, as can be clearly seen in Fig. 38.5, the GWO convergence for all trials begins much earlier at around the 5th iteration and the convergence point is attained near 1.8 MWh.

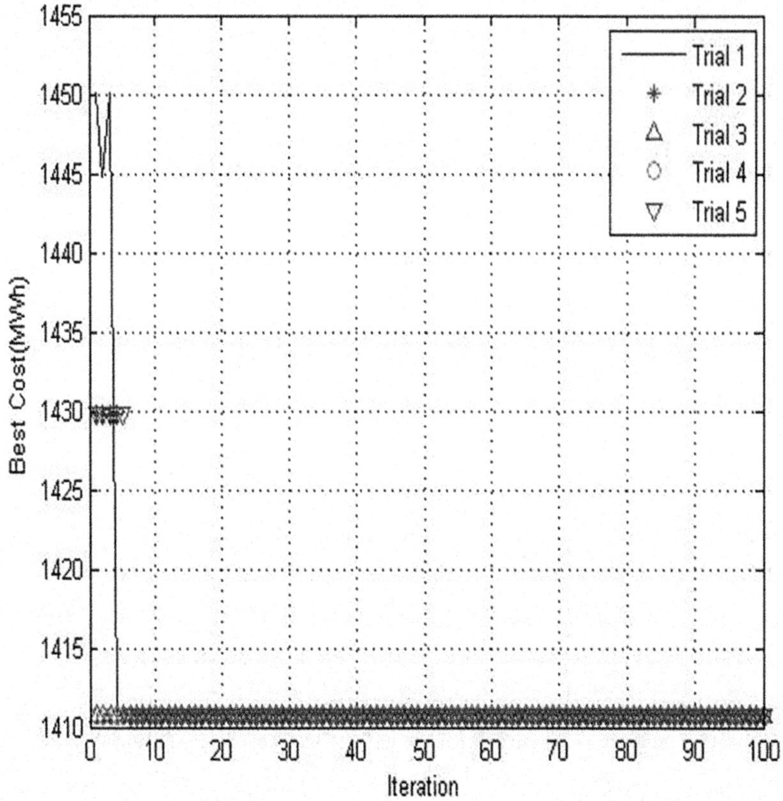

FIGURE 38.4 GWO-SIDER fitness response for Objective Function 1 using SEWA dataset depicting best cost in MWh versus iteration for five trials and showing rapid convergence to a stable minimum within the first few iterations (*GWO*, Grey wolf optimizer; *SIDER*, sparse integer distributed encoded representations).

TABLE 38.5 GWO rsults for Objective 1 using the PHEDC dataset (December, 2017).

Trial no.	Fitness (MWh)	Optimum time (hr)	MAPE	MSE	MAE
1	1.77	12	0.057	0.68	0.66
2	1.77	12	0.071	2.28	0.84
3	1.77	12	0.068	1.22	0.80
4	1.77	12	0.051	1.43	0.59
5	1.77	11	0.056	1.35	0.65
6	1.77	12	0.057	0.66	0.66
7	1.77	12	0.068	2.90	0.80
8	1.77	12	0.054	0.65	0.63
9	1.77	12	0.060	1.12	0.70
10	1.77	12	0.063	0.74	0.74
Mean	**1.77**	**12**	**0.061**	**1.30**	**0.71**

GWO, Grey wolf optimizer; *PHEDC*, Port-Harcourt Electricity Distribution Company; *MAPE*, Mean Absolute Percentage Error; *MSE*, Mean Squared Error; *MAE*, Mean Absolute Error.
Note: Bold values indicate the average values of the estimated metrics - fitness, optimum time, MAPE, MSE and MAE.

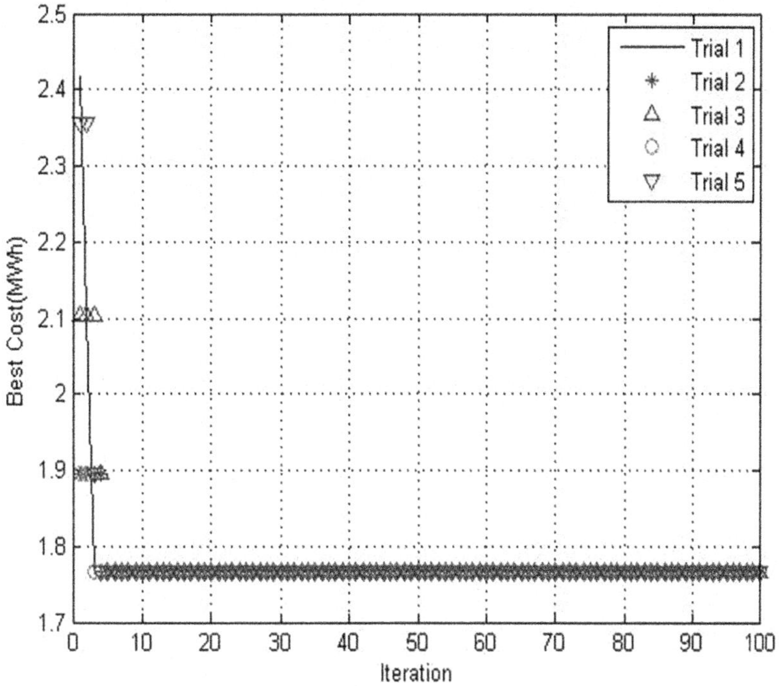

FIGURE 38.5 GWO fitness response for Objective Function 1 using PHEDC dataset depicting best cost in MWh versus iteration, showing five trials dropping steeply by iteration 10 and then flattening near 1.8 MWh through iteration 100 (*GWO*, Grey wolf optimizer; *PHEDC*, Port-Harcourt Electricity Distribution Company).

38.4.3.2 Grey wolf optimizer-sparse integer distributed encoded representations results using Objective Function 1

The results for 10 trial runs using the GWO-SIDER method for Objective Function 1 are shown in Table 38.6, considering the Trial number (Trial No.), Fitness, Optimum Time, MAPE, MSE, and MAE. The convergence response plots for the various trials (first 5 trial runs) are also shown in Fig. 38.6.

Just as in the case of GWO, the fitness response of GWO-SIDER is consistent at a value of 1.77 MWh. Also, the optimum time is consistent at around 12 h with an average MAPE, MSE, and MAE of 0.056, 0.82, and 0.65, respectively as highlighted in bold.

Furthermore, the GWO-SIDER convergence for all trials begins much earlier at around the 5th iteration, as shown in Fig. 38.6.

38.4.3.3 Results using Objective Function 2

The results for 10 trial runs using GWO and GWO-SIDER method for Objective Function 2 are as shown in Tables 38.7 and 38.8 respectively, considering the Trial number (Trial No.), Fitness, Optimum Time, MAPE, MSE, and MAE. Also, the fitness responses of the GWO and the GWO-SIDER methods are reported in Fig. 38.7 and Fig. 38.8, respectively.

As can be seen from Table 38.7, the fitness response of GWO is consistent, implying the convergence point is attained at the average value of 2924NMWh (as highlighted in bold). Also, just as in the case of Objective 1, the optimum time is consistent at 12 h with an average MAPE, MSE, and MAE of 0.054, 1.17, and 0.63, respectively as highlighted in bold. Interestingly, the results in Table 38.8 showed that GWO-SIDER can give several multiple predictions for a given trial run (trial runs 1, 4, 8, and 9), which approximates 11 h – the reference level, even though GWO has lower average error estimates.

38.4.4 Statistical analysis of GWO and GWO-SIDER methods considering the SEWA and PHEDC power demand datasets

This section presents the application of the Wilcoxon Signed-Rank (WSR) at 5% level and a one-tailed paired t-test at 5% and 1% levels on the optimum hour estimates obtained by the GWO and GWO-SIDER methods, considering the MAPE, MSE, and MAE for both the SEWA and PHEDC datasets. The purpose of the WSR significance tests was to validate whether the results from both methods come from an identical distribution with equivalent medians, while the t-test was

TABLE 38.6 GWO-SIDER results for Objective 1 using the PHEDC dataset (December, 2017).

Trial no.	Fitness (MWh)	Optimum time (hr)	MAPE	MSE	MAE
1	1.77	11	0.039	0.65	0.45
2	1.77	12	0.058	0.67	0.67
3	1.77	12	0.054	0.63	0.63
4	1.77	12	0.080	2.46	0.96
5	1.77	11	0.046	0.53	0.53
6	1.77	12	0.056	0.65	0.65
7	1.77	12	0.055	0.64	0.64
8	1.77	12	0.066	0.78	0.78
9	1.77	12	0.066	0.78	0.78
10	1.77	12	0.038	0.43	0.43
Mean	**1.77**	**12**	**0.056**	**0.82**	**0.65**

GWO, Grey wolf optimizer; *PHEDC*, Port-Harcourt Electricity Distribution Company; *SIDER*, sparse integer distributed encoded representations; *MAPE*, Mean Absolute Percentage Error; *MSE*, Mean Squared Error; *MAE*, Mean Absolute Error.
Note: Bold values indicate the average values of the estimated metrics - fitness, optimum time, MAPE, MSE and MAE.

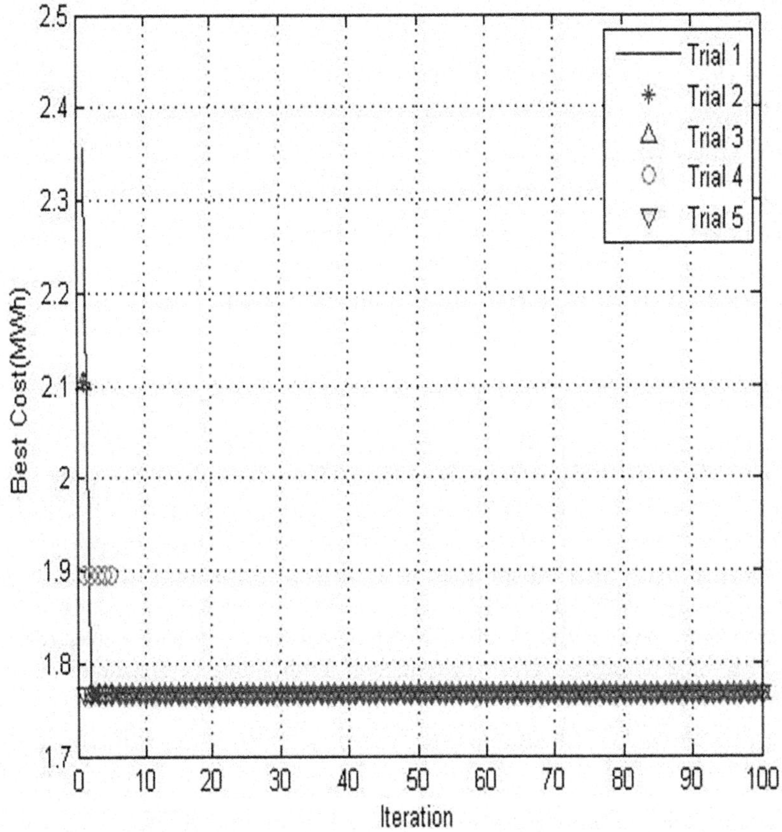

FIGURE 38.6 GWO-SIDER fitness response for Objective Function 1 using PHEDC dataset depicting best cost in MWh versus iteration, where five trials rapidly decrease within the first 10 iterations and then remain nearly constant through iteration 100 (*GWO*, Grey wolf optimizer; *PHEDC*, Port-Harcourt Electricity Distribution Company).

TABLE 38.7 GWO results for Objective 2 using the PHEDC Dataset (December, 2017).

Trial no.	Fitness (₦MWh)	Optimum time (hr)	MAPE	MSE	MAE
1	2924	12	0.054	0.93	0.63
2	2924	12	0.048	0.61	0.55
3	2924	12	0.073	3.16	0.86
4	2924	12	0.060	1.26	0.70
5	2924	11	0.044	1.23	0.51
6	2924	12	0.054	0.93	0.63
7	2924	11	0.047	0.84	0.54
8	2924	12	0.062	1.45	0.73
9	2924	12	0.065	0.88	0.76
10	2924	12	0.037	0.42	0.42
Mean	**2924**	**12**	**0.054**	**1.17**	**0.63**

GWO, Grey wolf optimizer; *PHEDC*, Port-Harcourt Electricity Distribution Company; *MAPE*, Mean Absolute Percentage Error; *MSE*, Mean Squared Error; *MAE*, Mean Absolute Error.
Note: Bold values indicate the average values of the estimated metrics - fitness, optimum time, MAPE, MSE and MAE.

TABLE 38.8 GWO-SIDER results for Objective 2 using the PHEDC dataset (December, 2017).

Trial no.	Fitness (₦MWh)	Optimum time (hr)	Optimum time (hr)[a]	MAPE	MSE	MAE
1	2924	21, 11	16	0.058	2.00	0.68
2	2924	12	12	0.076	2.47	0.91
3	2924	11	11	0.081	3.09	0.97
4	2924	7, 12	10	0.059	0.80	0.68
5	2924	11	11	0.076	2.59	0.91
6	2924	12	12	0.062	0.73	0.73
7	2924	11	11	0.056	1.07	0.65
8	2924	9, 12	11	0.055	0.98	0.64
9	2924	9, 11	10	0.068	1.24	0.80
10	2924	11	11	0.059	1.11	0.69
Mean	**2924**	11		0.0650	1.61	**0.77**

PHEDC, Port-Harcourt Electricity Distribution Company; *MAPE*, Mean Absolute Percentage Error; *MSE*, Mean Squared Error; *MAE*, Mean Absolute Error.
Note: Bold values indicate the average values of the estimated metrics - fitness, optimum time, MAPE, MSE and MAE.
[a] *Optimized Average.*

used to validate the notion of equal means of the optimizers. The statistical significance considering fitness response is not reported since, by inspection, the optimum fitness of both methods for each trial run is not different from each other.

Furthermore, Cohen's d (C_d) test is used to determine the relative superiority of the GWO over the GWO-SIDER. The results of these tests are as shown in Tables 38.9 and 38.10 for Objectives 1 and 2, respectively.

For Objective 1, the results in Table 38.9 clearly show that the GWO and GWO-SIDER methods are very similar in performance for both datasets, with P-values greater than the defined significance levels. Considering t-test P-values, we

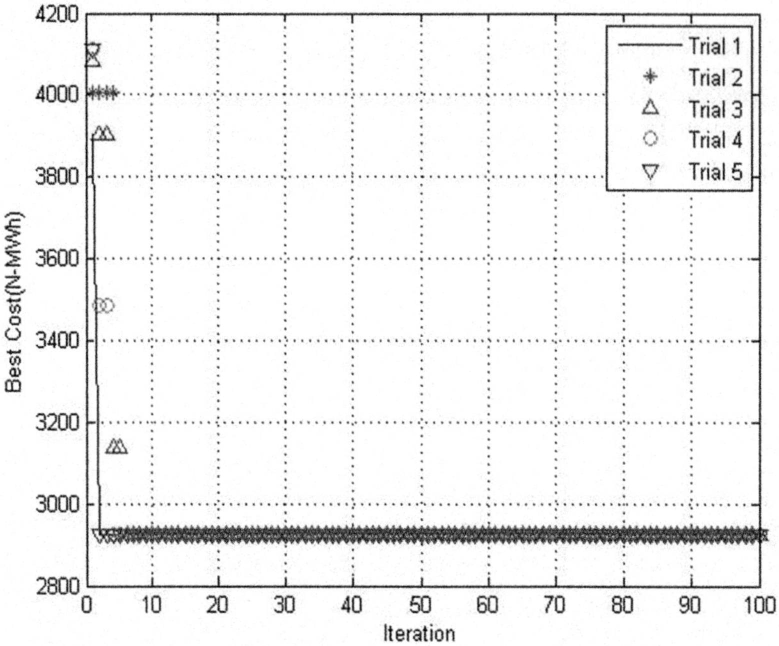

FIGURE 38.7 GWO fitness response for Objective Function 2 using PHEDC dataset depicting best cost in ₦MWh versus iteration for five trials, showing early drops and convergence near 2900 ₦MWh across iterations 0 to 100 (*GWO*, Grey wolf optimizer; *PHEDC*, Port-Harcourt Electricity Distribution Company).

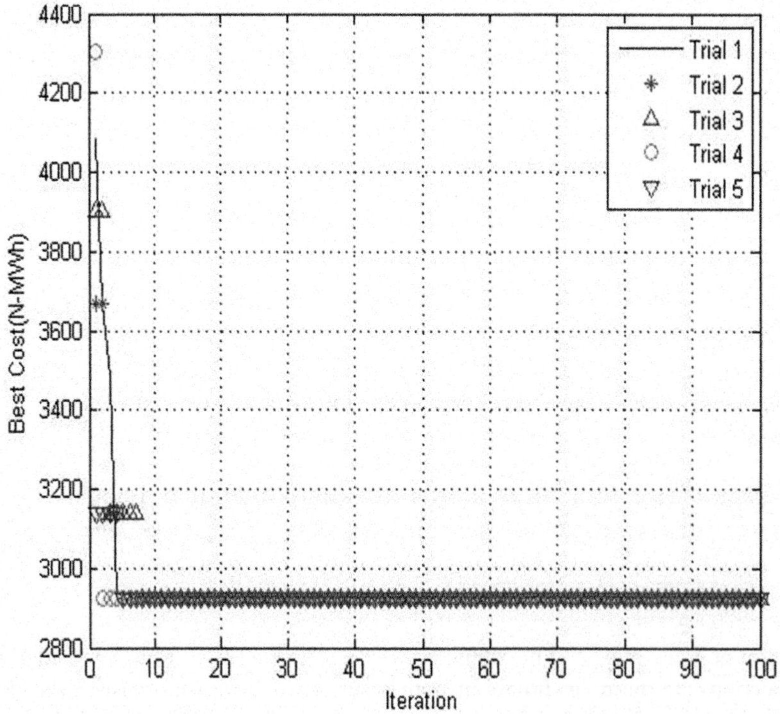

FIGURE 38.8 GWO-SIDER fitness response for Objective Function 2 using PHEDC dataset depicting best cost in ₦MWh versus iteration for five trials, showing sharp early decreases and convergence near 3000 ₦MWh by iteration 10 (*GWO*, Grey wolf optimizer; *PHEDC*, Port-Harcourt Electricity Distribution Company; *SIDER*, sparse integer distributed encoded representations).

TABLE 38.9 Wilcoxon signed-rank *P*-values, t-test *P-values* and Cohen's *d* obtained for Objective Function 1.

Metric (% -significance)	Numeric scores for datasets	
	SEWA	PHEDC
WSR *P*-value (MAPE) - 5%	0.65	0.28
WSR *P*-value (MSE) - 5%	0.57	0.11
WSR *P*-value (MAE) - 5%	0.65	0.28
t-test *P*-value (MAPE) - 5%	0.76 (-0.0049, 0.0065)	0.39 (-0.0069, 0.0163)
t-test *P*-value (MAPE) - 1%	0.76 (-0.0073, 0.0089)	0.39 (-0.0120, 0.0214)
t-test *P*-value (MSE) - 5%	0.54 (-0.1603, 0.2863)	0.13 (-0.1806, 1.1426)
t-test *P*-value (MSE) - 1%	0.54 (-0.2578, 0.3838)	0.13 (-0.4694, 1.4314)
t-test *P*-value (MAE) - 5%	0.81 (-0.0911, 0.1131)	0.42 (-0.0908, 0.2008)
t-test *P*-value (MAE) - 1%	0.81 (-0.1357, 0.1577)	0.42 (-0.1544, 0.2644)
C_d value (MAPE)	0.20	0.70
C_d value (MSE)	0.30	0.60
C_d value (MAE)	0.10	0.70

PHEDC, Port-Harcourt Electricity Distribution Company; *SEWA*, Sharjah Electricity and Water Authority.

TABLE 38.10 Wilcoxon signed-rank *P*-values, t-test *P-values* and Cohen's *d* obtained for Objective Function 2.

Metric (% -significance)	Numeric scores for PHEDC dataset
WSR *P*-value (MAPE) - 5%	0.02
WSR *P*-value (MSE) - 5%	0.19
WSR *P*-value (MAE) - 5%	0.02
t-test *P*-value (MAPE) - 5%	0.03 (-0.0197, -0.0015)
t-test *P*-value (MAPE) - 1%	0.03 (-0.0237, 0.0025)
t-test *P*-value (MSE) - 5%	0.12 (-1.0053, 0.1313)
t-test *P*-value (MSE) - 1%	0.12 (-1.2535, 0.3795)
t-test *P*-value (MAE) - 5%	0.03 (-0.2480, -0.0180)
t-test *P*-value (MAE) - 1%	0.03 (-0.2981, 0.0321)
C_d value (MAPE)	-1.00
C_d value (MSE)	-0.60
C_d value (MAE)	-1.00

PHEDC, Port-Harcourt Electricity Distribution Company.

see that the confidence bounds at 95% and 99% levels contain 0. Furthermore, the GWO exhibited a low-effect-sized superiority over GWO-SIDER for the SEWA dataset and a large-effect-sized superiority for the PHEDC dataset.

For Objective 2, the WSR and *t*-test *P*-values at 5% levels shown in Table 38.10 are indeed at variance with those of Objective 1, considering the PHEDC dataset. Apart from the MSE estimates, the MAPE and MAE WSR and t-test estimates at 5% level show that there are significant differences between the GWO and GWO-SIDER methods. However, the *t*-test

P-values at 1% level further reveal that there are indeed no significant differences between the GWO and GWO-SIDER methods. Furthermore, as clearly shown by the C_d values in Table 38.10, the GWO-SIDER exhibited a large-effect-sized superiority over GWO for the PHEDC dataset.

From these results and on the basis of the considered MAPE, MSE, and MAE metrics, it is clear that there is sufficient basis to accept the null hypothesis that there is generally no significant difference between the results generated by the two methods.

38.5 Conclusions and future Work

One of the benefits of metaheuristics optimization is their ability to search global solution spaces. However, real-world optimization problems are oftentimes constrained by the number of competing decision variables or constraints required in order to attain a good solution. The distribution network or distribution grid is an important part of the electrical power system, primarily responsible for the allocation of adequatte power to a teeming set of customers – the consumers of electrical energy, but this network is challenged by the power demand-supply schedule problem, for which, to an extent, only dynamic metaheuristic optimizers can solve.

In this paper, we have presented a more intuitive approach for optimal power scheduling considering the power supply and demand of the distribution network in a data-driven way. The GWO – an emerging metaheuristics and population-based machine learning technique combined with a continual learning neural-based consensus algorithm called the SIDER is employed in a data-driven solution for solving power system schedule problems using data from real distribution power networks.

More specifically, we have employed the potentials of using sequentially connected parallel sets of alpha GWOs in a GWO-SIDER solution for estimating the optimum hour for supply-demand scheduling, considering the SEWA and PHEDC datasets.

The proposed approach has been shown to attain promising results in terms of fitness, MAPE, MSE, and MAE for both datasets with respect to both a basic power-mismatch objective and an updated power-mismatch objective including several underlying energy demand constraints such as the cost of energy, demand peak, and off-peak hours, and customer size per zone. In particular, the GWO-SIDER method shows the capability to perform multiple predictions and is equally comparable to GWO. The ability to perform multiple predictions is an important function of intelligent agents, and as such, GWO-SIDER holds promise as a candidate machine intelligence solution in the field of real-time power scheduling.

However, there might be situations where suboptimality or early convergences in the predicted optimal hourly states occur; this is not unexpected, as the GWO is a stochastic problem solver. Indeed, such issues of suboptimality are verifiable from the statistical differences observed in the MAPE and MAE estimates at 5% significance level. Considering the fact that the GWO-SIDER method may generate multiple predictions and that the results may exhibit suboptimal states, it will be desirable to study the influence of a higher number of trial runs on the consensus estimates to determine if consistent patterns can be formed. Also, it may be helpful to employ higher search agents and maximum iterations, but this comes at the cost of increased computation size and simulation run-times.

References

[1] S.A. Adegoke, Y. Sun, Power system optimization approach to mitigate voltage instability issues: a review, Cogent Engineering 10 (1) (2023) 2153416.

[2] K Tazi, F Abdi, MF Abbou, Demand and energy management in smart grid: Techniques and implementation. in: 2017 International Renewable and Sustainable Energy Conference (IRSEC), IEEE, 2017, pp. 1-6.

[3] T. Yang, ICT technologies standards and protocols for active distribution network, Smart Power Distribution Systems, Academic Press, (2019), pp. 205–230.

[4] U. Assad, M.A.S. Hassan, U. Farooq, A. Kabir, M.Z. Khan, S.S.H. Bukhari, ... J. Popp, Smart grid, demand response and optimization: a critical review of computational methods, Energies 15 (6) (2022) 2003.

[5] D. Jacobson, L. Dickerman, Distributed intelligence: a critical piece of the microgrid puzzle, The Electricity Journal 32 (5) (2019) 10–13.

[6] M. Vukobratović, P. Marić, G. Horvat, Z. Balkić, S. Sučić, A survey on computational intelligence applications in distribution network optimization, Electronics 10 (11) (2021) 1247.

[7] S.S. Rao, Engineering Optimization: Theory and Practice, forth Ed., John Wiley & Sons, (2019).

[8] X.S. Yang, Nature-Inspired Metaheuristic Algorithms, Luniver Press, (2010).

[9] V. Basto-Fernandes, I. Yevseyeva, A. Deutz, M. Emmerich, A survey of diversity oriented optimization: problems, indicators, and algorithms. EVOLVE–A Bridge between Probability, Set Oriented Numerics and Evolutionary Computation VII (2017) 3–23.

[10] C.R. Çırak, H. Çalık, Hotspots in maximum power point tracking algorithms for photovoltaic systems–a comprehensive and comparative review, Engineering Science and Technology, an International Journal 43 (2023) 101436.

[11] A. Rajasekhar, N. Lynn, S. Das, P.N. Suganthan, Computing with the collective intelligence of honey bees–a survey, Swarm and Evolutionary Computation 32 (2017) 25–48.
[12] I. Koutsopoulos, L. Tassiulas, Optimal control policies for power demand scheduling in the smart grid, IEEE Journal on Selected Areas in Communications 30 (6) (2012) 1049–1060.
[13] G. Selvaraj, K. Rajangam, P. Vishnuram, M. Bajaj, I. Zaitsev, Optimal power scheduling in real-time distribution systems using crow search algorithm for enhanced microgrid performance, Scientific Reports 14 (1) (2024) 30982.
[14] S. Bharath, A. Vasuki, Adaptive energy loss optimization in distributed networks using reinforcement learning-enhanced crow search algorithm, Scientific Reports 15 (1) (2025) 12165.
[15] MP Anand, V Mohan, W Ongsakul, MR Suresh, Optimal day ahead scheduling of distributed EVs in a smart distribution network, in: 2015 IEEE Innovative Smart Grid Technologies-Asia (ISGT ASIA), IEEE, 2015, pp. 1-5.
[16] B. Hayes, Distribution generation optimization and energy management, Distributed Generation Systems (2017) 415–451.
[17] S.M. Sharifhosseini, T. Niknam, M.H. Taabodi, H.A. Aghajari, E. Sheybani, G. Javidi, et al., Investigating intelligent forecasting and optimization in electrical power systems: a comprehensive review of techniques and applications, Energies 17 (21) (2024) 5385.
[18] TI Ahamed, SD Maqbool, EA Al-Ammar, NH Malik, A simulated annealing algorithm for demand response, in: 2011 2nd IEEE PES International Conference and Exhibition on Innovative Smart Grid Technologies, IEEE, 2011, pp. 1-4.
[19] S Yue, D Zhu, Y Wang, M Pedram, Distributed load demand scheduling in smart grid to minimize electricity generation cost, in: 2014 IEEE PES General Meetingl Conference & Exposition, IEEE, 2014, pp. 1-5.
[20] A. Bosisio, A. Berizzi, D. Lupis, A. Morotti, G. Iannarelli, B. Greco, A tabu-search-based algorithm for distribution network restoration to improve reliability and resiliency, Journal of Modern Power Systems and Clean Energy 11 (1) (2022) 302–311.
[21] R. Quan, J. Jian, L. Yang, An improved priority list and neighborhood search method for unit commitment, International Journal of Electrical Power & Energy Systems 67 (2015) 278–285.
[22] C.A.C. Coello, Use of a self-adaptive penalty approach for engineering optimization problems, Computers in Industry 41 (2) (2000) 113–127.
[23] CR Chen, MJ Lan, CC Huang, YY Hong, SH Low, Demand response optimization for smart home scheduling using genetic algorithm, in: 2013 IEEE International Conference on Systems, Man, and Cybernetics, IEEE, 2013, pp. 1461-1465.
[24] S.L.L. Wynn, B. Marungsri, Performance comparison of swarm-intelligence optimization methods and their impact on the demand response program, International Energy Journal 23 (4) (2023).
[25] Q.P. Zheng, J. Wang, A.L. Liu, Stochastic optimization for unit commitment—a review, IEEE Transactions on Power Systems 30 (4) (2014) 1913–1924.
[26] B. Xu, J. Wang, M. Guo, J. Lu, G. Li, L. Han, A hybrid demand response mechanism based on real-time incentive and real-time pricing, Energy 231 (2021) 120940.
[27] L. Yao, W.H. Lim, Optimal purchase strategy for demand bidding, IEEE Transactions on Power Systems 33 (3) (2017) 2754–2762.
[28] A.B. Barnawi, Development and analysis of optimization algorithm for demand-side management considering optimal generation scheduling and power flow in grid-connected AC/DC microgrid, Sustainability 15 (21) (2023) 15671.
[29] S. Mirjalili, S.M. Mirjalili, A. Lewis, Grey wolf optimizer, Advances in Engineering Software 69 (2014) 46–61.
[30] E.N. Osegi, V. Anireh, AMI: an auditory machine intelligence algorithm for predicting sensory-like data, Computer Science 5 (2) (2020) 71–89.
[31] EN Osegi, Neuronal auditory machine intelligence (Neuro-AMI) in perspective. arXiv preprint arXiv:2401.02421, 2023. Available from: https://arxiv.org/abs/2401.02421.
[32] D. Webster, A. Popper, R. Fay (Eds.), The Mammalian Auditory Pathway: Neuroanatomy, Springer Handbook of Auditory Research, vol. 1, Springer-Verlag New York, Inc, (1992).
[33] Y. Cui, S. Ahmad, J. Hawkins, The HTM spatial pooler—a neocortical algorithm for online sparse distributed coding, Frontiers in cOmputational Neuroscience 111 (2017).
[34] S Ahmad, J Hawkins, Properties of sparse distributed representations and their application to hierarchical temporal memory. arXiv preprint arXiv:1503.07469, 2015.
[35] FMP, Data Collection Survey on Performance Improvement of Distribution Companies In The Federal Republic of Nigeria. Federal Ministry of Power (FMP) National Power Training Institute of Nigeria (NAPTIN), The Federal Republic of Nigeria, (2017).
[36] M.S. Jawad, C. Dhawale, A.R. Al Ali, A.A.B. Ramli, Power spectrum: a detailed dataset on electric demand and environmental interplays, Data in Brief 52 (2024) 109788.
[37] PHEDC, Port-harcourt electricity distribution company hourly load consumption data for december, 2017.

Glossary

Accuracy Fraction of correctly classified samples among all samples.

Adaptive Noise Cancellation A filtering approach that adapts filter coefficients online to remove noise using a correlated reference signal.

AI Artificial intelligence; computational methods that perform tasks typically requiring human intelligence (learning, reasoning, perception, and language).

Alpha Wolf The current best candidate solution (leader) that most strongly guides the position updates of the pack.

ANC Adaptive filtering that removes noise by continuously updating filter coefficients to minimize an error signal.

Ancillary Services Grid support services such as frequency control, voltage support, and reserves.

Artificial Intelligence Computational methods that perform tasks typically requiring human intelligence, such as perception, language, learning, and decision making.

AUC Area under the ROC curve; a threshold-independent measure of classifier discrimination.

AVOA A bio-inspired optimizer based on African vulture foraging behavior; sometimes hybridized with GWO/PSO in comparative studies.

BCDI A numerical index representing bridge condition/deterioration used as the target variable in predictive maintenance models.

Benchmark Functions Standard test problems used to compare optimizers under controlled settings (often unimodal/multimodal, separable/nonseparable).

Beta Wolf The second-best candidate solution that supports the alpha in guiding the search.

Binary GWO A GWO variant for binary decision variables that maps continuous updates to bit values using transfer functions or probability rules.

Boundary Handling Rules for dealing with candidate variables that leave the allowed domain (e.g., clipping, reflection, resampling).

CEC Often used to refer to CEC benchmark suites released around the IEEE Congress on Evolutionary Computation.

CNN A deep neural network that uses convolutional layers to learn spatial features (commonly used in image/time-series analysis).

Coefficient Vector A A GWO coefficient that scales the movement toward leaders; its magnitude controls exploration ($|A|>1$) versus exploitation ($|A|<1$).

Coefficient Vector C A GWO coefficient that randomizes the leaders' influence, helping diversify the search direction.

Constraint A feasibility requirement that candidate solutions must satisfy (equality, inequality, or domain restrictions).

Constraint Handling Techniques for dealing with infeasible solutions (e.g., penalties, repair operators, feasibility rules, or specialized encodings).

Convergence The tendency of an optimization run to stabilize as candidates move toward a (local or global) optimum.

Cross-Validation A resampling procedure for estimating generalization performance by training and testing on multiple data splits.

DE An evolutionary algorithm that generates new candidates by adding scaled differences between population members to another member (mutation) and then recombining (crossover).

Delta Wolf The third-best candidate solution that provides additional guidance to balance exploration and exploitation.

Diversity A measure of how spread out the population is; higher diversity helps exploration and reduces stagnation.

Droop Control A decentralized primary control method that shares load by adjusting power output in response to frequency/voltage deviations.

EIS	Enterprise Information System; integrates data and workflows across an organization to support operations and decisions.
ELM	A fast single-hidden-layer neural network where hidden-layer weights are randomly assigned and output weights are solved analytically.
EMS	Energy Management System; optimizes scheduling and dispatch of resources (often with economic objectives) under constraints.
Encircling Prey	The GWO position-update mechanism that moves candidates toward leaders using coefficient vectors that control step size and direction.
Energy Management System	A supervisory layer that schedules and coordinates resources (generation, storage, loads) to meet technical and economic objectives.
Energy Storage System	A device or set of devices that stores energy for later use to improve reliability, flexibility, or power quality.
Exploitation	Search behavior aimed at refining solutions near the current best candidates to improve quality.
Exploration	Search behavior aimed at covering new regions of the search space to avoid premature convergence.
Feature Selection	Selecting a subset of input variables to improve learning performance, reduce dimensionality, and enhance interpretability.
Filter Method	A feature-selection strategy that scores features using data statistics (independent of any specific predictive model).
Finite Impulse Response Filter	A digital filter whose impulse response settles to zero in finite time; widely used for stable linear filtering.
FIR	A stable digital filter implemented as a finite weighted sum of current and past input samples.
Fitness Function	An objective (sometimes including penalties/weights) used by a metaheuristic to rank and compare candidate solutions.
FOPIDSMC	A PID-SMC variant using fractional-order operators to improve robustness and reduce chattering.
Frequency Regulation	Control actions that keep system frequency close to its nominal value under disturbances.
GA	Genetic algorithm. An evolutionary algorithm that evolves a population using selection, crossover, and mutation operators.
Global Optimum	The best feasible solution over the entire search space for the chosen objective.
Grey Wolf Optimizer	A population-based metaheuristic inspired by grey-wolf hunting, where three leaders (alpha, beta, and delta) guide all candidates toward promising regions.
GSA	Gravitational search algorithm; a physics-inspired optimizer that models agents as masses that attract each other through a gravity-like interaction.
GWO	Abbreviation for grey wolf optimizer; a population-based metaheuristic inspired by grey-wolf hunting behavior.
GWOPSO	A hybrid method that combines GWO's leader-guided search with PSO's velocity/learning dynamics to improve convergence and robustness.
HESS	Hybrid energy storage system; combines complementary storage technologies to meet both fast power and longer energy needs.
High Voltage Direct Current	Long-distance power transmission using DC voltage, often favored for submarine cables and controllability.
Hunting	The GWO process of iteratively updating candidates toward the leaders to locate high-quality regions.
HVDC	High voltage direct current transmission; uses DC to transmit power efficiently over long distances or subsea cables.
Hybrid Energy Storage System	A combination of storage technologies (e.g., batteries plus fast storage) designed to meet both energy and power requirements.
Hybridization	Combining mechanisms from multiple algorithms (e.g., GWO + PSO) to leverage complementary strengths.
Hyperparameter	A model/algorithm setting chosen before training/optimization (e.g., C in SVM, population size).
Hyperparameter Tuning	Searching for hyperparameter settings that yield better validation performance.
IDS	Abbreviation for Intrusion Detection System; monitors activity to detect attacks or abnormal behavior.
Intrusion Detection System	A system that monitors activity and identifies malicious behavior or policy violations in networks or hosts.
Islanded Mode	Microgrid operation disconnected from the main grid, relying on local generation/storage for stability.
Iteration	One update step of an iterative optimization process in which all (or part of) the population is updated.
KNN	A nonparametric classifier/regressor that predicts based on the labels/values of the k closest training samples.
LFC	Abbreviation for load frequency control; keeps system frequency close to nominal by balancing generation and demand.

Load Frequency Control	A control function that maintains power-system frequency (and tie-line power) by adjusting generation or controllable loads.
Local Optimum	A solution better than nearby solutions but not necessarily the best over the entire search space.
LSTM	A recurrent neural network architecture designed to learn long-range dependencies via gated memory cells.
Machine Learning	Algorithms and statistical models that learn patterns from data to make predictions or decisions.
MAE	Mean of absolute errors; less sensitive to outliers than MSE/RMSE.
MATLAB	A numerical computing and simulation environment widely used for control, optimization, and signal processing.
Maximum Power Point Tracking	Control that adjusts operating conditions so a renewable source (e.g., PV) delivers maximum power under varying conditions.
Mean Absolute Error	A performance metric equal to the mean of absolute prediction errors.
Mean Squared Error	A performance metric equal to the mean of squared prediction errors.
Metaheuristic	A general, problem-independent search strategy that trades exactness for scalability and robustness on complex problems.
MG	Abbreviation for microgrid; a localized system of loads and resources that can run grid-connected or islanded.
Microgrid	A localized group of loads and energy resources that can operate connected to the main grid or in islanded mode.
ML	Machine learning; algorithms that learn patterns from data to make predictions or decisions without being explicitly programmed for each case.
MPPT	Control that adjusts operating point so a PV/wind system extracts maximum available power.
MSE	Mean of squared errors; common regression loss/metric.
Multimodal Function	An objective function with multiple local optima; challenging for optimizers due to trapping risk.
No Free Lunch Theorem	A result stating that averaged over all problems, no optimizer outperforms all others; performance is problem-dependent.
Objective Function	A quantitative function to be minimized or maximized; it maps a candidate solution to a scalar quality value.
Omega Wolves	The remaining candidate solutions that follow the leaders and help maintain population diversity.
Overfitting	When a model fits training data very well but performs poorly on unseen data due to learning noise or spurious patterns.
Parameter a	A control parameter in GWO that typically decreases from 2 to 0 across iterations to shift from exploration to exploitation.
Parameter Tuning	Choosing algorithm hyperparameters (e.g., population size, coefficients) to improve performance for a given problem class.
Pareto Front	The set of non-dominated solutions representing the best achievable trade-offs among objectives.
Penalty Function	A mechanism that adds a penalty to the objective/fitness when constraints are violated, discouraging infeasible solutions.
Permutation Encoding	Representing a solution as an ordered list (permutation) to model sequencing/scheduling problems.
Photoplethysmography	An optical technique that measures blood-volume changes in tissue, commonly used for pulse and oxygen saturation monitoring.
Photovoltaic	Technology that converts light directly into electrical energy using semiconductor devices (solar cells).
PI	A feedback controller combining proportional and integral actions; common in industrial control.
PID	A feedback controller combining proportional, integral, and derivative actions to reduce tracking error.
PIDSMC	A sliding-mode controller that incorporates PID-type terms in the sliding surface or control law to improve tracking and reduce steady-state error.
PMS	Power management system; coordinates generation, storage, and loads to meet operational targets and constraints.
Population	A set of candidate solutions evolved in parallel by a population-based optimizer.
Power Management System	A control/supervision system that allocates power among sources/loads to satisfy operational constraints and performance targets.
PPG	Abbreviation for photoplethysmography; an optical method that measures changes in blood volume to estimate pulse and related metrics.
Precision	Fraction of predicted positives that are true positives.
Premature Convergence	Early stagnation where the population collapses around a suboptimal region.
Proportional–Integral–Derivative Controller	A feedback controller combining proportional, integral, and derivative actions to reduce error and improve response dynamics.

PSH	A large-scale storage technology that pumps water to an upper reservoir when surplus power exists and generates when released.
PSO	Particle Swarm Optimization. A swarm-based optimizer where particles move through the search space guided by their own best position and the best position found by neighbors.
Pumped Storage Hydropower	Grid-scale storage that pumps water uphill when surplus power exists and generates electricity when released downhill.
PV	Photovoltaic generation; converts sunlight to electricity using solar cells.
RCGWO	A GWO variant that introduces random weighting and crossover-style recombination (elite-biased) to enhance diversity and convergence.
Recall	Fraction of true positives that are correctly identified (also called sensitivity/TPR).
Redox Flow Battery	A rechargeable battery where energy is stored in liquid electrolytes in external tanks and converted via electrochemical cells.
Renewable Energy Sources	Energy sources replenished naturally on human timescales (e.g., wind, solar, tidal).
RES	Renewable energy sources such as solar, wind, or tidal generation.
RFB	A battery where energy is stored in liquid electrolytes and power is delivered via electrochemical cells.
RMSE	Square root of mean squared error; emphasizes larger errors.
ROC Curve	A curve showing the trade-off between true positive rate and false positive rate over classification thresholds.
Root Mean Square Error	A performance metric equal to the square root of the mean of squared prediction errors.
Search Space	The set of all feasible candidate solutions, defined by variable domains and constraints.
Signal-to-Noise Ratio	A measure comparing signal power to noise power; higher SNR indicates cleaner measurements.
SMC	A robust control method that forces system trajectories to reach and stay on a designed sliding surface, improving disturbance rejection.
SMES	An energy storage device that stores energy in a magnetic field of a superconducting coil; provides very fast power support.
Solid Particle Erosion	Material loss caused by repeated impact of solid particles on a surface at high speed.
Superconducting Magnetic Energy Storage	A high-power storage technology that stores energy in the magnetic field of a superconducting coil.
SVM	A supervised learning method that finds a maximum-margin decision boundary; can use kernels for nonlinear separation.
Swarm Intelligence	Optimization methods inspired by collective behavior in nature (e.g., flocks, swarms, packs).
Ti6Al4V Alloy	A widely used titanium alloy (Ti-6Al-4V) valued for high strength-to-weight ratio and corrosion resistance.
TIDSMC	A sliding-mode controller that uses a tilt-integral-derivative structure (tilted proportional action) within the sliding-surface design.
Time Series	A sequence of measurements ordered in time, often modeled with temporal dependencies.
Unimodal Function	An objective function with a single optimum; often used to test exploitation capability.
Voltage Regulation	Control actions that keep bus voltages within acceptable limits.
Wind Energy	Electricity generation that converts wind kinetic energy into electrical power using turbines.
WOA	Whale optimization algorithm. A bio-inspired optimizer that models the bubble-net hunting strategy of humpback whales.
Wrapper Method	A feature-selection strategy that evaluates subsets using a predictive model's performance as the selection criterion.
WSN	A network of spatially distributed sensors that communicate wirelessly to monitor physical or environmental conditions.

Index

Note: Page numbers followed by "*f*" indicate figures, "*t*" indicate tables, and "*b*" indicate boxes.

A

Adaptive grey wolf optimization (AGWO), 2–3, 168–169
Ackley function, 517–518, 602
ACO. *See* Ant colony optimization (ACO)
Adaptive coefficient control for phased convergence, 88, 89*f*
Adaptive control parameter mechanisms, 76–77
Adaptive convergence pressure, 79
Adaptive grey wolf optimization (AGWO), 2–3, 168–169
Adaptive grey wolf-teaching-learning-based hybrid algorithm, 701–702
Adaptive Grey Wolf–Teaching-Learning-Based Optimization (AGW-TLBO), 697
Adaptive hybrid differential grey wolf optimization (AHDGWO), 600
Adaptive learning GWO (ALGWO), 395
Adaptive learning mechanism, 28–29
Adaptive noise canceller (ANC), 578
  design, 578*f*, 579–580
    baseline wander suppression, 579
    white Gaussian noise elimination, 579–580
  optimized ANC to enhance PPG signal, 578–580
  qualitative visualization of ANC effectiveness on PPG, 582, 582*f*
  quantitative assessment of ANC techniques on PPG, 582–584, 583*f*
Adaptive search GWO (ASMOGWO), 3
Adaptively balanced grey wolf optimization (ABGWO), 168–169
Adult-onset diabetes, 149
Adult-Pup Teaching–Learning Based Interactive GWO (AP-TLB-IGWO), 169–170
Advanced GWO (AGWO), 170
African Vulture Optimization Algorithm (AVOA), 150, 154
AGC. *See* Automatic generation control (AGC)
AHDGWO. *See* Adaptive hybrid differential grey wolf optimization (AHDGWO)
AHL. *See* Average hourly load (AHL)
AI. *See* Artificial intelligence (AI)
Algorithms, comparison of, 612
ALGWO. *See* Adaptive learning GWO (ALGWO)
Alpha assets, 468
Alpha wolves (AW), 121–122, 303, 404–405, 425–426, 659
Alternaria solani, 103, 105
Analysis of variance (ANOVA), 328, 339–342, 340*t*
ANC. *See* Adaptive noise canceller (ANC)
ANFIS-IA-GWO model, 447–448
Anomaly-based detection, 389
Anomaly-based IDS, 290
ANOVA. *See* Analysis of variance (ANOVA)
Ant colony optimization (ACO), 121, 261, 298, 315–316, 480, 599, 609–610, 610*f*, 628
Aquifers, 447
Artificial bee colony (ABC), 121, 261, 268, 276, 357, 600, 611–612, 612*f*
Artificial intelligence (AI), 104, 124, 327, 459, 479, 719
ASMOGWO. *See* Adaptive search GWO (ASMOGWO)
Asset classification, 464–465
Asymmetric double-depth grooves (AG), 329
ATE. *See* Average treatment effect (ATE)
Attack phase, 482
Attacking behavior, 660–661
Attacking phase, 607
Attacking prey, 4, 230, 302, 648
Automatic generation control (AGC), 476
Average convergence curves, 177
Average cost per group, 374
Average hourly load (AHL), 727
Average treatment effect (ATE), 356–357
AVOA. *See* African Vulture Optimization Algorithm (AVOA)
AW. *See* Alpha wolves (AW)

B

Banana function, 602
Base Station (BS), 377
Baseline Biogeography-based optimization (bBBO), 111
Baseline football optimization algorithm (bFbOA), 111
Baseline Genetic algorithm (bGA), 111
Baseline grey wolf optimizer (bGWO), 111
Baseline Multiverse optimizer (bMVO), 111
Baseline Particle swarm optimization (bPSO), 111
Baseline Sine cosine algorithm (bSBO), 111
Baseline wander (BW), 577, 579
Bayesian PDF (BPDF), 560
BBO. *See* Biogeography-based optimization (BBO)
BCDI. *See* Bridge condition deterioration index (BCDI)
Behavioral risk factor surveillance system (BRFSS), 150, 156–157
BEMA. *See* Binary exchange market algorithm (BEMA)
Benchmark functions, 171
  mathematical definitions of, 602–604
  used in experiments, 604*t*
Benchmark test functions, 613–614
Beta assets, 468
Beta expansion factor, 496
Beta wolf (BW), 121–122, 404–405, 466, 659
BGWO. *See* Binary grey wolf optimizer (BGWO)
Bi-level thresholding, 29
Bi-metric dimension (BMD), 628–629
  Bi-representation of G, 629*f*
  hybrid ACO-BGWO algorithm for, 636*f*
  hybrid ant colony optimization-BGWO algorithm for, 634
Bi-resolving set, 629
Bibliometric analysis
  data analysis, 124–143
  grey wolf optimizer, 121–123
  method, 123–124
    analysis tools used, 124
    database used, 123
    search criteria and publication year range, 123
Binary exchange market algorithm (BEMA), 151
Binary grey wolf optimization, 590
Binary grey wolf optimizer (BGWO), 54, 385, 628
  future direction, 644
  grey wolf optimizer algorithm, 630–631, 630*f*
  numerical results, 639–641
    EMD of some generalized antiprism graphs, 643*f*
    time and space complexity, 641
  problem definition, 628–630
    BMD, 629
    DMD, 628–629
    EMD, 629–630
    MD, 628
    MMD, 630
  proposed method, 631–634

application BGWO algorithm for MD problem, 633
hybrid ant colony optimization-BGWO algorithm for BMD problem, 634
hybrid ant colony optimization-BGWO algorithm for DMD problem, 634
modified BGWO algorithm for EMD problems, 634
modified BGWO algorithm for MMD problems, 634
Binary hybrid GWO models, 122–123
Bio-inspired optimization algorithms, 461
Biogeography-based optimization (BBO), 75
Bioinformatics, 510, 608
Biological inspiration, 121–122, 481, 659–660
BMD. *See* Bi-metric dimension (BMD)
Boxplot analysis, 203
BPDF. *See* Bayesian PDF (BPDF)
BRFSS. *See* Behavioral risk factor surveillance system (BRFSS)
Bridge condition database, 210
Bridge condition deterioration index (BCDI), 210
Brownian motion, 495–496
Budget constrained allocation, 357

C

Canadian Institute for Cyber security (CIC), 292–293
Canis lupus. See Grey wolves (*Canis lupus*)
Carrier sense multiple access with collision avoidance (CSMA/CA), 382
CastNet3D, 260–261
CATE. *See* Conditional average treatment effect (CATE)
Centro-symmetric friction model (CSFM), 418
CG-GWO, 173
CH lifetime index (CLI), 379
Chaos-enhanced GWO (CGWO), 54
Chaotic GWO (CGWO), 316
Chaotic perturbations, 169
"Chattering" phenomenon, 413
CI. *See* Cohort intelligence (CI)
Class frequency, 723
Classical adaptive algorithms, 577–578
Classical laminated plate theory (CLPT), 239
CLI. *See* CH lifetime index (CLI)
Cloud computing, 460
CLPT. *See* Classical laminated plate theory (CLPT)
Cluster Head (CH), 377
Cluster-based routing, 377
Clustering, 612
clustering-based fault tolerance techniques, 382
GWO-based clustering techniques, 379–382, 395–397
CMA. *See* Combines covariance matrix adaptation (CMA)
CNNs. *See* Convolutional neural networks (CNNs)
Coefficient of determination (R), 213
Coefficient of friction (COF), 329
COF. *See* Coefficient of friction (COF)
Cohen's d test, 733
Cohort intelligence (CI), 330
Combines covariance matrix adaptation (CMA), 318
Command velocity, look-ahead point respect to, 651
Commonality, 511
Composition functions, 184–190
convergence analysis on, 187–190, 189*f*
stability analysis on, 190
statistical analysis on, 187
Computational biology, 510
Computational complexity, 155, 365–366
analysis, 173, 443, 702
of GWOFSO, 497
and memory analysis, 5
of RCGWO, 688–690
Computational cost analysis, 584
Computational time analysis, 286, 369–370, 370*t*
Concurrent power distribution systems
applying GWO and GWO-SIDER approach to PHEDC power demand dataset, 728–731
experimental details, 727
methodology for optimal load scheduling, 720–727
related studies, 719–720
population based metaheuristics, 720
single point metaheuristics, 720
results, 727–736
using SEWA benchmark power demand dataset, 728
statistical analysis of GWO and GWO-SIDER methods considering SEWA and PHEDC power demand datasets, 728–729
Conditional average treatment effect (CATE), 356–357
Congress on Evolutionary Computation (CEC), 317–318
Conjugate gradient (CG), 555
Constant distance, look-ahead point respect to, 651
Control optimization, 609
Controllable energy sources, 475–476
Conventional filter-based techniques, 577
Conventional gradient-based LS algorithms, 275–276
Conventional optimization techniques, 683
Conventional SMC, 413
Convergence argument, 7
Convergence dynamics and stability, 76
Convergence goal (CG), 48, 98
Convergence outcomes (CG), 67
Conversion uplift modeling, 356
Convolutional neural networks (CNNs), 103, 450
Cooling schedule controls, 611
Correlation matrix, 566
Cost calculation, 494
Cost–performance–resilience trade-off model, 470, 471*f*
Coulomb-viscous model, 418
Coverage optimization, 378
GWO-based coverage optimization techniques, 392–395
role of GWO for coverage optimization in wireless sensor networks, 398–399
CP Ti, 327
CRM. *See* Customer relationship management (CRM)
Crop yield prediction, 105
Cross-dimensional insights and synthesis, 82–98
high-frequency and promising design pathways, 94–96
limitations, 97–98
mapping structural influence, 92–94
MM-centric behavioral and convergence pathways, 82–92
opportunities, 97–98
overview of analytical scope and path distribution, 82, 88*f*
strategic design patterns, 96–97
Crossover, 509, 590, 607–608
CSFM. *See* Centro-symmetric friction model (CSFM)
Current velocity, look-ahead point respect to, 651
Current–voltage curve (I–V curve), 196–197, 199
Curse of dimensionality, 606
Customer relationship management (CRM), 459
Cutting-edge optimization techniques, 557
Cybersecurity, 461

D

D-GWA. *See* Discrete GWO algorithm (D-GWA)
Daily optimization problems, common characteristics of, 663
Data
mining, 510
normalization, 154
preprocessing, 211
study selection and data extraction, 47–48
Data analysis, 124–143
citation analysis of publications based on work produced, 139–140
citation issues of publications at micro level, 133–134, 133*t*
coauthorship analysis, 137, 138*f*
country distribution of publications, 127–130, 130*t*
distribution
of institutions with group-authored publications, 136
of publications according to language, 135
of publications by research category, 127
of publications over years, 124
of WoS categories, 124, 125*f*
document type distribution of publications, 124–125, 126*t*
evaluation of most cited organizations, 138
funding institutions, 136

link analysis
between most cited journals, 142
between most used keywords, 142–143
linkage analysis of countries among most cited coauthored publications, 139
Meso distribution of publications' citation topics, 131–132, 132*t*
open access distribution of publications, 135–136
publications on sustainable development goals, 136–137
publisher distribution of publications, 130–131
research profiles, 127
WoS index distributions, 125–126, 127*t*
Database, 123, 210–211
categorical feature statistics for bridge, 213*t*
continuous feature statistics for bridge, 213*t*
description, 105–109, 292–293, 613–614
disease categories, 105
features and attributes of, 106
objective and importance of dataset, 106
overview of, 105
significance of weather-based prediction, 106–109, 106*f*
input and output variable descriptions, 211*t*
reference, 614
Dataset, 156, 156*t*, 290
DB. *See* Dynamic behavior (DB)
DBLP dataset, 709–710
DCR. *See* Direct current resistivity (DCR)
DD models. *See* Double-diode models (DD models)
DDR4 RAM, 32 GB of, 613
DE. *See* Differential evolution (DE)
Decision trees, 150
Decision-making, for optimal design, 547–548
Deep learning (DL), 104, 289–290
dataset description, 105–109
experimental setup, 112–113
evaluation metrics, 112–113
preprocessing, 112
training protocols and parameter settings, 112
feature selection, 111
integration of GWO with ML and DL classifiers, 291
literature review, 104–105
methodology, 109–111
predictive models, 109–110
hybrid grey wolf and football optimization algorithm, 110–111
K-nearest neighbors, 109
model selection, 110
neural network, 109
random forest, 109
support vector machine, 109
results, 113–117
feature selection performance, 113, 113*t*
performance of models after feature selection, 113, 115*t*
performance of models before feature selection, 113
techniques, 103
Delta assets, 468
Delta matrix, 634
Delta wolves (DW), 404–405, 466–467, 660
Demand-side management (DSM), 720
Demand-supply schedule problem, 719
Denavit-Hartenberg convention (D-H convention), 415
Dense low-depth grooves (DLDG), 329
Detection rate (DR), 389, 392
Deterministic models, 209
Detour metric dimension (DMD), 628–629
cycle graph, 628*f*
hybrid ant colony optimization-BGWO algorithm for, 633*f*, 634
Deviant adjust, 723
DHL. *See* Dimension learning-based hunting (DHL)
Diabetes, 150–151
evaluation and results, 155–162
dataset, 156, 156*t*
evaluation based on iteration, 157
evaluation based on number of features, 157–162
evaluation based on number of k, 157, 159*t*
proposed model, 151–155, 152*f*
binary solutions, 154
classification algorithm, 155
computational complexity, 155
creating initial population, 153–154
data normalization, 154
evaluation criteria, 155
fitness function, 155
update solutions, 154
Diabetes mellitus, 149–150
Differential evolution (DE), 67, 196, 261, 276, 298, 314, 344, 578, 599, 654
comparison of ANC methods optimized by, 583*t*
optimal control variables used for, 580*t*
performance comparison of, 615*t*
Digital technologies, 587
Dimension learning-based hunting (DHL), 279, 358
Dimensionality, 606
Direct current resistivity (DCR), 555–556, 567–570
Discrete GWO algorithm (D-GWA), 392
Distance-Based Stable Clustering using GWO (DBSC-GWO), 379
Distance-Based Stable Connected Dominating Set using GWO (DBSCDS-GWO), 379, 397
Distribution grid, 719, 727
Distribution network, 719, 727
Diversity-enhanced strategy grey wolf optimizer (DSGWO), 168–169, 173
DL. *See* Deep learning (DL)
DLDG. *See* Dense low-depth grooves (DLDG)
DMD. *See* Detour metric dimension (DMD)
Dominator lifetime index (DLI), 379
Double anchor SCAN (DASCAN), 386
Double-diode models (DD models), 195
obtained results for, 202–206
of photovoltaic module, 196–197
equivalent circuits of, 196*f*
DR. *See* Detection rate (DR)
DSGWO. *See* Diversity-enhanced strategy grey wolf optimizer (DSGWO)
DSM. *See* Demand-side management (DSM)
DW. *See* Delta wolves (DW)
Dynamic behavior (DB), 48
adaptive control parameter mechanisms, 76–77
convergence dynamics and stability, 76
of GWO variants, 76–78
leadership modeling and influence dynamics, 77
mechanisms, 67
memory, elite learning, and historical feedback, 77–78
population structure and diversity regulation, 78
reflection on A-F, 78
trajectory behavior and landscape sampling, 77
Dynamic model, 417, 418*t*
equation of motion, 417–418
of UR5 robot manipulator, 415–418
Dynamic performance analysis, 429–430

E

Economic dispatch control (EDC), 479–480
EDC. *See* Economic dispatch control (EDC)
Edge metric dimension (EMD), 628–630, 634, 637*f*
EDGWO. *See* Elite-driven GWO (EDGWO)
EECMIGWO. *See* Energy-efficient coverage method based on IGWO algorithm (EECMIGWO)
Efficient and robust GWO (ERGWO), 170
Efficient multiobjective optimization strategies, quest for, 529
EGWO. *See* Enhanced grey wolf optimizer (EGWO). *See* Experienced GWO (EGWO). *See* Extended grey wolf optimizer (EGWO)
EIS. *See* Enterprise information system (EIS)
Elastic settlement, 493
Electric motor, 533
Electric vehicles, 528–530
comprehensive sensitivity analysis, 538–540
decision variables in comprehensive sensitivity analysis, 539*f*
design parameters and their lower/upper bounds, 539*t*
results of, 540*t*
sensitivity analysis of objective functions, 540*f*
contributions, 529–530
general overview, 528–529
in-wheel powertrain configuration with hub-motors, 527*f*
powertrain configuration with central motor and MTU, 527*f*
initial sizing and power formulation, 530–533
complete sizing equation, 533

geometric definition of overlap area, 531–532
idealized power calculation, 531
initial electromagnetic design of motor, 530*f*
peak back-EMF derivation, 531
peak current and slot geometry, 532
three-phase in-wheel hub-motor, 533*t*
lack of knowledge, 529
dichotomy of modeling approaches, 529
lack of systematic comparative analysis of metaheuristic algorithms, 529
quest for efficient multiobjective optimization strategies, 529
modeling and performance (function) evaluation, 534–535
Ansys Electronics Desktop and EMDLAB software packages, 537*f*
FEA modeling of hub-motor using EMDLAB, 535*f*
full-load flux density of motor, 536*f*
optimization for best trade-off, 540–543
organization, 530
required performance criteria, 535–538
results
comparative analysis of Pareto fronts, 546–547
comparing initial and optimal designs, 548–549
decision-making for optimal design, 547–548
insights for metaheuristic community, 549–551
Electrical machines, 529
Electrical models, 556
Electrical parameter, 538
Electronic engineering, 124
Elite learning, and historical feedback, 77–78
Elite-driven GWO (EDGWO), 3
Elitism, 511–512, 634
ELM. *See* Extreme learning machine (ELM)
Embedded hybrid grey wolf optimizer, foundation of, 698
EMD. *See* Edge metric dimension (EMD)
EMS. *See* Energy management system (EMS)
Encircling behavior, 660–661
Encircling prey, 3–4, 229, 301, 313, 589–590, 648, 685
End-effector load variations, evaluating controller performance under, 435
comparative analysis of RMS torque under varying payloads, 437*f*
MAE values
of all controllers under different end-effector loads, 436*t*
of all joints under different end-effector loads for each control strategy, 437*f*
Energy harvesting WSNs (EH-WSNs), 385
Energy management, 670–671
Energy management system (EMS), 477
Energy Optimization Approach based on MAC/Routing Cross-Layer (EOAMRCL), 382, 397
Energy storage systems (ESS), 476
Energy systems, 47
Energy-efficient coverage method based on IGWO algorithm (EECMIGWO), 395
Engineering design, 302, 609, 612
Engineering optimization, 608
Enhanced grey wolf optimizer (EGWO), 170–171, 245
Ensemble-based optimizer with covariance matrix adaptation and restart (BOwithCMAR), 318
Enterprise asset prioritization, GWO social hierarchical model for, 466–467
Enterprise information system (EIS), 459, 463–464
background and context, 459
challenge of risk in, 459–460
conceptual framework and model integration, 470–471
grey wolf social order in, 467*t*
literature review, 461–464
meta-heuristic optimization and grey wolf optimizer, 460
research gap and chapter objectives, 461
risk management, 464–466, 470*f*
asset classification, 464–465
risk assessment procedures, 465–466
risk management optimization with GWO, 466–470
Enterprise resource planning (ERP), 459
Enterprise risk optimization
grey wolf hierarchical model for, 468
GWO encircling behavior adapted for, 468*f*
Environments, iterative grey wolf jellyfish optimization (EWFAIGF), 385
Equilibrium equations, 244
ERGWO. *See* Efficient and robust GWO (ERGWO)
ERP. *See* Enterprise resource planning (ERP)
ESS. *See* Energy storage systems (ESS)
Evapotranspiration (ET_0), 452–453
Experienced GWO (EGWO), 170
Experiment settings, 592
Exploitation, 302, 314, 507, 608
Exploration, 302, 314, 491, 507, 608
Exploration–exploitation trade-off in metaheuristics, 600, 600*f*
Extended grey wolf optimizer (EGWO), 246
Extreme learning machine (ELM), 210, 214, 216–217, 389

F

F1-score (F1), 389
FA. *See* Firefly algorithm (FA)
Factor of safety (FS), 493
Faraday's Law of Induction, 531
Fatal disease, 149
Fault tolerance, 377
GWO-based fault tolerance techniques, 382–385
mechanisms, 397–398
in wireless sensor networks, 397–398
Fault-tolerant and reliable green communication framework (FRGNWS), 385
Fault-tolerant sensor scheduling (FTSS), 385
FbOA. *See* Football optimization algorithm (FbOA)
FC. *See* Fuel cell (FC)
Feasibility, 513, 655
Feature selection (FS), 111, 289, 612
algorithms used for, 111
comparative analysis of FS techniques, 296–298, 297*f*
comparison and evaluation, 111
grey wolf optimization in FS for IDS, 290–291
importance of FS in IDS, 290
methods, 587
performance, 113, 113*t*
significance of FS in predictive modeling, 111
using grey wolf optimization algorithm, 293
Feature similarity index (FSIM), 28
FEs. *See* Function evaluations (FEs)
FES. *See* Functional electrical stimulation (FES)
Fiber laser treatment, 329
Filter methods, 587
Filtered FOPID controller, 228
Financial modeling, 609
Finite impulse response (FIR), 578
FIR. *See* Finite impulse response (FIR)
Firefly algorithm (FA), 385
Fireworks algorithm (FWA), 78
First-and second-order reliability methods (FORM), 275
Fitness function, 590–591, 655
Flying squirrel algorithm (FSO), 495–496
adaptive control mechanisms and implementation, 496
aerial exploration phase, 495
hybrid grey wolf optimizer, 494–497
local search phase, 495–496
problem statement, 492–494
cost calculation, 494
optimization problem, 494
quantity calculations, 493
results, 497–504
3D schematic representations of benchmark functions, 498*f*
parameters setting of algorithms, 499*t*
unimodal test functions, 497*t*
results of hybrid GWO-FSO on benchmark problems, 498–501, 500*f*
Wilcoxon test for benchmark problems, 501*t*
results of hybrid GWO-FSO on foundation problem, 501–504, 502*f*
optimal foundation design, 503*f*
study and Wang and Kulhawy, 503*t*
FOA. *See* Football optimization algorithm (FOA)
Football optimization algorithm (FbOA), 110–111
hybrid algorithm, 110–111
overview of grey wolf optimizer, 110
Football optimization algorithm (FOA), 103
FOPID. *See* Fractional order PID (FOPID)
FOPIDSMC structures, 420–421

FORM. *See* First-and second-order reliability methods (FORM)
FOTIDSMC, 431–435, 439–440
controller, 423
structures, 422–423, 423*f*
Foundation design, 491, 492*f*
Fractional order PID (FOPID), 225–226, 228, 420
Fractional order PID with filtered version (FOPIDF version), 226
Fractional orders
controllers, 235–236
SMC, 413–414
solving linear differential equations with, 302
steps for solving linear differential equations with, 302–303
Fractional-order PIλDμ controller (FOPID controller), 413
Fractional-order TID (FOTID), 414
Frequency control strategy, 479–483
grey wolf optimizer, 480–482
intelligent PMS, 479
objectives functions, 482–483
optimal frequency control model, 479–480
Friedman test, 174–175, 177, 321–324
FS. *See* Factor of safety (FS). *See* Feature selection (FS). *See* Safety factor (FS)
FSO. *See* Flying squirrel algorithm (FSO)
FTSS. *See* Fault-tolerant sensor scheduling (FTSS)
Fuel cell (FC), 477
Function evaluations (FEs), 174, 612
Functional electrical stimulation (FES), 225
advanced control structures for FES systems, 228
grey wolf optimizer, 229–230
simulation studies and results, 230–236, 232*t*
robustness analysis, 232–236
step response analysis, 231
system, 226–228, 227*f*
advanced control structures for, 228
filtered FOPID controller, 228
fractional-order PID controller, 228
GWO-tuned controller implementation in, 230
PID with filter controller, 228
Fuzzy AHP. *See* Fuzzy analytic hierarchy process (Fuzzy AHP)
Fuzzy analytic hierarchy process (Fuzzy AHP), 385
Fuzzy rule-based leader, 79
FuzzyGWO, 173, 191
FWA. *See* Fireworks algorithm (FWA)

G

GA. *See* Genetic algorithm (GA)
GABC, 268
GABGWO, 389
Gaining-sharing knowledge-based IMODE (APGSK-IMODE), 318
Gaussian noise, 71
Gauss–Newton technique, 555
gBest. *See* Global best (gBest)
GD. *See* Gradient descent (GD)
Generative AI-assisted technologies, declaration of, 596
Genetic algorithm (GA), 47, 67, 121, 195, 276, 298, 330, 389, 476, 507–509, 528, 599, 607–608, 654
comparative analysis of, 510–515
experimental design and implementation, 515–520
benchmark functions, 515*t*
GWO parameters on performance, 519*t*
hybrid parameters on performance, 520*t*
mean ± standard deviation of best fitness values and execution times, 516*t*
parameters on performance, 519*t*
sensitivity analysis, 516–520
three algorithms on Ackley function, 517*f*
three algorithms on Griewank function, 518*f*
three algorithms on Rastrigin function, 517*f*
three algorithms on Sphere function, 516*f*
Wilcoxon signed-rank test results and Cohen's d effect sizes, 518*t*
flowchart of, 608*f*
performance comparison of, 615*t*
theoretical foundations, 508–510
typical applications of, 511*f*
Global best (gBest), 609
Good point set (GPS), 386
GPS. *See* Good point set (GPS)
Gradient descent (GD), 170
Graph theory, 627
Graphical user interface (GUI), 221
Gravitational search algorithm (GSA), 196
Gray wolf optimization genetic algorithms (GWO-GA), 315–316
Gray wolves, 121–122
Grey wolf algorithm, 467, 647
Grey wolf hierarchy model (GWHM), 467
for enterprise asset classification and risk prioritization, 468*f*
for enterprise risk optimization, 468
Grey wolf jellyfish optimization (GWJFO), 385
Grey wolf optimization (GWO), 123, 258, 404–406, 587, 589–590
2D mesh-based NoC, 258*f*
algorithm, 264, 265*b*, 314, 683–684
background on, 165–171, 167*t*, 315–319
diversification and hybridization, 315–316
early developments, 315
recent advances, 316–317, 317*f*
biological motivation, 313
case study, 292–293
dataset description, 292–293
feature selection using, 293
initial data preprocessing, 293
challenges, limitations, and future prospects of, 298
comparative analysis of feature selection techniques, 296–298, 297*f*
practical advantages of GWO-based feature selection, 298
comparison algorithms, 171–174
computational complexity analysis, 173
hyperparameter settings, 174, 174*t*
declaration of generative AI-assisted technologies, 596
different evolution variants for comparative analysis, 317–319
ensemble-based optimizer with covariance matrix adaptation and restart, 318
gaining-sharing knowledge-based IMODE, 318
LSHADE with ensemble sinusoidal adaptation and covariance Matrix learning, 319
multioperator ensemble LSHADE with restart and local search, 318
multistrategy differential evolution, 319
orthogonal LSHADE with Cauchy and sinusoidal perturbations, 319
experiment result, 262*t*, 265–270, 293–296, 319–324, 320*t*, 591–596
comparison methods, 592
computational complexity analysis, 596
considered multilabel datasets, 591*t*
datasets, 591
evaluation criteria, 319
evaluation metrics, 591–592
experiment settings, 592
experimental, 319–321, 321*t*
result, 266–270, 266*f*, 592–593
setting, 265–266
statistical test results, 321–324
grey wolf optimization in FS for IDS, 290–291
integration of GWO with ML and DL classifiers, 291
application of GWO-based feature selection to specific attack types, 291
integrate GWO with classifier, 291, 295*t*
key characteristics, 314
mapping with GWO, 263–265
grey wolves in nature, 263
GWO modelization, 263
hunting behavior simulation, 263–264
improved grey wolves, 264–265
mathematical modeling, 313–314
modeling exploration of target or exploration, 405–406
modeling mapping problem, 261–262, 262*t*
modeling process of hunting, 405
network topology and mapping problem, 259
performance analysis framework, 171–175
benchmark functions, 171
performance evaluation, 367–374, 367*t*
average cost per group, 374
computational time analysis, 369–370, 370*t*
convergence analysis, 368–369
total uplift per group, 371–373
uplift distribution analysis, 367–368
preliminaries, 588–590
binary grey wolf optimization, 590
mutual information, 588–589
preliminaries and problem formulation, 359–360

problem formulation, 359–360
uplift modeling, 359
proposed method, 590–591
proposed solutions, 360–366
modeling casual impact, 360
related work, 259–261, 356–359, 588
budget constrained allocation, 357
metaheuristics, 357–359, 358*f*
recommender systems, 356
uplift modeling, 356–357
results, 175–191
composition functions, 184–190
performance of tested algorithms on hybrid functions, 181–184
performance of tested algorithms on unimodal and multimodal functions, 175–181
solving multichoice knapsack resource allocation problem, 360–365
computational complexity, 365–366, 366*f*
improved grey wolf optimizer, 362
levy flight grey wolf optimizer, 365
memory, evolutionary operator, local search, and LPSR-based GWO, 362–365
statistical analysis, 174–175
Friedman test, 174–175
Holm post hoc test, 175
and TLBO performance comparison, 404*f*
understanding basics of IDS, 290
variants and improvements of, 167–171
acceleration and convergence boosting, 170–171
chaotic and stochastic perturbations, 169
enhanced exploration and dimensionality handling, 170
hybridization with optimization techniques, 169–170
learning-based and reinforcement mechanisms, 170
parameter adaptation and dynamic control, 168–169
specialized improvements for large-scale and engineering problems, 170
variants, 171
Grey wolf optimizer (GWO), 1, 27, 30–31, 45, 67, 78, 103, 110, 121–123, 150, 165, 168, 196, 210, 215–216, 226, 229–230, 240, 276, 289–290, 301–302, 313, 330, 355, 357, 360–362, 377, 385–386, 389, 395, 405–406, 409–410, 414, 425–427, 447, 460, 480–482, 492, 494–495, 555, 557–559, 578, 580–581, 599, 606–607, 627–628, 659, 684–685, 697, 699–700, 719, 721–723
adopted algorithms for comparison, 198, 199*t*
advantages
and applications, 302
and limitations, 122
algorithm, 230, 245–247, 278, 301–302, 630–631, 630*f*, 647–649
attacking prey, 302
encircling prey, 301
hunting, 302
searching for new prey, 302
analysis of variance analysis of laser-texturing parameters, 339–342, 340*t*
application
across five optimization domains, 666*t*
AI models, usage frequency, and application field in related studies, 455*t*
in groundwater level prediction, 447–448, 449*f*
in lake water level modeling, 450–451
in pan evaporation estimation, 452
in reference crop evapotranspiration modeling, 452–453
in streamflow estimation, 448–449
in water infiltration estimation, 449–450
applications of GWO to optimization categories, 664–672
energy management, 670–671
resource allocation, 668–669
routing, 669–670
scheduling, 667–668
applying GWO and GWO-SIDER approach to PHEDC power demand dataset, 728–731
GWO results using objective function, 728–729
GWO-SIDER results using objective function, 731
results using objective function, 731
approaches real-life optimization problems successfully, 661
attacking phase, 495
attacking prey, 648
biological inspiration, 121–122, 481, 659–660
categorizes WSN-related methods, 396*f*
classification metrics, 378–379, 379*f*
comparative analysis of, 510–515
comparison
between traditional optimization methods and, 665*t*
of ANC methods optimized by, 583*t*
comprehensive overview of GWO applications across *vs.* WSN domains, 378*f*
computational complexity and memory analysis, 5
conceptual cost–performance–resilience trade-off model, 470
convergence outcomes and justifications, 78–82
adaptive convergence pressure, 79
diversity-preserving escape, 80
formal convergence proofs, 81
leadership-driven convergence acceleration, 81
memory-guided refinement, 80
multibehavior cooperative convergence, 81
phased convergence, 79
reflection on G1–G8, 81–82, 83*t*
trajectory stabilization, 80
core mechanisms of, 660–661
encircling, hunting, and attacking behaviors, 660–661
social hierarchy, 660
cross-dimensional insights and synthesis, 82–98
daily life problems as optimization tasks, 662–664
dynamic behavior of GWO variants, 76–78
encircling phase, 494–495
encircling prey, 648, 685
model for optimized risk mitigation, 469
enhanced and hybrid versions, 122–123
evidence, 58–59
experimental design and implementation, 515–520
benchmark functions, 515*t*
GA parameters on performance, 519*t*
hybrid parameters on performance, 520*t*
mean ± standard deviation of best fitness values and execution times, 516*t*
parameters on performance, 519*t*
sensitivity analysis, 516–520
three algorithms on Ackley function, 517*f*
three algorithms on Griewank function, 518*f*
three algorithms on Rastrigin function, 517*f*
three algorithms on Sphere function, 516*f*
Wilcoxon signed-rank test results and Cohen's d effect sizes, 518*t*
experimental setup and results, 654–655
algorithm selects the optimal look-ahead with obstacles, 655*f*
metaheuristic configurations and implementation, 654
objective weights in Eq. 34. 26 and tuning protocol, 654
results, 655
exploitation phase attacking prey, 685
exploration phase searching for prey, 685
flowchart of, 606*f*
fusion of, 559–560
future work, 399
for general optimization problems, 667*b*
grey wolf hierarchical model for enterprise risk optimization, 468
GWO Football Optimization Algori, 110–111
GWO-based approaches, 398
GWO-based clustering techniques, 379–382, 396
network parameters, 381*t*
solution parameters, 380*t*
GWO-based coverage optimization, 392–395, 399
GWO-based fault tolerance techniques, 382–385
GWO-based intrusion detection techniques, 388–392, 398
GWO-based localization, 385–388, 398
GWO-SIDER results, 728
GWO-tuned controller implementation in functional electrical stimulation systems, 230
hunting, 648, 685
operation, 722–723
phase, 495

hybrid flying squirrel optimizer-based, 496–497
implications for theory and practice, 60–61
learning-driven GWO hybrids, 699
materials and methods, 330–333
laser surface texturing, 331, 332*t*
materials, 330
reciprocating sliding wear test, 331, 331*f*
roughness characterization by noncontact laser profilometer, 332–333
solid particle erosion test, 331–332
mathematical model, 122, 229–230
and working mechanism, 481–482
attacking prey, 482
encircling prey, 481
flowchart of GWO algorithm, 483*f*
hunting, 482
search for prey, 482
social hierarchy, 481, 481*f*
mathematical principles, 3–4
attacking prey phase, 4
encircling prey phase, 3–4
hunting phase, 4
search for prey phase, 4, 5*f*
social hierarchy phase, 3
methodological approach, 68–69
categorization framework, 69, 69*f*
search methodology and selection criteria, 68–69
methodology, 276–280
enhanced grey wolf optimizer, 278–279
LS reliability method, 276–277, 277*f*
metaheuristic-based line sampling, 279–280
methods, 45–48
protocol and sources, 46–47
risk of bias and synthesis, 48, 51*f*
study selection and data extraction, 47–48, 49*t*
microgrid frequency with optimal AGC, 484*f*
microgrid generated power
and load with optimal AGC, 485*f*
and load without optimal AGC, 485*f*
MM of GWO variants, 70–75
numerical examples, 280–286, 280*t*
examples, 280–286, 282*t*
numerical results, 247–253, 249*t*, 303–310, 304*t*
optimal design problems, 249–253
comparison of meta-heuristic optimizers, 304*t*
offers efficient alternative, 664
optimal control variables used for, 580*t*
optimal frequency control using, 484
optimization of controller parameters using GWO-particle swarm optimization hybrid algorithm, 424–428
grey wolf optimizer algorithm, 425–426
hybrid grey wolf optimizer-particle swarm optimization algorithm, 426–428
overall optimization process, 425*f*
particle swarm optimization algorithm, 424–425
optimization problem, 247
path following, 649–651
differential drive kinematics equations, 649–650
PP algorithm, 650–651
performance analysis, 8–23, 15*t*
MaxIt impact on GWO convergence, 17–20, 18*t*
nonlinear methods impact on GWO convergence, 8–17, 13*f*
population size impact on GWO convergence, 15*t*, 17
problem scale impact on, 20–23
performance comparison of, 615*t*
prey encirclement operation, 722
problem formulation, 240–245, 241*f*
and optimization with, 342–352, 343*f*
computational and memory complexity of GWO and hybrids, 352
experimental setup, 345–352, 347*t*, 349*f*
procedural steps for joint inversion with, 557*f*
proof of GWO convergence, 5–8
probability analysis, 8
proposed methodology for parameter extraction, 197–198, 198*f*
pure pursuit with grey wolf optimization, 651–654
generating path using grey wolf optimizer, 652–653
look-ahead selection strategy, 654
research logical flow of systematic review, 46*f*
research method, 447, 448*f*
results, 199–206, 333–342
and synthesis, 48–57, 52*t*, 55*f*
mind-map of GWO variant categories, 58*f*
obtained results for double-diode model, 202–206
obtained results for single-diode model, 199–201, 200*t*
using objective function, 728, 728*t*, 729*f*
risk management optimization with, 466–470
role for clustering in wireless sensor networks, 395–397
role for coverage optimization in wireless sensor networks, 398–399
role for fault tolerance in wireless sensor networks, 397–398
role for intrusion detection in wireless sensor networks, 398
role for localization in wireless sensor networks, 398
roughness analysis of Ti6Al4V surface laser texturing, 333–339, 333*f*
search for prey, 648–649
single and double diode models of photovoltaic module, 196–197
social hierarchical model for enterprise asset prioritization, 466–467
grey wolf social order, 466*f*
social hierarchy, 301, 646–647, 684
social operation, 721–722
solving linear differential equations with fractional orders, 302
statistical analysis of GWO and GWO-SIDER methods considering SEWA and PHEDC power demand datasets, 728–729
GWO fitness response for objective function 2using PHEDC dataset, 734*f*
GWO results for objective 2 using PHEDC dataset, 733*t*
GWO-SIDER fitness response for objective function 2 using PHEDC dataset, 734*f*
GWO-SIDER results for objective 2 using the PHEDC dataset, 733*t*
steps for solving linear differential equations with fractional orders using, 302–303
pseudo code of GWO-analytical homotopy method algorithm, 303
strengths and limitations, 60, 662
theoretical foundations, 508–510
traditional optimization techniques and GWO-based approaches across, 665*t*
typical applications of, 509*f*
understanding, 659
Grey wolf optimizer for node Localization Problem in WSNs (GWO-LPWSN), 386
Grey wolf optimizer for station placement (GWO-SP), 386
Grey wolf optimizer integrated with two-phase mutation (GWO-TPM), 169
Grey wolf optimizer-based Cluster Head (GWO-CH), 379–380
Grey wolf optimizer-particle swarm optimization (GWOPSO), 398, 424, 555–556
BPDF distributions of, 564*f*
field examples, 567–574
application of joint inversion of DCR and MTT data, 570
application of joint inversion of MTT and DCR data, 567–569
application of joint inversion of MTT and RF data, 570–574
method, 556–561
forward modeling, 556
inverse modeling, 556–560
statistical method, 560–561
procedural steps for joint inversion with, 558*f*
results, 561–574
sample distribution of, 564*f*
synthetic examples, 561–567
application of joint inversion of synthetic DCR and MTT data, 561–562
application of joint inversion of synthetic MTT and RF data, 562–567
Grey wolves (*Canis lupus*), 30, 110, 165, 229–230, 263, 313, 482, 627–628, 648, 659
Grey wolves optimizer (GWO), 476
offshore microgrid model, 477–478
optimal power management and frequency control strategy, 479–483
simulation results, 483–488, 484*t*
combined multistage power management system-fuel cell, 487–488

intelligent power management system, 485–486
optimal frequency control using grey wolf optimizer, 484
Grid-type structures, 240–242
Griewank function, 602–604
Groundwater level prediction, application of grey wolf optimizer in, 447–448, 449*f*
GSA. *See* Gravitational search algorithm (GSA)
GUI. *See* Graphical user interface (GUI)
GWHM. *See* Grey wolf hierarchy model (GWHM)
GWJFO. *See* Grey wolf jellyfish optimization (GWJFO)
GWLBC, 382
GWO-GA. *See* Gray wolf optimization genetic algorithms (GWO-GA)
GWOFSO
computational complexity of, 497
optimization and unimodal benchmark function results obtained from, 499*t*
optimization foundation problem results obtained from, 501*t*
GWOTAB, 265

H

Hamming loss, 591, 592*t*
Harris Hawks Optimization (HHO), 75, 151, 276
Harris Hawks Optimization based on Dynamic Random Jump (DRM-HHO), 151
Healthcare, 47
Hebbian Learning rule (HL rule), 723
HESS. *See* Hybrid energy storage systems (HESS)
HHO. *See* Harris Hawks Optimization (HHO)
Hierarchical roles, 313
High-cost models, 529
High-dimensional problems, 606
High-fidelity, 529
High-frequency and promising design pathways, 94–96
dominant pathways, 94–95
underexplored but promising paths, 95–96
High-speed models, 529
Higher-order shear deformation theory (HSDT), 239
Hill model, 226
Hill muscle model, 226
Hillstrom dataset, 367
HL rule. *See* Hebbian Learning rule (HL rule)
Holm post hoc test, 175, 187
Homotopy analytical method (HAM), 302
numerical results, 303–310, 304*t*
comparison of meta-heuristic optimizers, 304*t*
solving linear differential equations with fractional orders, 302
steps for solving linear differential equations with fractional orders using GWO algorithm, 302–303
Hourly load scheduling problem, 724–727, 725*f*
assumptions, 726
datasets, 726–727
HSDT. *See* Higher-order shear deformation theory (HSDT)
Hub-motor, 534
Human health, 149
Hunting, 229–230, 278, 302, 648, 685
behavior, 263–264, 314, 660–661
modeling process of, 405
operation, 722–723
phase, 4, 607
Hybrid (DLDG AG), 329
Hybrid AGW-TLBO, 697, 701
Hybrid algorithm, 110–111
Hybrid cooperative search, 97
Hybrid energy storage systems (HESS), 476
Hybrid functions, performance of tested algorithms on, 181–184
convergence analysis on, 184
stability analysis on, 184
statistical analysis on, 181
Hybrid grey wolf, 110–111
hybrid algorithm, 110–111
overview of FbOA, 110
overview of grey wolf optimizer, 110
Hybrid grey wolf optimizer, 494–497
approaches, 57
computational complexity of GWOFSO, 497
construction of model, 214
data preprocessing, 211
database, 210–211
extreme learning machine, 214
FSO, 495–496
graphical user interface, 221
grey wolf optimizer, 215–216, 494–495
hybrid flying squirrel optimizer-based grey wolf optimizer, 496–497
hybrid GWO-particle swarm optimization algorithm, 426–428, 429*t*
algorithm, 426–427
approach, 414
flow chart of hybrid GWO-PSO algorithm, 427*f*
hybrid GWOFSO, 497
hybrid stochastic paint optimizer and GWO with ELM, 216–217
performance metrics, 213–214
coefficient of determination, 213
mean absolute error, 214
mean squared error, 213–214
root mean squared error, 214
problem statement, 492–494
cost calculation, 494
optimization problem, 494
quantity calculations, 493
results, 217–221, 219*f*, 497–504
3D schematic representations of benchmark functions, 498*f*
parameters setting of algorithms, 499*t*
unimodal test functions, 497*t*
results of hybrid GWO-FSO on benchmark problems, 498–501, 500*f*
Wilcoxon test for benchmark problems, 501*t*
results of hybrid GWO-FSO on foundation problem, 501–504, 502*f*
optimal foundation design, 503*f*
study and Wang and Kulhawy, 503*t*
stochastic paint optimizer, 214–215
Hybrid GWO-based sunflower optimization (HGWSFO), 380–382
Hybrid stochastic paint optimizer and GWO with ELM, 216–217
Hybrid techniques, 385
Hybrid versions, enhanced and, 122–123
Hybridization with optimization techniques, 169–170
Hybridized equation-level designs, 92
Hybridized mathematical models, 74–75
formal abstract model, 75
representative variants and mechanisms, 75
Hybridized models, 95
Hyperparameter settings, 174, 174*t*

I

IAE. *See* Integral of Absolute Error (IAE)
IBest. *See* Local best (IBest)
IC-HCL. *See* Intracrustal high-conductivity layer (IC-HCL)
ICEEWT-IGWO-GRU model, 449
IDS. *See* Intrusion detection system (IDS)
2017 IEEE Congress on Evolutionary Computation (CEC 2017), 2, 8
IEEE Xplore, SpringerLink, ScienceDirect (Elsevier), 68
IGWO. *See* Improved grey wolf optimizer (IGWO). *See* Inspired GWO (IGWO)
IGWO-CS. *See* Improved GWO with communication strategy (IGWO-CS)
ILP. *See* Integer linear programming (ILP)
Image processing, 609
Image segmentation, 27
IMDB dataset, performance analysis on, 705–708, 705*t*, 706*t*, 707*t*
convergence curves for each skill set for, 709*f*, 711*f*
team cost across skill set sizes for competing algorithms on, 708*f*, 710*f*
Improved grey wolf optimizer (IGWO), 169–170, 283, 358, 362, 382, 392, 395
Improved GWO with communication strategy (IGWO-CS), 386
In-wheel powertrain technology, 527–528
Industrial control systems, 460
Industrial sensor networks (ISNs), 392
Information system, 459, 463
Initial data preprocessing, 293
Initial designs, 548–549, 550*t*
Input variables, 210
Inspired GWO (IGWO), 170
Insulin-dependent diabetes mellitus, 149
Integer linear programming (ILP), 259–260
Integral of Absolute Error (IAE), 482
Integral of Squared Error (ISE), 482
Integral of Time multiplied Absolute Error (ITAE), 482

Integral of Time multiplied Squared Error (ITSE), 482
Intel Core i7–12700K, 613
Intellectual property (IP), 257
Intelligent control methods, 420
Intelligent PMS, 479
Intelligent power management system, 479, 485–486
  microgrid frequency
    with combined optimal PMS-FC, 487*f*
    with FC and with PMS, 486*f*
  microgrid generated power and load with intelligent PMS, 486*f*
Internet of Things (IoT), 47, 460
Interquartile range (IQR), 705
Intracrustal high-conductivity layer (IC-HCL), 573
Intrusion detection in wireless sensor networks, role of GWO for, 398
Intrusion detection system (IDS), 289, 377
  challenges, limitations, and future prospects of GWO in, 298
    challenges and limitations, 298
    future prospects, 298
    scalability and distributed deployment, 298
  grey wolf optimization in FS for, 290–291
    fitness function design, 291
    optimization flow, 291, 292*f*
    representation of candidate solutions, 291
  integration of GWO with ML and DL classifiers, 291
  understanding basics of, 290
    challenges in IDS datasets, 290
    importance of FS in, 290
    types of, 290
Intrusion detection techniques, GWO-based, 388–392
IOBL-GWO algorithm, 173
IoT. *See* Internet of Things (IoT)
IP. *See* Intellectual property (IP)
IQR. *See* Interquartile range (IQR)
ISE. *See* Integral of Squared Error (ISE)
ISNs. *See* Industrial sensor networks (ISNs)
ITAE. *See* Integral of Time multiplied Absolute Error (ITAE)
ITSE. *See* Integral of Time multiplied Squared Error (ITSE)

J

JAYA algorithm, 330
Joint torque inputs, evaluating controller performance under white noise disturbances in, 437–443
Juvenile-onset diabetes, 149

K

K-nearest neighbors (KNN), 104, 109, 150
Kapur's method, 29
Kinematic model, 415–417
  D-H convention of UR5, 415*f*
  DH parameters of UR5, 416*t*
  equation of motion, 417–418
  of UR5 robot manipulator, 415–418
Kirchhoff–Love hypothesis, 242
KNN. *See* K-nearest neighbors (KNN)

L

Lake water level modeling, application of GWO in, 450–451
Landscape sampling, trajectory behavior and, 77
Language, distribution of publications according to, 135
Laser powder bed fusion (LPBF), 330
Laser processing, 328, 337–339
Laser shock peening (LSP), 328
Laser surface texturing (LST), 327, 331, 332*t*
Laser surface treatment (LST), 327–329
Laser-texturing parameters, analysis of variance analysis of, 339–342, 340*t*
Leader influence reweighting and generalized hierarchy, 72–73
Leadership
  leadership-driven convergence acceleration, 81
  modeling and influence dynamics, 77
  reweighting
    and hierarchical control, 89
    and phasing, 96
Learner phase, 407
Learning, 73
Learning-based and reinforcement mechanisms, 170
Learning-driven grey wolf optimizer, 90–91
Levenberg–Marquardt technique (LM technique), 555
Lévy flight dynamics, 495
Levy flight grey wolf optimizer (LGWO), 358–359, 365
Levy function, 604
LFC. *See* Load frequency control (LFC)
LGWO. *See* Levy flight grey wolf optimizer (LGWO)
LIDS. *See* Lightweight IDS (LIDS)
Lightweight IDS (LIDS), 389
Likelihood function, 560
Line sampling (LS), 275–277, 277*f*
Linear differential equations
  solving linear differential equations
    with fractional orders, 302
    steps with fractional orders using GWO algorithm, 302–303
Linear population size reduction (LPSR), 358, 362–365
Linear programming (LP), 663
'Linspace' function, 726
LM technique. *See* Levenberg–Marquardt technique (LM technique)
Load frequency control (LFC), 476
Load-balanced clustering, 382
Local best (lBest), 609
Localization
  GWO-based localization techniques, 385–388
  role of GWO for localization in wireless sensor networks, 398
Long short-term memory network (LSTM network), 389
Look-ahead point
  respect to command velocity, 651
  respect to constant distance, 651
  respect to current velocity, 651
  selection of, 650–651
Look-ahead selection strategy, 654
Low power factor, 538
Lower-accuracy models, 529
LP. *See* Linear programming (LP)
LPBF. *See* Laser powder bed fusion (LPBF)
LPSR. *See* Linear population size reduction (LPSR)
LS. *See* Line sampling (LS)
LSHADE with ensemble sinusoidal adaptation and covariance Matrix learning, 319
LSP. *See* Laser shock peening (LSP)
LSTM-GWO hybrid model, 447–448
Lyapunov-based stability analysis, 424

M

MAC. *See* Medium access control (MAC)
Machine learning (ML), 104, 133–134, 151, 210, 290–291, 302, 510, 514, 608–609, 719
Machine learning with modified GWO (MLGWO), 389
Macro-F1, 591, 593*t*, 595*f*
MAE. *See* Mean absolute error (MAE)
Magnetic equivalent circuit (MEC), 528
Main Himalayan Thrust (MHT), 574
Markov chain formulation, 79
MAs. *See* Metaheuristic algorithms (MAs)
Mathematical inverse theory, 556
Mathematical modeling (MM), 67, 96, 313–314
  encircling prey, 313
  exploitation phase, 314
  exploration phase, 314
  functional redefinition of control parameters, 71–72
    formal abstract model, 71–72
    representative variants and mechanisms, 72
  of grey wolf optimizer variants, 70–75
    algebraic reformulation of position update rule, 70–71
  hierarchical roles, 313
  hunting behavior, 314
  leader influence reweighting and generalized hierarchy, 72–73
    formal abstract model, 72
    representative variants and mechanisms, 72–73
  MM-centric behavioral and convergence pathways, 82–92
    adaptive coefficient control for phased convergence, 88, 89*f*
    algebraic innovations driving path diversity, 88
    hybridized equation-level designs, 92

leadership reweighting and hierarchical control, 89
memory-augmented and learning-driven grey wolf optimizer, 90–91
stochastic search and probabilistic convergence models, 91–92
state-augmented models, 73
formal abstract model, 73
hybridized mathematical models, 74–75
probabilistic and stochastic process formulations, 74
reflection on MM1–MM6, 75
representative variants and mechanisms, 73
Mathematical modification (MM), 48
Matlab, 408
MaxHL. *See* Maximum Hourly Load (MaxHL)
Maximum Hourly Load (MaxHL), 727
Maximum iterations (MaxIter), 614
Maximum number of iterations (MaxIt), 8, 17–20, 18*t*
Maximum power point tracking (MPPT), 475–476
MaxIter. *See* Maximum iterations (MaxIter)
MCKP. *See* Multiple-choice knapsack problem (MCKP)
MCS method. *See* Monte Carlo simulation method (MCS method)
MD. *See* Metric dimension (MD)
Mean absolute error (MAE), 8, 213–214, 430–432, 439
Mean model, 561
Mean squared error (MSE), 213–214, 579–580
MEC. *See* Magnetic equivalent circuit (MEC)
Mechanical transmission unit (MTU), 526–527
Medical data, 150
Medium access control (MAC), 382
MELGWO. *See* Memory, evolutionary operator, LPSR based GWO (MELGWO)
Memory, 73
analysis, 5
computational and memory complexity of GWO and hybrids, 352
evolutionary operator, local search, and LPSR-based GWO, 362–365
and historical feedback, 77–78
memory-augmented models, 95
memory-augmented refinement and stabilization, 97
memory-augmented-driven grey wolf optimizer, 90–91
memory-guided refinement, 80
swarm, 362–365
Memory, evolutionary operator, LPSR based GWO (MELGWO), 358
Memory-based GWO (mGWO), 316
Meso distribution of publications' citation topics, 131–132, 132*t*
Metaheuristic algorithms (MAs), 1, 27, 45, 121, 154, 165, 276, 377, 389, 404, 460, 476, 514–515, 529, 683, 697
Metaheuristic(s), 357–359, 358*f*, 659, 683
algorithms overview, 606–612
ant colony optimization, 609–610
artificial bee colony, 611–612
genetic algorithm, 607–608
GWO, 606–607
particle swarm optimization, 608–609
simulated annealing, 610–611
background and motivation, 599
comparison of algorithms, 612
configurations and implementation, 654, 655*t*, 656*t*
contribution and objectives, 601
experimental results, 612–622
exploration–exploitation trade-off in, 600
insights for metaheuristic community, 549–551
literature review, 599–600
mathematical definitions of benchmark functions, 602–604
metaheuristic-based line sampling, 279–280
optimization, 301, 460, 491
organization, 601–602
population based metaheuristics, 720
properties, 604–606
simulation environment, 613–620
algorithms *vs*. number of FEs, 621*f*
all algorithms across selected benchmark functions, 623*t*
average computational for each algorithm, 616*f*
average ranks of algorithms based on Friedman test, 623*t*
benchmark test functions and dataset description, 613–614
best fitness values *vs*. computational time, 619*f*
best *vs*. mean fitness values, 617*f*
convergence behavior, 621
mean and standard deviation of final fitness values for all algorithms, 618*f*
mean fitness values for eight metaheuristic algorithms, 620*f*
mean fitness values *vs*. computational time, 619*f*, 620*f*
number of fitness evaluations, 616*f*
Pairwise statistical comparison, 623*t*
standard deviation *vs*. computational time, 618*f*
statistical comparison, 621–622
STD of fitness values across all algorithm-function pairs, 617*f*
trajectory of population diversity, 622*f*
single point metaheuristics, 720
Metric dimension (MD), 627–628, 633
MG. *See* Microgrid (MG)
mGWO. *See* Memory-based GWO (mGWO)
MGWO. *See* Modified GWO (MGWO)
Micro-F1, 591–592, 593*t*, 595*f*
Microgrid (MG), 475, 479
MILP. *See* Mixed-integer linear programming (MILP)
MinHL. *See* Minimum Hourly Load (MinHL)
Minimum Hourly Load (MinHL), 727
Minimum redundancy maximum relevance (mRMR), 587
Mixed metric dimension (MMD), 628, 630
modified BGWO algorithm for MMD problems, 634, 638*f*, 639*t*
of some generalized antiprism graphs, 643*f*
Mixed metric generator, 630
Mixed-integer linear programming (MILP), 357
ML. *See* Machine learning (ML)
MLGWO. *See* Machine learning with modified GWO (MLGWO)
MLP. *See* Multilayer perceptron (MLP)
mLSHADE-RL. *See* Multioperator ensemble LSHADE with restart and local search (mLSHADE-RL)
MLT. *See* Multilevel thresholding (MLT)
MM. *See* Mathematical modeling (MM). *See* Mathematical modification (MM)
MMD. *See* Mixed metric dimension (MMD)
Modality, 604
Modern digital ecosystem, 463
Modified GWO (MGWO), 315, 389
Modified PSO (MPSO), 408
MODOP. *See* Multiobjective design optimization problem (MODOP)
MOGWO. *See* Multiobjective grey wolf optimizer (MOGWO)
Monte Carlo simulation method (MCS method), 275
MOORA. *See* Multiobjective optimization method using ratio analysis (MOORA)
MOPSO. *See* Multiobjective particle swarm optimization (MOPSO)
Movement equations, 7
MPPT. *See* Maximum power point tracking (MPPT)
mRMR. *See* Minimum redundancy maximum relevance (mRMR)
MS-DE. *See* Multistrategy DE (MS-DE)
MSE. *See* Mean square error (MSE)
MSGWO. *See* Multistrategy GWO (MSGWO)
MTT data, application of joint inversion of, 561–562, 567–574
MTU. *See* Mechanical transmission unit (MTU)
Multilayer perceptron (MLP), 104
Multilevel thresholding (MLT), 27, 29–30
Multimodal functions, 604
performance of tested algorithms on, 175–181
convergence analysis on, 177–179, 179*f*
stability analysis on, 180–181, 180*f*
statistical analysis on, 177
Multiobjective design optimization problem (MODOP), 540–541
MOGWO solver for, 541
MOPSO solver for, 541–543
NSGA-II solver for, 543
Multiobjective grey wolf optimizer (MOGWO), 54, 315, 386, 529–530
implemented MOGWO algorithm, 542*f*
parameters and settings of, 546*t*
solver for MODOP, 541
Multiobjective optimization method using ratio analysis (MOORA), 330
Multiobjective particle swarm optimization (MOPSO), 529–530
implemented MOPSO algorithm, 544*f*

parameters and settings of, 546*t*
solver for MODOP, 541–543
Multioperator ensemble LSHADE with restart and local search (mLSHADE-RL), 318
Multiple disturbance strategy GWO (MDS-GWO), 386
Multiple-choice knapsack problem (MCKP), 355
Multipopulation grey wolf optimizer
with adaptive exchange and shrinkage, 31–33, 32*b*
grey wolf optimizer, 30–31
mathematical formulation of MLT problem, 29–30
results, 34–42, 35*f*
GWO and MP-GWO-AES across varying threshold values, 37*t*
statistical comparison of GWO and MP-GWO-AES, 41*t*
Multipopulation grey wolf optimizer with adaptive size reduction and solution exchange (MP-GWO-AES), 27, 34–36
Multistage power management system-fuel cell, 487–488
microgrid generated power and load with combined optimal PMS-FC, 487*f*
microgrid power deviation, 488*f*
Multistrategy DE (MS-DE), 319
Multistrategy GWO (MSGWO), 395
Mutual information, 588–589

N

Naive Bayes and Support Vector Machine (NBSVM), 392
NCOIGWO. *See* Node coverage optimization algorithm based on improved GWO (NCOIGWO)
Neighborhood function, 611
Network interfaces (NIs), 257
Network topology and mapping problem, 259
Network on chip (NoC), 257
Neural model based on SIDERs, 723
Neural network, 109, 117, 612
NeuroAMI. *See* Neuronal auditory machine intelligence (NeuroAMI)
Neuronal auditory machine intelligence (NeuroAMI), 723
model, 723–724
neural structure of, 723*f*
Newton–Raphson refinement technique (NR refinement technique), 196, 417
NIs. *See* Network interfaces (NIs)
NMI. *See* Normalized mutual information (NMI)
NoC. *See* Network-on-chip (NoC)
Node coverage optimization algorithm based on improved GWO (NCOIGWO), 392
Noncontact laser profilometer, roughness characterization by, 332–333
Nondominated Sorting Genetic Algorithm II (NSGA-II), 528–529
implemented NSGA-II algorithm, 545*f*
parameters and settings of, 546*t*
solver for MODOP, 543
Nonlinear methods on GWO convergence, impact of, 8–17, 13*f*, 14*f*
Nonseparable functions, 604–606
Normalized mutual information (NMI), 589
NR refinement technique. *See* Newton–Raphson refinement technique (NR refinement technique)
NSGA-II. *See* Nondominated Sorting Genetic Algorithm II (NSGA-II)
Null hypothesis (H_0), 175, 409–410
Numerical scoring system, 48

O

Objective function
GWO results using, 728–729, 728*t*, 729*f*
GWO-SIDER results using, 731
OBL. *See* Opposition-based learning (OBL)
Offshore microgrid model, 477–478
proposed offshore microgrid configuration, 477*f*
schematic diagram of, 478*f*
OGWO. *See* Opposition-based learning GWO (OGWO)
OLSHADE-CS. *See* Orthogonal learning-based DE (OLSHADE-CS)
Omega assets, 468
Omega wolves, 30, 425–426, 660
One-dimensional Earth model (1D Earth model), 556
1 TB NVMe solid-state drive, 613
Opposition-based learning (OBL), 75, 169–170, 382
Opposition-based learning GWO (OGWO), 2–3, 173, 382
Optical engineering, 302
Optimal designs, 548–549, 550*t*
decision-making for, 547–548
problems, 249–253
Optimal frequency control
microgrid frequency with optimal AGC, 484*f*
microgrid generated power
and load with optimal AGC, 485*f*
and load without optimal AGC, 485*f*
model, 479–480
frequency control of offshore microgrid, 480*f*
smart microgrid power management system, 479*f*
using grey wolf optimizer, 484
Optimal load scheduling, concurrent power distribution schedule systems methodology for, 720–727
GWO, 721–723
hourly load scheduling problem, 724–727
neural model based on SIDERs, 723
NeuroAMI model, 723–724
SIDERs model, 724
Optimal model, 556
Optimal power management, 479–483
grey wolf optimizer, 480–482
intelligent PMS, 479
objectives functions, 482–483
optimal frequency control model, 479–480
Optimization, 599
algorithms, 203, 507
applications of GWO to, 664–672
for best trade-off, 540–543
MOGWO solver for MODOP, 541
MOPSO solver for MODOP, 541–543
NSGA-II solver for MODOP, 543
optimization platform and settings, 543
flow, 291, 292*f*
problem, 247, 494
spread foundation assembly unit price, 494*t*
problem formulation and optimization with GWO, 342–352, 343*f*
process, 230, 426
tasks, 1
common characteristics of daily optimization problems, 663
in daily context, 662–663
daily life problems as, 662–664
GWO offers efficient alternative, 664
traditional methods fall short, 663
techniques, 507
Optimized risk mitigation, GWO encircling prey model for, 469
Orthogonal learning-based DE (OLSHADE-CS), 319
Orthogonal LSHADE with Cauchy and sinusoidal perturbations, 319
Otsu's method, 29
Output signal-to-noise ratio, 581, 584
Output weights, 210
Overlap area, geometric definition of, 531–532

P

Pabna dataset, 156
Pabna Diabetes Hospital (PDH), 156
Pan evaporation estimation, application of GWO in, 452
Parameter settings, 614, 614*t*
Pareto fronts
in 2-D, considering only two objectives, 547*f*, 548*f*, 549*f*
in 3-D, considering only three objectives, 550*f*
comparative analysis of, 546–547
Pareto-optimal solutions, 533
Particle erosion tests, 331–332
Particle swarm optimization (PSO), 47, 67, 121, 168–169, 196, 210, 261, 276, 298, 314, 330, 357, 389, 403, 414, 425, 476, 514, 555, 559, 578, 587, 599, 608–609, 654
algorithm, 424–425
comparison of ANC methods optimized by, 583*t*
flowchart of, 609*f*
fusion of, 559–560
optimal control variables used for, 580*t*
performance comparison of, 615*t*
procedural steps for joint inversion with, 558*f*
Path diversity, algebraic innovations driving, 88
pBest. *See* Personal best (pBest)

PCA. *See* Principal component analysis (PCA)
Peak back-EMF derivation, 531
Peak current, 532
Peak signal-to-noise ratio (PSNR), 27–28
Pearson correlation, 588
Performance improvements (PI), 584
Permanent magnet (PM), 530–531
Permanent magnet synchronous motor (PMSM), 528
Personal best (pBest), 609
Phased convergence, 79
PHEDC. *See* Port-Harcourt Electricity Distribution Company (PHEDC)
Photoplethysmography (PPG), 577
  algorithms employed, 580–581
    grey wolf optimizer, 580–581
  computational cost analysis, 584
  optimized ANC to enhance PPG signal, 578–580
  qualitative visualization of ANC effectiveness on, 582, 582*f*
  quantitative assessment of ANC techniques on, 582–584, 583*f*
  results, 581–584
  statistical test, 584
Photovoltaic module, single and double diode models of, 196–197
Photovoltaic technology (PV technology), 195
Phytophthora infestans, 103, 105
PI. *See* Performance improvements (PI)
PID controller. *See* Proportional-integral-derivative controller (PID controller)
PIDF. *See* Proportional-integral-derivative with filter (PIDF)
PIDSMC structures, 419–420
Piezoelectric materials, 239
Piezolaminated plates, 239–240
Pima dataset, 156
PM. *See* Permanent magnet (PM)
PMS. *See* Power management system (PMS)
PMSM. *See* Permanent magnet synchronous motor (PMSM)
Poisson's ratio, 493
Pollution-free electric motors, 526–527
Polynomial basis function, 109
Population based metaheuristics, 720
Population size, 513
Port-Harcourt Electricity Distribution Company (PHEDC), 726
  applying GWO and GWO-SIDER Approach to PHEDC power demand dataset, 728–731
  statistical analysis of GWO and GWO-SIDER methods considering SEWA and PHEDC power demand datasets, 728–729
  tariff band sequence, 726*t*
Position update rule, algebraic reformulation of, 70–71
  formal abstract model, 71
  representative variants and mechanisms, 71
Positive Predictive Value, 112–113
Posterior probability density function, 562
Potato, 103, 105
Power
  community, 719
  factor, 538
  generation units, 475
  idealized power calculation, 531
  system planning, 609
Power management system (PMS), 479
Power–voltage characteristic curves (P–V characteristic curves), 199
PP. *See* Pure pursuit (PP)
PPG. *See* Photoplethysmography (PPG)
Precision (P), 105, 112–113, 389
Prey
  encirclement operation, 722
  exploitation phase attacking, 685
  exploration phase searching for, 685
  search for, 4, 5*f*, 648–649
Principal component analysis (PCA), 290
Probabilistic convergence models, 91–92
Probabilistic models, 209
Probabilistic process formulations, 74
  formal abstract model, 74
  representative variants and mechanisms, 74
Probability analysis, 8
Probability density function, 560
Progressive disease, 149
Proportional-integral-derivative controller (PID controller), 225–226, 228, 413, 476
Proportional-integral-derivative with filter (PIDF), 225–226, 228
Proposed hybrid grey wolf and football optimization algorithm (bGWFbO), 103
PROSPERO, 46
PSH. *See* Pumped Storage Hydropower (PSH)
PSNR. *See* Peak signal-to-noise ratio (PSNR)
PSO. *See* Particle swarm optimization (PSO)
Pumped Storage Hydropower (PSH), 477
Pure pursuit (PP), 647
  algorithm, 650*f*
  experimental setup and results, 654–655
    algorithm selects the optimal look-ahead with obstacles, 655*f*
    metaheuristic configurations and implementation, 654
    objective weights in Eq. 34. 26 and tuning protocol, 654
    results, 655
  with grey wolf optimization, 651–654
  grey wolf optimizer algorithm, 647–649
    attacking prey, 648
    encircling prey, 648
    hunting, 648
    search for prey, 648–649
    social hierarchy, 647–646
  path following, 649–651
    calculation of velocity, 651
    differential drive kinematics equations, 649–650
    PP algorithm, 650–651
    selection of look-ahead point, 650–651
PV technology. *See* Photovoltaic technology (PV technology)
Python 3.10, 613

Q

QSVM. *See* Quantum support vector machine (QSVM)
Qualitative analysis, 465
Quality of service-aware GWO-based node deployment (QGND), 386
Quantitative analysis, 465
Quantity calculations, 493
Quantum support vector machine (QSVM), 392

R

Radial basis function (RBF), 109
Radio signal strength (RSS), 386
Random forest (RF), 104, 109, 291
Random trees, 150
Randomized balanced GWO (RBGWO), 169
Rastrigin function, 602
RBF. *See* Radial basis function (RBF)
RBGWO. *See* Randomized balanced GWO (RBGWO)
RCGWO
  bar chart of Friedman rank performance of, 689*f*, 690*f*
  for benchmark functions, 688*t*
  with compared methods on benchmark functions, 688*f*
  grey wolf optimizer, 684–685
  for IEEE CEC 2020 functions, 690*t*
  outcomes on benchmark functions, 687*t*
  proposed RCGWO approach, 685–690
    computational complexity of, 688–690
    pseudocode of, 686*f*
  quantitative outcomes on IEEE CEC'2020, 689*t*
  for real-world problems, 693*t*
  results, 693
  Wilcoxon signed rank test results using benchmark functions, 691*t*
  Wilcoxon signed rank test results using IEEE CEC 2020, 692*t*
Real-life optimization problems successfully, GWO approaches, 661
Received signal strength indicator (RSSI), 377
Receiver function (RF), 555–556
  application of joint inversion
    of MTT and, 570–574
    of synthetic MTT and, 562–567, 565*f*
Reciprocating sliding wear test, 331, 331*f*
Recommender systems (RS), 355
Recursive least squares (RLS), 577–578
Reinforcement learning (RL), 57
Relay nodes (RN), 385
Reluctance torque, 535–537
Renewable energy sources (RES), 195, 475, 514
Repulsion-based GWO (R-GWO), 386
RES. *See* Renewable energy sources (RES)
Revenue uplift modeling, 356
Reviewed methods, 395
RF. *See* Random forest (RF). *See* Receiver function (RF)
Risk assessment procedures, 465–466
RL. *See* Reinforcement learning (RL)
RLS. *See* Recursive least squares (RLS)

RMS. *See* Root mean square (RMS)
RMSE. *See* Root mean square error (RMSE)
RN. *See* Relay nodes (RN)
Robot manipulators, 413, 417
Robotics, 609
  dynamics, 418
  manipulators, 414
Robust control method, 430
Robustness analysis, 230–236
  robustness against
    disturbance, 233, 234*f*
    parameter change, 234–235
    reference signal, 231*t*, 235–236
Root mean square (RMS), 435, 561
Root mean squared error (RMSE), 195, 213–214, 302–303
Row uniqueness validation, 634
RS. *See* Recommender systems (RS)
RSS. *See* Radio signal strength (RSS)
RSSI. *See* Received signal strength indicator (RSSI)
RW-GWO algorithm, 173

S

S-Learner, 357
S-shaped transfer function, 154
S-wave. *See* Shear-wave (S-wave)
SA. *See* Simulated annealing (SA)
Safety factor (FS), 494
SCADA. *See* Supervisory control and data acquisition (SCADA)
Schwefel function, 604
SCM. *See* Supply chain management (SCM)
SD models. *See* Single-diode models (SD models)
SE. *See* Squeeze-and-excitation (SE)
Selection process, 607
Self-adaptive Bonomo optimizer, 240
Separability, 604–606
Separable functions, 604–606
Sequential sums of squares (Seq SS), 339–340
Series resistance (R_s), 196–197
Serviceability limit state (SLS), 492
SEWA. *See* Sharjah Electricity and Water Authority (SEWA)
SGPSO. *See* Single-directed PSO (SGPSO)
Sharjah Electricity and Water Authority (SEWA), 726
  results using SEWA benchmark power demand dataset, 728
    GWO results using objective function, 728
    GWO-SIDERs results using objective function, 728
  statistical analysis of GWO and GWO-SIDER methods considering SEWA and PHEDC power demand datasets, 728–729
Shear-wave (S-wave), 556
Shunt resistance (R_{sh}), 196–197
SI. *See* Swarm intelligence (SI)
SIDERs. *See* Sparse integer distributed encoded representations (SIDERs)
Sigma reduction factor, 496
Signature-based detection, 389
Signature-based IDS, 290
Signatures, 290
Simulated annealing (SA), 75, 268, 330, 392, 599, 610–611, 611*f*
Single diode models
  obtained results for, 199–201, 200*t*
  of photovoltaic module, 196–197
    equivalent circuits of, 196*f*
Single point metaheuristics, 720
Single-diode models (SD models), 195, 197
Single-directed PSO (SGPSO), 151
Single-hidden-layer feedforward neural networks (SLFNs), 210
Single-model approach, 357
6 degrees of freedom robot manipulators (6-DOF robot manipulators), 413
6R robot manipulators
  computational complexity analysis, 443
  dynamic performance analysis, 429–430
  evaluating controller performance
    under end-effector load variations, 435
    under white noise disturbances in joint torque inputs, 437–443
  kinematic and dynamic model of UR5 robot manipulator, 415–418
  optimization of controller parameters, 424–428
  proposed controller structures, 418–424
    FOPIDSMC structures, 420–421
    FOTIDSMC structures, 422–423
    PIDSMC structures, 419–420
    stability analysis, 423–424
    TIDSMC structures, 421–422
  rejection of external disturbances, 430–435, 432*t*
  simulation results and statistical analysis, 428–443, 430*f*
Sizing equation, 533
SLFNs. *See* Single-hidden-layer feedforward neural networks (SLFNs)
Sliding mode control (SMC), 413
Slot geometry, 532
SLS. *See* Serviceability limit state (SLS)
"Smart Grid" concept, 719
SMC. *See* Sliding mode control (SMC)
SMES. *See* Superconducting magnetic energy storage system (SMES)
Soc. *See* State of charge (Soc)
SoC. *See* System-on-chip (SoC)
Social operation, 721–722
Solar photovoltaic technology, 195
Solid particle erosion test, 331–332
Space complexity, 641
Sparse integer distributed encoded representations (SIDERs), 719
  GWO-SIDERs results using objective function, 728
  model, 724
  neural model based on, 723
Sphere function, 602
SPO. *See* Stochastic paint optimizer (SPO)
SPOGWO-ELM, 217
Spring constant (k_s), 234
Squeeze-and-excitation (SE), 104–105
Squirrel search algorithm (SSA), 169, 195
SSA. *See* Squirrel search algorithm (SSA)
SSM. *See* Supply-side management (SSM)
Stability
  analysis, 423–424
    on hybrid functions, 184
    on unimodal and multimodal functions, 180–181, 180*f*
  assessment, 190
Stagnation handling, 634
Standard deviation (std), 175
State of charge (Soc), 479
Statistical test, 584
Steepest Descent technique, 555
Stochastic averaging strategy, 71
Stochastic modeling approaches, 95
Stochastic paint optimizer (SPO), 210, 214–215
Stochastic paint optimizer algorithm (SPOGWO), 210
Stochastic perturbations, 169
Stochastic process formulations, 74
  formal abstract model, 74
  representative variants and mechanisms, 74
Stochastic search, 91–92
Stochastic trajectories with scheduling, 97
Storage devices, 476
Strategic design patterns, 96–97
  feedback-adaptive pressure, 96
  hybrid cooperative search, 97
  leadership reweighting and phasing, 96
  memory-augmented refinement and stabilization, 97
  stochastic trajectories with scheduling, 97
  time-programmed coefficient control, 96
Streamflow estimation, application of GWO in, 448–449
Structural reliability theory, 275
Structural similarity index (SSIM), 27–28
Subset accuracy, 591, 593*t*, 594*f*
Sunflower optimization (SFO), 380–382
Superconducting magnetic energy storage system (SMES), 477
Supervised machine learning models, 357
Supervisory control and data acquisition (SCADA), 392
Supply chain management (SCM), 459
Supply-side management (SSM), 720
Support vector machine (SVM), 104, 109, 150, 291, 382–385
Surface modifications, 327
Sustainable development goals, publications on, 136–137
SVM. *See* Support vector machine (SVM)
Swarm intelligence (SI), 647
Synthetic DCR, application of joint inversion of, 561–562
Synthetic MTT, application of joint inversion of, 562–567, 565*f*
System-on-chip (SoC), 257
Systematic comparative analysis of metaheuristic algorithms, lack of, 529

T

Teacher phase, 407
Teaching-learning-based optimization (TLBO), 75, 330, 407, 409–410, 697, 701
 learner phase, 407
 teacher phase, 407
Team formation, 697
Team formation optimization (TFO), 697
 literature review, 698–699
  contemporary developments, 699
  early hybridization trends, 698
  intelligent, multistage, and learning-driven GWO hybrids, 699
  transitional phase, 698–699
 mathematical modeling of methods and materials, 699–705
  AGW–teaching-learning-based hybrid algorithm, 701–702
  benchmark datasets and experimental setup, 704–705
  computational complexity analysis, 702
  GWO, 699–700
  overview of TFO problem, 704
  proposed adaptive GWO-TLBO hybrid algorithm, 703*f*
  TLBO, 701
 performance analysis on IMDB dataset, 705–708
 performance on DBLP dataset, 709–710
 results, 705–715
 statistical significance analysis, 710–715
Technique for order preference by similarity to ideal solution (TOPSIS), 330
TFO. *See* Team formation optimization (TFO)
THAvail. *See* Total Hourly Availability (THAvail)
Thin-walled plate element, 242
Three-dimensional mesh topology, 257
Three-dimensional NoC architectures (3D NoC architectures), 257
3D NoCs, 259
Through-silicon via technology (TSV technology), 257
Ti-6Al-4V, 327
 roughness analysis of Ti6Al4V surface laser texturing, 333–339
 titanium alloy, 330
TID controller. *See* Tilted-integral-derivative controller (TID controller)
TIDSMC structures, 421–422, 422*f*, 435
Tilted-integral-derivative controller (TID controller), 414, 421
Time complexity, 641
Time of arrival (ToA), 377
Time-programmed coefficient control, 96
Titanium alloy, 328
TLBO. *See* Teaching-learning-based optimization (TLBO)
TLS. *See* Total link strength (TLS)
TM mode. *See* Transverse magnetic mode (TM mode)
ToA. *See* Time of arrival (ToA)
TOPSIS. *See* Technique for order preference by similarity to ideal solution (TOPSIS)
Total Hourly Availability (THAvail), 727
Total link strength (TLS), 137–138
Total uplift per group, 371–373
Traditional control methods, 420
Traditional design approach, 491
Traditional manual tuning methods, 414
Trajectory stabilization, 80
Transverse magnetic mode (TM mode), 570
Traveling salesman problem (TSP), 403–404, 669–670
 methodology, 404–407
  grey wolf optimization, 404–406
  teaching-learning-based optimization, 407
 results, 408–410
  Att48 GWO and TLBO, 407*f*
  GWO and TLBO experiments, 406*t*
  Pr76 GWO and TLBO optimum path, 408*f*
  rd100 GWO and TLBO, 408*f*
TSP. *See* Traveling salesman problem (TSP)
TSV technology. *See* Through-silicon via technology (TSV technology)
Type 1 diabetes, 149
Type 2 diabetes mellitus, 149

U

ULS. *See* Ultimate limit state (ULS)
Ultimate limit state (ULS), 492
Unimodal functions, performance of tested algorithms on, 175–181
 convergence analysis on, 177–179, 179*f*
 stability analysis on, 180–181, 180*f*
 statistical analysis on, 177
Uplift distribution analysis, 367–368
Uplift modeling, 355–357, 359, 367
UR5, 415
 end-effector, 435
 kinematic and dynamic model of UR5 robot manipulator, 415–418
 manipulator, 428–429

V

Vehicle routing problem (VRP), 669
Velocity, 73
 calculation of, 651
 models, 556
VOSviewer, 124
VRP. *See* Vehicle routing problem (VRP)

W

Water infiltration estimation, application of GWO in, 449–450
Wavelet-based denoising methods, 577
Weather-based prediction, significance of, 106–109, 106*f*
 boxplots and violin plots of weather parameters segmented by disease type, 107*f*
 histograms showing distribution of numerical features in dataset, 107*f*
Web of Science (WoS), 121
 database, 123
 distribution of WoS categories, 124, 125*f*
 index distributions, 125–126, 127*t*
WEDM. *See* Wire electrical discharge machining (WEDM)
WGN. *See* White Gaussian noise (WGN)
Whale optimization algorithm (WOA), 75, 169, 344, 357, 654, 654
White Gaussian noise (WGN), 577, 579–580
White noise disturbances in joint torque inputs, evaluating controller performance under, 437–443
 average MAE values of controller sunder different noise powers, 441*f*
 joint position tracking performance of controllers under white noise, 442*f*
 MAE Values for different noise levels in joint torque inputs, 440*t*
 noise signal, 439*f*
 torque RMS values of controllers under different noise levels, 441*f*
Wilcoxon Signed-Rank (WSR), 731–733
Windows 10 Pro, 613
Wire electrical discharge machining (WEDM), 330
Wireless sensor networks (WSNs), 377, 382, 385, 398
 GWO's role
  for clustering in, 395–397, 397*f*
  for coverage optimization in, 398–399
  for fault tolerance in, 397–398
  for intrusion detection in, 398
  for localization in, 398
 routing, 612
WOA. *See* Whale optimization algorithm (WOA)
Wolf packs, 263
Wolf-influenced models, 560
Wolves, 263, 301
World Health Organization, 149–150
WoS. *See* Web of Science (WoS)
Wrapper methods, 587
WSNs. *See* Wireless sensor networks (WSNs)
WSR. *See* Wilcoxon Signed-Rank (WSR)

Z

Zakharov function, 604

Printed and bound by CPI Group (UK) Ltd, Croydon, CR0 4YY
21/09/2026
02220079-0001